자이스토리
중등 영문법 총정리
쉽고 빠른 개념 이해 + 최다 내신 문제

Xi STORY
중3

수경출판사

차 례

별책 부록

Workbook
Unit별 개념 확인 + 문법 복습 문제

- 2022 개정 교육과정의 10종 교과서와 본교재의 문법 연계를 정리했습니다.
- 학교에서 공부하고 있는 교과서 출판사와 대표 저자 이름을 확인하고 차례대로 공부하십시오.
- 본 자료는 학습에 도움을 주기 위해 분석한 것으로, 학교 진도와 선생님에 따라 진도가 다를 수 있습니다.

자이스토리 영문법 총정리 (중3)

A 문장의 기초	Unit 01 8품사와 문장의 구성 요소
	Unit 02 1형식 문장과 2형식 문장
	Unit 03 3형식 문장과 4형식 문장
	Unit 04 5형식 문장
B 문장의 종류	Unit 05 명령문, 제안문, 감탄문
	Unit 06 평서문, 의문문 (부가의문문, 간접의문문)
C 명사, 관사	Unit 07 셀 수 있는 명사의 복수형
	Unit 08 셀 수 없는 명사의 복수형
	Unit 09 명사의 소유격
	Unit 10 부정관사(a, an)와 정관사(the)
	Unit 11 주의해야 할 관사의 쓰임
D 대명사	Unit 12 지시대명사 this (these), that (those), it
	Unit 13 재귀대명사
	Unit 14 부정대명사
E 시제	Unit 15 시제의 종류
	Unit 16 현재시제, 과거시제
	Unit 17 동사의 과거–과거분사 불규칙 변화표
	Unit 18 미래시제
	Unit 19 진행시제
	Unit 20 완료시제
F 조동사	Unit 21 조동사의 특징과 조동사 do
	Unit 22 can (could), may (might)
	Unit 23 will (would), must (have to)
	Unit 24 shall, should, ought to, had better (not)
	Unit 25 used to, would, 조동사 + have + 과거분사
G 수동태	Unit 26 수동태의 개념 및 형태
	Unit 27 수동태의 시제
	Unit 28 조동사와 동사구의 수동태
	Unit 29 4형식, 5형식의 수동태
	Unit 30 주의해야 할 수동태와 관용표현
H 형용사	Unit 31 형용사의 종류, 쓰임, 어순
	Unit 32 부정 수량 형용사
	Unit 33 수사 형용사의 표현
I 부사	Unit 34 부사의 형태
	Unit 35 부사의 역할 및 위치
	Unit 36 그 밖의 중요 부사

새 교육과정이 반영된 10종 교과서와
본교재의 문법 연계표는
추후 교과서 분석 완료 시
QR코드를 통해 제공됩니다.

1. 능률 (김기택)
2. 동아 (윤정미)
3. 동아 (이병민)
4. 미래엔 (문영인)
5. 비상 (황종배)
6. 지학 (송미정)
7. 천재 (소영순)
8. 천재 (이상기)
9. YBM (시사 1) (박준언)
10. YBM (시사 2) (김은형)

문장의 5형식

1형식 – 주어(S)+동사(V) (S=Subject, V=Verb)
The wind blows. (바람이 분다.)

2형식 – 주어(S)+동사(V)+주격 보어(SC)
(SC=Subject Complement)
My sister became a lawyer.
(내 여동생은 변호사가 되었다.)

3형식 – 주어(S)+동사(V)+목적어(O) (O=Object)
He studied English last night.
(그는 어젯밤에 영어를 공부했다.)

4형식 – 주어(S)+동사(V)+간접목적어(IO)+직접목적어(DO)
(IO=Indirect Object, DO=Direct Object)
Mary gave him a book.
(Mary는 그에게 책 한 권을 줬다.)

5형식 – 주어(S)+동사(V)+목적어(O)+목적격 보어(OC)
(OC=Object Complement)
My family call the dog Lily.
(우리 가족은 그 개를 Lily라고 부른다.)

to부정사 (to+동사원형)

명사 역할 – To read a book is important.
(책을 읽는 것은 중요하다.)

형용사 역할 – I bought a book to read.
(나는 읽을 책을 샀다.)

부사 역할 – I came home to read the book.
(나는 그 책을 읽기 위해 집에 왔다.)

동명사 (동사원형+-ing)

주어 역할 – Swimming is my favorite sport.
(수영은 내가 가장 좋아하는 운동이다.)

보어 역할 – My favorite sport is swimming.
(내가 가장 좋아하는 운동은 수영이다.)

동사의 목적어 역할 – I like swimming.
(나는 수영하는 것을 좋아한다.)

전치사의 목적어 역할 – I am interested in swimming.
(나는 수영에 관심이 있다.)

시제

단순 시제

현재 (~한다)
I walk to school every day.
(나는 매일 학교에 걸어간다.)

과거 (~했다)
I walked to school yesterday.
(나는 어제 학교에 걸어갔다.)

미래 (~할 것이다)
I will walk to school tomorrow.
(나는 내일 학교에 걸어갈 것이다.)

진행 시제

현재진행 (~하고 있다)
I am walking to school.
(나는 학교에 걸어가고 있다.)

과거진행 (~하고 있었다)
I was walking to school yesterday.
(나는 어제 학교에 걸어가고 있었다.)

미래진행 (~하고 있을 것이다)
I will be walking to school.
(나는 학교에 걸어가고 있을 것이다.)

완료 시제

현재완료 (과거부터 지금까지~했다)
I have walked to school.
(나는 (과거부터 지금까지) 학교에 걸어갔다.)

과거완료 (더 오래전부터 과거까지~해왔다)
I had walked to school.
(나는 (더 오래전부터 과거까지) 학교에 걸어갔다.)

미래완료 (미래 ~까지 완료될 것이다)
I will have graduated from university by next year.
(나는 내년까지 대학을 졸업하게 될 것이다.)

분사

과거분사 (-ed) – 수동, 완료
He saw fallen leaves.
(그는 떨어진 나뭇잎을 봤다.)

현재분사 (-ing) – 능동, 진행
He saw falling leaves.
(그는 떨어지고 있는 나뭇잎을 봤다.)

비교

★ 원급: 형용사, 부사의 원급

원급 비교 – as+원급+as
She is as tall as he is.
(그녀는 그와 키가 같다.)

비교급 비교 – 원급+-er+than / more+원급+than
She is taller than he (is).
(그녀는 그보다 키가 크다.)
She is more creative than he (is).
(그녀는 그보다 더 창의적이다.)

– less+원급+than
She is less tall than he (is).
(그녀는 그보다 키가 덜 크다.)

최상급 비교 – 원급+-est / most+원급
She is the tallest in the class.
(그녀는 반에서 가장 키가 크다.)
She is the most creative in the class.
(그녀는 반에서 가장 창의적이다.)

[집필진]

구미순 서울 상계중학교	배윤경 서울 서운중학교	차덕원 서울 신일고등학교
김가영 서울 내곡중학교	유민정 서울 윤중중학교	홍민석 안양외국어고등학교
김다인 서울 서일중학교	이민지 서울 가재울중학교	수경 English Lab.
노윤희 서울 아주중학교	조용현 서울 바른스터디학원	

[감수진]

강두수 대전 더퍼스트영어	박민서 광명 포핀스헤리티지어학원	이 진 인천 (송도) 본질과방향
강라희 서울 대치탑영어학원	박서준 울산 해늘어학원	이진희 광주 이마스터학원
강민주 대구 글로리영어학원	박수진 부산 제이엔씨영어학원	이현일 서울 SEM영어학원
강성영 구미 외대어학원	박진석 제주 진리수	이현정 진주 니키잉글리쉬
강소윤 고양 (일산) 다른영어	방성모 대구 (범어) SM영어	이홍주 서울 쿠키영어교습소
강현욱 군포 링구아포럼외국어학원	방승희 인천 스마일잉글리쉬	이효명 구리 (갈매) 리드앤톡영어독서학원
고수복 제주 수에듀학원	배탐스 안양 삼성학원	이희우 시흥 와튼영어스쿨
고주희 양주 이지튜터학원	서정인 대구 서울입시학원	임서원 수원 외대영어
곽승호 군산 소망학원	신유정 청주 비타민영어클리닉학원	정영훈 부산 J&C영어전문학원
구본학 태백 엠스터디학원	신인철 부산 오아시스영어학원	조미영 서울 튼튼영어마스터클럽구로학원
김고은 인천 토북이교습소	심민후 서울 강서라임학원	조효숙 광주 눈높이첨단월계학원
김민경 김포 이규태시그니처학원	안혜정 부산 아발론랭콘해운대어학원	진주현 서울 (송파) EMC영어학원
김민정 서울 영동중학교	양용국 익산 마이엠영수학원	차희정 서울 Lisa리사영어
김비아 대구 김쌤영어	양진오 의정부 비앤비영어	최민우 서울 마이뉴영어
김수연 서울 수쌤잉글리쉬영어교습소	여민희 하남 꿈이룸영수학원	최민지 세종 윌그로우(세종고운점)
김수진 부산 잉투스어학원	오세훈 구리 레벨업학원	최서유 서울 (서초) 지승학원
김원기 서울 (노원) 탑노치영어학원	유홍상 부천 에이펙스영어학원	최재병 군포 (산본) PAX 어학원
김윤희 울산 하이지니어학원(동구캠퍼스)	윤세호 서울 PMP영어	최형욱 인천 (송도) 메가프라임학원
김은경 천안 천안서울학원	윤애리 인천 (송도) 이명학원 J관	최희정 성남 (분당) SJ클쌤영어
김종현 성남 (분당) 김진성열정어학원	윤정화 인천 BK영어전문학원	한기석 광주 이유국어영어전문학원
김좌현 서울 대치다원교육	이경채 서울 공릉중학교	한명숙 부산 (대신동) 벨라영어
김지선 안양 (평촌) 제임스M어학원	이광열 구리 열강영어교습소	허상은 대전 더프라임영어학원
김지영 대구 김지영영어	이보라 서울 윈썸영어교습소	홍문식 시흥 유니스영어학원
김현수 서울 (양천) 브레인학원	이상협 인천 더이룸학원	황규만 대전 대전한빛고등학교
김혜경 서울 이강영어교습소	이순옥 화성 아이윌잉글리시영어학원	황규진 서울 잉글리쉬잇업
남현욱 서울 스카이영어학원	이예원 서울 대치엠학원	황현성 순천 하이스트영재학원
박경진 부산 웅진프라임괴정학원	이용범 화성 (동탄) 로고스영어	
박계리 안양 글로리영어교습소	이정훈 아산 이엔에듀	

자이스토리 영문법 총정리(중3)

1. 현재완료시제

2. 수동태

3. 비교급

I'm tall.
I'm taller!

I'm the tallest!

그건 반칙이잖아!
It's not cheating. It's strategy!

Grammar는 A⁺지만, Honesty는 F네!

4. 관계사

와... 진짜 슬픈 유령이네.
옥상에 귀신이 있다는 이야기 들었어? Somebody who failed an Engilsh test became a ghost.

헐... 소름이다.
그 유령이 찾는 것은 바로, the test paper that everyone failed.

에이, 거짓말.
게다가 옆 반 영어 시간에 갑자기 전등이 꺼졌대. That's what I heard.

뭐야... 나 무서워...
그 일이 언제 일어났는지 알아? It happened on the day when the test papers disappeared!

구성과 특징

01 영문법 개념 + 개념 확인 문제 – 친절한 개념 설명과 개념 확인 문제로 영문법을 익힌다!

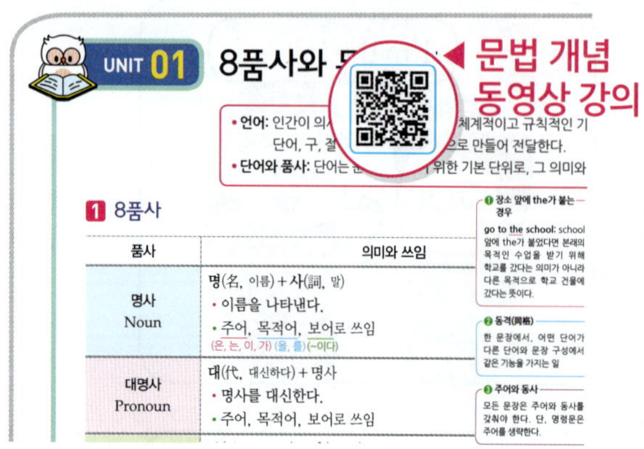

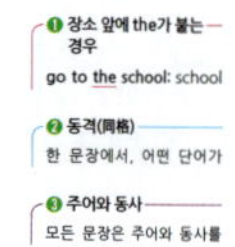

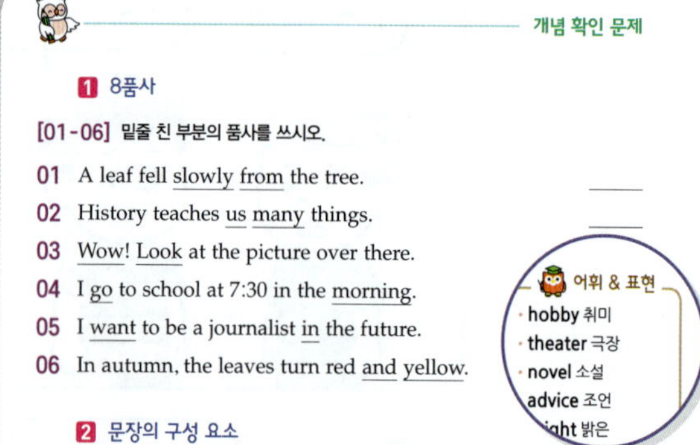

[영문법 개념 총정리]

- 표와 그림, 예문들을 통해 해당 Unit에서 배울 문법을 쉽게 이해할 수 있습니다.
- 명쾌한 문법 개념 동영상 강의로 개념 이해가 더욱 쉽습니다.
- **빨간색 박스**: 개념 보충 설명
  파란색 박스: 어려운 용어 설명
  보라색 박스: 예외 사항 설명

[개념 확인 문제]

- 다양한 개념 확인 문제들로 학습한 개념을 충분히 익힐 수 있습니다.
- 두 개 이상의 개념을 비교해서 공부할 수 있는 개념 혼합 문제들을 수록했습니다.

[어휘 & 표현]

해당 Unit에 나온 주요 어휘와 표현들을 한번 더 공부할 수 있습니다.

02 단원 평가 문제 – 학습한 문법 개념을 학교 시험 문제로 연습한다!

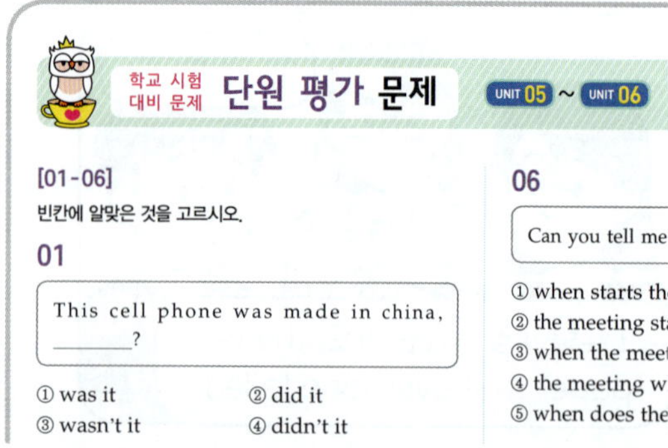

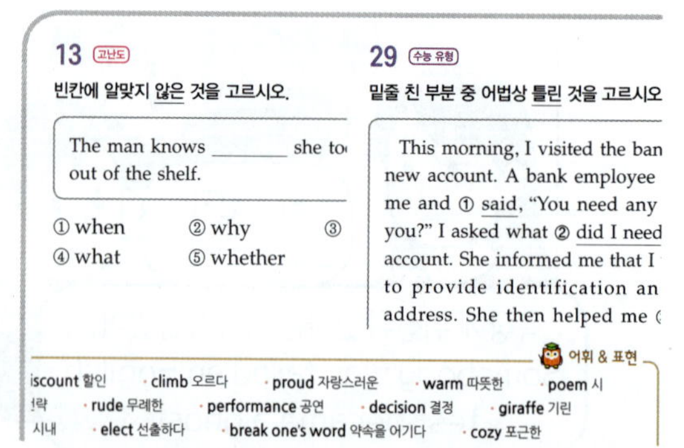

[문법 유형 문제]

- 학교 시험 대비 문제로 학습한 문법 개념에 대한 실력을 평가할 수 있습니다.
- 빈칸에 알맞은 말 고르기, 어법상 틀린 문장 고르기 등 다양한 학교 시험 유형 문제를 수록했습니다.

[고난도 문제 + 서술형 문제]

- Unit에서 공부한 문법 개념에 대한 서술형 문제들로 실력을 폭넓게 향상시킬 수 있습니다.
- 고난도 문제는 고난도 학교 시험 문제에 대한 대처 능력도 기르도록 다양한 유형으로 수록하였습니다.

[수능 유형 + 수능 맛보기]

- '수능 유형' 문제를 통해, 수능에 출제되는 어법 유형을 미리 공부할 수 있습니다.
- '수능 맛보기' 문제를 통해 다양한 수능 어법 유형을 대비할 수 있습니다.

03 실전 모의고사 – 단원별 모의고사로 학교 시험을 완벽히 대비한다!

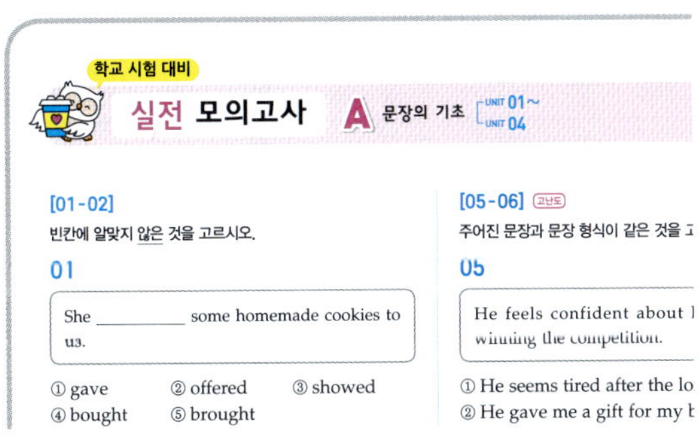

[자주 출제되는 단원별 문법 문제]

- 단원별 문법 개념에 대한 내신형 객관식 유형과 서술형 문제로 학교 시험에 충분히 대비할 수 있습니다.
- 고난도 문제들을 특별히 수록하여 어려운 내신 문제에 대한 대처 능력도 기르도록 하였습니다.

별책 부록

04 Workbook – 공부한 문법 개념과 어휘를 한 번 더 복습한다!

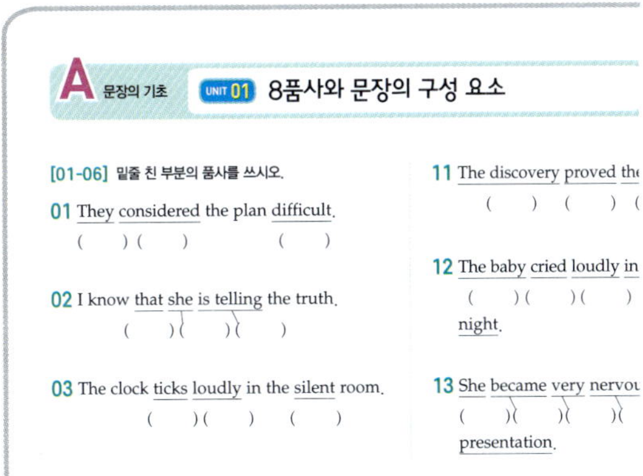

[Unit 개념별로 복습하는 워크북]

- 각 Unit에 해당하는 문제들로 앞에서 배운 내용을 반복해서 학습할 수 있습니다.
- 개념 확인 문제와 유사한 유형으로 문법 복습 문제들을 구성하였습니다.

---

05 자이스토리만의 명쾌한 해설 – 쉽게 이해되는 친절한 해설로 실력이 오른다!

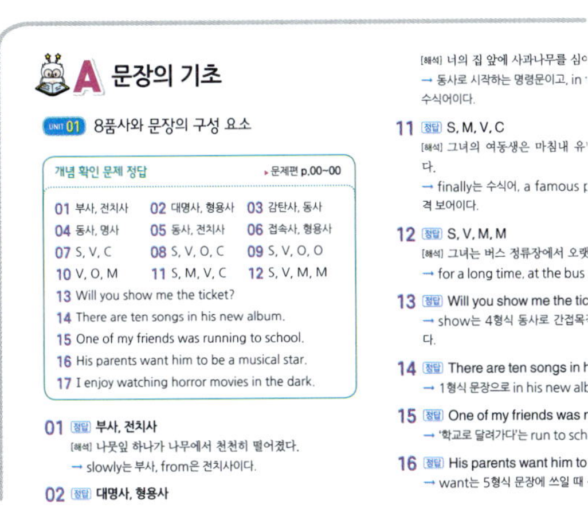

[혼자서도 쉽게 이해되는 친절한 해설]

- Unit별로 정답을 쉽게 확인할 수 있습니다.
- 틀린 문제를 확실히 이해할 수 있도록 쉽게 설명하였습니다.
- 모든 영문 선택지에 대해 우리말 해석을 제공하여 문제에 대한 이해를 도와드립니다.

Xi STORY 중등 영문법 총정리 학습 계획표 

★ Workbook과 함께 공부하면 영문법 실력이 더욱 더 탄탄해집니다.

단원	학습 내용	학습 날짜		확인	DAY
A 문장의 기초	Unit 01 8품사와 문장의 구성 요소	월	일		01
	Unit 02 1형식 문장과 2형식 문장	월	일		
	Unit 03 3형식 문장과 4형식 문장	월	일		
	Unit 04 5형식 문장	월	일		
	단원 평가 문제 [Unit 01~04]	월	일		02
B 문장의 종류	Unit 05 명령문, 제안문, 감탄문	월	일		03
	Unit 06 평서문, 의문문 (부가의문문, 간접의문문)	월	일		
	단원 평가 문제 [Unit 05~06]	월	일		
C 명사, 관사	Unit 07 셀 수 있는 명사의 복수형	월	일		04
	Unit 08 셀 수 없는 명사의 복수형	월	일		
	Unit 09 명사의 소유격	월	일		
	단원 평가 문제 [Unit 07~09]	월	일		
	Unit 10 부정관사(a, an)와 정관사(the)	월	일		05
	Unit 11 주의해야 할 관사의 쓰임	월	일		
	단원 평가 문제 [Unit 10~11]	월	일		
D 대명사	Unit 12 지시대명사 this (these), that (those), it	월	일		06
	Unit 13 재귀대명사	월	일		
	Unit 14 부정대명사	월	일		
	단원 평가 문제 [Unit 12~14]	월	일		07
E 시제	Unit 15 시제의 종류	월	일		08
	Unit 16 현재시제, 과거시제	월	일		
	Unit 17 동사의 과거−과거분사 불규칙 변화표	월	일		
	Unit 18 미래시제	월	일		
	단원 평가 문제 [Unit 15~18]	월	일		
	Unit 19 진행시제	월	일		09
	Unit 20 완료시제	월	일		
	단원 평가 문제 [Unit 19~20]	월	일		
F 조동사	Unit 21 조동사의 특징과 조동사 do	월	일		10
	Unit 22 can (could), may (might)	월	일		
	Unit 23 will (would), must (have to)	월	일		
	Unit 24 shall, should, ought to, had better (not)	월	일		
	Unit 25 used to, would, 조동사 + have + 과거분사	월	일		11
	단원 평가 문제 [Unit 21~25]	월	일		
G 수동태	Unit 26 수동태의 개념 및 형태	월	일		12
	Unit 27 수동태의 시제	월	일		
	Unit 28 조동사와 동사구의 수동태	월	일		
	단원 평가 문제 [Unit 26~28]	월	일		
	Unit 29 4형식, 5형식의 수동태	월	일		
	Unit 30 주의해야 할 수동태와 관용표현	월	일		13
	단원 평가 문제 [Unit 29~30]	월	일		
H 형용사	Unit 31 형용사의 종류, 쓰임, 어순	월	일		14
	Unit 32 부정 수량 형용사	월	일		
	Unit 33 수사 형용사의 표현	월	일		
	단원 평가 문제 [Unit 31~33]	월	일		15
I 부사	Unit 34 부사의 형태	월	일		16
	Unit 35 부사의 역할 및 위치	월	일		
	Unit 36 그 밖의 중요 부사	월	일		
	단원 평가 문제 [Unit 34~36]	월	일		17

 중등 영문법 `100점`을 위한 특별한 공부법

1. 중학교의 교과서 문법들을 체계적으로 공부하고
   개념 이해를 돕는 대표 예문들을 익힌다.

2. 문법 개념은 QR 코드 동영상 강의를 통해
   쉽고 명쾌하게 이해한다.

3. 개념 확인 문제로 공부한 문법 개념을 정확히 이해했는지 확인하고
   연습한다.

4. '어휘 & 표현' 코너를 통해 개념과 문제에서 나온 어휘와 표현들을 익힌다.

5. 단원 평가의 내신 대비 객관식, 서술형 문제, 고난도
   문제들을 통해 어려운 문제들도 풀 수 있는 능력을
   기른다.

6. Workbook을 통해 문법 개념이 확실히 이해되었는지
   테스트한다.

7. 틀린 문제는 확실히 이해해서 같은 개념의 문제는 다시
   틀리지 않도록 한다.

A

문장의 기초

완전한 의미를 갖추고
전달될 수 있는 말의 단위

Wow, the happy boy quickly ran to her and smiled.
감탄사　　　형용사　명사　부사　동사　전치사　대명사　접속사

(와, 그 행복한 소년이 그녀에게 빠르게 달려가 웃었다.)

He made the room clean after lunch.
주어　동사　목적어　보어　수식어

(그는 점심 식사 후에 방을 깨끗하게 만들었다.)

8품사와 문장의 구성 요소 

- **언어:** 인간이 의사소통을 위해 사용하는 체계적이고 규칙적인 기호의 집합이다.
  단어, 구, 절 등을 결합하여 문장으로 만들어 전달한다.
- **단어와 품사:** 단어는 문장을 만들기 위한 기본 단위로, 그 의미와 쓰임에 따라 분류한 것이 품사이다.

1 8품사

품사	의미와 쓰임	예시
명사 Noun	명(名, 이름) + 사(詞, 말) • 이름을 나타낸다. • 주어, 목적어, 보어로 쓰임 (은, 는, 이, 가) (을, 를) (~이다)	Minsu (민수), Seoul (서울), book (책), dog (개), happiness (행복)
대명사 Pronoun	대(代, 대신하다) + 명사 • 명사를 대신한다. • 주어, 목적어, 보어로 쓰임	he (그), she (그녀), it (그것), they (그들)
동사 Verb	동(動, 움직이다) + 사(詞, 말) • 행동이나 상태를 나타낸다. • be동사와 일반동사, 조동사가 있으며 시제를 표시함	run (달리다), eat (먹다), be (~이다)
형용사 Adjective	형용(形容, 모양 및 상태) + 사(詞, 말) • 명사·대명사의 성질이나 상태를 나타낸다. • 수식어, 보어로 쓰임	happy (행복한), blue (파란), tall (키가 큰)
부사 Adverb	부(副, 돕다) + 사(詞, 말) • 형용사, 동사, 부사, 문장 전체를 꾸민다. • 시간, 장소, 정도, 빈도, 방법 등을 나타냄	well (잘), quickly (빨리), here (여기), often (자주), very (매우)
접속사 Conjunction	접속(接續, 맞대서 이음) + 사(詞, 말) • 같은 문장 요소끼리 연결한다. (단어＋단어, 구＋구, 절＋절) • 문장 요소들을 연결해줌	and (그리고), but (하지만), because (왜냐하면)
전치사 Preposition	전치(前置, 앞에 두다) + 사(詞, 말) • 명사·대명사의 앞에 둔다. • 시간, 장소, 방향, 위치 등을 나타냄	in (~ 안에), on (~ 위에), at (~에서)
감탄사 Interjection	감탄(感歎, 느껴서 탄식함) + 사(詞, 말) • 감정을 표현한다. • 놀라움, 유감 등의 감정을 표현해줌	oh! (오!), wow! (와!), ouch! (아야!)

2 문장의 구성 요소

(1) 문장의 필수 구성 요소: 주어 (S), 동사 (V), 목적어 (O), 보어 (C)

- They named their dog Max.
  주어　동사　목적어　보어

  (그들은 그들의 개를 Max라고 이름지었다.)

(2) 수식어 (M): 문장의 필수 구성 요소 4개 이외에 다른 모든 것

- The man walked into the room. (그 남자가 방으로 들어왔다.)
  주어　동사　수식어

❶ 문장의 구성 요소

주어 (Subject)	• 동사가 나타내는 동작이나 상태의 주체가 되는 말 • '~은, ~는, ~이, ~가'
동사 (Verb)	• 주어의 동작·상태를 나타내는 말 • '~하다, ~이다'
목적어 (Object)	• 동사가 나타내는 동작이나 상태의 대상을 나타내는 말 • '~을, ~를, '~에게'
보어 (Complement)	• 주어나 목적어의 의미나 상태를 보충 설명하는 말 • 명사 상당어구나 형용사
수식어 (Modifier)	• 다른 말들을 꾸며주는 말 • 형용사적 수식어와 부사적 수식어

1 8품사

[01-06] 밑줄 친 부분의 품사를 쓰시오.

01 A leaf fell <u>slowly</u> <u>from</u> the tree.　______　______

02 History teaches <u>us</u> <u>many</u> things.　______　______

03 <u>Wow</u>! <u>Look</u> at the picture over there.　______　______

04 I <u>go</u> to school at 7:30 in the <u>morning</u>.　______　______

05 I <u>want</u> to be a journalist <u>in</u> the future.　______　______

06 In autumn, the leaves turn red <u>and</u> <u>yellow</u>.　______　______

2 문장의 구성 요소

[07-12] 밑줄 친 부분의 문장 구성 요소를 S, V, O, C, M으로 쓰시오.

07 <u>The tropical fruit</u> <u>tastes</u> <u>sour</u>.
　　(　) 　(　)(　)

08 <u>My daughter</u> <u>made</u> <u>me</u> <u>happy</u>.
　(　) 　(　)(　)(　)

09 <u>Mr. Kim</u> <u>will teach</u> <u>us</u> <u>Korean history</u>.
　(　) 　(　)(　) (　)

10 <u>Plant</u> <u>apple trees</u> <u>in front of your house</u>.
　(　)(　) 　　(　)

11 <u>Her sister</u> <u>finally</u> <u>became</u> <u>a famous pianist</u>.
　(　) (　)(　) (　)

12 <u>She</u> <u>waited</u> <u>for a long time</u> <u>at the bus stop</u>.
　(　)(　) (　) 　(　)

[13-17] 주어진 우리말과 일치하도록 괄호 안의 말을 바르게 배열하시오.

13 저에게 표를 보여주시겠어요? (will, show, the ticket, you, me)

　➡ ____

14 그의 새 앨범에는 10곡이 있다. (are, there, new, album, his, in, songs, ten)

　➡ ____

15 내 친구들 중의 한 명이 학교로 달려가고 있었다. (friends, to, my, was, one, school, running, of)

　➡ ____

16 그의 부모님은 그가 뮤지컬 스타가 되기를 원하신다. (be, him, want, a musical star, his parents, to)

　➡ ____

17 나는 어둠 속에서 공포 영화 보는 것을 즐긴다. (enjoy, the dark, horror movies, in, watching, I)

　➡ ____

> 🦉 **어휘 & 표현**
> · **name** 이름 짓다
> · **fall** 떨어지다
> · **journalist** 언론인
> · **autumn** 가을
> · **tropical** 열대의
> · **taste** 맛이 나다
> · **finally** 마침내
> · **become** ~이 되다
> · **famous** 유명한
> · **enjoy** 즐기다
> · **horror movie** 공포 영화

〈 정답과 해설 p. 2 〉

 **UNIT 02 1형식 문장과 2형식 문장** 

• **문장의 형식**: 문장이 구성되는 요소들의 배열 방식이나 문법적인 구조를 의미한다.
영어 문장은 1~5형식 문장으로 구분한다.

The actor ***appeared*** on the stage. (그 배우가 무대에 등장했다.)
1형식: S+V

He ***looked*** a bit tired. (그는 약간 피곤해 보였다.)
2형식: S+V+SC

1 1형식 문장: 주어(S) + 동사(V)

(1) 1형식에는 완전자동사가 쓰이며, 목적어나 보어를 필요로 하지 않는다.

- The baby sleeps. (아이가 잔다.)
  주어 / 동사
- I don't care. (나는 상관없다.)
  주어 / 동사

(2) 동사 뒤에 부사(구)를 수반하는 경우가 많다.

- She lives here. (그녀는 이곳에 산다.)
  동사 / 부사
- The sun rises in the east. (해가 동쪽에서 뜬다.)
  동사 / 부사구

(3) 1형식 문장에 쓰이는 be동사는 '~ 있다'라는 뜻이며, 뒤에 부사(구)가 와야 한다.

- Your glasses are on the desk. (네 안경은 책상 위에 있다.)
  be동사 / 부사구

(4) Here is[are] ~, There is[are] ~ 구문의 주어는 be동사 뒤에 온다.

- Here is a cup of coffee for you. (여기에 너를 위한 커피 한 잔이 있다.)
  be동사 / 주어
- There were several men near the tree. (몇 명의 남자들이 나무 근처에 있었다.)
  be동사 / 주어

❶ 1형식 문장
1형식은 '주어와 동사'로 이루어진 문장으로, 목적어나 보어를 필요로 하지 않는다는 사실을 기억해야 한다.

❷ Here / There 구문
'Here / There is ~'는 뒤에 단수 명사, 'Here / There are ~'는 뒤에 복수 명사가 따라 나오는 것에 유의해야 한다.

2 2형식 문장: 주어(S) + 동사(V) + 주격 보어(SC)

(1) 2형식에는 불완전자동사가 쓰이며, 보어를 필요로 한다.

be 동사 (~이다)	become 동사 (~이 되다)	seem 동사 (~인 것 같다)	감각동사
be, keep, stay 등	become, come, go, grow, turn, run, fall 등	seem, appear 등	look, feel, smell, taste, sound 등
The room is too small. 보어 (그 방은 너무 작다.)	Your dream will come true. 보어 (네 꿈은 실현될 것이다.)	She seems excited. 보어 (그녀는 흥분한 것 같다.)	It sounds good. 보어 (그것은 좋게 들린다.)

(2) 보어로는 명사(구)나 형용사가 온다.

- He became a soccer player. (그는 축구 선수가 되었다.)
  명사구(보어)
- You should stay calm. (너는 침착하게 있어야 한다.)
  형용사(보어)

❸ 보어가 될 수 없는 것
부사(구)는 보어로 쓸 수 없다.
- The waffle looks **delicious**. (○)
  (와플이 맛있어 보인다.)
- → The waffle looks **deliciously**. (×)

1　1형식 문장

[01-05] 빈칸에 알맞은 말을 〈보기〉에서 골라 쓰시오. (중복 사용 불가)

〈보기〉

| goes | matters | is | are | rises |

01 Here _______________ your ticket to the concert tonight.

02 The sun _______________ early in summer near the sea.

03 As long as you're happy, nothing else _______________.

04 There _______________ a lot of people in the park now.

05 Her older brother always _______________ to school by bike.

2　2형식 문장

[06-10] 괄호 안에서 알맞은 것을 고르시오.

06 He became (famously / a famous singer).

07 You'll feel (coolly / cooler) after a shower.

08 Anna's baby (had / fell) asleep on her back.

09 A few books keep (open / openly) on his desk.

10 These days the weather in Korea is (changing / getting) warmer.

1 + 2　1형식 문장과 2형식 문장

[11-14] 〈보기〉와 같이 문장의 구성 요소와 형식을 쓰시오.

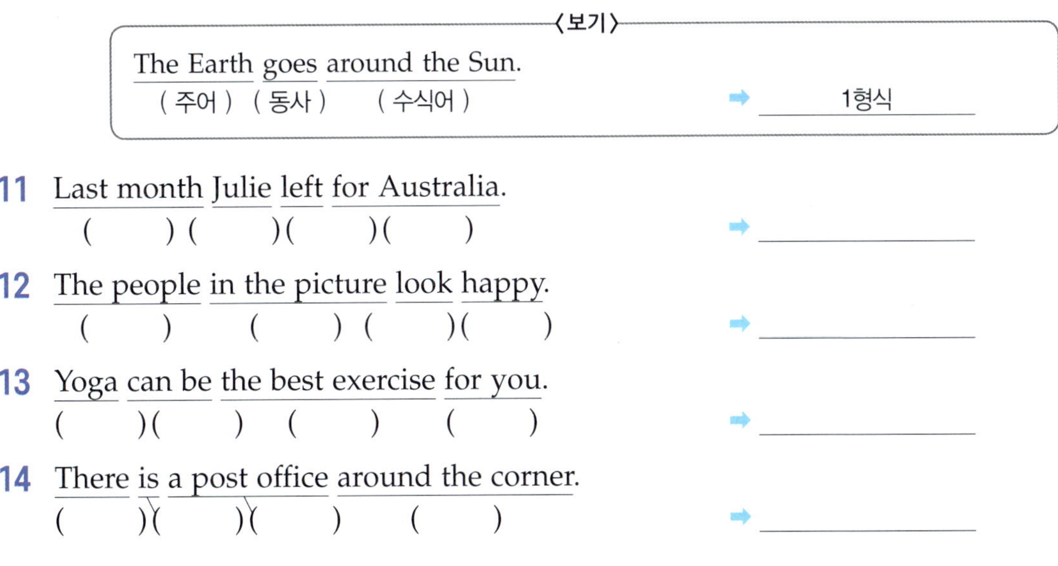

〈보기〉

The Earth goes around the Sun.
(주어) (동사) 　(수식어)　➡ ____ 1형식 ____

11 Last month Julie left for Australia.
(　　) (　　)(　　)(　　)　➡ _______________

12 The people in the picture look happy.
(　　　) 　(　　　) (　　)(　　)　➡ _______________

13 Yoga can be the best exercise for you.
(　　)(　　　) (　　　) 　(　　　)　➡ _______________

14 There is a post office around the corner.
(　　)(　　)(　　　) 　(　　　)　➡ _______________

어휘 & 표현

| ·**rise** (해가) 뜨다 | ·**several** 몇몇의 | ·**calm** 조용한 | ·**matter** 중요하다, 문제가 되다 | ·**asleep** 잠이 든 | ·**post office** 우체국 |

〈 정답과 해설 p. 2~3 〉

 **UNIT 03** # 3형식 문장과 4형식 문장 

1 3형식 문장: 주어(S) + 동사(V) + 목적어(O)

(1) 3형식에는 완전타동사가 쓰이며, 목적어로는 명사 상당어구가 온다. ❶

- My family visited the museum. (우리 가족은 박물관을 방문했다.)
  주어 / 동사 / 목적어

> ❶ **명사 상당어구**
> 상당어구란 '그에 준한다'라는 뜻으로, 명사 상당어구는 명사구, 대명사, 명사절 등을 말한다. 문장에서 명사 역할을 한다.

(2) 자동사로 착각하기 쉬운 타동사

전치사를 수반하는 자동사처럼 해석되지만 타동사이기 때문에 뒤에 목적어가 온다.

> **discuss** (~에 대해 논의하다),   **enter** (~에 들어가다),   **answer** (~에 대답하다),
> **resemble** (~와 닮다),   **reach** (~에 도착하다),   **marry** (~와 결혼하다) 등

- We discussed the plan at the meeting. (우리는 회의에서 그 계획에 대해 논의했다.)
- Do not enter this room without permission. (허락 없이 이 방에 들어가지 마세요.)

(3) 타동사 관용 구문

> **remind A of B** (A에게 B를 생각나게 하다),   **deprive A of B** (A에게서 B를 박탈하다),
> **provide A with B** (A에게 B를 공급하다),   **compare A with B** (A와 B를 비교하다),
> **thank A for B** (A에게 B를 감사하다),   **substitute A for B** (A를 B 대신 사용하다) 등

- The song reminds me of my childhood. (그 노래는 내 어린 시절을 떠올리게 한다.)
  A / B
- The company provided us with free samples. (그 회사는 우리에게 무료 샘플을 제공했다.)
  A / B

(4) 타동사처럼 해석되는 「자동사 + 전치사」

> **laugh at** (~을 비웃다), **put off** (~을 미루다), **look at** (~을 보다), **wait for** (~을 기다리다) 등

- They laughed at my attempt to dance. (그들은 내가 춤추려는 시도를 비웃었다.)

2 4형식 문장: 주어(S) + 동사(V) + 간접목적어(I.O) + 직접목적어(D.O)

(1) 4형식에는 수여동사가 쓰이며, 간접목적어와 직접목적어가 온다. ❷

- She showed me her new dress. (그녀는 나에게 그녀의 새 드레스를 보여주었다.)
  수여동사 / 간접목적어 / 직접목적어

> ❷ **수여동사**
> 간접목적어와 직접목적어를 가지는 4형식 문장에 쓰이는 동사를 말한다.
> • ask, buy, give, lend, offer, send, show, teach, tell, write 등

(2) 「주어 + 동사 + 간접목적어 + 직접목적어」의 4형식 문장을

「주어 + 동사 + 직접목적어 + 전치사 + 간접목적어」의 3형식 문장으로 바꿀 수 있다.

✪ 간접목적어 앞에 오는 전치사는 동사에 따라 to, for, of가 정해진다.

전치사 to가 필요한 동사	give, tell, send, bring, write, offer, teach, show 등
	• She showed me her new dress.
	→ She showed her new dress to me. (그녀는 나에게 그녀의 새 드레스를 보여주었다.)
전치사 for가 필요한 동사	buy, make, get, cook, find, build 등
	• Jack made me a tree house.
	→ Jack made a tree house for me. (Jack은 나에게 나무 위의 집을 만들어 주었다.)
전치사 of가 필요한 동사	ask, require, inquire, beg 등
	• Can I ask you a favor?
	→ Can I ask a favor of you? (제가 당신에게 부탁 하나 해도 될까요?)

1　3형식 문장

[01-06] 괄호 안에서 알맞은 것을 고르시오.

01 He (lay / laid / lied) his bag on the desk.

02 The company will provide its workers (at / to / with) houses.

03 Can I substitute oil (to / for / with) butter in your cookie recipe?

04 If you do your best, you can (reach / reach to / reach at) your goal.

05 My mom always compares me (my sister / of my sister / with my sister).

06 Whom did you (look up / look up at / look up to) when you were young?

2　4형식 문장

[07-10] 주어진 4형식 문장을 3형식 문장으로 바꿔 쓰시오.

07 Could you make us some snacks?

➡ ____

08 Ms. Lee sent her students Christmas gifts.

➡ ____

09 Can you show me the way to City Hall?

➡ ____

10 She cooked her mother a wonderful dinner.

➡ ____

1 + 2　3형식 문장과 4형식 문장

[11-14] 주어진 우리말과 일치하도록 괄호 안의 말을 이용하여 문장을 쓰시오.

11 그는 그의 할아버지를 많이 닮았다. (resemble, very much)

➡ ____

12 당신은 왕에게 사실을 이야기해야 한다. (should tell, the truth)

➡ ____

13 내가 너에게 너의 잃어버린 강아지를 찾아줄게. (find, lost puppy)

➡ ____

14 이 아름다운 경치가 나에게 내 고향을 생각나게 한다. (remind, this beautiful, scenery, hometown)

➡ ____

🦉 어휘 & 표현

- **permission** 허락　　· **substitute** 교체하다　　· **childhood** 어린 시절　　· **offer** 제공하다　　· **require** 요구하다
- **inquire** 문의하다　　· **beg** 간청하다　　· **reach** 도달하다　　· **compare** 비교하다　　· **snack** 간식　　· **scenery** 경치
- **hometown** 고향

〈 정답과 해설 p. 3~4 〉

UNIT 04 5형식 문장

The movie ***made*** her ***cry***. (그 영화는 그녀를 울렸다.)
사역동사   목적격 보어

He ***saw*** her ***cry*** during the movie.
지각동사   목적격 보어   (그는 그녀가 영화를 보는 중에 우는 것을 보았다.)

1 5형식 문장: 주어(S) + 동사(V) + 목적어(O) + 목적격 보어(OC)

– 목적격 보어 자리에는 명사 상당어구 또는 형용사 상당어구가 온다.

- The company appointed John manager. (회사는 John을 관리자로 임명했다.)
  주어   동사   목적어   목적격 보어(명사)
- The teacher made the students happy. (선생님은 학생들을 행복하게 만들었다.)
  주어   동사   목적어   목적격 보어(형용사)

2 목적격 보어 – 명사, 형용사

– 다음 동사는 목적격 보어로 명사나 형용사를 쓸 수 있다.

> make, choose, appoint, elect, drive, find, name, call, get, keep, leave, turn 등

- Everyone elected him team leader. (모두가 그를 팀 대표로 선출했다.)
                        목적격 보어(명사)
- He keeps the office organized. ❶ (그는 사무실을 정돈된 상태로 유지한다.)
                목적격 보어(형용사 - 과거분사)

❶ 목적격 보어로 쓰인 분사
목적격 보어로 분사가 올 수 있으며, 현재분사(-ing)는 능동과 진행을, 과거분사(p.p.)는 수동과 완료를 의미한다.

3 목적격 보어 – to부정사

– 주로 미래에 'to부정사의 동작'을 할 것을 요청, 요구, 권유하는 의미로 쓰인다.

> want, wish, order, tell, ask, advise, allow, force, expect, cause, encourage 등

- The coach encouraged the team to keep going. (코치는 팀에게 계속 나아가라고 격려했다.)
                권유
- His parents allowed him to enter the competition. (그의 부모님은 그가 대회에 참가하는 것을 허락했다.)
                허락

4 목적격 보어 – 원형부정사 ❷

– 사역동사와 지각동사는 목적격 보어로 원형부정사를 쓸 수 있다.
– 지각동사의 경우, 진행 중인 동작임을 강조할 때는 현재분사(-ing)를 쓰기도 한다.

❷ 원형부정사
원형부정사는 to부정사에서 to를 쓰지 않고 동사원형만 쓰는 부정사의 형태이다.

❸ 준사역동사 help
help는 준사역동사이며, 목적격 보어로 원형부정사와 to부정사를 모두 취할 수 있다.

사역동사 (시키다, 행하게 하다)	make, have, let, 준사역동사 help ❸
	• I had my sister pick me up at the airport. 　　　　　　　　원형부정사　(나는 언니에게 공항에 나를 데리러 오게 했다.)
	• He let his children play outside. (그는 자녀들이 밖에서 놀게 했다.) 　　　　　　　원형부정사
지각동사 (보다, 듣다, 느끼다 등)	see, watch, hear, listen to, feel, notice 등
	• We heard them argue[arguing] loudly. 　　　　　　　　현재분사 　(우리는 그들이 크게 논쟁하는[논쟁 중인] 것을 들었다.)
	• They watched the team practice for the game. 　　　　　　　　원형부정사 　(그들은 팀이 경기를 준비하는 것을 보았다.)

1 + **2** 목적격 보어 – 명사, 형용사

[01-07] 주어진 단어를 올바른 형태로 바꾸어 빈칸에 쓰시오.

01 They left the engine _______________ all night. (run)

02 He got his car _______________ at the garage. (repair)

03 The girls thought him _______________ and generous. (kindness)

04 The film left me _______________ and speechless. (shock)

05 She couldn't make herself _______________ in Spanish. (understand)

06 The babysitter kept the children _______________ for hours. (amuse)

07 The teacher kept the students _______________ in discussion. (engage)

3 + **4** 목적격 보어 – to부정사, 원형부정사

[08-13] 문장에서 <u>틀린</u> 부분을 찾아서 밑줄을 긋고 바르게 고쳐 쓰시오.

08 I saw him danced on the street. _______________

09 This dress makes me to look fat. _______________

10 I don't expect them come home early. _______________

11 She ordered them sat down and was quiet. _______________

12 Her parents won't allow her staying out late. _______________

13 He won't let his students to leave the classroom. _______________

1 + **2** + **3** + **4** 5형식 문장

[14-21] 괄호 안에서 알맞은 것을 고르시오.

14 We chose Paul (chairperson / be chairperson).

15 She felt a hand (touching / touched) her hair.

16 You should not let him (have / to have) his way.

17 I saw you (putting / to put) the key in your bag.

18 Banks (made / encouraged) people to borrow money.

19 We found the seats (be comfortable / very comfortable).

20 The mother (had / watched) her kids playing in the playground.

21 They don't expect him (becoming / to become) a successful director.

🦉 어휘 & 표현

· **advise** 조언하다　· **force** 강요하다　· **expect** 기대하다　· **argue** 논쟁하다　· **garage** 차고　· **generous** 관대한
· **chairperson** 의장　· **encourage** 용기를 북돋다　· **comfortable** 편한　· **director** 감독

[01-04]

빈칸에 알맞지 <u>않은</u> 것을 고르시오.

01

My father bought ________ pretty dolls.

① Minsu ② him ③ them
④ ours ⑤ my sister

02

The teacher considered him ________.

① a genius ② generous
③ kindness ④ a troublemaker
⑤ a good supporter

03

He made the wall ________.

① blue ② strong ③ high
④ green ⑤ widely

04

She ________ some homemade cookies to us.

① bought ② brought ③ gave
④ offered ⑤ showed

[05-09]

빈칸에 알맞은 것을 고르시오.

05

The dog barks ________ at strangers.

① loud ② happy ③ loudly
④ be loud ⑤ be loudly

06

The cake smells ________.

① well ② taste ③ sweetly
④ delicious ⑤ fabulously

07

I washed ________ this morning.

① clean ② through ③ careful
④ my pet ⑤ very good

08 고난도

The supervisor ________ all employees concentrate on their own work.

① wanted ② encouraged
③ got ④ made
⑤ ordered

09

His father ________ surprised at the news.

① made ② appeared
③ saw ④ gave
⑤ took

[10-16] 서술형

괄호 안의 단어를 이용하여 빈칸에 알맞은 말을 쓰시오.

10

He didn't allow me ________________ with the computer beyond 11 p.m. (play)

11

There ______________ a number of students in the classroom now. (be)

12

She encouraged me ______________ the English club. (join)

13

The old house in the mountain looked ______________. (attract)

14

I want to buy a nice car ______________. (he)

15

This cold drink makes us feel ______________. (fresh)

16 고난도

She heard her name ______________ by her teacher. (call)

[17-21]
주어진 문장과 형식이 같은 것을 고르시오.

17

My brother is happy with his new job.

① He seems tired after the long trip.
② He gave me a gift for my birthday.
③ Tom bought a new phone yesterday.
④ They visited the museum last weekend.
⑤ The teacher found the students studying in the library.

18

The children played happily in the park.

① The news made her upset.
② They offered us a big discount.
③ They arrived at the airport on time.
④ The weather became cold in the evening.
⑤ They are happy with the results of the research.

19

You can encourage them to work harder.

① The sun rises from the east.
② The tree became taller and taller.
③ She made a delicious cake for her son.
④ All the players did their best at the game.
⑤ Daniel felt something crawling on his arm.

20

The book reminds me of my childhood.

① Every cloud has a silver lining.
② The leaves on the trees turned red.
③ Friends in need are friends indeed.
④ She got her wallet stolen on the busy street.
⑤ The amount of the pollutant in the river has been on the increase.

21

Jessy found himself healthier than ever.

① My name is Christopher Lee.
② David used to send me a letter.
③ It's getting warmer and warmer.
④ Every morning, Britney runs 10 km.
⑤ She heard her father reading the storybook.

〈 정답과 해설 p. 5~6 〉

문장에서 <u>틀린</u> 부분을 찾아서 밑줄을 긋고 바르게 고치시오.

22

I really want to marry with you.

____

23

This lotion will make your skin softly.

____

24

Are you going to write a letter for the professor?

____

25

The painting reminded him his good old days.

____

26

I think him being a positive and outgoing person.

____

[27-28]

다음 글을 읽고 물음에 답하시오.

> One day, Tom's teacher ___(A)___ him to help his classmate, Jane, with her homework. Tom didn't want to at first, but he changed his mind and decided to help her. Tom heard Jane ___(B)___ about a difficult question. He explained it to her, and she ___(C)___ understood. Jane felt ___(D)___ and said, "Thank you, Tom!" Tom smiled because he realized that helping others is meaningful.

27

(A)와 (B)에 적절한 것을 고르시오.

	(A)		(B)
①	let	–	asking
②	asked	–	had
③	said	–	ask
④	ask	–	made
⑤	asked	–	ask

28

(C)와 (D)에 적절한 것을 고르시오.

	(C)		(D)
①	quickly	–	happy
②	quick	–	happy
③	quick	–	happiness
④	quickly	–	happily
⑤	quickly	–	happiness

[29-31] 서술형

주어진 문장을 괄호 안의 지시대로 바꿔 쓰시오.

29

My boss gave a challenging project to me.

(4형식으로)

➡ ______________________

____

30

She made her children chocolate cookies.

(3형식으로)

➡ ______________________

____

31

My mother doesn't allow me to stay up late.

(allow를 let으로 바꾸어서)

➡ ______________________

____

[32-33]

다음 글을 읽고 물음에 답하시오.

> One sunny afternoon, Mia went to the park with her dog. The weather was ⓐ perfect for a walk. As she was walking with her dog, she heard someone calling her name. It was her best friend, Lily. While they were talking, (A) Mia's dog chased a butterfly. Lily laughed and said, "Your dog is so fast!" Mia smiled and ⓑ let Lily throw the ball. They played together for a while. Later, Mia's mom called her to come home. Mia promised to meet Lily again, and they both went home.

32 고난도

ⓐ, ⓑ와 바꿔 쓸 수 있는 것으로 연결된 것을 고르시오.

	ⓐ	ⓑ		ⓐ	ⓑ
①	well	– made	②	nice	– helped
③	sunny	– wanted	④	good	– decided
⑤	much	– had			

33

(A)와 같은 형식의 문장을 고르시오.

① He handed me the keys to the house.
② The baby smiled as she saw her mother.
③ They felt nervous before the presentation.
④ She chose a red and green dress for the party.
⑤ The boys shouted across the playground during recess.

[34-35]

빈칸에 알맞지 <u>않은</u> 것을 고르시오.

34

> My bicycle broke down, so I ________ it repaired last night.

① had　　② let　　③ got
④ hoped　　⑤ made

35

> The soup in the bowl tastes ________.

① hot　　② good　　③ salty
④ sour　　⑤ sweetly

[36-38] 고난도

어법상 <u>틀린</u> 것을 고르시오.

36

① They'll get the book for us.
② He asked a question of her.
③ Who sent this package to Jake?
④ My father bought a smartphone to me.
⑤ Will you show the auditorium to them?

37

① I wanted to know the truth.
② Tom explained the problem to her.
③ You will be curious about the news.
④ He asked his neighbors a few questions.
⑤ The police found the boy safely with his parents.

38

① The young boy seems sleepy.
② Her latest bag looks very greatly.
③ He seems tired after the long journey.
④ She looked beautiful in the red dress.
⑤ The kids remained quiet during the movie.

〈 정답과 해설 p. 6~7 〉

(A) ~ (C)의 각 네모 안에서 어법에 맞는 표현으로 가장 적절한 것을 고르시오.

39

Some people (A) say / tell their children a tale that the Moon is made of green cheese. This popular myth can be traced back almost 500 years. Why did people say that? It's because the Moon (B) resembles / is resembled with cheese in some ways. The dark markings on the Moon are similar to the holes in cheese. The round shape of the Moon (C) reminds / reminds to us of the round shape of cheese. In addition, it has been said that "green cheese" is not green in color, but green in the sense of "young."

	(A)	(B)	(C)
①	say	resembles	reminds
②	tell	resembles	reminds
③	say	is resembled with	reminds to
④	tell	is resembled with	reminds to
⑤	tell	resembles	reminds to

40

I believe that school uniforms have some positive aspects. I look (A) neat and tidy / neatly and tidily in uniforms. Also, since I don't have to waste time deciding what to wear, I get ready (B) quick / quickly in the morning. However, it would be nice if students sometimes had a say in the uniform changes. If the design of the uniform changes each year, it will stay (C) fashionable / fashionably.

	(A)	(B)	(C)
①	neat and tidy	quick	fashionable
②	neat and tidy	quickly	fashionable
③	neat and tidy	quick	fashionably
④	neatly and tidily	quickly	fashionably
⑤	neatly and tidily	quick	fashionably

[41-42]

다음 글을 읽고 물음에 답하시오.

One afternoon, Sarah's mother had her ① clean the house. Sarah didn't want to, but her mother made her ② do it. Her mom promised her ③ go out for ice cream after cleaning. This made Sarah feel ④ better about cleaning. Her little brother, Jack, heard her ⑤ singing while cleaning and thought it was __________.

41 수능 유형

밑줄 친 부분 중 어법상 틀린 것을 고르시오.

①   ②   ③   ④   ⑤

42

빈칸에 알맞은 것을 고르시오.

① well   ② very   ③ funny
④ excited   ⑤ greatly

🦉 **어휘 & 표현**

- **consider** 여기다
- **troublemaker** 말썽꾸러기
- **supporter** 지지자
- **stranger** 낯선 사람
- **fabulously** 엄청나게
- **supervisor** 감독관
- **concentrate on** ~에 집중하다
- **a number of** 많은
- **research** 연구
- **crawl** 기다
- **pollutant** 오염 물질
- **storybook** 동화책
- **outgoing** 외향적인
- **challenging** 도전적인
- **auditorium** 강당
- **myth** 신화
- **neat** 단정한
- **have a say in** ~에 의견을 내다

B

문장의 종류
평서문, 명령문, 제안문, 감탄문, 의문문

Turn off your phone. Let's focus on the movie.
명령문 · 제안문

(휴대폰 꺼. 영화에 집중하자.)

What an exciting scene! (정말 짜릿한 장면이야!)
감탄문

The traffic light just turned red. Should we wait or go now?
평서문 · 의문문

(신호등이 막 빨간불로 바뀌었어. 기다릴까, 지금 갈까?)

 **UNIT 05 명령문, 제안문, 감탄문** 

Let's visit the National Museum. (국립박물관을 방문하자.)
제안문: 「Let's+동사원형 ~」

What a beautiful structure it is! (그것은 참 아름다운 건축물이구나!)
What 감탄문: 「What+a(n)+형용사+명사(+주어+동사)!」

1 명령문 – 상대방에게 명령, 요구, 충고, 금지 등을 나타낼 때 쓴다.

(1) 긍정 명령문과 부정 명령문

긍정 명령문	Be ~, 동사원형 ~
부정 명령문	Don't [Never] be ~, Don't [Never] + 동사원형 ~

- Be polite to your teacher. (너의 선생님께 공손해라.)
- Do your best all the time. (항상 최선을 다해라.)
- Don't be afraid to admit your mistakes. (너의 실수를 인정하는 것을 겁내지 마라.)
- Never give food to these animals. (이 동물들에게 절대 음식을 주지 마시오.)

(2) 명령문, and / or ~

① 명령문, and ~: …해라, 그러면 ~
- Start now, and you will catch the train. (지금 출발해라, 그러면 너는 기차를 탈 수 있을 것이다.)

② 명령문, or ~: …해라, 그렇지 않으면 ~
- Work hard, or you will not get a good grade.
(열심히 공부해라, 그렇지 않으면 너는 좋은 성적을 받지 못할 것이다.)

2 제안문 ❶ – 상대방에게 같이 무언가를 하자고 요청할 때 쓴다.

긍정 제안문	Let's + 동사원형
부정 제안문	Let's + not [never] + 동사원형

- Let's eat out tonight. (오늘 밤에는 외식하자.)
- Let's not [never] eat out tonight. (오늘 밤에는 외식하지 말자.)

> ❶ 제안문
>
> 제안문은 Shall we ~?, How[What] about ~?, Why don't we ~?와 같은 표현으로 바꿔쓸 수 있다.

3 감탄문 – 놀람이나 안타까움 등의 느낌을 표현하는 것으로,
how를 이용한 감탄문과 what을 이용한 감탄문이 있다.

	how를 이용한 감탄문	what을 이용한 감탄문
형태	How + 형용사[부사] + (주어 + 동사)!	What + a[an] + 형용사 + 명사(+ 주어 + 동사)!
쓰임	형용사나 부사 강조	명사 강조
예시	• This book is very interesting. → How interesting (this book is)! 형용사 (이 책은 정말 재미있구나!)	• This is a very wonderful world. → What a wonderful world (this is)! 형용사 + 명사 (얼마나 멋진 세상인가!)

03 DAY

1 + 2 명령문, 제안문

[01-07] 괄호 안에서 알맞은 것을 고르시오.

01 (Aren't / Don't) let them laugh at you.

02 Don't (be / let) her walk in the sun.

03 Tell me everything, (and / or) I will forgive you.

04 (Let / Let's) go to the theater to watch his new movie.

05 Don't eat a lot of meat, (and / or) you will be unhealthy.

06 How about (spend / spending) that money on our trip?

07 (Work / To work) hard to get good grades in the final exam.

3 감탄문

[08-12] 문장을 괄호 안의 지시대로 바꿔 쓰시오. (단, 주어와 동사를 생략하지 않을 것)

08 Usain Bolt runs very fast. (감탄문으로)

➡ _______________________________________

09 It is a very tall building. (감탄문으로)

➡ _______________________________________

10 What a difficult task it is! (평서문으로)

➡ _______________________________________

11 She has very good things in her house. (감탄문으로)

➡ _______________________________________

12 He takes care of his baby very carefully. (감탄문으로)

➡ _______________________________________

1 + 2 + 3 명령문, 제안문, 감탄문

[13-16] 주어진 우리말과 일치하도록 괄호 안의 말을 이용하여 문장을 완성하시오.

13 그녀는 참 좋은 가수구나! (good singer)

➡ What _________________________________!

14 안전벨트를 매라, 그렇지 않으면 너는 위험에 처할 것이다. (be in danger)

➡ Fasten your seatbelt, _______________________.

15 그에게 그 문제에 대해 조언을 구하자. (ask ~ for advice, about the problem)

➡ Let's _______________________________.

16 우리 잠시 쉬는 게 어때? (take a break, for a while)

➡ Why _______________________________?

어휘 & 표현
- **polite** 공손한
- **admit** 인정하다
- **mistake** 실수
- **eat out** 외식하다
- **laugh at** ~를 비웃다
- **forgive** 용서하다
- **spend** (시간이나 돈을) 들이다
- **task** 과제
- **fasten** 매다
- **seatbelt** 안전벨트
- **in danger** 위험에 직면해서
- **break** 쉬는 시간

〈 정답과 해설 p. 8~9 〉

 **UNIT 06** 평서문, 의문문 (부가의문문, 간접의문문) 

Tell me *why we should stretch* before exercising.
간접의문문

(운동 전에 왜 스트레칭을 해야 하는지 제게 말해 주세요.)

Stretching prevents injuries, *doesn't it?*
부가의문문

(스트레칭은 부상을 막아 줍니다, 그렇지 않나요?)

1 평서문 – 어떤 사실을 설명하는 문장으로, 「주어 + 동사」로 시작한다.

- I saw a shooting star while sitting on the porch.
주어 긍정 평서문(일반동사)

(나는 베란다에 앉아 있을 때 유성을 보았다.)

- He was not happy with his test results. (그는 시험 결과에 만족하지 않았다.)
주어 부정 평서문 (be동사)

- I don't❶ understand what you are talking about.
주어 부정 평서문 (일반동사)

(나는 네가 무슨 말을 하는지 이해하지 못하겠어.)

2 부가의문문 – 평서문 뒤에 붙는 의문문의 형태이다.

사실 여부를 확인하거나 상대방의 동의를 구할 때 쓴다.

(1) 일반 문장일 때

① 시제는 평서문의 시제와 동일하다.

② 주어는 주격 인칭대명사로 쓴다.

③ 부정형을 쓸 때 주로 축약형을 쓴다.❷

④ 평서문이 긍정일 때는 부정을, 부정일 때는 긍정을 쓴다.

＊부가의문문 만드는 법: 평서문 + 부가의문문?

평서문의 동사가	be동사일 때	평서문 + be동사 + 주어?
		• This cocoa is hot, isn't it? (이 코코아는 뜨거워요, 그렇지 않나요?)
	조동사일 때	평서문 + 조동사 + 주어?
		• Somin can speak English, can't she? (소민이는 영어를 할 수 있어요, 그렇지 않나요?)
	일반동사일 때	평서문 + do [does, did] + 주어?
		• The students didn't study yesterday, did they? (그 학생들은 어제 공부를 하지 않았어요, 그렇죠?)

(2) 명령문, 제안문일 때

① **명령문의 부가의문문** : 명령문 + will you?❸

- Close the window before you leave, will you?

(나가기 전에 창문 닫아, 알겠니?)

② **제안문의 부가의문문** : 제안문 + shall we?

- Let's take a break and get coffee, shall we? (우리 잠깐 쉬고 커피 마시자, 어때?)

---

❶ 부정 평서문 (일반동사) –

일반동사가 쓰인 부정 평서문은 동사 앞에 do not, does not, did not을 쓴다.

① 현재시제

- 3인칭 단수 주어(she, he, it) + **does not**

- 그 외 주어 + **do not**

② 과거시제

- 주어 + **did not**

❷ 부정형의 축약형

is not = isn't
are not = aren't
was not = wasn't
were not = weren't
do not = don't
does not = doesn't
did not = didn't

❸ 명령문의 부가의문문

긍정 명령문을 정중하게 권할 때는 부가의문문으로 won't you?를 쓰기도 한다.

- Wait here for a moment, won't you?

(여기서 잠깐만 기다려줘, 그래 줄래?)

03 DAY

1 평서문

[01-05] 괄호 안에서 알맞은 것을 고르시오.

01 (Missed I / I missed) the last train last night.

02 She (don't / doesn't) like crowded places at all.

03 They (planning / are planning) a trip to Jeju Island.

04 He didn't (answer / answered) any of my questions.

05 (My parents / My parents are) in the living room now.

2 부가의문문

[06-11] 빈칸에 알맞은 말을 〈보기〉에서 골라 부가의문문을 완성하시오. (중복 사용 불가)

〈보기〉
| can't | did | will | shall | doesn't | shouldn't |

06 She really enjoys spicy food, _______________ she?

07 They didn't go to school today, _______________ they?

08 Don't make so much noise tonight, _______________ you?

09 You can meet us at the station at 6, _______________ you?

10 Tom should apologize for being rude, _______________ he?

11 Let's go shopping after the movie ends, _______________ we?

1 + 2 평서문, 부가의문문

[12-15] 주어진 우리말과 일치하도록 괄호 안의 말을 바르게 배열하시오.

12 창문을 너무 많이 열지 마, 알겠니? (open, will, don't, too wide, the window, you)

➡ ____

13 너는 운동하기 위해 항상 오전 5시 전에 일어나지, 그렇지?

(wake up, you, to exercise, always, you, before 5 a.m., don't)

➡ ____

14 퀴즈 보기 전에 노트를 복습하자, 어때? (shall, we, our notes before the quiz, let's, review)

➡ ____

15 너는 내 핸드폰을 어디서도 본 적 없어, 그렇지? (you, seen, you, my phone anywhere, haven't, have)

➡ ____

🦉 어휘 & 표현
· **shooting star** 유성　· **porch** 베란다　· **crowded** 붐비는　· **spicy** 매운　· **noise** 소음　· **apologize** 사과하다
· **rude** 무례한　· **review** 복습하다

〈 정답과 해설 p. 9~10 〉

(3) 기타 문장일 때

① There is[are] ~로 시작하는 문장의 부가의문문 : There is[are] ~, 「is[are] (not) + there?」

　　• There is a problem with the computer, <u>isn't there</u>? (컴퓨터에는 문제가 있어, 그렇지 않아?)

② I am ~으로 시작하는 문장의 부가의문문 : I am ~, am I not 또는 aren't I?

　　• I'm supposed to be here early, <u>am I not[aren't I]</u>? (나 여기 일찍 와야 해, 그렇지 않니?)

3 간접의문문 – 의문문이 다른 문장의 일부가 될 때, 이를 간접의문문이라고 한다.

(1) 의문사가 없는 경우: 「if [whether] + 주어 + 동사 + ~」

　　• Do you know? + Has Rick been to Europe?
　　　　다른 문장의 일부(동사 know의 목적어)가 되는 의문문

　　→ Do you know if [whether] Rick has been to Europe?

　　　　　　　　(당신은 Rick이 유럽에 가 본 적이 있는지 알고 있나요?)

　　• Can you tell me? + Does the museum open today?
　　　　다른 문장의 일부(동사 can tell의 목적어)가 되는 의문문

　　→ Can you tell me if [whether] the museum opens today?

　　　　　　　　(당신은 오늘 박물관이 여는지 내게 말해주시겠어요?)

(2) 의문사가 있는 경우: 「의문사 + 주어 + 동사 + ~」

　　• Can you tell me? + How can I get to the bank?
　　　　다른 문장의 일부(동사 can tell의 목적어)가 되는 의문문

　　→ Can you tell me how I can get to the bank?

　　　　　　　　(당신은 은행에 어떻게 가는지 내게 말해주시겠어요?)

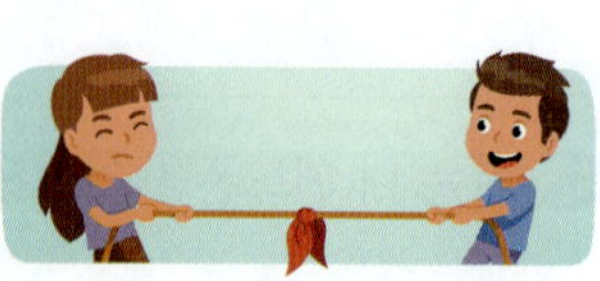

　　• Do you know? + What time does the meeting start?
　　　　다른 문장의 일부(동사 know의 목적어)가 되는 의문문

　　→ Do you know what time the meeting starts?

　　　　　　　　(당신은 회의가 몇 시에 시작하는지 아세요?)

　[주의] 의문사가 간접의문문의 주어로 쓰인 경우, 의문사=주어이므로 「의문사(= 주어) + 동사 + ~」 형태가 된다.

　　　• Do you know? + Who is coming to the party?
　　　　　다른 문장의 일부(동사 know의 목적어)가 되는 의문문

　　　→ Do you know who is coming to the party? (당신은 파티에 누가 오는지 아세요?)
　　　　　의문사 who = 간접의문문의 주어

(3) 의문사가 문장 앞으로 나오는 경우: think, believe, suppose, imagine 등에 의문사가 있는
　　　　　　　　　　　　　　　의문문이 연결될 때는 의문사가 문장의 맨 앞으로 나온다.

　　• Do you think? + Who will win?
　　　　다른 문장의 일부(동사 think의 목적어)가 되는 의문문

　　→ Who do you think will win? (너는 누가 이길 것이라고 생각하니?)
　　　　문장의 맨 앞으로 온 의문사

　　• Do you believe? + What is the best way to succeed?
　　　　다른 문장의 일부(동사 believe의 목적어)가 되는 의문문

　　→ What do you believe is the best way to succeed?
　　　　문장의 맨 앞으로 온 의문사
　　　　　　　　　　(너는 성공하는 가장 좋은 방법이 무엇이라고 믿니?)

03 DAY

2 부가의문문 (3) 기타 문장일 때

[16-18] 틀린 부분을 찾아 밑줄을 긋고 바르게 고치시오.

16 I am your close friend, amn't I? ➡ _______________________

17 There is a big tree in the middle of the square, aren't there? ➡ _______________________

18 There are new messages on your phone, is there? ➡ _______________________

3 간접의문문

[19-24] 문장을 간접의문문으로 바꿔 쓰시오.

19 I doubt. + Does he always tell the truth?

➡ _______________________

20 Do you think? + Who wrote this note?

➡ _______________________

21 I wonder. + Why can't he take part in the contest?

➡ _______________________

22 Do you imagine? + What does the blue bird look like?

➡ _______________________

23 Please tell me. + When did the thief break into the house?

➡ _______________________

24 Do you know? + Did a man donate one million dollars to the orphanage?

➡ _______________________

1 + **2** + **3** 평서문, 의문문 (부가의문문, 간접의문문)

[25-27] 주어진 우리말과 일치하도록 괄호 안의 말을 바르게 배열하시오.

25 영화는 8시에 시작하죠, 그렇지 않나요? (doesn't, at eight o'clock, starts, the movie, it)

➡ _______________________

26 나는 선생님이 시험지를 언제 돌려주실지 궁금하다.

(our test papers, when, the teacher, I, will return, wonder)

➡ _______________________

27 당신은 오늘 어느 팀이 가장 높은 점수를 받을 것이라고 생각하나요?

(will, think, you, the highest score today, do, which team, get)

➡ _______________________

🦉 어휘 & 표현

· **suppose** 가정하다　　· **square** 사각형, 광장　　· **doubt** 의심하다　　· **wonder** 궁금해하다　　· **take part in** ~에 참가하다
· **look like** ~같이 생기다　　· **thief** 강도　　· **break into** 침입하다　　· **donate** 기부하다　　· **orphanage** 고아원　　· **return** 돌려주다

〈 정답과 해설 p. 10~11 〉

[01-06]

빈칸에 알맞은 것을 고르시오.

01

> This cell phone was made in china, _________?

① was it

② did it

③ wasn't it

④ didn't it

⑤ hadn't it

02

> I wonder _________ he met his friend at the station.

① what

② whether

③ which

④ whose

⑤ who

03

> We should leave now, _________?

① aren't we

② don't we

③ haven't we

④ should we

⑤ shouldn't we

04

> You don't have any pets, _________?

① do you

② don't you

③ are you

④ aren't you

⑤ have you

05

> _________ go watch the horror movie together.

① Can

② Let's

③ Do you

④ Be

⑤ What

06

> Can you tell me _________?

① when starts the meeting

② the meeting starts when

③ when the meeting starts

④ the meeting when starts

⑤ when does the meeting start

[07-12] 서술형

틀린 부분을 찾아서 밑줄을 긋고 바르게 고쳐 쓰시오.

07

Koreans don't mind helping strangers, do we?

____

08

Can you tell me where is the post office?

____

09

Read the letter, or you'll know exactly how she feels.

____

10

How cute babies they are!

____

11

There was a big tree on the hill, wasn't it?

____

12

Please arrange the books alphabetically, do you? ________________

13 고난도

빈칸에 알맞지 <u>않은</u> 것을 고르시오.

> The man knows ________ she took the book out of the shelf.

① when　　② why　　③ how
④ what　　⑤ whether

[14-16] 서술형

문장을 괄호 안의 지시대로 바꿔 쓰시오.

14

I don't know. Where is he from?
(간접의문문으로)

➡ ________________________________

15

Your teacher is very strict. (how 감탄문으로)

➡ ________________________________

16

This rumor is very hard to believe.
(부가의문문을 추가하여)

➡ ________________________________

17

밑줄 친 부분 중 어법상 틀린 것을 고르시오.

① <u>How beautiful</u> the flowers are!
② Ron couldn't finish the job, <u>could he</u>?
③ <u>Never</u> give up on your plan so easily.
④ <u>What a great books</u> there are in the library!
⑤ <u>What about</u> going out for a walk after the meeting?

18

어법상 옳은 것을 고르시오.

① What intelligent he is!
② How clean this office is!
③ What a lovely girl is she!
④ What nice parents do you have!
⑤ How wonderful your house it is!

[19-23] 서술형

주어진 우리말과 일치하도록 빈칸에 알맞은 말을 쓰시오.

19

조용히 해, 그렇지 않으면 그가 우리를 찾아낼 거야.

➡ Be quiet, ________________ he will find us.

20

그가 무엇을 말할지 나는 확신하지 못한다.

➡ I am not sure ________________ he will say.

21

Jane은 책 읽는 것을 좋아해, 그렇지 않니?

➡ Jane likes to read books, ____________ she?

22

이 자료를 제출해, 그러면 처리가 빨리 될 거야.

➡ Submit this document, ________________ the process will go faster.

23 고난도

이번 주말에 할머니, 할아버지 뵈러 가는 게 어때?

➡ ________________________________ you visit your grandparents this weekend?

[24-25]

빈칸에 들어갈 말이 알맞게 짝지어진 것을 고르시오.

24

> • Bring me those boxes, ___(A)___ ?
> • Sean didn't do the dishes, ___(B)___ ?

　　　(A)　　　(B)　　　　(A)　　　(B)

① do you　 – is he　　② will you – did he
③ will you – was he　④ shall we – isn't he
⑤ shall we – does he

〈 정답과 해설 p. 11~12 〉

25

> • We were on time, ____(A)____ ?
> • You have never seen that movie, ____(B)____ ?

	(A)	(B)
①	was it	– have you
②	wasn't it	– don't you
③	wasn't it	– did you
④	weren't we	– haven't you
⑤	weren't we	– have you

26 고난도

주어진 대화에 관해 잘못 이야기한 학생을 고르시오.

> A: Let's go to the beach tomorrow and enjoy the sun.
> B: That sounds amazing! You will bring the sunscreen, will you?
> A: Of course! Don't forget to bring a towel, though.
> B: Thanks! What a fun day we're going to have tomorrow!

① 도아: Let's go to the beach ~.는 '~하자'를 뜻하는 제안문이야.

② 민우: 맞아. Shall we go to the beach ~?로 바꿔 쓸 수 있어.

③ 우영: will you는 상대방의 동의를 구할 때 쓰는 부가의문문인데, 여기서는 will이 잘못 쓰였어.

④ 은희: 맞아. 긍정 평서문이기 때문에 will you가 아닌 aren't you를 써야 해.

⑤ 연주: What a fun day ~는 감탄문으로, 여기서는 기대를 나타내고 있어.

[27-28] 서술형

다음 글을 읽고 물음에 답하시오.

> My friend Sujin came over to my house, and I asked ________ she would like to watch a movie. She enthusiastically responded, "Let's watch an action film!" I agreed, and we decided on an action movie. The movie was thrilling. Sujin shouted, "Wow! Wasn't it an amazing movie?"

27

빈칸에 알맞은 접속사 두 개를 쓰시오.

➡ ________________ , ________________

28

밑줄 친 부분을 What 감탄문으로 바꿔 쓰시오.

➡ What ________________________ it was!

29 수능 유형

밑줄 친 부분 중 어법상 틀린 것을 고르시오.

> This morning, I visited the bank to open a new account. A bank employee approached me and ① said, "You need any help, don't you?" I asked what ② did I need to open an account. She informed me that I would need to provide identification and proof of address. She then helped me ③ complete some paperwork. Within ④ a few minutes, my account was successfully established. "Wow, ⑤ how fast it was!" I exclaimed.

① ② ③ ④ ⑤

🦉 어휘 & 표현

· **mind** 언짢아하다　· **exactly** 정확하게　· **arrange** 배열하다　· **alphabetically** 알파벳순으로　· **strict** 엄격한
· **give up** 포기하다　· **go out for a walk** 산책하다　· **intelligent** 지능적인　· **process** 과정, 처리
· **sunscreen** 자외선 차단제　· **enthusiastically** 열광적으로　· **thrilling** 황홀한　· **account** 계좌　· **employee** 직원
· **inform** 알려주다　· **exclaim** 감탄하다

명사, 관사

名詞	冠詞
(이름 **명**, 말 **사**)	(갓 **관**, 말 **사**)
사람이나 사물의 이름을 나타내는 말	명사 앞에 놓이는 '갓'과 같은 말

We brought three cookies and two cups of coffee.
셀 수 있는 명사의 복수형　　　셀 수 없는 명사의 복수형

(우리는 쿠키 세 개와 커피 두 잔을 가져왔다.)

The teacher's books are on the shelf. (그 선생님의 책들이 선반 위에 있다.)
명사의 소유격

She put a letter in the mailbox. (그녀는 편지 한 통을 우체통에 넣었다.)
부정관사　　　정관사

 **UNIT 07** 셀 수 있는 명사의 복수형 

- **명사:** 사람, 사물, 장소, 동물 또는 개념 등을 나타내는 말로, 문장에서는 주어, 목적어, 보어의 역할을 한다.
- **명사의 복수형:** 두 개 이상의 명사를 나타내기 위해 사용하며, 명사 뒤에 -s, -es, -ies, -ves 등을 붙인다.

1 셀 수 있는 명사

보통명사	- 사람, 사물, 동물 등을 나타내며 복수 형태를 만들 수 있다. - engineer, passenger, instrument, vehicle, ox, ape 등
	• A passenger left a bottle on the train. (한 승객이 기차에 병을 두고 내렸다.)
집합명사 (단수, 복수 모두 취급)	- 여러 개체나 사람, 동물 등이 모여 하나의 단위를 이루는 명사이다. - 단수 (하나의 집합체로 볼 때), 복수 (개개의 구성원으로 볼 때) - family, team, group, class, audience, crowd, panel 등
	• The committee is discussing the new policy. (위원회는 새로운 정책을 논의하고 있다.) • The committees are meeting at different times today. (위원회들은 오늘 각기 다른 시간에 모일 예정이다.)
집합명사 (복수로만 취급)	- 항상 복수 취급한다. - cattle, people, police, clergy 등
	• The clergy were dressed in traditional robes. (성직자들은 전통적인 의복을 입고 있었다.)

2 셀 수 있는 명사의 복수형

(1) 규칙 변화

대부분의 명사	+ -s	chair → chairs, flower → flowers, house → houses • She has two houses. (그녀는 두 채의 집이 있다.)
-s, -x, -ch, -sh로 끝나는 명사	+ -es	class → classes, fox → foxes, match → matches • There are some foxes. (여우 몇 마리가 있다.)
-o로 끝나는 명사	+ -s + -es	zoo → zoos, piano → pianos, hero → heroes • Many zoos are closed. (많은 동물원이 문을 닫는다.)
「자음 + y」로 끝나는 명사	y를 i로 고치고 + -es	country → countries, duty → duties, party → parties • I visited six countries. (나는 여섯 국가를 방문했다.)
-f, -fe로 끝나는 명사	f, fe를 v로 고치고 + -es	shelf → shelves, life → lives, knife → knives • Two knives are left. (칼 두 개가 남아 있다.)

(2) 불규칙 변화

불규칙 명사	analysis → analyses, cactus → cacti, child → children, criterion → criteria, foot → feet, goose → geese, woman → women, mouse → mice, tooth → teeth
단수형과 복수형이 같은 명사	deer, fish, moose, salmon, series, sheep, species

• A deer is standing by the water. (사슴 한 마리가 물가에 서 있다.)

• Deer are commonly seen this time of year. (사슴들은 일 년 중 이맘때 흔히 보인다.)

04 DAY

1 셀 수 있는 명사

[01-04] 밑줄 친 명사의 종류를 고르시오.

01 The <u>class</u> was very noisy today. ➡ [보통명사 / 집합명사]

02 The crowd was excited about the <u>concert</u>. ➡ [보통명사 / 집합명사]

03 The team is practicing for the final <u>match</u>. ➡ [보통명사 / 집합명사]

04 The <u>cattle</u> were grazing peacefully in the field. ➡ [보통명사 / 집합명사]

2 셀 수 있는 명사의 복수형

[05-20] 주어진 명사의 복수형을 쓰시오.

05 thief ➡ __________

06 church ➡ __________

07 life ➡ __________

08 gallery ➡ __________

09 boss ➡ __________

10 volcano ➡ __________

11 echo ➡ __________

12 wheel ➡ __________

13 woman ➡ __________

14 species ➡ __________

15 analysis ➡ __________

16 tooth ➡ __________

17 crisis ➡ __________

18 sheep ➡ __________

19 cactus ➡ __________

20 criterion ➡ __________

[21-28] 괄호 안에서 알맞은 것을 고르시오.

21 We saw several (car / cars) on the street.

22 The police (is / are) investigating the crime.

23 There are several (cattle / cattles) on the farm.

24 The clergy (is / are) opposed to the new law.

25 The (lady / ladies) are having coffee in the garden.

26 She bought many (book / books) from the bookstore.

27 The designer (is / are) working hard to complete the project.

28 The people (is / are) planning a surprise party for her birthday.

[29-32] 밑줄 친 부분이 맞으면 ○로 표시하고, 틀리면 바르게 고치시오.

29 Bring those <u>box</u> to the front gate before they arrive. ➡ __________

30 He bought several <u>sandwich</u> for the picnic last weekend. ➡ __________

31 Her <u>shelves</u> are filled with old novels and photo albums. ➡ __________

32 We've received three different <u>diagnosis</u> from the hospital so far. ➡ __________

> 🦉 **어휘 & 표현**
> · **instrument** 기구
> · **ape** 유인원
> · **committee** 위원회
> · **cattle** (집합적으로) 소
> · **clergy** 성직자
> · **cactus** 선인장
> · **criterion** 기준
> · **species** 종(種)
> · **commonly** 흔히
> · **investigate** 조사하다
> · **oppose to** ~에 반대하다
> · **diagnosis** 진단

〈 정답과 해설 p. 13~14 〉

(3) 셀 수 있는 명사 중 주의해야 할 복수형

① 항상 복수로 쓰는 명사 – gloves, pants, scissors, socks, trousers 등

- My antique scissors are displayed in a glass case. (나의 골동품 가위는 유리 전시장에 진열되어 있다.)

② 복수 형태지만 단수 취급하는 명사 – 일부 과목명, 질병 이름, 국가명

- Economics is my favorite subject. (경제학은 내가 가장 좋아하는 과목이다.)
- Diabetes demands care. (당뇨병은 관리가 필요하다.)
- The Philippines is a country in Asia. (필리핀은 아시아에 있는 나라이다.)

❶ 한 쌍을 이루는 명사의 수량 표현

단위명사인 pair를 이용하여, 한 쌍을 이루는 명사의 수량을 표현할 수 있다.
- I need two pairs of gloves. (난 장갑 두 켤레가 필요해.)

③ 복수 형태가 될 때 뜻이 달라지는 명사

단수형	good (좋음)	wood (목재)	cloth (천)	custom (관습)	manner (방법)	work (일)
복수형	goods (상품)	woods (숲)	clothes (옷)	customs (세관)	manners (예절)	works (작품)

UNIT 08 셀 수 없는 명사의 복수형

I want **two bottles of** water. (나는 물 두 병을 원해.)
셀 수 없는 명사의 수량 표현

I only have **one cup of** water. (나에게는 물 한 컵만 있어.)
셀 수 없는 명사의 수량 표현

1 셀 수 없는 명사

물질명사	– 재료나 물질 자체를 나타내는 명사이다. – water, air, sand, gold, money, salt, oil, coffee, milk, bread 등
	• We need to buy some flour for the cake. (케이크를 만들기 위해 밀가루를 좀 사야 한다.)
추상명사	– 형태나 존재가 없는 개념, 상태, 감정, 특성, 질 등을 나타내는 명사이다. – love, happiness, freedom, courage, justice, knowledge, peace 등
	• The courage of the firefighters saves many lives. (소방관들의 용기가 많은 생명을 구한다.)
고유명사	– 특정한 사람, 장소, 사물, 기관, 월, 요일 등을 나타내는 명사로, 항상 대문자로 시작한다. – John, Paris, Samsung, Apple, Korea, Beethoven, NASA 등
	• NASA plans to launch a new satellite. (NASA는 새로운 위성을 발사하려고 계획한다.)
집합명사	– 여러 개의 개체가 모여 하나의 집합이나 단체를 형성할 때 사용되는 명사이다. – equipment, clothing, furniture, machinery, jewelry 등
	• Your furniture is exactly what we need. (당신의 가구는 우리가 딱 필요로 하는 것이다.)

04 DAY

2 셀 수 있는 명사의 복수형 (3) 셀 수 있는 명사 중 주의해야 할 복수형

[33-37] 괄호 안에서 알맞은 것을 고르시오.

33 Let's buy some (cloth / clothes) for the costume party this weekend.

34 Did he go into the (wood / woods) to gather firewood for the winter?

35 China became the largest luxury (good / goods) market in the world.

36 The (custom / customs) of giving chocolate on Valentine's Day was first promoted in Japan.

37 She told me that it is bad (manner / manners) to have my elbows on the table during a meal.

1 셀 수 없는 명사

[01-04] 〈보기〉의 명사를 종류에 따라 분류하시오. (중복 사용 불가)

〈보기〉
clothing, water, ambition, Paris, air, courage,
New York, sugar, Amazon, freedom, milk, Seoul, jewelry,
salt, London, furniture, happiness, wisdom, machinery

01 물질명사 ➡ ___________, ___________, ___________, ___________, ___________

02 추상명사 ➡ ___________, ___________, ___________, ___________, ___________

03 고유명사 ➡ ___________, ___________, ___________, ___________, ___________

04 집합명사 ➡ ___________, ___________, ___________, ___________

[05-12] 밑줄 친 부분이 맞으면 ○로 표시하고, 틀리면 바르게 고치시오.

05 We are traveling to <u>Jeju Island</u> next weekend. ➡ ___________

06 The chair is made of <u>iron</u>, so it is very heavy. ➡ ___________

07 The factory uses <u>a new machinery</u> for production. ➡ ___________

08 <u>A kindness</u> makes the world a better place to live. ➡ ___________

09 December is usually a very cold month in <u>a Korea</u>. ➡ ___________

10 She poured some <u>milks</u> into the glass for her brother. ➡ ___________

11 Success <u>require</u> hard work, patience, and determination. ➡ ___________

12 The living room has modern and comfortable <u>furnitures</u>. ➡ ___________

🦉 어휘 & 표현

· **economics** 경제학   · **diabetes** 당뇨병   · **launch** 발사하다   · **satellite** 위성   · **machinery** 기계
· **gather** 모이다, 모으다   · **firewood** 장작   · **promote** 홍보하다   · **elbow** 팔꿈치   · **ambition** 야망
· **determination** 결단력   · **comfortable** 편안한

2 셀 수 없는 명사의 복수형 ❶

– 측정 단위나 담는 용기, 모양 등을 이용하여 「수 + 단위명사 + of + 셀 수 없는 명사」의 어순으로 나타낸다.

단위명사	의미	예시
bottle bottles	병	a bottle of **beer** (맥주 한 병), two bottles of **wine** (와인 두 병), several bottles of **hot sauce** (매운 소스 여러 병)
cup cups	컵 (잔)	a cup of **coffee** (커피 한 잔), two cups of **milk** (우유 두 컵), several cups of **tea** (차 여러 잔)
glass glasses	잔	a glass of **milk** (우유 한 잔), two glasses of **juice** (주스 두 잔), several glasses of **water** (물 여러 잔)
jar jars	병	a jar of **honey** (꿀 한 병), two jars of **jam** (잼 두 병), several jars of **tomato sauce** (토마토소스 여러 병)
loaf loaves	덩어리	a loaf of **bread** (빵 한 덩어리), two loaves of **dough** (반죽 두 덩어리), several loaves of **cheese** (치즈 여러 덩어리)
bar bars	막대	a bar of **gold** (금 막대 하나), two bars of **soap** (비누 바 두 개), several bars of **chocolate** (초콜릿 바 여러 개)
bowl bowls	그릇	a bowl of **rice** (쌀 한 그릇), two bowls of **noodle** (국수 두 그릇), several bowls of **cereal** (시리얼 여러 그릇)
sheet sheets	장	a sheet of **paper** (종이 한 장), two sheets of **fabric** (천 두 장), several sheets of **cotton** (면 여러 장)
slice ❷ slices	조각	a slice of **pizza** (피자 한 조각), two slices of **bacon** (베이컨 두 조각), several slices of **pie** (파이 여러 조각)
piece ❷ pieces	조각	a piece of **advice** (충고 하나), two pieces of **furniture** (가구 두 점), several pieces of **cake** (케이크 여러 조각)
bunch bunches	다발	a bunch of **parsley** (파슬리 한 다발), two bunches of **balloons** ❸ (풍선 두 다발), several bunches of **flowers** ❸ (꽃 여러 다발)
spoonful spoonfuls	스푼	a spoonful of **sugar** (설탕 한 스푼), two spoonfuls of **flour** (밀가루 두 스푼), several spoonfuls of **butter** (버터 여러 스푼)
pound pounds	파운드	a pound of **chicken breast** (닭가슴살 1파운드), two pounds of **cheese** (치즈 2파운드), several pounds of **mud** (진흙 여러 파운드)

❶ 셀 수 없는 명사의 양을 나타내는 표현

(1) 적은
- (a) little

(2) 많은
- much
- lots[a lot] of
- plenty of
- a great[good] deal of
- a huge amount of
- an enormous amount of

(3) 조금, 몇몇
- some

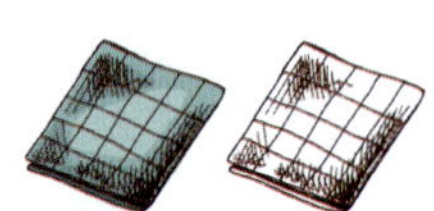

❷ slice vs. piece
- **slice**: 얇게 썬 조각
- **piece**: 모양과 상관없는 한 부분

❸ 셀 수 있는 명사와 쓰이는 단위명사

bunch, stack, pile 등의 단위명사는 셀 수 있는 명사와 함께 쓰일 수 있다.
- a bunch of sticks (한 다발의 막대)
- two stacks of diaries (두 무더기의 일기들)
- three piles of applications (세 더미의 지원서들)

- Mom bought two loaves of bread for breakfast. (엄마는 아침을 위해 빵 두 덩이를 샀다.)
- He gave her a bunch of flowers for the proposal. (그는 그녀에게 프로포즈로 꽃다발을 주었다.)

참고 음식이나 음료 이름은 주로 셀 수 없는 명사로 a cup of 등의 단위명사를 붙여 수량을 나타내지만,
음식을 주문하는 내용의 대화에서는 a[one], two, three 등을 붙여 쓴다.
A: Are you ready to order? (주문하시겠어요?)
B: Sure. I'd like an orange juice, please. (네. 오렌지 주스 한 잔 주세요.)

2 셀 수 없는 명사의 복수형

[13-19] 문장에서 틀린 부분을 찾아 밑줄을 긋고 바르게 고치시오.

13 She bought two loafs of beef to make steak. _______________

14 She devotes a plenty of time to her makeup. _______________

15 I need several slice of cheese to make sandwiches. _______________

16 Can you go to the supermarket and buy bottle of salt? _______________

17 Add a spoonful of soy sauces and boil for 10 minutes. _______________

18 A little boy messed up the room cutting lots of paper with a scissors. _______________

19 There are lots of people who are willing to spend good deals of money on a space trip.

____

[20-25] 괄호 안에서 알맞은 것을 고르시오.

20 What a lovely (bunch / bunches) of tulips you brought me!

21 Please pull out (a / two) sheet of torn paper from the printer.

22 How many pounds of (meat / meats) did you buy at the market?

23 You need to open two (jar / jars) of strawberry jam before breakfast.

24 She served (a / three) bowls of spicy noodle soup and offered us some tea.

25 I found a (bar / bars) of chocolate in the back of the fridge. Who put it there?

[26-29] 주어진 우리말과 일치하도록 괄호 안의 말을 바르게 배열하시오.

26 우리는 그들을 먹일 많은 빵과 우유가 필요하다.
(a great deal of, them, need, and milk, feed, we, to, bread)

➡ ____

27 한 상자에는 여섯 개의 비누가 있다. (a box, are, soap, six, in, there, bars of)

➡ ____

28 아보카도 버거 세 개, 밀크셰이크 하나, 콜라 두 잔 주세요.
(colas, three, and, milkshake, two, a, avocado hamburgers)

➡ _______________________________________, please.

29 저는 후식으로 커피 한 잔과 치즈케이크 하나를 먹을게요.
(like, and a cheesecake, I'd, a coffee)

➡ _______________________________ for dessert.

🦉 어휘 & 표현

· **proposal** 제안, 청혼 · **devote** 바치다 · **makeup** 화장 · **soy sauce** 간장 · **mess up** 엉망으로 만들다
· **be willing to** 기꺼이 ~하다 · **torn paper** 찢어진 종이 · **serve** 대접하다 · **offer** 내놓다, 제공하다 · **fridge** 냉장고
· **feed** 먹이다

〈 정답과 해설 p. 15~16 〉

UNIT 09 명사의 소유격

> **핵심 개념**
> • **명사의 소유격:** '(명사)의'라는 뜻으로, 명사가 무언가를 가지고 있음을 뜻한다.

1 아포스트로피(')를 붙이는 경우 – 사람이나 동물을 나타내는 명사

단수 명사	+ 's	cat's tail (고양이의 꼬리), dog's nose (개의 코), elephant's trunk (코끼리의 코), Ryan's hand (Ryan의 손), actor's name (배우의 이름)
		• The elephant's trunk is also used to drink water. (코끼리의 코는 물을 마시는 데에도 사용된다.)
		• Do you know the actor's name in the movie? (너는 그 영화에서 배우의 이름을 알아?)
-s로 끝나는 복수 명사	+ '	birds' song (새들의 노래), cats' owner (고양이들의 주인), ladies' room (여자 화장실), students' book (학생들의 책), teachers' room (교무실)
		• I met the cats' owner at the park yesterday. (어제 공원에서 그 고양이들의 주인을 만났다.)
		• The writers' novels were adapted into successful movies. (그 작가들의 소설들은 성공적인 영화들로 각색되었다.)
-s로 끝나지 않는 복수 명사	+ 's	children's hat (아이들의 모자), men's fashion (남성 패션), women's university (여대), people's idea (사람들의 생각), geese's feather (거위들의 깃털)
		• Men's fashion is focusing on comfort as well as style. (남성 패션은 스타일뿐만 아니라 편안함에도 집중하고 있다.)
		• The pillow is filled with geese's feathers. (그 베개는 거위의 깃털로 채워져 있다.)

2 아포스트로피(')를 붙이지 않는 경우 – 무생물 명사

of + 무생물 명사 ❶	end of a hall (복도의 끝), top of a hill (언덕의 꼭대기), cover of a book (책의 표지), size of a box (상자의 크기), title of the play (연극의 제목)
	• The roof of the house needs repairing after the storm. (그 집의 지붕은 폭풍 후에 수리가 필요하다.)
	• The knob of the door is broken. (그 문의 손잡이가 부러졌다.)

> **❶ 시간을 나타내는 명사**
> 시간을 나타내는 명사는 무생물 명사이지만 's를 이용하여 소유격을 나타낸다.
> • Last week's weather was warm.
> (지난주의 날씨는 따뜻했다.)

3 생략 가능한 경우 – 반복해서 나오는 경우, 소유격 뒤에 오는 명사는 생략 가능

• The toys scattered around are my children's (toys).
(흩어져 있는 장난감들은 내 아이들의 것이다.)

• The cookies on the table are my grandmother's (cookies).
(테이블 위에 있는 쿠키는 내 할머니의 것이다.)

1 아포스트로피(')를 붙이는 경우

[01-06] 괄호 안의 단어의 소유격을 빈칸에 쓰시오.

01 The _______________ (doctors) conference is next week.

02 The _______________ (teachers) meeting was postponed.

03 The _______________ (team) performance was outstanding.

04 The _______________ (company) policy changed recently.

05 The _______________ (professor) lecture was very informative.

06 The _______________ (children) laughter echoed through the hall.

1 + 2 아포스트로피(')를 붙이는 경우와 붙이지 않는 경우

[07-12] 문장에서 <u>틀린</u> 부분을 찾아 밑줄을 긋고, 바르게 고치시오.

07 The edges' the roof are about to collapse.　　➡ _______________

08 The parents's advice was incredibly helpful.　　➡ _______________

09 The athletes uniforms are in the locker room.　　➡ _______________

10 The girls of dresses are hanging in the closet.　　➡ _______________

11 The pages' the book have started to turn yellow.　　➡ _______________

12 The color's the leather boots is too bright for me.　　➡ _______________

1 + 2 + 3 명사의 소유격

[13-17] 주어진 우리말과 일치하도록 괄호 안의 단어를 이용하여 빈칸에 알맞은 말을 쓰시오.

13 그 소년들의 자전거가 밖에 주차되어 있다. (the boys, bicycles)

➡ _______________________________ are parked outside.

14 여행자들의 짐이 컨베이어 벨트 위로 던져졌다. (the travelers, luggage)

➡ _______________________________ was thrown on the conveyor belt.

15 그 제품의 가격은 최근에 급증했다. (the product, the price)

➡ _______________________________ has soared recently.

16 모두가 수영장의 시설에 대해 좋은 댓글을 남겼다. (the pool, the facility)

➡ Everyone left good comments about _______________________________.

17 Gilbert의 계획은 이사회에서 승인되었지만, Eric의 계획은 그렇지 않았다. (Eric)

➡ Gilbert's plan was approved by the board, but _______________ wasn't.

🦉 **어휘 & 표현**

- **adapt** 적응하다, 각색하다　　- **comfort** 편안함　　- **scatter** (흩)뿌리다　　- **conference** 회의　　- **postpone** 미루다
- **outstanding** 눈에 띄는　　- **recently** 최근에　　- **informative** 유익한　　- **collapse** 붕괴하다　　- **incredibly** 믿을 수 없게
- **athlete** 운동선수　　- **soar** 급증하다　　- **facility** 시설　　- **board** 이사회

〈 정답과 해설 p. 16 〉

[01-02]

빈칸에 알맞지 <u>않은</u> 것을 고르시오.

01

> Having a pet gives you _________ pleasure.

① much
② lots of
③ plenty of
④ a great many
⑤ a huge amount of

02

> Nick threw away a pair of unused _________.

① shoes
② glass
③ socks
④ gloves
⑤ chopsticks

[03-08]

괄호 안에서 알맞은 것을 고르시오.

03

I have to get some information on the life and (work / works) of Michelangelo.

04

(The fish' fins / The fish's fins) help it swim efficiently.

05

There are (many / much) errors on papers.

06

(The oxen's yokes / The oxen' yokes) are stored in the barn.

07

Long ago, people believed there lived evil things in the (wood / woods).

08

The (kids' / kids's) jokes kept everyone laughing for hours.

09

빈칸에 들어갈 말이 알맞게 짝지어진 것을 고르시오.

> • Carrie said hello in a friendly _________.
> • The shop carries leather _________ such as shoes and bags.
> • When you arrive in the UK, you'll have to go through _________.

① manner   − goods   − custom
② manner   − good   − customs
③ manners   − good   − custom
④ manner   − goods   − customs
⑤ manners   − goods   − customs

[10-14] (서술형)

〈보기〉와 같이 주어진 단어를 이용하여 빈칸에 알맞은 말을 쓰시오.

> ───〈보기〉───
> We need <u>three cups of</u> coffee. (three, cup)

10

I went to the supermarket and bought _________________ cereal. (three, box)

11

Can you give me _________________ information on it? (several, piece)

12

He likes chocolate, so he eats _________ chocolate every day. (five, bar)

13

I put _________________ ham on my sandwich. (two, slice)

14

She likes to wear jeans. She has _________ _________ jeans now. (ten, pair)

[15-17] 서술형

주어진 우리말과 일치하도록 괄호 안의 어구를 이용하여 빈칸에 알맞은 말을 쓰시오.

15

남자들의 재킷이 옷장에 걸려 있다.

(jackets, the men)

➡ _________________________ are hung in the closet.

16

쥐들의 보금자리가 다락방에서 발견되었다.

(the mice, nests)

➡ _________________________ were found in the attic.

17 고난도

거위들의 이동이 올해는 더 일찍 일어나고 있다.

(migration, the geese)

➡ _________________________ is happening earlier this year.

[18-20] 서술형

주어진 우리말과 일치하도록 괄호 안의 말을 바르게 배열하시오.

18

집을 고치는 데는 엄청난 비용이 든다.

(huge, to fix, money, costs, a, it, house, amount of, the)

➡ _________________________

19

그는 빵 한 덩어리로 굶주림을 달랬다.

(eased, a loaf of, hunger, bread, he, with, his)

➡ _________________________

20

그들은 우유 두 잔과 치즈샌드위치 두 개를 주문했다.

(glasses, two, sandwiches, two, of, milk, and, cheese)

➡ They ordered _________________________

_________________________.

[21-22]

다음 글을 읽고 물음에 답하시오.

> One morning, a group of people set off on an adventure into the deep ① woods. As they ventured through the forest, they encountered a family of ② mouses scurrying under the (A) leaf. The wolves were howling in the distance, and the ③ deer were grazing peacefully by the river. Suddenly, a group of birds flapped their wings and sang in harmony. The men in the group decided to climb higher to get a better view, while the ④ women stayed below, watching a (B) fox play by the ⑤ bushes.
>
> *scurry 총총 가다

21 수능 유형

밑줄 친 부분 중 어법상 틀린 것을 고르시오.

①   ②   ③   ④   ⑤

22

(A)와 (B)의 복수형이 알맞게 짝지어진 것을 고르시오.

	(A)	(B)		(A)	(B)
①	leaf	– fox	②	leafs	– foxs
③	leaves	– foxs	④	leaves	– foxes
⑤	leafs	– foxes			

🦉 어휘 & 표현

- **fin** 지느러미 ・ **yoke** 멍에 ・ **store** 보관하다 ・ **barn** 곳간, 헛간 ・ **evil** 악마 ・ **go through** 통과하다
- **migration** 이주, 이동 ・ **cost** 비용이 들다 ・ **ease** 완화하다, 덜어주다 ・ **hunger** 굶주림 ・ **set off** 출발하다
- **venture** (위험을 무릅쓰고) 가다 ・ **encounter** 마주하다 ・ **howl** 울부짖다 ・ **graze** 풀을 뜯다 ・ **flap** (날개를) 파닥거리다

 **UNIT 10** 부정관사(a, an)와 정관사(the) 

❶ 관사의 뜻과 종류

(1) **관사**: 명사 앞에 위치하며, 명사를 한정해 주는 말이다. 부정관사와 정관사가 있다.

(2) **부정관사 (a, an)**: 수식하는 명사가 일반적인 명사임을 나타낸다.
　　　　　　　　　새로운 정보를 제시하거나 특정하지 않은 대상을 언급할 때 쓴다.

(3) **정관사 (the)**: 수식하는 명사가 특정한 명사임을 나타낸다.
　　　　　　　　대화하는 사람(글을 읽는 사람)이 그 명사가 가리키는 특정 대상을 언급할 때 쓴다.

❷ 부정관사 a, an의 쓰임 ❶

(1) **정해지지 않은 막연한 것 (certain), 얼마간의 (some)**

　　• I want to purchase a new computer. (나는 새 컴퓨터를 구입하고 싶다.)
　　　　　　　　　　　 = certain

　　• Let's watch a movie tonight. (오늘 밤에 영화 보자.)
　　　　　　　　　 = some

(2) **하나 (one), ~당, ~마다 (per), 같은 (the same)**

　　• I saw a bird on the tree. (나는 나무 위에 새 한 마리를 봤다.)
　　　　　　 = one

　　• They're two of a kind, and they call each other twice a day.
　　　　　　　　　 = the same　　　　　　　　　　　　　　　　 = per
　　　　　　　　　　　　　(그들 둘은 아주 비슷하고, 하루에 두 번씩 서로 전화한다.)

(3) **직업, 신분, 국적 앞**

　　• We met a Canadian who is an English literature teacher. (우리는 영문학 선생님인 캐나다인을 만났다.)
　　　　　　　 국적 앞　　　　　　　　　　 직업, 신분

(4) **종족 전체 ❷**

　　• An elephant is the largest land animal. (코끼리는 가장 큰 육상 동물이다.)
　　　 종족 전체

❸ 정관사 the의 쓰임

(1) **정해진 것**

　　• The dog barked fiercely. (그 개가 사납게 짖었다.)
　　　 정해진 것

(2) **이미 언급된 명사를 다시 언급, 서로 알고 있는 것**

　　• He dropped by the store to buy some bread. (그는 빵을 사러 그 가게에 들렀다.)
　　　　　　　　　 서로 알고 있는 것

(3) **최상급, 서수, next, same, only 앞**

　　• She is the best player on the team. (그녀는 팀에서 가장 뛰어난 선수이다.)
　　　　　　 최상급

　　• The first chapter was exciting, but the next one was even better.
　　　 서수 앞　　　　　　　　　　　　　 next 앞
　　　　　　　　　　　　　(첫 번째 장은 흥미로웠지만, 다음 장은 훨씬 더 좋았다.)

　　• That was the only time we had the same idea. (그건 우리가 같은 생각을 했던 유일한 순간이었다.)
　　　　　　　 only 앞　　　　　　　 same 앞

(4) **유일한 것, 종족 전체**

　　• The sun rises in the east and sets in the west. (태양은 동쪽에서 뜨고 서쪽에서 진다.)
　　　 유일한 것

　　• The dolphin is very intelligent. (돌고래는 매우 지능이 높다.)
　　　 종족 전체

(5) **악기 이름, 사람을 지칭하는 형용사 앞**

　　• The elderly find comfort in the sound of the piano. (노인들은 피아노 소리에서 위안을 찾는다.)
　　　 사람을 지칭하는 형용사 앞　　　　　　　　　　　　　 악기 이름 앞

---

❶ a, an 구분

a+자음	an+모음
첫 소리가 자음	첫 소리가 모음
• a door　a boy	• an egg　an apple
철자가 모음이지만 발음이 자음	철자가 자음이지만 발음이 모음
• a uniform　a university	• an hour　an honor

❷ 부정관사와 정관사 둘 다 가능한 경우

종족 전체를 나타낼 때는 부정관사 a, an과 정관사 the를 모두 쓸 수 있다.

1 + 2 부정관사 a, an의 쓰임

[01-06] 빈칸에 부정관사 a나 an을 쓰시오.

01 I go hiking with my father once _____________ week.

02 Excuse me, but where can I find _____________ bus stop?

03 Step back from the painting. It looks better at _____________ distance.

04 Emily and I are of _____________ age, so we became very good friends quite quickly.

05 He broke his glasses on purpose because he wanted _____________ pair of new ones.

06 _____________ rose, which blooms between May and June, is called the queen of all the flowers.

3 정관사 the의 쓰임

[07-13] 괄호 안에서 알맞은 것을 고르시오.

07 (An / The) lion is known as the king of the jungle.

08 How beautiful! Look at the shining stars in (a / the) sky.

09 The fact is that (a / the) Moon goes around (a / the) Earth.

10 I met (a / the) man at the library. (A / The) man was a famous writer.

11 (A / The) tea in the cup is so hot that I burned (a / the) roof of my mouth.

12 I can't concentrate on my study. Can you turn off (a / the) radio, please?

13 (A / An) chimpanzee is known as (a / the) smartest animal, having almost (a / the) same intelligence as human beings.

1 + 2 + 3 부정관사(a, an)와 정관사(the)

[14-18] 문장에서 틀린 부분을 찾아 밑줄을 긋고 바르게 고치시오.

14 We want to create jobs for an unemployed. _____________

15 He stayed at an expensive hotel, but he doesn't remember a name. _____________

16 Are you acquainted with an area? Where is the best restaurant near it? _____________

17 I try to drink more than eight glasses of water the day, but it is quite difficult.

____

18 I've known hundreds of musicians, but he is a greatest musician that I've ever met.

____

〈 정답과 해설 p. 18 〉

They go to *church* on Sundays. (그들은 일요일마다 교회에 간다.)
교회 본래의 목적으로 쓰일 때는 관사를 쓰지 않음

We visited *the* famous old *church*.
교회의 본래 목적이 아닐 때는 관사를 씀
(우리는 유명한 오래된 교회를 방문했다.)

1 주의해야 할 관사의 위치

(1) all, both, half, double 등 + 관사 + 명사
- Both the shirts are on sale. (두 셔츠가 모두 세일 중이다.)
- She gave her brother half the chocolate. (그녀는 남동생에게 초콜릿 절반을 주었다.)

(2) so, too + 형용사 + 부정관사 + 명사
- It's too complicated a problem to solve in one day. (하루 만에 해결하기에 이것은 너무 복잡한 문제이다.)

(3) what, such, quite + 부정관사 (+형용사) + 명사
- It's quite a long journey to get there. (그곳에 가는 것은 꽤 긴 여행이다.)

2 관사를 쓰지 않는 경우

구분	예
과목명, 월, 계절 ❶	mathematics (수학), science (과학), January (1월), spring (봄) • She studied biology in university. (그녀는 대학에서 생물학을 공부했다.)
운동 경기	badminton (배드민턴), baseball (야구), basketball (농구) • Jogging is a great exercise. (조깅은 좋은 운동이다.)
식사	breakfast (아침), lunch (점심), dinner (저녁) • I had lunch at home. (나는 집에서 점심을 먹었다.)
가족 구성원	mother (엄마), nephew (남자 조카), niece (여자 조카), son (아들) • I planned a party for Dad. (나는 아빠를 위한 파티를 계획했다.)
관직, 신분	Ambassador (대사), CEO (대표이사), Doctor (박사) • Professor Lee writes important papers. (이 교수는 중요한 논문을 쓴다.)
국가, 도시, 사람 ❷	South Korea (대한민국), Paris (파리), Max • Noah will go to Switzerland. (Noah는 스위스에 갈 것이다.)
by + ┌ 교통 수단 └ 통신 수단	by boat (배로), by bus (버스로), by email (이메일로) • She prefers to travel by airplane rather than by train. (그녀는 기차보다는 비행기를 타고 여행하는 것을 선호한다.)
본래 목적으로 쓰이는 시설물, 사물 ❸	go to church ((예배 보러) 교회에 가다), go to bed (잠자리에 들다) • I go to school by bus. (나는 버스를 타고 학교에 간다.)
관용적인 표현	listen to music (음악을 듣다), watch TV (TV를 보다) • I visited my friend in hospital. (나는 입원 중인 친구를 방문했다.)

❶ 계절과 관사

일반적인 계절 spring, summer, autumn, fall, winter는 관사를 쓰지 않고, 특정 해의 계절을 지칭할 때는 관사 the를 쓴다.
- in the summer (그해 여름)

❷ 이름 앞에 a(n)을 쓰는 경우

보통 일반적인 사람 이름 앞에 a(n)을 쓸 수 없지만, 유명인의 이름 앞에 a(n)이 오면 '그와 같은 사람'을 의미한다.
- a Mozart (모차르트 같은 사람)
- an Einstein (아인슈타인 같은 사람)

❸ 본래 목적과 관계없을 때

건물이나 장소의 본래 목적과 관계없을 때는 관사를 쓴다.
- He visited a school for a survey. (그는 설문 조사를 위해 한 학교를 방문했다.)

1 주의해야 할 관사의 위치

[01-05] 주어진 우리말과 일치하도록 괄호 안의 말을 바르게 배열하시오.

01 너무 비싼 선물은 나를 불편하게 만든다. (uncomfortable, gift, so, me, a, makes, expensive)

➡ ____

02 그는 그의 사촌 집에 꽤 오랫동안 머물렀다. (stayed, long, cousin's, he, quite, house, time, at, a, his)

➡ ____

03 그녀는 노래 경연 대회에 여섯 번 참가했다.

(half, taken part in, times, she, a, singing contests, dozen, has)

➡ ____

04 나는 평생 그렇게 강인한 여자는 본 적이 없다.

(strong, a, life, I've, such, my, seen, in, never, woman)

➡ ____

05 이것은 공유하기에는 너무 좋은 요리 비법이다. (secret recipe, too, this, good, share, to, a, is)

➡ ____

2 관사를 쓰지 않는 경우

[06-11] 문장에서 필요 없는 관사를 찾아 밑줄을 그으시오.

06 You've just followed the instructions step by the step.

07 A last summer, I traveled across Europe by train and the bus.

08 My dad is at the work, and I'm going to the office to meet him.

09 He caught a severe cold and he's been sick in the bed for the days.

10 My friends and I met at the school playground to play the basketball.

11 I'm a senior in a high school, so I'm going to go to a college next year.

1 + **2** 주의해야 할 관사의 쓰임

[12-16] 빈칸에 알맞은 관사를 쓰고, 필요 없는 경우에는 ×표 하시오.

12 When I lost my ID card, I felt like such ___________ idiot.

13 In ___________ spring, lots of people go on ___________ picnic.

14 She was successful both as ___________ lawyer and as ___________ politician.

15 I'd like to learn ___________ Spanish, because I'm planning to travel widely in ___________ South America.

16 ___________ game was stopped because of a sudden shower, but it restarted in half ___________ hour.

어휘 & 표현
- **complicated** 복잡한
- **biology** 생물학
- **uncomfortable** 불편한
- **instruction** 지시
- **severe** 심한
- **politician** 정치인
- **shower** 소나기
- **restart** 다시 시작하다

〈 정답과 해설 p. 19 〉

[01-06]

괄호 안에서 알맞은 것을 고르시오.

01

It's time to get out of (bed / the bed).

02

She is wearing (a / an) red dress.

03

He said to me, "(What a / A what) nice car you have!"

04

It looks like (such interesting a job / such an interesting job) to do.

05

She is studying (a / the / 관사 없음) computer engineering at MIT.

06 고난도

(A / The / 관사 없음) United Nations has been a key player in international diplomacy for decades.

07

어법상 **틀린** 부분을 바르게 고친 것을 고르시오.

> This is too a difficult problem for me. I haven't solved it yet.

① This is → One is
② too a difficult → too difficult a
③ for me → to me
④ haven't solved → didn't solve
⑤ it → one

[08-09] 고난도

주어진 문장의 밑줄 친 a와 쓰임이 같은 것을 고르시오.

08

> Take pills three times <u>a</u> day.

① Give me <u>a</u> minute.
② Birds of <u>a</u> feather flock together.
③ There is <u>a</u> cook book on the shelf.
④ You can use this program twice <u>a</u> week.
⑤ <u>A</u> horse is usually described as a holy animal.

09

> The couple always walk at <u>a</u> distance.

① We are of <u>a</u> mind on the refugee issue.
② A morning glory blooms in the morning.
③ She could have gone out for <u>a</u> minute.
④ This car can run at 240 kilometers <u>an</u> hour.
⑤ <u>A</u> Bill came to see you while you were out.

[10-12] 서술형

문장에서 **틀린** 부분을 찾아 밑줄을 긋고 바르게 고치시오.

10

When I saw a doctor, he advised me to eat an apple the day.

➡ ___________

11

The Earth moves around Sun every day without any exception.

➡ ___________

12

We should always respect a elderly.

➡ ________________

13

빈칸에 관사가 필요한 것을 고르시오.

① What did you have for __________ lunch?
② The vase was broken by __________ accident.
③ Have you played __________ volleyball before?
④ He was sent to __________ prison for three years.
⑤ I heard my mother talking on __________ phone.

14

대화의 빈칸에 알맞은 것을 고르시오.

> A: How do you get paid?
> B: Well, the firm pays me only minimum wage once __________.

① month   ② a month
③ the month   ④ an month
⑤ month by month

[15-17] 서술형

주어진 우리말과 일치하도록 괄호 안의 단어를 바르게 배열하시오.

15

나는 일주일에 네 번 영어 수업을 받는다. (lesson, take, a, times, I, English, week, four, an)

➡ ____

16

이것이 너의 승진을 위한 마지막 단계이므로, 최선을 다해야 한다.
(promotion, the, step, your, for, last)

➡ This is ________________________________,
so you must do your best.

17

그녀는 그 다락방에 있는 오래된 상자에서 숨겨진 보물을 발견했다.
(a, an, old, box, hidden treasure, in)

➡ She discovered ________________________________
in the attic.

[18-20]

밑줄 친 부분 중 어법상 틀린 것을 고르시오.

18

① My cousin is a very pretty girl.
② Brown is such an intelligent boy.
③ My little brother is quite a handsome boy.
④ This is too good an opportunity to miss.
⑤ The all paper is scattered on the floor.

19

① There is a boring book on the table.
② His opinion makes sense in a sense.
③ I am full because I had a good lunch.
④ I went there by a taxi because I was late.
⑤ A snake is usually described as evil in a fairy tale story.

20

① The only person I love is you.
② We should not ignore the poor.
③ He usually plays the soccer when he is free.
④ The Sun is a star and the Moon is a satellite.
⑤ My wedding anniversary is the same as yours.

[21-23]

밑줄 친 부분과 바꿔쓸 수 있는 것을 고르시오.

21

> He was required to complete an online training <u>a</u> week to maintain his certification.

① per ② an ③ same
④ certain ⑤ the

22

> <u>An</u> eagle, unlike many other birds, is able to spot its prey from a distance.

① Per ② One ③ Same
④ Certain ⑤ The

23

> Emergency workers helped <u>injured people</u> after the accident.

① injury ② injured ③ a injured
④ an injured ⑤ the injured

24

빈칸에 알맞게 〈보기〉의 단어들을 배열한 것을 고르시오.

> Elvis Aaron Presley was an American singer and actor. Regarded as one of the most significant cultural icons of the 20th century, he is often referred to as the "King of Rock." On July 5, 1954 he recorded his first single, which had ____________ pop music. After that, he was commercially successful in many genres, including pop, country, blues, and gospel, and became the best-selling solo artist in the history of recorded music.

〈보기〉

tremendous	such	on	a(n)	effect

① a such tremendous effect on
② such tremendous an effect on
③ such a tremendous effect on
④ such a tremendous on effect
⑤ on such a tremendous effect

[25-26]

다음 글을 읽고 물음에 답하시오.

> ① <u>Quite a few</u> people enjoy saunas, spas, and hot tubs which help them relax and relieve muscle pains. However, there is something that you should ② <u>keep in mind</u>. You might feel dizzy when you stay in hot water because ③ <u>such a hot water</u> makes blood rush to the body so fast that ④ <u>not enough blood reaches</u> __(A)__ brain. When people stand up after __(B)__ long bath, they might get dizzy and pass out. This could result in them falling and hitting the floor. Be careful when ⑤ <u>getting in and out</u> of the hot tub and be with someone else in case of fainting or other problems.

25 수능 유형

밑줄 친 부분 중 어법상 틀린 것을 고르시오.

①　　②　　③　　④　　⑤

26

빈칸에 들어갈 말이 알맞게 짝지어진 것을 고르시오.

	(A)	(B)			(A)	(B)
①	the	a		②	×	a
③	the	×		④	a	×
⑤	the	the				

🦉 **어휘 & 표현**

· **international** 국제적인　· **diplomacy** 외교　· **flock** 모이다　· **holy** 신성한　· **refugee** 난민　· **morning glory** 나팔꽃
· **exception** 예외　· **minimum wage** 최저 임금　· **attic** 다락방　· **scatter** 흩어지게 하다　· **anniversary** 기념일
· **certification** 증명서　· **significant** 상당한　· **refer to** ~을 언급하다[지칭하다]　· **tremendous** 매우 큰, 굉장한
· **relieve** 완화시키다　· **dizzy** 어지러운　· **faint** 기절하다

대명사

代名詞

(대신할 내, 이름 띵, 말 사)
명사를 대신하는 말

UNIT 12 지시대명사 this (these),
that (those), it

UNIT 13 재귀대명사
再歸 (두 번째 재, 돌아갈 귀)
'~ 자신'을 가리키는 대명사

UNIT 14 부정대명사
不定 (아닐 부, 정해진 정)
정해지지 않은 명사를 가리키는 대명사

These are my bags, and those are yours.
지시대명사 these   지시대명사 those

(이건 내 가방들이고, 저건 네 것들이야.)

I forgot to lock the door. That was careless of me.
지시대명사 that

(나는 문을 잠그는 걸 잊었어. 그건 내 부주의였어.)

Keep this in mind: the exam starts at 9 a.m.
지시대명사 this

(이걸 기억해. 시험은 오전 9시에 시작해.)

She made the cake herself, but nobody ate it.
재귀대명사   부정대명사   대명사 it

(그녀는 그 케이크를 직접 만들었지만, 아무도 먹지 않았다.)

 **UNIT 12 지시대명사 this (these), that (those), it** 

This is my dog, and ***that*** is my friend's dog.
가까이 있는 것을 가리킴　　멀리 떨어져 있는 것을 가리킴
(이것은 나의 개고, 저것은 내 친구의 개다.)

It is their ball. (그것은 그들의 공이다.)
단수 명사를 받는 지시대명사

1 지시대명사 this (these)와 that (those) ❶

this (these)	**that** (those)
(1) 가까이 있는 사람이나 사물을 가리킬 때 • This smells really good. (이것은 냄새가 정말 좋다.) • I made these myself. (내가 이것들을 직접 만들었어.)	**(1)** 멀리 있는 사람이나 사물을 가리킬 때 • Don't touch that! (그거 만지지 마!) • Can you hand me those? (저것들 좀 건네줄래?)
(2) 뒤 절을 대신할 때 • Be aware of this; the road is slippery. 　　　　　　(이 점을 알아둬. 길이 미끄러워.)	**(2)** 앞에 나온 명사(구)가 반복되면서 수식어구의 수식을 받을 때 • The climate of Russia is colder than that of Korea. (러시아의 기후는 한국의 기후보다 더 춥다.) • The prices today are lower than those last week. (오늘 가격이 지난주 가격보다 낮다.) = the prices
(3) 앞 절이나 문장을 대신할 때 • She failed the test. This was unfortunate. 　　(그녀는 시험에 떨어졌다. 그것은 운이 없었다.)	**(3)** 앞 절이나 문장을 대신할 때 • He left early. That bothered me. 　　　　(그는 일찍 떠났다. 그게 날 불편하게 했다.)
	(4) those who : '~한 사람들' • Those who exercise regularly are mostly healthy. (규칙적으로 운동하는 사람들은 대부분 건강하다.)

2 it의 쓰임

❶ 지시대명사와 지시형용사

this, these, that, those는 뒤에 오는 명사를 수식하는 지시형용사로도 쓰인다.
• Enjoy this beautiful sunset. (이 아름다운 석양을 즐기세요.)

(1) **3인칭 대명사** : 앞에 나온 단수 명사를 대신할 때 쓰며, '그것', '그 사람'이라는 뜻이다.
　• I saw a movie last night, and it was amazing.
　　　　　　　　　　　= a movie
　　　　　　(어젯밤에 영화를 봤는데, 그것은 정말 훌륭했다.)

(2) **비인칭주어** : 시간, 날짜, 요일, 날씨, 명암, 거리 등을 나타낼 때 쓴다.
　• It is the 15th of September today. (오늘은 9월 15일이다.)
　　날짜
　• It's really humid this time of year. (이 시기에는 정말 습하다.)
　　날씨

(3) **가주어 it** : to부정사(구), 동명사(구), 명사절을 진주어로 대신할 때 쓴다.
　• It is hard to believe that he passed the exam. (그가 시험에 합격했다는 것은 믿기 어렵다.)
　　가주어　　　　　　진주어(to부정사구)

가목적어 it : to부정사(구), 동명사(구), 명사절을 진목적어로 대신할 때 쓴다.
　• I found it hard saying no to her request. (나는 그녀의 부탁을 거절하는 것이 어렵다는 걸 알았다.)
　　　가목적어　　　　진목적어(동명사구)

(4) **It is[was] ~ that ... 강조 구문** : 강조하는 말을 It is[was]와 that 사이에 쓴다.
　• It is kindness that makes the world a better place. (세상을 더 나은 곳으로 만드는 것은 친절이다.)
　　　강조하는 말

1 지시대명사 this (these)와 that (those)

[01-08] 괄호 안에서 알맞은 것을 고르시오.

01 He makes mistakes, and (that / those) is very often.

02 He hasn't come home yet. (This / These) worries me.

03 I think they are (that / those) who can never be forgiven.

04 What he told me is (this / that); he wanted to go to England.

05 My daughter's mental age is higher than (that / this) of her friends.

06 The number of unmarried people has been increasing (these / those) days.

07 The earthquake that struck Chile was far stronger than (this / that) of Haiti.

08 She is overweight and has knee pain. (That / Those) is why she wants to lose weight.

2 it의 쓰임

[09-15] 밑줄 친 부분의 쓰임을 〈보기〉에서 골라 쓰시오. (중복 사용 가능)

〈보기〉
| 앞에 나온 단수 명사 대신 | 가주어 | 가목적어 | 비인칭주어 | 강조 구문 |

09 It is the 14th of July today. ＿＿＿＿＿＿＿

10 It is hard to predict the future. ＿＿＿＿＿＿＿

11 It was her sister that I visited yesterday. ＿＿＿＿＿＿＿

12 The thick fog makes it difficult to drive. ＿＿＿＿＿＿＿

13 It is today that we create the world of the future. ＿＿＿＿＿＿＿

14 As we went deeper into the cave, it became darker. ＿＿＿＿＿＿＿

15 My family went to the aquarium and it was very crowded. ＿＿＿＿＿＿＿

1 + **2** 지시대명사 this (these), that (those), 대명사 it

[16-20] 자연스러운 의미가 되도록 바르게 연결하시오.

16 My grades were much lower than •   • ⓐ that told us to read the story.

17 It is impossible for him   •   • ⓑ for her to go there.

18 It was our English teacher   •   • ⓒ to join the race next week.

19 I don't like those   •   • ⓓ those of my twin brother.

20 It'll take about two hours   •   • ⓔ who are rude to the elderly.

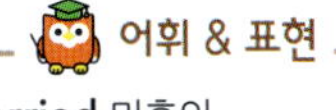 어휘 & 표현

- **climate** 기후　　· **bother** 괴롭히다　　· **humid** 습한　　· **request** 부탁, 요청　　· **mental** 정신의　　· **unmarried** 미혼의
- **earthquake** 지진　　· **strike** 때리다　　· **overweight** 과체중의　　· **predict** 예측하다　　· **thick** 두꺼운　　· **aquarium** 수족관
- **rude** 무례한

〈 정답과 해설 **p. 21~22** 〉

UNIT 13 재귀대명사

• **재귀대명사**: 앞에 나온 명사를 다시 나타내거나,
'~ 자신, ~ 것 자체'라는 뜻으로 자신을 가리키는 대명사이다.(-self, -selves)

She is looking at *herself* in the mirror.
재귀 용법 (전치사 at의 목적어 역할)　(그녀는 거울 속의 자신을 바라보고 있다.)

She *herself* is brushing her hair. (그녀는 직접 머리를 빗질하고 있다.)
강조 용법 (주어 She 강조)

1 재귀대명사의 종류

인칭	단수	복수
1인칭	I → myself (나 자신)	we → ourselves (우리들 자신)
2인칭	you → yourself (너 자신)	you → yourselves (너희들 자신)
3인칭	he → himself (그 자신) she → herself (그녀 자신) it → itself (그것 자체)	they → themselves (그들 자신)

2 재귀대명사의 쓰임

(1) **강조 용법**: 재귀대명사를 써서 주어, 목적어, 보어를 강조하며, 생략 가능하다.

　• We will handle it ourselves. (우리는 그것을 우리 스스로 처리할 것이다.)
　　　　　　　　　주어 We 강조
　• He repaired the engine itself. (그는 엔진 자체를 수리했다.)
　　　　　　　　　목적어 the engine 강조

(2) **재귀 용법**: 동사나 전치사의 목적어로 쓰인 대명사가 주어와 동일한 사람이나
　　사물을 가리킬 때 쓴다. 재귀 용법의 재귀대명사는 생략할 수 없다. ❶

> ❶ **재귀대명사 생략 가능 여부**
> 재귀대명사 앞에 동사나 전치사가 있을 때는 생략이 불가능하고, 명사가 있을 때는 생략 가능하다.

enjoy oneself 즐거운 시간을 보내다	talk to oneself 혼잣말하다
help oneself to ~을 마음껏 먹다	look at oneself in a mirror 거울을 보다
make oneself at home 편하게 지내다	make oneself understood (자신의 말을) 남에게 이해시키다

　• I enjoyed myself at the party. (나는 파티에서 즐거운 시간을 보냈다.)
　　　　　　=I
　• Harry is talking to himself. (Harry는 혼잣말을 하고 있다.)
　　　　　　　= Harry

3 전치사와 함께 쓰이는 관용표현

in itself 그 자체가, 본래	by[of] itself 저절로	by oneself 홀로, 혼자서
beside oneself 제정신이 아닌	for oneself 혼자 힘으로, 스스로	
in spite of oneself 자기도 모르게, 무심코	between ourselves 우리끼리 이야기지만	

　• My parents were beside themselves with joy when I passed the exam.
　　　　　　　　　(내가 시험에 통과했을 때 부모님은 기쁨에 넘쳐 어쩔 줄 몰랐다.)

　• Between ourselves, I think she's the best candidate for the job.
　　　　　　　　　(우리끼리 말인데, 나는 그녀가 이 일에 가장 적합한 후보라고 생각한다.)

1 + 2 재귀대명사의 종류와 쓰임

[01-06] 괄호 안에 주어진 재귀대명사가 들어가기에 알맞은 곳에 ✓표 하시오.

01 I built this house and my family moved into it last month. (myself)

02 Jessica wanted to talk to her homeroom teacher. (himself)

03 Riding a roller coaster at an amusement park is a thrill. (itself)

04 The heel broke off her shoe, but she repaired it with a glue. (herself)

05 Instead of buying a dog house, we built one for our dog. (ourselves)

06 I'm not good at math, so mom taught me math. (herself)

[07-14] 괄호 안에서 알맞은 것을 고르시오.

07 You can help (yourself / itself) to whatever you like.

08 Can I ask you briefly to introduce (myself / yourself)?

09 He bought (him / himself) a new jacket for his own birthday.

10 She fell down on the ice, but she didn't hurt (her / herself) at all.

11 It's not your fault. I don't think you should blame (myself / yourself).

12 My brother made me angry, but I tried to calm (himself / myself) down.

13 Don't worry about Peter. His mom is going to take good care of (him / himself).

14 Wendy forgot where she put her glasses, so she was looking for (them / themselves).

3 전치사와 함께 쓰이는 관용표현

[15-20] 빈칸에 알맞은 것을 〈보기〉에서 골라 쓰시오. (중복 사용 불가)

〈보기〉

beside himself	by itself	between ourselves
in itself	in spite of myself	for himself

15 The actor wanted to perform the action scenes ___________________.

16 I didn't see anyone coming in. I think the door opened ___________________.

17 I revealed Melissa's secret ___________________.

18 Leave him alone. He's ___________________ with anger.

19 The brain ___________________ feels no pain.

20 ___________________, he liked her when they were in school together.

🦉 어휘 & 표현

· **handle** 처리하다　· **candidate** 후보　· **amusement park** 놀이동산　· **thrill** 전율　· **break off** 부러뜨리다
· **briefly** 짧게　· **blame** 비난하다　· **perform** 수행하다, 연기하다　· **reveal** 드러내다　· **anger** 분노, 화　· **pain** 고통

〈 정답과 해설 p. 22~23 〉

 **UNIT 14** 부정대명사 

• **부정대명사**: 정해지지 않은 사람이나 사물을 가리키는 대명사이다.

1 one, ┌ one ~ the other, ┌ some ~ others
       └ another   └ some ~ the others

부정대명사	의미	예문	
one	~ 하나	(1) 앞에 나온 셀 수 있는 명사를 가리키며, 불특정한 것을 나타낸다. • If you have frying pans, can you lend me one? (프라이팬이 있으면, 하나 빌려 주시겠어요?) 앞에 나온 frying pans 중 불특정한 하나 (2) 명사가 복수형일 때는 ones를 쓴다. • Black rocks are on the left and white ones are on the right. 앞에 나온 rocks 중 불특정한 여러 개 (검은 돌들은 왼쪽에 있고 흰 돌들은 오른쪽에 있다.) (3) 일반적인 사람을 나타낼 때도 쓸 수 있다. • One can't always get what one wants. 일반적인 사람 일반적인 사람 (누구나 자신이 원하는 것을 항상 가질 수는 없다.)	one
another	또 다른 하나 (단수)	• This one is too big for me. Can you show me another? (이것은 제게 너무 커요. 다른 것을 보여주시겠어요?)	one another 여럿 중 다른 하나
one, another, the other	하나, 또 다른 하나, 나머지 하나	• There are three pens. One is mine, another is my brother's, and the other is my father's. (세 개의 펜이 있다. 하나는 내 것이고, 또 다른 하나는 내 남동생의 것이고, 나머지 하나는 나의 아버지의 것이다.)	one another the other 또 다른 하나 나머지 하나
some ~ others	몇몇 …, 나머지 일부 (복수)	• Some like tea, and others like coffee. (어떤 사람들은 차를 좋아하고, 다른 몇몇 사람들은 커피를 좋아한다.) • Some went inside but others went outside. (몇몇은 들어갔고 다른 몇몇 사람들은 나갔다.)	some others 여럿 중 다른 여럿
some ~ the others	몇몇 …, 나머지 전부 (복수)	• Some of the fruits are oranges, and the others are apples. (과일들 중 일부는 오렌지이고, 나머지 전부는 사과이다.) • Only some work, and the others rest. (몇몇만 일하고 나머지 전부는 쉰다.)	some the others 여럿 중 나머지 전부

1 one, another, the other(s), some, others

[01-06] 괄호 안에서 알맞은 것을 고르시오.

01 I had to take a taxi, so I called (one / it).

02 I've lost my wallet, so I should buy a new (one / it).

03 Small peppers are often hotter than big (one / ones).

04 If this book isn't interesting, read another (one / ones).

05 These days the young (one / ones) seem to be addicted to smart devices.

06 If other things are equal, most people prefer the cheaper (them / ones).

[07-11] 빈칸에 알맞은 것을 〈보기〉에서 골라 쓰시오. (중복 사용 불가)

〈보기〉

| one | another | the other | others | some | the others |

07 I have three sons. ＿＿＿＿＿＿＿ is a teacher, ＿＿＿＿＿＿＿ is a pilot, and the other is a businessman.

08 There are five pieces of cake. I ate one and he ate ＿＿＿＿＿＿＿.

09 I bought flowers for my mom. ＿＿＿＿＿＿＿ of them are white and the others are red.

10 He brought two useful tools. One is a hammer and ＿＿＿＿＿＿＿ is a screwdriver.

11 Some people in the world use English as their first language, and ＿＿＿＿＿＿＿ use it as their second language.

[12-15] 주어진 우리말과 일치하도록 빈칸에 알맞은 말을 쓰시오.

12 나는 이 점잖은 모자를 골랐어. 너도 분위기에 맞는 하나를 골라 봐.

➡ I picked this elegant hat. Choose ＿＿＿＿＿＿＿ that fits the mood.

13 사람은 누구나 실수할 수 있는데, 그것을 인정하는 게 왜 어려울까요?

➡ ＿＿＿＿＿＿＿ may make a mistake — why is it so hard to admit that?

14 몇몇은 이미 신분증을 제출했어요. 나머지 다른 사람들도 제출했나요?

➡ ＿＿＿＿＿＿＿ have already submitted their ID card. Have ＿＿＿＿＿＿＿ done so?

15 세 개의 가방이 있다. 하나는 가볍고, 다른 하나는 무겁고, 나머지 하나는 비어 있다.

➡ There are three bags. ＿＿＿＿＿＿＿ is light, ＿＿＿＿＿＿＿ is heavy, and ＿＿＿＿＿＿＿ is empty.

🦉 어휘 & 표현

·**addicted** 중독된　·**device** 장치　·**pilot** 비행기 조종사　·**businessman** 사업가　·**useful** 유용한　·**language** 언어
·**elegant** 점잖은　·**fit** 맞다　·**mood** 분위기　·**admit** 인정하다　·**submit** 제출하다　·**empty** 빈

〈 정답과 해설 p. 24 〉

2 some (some-), any (any-), no-

(1) some, some- : 긍정문, 권유를 나타내는 의문문, 긍정적인 대답을 예상하는 의문문에 쓰인다.

부정대명사	의미	예문
some	조금, 약간, 일부, 몇몇	− 대명사와 형용사로 쓰인다. • I like coriander, but some hate it. 대명사 (나는 고수를 좋아하지만, 몇몇은 그것을 싫어한다.) • There are some students waiting outside. 형용사 (밖에서 기다리는 몇몇 학생들이 있다.)
someone (= somebody)	어떤 사람, 누군가	− 대명사로 쓰인다. • Shall we ask someone to join us for dinner tonight? (오늘 저녁에 누군가를 초대해볼까?) • Have you recommended somebody for the position? (너는 그 자리에 누군가를 추천했니?)
something	무언가	− 대명사로 쓰인다. • Did you bring something for the presentation? (발표를 위해 무언가를 가져왔군요?)

(2) any, any- : 부정문, 의문문, 긍정문(아무나, 무엇이든), 조건을 나타내는 부사절에 쓰인다.

부정대명사	의미	예문
any	조금, 약간, 일부	− 대명사와 형용사로 쓰인다. • I looked for tickets, but I couldn't find any. 대명사 (나는 표를 찾아다녔지만, 어떤 것도 찾을 수 없었다.) • You can choose any book you like. 형용사 (네가 원하는 어느 책이든 골라도 돼.)
anyone (= anybody)	누구, 아무나	− 대명사로 쓰인다. • Has anyone seen my phone? (아무나 내 핸드폰 본 사람 있어?) • Anybody can join our team if they're interested. (관심이 있다면 누구라도 우리 팀에 합류할 수 있다.)
anything	어떤 것, 아무거나	− 대명사로 쓰인다. • If you need anything else, just let me know. (혹시 다른 무엇이든 필요하면, 내게 말만 해줘.)

(3) no- : 부정문에 쓰인다.

부정대명사	의미	예문
nobody (= no one) (= not anyone) (= not anybody)	아무도 ~ 아닌	• Nobody was in the classroom when I arrived. (내가 도착했을 때 아무도 교실에 없었다.) • No one answered the phone when it rang. (전화가 울렸을 때 아무도 받지 않았다.) • Isn't anybody coming here? (아무도 여기 안 오는 거야?)
nothing (= not anything)	아무것도 ~ 아닌	• Nothing has been decided yet, so don't make anything public. (아직 아무것도 결정되지 않았으니, 아무것도 공개하지 마.)

❷ some (some-), any (any-), no-

[16-22] 괄호 안에서 알맞은 것을 고르시오.

16 We didn't bring (some / any) water for the hiking.

17 I tried (some / any) of the exercises, but skipped the rest.

18 Do you see (some / any) light coming through the window?

19 Marie baked cookies, but I didn't get (some / any).

20 Are there (some / any) seats left near the front? — No, they're all taken.

21 I think (some / any) of the tools are missing from the box.

22 All the kids joined the game, but (some / any) left early.

[23-26] 빈칸에 알맞은 말을 〈보기〉에서 골라 쓰시오. (중복 사용 가능)

> 〈보기〉
> somebody   anybody   nobody

23 I rang the doorbell several times, but ________________ came to answer it.

24 Please don't tell ________________ about the surprise party we're planning.

25 Is there ________________ around here who can help me lift this heavy box?

26 ________________ probably left their phone on the table during the meeting.

[27-30] 빈칸에 알맞은 말을 〈보기〉에서 골라 대화를 완성하시오. (중복 사용 불가)

> 〈보기〉
> something   anything   nothing   anyone

27 A: I'm starving right now!

B: Then eat ________________ before we head out together.

28 A: You didn't tell ________________, right?

B: Of course not! I would never do such a thing.

29 A: What did you find in the old basement?

B: ________________ at all. It was completely dark and empty.

30 A: Look at what I randomly found in the drawer!

B: Wow, I've never seen ________________ like that since I moved here!

🦉 **어휘 & 표현**

- **coriander** ((식물 이름)) 고수   · **recommend** 추천하다   · **position** 위치, 자리   · **public** 공개된   · **skip** 생략하다
- **doorbell** 초인종   · **starve** 굶주리다   · **basement** 지하실   · **completely** 완전히   · **empty** 빈
- **randomly** 우연히, 무작위로   · **drawer** 서랍

〈 정답과 해설 p. 24~25 〉

3 **each, every:** each는 대명사와 형용사로 쓰이지만, every는 형용사로만 쓰인다.

부정대명사	의미	형태 & 예문
each	각각(의)	대명사 : 「each of + 복수 명사」 + 단수 동사 • Each of the proposals seems reasonable. (각각의 제안들이 타당해 보인다.) • Each of the artists was praised. (각각의 예술가들이 칭찬받았다.) 형용사 : 「each + 단수 명사」 + 단수 동사 • Each assignment demands full attention. (각 과제는 완전한 집중을 요구한다.) • Each member holds a unique role. (각 구성원은 독특한 역할을 맡는다.)
every	모든	형용사 : 「every + 단수 명사」 + 단수 동사 • Every citizen obeys the new policy. (모든 시민은 새 정책을 따른다.) • Every child deserves equal opportunity. (모든 아이는 평등한 기회를 누릴 자격이 있다.)

❶ 「부정대명사 + of + 복수 명사」와 수식어

부정대명사 each, all, both, none이 of와 함께 쓰일 때, 복수 명사의 앞에 수식어(소유격, 관사)가 와야 한다.
• Each of the boys is ready. (소년들 각각은 준비되어 있다.)
• All of my friends came. (내 친구들 모두가 왔다.)

❷ everyone, everybody

everyone, everybody도 every와 마찬가지로 단수 취급한다.
• Everyone has to wear a uniform. (모두 유니폼을 입어야 한다.)

4 **all (of), both:** 대명사와 형용사로 쓰인다.

부정대명사	의미	형태 & 예문
all	모두	대명사 : 「all (of) + 단수[복수] 명사」 + 단수[복수] 동사 • All (of) the information is confidential. (그 모든 정보가 기밀이다.) [관사 / 단수 명사 / 단수 동사] • All (of) her ideas were adopted. (그녀의 모든 아이디어가 채택되었다.) [소유격 / 복수 명사 / 복수 동사] [참고] all 뒤에 인칭대명사가 오는 경우는 of를 꼭 써야 한다. • All you are invited. (X) → All of you are invited. (O) [인칭대명사] (여러분 모두가 초대되었습니다.) 형용사 : 「all + 단수[복수] 명사」 + 단수[복수] 동사 • All music tells a story. (모든 음악은 이야기를 전한다.) [단수 명사 / 단수 동사] • All students need clear rules. (모든 학생들은 명확한 규칙이 필요하다.) [복수 명사 / 복수 동사]
both	둘 다	대명사 : 「both of + 복수 명사」 + 복수 동사 • Both of my parents work. (우리 부모님 두 분 다 일하신다.) 형용사 : 「both + 복수 명사」 + 복수 동사 • Both movies feel realistic. (두 영화 모두 현실감 있다.)

[참고] **부분 부정**: 전체를 나타내는 말(all, both, every 등)이 부정어와 함께 쓰이면 '모두 ~인 것은 아니다'를 뜻하는 부분 부정이 된다. <UNIT 78 참고>

• Not all of the information was accurate. (모든 정보가 정확했던 것은 아니다.)

3 each, every

[31-36] 괄호 안에서 알맞은 것을 고르시오.

31 We gave (each / every) of the children a small gift after the event.

32 Each of the students (was / were) separated into different classrooms.

33 I read (each / every) of the articles, but only one of them stood out.

34 Bella greeted every (guest / guests) with a warm smile and handshake.

35 Everyone (was / were) asked to present their ideas, but no one answered.

36 Each of the (option / options) you gave me seems reasonable in its own way.

4 all (of), both

[37-39] 주어진 우리말과 일치하도록 괄호 안의 말을 이용하여 빈칸에 알맞은 말을 쓰시오. (필요시 형태를 변형할 것)

37 남자아이들은 전부 운동장에 있다. (all of, boys, be, the, in the playground)

➡ ____

38 이 재킷들은 둘 다 비싸지 않다. (these, both of, jackets, be, expensive)

➡ ____

39 우리 모두는 환경 보호를 위해 더 많은 노력을 해야 한다. (all of, have to, us, make more effort)

➡ ______________________________ in protecting the environment.

3 + 4 each, every, all (of), both

[40-43] 주어진 우리말과 일치하도록 빈칸에 알맞은 것을 〈보기〉에서 골라 쓰시오. (중복 사용 불가)

〈보기〉

each	every	all	both

40 두 정당 모두 이 법안을 반대했고, 서로 다른 대안을 제시했다.

➡ ______________ political parties opposed the bill and proposed different alternatives.

41 그의 모든 경제 분석이 완전히 정확한 것은 아니었다.

➡ Not ______________ of his economic analyses were entirely accurate.

42 모든 과학 이론은 끊임없는 검증을 통해 발전해 왔다.

➡ ______________ scientific theory has evolved through constant testing.

43 각각의 생물 종은 생태계에서 고유한 역할을 담당한다.

➡ ______________ of the species plays a unique role in the ecosystem.

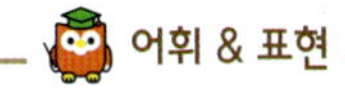 어휘 & 표현

- **proposal** 제안
- **reasonable** 타당한
- **obey** 준수하다, 따르다
- **deserve** ~할 자격이 있다
- **confidential** 기밀의
- **adopt** 채택하다
- **greet** 인사하다
- **political parties** 정당
- **oppose** 반대하다
- **alternative** 대안
- **evolve** 발전하다

〈 정답과 해설 p. 25 〉

01

빈칸에 any[Any]를 쓸 수 <u>없는</u> 것을 고르시오.

① If you need __________ help, call me.
② Do you have __________ plans this weekend?
③ __________ child can understand the principle.
④ Would you like to have __________ more cake?
⑤ There isn't __________ water in the bottle.

[02-09]

빈칸에 알맞은 대명사를 〈보기〉에서 골라 쓰시오.

(중복 사용 불가)

┌─────〈보기〉─────┐
it   one   those   ones
└──────────────────┘

02

There were three apples on the table. __________ is here. Where are the others?

03

What's the secret for __________ who pass the exam?

04

I dropped my chopsticks on the floor. Can you bring me new __________?

05

Is __________ her that you want to invite?

┌─────〈보기〉─────┐
someone   anyone   each   all
└──────────────────┘

06

__________ who is interested in taking pictures can join our club.

07

__________ of us is going to kiss mom before taking the train.

08

__________ of his money was stolen on the train.

09

There seems to be __________ behind the door.

10

〈보기〉의 밑줄 친 재귀대명사의 용법과 같은 것을 고르시오.

┌──────────────〈보기〉──────────────┐
The lawyer reminded <u>herself</u> to check the documents.
└────────────────────────────────┘

① She <u>herself</u> admitted her mistake.
② We completed the project <u>ourselves</u>.
③ He <u>himself</u> gave the opening speech.
④ The dog scratched <u>itself</u> behind the ear.
⑤ They organized the entire event <u>themselves</u>.

11

빈칸에 알맞은 것으로 바르게 짝지어진 것을 고르시오.

┌────────────────────────────────┐
• The position of the stars in this painting is similar to __________ of the actual sky.
• Only __________ who registered in advance can participate.
└────────────────────────────────┘

① it – those   ② that – it
③ this – that   ④ this – those
⑤ that – those

괄호 안에서 알맞은 것을 고르시오.

12

I tried to read the books through, but (that / those) was not easy.

13

His presence (himself / itself) was torture to me.

14

Would you like to eat (some / any) more cookies?

15

A giraffe's neck is much longer than (that / this) of a deer.

16

The microwave will start (in itself / by itself) in a few seconds.

17

밑줄 친 부분 중 생략할 수 있는 것을 고르시오.

① Peter is ashamed of <u>himself</u>.
② Students repainted the wall <u>themselves</u>.
③ Jenny talked to <u>herself</u> not to break promises.
④ Why don't you introduce <u>yourself</u> to the audience?
⑤ He was very proud of <u>himself</u> for giving a successful speech.

18

주어진 문장의 밑줄 친 It과 쓰임이 같은 것을 고르시오.

> <u>It</u> is a glass of water that he asks for.

① <u>It</u> is Sunday today.
② <u>It</u> is not that far from here.
③ <u>It</u> was yesterday that I met her.
④ <u>It</u> is important to keep ourselves healthy.
⑤ This will make <u>it</u> possible to draw the map.

[19-21] 서술형

문장을 괄호 안의 지시대로 다시 쓰시오.

19

Johnson had a car accident this morning.
　　　　　　　(this morning을 강조하여)

➡ ______________________________

____

20

I have something to do tonight.
　　　　　　　(-thing 활용하여 부정문으로)

➡ ______________________________

____

21 고난도

Among 17 people in our team, 6 people enjoy working out in the morning, while 11 people prefer to exercise in the evening.
　　　　　　　(부정대명사를 사용하여)

➡ Among 17 people in our team, __________ ______________________ in the morning, while ______________________ in the evening.

〈 정답과 해설 p. 26~27 〉

[22-26]

문장에서 <u>틀린</u> 부분을 찾아서 밑줄을 긋고 바르게 고치시오.

22

This toys are popular among kids. If you don't buy them, you'll regret it.

____

23

Jack cut him while he was shaving.

____

24

The Internet has made this easier to search for information.

____

25

He didn't make some mistakes.

____

26

It was regular exercise that it made me healthy.

____

[27-28]

빈칸에 알맞은 것을 고르시오.

27

To kill animals for food seems inevitable, but __________ is not acceptable to hunt animals for the simple pleasure of taking life.

① it   ② that   ③ all
④ what   ⑤ each

28

The weather today is beautiful, and I want to believe that __________ will stay like this all week.

① it   ② one   ③ what
④ these   ⑤ those

[29-31]

대화의 빈칸에 알맞은 것을 고르시오.

29

A: Could I have __________ more salad, please?
B: Sure, but that will cost extra money, sir.

① no   ② each   ③ some
④ others   ⑤ the other

30

A: I really like this shirt, but it is too tight.
B: Would you like to try __________ size?

① one   ② any   ③ some
④ another   ⑤ the others

31

A: I have two meetings today.
B: I only have one, but I'll join you for __________.

① one   ② any   ③ some
④ both   ⑤ the other

32 고난도

〈보기〉의 those와 같은 의미로 쓰인 것을 고르시오.

〈보기〉
Heaven helps those who help themselves.

① I think those are my earrings.
② Those books you lent me were very useful.
③ Selfish behavior is likely to cause real damage to those who are around us.
④ His sales in this year increased greatly, compared with those of last year.
⑤ I understand there are several projects going on. Could you tell us about those?

[33-37]

〈보기〉에서 알맞은 말을 골라 빈칸에 쓰시오. (중복 사용 불가)

〈보기〉
for　between　beside　of　in

33

_____________ ourselves, I really don't want to be friends with her.

34

When he heard of the news, the boy was _____________ himself with fear.

35

I didn't help my brother do his homework because I wanted him to do it _____________ himself.

36

Everyone felt shocked as the door opened _____________ itself.

37

To exchange a few words with him is _____________ itself such a honor.

38

밑줄 친 재귀대명사의 용법이 나머지 넷과 다른 것을 고르시오.

① I myself cooked this food.
② The lady is innocence itself.
③ I would like to see him myself.
④ The girl dislikes herself for no reason.
⑤ She herself is taking care of the baby.

39

밑줄 친 It의 쓰임이 나머지 넷과 다른 것을 고르시오.

① It is she that likes me very much.
② It is important that you study hard.
③ It was my mother that you met on the street.
④ It was yesterday that I happened to meet him.
⑤ It was at the coffee shop that she met her boyfriend.

[40-41] 서술형

대화의 빈칸에 알맞은 대명사를 쓰시오.

40

A: What's the difference between these two coffee makers?
B: Well, this one is more difficult to use than _____________.

41

A: My digital camera does not work well.
B: Why don't you get a new _____________?

주어진 우리말과 일치하도록 괄호 안의 말을 바르게 배열하시오.

42

그 여자들은 둘 다 프랑스인이었다.
(both, were, the women, of, French)

➡ ________________________________

____

43

내가 어제 만난 사람은 그의 삼촌이었다.
(I, met, it, his uncle, was, that, yesterday)

➡ ________________________________

____

44

이 음악은 내가 모든 것을 잊는 것을 가능하게 해 준다.
(makes, this music, it, to forget, for me, everything, possible)

➡ ________________________________

____

45

너는 우리 집에 와서 편히 쉴 수 있어.
(at home, my house, you, come to, can, and, make yourself)

➡ ________________________________

____

[46-47]

다음 글을 읽고 물음에 답하시오.

> Has (A) someone / anyone ever been a little late picking you up from school or (B) anything / something ? NASA astronaut Chris Baker found ⓐ in a similar situation this week. Chris has been living on the International Space Station(ISS) since July. He had been scheduled to return to Earth aboard the space shuttle Discovery, but his return has been delayed. ⓑ was due to thunderstorms that Discovery was unable to be launched at its scheduled time on Tuesday. Until Discovery arrives to take him home, Chris and five (C) other / another astronauts currently live on the ISS.

46 수능 맛보기

(A), (B), (C)의 각 네모 안에서 어법에 맞는 표현으로 가장 적절한 것을 고르시오.

	(A)	(B)	(C)
①	someone	something	other
②	someone	anything	another
③	anyone	anything	other
④	anyone	something	another
⑤	anyone	anything	another

47

ⓐ와 ⓑ에 알맞은 대명사로 연결된 것을 고르시오.

	ⓐ	ⓑ
①	his	It
②	himself	It
③	himself	That
④	themselves	It
⑤	themselves	That

🦉 어휘 & 표현

- **organize** 정리하다
- **presence** 존재
- **torture** 고문
- **microwave** 전자레인지
- **ashamed** 부끄러워하는
- **shave** 면도하다
- **inevitable** 불가피한
- **acceptable** 수용 가능한
- **damage** 피해를 주다
- **exchange** 교환하다
- **astronaut** 우주비행사
- **space shuttle** 우주 왕복선
- **thunderstorm** 뇌우

E

시제

時制

(때 시, 지을 제)

동사의 행동이 언제 일어났는지를
나타내는 것

UNIT 15 시제의 종류

동사의 행동이 지금 일어남

UNIT 16 현재시제, 과거시제

동사의 행동이 과거에 일어났음

UNIT 17 동사의 과거–과거분사 불규칙 변화표

UNIT 18 미래시제

동사의 행동이 앞으로 일어날 것임

UNIT 19 진행시제

동사의 행동이 일어나고 있는 중임

UNIT 20 완료시제

동사의 행동이 어떤 시점보다 먼저 완료되었음

She looks happy because she has finished her project.
현재시제 　　　　　　　　　　　　완료시제
(그녀는 프로젝트를 끝냈기 때문에 행복해 보인다.)

We were tired because we were working all day.
과거시제 　　　　　　　　　　진행시제
(우리는 종일 일하고 있어서 피곤했다.)

She is going to visit her grandmother this weekend.
미래시제
(그녀는 이번 주말에 할머니를 방문할 거야.)

★ 시제의 종류

종류	개념	형태 및 예문
현재 (Present Tense)	일반적인 사실, 반복적인 행동, 상태 등을 나타냄	동사원형 또는 3인칭 단수형(동사원형 + -s[es]) • I eat breakfast every morning. (나는 매일 아침을 먹는다.)
현재진행 (Present Continuous)	현재 일어나고 있는 동작이나 가까운 미래의 계획을 나타냄	am, are, is + -ing • I am eating breakfast now. (나는 지금 아침을 먹는 중이다.)
현재완료 (Present Perfect)	과거에 일어난 일이 현재에 영향을 미친 경우나 완료된 일을 나타냄	have[has] + 과거분사 • I have just eaten breakfast. (난 방금 아침을 먹었다.)
현재완료진행 (Present Perfect Continuous)	과거부터 현재까지 계속되어 온 동작이나 상태를 나타냄	have[has] been + -ing • I have been eating breakfast for 30 minutes. (나는 30분 동안 아침을 먹고 있는 중이다.)
과거 (Past Tense)	과거에 일어난 일을 나타냄	동사의 과거형 • I ate breakfast this morning. (나는 오늘 아침에 아침을 먹었다.)
과거진행 (Past Continuous)	과거의 특정 시간에 진행 중이었던 동작이나 상태를 나타냄	was, were + -ing • I was eating breakfast when you called. (나는 네가 전화했을 때 아침을 먹고 있었다.)
과거완료 (Past Perfect)	과거의 어느 시점보다 이전에 일어난 일을 나타냄	had + 과거분사 • I had eaten breakfast before I left. (나는 떠나기 전에 아침을 먹었다.)
과거완료진행 (Past Perfect Continuous)	과거의 어느 시점부터 다른 시점까지 계속되었던 동작이나 상태를 나타냄	had been + -ing • I had been eating breakfast when you called. (나는 네가 전화했을 때 아침을 먹고 있었던 중이었다.)
미래 (Future Tense)	미래에 일어날 일을 나타냄	will + 동사원형, be going to + 동사원형 • I will eat breakfast tomorrow. (나는 내일 아침을 먹을 것이다.)
미래진행 (Future Continuous)	미래의 특정 시간에 진행될 동작이나 상태를 나타냄	will be + -ing • I will be eating breakfast at 8 AM. (나는 오전 8시에 아침을 먹고 있을 것이다.)
미래완료 (Future Perfect)	미래의 특정 시점까지 완료될 동작을 나타냄	will have + 과거분사 • I will have eaten breakfast by the time you arrive. (당신이 도착할 때까지 나는 아침을 다 먹었을 것이다.)
미래완료진행 (Future Perfect Continuous)	미래의 특정 시점까지 계속될 동작이나 상태를 나타냄	will have been + -ing • I will have been eating breakfast for 30 minutes by the time you arrive. (당신이 도착할 때까지 나는 아침을 30분 동안 먹고 있을 것이다.)

⭐ 시제의 종류

[01-07] 밑줄 친 부분의 시제를 쓰시오.

01 The kids <u>are playing</u> outside. ➡ ______________

02 We <u>have lived</u> here for five years. ➡ ______________

03 I <u>visited</u> my grandmother last weekend. ➡ ______________

04 I <u>will have finished</u> my homework by 7 p.m. ➡ ______________

05 He <u>was studying</u> when his friend came over. ➡ ______________

06 He <u>will be playing</u> football tomorrow afternoon. ➡ ______________

07 We <u>have been waiting</u> for you for over an hour. ➡ ______________

[08-12] 문장에서 틀린 부분을 찾아 밑줄을 긋고 바르게 고치시오.

08 Blood circulated through the body. ➡ ______________

09 I will waiting for you until you arrive. ➡ ______________

10 By 2028, they will had built the new bridge. ➡ ______________

11 She have been practicing the piano for an hour. ➡ ______________

12 He was studied for two hours before he went out. ➡ ______________

[13-18] 주어진 우리말과 일치하도록 괄호 안의 단어를 알맞은 형태로 바꿔 쓰시오.

13 그녀는 현재까지 파리를 세 번 방문했다. (visit)

➡ She ______________ Paris three times so far.

14 나는 2020년에 대학을 졸업했다. (graduate)

➡ I ______________ from college in 2020.

15 그들은 다음 여름에 로마로 여행을 갈 것이다. (travel)

➡ They ______________ to Rome next summer.

16 우리가 대화를 나누고 있었을 때 갑자기 불이 꺼졌다. (have)

➡ The lights suddenly went out when we ______________ a conversation.

17 그녀는 매 학기 다양한 학교 활동에 참여한다. (participate)

➡ She ______________ in various school activities every semester.

18 우리는 내일 같은 시간에 영화를 보고 있을 것이다. (watch)

➡ We ______________ a movie at the same time tomorrow.

🦉 **어휘 & 표현**

· **come over** 들르다   · **blood** 피, 혈액   · **circulate** 순환하다   · **graduate** 졸업하다   · **college** 대학
· **go out** (전기가) 나가다   · **conversation** 대화   · **participate** 참가[참여]하다   · **semester** 학기

〈 정답과 해설 p. 29 〉

 **UNIT 16** 현재시제, 과거시제 

1 현재시제

(1) 현재의 사실이나 상태, 습관, 반복, 불변의 진리, 속담, 격언을 나타낼 때 사용한다.
가까운 미래나 시간과 조건의 부사절에서 미래를 나타낼 때도 사용된다.

- The speed of light is approximately 299,792 kilometers per second.
  현재의 상태
  (빛의 속도는 1초당 약 299,792킬로미터이다.)

- The Earth has one natural satellite, the Moon. (지구는 하나의 자연 위성, 즉 달을 가지고 있다.)
  불변의 진리

- If he studies hard, he will pass the exam. (그는 열심히 공부하면, 시험에 합격할 것이다.)
  조건의 부사절(미래)

(2) 주어가 3인칭 단수, 현재시제를 나타낼 때 〈3인칭 단수형 동사 변화 규칙〉

동사	규칙	예시
대부분의 동사	동사원형 + -s	think → thinks, use → uses, find → finds, love → loves, look → looks, eat → eats, believe → believes, know → knows 등
-o, -s, -x, -sh, -ch로 끝나는 동사	동사원형 + -es	do → does, miss → misses, fix → fixes, wish → wishes, watch → watches 등
「자음 + -y」로 끝나는 동사	y를 i로 바꾸고 + -es	cry → cries, worry → worries, study → studies, apply → applies, carry → carries, satisfy → satisfies, dry → dries 등
불규칙 동사	규칙 없음	have → has

2 과거시제

(1) 과거에 이미 끝난 동작이나 상태, 역사적 사실을 나타낼 때 사용된다.

- We watched a documentary about space last night. (우리는 어젯밤 우주에 관한 다큐멘터리를 봤다.)
  과거에 이미 끝난 동작

- The printing press was invented by Johannes Gutenberg in the 15th century.
  역사적 사실
  (인쇄기는 15세기에 Johannes Gutenberg에 의해 발명되었다.)

(2) 〈과거시제 동사 변화 규칙〉

동사	규칙	예시
대부분의 동사	동사원형 + -ed	help → helped, listen → listened, respect → respected, call → called, work → worked, play → played 등
-e로 끝나는 동사	동사원형 + -d	like → liked, live → lived, taste → tasted, hate → hated, smile → smiled, arrive → arrived, receive → received 등
「자음 + -y」로 끝나는 동사	y를 i로 바꾸고 + -ed	try → tried, study → studied, reply → replied, marry → married, carry → carried, worry → worried 등
「단모음+단자음」으로 끝나는 동사	마지막 자음을 한 번 더 쓰고 + -ed	stop → stopped, drop → dropped, plan → planned, chat → chatted 등

1 현재시제

[01-05] 괄호 안에서 알맞은 것을 고르시오.

01 The water in rivers (flow / flows) toward the ocean.

02 Now she (trys / tries) to finish her homework on time.

03 The city tour bus (departs / departes) every hour from the central station.

04 It always (astonishes / astonishs) me how much he knows about history.

05 She (analyze / analyzes) data carefully every time she prepares presentation.

08^{DAY}

2 과거시제

[06-11] 빈칸에 알맞은 동사를 〈보기〉에서 골라 쓰시오. (중복 사용 불가, 필요시 형태를 변형할 것)

〈보기〉

clean   discover   answer   plan   save   develop

06 Albert Einstein ________________ the theory of relativity.

07 We ________________ our vacation last week.

08 She definitely ________________ the report before dawn.

09 The students ________________ their classroom yesterday.

10 She ________________ all the questions correctly last night.

11 Christopher Columbus ________________ America in 1492.

1 + **2** 현재시제, 과거시제

[12-16] 주어진 우리말과 일치하도록 괄호 안의 말을 바르게 배열하시오. (필요시 형태를 변형할 것)

12 그는 매주 일요일 아침 가족과 함께 시간을 보낸다. (family, spend, with, time, his)

➡ He ________________________ every Sunday morning.

13 감독은 어제 새로운 공포영화를 추천했다. (new, a, horror, recommend, movie)

➡ The director ________________________ yesterday.

14 그 요리사는 매달 새로운 요리법을 개발한다. (develop, a, recipe, new)

➡ The chef ________________________ every month.

15 내 할아버지는 매일 아침에 신문을 읽으신다. (every, the, morning, read, newspaper)

➡ My grandfather ________________________.

16 그들은 지난달에 새로운 집으로 이사했다. (to, new, house, a, move)

➡ They ________________________ last month.

어휘 & 표현

- **approximately** 거의, 약 · **satellite** 위성 · **depart** 출발하다 · **astonish** 놀래키다 · **analyze** 분석하다
- **develop** 개발하다, 발전시키다 · **theory of relativity** 상대성 이론 · **discover** 발견하다 · **recommend** 추천하다

〈 정답과 해설 p. 30 〉

동사의 과거-과거분사 불규칙 변화표

1 A – A – A형 (원형, 과거, 과거분사가 모두 같은 경우)

뜻	원형	과거	과거분사
내기하다	bet	bet	bet
방송하다	broadcast	broadcast	broadcast
비용이 들다	cost	cost	cost
자르다	cut	cut	cut
치다	hit	hit	hit
다치다	hurt	hurt	hurt
~하게 하다	let	let	let

뜻	원형	과거	과거분사
놓다	put	put	put
그만두다	quit	quit	quit
읽다	read	read	read
재설정하다	reset	reset	reset
놓다	set	set	set
닫다	shut	shut	shut
퍼지다	spread	spread	spread

2 A – B – B형 (과거와 과거분사가 같은 경우)

뜻	원형	과거	과거분사
구부리다	bend	bent	bent
묶다	bind	bound	bound
가져오다	bring	brought	brought
짓다	build	built	built
사다	buy	bought	bought
잡다	catch	caught	caught
거래하다	deal	dealt	dealt
먹이다	feed	fed	fed
느끼다	feel	felt	felt
찾다	find	found	found
얻다	get	got	got, gotten
갈다	grind	ground	ground
가지다	have	had	had
듣다	hear	heard	heard
지니다	hold	held	held
유지하다	keep	kept	kept
놓다, 낳다	lay	laid	laid
인도하다	lead	led	led
떠나다	leave	left	left
빌려주다	lend	lent	lent
잃어버리다	lose	lost	lost

뜻	원형	과거	과거분사
만들다	make	made	made
의미하다	mean	meant	meant
만나다	meet	met	met
지불하다	pay	paid	paid
말하다	say	said	said
팔다	sell	sold	sold
보내다	send	sent	sent
쏘다	shoot	shot	shot
앉다	sit	sat	sat
자다	sleep	slept	slept
냄새를 맡다	smell	smelt	smelt
흘리다	spill	spilt	spilt
소비하다	spend	spent	spent
서다	stand	stood	stood
때리다, 치다	strike	struck	struck
쓸다	sweep	swept	swept
가르치다	teach	taught	taught
말하다	tell	told	told
생각하다	think	thought	thought
이해하다	understand	understood	understood
이기다	win	won	won

1 + 2 A － A － A형, A － B － B형

[01-26] 주어진 동사의 과거형과 과거분사형을 순서대로 쓰시오.

01 bet — ___________ — ___________

02 hear — ___________ — ___________

03 quit — ___________ — ___________

04 find — ___________ — ___________

05 reset — ___________ — ___________

06 catch — ___________ — ___________

07 bend — ___________ — ___________

08 lay — ___________ — ___________

09 hurt — ___________ — ___________

10 leave — ___________ — ___________

11 bind — ___________ — ___________

12 sell — ___________ — ___________

13 deal — ___________ — ___________

14 feed — ___________ — ___________

15 mean — ___________ — ___________

16 grind — ___________ — ___________

17 hold — ___________ — ___________

18 shoot — ___________ — ___________

19 shut — ___________ — ___________

20 spread — ___________ — ___________

21 bring — ___________ — ___________

22 spill — ___________ — ___________

23 strike — ___________ — ___________

24 lead — ___________ — ___________

25 lose — ___________ — ___________

26 win — ___________ — ___________

[27-34] 주어진 문장을 과거시제 문장으로 바꿔 쓰시오.

27 The ball hits the wall hard.

➡ The ball ___________ the wall hard.

28 She hurts her ankle while jogging.

➡ She ___________ her ankle while jogging.

29 He bends the metal with his hands.

➡ He ___________ the metal with his hands.

30 They sweep the garage after school.

➡ They ___________ the garage after school.

31 He pays all his money for the game.

➡ He ___________ all his money for the game.

32 The channel broadcasts the match live.

➡ The channel ___________ the match live.

33 We smell something strange in the hallway.

➡ We ___________ something strange in the hallway.

34 She spends the weekend cleaning the basement alone.

➡ She ___________ the weekend cleaning the basement alone.

어휘 & 표현
- **broadcast** 방송하다
- **ankle** 발목
- **jog** 조깅하다
- **metal** 금속
- **garage** 차고
- **strange** 이상한, 낯선
- **hallway** 복도
- **basement** 지하

〈 정답과 해설 p. 30~32 〉

3 A－B－A형 (원형과 과거분사가 같은 경우)

뜻	원형	과거	과거분사
되다	become	became	become
오다	come	came	come
극복하다	overcome	overcame	overcome
달리다	run	ran	run

4 A－B－C형 (원형, 과거, 과거분사가 모두 다른 경우)

뜻	원형	과거	과거분사	뜻	원형	과거	과거분사
발생하다	arise	arose	arisen	자라다	grow	grew	grown
깨다	awake	awoke	awoken	숨다	hide	hid	hidden
～이다	be	was, were	been	알다	know	knew	known
낳다, 견디다	bear	bore	born(e)	눕다	lie	lay	lain
시작하다	begin	began	begun	타다	ride	rode	ridden
물다	bite	bit	bitten	울리다	ring	rang	rung
불다	blow	blew	blown	오르다	rise	rose	risen
깨뜨리다	break	broke	broken	보다	see	saw	seen
선택하다	choose	chose	chosen	흔들다	shake	shook	shaken
하다	do	did	done	노래하다	sing	sang	sung
그리다	draw	drew	drawn	가라앉다	sink	sank	sunk
마시다	drink	drank	drunk	말하다	speak	spoke	spoken
운전하다	drive	drove	driven	훔치다	steal	stole	stolen
먹다	eat	ate	eaten	수영하다	swim	swam	swum
떨어지다	fall	fell	fallen	잡다	take	took	taken
잊다	forget	forgot	forgotten	찢다	tear	tore	torn
날다	fly	flew	flown	던지다	throw	threw	thrown
얼다	freeze	froze	frozen	깨다	wake	woke	woken
주다	give	gave	given	입다	wear	wore	worn
가다	go	went	gone	쓰다	write	wrote	written

1 + 2 + 3 + 4 동사의 과거 – 과거분사 불규칙 변화

[35-64] 주어진 동사의 과거형과 과거분사형을 순서대로 쓰시오.

35 do — __________ — __________		**50** bear — __________ — __________
36 cost — __________ — __________		**51** break — __________ — __________
37 eat — __________ — __________		**52** shake — __________ — __________
38 pay — __________ — __________		**53** wear — __________ — __________
39 ring — __________ — __________		**54** drink — __________ — __________
40 choose — __________ — __________		**55** run — __________ — __________
41 buy — __________ — __________		**56** rise — __________ — __________
42 teach — __________ — __________		**57** overcome — __________ — __________
43 arise — __________ — __________		**58** smell — __________ — __________
44 send — __________ — __________		**59** sit — __________ — __________
45 let — __________ — __________		**60** stand — __________ — __________
46 build — __________ — __________		**61** wake — __________ — __________
47 throw — __________ — __________		**62** hit — __________ — __________
48 awake — __________ — __________		**63** bite — __________ — __________
49 write — __________ — __________		**64** tear — __________ — __________

08 DAY

[65-70] 주어진 우리말과 일치하도록 괄호 안의 단어를 알맞은 형태로 바꿔 쓰시오.

65 나는 지난주에 Barack Obama의 자서전을 읽었다. (read)

➡ I ____________ Barack Obama's autobiography last week.

66 내 전화기가 방금 수영장의 바닥으로 가라앉았다. (sink)

➡ My phone has just ____________ to the bottom of the pool.

67 Mahatma Gandhi는 1947년에 인도를 독립으로 이끌었다. (lead)

➡ Mahatma Gandhi ____________ India to independence in 1947.

68 산업 혁명은 18세기 말에 시작되었다. (begin)

➡ The Industrial Revolution ____________ in the late 18th century.

69 내가 안 보고 있었을 때 낯선 사람이 내 가방을 훔쳤다. (steal)

➡ A stranger ____________ my bag when I wasn't looking.

70 그들은 운동 경기 동안 맞춘 유니폼을 입었다. (wear)

➡ They ____________ matching uniforms during the sports competition.

〈 정답과 해설 p. 32~33 〉

 **UNIT 18 미래시제** 

He ***will graduate*** from the university soon.
미래에 대한 예상

(그는 곧 대학을 졸업할 것이다.)

He ***is going to be*** a doctor. (그는 의사가 되려고 한다.)
현재 상황을 바탕으로 미래에 일어날 일을 예상

1 미래시제의 쓰임

미래시제는 현재보다 나중에 하는 일을 나타낼 때 쓴다.

- They will marry each other in October. (그들은 10월에 서로 결혼할 것이다.)
- No one can expect what will surpass the role of AI in the next century.

(아무도 다음 세기에 무엇이 AI의 역할을 능가할지 예상할 수 없다.)

- Experts don't know what technologies will be helpful in slowing down global warming in the future. (전문가들은 미래에 지구 온난화를 늦추기 위해 어떤 기술들이 도움이 될 것인지 알지 못한다.)

[참고] 시간 및 조건의 부사절에서는 현재시제로 미래를 나타낸다.
- I'll call you when I arrive at the airport. (공항에 도착할 때, 너에게 전화할게.)
  시간을 나타내는 접속사
- As the ceremony begins, the lights will dim. (행사가 시작할 때, 조명이 어두워질 거야.)
  시간을 나타내는 접속사
- If it rains tomorrow, we'll stay home all day. (내일 비가 오면, 우리는 하루 종일 집에 있을 거야.)
  조건을 나타내는 접속사

2 미래시제의 종류

will + 동사원형 (~할 것이다, ~일 것이다)	(1) 즉흥적인 결정 • I'll answer the phone. (제가 전화를 받을게요.)
	(2) 예상이나 예측 • It will snow tomorrow. (내일 눈이 올 것이다.)
be going to + 동사원형 (~일 것이다, ~하려고 하다)	(1) 이미 계획된 일 • I'm going to visit my friend tomorrow. (나는 내일 내 친구를 방문할 것이다.)
	(2) 현재 상황을 바탕으로 미래에 일어날 것으로 예상되는 일 • Look at those clouds. It's going to rain. (저 구름을 봐. 비가 올 거야.)
be about to + 동사원형 (막 ~하려고 하다)	(1) 곧 일어날 확실한 일 • They are about to announce the result. (그들은 결과를 막 발표하려 한다.)
	(2) 즉시 시작될 행동 • I was about to call you when you texted me. (네가 문자를 보냈을 때, 나는 막 너에게 전화하려고 했었다.)

[참고] will, be going to, be about to 비교
- I will travel to Paris. (나는 파리로 여행할 것이다.)
  → 즉흥적으로 파리로 여행할 것이라는 결정 또는 막연한 예상
- I'm going to travel to Paris next summer. (나는 내년 여름에 파리로 여행할 것이다.)
  → 파리로 여행하기로 이미 계획된 일이나 근거가 있는 예측
- I'm about to travel to Paris this summer. (나는 올해 여름에 파리로 여행할 것이다.)
  → 곧 다가오는 여름에 파리를 여행하기로 확실히 정해진 계획

❶ + ❷ 미래시제

[01-06] 괄호 안에서 알맞은 것을 고르시오.

01 I'm about (leave / to leave) for the airport.

02 He's going (run / to run) for election next year.

03 They will (finish / to finish) the project by Friday.

04 We will not (be / to be) able to attend the meeting.

05 She's (go / going) to be promoted to team leader soon.

06 I'm about (move / to move) to a new apartment next month.

08 DAY

[07-12] 주어진 우리말과 일치하도록 괄호 안의 말을 이용하여 빈칸에 알맞은 말을 쓰시오.

07 나는 장을 보러 가는 것을 잊지 않을 것이다. (forget, will)

→ I _________________ to buy the groceries.

08 그들은 이제 새로운 제품을 출시하려고 한다. (about, launch)

→ They _________________ a new product.

09 그는 내년에 유학을 갈 것이다. (go, study)

→ He _________________ abroad next year.

10 대통령은 내일 새로운 정책을 발표할 것이다. (will, announce)

→ The president _________________ the new policy tomorrow.

11 Reina는 그녀의 최신 발명품을 막 공개하려고 했다. (about, unveil)

→ Reina _________________ her latest invention.

12 그녀는 그 파란 드레스를 사려고 했었는데, 벌써 매진됐다. (go, buy)

→ She _________________ the blue dress, but it was sold out already.

[13-16] 문장에서 <u>틀린</u> 부분을 찾아 밑줄을 긋고 바르게 고치시오.

13 I'll book the tickets as soon as she will confirm the schedule.　→ _____________

14 The students will leave the hall when the clock will strike noon.　→ _____________

15 Before the sun is going to set, the hikers will go down the mountain.　→ _____________

16 The outdoor concert will be canceled if the weather will worsen in the evening.

→ _____________

🦉 **어휘 & 표현**

- **surpass** 능가하다
- **expert** 전문가
- **technology** 기술
- **slow down** 늦추다
- **global warming** 지구 온난화
- **announce** 발표하다
- **election** 선거
- **promote** 승진하다
- **launch** 출시하다
- **unveil** 공개하다
- **invention** 발명품
- **confirm** 확인하다
- **worsen** 악화되다

〈 정답과 해설 p. 33~34 〉

[01-02]

동사의 원형-과거-과거분사 형태가 바르게 연결된 것을 고르시오.

01

① speak – spoke – spoke
② shut – shutted – shutted
③ put – putted – putted
④ build – built – built
⑤ stand – stood – stand

02

① hide – hid – hiden
② lend – lent – lend
③ freeze – froze – frozen
④ catch – catched – catched
⑤ spread – spreaded – spreaded

[03-05]

빈칸에 공통으로 들어갈 것을 고르시오.

03

- She _________ a shower every morning.
- It _________ about an hour to get to the airport.

① take　　② taken　　③ takes
④ to take　　⑤ taking

04

A: I _________ send you the documents as soon as I get home.
B: Great, I _________ wait for your email.

① will
② was going to
③ was about to
④ be going to
⑤ be about to

05

- We _________ a meeting at 3 p.m. yesterday.
- We _________ a great time at the art expo last weekend.

① has　　② had　　③ have
④ having　　⑤ to have

[06-07] 고난도

어법상 틀린 것을 고르시오.

06

① The train leave in five minutes.
② He taught English in his thirties.
③ Yesterday's message meant a lot to me.
④ I met a lot of new people at the conference.
⑤ It'll take me about an hour to solve this math problem.

07

① He ran five kilometers yesterday.
② She will join the new team next week.
③ I wrote a letter to my friend last week.
④ She was taking the bus to work these days.
⑤ You will need a visa to travel to that country.

08

대화의 빈칸에 들어갈 말이 알맞게 짝지어진 것을 고르시오.

M: She ___(A)___ at E. I. software company now.
W: Oh, really? I ___(B)___ in the marketing department at the same company.

	(A)	(B)		(A)	(B)
①	work	– work	②	work	– works
③	works	– work	④	works	– works
⑤	working	– working			

[09-11] 서술형

밑줄 친 부분을 바르게 고쳐 빈칸에 쓰시오.

09

The Earth <u>be</u> the third planet from the Sun.

➡ The Earth ______________ the third planet from the Sun.

10

The first successful vaccine <u>be</u> developed by Edward Jenner in 1796.

➡ The first successful vaccine ______________ developed by Edward Jenner in 1796.

11

The Wright brothers <u>make</u> the first powered flight in 1903.

➡ The Wright brothers ______________ the first powered flight in 1903.

[12-13] 고난도

빈칸에 알맞지 <u>않은</u> 것을 고르시오.

12

Flora ______________ a beautiful voice.

① has   ② had   ③ hear
④ hears   ⑤ heard

13

Ladies and gentlemen, the musical *Frankenstein* ______________ soon.

① starts   ② starting   ③ is starting
④ will start   ⑤ is about to start

14

빈칸에 들어갈 말로 알맞은 것을 고르시오.

In 2003, archaeologists ______________ a 4000-year-old pyramid in Egypt.

① finds   ② discovers   ③ discovered
④ is finding   ⑤ has found

[15-16]

다음 글을 읽고 물음에 답하시오.

Two hours ago, Lily and her dog ___(A)___ for a walk in the park. They found a beautiful flower and ___(B)___ to smell it. Suddenly, Lily's dog ① run after a butterfly. She laughed and ② chased after him. After a while, they ③ rested under a tree and ④ enjoyed the peaceful afternoon. On their way home, Lily thought it ⑤ was the best walk they'd ever had.

15

(A)와 (B)에 들어갈 말이 알맞게 짝지어진 것을 고르시오.

(A)	(B)	(A)	(B)
① go	– stops	② go	– stopped
③ goes	– stops	④ went	– stop
⑤ went	– stopped		

16 수능 유형

밑줄 친 부분 중 어법상 틀린 것을 고르시오.

①   ②   ③   ④   ⑤

어휘 & 표현

· **shut** 닫다   · **freeze** 얼다   · **spread** 퍼지다   · **conference** 회의   · **department** 부서   · **planet** 행성
· **successful** 성공적인   · **vaccine** 백신   · **archaeologist** 고고학자   · **discover** 발견하다   · **chase** 쫓다

〈 정답과 해설 p. 34~35 〉

I**'m speaking** English now. (나는 지금 영어를 말하고 있다.)
현재진행시제: 현재 진행 중인 일

We **were cleaning** the classroom then.
과거진행시제: 과거에 진행 중이었던 일

(우리는 그때 교실을 청소하고 있었다.)

1 진행시제의 종류와 형태

	현재진행시제❶	과거진행시제❷	미래진행시제
형태	am[are, is] + -ing	was[were] + -ing	will be + -ing
쓰임	현재 진행 중이거나 일시적으로 반복되는 습관적 동작을 나타냄	과거에 진행 중이었거나 일시적으로 반복되었던 동작을 나타냄	미래의 어느 때 진행 중인 동작을 나타냄

- Emma is focusing on her upcoming presentation.
  현재진행시제
  (그녀는 곧 있을 그녀의 발표에 집중하고 있다.)
- I was watching TV when my parents came home.
  과거진행시제
  (부모님이 집에 오셨을 때 나는 TV를 보고 있었다.)
- He will be traveling at this time tomorrow.
  미래진행시제
  (그는 내일 이 시간에 여행을 하고 있을 것이다.)

❶ 현재진행시제의 쓰임

가다(go), 오다(come), 출발하다(depart), 도착하다(arrive) 등 이동을 나타내는 동사가 현재진행시제로 쓰이면 가까운 미래를 나타낼 수 있다.
- We are arriving in Paris next week.
(우리는 다음 주에 파리에 도착할 것이다.)

❷ 과거진행시제의 쓰임

과거시제는 행동이 완료된 상황을 표현하는데 비해, 과거진행시제는 과거 행동의 중간을 표현한다.

2 진행형을 쓰지 않는 동사

(1) 상태를 나타내는 동사는 진행형으로 쓰지 않는다.

like	love	hate	want	know	realize	understand
think	contain	consist of	own	have❸(가지고 있다)		

- I'm thirsty. I want something to drink.
  ~~am wanting~~
  (나는 목이 마르다. 나는 마실 것을 원한다.)
- Do you understand what I'm saying? (너는 내가 말하는 것을 이해하니?)
  ~~Are you understanding~~

(2) 주어의 의도나 의지가 포함되지 않은 지각동사는 진행형으로 쓰지 않는다.

see	hear	smell	taste

- Do you see the dog over there? (너는 저기 있는 개가 보이니?)
  ~~Are you seeing~~
- Do you hear that noise outside? (너는 밖에서 나는 저 소리가 들리니?)
  ~~Are you hearing~~

❸ 소유동사 have

have가 '가지고 있다'라는 뜻을 가지는 소유동사일 때는 진행형으로 쓸 수 없는데, 이와 같은 종류의 동사로 belong, own, possess가 있다.

참고 동사들이 상태나 지각을 나타내는 뜻으로 쓰이지 않거나, 지각동사가 주어의 의도나 의지를 포함하고 있는 경우에는 진행형으로 사용할 수 있다.

- We are having lunch and having a good time here. We are thinking of visiting
  = are eating   = spending   = are considering
  here again. (우리는 이곳에서 점심을 먹으며 좋은 시간을 보내고 있다. 우리는 여기를 다시 들르는 것을 생각하는 중이다.)
- I'm seeing the police officer this afternoon. (나는 오늘 오후에 그 경찰관을 만날 것이다.)
  = 'm meeting

1 진행시제의 종류와 형태

[01-05] 괄호 안에서 알맞은 것을 고르시오.

01 When you get home, I (am flying / will be flying) over the East Sea.

02 You (are working / will be working) in your new job at this time next week.

03 Tom (surfs / was surfing) the Internet when I arrived.

04 While I (work / was working) alone, I heard a strange sound.

05 James and I (went / were going) to the movies last Sunday, but we didn't enjoy it very much.

2 진행형을 쓰지 않는 동사

[06-09] 주어진 우리말과 일치하도록 괄호 안의 말을 이용하여 문장을 쓰시오.

06 나는 그들이 진실을 말하고 있지 않다고 생각한다. (I, think, that, are not, tell, the truth)

➡ ____

07 내가 그의 방에 들어갔을 때, 그는 간식을 먹고 있었다. (enter, his room, have, snacks, when)

➡ ____

08 물은 수소와 산소로 이루어져 있다. (water, consist of, hydrogen, oxygen)

➡ ____

09 나는 이 음식을 전에 한 번도 본 적이 없지만, 그것은 정말 맛있다. (see, never, taste, food, really good)

➡ ____

1 + 2 진행시제

[10-13] 주어진 단어를 이용하여 알맞은 시제로 대화를 완성하시오.

10 A: What ____________ you ____________ at this time yesterday? (do)

B: I ____________ ____________ TV. (watch)

11 A: Why ____________ you ____________ those old clothes? (wear)

B: I'm going to paint the fence and roof.

12 A: Where is Barbara?

B: She ____________ ____________ on the phone right now. (talk)

13 A: ____________ you ____________ a good time? (have)

B: Yes, I am enjoying myself very much.

🦉 어휘 & 표현

- **upcoming** 곧 있을
- **have a good time** 좋은 시간을 보내다
- **surf** 인터넷을 검색하다
- **strange** 이상한, 수상한
- **consist of** ~로 이루어지다
- **hydrogen** 수소
- **oxygen** 산소
- **fence** 울타리
- **roof** 지붕

〈 정답과 해설 **p. 35~36** 〉

UNIT 20 완료시제

핵심 개념

1 현재완료시제

(1) 현재완료시제 : (1, 2인칭 단수 · 복수, 3인칭 복수) **have**
(3인칭 단수) **has** ┘ + 과거분사

과거시제	현재완료시제
과거에 초점을 두고, 현재와 상관없이 과거에 끝난 일을 나타냄	현재에 초점을 두고, 과거에 일어난 일이 현재까지 이어짐을 나타냄
• We knew each other in kindergarten. (우리는 유치원 때 서로를 알았다.)	• We have known each other since kindergarten. (우리는 유치원 때부터 서로를 알아 왔다.)
− 과거시제는 과거 상태만 나타낸다. − 이 문장만으로는 현재 서로 아는 사이인지 알 수 없다. 다른 문장이 더 있어야 알 수 있다. (+We still know each other.) (우리는 여전히 서로 안다.)	− 현재완료시제는 한 문장으로도 과거와 현재 상태를 나타낼 수 있다.

참고 현재완료는 현재를 포함하고 있으므로, yesterday, ago, last ~ 등의 명백한 과거를 나타내는 부사구나
의문사 when, what time과 함께 쓸 수 없다.

• I have just met her for the first time yesterday. (×) (나는 어제 처음으로 그녀를 만났다.)
yesterday가 과거를 나타내는 부사이므로 현재완료시제 have met은 쓸 수 없음

(2) 현재완료시제의 용법

용법	의미와 예문
계속	'~해 오고 있다' − 과거에 일어난 일이 현재까지 계속됨 for, since, how long, so far 등과 함께 쓰인다. • We have known each other for more than a decade. (우리는 10년 이상 서로 알고 지냈다.)
경험	'(지금까지) ~해 본 적이 있다' − 과거부터 지금까지 경험한 적이 있음 ever, never, before, ~ times 등과 함께 쓰인다. • I have never eaten such a delicious food before. (나는 전에 그렇게 맛있는 음식을 먹어본 적이 없다.)
완료	'(지금 막) ~했다' − 과거에 시작한 일이 현재 완료되었음 just, yet, already, recently 등과 함께 쓰인다. • She has just left the room to grab some coffee. (그녀는 커피를 사기 위해 막 방을 나섰다.)
결과	'~해버렸다, (그 결과) …하다' − 과거의 일의 결과가 현재에 영향을 미침 • He has gone❶ on vacation, so nobody here can answer your question. (그는 휴가를 가버려서, 여기서 누구도 당신의 질문에 대답할 수 없다.)

❶ **have gone to** *vs.* **have been to**
• **have gone to(결과):** 현재 가버리고 없음
• **have been to(경험):** 가본 적 있음

1 현재완료시제

[01-04] 주어진 우리말과 일치하도록 괄호 안의 단어를 알맞은 형태로 바꿔 쓰시오.

01 나는 어제 박물관에서 그 유명한 화가를 처음으로 직접 만났다. (meet)

➡ I _____________ the famous painter in person at the museum yesterday.

02 우리는 대학 입학 이후로 줄곧 서로에게 문자를 보내며 지내 왔다. (text)

➡ We _____________ to each other regularly since we entered college.

03 그는 2020년에 회사를 떠났고, 유럽으로 여행을 갔다. (leave)

➡ He _____________ the company in 2020 and went on a trip to Europe.

04 그들은 고객센터에 지금까지 세 번 전화했다. (call)

➡ They _____________ the customer service center three times so far.

[05-12] 밑줄 친 현재완료시제의 용법으로 알맞은 것을 〈보기〉에서 고르시오. (중복 사용 가능)

〈보기〉

① 계속: ~해 오고 있다　　② 경험: (지금까지) ~해 본 적이 있다
③ 완료: (지금 막) ~했다　　④ 결과: ~해버렸다, (그 결과) …하다

05 Have you ever traveled abroad with your family? _____________

06 She has just finished editing her presentation slides. _____________

07 I have never heard such an inspiring speech before. _____________

08 Don't delete the file! I have not saved the changes yet. _____________

09 We have waited for more than an hour. Let's just leave. _____________

10 Look! The volcano has erupted, and the sky is full of smoke. _____________

11 My grandfather has collected rare coins since he was a teenager. _____________

12 Has he broken another window again? His parents must be furious. _____________

[13-16] 괄호 안에서 알맞은 것을 고르시오.

13 Yesterday, the government (announced / has announced) a new plan for forest fire areas.

14 Artists in many cultures (have explored / explored) identity and conflict for decades.

15 Isaac (didn't visit / haven't visited) the ancient palace ruins in that region yet.

16 What a match! The team (showed / has shown) the best performance so far.

🦉 어휘 & 표현

· **kindergarten** 유치원　　· **decade** 10년　　· **customer service center** 고객센터　　· **inspiring** 감동적인, 인상적인
· **delete** 삭제하다　　· **erupt** 분출하다　　· **furious** 몹시 화난　　· **government** 정부　　· **identity** 정체성　　· **conflict** 갈등
· **ancient** 고대의　　· **ruins** 유적　　· **region** 지역

〈 정답과 해설 p. 36~37 〉

(3) 현재완료진행시제 : have[has] been + -ing

① 주로 for, since와 함께 쓰여 과거에 시작된 일이 현재까지 계속 진행되고 있음을 나타낸다.

- I have been reading this book for hours, and I'm almost done.

  (나는 이 책을 몇 시간 동안 읽어 왔고, 거의 다 읽었다.)

- We have been traveling around Europe for two weeks until now.

  (우리는 지금까지 2주 동안 유럽을 여행하고 있다.)

② 현재완료시제 〈계속〉 용법과 비슷하지만, 진행 중임을 좀 더 강조한다.

- She has looked for her phone since yesterday. (그녀는 어제부터 핸드폰을 찾아왔다.)

- She has been looking for her phone since yesterday. (그녀는 어제부터 핸드폰을 찾고 있다.)

2 과거완료시제

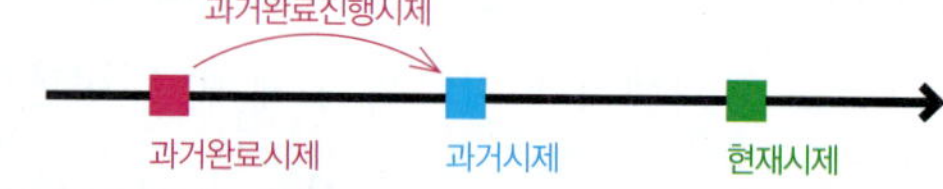

과거완료시제	과거완료진행시제
had + 과거분사	had been + -ing
과거의 특정 시점을 기준으로 그 이전에 일어난 일이 기준 시점까지 영향을 주었음을 나타냄	과거의 특정 시점을 기준으로 그 이전에 일어난 일이 기준 시점까지 진행되고 있음을 나타냄

went보다 전에 일어난 일

- I had finished my homework before I went out. (나는 외출하기 전에 숙제를 끝냈다.)

called 시점에서 진행 중이었던 일

- I had been studying for hours when my friend called.

  (내 친구가 전화했을 때 나는 몇 시간 동안 공부하고 있었다.)

3 미래완료시제

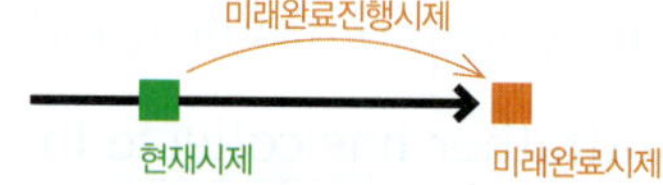

미래완료시제	미래완료진행시제
will + have + 과거분사	will + have been + -ing
미래의 특정 시점을 기준으로 그 이전에 일이 완료될 것임을 나타냄	미래의 특정 시점을 기준으로 그 이전부터 일어난 일이 계속 진행되고 있음을 나타냄

next year 이전에 완료될 일

- By next year, I will have finished my degree. (내년까지 나는 학위를 마칠 것이다.)

2030년을 기준으로 계속 진행되고 있는 일

- By 2030, she will have been working as a lawyer for seven years.

  (2030년까지 그녀는 변호사로 7년 동안 일하고 있을 것이다.)

1 현재완료시제 (3) 현재완료진행시제

[17-21] 괄호 안의 지시대로 주어진 동사를 이용하여 문장을 완성하시오.

17 I ________________ Minsu since I was a high school student. (see, 현재완료진행시제)

18 Jane ________________ to Sydney. (go, 현재완료시제)

19 She ________________ for the exam since this morning. (study, 현재완료진행시제)

20 It ________________ cloudy since yesterday. (be, 현재완료시제)

21 Tony ________________ a medical checkup several times. (receive, 현재완료시제)

2 과거완료시제

[22-28] 문장의 빈칸에 알맞은 말을 〈보기〉에서 골라 알파벳을 쓰시오. (중복 사용 불가)

〈보기〉
ⓐ until I moved to Jeju Island.
ⓑ because he had already seen the film.
ⓒ the train had already been leaving.
ⓓ she had been doing so much work.
ⓔ I mailed it.
ⓕ and it was finally working.
ⓖ the test was still difficult.

22 She felt tired because ________________

23 When he reached the station, ________________

24 Jimmy didn't go to the movies ________________

25 I had lived in Busan ________________

26 He had been fixing the car, ________________

27 Even though I had studied hard, ________________

28 The moment I had finished the letter, ________________

3 미래완료시제

[29-33] 문장에서 틀린 부분을 찾아 밑줄을 긋고 바르게 고치시오.

29 By 2 p.m., he will be finishing his homework. ________________

30 They will finish their work by the time the teacher comes back. ________________

31 By the time you arrive, I'll cook for two hours. ________________

32 He'll be working at this factory for 20 years by then. ________________

33 In ten minutes, I will be waiting for him for two hours. ________________

🦉 **어휘 & 표현**

· **degree** 학위　　· **lawyer** 변호사　　· **receive** 받다　　· **medical checkup** 건강 검진　　· **reach** 도달하다　　· **factory** 공장

〈 정답과 해설 p. 37 〉

01

빈칸에 알맞지 <u>않은</u> 것을 고르시오.

> I can't believe that Bill is __________ Korea next week.

① leaving　　② gone to　　③ coming to
④ traveling to　⑤ moving to

[02-06]

괄호 안에서 알맞은 것을 고르시오.

02

I (am walking / have been walking) for exercise since then.

03

The cake (tastes / is tasting) very good.

04

How long (did you study / have you studied) Chinese?

05

He arrived at the airport, but his flight (has already left / had already left).

06

I'm going to watch TV from 10:00 p.m. until 11:00 p.m. So, at 10:30 I (will watch / will be watching) TV.

[07-11] 서술형

〈보기〉의 단어를 이용하여 알맞은 시제로 다음 문장을 완성하시오. (중복 사용 불가)

> 〈보기〉
> miss　use　wash　be married　see

07

These are the dictionaries that I __________ __________ since I was twelve.

08

I could find him easily because I __________ __________ him before.

09

Emma __________ her hair when the phone rang.

10

We realized that we __________ the bus, so we waited for the next bus.

11

Tony and Julie __________ for ten years. Next year, they __________ __________ for eleven years.

12

대화의 빈칸에 알맞은 것을 고르시오.

> A: I finally saw the movie that you had told me about. Do you know it's based on a novel?
> B: Yes, I __________ before.

① am reading it　　　② have read it
③ have read it yet　　④ had not read it
⑤ have been reading it

13

주어진 문장의 밑줄 친 부분과 쓰임이 같은 것을 고르시오.

> She <u>has visited</u> the art gallery once.

① They <u>have lived</u> here for 5 years.
② He <u>has lost</u> his key to the classroom.
③ Tom <u>has never seen</u> the dolphin show.
④ She <u>has just finished</u> cleaning the room.
⑤ I <u>have helped</u> to build houses for the poor since 2010.

밑줄 친 부분을 바르게 고쳐 쓰시오.

14

Kevin is liking to play tennis with his uncle.

____

15

My family is consisting of five people, including a little puppy. _______________

16

They still live in the house that they have bought twenty years ago. _______________

17

If I travel Australia one more time, I have been there three times. _______________

18

He has been knowing you since you entered school. _______________

19

빈칸에 들어갈 말이 알맞게 짝지어진 것을 고르시오.

- I have been studying English __________ I was young.
- Sean had been playing outside __________ two hours when his mother arrived.

① since – as   ② before – to   ③ after – for
④ when – as   ⑤ since – for

20

괄호 안의 동사 형태로 알맞은 것을 고르시오.

I (know) nothing about her until I met her in person.

① have known   ② had known
③ will have known   ④ have been knowing
⑤ had been knowing

[21-24] (서술형)

두 문장을 한 문장으로 쓸 때, 빈칸에 알맞은 말을 쓰시오.

21

She was talking on the phone an hour ago. She is still on the phone.

➡ She ________________ talking on the phone for an hour.

22

Chris is washing his father's car. It'll take him about one hour to finish it.

➡ Chris ________________ washing his father's car about one hour later.

23

My cousin left for Chicago two years ago. He still lives there now.

➡ My cousin ______________ in Chicago for two years.

24

Jenny went to the library. She hasn't returned yet.

➡ Jenny ______________ to the library.

[25-26] (서술형)

대화의 괄호 안의 말을 알맞은 형태로 바꿔 쓰시오.

25

A: Are you going to swim at the gym?
B: No, I ________________ (already swim) this week at the gym.
A: Really? When?
B: I swam there two days ago.

26

A: You must have some problem. What's the matter?
B: I ________________ (think) about my future now. I am not sure if it will be fine.

〈 정답과 해설 p. 38~39 〉

27 고난도

밑줄 친 부분의 쓰임이 나머지 넷과 다른 것을 고르시오.

① He <u>has been</u> ill since last week.
② The baby <u>has just started</u> walking.
③ They <u>have been married</u> for 30 years.
④ We <u>have been</u> friends since we were at school.
⑤ I <u>have worked</u> for this company for 10 years.

28

대화의 밑줄 친 부분 중 어법상 어색한 것을 고르시오.

A: ① <u>Have you ever been</u> to America?
B: No. I ② <u>have never been</u> there. ③ <u>What about you?</u>
A: I've been there ④ <u>three times</u>. My uncle lives there. He ⑤ <u>lived</u> there for 10 years.

[29-30] 서술형

주어진 우리말과 일치하도록 괄호 안의 단어를 알맞게 쓰시오.

29

우리는 20분 동안 버스를 기다리고 있다. (wait)

➡ We ＿＿＿＿＿ ＿＿＿＿＿ ＿＿＿＿＿
for the bus for 20 minutes.

30

우리는 휴게소를 찾기 전 몇 시간 동안 운전하고 있었다. (drive)

➡ We ＿＿＿＿＿ ＿＿＿＿＿ ＿＿＿＿＿
for hours before we found a rest stop.

31 수능 맛보기

(A), (B), (C)의 각 네모 안에서 어법에 맞는 표현으로 가장 적절한 것을 고르시오.

I need your advice. I am very worried about my 13-year-old daughter. She used to look very healthy, but lately she decided to go on a diet. For over three weeks, she (A) | has been eaten / has been eating | only fruit and water. As a result, she (B) | is losing / has lost | so much weight and she is satisfied with this. I think she (C) | looked / looks | much better before. Now she looks tired and ill. I want to persuade her to start eating normally again.

	(A)	(B)	(C)
①	has been eaten	– is losing	– looked
②	has been eaten	– has lost	– looked
③	has been eaten	– has lost	– looks
④	has been eating	– has lost	– looked
⑤	has been eating	– is losing	– looks

32 수능 유형 고난도

밑줄 친 부분 중 어법상 틀린 것을 고르시오.

Jane ① <u>has traveled</u> to many countries over the past few years. Before she went to Italy, she ② <u>has always wanted</u> to see the Colosseum. When she finally arrived in Rome, she had already booked tickets for the Colosseum. She ③ <u>explored</u> the ancient ruins and took many photos. By the time she finished the tour, she ④ <u>had learned</u> so much about Roman history. She has been to several places in Rome, but the Colosseum ⑤ <u>was</u> definitely the highlight of her trip.

①　②　③　④　⑤

어휘 & 표현

- **dictionary** 사전　· **art gallery** 미술관　· **consist of** ~로 구성되다　· **including** ~을 포함하여　· **rest stop** 휴게소
- **go on a diet** 다이어트를 하다　· **satisfied** 만족하는　· **ill** 아픈　· **persuade** 설득하다　· **normally** 정상적으로
- **ancient ruins** 고대 유적　· **definitely** 절대, 분명히

F

조동사
助動詞
(도울 조, 움직일 동, 말 사)

동사의 의미를 보조하거나
문법적 요소를 추가하는 역할

UNIT 21 조동사의 특징과 조동사 do

UNIT 22 can (could), may (might)

UNIT 23 will (would), must (have to)

UNIT 24 shall, should, ought to, had better (not)

UNIT 25 used to, would, 조동사 + have + 과거분사

You can eat now, or you may wait for the others.
~할 수 있다　　　　　　　~해도 된다

(너는 지금 먹을 수 있고, 아니면 다른 사람들을 기다려도 돼.)

We will win, and we must not give up now.
~할 것이다　　　　~해야 한다

(우린 이길 거야, 그리니 지금 포기해서는 안 돼.)

You had better be careful. People used to get into accidents there.
~하는 편이 낫다　　　　　~하곤 했다

(너는 조심하는 게 좋아. 예전에는 그곳에서 사고가 자주 났거든.)

They should have brought more food. (그들은 음식을 더 가져왔어야 했는데.)
~했어야 했는데

 **UNIT 21** 조동사의 특징과 조동사 do 

He said he *did* practice the piano. (그는 정말로 피아노를 연습했다고 말했다.)
동사 practice의 의미를 강조

Never *did* I hear him playing the piano.
부정어 never가 문두에 온 도치 구문에서 사용됨
(나는 그가 피아노를 치는 것을 전혀 듣지 못했다.)

1 조동사의 특징

(1) 조동사 뒤에는 동사원형이 온다. 「조동사 + 동사원형」

- You can trust him to get the job done. (당신은 그를 믿고 일을 맡길 수 있다.)
  조동사 + 동사원형

참고 조동사 뒤에 조동사를 써야 할 때는 뒤에 오는 조동사의 대체 어구를 사용한다.

조동사의 대체 어구: can → be able to, will → be going to, must → have to

- I will be able to visit you next weekend. (나는 다음 주말에 너를 방문할 수 있을 것이다.)

(2) 조동사는 주어의 인칭이나 수에 따라 형태가 변하지 않는다.

단, 조동사 do와 have to는 주어의 인칭이나 수에 따라 형태가 변한다.

- She may come to the party if she finishes her work early. (그녀는 일을 일찍 끝내면 파티에 올 수 있다.)

- She does not understand the instructions. (그녀는 지시 사항을 이해하지 못한다.)
  3인칭 단수

- Tony has to do his homework by 4:00. (Tony는 4시까지 숙제를 해야 한다.)
  3인칭 단수

(3) 조동사의 부정문 : 「조동사 + not + 동사원형」

- You should accept the offer. (너는 그 제안을 받아들여야 한다.)

→ You should not accept the offer. (너는 그 제안을 받아들이면 안 된다.)

(4) 조동사의 의문문 : 「(의문사) + 조동사 + 주어 + 동사원형」

- May I help you? (도와 드릴까요?)
  조동사 + 주어 + 동사원형
  (의문사 없음)

- What can you do for me? (넌 날 위해 무엇을 할 수 있니?)
  의문사 + 조동사 + 주어 + 동사원형

2 조동사 do

일반동사의 의문문을 만듦	do[does, did] + 주어 + 동사원형 • Does she like sweet desserts? (그녀는 달콤한 후식을 좋아하나요?)
일반동사의 부정문을 만듦	do[does, did] + not + 동사원형 • I don't know him. (나는 그를 알지 못한다.)
일반동사를 강조함	do[does, did] + 동사원형 • I did try my best, even if I failed. (나는 실패했지만, 정말 최선을 다했다.)
대동사로 사용됨	동사 대신 do[does, did]를 씀 (대동사) • Who won the game? – We did. (누가 경기에서 이겼어? - 우리가 이겼어.)
도치구문에 사용됨	부정어구 + do[does, did] + 주어 + 동사원형 • Never did I see such a brave man. (나는 그렇게 용감한 사람을 보지 못했다.)

1 조동사의 특징

[01-06] 괄호 안에서 알맞은 것을 고르시오.

01 (Do you will / Will you) go to Jenny's party this Friday?

02 They should (prepare / to prepare) for the first day of class.

03 He said to me that he would (can / be able to) fix this computer.

04 The parrot can memorize lots of words and (talk / talks) with his owner.

05 You (don't should / should not) share your personal information with anyone else.

06 Because of the volcano's eruption, they (could not travel / could travel not) to that country.

2 조동사 do

[07-12] 문장을 do동사를 이용하여 괄호 안의 지시대로 바꾸어 쓰시오.

07 Paul goes to church every Sunday. (의문문으로)

➡ ____

08 We went to the station by taxi. (부정문으로)

➡ ____

09 His nephew stayed with him for a long time. (의문문으로)

➡ ____

10 My older brother rarely goes out. (부사 **rarely**를 문두에 써서)

➡ ____

11 I know what I should do. (동사를 강조하여)

➡ ____

12 She earns as much money as he earns. (대동사를 사용하여)

➡ ____

1 + **2** 조동사의 특징과 조동사 do

[13-16] 틀린 부분을 찾아서 밑줄을 긋고 바르게 고치시오.

13 You may going wherever you want. _______________

14 He will travels around the world next year. _______________

15 My brother knows more about Jessica than I does. _______________

16 He did trusted her. She never lied to him or anyone. _______________

🦉 **어휘 & 표현**

· **instruction** 지시 사항　· **accept** 받아들이다　· **brave** 용감한　· **memorize** 암기하다　· **personal** 개인적인
· **volcano** 화산　· **eruption** 분출　· **go out** 외출하다　· **earn** 돈을 벌다

〈 정답과 해설 p. 40~41 〉

 **UNIT 22** can (could), may (might) 

The ostrich ***can*** run fast. (타조는 빨리 달릴 수 있다.)
능력의 조동사 can

The duck ***can't*** run fast. (오리는 빨리 달릴 수 없다.)
can의 부정형

1 can (could)

	can은 현재를, **could**는 과거를 나타낸다.
능력	• She can bake fruit cookies. (그녀는 과일 쿠키를 구울 수 있다.) 현재 능력을 나타냄 • She could bake fruit cookies. (그녀는 과일 쿠키를 구울 수 있었다.) 과거 능력을 나타냄 참고 능력을 나타내는 can, could가 다른 조동사 뒤에 올 때는 be able to의 형태로 온다. • We may be able to live to be 120 years old. (우리는 120살까지 살 수 있을지도 모른다.)
	could는 can보다 더 공손한 표현이다.
요청, 허가	요청 Can[Could] you move my bag? (내 가방을 옮겨 줄 수 있니?) 허가 Can[Could] I borrow your bicycle? (네 자전거를 빌릴 수 있을까?)
	– 주로 be동사와 함께 나타낸다. – can [could] be (~일지도 모른다), cannot [could not] be (~일 리 없다)
추측	• Traffic can be terrible on Friday. (금요일에 교통은 최악일 수 있다.) • It couldn't be true that he didn't know about the surprise party! (그가 깜짝 파티에 대해 몰랐다는 건 있을 수 없어!)

2 may❶ (might)

❶ **may의 부정문**

may에 not을 붙여서 부정문으로 만들면 '~하면 안 된다'는 약한 금지를 나타낸다.
• Visitors may not feed the animals.
(방문객은 동물들에게 먹이를 주어서는 안 됩니다.)

불확실한 추측	**might**는 may보다 더 불확실함을 나타낸다. • The rumor may[might] be true. (그 소문은 사실일지도 모른다.)
허가	**might**는 may보다 더 공손한 표현이다. • May[Might] I have another cup of coffee? (커피 한 잔 더 마셔도 될까요?)
기원	**may**는 기원을 나타낼 때 쓰인다. • May God bless you! (신의 은총이 함께 하기를!)
관용표현	**may[might] well** (~하는 것도 당연하다) — • They may well disagree with you. (그들이 네 의견에 동의하지 않는 것도 당연하다.) **may[might] as well** (~하는 것이 낫다) — • You might as well give up your seat. (너는 네 자리를 포기하는 것이 낫다.)

1 can (could)

[01-04] 밑줄 친 조동사의 쓰임으로 알맞은 것에 ✓표 하시오.

01 He <u>can</u> speak more than five languages. ☐ 능력 ☐ 요청

02 <u>Could</u> you help me download MP3 files? ☐ 추측 ☐ 요청

03 The person you saw there <u>cannot</u> be Jane. ☐ 능력 ☐ 추측

04 The furniture was so heavy that he <u>could not</u> move it by himself. ☐ 불허 ☐ 불가

2 may (might)

[05-09] 밑줄 친 조동사의 쓰임에 유의하여 다음 문장을 우리말로 해석하시오.

05 You <u>might as well</u> give the gift to him.

➡ ____

06 <u>May</u> I call you at a more convenient time?

➡ ____

07 She's always late. He <u>may well</u> lose his temper.

➡ ____

08 You <u>may</u> not smoke in this building at any time.

➡ ____

09 <u>May</u> peace and happiness be yours in the New Year.

➡ ____

1 + 2 can (could), may (might)

[10-13] 문장에서 틀린 부분을 찾아서 밑줄을 긋고 바르게 고치시오.

10 We will be taking off soon. May you fasten your seat belt, please?

➡ ______________________________

11 The space scientist says we will can travel to Mars sooner or later.

➡ ______________________________

12 It was minus 10 degrees yesterday. It was so cold that we can't go outside.

➡ ______________________________

13 Mike's uncle won the lottery. Mike can well buy a lottery ticket every week.

➡ ______________________________

어휘 & 표현

· **bake** 굽다　· **disagree** 반대하다　· **give up** 포기하다　· **furniture** 가구　· **convenient** 편리한
· **lose one's temper** 화를 내다　· **happiness** 행복　· **take off** 이륙하다　· **Mars** 화성　· **lottery** 복권

〈 정답과 해설 p. 41 〉

 **UNIT 23** ## will (would), must (have to) 

You ***must*** park your car there. (당신은 차를 저기에 주차해야 한다.)
의무: '~해야 한다'

You ***must not*** park your car here.
금지: '~해서는 안 된다'

(당신은 차를 여기에 주차해서는 안 된다.)

1 will (would)

단순 미래	**will**은 현재 시점에서 미래를, **would**는 과거 시점에서 미래를 나타낸다.
	• I will be seventeen next year. (나는 내년에 17살이 될 것이다.) • She said she would call me later. (그녀는 내게 나중에 전화하겠다고 말했다.)
요청	**would**는 will보다 더 공손한 표현이다.
	• Will[Would] you pass me the salt? (소금을 건네주시겠어요?)
주어의 고집	• He would not listen to the doctor's advice. (그는 의사의 충고를 들으려고 하지 않았다.)

would	과거의 반복적인 동작 또는 습관	• When I was young, I would skip breakfast. (어렸을 때 나는 아침 식사를 거르곤 했다.)
	would like (to) ~ (~하고 싶다)	• I would like to hear more about your ideas. (당신의 아이디어에 대해 더 듣고 싶어요.)
	would rather A than B (B 하느니 차라리 A 하겠다)	• I would rather sleep than watch it again. (나는 그것을 또 보느니 차라리 잠을 자겠다.)

2 must (have to)

추측	**must**는 추측을 나타낸다.
	• You must be a good teacher. (당신은 좋은 선생님임에 틀림없다.)
❶ 의무, 필요	– **must**는 법이나 규율처럼 강제성이 있는 의무를 나타내거나 꼭 해야 할 필요가 있는 것을 나타낼 때 쓴다. – 의무나 필요를 나타내는 must는 have to와 바꾸어 쓸 수 있다.
	• Every citizen must obey the law. (모든 시민은 법을 지켜야 한다.) 의무 • Must he come home by 10:00? (그가 10시까지 집에 와야 하나요?) 필요 = Does he have to come home by 10:00? 필요

부정	must not: 금지 (~해서는 안 된다)	• You must not leave the house tomorrow. (너는 내일 집을 떠나서는 안 된다.)
	don't have to: ❷ 불필요 (~할 필요가 없다)	• You don't have to get up early tomorrow. (너는 내일 일찍 일어날 필요가 없다.)

❶ **must의 과거형과 미래형**

의무를 나타내는 must의 과거형은 had to로 쓰고, 미래형은 will have to로 쓴다.

❷ **don't have to 와 need not**

불필요를 나타내는 don't have to는 need not으로 바꾸어 쓸 수 있다. 이때 need는 조동사이므로 인칭이나 수에 따라 형태가 변하지 않는다.

1 will (would)

[01-05] 괄호 안에서 알맞은 것을 고르시오.

01 She thought that they (will / would) go home.

02 She (will / would) like to break up with him.

03 (May / Will) you turn on the computer for me?

04 I (could / would) rather ask him for help than give it up.

05 He (will / would) not read the user's manual and finally broke the toaster.

10 DAY

2 must (have to)

[06-10] 빈칸에 알맞은 말을 〈보기〉에서 골라 쓰시오. (중복 사용 불가)

〈보기〉
| must | must not | have to | need not | not have to |

06 Do I ＿＿＿＿＿＿＿ fill in this application form again?

07 She is full of energy today. She ＿＿＿＿＿＿＿ be happy.

08 He was very rich. He did ＿＿＿＿＿＿＿ work for a living.

09 Tom has got well from his illness. He ＿＿＿＿＿＿＿ go to see a doctor anymore.

10 If you park here, the police will give you a ticket. You ＿＿＿＿＿＿＿ park here.

1 + **2** will (would), must (have to)

[11-14] 주어진 어구를 이용하여 다음 우리말을 영어로 쓰시오.

11 나는 그 경연 대회에 참가하고 싶다. (would, take part in, the contest, like)

➡ ＿＿＿＿＿＿＿＿＿＿＿＿＿＿＿＿＿＿＿＿

12 너는 오늘 그 일을 끝낼 필요가 없었다. (have to, finish, the work, today)

➡ ＿＿＿＿＿＿＿＿＿＿＿＿＿＿＿＿＿＿＿＿

13 그녀는 그것이 가능한지 의심함에 틀림없다. (must, doubt, if, possible)

➡ ＿＿＿＿＿＿＿＿＿＿＿＿＿＿＿＿＿＿＿＿

14 너희들 우리 집에 저녁 먹으러 올래? (will, come, to my house, for dinner)

➡ ＿＿＿＿＿＿＿＿＿＿＿＿＿＿＿＿＿＿＿＿

🦉 어휘 & 표현

· **advice** 충고　· **skip** 거르다　· **citizen** 시민　· **break up** 결별하다　· **manual** 설명서　· **application form** 신청서
· **get well** 병이 낫다　· **illness** 질병　· **take part in** 참여하다　· **doubt** 의심하다　· **possible** 가능한

〈 정답과 해설 p. 41~42 〉

UNIT 24 — shall, should, ought to, had better (not)
~해야 한다

You ***should*** wear a helmet. (너는 헬멧을 써야 한다.)
의무: '~해야 한다'

You ***had better not*** ride a bike on the busy road.
had better의 부정형: '~하지 않는 것이 좋다'
(교통량이 많은 도로에서는 자전거를 타지 않는 것이 좋다.)

1 shall, should, ought to

shall	주로 미래의 행동, 제안, 제시, 또는 의도를 표현할 때 사용된다.
	• Shall we go to the movies tonight? (오늘 밤 영화 보러 갈까?) 제안
	• I shall return the book to the library tomorrow. 미래의 행동 (내일 도서관에 그 책을 반납할게.)
should, ought to ❷	− 조언, 권유, 의무, 또는 기대를 표현할 때 사용된다. − must나 have to처럼 강한 의무감을 주지는 않는다.
	• Should I bring anything to the party? 조언 (파티에 무언가를 가져가야 할까?)
	• We ought to leave early to avoid traffic. 권유 (교통체증을 피하려면 일찍 떠나는 게 좋겠다.)

❶ shall의 사용
영국 영어에서 더 많이 쓰고, 공식적이고 격식 있는 문장에서 많이 사용된다.

❷ ought to의 부정
다른 조동사들과 달리, ought to는 다음과 같은 형태를 따른다.
- **ought to의 부정문:**
  ought+not+to+동사원형
- **ought to의 의문문:**
  ought+주어+to+동사원형

2 should의 생략

(1) 주장, 명령, 충고, 제안, 요구, 필요를 나타내는 동사나 형용사가 주절에 쓰였을 때, 종속절의 동사에 should를 쓰는데 이때 should는 생략할 수 있다.

> 동사 : insist, order, advise, propose, suggest, demand, require, ask 등
> 형용사 : necessary, essential, important, urgent 등

• He insisted that Nick (should) apply for the job. (그는 Nick이 그 일에 지원해야 한다고 주장했다.)
주장을 나타내는 동사   should 생략 가능

• It is essential that we (should) protect the environment. (우리가 환경을 보호하는 것은 필수적이다.)
필요를 나타내는 형용사   should 생략 가능

(2) 해당 동사나 형용사가 그 외의 의미일 때, 종속절의 동사는 문맥에 맞게 사용한다.

• Her words suggest that she likes him. (그녀의 말은 그녀가 그를 좋아한다는 것을 암시한다.)
'암시하다'라는 뜻의 동사   주어 she에 맞게 likes가 옴

• It's more important that we are happy now. (우리가 지금 행복하다는 것이 더 중요하다.)
단순히 '중요한'을 의미하는 형용사   주어 we에 맞게 are가 옴

3 had better, had better not

had better (= 'd better)	'~하는 편이 좋겠다'
	• You'd better exercise regularly. (너는 규칙적으로 운동하는 것이 좋겠다.)
had better not (= 'd better not)	'~하지 않는 편이 좋겠다'
	• They'd better not leave their bags unattended. (그들은 가방을 아무렇게나 두지 않는 것이 좋겠다.)

1 shall, should, ought to

[01-05] 자연스러운 의미가 되도록 다음 빈칸에 알맞은 말을 〈보기〉에서 골라 알파벳을 쓰시오. (중복 사용 불가)

> ─〈보기〉─
> ⓐ this project by Friday.
> ⓑ you should wear a seat belt.
> ⓒ He should get up earlier.
> ⓓ She ought to exercise more.
> ⓔ What shall I do?

01 I shall finish ________________________

02 While driving, ________________________

03 She is disappointed at me. ________________________

04 He is always late for school. ________________________

05 Jenny wants to lose weight. ________________________

2 should의 생략

[06-08] 주어진 어구를 바르게 배열하여 문장을 완성하시오.

06 (necessary, attend, that, it's, we, the meeting)

➡ ________________________

07 (he, all the evidence, is, that, innocent, suggests)

➡ ________________________

08 (in bed, insisted, my, stay, I, family doctor, that)

➡ ________________________

3 had better, had better not

[09-14] 문장에서 **틀린** 부분을 찾아 밑줄을 긋고 바르게 고치시오.

09 Look at those clouds. You have better bring your umbrella with you. ________________

10 Your room is a mess. You'd better to clean up your room. ________________

11 We have better start now, or we'll miss the train. ________________

12 You had not better be late for the meeting. ________________

13 You look pale. I think you had better to go to see a doctor. ________________

14 You had not better answer the phone. ________________

🎓 어휘 & 표현

· **avoid** 피하다	· **insist** 주장하다	· **apply for** 지원하다	· **essential** 필수적인	· **protect** 보호하다	· **environment** 환경
· **disappointed** 실망한	· **lose weight** 살을 빼다	· **evidence** 증거	· **innocent** 순진한, 무죄의	· **pale** 창백한	

〈 정답과 해설 p. 42~43 〉

UNIT 25 used to, would, 조동사 + have + 과거분사
~하곤 했다

There **used to** be a big tree here. (여기에 커다란 나무가 한 그루 있었다.)
과거의 상태

When young, I **used to** play under the tree.
과거의 반복적인 동작

(어렸을 적에 나는 그 나무 밑에서 놀곤 했다.)

1 used to, would

used to, would (둘 다 가능)	'～하곤 했다' – 과거의 반복적이었던 행동을 나타낸다. • I used to(= would) jog in the morning. (나는 아침에 조깅을 하곤 했다.)
used to (would는 사용 불가)	'～이 있었다' – 행위가 아닌, 과거의 상태를 나타낸다. • There used to be a bakery on that corner. (저 모퉁이에 빵집이 있었다. → 지금은 없다.) '～하곤 했다' – 과거의 습관이었지만, 지금은 하지 않는 것을 나타낸다. • As a child, I used to read books all day long. 지금은 읽지 않는다는 의미를 포함 (어렸을 때, 나는 하루 종일 책을 읽곤 했다.)

[참고] be [become, get] used to + 명사, 동명사: ~에 익숙하다

• My friend Paul got used to Korean food. (내 친구 Paul은 한국 음식에 익숙해졌다.)

• She wasn't used to working at a desk all day.

(그녀는 하루 종일 책상에서 일하는 것에 익숙하지 않았다.)

2 조동사 + have + 과거분사: 과거 일에 대한 추측 또는 유감이나 후회를 나타낸다.

표현	예문
would have + 과거분사 (～했을 텐데)	• He would have helped you, but he was too busy. (그는 너를 도왔을 텐데, 그는 너무 바빴다.)
could have + 과거분사 (～할 수 있었을 텐데)	• She could have been to Venice. (그녀는 베니스에 갈 수 있었을 텐데.)
cannot[couldn't] have + 과거분사 (～했을 리가 없다)	• Can she not have received the invitation? 영국식 표현 • Can't she have received the invitation? 미국식 표현 (그녀는 초대장을 받았을 리가 없지?)
may[might] have + 과거분사 (～했을지도 모른다)	• They might have been waiting for us at the restaurant. (그들은 레스토랑에서 우리를 기다리고 있었을지도 모른다.)
must have + 과거분사 (～했음에 틀림없다)	• He must have passed the test. (그는 시험에 합격했음에 틀림없다.)
should[ought to] have + 과거분사 (～했어야 했다)	• You should have come to the party. (당신은 파티에 왔어야 했다.)

① used to, would

[01-04] 문장에서 **틀린** 부분을 찾아 밑줄을 긋고 바르게 고치시오. (단, 틀린 부분이 없다면 ○로 표시할 것)

01 Sometimes I would play baseball with him. ___________

02 My American friend used to eating with chopsticks. ___________

03 She was used to teach children English on Sundays. ___________

04 Though he is 70 years old, he is as energetic as he would be. ___________

② 조동사 + have + 과거분사

[05-09] 괄호 안에서 알맞은 것을 고르시오.

05 She lost one of her earrings. She (must / should) have dropped it somewhere.

06 You missed a chance to meet the President. You (would / should) have come here.

07 She (can / may) have left for her house yesterday if she had got a plane ticket.

08 You (could have seen / cannot have seen) her there. She was here with me at that time.

09 World history (should have been changed / might have been changed) if they had conquered the country.

① + ② used to, would, 조동사 + have + 과거분사

[10-15] 밑줄 친 조동사 어구에 유의하여 다음 문장을 우리말로 해석하시오.

10 I <u>should have been</u> a little more careful.

➡ ____

11 When I was young, summers <u>didn't use to</u> be as hot as they are now.

➡ ____

12 He looked happy. The movie <u>must have been</u> interesting.

➡ ____

13 We've already been waiting for 30 minutes. We <u>ought to have reserved</u> a table.

➡ ____

14 This area <u>used to</u> be a large field, not apartment complexes.

➡ ____

15 He <u>may have seen</u> the movie.

➡ ____

 어휘 & 표현

- **all day long** 하루 종일 · **receive** 받다 · **invitation** 초대장 · **chopsticks** 젓가락 · **energetic** 활기찬 · **conquer** 정복하다
- **careful** 조심하는 · **already** 이미 · **reserve** 예약하다 · **field** 들판 · **apartment complex** 아파트 단지

〈 정답과 해설 p. 43~44 〉

[01-03]

대화의 빈칸에 알맞은 것을 고르시오.

01

> A: What a scary dog she is!
> B: You _________ be afraid of her. She never bites humans.

① should
② could
③ had better
④ ought to
⑤ don't have to

02

> A: I'm feeling awful today. What time will the meeting finish?
> B: You _________ go home now and take a rest.

① can
② might not
③ should not
④ must not
⑤ don't have to

03

> A: He got a perfect score again on the exam.
> B: _________________________

① He had better study all night.
② He must have studied all night.
③ He cannot have studied all night.
④ He should have studied all night.
⑤ He ought to have studied all night.

[04-08]

빈칸에 must와 cannot 중 알맞은 것을 쓰시오.

04

Jenny has gone to Italy. She ____________ be in Korea now.

05

She is putting on her makeup.
She ____________ be going out.

06

Joe had brunch an hour ago.
He ____________ be hungry.

07

Peter was sick yesterday. He ____________ have done his homework.

08

He walked all day long. He ____________ be tired now.

[09-10] 고난도

밑줄 친 부분이 어법상 **틀린** 문장을 고르시오.

09

① I would like to help my old friend.
② You had better not to meet her again.
③ My cousin Jane is used to Japanese food.
④ She would not listen to the doctor's advice.
⑤ You don't have to get up early tomorrow morning.

10

① I do enjoy spending time with my family.
② You can always count on me.
③ They won't be able attend the meeting next week.
④ He shall return your call as soon as he's available.
⑤ We need not worry about the weather; it's going to be fine.

[11-16]

빈칸에 알맞은 말을 〈보기〉에서 골라 문장을 완성하시오.

(중복 사용 불가)

〈보기〉

| cannot | might | has to |
| used to | had better not | will |

11

She thought the ring ______________ be a fake.

12

David ______________ do his homework by himself.

13

We ______________ be high school students next year.

14

You ______________ enter the room without permission.

15

I ______________ find my wallet. I must have dropped it somewhere.

16

My father ______________ cook on Sunday afternoons when I was young.

[17-19] (서술형)

대화를 읽고 밑줄 친 우리말과 일치하도록 빈칸에 알맞은 말을 쓰시오. (단, 조동사와 주어진 동사를 사용할 것)

17

A: I was wondering why John didn't come to the party last night.
B: He wouldn't have missed it unless there was a good reason. 그는 뭔가 일이 생겼음에 틀림없어. (have)

➡ He ______________ something come up.

18

A: It looks like we got lost.
B: I know. What should we do now?
A: I have no idea. We did not listen to the teacher. We should have listened to him.
B: Don't cry over spilt milk. 누군가가 와서 우리를 도와줄 것임에 틀림없어. (come)

➡ Someone ______________ and help us.

19

A: Tom has a serious health problem.
B: Is that true? He looked all right before.
A: But he hasn't been sleeping at night recently. 의사는 그가 밤에 잠을 자야 한다고 주장했지만, 그는 충고를 따르지 않았어. (sleep)
B: No doubt he has a health problem.

➡ His doctor insisted that he ______________ ______________ at night, but he did not follow the advice.

[20-21]

밑줄 친 부분의 의미가 나머지 넷과 다른 것을 고르시오.

20

① My brother <u>can</u> speak Spanish.
② Who <u>can</u> answer this question?
③ He <u>can</u> run 100 meters in 13 seconds.
④ They <u>can</u> help you carry these books.
⑤ John doesn't look good. He <u>can</u> be sick.

21

① You <u>must</u> be quiet here.
② Mr. Kim <u>must</u> be a good teacher.
③ You <u>must</u> call your parents right now.
④ You <u>must</u> drink water at least twice a day.
⑤ Every student <u>must</u> obey and follow the rules.

〈 정답과 해설 p. 44~45 〉

자연스러운 대화가 되도록 괄호 안에서 알맞은 것을 고르시오.

22

A: I used to (go / going) to the gym every morning, but I lost the routine after a while.

B: It happens.

23

A: I'm not sure what to do about the presentation tomorrow.

B: Don't worry. You (shall / had better) do great! You've prepared well.

24

A: I've been thinking about starting a new hobby, like painting.

B: That's a great idea! You (must / should) have done that sooner.

[25-26]
not이 들어갈 알맞은 위치를 고르시오.

25

> They (①) must (②) share (③) their (④) passwords (⑤) with anyone.

26

> You (①) had (②) better (③) ignore (④) the warning signs on (⑤) the road.

[27-28]
어법상 틀린 것을 고르시오.

27

① You'd better call the police, first.
② May I help him with his homework?
③ You have to make her come back here.
④ It might be true that he lived in the U.S.
⑤ She used to got up early in the morning.

28 고난도

① She can speak three languages fluently.
② We ought finish this project by tomorrow.
③ You might as well reconsider that decision.
④ I insist that he be more careful with his spending.
⑤ They could have arrived earlier if they had taken a shortcut.

29

주어진 우리말과 일치하도록 바르게 영작한 것을 고르시오.

> 당신은 내가 한 말을 오해했음에 틀림없다.

① You can have misunderstood what I said.
② You must have misunderstood what I said.
③ You might have misunderstood what I said.
④ You should have misunderstood what I said.
⑤ You ought to have misunderstood what I said.

[30-32] 서술형
문장을 괄호 안의 지시대로 바꿔 쓰시오.

30

They encouraged her to reveal her true feelings. (동사를 강조하여)

➡ ______________________

31

She can't force her son to eat what he doesn't like. (be able to를 이용하여)

➡ ______________________

32

The students need not wear their uniform on Saturday. (have to를 이용하여)

➡ ______________________

두 문장의 의미가 <u>다른</u> 것을 고르시오.

33

① Can I ask you a favor?
= May I ask you a favor?
② I would like to reserve a room.
= I want to reserve a room.
③ You don't have to hand in the report.
= You need not hand in the report.
④ She can make a chocolate cake.
= She is able to make a chocolate cake.
⑤ They should have told the truth to their parents.
= They may have told the truth to their parents.

34

① She used to live in New York.
= She would live in New York.
② You should take an umbrella.
= You ought to take an umbrella.
③ You must respect the rules.
= You have to respect the rules.
④ I might go to the gym tomorrow.
= I may go to the gym tomorrow.
⑤ You don't have to use your phone while driving.
= You had better not use your phone while driving.

[35-37] 서술형

대화가 자연스럽도록 주어진 단어와 조동사 표현을 이용하여 빈칸에 알맞은 말을 쓰시오.

35

A: I couldn't go to the party last night. How was it?
B: It was fantastic. You ________________ ________________ to the party. (come)

36

A: Rise and shine! It's 7 o'clock.
B: I'm not working today, so I ________________ ________________ early. (get up)

37

A: I decided to stop eating junk food for my health.
B: Good. You ________________________ ________________ junk food any more. (eat)

[38-39] 고난도

대화의 밑줄 친 부분 중 어법상 <u>어색한</u> 것을 고르시오.

38

A: ① <u>Can</u> Mary speak Japanese well?
B: No, she ② <u>can't</u> speak Japanese well. She ③ <u>has studied</u> it only for a year.
A: But she ④ <u>will</u> go to Japan this winter, right?
B: Right. That's why she hopes that she ⑤ <u>can be able to speak</u> it very well.

39

A: I ① <u>can't</u> find my keys anywhere!
B: You ② <u>may have left</u> them at the office.
A: Oh no, you're probably right. I ③ <u>should have checked</u> before leaving.
B: Don't worry, we ④ <u>can</u> go back and grab them.
A: Wait, I ⑤ <u>ought to have left</u> them in the car.
B: Maybe. Let's check there first.

〈 정답과 해설 p. 45~46 〉

문장의 밑줄 친 부분과 바꿔 쓸 수 있는 말을 고르시오.

40

> You <u>ought to</u> obey the advice that your doctor gave you.

① can   ② may   ③ have
④ should   ⑤ would

41

> You <u>don't have to</u> answer my call if you don't want to.

① cannot   ② need not   ③ should not
④ must not   ⑤ will not

42

> I didn't get your reply. It <u>may have ended</u> up in my spam folder.

① could have ended
② might have ended
③ would have ended
④ should have ended
⑤ ought to have ended

43

주어진 문장의 밑줄 친 do동사와 쓰임이 같은 것을 고르시오.

> I <u>do</u> want to go to the concert this Sunday.

① <u>Do</u> you have a stopwatch?
② Did you <u>do</u> the dishes, Sally?
③ She <u>did</u> do her homework last night.
④ Never <u>did</u> I see such a strange person.
⑤ You <u>do</u> not have to bring your camera.

44 수능 유형 고난도

밑줄 친 부분 중 어법상 <u>틀린</u> 것을 고르시오.

> My 70-year-old grandma always tells me what I ① <u>should</u> and shouldn't do. She insists that the cupboard doors ② <u>are</u> closed at all times. She says if I leave the cupboard doors open, it ③ <u>will</u> bring bad luck to my family. When I heard this as a young girl, I believed it ④ <u>was</u> related to something superstitious. Now I know that it ⑤ <u>has made</u> me develop a good habit.

①   ②   ③   ④   ⑤

다음 글을 읽고 물음에 답하시오.

> Tom doesn't like flying, but he ① <u>will have to take</u> a plane for his business trip next week. His colleague _____________ him, but she has a family event and can't make it. Tom ② <u>would rather drive</u>, but the trip is too far to travel by car. He ③ <u>should book</u> his flight soon to get the best price. Since he doesn't want to be late, he ④ <u>has to leave</u> earlier than planned. "I ⑤ <u>had better to stay</u> focused during the trip," he thought, preparing for the busy week ahead.

45 수능 유형

밑줄 친 부분 중 어법상 <u>틀린</u> 것을 고르시오.

①   ②   ③   ④   ⑤

46

빈칸에 적절한 것을 고르시오.

① will join   ② must join
③ have to join   ④ could have joined
⑤ would like to joined

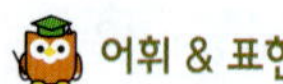

어휘 & 표현

- **scary** 무서운   • **bite** 물다   • **awful** 끔찍한   • **fake** 모조품   • **warning** 경고   • **fluently** 유창하게   • **shortcut** 지름길
- **misunderstand** 오해하다   • **hand in** 제출하다   • **cupboard** 찬장   • **superstitious** 미신적인   • **colleague** 동료

수동태

受動態

(받을 수, 움직일 동, 형태 태)

주어가 동사의 동작을 당함

The patient may be taken care of by the nurse.

조동사와 동사구의 수동태

(환자는 간호사에게 돌봄을 받을지도 모른다.)

[능동태] The actor gave the fan an autograph.

간접목적어 　 직접목적어

(그 배우가 팬에게 사인을 해줬다.)

[4형식 수동태] The fan was given an autograph by the actor.

간접목적어를 주어로

(그 팬은 그 배우에 의해 사인을 받았다.)

An autograph was given to the fan by the actor.

직접목적어를 주어로

(사인은 그 배우에 의해 그 팬에게 주어졌다.)

[능동태] They elected Sarah the new leader after the final vote.

(그들은 최종 투표 후에 Sarah를 새로운 리더로 선출했다.)

[5형식 수동태] Sarah was elected the new leader after the final vote

과거시제 수동태

by them.

(Sarah는 최종 투표 후 그들에 의해 새로운 리더로 선출되었다.)

 **UNIT 26** 수동태의 개념 및 형태 

능동태: A hunter caught the rabbit.
주어 / 능동태 동사 / 목적어
(사냥꾼이 토끼를 잡았다.)

수동태: The rabbit was caught by a hunter. 
주어 / 수동태 동사 / 「by + 행위자」
(토끼는 사냥꾼에게 잡혔다.)

1 능동태와 수동태

능동태는 주어가 어떤 동작이나 작용을 스스로 하였을 때의 동사 형태이고,
수동태는 주어가 어떤 동작의 대상이 되어 그 작용을 받을 때의 동사 형태이다.

> ③ 주어 ② 동사 ① 목적어
> [능동태] They build a new house. (그들은 새집을 짓는다.)
>
> [수동태] A new house is built by them. (새집은 그들에 의해 지어진다.)
> ① 주어 ② 동사 ③ 「by + 목적격」
>
> ① 능동태 문장의 목적어 → 수동태 문장의 주어로 옮긴다.
> ② 능동태 문장의 동사 → 「be동사 + 과거분사」로 바꾼다.
> ③ 능동태 문장의 주어 → 「by + 목적격(행위자)」으로 바꾼다.
> [참고] 「by + 목적격(행위자)」은 생략되기도 한다.

❶ 「by+행위자」를 생략하는 경우

행위자가 people이나 we와 같이 일반인이거나 정확하지 않은 경우, 불분명한 경우, 또 물건이나 건물의 위치를 나타내는 경우에는 「by+행위자」를 생략한다.

[능동태] She edited the report. (그녀는 보고서를 수정했다.)
[수동태] The report was edited by her. (그 보고서는 그녀에 의해 수정되었다.)
능동태의 동사가 과거이므로 수동태의 동사도 과거로 씀

2 수동태의 부정문: 능동태의 동사 → 「be동사 + not + 과거분사」

[능동태] I didn't clean my room. (나는 방을 청소하지 않았다.)
[수동태] My room wasn't cleaned (by me). (내 방은 (나에 의해) 청소되지 않았다.)

❷ 의문사 who가 주어인 경우

의문사 who가 주어인 경우에는 「by+행위자」의 '행위자'에 해당하는 것이 who이므로 수동태 문장이 By whom으로 시작하는 것에 유의해야 한다.

3 수동태의 의문문

(1) 의문사가 없는 의문문의 수동태: be동사 + 주어 + 과거분사 + by + 목적격?

[능동태] Did she write the letter? (그녀가 편지를 썼니?)
[수동태] Was the letter written by her? (그 편지가 그녀에 의해 쓰였니?)

(2) 의문사 who가 주어인 의문문의 수동태: By whom + be동사 + 주어 + 과거분사?

[능동태] Who invented the computer? (컴퓨터를 누가 발명했니?)
[수동태] By whom was the computer invented? (컴퓨터는 누구에 의해 발명되었니?)

(3) 그 외 의문사가 있는 의문문의 수동태: 의문사 + be동사 + 주어 + 과거분사 + by + 목적격?

[능동태] Where did they build the bridge? (그들은 그 다리를 어디에 지었니?)
[수동태] Where was the bridge built by them? (그 다리는 그들에 의해 어디에 지어졌니?)

1 능동태와 수동태

[01-06] 문장을 수동태 문장으로 바꿔 쓰시오.

01 The company fired them. ➡ ____

02 He visited his grandparents. ➡ ____

03 Robots do the dangerous work. ➡ ____

04 She missed the last train. ➡ ____

05 The young man took the front seat. ➡ ____

06 The earthquake destroyed lots of buildings. ➡ ____

2 수동태의 부정문

[07-11] 괄호 안에서 알맞은 것을 고르시오.

07 This message was (not / don't) sent by me last night.

08 The room (not is / is not) cleaned by Jane every day.

09 The machine was not developed (by he / by him).

10 The suspects (did not arrest / were not arrested) by the police.

11 The glass (did not break / was not broken) by Nick.

3 수동태의 의문문

[12-14] 그림을 보고 주어진 어구를 이용하여 수동태 문장을 완성하시오. (단, 과거형으로 쓸 것)

12 

(the picture, take)
Where ____?

13 

(that window, break)
By whom ____?

14 

(this house, design, you)
Was ____?

🦉 어휘 & 표현

- **edit** 수정하다 · **invent** 발명하다 · **company** 회사 · **fire** 해고하다 · **earthquake** 지진 · **destroy** 파괴하다
- **develop** 개발하다 · **suspect** 용의자 · **arrest** 체포하다

〈 정답과 해설 **p. 47~48** 〉

In 1876, the telephone ***was invented*** by Alexander Graham Bell.
과거시제 수동태
(1876년에 전화기가 Alexander Graham Bell에 의해 발명되었다.)

Since then, it ***has been used*** by billions of people.
현재완료시제 수동태
(그때 이후로 그것은 수십억 명의 사람들에 의해 사용되어져 왔다.)

1 수동태의 현재, 과거, 미래시제

현재시제	am / is / are + 과거분사	[능동태] This machine detects tiny vibrations. (이 기계는 아주 작은 진동을 감지한다.) [수동태] Tiny vibrations are detected by this machine. (아주 작은 진동이 이 기계에 의해 감지된다.)
과거시제	was / were + 과거분사	[능동태] The flood shut down the entire network. (홍수가 전체 네트워크를 정지시켰다.) [수동태] The entire network was shut down by the flood. (전체 네트워크가 홍수에 의해 정지되었다.)
미래시제	will / be going to + be + 과거분사	[능동태] They will release a new movie next week. (그들은 다음 주에 새 영화를 개봉할 것이다.) [수동태] A new movie will be released by them next week. (새 영화가 다음 주에 그들에 의해 개봉될 것이다.)

2 수동태의 진행형

현재진행시제	am / is / are + being + 과거분사	[능동태] They are cleaning the classroom. (그들은 교실을 청소하고 있다.) [수동태] The classroom is being cleaned by them. (교실이 그들에 의해 청소되고 있다.)
과거진행시제	was / were + being + 과거분사	[능동태] The architect was designing a revolutionary structure. (그 건축가는 혁신적인 구조물을 설계하고 있었다.) [수동태] A revolutionary structure was being designed by the architect. (혁신적인 구조물이 그 건축가에 의해 설계되고 있었다.)

3 수동태의 완료형

현재완료시제	have / has + been + 과거분사	[능동태] Experts have proposed an alternative solution. (전문가들이 대안을 제안해왔다.) [수동태] An alternative solution has been proposed by experts. (대안이 전문가들에 의해 제안되어왔다.)
과거완료시제	had + been + 과거분사	[능동태] He had repaired the car before the trip. (그는 여행 전에 차를 수리했었다.) [수동태] The car had been repaired by him before the trip. (차가 여행 전에 그에 의해 수리되었었다.)

1 수동태의 현재, 과거, 미래시제

[01-04] 주어진 우리말과 일치하도록 괄호 안의 말을 이용하여 영작하시오.

01 이 물은 마을 사람들에 의해 마셔진다. (this water, the villagers, drink)

➡ ____

02 그 이메일은 경찰관들에 의해 쓰여졌다. (the email, the police officers, write)

➡ ____

03 영어는 전 세계의 많은 사람들에 의해 사용된다. (many people around the world, speak, English)

➡ ____

04 그 문서들은 나중에 인쇄될 예정이다. (the documents, print, later)

➡ ____

12^{DAY}

2 수동태의 진행형

[05-09] 문장을 수동태 문장으로 바꿔 쓰시오.

05 Two men are painting the roof of my house.

➡ ____

06 An old woman was collecting empty boxes.

➡ ____

07 The famous pianist is playing symphonies.

➡ ____

08 The waitress was serving hot food.

➡ ____

09 The students are singing cheerful songs.

➡ ____

> **어휘 & 표현**
> - **detect** 감지하다
> - **tiny** 아주 작은
> - **vibration** 진동
> - **flood** 홍수
> - **entire** 전체의
> - **architect** 건축가
> - **revolutionary** 혁신적인
> - **structure** 구조(물)
> - **alternative** 대안이 되는
> - **villager** 마을 사람
> - **symphony** 교향곡
> - **supply** 공급하다
> - **tough** 질긴
> - **allowance** 용돈

3 수동태의 완료형

[10-15] 괄호 안에서 알맞은 것을 고르시오.

10 Some friends (have inviting / had been invited) to the party by me.

11 The carpenter (has used / has been used) solid wood to make tables.

12 These products (have been supplied / have being supplied) by his company.

13 The steak (has been cooked / had been cooked) too long, so it was very tough.

14 Her allowance (has usually spent / has usually been spent) on snacks.

15 When we arrived at the theater, we found that the movie (has been canceled / had been canceled).

〈 정답과 해설 p. 48~49 〉

 **UNIT 28** 조동사와 동사구의 수동태 

The damaged car **_must be repaired_** by a mechanic.
조동사 must의 수동태
(그 부서진 차는 정비사에 의해 수리되어야 한다.)

It should **_be taken care of_** before the trip.
동사구 take care of의 수동태
(그것은 여행 전에 수습되어야 한다.)

1 조동사가 있는 수동태 ❶

(1) 조동사가 있는 수동태: 조동사 + be + 과거분사

> 능동태 We will elect a new president. (우리는 새 대통령을 선출할 것이다.)
>
> 수동태 A new president will be elected by us.
>
> (새 대통령이 우리에 의해 선출될 것이다.)

(2) 조동사가 있는 수동태의 부정문: 조동사 + not be + 과거분사

> 능동태 You can't take photos without permission.
>
> (당신은 허가 없이 사진을 찍을 수 없다.)
>
> 수동태 Photos can't be taken without permission.
>
> (사진은 허가 없이 찍힐 수 없다.)

(3) 조동사가 있는 수동태의 의문문: 조동사 + 주어 + be + 과거분사 ~?

> 능동태 Can the scientists discover a cure for cancer?
>
> (과학자들이 암 치료제를 발견할 수 있을까?)
>
> 수동태 Can a cure for cancer be discovered by the scientists?
>
> (암 치료제가 그 과학자들에 의해 발견될 수 있을까?)

> ❶ **수동태에 사용되지 않는 조동사**
>
> 다른 조동사들은 수동태로 만들 수 있지만, 조동사 do는 수동태 문장에 사용되지 않는다.

2 동사구의 수동태 ❷

「동사+전치사」, 「동사+부사」 등 두 개 이상의 단어로 이루어진 동사구의 수동태는 동사구를 하나의 단위로 취급하여 수동태로 바꾼다.

give up 포기하다	① bring up 양육하다	run over (차가) 치다
laugh at 비웃다	② take care of 돌보다	make up 구성하다
deal with 다루다	③ put off 연기하다	fill in (여백 등을) 메우다

> ❷ **동사구의 수동태를 만들 때**
>
> 동사구의 수동태를 만드는 경우에는 「be동사+과거분사」 뒤에 나머지 동사구가 이어지므로 동사의 과거분사 형태에 유의해야 한다.

① 능동태 My grandmother brought me up. (할머니가 나를 키우셨다.)
   수동태 I was brought up by my grandmother. (나는 할머니에 의해 키워졌다.)

② 능동태 Jenny takes care of the patient. (Jenny가 그 환자를 돌본다.)
   수동태 The patient is taken care of by Jenny. (그 환자는 Jenny에 의해 돌보아진다.)

③ 능동태 We put off the field trip. (우리는 현장 학습을 연기했다.)
   수동태 The field trip was put off by us. (현장 학습은 우리에 의해 연기됐다.)

❶ 조동사가 있는 수동태

[01-05] 문장을 수동태로 고칠 때 빈칸에 알맞은 말을 쓰시오.

01 We can't see the sun at night.

→ The sun ___________________________ at night by us.

02 You may hear the beep sound.

→ The beep sound ___________________________ by you.

03 The workers should wear helmets.

→ ___________________________ by the workers.

04 They did not provide the solution.

→ The solution ___________________________ by them.

05 They will teach students at this school in English.

→ Students at this school ___________________________ in English by them.

❷ 동사구의 수동태

[06-10] 빈칸에 들어갈 말을 〈보기〉에서 골라 알맞은 형태의 수동태 문장을 완성하시오. (중복 사용 불가)

> 〈보기〉
> run over   put off   fill in   laugh at   make up of

06 The driver's license test ___________________________ the written test and driving test.

07 Yesterday his funny hat ___________________________ by his classmates.

08 The police officer reported that a deer had ___________________________ by an overspeeding car.

09 All the blanks on this form should ___________________________.

10 Their game had ___________________________ because of heavy rain, but it was played the next day.

❶ + ❷ 조동사와 동사구의 수동태

[11-14] 문장에서 **틀린** 부분을 찾아 밑줄을 긋고 바르게 고치시오.

11 The package is can be delivered by the postman.   ___________________

12 One of the Shakespeare's plays will are performed by them.   ___________________

13 Most people think this project should stop by them right away.   ___________________

14 Our customer's complaints are dealt by the department.   ___________________

🦉 **어휘 & 표현**

· **cure** 치료제   · **cancer** 암   · **patient** 환자   · **field trip** 현장 학습   · **driver's license** 운전 면허증   · **overspeeding** 과속
· **heavy rain** 폭우   · **package** 소포   · **postman** 우편집배원   · **complain** 불만   · **department** 부서

〈 정답과 해설 p. 49 〉

[01-02]

빈칸에 알맞은 것을 고르시오.

01

> This poem __________ by Robert Burns in 1788.

① write
② wrote
③ was written
④ will write
⑤ has been written

02

> __________ was the antique car purchased?

① What
② Who
③ Which
④ Who
⑤ By whom

[03-04] (서술형)

주어진 우리말과 일치하도록 괄호 안의 단어를 알맞은 형태로 바꿔 빈칸에 쓰시오.

03

그는 어제 그 사고에서 심하게 부상당했다. (injure)

➡ He __________ badly at the accident yesterday.

04

이 사진은 그에 의해 찍히지 않았다. (take)

➡ This picture __________ by him.

05

주어진 문장을 수동태로 알맞게 바꾼 것을 고르시오.

> The mother didn't hear the baby's cry.

① The baby was not heard cry by the mother.
② The mother was not hear the baby's cry.
③ The baby's cry was not heard by the mother.
④ Cry was not heard the baby by the mother.
⑤ The baby's cry didn't heard by the mother.

[06-09] (서술형)

그림을 보고 〈보기〉의 단어와 주어진 시제로 문장을 완성하시오. (중복 사용 불가)

〈보기〉

grow　　　catch

06

Various flowers __________ on the grass by her. (현재시제)

07

A few fish __________ by the two boys. (현재진행시제)

〈보기〉

buy　　　wrap

08

Each bunch of grapes __________ by yellow paper. (과거시제)

09

A bag of apples __________ by a woman. (과거진행시제)

[10-13]

문장에서 틀린 부분을 찾아 밑줄을 긋고 바르게 고치시오.

10

While she was walking her dog, she saw a man run by a car. ________________

11

I was scolded for my carelessness from my teacher. ________________

12

When I asked by my grandfather, I replied, "Yes, I'll take care of her until you return." ________________

13

He was not listened by anyone in the classroom. ________________

14 고난도

어법상 틀린 것을 고르시오.

① His room was painted in blue and yellow.
② The result had better be told at once to Eric.
③ The weeds have to be pulled up for roses to grow.
④ The questions are going to be answered by midnight.
⑤ When the dinner made, John called me to eat.

[15-16] 서술형

주어진 우리말과 일치하도록 괄호 안의 말을 이용하여 영작하시오.

15

그녀의 빵집이 누군가의 침입을 받았다.
(bakery, break into, someone)

➡ ________________________________

16

그녀는 나에게 면접을 받을 것이다.
(be going to, interview)

➡ ________________________________

17

문장을 수동태로 고칠 때 빈칸에 알맞은 것을 고르시오.

> We may see a rainbow after the rain stops.
> → A rainbow ________ after the rain stops.

① is may seen
② may be seeing
③ may be seen
④ may have seen
⑤ may have been seen

18 수능 유형

밑줄 친 부분 중 어법상 틀린 것을 고르시오.

> The Korean turtle ship, also ① known as Geobukseon, is the first ironclad warship in world history. It is ② called the turtle ship because it is shaped like a turtle. Admiral Yi Soonshin ③ considered a great figure who invented this great warship. The turtle ships ④ had advanced weapons. They ⑤ were used in the wars against the Japanese navy, leading to many victories in battle.
>
> *ironclad 철갑의

①　②　③　④　⑤

🦉 어휘 & 표현

· **poem** 시　· **antique** 골동품의　· **injure** 부상을 입히다　· **wrap** 포장하다　· **scold** 혼내다　· **weed** 잡초
· **break into** 침입하다　· **warship** 군함　· **figure** 인물　· **advanced** 진보된　· **weapon** 무기　· **victory** 승리

〈 정답과 해설 p. 50~51 〉

UNIT 29 · 4형식, 5형식의 수동태

Spaghetti **was made** for them by the woman.
「직접목적어+be동사+과거분사+전치사+간접목적어」
(스파게티가 그들을 위해 그 여자에 의해 만들어졌다.)

The girls **were heard to say** "Thank you" to their mom.
지각동사의 수동태: 목적격 보어(원형부정사) → to부정사
(소녀들이 엄마에게 "고마워요"라고 말하는 것이 들렸다.)

1 4형식 문장의 수동태 전환

(1) 간접목적어와 직접목적어 각각을 주어로 하는 두 개의 수동태를 만들 수 있다.

① **간접목적어가 주어: 간접목적어 + be동사 + 과거분사 + 직접목적어 + (by + 행위자)**

② **직접목적어가 주어: 직접목적어 + be동사 + 과거분사 + to[for, of] + 간접목적어 + (by + 행위자)**

간접목적어와 직접목적어 둘 다 수동태의 주어가 되는 동사	ask, award, give, lend, send, show, teach, tell, offer 등 능동태 I gave him my coat. (나는 그에게 내 외투를 주었다.) 동사 / 간접목적어 / 직접목적어 간접목적어가 주어 수동태 He was given my coat by me. 주어가 된 간접목적어 (그는 나에 의해 내 외투를 받았다.) 직접목적어가 주어 수동태 My coat was given *to him* by me. 주어가 된 직접목적어 (내 외투는 나에 의해 그에게 주어졌다.)
직접목적어만 수동태의 주어가 되는 동사	buy, cook, get, make, read, pass, prepare, sell, sing, write 등 간접목적어 / 직접목적어 능동태 Mom bought me an umbrella. (엄마가 내게 우산을 사 주셨다.) 직접목적어만 수동태의 주어가 되는 동사 직접목적어가 주어 수동태 An umbrella was bought *for me* by Mom. 주어가 된 직접목적어 (우산이 나를 위해 엄마에 의해 구매되었다.) 간접목적어 / 직접목적어 능동태 Someone wrote her a letter last week. 직접목적어만 수동태의 주어가 되는 동사 (누군가가 지난주 그녀에게 편지를 썼다.) 직접목적어가 주어 수동태 A letter was written *to her* last week. 주어가 된 직접목적어 (지난주 그녀에게 편지가 쓰여졌다.)

(2) **직접목적어가 주어가 될 때 간접목적어 앞에 붙는 전치사**

to	give, offer, read, sell, send, teach, tell, write, lend, show, pay, pass 등 • An email is sent to his boss by him. (이메일이 그의 상사에게 그에 의해 보내졌다.) • The answer was told to us by the guide. (그 답은 가이드에 의해 우리에게 말해졌다.)
for	buy, find, cook, get, make, prepare 등 • The cake was made for her by them. (그 케이크는 그녀를 위해 그들에 의해 만들어졌다.) • The room was prepared for guests last night. (그 방은 어젯밤 손님들을 위해 준비되었다.)
of	ask, require 등 • A favor was asked of me by her. (부탁이 그녀에 의해 나에게 요청되었다.) • A response was required of him by the court. (답변이 법원에 의해 그에게 요구되었다.)

1 4형식 문장의 수동태 전환

[01-05] 문장을 수동태로 고쳐 쓰시오.

01 Our English teacher gave us a lot of homework.

➡ ____

➡ ____

02 The librarian read young children an interesting storybook.

➡ ____

03 My mother made me a doll.

➡ ____

04 Ella's older brother teaches them English and math.

➡ ____

➡ ____

05 He bought me a brand-new smartphone.

➡ ____

[06-09] 문장을 수동태로 바꿔 쓸 때, 빈칸에 알맞은 말을 쓰시오.

06 The school awarded her a special prize.

➡ ______________________ a special prize by the school.

07 The students gave the teacher a touching letter.

➡ A touching letter ______________________ by the students.

08 His father bought him a new bicycle.

➡ A new bicycle ______________________ by his father.

09 The company offered the workers better conditions.

➡ ______________________ to the workers by the company.

[10-13] 주어진 우리말과 일치하도록 괄호 안의 단어를 이용하여 빈칸에 알맞은 말을 쓰시오.

10 열쇠는 그들에 의해 우리에게 전달되었다. (pass)

➡ The keys ______________________ us by them.

11 깜짝 파티가 그들에 의해 그녀를 위해 준비되었다. (prepare)

➡ A surprise party ______________________ her by them.

12 오늘 아침 나를 위해 커피가 만들어졌다. (make)

➡ Coffee ______________________ me this morning.

13 그 회의 시간은 그녀에 의해 그에게 물어졌다. (inquire)

➡ The meeting time ______________________ him by her.

〈 정답과 해설 **p. 51~52** 〉

2 5형식 문장의 수동태 전환

- 5형식 문장: 주어＋동사＋목적어＋목적격 보어
- 5형식 문장의 목적어는 수동태의 주어가 되고, 목적격 보어는 주격 보어가 된다.

(1) 목적격 보어가 명사, 형용사, to부정사인 경우

능동태: 「주어＋동사＋목적어＋목적격 보어」

수동태: 「주어＋「be동사＋과거분사」(수동태)＋주격 보어＋(by＋목적격)」

능동태 The company named him CEO. (그 회사는 그를 CEO로 임명했다.)
목적격 보어(명사)

수동태 He was named CEO by the company.
그대로 옴

(그는 그 회사에 의해 CEO로 임명되었다.)

능동태 They found the book interesting. (그들은 그 책이 흥미롭다고 생각했다.)
목적격 보어 (형용사)

수동태 The book was found interesting by them.
그대로 옴

(그 책은 그들에 의해 흥미롭다고 여겨졌다.)

능동태 They ask us to help them. (그들은 우리에게 그들을 도와달라고 요청한다.)
목적격 보어 (to부정사)

수동태 We are asked to help them by them.
그대로 옴

(우리는 그들에 의해 그들을 도와달라고 요청받았다.)

> ❶ 사역동사, 준사역동사, 지각동사
> - **사역동사:** 시키다, ~하게 하다 (let, have, make)
> - **준사역동사:** ~하도록 돕다 (help)
> - **지각동사:** 보다, 듣다, 느끼다 등 (see, hear, feel, watch, listen to 등)

(2) 사역동사, 지각동사가 쓰인 경우: 사역동사, 지각동사는 목적격 보어로 원형부정사를 취한다. ❶
목적격 보어인 원형부정사를 to부정사로 바꾼다. ❷

능동태: 「주어＋동사＋목적어＋목적격 보어」
(지각, 사역)

수동태: 「주어＋「be동사＋과거분사」(수동태)＋주격 보어＋(by＋목적격)」

능동태 I saw him leave the house. (나는 그가 집을 떠나는 것을 봤다.)
지각동사   목적격 보어 (원형부정사)

수동태 He was seen to leave the house by me.
to부정사로 옴

(그가 집을 떠나는 것이 나에 의해 목격되었다.)

능동태 She helped me (to) carry the bags.
준사역동사   목적격 보어 (원형부정사 또는 to부정사)

(그녀는 내가 가방을 들도록 도와주었다.)

수동태 I was helped to carry the bags by her.
to부정사로 옴

(나는 그녀에 의해 가방을 드는 것을 도움받았다.)

> ❷ 목적격 보어인 현재분사
> 지각동사의 목적격 보어로 현재분사가 오면 수동태 문장에서도 이를 그대로 쓴다.
> · I heard a bird singing. (나는 새가 노래하는 것을 들었다.)
> → A bird was heard singing by me. (새가 노래하는 것이 나에 의해 들렸다.)

[참고] 사역동사 let과 have: 사역동사 let과 have는 수동태 동사로 쓰일 수 없다. 비슷한 의미를 나타내기 위해 let은 allow, have는 make로 바꾸어 쓴다.

능동태 He had the workers rearrange the entire office. (그는 직원들에게 사무실 전체를 재배치하게 했다.)

수동태 The workers were had to rearrange the entire office by him. (X)

수동태 The workers were made to rearrange the entire office by him. (O)

(직원들은 그에 의해 사무실 전체를 재배치하게 되었다.)

② 5형식 문장의 수동태 전환

[14-17] 문장을 수동태로 바꿔 쓸 때, 빈칸에 알맞은 말을 쓰시오.

14 We made her the leader of the group.

➡ _________________________ the leader of the group by us.

15 She made him wash the car.

➡ _________________________ the car by her.

16 She saw him making a delicious sandwich.

➡ _________________________ a delicious sandwich by her.

17 The coach helped the players improve their skills.

➡ _________________________ their skills by the coach.

[18-25] 괄호 안에서 알맞은 것을 고르시오.

18 I was encouraged (take / to take) part in the race by my teacher.

19 We can be made (strong / being strong) by eating healthy food.

20 Many people were seen (watch / watching) the concert by her.

21 The customer was recommended (to buy / him to buy) this computer by the salesperson.

22 The police (think / are thought) him guilty.

23 The island (called / is called) heaven on earth because of its fine view.

24 They (were heard sing / were heard to sing) a song by us.

25 The employees were made (to work / work) on the weekend.

①+② 4형식, 5형식의 수동태

[26-32] 문장에서 **틀린** 부분을 찾아 밑줄을 긋고 바르게 고치시오.

26 The text message will be sent for the wrong person by Sara. _____________

27 We were asked call the police by the man. _____________

28 My photo albums were shown him by my parents. _____________

29 A couple of suspicious men were watched run out of the building. _____________

30 The report requires to be done by next Monday by the teacher. _____________

31 She was watched dance at the party by them. _____________

32 The wind is feeling blowing through the trees by me. _____________

🦉 어휘 & 표현

- **name** 임명하다
- **rearrange** 재배치하다
- **improve** 개선시키다
- **salesperson** 판매원
- **guilty** 유죄의
- **employee** 직원
- **a couple of** 두세 개의
- **suspicious** 의심스러운
- **run out of** ~로부터 달아나다
- **blow** (바람이) 불다

〈 정답과 해설 p. 52~53 〉

UNIT 30 주의해야 할 수동태와 관용표현

1 주의해야 할 수동태

(1) 「by+행위자」의 생략 : 행위자가 they, people, we, someone 등일 경우

- Korean is spoken in Korea (by them/by us/by Koreans). (한국어는 한국에서 사용된다.)

(2) 수동태로 바꾸어 쓸 수 없는 타동사 : have(가지고 있다), resemble(닮다), become(~에 어울리다)

- Black dress really becomes her. (검정 드레스가 그녀에게 정말 어울린다.)

(3) 능동의 형태로도 수동의 의미를 가질 수 있는 동사 ❶

open 열리다	sell 팔리다	peel 벗겨지다	tear 찢어지다
cut 잘리다	change 바뀌다	say ~라고 쓰여 있다	read ~라고 읽힌다

❶ **수동의 의미를 가지는 동사**
동사의 우리말 뜻이 '팔리다', '벗겨지다' 등처럼 수동태의 의미를 포함하고 있으므로 「be동사+과거분사」로 쓰지 않도록 해야 한다.

- The shirt sells well. (그 셔츠는 잘 팔린다.)

(4) 다음 동사들의 목적어가 that절인 경우, 가주어 it이나 that절의 주어를 수동태의 주어로 할 수 있다.

believe	consider	expect	know	report	say	suppose	think	understand

① 가주어 it이 수동태의 주어인 경우: 「It + be동사 + 과거분사 + that ~」

② that절의 주어가 수동태의 주어인 경우: 「that절의 주어 + be동사 + 과거분사 + to부정사 ~」

- They know that the situation is going to be changed. ❷ (그들은 상황이 바뀔 것임을 안다.)

→ ① It is known that the situation is going to be changed.
   가주어 It을 수동태의 주어로 전환
→ ② The situation is known to be going to be changed.
   that절의 주어를 수동태의 주어로 전환

❷ **that절의 시제**
that절의 시제가 주절의 시제보다 과거일 때, to부정사는 「to have + 과거분사」의 형태로 쓴다.
- They say that she left. (그들은 그녀가 떠났다고 말한다.)
→ She is said to have left. (그녀는 떠났다고 한다.)

2 by 이외의 전치사를 사용하는 관용표현 ❸

① be interested in ~에 관심이 있다
be tired of ~에 싫증나다
② be satisfied with ~에 만족하다
be pleased with ~에 기뻐하다
be surprised at[by] ~에 놀라다
be worried about ~에 대해 걱정하다
be concerned about ~에 대해 걱정하다
③ be based on ~에 기초를 두다

be covered with ~으로 덮여 있다
④ be filled with ~으로 가득하다
⑤ be composed of ~으로 구성되어 있다
be excited about ~에 흥분하다
be known to ~에게 알려져 있다
⑥ be known for ~으로 유명하다
be known as ~으로 알려져 있다
be[get] married to ~와 결혼하다

❸ **be made of vs. be made from**
be made of와 be made from은 둘 다 '~로 만들어지다'라는 뜻이지만 be made of는 물리적 변화를 통해, be made from은 화학적 변화를 통해 만들어진 것을 나타낸다.

① He is interested in space exploration. (그는 우주 탐사에 관심이 있다.)

② We are satisfied with the hotel's facilities. (우리는 그 호텔의 시설에 만족한다.)

③ This movie is based on real events. (이 영화는 실제 사건에 기반을 두고 있다.)

④ The classroom was filled with laughter. (교실은 웃음소리로 가득했다.)

⑤ It is composed of spare parts. (그것은 예비 부품으로 구성되어 있다.)

⑥ She is known for fast typing. (그녀는 빠른 타자 치기로 유명하다.)

1 주의해야 할 수동태

[01-07] 괄호 안에서 알맞은 것을 고르시오.

01 I heard Michael's uncle (had / was had) a nice yacht.

02 Though there was no wind, the door (opened / was opened) by itself.

03 Look at the sign. It (says / is said) no swimming.

04 My younger sister (resembles / is resembled by) my grandmother.

05 The article (reads / be read) very well.

06 The scissors are dull, so they (aren't cut / don't cut) very well.

07 The paint on the wall (is peeling / is peeled).

2 by 이외의 전치사를 사용하는 관용표현

[08-13] 주어진 단어를 이용하여 수동태 문장을 완성하시오.

08 When she was in high school, she ___________________ gaining weight. (worry)

09 In 2018, we ___________________ the result of the Winter Olympics. (surprise)

10 Are you ___________________ taking photos? (interest)

11 The fact that Yoga is good for health ___________________ many people. (know)

12 All the students will ___________________ the after-school programs. (satisfy)

13 My parents ___________________ in the spring of 2000. (marry)

1 + 2 주의해야 할 수동태와 관용표현

[14-19] 주어진 우리말과 일치하도록 괄호 안의 말을 이용하여 영작하시오.

14 Jane은 그녀의 친구의 결정에 기뻐했다. (friend's decision, please)

➡ ____

15 아이스크림은 이렇게 더운 날에 잘 팔린다. (ice cream, on such a hot day, sell, well)

➡ ____

16 그의 눈에는 눈물이 가득하다. (eyes, tears, fill)

➡ ____

17 이탈리아는 스파게티와 피자로 유명하다. (Italy, spaghetti, pizza, know)

➡ ____

18 책장의 맨 윗부분은 먼지로 덮여 있다. (the top of the bookcase, dust, cover)

➡ ____

19 신선한 과일이 우리의 건강에 좋다고 한다. (say, fresh fruit, good for, health)

➡ It ____ .

➡ Fresh fruit ____ .

🦉 어휘 & 표현
- **resemble** 닮다
- **peel** 껍질을 벗기다
- **yacht** 요트
- **dull** 둔한, 뭉뚝한
- **gain weight** 살이 찌다
- **dust** 먼지

〈 정답과 해설 p. 53~54 〉

01

주어진 우리말과 일치하도록 빈칸에 알맞은 것을 고르시오.

> Tommy가 그의 개와 함께 조깅하는 것이 목격되었다.
> → Tommy was ___________ with his dog.

① saw jogging ② seen jogged
③ seen to jog ④ seen jog
⑤ saw to be jogged

[02-03] 서술형

괄호 안의 지시대로 빈칸에 알맞은 말을 쓰시오.

02

My uncle bought me a nice bicycle.
(직접목적어를 주어로 하는 수동태로)

➡ A nice bicycle _______________ by my uncle.

03

The teacher gave me some lessons.
(간접목적어를 주어로 하는 수동태로)

➡ I _______________ by the teacher.

04

빈칸에 들어갈 단어가 나머지 넷과 다른 것을 고르시오.

① She was pleased _______ the present.
② People were satisfied _______ the result.
③ Government is worried _______ the pollution.
④ The warehouse is filled _______ dust.
⑤ The village was covered _______ white snow.

[05-06] 서술형

주어진 우리말과 일치하도록 괄호 안의 단어를 이용하여 빈칸에 알맞게 쓰시오.

05

그는 할아버지에 의해 Henry라고 이름 지어졌다.
(name, Henry)

➡ He _______________ by his grandfather.

06

큰 태풍이 다가오고 있는 것이 과학자들에 의해 발견되었다. (find, approach)

➡ A huge typhoon _______________ by the scientists.

07

주어진 문장을 수동태로 알맞게 바꾼 것을 고르시오.

> They say the item is at Joy's shop.

① It says the item is at Joy's shop.
② They are said to be at Joy's shop.
③ It is said the item be at Joy's shop.
④ The item is said to be at Joy's shop.
⑤ The item be said to be at Joy's shop..

[08-09] 서술형

문장에서 틀린 부분을 찾아 밑줄을 긋고 바르게 고치시오.

08

Recently, many teenagers are concerned by gaining weight. _______________

09

Mt. Titlis is covered by snow all through the year. _______________

10 고난도

어법상 틀린 것을 고르시오.

① The donut is covered with sugar.
② I am tired this work.
③ He is known as a singer and actor.
④ They were satisfied with their decision.
⑤ Are you interested in traditional Korean dance?

11

어법상 옳은 것을 고르시오.

① My elder sister is resembled by me.
② All the streets were covered by snow.
③ The dogs were taken care by her.
④ Her new album is being looked forward to by many fans.
⑤ Even though it has difficult vocabulary, this book is read well.

12

밑줄 친 부분 중 생략할 수 있는 것을 고르시오.

① The window was broken <u>by Sean</u>.
② That movie has been loved <u>by people</u>.
③ The book was torn out <u>by my brother</u>.
④ The cake was eaten <u>by Jake</u>.
⑤ The show was produced <u>by the actor</u>.

13

빈칸에 들어갈 말이 알맞게 짝지어진 것을 고르시오.

- The email was sent __________ her by Mike.
- The cheesecake was made __________ James by his mom.

① to – to
② to – for
③ for – to
④ for – of
⑤ of – for

14

문장을 수동태로 고친 것 중 옳지 <u>않은</u> 것을 고르시오.

① What did he do?
  → What was done by him?
② We elected him leader of our class.
  → He was elected leader of our class by us.
③ She is drawing a picture of her mother.
  → A picture of her mother is being drawn by her.
④ A bus ran over the old lady.
  → The old lady was run over by a bus.
⑤ My father bought me a book.
  → I was bought a book by my father.

[15-19]

빈칸에 알맞은 말을 〈보기〉에서 골라 쓰시오. (중복 사용 불가)

〈보기〉
| of | with | in | about | to |

15

The team is composed __________ ten players.

16

I'm not satisfied __________ my job as a tour guide.

17

She's just worried __________ her big presentation at school tomorrow.

18

He was married __________ the woman of his dreams.

19

Jerome is not interested __________ any sports.

〈 정답과 해설 p. 54~55 〉

20

빈칸에 들어갈 말이 알맞게 짝지어진 것을 고르시오.

> • Can my cat be looked __________ by you
>   for an hour?
> • The bottle is filled __________ milk.

① in – up
② after – up
③ on – up
④ after – with
⑤ before – with

[21-23]

주어진 우리말과 일치하도록 괄호 안의 말을 바르게 배열하시오.

21

신선한 채소가 우리의 건강에 좋다고 믿어진다.

(it, that, fresh, is believed, vegetables, good, our health, are, for)

➡ _______________________________

____

22

그녀는 나에 의해 문서를 치게 되었다. (was made, the document, me, by, to type, she)

➡ _______________________________

____

23

그가 다른 친구들과 바이올린을 연주하는 것이 들렸다. (he, playing, the violin, was heard, along with, other friends)

➡ _______________________________

____

24 수능 유형

밑줄 친 부분 중 어법상 **틀린** 것을 고르시오.

> I ① have a few healthy habits, which include hiking in a nearby mountain with my mother. When I ② am asked why I go hiking in the mountains, I say it's because I like everything about mountains. When I go to the mountains, I am allowed ③ enjoy clean air and mountain breezes. Squirrels can be seen ④ to run up and down the trees. Most of all, when I ⑤ am done, I feel I made it after all.

①　　②　　③　　④　　⑤

[25-26]

다음 글을 읽고 물음에 답하시오.

> My mother baked a pretty cake. It was decorated ① by colorful chocolate and candy bits. A few candles ② were put on the cake by my mother to celebrate my birthday. (A) My friends gave me the presents during the party. The party was enjoyed by everyone, and many pictures ③ were taken. The house ④ was cleaned by my family after the party ended. A thank-you note ⑤ will be written by me to express my gratitude to everyone.

25 수능 유형 고난도

밑줄 친 부분 중 어법상 **틀린** 것을 고르시오.

①　　②　　③　　④　　⑤

26 서술형

밑줄 친 (A)를 수동태로 바꿀 때, 빈칸에 알맞은 말을 쓰시오.

➡ The presents __________ by my friends during the party.

형용사

形容詞

(모양 형, 얼굴 용, 말 사)

명사(사람·사물)의 상태, 특징 등을 나타내는 말

UNIT 31 형용사의 종류, 쓰임, 어순

UNIT 32 부정 수량 형용사
不定 (아닐 부, 정할 정)
정확한 수량이 정해지지 않은 명사 앞에 쓰는 형용사

UNIT 33 수사 형용사의 표현
명사의 정확한 수나 순서를 나타내는 형용사

The broken phone is useless now. (그 고장 난 휴대폰은 지금 쓸모가 없다.)
형용사의 한정적 쓰임   형용사의 서술적 쓰임

I have very few books, but she has a lot of books.
──── 부정 수량 형용사 ────

(나는 아주 적은 책을 가지고 있지만, 그녀는 많은 책을 가지고 있다.)

We found three old paintings, and the second one is a masterpiece.
──── 수사 형용사 ────

(우리는 세 개의 오래된 그림을 발견했고, 두 번째 그림은 걸작이다.)

 **UNIT 31** 형용사의 종류, 쓰임, 어순 

1 형용사의 종류와 쓰임

성질·상태 형용사	명사의 성질이나 상태를 나타냄 – happy, tall, strong, old 등 beautiful house (아름다운 집), cold water (차가운 물) 등
수량 형용사	명사의 수나 양을 나타냄 – some, much, few 등 many books (많은 책들), several activities (몇 개의 활동들) 등
수사 형용사	명사의 정확한 수나 순서를 나타냄 – two, first, second 등 one point (일 점), second day (둘째 날) 등
지시 형용사	명사가 특정한 것임을 나타냄 – this, that, these, those 등 this cat (이 고양이), those people (저 사람들) 등
소유 형용사	명사가 소유하는 것임을 나타냄 – my, your, his, her 등 my car (나의 차), your family (너의 가족) 등
의문 형용사	질문을 할 때 쓰임 – what, which, whose 등 which book (어떤 책), whose jacket (누구의 재킷) 등
한정 형용사	명사의 의미를 한정함 – only, every, each 등 every morning (모든 아침), any question (어떤 질문) 등

(1) 한정적 쓰임: 명사나 대명사 앞·뒤에서 명사나 대명사를 꾸며준다.

- **Each student** must submit their homework today. (각각의 학생은 오늘 그들의 숙제를 제출해야 한다.)
  형용사　명사

한정적 쓰임으로만 쓰이는 형용사	chief (주요한), daily (매일의), elder (나이가 많은), former (이전의), inner (안쪽의), live (살아 있는), main (주요한), mere (겨우), only (유일한) 등

- His **former teacher** retired last month. (그의 이전 선생님은 지난달에 은퇴하셨다.)
  형용사　명사

(2) 서술적 쓰임: 주격 보어 또는 목적격 보어로 사용되어 주어 또는 목적어에 대한 설명을 한다.

① 주격 보어: The cake smells delicious. (그 케이크는 맛있는 냄새가 난다.)

② 목적격 보어: I consider him talented. (나는 그가 재능 있다고 생각한다.)

서술적 쓰임으로만 쓰이는 형용사	afraid (두려운), alike (비슷한), alive (살아 있는), alone (혼자), asleep (잠든), awake (깨어 있는), aware (알고 있는), content (만족하는), glad (기쁜), worth (가치 있는) 등

- She seemed **content** with her score. (그녀는 그녀의 점수에 만족해 보였다.)
  주격 보어

2 형용사의 어순

(1) 두 개 이상의 형용사가 하나의 명사를 수식할 경우

전치한정사 + [관사 / 지시형용사 / 인칭대명사의 소유격] + **수량 형용사** + **일반 형용사** + **명사**

- **All her three cheerful children** are always laughing. (그녀의 세 명랑한 아이들 모두 항상 웃고 있다.)
  전치한정사　인칭대명사의 소유격　수량 형용사　일반 형용사　명사

(2) 일반 형용사의 어순: 일반 형용사는 OSASCOMP 순서로 쓴다.

Opinion (의견, 날씨, 맛, 감정, 성격, 상태 등) → **S**ize (크기) → **A**ge (나이) → **S**hape (모양) → **C**olor (색깔) → **O**rigin (출신) → **M**aterial (재료) → **P**urpose (용도)

- They saw a **large old wooden** chair. (그들은 크고 오래된 나무 의자를 보았다.)
  크기　나이　재료

> **주의** **주의해야 할 형용사의 어순**
>
> 「-thing, -one, -body」로 끝나는 단어는 형용사가 뒤에서 수식한다.
> - I'm not busy with anything special. (나는 바쁜 특별한 일이 없다.)

1 형용사의 종류와 쓰임

[01-05] 밑줄 친 형용사의 종류로 알맞은 것을 〈보기〉에서 고르시오. (중복 사용 불가)

〈보기〉
성질·상태 형용사	수량 형용사	수사 형용사
지시 형용사	소유 형용사	의문 형용사	한정 형용사

01 What time does the train leave? ➡ ____________

02 I need a little time to finish this. ➡ ____________

03 This is my first time visiting Paris. ➡ ____________ , ____________

04 This book contains valuable information. ➡ ____________ , ____________

05 Every student in the class passed the exam. ➡ ____________

[06-13] 밑줄 친 형용사의 쓰임을 〈보기〉에서 찾아 쓰시오. (중복 사용 가능)

〈보기〉
ⓐ 명사 수식 (한정적)　　ⓑ 주격 보어 (서술적)　　ⓒ 목적격 보어 (서술적)

06 The bad weather kept us worried. ➡ ____________

07 The large library on the corner was quiet. ➡ ____________

08 The young girl was cheerful and energetic. ➡ ____________

09 The dangerous experience left me confused. ➡ ____________

10 Her performance made the audience amazed. ➡ ____________

11 The small café near the park was welcoming. ➡ ____________

12 The tall man standing by the door was serious. ➡ ____________

13 The news of his promotion made everyone proud. ➡ ____________

2 형용사의 어순

[14-17] 괄호 안의 말을 바르게 배열하시오.

14 ____________________ are always hopping around. (playful, four, his, rabbits)

15 I want to have ____________________. (very, light and simple, something)

16 She bought ____________________ for the living room.
(round, wooden, table, a, small)

17 ____________________ are always perfect for a morning coffee.
(three, our, spacious, balconies)

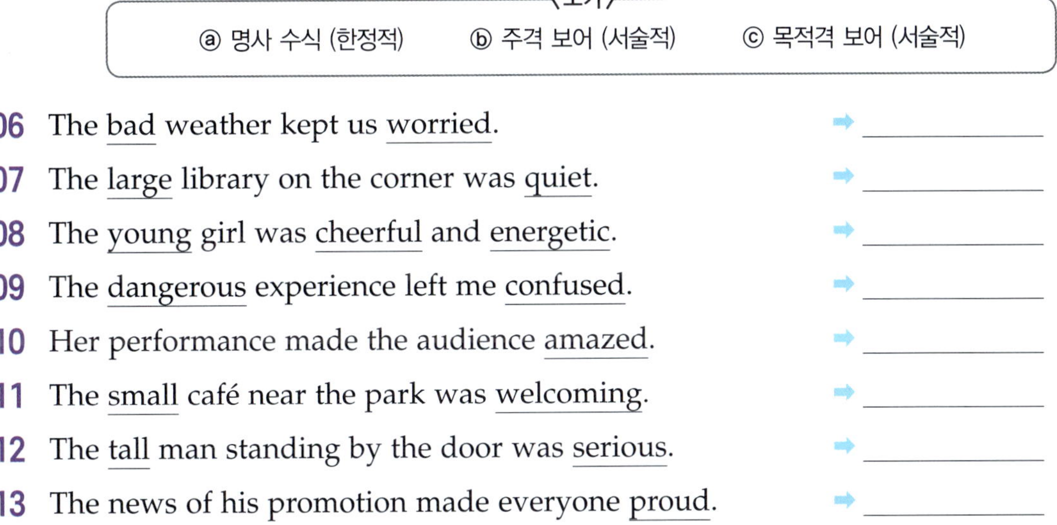

어휘 & 표현

·**submit** 제출하다　·**former** 이전의　·**retire** 은퇴하다　·**talented** 재능 있는　·**content** 만족한　·**valuable** 가치 있는
·**confused** 혼란스러운　·**audience** 관객　·**promotion** 승진　·**hop around** 깡충깡충 뛰다　·**spacious** 넓은

〈 정답과 해설 p. 56 〉

 **UNIT 32** 부정 수량 형용사 

정해지지 않은 수량을 나타내는 형용사

⭐ 부정 수량 형용사

(1) 많은 – many, much, a lot of

many [a number of] ❶	**many + 셀 수 있는 명사** • Many[A number of] robots now assist surgeons. 셀수있는 명사 (많은 로봇들이 이제 외과 의사를 보조한다.)
much [a great deal of]	**much + 셀 수 없는 명사** • Much[A great deal of] attention is given to AI ethics. 셀 수 없는 명사 (많은 관심이 AI 윤리에 주어진다.)
a lot of [lots of, plenty of]	**a lot of + 셀 수 있는 명사, 셀 수 없는 명사** • A lot of volunteers helped the injured. ❷ 셀 수 있는 명사 (많은 자원봉사자들이 부상자들을 도왔다.) • Lots of creativity is required in sustainable fashion 셀 수 없는 명사 design. (많은 창의성이 지속 가능한 패션 디자인에 필요하다.)

❶ a number of와 the number of 등
- a number of: '많은' → 복수 취급
- the number of: '~의 수' → 단수 취급
- an amount of: ~ 양 (막연한 양)
- the amount of: 그 양 (정해진 양)
- a great amount of: 많은 양

주의 **❷ the + 형용사**
'~한 사람들'로 해석하며, 복수 명사처럼 쓰인다.
- The elderly need more care.
(노인들은 더 많은 돌봄이 필요하다.)

(2) 약간의 – a few, a little

a few	**a few + 셀 수 있는 명사** • She bought a few souvenirs from the trip. (그녀는 여행에서 몇 개의 기념품을 샀다.) 셀 수 있는 명사
a little	**a little + 셀 수 없는 명사** • The poor received a little aid after the flood. ❷ (홍수 이후에 가난한 사람들은 약간의 지원을 받았다.) 셀 수 없는 명사

(3) 거의 없는 – few, little

few	**few + 셀 수 있는 명사** • He has (only a) ❸ few friends to trust. (그가 믿을 친구가 거의 없다.) 셀 수 있는 명사
little	**little + 셀 수 없는 명사** • The speech had little impact on me. (그 연설은 내게 거의 영향이 없었다.) 셀 수 없는 명사

❸ 부사 + a few[little]
- only a few[little]: '거의 없는'
- She made only a few mistakes.
(그녀는 거의 실수하지 않았다.)
- quite a few[little]: '많은, 상당한'
- They poured quite a little water on the fire.
(그들은 불에 많은 물을 부었다.)

(4) 약간의 – some, 어떤 – any
– 셀 수 있는 명사, 셀 수 없는 명사 앞에 모두 쓸 수 있다. UNIT 14 참고

some	긍정문	• I picked some strawberries from the garden. (나는 정원에서 딸기 몇 개를 땄다.) 긍정문 **(약간의, 몇몇의)**
	권유의 의문문	• Would you like some coffee before your interview? (면접 전에 커피 좀 드실래요?) 권유의 의문문 **(~ 좀)**
any	긍정문	• You can ask any question during the Q&A session. 긍정문 **(어떤 ~도)** (질의응답 시간엔 어떤 질문이든 하셔도 됩니다.)
	의문문, 조건문	• Do you have any ideas for our science project? 의문문 **(어떤 ~라도)** (우리 과학 프로젝트에 대한 어떤 아이디어라도 있니?) • If you notice any errors in the report, let me know. 조건문 **(어떤 ~라도)** (보고서에서 어떤 오류라도 발견하면, 나한테 알려줘.)
	부정문	• They didn't show any interest in the proposal. 부정문 **(전혀, 조금의)** (그들은 그 제안서에 전혀 관심을 보이지 않았다.)

⭐ 부정 수량 형용사

[01-04] 주어진 우리말과 일치하도록 빈칸에 알맞은 것을 〈보기〉에서 골라 쓰시오. (중복 사용 불가)

〈보기〉

| a few | any | many | a great deal of |

01 도움이라도 필요하시면, 저에게 말씀만 하세요.

➡ If you need ＿＿＿＿＿＿ help, just let me know.

02 많은 과학자들이 청정에너지의 가능성을 믿는다.

➡ ＿＿＿＿＿＿ scientists believe in the potential of clean energy.

03 그녀는 차에 레몬즙 몇 방울을 넣었다.

➡ She added ＿＿＿＿＿＿ drops of lemon juice to the tea.

04 유아들을 다룰 때는 많은 인내가 필요하다.

➡ ＿＿＿＿＿＿ patience is needed when dealing with toddlers.

14 DAY

[05-09] 밑줄 친 부분이 맞으면 ○로 표시하고, 틀리면 바르게 고치시오.

05 There was lots of cars on the road yesterday.　　➡ ＿＿＿＿＿＿

06 We need plenty of volunteer to help with the event.　　➡ ＿＿＿＿＿＿

07 A number of people attended the concert last night.　　➡ ＿＿＿＿＿＿

08 It requires a great deal of efforts to complete the task.　　➡ ＿＿＿＿＿＿

09 I spent a number of time preparing for the presentation.　　➡ ＿＿＿＿＿＿

[10-17] 괄호 안에서 알맞은 것을 고르시오.

10 How (many / much) money do you need?

11 (Few / Little) people can understand his presentation.

12 Did you have (any / some) questions before the meeting?

13 She has (a little / few) time before the meeting starts.

14 We have (little / a few) minutes before the bus arrives.

15 A great (deal / number) of attention was given to detail in the design.

16 Lots of (child / children) were playing in the park during the afternoon.

17 The injured often (experience / experiences) emotional trauma in addition to physical pain.

 어휘 & 표현

- **surgeon** 외과 의사　· **ethics** 윤리　· **creativity** 창의성　· **sustainable** 지속 가능한　· **souvenir** 기념품
- **potential** 잠재력, 가능성　· **toddler** 걸음마를 배우는 아기　· **trauma** 정신적 외상　· **physical** 육체적인

〈 정답과 해설 p. 57 〉

 **UNIT 33** 수사 형용사의 표현 

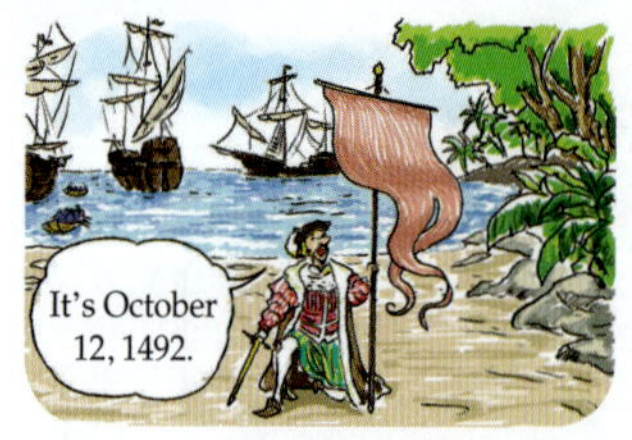

Columbus discovered the Americas on ***October 12, 1492.***
날짜는 월, 일, 연도 순으로 읽는다.
(콜럼버스는 1492년 10월 12일에 아메리카 대륙을 발견했다.)

He sailed for India ***four times.*** (그는 인도를 향해 네 번 항해했다.)
'네 번'은 기수 뒤에 times를 붙인다.

1 기수와 서수

- **기수** : '개수'를 나타내는 말   - **서수** : '순서'를 나타내는 말

기수	서수	기수	서수
1: one	1st: first	15: fifteen	15th: fifteenth
2: two	2nd: second	19: nineteen	19th: nineteenth
3: three	3rd: third	20: twenty	20th: twentieth [1]
4: four	4th: fourth	21: twenty-one	21st: twenty-first
5: five	5th: fifth	22: twenty-two	22nd: twenty-second
6: six	6th: sixth	23: twenty-three	23rd: twenty-third
7: seven	7th: seventh	100: a[one] hundred	100th: one hundredth
8: eight	8th: eighth	1,000: a[one] thousand	1,000th: one thousandth
9: nine	9th: ninth	1,000,000(백만): a[one] million	1,000,000th(백만 번째): one millionth
10: ten	10th: tenth	1,000,000,000(십억): a[one] billion	1,000,000,000th(십억 번째): one billionth

❶ -ty로 끝나는 기수의 서수
-ty로 끝나는 기수의 서수는 -tieth로 표현한다.

2 숫자

정수	• 세 자리씩 천 단위로 끊어 읽는다. – hundred 뒤의 and는 생략할 수 있다. • 345 → three hundred (and) forty-five • 2,863 → two thousand eight hundred (and) sixty-three
소수	• 소수점은 point로 읽고, 소수점 이하는 한 자리씩 따로따로 읽는다. – 소수점 앞의 수가 0이면 0(zero)을 생략하고 point부터 읽기도 한다. • 1.264 → one point two six four • 0.4 → zero point four 또는 point four
분수	• 분자는 기수(개수)로 읽고, 분모는 서수(순서)로 읽는다. – 분자가 2 이상이면 분모에 -s를 붙인다. – 정수와 분수가 있으면 「정수＋and＋분수」로 구분하여 읽는다. • $\frac{1}{6}$ → a sixth 또는 one-sixth • $\frac{1}{2}$ → a half 또는 one-half • $\frac{1}{4}$ → a quarter 또는 one-quarter • $4\frac{2}{3}$ → four and two-thirds
배수	몇 배가 되는지를 나타내는 수로, 3배부터는 「기수＋times」로 읽는다. once (1배), twice (2배), three times (3배), four times (4배), ten times (10배)

❷ half와 quarter
half는 2분의 1(절반)을, quarter는 4분의 1을 뜻한다.

1 기수와 서수

[01-10] 기수는 서수로, 서수는 기수로 바꿔 쓰시오. (단, 영어로 쓸 것)

01 three ⇒ ________________

02 seven ⇒ ________________

03 fifteen ⇒ ________________

04 sixty ⇒ ________________

05 ten ⇒ ________________

06 thirtieth ⇒ ________________

07 ninety-ninth ⇒ ________________

08 one hundredth ⇒ ________________

09 forty-fourth ⇒ ________________

10 sixteenth ⇒ ________________

2 숫자

[11-20] 수를 알맞게 읽으시오.

11 $\dfrac{2}{3}$ ⇒ ________________

12 6.07 ⇒ ________________

13 $\dfrac{4}{9}$ ⇒ ________________

14 0.25 ⇒ ________________

15 357 ⇒ ________________

16 $1\dfrac{3}{5}$ ⇒ ________________

17 3.14 ⇒ ________________

18 $\dfrac{5}{8}$ ⇒ ________________

19 42,350 ⇒ ________________

20 $7\dfrac{2}{7}$ ⇒ ________________

1 + 2 기수와 서수, 숫자

[21-26] 주어진 우리말과 일치하도록 빈칸에 알맞은 말을 쓰시오. (단, 영어로 쓸 것)

21 그는 아홉 번째 시도에서 마침내 시험에 합격했다.

⇒ He finally passed the test on his ______________ attempt.

22 그 연구는 백만 분의 일 단위로 측정된 데이터를 사용했다.

⇒ The study used data measured in ______________ units.

23 이 책의 3분의 2는 환경 문제에 대해 다루고 있다.

⇒ ______________ of this book deals with environmental issues.

24 그는 지난달에 87달러를 전기 요금으로 냈다.

⇒ He paid ______________ dollars for electricity last month.

25 그 조리법에는 약 0.33킬로그램의 설탕이 필요하다.

⇒ The recipe requires about ______________ kilograms of sugar.

26 그 우승자는 경쟁자보다 정확히 일곱 배 많은 점수를 받았다.

⇒ The winner received exactly ______________ more points than the competitor.

> **어휘 & 표현**
> - **attempt** 시도
> - **measure** 측정하다
> - **deal with** ~을 다루다
> - **environmental** 환경의
> - **electricity** 전기
> - **recipe** 조리[요리]법
> - **require** 필요로 하다
> - **competitor** 경쟁자

〈 정답과 해설 p. 58~59 〉

3 시각 읽기

(1) 시간 → 분 순서로 읽는다.
- 9:14 → nine fourteen　• 10:21 → ten twenty-one　• 11:30 → eleven thirty

(2) 10분 미만이라면 중간에 'o'를 붙일 수 있고, "오"로 읽는다. (0 = 'o')
- 1:08 → one-(o)-eight　　　　• 3:02 → three-(o)-two

(3) 정각에는 o' clock을 붙일 수 있다.
- 4:00 → four (o' clock)　　　　• 5:00 → five (o' clock)

(4) 전치사 after, past, to를 이용하여 표현할 수 있다.
- 분 **after** 시 : 시로부터 분 지난
  = past
- 분 **to** 시 : 시가 되기 분 전
- 2:15 → two fifteen 또는 a quarter❶ after[past] two
- 4:30 → four thirty 또는 a half❶ after[past] four (※ a half to ~는 잘 쓰이지 않음)
- 2:45 → two forty-five 또는 a quarter to three

> ❶ **quarter와 half**
> quarter는 15분, half는 30분을 나타낸다.

4 연도와 날짜

연도	– 두 자리씩 끊어서 읽는다. (2000년 이후는 정수를 읽는 것처럼 읽을 수 있다.)
	• 1999년 → nineteen ninety-nine　• 1856년 → eighteen fifty-six • 719년 → seven (hundred and) nineteen • 2025년 → two thousand (and) twenty-five
날짜	– 날짜(일)는 서수로 읽는다. • 7월 21일 → July (the) twenty-first 또는 the twenty-first of July • 9월 12일 → September (the) twelfth 또는 the twelfth of September
	– 연도는 월과 일보다 나중에 읽는다. • 1972년 11월 21일 → November (the) twenty-first, nineteen seventy-two
	– 월을 나타내는 말 1월 January　　2월 February　　3월 March 4월 April　　5월 May　　6월 June 7월 July　　8월 August　　9월 September 10월 October　　11월 November　　12월 December

5 전화번호

(1) 전화번호는 한 자리씩 읽는다.
- 같은 숫자가 나란히 나오면 double을 쓰기도 한다. 0은 o[ou], zero라고 읽기도 한다.
  - 123-4506 → one two three, four five o[zero] six
  - 123-4556 → one two three, four five five[double five] six

(2) 지역 번호는 area code를 붙여 읽는다.
- 첫 자리가 0이면 zero라고 읽는다.
  - (02) 123-4567 → area code zero two, one two three, four five six seven

(3) 휴대폰 앞 자리는 주로 zero라고 읽는다.
- 010-1234-5678 → zero one zero, one two three four, five six seven eight

3 시각 읽기

[27-32] 알맞은 영어 표기법을 고르시오.

27 5:55 ➡ (five fifty / five to six)

28 9:50 ➡ (nine fifteen / ten to ten)

29 12:30 ➡ (twelve thirty / a half past one)

30 6:45 ➡ (six forty-five / a quarter to six)

31 4:20 ➡ (four twenty / twenty past five)

32 3:15 ➡ (a quarter past four / a quarter after three)

> **어휘 & 표현**
> · forget 잊다
> · uncle 삼촌
> · triple 3배의
> · price 가격
> · population 인구
> · daughter 딸

4 + **5** 연도와 날짜, 전화번호

[33-39] 연도와 날짜, 전화번호를 영어로 읽을 때의 표기법을 쓰시오.

33 2월 14일 ➡ _______________________________

34 3월 3일 ➡ _______________________________

35 12월 24일 ➡ _______________________________

36 1786년 1월 4일 ➡ _______________________________

37 3480-9927 ➡ _______________________________

38 010-2345-6789 ➡ _______________________________

39 (051) 2468-1357 ➡ _______________________________

1 + **2** + **3** + **4** + **5** 수사 형용사의 표현

[40-44] 문장에서 틀린 부분을 찾아 밑줄을 긋고 바르게 고치시오.

40 I won't forget July 21th, 1999. ➡ _______________

41 My uncle is triple times my age. ➡ _______________

42 The price of most items in this store is nine dollar and ninety-nine cents.

➡ _______________

43 The population of Brazil is about fourth times as large as that of Korea.

➡ _______________

44 The twelfth on December is my daughter's birthday.

➡ _______________

〈 정답과 해설 p. 59 〉

[01-03]

숫자를 영어로 읽을 때 <u>잘못</u> 읽은 것을 고르시오.

01

① $\frac{1}{3}$: a thirds

② 0.05: zero point zero five

③ 10월 20일: the twentieth of October

④ 오후 3시 25분: twenty-five past three in the afternoon

⑤ 2037년: twenty thirty-seven

02

① $3\frac{4}{5}$: three and four-fifths

② 3배: third times

③ 36.09: thirty-six point zero nine

④ 1:45: a quarter to two

⑤ ☎ 012–345–6789: zero one two, three four five, six seven eight nine

03

① 4,380: four thousand, three hundred and eighty

② 0.056: zero point zero five six

③ $\frac{4}{9}$: four-ninths

④ 11:30: half to eleven

⑤ 1643년: sixteen forty-three

[04-09] (서술형)

다음을 알맞게 읽으시오.

04

$\frac{4}{7}$ ➡ _______________

05

0.493 ➡ _______________

06

108.5 ➡ _______________

____

07

6,329,765 ➡ _______________

____

08

553–8925 ➡ _______________

09

11시 5분 ➡ _______________

10

빈칸에 들어갈 말이 알맞게 짝지어진 것을 고르시오.

- There are ___(A)___ people at the concert today. It's not very crowded.
- We still have ___(B)___ time left before the bus arrives, so don't worry.

	(A)		(B)
①	few	–	lots of
②	little	–	few
③	many	–	a number of
④	much	–	many
⑤	plenty of	–	a few

괄호 안에서 알맞은 것을 고르시오.

11

I need (some / a few) help with my homework.

12

I was able to find (things interesting / interesting things) about chocolate in this book.

13

Can you show me (cheaper something / something cheaper)?

14

I have (many / much) small change for the vending machine.

15

밑줄 친 부분이 어법상 틀린 것을 고르시오.

① I have little knowledge about it.
② Every year the number of students go to university.
③ He is so weak that he's absent from school several times a month.
④ There were a great many people in the concert hall.
⑤ It took a great amount of money to build the skyscraper.

[16-18] 서술형

빈칸에 알맞은 관사를 쓰시오. (단, 관사가 필요 없을 경우 '없음'으로 쓸 것)

16

A: How crowded was the stadium yesterday?

B: ______________ number of attendees was higher than expected.

17

A: Did many applicants meet the qualifications?

B: No, only __________ few had the required experience.

18 고난도

A: Why didn't you react to the announcement at all?

B: I had ______________ little interest in what they were saying.

[19-20]

어순이 올바른 문장을 고르시오.

19

① He has a round nice oak table.
② She wants expensive this long red dress.
③ Is this round large chair yours?
④ How much is that new brown leather bag?
⑤ The old small restaurant has a history of forty years.

20

① I saw a white cute fluffy puppy in the park.
② The metal old rusty bike was left in the yard.
③ They bought a black modern sleek car last week.
④ He gave her a beautiful blue silk scarf as a gift.
⑤ She was hiding important something that I needed to know.

〈 정답과 해설 p. 60~61 〉

[21-22]
밑줄 친 부분과 바꿔 쓸 수 있는 것을 고르시오.

21

> The event should wrap up by a half past five, but some activities might run a little longer.

① five thirty
② four thirty
③ five thirteen
④ a half after four
⑤ five forty-five

22

> A number of countries have signed the peace agreement.

① Much
② A few
③ A little
④ Plenty of
⑤ The number of

[23-25]
괄호 안의 말을 바르게 배열하시오.

23

I found ________________________

________________________ in the attic.

(wooden, this, chest, old, large)

24

My dog, Molly, gave birth to ____________

________________________________.

(black, three, puppies, cute, little)

25

He was wearing ________________________

________________________ on top of a gray shirt

with a hood. (jacket, leather, a, black)

[26-29]
밑줄 친 형용사의 쓰임을 구분하시오.

26

The cake looks so delicious that I can't wait
to taste it. ➡ [한정적 / 서술적] 쓰임

27

The warm weather made it perfect for a
picnic in the park. ➡ [한정적 / 서술적] 쓰임

28

The teacher made the lesson interesting by
using real-world examples.

➡ [한정적 / 서술적] 쓰임

29

The movie had a thrilling plot that kept us
on the edge of our seats.

➡ [한정적 / 서술적] 쓰임

[30-31]
다음 글을 읽고 물음에 답하시오.

> After the earthquake, there was ___(A)___ damage reported across the region. Emergency teams were sent out, but ___(B)___ support was available in the first few hours. Because most of the roads and bridges had been damaged as well. The chaotic situation caused ___(C)___ concern, especially for the elderly and children.

30

빈칸 (A), (B)에 들어갈 말이 알맞게 짝지어진 것을 고르시오.

　　(A)　　　　　(B)
① some　－　few
② some　－　little
③ a few　－　a little
④ many　－　a number of
⑤ many　－　quite a little

31

빈칸 (C)에 적절하지 <u>않은</u> 것을 고르시오.

① a lot of
② many
③ lots of
④ plenty of
⑤ a great deal of

빈칸에 알맞지 <u>않은</u> 것을 고르시오.

32

He made _________ progress in just one week of practice sessions.

① some ② a few ③ a little
④ plenty of ⑤ a great deal of

33

According to the report, _________-tenths of the city's population are under 50.

① one ② two ③ three
④ five ⑤ eight

34

There were many _________ about the new company policy yesterday.

① opinions ② concerns
③ questions ④ complaints
⑤ information

[35-37] 서술형

어법상 <u>틀린</u> 곳을 찾아 바르게 고치시오.

35

Three-fourth of the work is finished, but the rest is still pending.

➡ _________________ → _________________

36

She noticed unexpected something in her email inbox.

➡ _________________ → _________________

37

Would you like any tea before we head out?

➡ _________________ → _________________

[38-39]

대화의 빈칸에 들어갈 알맞은 것을 고르시오.

38

A: I have _________ experience with coding, but I'm eager to learn.
B: Don't worry, a little practice will make you more confident soon.

① few ② little ③ a few
④ many ⑤ a number of

39

A: I need _________ more minutes to finish this task before lunch.
B: No worries. I'll wait.

① a few ② a little ③ little
④ much ⑤ a great deal of

[40-41]

밑줄 친 형용사의 쓰임이 나머지 넷과 <u>다른</u> 것을 고르시오.

40

① She wore a <u>red</u> dress to the party.
② The sky looks so <u>pink</u> during sunset.
③ He lives in a <u>tiny</u> apartment in the city.
④ The <u>white</u> sand on the beach was so calming.
⑤ The <u>bright</u> sun made the beach look even more beautiful.

〈 정답과 해설 p. 61~62 〉

41

① The wide river is <u>perfect</u> for canoeing.
② Everyone is <u>ready</u> to begin the game.
③ The cake looks huge, but it's surprisingly <u>light</u>.
④ She remained <u>alone</u> after everyone had failed.
⑤ I bought a <u>small</u> coffee because I wasn't that hungry.

[42-43]

다음 글을 읽고 물음에 답하시오.

A ① 3-year-old British boy, William Potter joined Mensa. This ② <u>genius little boy</u> with IQ of 140 likes to play outside just like other kids. However, there is ③ <u>special something</u> about him. When he was 24 months old, he could count up to 20, and knew all the colors and alphabets. "I was amazed to see him remember ④ <u>some</u> random characters in children's movies when he was only 18 months," said his mother. Now, he enjoys reading maps and solving ⑤ <u>difficult word puzzles</u> on his computer. This would impress (A) many / much young learners interested in learning.

42 수능 유형 고난도

밑줄 친 부분 중 어법상 틀린 것을 고르시오.

①   ②   ③   ④   ⑤

43

(A)에 알맞은 것을 고르시오.

➡ _______________

[44-45]

다음 글을 읽고 물음에 답하시오.

On a rainy afternoon, Sarah decided to go to the library to work on her project. <u>그녀는 그녀의 큰 갈색 가방을 챙겼다.</u> The library had a quiet corner with (A) live / alive plants that made the space feel more relaxed. As she started reading, she came across (B) a few / a little useful articles that would help with her research. After several hours of focused work, she felt a sense of accomplishment and (C) a number of / a great deal of happiness with her progress.

44

밑줄 친 우리말과 같도록 괄호 안의 말을 바르게 배열하시오.

(brown, she, bag, packed, her, large)

➡ _______________

45 수능 맛보기

(A), (B), (C)의 각 네모 안에서 어법에 맞는 표현으로 가장 적절한 것을 고르시오.

	(A)	(B)	(C)
①	alive	a few	a number of
②	alive	a little	a great deal of
③	live	a few	a number of
④	live	a few	a great deal of
⑤	live	a little	a great deal of

부사

副詞

(도울 부, 말 사)

동사, 형용사, 문장 전체, 지신 이외의 부사를 수식하는 말

UNIT 34 **부사의 형태**

UNIT 35 **부사의 역할 및 위치**

UNIT 36 **그 밖의 중요 부사**

Unfortunately, the concert was canceled due to the heavy rain.
문장 전체 수식

(불행하게도, 폭우로 인해 콘서트가 취소되었다.)

I always drink coffee in the morning to wake up.
빈도부사는 일반동사 앞에 위치함

(나는 항상 아침에 일어나기 위해 커피를 마신다.)

I was still waiting for his response, but he hadn't replied yet.
부사 (여전히)   부사 (아직)

(나는 여전히 그의 답장을 기다리고 있었지만, 그는 아직 답하지 않았다.)

UNIT 34 부사의 형태

Sally exercises ***regularly*** every morning.
부사 (exercises 수식)

(Sally는 매일 아침 규칙적으로 운동한다.)

Truly, this regular exercise helps her maintain her health.
부사 (문장 전체 수식)

(정말로, 이 규칙적인 운동이 그녀가 건강을 유지하는 데 도움이 된다.)

1 부사의 종류

시간, 때	now, soon, yet, then 등	장소	there, near, up, down 등
방법	well, carefully, quickly 등	정도	hardly, quite, too, very 등
빈도	always, usually, often, frequently, never 등		

2 형용사를 부사로 만드는 규칙

형용사	규칙	예시와 예문
대부분의 형용사	+ -ly	careful → carefully, loud → loudly, smooth → smoothly • She clearly explained the directions. (그녀는 길을 분명하게 설명했다.) • He quickly tied his shoelaces. (그는 빠르게 신발 끈을 묶었다.)
「자음＋y」로 끝나는 형용사	y를 ily로 고치기	easy → easily, happy → happily, lucky → luckily, steady → steadily • They chatted cozily by the door. (그들은 문 옆에서 편안하게 이야기를 나누었다.) • She merrily waved at her friend. (그녀는 친구에게 기쁘게 손을 흔들었다.)
-le로 끝나는 형용사	le를 ly로 고치기	gentle → gently, simple → simply, probable → probably • We could possibly meet tomorrow. (우리는 어쩌면 내일 만날 수 있다.) • He gently closed the old book. (그는 오래된 책을 살살 덮었다.)
-ll로 끝나는 형용사	+ -y	dull → dully, full → fully • The restaurant was fully booked. (그 식당은 예약이 꽉 찼다.) • The knife glinted dully in the light. (칼이 빛 속에서 흐릿하게 반짝였다.)
-ue로 끝나는 형용사	ue를 uly로 고치기	true → truly • I truly believe in the power of kindness. (나는 친절의 힘을 진심으로 믿는다.)
-ic로 끝나는 형용사	+ -ally	basic → basically, automatic → automatically • My mom manages the household finances economically. (엄마는 가정 재정을 경제적으로 관리한다.) • Basically, we agree with the idea. (기본적으로 우리는 그 생각에 동의해.)
불규칙		shy → shyly, sly → slyly, public → publicly, unique → uniquely • She shyly handed him a small gift. (그녀는 수줍게 그에게 작은 선물을 건넸다.) • He publicly apologized for the mistake. (그는 그 실수에 대해 공개적으로 사과했다.)

1 부사의 종류

[01-05] 문장에서 부사를 찾아 밑줄을 긋고, 어떤 종류인지 〈보기〉에서 골라 기호를 쓰시오. (중복 사용 불가)

> 〈보기〉
> ⓐ 시간, 때　　ⓑ 장소　　ⓒ 방법　　ⓓ 정도　　ⓔ 빈도

01 As she leaned near, I could smell her perfume.　➡ _______________

02 She plans to start her own bakery soon.　➡ _______________

03 I never eat breakfast when I have to hurry.　➡ _______________

04 The robot moved smoothly across the glass floor.　➡ _______________

05 The school uniform was very expensive for the student.　➡ _______________

2 형용사를 부사로 만드는 규칙

[06-25] 주어진 형용사의 부사형을 쓰시오.

06 sly _______________   **16** classic _______________

07 true _______________   **17** smooth _______________

08 dull _______________   **18** sudden _______________

09 easy _______________   **19** psychic _______________

10 silly _______________   **20** probable _______________

11 quiet _______________   **21** steady _______________

12 actual _______________   **22** public _______________

13 gentle _______________   **23** automatic _______________

14 happy _______________   **24** basic _______________

15 subtle _______________   **25** fortunate _______________

[26-30] 괄호 안에서 알맞은 것을 고르시오.

26 He (truly / honesty) admitted that he had made a mistake.

27 The restaurant was (full / fully) booked on Christmas day.

28 She spoke (shyly / friendly) to the new student in the hallway.

29 The river flowed (smooth / smoothly) through the valley after the rain.

30 She (public / publicly) apologized for her mistake during the press conference.

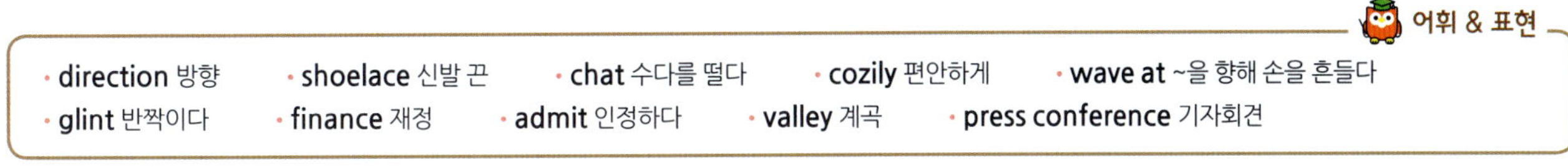

🦉 **어휘 & 표현**

- **direction** 방향　　• **shoelace** 신발 끈　　• **chat** 수다를 떨다　　• **cozily** 편안하게　　• **wave at** ~을 향해 손을 흔들다
- **glint** 반짝이다　　• **finance** 재정　　• **admit** 인정하다　　• **valley** 계곡　　• **press conference** 기자회견

〈 정답과 해설 p. 63~64 〉

3 형용사와 형태가 동일한 부사

① high 형 높은 부 높이 enough 형 충분한 부 충분히 ② fast 형 빠른 부 빠르게
far 형 먼 부 멀리 ③ early 형 이른 부 일찍 ④ late 형 늦은 부 늦게
⑤ low 형 낮은 부 낮게 ⑥ long 형 오래된 부 오래 ⑦ near 형 가까운 부 가까이
last 형 마지막인 부 마지막으로 hard 형 단단한, 어려운, 열심인 부 열심히

① ┌ He has high expectations for his students. (그는 학생들에게 높은 기대를 가지고 있다.)
  └ She jumped high during the competition. (그녀는 대회에서 높이 점프했다.)

② ┌ He bought a fast car with excellent acceleration. (그는 가속이 뛰어난 빠른 차를 샀다.)
  └ The athlete ran fast enough to win the gold medal. (그 운동선수는 금메달을 딸 만큼 빠르게 달렸다.)

③ ┌ The early train is always less crowded. (이른 기차는 항상 덜 붐빈다.)
  └ She arrived early to prepare for the presentation. (그녀는 발표 준비를 위해 일찍 도착했다.)

④ ┌ The bus was late because of the traffic. (교통 체증 때문에 그 버스는 늦었다.)
  └ He arrived late and quietly took a seat in the back. (그는 늦게 도착해 조용히 뒤쪽에 자리를 잡았다.)

⑤ ┌ The low clouds made it difficult to see the mountains. (낮은 구름 때문에 산이 잘 보이지 않았다.)
  └ The helicopter flew low over the forest. (헬리콥터는 숲 위를 낮게 날았다.)

⑥ ┌ They had a long talk after the meeting. (그들은 회의 후에 긴 대화를 나눴다.)
  └ We didn't have to wait long before the show began. (공연이 시작되기까지 오래 기다릴 필요는 없었다.)

⑦ ┌ Victory seemed near. (승리가 가까워 보였다.)
  └ She stood near and listened without interrupting. (그녀는 가까이 서서 방해하지 않고 들었다.)

4 형용사와 형태가 동일한 부사에 **-ly**를 붙이면 뜻이 달라지는 부사

① near (가까이) — nearly (거의) ② late (늦게) — lately (최근에) ③ short (짧게) — shortly (곧)
④ high (높이) — highly (대단히) ⑤ hard (열심히) — hardly (거의 ~않는)

① ┌ She came near and whispered something in my ear. (그녀는 가까이 다가와서 내 귀에 뭔가를 속삭였다.)
  └ He nearly hit the wall while backing the car. (그는 차를 후진하다가 거의 벽에 부딪칠 뻔했다.)

② ┌ She arrived late and missed the opening remarks. (그녀는 늦게 도착해 개회사 내용을 놓쳤다.)
  └ He's been working on a new project lately. (그는 최근에 새 프로젝트에 매달리고 있다.)

③ ┌ The speaker paused short when someone interrupted. (그 연사는 누군가 방해하자 잠시 멈췄다.)
  └ The announcement will be made shortly after the break. (그 발표는 휴식 후에 곧 있을 예정이다.)

④ ┌ The eagle flew high above the cliffs. (독수리는 절벽 위로 높이 날아올랐다.)
  └ She is highly respected in her field. (그녀는 자신의 분야에서 대단히 존경받는다.)

⑤ ┌ He worked hard to earn their trust. (그는 그들의 신뢰를 얻기 위해 열심히 일했다.)
  └ She could hardly believe what she heard. (그녀는 자신이 들은 것을 거의 믿을 수 없었다.)

3 형용사와 형태가 동일한 부사

[31-36] 밑줄 친 부분이 형용사인지, 부사인지 구분하시오.

31 The eagle flew <u>high</u> in the sky. ➡ [형용사 / 부사]

32 She is an <u>early</u> riser. ➡ [형용사 / 부사]

33 We don't have <u>enough</u> food for everyone. ➡ [형용사 / 부사]

34 The train arrived <u>late</u>. ➡ [형용사 / 부사]

35 He is a <u>fast</u> runner. ➡ [형용사 / 부사]

36 Come <u>near</u> and take a look. ➡ [형용사 / 부사]

4 형용사와 형태가 동일한 부사에 -ly를 붙이면 뜻이 달라지는 부사

[37-41] 괄호 안에서 알맞은 것을 고르시오.

37 The hunter moved (near / nearly) without making a sound.

38 The film was (high / highly) regarded among international critics.

39 She will join us (short / shortly) after the meeting starts.

40 She (hard / hardly) touched her food, distracted by the unfolding news.

41 He showed up unusually (late / lately) so that no one would notice him.

3 + **4** 부사의 형태

[42-50] 밑줄 친 부분의 품사를 고르시오.

42 He ran <u>fast</u> to catch the last bus before it left. ➡ [형용사 / 부사]

43 That's a <u>fast</u> car with excellent handling on sharp turns. ➡ [형용사 / 부사]

44 I didn't stay <u>long</u> because I had another appointment later. ➡ [형용사 / 부사]

45 We had a <u>long</u> meeting discussing plans for the summer event. ➡ [형용사 / 부사]

46 The doctor will see you <u>shortly</u>, so please wait here. ➡ [형용사 / 부사]

47 He gave a <u>short</u> speech before the award ceremony began. ➡ [형용사 / 부사]

48 Come <u>near</u> if you want to see the tiny details clearly. ➡ [형용사 / 부사]

49 The <u>near</u> building was closed for repairs after the storm. ➡ [형용사 / 부사]

50 She <u>nearly</u> fell asleep during the long, boring lecture. ➡ [형용사 / 부사]

🦉 어휘 & 표현

- acceleration 가속　　· athlete 운동선수　　· interrupt 방해하다　　· whisper 속삭이다　　· opening remarks 개회사
- break 휴식　　· eagle 독수리　　· cliff 절벽　　· field 분야　　· international 국제의　　· critic 평론가
- distract (주의를) 딴 데로 돌리다　　· unfolding 펼쳐지는[밝혀지는], 새로 들어오는　　· appointment 약속　　· discuss 상의하다

〈 정답과 해설 p. 64~65 〉

UNIT 35 부사의 역할 및 위치

1 부사의 역할: 형용사, 다른 부사, 동사, 또는 문장 전체를 꾸며주는 역할을 한다.

- This problem seems quite difficult. (이 문제는 상당히 어려운 것 같다.)
  형용사 수식
- The signal vanished almost completely. (신호가 거의 완전히 사라졌다.)
  다른 부사 수식 동사 vanished 수식
- Honestly, I didn't mean to hurt your feelings. (솔직히 말하자면, 당신의 기분을 상하게 할 의도가 없었다.)
  문장 전체 수식

2 부사의 위치

(1) 형용사, 다른 부사, 동사를 수식할 때 : 형용사, 다른 부사의 ❶앞, 동사 (동사 의미 단위)의 뒤에 위치

- The movie was very entertaining. (그 영화는 매우 재미있었다.)
  형용사 entertaining 수식
- She answered quite confidently. (그녀는 꽤 자신감 있게 답했다.)
  부사 confidently 수식
- He walked quickly without looking back. (그는 돌아보지 않고 빨리 걸었다.)
  동사 walked 수식

(2) 문장 전체를 수식할 때 : 주로 문장 앞에 위치

- Unfortunately, we missed the important meeting.
  문장 전체 수식
  (불행히도, 우리는 그 중요한 회의를 놓쳤다.)

> **❶ 부사의 위치 예외**
> - enough는 꾸미는 단어 뒤에 온다.
> - He is rich enough to buy it.
>   (그는 그것을 살 만큼 충분히 부유하다.)
> - enough to부정사로 명사 뒤에서 수식하는 형용사로 쓰일 수 있다.
> - He has money enough to buy it. (명사 / 형용사)
>   (그는 그것을 살 만큼 충분한 돈을 가지고 있다.)

(3) 「타동사＋부사」 형태로 올 때

목적어가 명사일 때	목적어가 대명사일 때
「타동사＋부사＋명사」 ┐ 둘 다 가능 「타동사＋명사＋부사」 ┘ ・He brought up the topic. → He brought the topic up. (그는 그 주제를 꺼냈다.)	「타동사＋대명사＋부사」 만 가능 ・He brought it up. (O) → He brought up it. (×) (그는 그것을 꺼냈다.)

자주 쓰이는 「타동사＋부사」와 예문	turn on (켜다), turn off (끄다), pick up (줍다, 태우다), look up (찾다), put off (미루다), break down (분석하다), give up (포기하다) 등
	・She picked the phone up. (O) → She picked up the phone. (O) ・She picked it up. (O) → She picked up it. (×) (그녀는 전화를 받았다.)

(4) 빈도부사의 위치 ❷

always (항상) >	usually (보통) >	often (자주) >	sometimes (때때로) >	hardly, rarely, seldom (거의 ~없는, ~않는) >	never (절대 ~않는)

① be동사 + 빈도부사
- They are never rude to others. (그들은 결코 다른 사람들에게 무례하지 않다.)
  빈도부사 never가 be동사 are 뒤에 위치함

② 빈도부사 + 일반동사
- She seldom complains about her work. (그녀는 자신의 일에 대해 드물게 불평한다.)
  빈도부사 seldom이 일반동사 complains 앞에 위치함

③ 조동사 + 빈도부사 + 일반동사
- They might sometimes forget to lock the door. (그들은 가끔 문 잠그는 걸 잊을 수 있다.)
  빈도부사 sometimes가 조동사 might와 일반동사 forget 사이에 위치함

> **❷ 빈도부사**
> 빈도부사는 어떤 일이 얼마나 자주 일어나는지를 나타내는 부사이다.

1 부사의 역할

[01-07] 〈보기〉와 같이 부사에 밑줄을 긋고, 부사가 수식하는 대상을 찾아 빈칸에 쓰시오.

〈보기〉

He ran <u>quickly</u> to catch the bus this morning. ➡ 동사 ran

01 Fortunately, we found the missing keys. ➡ ___________

02 That was an incredibly difficult challenge. ➡ ___________

03 Luckily, she arrived in time for the meeting. ➡ ___________

04 The children waited eagerly for the circus to start. ➡ ___________

05 The concert was absolutely fantastic from start to finish. ➡ ___________

06 The artist creatively decorated the walls with colorful murals. ➡ ___________

07 They worked hard to complete the project before the deadline. ➡ ___________

2 부사의 위치

[08-11] 주어진 부사가 들어가기에 알맞은 곳에 ✓표 하시오.

08 The streets are icy this morning. (really)

09 I hadn't trained for the match. (enough)

10 If the heater isn't working, try to turn it again. (on)

11 These big problems are scary, but let's break them. (down)

[12-14] 주어진 우리말과 일치하도록 알맞은 부사를 〈보기〉에서 골라 문장을 다시 쓰시오. (중복 사용 불가)

〈보기〉

always   usually   never

12 그는 항상 마감 전에 일을 끝낸다.

He finishes his work before the deadline.

➡ ___________

13 산림 파괴는 결코 토지 개발을 위한 지속 가능한 해결책이 아니다.

Deforestation is a sustainable solution for land development.

➡ ___________

14 그들은 보통 힘든 시기에도 서로를 매우 지지한다.

They have been very supportive of each other during tough times.

➡ ___________

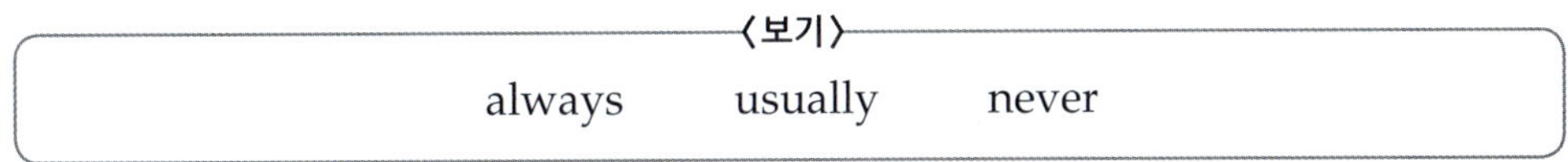

🦉 어휘 & 표현

· **entertaining** 재미있는   · **confidently** 자신감 있게   · **decorate** 장식하다   · **mural** 벽화   · **deadline** 마감 시간[일자]
· **deforestation** 산림 파괴   · **sustainable** 지속 가능한   · **development** 개발   · **supportive** 지지하는

〈 정답과 해설 p. 65 〉

UNIT 36 그 밖의 중요 부사

1 ago, before

ago	~ 전에	단순 과거시제	• I went there two years <u>ago</u>. (나는 2년 전에 그곳에 갔다.) 　　단순 과거시제
before		완료시제	• I have visited that museum <u>before</u>. 　　현재완료시제 　　　　　　　　　　　　　(나는 전에 그 박물관을 방문한 적이 있다.)

2 too, either, neither

too	또한, 역시	긍정문	• She loves ice cream, and I do <u>too</u>. 　　긍정문 　　　　　　　　　　　　(그녀는 아이스크림을 좋아하고, 나도 그렇다.)
either		부정문	• I can't speak French, and my friend can't <u>either</u>. 　　부정문 　　　　　　　　　　(나는 프랑스어를 할 수 없고, 내 친구도 할 수 없다.)
neither	~도 아니다	부정문	− not ~ either 대신 쓸 수 있다. • I don't feel like going out. – I don't either. (= Me neither.) 　　　　　　　　　　(나는 외출할 기분이 아니다. – 나도 그렇지 않다.)

3 very, much

very	매우	형용사나 부사의 원급 수식	• This is a <u>very</u> sad story. (이것은 매우 슬픈 이야기이다.) 　　　　　　　형용사의 원급
much	훨씬	형용사나 부사의 비교급 수식	• This story is <u>much</u> sadder than I expected. 　　　　　　　형용사의 비교급 　　　　　　(이 이야기는 내가 예상했던 것보다 훨씬 더 슬프다.)

4 already, yet, still

already ❶	이미	긍정문	• He is <u>already</u> asleep. (그는 이미 잠들었다.)
	벌써	의문문	• Is it bedtime <u>already</u>? (벌써 취침시간인가요?)
yet	아직	부정문	• I haven't eaten <u>yet</u>. (나는 아직 밥을 먹지 않았다.)
	벌써	의문문	• Have you met her <u>yet</u>? (벌써 그녀를 만났나요?)
still	여전히	긍정문	• She is <u>still</u> cheerful despite the rain. (그녀는 비가 오는데도 여전히 활기차다.)
		의문문	• Is the store <u>still</u> open at this hour? (그 가게는 이 시간에도 여전히 영업하나요?)
		부정문	• They <u>still</u> don't believe me. (그들은 여전히 나를 믿지 못한다.)

❶ 의문문에 쓰이는 already
놀람을 나타낼 때는 already도 의문문에 쓰일 수 있다.

5 even, else

even	~도, ~조차	강조하려는 말의 앞에 쓰임	• Mary didn't <u>even</u> try to help. 　　　　　　　(Mary는 도와주려 하지도 않았다.)
else	또 다른, 그 밖에	수식하려는 말의 뒤에 쓰임	• They will move to somewhere <u>else</u>. 　　　　　　(그들은 또 다른 곳으로 이사를 갈 것이다.)

[참고] else가 의문대명사나 부정대명사 뒤에 쓰였다면 **형용사로 쓰인 것**이다.

• What <u>else</u> can we do?　　　　　　　　　• Does anyone <u>else</u> come to the party?
　의문대명사　　　　　　　　　　　　　　　　부정대명사
　　　　(우리가 그 밖에 무엇을 할 수 있니?)　　　　　　　　(또 다른 누군가가 파티에 오니?)

1 + 2 ago, before, too, either, neither

[01-07] 괄호 안에서 알맞은 것을 고르시오.

01 I have seen this statue somewhere (ago / before).

02 He booked a plane ticket three months (ago / before).

03 A: I don't like spicy food. It gives me a stomachache.

　　B: I don't like it (either / neither). I prefer milder flavors.

04 A: I'll skip the meeting today. I'm just not feeling up to it.

　　B: I'm thinking the same thing. I might skip it (either / too).

05 A: I don't like the new design of the website. It's hard to navigate.

　　B: (Neither / Either) do I. It's way more confusing than the old one.

06 She said that she had never seen the man (ago / before).

07 The Korean War ended over sixty years (ago / before).

3 + 4 + 5 very, much, already, yet, still, even, else

[08-13] 빈칸에 알맞은 말을 〈보기〉에서 골라 쓰시오. (중복 사용 불가)

〈보기〉

| even | already | much | very | else | yet |

08 His story is always ＿＿＿＿＿＿＿＿ interesting.

09 Do you want something ＿＿＿＿＿＿＿＿ for dessert?

10 I have not received a salary this month ＿＿＿＿＿＿＿＿.

11 I can't ＿＿＿＿＿＿＿＿ imagine how difficult it must have been.

12 When I arrived, he had ＿＿＿＿＿＿＿＿ finished his homework.

13 The blockbuster movie was ＿＿＿＿＿＿＿＿ more interesting than I thought.

[14-18] 괄호 안에서 알맞은 것을 고르시오.

14 I haven't received a postcard from my father (yet / else).

15 (Even / Else) the teacher was surprised by his clever answer.

16 We should listen to the doctor's advice (very / else) carefully.

17 I went to the train station, and the train had (still / already) left.

18 They booked a hotel somewhere (else / much) after seeing the bad reviews.

🦉 어휘 & 표현

· **despite** ~에도 불구하고　　· **statue** 조각상　　· **stomachache** 복통　　· **mild** 순한, 부드러운　　· **flavor** 맛　　· **skip** 건너뛰다
· **navigate** 길을 찾다　　· **confusing** 혼란스러운　　· **dessert** 후식　　· **salary** 월급　　· **blockbuster** 블록버스터(크게 성공한 책이나 영화)

〈 정답과 해설 p. 65~66 〉

[01-03]

형용사와 부사의 형태가 옳은 것을 고르시오.

01

① shy – shily　② nice – nicly
③ true – truely　④ heavy – heavyly
⑤ careful – carefully

02

① noble – noblely　② simple – simplely
③ unique – uniquly　④ precise – precisely
⑤ terrible – terriblely

03

① sly – slyly　② basic – basicly
③ angry – angryly　④ public – publically
⑤ fantastic – fantasticly

[04-07]

괄호 안에서 알맞은 것을 고르시오.

04

He is not ready to leave (already / yet).

05

The crowd cheered (loud / loudly) after the team scored a goal.

06

The storm started much earlier this morning, around three hours (ago / before).

07

Fresh fruits and vegetables are (very / much) more nutritious than processed foods.

[08-10]

어법상 틀린 것을 고르시오.

08

① She sings beautifully.
② He works hard every day.
③ She was dancing gracefully.
④ The children played outside happy.
⑤ The sun sets slowly in the evening.

09

① He apologized sincere.
② The dog barked loudly.
③ He arrived late to the party.
④ The teacher spoke very clearly.
⑤ They were walking quietly down the street.

10 고난도

① I usually go skiing in winter.
② She always takes the eight o'clock bus.
③ I will never forget what you said to me.
④ Susan is rich enough to buy this expensive car.
⑤ I will think always of you when I hear this music.

[11-12]

대화의 빈칸에 알맞은 것을 고르시오.

11

> A: Hey, could you turn on the lights? It's getting dark in here.
> B: Sure! I'll ___________. There we go!

① turn it on　② turn on it
③ turn them on　④ turn on them
⑤ turn them off

12

> A: I finished reading that book a week
> ___________, and it was amazing.
> B: I read it a few weeks ago, but I didn't
> find it interesting.

① yet   ② ago
③ much   ④ already
⑤ sometimes

13 [고난도]

밑줄 친 부분에 관해 <u>잘못</u> 이야기한 학생을 고르시오.

> ⓐ I forget <u>always</u> my keys at home.
> ⓑ She eats <u>much</u> healthier than I do.
> ⓒ I haven't finished my homework <u>yet</u>.
> ⓓ I saw her two weeks <u>ago</u>, and we had a
> great conversation.
> ⓔ <u>Fortunately</u>, the power came back on after
> only a brief outage.

① 다나: ⓐ의 빈도부사 always는 일반동사 forget
뒤가 아니라 앞에 와야 해.
② 호영: ⓑ처럼 much는 비교급을 수식할 수 있어.
③ 예지: ⓒ는 부정문이니까 yet이 온 것은 적절해.
④ 승준: ⓓ는 과거시제에서 '~ 전에'를 의미하는 ago가
적절하게 사용되었어.
⑤ 이서: Fortunately는 문장 전체를 수식하기 때문
에 맨 뒤에 와야 해.

14

빈칸에 알맞은 것을 고르시오.

> I have heard that song ___________, but I
> don't remember the lyrics.

① ago   ② very
③ after   ④ always
⑤ before

[15-16]

괄호 안에 주어진 부사가 들어가기에 알맞은 곳을 고르시오.

15

> This field (①) is (②) large (③) for
> all my friends (④) to play soccer and
> baseball (⑤). (enough)

16

> However unhappy, (①) we (②)
> should (③) remember happiness (④)
> is not far away (⑤). (always)

[17-18] [서술형]

어법상 틀린 곳을 찾아 바르게 고치시오.

17

> It's near impossible to find a parking spot in
> this area.

➡ ___________ → ___________

18

> I will be leaving short, so please wrap up
> the meeting.

➡ ___________ → ___________

[19-20]

어순이 옳은 문장을 고르시오.

19

① Bob rarely arrives on time.
② I have been always thinking of you.
③ She thinks she never will walk again.
④ My computers sometimes are out of order.
⑤ Do you have often a fight with your
brother?

〈 정답과 해설 p. 66~68 〉

20

① I rarely should skip breakfast.
② He usually is very busy at work.
③ She eats never dessert after dinner.
④ I always must be on time for meetings.
⑤ He sometimes forgets to bring his lunch.

[21-24]

밑줄 친 부사가 수식하는 대상에 따라 문장을 분류하시오.

> ⓐ Luckily, we found our way back before it got dark.
> ⓑ The global temperature is rising <u>alarmingly</u> fast.
> ⓒ <u>Thankfully</u>, no one was hurt during the accident.
> ⓓ He <u>always</u> remembers to call his mom on Sundays.
> ⓔ The weather is <u>surprisingly</u> warm for this time of year.
> ⓕ They worked <u>incredibly</u> hard to finish the project on time.
> ⓖ The movie was <u>absolutely</u> fantastic, and everyone loved it.
> ⓗ I <u>rarely</u> eat fast food because I prefer home-cooked meals.

21

동사 수식: ____________

22

형용사 수식: ____________

23

부사 수식: ____________

24

문장 전체 수식: ____________

[25-26] 서술형

빈칸에 공통으로 들어갈 말을 쓰시오.

25

> • She stopped to pick __________ a book she dropped while walking.
> • After hours of trying to solve the puzzle, she decided to give it __________.

➡ ____________

26

> • Please turn __________ the oven once the timer goes off.
> • I keep putting __________ going to the gym because I'm so busy.

➡ ____________

[27-30]

밑줄 친 부분의 품사가 나머지 넷과 다른 것을 고르시오.

27

① I didn't get <u>enough</u> sleep last night.
② He didn't study <u>enough</u> to pass the exam.
③ She didn't bring <u>enough</u> food for the picnic.
④ There's <u>enough</u> room in the car for all of us to fit.
⑤ I didn't pack <u>enough</u> clothes for the trip, so I had to buy more.

28

① These are <u>hard</u> questions.
② He faced a <u>hard</u> decision.
③ It was a <u>hard</u> day at work.
④ He worked <u>hard</u> on the project.
⑤ The material is too <u>hard</u> to bend.

29

① He finished the project <u>early</u>.
② We left <u>early</u> to avoid traffic.
③ We had an <u>early</u> dinner today.
④ The store opens <u>early</u> on Sundays.
⑤ The train departed <u>early</u> this morning.

30

① The cheetah is the <u>fast</u> animal on land.
② The car sped <u>fast</u> through the intersection.
③ I can type <u>fast</u>, but I still make a few mistakes.
④ The storm moved <u>fast</u>, and we had little time to prepare.
⑤ He made decisions <u>fast</u> and managed to close the deal quickly.

[31-33]

주어진 단어가 들어갈 알맞은 위치를 고르시오.

31

> up

She (①) saw (②) a pencil on the floor and picked (③) it (④) to use (⑤) for the test.

32

> enough

The soup (①) wasn't (②) hot (③) for (④) the baby (⑤) to eat safely.

33

> it

She found an application form and (①) filled (②) out (③) before the (④) deadline (⑤).

[34-35]

빈칸에 들어갈 말이 알맞게 짝지어진 것을 고르시오.

34

W: There was a loud noise outside three nights ___(A)___ . Did you hear that?
M: Yes, I woke up because of the noise, and ___(B)___ sleep after that. Do you know what happened?

	(A)		(B)
①	ago	–	hardly could
②	ago	–	could hardly
③	ago	–	usually could
④	before	–	hardly could
⑤	before	–	could usually

35 고난도

W: Have you seen the new movie? Everyone's been talking about it ___(A)___ .
M: Yes, I've heard it's ___(B)___ recommended. I plan to watch it this weekend.

	(A)		(B)
①	late	–	high
②	late	–	highly
③	lately	–	high
④	lately	–	highly
⑤	recent	–	highly

36 고난도

밑줄 친 부분의 쓰임이 어색한 것을 고르시오.

① I haven't eaten breakfast <u>yet</u>.
② We can go somewhere <u>else</u> after lunch.
③ He didn't call me, and I didn't call him <u>either</u>.
④ I didn't go to the party, and she didn't <u>neither</u>.
⑤ They had <u>already</u> left the house when I finally arrived.

〈 정답과 해설 p. 68~69 〉

주어진 우리말과 일치하도록 바르게 영작한 것을 고르시오.

37

> 그녀는 아직도 내 메시지에 답이 없다.

① She hasn't responded to my message else.
② She still hasn't responded to my message.
③ She hasn't responded even to my message.
④ She hasn't much responded to my message.
⑤ She hasn't responded to my message already.

38

> 그는 준비되지 않았고, 그의 팀도 마찬가지였다.

① He wasn't ready, and his team did too.
② He wasn't ready, and his team wasn't too.
③ He wasn't ready, and his team didn't either.
④ He wasn't ready, and his team wasn't either.
⑤ He wasn't ready, and his team wasn't neither.

[39-42] 서술형

주어진 우리말과 일치하도록 〈보기〉에서 알맞은 단어를 골라 괄호 안의 동사와 함께 빈칸을 완성하시오. (중복 사용 불가)

〈보기〉
always   usually   often   never

39

밤에는 부엉이 우는 소리를 자주 들을 수 있다. (can hear)

➡ You ＿＿＿＿＿＿＿＿＿ owls hooting at night.

40

고양이는 하루에 보통 12~16시간 정도 잠을 잔다. (sleep)

➡ Cats ＿＿＿＿＿＿＿＿＿ for around 12 to 16 hours a day.

41

공룡은 인간과 절대 같은 시대에 살지 않았다. (were)

➡ Dinosaurs ＿＿＿＿＿＿＿＿＿ alive at the same time as humans.

42

빛이 소리보다 빠르기 때문에 번개는 항상 천둥보다 먼저 발생한다. (occurs)

➡ Lightning ＿＿＿＿＿＿＿＿＿ before thunder because light travels faster than sound.

43 수능 유형

밑줄 친 부분 중 어법상 틀린 것을 고르시오.

> Sarah ① saw seldom her friends because she had busy schedules. Despite feeling ② lonely, she had not given up on finding a way to spend more time with her friends. ③ Luckily, one weekend, her friends invited her to join them on a hiking trip. She knew this was ④ enough to make up for the time they had missed. Sarah was ⑤ happy that they had finally managed to spend time together.

①   ②   ③   ④   ⑤

🦉 어휘 & 표현

· **nutritious** 영양가 있는   · **processed** 가공한   · **conversation** 대화   · **outage** 정전   · **lyric** 가사   · **out of order** 고장 난
· **alarmingly** 놀랄 만큼   · **temperature** 온도   · **go off** 울리다   · **material** 물질   · **depart** 출발하다   · **speed** 빨리 가다(- sped - sped)
· **intersection** 교차로   · **application form** 지원서   · **owl** 부엉이   · **hoot** 부엉부엉 울다   · **dinosaur** 공룡   · **thunder** 천둥

J

비교급
比較級
(견줄 비, 견줄 교, 등급 급)
두 대상, 또는 그 이상을 견주어
한쪽의 더하거나 덜한 정도를 나타내는 것

This dress is as beautiful as the one I saw online.
원급
(이 드레스는 내가 온라인에서 본 것만큼 아름답다.)

This book is more informative than the previous one I read.
비교급
(이 책은 내가 읽은 이전 책보다 더 유익하다.)

This is the most comfortable chair in the whole store.
최상급
(이것은 가게 전체에서 가장 편안한 의자이다.)

UNIT 37 원급 

> **핵심 개념**
> •**원급**: 양측의 성질이나 상태가 비슷하거나 같음을 나타내는 것이다. 동등 비교라고도 한다.

1 원급: 둘 사이를 비교해서 정도가 비슷하거나 같음을 표현한다.

(1) **기본 형태: as + 형용사 [부사]의 원급 + as** '···만큼 ～한 [하게]'
- The movie was as interesting as the book was.
  (그 영화는 그 책만큼 재미있었다.)

(2) **부정형: not as [so] + 형용사 [부사]의 원급 + as** '···만큼 ～하지 않는 [하지 않게]'
- She does not sing as[so] cheerfully as I do. (그녀는 나만큼 쾌활하게 노래 부르지 않는다.)

(3) 비교 대상이 주어일 경우, as 뒤의 be동사 또는 대동사 do를 생략하거나 목적격으로 바꾸어 쓸 수 있다.
- He is as thin as I (am). = He is as thin as me. (그는 나만큼 날씬하다.)
  be동사 생략 / 목적격
- She studies as hard as I (do). = She studies as hard as me. (그녀는 나만큼 열심히 공부한다.)
  대동사 do 생략 / 목적격

2 다양한 원급 표현

(1) **as[so] long as** : '～하는 동안, ～하는 한'
- I will help you as[so] long as you promise to be careful.
  (네가 조심한다고 약속하는 한 나는 너를 도울 것이다.)

(2) **as + 원급 + as + possible (= as + 원급 + as + 주어 + can [could])** : '가능한 한 ～한[하게]'
- I want to make this process as simple as possible.
  = I want to make this process as simple as I can.
  (나는 이 과정을 가능한 한 간단하게 만들고 싶다.)

(3) **배수사 + as + 원급 + as** : '···의 몇 배 ～한[하게]'
- His luggage is twice as heavy as mine. (그의 짐은 내 것의 두 배만큼 무겁다.)

3 원급 관용표현

> ① as busy as a bee 아주 바쁜　　　　as smart as a fox 아주 약삭빠른
> 　as proud as a peacock 아주 뽐내는　② as brave as a lion 아주 용감한
> ③ as happy as a lark 아주 즐거운　　　as wise as an owl 아주 현명한
> 　as stubborn as a donkey[mule] 아주 고집이 센
> ④ as like as two peas (in a pod) 아주 똑같은

① She is always as busy as a bee. (그녀는 항상 아주 바쁘다.)

② Jiho was as brave as a lion when he gave his speech in front of the whole school.
  (지호는 전교생 앞에서 발표할 때 아주 용감했다.)

③ After finishing all her exams, she looked as happy as a lark.
  (시험이 다 끝난 후, 그녀는 아주 즐거워 보였다.)

④ The brothers are as like as two peas in a pod. (그 형제들은 아주 똑같이 생겼다.)

1 원급

[01-05] 괄호 안에서 알맞은 것을 고르시오.

01 The company is not doing as (good / well) as last year.

02 After hearing the news, she was as excited as (I / my).

03 She reads (as many as / as much as) three books every week.

04 His new movie is (not so / so not) interesting as his previous ones.

05 Jamies' eyes are (as / so) big as his mother's.

2 다양한 원급 표현

[06-10] 자연스러운 문장이 되도록 연결하시오.

06 He has three times as   •   • ⓐ to catch the bus.

07 You'd better go home as   •   • ⓑ much money as I have.

08 I tried to run as fast as I could   •   • ⓒ bananas as he could.

09 English has about twice   •   • ⓓ soon as you can.

10 The monkey tried to catch as many   •   • ⓔ as many words as Spanish.

3 원급 관용표현

[11-15] 주어진 우리말과 일치하도록 괄호 안의 말을 이용하여 원급 문장을 완성하시오.

11 그녀는 아주 고집이 세서 누구의 말도 들으려고 하지 않는다.
(stubborn, is, a mule, doesn't, so, anyone, listen to)

➡ She ________________________________.

12 그는 졸업식 날 아주 즐거워 보였다. (happy, on the day, looked, a lark, of his graduation)

➡ He ________________________________.

13 그 소방관은 불타는 건물에 들어갈 때 아주 용감했다.
(entered, was, he, brave, the burning building, a lion, when)

➡ The firefighter ________________________________.

14 그녀는 까다로운 문제를 푸는 데 있어서 아주 약삭빠르다.
(smart, is, a fox, solving, when, comes to, it, tricky problems)

➡ She ________________________________.

15 나의 아버지는 주말에도 아주 바쁘시다. (busy, a bee, even on the weekend)

➡ My father ________________________________.

 어휘 & 표현

• **promise** 약속하다	• **process** 과정	• **luggage** 짐	• **peacock** 공작	• **lark** 종달새	• **stubborn** 완고한	• **mule** 노새
• **pea** 완두콩	• **pod** (콩 따위의) 깍지	• **speech** 발표, 연설	• **graduation** 졸업	• **tricky** 까다로운	

〈 정답과 해설 p. 69~70 〉

비교급, 최상급 형태 

- **비교급 형태**: 형용사 또는 부사 뒤에 '**-er**'을 또는 앞에 '**more**'를 붙여 사용한다.
- **최상급 형태**: 형용사 또는 부사 뒤에 '**-est**'를 또는 앞에 '**most**'를 붙여 사용한다.

❶ 「모음+y」로 끝나는 단어

일반적인 경우처럼 단어 뒤에 -er과 -est를 붙인다.
예) gray - grayer - grayest

1 규칙 변화

(1) 대부분 1 음절 단어와 일부 2음절 단어 (narrow, sleepy, happy, simple, clever, quiet 등)

– [비교급]: **원급 + -er,** [최상급]: **원급 + -est**

구분	규칙		원급	비교급	최상급
대부분	[비교급] **원급 + -er**		low 낮은	lower 더 낮은	lowest 가장 낮은
	[최상급] **원급 + -est**		tall 키가 큰	taller 키가 더 큰	tallest 키가 가장 큰
	[비교급] The weather is getting colder these days. (요즘 날씨가 더 추워지고 있다.)				
	[최상급] The coldest hours are just before dawn. (가장 추운 시간은 동트기 직전이다.)				
-e로 끝날 때	[비교급] **원급 + -r**		wide 넓은	wider 더 넓은	widest 가장 넓은
	[최상급] **원급 + -st**		wise 현명한	wiser 더 현명한	wisest 가장 현명한
	[비교급] Safer options are also available. (더 안전한 선택도 가능하다.)				
	[최상급] This is the safest route to take. (이것이 갈 수 있는 가장 안전한 길이다.)				
「자음+y」로 ❶ 끝날 때	[비교급] **y를 i로 고치고 + -er**		easy 쉬운	easier 더 쉬운	easiest 가장 쉬운
	[최상급] **y를 i로 고치고 + -est**		sleepy 졸린	sleepier 더 졸린	sleepiest 가장 졸린
	[비교급] Nothing makes me happier than you. (당신보다 나를 더 행복하게 만드는 것은 없다.)				
	[최상급] Thank you for the happiest year. (가장 행복한 한 해에 감사드립니다.)				
「단모음+단자음」으로 끝날 때	[비교급] **단자음을 한 번 더 쓰고 -er**		thin 마른	thinner 더 마른	thinnest 가장 마른
	[최상급] **단자음을 한 번 더 쓰고 -est**		hot 더운	hotter 더 더운	hottest 가장 더운
	[비교급] The autumn leaves gradually turned redder. (가을 단풍이 점점 더 붉어졌다.)				
	[최상급] He picked the reddest rose for me. (그는 나를 위해 가장 붉은 장미를 골랐다.)				

(2) 대부분 2음절 (-ous, -ful, -ish, -less, -able, -ive, -ly)과 2음절 이상의 원급, 분사 형태의 형용사, 「형용사 + ly」 형태의 부사 ⌐ [비교급]: **more + 원급,** [최상급]: **most + 원급**

구분	원급	비교급	최상급
대부분 2음절 이상의 원급	anxious 불안한 famous 유명한	more anxious 더 불안한 more famous 더 유명한	most anxious 가장 불안한 most famous 가장 유명한
	[비교급] It was more annoying than I thought. (그것은 내가 생각했던 것보다 더 성가셨다.)		
	[최상급] It is the most annoying thing in the world. (그것은 세상에서 가장 귀찮은 것이다.)		
두 개의 비교급을 갖는 경우	friendly 친근한	friendlier, more friendly ⌐ 더 친근한	friendliest, most friendly ⌐ 가장 친근한
	[비교급] The new design is simpler[more simple] than the old one. (새 디자인은 옛날 것보다 더 간단하다.)		
	[최상급] This is the simplest[most simple] solution to the problem. (이것이 그 문제에 대한 가장 간단한 해결책이다.)		

1 규칙 변화

[01-20] 형용사 또는 부사의 비교급과 최상급을 쓰시오.

	원급	비교급	최상급		원급	비교급	최상급
01	sunny	— ________	— ________	11	annoying	— ________	— ________
02	lazy	— ________	— ________	12	happy	— ________	— ________
03	humble	— ________	— ________	13	wet	— ________	— ________
04	flexible	— ________	— ________	14	intelligent	— ________	— ________
05	lovely	— ________	— ________	15	close	— ________	— ________
06	logical	— ________	— ________	16	thin	— ________	— ________
07	funny	— ________	— ________	17	gentle	— ________	— ________
08	busy	— ________	— ________	18	cold	— ________	— ________
09	responsible	— ________	— ________	19	challenging	— ________	— ________
10	big	— ________	— ________	20	rude	— ________	— ________

[21-29] 주어진 우리말과 일치하도록 괄호 안의 단어를 이용하여 빈칸을 완성하시오.

21 그는 팀에서 가장 용감한 소방관이다. (brave)

➡ He is the _______________ firefighter in the team.

22 그녀는 컴퓨터로 나보다 더 빠르게 타자를 친다. (quick)

➡ She types _______________ than I do on the computer.

23 그는 이제 선생님들에게 더 예의를 갖춘다. (respectful)

➡ He is _______________ toward his teachers now.

24 그는 내가 들은 것 중 가장 단순한 설명을 해줬다. (simple)

➡ He gave the _______________ explanation I've ever heard.

25 그 운동선수는 경기에 지고 나서 더 열심히 훈련했다. (hard)

➡ The athlete trained _______________ after losing the match.

26 그는 전체 토론 중 가장 고귀한 답변을 했다. (noble)

➡ He gave the _______________ answer in the entire debate.

27 아기를 깨우지 않으려고 그녀는 평소보다 더 조용한 목소리로 말했다. (quiet)

➡ She spoke in a _______________ voice than usual not to wake the baby.

28 이것은 올해 우리가 받은 가장 정확한 보고서이다. (accurate)

➡ This is the _______________ report we've received this year.

29 온라인 학습은 전통적인 교실 수업보다 더 유연하다. (flexible)

➡ Online learning is _______________ than traditional classroom education.

> **🦉 어휘 & 표현**
> · **available** 사용 가능한
> · **route** 길
> · **gradually** 점진적으로
> · **celebrity** 유명 인사
> · **respectful** 예의를 갖추는
> · **entire** 전체
> · **debate** 토론
> · **accurate** 정확한
> · **flexible** 유연한
> · **education** 교육

〈 정답과 해설 p. 70~72 〉

원급	비교급	최상급	예문
good 좋은	better 더 좋은, 더 잘	best 가장 좋은, 가장 잘	[비교급] I feel better today than I did yesterday. (나는 어제보다 오늘 기분이 더 좋다.) [최상급] Laughter is the best medicine. (웃음이 가장 좋은 약이다.)
well 잘			[비교급] The changed plan worked better. (수정된 계획이 더 잘 작용했다.)
bad 나쁜	worse 더 나쁜, 더 아픈	worst 가장 나쁜, 가장 아픈	[비교급] The situation is worse than we imagined. (상황은 우리가 상상했던 것보다 더 나쁘다.) [최상급] He had the worst day at work today. (그는 오늘 직장에서 가장 힘든 하루를 보냈다.)
ill 아픈			[최상급] It's the worst flu I've ever had. (내가 앓았던 최고로 아픈 독감이다.)
many [수] 많은	more 더 많은	most 가장 많은	[비교급] There are more people in the park today. (오늘 공원에 더 많은 사람들이 있다.)
much [양] 많은			[최상급] Jack has the most energy in his class. (Jack은 그의 반에서 가장 많은 에너지를 갖고 있다.)
few [수] 적은	fewer 더 적은	fewest 가장 적은	[최상급] David received the fewest votes. (David가 가장 적은 표를 받았다.)
little [양] 적은	less 더 적은	least 가장 적은	[비교급] There was less traffic on the roads. (도로에 교통량이 더 적었다.)
far [물리적인 거리] 먼, 멀리	farther 더 먼	farthest 가장 먼	[최상급] He threw the ball to the farthest corner. (그는 공을 가장 먼 구석으로 던졌다.)
far [추상적 의미, 정도] 더욱	further 더 깊이	furthest 가장 깊이	[비교급] Further investigation revealed new evidence. (추가 조사가 새로운 증거를 드러냈다.)
late [시간] 늦은, 늦게	later 이후의	latest 최신의	[비교급] Let's grab a coffee later in the afternoon. (이따 오후에 커피를 마십시다.)
late [순서] 늦은, 늦게	latter 후자의	last 마지막의	[최상급] This is the last train to the city. (이것이 도시로 가는 마지막 기차이다.)
old 오래된, 나이든	older ❶ 더 오래된	oldest 가장 오래된	[비교급] My brother is two years older than me. (내 형은 나보다 두 살 더 많다.) [최상급] This building is the oldest building in town. (이 건물은 마을에서 가장 오래된 건물이다.)
old 연상의	elder 더 연상의	eldest 가장 연상의	[비교급] My elder brother is my best friend. (형은 나의 가장 친한 친구이다.) [최상급] She is the eldest child in her family. (그녀는 가족 중에서 맏이다.)

❶ **older vs. elder**
oldest vs. eldest

elder, eldest는 사람의 나이를 나타낼 때만 쓰이지만, older, oldest는 사물에도 쓸 수 있다.

2 불규칙 변화

[30-41] 형용사 또는 부사의 원급, 비교급, 최상급을 쓰시오.

	원급	비교급	최상급		원급	비교급	최상급
30	__________	__________	eldest	36	__________	further	__________
31	good	__________	__________	37	__________	later	__________
32	bad	__________	__________	38	__________	latter	__________
33	many	__________	__________	39	little	__________	__________
34	__________	fewer	__________	40	ill	__________	__________
35	__________	__________	farthest	41	__________	older	__________

1 + **2** 비교급, 최상급 형태

[42-51] 주어진 문장이 맞으면 O로 표시하고, <u>틀리면</u> 바르게 고쳐 문장을 다시 쓰시오.

42 He became lazyer after the vacation ended.

➡ _______________________________________

43 Neptune is the furthest planet in our solar system.

➡ _______________________________________

44 The most popular sport in the world is football.

➡ _______________________________________

45 That street is narrower than it looks on the map.

➡ _______________________________________

46 Cats can be friendlier than dogs in some situations.

➡ _______________________________________

47 Drinking water is gooder than drinking soda for staying healthy.

➡ _______________________________________

48 The student who studied least got the lowest test score.

➡ _______________________________________

49 The forest became denser as we walked deeper into the woods.

➡ _______________________________________

50 He acted the carefullyest in the dangerous situation to stay safe.

➡ _______________________________________

51 The ground is weter than usual due to last night's heavy rainfall.

➡ _______________________________________

 어휘 & 표현

- **laughter** 웃음
- **imagine** 상상하다
- **vote** 표
- **investigation** 조사
- **lazy** 게으른
- **Neptune** 해왕성
- **solar system** 태양계
- **narrow** 좁은
- **forest** 숲
- **dense** 빽빽한, 밀도 높은
- **ground** 땅, 지면
- **rainfall** 강수

〈 정답과 해설 p. 72 〉

 **UNIT 39** 비교급 

The tiger is *stronger than* the cheetah.
우등 비교(~보다 더 …하다)
(호랑이는 치타보다 더 강하다.)

The tiger is *less fast than* the cheetah.
열등 비교(~보다 …하지 않다)
(호랑이는 치타보다 더 빠르지 않다.)

Which do you *like better, a tiger or a cheetah*?
which ~ 비교급, A or B: A와 B 중 어느 쪽이 더 ~한가?
(호랑이와 치타 중 어느 것이 더 좋은가?)

1 **비교급:** 둘 사이를 비교해서 한쪽이 다른 한쪽보다 낫거나 열등함을 표현한다.
두 개를 비교해서 한쪽이 더 좋거나 우수함을 표현하는 우등 비교와
나쁘거나 덜 우수한 것을 표현하는 열등 비교가 있다.

(1) 우등 비교: **형용사[부사]의 비교급 + than** '~보다 더 …한[하게]'
  - This test was easier than the last one. (이번 시험은 지난 시험보다 더 쉬웠다.)

(2) 열등 비교: **less + 형용사[부사]의 원급 + than** '~보다 덜 …한[하게]'
  - This test was less difficult than the last one. (이 시험은 지난 시험보다 덜 어려웠다.)

(3) 비교급 강조: 비교급 앞에 부사 much, still, far, even, a lot 등을 써서
  '훨씬'의 뜻으로 비교급을 강조한다.
  - My house is a lot closer to the school than yours.
    (내 집은 너의 집보다 학교에 훨씬 더 가깝다.)

❶ 비교급 강조 부사
much, even, still, far, a lot은 비교급을 강조하며, very는 원급을 강조한다.

2 **다양한 비교급 표현**

(1) **비교급 + and + 비교급:** '점점 더 ~한'
  - The weather is getting warmer and warmer every day. (날씨가 매일매일 점점 더 따뜻해지고 있다.)

(2) **the + 비교급, the + 비교급:** '~할수록 더 …한'
  - The more you practice, the better you get. (더 많이 연습할수록, 더 잘하게 된다.)

(3) **배수사 비교급 + than:** '~보다 몇 배 더 …한'
  - He is four times more hardworking than his colleagues. (그는 동료들보다 네 배 더 열심히 일한다.)

(4) **no more than:** '겨우, 단지, ~ 이하의'
  - You should spend no more than $50 on the gift. (선물에 50달러 이하로 써야 한다.)

(5) **no less than:** '~만큼이나, ~ 이상의'
  - The project will cost no less than $1,000. (그 프로젝트는 1,000달러 이상 비용이 들 것이다.)

(6) **What [Who, Which] ~ 비교급, A or B?:** 'A와 B 중 어느 쪽이 더 ~한가?'
  - Which do you prefer more, Harry Potter or The Lord of the Rings?
    (해리포터와 반지의 제왕 중 어떤 것을 더 선호하니?)

(7) **라틴어에서 온 단어들의 비교급:** than이 아닌 to로 비교 대상을 나타낸다.
  - Tom is junior to Mark in terms of experience.
    (Tom은 경험 면에서 Mark보다 더 후배이다.)

❷ 라틴어에서 온 단어
superior to: ~보다 우월한
inferior to: ~보다 열등한
senior to: ~보다 손위의
junior to: ~보다 손아래의
prior to: ~보다 이전의

1 비교급

[01-05] 주어진 우리말과 일치하도록 괄호 안의 말을 이용하여 비교급 문장을 완성하시오.

01 Tom은 Steve보다 더 부지런하다. (diligent)

➡ Tom is ___________________________________.

02 미국에서 축구는 야구보다 인기가 덜하다. (popular, baseball)

➡ In America, soccer is ___________________________________.

03 그의 휴대 전화가 내 것보다 훨씬 더 비싸다. (much, expensive, mine)

➡ His cellphone is ___________________________________.

04 서울은 부산보다 더 많은 인구를 가지고 있다. (a big population, Busan)

➡ Seoul has ___________________________________.

05 이 새 차가 구 모델보다 더 세련됐다. (stylish, the old model)

➡ This new car is ___________________________________.

2 다양한 비교급 표현

[06-09] 주어진 말을 바르게 배열하여 비교급 문장을 완성하시오.

06 (than, twice, mine, bigger)

➡ His foot is ___________________________________.

07 (which, more, is, comfortable)

➡ ___________________________________, this sofa or that armchair?

08 (the, questions, more, have, they)

➡ The more students learn, ___________________________________.

09 (cooler, get, cooler, is going to, and)

➡ The weather ___________________________________ every day.

[10-13] 주어진 우리말과 일치하도록 괄호 안의 말을 이용하여 비교급 문장을 완성하시오.

10 상황이 점점 더 나빠지고 있다. (is becoming, bad)

➡ The situation ___________________________________.

11 그는 기타를 치는 데 있어서 초보자에 불과하다. (no, than, a beginner, much)

➡ He is ___________________________________ at playing the guitar.

12 이 작업은 이전 작업보다 5배 더 어렵다. (hard, the previous one, than, times, five)

➡ This task is ___________________________________.

13 그 회사는 새로운 제품을 출시하기 전에 설문 조사를 진행했다. (launching, prior)

➡ The company conducted a survey ___________________________________ the new product.

〈 정답과 해설 p. 73 〉

어휘 & 표현

- **hardworking** 열심히 일하는
- **colleague** 동료
- **diligent** 부지런한
- **armchair** 안락의자
- **question** 질문
- **beginner** 초보자
- **launch** 출시하다, 착수하다
- **conduct** 시행하다
- **survey** 설문 조사
- **product** 제품

18 DAY

최상급

1 최상급: 셋 이상을 비교하여 그중에서 정도가 가장 높은 것을 표현한다.

(1) 기본 형태: the + 형용사 [부사]의 최상급 '가장 ~한[하게]'

- Mount Everest is the <u>highest</u> mountain in the world. (Everest 산은 세계에서 <u>가장 높은</u> 산이다.)

(2) 최상급에 the를 붙이지 않는 경우

① 부사의 최상급 앞

- We must work <u>hardest</u> during the final week. (우리는 마지막 주에 가장 열심히 일해야 한다.)

② 최상급 앞에 소유격이 있을 때

- My <u>best</u> choice was to study abroad. (내 <u>가장 좋은</u> 선택은 해외에서 공부하는 것이었다.)

③ 동일한 사람이나 사물의 성질 또는 상태를 비교할 때 (be + 보어로 쓰인 경우)

- The cake is <u>fluffiest</u> when baked for 30 minutes. (그 케이크는 30분 동안 구웠을 때 가장 부드럽다.)

(3) 최상급 뒤에 「of + 복수 명사」나 「in + 단체/장소」를 써서 비교 범위를 나타낸다.

- He is the <u>most experienced of the members.</u> (그는 팀원들 중에서 가장 경험이 많다.)
- This is the <u>most valuable painting in the gallery.</u> (이것은 이 <u>미술관에서 가장 가치 있는</u> 그림이다.)

2 다양한 최상급 표현

(1) one of the + 최상급 + 복수 명사 : '가장 ~한 것 중 하나'

- The Louvre is <u>one of the most famous museums.</u> (루브르는 가장 유명한 박물관 중 하나이다.)

(2) the + 최상급 + 명사 (+that) + 주어 + have[has] (ever) + 과거분사 : '(지금까지) ~한 것 중 가장 …한'

- That was the <u>most beautiful sunset I've ever seen.</u> (그것은 내가 본 가장 아름다운 일몰이었다.)

3 원급, 비교급을 이용한 최상급 표현

① **비교급 + than any other + 단수 명사:** '다른 어떤 …보다 더 ~하다'

② **비교급 + than all the other + 복수 명사:** '다른 모든 …보다 더 ~하다'

③ **no (other) 단수 명사 + 비교급 + than:** '어느 무엇도 …보다 더 ~하지 않다'

④ **no (other) 단수 명사 + as[so] + 원급 + as:** '어느 무엇도 …만큼 ~하지 않다'

⑤ **There is nothing + 비교급 + than:** '…보다 ~한 것은 없다'

① This laptop is <u>lighter</u> than any other <u>model</u> in the store.
　　　　　　　　　비교급　　　　　　　　단수 명사
(이 노트북은 매장에서 다른 어떤 모델보다 더 가볍다.)

② This laptop is <u>lighter</u> than all the other <u>models</u> in the store.
　　　　　　　　　비교급　　　　　　　　복수 명사
(이 노트북은 매장에서 다른 모든 모델보다 더 가볍다.)

③ No (other) <u>model</u> in the store is <u>lighter</u> than this laptop.
　　　　　단수 명사　　　　　　　비교급
(매장에 있는 어느 노트북도 이 노트북보다 더 가볍지 않다.)

④ No (other) <u>model</u> in the store is as[so] <u>light</u> as this laptop.
　　　　　단수 명사　　　　　　　　원급
(매장에 있는 어느 노트북도 이 노트북만큼 가볍지 않다.)

⑤ There is nothing <u>lighter</u> than this laptop in the store. (매장에서 이 노트북보다 가벼운 것은 없다.)
　　　　　　　　　비교급

1 최상급

[01-05] 문장에서 **틀린** 부분을 찾아 밑줄을 긋고 바르게 고치시오.

01 He has the biggest company of this country. _______________

02 The my eldest brother is older than my uncle. _______________

03 Who is the most fastest boy in your school? _______________

04 Being a parent is more difficult job in the world. _______________

05 I think my boyfriend is the diligentest boy in my neighborhood. _______________

2 다양한 최상급 표현

[06-09] 주어진 말을 바르게 배열하여 최상급 문장을 완성하시오.

06 _______________________________________ is 29 inches.

(the shortest, in, men, of, one, the world)

07 *The Catcher in the Rye* is _______________________________.

(my, books, of, most, one, cherished)

08 What's _______________________________?

(ever, the most, you've, foolish, done, thing)

09 It is _______________________________.

(watched, most, I've, movie, boring, ever, the)

3 원급, 비교급을 이용한 최상급 표현

[10-13] 두 문장의 의미가 같도록 빈칸에 알맞은 말을 쓰시오.

10 The Himalayas are the highest mountain range in the world.

➡ The Himalayas are _______________ any other mountain range in the world.

11 Mercury is nearer than any other planet to the Sun in our solar system.

➡ Mercury is _______________ planet to the Sun in our solar system.

12 The mosquito is the most dangerous insect in the world.

➡ _______________ insect in the world is more dangerous _______________ the mosquito.

13 The Burj Khalifa is the tallest building in the world.

➡ No other building in the world is _______________ tall _______________ the Burj Khalifa.

🦉 **어휘 & 표현**

· **abroad** 해외에(서)　· **fluffy** 푹신한, 솜털의　· **valuable** 가치 있는, 소중한　· **neighborhood** 이웃, 근처　· **cherish** 아끼다
· **foolish** 어리석은　· **range** 범위　· **Mercury** 수성　· **solar system** 태양계　· **mosquito** 모기　· **insect** 곤충

〈 정답과 해설 **p. 73~74** 〉

[01-04]

빈칸에 알맞은 것을 고르시오.

01

> I am as ___________ as my brother.

① tall
② taller
③ tallest
④ more tall
⑤ most tall

02

> The lion is not ___________ than the tiger.

① strong
② stronger
③ strongest
④ more strong
⑤ most strong

03

> That parking lot is the ___________ in this area.

① large
② larger
③ largest
④ more large
⑤ most large

04

> The new hamburger is popular because it has ___________ fat than the others.

① low
② less
③ few
④ small
⑤ a few

05

빈칸에 알맞지 <u>않은</u> 것을 고르시오.

> This chair is ___________ more comfortable than your sofa.

① much
② very
③ far
④ even
⑤ a lot

[06-07] 서술형

두 문장의 뜻이 같도록 빈칸에 알맞은 말을 쓰시오.

06

The tiger is the most dangerous animal in the world.

➡ No ___________ ___________ in the world is more dangerous than the tiger.

07

Meeting my husband was the best thing in my life.

➡ There was ___________ ___________ in my life than meeting my husband.

[08-10]

두 문장의 뜻이 같도록 빈칸에 알맞게 짝지어진 것을 고르시오.

08

> My room is not so clean as yours.
> = My room is ___________ clean ___________ yours.

① as − as
② not − than
③ more − than
④ less − than
⑤ not − so

09

> As the prices are cheaper, people will buy them more.
> = ___________ the prices are, ___________ people will buy them.

① Cheaper − more
② Cheaper − most
③ The cheaper − more
④ Cheaper − the most
⑤ The cheaper − the more

10

> Rachel is the fastest student in my class.
> = ___________ student in my class is
> ___________ Rachel.

① As – fast as   ② Not – fast than
③ No – as fast   ④ No – faster than
⑤ No – so fast

[11-12] 고난도

밑줄 친 부분 중 어법상 **틀린** 것을 고르시오.

11

① A snake is not as <u>dangerous as</u> a lion.
② Math is <u>a lot more difficult</u> than English.
③ This is <u>the fastest train</u> I have ever taken.
④ This bridge is <u>three times shorter</u> than that one.
⑤ Lim is <u>one of the most famous director</u> in the world.

12

① Dave ran away <u>as fast as he could</u>.
② Send me the mail <u>as soon as possible</u>.
③ The weather is getting <u>hotter and hotter</u>.
④ Her little sister is <u>the smartest of the girls</u>.
⑤ The Nile is longer than <u>any other rivers</u> in the world.

[13-15] 서술형

자연스러운 대화가 되도록 괄호 안의 단어를 알맞은 형태로 쓰시오.

13

A: Mom, can I invite some of my friends to the party?

B: Sure, you can. The more, the ___________.
(merry)

14

A: Were there many guests at the wedding?

B: Well, there weren't as ___________ guests as I expected. (many)

15

A: You're speaking too fast. I can hardly understand what you're saying.

B: Do you want me to speak ___________? (slowly)

16

밑줄 친 even과 같은 의미로 쓰인 것을 고르시오.

> I think I'll get <u>even</u> better grades than last semester.

① The two players were pretty <u>even</u>.
② She smiled, showing her <u>even</u> teeth.
③ Two, four, and six are <u>even</u> numbers.
④ <u>Even</u> the boy threw waste on the street.
⑤ Taking a bus is <u>even</u> faster to get there.

[17-18]

주어진 우리말과 일치하도록 바르게 영작한 것을 고르시오.

17

> Mary의 집은 우리 집보다 두 배 더 넓다.

① Mary's house is twice large as my house.
② Mary's house is twice largest than my house.
③ Mary's house is twice as large as my house.
④ Mary's house is more twice large as my house.
⑤ Mary's house is more twice larger than my house.

〈 정답과 해설 p. 74~75 〉

19 DAY

18

Flex는 우리 반에서 가장 성실한 남학생 중 한 명이다.

① Flex is the most hardworking boy in my class.
② Flex is one most hardworking boy of my class.
③ Flex is one of the hardworking boy of my class.
④ Flex is one of the hardworking most boys in my class.
⑤ Flex is one of the most hardworking boys in my class.

19

주어진 문장과 의미가 다른 것을 고르시오.

Chris is the funniest student in my class.

① No one in my class is funnier than Chris.
② No student in my class is funnier than Chris.
③ No student in my class is as funny as Chris.
④ Chris is not as funny as any other student in my class.
⑤ Chris is funnier than any other student in my class.

20 고난도

어법상 옳은 것을 고르시오.

① Pick up garbage as much as you do.
② People are not as happier as before.
③ The situation got badder than last year.
④ China is one of the most crowded country in the world.
⑤ It's already 2 o'clock in the morning. You should have gotten back earlier.

21

문장의 뜻이 같도록, 빈칸에 알맞은 말로 바르게 짝지어진 것을 고르시오.

His watch is much nicer than mine.
→ My watch is ___________ than his.
→ My watch is ___________ as his.

① less nice – as nice
② less nicer – so nice
③ less nice – not as nice
④ less nicer – not as nicer
⑤ less nicer – not so nicer

[22-29] 서술형

문장에서 틀린 부분을 찾아 밑줄을 긋고 바르게 고치시오.

22

This is most expensive restaurant I've ever been to.

23

I answered all the questions more well than the other students.

24

I want to read as many books as I could.

25

The population of Seoul is about four times large as that of Busan.

26

The woman who weighs 1,215 pounds is one of the fat women in the world.

27

This year we spent less money on eating out as last year.

28

The more I think about the problem, more difficult it feels.

____

29

She seems to be as happily as a dog with two tails.

____

30

두 문장의 의미가 <u>다른</u> 것을 고르시오.

① Speak as loudly as possible.
→ Speak as loudly as you can.
② This river is the largest river in the world.
→ No river in the world is larger than this one.
③ The station was nearer than I thought.
→ The station was as far as I thought.
④ It is still cold, but it was colder yesterday.
→ It isn't as cold as it was yesterday.
⑤ Jupiter is the largest planet in the solar system.
→ Jupiter is larger than any other planet in the solar system.

[31-34] 서술형

주어진 문장을 괄호 안의 지시대로 바꾸어 쓰시오.

31

Keeping kids safe in school is the most important thing. (비교급으로)

➡ _______________

____

32

There are not as many jobs as we need.
(fewer를 사용하여)

➡ _______________

____

33

As you read more, you become more knowledgeable.
(the+비교급 ~, the+비교급 표현으로)

➡ _______________

____

34

No student in my class is as intelligent as Andy. (최상급으로)

➡ _______________

____

[35-39]

괄호 안에서 알맞은 것을 고르시오.

35

He is not so (clever / cleverer) as he looks.

36

Jennifer is the most generous (between / of) the girls.

37

Don't stand in front of the entrance. Can you move a bit (farther / farthest) back, please?

38

No one is richer than (he is / his) in this country.

39

As she grew older, she became (wiser and wiser / more and more wiser).

[40-41] (서술형)

주어진 우리말과 일치하도록 괄호 안의 말을 이용하여 빈칸을 완성하시오.

40

Micky는 Cindy보다 두 배 더 많은 책들을 읽는다.
(twice, Cindy, as, many, books)

➡ Micky reads __________________

__________________ .

41

Usain Bolt는 세계의 어떤 단거리 선수들보다 빠르다.

(faster, in the world, any other sprinter)

➡ Usain Bolt is __________________

__________________ .

42 (수능 유형)

밑줄 친 부분 중 어법상 틀린 것을 고르시오.

The ocean can be very cold, especially at ① greater depths. Divers who dive deeper into the ocean should keep this in mind. At the surface, the water seems warmer, but as they descend, the temperature drops ② lower and lower. In fact, the ③ deepest they go, the colder it gets. The temperature at the deepest parts of the ocean is ④ the coldest. Along with the temperature, the water pressure becomes stronger. The pressure at the deepest points of the ocean is the most intense, and this can be dangerous without proper equipment. Therefore, divers must wear the ⑤ most protective equipment to ensure their safety in the harshest conditions.

①   ②   ③   ④   ⑤

[43-44]

다음 글을 읽고 물음에 답하시오.

Recently unusual things have happened on Earth. In Pakistan, floods have covered nearly a third of the country since July, causing ⓐ 적어도 1,500명이나 되는 사망자를 and forcing ① more than 4 million people to flee their homes. In Russia, heat waves have caused widespread drought and uncontrollable fires. Summer temperatures are averaging ② 30 degrees higher than normal in Moscow, Russia. In Greenland, the heat has caused an enormous chunk of ice ③ as four times big as the island of Manhattan to break off the Petermann Glacier. This is ④ the largest glacier break ever recorded. Scientists warn that extreme weather events like these caused by global warming may be ⑤ a lot worse in the future.

43

밑줄 친 ⓐ를 바르게 영작한 것을 고르시오.

① less than 1,500 deaths
② no less than 1,500 deaths
③ no little than 1,500 deaths
④ no more than 1,500 deaths
⑤ no many than 1,500 deaths

44 (수능 유형)

밑줄 친 부분 중 어법상 틀린 것을 고르시오.

①   ②   ③   ④   ⑤

어휘 & 표현

- **semester** 학기   · **garbage** 쓰레기   · **population** 인구   · **Jupiter** 목성   · **knowledgeable** 아는 것이 많은
- **sprinter** 단거리 주자   · **depth** 깊이   · **descend** 내려오다   · **pressure** 압박   · **ensure** 반드시 ~하게 하다
- **widespread** 광범위한   · **drought** 가뭄   · **enormous** 막대한   · **chunk** 덩어리   · **glacier** 빙하

K

접속사

接續詞

(이을 접, 이을 속, 말 사)

두 개 이상의 단어와 단어, 구와 구,
절과 절, 문장과 문장을 이어주는 말

I went to the store, and I bought some fruit. (나는 가게에 갔고, 과일을 좀 샀다.)
등위접속사

Both my brother and my sister like to swim. (내 남동생과 여동생은 수영하는 것을 좋아한다.)
상관접속사

She believes that it will rain tomorrow. (그녀는 내일 비가 올 것이라고 믿는다.)
명사절을 이끄는 종속접속사

Since it's your birthday, I'll buy you a gift. (네가 생일이니까, 내가 선물을 사줄게.)
부사절을 이끄는 종속접속사

He forgot his umbrella. Thus, he got wet in the rain.
접속부사

(그는 우산을 잊어버렸다, 그래서 비에 젖었다.)

  **등위접속사** 

핵심 개념

- **접속사**: 단어와 단어, 구와 구, 절과 절, 문장과 문장을 연결해 주는 말로, 등위접속사, 상관접속사, 종속접속사가 있다.
- **등위접속사**: 비슷하거나 같은 단위의 문장 성분을 동등하게 연결해 주는 접속사 (and, but, or, so, for)이다.

---

1 등위접속사의 개념: 문법적으로 대등한 둘 이상의 단어, 구, 절을 연결하는 접속사이다.

– 세 개 이상의 항목을 나열할 때는 원칙적으로 마지막 항목 앞에만 쓴다.

- Would you like tea or coffee? (차를 원하세요, 또는 커피를 원하세요?)
  단어 접속사 단어

- Getting up early and preparing for school are part of my routine.
  구   접속사   구
  (일찍 일어나고 학교 갈 준비를 하는 것은 내 일상의 일부이다.)

- My brother doesn't get up early, so my mom wakes him up every day.
  절   접속사   절
  (내 동생은 일찍 일어나지 않아서, 엄마는 매일 그를 깨운다.)

2 등위접속사의 종류와 쓰임

and	그리고, ~과, ~와	앞뒤의 내용이 대등한 것을 연결한다.
		• I've already had a meal and a nap. (나는 이미 식사를 했고 낮잠을 잤다.)
		시간적인 순서를 나타낼 때 사용한다.
		• I finished my work, and now I can relax. (나는 일을 마쳤고, 이제 쉴 수 있다.)
but	그러나, 하지만	앞뒤의 반대되는 내용을 연결한다.
		• I want to go out, but it's too hot. (나는 밖에 나가고 싶지만, 너무 덥다.)
or	또는, 혹은	둘 또는 그 이상의 선택해야 할 것을 연결한다.
		• Would you like still or sparkling water? (생수나 탄산수 드실래요?)
so	그래서	절과 절을 이어 주며, so의 앞의 절이 원인, 뒤의 절이 결과를 나타낸다.
		• It was raining, so I stayed at home. (비가 와서 나는 집에 있었다.)
for	왜냐하면, ~하니까	• 절과 절을 이어 주며, for의 앞의 절이 결과, 뒤의 절이 원인·이유를 나타낸다. • 항상 콤마 (,) 와 같이 쓰인다.
		• I didn't go to the party, for I was feeling tired. (나는 파티에 가지 않았는데, 왜냐하면 피곤했기 때문이다.)
yet	그러나, 그런데도	앞뒤의 대조되는 내용을 연결하며, but보다 강한 대조를 나타낼 때 사용한다.
		• Carbon fiber is light, yet it's amazingly strong. (탄소 섬유는 가벼운데도, 놀라울 만큼 튼튼하다.)

3 명령문 + and, 명령문 + or

명령문 + and	~해라, 그러면	• Run as fast as you can, and you will get to the exit. 　명령문 (가능한 한 빨리 달려라, 그러면 출구에 도착할 것이다.)
명령문 + or	~해라, 그렇지 않으면	• Close the door, or the cat will escape. 　명령문 (문을 닫아라, 그렇지 않으면 고양이가 탈출할 것이다.)

1 등위접속사의 개념

[01-07] 괄호 안에서 알맞은 것을 고르시오.

01 You can go to the store (but / now) or later.

02 She didn't study, so (she failed / to fail) the test.

03 He is talented, (or / but) he doesn't practice enough.

04 He didn't go to work, (but / for) he was severely sick.

05 I was tired, (or / yet) I stayed up late to finish the project.

06 She hates pineapple pizza, (or / so) she always picks the potato one.

07 The task seemed impossible, (yet / or) she finally managed to complete it.

2 등위접속사의 종류와 쓰임

[08-12] 빈칸에 알맞은 것을 〈보기〉에서 골라 쓰시오. (중복 사용 불가)

〈보기〉
| and | so | yet | for | or |

08 I was exhausted, ____________ I fell asleep right away.

09 The sun was shining, ____________ the birds were singing.

10 Are you looking for something casual ____________ more formal?

11 I took an umbrella, ____________ it looked like it was going to rain.

12 She was inexperienced, ____________ she handled the situation well.

1 + 2 + 3 등위접속사

[13-16] 주어진 우리말과 일치하도록 괄호 안의 말과 등위접속사를 이용하여 문장을 완성하시오.

13 영화는 길었지만 정말 흥미로웠다. (it, be, really, interesting)

➡ The movie was long, ____________________________.

14 그녀는 파티에 가지 않았다, 왜냐하면 그녀는 아팠기 때문이다. (she, be, sick)

➡ She didn't go to the party, ____________________________.

15 매일 연습해라, 그러면 너는 기술을 향상시킬 것이다. (you, improve, your skills)

➡ Practice every day, ____________________________.

16 저녁을 다 먹어라, 그렇지 않으면 디저트를 먹을 수 없다. (finish, your dinner)

➡ ____________________________ you won't be allowed to have dessert.

🦉 어휘 & 표현

· **nap** 낮잠　· **sparkling water** 탄산수　· **carbon** 탄소　· **fiber** 섬유　· **escape** 탈출하다　· **severely** 심각하게
· **exhausted** 지친　· **casual** 편한　· **inexperienced** 미숙한　· **handle** 다루다　· **improve** 향상시키다

〈 정답과 해설 p. 77~78 〉

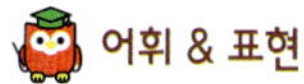

> **핵심 개념**
> • **상관접속사**: 서로 연결되어 같이 쓰는 접속사로, 문법적으로 대등한 단어와 단어,
>   구와 구, 절과 절을 연결한다.

1 상관접속사의 개념과 종류

(1) **개념**: 둘 이상의 단어가 짝을 이루어 하나의 접속사 역할을 하며,
   문법적으로 대등한 문장 성분(단어와 단어, 구와 구, 절과 절)을 연결한다.

(2) **종류**

both A and B	A와 B 둘 다	• Both talent and effort are essential for success. (재능과 노력 둘 다 성공에 필수적이다.)
either A or B	A 또는 B 둘 중 하나	• Either Tom or Jane will answer the phone. (Tom이나 Jane 둘 중 한 명이 전화를 받을 것이다.)
neither A nor B	A, B 둘 다 아닌	• Neither I nor my sister can speak French. = Either my sister or I can't speak French. (나도 내 여동생도 프랑스어를 못한다.)
not A but B	A가 아니라 B	• Her parents are not angry, but disappointed. (그녀의 부모님은 화난 것이 아니라 실망했다.)
not only A but also B **= B as well as A** also는 생략 가능	A뿐만 아니라 B도	• He is not only my boss, but also my mentor. = He is my mentor as well as my boss. (그는 내 상사일 뿐만 아니라, 내 멘토이다.)

2 상관접속사의 수 일치

(1) **항상 복수 취급함** : 항상 복수 동사가 옴

both A and B	• Both my brother and my sister are going to the party. (내 남동생과 여동생 모두 파티에 간다.)

(2) **B에 동사의 수를 일치시킴** : **B**가 단수면 단수 동사, 복수면 복수 동사가 옴

either A or B	• Either the manager or the employees are responsible for the fault. (매니저 또는 직원들이 그 잘못에 책임이 있다.)
neither A nor B	• Neither my brothers nor my sister likes that movie. (내 형들도, 누나도 그 영화를 좋아하지 않는다.)
not A but B	• Not the tools but the machine needs repair. (도구들이 아니라 기계가 수리가 필요하다.)
not only A but also B	• Not only she but also her parents are coming to the concert. (그녀뿐만 아니라 부모님도 콘서트에 오신다.)
B as well as A	• Her parents as well as she are coming to the concert. (그녀뿐만 아니라 부모님도 콘서트에 오신다.)

1 상관접속사의 개념과 종류

[01-05] 빈칸에 알맞은 것을 〈보기〉에서 골라 쓰시오. (중복 사용 불가)

> 〈보기〉
> either but but also both neither

01 _______________ John nor his friends have the correct answer.

02 _______________ my mother or my father is going to the market.

03 Not the red dress _______________ the blue one looks better on you.

04 Not only I _______________ my friends are attending the meeting.

05 _______________ the team and the coach are ready for the competition.

2 상관접속사의 수 일치

[06-12] 괄호 안의 말을 이용하여 문장을 완성하시오. (현재시제로 쓸 것)

06 Both the teacher and the writer _______________ the idea. (like)

07 Not the cake but the cookies _______________ for dessert. (be)

08 Not history itself but its meaning _______________ something crucial. (be)

09 Either my brother or my friends _______________ me with the project. (help)

10 Tom as well as his brothers _______________ interested in learning Spanish. (be)

11 In a textbook, not only text but also pictures _______________ the meaning. (deliver)

12 Neither the players nor the coach _______________ the result of the game. (accept)

1 + **2** 상관접속사

[13-18] 문장에서 틀린 부분을 찾아 밑줄을 긋고 바르게 고치시오.

13 I think he must be either Chinese but Japanese.   _______________

14 What I want is not your possessions or you.   _______________

15 He as well as his brothers are good at sports.   _______________

16 His doctor allows him neither to smoke or to drink.   _______________

17 Both English and Chinese is spoken in Hong Kong.   _______________

18 Not only Great Britain and the United States, also Australia and New Zealand use English as their first language.   _______________

20DAY

🦉 어휘 & 표현

- **essential** 필수적인   - **disappointed** 실망한   - **mentor** 멘토, 조언자   - **responsible** 책임 있는   - **attend** 참석하다
- **competition** 대회   - **crucial** 중대한   - **deliver** 전달하다   - **accept** 수용하다   - **possession** 소유

〈 정답과 해설 p. 78~79 〉

 **UNIT 43** 명사절을 이끄는 종속접속사 

1 명사절을 이끄는 종속접속사의 개념

- 하나의 문장에 다른 문장(종속절)을 연결하여, 연결한 문장이 전체 문장의 주어, 목적어, 보어 역할을 하도록 만드는 접속사를 말한다.
  - that이 붙음으로써 목적어 역할을 하는 명사절이 됨
  - I believe that she is telling the truth. (나는 그녀가 진실을 말하고 있다고 믿는다.)
    주절 / 종속절

2 명사절을 이끄는 종속접속사의 종류와 역할

that (~하기, ~라는 것)	주어	– 주어로 쓰일 때는 가주어–진주어 구문으로 바꿀 수 있다. • That we won the game surprised everyone. = It surprised everyone that we won the game. (우리가 게임에서 이겼다는 것은 모두를 놀라게 했다.)
	목적어	– that절이 목적어일 때 that은 생략할 수 있다. – 목적어로 쓰일 때는 가목적어–진목적어 구문으로 바꿀 수 있다. • They realized (that) his decision was a big mistake. (그들은 그의 결정이 큰 실수였다는 것을 깨달았다.)
	보어	– 2형식 문장의 주격 보어로 쓰인다. • Her concern is that people hate her. (그녀의 걱정은 사람들이 그녀를 싫어한다는 것이다.)
whether, **if** (~인지 아닌지)		– 불확실하거나 의문시되는 사실을 이야기할 때 쓴다. – whether는 주어, 목적어, 보어절을 모두 이끌지만 if는 목적어절만 이끈다. – or not이 뒤에 이어지기도 한다. – whether는 to부정사와 함께 쓰일 수 있다.
	주어	• Whether he likes it or not is what I want to know. (그가 그것을 좋아하는지 아닌지가 바로 내가 알고 싶은 것이다.)
	목적어	• I wonder whether[if] they will accept our offer. (그들이 우리의 제안을 받아들일지 궁금하다.)
	보어	• The question is whether she will attend the meeting (or not). (문제는 그녀가 그 회의에 참석할지 (아닐지)이다.)
의문사		– 의문사가 있는 절이 문장의 종속절로 쓰이면, 이것을 간접의문문이라고 한다.
	who / 누가	• I can't remember who told me that. (나는 누가 그 말을 했는지 기억이 나지 않는다.)
	when / 언제	• When I can meet her depends on my schedule. (내가 그녀를 언제 만날 수 있는지는 내 일정에 달려 있다.)
	where / 어디에	• Can you tell me where the nearest station is? (가장 가까운 역이 어디인지 내게 말해 줄 수 있니?)
	what / 무엇이, 무엇을	• She asked what I wanted for lunch. (그녀는 내가 점심으로 무엇을 원하는지 물었다.)
	how / 어떻게	• We're trying to figure out how they solved the problem. (우리는 그들이 그 문제를 어떻게 해결했는지 알아내려 하고 있다.)
	why / 왜	• I wonder why she is so upset. (나는 그녀가 왜 그렇게 화가 났는지 궁금하다.)

❶ whether or not

whether는 바로 뒤에 or not을 쓰기도 하지만, if는 if or not으로 쓸 수 없다.
  • He asked whether or not she agreed. (O)
    He asked if or not she agreed. (X)
    (그는 그녀가 동의하는지 아닌지 물었다.)

❷ whether + to부정사

whether는 바로 뒤에 to부정사가 올 수 있지만, if는 'if + to부정사'로 쓸 수 없다.
  • She debated whether to stay. (O)
    She debated if to stay. (X)
    (그녀는 머물지 고민했다.)

❸ 간접의문문

의문사는 접속사처럼 주절에 종속절(간접의문문)을 연결한다.
  • 간접의문문의 어순:
「의문사 + 주어 + 동사 + ~」,
「의문사(= 주어) + 동사 + ~」
(의문사가 주어일 때)

1 명사절을 이끄는 종속접속사의 개념

[01-05] 밑줄 친 부분에 해당하는 문장 구성 요소를 〈보기〉에서 골라 쓰시오. (중복 사용 불가)

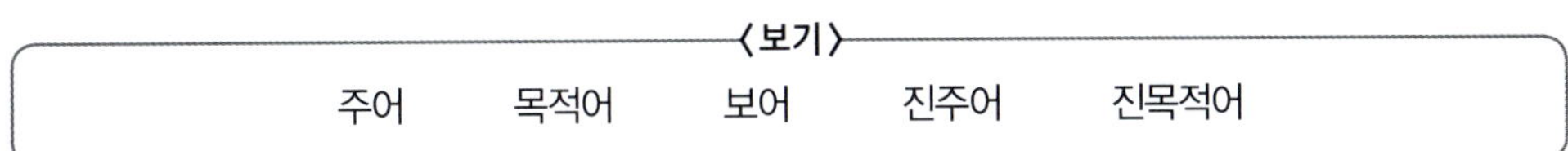

01 When she will arrive is still unknown.   ➡ ___________

02 The point is whether she accepts the suggestion.   ➡ ___________

03 They found it strange that he didn't reply to the message.   ➡ ___________

04 I'm concerned about whether they are interested in the project.   ➡ ___________

05 It is still vague that the results from innovation team are accurate.   ➡ ___________

1 + **2** 명사절을 이끄는 종속접속사

[06-12] 괄호 안에서 알맞은 것을 고르시오.

06 (If / Whether) she will come or not is not important.

07 I want to know (that / if) he is going to retire or not.

08 They don't care (who / whom) wins the election.

09 You cannot change (if / that) your pet died.

10 It is important (what / that) you did your best.

11 (How / Who) he made it in time is a mystery.

12 Did she ask him (if / that) he had called his grandparents?

[13-16] 주어진 우리말과 일치하도록 괄호 안의 말을 바르게 배열하시오.

13 네가 떠나는지 아닌지는 중요하지 않다. (doesn't, whether, leave, you, or not, it, matter)

➡ _______________________________________

14 그는 내가 그를 얼마나 신경 쓰는지 알고 있다. (how much, knows, he, I, him, care about)

➡ _______________________________________

15 그들이 법을 어겼다는 것은 확실하지 않다. (it, they, the law, not certain, is, broke, that)

➡ _______________________________________

16 Felix가 내게 무엇을 말했는지 정말로 궁금하지 않니?

(really, what, said, Felix, to me, wonder, you, don't)

➡ _______________________________________

 어휘 & 표현

· **concern** 걱정, 관심   · **figure out** 알아내다   · **concerned** 걱정하는   · **vague** 희미한, 애매한   · **innovation** 혁신
· **accurate** 정확한   · **retire** 은퇴하다   · **election** 선거   · **matter** 중요하다   · **care about** ~에 신경 쓰다

〈 정답과 해설 p. 79~80 〉

 **UNIT 44** 부사절을 이끄는 종속접속사 

1 시간 부사절 접속사 ❶

when	~할 때	• I was cooking dinner when the phone rang. (전화가 울렸을 때 나는 저녁을 요리하고 있었다.)
while	~하는 동안	• She listened to music while she was doing her homework. (그녀는 숙제를 하는 동안 음악을 들었다.)
as	~할 때, ~하면서	• As I walked into the room, everyone looked at me. (내가 방에 들어섰을 때, 모두가 나를 바라보았다.)
until	~할 때까지	• We waited until the rain stopped. (우리는 비가 그칠 때까지 기다렸다.)
before	~ 전에	• Finish your meal before you leave the table. (식탁에서 일어나기 전에 식사를 마쳐라.)
after	~ 후에	• He went to bed after he finished the report. (그는 보고서를 끝낸 후에 잠자리에 들었다.)
since	~한 이래로	• He has worn glasses since he was nine. (그는 9살 이후로 안경을 썼다.)
as soon as	~하자마자	• I called her as soon as I got the news. (나는 소식을 듣자마자 그녀에게 전화했다.)

❶ **부사절**

동사, 형용사, 부사 또는 전체 문장을 수식하는 절이다. 시간, 이유, 조건, 양보, 목적, 결과 등의 뜻을 덧붙인다.

2 조건 부사절 접속사

if	~한다면	• If it rains tomorrow, we'll cancel the picnic. (만약 내일 비가 오면, 우리는 소풍을 취소할 거야.)
unless	~하지 않는다면	• You won't pass the test unless you study harder. (더 열심히 공부하지 않으면 시험에 통과하지 못할 거야.)
once	일단 ~하면	• Once you learn the basics, programming becomes easier. (일단 기초를 배우면, 프로그래밍은 더 쉬워진다.)

❷ **so that**

결과의 의미일 때는 so 앞에 콤마를 쓴다.
• His leg was broken, so that he couldn't play soccer.
(다리가 부러져서 그는 축구를 할 수 없었다.)

3 목적 부사절 접속사

so that ❷	~하도록, ~하기 위하여	• I lent him my cellphone so that he could make a call. (나는 그가 전화를 할 수 있도록 내 휴대 전화를 그에게 빌려주었다.)
in order that		• He lowered his voice in order that no one would hear him. (그는 아무도 듣지 못하게 하기 위해 목소리를 낮췄다.)

❸ **because vs. because of**

because 뒤에는 주어와 동사로 이루어진 절이 오지만, 전치사 because of 뒤에는 명사(구)가 와야 한다.

4 이유 부사절 접속사

because ❸	~하기 때문에	• She stayed home because she was feeling sick. (그녀는 몸이 안 좋아서 집에 머물렀다.)
as ❹		• As it was getting dark, they decided to go back. (어두워지고 있었기 때문에 그들은 돌아가기로 결정했다.)
since		• Since he is under eighteen, he can't vote. (그는 18세가 안 되었기 때문에 투표를 할 수 없다.)

❹ **as**

비례(~함에 따라), 양태(~대로), 비교(~만큼)의 의미로도 쓰인다.
• As she grew older, she became wiser. (비례)
(나이가 들어감에 따라, 그녀는 더 현명해졌다.)
• Do as you are told. (양태) (네가 들은대로 해라.)
• He is as tall as his father (is). (비교) (그는 그의 아버지만큼 키가 크다.)

5 양보 부사절 접속사

(al)though	비록 ~일지라도	• (Al)though he was tired, he kept working until midnight. (그는 피곤했지만 자정까지 계속 일했다.)
even though		• Even though he's rich, he lives very simply. (그는 부자임에도 아주 검소하게 산다.)
even if		• I'll support you even if everyone else disagrees. (다른 모든 사람이 반대하더라도 나는 널 지지할게.)

6 결과 부사절 접속사

so + 형용사[부사] + that	매우 ~해서 ...하다	• He speaks so fast that I can't understand him. (그는 매우 빨리 말해서 나는 그를 이해할 수 없다.)
such + a(n) + 형용사 +명사 + that		• She is such a talented singer that everyone admires her. (그녀는 매우 재능 있는 가수라서 모두가 그녀를 존경한다.)

1 + **2** + **3** 시간, 조건, 목적 부사절 접속사

[01-06] 자연스러운 의미가 되도록 바르게 연결하시오.

01 I was walking to the bus stop •   • ⓐ make sure you have packed your bag.

02 Before you leave for school,   •   • ⓑ while I was on vacation.

03 Once you choose,   •   • ⓒ when it suddenly started to rain.

04 I relaxed a lot   •   • ⓓ unless the train is delayed.

05 I'll be there at seven,   •   • ⓔ that they could catch the ice cream truck.

06 They ran fast in order   •   • ⓕ you can't change your mind
about your decision.

4 + **5** + **6** 이유, 양보, 결과 부사절 접속사

[07-11] 주어진 우리말과 일치하도록 괄호 안의 말을 이용하여 문장을 완성하시오.

07 낮이 길어짐에 따라 나는 잠을 덜 잔다. (as, the days, get longer)

➡ ___________________________, I get less sleep.

08 비가 많이 와서 우리는 외출할 수 없었다. (as, rain, a lot)

➡ ___________________________, we couldn't go out.

09 그녀는 감기에 걸린 이후로 아파서 침대에 누워 있다. (since, have a cold)

➡ She has been sick in bed ___________________________.

10 그녀는 대회에서 이기지 않았지만 웃었다. (although, win the contest)

➡ She smiled ___________________________.

11 그것은 아주 흥미진진한 소설이어서 모든 사람들이 좋아한다. (such, interesting, that, novel)

➡ It is ___________________________ everyone loves it.

> **🦉 어휘 & 표현**
> · cancel 취소하다
> · vote 투표하다
> · midnight 자정
> · disagree 반대하다
> · delay 미루다, 늦추다
> · novel 소설
> · burst into tears 갑자기 울음을 터뜨리다
> · firm 단단한, 확고한
> · solve 풀다

21 DAY

1 + **2** + **3** + **4** + **5** 부사절을 이끄는 종속접속사

[12-16] 빈칸에 알맞은 것을 〈보기〉에서 골라 쓰시오. (중복 사용 불가)

〈보기〉

because   although   so that   if   as soon as

12 I couldn't go to the amusement park _______________ I caught a cold.

13 The little boy burst into tears _______________ he saw his mom.

14 _______________ they tell us something, we'll stand firm in what we believe.

15 _______________ you study hard every day, you will be able to get good grades.

16 He gave us enough time _______________ we could solve the questions.

〈 정답과 해설 p. 80 〉

 **UNIT 45** 접속부사 

1 접속부사의 개념: 접속사가 아닌 부사이다.

– 절과 절을 연결하지 못하고, 뒤에 콤마(,)를 찍는다.
– 앞에 완전한 문장이 나온 뒤 새 문장이나 동사가 온다.

2 접속부사의 종류와 쓰임

for example (for instance)	예를 들면	• Many animals sleep during the day. For example, owls and bats are active at night. (많은 동물들이 낮에 잠을 잔다. 예를 들어, 부엉이와 박쥐는 밤에 활동적이다.) • I enjoy outdoor activities. For instance, I often go hiking. (나는 야외 활동을 좋아한다. 예를 들어, 나는 자주 등산을 간다.)
however (nevertheless)	그러나	• I studied hard for the test. However, I still didn't do well. (나는 시험을 위해 열심히 공부했다. 그러나 여전히 결과가 좋지 않았다.) • It was raining. Nevertheless, we played soccer outside. (비가 오고 있었다. 하지만 우리는 밖에서 축구를 했다.)
in addition (moreover, besides)	게다가	• He is good at math. In addition, he plays the piano very well. (그는 수학을 잘한다. 게다가 피아노도 매우 잘 친다.) • The book is interesting. Moreover, it's very informative. (그 책은 흥미롭다. 더욱이 매우 유익하다.) • I don't want to go out. Besides, I have a lot of homework. (나는 나가고 싶지 않다. 게다가 숙제도 많다.)
therefore (thus, consequently)	그러므로, 결과적으로	• He studied hard. Therefore, he did well. (그는 열심히 공부했다. 그러므로 그는 잘 했다.) • He broke the rules. Thus, he was punished. (그는 규칙을 어겼다. 따라서 벌을 받았다.) • The road was icy. Consequently, there were several accidents. (도로가 얼어 있었다. 결과적으로 여러 사고가 발생했다.)
in contrast (on the contrary)	그와 대조적으로	• My sister loves spicy food. In contrast, I prefer sweet dishes. (내 여동생은 매운 음식을 좋아한다. 그와 대조적으로 나는 단 음식을 선호한다.) • She looks quiet. On the contrary, she talks a lot. (그녀는 조용해 보인다. 그와 대조적으로, 그녀는 말이 정말 많다.)
on the other hand	반면에, 한편으로는	• Online classes are convenient. On the other hand, it's hard to focus at home. (온라인 수업은 편리하다. 반면에 집에서는 집중하기 어렵다.)
in other words	다시 말해서	• She is bilingual. In other words, she can speak two languages fluently. (그녀는 이중 언어 사용자이다. 다시 말해, 그녀는 두 언어를 유창하게 한다.)
as a result	그 결과	• He didn't sleep at all last night. As a result, he was very tired today. (그는 어젯밤에 전혀 잠을 자지 않았다. 그 결과 오늘 매우 피곤했다.)
finally	결국	• He tried several passwords. Finally, he got into his account. (그는 여러 개의 비밀번호를 시도했다. 결국 그는 자신의 계정에 접속했다.)

1 + 2 접속부사

[01-06] 주어진 우리말과 일치하도록 괄호 안에서 알맞은 것을 고르시오.

01 우리는 도쿄에 있었다. 그와는 반대로, Liam은 서울에 있었다.

➡ We were in Tokyo. (In contrast / For example), Liam was in Seoul.

02 Emma는 이미 도착했다. 그러나, 우리는 그녀를 못 봤다.

➡ Emma had already arrived. (Therefore / However), we didn't see her.

03 나는 지금 회의 중이다. 반면에, Jacob은 통화 중이다.

➡ I'm in a meeting now. (On the other hand / In addition), Jacob is on a call.

04 Olivia는 밤새 일했다. 그 결과, 그녀는 마감에 맞췄다.

➡ Olivia worked all night. (As a result / On the contrary), she met the deadline.

05 Daniel은 일정을 확인하지 않았다. 그러므로, 그는 약속을 잊었다.

➡ Daniel didn't check his schedule. (Therefore / However), he forgot the appointment.

06 우리는 두 시간 넘게 기다렸다. 결국, 우리는 콘서트 티켓을 얻었다.

➡ We waited for over two hours. (For example / Finally), we got tickets to the concert.

[07-11] 주어진 우리말과 일치하도록 빈칸에 알맞은 것을 〈보기〉에서 골라 쓰시오. (중복 사용 불가)

〈보기〉

In other words   For example   However   In addition   Consequently

---

07 그는 수면 시간이 줄어들었다. 그러나 집중력은 유지되고 있다.

➡ His sleep duration has decreased. ＿＿＿＿＿＿＿, his focus remains steady.

08 우리는 이미 새로운 소프트웨어를 업로드했다. 게다가 사용자 가이드를 업데이트했다.

➡ We have already uploaded the new software. ＿＿＿＿＿＿＿, we updated the user guide.

09 연구팀은 새로운 물질을 발견했다. 그 결과, 논문이 발표될 예정이다.

➡ The research team discovered a new material. ＿＿＿＿＿＿＿, a paper will be published.

10 나는 자연과학에 흥미가 많다. 예를 들면 천문학을 자주 공부한다.

➡ I have a strong interest in the natural sciences. ＿＿＿＿＿＿＿, I frequently study astronomy.

11 이 이론은 지금까지 사람들이 생각하던 것과 다르다. 다시 말해, 새로운 아이디어를 제안한다.

➡ The theory is different from what people used to think. ＿＿＿＿＿＿＿, it suggests a new idea.

🎓 어휘 & 표현

· **informative** 유익한   · **punish** 벌을 주다   · **convenient** 편리한   · **bilingual** 이중 언어를 사용하는   · **fluently** 유창하게, 능숙하게
· **account** 계정   · **sleep duration** 수면 시간   · **decrease** 감소하다   · **steady** 꾸준한   · **frequently** 자주   · **astronomy** 천문학

〈 정답과 해설 p. 81 〉

[01-03]

빈칸에 알맞은 것을 고르시오.

01

> We recently revised our menu. __________, we added vegetarian options.

① However   ② Besides
③ In contrast   ④ But
⑤ On the contrary

02

> The project was delayed, __________ we did not receive the materials in time.

① or   ② but   ③ for
④ yet   ⑤ so

03

> Call me immediately, __________ I'll be late for the meeting.

① or   ② and   ③ when
④ yet   ⑤ so

04

밑줄 친 if 대신 쓸 수 있는 것을 고르시오.

> Please let me know as soon as possible <u>if</u> your answer is yes or no.

① unless   ② while   ③ until
④ since   ⑤ whether

05

빈칸에 알맞은 말로 바르게 짝지어진 것을 고르시오.

> • The players warmed up ______(A)______ the soccer match started.
> • I don't want to be interrupted ______(B)______ I'm working.
> • You'll be asked ______(C)______ you want to join this experiment.

	(A)	(B)	(C)
①	before	while	if
②	after	since	that
③	because	when	if
④	although	until	that
⑤	as long as	because	whether

[06-09]

주어진 우리말과 일치하도록 괄호 안의 말을 바르게 배열하여 문장을 완성하시오.

06

네가 얼마나 오랫동안 나를 기다렸는지 궁금해.

(have, long, waiting, how, you, been)

➡ I wonder ______________________________
________________________________ for me.

07

그들은 그 과제가 쉽지 않다는 것을 안다.

(not, task, easy, that, is, the)

➡ They know ______________________________
________________________________.

08

내가 집에 돌아가자마자 네게 전화할게.

(get, as soon as, I, home, back)

➡ I'll call you ___________________________

___________________________ .

09

그는 아주 현명해서 모든 사람이 그에게 조언을 구하고 싶어 한다. (wise, advice, to, that, so, from, everyone, get, him, wants, some)

➡ He is ___________________________

___________________________ .

10 고난도

주어진 문장의 밑줄 친 As와 같은 의미로 쓰인 것을 고르시오.

> As it gets hotter and hotter, many people are looking for something cool to drink.

① As balloons popped, the baby started to cry.
② As the alarm went off, the robber rushed into his car.
③ As he was a college student, he wanted to try challenging things.
④ As you know, the skiing and snowboarding are different in many ways.
⑤ As the technology develops rapidly, people try to adapt themselves to the change.

[11-16] 서술형

두 문장을 주어진 접속사를 이용하여 한 문장으로 쓰시오.

11

I'll let you know. I get the news. (as soon as)

➡ ___________________________

____

12

Jessica and Amy are not so close. They've known each other for a long time. (although)

➡ ___________________________

____

13

There was heavy fog at the airport. The planes were redirected to other airports.

(because)

➡ ___________________________

____

14

I was waiting at the bus stop. Three buses went by in the opposite direction. (while)

➡ ___________________________

____

15

We will refund your payment right away. You are not satisfied with our service for any reason. (if)

➡ ___________________________

____

16

He speaks with a convincing voice. Everyone is impressed. (such ~ that)

➡ ___________________________

____

17 서술형

두 문장이 같도록 빈칸에 알맞은 말을 쓰시오.

Art galleries display not only antiques but also modern art pieces.
= Art galleries display modern art pieces ______________ antiques.

18

어법상 <u>틀린</u> 것을 고르시오.

① He is neither tall nor short.
② Not only you but also Linda is beautiful.
③ Either Italian or French restaurant are fine.
④ Both his mother and father are joining the program.
⑤ A strawberry as well as a kiwi contains lots of vitamin C.

[19-24]

괄호 안에서 알맞은 것을 고르시오.

19

It was (so / such) a boring movie that I fell asleep while I was watching it.

20

(It / Who) is right is not clear.

21

I'd like (either / neither) a cheeseburger or a pizza for lunch.

22

Did you hear (that / whether) Joseph agreed with us or not?

23

I don't want to be disturbed, so don't call me (if / unless) it's something important.

24

(So that / Once) you learn how to ride a bike, you never forget it.

[25-29]

빈칸에 알맞은 것을 고르시오.

25

As soon as he ________ up, I will start the game.

① show
② shows
③ will show
④ showed
⑤ will be shown

26

I'm going to ________ get my computer fixed or buy a new one.

① either
② both
③ neither
④ not only
⑤ as well as

27

> I'm looking for what helps me to be both
> happy and ________.

① success
② succeed
③ successful
④ successfully
⑤ successor

28

> Neither plastic nor paper cups ________
> recycled in my town.

① is
② was
③ be
④ are
⑤ has been

29

> We didn't expect ________ she would accept
> his proposal.

① as
② that
③ if
④ since
⑤ while

[30-32] 서술형
주어진 우리말과 일치하도록 문장에서 <u>틀린</u> 부분을 찾아 바르게 고치시오.

30

Jason은 공항에 일찍 도착했지만, 대합실에서 잠들었기 때문에 비행기를 놓쳤다.
Jason arrived at the airport early, but he missed his flight so he fell asleep in the waiting area.

________ ➡ ________

31

그들은 햇빛에서 많은 시간을 보내기 때문에 피부가 갈색이다.
Their skin is brown because of they spend a lot of time in the sunlight.

________ ➡ ________

32

그는 매년 다른 나라를 여행한다. 예를 들면 작년에는 페루에 갔다.
He travels to different countries every year. In other words, last year he went to Peru.

________ ➡ ________

[33-35]
주어진 두 문장이 같은 뜻이 되도록 빈칸에 알맞은 것을 고르시오.

33

> Whether he is tall or not is not important to me.
> = It is not important to me ________ he is tall or not.

① whether
② when
③ as
④ while
⑤ since

34

> If you don't give up, your dream will come true.
> = ________ you give up, your dream will come true.

① Whether
② Unless
③ Though
④ When
⑤ As

<정답과 해설 p. 83 >

35

> She can swim, and she can dive, too.
> = She can dive ________ swim.

① or   ② both   ③ as
④ as well as   ⑤ but

[36-39] 서술형

문장에서 어법상 틀린 부분을 찾아 밑줄을 긋고 바르게 고치시오.

36

> My parents enjoy both classical or pop music.

➡ ________________

37

> His uncle neither drinks nor smoking.

➡ ________________

38

> We wore warm clothes that we wouldn't get cold.

➡ ________________

39

> Although I opened the window, a cool breeze came into the room.

➡ ________________

40 고난도

밑줄 친 that의 쓰임이 나머지 넷과 다른 것을 고르시오.

① That he didn't pass the audition disappointed everyone.
② His final goal is that his team wins in the national league.
③ Who can imagine that the director made this movie only with $1 million?
④ It was not surprising that he wasn't there at that time.
⑤ David lost the watch that his grandfather had given to him.

[41-42]

빈칸에 공통으로 알맞은 것을 고르시오.

41

> • Are you upset ________ I didn't call you yesterday?
> • ________ it was cold, I caught a cold.

① whether   ② that   ③ as
④ while   ⑤ until

42

> • I wonder ________ she will remember my birthday this year.
> • ________ this road is closed, we'll have to find another route.

① if   ② how   ③ once
④ finally   ⑤ whether

43

밑줄 친 부분을 생략할 수 없는 것을 고르시오.

① The students thought that the exam was over.
② I know that she will come here soon.
③ This is the dog that I like so much.
④ Can you believe that she won a gold medal at the Winter Olympics?
⑤ What I heard on the news was that there was an earthquake in Japan.

밑줄 친 부분 중 어법상 틀린 것을 고르시오.

44

① They will take you to Seoul <u>when</u> you visit Korea.
② You can order either Chinese food <u>nor</u> Japanese food here.
③ I was not only embarrassed <u>but</u> quite shocked at what had happened.
④ I'm not sure <u>if</u> the movie would be too boring for you or not.
⑤ It is true <u>that</u> your answer is right.

45

① You won't be late <u>unless</u> you run.
② Do it right now <u>before</u> you forget.
③ <u>While</u> we were watching the movie, he fell asleep.
④ <u>As</u> tomorrow is the school anniversary, I don't have to go to school.
⑤ It was yesterday <u>that</u> I met him in the park.

46

① Both Tom and Lisa <u>are</u> here.
② Neither I nor he <u>was</u> invited.
③ Either you or he <u>takes</u> the lead.
④ My cat as well as my dogs <u>needs</u> regular checkups.
⑤ Not his friends but John himself <u>were</u> responsible for the mistake.

47

밑줄 친 It의 쓰임이 나머지 넷과 다른 것을 고르시오.

① <u>It</u>'s going to rain tomorrow.
② <u>It</u> is obvious that she is upset.
③ <u>It</u> was midnight, but I was awake.
④ <u>It</u> takes about 30 minutes to get there.
⑤ <u>It</u> is getting warmer as the season changes.

[48-51]

빈칸에 알맞은 것을 〈보기〉에서 골라 쓰시오. (중복 사용 불가)

> 〈보기〉
> or   as a result
> yet   for instance

48

He studied diligently, __________ he failed to achieve the desired result.

49

Would you prefer reading novels __________ watching movies tonight?

50

Lena has practiced abstract painting for years. ______________, her work now appears in several modern art galleries.

51

Online learning can be effective in some cases. ______________, students can review lectures at their own pace.

[52-54] 서술형

주어진 우리말과 일치하도록 빈칸에 알맞은 말을 쓰시오.

52

영화관에 있는 대부분의 사람들은 그 영화가 시작하자마자 휴대폰 전원을 껐다.

➡ Most people in the movie theater turned off their cell phones ______________ the movie started.

〈 정답과 해설 p. 83~85 〉

53

그는 외출할 생각이 없었기 때문에 하루 종일 집에 머물렀지만, 여전히 단정한 옷차림을 유지했다.

➡ He stayed home all day, for he didn't think of going out, _______________ he still remained well-dressed.

54

나는 그 연극의 연출과 연기 둘 다 인상적이었다고 느꼈다.

➡ I felt that _________ the direction of the play _________ the acting were impressive.

[55-57]

다음 글을 읽고 물음에 답하시오.

> I lost my dog Kelly. _____ⓐ_____ I looked everywhere, I couldn't find it, _____ⓑ_____ I shed tears. I made a lot of posters _____ⓒ_____ I could put them up all around my neighborhood. The next day, I got a call. The caller said, "I found a poodle, but how do I know that it's your poodle?" I told him, "There is a good way to prove it. Whistle 'Jingle Bells' to the poodle." After a moment, he got back on the phone and said, "The dog started running in circles." "Then it's certainly Kelly!" said I.

55

ⓐ와 ⓑ에 들어갈 말이 알맞게 짝지어진 것을 고르시오.

	ⓐ	ⓑ		ⓐ	ⓑ
①	Once	– or	②	Unless	– or
③	Though	– so	④	Because	– so
⑤	As long as	– so			

56 서술형

빈칸 ⓒ에 문맥과 어법상 알맞은 말을 쓰시오. (2단어)

____

57 서술형

밑줄 친 접속사에 유의하여 질문에 알맞은 답을 영어로 쓰시오.

> What did the dog do <u>after</u> listening to the caller's whistle?

➡ It _______________________________.

58 수능 유형

밑줄 친 부분 중 어법상 <u>틀린</u> 것을 고르시오.

> In general, ① <u>when</u> insects such as a ladybug and a cicada are dead, they lie on their backs with their legs curled up against their chest. They have three pairs of legs, ② <u>with</u> six in total. They have such many legs ③ <u>if</u> they can distribute their body weight evenly and move easily. ④ <u>As</u> they begin to die, the muscles in their legs contract. ⑤ <u>When</u> their legs no longer support their body weight, the bugs start to turn upside down.
>
> *ladybug 무당벌레 **cicada 매미

① ② ③ ④ ⑤

전치사

前置詞

(앞 전, 둘 치, 말 사)

명사·대명사의 앞에 위치하여
다른 말과 관계를 나타내는 말

The concert is at the stadium on Sunday afternoon.
장소를 나타내는 전치사　　시간을 나타내는 전치사

(콘서트는 일요일 오후에 경기장에서 열릴 것이다.)

The car drove through the tunnel. (차는 터널을 지나갔다.)
방향을 나타내는 전치사

The book on the shelf belongs to my grandmother.
동사 + 전치사

(선반에 있는 책은 내 할머니의 것이다.)

He is good at playing chess. (그는 체스를 잘 둔다.)
형용사 + 전치사

1 at, on, in : '~에'

at	① 구체적인 시각 [1]	The meeting is scheduled at 9:00 AM. (회의는 오전 9시에 예정되어 있다.)
	② 특정한 시점	She always goes to bed at midnight. (그녀는 항상 자정에 잠자리에 든다.)
on	① 날짜	My son was born on July 14th. (내 아들은 7월 14일에 태어났다.)
	② 요일	The store is closed on Monday. (그 가게는 월요일에 문을 닫는다.)
	③ 특정한 날	We are going on vacation on Christmas Day. (우리는 크리스마스 날에 휴가를 간다.)
in	① 월, 연도	He moved to the United States in 2010. (그는 2010년에 미국으로 이사를 갔다.)
	② 계절	In fall, leaves turn bright colors. (가을에 나뭇잎은 밝은색으로 변한다.)
	③ 세기	Art grew in the 15th century. (예술은 15세기에 성장했다.)
	④ 비교적 긴 시간	The birds sing in the morning. (그 새들은 아침에 노래한다.)

❶ 전치사의 특징

전치사는 명사 앞에 쓰여 문장에 시간, 장소, 방향 등을 알려준다.
- at night (밤에) — 시간
- in Korea (한국에서) — 장소
- into the room (방으로) — 방향

2 for, during : '~ 동안'

for	숫자가 포함된 구체적인 길이의 시간 앞 for two hours (두 시간 동안), for a week (한 주 동안) 등
	• I have lived in this city for five years. (나는 이 도시에 5년 동안 살았다.) • He meditated for ten days in complete silence. (그는 열흘 동안 완전한 침묵 속에서 명상했다.)
during	특정한 기간 앞 during the night (밤 동안), during the summer (여름 동안) 등
	• The store is closed during lunchtime. (그 가게는 점심시간 동안 문을 닫는다.) • Ancient people feared the wrath of the god during the eclipse. (고대 사람들은 일식 동안 신의 분노를 두려워했다.)

3 from, since : '~부터'

from	'A부터 B까지'라는 표현의 「from A to B」로 자주 쓰임 from January (1월부터), from Monday to Friday (월요일부터 금요일까지) 등
	• Michel studied abroad from 2016 until 2019. (Michel은 2016년부터 2019년까지 해외에서 공부했다.) • Usually, she works from 9 AM to 6 PM. (그녀는 보통 오전 9시부터 오후 6시까지 일한다.)
since	주로 완료시제와 함께 쓰여 행위가 지속됨을 나타냄 since the beginning (시작부터 줄곧), since last year (작년부터) 등
	• It seems the mice have lived here since the day this house was built. (그 쥐들은 이 집이 지어진 날부터 여기 살아왔던 것 같다.) • The company had improved a lot since the arrival of the new CEO. (그 회사는 새로운 CEO의 도착 이후로 많이 개선되었다.)

1 + 2 at, on, in, for, during

[01-06] 괄호 안에서 알맞은 것을 고르시오.

01 The train is scheduled to arrive (in / at) 7:45 exactly, so don't be late.

02 Please remember the store closes (for / during) lunchtime every weekday.

03 They have been waiting (for / during) an hour outside in the freezing cold.

04 What a tragic traffic accident there was (for / during) the rush hour today!

05 Can you believe my birthday is (at / on) January 2nd, right after the holiday?

06 The entire restoration project will be finished (in / at) two weeks, as scheduled.

2 + 3 for, during, from, since

[07-10] 빈칸에 알맞은 것을 〈보기〉에서 골라 쓰시오. (중복 사용 불가)

> 🦉 **어휘 & 표현**
> · **meditate** 명상하다
> · **silence** 침묵
> · **wrath** 분노
> · **eclipse** 일식
> · **tragic** 비극적인
> · **restoration** 복원
> · **embassy** 대사관
> · **application** 신청서
> · **exhibition** 전시
> · **recover** 회복하다

〈보기〉

for	during	from	since

07 Please take your test ____________ 9:00 sharp to 11:30.

08 He fell asleep ____________ the keynote speech.

09 She has worked at the embassy ____________ 2019.

10 I have studied environmental law ____________ three years.

1 + 2 + 3 at, on, in, for, during, from, since

22 DAY

[11-16] 주어진 우리말과 일치하도록 빈칸에 알맞은 말을 쓰시오.

11 신청서는 다음 주부터 온라인으로만 접수될 것이다.

   ➡ Applications will only be accepted online ____________ next week.

12 당신은 폐막식 이후로 그와 연락을 해왔나요?

   ➡ Have you been in touch with him ____________ the closing ceremony?

13 우리는 회의 동안 창의적인 아이디어를 많이 공유했다.

   ➡ We shared many creative ideas ____________ the meeting.

14 그 전시는 토요일에 지역 미술관에서 열린다.

   ➡ The exhibition opens ____________ Saturday at the local art museum.

15 그는 회복하기 위해 며칠 동안 병원에 머물렀다.

   ➡ He stayed in the hospital ____________ several days to recover.

16 식사는 오후 6시에 시작될 예정이다.

   ➡ The meal is scheduled to begin ____________ 6 p.m.

〈 정답과 해설 **p. 85~86** 〉

4 until, by, within

until, till	~까지	특정 시점까지 행위나 상황이 지속됨 until sunset (해질 때까지), till midnight (자정까지) 등
		내일 내일까지 계속 머무를 수 있음 • You can stay here until tomorrow. (너는 내일까지 여기에 머물러도 돼.)
by	~까지	특정 시점까지 행위나 상황이 완료됨 by next week (다음 주까지), by noon (정오까지) 등
		내일 지속 여부와 상관없이 내일까지 완료되어야 함 • She promised to return the book by tomorrow. (그녀는 내일까지 그 책을 반납하겠다고 약속했다.)
within	~ 이내에	특정 기간 이내에 행위나 상황이 완료됨 • You should submit the form within three days. (너는 그 양식을 3일 이내에 제출해야 한다.)

5 before, after

before	~하기 전에	before sunrise (해뜨기 전에), before bedtime (잠들기 전에), before the exam (시험 전에) 등
		• You should stretch your muscles before intense exercise. (강도 높은 운동 전에 근육을 스트레칭하는 것이 좋다.) • Finish your homework before dinner. (저녁 먹기 전에 숙제를 끝내렴.)
after	~한 후에	after lunch (점심식사 후에), after the movie (영화 본 후에), after the rain (비 온 뒤) 등
		• The air feels fresher after a summer thunderstorm. (여름 폭풍우 뒤에는 공기가 더 상쾌하다.) • I'll call you after lunch if I'm not too busy. (내가 점심 먹은 후에 너무 바쁘지 않으면 전화할게.)

참고 접속사로도 쓰이는 before와 after

before와 after는 문장에서 접속사로도 쓰이기 때문에 뒤에 절이 올 수도 있다.

• Before the storm arrived, they closed the windows. (폭풍이 오기 전에 그들은 창문을 닫았다.)
　　접속사　　　　　절
• After the party ended, they cleaned up the mess. (파티가 끝난 후, 그들은 엉망진창인 것을 치웠다.)
　　접속사　　　　절

4 until, by, within

[17-22] 빈칸에 until, by, within 중 알맞은 것을 쓰시오.

17 All event attendees are required to check in ＿＿＿＿＿＿＿ 9:30 a.m. at the latest.

18 The report must be submitted ＿＿＿＿＿＿＿ 48 hours after receiving the request.

19 We will have a short break ＿＿＿＿＿＿＿ noon, so please return to your seats on time.

20 She had waited ＿＿＿＿＿＿＿ midnight for the final approval, but no message ever came.

21 Have you completed all your visa documents ＿＿＿＿＿＿＿ the deadline?

22 You must respond to the publisher's offer ＿＿＿＿＿＿＿ seven days to secure the contract.

5 before, after

[23-26] 주어진 우리말과 일치하도록 괄호 안의 단어를 before나 after와 함께 쓰시오.

23 그녀는 긴 출장 전에 Ian에게 그녀의 앵무새를 돌볼 것을 부탁했다. (her long business trip)

➡ She asked Ian to take care of her parrot ＿＿＿＿＿＿＿＿＿＿＿＿＿＿＿＿.

24 학생들은 기말고사 후에 도서관 대신 카페에 모였다. (the final exam)

➡ The students gathered in the cafe instead of the library ＿＿＿＿＿＿＿＿＿＿＿＿＿＿.

25 건강검진 전에, 환자는 금식을 포함한 여러 가지 준비 절차를 따라야 한다. (the medical checkup)

➡ ＿＿＿＿＿＿＿＿＿＿＿＿＿＿＿＿, the patient must follow several rules including fasting.

26 공연 후에, 관객들은 극단에 큰 박수를 보냈다. (the performance)

➡ ＿＿＿＿＿＿＿＿＿＿＿＿＿＿＿＿, the audience gave the troupe a big applause.

4 + 5 until, by, within, before, after

[27-30] 주어진 우리말과 일치하도록 괄호 안에서 알맞은 것을 고르시오.

27 식물 성장 사진을 금요일까지 단체 대화방에서 공유해 주세요.

➡ Please share your plant growth photos in the group chat (by / until) Friday.

28 우리는 올해 1분기 이내에 상당한 진전을 기대한다.

➡ We expect significant progress (until / within) the first quarter of this year.

29 구조팀은 마지막 생존자를 찾기 위해 새벽까지 계속 일했다.

➡ The rescue team kept working to find the last survivor (by / until) dawn.

30 그는 수술 전에 장비가 제대로 작동하는지 꼼꼼히 점검했다.

➡ He checked if the equipment was functioning properly (before / after) the surgery.

어휘 & 표현

· **intense** 강도 높은　· **attendee** 참석자　· **request** 요청하다, 요청　· **approval** 동의　· **secure** 확보하다　· **contract** 계약
· **gather** 모이다　· **fasting** 금식　· **significant** 의미 있는, 상당한　· **rescue** 구조　· **function** 기능하다　· **surgery** 수술

〈 정답과 해설 p. 86 〉

UNIT 47 장소를 나타내는 전치사

1 at, on, in → 장소를 나타내는 전치사 at, on, in과 함께 쓰이는 명사(구)

at	① 비교적 좁은 장소나 지점 ② 건물의 용도에 맞는 일 ③ 행사나 모임	at school, at home, at a party, at a meeting, at the restaurant, at the beach, at the movies, at the cafe, at the airport 등 ① Wait <u>at</u> the bus stop until the next one arrives. (다음 버스가 올 때까지 버스 정류장에서 기다려.) ② Neal has learned basic English grammar <u>at</u> school. (Neal은 학교에서 기초 영어 문법을 배워왔다.) ③ Eddie showed a new theory <u>at</u> the physics conference. (Eddie는 물리학 학회에서 새로운 이론을 제시했다.)
on	① 표면에 접촉했을 때 ❶ ② 교통수단, 통신수단 ③ 길	on a bus, on a plane, on a subway, on a ferry, on a bike, on a highway, on a street, on the roof, on the desk, on the mat, on the way 등 ① She placed the glass carefully <u>on</u> the upper shelf. (그녀는 유리를 윗선반에 조심스럽게 올려두었다.) ② They watched the news <u>on</u> TV. (그들은 TV로 뉴스를 봤다.) ③ I bought some bread <u>on</u> the way back home. (나는 집에 돌아오는 길에 빵을 조금 샀다.)
in	① 넓은 장소나 지역 ② 내부나 테두리 안에 있을 때 ③ 우주나 하늘	in Seoul, in class, in a city, in a town, in a car, in a taxi, in a hospital, in a university, in a theater, in a conference room 등 ① I studied economics <u>in</u> Melbourne. (나는 멜버른에서 경제학을 공부했다.) ② The keys are <u>in</u> the drawer under the files. (열쇠는 서류 아래 서랍 안에 있다.) ③ A lot of crows are flying <u>in</u> the sky. (많은 까마귀가 하늘에 날아다니고 있다.)

> **❶ 전치사의 특징**
> 전치사는 형용사구나 부사구를 이끈다.
> • The cellphone on the desk is mine. (형용사구)
> (책상 위의 휴대 전화는 내 것이다.)
> • I put my bag on the desk. (부사구)
> (나는 내 가방을 책상 위에 두었다.)

> **❷ 비유적인 표현의 over**
> over는 '~ 위에'의 뜻도 있지만, 시간, 비용 등과 함께 쓰여 '~ 이상'의 뜻을 갖는다.
> • The driver goes over the speed limit.
> (그 운전자는 제한 속도 이상으로 간다.)

2 over, above  ❷

over	덮여 있듯 바로 위에	over the horizon, over the mountains 등 • A chandelier is hanging <u>over</u> the large dining table. (샹들리에가 큰 식탁 위에 걸려 있다.) • The sun was rising <u>over</u> the horizon. (수평선 위로 태양이 떠오르고 있었다.)
above	조금 떨어진 위에	above the building, above the clouds 등 • Is the mirror still <u>above</u> the fireplace? (그 거울은 아직도 벽난로 위에 있니?) • The helicopter was hovering <u>above</u> the sea. (헬리콥터가 바다 <u>위</u>를 맴돌고 있다.)

1 at, on, in

[01-03] 빈칸에 공통으로 들어갈 말을 쓰시오.

01 Don't get lost ＿＿＿＿＿＿＿＿ the forest after sunset.

Thousands of satellites are currently being tracked ＿＿＿＿＿＿＿＿ space.

02 The ancient map was spread ＿＿＿＿＿＿＿＿ the stone table.

A bronze sculpture stood proudly ＿＿＿＿＿＿＿＿ a pedestal.

03 A flag was raised ＿＿＿＿＿＿＿＿ the highest tower of the castle.

There's a carved emblem just ＿＿＿＿＿＿＿＿ the central archway.

2 over, above

[04-06] 자연스러운 대화가 되도록 빈칸에 over와 above 중 알맞은 것을 쓰시오.

04 A: Did you see that plane flying ＿＿＿＿＿＿＿＿ the beach just now?

B: Yeah, it was so low that I thought it might land right there!

05 A: Wow, that painting is hanging a bit too high.

B: I know. It's way ＿＿＿＿＿＿＿＿ the shelf. It's hard to even see the details.

06 A: What's that strange cloud ＿＿＿＿＿＿＿＿ the mountain?

B: I think it's just fog rolling in from the other side.

1 + 2 at, on, in, over, above

[07-11] 괄호 안에서 알맞은 것을 고르시오.

07 I noticed a stranger roaming (on / in) the botanical garden.

08 Shall we meet (at / on) the historical archive around noon?

09 Ask the curator if she can place that ornament (in / over) the post.

10 There's a detailed map attached (on / over) the wall near the entrance.

11 The drone will be hovering (on / above) the exhibition area for security purposes.

🦉 **어휘 & 표현**

· **grammar** 문법　· **physics** 물리학　· **conference** 학회　· **economics** 경제학　· **hang** 걸려 있다　· **horizon** 수평선
· **hover** 맴돌다　· **satellite** 위성　· **currently** 현재　· **spread** 퍼지다　· **bronze** 청동　· **sculpture** 조각품
· **pedestal** 받침대　· **carve** 새기다　· **emblem** 상징　· **archway** 아치형 입구　· **roam** 돌아다니다　· **botanical** 식물의
· **archive** 기록 보관소　· **curator** 큐레이터 (박물관·미술관 등의 전시 책임자)　· **ornament** 장식(품)　· **security** 보안

〈 정답과 해설 **p. 86~87** 〉

3 beneath, under, below

beneath	접촉하여 아래에	beneath the surface, beneath her feet 등
		• There was a storage room beneath the kitchen. (주방 아래에 창고가 하나 있었다.)
under	바로 아래에	under the bed, under the table, under the tree 등
		• The dog was sleeping under the table when I came in. (내가 들어왔을 때 개가 탁자 아래에서 자고 있었다.)
below	조금 떨어져 아래에	below ground level, below the boat, below the horizon 등
		• They have placed a wooden chest below the staircase. (그들은 계단 아래에 나무 상자 하나를 두었다.)

> **[주의] 전치사의 특징**
> 전치사 뒤에는 명사나 대명사의 목적격, 명사 상당어구(동명사, 의문사절)가 온다.
> • The garden is behind the house.
>   명사
> (정원은 집 뒤에 있다.)
> • Jane is sitting next to him.
>   대명사의 목적격
> (Jane은 그의 옆에 앉아 있다.)

4 by, beside, next to, in front of, behind, near

by, beside, next to	~ 옆에	by the window, beside the bed, next to him 등
		• The apartment is located by(= beside) the central subway station. (그 아파트는 중심 지하철역 근처에 있다.)
		• Stand next to(= beside) the entrance until you're called. (이름이 불릴 때까지 입구 옆에 서 있어라.)
in front of	~ 앞에	in front of me, in front of the house, in front of the mirror 등
		• I put some oranges in front of apples. (나는 몇몇 오렌지를 사과 앞에 두었다.)
behind	~ 뒤에	behind us, behind the couch, behind the curtains 등
		• The delivery truck was idling behind(⇔ in front of) the building when I arrived. (내가 도착했을 때 배달 트럭이 건물 뒤에서 공회전 중이었다.)
near	~ 가까이에	near the bank, near the shop, near the building 등
		• He set up his telescope near the cliff to watch the shooting star. (그는 유성을 보기 위해 절벽 근처에 망원경을 설치했다.)

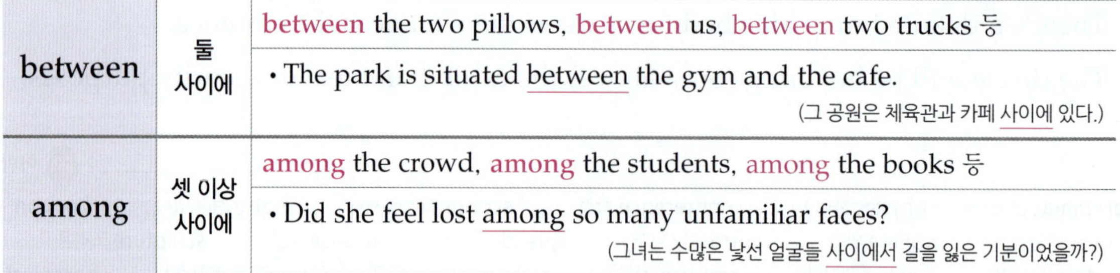

5 between, among

between	둘 사이에	between the two pillows, between us, between two trucks 등
		• The park is situated between the gym and the cafe. (그 공원은 체육관과 카페 사이에 있다.)
among	셋 이상 사이에	among the crowd, among the students, among the books 등
		• Did she feel lost among so many unfamiliar faces? (그녀는 수많은 낯선 얼굴들 사이에서 길을 잃은 기분이었을까?)

3 beneath, under, below

[12-13] 주어진 우리말과 일치하도록 괄호 안에 주어진 말을 바르게 배열하시오.

12 고대 유적은 종종 현대적인 도시 바로 아래에서 발견된다.
(found, are, the ancient remains, beneath, often, the modern city)

➡ ____

13 그 작은 검은 고양이는 나무 탁자 아래에서 자고 있다.
(under, sleeping, the little black cat, is, the wooden table)

➡ ____

4 by, beside, next to, in front of, behind, near

[14-15] 주어진 우리말과 일치하도록 괄호 안에서 알맞은 것을 고르시오.

14 다 읽은 책들은 책상 옆에 두세요.

➡ Leave your books you finished (next to / behind) the desk.

15 우체국은 경찰서 앞에 있나요?

➡ Is the post office (in front of / behind) the police station?

5 between, among

[16-19] 빈칸에 between과 among 중에서 알맞은 것을 쓰시오.

16 Tensions ______________ the two Koreas decreased in 2018.

17 The secret door was located ______________ the two bookshelves.

18 Worries spread ______________ all the students after the midterm exam.

19 My meerkat was searching for his toy ______________ numerous clothes.

1 + **2** + **3** + **4** + **5** 장소를 나타내는 전치사

[20-24] 그림을 보고 빈칸에 알맞은 전치사를 넣어 문장을 완성하시오.

- telescope 망원경
- cliff 절벽
- shooting star 유성
- remains 유적
- decrease 감소하다
- spread 퍼지다
- numerous 수많은
- stream 개울

20 A man sits ______________ a cat and a woman.

21 Four children are ______________ the mat ______________ the tree.

22 A woman with a hat on walks across the bridge ______________ the stream.

23 A cat is sleeping ______________ the grass ______________ the bench.

24 Fish are swimming ______________ the stream.

1 방향 전치사

up	~ 위로	• The drone is flying up the observation deck. (드론이 전망대 위로 비행하고 있다.)
down	~ 아래로	• He followed the path down the hillside after the meeting. (그는 회의 후 언덕 아래로 이어진 길을 따라갔다.)
into	~ 안으로	• Water has already been poured into the vase. (물이 이미 꽃병 속으로 부어졌다.)
out of	~ 밖으로	• She stepped out of the elevator with a sigh. (그녀는 한숨을 쉬며 엘리베이터 밖으로 나왔다.)
onto	~ 위로	• He climbed onto the roof to fix the antenna. (그는 안테나를 고치기 위해 지붕 위로 올라갔다.)
off	~에서 떨어져	• The bird flew off the roof. (새가 지붕에서 날아갔다.)
to	~로, ~에	• We're heading to the airport now. (우리는 지금 공항으로 가는 중이다.)
for ❶	~을 향해	• The new satellite will be heading for the launch site in September. (새로운 인공위성은 9월에 발사장으로 향하는 중일 것이다.)
toward ❶	~을 향해, ~쪽으로	• They rushed toward the hut as the rain began. (비가 오기 시작하자 그들은 오두막 쪽으로 달려갔다.)
across	~을 가로질러 (횡단을 의미)	• Walk across the plaza and find the building without any windows. (광장을 가로질러 걷고 아무 창문도 없는 건물을 찾으세요.)
through	~을 통하여 (통과를 의미)	• The parade passed through the narrow alley. (퍼레이드는 좁은 골목을 통과해 지나갔다.)
along	~을 따라서	• Let's stroll along the river before it gets dark. (어두워지기 전에 강을 따라 산책하자.)
around, round ❷	~ 주위에	• There are elegant villas around the hillside. (그 언덕 주위에는 우아한 별장들이 있다.) • She led the tourists round the historic castle. (그녀는 관광객들을 성 주변을 돌며 안내했다.)

❶ **for와 toward**

for와 toward는 '~을 향해'의 뜻을 가진다. for는 뒤에 정확한 목표 대상이 나오고 toward는 나아가는 방향이 나온다는 차이가 있다.

❷ **around와 round**

around와 round는 '주변에'의 뜻을 가진다. around는 대상 주위의 존재에 집중하고, round는 원형이나 곡선을 이루며 주변을 도는 행위에 집중한다는 차이가 있다.

■ 방향 전치사

[01-06] 그림을 보고, 빈칸에 알맞은 말을 〈보기〉에서 골라 쓰시오. (중복 사용 불가)

〈보기〉

up	down	into	out of	off	along

01

➡ She is going ＿＿＿＿＿ the stairs with a folder in her hand.

02

➡ When he got ＿＿＿＿＿ the room, he saw something astonishing.

03

➡ A mole went ＿＿＿＿＿ the soil.

04

➡ My grandfather can't walk ＿＿＿＿＿ the stairs without the handrail.

05

➡ Baby penguins are walking ＿＿＿＿＿ their mother.

06

➡ My daughter is in the hospital, for she fell ＿＿＿＿＿ the bike yesterday.

[07-10] 주어진 우리말과 일치하도록 괄호 안에서 알맞은 것을 고르시오.

07 젤리를 접시 위로 떨어뜨리지 않게 조심하세요.

➡ Be careful not to drop the jelly (onto / through) the plate.

08 그는 왜 부산행 대신 군산행 버스를 탔나요?

➡ Why did he take the bus (for / toward) Gunsan, instead of Busan?

09 낚시꾼들이 강을 가로질러 그들의 배를 저었다.

➡ The fishermen rowed their boats (across / along) the river.

10 그녀는 해가 지고 있을 때 지평선 쪽을 바라보고 있었다.

➡ She was looking (for / toward) the horizon as the sun was setting.

 어휘 & 표현

- **hillside** 언덕
- **pour** 붓다
- **sigh** 한숨
- **satellite** 인공위성
- **launch** 발사
- **rush** 달려가다, 서두르다
- **alley** 골목
- **soil** 토양
- **row** 노를 젓다
- **horizon** 지평선, 수평선

〈 정답과 해설 p. 88 〉

with	① (도구) ~로	• Children cut the paper with scissors. (어린이들은 가위로 종이를 잘랐다.)
	② ~와 함께	• Tom went to the movies with his friends. (Tom은 친구들과 함께 영화를 보러 갔다.)
	③ ~을 가진	• We need someone with new ideas. (우리는 새로운 생각을 가진 사람이 필요하다.)
	④ ~의 몸에 지니고	• Despite the heavy rain, Olivia walked to the gallery with her camera. (많은 비에도 불구하고, Olivia는 카메라를 가지고 미술관으로 걸어갔다.)
	⑤ ~에 대하여	• We thought that the manager was happy with our work. (우리는 매니저가 우리의 일에 대해 만족했다고 생각했다.)
	⑥ ~와, ~에 찬성하여	• They all agreed with the teacher's explanation. (그들은 모두 선생님의 설명에 동의했다.)
without	① ~ 없이	• She went to school without her backpack. (그녀는 가방 없이 학교에 갔다.)
	② ~하지 않고	• He left the room without saying goodbye. (그는 인사하지 않고 방을 나갔다.)
❶ of	① (재료) ~로	• The sculpture is carved of marble. (그 조각상은 대리석으로 조각되었다.)
	② (원인) ~(으)로	• He died of heart disease. (그는 심장병으로 죽었다.)
from ❶	① (재료) ~로	• The wine is made from grape. (그 와인은 포도로 만들어졌다.)
	② (원인) ~(으)로	• The problem arose from miscommunication. (그 문제는 의사소통 오류에서 발생했다.)
by ❷	① (수단) ~로	• She communicated by email. (그녀는 이메일로 소통했다.)
	② ~에 의해	• The discovery was made by Marie Curie. (그 발견은 마리 퀴리에 의해 이루어졌다.)
	③ ~로	• The team won the basketball game by 10 points. (그 팀은 농구 경기에서 10점 차로 이겼다.)
	④ ~함으로써	• You can save time by completing small tasks right after meetings. (회의 직후에 작은 작업들을 완료함으로써 시간을 절약할 수 있다.)
in ❷	① (수단) ~로	• The artist painted the picture in oil. (그 예술가는 그 그림을 유화로 그렸다.)
	② ~을 입고 있는	• The man in black walked silently. (검은 옷을 입은 남자가 말없이 걸었다.)
for	(목적) ~ 때문에	• He is studying for his English exams. (그는 영어 시험 때문에 공부하고 있다.)

❶ be made of, be made from

be made of: 원재료가 바뀌지 않을 때
• The necklace is made of gold.
금이 다른 물질로 바뀌지 않음
(그 목걸이는 금으로 만들어졌다.)

be made from: 원재료가 바뀔 때
• The cheese is made from milk.
우유가 치즈로 바뀌었음
(그 치즈는 우유로 만들어졌다.)

❷ by와 in

by와 in은 '~로'의 뜻을 가지며 수단을 나타낸다. by는 교통수단 앞에 쓰이고, in은 행위의 수단이나 재료 앞에 쓰인다는 차이가 있다.

2 기타 전치사

[11-13] 그림을 보고, 빈칸에 알맞은 전치사를 쓰시오.

11 

➡ She was with a man __________ a bright smile.

12 

➡ We traveled around the city __________ train during our vacation.

13 

➡ The woman __________ red is Tina, my best friend.

[14-19] 빈칸에 알맞은 것을 〈보기〉에서 골라 쓰시오. (중복 사용 불가)

〈보기〉

in	for	by	of	as	with

14 He got an award __________ his hard work.

15 She died __________ a serious illness last year.

16 The man __________ the blue jacket is our new coach.

17 He is working __________ a volunteer at the animal shelter.

18 The painting was drawn __________ a famous artist from France.

19 She plays __________ her dog in the backyard every afternoon.

1 + 2 방향 및 기타 전치사

[20-23] 빈칸에 공통으로 들어갈 말을 쓰시오.

20
- I went to the concert ______ my friend.
- James opened the door ______ a key.

➡ __________

21
- She was praised ______ her kindness.
- He left ______ Paris this morning.

➡ __________

22
- This book was written ______ a famous author.
- They paid ______ credit card.

➡ __________

23
- He ate lunch ______ his friends.
- She walked away ______ answering the question.

➡ __________

🦉 어휘 & 표현

- **sculpture** 조각상　· **carve** 조각하다　· **marble** 대리석　· **disease** 병　· **miscommunication** 의사소통 오류
- **discovery** 발견　· **silently** 말없이　· **illness** 병　· **volunteer** 자원봉사자　· **backyard** 뒷마당

〈 정답과 해설 p. 88~89 〉

on	(목적) ~하러	• The researcher works on improving skills. (연구자는 기술 향상을 위해 일하고 있다.)
as	~로(서)	• A flat stone is used as a table. (평평한 돌은 식탁으로 사용된다.)
about	~에 대해	• He was talking about his trip to Italy. (그는 그의 이탈리아 여행에 대해 이야기하고 있었다.)
like	~처럼	• She dresses like a fashion model. (그녀는 패션 모델처럼 옷을 입는다.)
	~와 같은	• They visited famous landmarks like the Eiffel Tower. (그들은 에펠탑과 같은 유명한 랜드마크를 방문했다.)
against	~에 반대하는	• The players spoke out against the unfair decision. (선수들은 그 불공정한 판정에 반대하여 공개적으로 말했다.)
except (for)	~을 제외하고	• Everyone came to the party except for Tom. (Tom을 제외하고 모두 파티에 왔다.)
including	~을 포함하여	• Everyone was invited including Peter and Mary. (Peter와 Mary를 포함하여 모두가 초대되었다.)
due to (=because of)	~ 때문에	• The flight was delayed due to heavy rain. (비행기가 폭우 때문에 지연되었다.) • Because of the deadline, he skipped lunch. (마감 때문에 그는 점심을 걸렀다.)
according to	~에 따르면	• According to the news, it will snow tomorrow. (뉴스에 따르면 내일 눈이 올 것이다.)
❶ instead of	~ 대신에	• We had pizza instead of rice for dinner. (우리는 저녁으로 밥 대신에 피자를 먹었다.)
such as	~와 같은	• I like fruits such as apples, bananas, and grapes. (나는 사과, 바나나, 포도 같은 과일을 좋아한다.)
despite (=in spite of)	~에도 불구하고	• Despite the rain, they continued playing. (비가 내렸음에도 불구하고, 그들은 계속 경기를 했다.) • In spite of the glitch, the game felt real. (오류에도 불구하고, 그 게임은 현실처럼 느껴졌다.)

❶ instead

instead가 단독으로 쓰이면 부사로서 '대신에'라는 뜻을 가진다. 주로 동사나 문장 전체를 수식할 때 쓰인다.
• He lost his pencil, so I gave mine instead.
(그가 연필을 잃어버려서, 나는 내 것을 대신 줬다.)
• Sorry, I can't go. Instead, my father will go.
(미안, 나는 못 가. 대신에, 우리 아빠가 갈 거야.)

2 기타 전치사

[24-27] 괄호 안에서 알맞은 것을 고르시오.

24 She drank juice (instead of / despite) coffee.

25 The game was canceled (such as / due to) heavy snow.

26 The museum is open every day (except / against) Monday.

27 (Because of / According to) the weather forecast, the weather will be sunny tomorrow.

[28-33] 빈칸에 알맞은 것을 〈보기〉에서 골라 쓰시오. (중복 사용 불가)

〈보기〉
| by | against | due to | such as | like | except for |

28 He was kind to everyone, _____________ the stranger.

29 The city received a warning _____________ severe air pollution.

30 Many scientists have publicly argued _____________ the theory.

31 Was the data analyzed _____________ the new software you installed?

32 The children brought fruits _____________ apples, pears, and cherries.

33 The child dressed _____________ a movie character at the costume party.

1 + 2 방향 및 기타 전치사

[34-39] 주어진 우리말과 일치하도록 괄호 안에서 알맞은 것을 고르시오.

34 그 책은 유명한 작가에 의해 쓰였다.

➡ The book was written (by / for) a famous author.

35 그녀는 버스를 타기 위해 길을 가로질러 달렸다.

➡ She ran (through / across) the street to catch the bus.

36 나는 컴퓨터 없이는 숙제를 할 수 없다.

➡ I can't do my homework (about / without) a computer.

37 불이 나자 그는 창문 밖으로 뛰어내렸다.

➡ He jumped (out of / onto) the window when the fire started.

38 내 남동생을 포함하여 다섯 명이 수업에 늦었다.

➡ Five people, (including / against) my brother, were late for class.

39 그녀는 프로 가수처럼 노래한다.

➡ She sings (as / like) a professional singer.

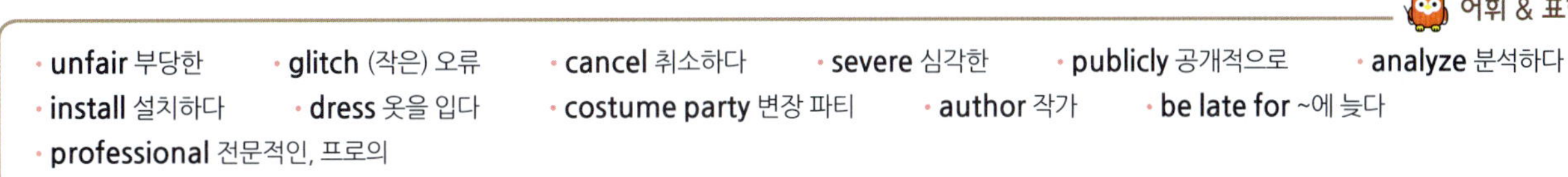

🦉 **어휘 & 표현**

- **unfair** 부당한   · **glitch** (작은) 오류   · **cancel** 취소하다   · **severe** 심각한   · **publicly** 공개적으로   · **analyze** 분석하다
- **install** 설치하다   · **dress** 옷을 입다   · **costume party** 변장 파티   · **author** 작가   · **be late for** ~에 늦다
- **professional** 전문적인, 프로의

〈 정답과 해설 **p. 89** 〉

UNIT 49 동사 + 전치사

1 동사 + 전치사 ❶

look for	~을 찾다	• I'm looking for my math book. (나는 수학책을 찾고 있다.)
wait for	~을 기다리다	• We waited for the bus for 20 minutes. (우리는 20분 동안 버스를 기다렸다.)
apply for	~에 지원하다	• He applied for a part-time job at the bookstore. (그는 서점에서의 아르바이트에 지원했다.)
belong to	~에 속하다	• This red pen belongs to my sister. (이 빨간 펜은 내 여동생의 것이다.)
listen to	~을 듣다	• She listens to music every evening. (그녀는 매일 저녁 음악을 듣는다.)
lead to	~로 이끌다	• Too much stress may lead to serious illness. (너무 많은 스트레스는 심각한 질병으로 이어질 수 있다.)
depend on	~에 의지하다, ~에 달려 있다	• Babies depend on their parents for everything. (아기들은 모든 것을 부모에게 의지한다.)
put on	~을 입다	• He put on his jacket and went outside. (그는 재킷을 입고 밖으로 나갔다.)
focus on	~에 집중하다	• Please focus on your homework, not your phone. (너의 휴대폰이 아니라 너의 숙제에 집중해라.)
agree with	~에 동의하다	• I agree with your idea. It sounds great. (나는 네 생각에 동의해. 좋은 생각이야.)
deal with	~을 다루다	• The teacher helped us deal with the problem. (선생님이 우리가 그 문제를 처리하는 걸 도와주셨다.)
die of ❷	~로 죽다 (노령, 병으로 인해)	• His grandfather died of cancer. (그의 할아버지는 암으로 돌아가셨다.)
die from ❷	~로 죽다 (사고, 부주의로 인해)	• The man died from a car accident. (그 남자는 교통사고로 죽었다.)
laugh at	~을 비웃다	• Don't laugh at others when they make mistakes. (다른 사람들이 실수할 때 비웃지 말아라.)
believe in	~을 믿다	• I believe in myself and my dreams. (나는 내 자신과 나의 꿈을 믿는다.)

2 동사 + 명사 + 전치사

take care of (= look after, care for)	~을 돌보다	• She takes care of her brother every day. (그녀는 매일 그녀의 남동생을 돌본다.)
take advantage of	~을 이용하다	• He took advantage of the good weather to play soccer. (그는 좋은 날씨를 이용해서 축구를 했다.)
make fun[a fool] of	~을 놀리다	• Don't make fun of your friends. It's not nice. (네 친구들을 놀리지 마. 그건 좋지 않아.)
make use of	~을 이용하다	• We should make use of our free time wisely. (우리는 자유 시간을 현명하게 이용해야 한다.)
take the place of	~을 대신하다	• John took the place of his friend in the game. (John은 게임에서 친구를 대신했다.)
take pride in	~을 자랑하다	• She takes pride in her artwork. (그녀는 자신의 미술 작품을 자랑한다.)
take part in	~에 참가하다	• I want to take part in the school festival. (나는 학교 축제에 참여하고 싶다.)
pay attention to	~에 주의를 기울이다	• You must pay attention to the teacher in class. (너는 수업 시간에 선생님 말씀에 주의를 기울여야 해.)

1 동사+전치사

[01-07] 괄호 안에서 알맞은 것을 고르시오.

01 I like to listen (for / to) music when I study.

02 I applied (from / for) a science camp last week.

03 Plants depend (on / of) sunlight and water to grow.

04 Eating too much junk food can lead (to / with) obesity.

05 They waited (in / for) their teacher outside the classroom.

06 She is trying to look (to / for) her lost keys.

07 It's hard to focus (on / with) studying when it's noisy.

1 + **2** 동사+전치사, 동사+명사+전치사

[08-14] 빈칸에 알맞은 것을 〈보기〉에서 골라 쓰시오. (중복 사용 불가)

〈보기〉

at	for	from	of	on	to	with

08 He applied ____________ a scholarship to study abroad.

09 The lack of sleep can lead ____________ health problems.

10 They took advantage ____________ the free Wi-Fi at the cafe.

11 He died ____________ a heart attack last year.

12 Don't laugh ____________ people just because they are different.

13 I need to put ____________ some sunscreen before going outside.

14 She agrees ____________ the new policy that was introduced last week.

[15-22] 문장의 빈칸에 알맞은 전치사를 쓰시오.

15 My brother takes care ____________ our dog every morning.

16 That red bike belongs ____________ my cousin.

17 You should take advantage ____________ this chance to learn.

18 Let's make use ____________ the old boxes for storage.

19 The baby paid attention ____________ the colorful toy.

20 He takes pride ____________ helping others.

21 He had to deal ____________ a lot of stress at work.

22 It's important to believe ____________ yourself.

어휘 & 표현
- **advantage** 장점
- **grow** 자라다
- **obesity** 비만
- **scholarship** 장학금
- **lack** 부족
- **heart attack** 심장마비
- **policy** 정책
- **bike** 자전거
- **cousin** 사촌
- **storage** 보관
- **colorful** 형형색색의

〈 정답과 해설 p. 89~90 〉

 **UNIT 50** 형용사 + 전치사, 주의해야 할 전치사 

1 be동사 + 형용사 + 전치사

be afraid of	~을 두려워하다	• She is afraid of big, hairy spiders. (그녀는 크고 털 많은 거미를 두려워한다.)
be ashamed of	~을 부끄러워하다	• He was ashamed of his rude behavior. (그는 무례한 행동을 부끄러워했다.)
be proud of	~을 자랑스러워하다	• I am proud of my younger brother. (나는 내 남동생이 자랑스럽다.)
be fond of	~을 좋아하다	• She is fond of cute animals. (그녀는 귀여운 동물들을 좋아한다.)
be capable of	~을 할 수 있다	• He is capable of solving hard math problems. (그는 어려운 수학 문제들을 해결할 수 있다.)
be jealous of	~을 질투하다	• Tom is jealous of his friend's expensive phone. (Tom은 친구의 비싼 휴대폰을 질투한다.)
be full of	~로 가득 차다	• The box is full of old books. (그 상자는 오래된 책들로 가득 찼다.)
be good at	~을 잘하다	• She is good at drawing people. (그녀는 사람들을 그리는 것을 잘한다.)
be poor at	~을 못하다	• I am poor at speaking English fluently. (나는 영어를 유창하게 말하는 것을 못한다.)
be related to	~와 관련 있다	• This book is related to ancient Korean history. (이 책은 고대 한국 역사와 관련이 있다.)
be familiar to	~에 대해 잘 알고 있다	• Her soft voice was familiar to me. (그녀의 부드러운 목소리는 내가 잘 알고 있다.)
be familiar with	~에게 친숙하다	• I am familiar with this game and its rules. (나는 이 게임과 그 규칙에 친숙하다.)
be crowded with	~로 가득하다	• The street was crowded with tourists. (거리는 관광객들로 가득했다.)
be based on	~에 근거하다	• This movie is based on a true crime story. (이 영화는 실제 범죄 이야기에 근거한다.)
be responsible for	~에 책임이 있다	• You are responsible for cleaning the kitchen floor. (너는 부엌 바닥 청소에 책임이 있다.)
be famous for	~로 유명하다	• Paris is famous for art, food, and fashion. (파리는 예술, 음식, 그리고 패션으로 유명하다.)
be known for	~로 알려지다	• He is known for his great cooking skills. (그는 훌륭한 요리 실력으로 알려져 있다.)
be different from	~와 다르다	• My idea is different from yours and hers. (내 생각은 너와 그녀의 생각과 다르다.)

2 주의해야 할 전치사 – 의미가 같은 전치사와 접속사

의미	전치사 – 뒤에 명사(구)가 온다.	접속사 – 뒤에 「주어 + 동사」의 절이 온다.
~ 때문에	**because of, due to** • The flight was delayed because of heavy snow. (폭설 때문에 비행기가 지연되었다.)	**because** • The game was canceled because it was raining. (비가 오고 있었기 때문에 경기가 취소되었다.)
~에도 불구하고	**despite, in spite of** • He went out despite the bad weather. (나쁜 날씨에도 불구하고 그는 외출했다.)	**although, though** • Although he was tired, he kept working. (그는 피곤함에도 불구하고 계속 일했다.)
~인 경우에 대비하여	**in case of** • In case of fire, use the stairs, not the elevator. (화재인 경우에 대비하여 엘리베이터가 아닌 계단을 이용하세요.)	**in case (that)** • Take an umbrella in case (that) it rains. (비가 올 경우를 대비해서 우산을 가져가.)
~ 동안	**during** • No one is allowed to talk during the test. (시험 동안에 아무도 말하면 안 된다.)	**while** • She listened to music while she was studying. (그녀는 공부하는 동안 음악을 들었다.)

1 be동사 + 형용사 + 전치사

[01-05] 괄호 안에서 알맞은 것을 고르시오.

01 I am responsible (of / for) organizing the event.

02 He was ashamed (of / for) his outfit at the party.

03 Paris is famous (for / with) its beautiful architecture.

04 This machine is capable (at / of) processing large amounts of data.

05 The name is familiar (in / to) me, but I can't remember where I heard it.

[06-12] 빈칸에 알맞은 것을 〈보기〉에서 골라 쓰시오. (중복 사용 불가)

〈보기〉
| of | on | to | from | for | at | with |

06 I'm poor _____________ remembering names.

07 This book is based _____________ real events.

08 My opinion is different _____________ yours.

09 He is accustomed _____________ staying up late.

10 I'm familiar _____________ this type of question.

11 He is known _____________ a kind teacher.

12 I am afraid _____________ swimming in deep water.

2 주의해야 할 전치사

[13-20] 문장에서 틀린 부분을 찾아서 밑줄을 긋고 바르게 고쳐 쓰시오.

13 In case technical failure, backup generators will operate. _____________

14 Submit the report during the committee is still in session. _____________

15 In case unexpected delays, please inform your supervisor. _____________

16 The concert was canceled because a sudden power outage. _____________

17 Did the judge admit the evidence despite it lacked credibility? _____________

18 The conference was postponed because the weather conditions. _____________

19 In spite of he was tired, he kept working. _____________

20 During she was giving her presentation, I took notes. _____________

🦉 어휘 & 표현

- **behavior** 행동   - **organize** 준비하다   - **architecture** 건축학[술]   - **process** 처리하다   - **stay up late** 밤늦게까지 깨어 있다
- **operate** 작동하다   - **committee** 위원회   - **outage** 정전   - **evidence** 증거   - **credibility** 신뢰성

〈 정답과 해설 p. 90~91 〉

[01-04]

빈칸에 공통으로 알맞은 전치사를 고르시오.

01

- He suffers __________ diabetes.
- I'm going to live here __________ next week.

① on ② in ③ from
④ by ⑤ because of

02

- We are going on vacation ________ the summer.
- She finished the assignment ________ three hours.

① at ② on ③ in
④ by ⑤ for

03

- They need to be at the airport ________ 8 a.m.
- He commutes to work ________ subway every day.

① by ② for ③ from
④ until ⑤ while

04

- Smith felt nervous ________ the presentation.
- Hana practiced yoga ________ her lunch break.

① for ② from ③ until
④ during ⑤ while

05

밑줄 친 전치사의 쓰임이 <u>잘못된</u> 것을 고르시오.

① She waited for him <u>until</u> noon.
② Music festivals were held <u>for</u> the fall.
③ A man is walking <u>through</u> the forest.
④ We're supposed to meet <u>at</u> 10 o'clock.
⑤ My holidays can be spoiled <u>because of</u> a heavy snowfall.

[06-15]

빈칸에 알맞은 전치사를 <보기>에서 골라 쓰시오.

(중복 사용 불가)

─────〈보기〉─────
with within for by against

06

I'm sorry, but can you hold the door __________ me?

07

Most online purchase can be returned __________ seven days from the date of receiving it.

08

It is __________ the law to smoke in this building.

09

In India, you should eat __________ your right hand.

10

If we send you this package __________ airmail today, you'll receive it before Friday.

<보기>

like   from   about   in   by

11

According to the agreement, the country has to import thousands of tons of rice ___________ 2020.

12

Can you make yourself understood ___________ English?

13

When she laughs, she sounds ___________ a little girl.

14

The toilet paper is made ___________ recycled paper.

15

He enjoys watching documentaries ___________ marine animals.

[16-19] 서술형

괄호 안의 말과 전치사를 이용하여 주어진 우리말을 영어로 쓰시오.

16

다섯 명의 소년들이 헤엄쳐서 개울을 건너고 있다.
(swim, the stream)

➡ ___________________________________

____

17

그녀의 친구들 중의 한 명은 유명한 가수가 되었다.
(one, become, famous singer)

➡ ___________________________________

____

18

그 두 건물 사이에는 작은 공원이 있다.
(there, a small park, the two buildings)

➡ ___________________________________

____

19

그 서비스는 자정까지 중단될 것이다.
(service, stop, midnight)

➡ ___________________________________

____

20

빈칸에 알맞은 말로 바르게 짝지어진 것을 고르시오.

- The road is still ___________ construction.
- Lisa is the tallest ___________ the three girls.

① on – among　　　② by – among
③ in – between　　④ for – between
⑤ under – among

21 고난도

밑줄 친 전치사의 쓰임이 바르지 못한 것을 고르시오.

Kelly likes to look at the stars ① in the sky ② at night. ③ After dinner she lies ④ on the grass looking up at the sky ⑤ during ten minutes.

22

빈칸에 들어갈 전치사가 나머지 넷과 다른 것을 고르시오.

① Nobody is ___________ the classroom now.
② We have many kinds of fruits ___________ summer.
③ Both my brother and I were born ___________ July.
④ I'm sorry but we are closed ___________ Sundays.
⑤ You can get a discount when paying ___________ cash.

<정답과 해설 p. 91~92>

밑줄 친 전치사가 옳으면 ○로 표시하고, 틀리면 바르게 고치시오.

23

She was hiding her face <u>except for</u> around the eyes.

____

24

The rain changed <u>from</u> snow.

____

25

They will have to visit their grandfather <u>during</u> the Christmas holidays.

____

26

Because he doesn't have a cellphone, we can contact him only <u>in</u> e-mail.

____

27

He's usually in the office <u>at</u> 9:00 a.m. to 6:00 p.m.

____

28

Thank you <u>about</u> giving me the chance to see you.

____

[29-31] 고난도

빈칸에 들어갈 수 없는 것을 고르시오.

29

> My dad was standing _______ the door when I arrived.

① on　　　② beside　　　③ behind
④ close to　　　⑤ in front of

30

> The children are playing _______ the pine tree.

① near　　　② from　　　③ behind
④ around　　　⑤ close to

31

> They walked _______ the street to reach the store.

① on　　　② in　　　③ down
④ across　　　⑤ through

[32-34]

대화가 자연스럽도록 빈칸에 알맞게 짝지어진 것을 고르시오.

32

> A: Can you deal _______ this problem?
> B: Sure! But I'm busy _______ the next few hours.

① with – by　　　② from – for
③ from – by　　　④ with – for
⑤ for – since

33

> A: The dog is sitting _______ the door, waiting to go out.
> B: I saw the cat _______ the couch, sneaking up on the dog!

① in – from　　　② at – for
③ beside – from　　　④ before – beside
⑤ in front of – behind

34

> A: We drove _______ the forest to get to the cabin.
> B: That sounds wonderful! Did you go _______ the river, too?

① beside – next　　　② from – beside
③ next – around　　　④ through – across
⑤ in front of – behind

빈칸에 알맞은 전치사를 〈보기〉에서 골라 쓰시오.
(중복 사용 불가)

〈보기〉
between　with　since　at　on　from

35
He's been working out hard _____________ last month.

36
She was standing _____________ Tom and Jenny.

37
Your desk is crowded _____________ papers and notebooks.

38
The speaker asked the audience to focus _____________ the presentation.

39
The injured bird flew _____________ the rooftop and disappeared into the woods.

40
The seminar will begin precisely _____________ 9:30 in the morning, so don't be late.

[41-42] 서술형 고난도
어법상 틀린 부분을 찾아 바르게 고쳐 쓰시오. (두 군데)

41

On this time tomorrow, we'll be in New York. So can you finish the work until 6 o'clock today?

① _______________ → _______________
② _______________ → _______________

42

She was ashamed by her behavior during the meeting, but she knew she was also responsible to the confusion that followed.

① _______________ → _______________
② _______________ → _______________

[43-46]
빈칸에 알맞은 말을 〈보기〉에서 골라 쓰시오. (중복 사용 불가)
〈보기〉
to　at　on　for

43
She's always been good _________ singing in front of others.

44
We've waited _________ the bus for thirty minutes.

45
He depended _________ his team to finish the task.

46
I listened _________ your advice before making a choice.

47
어법상 틀린 것을 고르시오.

① I'm fond of reading mystery novels.
② She is jealous of her sister's talent.
③ We're proud of our team's progress.
④ They are accustomed to waking up early.
⑤ He is capable to solving difficult math problems.

〈 정답과 해설 p. 92~94 〉

[48-50] 서술형

두 문장이 같은 뜻이 되도록 괄호 안에 주어진 말을 이용하여 쓰시오.

48

He didn't study much, so he failed the exam. (depend)

= His success on the exam ________________ how much he studied.

49

They joined the environmental campaign last weekend. (take part)

= They ________________________________ last weekend.

50

I was really embarrassed by my careless mistake. (ashamed)

= I was ______________ my careless mistake.

[51-52] 고난도

밑줄 친 부분의 쓰임이 나머지 넷과 다른 것을 고르시오.

51

① She apologized to her coworker.
② She agreed to address the issue.
③ We walked to the nearest station.
④ I talked to my professor about the exam.
⑤ He listened to the announcement carefully.

52

① I believe in about 90% of your potential.
② He stood about five feet from the curtain.
③ Let's talk about the budget for this month.
④ They came with about ten of their relatives.
⑤ She spends about three hours on homework.

53

빈칸에 들어갈 전치사로 알맞은 것을 고르시오.

> She's really good ________ organizing events and working with people.

① on　②for　③at　④by　⑤to

54 고난도

밑줄 친 on의 쓰임이 옳지 않은 것을 모두 고르시오.

① She depends on her teammates for support.
② The cat jumped on the table when no one was watching.
③ We arrived on the train station an hour ago.
④ The test is scheduled on Monday morning.
⑤ I'm proud on your achievements.

55 고난도

밑줄 친 for의 의미가 '~을 위해'가 아닌 것을 모두 고르시오.

① He left for Germany last night.
② I've waited for over two hours.
③ This letter is for my grandparents.
④ It's important for personal growth.
⑤ She prepared dinner for the invited guests.

56

밑줄 친 부분이 '원인'을 의미하는 것을 고르시오.

① The bag is on the floor.
② He ran across the street.
③ She died of a serious illness.
④ It's made of metal and plastic.
⑤ We waited for the bus in the rain.

57

주어진 문장과 뜻이 같은 것을 고르시오.

> She entered the museum quietly.

① She exited the museum quickly.
② She walked on the museum slowly.
③ She ran over the museum building.
④ She walked into the museum silently.
⑤ She moved beneath the museum with care.

주어진 우리말과 일치하도록 괄호 안의 말을 바르게 배열하시오.

58

그들은 국제선 터미널에 일찍 도착했다. (arrived, they, early, at, the, terminal, international)

➡ _______________________________________

59

그녀는 남동생과 말다툼을 벌였다. (with, she, her, had, brother, a quarrel)

➡ _______________________________________

60

그 방은 토론을 준비하는 학생들로 이미 가득 차 있었다. (was, of, already, full, students, the room)

➡ _______________________________________

preparing for the discussion.

[61-62]

각 빈칸에 들어갈 말이 알맞게 짝지어진 것을 고르시오.

61

Yumi got anxious because she was going to the Australia ___(A)___ the winter. 'I'll be alone ___(B)___ someone with no friends on a desert island. I don't know what to do there,' she thought. Before she left for Australia, Yumi wanted to know more about the country. She surfed the Internet and luckily found a great website. At the site, she found a link for ___(C)___ people there and sent an e-mail. Soon, she got a helpful reply.

	(A)		(B)		(C)
①	for	–	as if	–	contact
②	for	–	just like	–	contacting
③	during	–	just like	–	contacting
④	during	–	just like	–	contact
⑤	during	–	as if	–	contact

62

Emily walked ___(A)___ the classroom quietly, hoping not to disturb anyone. She took a seat right ___(B)___ front of the blackboard and smiled politely. The class was scheduled to begin ___(C)___ 9:00 a.m., and the teacher arrived on time.

	(A)		(B)		(C)			(A)		(B)		(C)
①	up	–	on	–	at		②	into	–	in	–	by
③	into	–	in	–	at		④	up	–	on	–	by
⑤	into	–	on	–	at							

[63-64]

다음 글을 읽고 물음에 답하시오.

> *A Birthday Party!*
>
> For: Miya Edwards
> Date: August 18th
> Time: 6:45 p.m.
> Place: David Restaurant
> Given by: The ABC Society
> RSVP: Sophie Yu 010-1234-5678
>
> *RSVP: 프랑스 어 "Répondez s'il vous plaît."의 줄임말.
> '회신 바랍니다.'의 뜻.

63

어법상 옳지 <u>않은</u> 것을 고르시오.

① Miya is waiting for her birthday.
② People can have dinner at the party.
③ The ABC Society is the organizer of the party.
④ Sophie Yu is responsible for managing the party.
⑤ Miya may want the party to be crowded in her friends.

64 서술형

위 글의 내용과 일치하도록 다음 문장의 빈칸에 알맞은 전치사를 쓰시오.

> The birthday party for Miya will be held _________ David Restaurant _________ August 18th _________ 6:45 p.m.

〈 정답과 해설 p. 94~95 〉

[65-66]

다음 글을 읽고 물음에 답하시오.

Good quality sleep is essential ① for maintaining overall health and well-being. Poor sleep ⓐ 심각한 건강 문제를 초래할 수 있다, such as heart disease and diabetes. It is important to avoid caffeine ② before bed to improve sleep quality. Many people struggle ③ of insomnia, which makes it difficult to fall asleep. Exercising regularly can help you sleep better at night. The light ④ from screens can interfere ⑤ with your sleep if used too late at night. Sleeping in a cool, quiet environment can improve the quality of your rest.

65 수능 유형

밑줄 친 부분 중 어법상 틀린 것을 고르시오.

①　　　②　　　③　　　④　　　⑤

66 서술형

밑줄 친 ⓐ에 주어진 우리말을 참고하여 괄호 안의 말을 알맞게 배열하시오.

ⓐ (serious, to, can, health, problems, lead)

____

____

[67-68]

다음 글을 읽고 물음에 답하시오.

The Louvre Museum is located in Paris, France. It is one of the most famous museums ① in the world. The museum has a vast collection of art, including works by famous artists ② from Leonardo da Vinci and Vincent van Gogh. Many visitors come ③ to the Louvre every day to admire its masterpieces. ⓐ 박물관의 개장 시간은 오전 9시부터 오후 6시까지이다, except ④ on Tuesdays. The Mona Lisa is displayed ⑤ in a special gallery in the museum. ⓑ 사람들은 종종 박물관의 유리 피라미드 앞에서 사진을 찍는다, which is a modern architectural feature.

67 수능 유형

밑줄 친 부분 중 어법상 틀린 것을 고르시오.

①　　　②　　　③　　　④　　　⑤

68 서술형

밑줄 친 ⓐ와 ⓑ에 주어진 우리말을 영작하시오.

ⓐ _______________________________________

ⓑ _______________________________________

_______________________________ at the museum.

부정사

不定詞

(아닐 **부**, 정해진 **정**, 말 **사**)

'to + 동사원형' 또는 '동사원형'의 형태로 동사의
성질을 가지고 있고, 명사, 형용사, 부사로 쓰이는 말

UNIT 51 to부정사의 **명사적 용법**
주어, 목적어, 보어 역할

UNIT 52 to부정사의 **형용사적 용법**
명사 또는 대명사 수식, 보어 역할

UNIT 53 to부정사의 **부사적 용법**
목적, 결과, 이유, 원인 등을 나타냄

UNIT 54 원형부정사, to부정사의 의미상 주어

UNIT 55 to부정사의 시제, 부정, 수동태, 대부정사
동사나 to부정사의 반복을 피해 to만 쓰는 것

UNIT 56 to부정사의 관용표현

To exercise is important, and I need a routine to follow to stay healthy.
명사적 용법 / 형용사적 용법 / 부사적 용법

(운동하는 것은 중요하며, 나는 건강을 유지하기 위해 따를 루틴이 필요하다.)

It's important for her not to lie. (그녀가 거짓말하지 않는 것이 중요하다.)
to부정사의 의미상 주어 / to부정사의 부정

I heard her sing a beautiful song at the concert.
원형부정사

(나는 콘서트에서 그녀가 아름다운 노래를 부르는 것을 들었다.)

To begin with, let's discuss the main issues. (우선, 주요 문제를 논의하자.)
to부정사의 관용표현

 **UNIT 51** to부정사의 명사적 용법 

1 to부정사의 개념

- 「to+동사원형」의 형태로, 동사의 뜻(상태나 동작)을 가진다.
- 문장에서는 명사, 형용사, 부사로 쓰인다.

2 to부정사의 명사적 용법: to + 동사원형

(1) 주어 역할 (~하기, ~하는 것) : 주어 역할을 하며, 단수 취급한다.

- To learn new skills is important for personal growth.
  <u>주어</u>

  (새로운 기술을 배우는 것은 개인 성장에 중요하다.)

⭐ **가주어 – 진주어 구문:** 주어 역할을 하는 to부정사가 길어지면, 주어 자리에 가주어 it을 쓰고 진주어인 to부정사를 뒤로 보낸다.

- To follow the rules is necessary.
  <u>주어</u>
- = It is necessary to follow the rules. (규칙을 따르는 것은 필요하다.)
  <u>가주어</u> <u>진주어</u>

(2) 목적어 역할 ❶ (~하는 것을, ~하기를) : 타동사 다음에 와서 목적어 역할을 한다.

- They decided to postpone the meeting until next week.
  <u>목적어</u>

  (그들은 회의를 다음 주로 연기하는 것을 결정했다.)

⭐ **가목적어 – 진목적어 구문:** 5형식 문장은 목적어 자리에 가목적어 it을 쓰고 진목적어인 to부정사를 뒤로 보낸다.

- I found to work together important. (×)
  <u>목적어</u>
- = I found it important to work together. (나는 함께 일하는 것이 중요하다는 것을 알게 되었다.)
  <u>가목적어</u> <u>진목적어</u>

(3) 보어 역할

① 주격 보어 역할 (~하는 것이다): 불완전자동사 다음에 와서 주어의 상태나 성질 등을 보충 설명한다.

- My dream is to start my own business. (내 꿈은 내 사업을 시작하는 것이다.)
  <u>주격 보어</u>

② 목적격 보어 역할 ❷: 불완전타동사의 목적어 뒤에 와서 목적어를 보충 설명한다.

- We expect him to arrive at 10 AM. (우리는 그가 오전 10시에 도착하기를 기대한다.)
  <u>목적격 보어</u>

(4) 「의문사 + to부정사」 ❸ : 문장 안에서 명사처럼 쓰인다.

(단, 「why + to부정사」는 쓰지 않는다.)

what + to부정사 : 무엇을 ~할지	where + to부정사 : 어디에서 ~할지
how + to부정사 : 어떻게 ~할지	who(m) + to부정사 : 누구를 ~할지
when + to부정사 : 언제 ~할지	

- What to eat for dinner is always a difficult decision.
  <u>주어</u>

  (저녁으로 무엇을 먹을지가 항상 어려운 결정이다.)

- He explained how to use the app. (그는 그 앱을 어떻게 사용하는지를 설명했다.)
  <u>목적어</u>

---

❶ to부정사를 목적어로 취하는 동사

want (원하다),
hope (희망하다),
plan (계획하다),
decide (결정하다),
wish (바라다),
need (필요하다),
expect (기대하다),
choose (선택하다),
offer (제안하다, 제공하다)
promise (약속하다),
ask (요청하다),
agree (동의하다),
refuse (거절하다),
fail (실패하다),
learn (배우다),
try (노력하다),
hope (희망하다),
pretend (가장하다) 등

❷ to부정사를 목적격 보어로 취하는 동사

advise (조언하다),
allow (허락하다),
ask (묻다, 요청하다),
cause (야기하다),
enable (가능하게 하다),
order (명령하다),
tell (시키다),
want (원하다),
warn (경고하다) 등

❸ 「의문사+to부정사」에 쓰이는 동사

「의문사 + to부정사」 앞에는 주로 know, show, tell, learn, decide, explain 등의 동사가 온다.

2 to부정사의 명사적 용법

[01-07] 밑줄 친 to부정사가 문장에서 주어, 목적어, 보어 중 어떤 역할을 하는지 쓰시오.

01 To master foreign languages is a difficult thing. ➡ ________________

02 My job is to make books for middle school students. ➡ ________________

03 It is impossible to survive in the desert without water. ➡ ________________

04 Poor eating habits will make it difficult to stay healthy. ➡ ________________

05 His parents have to teach him how to control his anger. ➡ ________________

06 He wants her to take part in the English speaking contest. ➡ ________________

07 She decided to share the house with one of her classmates. ➡ ________________

[08-11] 〈보기〉에서 적절한 동사를 찾아 알맞은 형태로 문장을 완성하시오. (중복 사용 불가)

〈보기〉

| accept | move | skip | save |

08 They refused ________________ the terms of the new contract.

09 She chose ________________ dessert because she was already full enough.

10 We are planning ________________ money and buy a new gaming console.

11 They decided ________________ to a bigger city for better opportunities.

[12-16] 주어진 우리말과 일치하도록 괄호 안의 말을 바르게 배열하시오.

12 미래를 위해 계획하는 것은 필수적이다. (plan, is, to, essential, it)

➡ ________________________ for your future.

13 그는 그 문제를 이해하기가 쉽다는 것을 느꼈다. (easy, it, understand, to)

➡ He found ________________________ the problem.

14 가장 가까운 버스 정류장을 어디에서 찾는지 말해줄 수 있니? (where, tell, to, me, find)

➡ Can you ________________________ the nearest bus stop?

15 비밀번호를 재설정하는 방법을 보여줄 수 있나요? (how, reset, to, the password)

➡ Can you show me ________________________?

16 그들은 재생 가능 에너지에 투자하는 것이 중요하다고 생각한다. (invest, important, to, it)

➡ They consider ________________________ in renewable energy.

🦉 **어휘 & 표현**

- **personal** 개인적인
- **necessary** 필수적인
- **postpone** 미루다, 연기하다
- **foreign language** 외국어
- **survive** 생존하다
- **desert** 사막
- **anger** 분노, 화
- **refuse** 거절하다
- **contract** 계약
- **console** 장치, 기구
- **opportunity** 기회
- **essential** 필수적인
- **invest** 투자하다
- **renewable** 재생 가능한

〈 정답과 해설 p. 95~96 〉

 to부정사의 형용사적 용법 

There are lots of skills *to master* for soccer.
명사를 수식하는 형용사적 용법의 to부정사
(축구를 위해 익혀야 할 많은 기술들이 있다.)

He needs a soccer ball *to practice with*.
명사가 전치사의 목적어이므로 전치사가 이어짐
(그는 연습할 공이 필요하다.)

He is *to join* the soccer team tomorrow.
'예정'을 나타내는 be to 용법의 to부정사
(그는 내일 축구팀에 합류할 것이다.)

1 **to부정사의 형용사적 용법:** to + 동사원형

– to부정사가 명사를 수식하는 형용사 역할을 하는 것이다.

2 「**명사**(대명사) **+ to부정사**」(한정적 쓰임): '~할, ~해야 할'

– 명사 뒤에서 명사를 꾸미는 형용사 역할을 한다.

· I have a report to finish before the meeting starts.

(나는 회의가 시작되기 전에 끝내야 하는 보고서가 있다.)

· We need a plan to improve our marketing strategy. (우리는 마케팅 전략을 개선할 계획이 필요하다.)

참고 -thing, -body, -one으로 끝나는 대명사 뒤에 형용사가 올 때, to부정사는 형용사 뒤에 온다.
-thing, -body, -one + 형용사 + to부정사

· She wanted to buy anything expensive to eat. (그녀는 아무거나 비싼 먹을 것을 사길 원했다.)

3 「**명사**(대명사) **+ to부정사 + 전치사**」(한정적 쓰임): '~할, ~해야 할'

– to부정사가 수식하는 명사가 전치사의 목적어일 경우 to부정사 뒤에 전치사를 반드시 쓴다.

· He is looking for a company to invest. (×)

→ He is looking for a company to invest in. (○) (그는 투자할 회사를 찾고 있다.)

4 「**be동사 + to부정사**」(서술적 쓰임)

– '예정, 가능, 의도, 의무, 운명'의 의미를 나타낸다.
– 주로 일상적인 상황보다는 격식을 갖춘 상황에 사용된다.

예정	~할 예정이다	· The exhibition is to open on Friday. (그 전시회는 금요일에 열릴 예정이다.) = is going to open
가능	~할 수 있다	· The event is to be canceled due to the weather. = is able to be canceled　(그 행사는 날씨 때문에 취소될 수도 있다.)
의도	~하려고 한다	· He is to finish the assignment by tomorrow. = intends to finish　(그는 내일까지 과제를 끝내려고 한다.)
의무	~해야 한다	· All employees are to attend the meeting at 3 PM. = have to attend　(모든 직원은 오후 3시에 회의에 참석해야 한다.)
운명	~할 운명이다	· They are to inherit their parents' business. = are destined to inherit　(그들은 부모의 사업을 물려받을 운명이다.)

1 + **2** + **3** 「명사 + to부정사 (+ 전치사)」

[01-05] 괄호 안의 말을 바르게 배열하시오.

01 I need a ___________________ in my office. (desk, at, to, work)

02 He found a ___________________ near the university. (live, place, to)

03 She wants a ___________________ happiness at home. (bring, her, pet, to)

04 He has a lot of ___________________ before the deadline. (finish, work, to)

05 I need a ___________________ during my vacation next week. (to, read, book)

[06-10] 주어진 어구와 to부정사를 이용하여 영어 문장을 완성하시오. (필요시 전치사를 사용할 것)

06 두려워할 것은 아무것도 없다. (there, nothing, is, afraid of)

➡ ____

07 그들은 먹을 것을 거의 가지고 있지 않다. (have, they, little, eat)

➡ ____

08 나는 쓸 종이 한 장이 필요하다. (need, a piece of paper, I, write)

➡ ____

09 그녀는 가지고 쓸 펜을 빌리고 싶어 한다. (wants, borrow, a pen, she, write)

➡ ____

10 그는 방과 후에 같이 놀 친구들이 많다. (has, lots of, he, friends, play)

➡ _______________________________ after school.

4 「be동사 + to부정사」

[11-14] 문장의 뜻이 같도록 알맞은 것을 〈보기〉에서 골라 문장을 완성하시오. (중복 사용 불가)

〈보기〉
be going to   be able to   have[has] to   be destined to

11 She was to marry him as her parents wished.

➡ She ____ .

12 The CEO is to visit the headquarters tomorrow.

➡ The CEO _______________________________________ .

13 The students are to follow the rules during the exam.

➡ The students ____________________________________ .

14 There is a possibility that they are to cancel the event.

➡ There is a possibility that they _______________________ .

어휘 & 표현
· **improve** 개선하다
· **strategy** 전략
· **exhibition** 전시회
· **assignment** 과제
· **inherit** 물려받다, 상속받다
· **deadline** 마감 기한
· **headquarter** 본사

〈 정답과 해설 p. 96 〉

UNIT 53 to부정사의 부사적 용법

He got up early *to practice* soccer.
'목적'을 나타내는 부사적 용법의 to부정사
(그는 축구를 연습하기 위해 일찍 일어났다.)

His coach was surprised *to see* him. (그의 감독은 그를 보고 놀랐다.)
'원인, 이유'를 나타내는 부사적 용법의 to부정사

He grew up *to be* a famous soccer player.
'결과'를 나타내는 부사적 용법의 to부정사
(그는 자라서 유명한 축구 선수가 되었다.)

1 목적 : ~하기 위해

– 「so as to + 동사원형」, 「in order to + 동사원형」,
　「so that + 주어 + can[could] + 동사원형」으로도 바꾸어 쓸 수 있다.

• She went to the store to buy some milk. (그녀는 우유를 사기 위해 가게에 갔다.)

　= She went to the store so as to buy some milk.
　　　　　　　　　　　형식적, 문어체 표현

　= She went to the store in order to buy some milk.
　　　　　　　　　　　격식 있는 표현

　= She went to the store so that she could buy some milk.
　　　　　　　　　　　일상적인 표현

• He avoids eating junk food (so as) not to gain weight. ❶
　　　　　　　　　　　부정 표현

　　　　　　　　　(그는 살이 찌지 않기 위해 정크 푸드를 피한다.)

2 원인, 이유 : (감정의 원인) ❷ ~해서, ~하기 때문에

• They were surprised to see the new building. (그들은 새 건물을 보고 놀랐다.)

• We were relieved to find out the test was canceled.

　　　　　　　　　(우리는 시험이 취소된 것을 알고 안도했다.)

3 판단의 근거 : ~하다니

• She must be tired to fall asleep so early.

　　　　　　　(그녀는 그렇게 일찍 자는 걸 보니 피곤함에 틀림없다.)

• They must be in a hurry to leave without saying goodbye.

　　　　　　　(그들이 작별 인사도 없이 떠나다니 급한가 보다.)

4 형용사 수식 (정도) ❸ : ~하기에 ~한

– 뒤에서 형용사를 수식한다.

• This task is too hard to complete in one day.

　　　　　　　(이 작업은 하루 만에 끝내기에는 너무 어렵다.)

5 결과 : 결국 ~하게 되는

• Jane lived to be a hundred years old. (Jane은 결국 100세까지 살았다.)

[참고] to 앞에 only를 써서 〈실망〉을 나타내기도 한다.

　• They worked all night, only to realize they had made a mistake.

　　　　　　　(그들은 밤새워 일했지만 결국 실수를 했던 것을 깨달았다.)

---

❶ 부정 표현

to부정사가 목적을 나타내는 부사적 용법으로 쓰였을 때 부정 표현은 「not to + 동사원형」, 「in order[so as] + not to + 동사원형」으로 나타낸다.

❷ 감정의 형용사

pleased, happy, glad, surprised, excited, sad, shocked 등

❸ 정도를 나타내는 부사적 용법의 to부정사

주관적 판단을 의미하는 형용사(difficult, hard, easy 등) 뒤에 온다.

1 + 2 + 3 + 4 + 5 to부정사의 부사적 용법

[01-06] 밑줄 친 to부정사의 쓰임으로 알맞은 것에 ✓표 하시오.

01 She is so smart to say so. □ 결과 □ 판단의 근거

02 My grandmother lived to be 91. □ 원인, 이유 □ 결과

03 This computer program is easy to use. □ 결과 □ 형용사 수식

04 I'm excited to watch the final match in person. □ 원인, 이유 □ 목적

05 The detective drank a lot of coffee to keep awake. □ 목적 □ 판단의 근거

06 Parents should talk with their kids to know each other better. □ 목적 □ 결과

[07-11] 문장을 해석하고 밑줄 친 to부정사의 쓰임을 〈보기〉에서 골라 쓰시오. (중복 사용 불가)

〈보기〉
| 목적 | 원인, 이유 | 판단의 근거 | 형용사 수식 | 결과 |

07 He is not strong enough to lift the box.

➡ ______________________________ ( )

08 We should leave early to avoid the traffic.

➡ ______________________________ ( )

09 She must be excited to shout like that.

➡ ______________________________ ( )

10 My grandmother was sad to leave my hometown.

➡ ______________________________ ( )

11 I tried to fix the computer, only to make it worse.

➡ ______________________________ ( )

[12-14] 우리말과 뜻이 같도록 괄호 안의 어구를 이용하여 문장을 완성하시오.

12 그는 비행기가 취소된 것을 알고 속상했다. (upset, find out)

➡ He was ______________________ that his flight was canceled.

13 그는 다음 달에 승진할 예정이라 흥분하고 있다. (excited, promote)

➡ He is ______________________ next month.

14 그녀는 유기견들을 돕기 위해 동물 보호소에서 자원봉사를 한다. (help, dogs)

➡ She volunteers at the animal shelter ______________ abandoned ______________.

 어휘 & 표현

- **junk food** 정크 푸드, 즉석식품
- **gain weight** 살이 찌다
- **relieved** 안도하는
- **complete** 완성하다
- **detective** 탐정
- **avoid** 피하다
- **shout** 소리치다
- **promote** 승진하다
- **shelter** 보호소
- **abandoned** 버려진, 유기된

〈 정답과 해설 p. 97 〉

[01-05]

문장에서 밑줄 친 to부정사의 역할(주어, 목적어, 보어)을 쓰시오.

01

It is hard <u>to park</u> around this area.

➡ _______________

02

We expected <u>to meet</u> the author again.

➡ _______________

03

I think it is our duty <u>to investigate</u> the truth.

➡ _______________

04

The reason for studying history is <u>to learn</u> from the past. ➡ _______________

05

The only thing we should remember is <u>to appreciate</u> what we have now.

➡ _______________

[06-08]

빈칸에 알맞은 것을 고르시오.

06

She was surprised _______ him there.

① see ② saw ③ sees
④ to see ⑤ to be seen

07 고난도

_______ for dinner is still undecided.

① Eat ② To eats ③ To eating
④ Not to eat ⑤ What to eat

08

It is dangerous _______ without wearing a seatbelt.

① drive ② to drive
③ not to drive ④ how to drive
⑤ that you driving

[09-11]

밑줄 친 to부정사의 용법이 나머지 넷과 다른 것을 고르시오.

09

① She is happy <u>to help</u> others.
② She was too tired <u>to go</u> out.
③ He studied hard <u>to pass</u> the exam.
④ They went to the park <u>to play</u> soccer.
⑤ I plan <u>to visit</u> the museum tomorrow.

10

① Her suggestion is <u>to take</u> a break.
② I have a lot of work <u>to finish</u> today.
③ <u>To help</u> others is a noble thing to do.
④ We expect him <u>to finish</u> the report by Friday.
⑤ Do you know <u>when to leave</u> for the airport?

11

① I hope <u>to meet</u> you soon.
② Minju loves <u>to read</u> mystery novels.
③ They decided <u>to go</u> hiking this weekend.
④ Jane wants <u>to learn</u> how to play the piano.
⑤ He was happy <u>to see</u> his friends at the party.

우리말과 뜻이 같도록 「It ~ to-v」 구문과 괄호 안의 말을 사용하여 문장을 완성하시오.

12

이 문제를 혼자 해결하는 것은 어렵다.
(difficult, solve this matter alone)

➡ ___________________________

____

13

아침 식사를 거르는 것은 좋은 생각이 아니다.
(a good idea, skip breakfast)

➡ ___________________________

____

14

오토바이를 타는 것은 종종 위험하다.
(often dangerous, ride a motorbike)

➡ ___________________________

____

15

선택지를 모두 사용해서 문장을 만들 때, ⓒ에 들어갈 알맞은 것을 고르시오.

> 그는 누구도 방해하지 않기 위해 살금살금 방으로 들어갔다.
> = He tiptoed into the room (ⓐ)(ⓑ)
> (ⓒ)(ⓓ)(ⓔ) anyone.

① to　　　　② in　　　　③ order
④ not　　　　⑤ disturb

16

밑줄 친 to부정사가 부사적 용법이 아닌 것을 고르시오.

① I am glad to meet you all.
② It is better to do well than to say well.
③ She got up early to catch the first train.
④ What should I do to register this course?
⑤ We worked very hard to get a good result.

밑줄 친 부분 중 어법상 틀린 것을 고르시오.

17

> I would say my mother is ① to be the wisest woman in the world, but she is sometimes forgetful. Several weeks ago, my mother and I were ready ② to go out. My mother said she would wait for me at the parking lot ③ to give me a ride to the station. But when I went down, she was nowhere. I ended up having to take a bus to the station in time ④ not so as to miss my train. I tried ⑤ to call my mother, but her phone was off.

①　　　②　　　③　　　④　　　⑤

18

> Six months ago, Evan came to Korea ① to study Korean. Evan needed ② to buy some T-shirts and shorts because he didn't take enough summer clothes. However, he didn't know ③ to where go shopping. He asked some of his Korean friends ④ where he could get good-quality clothes at a low price. They recommended an outlet mall and told him ⑤ to go with them if he wanted to.

①　　　②　　　③　　　④　　　⑤

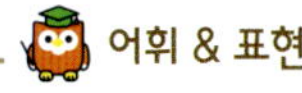

어휘 & 표현

- **park** 주차하다
- **investigate** 조사하다
- **appreciate** 감사하다
- **seatbelt** 안전벨트
- **suggestion** 제안
- **noble** 상류층의
- **skip** 거르다
- **motorbike** 오토바이
- **tiptoe** 살금살금 걷다
- **disturb** 방해하다
- **register** 등록하다
- **recommend** 추천하다
- **good-quality** 품질이 좋은

〈 정답과 해설 p. 97~98 〉

 **UNIT 54** 원형부정사, to부정사의 의미상 주어 

It's easy ***for him*** to solve the problem. (그가 그 문제를 푸는 것은 쉽다.)
　　　to solve의 의미상 주어

I saw him ***study*** all night. (나는 그가 밤새 공부하는 것을 보았다.)
지각동사 see의 목적격 보어

---

1 원형부정사 : ~~to~~ + 동사원형

to 없이 동사원형만 쓰이며, 지각동사와 사역동사의 목적격 보어로 쓰인다.

(1) 사역동사 : 사역동사 + 목적어 + 목적격 보어 (원형부정사)

> make, have, let, 준사역동사 help (to를 쓸 수도 있음)

- I made him apologize for the mistake. (나는 그가 실수에 대해 사과하게 만들었다.)
  사역동사　　　　목적격 보어　　　　　　　　　　　　원형부정사
- She helped me (to) use her computer.
  준사역동사　　　목적격 보어
  　　　　　　　　　　　　　　(그녀는 내가 그녀의 컴퓨터를 사용하게 도와주었다.)

(2) 지각동사 : 지각동사 + 목적어 + 목적격 보어 (원형부정사)

> see, watch, look at, hear, listen to, feel, notice 등

- They watched the player score a goal in the final match.
  지각동사　　　　　　　　목적격 보어 (원형부정사)
  　　　　　　　　　　(그들은 마지막 경기에서 선수가 골을 넣는 것을 봤다.)
- He noticed her leave the office early yesterday.
  지각동사　　　목적격 보어 (원형부정사)
  　　　　　　　　(그는 그녀가 어제 사무실을 일찍 떠나는 것을 알아차렸다.)

2 to부정사의 의미상 주어 : to부정사가 나타내는 동작의 주체를 의미한다.

(1) 대부분의 경우 :「for + 목적격 + to부정사」

- It can be frustrating for him to deal with difficult customers.
  　　　　　　　　　　　　의미상 주어
  　　　　　　(그가 까다로운 고객을 상대하는 것은 짜증 날 수 있다.)

(2) 성격이나 성질을 나타내는 형용사와 함께 쓰일 때 :「of + 목적격 + to부정사」

- It is brave of you to speak in front of such a large audience.
  　　　　형용사　　의미상 주어
  　　　　　　(그렇게 큰 청중 앞에서 네가 말하는 것은 용감하다.)

(3) 의미상 주어를 쓰지 않는 경우

① 의미상 주어가 막연한 일반인인 경우

- It takes 30 minutes to finish this test. (이 시험을 끝내는 데 30분 걸린다.)
  　　　　　　　　　　to finish의 의미상 주어가 막연한 일반인임

② 의미상 주어가 문장의 주어와 같은 경우

- She was surprised to see her name on the list. (그녀는 명단에서 자기 이름을 보고 놀랐다.)
  　　　　　　　　to see의 의미상 주어가 문장의 주어인 She임

③ 의미상 주어가 문장의 목적어와 같은 경우

- I want you to speak more confidently in class. (나는 당신이 수업 시간에 더 자신 있게 말하길 바란다.)
  　　　　　to speak의 의미상 주어가 문장의 목적어인 you임

---

❶ 사역동사, 지각동사
- 사역동사: ~하게 하다
- 지각동사: 보다, 느끼다 등

❷ 사역동사 get
get은 사역의 의미가 있지만 목적격 보어로 원형부정사가 아닌 to부정사를 쓴다.
- She got the kids to clean their room.
(그녀는 아이들이 방을 청소하게 했다.)

❸ 지각동사의 목적격 보어
동작이 진행 중인 것을 강조하는 경우에는 지각동사의 목적격 보어로 현재분사를 쓰기도 한다.

❹ 성격을 나타내는 형용사
brave (용감한),
clever (영리한),
honest (정직한),
kind (친절한),
nice (좋은),
silly (어리석은),
generous (관대한),
rude (무례한),
foolish (어리석은),
wise (현명한),
polite (예의 바른),
stupid (어리석은) 등

1 원형부정사

[01-04] 괄호 안의 말을 바르게 배열하시오.

01 (heard, I, yell, her)

→ _______________________________ a few minutes ago.

02 (see, leave, him, the building, didn't, I)

→ ____

03 (grow, the plants, sunlight, let, will, better, enough)

→ ____

04 (helped, the team, to clean up)

→ Volunteers _______________________________ after the big event.

2 to부정사의 의미상 주어

[05-11] 빈칸에 for 또는 of 중 알맞은 것을 쓰시오.

05 It is difficult _______________ him to write a good hand.

06 It was foolish _______________ you to fail such an easy test.

07 It is not okay _______________ them to treat their children badly.

08 It is impossible _______________ them to come back by tomorrow.

09 It is really hard _______________ me to get up early on the weekend.

10 It was very generous _______________ him to forgive his friend's mistake.

11 It was selfish _______________ her to leave all the work to you and go home.

1 + 2 원형부정사, to부정사의 의미상 주어

[12-18] 문장에서 틀린 부분을 찾아 밑줄을 긋고 바르게 고치시오.

12 It's time of them to move on. → _______________

13 She had her assistant to print all the reports. → _______________

14 How many people did you see to get on the car? → _______________

15 It was very smart of him invest his money in gold. → _______________

16 It was wise for you to have some time to think it over. → _______________

17 I listened to my favorite singer to singing *I Had a Dream*. → _______________

18 The camp counselor got the kids clean their room before dinner. → _______________

🦉 어휘 & 표현

· **apologize** 사과하다	· **frustrating** 좌절하는, 짜증 나는	· **deal with** 다루다, 상대하다	· **confidently** 자신감 있게
· **write a good hand** 글씨를 잘 쓰다	· **selfish** 이기적인	· **assistant** 조수	· **invest** 투자하다	· **counselor** (캠프의) 지도자

〈 정답과 해설 **p. 98~99** 〉

to부정사의 시제, 부정, 수동태, 대부정사

They claim **to have completed** the project.
to부정사의 과거 (to have + 과거분사)
(그들은 그 프로젝트를 완료했다고 주장한다.)

They deserve **to be recognized**. (그들은 인정받을 자격이 있다.)
to부정사의 수동태 (to be + 과거분사)

1 to부정사의 시제

단순부정사	to + 동사원형	– to부정사의 시제가 주절의 시제와 같거나 미래일 때
		• We need to solve the problem quickly. 주절의 시제와 같음 (우리는 그 문제를 빨리 해결해야 한다.) • She plans to attend the meeting tomorrow. 주절의 시제보다 미래 (그녀는 내일 회의에 참석할 계획이다.)
완료부정사	to have + 과거분사	– to부정사의 시제가 주절의 시제보다 과거일 때
		• The suspect is thought to have escaped through the back door. 주절의 시제보다 과거 = People think that the suspect escaped through the back door. (사람들은 그 용의자가 뒷문을 통해 도망쳤다고 생각한다.)

2 to부정사의 부정 : not[never] + to부정사

- I decided **not to do** the work. (나는 그 일을 하지 않기로 결정했다.)
- He warned me **never to trust** her. (그는 나에게 그녀를 절대 믿지 말라고 경고했다.)

3 to부정사의 수동태 : 「to be + 과거분사」, 「to have been 과거분사」

- The plan is **to be implemented** immediately after being approved.
  (이 계획은 승인된 후 즉시 실행될 예정이다.)
- It is unfortunate **to have been misunderstood** in such an important meeting.
  (그렇게 중요한 회의에서 오해를 받았던 것은 유감이다.)

4 대부정사 : 동일한 동사 또는 to부정사가 반복될 때, to부정사를 대신하여 **to만 쓴다.**

- You may go home if you want **to**. (네가 원한다면 집에 가도 된다.)
  = to go home
- They said they would help, but they never tried **to**.
  = to help
  (그들이 도와준다고 했지만, 시도조차 안 했다.)
- Would you like to go swimming? (너 수영하러 가고 싶니?)
  – Yes, I'd love **to**. (응, 그러고 싶어.)
  = to go swimming

1 to부정사의 시제

[01-06] 두 문장의 뜻이 같도록 빈칸에 알맞은 to부정사를 쓰시오.

01 I hope that I will catch the train on time.

= I hope ________________ the train on time.

02 Nobody believed that he had done such a thing.

= Nobody believed him ________________ such a thing.

03 She was pleased that she won the gold medal.

= She was pleased ________________ the gold medal.

04 He is the only person who won the award twice.

= He is the only person ________________ the award twice.

05 He promised he would call me back, but he couldn't.

= He promised ________________ me back, but he couldn't.

06 They thought that the fake luxury bags had come from China.

= The fake luxury bags were thought ________________ from China.

> **어휘 & 표현**
> - **attend** 참석하다
> - **suspect** 용의자
> - **escape** 도망가다
> - **implement** 실행하다
> - **immediately** 즉시
> - **unfortunate** 유감인
> - **award** 상
> - **conclusion** 결론

2 + 3 to부정사의 부정과 수동태

[07-13] 괄호 안에서 알맞은 것을 고르시오.

07 You should hurry up (to / not to) miss the train.

08 I was waiting for my name (to call / to be called).

09 Be careful (to not / never to) jump to a conclusion.

10 What questions can we expect (to / to be) answered?

11 He has studied hard (not to fail / to not fail) the exam.

12 You were lucky (not to have hurt / not to have been hurt) seriously.

13 In Korea, most students hope (to enter / to be entered) a good university.

4 대부정사

[14-19] 문장에서 밑줄 친 to 뒤에 생략된 것을 쓰시오.

14 Do you want to go hiking? – Yes, I'd like <u>to</u>. ________________

15 You can take a picture with him if you want <u>to</u>. ________________

16 It's hard to believe it, but it would be stupid not <u>to</u>. ________________

17 You don't need to do the work if you don't want <u>to</u>. ________________

18 He opened the window, though I had told him not <u>to</u>. ________________

19 I wanted to make curry and rice, but I didn't know how <u>to</u>. ________________

⟨ 정답과 해설 p. 99~100 ⟩

 **UNIT 56 to부정사의 관용표현** 

1 **seem + to부정사 :** ~인 것 같다 (= it seems that S + V ~)

- It seems to rain a lot during the winter here. (여기 겨울에는 비가 많이 오는 것 같다.)
  = It seems that it rains a lot during the winter here.
- They seemed to have forgotten[1] about the meeting.
  (그들은 그 회의에 대해 잊어버렸던 것 같았다.)
  = It seemed that they had forgotten about the meeting.

> **❶ seem to have + 과거분사**
> '~이었던 것 같다'라는 뜻으로 주절보다 앞선 일에 대한 추측을 나타낼 때는 seem(s) 뒤에 완료부정사(to have + 과거분사)를 쓴다.

2 **기타 관용표현**

too ~ to부정사	너무 ~해서 …할 수 없다 = so ~ that + 주어 + can't[couldn't] + 동사원형 …
	• He was too sad to say anything. (그는 너무 슬퍼서 아무 말도 하지 못했다.) = He was so sad that he couldn't say anything.
enough + to부정사	…할 정도로 충분히 ~하다 = so ~ that + 주어 + can[could] + 동사원형 …

	• She is kind enough to carry your luggage.
	  = She is so kind that she can carry your luggage.
	  (그녀는 너의 짐을 옮겨 줄 정도로 충분히 친절하다.)

It takes + 목적어 + 시간 + to부정사	…이 ~하는 데 시간이 걸리다
	• It takes us ten minutes to walk to the station. (우리가 역까지 걸어가는 데 10분 걸린다.)

> 참고 so ~ that을 이용한 표현을 「too ~ to부정사」, 「enough + to부정사」로 바꿀 때,
> to부정사의 목적어가 주어와 일치하는 경우, to부정사 뒤에 목적어를 쓰지 않는다.
>
> - The problem is so difficult that we can't solve it. (문제가 너무 어려워서 우리는 그것을 풀 수 없다.)
>   = the problem
>   → The problem is too difficult for us to solve. (○)
>   → The problem is too difficult for us to solve it. (×)

3 **독립부정사 :** 대부분 문장 맨 앞에 위치해서 문장 전체를 수식한다.

① **to begin with** 우선, 먼저 **so to speak** 말하자면 **to make a long story short** 요약하면 ② **to tell (you) the truth** 사실을 말하자면	**to be sure** 확실히 ③ **to make matters worse** 설상가상으로 ④ **not to mention** 말할 것도 없고 ⑤ **to be frank[honest] (with you)** 솔직히 말하자면

① To begin with, the hotel didn't have our reservation. (우선, 호텔에 우리 예약이 없었어요.)

② To tell you the truth, I really hate group projects. (사실을 말하자면, 저는 조별 과제를 정말 싫어해요.)

③ To make matters worse, my phone rang in the middle of the test.

(설상가상으로, 시험 도중에 제 휴대전화가 울렸어요.)

④ Not to mention, he showed up 30 minutes late. (말할 것도 없이, 그는 30분이나 늦게 왔어요.)

⑤ To be honest, I'm not really a fan of spicy food. (사실, 저는 매운 음식을 그다지 좋아하지 않아요.)

1 seem + to부정사

[01-05] 문장을 접속사 that을 이용하여 다시 쓰시오.

01 You seem to take a different view.

➡ _______________________________________

02 You seem to know a lot about him.

➡ _______________________________________

03 He doesn't seem to have been rich.

➡ _______________________________________

04 She seemed to have misunderstood the question.

➡ _______________________________________

05 They seemed to have had a good time in Disneyland.

➡ _______________________________________

2 기타 관용표현

[06-09] 두 문장의 뜻이 같도록 빈칸에 알맞은 말을 쓰시오.

06 It is so late that I can't cancel my flight.

= It is too late for me _________________ my flight.

07 The water is so warm that we can swim in.

= The water is _____________________ for us to swim in.

08 Her pet is small enough to be put in a pocket.

= Her pet is _________________ that it _________________ in a pocket.

09 He was too nervous to make a speech in public.

= He was _________________ that he _________________ a speech in public.

3 독립부정사

[10-13] 괄호 안에서 알맞은 것을 고르시오.

10 The idea was, (so / as) to speak, ahead of its time.

11 To make a long story (short / shortly), it was all my fault.

12 He is intelligent, (to sure / to be sure), but he's also very lazy.

13 The roof leaked here and there. To make matters (better / worse), it started to rain.

🦉 어휘 & 표현

- **luggage** 짐   - **matter** 문제   - **frank** 솔직한   - **misunderstand** 오해하다   - **nervous** 긴장한   - **speech** 연설
- **in public** 사람들 앞에서   - **fault** 잘못   - **intelligent** 지적인, 똑똑한   - **roof** 지붕   - **leak** 새다

〈 정답과 해설 p. 100~101 〉

[01-02]

빈칸에 알맞은 것을 고르시오.

01

> The manager politely asked the children __________ in the hall.

① not run
② run not
③ to not run
④ not to run
⑤ to run not

02

> The player made reporters __________ over an hour.

① wait
② to wait
③ waiting
④ waited
⑤ have waited

[03-06]

빈칸에 알맞지 <u>않은</u> 것을 고르시오.

03

> Our baseball team coach __________ us exercise regularly.

① makes
② helps
③ has
④ watches
⑤ allows

04

> It's __________ of you to say what you think.

① easy
② rude
③ careless
④ foolish
⑤ thoughtless

05

> He __________ the ground shake during the earthquake.

① saw
② felt
③ knew
④ watched
⑤ noticed

06

> It was __________ for them to solve the problem quickly.

① easy
② necessary
③ difficult
④ important
⑤ thoughtless

07

괄호 안에 주어진 동사를 어법상 알맞게 바꾸어 쓴 것을 고르시오.

> One of the best ways of learning English is __________ more books in English. (read)

① read
② to read
③ reads
④ be read
⑤ to be read

[08-10] 서술형

주어진 문장을 괄호 안의 지시대로 바꿔 쓰시오.

08

The room seemed to have been cleaned.

(that절 사용)

➡ __________________________________

____

09

We were asked to vote for him.

(to부정사의 부정형 사용)

➡ __________________________________

____

10

He is so foolish that he can't do such a thing.
(too ~ to부정사 사용)

➡ ________________________________

____

[11-15]

괄호 안에서 알맞은 것을 고르시오.

11

I am waiting (to serve / to be served).

12

My parents never let me (to go / go) out at night.

13

A lot of exercise helps me (keeping / keep) in shape.

14

I heard Joe (sing / sung) a beautiful song at the audition.

15

Jessie wants some movies (to download / to be downloaded).

16 고난도

빈칸에 들어갈 말이 나머지 넷과 다른 것을 고르시오.

① It is impossible ________ her to call us back now.
② It was really hard ________ me to get up this early.
③ It is difficult ________ me to have a good handwriting.
④ It was so generous ________ him to forgive your mistake.
⑤ It is not okay ________ them to submit the assignment late.

[17-18] 고난도

어법상 옳은 것을 고르시오.

17

① We expect meet again next year.
② They promised taking me to the aquarium tomorrow.
③ Are you planning doing something for your summer vacation?
④ I want them form study groups to finish this project faster.
⑤ I'm sure the book you bought will help you do your homework easily.

18

① We heard Sam's dog to bark last night.
② It was so stupid for Rebecca to leave her umbrella again.
③ To tell the truth, Yumi had never expected to win the contest.
④ Cathy was really astonished to elect as the captain.
⑤ He got the mechanic repairing the elevator as soon as possible.

[19-20] 서술형

다음 글에서 어법상 틀린 부분을 두 개 찾아, 바르게 고쳐 쓰시오.

> Jinsu is my classmate who is really good at math. Yesterday, I was having difficulty solving a math problem, so I asked him. It seemed very easy for he to solve the problem. He kindly explained to me how he got the answer. It was nice for him to help me.

19

________ ➡ ________

20

________ ➡ ________

〈 정답과 해설 p. 101~103 〉

21

주어진 문장과 같은 뜻의 문장을 고르시오.

> The temperature is so high that people can't work at midday.

① The temperature is high enough for people to work at midday.
② The temperature is not that high, so people can work at midday.
③ The temperature is very high, but people can work at midday.
④ The temperature is too high for people to work at midday.
⑤ Even though the temperature is very high, people can work at midday.

[22-25]

주어진 문장의 의미가 자연스럽도록 〈보기〉에서 알맞은 표현을 골라 쓰시오. (중복 사용 불가)

> 〈보기〉
> to tell the truth   so to speak
> not to mention   to make matters worse

22

I suffered from motion sickness during the journey. _________________, I lost my wallet.

23

I pretended to be confident. But ____________, I don't know if I can handle this job.

24

Ms. Park is, _________________, a walking dictionary. She knows everything.

25

James is rich, and _________________, generous too!

[26-27] 서술형

두 문장의 뜻이 같도록 빈칸에 알맞은 말을 쓰시오.

26

He was so sick that he couldn't go to school.

= He was __________ sick __________ go to school.

27

My camera is so small that you can carry it in your pocket.

= My camera is __________ __________ for you to carry in your pocket.

[28-30]

두 문장의 뜻이 같도록 빈칸에 알맞은 것을 고르시오.

28

> It seems that she was upset.
> = She seems __________ upset.

① be   ② to be   ③ to being
④ to have been ⑤ having been

29

> It seems that he doesn't have a chance to speak.
> = He seems __________ a chance to speak.

① to not have   ② to have not
③ not to have   ④ to not have had
⑤ not to have had

30

> It seemed that the audience was impressed by the play.
> = The audience seemed __________ by the play.

① impress   ② to impress
③ be impress   ④ to be impressed
⑤ to have impressed

31

괄호 안에 주어진 단어들을 빈칸에 어법상 맞게 배열한 것을
고르시오.

> I think John is __________ responsibility for
> his decisions. (enough, to, old, take)

① old enough take to
② take to old enough
③ to take old enough
④ old enough to take
⑤ enough old to take

[32-34] 고난도 서술형

〈보기〉와 같이 to부정사를 이용하여 의미가 같은 문장으로 쓰
시오.

> ───〈보기〉───
> I was ashamed that I had forgotten the
> exam date.
> = I was ashamed to have forgotten the exam
> date.

32

It seems that she is quite busy now.

= ____

____

33

It seemed that her secretary made a big
mistake.

= ____

____

34

We hope that everyone will arrive on time.

= ____

____

[35-36] 서술형

대화의 내용을 한 문장으로 요약할 때 빈칸에 알맞은 말을 쓰
시오. (각 4단어)

35

> Tim: Can I play computer games?
> Mom: No, you can't. You need to finish your
>   homework first.
> Tim: Okay.

➡ Mom made Tim ________________________

____ .

36

> Lisa: Can I work by myself? I always do
>   better when I work alone.
> Mr. Jackson: No, you can't. You need to
>   work in a group today.

➡ Mr. Jackson had Lisa ________________

____ .

37

(A) ~ (C)에 들어갈 말이 알맞게 짝지어진 것을 고르시오.

> • I had my little brother (A) book / booked
>   the movie ticket.
> • Mr. Kim got us (B) make / to make a
>   presentation about the current social
>   issues.
> • Thankfully, the police officer helped me (C)
>   find / finding the place.

	(A)	(B)	(C)
①	book	– make	– find
②	book	– to make	– find
③	book	– to make	– finding
④	booked	– make	– finding
⑤	booked	– make	– find

〈 정답과 해설 **p. 103** 〉

38

어법상 <u>틀린</u> 것을 고르시오.

① I decided not to go out tonight.
② The doctor advised her to take a rest.
③ Brian tried not to be laughed at her joke.
④ He is believed to have stolen the money.
⑤ They won't allow me to go camping with you.

[39-40] 고난도

밑줄 친 부분 중 어법상 <u>틀린</u> 것을 고르시오.

39

① She made me <u>paint</u> the fence.
② I feel the house <u>shake</u> right now.
③ Did anyone see Tom <u>to break</u> into that house?
④ We heard someone <u>ring</u> the doorbell last night.
⑤ Jenny will help me <u>write</u> the report in English.

40

① It takes me 30 minutes <u>to get</u> to school.
② She seems <u>to be respected</u> by everyone.
③ He's the backbone of the team, <u>so to speaking</u>.
④ This book is known <u>to be written</u> by a famous author.
⑤ The movie was interesting enough <u>to watch</u> it again later.

[41-42] 수능 유형

밑줄 친 부분 중 어법상 <u>틀린</u> 것을 고르시오.

41

① <u>To use</u> your phone wisely is important for your health and studies. It is not good ② <u>to use</u> your phone during class unless it's for studying. ③ <u>To not get</u> addicted to games or social media is necessary for your future success. The phone should be put away during class hours so that students can focus on their studies. Learning ④ <u>how to use</u> your phone responsibly can help you ⑤ <u>improve</u> your academic and social life.

①   ②   ③   ④   ⑤

42

① <u>To experience</u> the white nights is a unique and exciting event. In places like St. Petersburg, the sun doesn't set for several weeks during the summer. It is difficult ② <u>of us</u> to sleep during the white nights because the sky is always bright. The white nights are caused by the Earth's tilt and its position relative to the sun. ③ <u>To understand</u> this phenomenon, we need ④ <u>to study</u> the Earth's rotation and orbit. It is common ⑤ <u>to celebrate</u> the white nights with festivals in northern regions.

*tilt 기울기

①   ②   ③   ④   ⑤

🦉 어휘 & 표현

- **politely** 예의 바르게
- **thoughtless** 배려심 없는
- **earthquake** 지진
- **vote** 투표하다
- **handwriting** 손글씨
- **aquarium** 수족관
- **astonished** 놀란
- **mechanic** 정비공
- **midday** 한낮, 정오
- **suffer** 고통받다
- **motion sickness** 멀미
- **pretend to** ~인 척하다
- **dictionary** 사전
- **impressed** 감명받은
- **responsibility** 책임
- **ashamed** 부끄러운
- **doorbell** 초인종
- **academic** 학술적인
- **phenomenon** 현상
- **rotation** 회전
- **northern** 북쪽의
- **region** 지역

동명사

動名詞

(움직일 동, 이름 명, 말 사)

동사의 성질과 의미를 가지고 명사로 쓰이는 말

Traveling around the world is one of my dreams.
동명사
(전 세계를 여행하는 것은 내 꿈 중 하나이다.)

He started working(= to work) on the report.
동명사와 to부정사를 목적어로 취하는 동사
(그는 보고서 작업을 시작했다.)

She is good at solving problems quickly.
전치사의 목적어로 쓰인 동명사
(그녀는 문제를 빠르게 해결하는 데 능숙하다.)

My parents are busy packing for their trip.
동명사의 관용표현
(내 부모님은 여행을 위한 짐을 싸는 데 바쁘다.)

 **UNIT 57** 동명사 

1 **동명사 :** 「동사원형 + -ing」의 형태로, 동사의 뜻(상태나 동작)을 가진다.

– 문장에서는 주어❶, 보어, 목적어의 역할을 한다.

(1) 주어 역할 (~하기, ~하는 것) : 주어 역할을 하며, 단수 취급한다.

- Traveling around the world broadens your perspective.
  <u>주어</u>
  (세계를 여행하는 것은 당신의 시야를 넓혀 준다.)

(2) 보어 역할 (~하는 것이다) : 불완전자동사 다음에 온다.

- His dream is becoming a professional athlete.
  <u>주격 보어</u>
  (그의 꿈은 프로 운동선수가 되는 것이다.)

(3) 동사의 목적어 역할 : 동사의 목적어로 동사를 써야 할 때, 동명사 형태로 쓴다.

  (enjoy, stop, begin, hate 등) ◁ UNIT 58 참고

- They hate waiting in long lines. (그들은 긴 줄에서 기다리는 것을 싫어한다.)
  <u>동사의 목적어</u>

(4) 전치사의 목적어 역할 : 전치사의 목적어로 동사를 써야 할 때, 동명사 형태로 쓴다.

  (by -ing, about -ing 등) ◁ UNIT 59 참고

- They are passionate about designing eco-friendly products.
  <u>전치사의 목적어</u>
  (그들은 친환경 제품을 디자인하는 데 열정적이다.)

주의 동명사는 목적격 보어로는 쓸 수 없다. 목적격 보어로 쓰이는 -ing는 현재분사이다.

- They watched their dog running in the yard. (그들은 그들의 개가 마당에서 뛰는 것을 지켜봤다.)

2 **동명사의 부정 :** not[never] + 동명사

- He regrets not studying harder for the exam. (그는 시험을 위해 더 열심히 공부하지 않은 것을 후회한다.)

- He was angry about her never helping him. (그는 그녀가 자신을 결코 돕지 않은 것에 화가 났다.)

3 **동명사의 의미상 주어 :** 동명사가 나타내는 동작의 주체를 의미한다.

(1) 대부분의 경우: 소유격 또는 목적격❷

- We were shocked by his[him] not quitting❸ the job.
  <u>의미상 주어</u>
  (우리는 그가 직장을 그만두지 않은 것에 충격을 받았다.)

(2) 의미상 주어를 쓰지 않는 경우

① 의미상 주어가 막연한 일반인인 경우

- Learning English takes patience and a lot of time.
  <u>Learning</u>의 의미상 주어가 막연한 일반인임
  (영어를 배우는 것은 인내심과 많은 시간이 필요하다.)

② 의미상 주어가 문장의 주어와 같은 경우

- He admitted breaking the window during soccer practice.
  <u>breaking</u>의 의미상 주어가 문장의 주어인 He임
  (그는 축구 연습 중에 창문을 깼다고 인정했다.)

③ 의미상 주어가 문장의 목적어와 같은 경우

- He congratulated her for passing the final exam.
  <u>passing</u>의 의미상 주어가 문장의 목적어인 her임
  (그는 그녀가 기말시험에 합격한 것을 축하했다.)

---

❶ 주어로 쓰이는 동명사

동명사가 주어로 쓰일 때는 단수로 취급한다. 또한, 보통 to부정사가 진주어로 많이 쓰이지만 동명사가 진주어로 쓰이기도 한다.

❷ 동명사의 의미상 주어

동명사의 의미상 주어는 보통 소유격으로 쓰지만 구어체에서는 목적격으로 쓰는 경우가 많다. 또한, 의미상 주어가 부정대명사, 무생물, 추상명사일 때는 목적격으로 쓴다.

❸ 부정과 의미상 주어

동명사의 부정형에 의미상 주어가 올 때는 not 또는 never의 앞에 의미상 주어가 온다.

1 동명사

[01-07] 밑줄 친 동명사의 역할을 주어, 동사의 목적어, 전치사의 목적어, 보어로 구분하여 쓰시오.

01 I don't enjoy <u>walking</u> as much as I used to. ___________

02 You can improve your English by <u>reading</u> a lot. ___________

03 The workers complained of <u>being</u> overworked. ___________

04 <u>Meeting</u> new people is difficult for some people. ___________

05 I think I should give up <u>trying</u> to look good to her. ___________

06 It is said that <u>playing</u> chess helps children excel in maths. ___________

07 What I enjoy most about my job is <u>traveling</u> many countries. ___________

2 + 3 동명사의 부정과 의미상 주어

[08-12] 괄호 안에서 알맞은 것을 고르시오.

08 I can't believe (she / her) becoming a lawyer.

09 I was excited about (he / his) getting an award.

10 He is tired of (her / hers) asking questions about the soccer rules.

11 I can't understand (not his inviting / his not inviting) me to his birthday party.

12 There's no greater poverty than (knowing / not knowing) how to read and write.

1 + 2 + 3 동명사

[13-16] 주어진 우리말과 일치하도록 괄호 안의 말을 바르게 배열하시오.

13 악수하는 것은 누군가와 인사를 하는 한 방법이다. (a way, hands, greeting, of, someone, is, shaking)
➡ ____

14 그들은 바다에 가는 대신 산으로 갔다. (going, the mountain, to, instead of, to, went, the sea)
➡ They ______________________________________.

15 내가 너의 의견을 물어봐도 되겠니? (mind, opinion, asking, you, would, your, my)
➡ ____

16 너는 그녀가 거기에 가지 않은 것을 용서해야 한다. (excuse, not, her, should, there, you, going)
➡ ____

🦉 **어휘 & 표현**

- **broaden** 넓히다　· **perspective** 시야, 관점　· **professional** 전문적인　· **passionate** 열정적인　· **eco-friendly** 친환경적인
- **patience** 인내심　· **admit** 인정하다　· **congratulate** 축하하다　· **complain** 불평하다, 항의하다　· **overwork** 추가 근무하다
- **excel** 뛰어나다　· **poverty** 가난　· **opinion** 의견　· **excuse** 용서하다

〈 정답과 해설 **p. 104~105** 〉

 **UNIT 58** 　동사의 목적어로 쓰이는 동명사, to부정사 

1 동명사를 목적어로 취하는 동사 : 동사 + 동명사

avoid(피하다),	consider(고려하다),
deny(거부하다),	dislike(싫어하다),
enjoy(즐기다),	escape(모면하다),
finish(끝내다),	imagine(상상하다),
mind(언짢아하다),	postpone(미루다),
practice(연습하다),	suggest(제안하다),
stop(멈추다),	quit(그만두다),
give up(포기하다),	put off(연기하다) 등

· She avoids talking about her mistakes.
　　　　　　　동명사
　　　　　　(그녀는 실수에 대해 말하는 걸 피한다.)

· Can you imagine living on another planet?
　　　　　　　　　　동명사
　　　　　　(넌 다른 행성에 사는 걸 상상할 수 있어?)

· Do you mind opening the window a bit?
　　　　　　　동명사
　　　　　　(창문 좀 열어도 괜찮을까요?)

· I suggested going there early next time.
　　　　　　　동명사
　　　　　　(다음엔 거기에 일찍 가자고 제안했다.)

2 to부정사를 목적어로 취하는 동사 : 동사 + to부정사

afford(~할 여유가 되다),	
agree(동의하다),	choose(선택하다),
decide(결정하다),	desire(갈망하다),
expect(예상하다),	fail(실패하다),
hope(바라다),	learn(배우다),
need(필요로 하다),	plan(계획하다),
promise(약속하다),	refuse(거절하다),
want(원하다),	wish(소망하다) 등

· I decided to join the soccer team.
　　　　　　　to부정사
　　　　　　(나는 축구팀에 들어가기로 했다.)

· I hope to see you again very soon. (곧 다시 만나길 바라.)
　　　　　to부정사

· They plan to visit Jeju Island this summer.
　　　　　　　to부정사
　　　　　　(그들은 이번 여름 제주도를 방문할 계획이다.)

· Do you want to come with us tomorrow?
　　　　　　　to부정사
　　　　　　(내일 우리랑 같이 갈래?)

3 동명사와 to부정사를 목적어로 취할 때 의미가 같은 동사 : 동사 + [동명사 / to부정사]

begin(시작하다),
continue(계속하다), hate(싫어하다),
like(좋아하다), love(좋아하다),
prefer(선호하다), start(시작하다) 등

· He began writing(= to write) his novel.
　　　　　동명사　　　to부정사
　　　　　　(그는 소설을 쓰기 시작했다.)

· He hates waiting(= to wait) in long lines.
　　　　　동명사　　　to부정사
　　　　　　(그는 긴 줄에서 기다리는 걸 싫어한다.)

4 동명사와 to부정사를 목적어로 취할 때 의미가 다른 동사

try	+ 동명사	'시험 삼아 ~해보다'	· Try adding salt to the soup. (수프에 소금을 넣어봐.)
	+ to부정사	'~하려고 노력하다'	· They tried to open the door. (그들은 문을 열려고 했다.)
regret	+ 동명사	'~한 것을 후회하다'	· I regret saying that to her. (그녀에게 그렇게 말한 걸 후회해.)
	+ to부정사	'~하게 되어 유감이다'	· I regret to tell you the bad news. (나쁜 소식을 전하게 되어 유감입니다.)
remember	+ 동명사	'~했던 것을 기억하다'	· He remembers meeting her last year. (그는 작년에 그녀를 만난 걸 기억한다.)
	+ to부정사	'~할 것을 기억하다'	· Remember to lock the door. (문 잠그는 거 기억해.)
forget	+ 동명사	'~했던 것을 잊다'	· I'll never forget visiting Bangkok. (방콕에 갔던 걸 절대 잊지 못할 거야.)
	+ to부정사	'~할 것을 잊다'	· I forgot to send the email. (이메일 보내는 걸 깜빡했어.)

1 + **2** 동명사 또는 to부정사만 목적어로 취하는 동사

[01-07] 괄호 안에서 알맞은 것을 고르시오.

01 We agreed (meeting / to meet) again on Sunday.

02 The girls admitted (speaking / to speak) ill of Lisa.

03 He delayed (to tell / telling) his parents the news.

04 They decided (climbing / to climb) Mt. Halla within this year.

05 Would you mind (my smoking / for me to smoke) in this room?

06 The factory owner is considering (hiring / to hire) more workers.

07 My father promised (buying / to buy) me a teddy bear this Christmas.

3 + **4** 동명사와 to부정사 둘 다 목적어로 취하는 동사

[08-11] 밑줄 친 부분에 유의하여 문장을 해석하시오.

08 I will <u>remember to call</u> you back later this evening.

➡ ____

09 I will never <u>forget meeting</u> you at the party last night.

➡ ____

10 The counselor <u>continued listening</u> to what he was saying.

➡ ____

11 Chris is <u>trying</u> hard <u>to fix</u> this radio, but it doesn't seem easy.

➡ ____

1 + **2** + **3** + **4** 동명사와 to부정사를 목적어로 취하는 동사

[12-16] 빈칸에 들어갈 말을 〈보기〉에서 골라 알맞은 형태로 쓰시오. (중복 사용 불가)

〈보기〉

write	feed	bring	shake	be

12 Stop _______________ your leg while eating.

13 I remember _______________ her a letter last year.

14 Don't forget _______________ your textbook tomorrow.

15 People always try _______________ on a diet, but many of them fail.

16 She forgot _______________ her dog and refilled the bowl with dog food.

26 DAY

〈 정답과 해설 p. 105~106 〉

UNIT 59 전치사의 목적어로 쓰인 동명사, 관용표현

1 전치사의 목적어로 쓰인 동명사

① accuse of -ing: ~을 고발하다	apologize for -ing: ~에 대해 사과하다
be capable of -ing: ~을 할 수 있다	be afraid of -ing: ~을 두려워하다
be good at -ing: ~을 잘하다	be interested in -ing: ~에 관심이 있다
② be in favor of -ing: ~에 찬성하다	be tired of -ing: ~에 지치다
be proud of -ing: ~을 자랑스럽게 생각하다	
be used to -ing②: ~에 익숙하다	believe in -ing: ~을 믿다
③ by -ing: ~함으로써	care for -ing: ~을 돌보다, ~을 좋아하다
feel like -ing: ~하고 싶다	focus on -ing: ~에 집중하다
go on -ing = keep (on) -ing: 계속 ~하다	
④ instead of -ing: ~ 대신에	on -ing: ~하자마자
prevent from -ing: ~을 막다, 방해하다	
thank for -ing: ~에 대해 감사하다	use … for -ing: ~하는 데 …을 쓰다
⑤ warn against -ing: ~에 대해 경고하다	⑥ without -ing: ~하지 않고

❶ 전치사의 목적어
전치사의 목적어로 보통 명사를 쓰지만 동사의 의미를 나타내기 위해서 동명사를 쓴다.

❷ be used to
- used to부정사: ~하곤 했다
- be used to부정사: ~하는 데 사용되다

① The government accused the company of polluting the river.

(정부는 그 회사가 강을 오염시킨 것에 대해 고발했다.)

② Most students were in favor of extending the lunch break.

(대부분의 학생들이 점심시간을 연장하는 것에 찬성했다.)

③ You can improve your writing by reading more books.

(책을 더 많이 읽음으로써 글쓰기 실력을 향상시킬 수 있다.)

④ She took a walk instead of watching TV. (그녀는 TV를 보는 대신에 산책했다.)

⑤ Doctors warned against eating undercooked meat. (의사들은 덜 익힌 고기를 먹지 말라고 경고했다.)

⑥ He left the house without locking the door. (그는 문을 잠그지 않은 채 집을 나갔다.)

2 동명사의 관용표현

be busy -ing: ~하느라 바쁘다	① be worth -ing: ~할 가치가 있다
go -ing: ~하러 가다	② cannot help -ing: ~하지 않을 수 없다
③ It is no use -ing: ~해도 소용없다	need[want] -ing: ~될 필요가 있다
④ spend + 시간(돈) + -ing: ~하는 데 시간(돈)을 소비하다	
⑤ have difficulty[trouble] (in) -ing: ~하는 데 어려움을 겪다	
look forward to -ing: ~하기를 고대하다	

① The movie is worth watching for its amazing visuals.

(그 영화는 놀라운 시각 효과 때문에 볼 가치가 있다.)

② I cannot help laughing whenever I watch that comedy.

(나는 그 코미디를 볼 때마다 웃지 않을 수 없다.)

③ It is no use arguing with someone who refuses to listen.

(말을 들으려 하지 않는 사람과 논쟁해도 소용없다.)

④ She spent three hours being questioned by the police.

(그녀는 경찰에게 심문을 받는 데 세 시간을 소비했다.)

⑤ They had difficulty finding a restaurant that serves vegetarian food.

(그들은 채식 요리를 파는 식당을 찾는 데 어려움을 겪었다.)

❸ 동명사의 수동태
「being + 과거분사」로 쓴다.
• He is proud of being chosen for the team.
(그는 팀에 선발된 것을 자랑스러워한다.)

1 전치사의 목적어로 쓰인 동명사

[01-06] 주어진 우리말과 일치하도록 괄호 안의 단어를 이용하여 문장을 완성하시오.

01 그녀는 사과 한마디 없이 회의실을 나갔다. (without, apologize)

➡ She left the meeting room ________________ at all.

02 과학자들은 데이터를 분석하는 데 인공지능 시스템을 사용했다. (use, for, analyze)

➡ The scientists ____________ an AI system ____________ the data.

03 그들은 공동체가 함께 행동함으로써 변화를 이끌 수 있다고 믿는다. (believe in, act)

➡ They ________________ together as a community to create change.

04 많은 시민들이 대중교통 요금 인하에 찬성했다. (be in favor of, reduce)

➡ Many citizens ________________ public transportation fees.

05 그녀는 낯선 도시를 혼자 탐험함으로써 큰 용기를 얻었다. (by, explore)

➡ She gained great courage ________________ a strange city on her own.

06 그는 타인의 지시를 따르는 대신에 스스로 문제를 해결했다. (instead of, follow)

➡ He solved the problem by himself ________________ others' instructions.

2 동명사의 관용표현

[07-12] 주어진 우리말과 일치하도록 빈칸에 알맞은 것을 〈보기〉에서 골라 주어진 동사를 활용해 문장을 완성하시오.
(중복 사용 불가)

〈보기〉
be afraid of   insist on   be worth   it is no use   need   look forward to

07 이 보고서는 전문가들에 의해 검토될 필요가 있다. (review)

➡ This report ________________ by experts.

08 그 다큐멘터리는 밤을 새워서라도 볼만한 가치가 있었다. (stay)

➡ The documentary ________________ up all night to watch.

09 기차가 떠난 뒤에 승강장을 뛰어다녀봐야 아무 소용이 없다. (run)

➡ ________________ around the platform after the train has left.

10 그는 국제회의에서 연설하기를 고대하고 있다. (speak)

➡ He ________________ at the international conference.

11 그들은 차를 타는 대신 기차를 타는 것을 고집했다. (take)

➡ They ________________ the train instead of driving.

12 그녀는 다른 사람들에 의해 판단받는 것을 두려워했다. (judge)

➡ She ________________ by others.

〈 정답과 해설 p. 106 〉

어휘 & 표현
- **extend** 연장하다
- **undercooked** 덜 익은
- **vegetarian food** 채식 요리
- **public transportation** 대중교통
- **courage** 용기
- **instruction** 지시
- **platform** 승강장
- **international** 국제적인
- **conference** 회의

26 DAY

[01-04]

빈칸에 알맞은 것을 고르시오.

01

> James stopped ________ the program by himself and decided to ask Jack for help.

① install
② to install
③ installing
④ being installed
⑤ to be installed

02

> We could not help ________ for bringing food to the concert hall.

① apologize
② to apologize
③ apologizing
④ apologized
⑤ to have apologized

03

> Some people are interested in ________ the future.

① foretell
② to foretell
③ foretelling
④ being foretold
⑤ to have foretold

04

> The captain of the ship tried to avoid ________ into the iceberg.

① crash
② crashing
③ to crash
④ crashed
⑤ having been crashed

[05-13] 서술형

괄호 안의 동사를 알맞은 형태로 바꿔 문장을 완성하시오.

05

He refused ______________ in court. (testify)

06

I didn't expect ______________ this in this shop. (find)

07

Have you finished ______________ that magazine? (read)

08

He wants to put off ______________ to see the surgeon until next week. (go)

09

Emma dreams of ______________ a singer, but she can't sing very well. (be)

10

On ______________ a fire alarm ringing, please walk to the nearest fire exit. (hear)

11

As time went by, I got used to ______________ my room with my sister. (share)

12

Sandra recommended ______________ in Jumbo restaurant while we're in Hong Kong. (eat)

13

A: Did you forget to turn off the heater again?

B: What are you talking about? I am absolutely sure I turned off the heater. I clearly remember ______________ it off. (turn)

밑줄 친 부분 중 어법상 틀린 것을 고르시오.

14

① The cat tried to catch a mouse.
② Many people choose not to marry.
③ He continued to ignore everything I said.
④ Ryan gave up to write his books in serials.
⑤ The officer promised to look into the matter.

15

① I quit smoking about a year ago.
② She decided majoring in business.
③ Do you mind sharing the table with us?
④ He enjoyed fishing when he was young.
⑤ They began screaming at the ghost house.

16

① I'm used to using chopsticks.
② He could not help burst into a laugh.
③ I'm looking forward to seeing you soon.
④ She is accustomed to driving at night.
⑤ He is proud of teaching the students.

[17 - 18]

빈칸에 알맞지 않은 것을 고르시오.

17

It's been issued that many companies ________ hiring married women.

① began　　② stopped　　③ decided
④ minded　　⑤ considered

18

My parents ________ talking about my entering talent shows.

① avoided　　② continued
③ stopped　　④ began
⑤ wanted

[19 - 26]

괄호 안에서 알맞은 것을 고르시오.

19

Do you want to go on (learn / learning) Chinese?

20

I feel like (go / going) to the beach during summer break.

21

Would you mind (to not turn / not turning) up the volume?

22

My mom spends many hours (talk / talking) on the phone.

23

There are no articles worth (read / reading) in this newspaper.

24

Amy has refused (to speak / speaking) to me since the argument.

25

According to news reports, both companies agreed (to sign / signing) up for the contract.

〈 정답과 해설 p. 106~108 〉

26

Practicing (to make / making) a speech in front of the mirror will help you do well at the speech contest.

[27-30]

두 문장의 뜻이 같도록 동명사를 이용하여 문장을 완성하시오.

27

Eric suggested that we go to the movies.

= Eric suggested ___________________

___________________.

28

He doesn't remember that he met her the other day.

= He doesn't remember ___________

___________________.

29

My dream is to travel around the world before I get too old.

= My dream is ___________________

___________________ before I get too old.

30

It is necessary to wear uniforms while you are at work.

= ___________________

is necessary.

[31-32]

밑줄 친 부분의 쓰임이 나머지 넷과 다른 것을 고르시오.

31

① I'm <u>learning</u> how to play the guitar.
② His concern is <u>protecting</u> his property.
③ My hobby is <u>reading</u> a fashion magazine.
④ His wish is <u>seeing</u> his grandchildren again.
⑤ Her goal is <u>becoming</u> a famous songwriter.

32

① <u>Changing</u> your study habits won't be easy.
② <u>Returning</u> from the trip, we couldn't forget the taste of seafood paella.
③ <u>Playing</u> computer games too much might tire your eyes.
④ <u>Eating</u> a balanced diet can help you lose weight.
⑤ Ted likes not only <u>playing</u> the violin but also drawing pictures.

[33-34]

밑줄 친 부분이 어법상 옳은 것을 고르시오.

33

① I chose <u>studying</u> architecture in Paris.
② She pretended not <u>being</u> happy.
③ He minds <u>inviting</u> his friends home.
④ Sarah wants <u>living</u> in a foreign country.
⑤ Please prepare <u>getting</u> off the train.

34

① We promised <u>sending</u> them some toys.
② My sister never gives up <u>to eat</u> sweets.
③ Try to avoid <u>to hurt</u> someone's feelings.
④ He denied <u>to threaten</u> them.
⑤ I look forward to <u>visiting</u> her.

[35-37]

주어진 우리말과 일치하도록 빈칸에 알맞은 것을 〈보기〉에서 골라 주어진 동사를 활용해 문장을 완성하시오.

(중복 사용 불가)

〈보기〉

focus on	keep	succeed in

35

그 의사는 그 질병의 치료법을 계속 연구했다.

(research)

➡ The doctor ___________________ a cure for the disease.

36

그들은 프로젝트를 위한 충분한 자금을 모으는 데 성공했다. (raise)

➡ They _________________ enough funds for the project.

37

정부는 시민들에게 의료 서비스를 제공하는 데 집중하고 있다. (provide)

➡ The government _________________ healthcare to its citizens.

38 서술형

다음 대화를 읽고 대화 속의 단어를 활용하여 주어진 질문에 답하시오.

Mike: Sumi, why the long face?
Sumi: I'm worried that I might make a mistake during the singing contest.

What is Sumi worried about?

➡ She is worried about _________________

_________________.

39 서술형

기차에서 지켜야 할 사항에 관한 다음 글을 읽고, 주어진 두 문장이 같은 뜻이 되도록 빈칸에 알맞은 말을 쓰시오.

On the train

1. Do not talk loudly on your cell phones.
   ➡ Please stop _________________
   _________________.

2. You should take all your belongings with you.
   ➡ Don't forget _________________
   _________________.

[40-42] 서술형

각 문장에서 어법상 **틀린** 부분을 찾아 바르게 고치시오.

(A) Sam enjoys to walk along the river every day.
(B) Mary regrets studying not enough for the test.
(C) We are capable of create a better future for everyone.

40

(A) _________________ ➡ _________________

41

(B) _________________ ➡ _________________

42

(C) _________________ ➡ _________________

43

각 빈칸에 들어갈 말이 알맞게 짝지어진 것을 고르시오.

· I look forward to ___(A)___ from you about the final decision.
· She got used to ___(B)___ out of this kind of trouble.
· The congress member was in favor of ___(C)___ rice.

	(A)	(B)	(C)
①	hear	getting	import
②	hearing	getting	import
③	hear	being gotten	import
④	hearing	getting	importing
⑤	hear	being gotten	importing

44 고난도

어법상 **틀린** 것을 고르시오.

① He tries to avoid being criticized.
② I've just finished to read your article.
③ Dr. Kim told me to stop drinking coffee.
④ They forgot to do what their mom told them.
⑤ Don't expect to learn a foreign language in a few months.

45 고난도

(A) ~ (C)에 들어갈 말이 알맞게 짝지어진 것을 고르시오.

- I believe he won't give up (A) | to finish / finishing | a marathon.
- Vicky decided to quit (B) | to have / having | fast food to be healthy.
- The article says that this short story is worth (C) | to be published / being published |.

　　　(A)　　　　　(B)　　　　　(C)
① to finish　−　to have　−　to be published
② to finish　−　having　−　being published
③ finishing　−　to have　−　to be published
④ finishing　−　having　−　being published
⑤ finishing　−　having　−　to be published

[46-47] 수능 유형

밑줄 친 부분 중 어법상 **틀린** 것을 고르시오.

46

Kim Yuna is a Korean figure skater who won the gold medal in figure skating at the 2010 Winter Olympics in Vancouver. ① Suffering from leg injuries and financial problems, she had never given up until she became a gold medalist at the Olympics. Her mother once said she used ② to cry all the time. It shows how stressful it had been for her to go on ③ skating until she won the medal. After ④ performance her free-skating program at the Olympics, "Crying for the first time (at the game), I still don't know why I did," she said. Her tears that she ⑤ had shed before have made her Korea's first Olympic champion in figure skating.

①　　②　　③　　④　　⑤

47

Jeju Olle Trail is a fantastic place ① to visit for anyone who loves nature. ② Walking along the scenic paths gives you a chance to enjoy the island's breathtaking views. Many people choose ③ hiking the trail to experience the beauty of Jeju's coastline and rural landscapes. It is said that ④ exploring the various routes helps you connect with nature and find peace. If you plan to visit Jeju, don't miss the chance ⑤ to walk on this famous trail. Taking a leisurely stroll or challenging yourself with longer sections, either way, the trail offers something for everyone.

①　　②　　③　　④　　⑤

🦉 **어휘 & 표현**

- **captain** 선장
- **iceberg** 빙산
- **testify** 증명하다
- **court** 법정
- **surgeon** 외과 의사
- **ignore** 무시하다
- **scream** 소리지르다
- **argument** 말다툼
- **property** 재산, 소유물
- **songwriter** 작사가
- **threaten** 위협하다
- **fund** 자금
- **healthcare** 의료 서비스
- **citizen** 시민
- **belongings** 소지품
- **congress** 국회
- **criticize** 비판하다
- **publish** 출판하다
- **financial** 재정적인
- **scenic** 경치가 좋은
- **breathtaking** 숨이 막히는
- **coastline** 해안선

0

분사

동사의 성질과 의미를 가지고,
형용사로 쓰이는 말

The broken glass lying on the floor needs to be cleaned.
과거분사　　　　　현재분사
(바닥에 놓여 있는 부서진 유리는 청소가 필요하다.)

Running every day can be exhausting. (매일 달리는 것은 피곤할 수 있다.)
동명사　　　　　　　　　현재분사

Hearing the news, they all rushed to the hospital.
분사구문
(그 소식을 듣고, 그들은 모두 병원으로 달려갔다.)

He entered the room with his hands waving.
주의해야 할 분사구문 (with + 명사 + 분사)
(그는 손을 흔들고 있는 채로 방에 들어왔다.)

 **UNIT 60** 분사의 종류와 역할 

- **분사**: 동사에 -ing(현재분사) 또는 -ed(과거분사)를 붙여 만든 것으로,
  동사의 성질과 의미를 가지고 형용사 역할을 한다.

1 분사의 종류

현재분사 (동사원형 + -ing)		과거분사 (동사원형 + -ed)	
① '~하는' (능동)	– **명사 수식**: 수식하는 명사와의 관계가 능동일 때 • shocking news (충격을 주는 소식)	① '~된' (수동)	– **명사 수식**: 수식하는 명사와의 관계가 수동일 때 • bored kids (지루함을 느끼는 아이들)
	– **주격 보어**: 주어와의 관계가 능동일 때 • The movie was boring. (영화는 지루했다.)		– **주격 보어**: 주어와의 관계가 수동일 때 • He looked confused. (그는 혼란스러워 보였다.)
	– **목적격 보어**: 목적어와의 관계가 능동일 때 • I saw you running down the street. (나는 당신이 거리를 내려가는 것을 보았다.)		– **목적격 보어**: 목적어와의 관계가 수동일 때 • I heard the news reported. (나는 소식이 보도되는 것을 들었다.)
			– **동사 완성**: be동사와 함께 수동태를 만들 때 • The cake was baked by him. (케이크가 그에 의해 만들어졌다.)
② '~하고 있는' (진행)	– **명사 수식**: 수식하는 명사가 행동을 진행 중일 때 • a crying baby (울고 있는 아기)	② '~한' (완료)	– **명사 수식**: 수식하는 명사의 행동이 완료됐을 때 • a painted wall (도색된 벽)
	– **동사 완성**: be동사와 함께 진행형을 만들 때 • They are playing in the backyard. (그들은 뒷마당에서 놀고 있다.)		– **동사 완성**: have 동사와 함께 완료시제를 만들 때 • We have seen this movie already. (우리는 이미 이 영화를 봤다.)

2 분사의 역할

(1) 명사 앞 또는 뒤에서 명사를 수식 : 분사는 형용사처럼 명사를 수식할 수 있다.

- The burning candle smells great. (타고 있는 촛불은 좋은 향이 난다.)
  단독으로 수식할 경우 명사 앞에 옴
- The books published last year were bestsellers. (작년에 출판된 책들은 베스트 셀러였다.)
  구를 이루며 수식할 경우 명사 뒤에 옴

(2) 주격 보어 역할 : 주어의 상태나 행위를 보충 설명한다.

- The music was calming after a stressful day. (힘든 하루가 끝난 후, 음악은 마음을 진정시켜 주었다.)
  능동 관계 (현재분사)
- My phone was lost during the trip to Spain. (내 휴대폰은 스페인 여행 중에 분실되었다.)
  수동 관계 (과거분사)

(3) 목적격 보어 역할 : 목적어의 상태나 행위를 보충 설명한다.

- I heard the dog barking outside. (나는 개가 밖에서 짖는 것을 들었다.)
  능동 관계 (현재분사)
- She saw the car parked outside. (그녀는 차가 밖에 주차되어 있는 것을 보았다.)
  수동 관계 (과거분사)

1 분사의 종류

[01-05] 괄호 안의 단어를 알맞은 분사 형태로 쓰시오.

01 The cat ________________ under the tree looks sleepy. (lie)

02 The police are looking for the ________________ child. (miss)

03 Many people use products ________________ in China. (make)

04 Can you delete my photos ________________ on your blog? (upload)

05 Some people say ________________ vegetables are even better than raw ones. (cook)

[06-16] 괄호 안에서 알맞은 것을 고르시오.

06 The man (driving / driven) the car is our teacher.

07 I saw some books (placing / placed) on the table.

08 She wore a (shining / shined) necklace at the party.

09 The boy (carrying / carried) a big box is my brother.

10 They helped the (injuring / injured) people after the accident.

11 The girl (sitting / sat) on the bench is my cousin.

12 He saw a dog (chasing / chased) by a group of kids.

13 Who is the girl (slept / sleeping) on the sofa?

14 I saw a man (arrested / arresting) by the police.

15 Tina saw him (repaired / repairing) my watch.

16 She was (listened / listening) to music with earphones.

2 분사의 역할

[17-21] 밑줄 친 분사의 역할을 〈보기〉에서 골라 기호를 쓰시오. (중복 사용 가능)

〈보기〉
ⓐ 명사 수식   ⓑ 주격 보어   ⓒ 목적격 보어

17 The smoke <u>rising</u> from the chimney is thick. ________________

18 The concert hall was full of the <u>excited</u> fans. ________________

19 She had her hair <u>cut</u> by a professional stylist. ________________

20 The movie was so <u>interesting</u> that I watched it twice. ________________

21 I saw the robot <u>assembling</u> itself without any human help. ________________

🦉 어휘 & 표현

· **confused** 혼란스러운   · **backyard** 뒷마당   · **publish** 출판하다   · **calming** 진정시키는   · **bark** 짖다
· **delete** 삭제하다   · **raw** 날것의   · **injure** 부상을 입다[입히다]   · **arrest** 체포하다   · **repair** 고치다   · **chimney** 굴뚝
· **professional** 전문적인   · **assemble** 조립하다

〈 정답과 해설 p. 109~110 〉

 **UNIT 61** 현재분사와 동명사, 감정을 나타내는 분사 

■ 현재분사와 동명사 비교

현재분사 (+ -ing)	동명사 (+ -ing)
– ~하는, ~하고 있는 – 명사의 앞·뒤에서 명사를 수식하는 **형용사 역할**	– ~하기, ~하는 것 – 주어, 목적어, 보어 자리에서 **명사 역할**
• The smiling woman greeted us. 　　woman을 앞에서 수식 　　　　　(미소 짓고 있는 여성이 우리를 맞이했다.) • The song playing on the radio is my favorite.　The song을 뒤에서 수식 　　　(라디오에서 나오는 노래는 내 가장 좋아하는 노래이다.)	• Reading regularly to children improves 　주어 역할 　their vocabulary. (어린이에게 규칙적으로 읽어주는 것은 그들의 어휘력을 향상시킨다.) • We consider moving to a new city. 　　　　목적어 역할 　(우리는 새로운 도시로 이사하는 것을 고려한다.) • The best thing is learning from mistakes. 　　　　　　보어 역할 　　(가장 좋은 것은 실수에서 배우는 것이다.)
① be동사 + 현재분사	**① be동사 + 동명사**
– (~하는 중이다) 진행시제를 나타낸다.	– (~하는 것이다) 주격 보어를 나타낸다.
• The children are playing in the park. 　　　　　　(아이들이 공원에서 노는 중이다.)	• My dream is becoming an author. 　　　　　　(나의 꿈은 작가가 되는 것이다.)
② 현재분사 + 명사	**② 동명사 + 명사**
동작이나 상태를 나타낸다. (명사 수식)	용도와 목적을 나타낸다. (복합명사)
swimming boy (수영하고 있는 소년) dancing woman (춤추는 여자) singing man (노래하는 남자) shining diamond (빛나는 다이아몬드) flying drone (날아가는 드론)　running water (흐르는 물) burning candle (타고 있는 초)	answering machine (자동응답기) dinning room (식당)　waiting room (대기실) hiking boots (등산화)　reading glasses (돋보기) jumping rope (줄넘기) running shoes (런닝화) swimming pool (수영장)

■ 감정을 나타내는 분사: 감정의 원인을 나타낼 때는 현재분사를 쓰고,
　　　　　　　　　　　사람이 주어가 되어 감정을 느낄 때는 과거분사를 쓴다.

현재분사 : 느끼게 하는 (동사원형 + -ing)	과거분사 : 느끼는 (동사원형 + -ed)
amazing (놀라운)　　fascinating (매력적인) ①confusing (혼란스러운)　　exciting (신나는) ③surprising (놀라운)　interesting (재미있는) shocking (충격적인)　satisfying (만족시키는) boring (지루한)　disappointing (실망스러운) 등	amazed (놀란)　　fascinated (매료된) ②confused (혼란스러운)　　excited (신이 난) ④surprised (놀란)　interested (관심 있어 하는) shocked (충격을 받은)　satisfied (만족스러운) bored (지루한)　disappointed (실망한) 등

① The map was so confusing that we got lost. (그 지도는 너무 헷갈려서 우리는 길을 잃었다.)
　　　　　　　　현재분사

② She looked confused when I asked the question. (내가 질문했을 때 그녀는 혼란스러워 보였다.)
　　　　　　과거분사

③ Her decision was truly surprising to all of us. (그녀의 결정은 우리 모두에게 정말 놀라웠다.)
　　　　　　　　　　현재분사

④ They were surprised at the unexpected results. (그들은 예상치 못한 결과에 놀랐다.)
　　　　　　과거분사

1 현재분사와 동명사 비교

[01-03] 밑줄 친 부분이 현재분사로 쓰인 문장에 ✓표 하시오.

01 ☐ a. Who is the woman <u>standing</u> over there?

☐ b. <u>Standing</u> long at one place must be hard.

02 ☐ a. I saw my son <u>swimming</u> in the pool.

☐ b. My favorite summer activity is <u>swimming</u>.

03 ☐ a. Her dream is <u>writing</u> a great novel.

☐ b. She was <u>writing</u> a diary in English when I entered her room.

[04-09] 밑줄 친 부분을 동명사와 현재분사로 구분하시오.

04 <u>Sleeping</u> babies look very peaceful. ______________

05 Don't forget to bring your <u>sleeping</u> bag. ______________

06 Is there a <u>smoking</u> room in this building? ______________

07 The <u>following</u> example will show us how it works. ______________

08 Do you know who the man wearing <u>reading</u> glasses is? ______________

09 He knows his field from A to Z; he is a <u>walking</u> dictionary. ______________

2 감정을 나타내는 분사

[10-14] 주어진 우리말과 일치하도록 괄호 안의 말을 바르게 배열하시오.

10 그녀는 여행에 관한 놀라운 이야기를 우리에게 들려주었다.

(about, she, amazing, an, told, us, story, her trip)

➡ ____

11 우리는 그가 떠난다는 소식을 듣고 놀랐다. (leaving, to hear, that, were, surprised, we, he, is)

➡ ____

12 그녀는 저녁에 신나는 영화를 보는 것을 좋아한다.

(watching, the evening, exciting, she, in, likes, movies)

➡ ____

13 공연이 취소되었을 때 모두가 실망했다.

(disappointed, when, was, was, the concert, everyone, canceled)

➡ ____

14 나는 설명서를 확인했지만, 그것들은 매우 혼란스러웠다.

(the manuals, I, they, confusing, but, were, checked out, very)

➡ ____

어휘 & 표현

- **greet** 인사하다, 맞이하다 · **regularly** 규칙적으로 · **improve** 향상시키다 · **vocabulary** 어휘 · **author** 작가
- **unexpected** 예상치 못한 · **peaceful** 평화로운 · **dictionary** 사전 · **manual** 설명서

01 서술형

괄호 안의 동사를 알맞은 분사 형태로 쓰시오.

> They started selling an amazing machine __________ a tablet PC. (call)

[02-06]

빈칸에 알맞은 것을 고르시오.

02

> Can you name any word ________ with the letter Q?

① begin ② began ③ beginning
④ being begun ⑤ has begun

03

> We need to have this knife ________. It's too dull.

① sharpen ② sharpening
③ sharpened ④ to sharpen
⑤ being sharpened

04

> Is this the guidebook ________ for the travellers from Germany?

① translate ② translating
③ translated ④ being translated
⑤ to translate

05

> I'd like to interview a 16-year-old tennis player ________ the Olympics this year.

① enter ② entering ③ entered
④ being entered ⑤ to be entered

06

> Among a lot of fashion magazines ________ recently, this is the best.

① publish ② published
③ publishing ④ are published
⑤ have published

[07-13]

괄호 안에서 알맞은 것을 고르시오.

07

There are a lot of (injuring / injured) soldiers.

08

Yesterday, we walked on the (falling / fallen) leaves in the park.

09

This is the list of (leading / lead) companies in India.

10

She heard her name (call / called) from somewhere.

11

Kelly sprained her wrist (played / playing) tennis.

12

The girl listened to music, with her eyes (closing / closed).

13

We'll paint the walls, weather (permitted / permitting).

〈보기〉에서 알맞은 말을 골라 적절한 분사 형태로 쓰시오.
(중복 사용 불가)

〈보기〉
kidnap   name   blow

14

There was a cold wind ＿＿＿＿＿＿＿＿ in from the sea.

15

The police are putting tremendous efforts in order to find the ＿＿＿＿＿＿＿ boy.

16

I have a friend ＿＿＿＿＿＿＿＿ Isabella, which means "devoted to God."

[17-20]

밑줄 친 부분의 쓰임이 나머지 넷과 다른 것을 고르시오.

17

① What do I need a sleeping bag for?
② He saw a car passing through the tunnel.
③ There are two women crossing the street.
④ We didn't want to wake the sleeping baby up.
⑤ They know the singer practicing on the stage.

18

① There is a dog barking at strangers.
② Speaking English fluently is not easy.
③ He is very good at reading others' feelings.
④ Do you mind my opening all the windows?
⑤ Volunteering at children's hospital was a great experience.

19

① I found the lost key in my bag.
② The broken vase was on the table.
③ The letter sent yesterday was important.
④ He has broken his leg while playing soccer.
⑤ The tired workers took a break after the shift.

20

① The damaged car was towed away.
② She has visited Sydney three times.
③ The finished product is ready for delivery.
④ They watched the carved wooden sculpture.
⑤ He showed off his polished shoes at the interview.

괄호 안의 단어를 알맞은 분사 형태로 쓰시오.

21

We stood ＿＿＿＿＿＿＿ for the taxi. (wait)

22

David hurt his back ＿＿＿＿＿＿ taegwondo. (do)

23

The key ＿＿＿＿＿＿＿ under the sofa belongs to Jake. (find)

24

I live in an apartment ＿＿＿＿＿＿＿＿ a beautiful garden. (overlook)

〈 정답과 해설 p. 111~113 〉

25

The glass ________________ with apple juice stood on the table. (fill)

26

My wife wants our baby boy to have a name ________________ in "Jun." (end)

[27-31]

밑줄 친 부분이 어법상 틀린 것을 고르시오.

27

① The <u>running</u> water is very cold.
② I felt the car <u>moved</u> under my feet.
③ The <u>cleaned</u> office looked so much better.
④ We watched the couple <u>dancing</u> at the party.
⑤ The baby <u>crying</u> on the bed needs attention.

28

① The <u>barking</u> dog woke everyone up.
② We enjoyed the water <u>running</u> in the stream.
③ The guests <u>invited</u> by my mother arrived late.
④ She watched the ball <u>bounced</u> in the playground.
⑤ The instructions <u>translated</u> into French were clear.

29

① He was <u>surprised</u> by the play.
② The noise is very <u>annoyed</u> to me.
③ Jessy wasn't <u>satisfied</u> with the grade.
④ I'm <u>interested</u> in watching all types of movies.
⑤ The navigation was so <u>confusing</u> that it didn't help.

30

① I have <u>shocking</u> news to tell you.
② She was <u>disappointing</u> at the result.
③ It's <u>amazing</u> that he became a doctor.
④ It is an <u>exciting</u> movie about adventure.
⑤ The teacher's explanation is very <u>interesting</u>.

31

① I heard my mother <u>talking</u> on the phone.
② The picture <u>stolen</u> from a museum was not found yet.
③ The bus crashed into <u>parked</u> cars on the street this morning.
④ There are a few highly <u>experiencing</u> engineers in the repair shop.
⑤ He told me the most <u>entertaining</u> story about his days as a soccer player.

[32-35] (서술형)

두 문장이 같은 뜻이 되도록 빈칸에 알맞은 분사를 쓰시오.

32

I'm looking for a book. It was written by John Grisham.
= I'm looking for a book ____________ by John Grisham.

33

The old lady was injured in the accident. She was taken to the hospital.
= The old lady ____________ in the accident was taken to the hospital.

34

There are some children in the park. They are playing hide-and-seek.
= There are some children ____________ hide-and-seek in the park.

35

A new movie theater has just opened in the city center. The theater accommodates 200 people.

= A new movie theater ________________ 200 people has just opened in the city center.

[36-37]

주어진 우리말과 일치하도록 괄호 안의 말을 이용하여 분사 형태로 쓰시오.

36

나를 보고 미소 짓고 있는 그 아기를 보아라.
(at, smile, the baby, at)

➡ Look ______________________________ .

37

나는 100년 전에 설립된 회사에서 일한다.
(work, found, 100 years ago, at a company)

➡ I __________________________________

_______________________________________ .

38

밑줄 친 부분 중 어법상 옳은 것을 고르시오.

① I saw various colors of maple tree leaves to fall.

② Did you get a pair of scissors making for left-handed people?

③ The lights must turn off if they are not in use.

④ I was so exciting to visit the amusement park for the first time.

⑤ We will attend the opening ceremony to be held in Seoul.

[39-40]

밑줄 친 부분 중 어법상 틀린 것을 고르시오.

39

It has been ① known that carbonated drinks like cola are harmful to the teeth. Acid is one of the ingredients. It weakens the surface of the teeth by ② eroding protective coating ③ calling enamel in the long run. In addition, ④ being extremely small, sugar in the sodas can last longer on the surface. Finally, the whole structure of the teeth is ⑤ weakened by sugary sodas.

*carbonated drink 탄산음료 **coating (막 같이 두른) 칠

① ② ③ ④ ⑤

40

Antoni Gaudí was a famous Spanish architect, ① known for his unique style, which was inspired by nature. It was ② characterized by complex curves and organic forms, creating a sense of harmony with the environment. Gaudí designed many iconic buildings in Barcelona, such as the Sagrada Familia, Casa Batlló, and Park Güell. His works are now ③ protected as UNESCO World Heritage sites. For example, the Sagrada Familia and Park Güell, ④ designed by Gaudí, were listed as UNESCO World Heritage sites in 1984. Also, Casa Batlló and Casa Milà, ⑤ recognizing for their unique design, were included in 2005.

① ② ③ ④ ⑤

🦉 어휘 & 표현

- dull 무딘, 둔한　・ sharpen 날카롭게 하다　・ translate 번역하다　・ sprain 삐다, 접질리다　・ wrist 손목, 팔목
- kidnap 납치하다　・ tremendous 엄청난　・ tow away 견인하다　・ polish 닦다, 광을 내다　・ overlook 내려다보다
- entertaining 재미있는　・ hide-and-seek 숨바꼭질　・ accommodate 수용하다　・ amusement park 놀이공원
- ingredient 재료, 성분　・ erode 부식시키다　・ inspire 영감을 주다　・ heritage 유산

 **UNIT 62** 분사구문 

> • **분사구문**: 현재분사 또는 과거분사를 포함하고 구 또는 절로 이루어진 형태로,
> 시간, 이유, 양보, 조건, 동시동작 등을 나타낸다.

1 분사구문 만드는 법

접속사 · 주어 · 동사

• When I knocked on the door, I heard nothing inside.

부사절 / 주절

(내가 문을 두드렸을 때, 나는 안에서 어떤 소리도 듣지 못했다.)

~~When~~ I knocked on the door, I heard nothing inside.
→ ① 부사절의 **접속사**를 없앤다.❶

~~When~~ ~~I~~ knocked on the door, I heard nothing inside.
② 같은 주어
→ ② 부사절의 **주어**와 주절의 주어가 같으면 부사절의 **주어**를 없앤다.

~~When~~ ~~I~~ ~~knocked~~ on the door, I heard nothing inside.
③ 같은 시제 (→ knocking)
→ ③ 부사절의 **동사**를 현재분사의 형태(-ing)로 바꾼다. being은 종종 생략된다.

분사구문 **Knocking on the door**, I heard nothing inside.

분사구문

(**문을 두드렸을 때**, 나는 안에서 어떤 소리도 듣지 못했다.)

❶ **접속사를 없애지 않는 경우**

접속사의 의미를 분명히 하고자 할 때, 분사구문에서 접속사를 생략하지 않기도 한다.

2 분사구문의 쓰임

시간	when (~할 때), after (~ 후에), before (~ 전에) 등	• After he finished his homework, he went out. → Finishing his homework, he went out. 분사구문 (숙제를 끝낸 후, 그는 나갔다.) • Before I had dinner, I washed my hands. → Having dinner, I washed my hands. 분사구문 (저녁을 먹기 전에, 나는 손을 씻었다.)
이유, 원인	as, because, since (~ 때문에) 등	• Since he met her, he's been much happier. → Meeting her, he's been much happier. 분사구문 (그녀를 만나서, 그는 훨씬 더 행복해졌다.)
조건	if (~한다면) 등	• If you turn on the radio, you will hear the song. → Turning on the radio, you will hear the song. 분사구문 (라디오를 켜면, 너는 그 노래를 듣게 될 것이다.)
양보	even though, although, though (~할지라도) 등	• Though he was sleepy, he tried to stay awake. → Being sleepy, he tried to stay awake. 분사구문 (졸렸지만, 그는 깨어 있으려고 노력했다.)
동시 동작	while (~하는 동안), as (~하면서) 등	• While she was studying❷ for the test, she listened to music. → Studying for the test, she listened to music. 분사구문 (시험 공부를 하면서, 그녀는 음악을 들었다.) • As I walked to school, I saw a rainbow. → Walking to school, I saw a rainbow. 분사구문 (학교에 걸어가면서, 나는 무지개를 봤다.)

❷ **부사절에 진행형이 포함됐을 때**

동시동작을 나타내는 부사절에 진행형이 포함됐더라도, 분사구문에서 「being+ -ing」 형태로 쓰지는 않는다.

1 분사구문 만드는 법

[01-04] 밑줄 친 부사절을 분사구문으로 바꿔 쓰시오.

01 <u>As I was tired</u>, I came home early.

→ ___________________________, I came home early.

02 <u>If you win the game</u>, you can make the top 16.

→ ___________________________, you can make the top 16.

03 <u>Though he won the prize</u>, he wasn't satisfied with it.

→ ___________________________, he wasn't satisfied with it.

04 <u>Because he wants to travel to America</u>, he studies English hard.

→ ___________________________, he studies English hard.

2 분사구문의 쓰임

[05-08] 밑줄 친 분사구문을 부사절로 바꿔 쓰시오.

05 <u>Being out of breath</u>, he keeps running.

→ ___________________________, he keeps running.

06 <u>Feeling sick</u>, she left school early.

→ ___________________________, she left school early.

07 <u>Having lunch</u>, we talked about our vacation plan.

→ ___________________________, we talked about our vacation plan.

08 <u>Patting him on the shoulder</u>, she tried to cheer him up.

→ ___________________________, she tried to cheer him up.

1 + 2 분사구문

[09-14] 문장에서 틀린 부분을 찾아 밑줄을 긋고 바르게 고치시오.

09 I eating breakfast, I went to school. ___________

10 Talked on the phone, she ate snacks. ___________

11 Accept my offer, you will earn a lot of money. ___________

12 To go one more block, you will see the station. ___________

13 Gotten the bad result, I was very disappointed. ___________

14 Waiting for the bus, and I found I left my wallet at home. ___________

〈 정답과 해설 p. 114~115 〉

UNIT 63 주의해야 할 분사구문

1 완료형 분사구문: 부사절의 시제가 주절보다 한 시제 앞선 경우에, 「having + 과거분사」 분사구문

- Because I lost my wallet, I have no money. (지갑을 잃어버려서, 나는 돈이 없다.)
- → Having lost my wallet, I have no money. 분사구문
  과거분사

2 수동형 분사구문: 「being[having been] + 과거분사」 (being과 having been을 생략 가능)

- When he was left alone, he began to weep. (홀로 남겨지자, 그는 울기 시작했다.)
- → (Being) Left alone, he began to weep. 분사구문
  과거분사

3 부정형 분사구문: not[never] + 분사

- Because I didn't know the answer, I said nothing. (답을 몰라서, 나는 아무 말도 못했다.)
- → Not[Never] knowing the answer, I said nothing. 분사구문
  현재분사

4 「with + 명사 + 분사」: 동시동작을 나타내며 '~한 채로, ~하면서'의 의미이다.

① 명사와 분사의 관계가 능동이면 현재분사, 수동이면 과거분사를 쓴다.
  현재분사
- The streets became slippery with the rain falling. (비가 내리면서 거리가 미끄러워졌다.)
  과거분사
- He went home early with his work completed. (그의 일이 끝나자, 그는 일찍 집에 갔다.)

② 상황이 진행ㆍ지속 중일 때 현재분사, 완료된 상황이면 과거분사를 쓴다.
- She sat on the bench, with birds singing in the trees.
  현재분사
  (그녀는 나무에서 새들이 지저귀는 채로 벤치에 앉아 있었다.)
- He walked into the room, with his homework finished. (그는 숙제가 끝난 상태에서 방에 들어왔다.)
  과거분사

5 주어를 생략하지 않는 분사구문: 부사절과 주절의 주어가 다를 때는 부사절의 주어를 생략하지 않는다.

  주어   주어
- If it is fine tomorrow, I'll go to the beach. (내일 날씨가 맑으면, 나는 해변에 갈 것이다.)
      부사절   주절
- → It being fine tomorrow, I'll go to the beach. 분사구문

6 분사구문의 관용적 표현: 분사구문의 주어가 일반인일 때, **주어를 생략하고 쓰는 표현**

① frankly speaking 솔직히 말해서   ② generally speaking 일반적으로 말해서
  compared with ~와 비교해 보면   considering that ~을 고려해 보면
  judging from ~으로 판단하건대   speaking of ~에 대해 말하자면

① Frankly speaking, I was a little disappointed by the result. 분사구문
  (솔직히 말해서, 나는 그 결과에 조금 실망했다.)

② Generally speaking, people prefer to live in cities for better job opportunities. 분사구문
  (일반적으로 말하자면, 사람들은 더 나은 직업 기회를 위해 도시에서 사는 것을 선호한다.)

1 + **2** + **3** 완료형, 수동형, 부정형 분사구문

[01-07] 괄호 안에서 알맞은 것을 고르시오.

01 (Not feeling / Feeling not) well, I declined the invitation.

02 An apple (eaten / eating) daily, you can improve your health.

03 (Being / Been) flattered by the fox, the stupid crow began to sing.

04 (Having met / Not having met) her before, I couldn't easily recognize her.

05 (Arrived / Having arrived) at the coffee shop, he found his girlfriend gone.

06 (Not knowing / Having known) the rules of the game, I couldn't enjoy the game.

07 (Having been burnt / Having burnt) down the house, the fire was brought under control.

4 + **5** + **6** 분사구문, 분사구문의 관용적 표현

[08-12] 밑줄 친 부분을 분사구문으로 바꿔 쓰시오.

08 She fell asleep <u>while the radio was turned on</u>.

→ She fell asleep with ___________________________.

09 <u>As the water is cut off</u>, I can't take a shower.

→ ___________________________, I can't take a shower.

10 <u>Although he didn't arrive yet</u>, we started the party.

→ ___________________________, we started the party.

11 <u>If I speak frankly</u>, the work seems to be beyond his ability.

→ ___________________________, the work seems to be beyond his ability.

12 <u>As night approached</u>, bright stars showed up in the sky.

→ With ___________________________, bright stars showed up in the sky.

1 + **2** + **3** + **4** + **5** + **6** 주의해야 할 분사구문

[13-17] 문장에서 틀린 부분을 찾아 밑줄을 긋고 바르게 고치시오.

13 Knowing not what to do, he stood still. _______________

14 Traveled in Australia, I tried eating kangaroo meat. _______________

15 His having a cup of coffee, he is reading a newspaper. _______________

16 She was checking her smartphone with her leg crossing. _______________

17 Having failing the test twice, he decided not to try it again. _______________

〈 정답과 해설 p. 115~116 〉

[01-02]

대화의 빈칸에 알맞은 것을 고르시오.

01

> A: Is this your first time in Paris?
> B: No, __________ it two years ago, I know my way around.

① visiting
② To visit
③ visited
④ having visited
⑤ being visited

02

> A: __________ by a famous filmmaker, the movie was full of great scenes.
> B: That sounds amazing!

① Directing
② Direct
③ Be directed
④ Having directed
⑤ Having been directed

[03-06]

괄호 안에서 알맞은 것을 고르시오.

03

(Speaking frankly / Frankly speaking), this is nonsense.

04

(While going / Being gone) to the station, I met a friend of mine.

05

(Being / Having been) only sixteen, I can't get a driver's license.

06

(Not talking / Talking not) much, we are able to know what the other thinks.

[07-08]

두 문장의 뜻이 같도록 빈칸에 알맞은 것을 고르시오.

07

> After I finished writing an article, I left for New York.
> = __________________, I left for New York.

① I finishing writing an article
② After finished writing an article
③ Being finished writing an article
④ After finishing writing an article
⑤ Having been finished writing an article

08

> Looking out the window, she saw lightning flashing in the sky.
> = __________________, she saw lightning flashing in the sky.

① Before she looked out the window
② When she looked out the window
③ Unless she looked out the window
④ Although she looked out the window
⑤ Even though she looked out the window

09

주어진 우리말과 일치하도록 빈칸에 알맞은 것을 고르시오.

> 솔직히 말하자면, 나는 그의 선물이 마음에 들지 않았다.
> ➡ __________________, I didn't like his present.

① To be sure
② Strange to say
③ To begin with
④ Frankly speaking
⑤ Roughly speaking

10

밑줄 친 부분을 어법상 알맞은 형태로 바꾼 것끼리 짝지어진 것을 고르시오.

> • <u>Surprise</u>, she dropped the phone and stepped back.
> • <u>Carry</u> a heavy box, he struggled to open the door.

① Surprise – Carrying
② Surprising – Carrying
③ Surprising – Carried
④ Surprised – Carrying
⑤ Surprised – Carried

[11-15] 서술형

주어진 문장을 분사구문을 이용하여 다시 쓰시오. (단, 접속사는 생략할 것)

11

As she felt tired, she lay down on the bed.

➡ ________________________, she lay down on the bed.

12

While I was walking my dog, I came across an old friend of mine.

➡ ________________________, I came across an old friend of mine.

13

Although she was an hour late, she didn't say a word of apology.

➡ ________________________, she didn't say a word of apology.

14

Because I didn't know where to go, I stopped to ask for directions.

➡ ________________________ where to go, I stopped to ask for directions.

15

After Elly had dinner with me, she went back home.

➡ ________________________ dinner with me, Elly went back home.

16

밑줄 친 분사구문에서 생략된 접속사의 의미가 나머지 넷과 다른 것을 고르시오.

① <u>Being poor</u>, she never loses her smile.
② <u>Being so young</u>, she is a world-famous painter.
③ <u>Reading a newspaper in the sofa</u>, I felt relaxed.
④ <u>Written by a child</u>, the article was well-written and persuasive.
⑤ <u>Not knowing how to solve the puzzle</u>, he pretends to know about it.

[17-20]

밑줄 친 부분과 바꿔 쓸 수 있는 것을 고르시오.

17

> <u>Tired</u> from the work all day long, he couldn't stop packing his suitcase.

① If he was tired
② Since he was tired
③ After he was tired
④ Because he was tired
⑤ Even though he was tired

18

> <u>Getting off the bus</u>, I noticed I had left my bag.

① When I got off the bus
② Though I got off the bus
③ Because I got off the bus
④ Although I got off the bus
⑤ Even though I got off the bus

〈 정답과 해설 p. 116~117 〉

19

> Handing in my assignment, I played computer games.

① If I handed in my assignment
② After I handed in my assignment
③ While I handed in my assignment
④ Though I handed in my assignment
⑤ Although I handed in my assignment

20

> Not knowing what to say, everyone kept silent.

① If they didn't know what to say
② As they didn't know what to say
③ After they didn't know what to say
④ Before they didn't know what to say
⑤ Though they didn't know what to say

[21-24] 서술형

밑줄 친 분사구문은 부사절로, 부사절은 분사구문으로 알맞게 바꿔 쓰시오.

21

You'd better not speak <u>while your back is turned</u>.

➡ You'd better not speak with ____________ ____________.

22

<u>After I checked in the hotel</u>, I called Mom.

➡ ____________________, I called Mom.

23

<u>As he saw the advertisement</u>, he knows about the festival.

➡ ____________________, he knows about the festival.

24 고난도

<u>If there are no empty seats on the train</u>, you have to keep standing.

➡ ____________________, you have to keep standing.

[25-26]

주어진 우리말과 일치하도록 빈칸에 알맞은 것을 고르시오.

25

> 영어로 쓰여 있기 때문에, 그 책은 아이들이 읽기 어려웠다.
> ➡ ____________________, the book was difficult for children to read.

① Writing in English
② Written in English
③ Be written in English
④ Been written in English
⑤ Being writing in English

26

> 어디로 가야 할지 몰라서, 나는 주변을 둘러보았다.
> ➡ ____________________, I looked all around.

① Not know where to go
② Not known where to go
③ To know not where to go
④ Knowing not where to go
⑤ Not knowing where to go

[27-31] 서술형

주어진 우리말과 일치하도록 괄호 안의 지시대로 문장을 완성하시오.

27

TV 앞에 앉아서, 그는 저녁을 먹었다. (분사구문으로)
➡ ____________ in front of the TV, he had dinner.

28

비가 내리기 시작했기 때문에, 우리는 택시를 탔다.
(부사절로)

➡ ___________ ___________ ___________

___________, we took a taxi.

29

전화번호가 맞는지 확인한 후에, Jane은 다시 전화를 걸었다. (분사구문으로)

➡ After ___________ if she had the right number, Jane phoned again.

30

김 선생님은 손가락으로 서류를 가리키며 그를 바라보고 있었다. (분사구문으로)

➡ Ms. Kim was staring at him with her finger ___________ at the document.

31

이력서로 판단하건대, 그녀는 충분히 자격이 있다.
(비인칭 독립분사구문으로)

➡ ___________ ___________ her résumé,

she's highly qualified.

[32-33]

밑줄 친 부분 중 어법상 틀린 것을 고르시오.

32

① It getting dark fast, we had to hurry.
② Barking loudly, the dog ran toward me.
③ Being sick, I could not go to work today.
④ You being uncooperative, we can't finish this project in time.
⑤ Being giving a gift on his birthday, Jack felt so good.

33

① Try not to speak with your mouth full.
② James was talking with his arms crossing.
③ She spoke with tears rolling down her face.
④ Do you often sleep with the television on?
⑤ He was thinking about something with his back against the wall.

34

빈칸에 들어갈 말이 알맞게 짝지어진 것을 고르시오.

> ___(A)___ as the son of a slave, John didn't have many chances to learn. However, he got eleven degrees and learned six languages in his life. He never stopped ___(B)___. He said, "It's always such a great pleasure for me to learn."

	(A)		(B)
①	Born	–	to learn
②	Born	–	learning
③	Having born	–	to learn
④	Being having born	–	learning
⑤	Having being born	–	to learn

[35-36]

밑줄 친 부분이 어법상 옳은 것을 고르시오.

35

① People looked at the fire burned furiously.
② Do you know the building calling 'Miracle'?
③ What is the first language speaking in your country?
④ They left the house with the dog barking fiercely.
⑤ Most of the questioning people hesitated to answer the survey.

‹ 정답과 해설 p. 117~118 ›

36

① Turning red, you can't cross the street.
② Being rainy, we decided to stay at home.
③ Having not his hearing aid, John couldn't hear what I said.
④ The woman is sitting on the bench with her hair blown in the wind.
⑤ Judging from his accent, Mr. Park must be from Australia.

37 서술형

주어진 우리말과 일치하도록 〈조건〉에 맞게 영작하시오.

〈조건〉
• With로 문장을 시작할 것
• cry를 활용할 것
• 4단어로 적을 것

아기가 울고 있어서, 그들은 전화를 일찍 끊어야 했다.

➡ ____________________, they had to end the call early.

38 고난도

밑줄 친 부분에 관해 잘못 이야기한 학생을 고르시오.

• ⓐ Not knowing what to say, I just nodded.
• ⓑ Speaking of birthdays, mine is next week!
• ⓒ With everyone watched, he made a mistake.

① 지혜: ⓐ는 부정형 분사구문으로, 분사 앞에 not을 쓴 건 적절해.
② 준호: 맞아. not 대신 never를 부정형에 쓰기도 해.
③ 은지: ⓑ는 '~에 대해 말하자면'이라는 뜻의 분사구문의 관용적 표현이야.
④ 지민: 분사구문의 관용적 표현은 주어가 you일 때 생략하고 쓰는 표현이야.
⑤ 이서: ⓒ에서 everyone과 watch의 관계가 능동이므로 watching으로 고쳐야 해.

[39-40] 수능 유형

밑줄 친 부분 중 어법상 틀린 것을 고르시오.

39

When Ronald Reagan was the governor of California, he made a speech in Mexico City. ① Finished speaking, he took his seat. But the audience didn't give him an applause, so he felt ② embarrassed. The next speaker spoke in Spanish, which Reagan didn't understand. And the speaker was ③ applauded about every paragraph. To protect his pride, Reagan started ④ clapping before everyone else and longer than anyone else. Then the U.S. ambassador went to him and said quietly, "Sir, if I were you, I wouldn't do that. He is ⑤ translating your speech into Spanish."

①   ②   ③   ④   ⑤

40

The Eden Project in Cornwall, England, is a unique collection of biomes, ① designed to blend with nature. It showcases the relationship between humans and the environment, ② housing thousands of plant species from different climates. ③ Built in an old clay pit, the biomes appear to grow naturally from the land. Visitors walk through lush rainforests, ④ surrounded by vibrant plants and trees. The transparent domes, ⑤ making with hexagonal panels, let sunlight in, creating ideal conditions for various ecosystems.

*biome 생물 군계 **hexagonal 육각형의

①   ②   ③   ④   ⑤

어휘 & 표현

• **filmmaker** 영화 제작자 • **nonsense** 터무니 없는 생각 • **flash** 반짝이다 • **struggle** 고군분투하다 • **come across** 우연히 만나다
• **apology** 사과 • **persuasive** 설득력 있는 • **silent** 침묵하는 • **advertisement** 광고 • **empty** 빈 • **résumé** 이력서
• **qualified** 자격이 있는 • **uncooperative** 비협조적인 • **slave** 노예 • **furiously** 맹렬하게 • **hesitate** 망설이다
• **governor** 주지사 • **applaud** 박수를 치다 • **ambassador** 대사 • **vibrant** 생기가 넘치는 • **transparent** 투명한

P

관계사

關係詞

(관계할 관, 맬 계, 말 사)
선행사를 대신하여
접속사처럼 두 문장을 연결하는 말

The car that he bought last week is very expensive.
관계대명사 that
(그가 지난주에 산 차는 매우 비싸다.)

What they did was absolutely amazing. (그들이 한 일은 정말 놀라웠다.)
관계대명사 what

Do you know a restaurant where we can sit outside?
관계부사 where
(야외에서 앉을 수 있는 식당 알아?)

Whatever happens, I will always be here for you.
복합관계대명사
(무슨 일이 있더라도 나는 항상 너를 위해 여기 있을 거야.)

I'll visit you whenever I'm in town. (나는 도시에 있을 때마다 너를 방문할 거야.)
복합관계부사

 UNIT **64** 관계대명사 

> • **관계대명사**: 선행사를 대신하는 대명사와 두 문장을 연결하는 접속사 역할을 동시에 한다.
> who, which, that, what 등이 있다.

1 관계대명사의 역할: 선행사를 수식하며 「접속사 + 대명사」의 역할을 한다.

❶ 선행사
앞에 있는 명사

- There are many people and they want to join the team.
  선행사　　　「접속사 + 대명사」

  (많은 사람들이 있는데, 그들은 그 팀에 합류하고 싶어 한다.)

  → There are many people who want to join the team. (그 팀에 합류하고 싶어 하는 많은 사람들이 있다.)
  선행사　　　형용사절을 이끄는 관계대명사

2 관계대명사의 종류

– 관계대명사가 관계대명사절에서 하는 역할에 따라 주격, 목적격, 소유격으로 구분한다.

선행사 ＼ 관계대명사의 격	❷ 주격	❸ 목적격	❹ 소유격
사람	who	who, whom	whose
사물, 동물	which	which	whose
사람, 사물, 동물	that	that	–
없음	what	what	–

❷ 주격 관계대명사
관계대명사절 안에서 주어 역할을 한다.

❸ 목적격 관계대명사
관계대명사절 안에서 목적어 역할을 한다.

❹ 소유격 관계대명사
관계대명사 뒤에 나오는 명사와 소유 관계를 나타낸다.

3 who, who(m), whose – 선행사가 사람일 때

who (주격)	• I know the person. The person is in charge of the finance. (나는 그 사람을 안다. 그 사람은 재정을 담당한다.) → I know the person who is in charge of the finance. (나는 재정을 담당하는 그 사람을 안다.) 주어 역할
who(m) (목적격)	• The people all showed up. We invited them. (사람들은 모두 나타났다. 우리는 그들을 초대했다.) → The people who(m) we invited all showed up. (우리가 초대한 사람들은 모두 왔다.) 목적어 역할
whose (소유격)	• The man calls the police. His car was stolen. (그 남자는 경찰에 신고한다. 그의 차는 도난당했다.) → The man whose car was stolen calls the police. (차를 도난당한 그 남자는 경찰에 신고한다.) 소유 관계를 나타냄

4 which, whose – 선행사가 사물, 동물일 때

which (주격)	• She likes the cake. The cake has mangoes on top. (그녀는 그 케이크를 좋아한다. 그 케이크는 망고가 위에 올라가 있다.) → She likes the cake which has mangoes on top. 주어 역할 (그녀는 망고가 위에 올라간 케이크를 좋아한다.)
which (목적격)	• The dress is beautiful. She chose it for the wedding. (그 드레스는 아름답다. 그녀는 결혼식을 위해 그것을 골랐다.) → The dress which she chose for the wedding is beautiful. 목적어 역할 (그녀가 결혼식을 위해 고른 그 드레스는 아름답다.)
whose (소유격)	• This is the book. Its cover is torn. (이것은 책이다. 그것의 표지는 찢어졌다.) → This is the book whose cover is torn. (이것은 표지가 찢어진 책이다.) 소유 관계를 나타냄

1 + **2** 관계대명사

[01-04] 두 문장을 한 문장으로 쓸 때, 빈칸에 알맞은 관계대명사를 〈보기〉에서 골라 쓰시오. (중복 사용 불가)

〈보기〉
whose   which   who   whom

01 I hired an intern. The intern speaks fluently in Chinese.

➡ I hired an intern ＿＿＿＿＿＿＿ speaks fluently in Chinese.

02 She adopted a parrot. Its feathers are bright green and blue.

➡ She adopted a parrot ＿＿＿＿＿＿＿ feathers are bright green and blue.

03 He greeted the guests. He had met them during his summer vacation.

➡ He greeted the guests ＿＿＿＿＿＿＿ he had met during his summer vacation.

04 The box had plenty of candy. It was delivered to me this morning.

➡ The box ＿＿＿＿＿＿＿ was delivered to me this morning had plenty of candy.

3 who, who(m), whose

[05-07] 두 문장을 관계대명사(who(m), whose)로 연결하여 쓰시오.

05 The person is my boss. + You called him.

➡ The person ＿＿＿＿＿＿＿＿＿＿＿＿＿＿＿＿ .

06 The student is very smart. + He solved the problem.

➡ The student ＿＿＿＿＿＿＿＿＿＿＿＿＿＿＿ .

07 The team is struggling this season. + Its coach was fired.

➡ The team ＿＿＿＿＿＿＿＿＿＿＿＿＿＿＿＿ .

4 which, whose

[08-10] 밑줄 친 부분의 역할을 〈보기〉에서 골라 쓰시오. (중복 사용 불가)

〈보기〉
주격 관계대명사   목적격 관계대명사   소유격 관계대명사

08 The car which makes that strange noise needs to be fixed.   ＿＿＿＿＿＿＿

09 She found a cat whose leg was broken badly.   ＿＿＿＿＿＿＿

10 I found a letter which my grandfather had written in 1950.   ＿＿＿＿＿＿＿

🦉 **어휘 & 표현**

· **in charge of** ~를 맡아서   · **finance** 재정   · **tear** 찢다(- tore - torn)   · **adopt** 입양하다   · **parrot** 앵무새
· **feather** 깃털   · **struggle** 애쓰다   · **fire** 해고하다   · **strange** 이상한, 수상한   · **noise** 소음

〈 정답과 해설 **p. 119** 〉

 **UNIT 65** 관계대명사 that, what 

Neil Armstrong was the first person ***that*** walked on the moon.
the first person을 선행사로 하는 주격 관계대명사
(Neil Armstrong은 달에서 걸어 다닌 최초의 사람이었다.)

What he wanted was to go into space.
선행사가 포함된 관계대명사

(그가 원했던 것은 우주에 가는 것이었다.)

1 that – 선행사가 사람, 사물, 동물일 때

(1) 관계대명사 who, whom, which 주격과 목적격을 대신할 수 있다.

• She is the person who(m)[that] I admire the most.
who(m) 대신 that을 쓸 수 있음

(그녀는 내가 가장 존경하는 사람이다.)

• There is a house which[that] we used to live in. (우리가 살던 집이 있다.)
which 대신 that을 쓸 수 있음

❶ 관계사절의 「동사+전치사」

관계사절에서 「동사+전치사」는 그대로 쓰거나, 전치사를 관계대명사 앞에 쓰는 것 모두 가능하다. 단, 전치사가 관계대명사 앞에 올 때 that은 쓸 수 없다.

(2) 선행사에 다음이 포함되어 있을 때는 주로 that을 쓴다.

사람 + 사물, 동물	• The teacher and the book that inspired me are both famous. (나에게 영감을 준 선생님과 책은 둘 다 유명하다.)
서수, 최상급, the only, very, same	• She is the best singer that I have ever heard. (그녀는 내가 지금까지 들었던 최고의 가수이다.) • This is the only restaurant that serves vegetarian food. (이것은 채식 음식을 제공하는 유일한 레스토랑이다.)
-thing	• I need something that helps me finish this project. (나는 이 프로젝트를 끝내는 데 도움이 될 무언가가 필요해.)
all, much, little, no	• All that I could do was apologize. (내가 할 수 있는 모든 것은 사과하는 것이었다.)
who, which, what 으로 시작하는 의문문	• Who is the person that called me earlier? (나에게 아까 전화한 사람은 누구인가요?)

주의 관계대명사 that을 쓸 수 없는 경우

- 관계대명사가 전치사 바로 뒤에서 목적어로 쓰일 때
- 소유격 관계대명사를 대신해야 할 때
- 관계대명사가 계속적 용법으로 쓰일 때

2 what – 선행사가 없을 때

(1) 선행사를 포함하고 있으므로 앞에 선행사가 없다.

the thing(s) which[that]로 바꿔쓸 수 있다. ('~하는 것(들)'으로 해석)

• This is exactly what I was looking for! (이것이 바로 내가 찾고 있던 것이야!)
= the thing which[that]

(2) 주어, 목적어, 보어가 되는 명사절 역할을 한다. (소유격은 쓰지 않는다.)

주어	• What you should focus on is building consistent habits. 문장의 주어 (당신이 집중해야 할 것은 꾸준한 습관을 만드는 것이다.)
목적어	• I'll never forget what happened that day. (나는 그날 일어난 것을 절대 잊지 않을 거야.) 문장의 목적어
보어	• The truth is what nobody wants to admit. (진실은 아무도 인정하고 싶어 하지 않는 것이다.) 문장의 보어

1 that

[01-07] 괄호 안에서 알맞은 것을 고르시오.

01 What is it (which / that) is behind the tree?

02 Do you know the man (whom / that) is smiling at you?

03 My mom has a friend (that / whose) husband is a doctor.

04 There's a saying that all (which / that) glitters is not gold.

05 Do you know anything (which / that) makes me lose my appetite?

06 Can you remember the man (which / that) you picked up at the airport?

07 Mina and her dog (that / which) were dressed in pink drew people's attention.

2 what

[08-12] 주어진 우리말과 일치하도록 관계대명사 what과 주어진 말을 이용하여 빈칸을 완성하시오.

08 나는 그가 하고 있는 말을 이해할 수 없다. (say)

➡ I can't understand ______________________________________.

09 네 손에 가지고 있는 것을 내게 보여 줘. (have, in your hand)

➡ Show me ______________________________________.

10 그가 원하는 것은 네 마음으로부터 우러난 사과이다. (want)

➡ ______________________________ is an apology from the bottom of your heart.

11 그것은 내가 너에게 해 달라고 부탁했던 것이 아니다. (ask, you, to do)

➡ That is not ______________________________________.

12 그는 내게 그가 개울에서 찾아낸 것을 주었다. (had found, in the stream)

➡ He gave me ______________________________________.

1 + 2 관계대명사 that, what

[13-18] 문장에서 틀린 부분을 찾아 밑줄을 긋고 바르게 고치시오.

13 Anyone whom is interested in music is welcome. ______________

14 I feel awfully sorry for that I have done. ______________

15 The promises what I made to my mother were not kept. ______________

16 That we need is a pair of scissors and three pieces of colored paper. ______________

17 He has a watch what costs 1,000 dollars. ______________

18 She was the last person whom I had an interview with. ______________

〈 정답과 해설 p. 119~120 〉

UNIT 66 관계대명사의 계속적 용법과 생략

1 관계대명사의 계속적 용법: 관계대명사 앞에 콤마(,)를 붙여 선행사에 관한 추가 정보를 덧붙인다.

(1) 「**접속사 + 대명사**」로 바꾸어 쓸 수 있다. (접속사: and, but, because 등)

- They moved to Canada, which has better natural environments.
  (= and it)
  (그들은 캐나다로 이사했는데, 그곳은 자연환경이 더 좋다.)

(2) 계속적 용법의 관계대명사 who(m), which는 that으로 바꿔쓸 수 없다.

- He bought a new phone, ~~that~~(→ which) has better performance than his PC.
  (그는 새로운 휴대폰을 샀는데, 그것은 그의 컴퓨터보다 더 좋은 성능을 갖고 있다.)

(3) 선행사가 고유명사 또는 특정 인물[사물]일 때 쓴다.

- Einstein, who developed the theory of relativity, was a genius.
  (관계사절 없이도 의미를 알 수 있을 때)
  (아인슈타인은 상대성 이론을 발전시킨 사람인데, 그는 천재였다.)

(4) 앞의 절에 부가적인 설명을 덧붙일 때 쓴다.

- He hurt his ankle, which made him sidelined from the final match.
  (앞의 절 전체가 선행사임)
  (그는 발목을 다쳤고, 그것은 그가 결승 경기에서 빠지게 했다.)

2 관계대명사의 생략

(1) **목적격 관계대명사 who(m), which, that은 생략할 수 있다.**

- They hired a new employee (who(m)) the manager recommended.
  (생략 가능)
  (그들은 매니저가 추천한 신입 직원을 고용했다.)

> **[참고] 전치사와 관계대명사**
>
> (1) 전치사가 관계대명사 앞에 올 경우 목적격 관계대명사는 생략할 수 없다.
> - The country in which he was born is beautiful. (그가 태어난 나라는 아름답다.)
>   (which 생략 불가)
>
> (2) 전치사 뒤에 목적격 관계대명사 who는 올 수 없다.
> - The man with whom I had a meeting is our new manager.
>   (who는 불가)
>   (내가 회의를 함께 했던 남자는 우리의 새 매니저이다.)
>
> (3) 관계대명사 that은 「전치사 + that」의 형태로 쓸 수 없다.
> - The laptop on that she is working is brand new. (×)
> - → The laptop on which she is working is brand new. (그녀가 작업하고 있는 노트북은 새것이다.)

(2) **「주격 관계대명사 + be동사 + 분사」일 때, 「주격 관계대명사 + be동사」는 생략할 수 있다.**

- The train (that is) approaching the station will depart in five minutes.
  (생략 가능) (현재분사)
  (역으로 다가오고 있는 기차는 5분 후에 출발할 것이다.)

The car (*that*) she drove was red. (그녀가 운전한 차는 빨간색이었다.)
(목적격 관계대명사의 생략)

The woman (*who was*) driving the red car was Julie.
(「주격 관계대명사+be동사」의 생략)
(빨간 차를 운전하던 여자는 Julie였다.)

1 관계대명사의 계속적 용법

[01-06] 괄호 안에서 알맞은 것을 고르시오.

01 We met the tour guide, (who / it) lives near the castle.

02 Lisa called Ethan, (whom / as) she hadn't seen in years.

03 My dad named me Aiden, (which / that) means 'little fire.'

04 She showed me a violin, (that / and it) was made in 1984.

05 He forgot his homework, (that / which) surprised the teacher a lot.

06 While washing the dishes, I broke the cup, (which / and) my mother likes most.

2 관계대명사의 생략

[07-12] 문장에서 생략할 수 있는 부분에 밑줄을 그으시오. (단, 없을 경우 문장 옆에 '없음'을 쓸 것)

07 The man who is reading a newspaper at the door is my uncle.

08 Is that the book which the librarian recommended us to read?

09 I'm looking for a man whom I owed a big favor when I was young.

10 In Australia, people use a special Australian English that is called 'Strine.'

11 Robert Edwin Peary was the first American that explored the North Pole.

12 The scholar has tried to decode the letter which was written 2,000 years ago.

[13-17] 빈칸에 알맞은 것을 〈보기〉에서 골라 쓰시오. (중복 사용 불가)

〈보기〉

with whom　　on which　　for which　　with which　　from which

13 I need a pencil ______________ I can write.

14 Do you have a friend ______________ you go to the school festival?

15 Is this the university ______________ you graduated?

16 The company ______________ they work has financial problems.

17 The site ______________ the apartment complex was built was not big.

〈정답과 해설 p. 120~121〉

[01-03]

빈칸에 알맞은 것을 고르시오.

01

> The patient met a doctor. + He specializes in heart surgery.
> ➡ The patient met a doctor ____________ specializes in heart surgery.

① who ② which ③ of which
④ whose ⑤ whom

02

> The writer is giving a lecture today. + Her book became a bestseller.
> ➡ The writer ____________ book became a bestseller is giving a lecture today.

① who ② that ③ which
④ whose ⑤ whom

03

> I have two sisters, and they are elementary students.
> ➡ I have two sisters, ________ are elementary students.

① who ② that ③ which
④ whose ⑤ whom

[04-07]

괄호 안에서 알맞은 것을 고르시오.

04

She blames someone else for anything (which / that) goes wrong.

05

Frankly speaking, I didn't like (that / what) I got from Mom on my birthday.

06

He gave me some advice, (that / which) I didn't listen to.

07

The patient (whose / whom) she had taken care of got better.

[08-11]

빈칸에 알맞은 것을 고르시오.

08

> She is the kind girl about ________ I spoke.

① which ② whom ③ whose
④ that ⑤ of which

09

> The fire fighter saved the old woman ________ life was in danger.

① who ② that ③ which
④ whose ⑤ whom

10

> I bought a blue jacket ________ I wanted to have.

① who ② whom ③ which
④ whose ⑤ what

11

> Choose ________ you want to eat from the menu.

① what ② who ③ which
④ whom ⑤ that

[12-15]
빈칸에 알맞은 것을 〈보기〉에서 골라 쓰시오. (중복 사용 불가)

〈보기〉
who   which   whom   what

12

______________ I wanted to find out first was how long it was going to take.

13

The man ______________ robbed the bank was wearing a mask.

14

The woman to ______________ I was introduced was very helpful.

15

My father's car, ______________ is in excellent condition, was made 10 years ago.

16

어법상 틀린 것을 고르시오.

① This is the woman with that he fell in love.
② I don't want to remember what they said to me.
③ The flight was delayed for another 1 hour, which made me in trouble.
④ This is the same cell phone that I lost two weeks ago.
⑤ The man and the dog that you know are waiting for you in front of the main gate.

[17-19] 고난도
문장에서 생략된 관계대명사를 올바른 위치에 써 넣으시오.
(필요시 동사도 함께 쓸 것)

17

She read the novel written by a famous writer.

18

The museum we visited last month is closed now.

19

The boy sitting next to me chattered non-stop all the way.

20

밑줄 친 that의 쓰임이 나머지 넷과 다른 것을 고르시오.

① All that I want is that you are with me.
② This is the company that I used to work for.
③ The man that is smiling at the children is the teacher of this school.
④ Did you hear that the field trip is going to be canceled because of the bad weather?
⑤ What is the TV program that people are most interested in?

[21-22] 서술형
주어진 우리말과 일치하도록 괄호 안의 말을 두 가지 형태로 바르게 배열하시오.

그녀가 두려워하는 것은 거의 없다.
There are very few things (she, which, afraid, is, of)

21

There are very few things ______________
______________.

22

There are very few things ______________
______________.

〈 정답과 해설 p. 121~122 〉

30 DAY

23

밑줄 친 부분 중 생략할 수 없는 것을 고르시오.

① This is the camera that my father bought for my birthday.
② Have you read any books which are written in English?
③ Do you know the girl who is wearing a pair of red shoes?
④ Ten students came in late this morning, which really irritated the teacher.
⑤ King Sejong is the man whom I admire most in Korean history.

[24-26] (서술형)

주어진 문장에 이어질 알맞은 문장을 〈보기〉에서 고르고, 관계대명사를 이용하여 한 문장으로 쓰시오. (중복 사용 불가)

┌─────〈보기〉─────┐
This meant he had to stay there.
It was very thankful.
This made me miss the first class.
└──────────────┘

24

I was late for school, ___________

___________________________.

25

Joseph didn't catch the last train, ___________

___________________________.

26

Judy lent me some money, ___________

___________________________.

[27-28]

밑줄 친 부분 중 어법상 틀린 것을 고르시오.

27

① I don't know which he wants.
② He is the one that I was talking about.
③ You should focus on what really matters.
④ The phone which I bought is broken.
⑤ The dog whose owner moved away is now at the shelter.

28

① This is the house that I used to live in.
② I have a cat which loves to sleep all day.
③ Do you know the person who wrote this book?
④ The man which car was stolen called the police.
⑤ This is the book that I borrowed from the library.

[29-31] (서술형)

〈보기〉에서 알맞은 말을 골라 두 문장을 한 문장으로 쓰시오. (중복 사용 불가)

┌────────〈보기〉────────┐
that   what   whose
└──────────────────────┘

29

┌────────────────────────────┐
· She owns a company.
· Its products are sold in more than fifty countries worldwide.
└────────────────────────────┘

➡ ___________________________

____

30 (고난도)

┌────────────────────────────┐
· She didn't tell me the thing.
· The thing happened at the meeting.
└────────────────────────────┘

➡ ___________________________

____

31

┌────────────────────────────┐
· The very comedy novel is really exciting.
· I was looking for the very comedy novel.
└────────────────────────────┘

➡ ___________________________

____

[32-34]
주어진 우리말과 일치하도록 괄호 안의 말을 바르게 배열하시오.

32

안경을 쓰고 있는 소년이 Tom이다.
(is, the boy, glasses, wearing, is, who, Tom)

➡ ____

33

나를 회의에 참석하지 못하게 한 것은 겨우 고양이 한 마리였다. (kept, what, from, me, the meeting, attending)

➡ ____

　　was just a cat.

34

우리가 논의하고 있는 그 마지막 주제는 매우 중요하다.
(are, that, very, discussing, we, is, important)

➡ The last subject _______________________________

_______________________________________.

[35-36]
다음 글을 읽고 물음에 답하시오.

Think carefully about ___(A)___ makes your teacher dislike you. Is it because you don't say hello in the morning? Is it because you make noise in class? If so, change your bad habit and try to pay more attention in class. In addition, ask your friends. Do they think ⓐ that she hates them, too? If they agree with you, your teacher is just a tough teacher ___(B)___ is not easy to please.

35

(A), (B)에 들어갈 말이 알맞게 짝지어진 것을 고르시오.

	(A)	(B)		(A)	(B)
①	who	– whom	②	that	– who
③	whose	– which	④	which	– whose
⑤	what	– that			

36

ⓐ와 용법이 같은 것을 고르시오.

① I believe that she told me the truth.
② Sally is a student that everybody likes.
③ Can you see that small star in the sky?
④ My grandfather is working in that building.
⑤ This is the shop that I bought my shorts from.

37 수능 유형

밑줄 친 부분 중, 어법상 틀린 것을 고르시오.

Teenage hearing loss ① is a big problem. A lot of teenagers use earphone, whether wireless or not, to listen to music or watch videos, ② that leads teenagers to develop some kind of hearing loss. Experts advise teenagers ③ to turn down the volume on their listening devices in order to avoid hearing loss. ④ It can be more dangerous to use the devices in crowded areas because they have to turn the volume up higher. That's why they are likely to wear hearing aids ⑤ earlier than they are supposed to.

①　　②　　③　　④　　⑤

🦉 어휘 & 표현

· **specialize in** ~을 전문으로 하다　· **surgery** 수술　· **elementary student** 초등학생　· **frankly** 솔직하게　· **rob** 도둑질하다
· **chatter** 수다를 떨다　· **irritate** 짜증 나게 하다　· **shelter** 쉼터　· **worldwide** 전 세계적으로　· **teenage** 십대의
· **loss** 손상, 손실　· **hearing aid** 보청기　· **crowded** 붐비는　· **be supposed to** ~하기로 되어 있다

〈 정답과 해설 p. 123~124 〉

30 DAY

UNIT 67 관계부사

The day **when** he was born is celebrated in the world.
The day를 선행사로 하는 관계부사
(그가 태어난 날은 세계에서 기념된다.)

The place **where** he was born was a stable.
The place를 선행사로 하는 관계부사
(그가 태어난 곳은 마구간이었다.)

1 관계부사의 역할: 선행사를 수식하며 「접속사 + 부사」의 역할을 한다.

- I remember the day and we first met on the day. (나는 그날을 기억하는데 우리는 그날 처음 만났다.)
  선행사 「접속사+부사」

→ I remember the day when we first met. (나는 우리가 처음 만났던 날을 기억한다.)
  선행사 형용사절을 이끄는 관계부사

2 관계부사의 종류

– 선행사에 따라 where, when, why, how를 쓴다.
– 「전치사＋관계대명사」로 바꿔쓸 수 있다.

선행사		관계부사	전치사 + 관계대명사
(1) 장소	the place, the city, the case, the point	where	= in[at] + which
(2) 시간	the time, the day	when	= on[at] + which
(3) 이유	the reason	why	= for which
(4) 방법	the way	how	= in which

(1) He works at a company. They make electric cars at the company.
(그는 한 회사에서 일한다. 그들은 그 회사에서 전기차를 만든다.)

→ He works at a company where[at which] they make electric cars.
(그는 전기차를 만드는 한 회사에서 일한다.)

(2) He moved abroad on the day. He graduated from university then.
(그는 그 날 해외로 이사했다. 그는 그때 대학을 졸업했다.)

→ He moved abroad on the day when[on which] he graduated from university.
(그는 대학을 졸업한 날에 해외로 이사했다.)

(3) Can you explain the reason? You were late for the reason.
(이유를 설명해 줄 수 있니? 너는 그 이유로 늦었어.)

→ Can you explain the reason why[for which] you were late?
(네가 늦은 이유를 설명해 줄 수 있니?)

(4) This book explains the way. The human brain works in the way.
(이 책은 방법을 설명한다. 인간의 두뇌는 그 방법으로 작동한다.)

→ This book explains the way (또는 how) the human brain works.
(이 책은 인간의 두뇌가 어떻게 작동하는지 설명한다.)

주의 the way와 how는 동시에 사용하지 않는다.

❶ 관계부사 how
방법을 나타내는 관계부사 how는 선행사 the way와 같이 쓰지 않고, 반드시 둘 중 하나만 쓴다. 단, in which는 선행사 the way와 함께 쓰일 수 있다.

1 + **2** 관계부사

[01-07] 괄호 안에서 알맞은 것을 고르시오.

01 The season (where / when) I arrived at London was winter.

02 Do you know the time (at which / in which) the train arrives?

03 1914 was the year (in which / on which) World War I broke out.

04 She remembers the moment (when / in when) her son first said 'Mommy.'

05 Make sure you can't turn back time (which / when) you're wasting now.

06 I can't forget the moment (during which / at which) I ate sushi for the first time.

07 Christmas is the holiday (which / when) Christians celebrate the birth of Jesus.

[08-12] 두 문장이 같은 뜻이 되도록 빈칸에 알맞은 말을 쓰시오.

08 This is the floor where your father works.

= This is the floor ＿＿＿＿＿＿ ＿＿＿＿＿＿ your father works.

09 I went to the city in which I could meet a lot of people.

= I went to the city ＿＿＿＿＿＿ I could meet a lot of people.

10 The place where I was born has some ancient monuments.

= The place ＿＿＿＿＿＿ ＿＿＿＿＿＿ I was born has some ancient monuments.

11 The department store which Tom is working at is the biggest store in this city.

= The department store ＿＿＿＿＿＿ Tom ＿＿＿＿＿＿ ＿＿＿＿＿＿ is the biggest store in this city.

12 The hotel where they are staying is famous for its elegant interior design.

= The hotel ＿＿＿＿＿＿ they are staying ＿＿＿＿＿＿ is famous for its elegant interior design.

[13-17] 문장에서 <u>틀린</u> 부분을 찾아 밑줄을 긋고 바르게 고치시오.

13 This is the way in how I lost weight. ＿＿＿＿＿＿

14 Let me know the reason what you don't use this vending machine. ＿＿＿＿＿＿

15 Tell me the reason which you want to be a billionaire. ＿＿＿＿＿＿

16 Can you tell me the reason how you didn't show up? ＿＿＿＿＿＿

17 I'm sure he won't tell you the way how he passed the test. ＿＿＿＿＿＿

31 DAY

🦉 어휘 & 표현

· **electric car** 전기차　· **World War I** 제1차 세계대전　· **break out** (사건 등이) 발생하다　· **ancient** 고대의
· **monument** 기념물　· **elegant** 우아한　· **vending machine** 자판기　· **billionaire** 억만장자

〈 정답과 해설 **p. 124~125** 〉

 **UNIT 68** 관계부사의 계속적 용법과 생략 

1 **관계부사의 계속적 용법:** 관계부사 앞에 **콤마(,)**를 붙여 선행사에 관한 추가 정보를 덧붙인다.

(1) 관계부사 when과 where는 계속적 용법으로 쓸 수 있다.

(2) 「접속사 + 부사」로 바꾸어 쓸 수 있다.

I was in Ukraine in 2022, when Russia invaded the country.
계속적 용법(= and then)
(나는 2022년에 우크라이나에 있었는데, 그 해에 러시아가 그 나라를 침공했다.)

I was in Ukraine in 2022 when Russia invaded the country.
제한적 용법
(나는 러시아가 침공한 2022년에 우크라이나에 있었다.)

❶ 제한적 용법
제한적 용법은 관계사가 선행사 바로 뒤에서 선행사를 형용사처럼 수식하는 것을 말한다.

[참고] **헷갈리기 쉬운 제한적 용법과 계속적 용법**

관계사 앞에 콤마가 있다고 해서 반드시 계속적 용법인 것은 아니다. 문장 중간에 삽입되는 제한적 용법의 관계사절은 문맥을 쉽게 파악하기 위해 관계사절 앞뒤에 콤마를 붙이기도 한다.

• The museum, where rare fossils were displayed, attracted many researchers.
문장 중간에 삽입된 제한적 용법의 관계부사절
(희귀 화석들이 전시된 그 박물관은 많은 연구자들을 끌어모았다.)

2 **관계부사의 생략:** 선행사의 생략, 관계부사의 생략이 가능하다.

(1) **선행사의 생략:** 관계부사의 선행사가 the time, the place, the reason 같이 일반적인 경우에는 선행사를 생략할 수 있다.

• I visited the place where I spent my childhood. (나는 내가 어린 시절을 보낸 그곳을 방문했다.)
생략 가능

(2) **관계부사 when, why의 생략:** 선행사가 the time, the reason일 때 when, why를 생략할 수 있다.

• The time when I lived abroad was full of challenges. (내가 해외에 살았던 시기는 도전으로 가득했다.)
생략 가능

• The reason why he was crying was unknown. (그가 울고 있었던 이유는 알려지지 않았다.)
생략 가능

(3) **선행사 the way와 관계부사 how의 생략:** 선행사 the way와 how는 같이 쓸 수 없으며, 둘 중 하나는 생략해야 한다.

• I was surprised at the way (또는 how) he handled the situation.
둘 중 하나만 써야 함
(나는 그가 상황을 어떻게 처리했는지에 놀랐다.)

(4) **관계부사 where의 생략:** 보통은 생략될 수 없지만, 다음과 같은 경우에 where를 생략할 수 있다.

① where를 「전치사 + 관계대명사」 형태로 바꾸고, 전치사를 맨 뒤로 보낸 후 남은 목적격 관계대명사는 생략할 수 있다.

• This is the city where I grew up. (이곳이 내가 자란 도시이다.)

= This is the city in which I grew up.
전치사+관계대명사

= This is the city (which) I grew up in.
생략 가능　　　전치사

② 선행사가 somewhere, anywhere, everywhere, nowhere, place이면, where를 생략할 수 있다.

• I looked everywhere where I thought it might be. (난 그게 있을 법한 모든 곳을 찾아봤다)
생략 가능

3 **관계대명사와 관계부사의 차이**

– **관계대명사:** 뒤에 불완전한 문장이 옴 (주어 또는 목적어가 없음), 대명사 역할

– **관계부사:** 뒤에 완전한 문장이 옴 (주어, 목적어 등 문장 형식에 맞는 필수 요소가 모두 있음), 부사 역할

• The girl who lives next door is my friend. (옆집에 사는 소녀는 내 친구야.)
관계대명사 주어가 없는 불완전한 절이 옴

• Tell me the reason why you are upset. (네가 왜 화가 났는지 이유를 내게 말해봐.)
관계부사　　　완전한 절이 옴

1 관계부사의 계속적 용법

[01-04] 두 문장의 의미가 같도록 알맞은 관계부사를 사용하여 빈칸을 채우시오.

01 We came home at 8 o'clock, and then we started to have dinner.

→ We came home at 8 o'clock, ____.

02 I decided to move back to Busan and there I spent my childhood.

→ I decided to move back to Busan, ____.

03 I still clearly remember March 3, 2008, and then the accident happened.

→ I still clearly remember March 3, 2008, ________________________________.

04 Our ship is nearing to the glacier, and here we notice two polar bears swimming.

→ Our ship is nearing to the glacier, ____.

2 관계부사의 생략

[05-09] 주어진 단어를 바르게 배열하여 다음 문장을 완성하시오.

05 This is (feel, I, would, nowhere, comfortable).

→ This is ____.

06 That's (in, born, the hospital, was, she).

→ That's ____.

07 Please tell me (you, why, tell, didn't, him, the truth).

→ Please tell me ____.

08 I want to know (I, in front of, show up, when, have to, him).

→ I want to know ____.

09 What is the reason (are, sleepy, and tired, you, always)?

→ What is the reason ____?

3 관계대명사와 관계부사의 차이

[10-14] 빈칸에 알맞은 말을 〈보기〉에서 골라 쓰시오. (중복 사용 불가)

〈보기〉

which	who	where	why	when

10 This is the museum ______________ Van Gogh's works are displayed.

11 That's the reason ______________ many students choose online classes.

12 We are waiting for the day ______________ the results will be announced.

13 He bought a camera ______________ can record in 4K resolution at night.

14 The scientist ______________ received the Nobel Prize teaches at my university.

〈정답과 해설 **p. 125~126**〉

어휘 & 표현

· **invade** 침공하다
· **fossil** 화석
· **display** 전시하다
· **handle** 처리하다
· **glacier** 빙하
· **polar bear** 북극곰
· **comfortable** 편안한
· **announce** 발표하다
· **resolution** 해상도
· **the Nobel Prize** 노벨상

 **UNIT 69** 복합관계대명사, 복합관계부사 

1 **복합관계대명사** –「관계대명사 + -ever」형태, 명사절과 양보의 부사절을 이끈다.

복합관계대명사	명사절 (선행사+관계대명사)	양보의 부사절 (no matter+관계대명사)
(1) whoever ❶ (주격)	~하는 사람은 누구든지 = anyone who	누가 ~하더라도 = no matter who
(2) whomever (목적격)	~하는 사람은 누구든지 = anyone whom	누구를 ~하더라도 = no matter whom
(3) whichever ❷	~하는 것은 어느 것이나 = anything that	어느 것을 ~하더라도 = no matter which
(4) whatever ❷	~하는 것은 무엇이나 = anything that	무엇을 ~하더라도 = no matter what

❶ **whoever의 소유격**
복합관계대명사 whoever의 소유격은 whosever로 쓴다.

❷ **whichever와 whatever의 차이**
· whichever: 어느 것
(정해진 범위가 있는 상태)
· whatever: 무엇
(정해진 범위가 없는 상태)

(1) We will hire whoever is qualified. (우리는 자격이 있는 사람은 누구든 고용할 것이다.)
= anyone who

Whoever comes to the door, don't open it. (문에 누가 오더라도, 열지 마.)
= No matter who

(2) Let whomever you trust handle the money. (네가 믿는 사람 누구든 그 돈을 맡겨.)
= anyone whom

Whomever you choose, I'll support your decision. (네가 누구를 선택하더라도, 나는 네 결정을 지지할게.)
= No matter whom

(3) Whichever comes first will be accepted. (먼저 오는 것은 어느 것이나 받아들여질 것이다.)
= Anything that

Whichever team wins, the fans will be happy. (어느 팀이 이기더라도 팬들은 기뻐할 것이다.)
= No matter which

(4) Do whatever makes you happy. (너를 행복하게 하는 건 무엇이든 해.)
= anything that

Whatever you decide, think carefully. (네가 무엇을 결정하더라도, 신중히 생각해.)
= No matter what

2 **복합관계부사** –「관계부사 + -ever」형태, 시간, 장소, 양보의 부사절을 이끈다.

복합관계부사	시간, 장소의 부사절 (선행사+관계부사)	양보의 부사절 (no matter+관계부사)
(1) wherever	~하는 곳은 어디든지 = at[in, to] any place where	어디에서 ~하더라도 = no matter where
(2) whenever	~할 때는 언제든지 = at any time when	언제 ~하더라도 = no matter when
(3) however ❸	–	아무리 ~하더라도 = no matter how

❸ **복합관계부사 however**
wherever나 whenever와 달리, however는 양보의 부사절만 이끌기 때문에「선행사+관계부사」로는 바꿔쓸 수 없다.
· You can do it however often you fail.
(네가 아무리 자주 실패하더라도 너는 그것을 할 수 있다.)
= You can do it no matter how often you fail.

(1) Wherever she goes, she takes her dog with her. (그녀는 어디를 가든 개를 데리고 다닌다.)
= In[At, To] any place where

She feels at home wherever she travels. (그녀는 어디를 여행하더라도 편안함을 느낀다.)
= no matter where

(2) We go hiking whenever the weather is nice. (날씨가 좋을 때는 언제든 우리는 등산을 간다.)
= at any time when

She answers the phone whenever I call. (내가 언제 전화를 해도, 그녀는 전화를 받는다.)
= no matter when

(3) However fast we run, we can't catch the bus. (아무리 우리가 빨리 달려도 버스를 잡을 수 없다.)
= No matter how

① 복합관계대명사

[01-06] 밑줄 친 복합관계대명사에 유의하여 〈보기〉와 같이 바꾸어 쓰시오.

> 〈보기〉
> I respect whoever helps others. → I respect anyone who helps others.
> Whatever he does, I'll help him. → No matter what he does, I'll help him.

01 You can give the clothes to whoever wants it.
→ You can give the clothes to ________________________________.

02 Take whichever you want among these colors.
→ Take ____________________ among these colors.

03 He'll buy you whatever you want.
→ He'll buy you ________________________________.

04 Whoever is right or wrong, you shouldn't have a fight with each other.
→ ________________________________, you shouldn't have a fight with each other.

05 Whatever happens, he'll protect the young girl.
→ ________________________________, he'll protect the young girl.

06 Whosever keys were left on the counter should come get them before we lock up.
→ ________________________________ on the counter should come get them before we lock up.

② 복합관계부사

[07-12] 빈칸에 알맞은 것을 〈보기〉에서 골라 쓰시오. (중복 사용 불가)

> 〈보기〉
> when   wherever   however   where   how   whenever

07 You can stay ____________ you want to.

08 No matter ____________ you start, it's never too late to learn.

09 No matter ____________ you live, internet access is now essential.

10 ____________ they come to you with a problem, let them know there is a way out.

11 ____________ much he earned, he couldn't keep up with rising house prices.

12 No matter ____________ carefully he drives, accidents still happen sometimes.

🦉 어휘 & 표현

- **qualify** 자격을 부여하다   · **handle** 다루다, 처리하다   · **support** 지지하다   · **decision** 결정   · **accept** 받아들이다
- **carefully** 신중하게   · **protect** 보호하다   · **access** 접속, 접근   · **essential** 필수적인   · **earn** (돈을) 벌다
- **keep up with** 따라잡다   · **accident** 사고

〈 정답과 해설 p. 126 〉

[01-04]
두 문장이 같은 뜻이 되도록 빈칸에 알맞은 것을 고르시오.

01

> Give it to whoever likes it.
> = Give it to ___________ likes it.

① anything that　　② anyone whom
③ no matter what　　④ anyone who
⑤ no matter whom

02

> He flatters whosever position is high.
> = He flatters ___________ position is high.

① anyone whose　　② anyone whom
③ anything that　　④ no matter who
⑤ no matter what

03

> No matter where you go, I will be there for you.
> = ___________ you go, I will be there for you.

① Wherever　　② Whenever
③ However　　④ Whoever
⑤ Whichever

04

> Whatever the reason is, whales rarely land on boats when they jump.
> = ___________ the reason is, whales rarely land on boats when they jump.

① No matter what　　② Anyone who
③ Anyone whom　　④ No matter who
⑤ No matter whom

05
빈칸에 알맞은 것을 고르시오.

> I'll have finished the work by the time ___________ you return.

① when　　② why　　③ where
④ in which　　⑤ how

[06-09]
괄호 안에서 알맞은 것을 고르시오.

06

I need a piece of paper (with which / on which) I can write.

07

Can you tell me (how / where) I can get to the bank?

08

(Whatever / However) good this room is, I like my own room better.

09

If you feel hungry, you can have some food (whatever / whenever) you want.

[10-12] 서술형
문장에서 생략된 선행사나 관계부사를 올바른 위치에 써 넣으시오.

10

This is where we can use Wi-Fi.

11

What is the reason you want to go to the U.S.?

12

This is when watermelons taste most delicious.

[13-14] `서술형`

주어진 두 문장이 같은 뜻이 되도록 빈칸에 알맞은 말을 쓰시오.

13

I visited Italy, where I came across a famous K-pop singer.

= I visited Italy, _____________ _____________ I came across a famous K-pop singer.

14

I don't want to see them whoever they are.

= I don't want to see them _____________ _____________ _____________ they are.

[15-18]

빈칸에 알맞은 것을 고르시오.

15

> I don't know the time __________ they left for the station.

① when   ② where   ③ why
④ how   ⑤ what

16

> All students arrived at the palace __________ the king lived.

① which   ② where   ③ that
④ how   ⑤ why

17

> I know the __________ why they are angry.

① house   ② time   ③ way
④ reason   ⑤ man

18

> What makes our lives good or bad depends on __________ we make up our mind.

① why   ② what   ③ how
④ when   ⑤ where

19

밑줄 친 부분의 쓰임이 옳지 <u>않은</u> 것을 고르시오.

① You can do <u>whatever</u> you please.
② <u>Whomever</u> comes with you is welcome.
③ <u>Whichever</u> they choose, I'll give it to them.
④ Don't forget to pack your passport <u>wherever</u> you go.
⑤ <u>However</u> hard I worked, my parents were not satisfied.

[20-21] `고난도`

어법상 <u>틀린</u> 것을 고르시오.

20

① Do you know the time when the test began?
② Nobody knows the reason why the baby is crying.
③ Please tell me the way how he became tall.
④ The museum where we saw a lot of antiques was excellent.
⑤ What is the name of the restaurant where I ate a delicious spaghetti?

21

① The day which she will leave is still undecided.
② I'll never forget the summer we traveled across Northern Europe.
③ The museum Van Gogh's works are displayed attracts many tourists.
④ The novel, where the ending surprised everyone, became a bestseller.
⑤ She finally found the moment when everything started to make sense.

〈 정답과 해설 p. 127~128 〉

[22-24]
빈칸에 알맞지 <u>않은</u> 것을 고르시오.

22

> Can you tell me _______________ ?

① the time he will finish his homework
② the place where they live
③ when will you see me
④ the way you solved the question
⑤ the reason why this is happening to me

23

> He brings a gift _______________ .

① whenever he visits us
② when he meets a client
③ every time he attends a party
④ at any time he visits
⑤ no matter when he returns from a trip

24

> The lab, _______________ , was locked without any notification.

① where the test had taken place
② where sensitive data was stored
③ whenever the lights were turned off
④ which no one had entered for hours
⑤ where Dr. Hall conducted a project

[25-26]
밑줄 친 부분을 생략할 수 <u>없는</u> 것을 고르시오.

25

① Can you explain <u>how</u> this machine works?
② Can you tell me the reason <u>why</u> he left?
③ This is the moment <u>when</u> everything changed.
④ I wonder the reason <u>why</u> the meeting was canceled.
⑤ This is <u>the place</u> where I spent most of my childhood.

26

① The reason <u>why</u> I could finish the project is that I ran out of time.
② Do you remember the park <u>which</u> we used to play in?
③ I want to visit the country <u>which</u> invented pizza.
④ Do you remember the time <u>when</u> we traveled to Paris?
⑤ This is <u>the place</u> where I used to play soccer.

[27-31]
빈칸에 알맞은 것을 〈보기〉에서 골라 쓰시오. (중복 사용 불가)

> 〈보기〉
> whenever   however   wherever   whosever   whichever

27

_______________ Tom lives, we'll miss him so much.

28

He tries to calm down _______________ he is in trouble.

29

_______________ undesirable the rule may be, you should follow it.

30

She can choose _______________ she wants.

31

_______________ phone keeps ringing, please turn it off.

[32-33] 고난도

두 문장을 한 문장으로 바꾸어 쓴 것 중 **틀린** 것을 고르시오.

32

> I like the place. I was born in it.

① I like the place I was born in.
② I like the place where I was born.
③ I like the place where I was born in.
④ I like the place in which I was born.
⑤ I like the place which I was born in.

33

> She still remembers the moment. She saw the shooting star at that moment.

① She still remembers when she saw the shooting star.
② She still remembers the moment she saw the shooting star.
③ She still remembers the moment when she saw the shooting star.
④ She still remembers the moment at when she saw the shooting star.
⑤ She still remembers the moment at which she saw the shooting star.

[34-36] 서술형

주어진 우리말과 일치하도록 괄호 안의 말을 이용하여 알맞게 쓰시오. (관계부사를 꼭 사용할 것)

34

이것이 내가 회의에 참석하지 않은 이유이다.
(the reason, attend, is, the meeting, I, didn't)

➡ This ________________

________________________ .

35

그는 외계 생명체가 처음으로 그와 접촉한 밤을 기억했다. (the alien, the night, first contacted, him)

➡ He remembered ________________

________________________ .

36

처음 그 영화를 봤던 장소로 다시 가 봐.
(saw, first, the place, you, the movie)

➡ Go back to ________________

________________________ .

37 고난도

밑줄 친 부분에 관해 잘못 이야기한 학생을 고르시오.

> - The museum ⓐ where they discovered the fossil was once a royal bathhouse.
> - She remembers the year ⓑ when her village vanished into the sand.
> - That's the reason ⓒ why scholars still debate his final theory.
> - He always competes fairly, ⓓ why he's respected among rivals.
> - They distributed the latest update at dawn, ⓔ when they finished fixing errors.

① 다정: ⓐ는 in which로도 바꿔 쓸 수 있어.
② 석영: ⓑ도 in which로 바꿔 쓸 수 있어.
③ 태희: ⓒ는 선행사가 the reason이기 때문에 생략할 수 있어.
④ 효철: ⓓ는 계속적 용법의 관계부사 why가 알맞게 쓰였어.
⑤ 대한: ⓔ는 계속적 용법으로 쓰였으므로 that으로 바꿔 쓸 수 없어.

[38-40] 서술형

빈칸에 공통으로 들어갈 말을 쓰시오.

38

> - That's the hour ________ the sky turns a strange shade of green before a storm.
> - Hana remembers the exact second ________ the power suddenly went out.

➡ ________________

〈 정답과 해설 p. 128~129 〉

39

- This is the room _________ we together saw the lunar eclipse.
- She visited the place _________ she saw the glowing statue.

➡ _________________

40

- _________ strange it looked, they touched the mirror.
- There was a loud noise. _________, no one checked what it was.

➡ _________________

[41-42]

다음 글을 읽고, 물음에 답하시오.

The café ① where we first crossed each other's paths has now expanded and opened an elegant new branch in the heart of the city. I often miss the moment ② when we sat there for hours, and ⓐ how we discussed everything. We can visit the newly opened branch ③ whenever we want, though we may long for the intimate charm of the original location. ④ Whoever much time passes, the unforgettable taste of their coffee will linger in our memories. ⑤ Wherever I go, the memories of that special place stay with me.

41 수능 유형

밑줄 친 부분 중 어법상 틀린 것을 고르시오.

①   ②   ③   ④   ⑤

42

밑줄 친 ⓐ how와 쓰임이 같은 것을 고르시오.

① How do you usually start your day?
② How beautiful the stars look tonight!
③ She explained how to operate the machine in detail.
④ I wonder how often the hacker tried to breach the security system.
⑤ This is how traditions are passed down from one generation to the next.

43 수능 맛보기

(A), (B), (C)의 각 네모 안에서 어법에 맞는 표현으로 가장 적절한 것을 고르시오.

I studied Early Childhood Education in the United States. I worked as a student teacher in one kindergarten, (A) which / where I learned teaching skills from the kindergarten teachers. Although, as a Korean, I was a foreigner to them, I felt that we got along really well. I belonged to one of the classes for 6-year-olds. In that class, there was a Kelly. She was a Chinese-American girl (B) who / whom was born and raised in the United States. One day, a boy in the class asked me, "Are you Kelly's mom?" I realized children can distinguish different races (C) however / whatever old they are.

	(A)		(B)		(C)
①	which	−	who	−	whatever
②	where	−	whom	−	however
③	which	−	who	−	however
④	where	−	who	−	however
⑤	which	−	whom	−	whatever

🦉 **어휘 & 표현**

- **flatter** 아첨하다
- **notification** 공지
- **undesirable** 바람직하지 않은
- **shooting star** 유성
- **bathhouse** 대중목욕탕
- **vanish** 사라지다
- **debate** 토론하다
- **distribute** 분배하다
- **lunar eclipse** 월식
- **expand** 확장하다
- **intimate** 분위기 있는
- **charm** 매력
- **unforgettable** 잊을 수 없는
- **linger** 남다[계속되다]
- **breach** (방어벽 등에) 구멍을 뚫다, 침해하다
- **distinguish** 구별하다
- **race** 인종

가정법

假定法

(거짓 가, 정할 정, 법 법)
사실이 아닌 일이나
일어날 가능성이 없는 일을 가정하는 것

UNIT 70 **가정법 과거**
현재 사실과 반대되는 상황을 가정하는 것

UNIT 71 **가정법 과거완료**
과거 사실과 반대되는 상황을 가정하는 것

UNIT 72 **가정법의 다양한 형태**

If I were taller, I would play basketball better than now.
가정법 과거

(만약 내가 더 키가 크다면, 지금보다 농구를 더 잘할 텐데.)

If we had booked a table, we wouldn't have waited for an hour.
가정법 과거완료

(만약 우리가 예약을 했더라면, 한 시간이나 기다리지 않았을 텐데.)

Were I you, I would say no. (내가 너라면, 나는 거절할 거야.)
가정법의 다양한 형태 (if 생략)

 **UNIT 70** 가정법 과거 

- **가정법**: 사실을 말하는 문장은 직설법이고,
  사실이 아닌 일이나 일어날 가능성이 없는 일을 가정하거나 소망하는 문장은 가정법이다.
- **가정법 과거**: 현재 사실에 반대되거나 실현 가능성이 거의 없는 상황을 가정할 때 쓴다.

1 if의 쓰임: '~한다면, ~라면'

'만약 ~라면' (가정법)	현재나 과거 사실에 반대되는, 실현 가능성이 거의 없는 상황을 가정할 때 쓴다.
	• If I were a bird, I would fly to you. (만약 내가 새라면, 너에게 날아갈 텐데.) 나는 새가 아님
'~인지 아닌지' (명사절 접속사)	불확실하거나 의문시되는 사실을 이야기할 때 쓴다.
	• I don't know if she is coming. (나는 그녀가 올지 안 올지 몰라.) 올지 안 올지 의문시됨
'~한다면' (부사절 접속사)	실현 가능성이 있는 일에 대한 조건을 이야기할 때 쓴다.
	• If it rains, we will stay home. (비가 오면, 우리는 집에 있을 거야.) '비가 온다'라는 조건을 제시함

2 if 가정법 과거   If + 주어 + 동사의 과거형, 주어 + would[could, might, should] + 동사원형

(만약 ~라면)   (…할 텐데)

– 현재 사실에 반대되는 일, 또는 실현 가능성이 거의 없는 상황을 가정할 때 쓴다.

[가정법 과거] If he were ❶ very distracted, he couldn't pass the test.
    if절의 동사 (동사의 과거형)   주절의 동사 (could not + 동사원형)

(만약 그의 주의가 많이 흐트러진다면, 시험을 통과할 수 없을 텐데.)

[현재 사실] As he is not very distracted, he can pass the test.

(그의 주의가 많이 흐트러지지 않기 때문에, 시험에 통과할 수 있다.)

❶ if절의 be동사

if절의 동사로 be동사가 오면, 주어에 상관없이 were를 쓴다.
- If I were rich, I would travel the world.
(내가 부자라면, 세상을 여행할 텐데.)

3 I wish 가정법 과거   I wish + 주어 + 동사의 과거형 (~라면 좋을 텐데)

– 현재 사실과 반대되는 일, 또는 현재의 일에 대한 아쉬움을 나타낼 때 쓴다.

[가정법 과거] I wish some company offered me a job.
      동사의 과거형

(어느 한 회사나 나에게 일을 제안해 주면 좋을 텐데.)

[현재 사실] I'm sorry no company offers me a job. (아무 회사도 나에게 일을 제안해 주지 않아서 유감이다.)

❷ 직설법 문장의 접속사

가정법을 직설법으로 전환할 때, 이유나 원인을 나타내는 부사절 접속사로 as, because, since를 쓸 수 있다.

4 as if 가정법 과거   as if + 주어 + 동사의 과거형 (~인 것처럼)

– 주절의 시제와 동일한 시제의 반대되는 일을 사실인 척 나타낼 때 쓴다.

[가정법 과거] He acts as if he were the CEO of the company. (그는 마치 그가 회사의 CEO인 것처럼 행동한다.)
      동사의 과거형

[현재 사실] In fact, he is not the CEO of the company. (사실, 그는 회사의 CEO가 아니다.)

5 without 가정법 과거 ❸   Without + 명사(구), 주어+would[could, might, should] + 동사원형

(~이 없다면)   (…할 것이다)

– 현재 무언가가 없는 상황을 가정할 때 쓰인다.

가정법 문장의 if절, 「If it were not for + 명사(구)」를 대신한다.

[가정법 과거] Without me, you would be lost in these woods.
      주절의 동사 (would + 동사원형)
= If it were not for me, you would be lost in these woods.

(내가 없다면, 너는 숲에서 길을 잃을 것이다.)

❸ without을 대신하는 but for

without과 but for 모두 같은 뜻으로 쓰이지만, but for가 좀 더 격식 있는 표현이다.

1 + 2 if 가정법 과거

[01-03] 두 문장의 뜻이 같도록 빈칸에 알맞은 말을 쓰시오.

01 As I am not in your shoes, I ___________________ to her.

= If I ______________ in your shoes, I would apologize to her.

02 Because she is super timid, she never ______________ in front of the class.

= If she ______________ super timid, she would speak in front of the class.

03 If he ______________ hectic in September, he would visit his parents more often.

= As he is hectic in September, he ___________________ his parents more often.

3 + 4 + 5 I wish / as if / without 가정법 과거

[04-08] 두 문장의 뜻이 같도록 빈칸에 알맞은 말을 쓰시오.

04 She acts as if she liked him.

= In fact, ___________________________________.

05 In fact, he isn't a teacher at the school.

= He talks ___________________________________ at the school.

06 If it were not for the trainer, my dog wouldn't be so active.

= But ___________________________________, my dog wouldn't be so active.

07 I'm sorry I'm sitting in a classroom instead of lying on the beach.

= I wish I ___________________________________ instead of sitting in a classroom.

08 Without his alarm clock, he would miss the first class every day.

= If ___________________________________, he would miss the first class every day.

2 + 3 + 4 + 5 가정법 과거

[09-12] 주어진 우리말과 일치하도록 괄호 안의 동사를 이용하여 빈칸에 알맞은 말을 쓰시오.

09 그들이 답을 안다면, 그들은 우리에게 말할 텐데. (know)

➡ If they ______________ the answer, they would tell us.

10 지금 비가 오지 않는다면, 우리는 산책할 수 있을 텐데. (be raining)

➡ If it ______________, we could go for a walk.

11 네가 없다면 나는 이 나라에서 살 수 없을 거야. (be)

➡ If it ______________, I could not live in this country.

12 우리 부모님이 내가 수학여행을 가도록 허락해 주시면 좋을 텐데. (allow)

➡ I wish my parents ______________ me to go on the school trip.

> **🦉 어휘 & 표현**
> · **distracted** 주의가 산만한
> · **apologize** 사과하다
> · **timid** 소심한
> · **hectic** 정신없이 바쁜
> · **active** 활발한
> · **go for a walk** 산책하다
> · **school trip** 수학여행

〈 정답과 해설 **p. 130** 〉

 **UNIT 71** 가정법 과거완료 

• **가정법 과거완료**: 과거 사실에 반대되거나 실현 가능성이 거의 없는 상황을 가정할 때 쓴다.

I flew *as if* I *had become* a bird. (나는 마치 새가 됐던 것처럼 날았다.)
주절의 시제보다 앞선 시제의 반대되는 일을 사실인 척 나타냄

If I *hadn't flown* too high, I *wouldn't have fallen* down.
과거 사실에 반대되는 일을 나타냄
(내가 너무 높게 날지 않았다면, 떨어지지 않았을 텐데.)

1 if 가정법 과거완료

If + 주어 + had + 과거분사, 주어 + would[could, might, should] + have + 과거분사
(만약 ~였다면)   (…했을 텐데)

– 과거 사실에 반대되는 일, 또는 실현 가능성이 거의 없는 상황을 가정할 때 쓰인다.

[가정법 과거완료] If the king had listened to him, the war might have stopped.
if절의 동사 (had + 과거분사)   주절의 동사 (might + have + 과거분사)
(왕이 그의 말을 들었더라면, 전쟁이 멈췄을 텐데.)

[과거 사실] As the king didn't listen to him, the war didn't stop.
(왕이 그의 말을 듣지 않았기 때문에, 전쟁은 멈추지 않았다.)

2 I wish 가정법 과거완료   I wish + 주어 + had + 과거분사 (~했더라면 좋을 텐데)

– 과거 사실과 반대되는 일, 또는 과거의 일에 대한 아쉬움을 나타낼 때 쓴다.

[가정법 과거완료] I wish I had been more careful with my children.
had + 과거분사
(내가 내 아이들을 더 신경 썼더라면 좋을 텐데.)

[과거 사실] I regret that I was not more careful with my children.
(나는 내 아이들을 더 신경 쓰지 않았던 것을 후회한다.)

3 as if 가정법 과거완료   as if + 주어 + had + 과거분사 (~였던 것처럼)

– 주절의 시제보다 더 과거에 일어난 사실과 반대되는 일을 사실인 척 나타낼 때 쓴다.

[가정법 과거완료] She acted as if she had won the competition. (그녀는 마치 그 대회에서 이겼던 것처럼 행동했다.)
had + 과거분사

[과거 사실] In fact, she didn't win the competition. (사실, 그녀는 그 대회에서 이기지 않았다.)

4 without 가정법 과거완료

Without + 명사(구), 주어+would[could, might, should] + have + 과거분사
(~이 없었다면)   (…했을 것이다)

– 과거에 무언가가 없는 상황을 가정할 때 쓰인다.

가정법 문장의 if절, 「If it had not been for + 명사(구)」를 대신한다.

[가정법 과거완료] Without her advice, I would have made a big mistake.
주절의 동사 (would + have + 과거분사)

= If it had not been for her advice, I would have made a big mistake.
(그녀의 조언이 없었다면, 나는 큰 실수를 했었을 것이다.)

1 + **2** if 가정법 과거완료, I wish 가정법 과거완료

[01-05] 직설법 문장을 가정법 문장으로 바꿀 때, 빈칸에 알맞은 말을 쓰시오.

01 As they didn't invite me, I didn't go to the wedding.
 ➡ If they _________________ me, I would _________________ to the wedding.

02 She failed the course since she didn't submit the final paper.
 ➡ If she _________________ the final paper, she would _________________ the course.

03 He missed the opportunity because he didn't respond promptly.
 ➡ If he _________________ promptly, he would _________________ the opportunity.

04 I regret that I didn't witness an ocean of stars last night.
 ➡ I wish I _________________ an ocean of stars last night.

05 I regret that my instincts didn't guide me more clearly during last expedition.
 ➡ I wish my instincts _________________ me more clearly during last expedition.

3 as if 가정법 과거완료

[06-08] 괄호 안에서 알맞은 것을 고르시오.

06 He spoke about quantum physics as if he (has known / had known) it perfectly.

07 She debated with the philosophers as if she (formulates / had formulated) the theories herself.

08 He looked as if he (had hidden / has hidden) something about the accident.

4 without 가정법 과거완료

[09-11] 주어진 우리말과 일치하도록 괄호 안의 말을 이용하여 문장을 완성하시오. (단, 주절의 조동사는 would만 사용할 것)

09 비상 보급품이 없었다면, 그 등산객들은 폭풍우에서 살아남지 못했을 것이다. (survive)
 ➡ Without emergency supplies, the hikers _________________ the storm.

10 네 도움이 없었더라면, 나는 시험에 떨어졌을 것이다. (fail)
 ➡ Without your help, I _________________ the exam.

11 그 기회가 없었다면, 나는 너를 만나지 못했을 것이다. (meet)
 ➡ Without that opportunity, I _________________ you.

32 DAY

🦉 어휘 & 표현

· **submit** 제출하다   · **opportunity** 기회   · **promptly** 즉시   · **witness** 목격하다   · **instinct** 본능   · **expedition** 탐험
· **quantum physics** 양자 물리학   · **formulate** 만들어 내다   · **emergency supplies** 비상 보급품

〈 정답과 해설 p. 131 〉

 **UNIT 72 가정법의 다양한 형태** 

1 혼합 가정법: 과거 사실과 반대되는 일이 현재까지 영향을 미칠 때를 나타낸다.

┌─ 가정법 과거완료 if절 ─┐ ┌─ 가정법 과거 주절 ─┐
If + 주어 + had + 과거분사, 주어 + would[could, might, should] **+ 동사원형**
(만약 ~였다면)　　　　　　　　　　　　(…할 텐데)

[가정법 과거완료] If I had known about the event, I would be there now.
\+ [가정법 과거]　　　　　if절의 동사 (had + 과거분사)　　　주절의 동사 (would + 동사원형)
(내가 그 행사에 대해 알았더라면, 지금 거기에 있을 텐데.)

[과거 사실] As I didn't know about the event, I can't be there now. ❶
\+ [현재 사실]　　　　과거에 관한 내용　　　　　　　　　　현재에 관한 내용
(나는 그 행사에 대해 몰랐기 때문에, 지금 거기에 있을 수 없다.)

❶ **혼합 가정법의 단서**
혼합 가정법 문장의 주절에는 현재를 나타내는 표현, 즉 now, this time, today 등이 함께 쓰인다.

[가정법 과거완료] If they had taken care of the car, it would run smoothly now.
\+ [가정법 과거]　　　　if절의 동사 (had + 과거분사)　　　주절의 동사 (would + 동사원형)
(그들이 차를 관리했더라면, 지금도 잘 굴러갈 텐데.)

[과거 사실] As they didn't take care of the car, it can't run smoothly now. ❶
\+ [현재 사실]　　　　과거에 관한 내용　　　　　　　　　　현재에 관한 내용
(그들이 차를 관리하지 않았기 때문에, 지금 잘 굴러갈 수 없다.)

2 if의 생략

If + 주어 + were ~, …　　　→ Were + 주어 + ~, …
If + 주어 + had + 과거분사 ~, … → Had + 주어 + 과거분사 ~, …

– 가정법 문장의 if절에 were 또는 「had + 과거분사」가 있을 때, if를 생략하고 if절의 주어와 were/had를 도치❷하여 「Were/had + 주어」로 쓸 수 있다.

[가정법 과거] If he were to accept the offer, it would alter his future.
　　　　→ Were he to accept the offer, it would alter his future.
(그가 그 제안을 수락한다면, 그의 미래가 달라질 것이다.)

❷ **도치**(倒置, 넘어질 도, 둘 치)
문장 안에서 어순을 바꾸는 것을 뜻한다. 주로 문장의 주어와 동사의 위치를 서로 바꿀 때를 가리킨다.

[가정법 과거완료] If circumstances had permitted, we might have won.
　　　　→ Had circumstances permitted, we might have won.
(상황이 허락했더라면, 우리는 이겼을지도 모른다.)

3 It's time (that) + 가정법 과거 '~해야 할 때이다'를 뜻한다.

= 「It's time to + 동사원형」 = 「It's time (that) + 주어 + should + 동사원형」

• It's time (that) you took responsibility for your actions.
　= It's time to take responsibility for your actions.
　= It's time (that) you should take responsibility for your actions.
(너의 행동에 대해 책임질 때이다.)

1 혼합 가정법

[01-05] 자연스러운 의미가 되도록 바르게 연결하시오.

01 If I had married Helen, •

02 If he had gone to bed early, •

03 If you had brought an umbrella, •

04 If she had gone to Paris, •

05 If they had taken the taxi, •

• ⓐ they would be here by now.

• ⓑ he would not be tired now.

• ⓒ she would be able to speak French.

• ⓓ I would be living in London now.

• ⓔ you would not have to worry about the acid rain now.

2 if의 생략

[06-09] 주어진 우리말과 일치하도록 괄호 안의 말을 이용하여 문장을 완성하시오. (단, 주절의 조동사는 would만 사용할 것)

06 내가 식물학자라면, 그 식물의 생존 가능성을 판단할 텐데. (be, assess)

➡ ______________ I a botanist, I ______________ the plant's chance of survival.

07 그가 더 조심했더라면, 그는 박제된 호랑이를 진짜라고 착각하지 않았을 텐데. (be, mistake)

➡ __________ he __________ more careful, he ______________ the stuffed tiger for a real one.

08 이 정보가 사실이라면, 결과가 다를 텐데. (be)

➡ ______________ this information true, the results ______________ different.

09 우리가 지도를 가져왔더라면, 우리는 길을 잃지 않았을 텐데. (bring, get)

➡ ______________ we ______________ a map, we ______________________________ lost.

3 It's time (that) + 가정법 과거

[10-13] 빈칸에 알맞은 것을 〈보기〉에서 골라 문장을 쓰시오. (중복 사용 불가)

〈보기〉

| to | time | that | should |

10 It's ______________ they left for their house.

11 It's time that he ______________ do something for his family.

12 It's time ______________ put down their smartphones before going to sleep.

13 It's time ______________ you should start studying seriously.

어휘 & 표현

· **circumstance** 상황　· **permit** 허락하다　· **responsibility** 책임　· **acid rain** 산성비　· **botanist** 식물학자
· **assess** 판단하다, 평가하다　· **survival** 생존　· **stuffed** 박제된　· **information** 정보

〈 정답과 해설 p. 131~132 〉

[01-05]

빈칸에 알맞은 것을 고르시오.

01

> If you __________ to the mountain, you would feel better.

① goes ② went ③ gone
④ have gone ⑤ has gone

02

> If it had stopped raining, we __________ hiking.

① go ② would have gone
③ went ④ will have gone
⑤ had gone

03

> __________ I you, I would study English hard.

① If ② Were ③ Had
④ Should ⑤ Without

04

> __________ my math teacher, I would fail the exam.

① Without ② If ③ Had
④ Should ⑤ But

05

> It's time you __________ eating junk food.

① stops ② stopped
③ will stop ④ had stopped
⑤ would stop

06

빈칸에 알맞은 말로 바르게 짝지어진 것을 고르시오.

> A: Did you go to the library yesterday?
> B: No. It was too cold. If it __________ cold, I might have gone there.
> A: Yes, it is still cold today. I wish it __________ warmer.

① isn't – will get
② weren't – got
③ hadn't been – got
④ weren't – had gotten
⑤ hadn't been – will get

07

두 문장의 뜻이 같도록 빈칸에 알맞은 것끼리 짝지은 것을 고르시오.

> My mother is very busy today, so she doesn't play with me.
> = If my mother __________ so busy today, she __________ with me.

① isn't – will play
② was – would play
③ was – played
④ weren't – would play
⑤ were – would play

08

두 문장의 의미가 같도록 빈칸에 알맞은 것을 고르시오.

> He tells __________ me with the housework.
> = In fact, he doesn't help me with the housework.

① as if he helps ② as if he helped
③ even if he helps ④ even if he helped
⑤ as if he had helped

[09-12] 고난도

어법상 옳은 것을 고르시오.

09

① I wish he comes to the party.
② She talks as if she is older than me.
③ If I were you, I would buy this jacket.
④ If you hurried up, you can see him.
⑤ The boy looked as if he loses his toy.

10

① What would happen if I pushed this button?
② With your help, we couldn't have done it.
③ If I have enough money, I could have bought you a laptop computer.
④ If we left at 10, we will arrive in time.
⑤ I wish I can go to the concert with you.

11

① You talked as if you are familiar with him.
② If I had seen her email, I will send her the message.
③ If I didn't have to clean the school, I could go home earlier.
④ I wish I have a motor bike.
⑤ If you know that, you wouldn't go there.

12

① If I were you, I will tell the truth.
② If he had time, he won't skip the meal.
③ If we hurried, we could have caught the train.
④ If she were healthy, she would have finished the race.
⑤ If he had followed my advice, he would be more successful now.

[13-19]

괄호 안에서 알맞은 것을 고르시오.

13

If it had not been (of / for) my teacher, I wouldn't have been able to write novels.

14

They say they are very hungry. I wish they (had / have had) something to eat.

15

He has never been to Africa. However, he speaks as if he (were / had been) there before.

16

(With / Without) electricity, their life would have been much harder.

17

On Mike's birthday, his girlfriend was beyond the sea. I wish she (were / had been) with him.

18

It's time they (go / went) for a walk.

19

(Without / But) for their support, he could not have won the election.

20

주어진 문장과 의미가 <u>다른</u> 것을 고르시오.

> As there is water, creatures can exist on Earth.

① Without water, no creatures could exist on Earth.
② But for water, no creatures could exist on Earth.
③ Were it not for water, no creatures could exist on Earth.
④ If it were not for water, no creatures could exist on Earth.
⑤ Had it not been for water, no creatures could exist on Earth now.

〈 정답과 해설 p. 132~134 〉

33 DAY

괄호 안에 주어진 동사를 알맞은 형태로 바꾸어 빈칸에 쓰시오.

21

If she ___________ hungry, she would be having lunch with you. (be)

22

You are eating too much candy. I wish you ___________ so much candy. (not eat)

23

What ___________ if Japan had not invaded Pearl Harbor? (happen)

24

He's only fifteen, but he walks as if he ___________ an old man. (be)

25

If I were a doctor, I ___________ you to stop smoking. (advise)

26

If you ___________ our dance club, we would win the first prize. (join)

27

주어진 문장을 가정법 문장으로 바르게 고친 것을 고르시오.

> As they didn't take the early train, they could not arrive on time.

① If they take the early train, they could arrive on time.
② If they took the early train, they could arrive on time.
③ If they took the early train, they could have arrived on time.
④ If they had taken the early train, they could arrive on time.
⑤ If they had taken the early train, they could have arrived on time.

두 문장의 뜻이 같도록 빈칸에 알맞은 말을 쓰시오.

28

But for your effort, we couldn't do the work.
➡ Were it ___________ your effort, we couldn't do the work.

29

As I didn't finish my homework yesterday, I can't take a rest now.
➡ If I ___________ my homework yesterday, I could take a rest now.

30

It's time for him to get up.
➡ It's time he ___________ up.

31

As I didn't take my trainer's advice, I'm not in good shape now.
➡ If I ___________ my trainer's advice, I ___________ in good shape now.

주어진 우리말과 일치하도록 괄호 안에 주어진 말을 이용하여 쓰시오.

32

내가 그때 애플파이를 먹었더라면 좋았을 텐데.
(have, the apple pie, then)
➡ I wish ___________

____

33

그가 너를 돕게 내버려 두었다면, 너는 그 일을 완료할 수 있었을 텐데. (let, help, complete, the task)
➡ If you ___________

____

다음 글을 읽고 물음에 답하시오.

Dear Alison,
Hi, I'm a 23-year-old woman. I have a problem with my parents. I have majored in law, but I'm a painter. I like drawing pictures and I love my job. ⓐ Unfortunately, my parents wish I will be a lawyer. To tell the truth, ⓑ I'm really not interested in law and I want to be a well-known painter. What should I do?

from Maria

34

밑줄 친 ⓐ에서 어법상 틀린 부분을 찾아 바르게 고쳐 쓰시오.

➡ ________________

35

밑줄 친 ⓑ를 가정법 문장으로 바꿀 때, 빈칸에 알맞은 말을 쓰시오.

If I __________ really interested in law, I __________ not want to be a well-known painter.

[36-37]

다음 글을 읽고 물음에 답하시오.

Your best friend Susan is excited to go to a party, but her dress and make-up look terrible. Susan asks you ⓐ if she looks good. What would you say to her? If you ___ ⓑ ___ the truth, her feelings might not be hurt. Wait a minute! Let's see this way. Telling the truth can mean that she has a second chance at making things better. For example, she can go home and change her dress and make-up.

36

밑줄 친 ⓐ와 쓰임이 같은 것을 고르시오.

① If I were you, I would go there with him.
② I don't understand if she is upset with me.
③ What would you do if you were in my shoes?
④ If I were in Japan, I could attend my aunt's wedding.
⑤ If I had enough time, I would go to the amusement park.

37

빈칸 ⓑ에 알맞은 것을 고르시오.

① didn't tell   ② told
③ have not told   ④ had told
⑤ had been told

[38-39]

다음 글을 읽고 물음에 답하시오.

What time do you usually go to bed? Do you dream a lot? If your answer is yes, you will be surprised to know this fact: when you dream, your eyes move around ⓐ 마치 당신이 영화 한 편을 보고 있는 것처럼. Scientists call it "REM(rapid eye movement)." Next time when you see someone sleeping, check if his or her eyes are moving. If they are moving, you will know that the person is dreaming. I wish you ⓑ see it in person.

38 서술형 고난도

밑줄 친 ⓐ의 우리말을 as if와 주어진 단어를 사용하여 영어로 쓰시오. (watch, a movie)

➡ as if ________________ ________________ ________________

________________ ________________

39 서술형

밑줄 친 ⓑ를 어법상 알맞게 고쳐 쓰시오.

(조동사 can을 함께 쓸 것)

________________ ________________

주어진 우리말과 일치하도록 빈칸에 알맞은 것끼리 짝지은 것을 고르시오.

40

내가 너라면, 그 휴대폰을 사지 않을텐데.
➡ If I __________ you, I __________ buy the cell phone.

① were – would
② am – would
③ were – would have
④ am – won't
⑤ were – would not

41

비가 오고 있지 않다면, 우리는 축구를 할 수 있을 텐데.
➡ If it __________ raining, we __________ soccer.

① were not – can play
② is not – could not play
③ is – can play
④ was not – could not play
⑤ were not – could play

42

내가 여자 친구가 있다면, 나는 그녀와 함께 영화관에 갈 텐데.
➡ If I __________ a girl friend, I __________ to the theater with her.

① have – would go
② have not – would not go
③ had – went
④ had – would go
⑤ had not – would go

[43-44] 서술형

주어진 두 문장이 같은 뜻이 되도록 빈칸에 알맞은 말을 쓰시오.

43

As I don't bring an umbrella, I can't go to see a movie.
= __________________________________, I could go to see a movie.

44

As she didn't ask me twice, I didn't help her.
= __________________________________, I would have helped her.

45 수능 유형

밑줄 친 부분 중 어법상 틀린 것을 고르시오.

What would you do if your children ① lost their temper and became uncontrollable in public? One day, on my way home, I saw a lady and her little boy. The boy was crying out loud for a candy, but his mom would not ② give it to him. What bothered me was the mom's attitude. She kept yelling at him, "Stop it! Stop!" However, he acted as if he ③ hasn't heard her. His crying and screaming got louder and louder, and he didn't want to stop. When ④ returning home, I thought about the lady and her little boy. If I ⑤ had been her, I wouldn't have yelled at him and would have waited until he became calm.

①　　②　　③　　④　　⑤

🦉 어휘 & 표현

- **junk food** 즉석식품　· **housework** 가사, 집안일　· **successful** 성공적인　· **electricity** 전기　· **election** 선거
- **creature** 생명체　· **exist** 존재하다　· **invade** 침략하다　· **effort** 노력　· **major in** ~을 전공하다
- **unfortunately** 불행하게도　· **movement** 움직임　· **lose one's temper** 화를 내다　· **bother** 괴롭히다　· **attitude** 태도

일치, 화법
一致　　話法
(하나 일, 이를 치)　(말씀 화, 법 법)

UNIT 73 **주어와 동사의 수 일치**
주어에 동사의 수를 맞춰 쓰는 것

UNIT 74 **시제 일치**
주절에 종속절의 시제를 맞춰 쓰는 것

UNIT 75 **화법**
직접화법과 간접화법

Speaking English fluently takes practice.
단수 주어 (동명사)　　　　　　　단수 동사

(영어를 유창하게 말하는 것은 연습이 필요하다.)

He hoped that everything would be fine.
주절 (과거)　　　　　　　　종속절 (과거)

(그는 모든 게 잘 되길 바랐다.)

He said to his friend, "I will call you tomorrow."
직접화법

(그는 친구에게 "내가 내일 너에게 전화할게."라고 말했다.)

He told his friend that he would call him the next day.
간접화법

(그는 친구에게 다음 날 전화하겠다고 말했다.)

주어와 동사의 수 일치

Every student is sitting in the auditorium.
「every+단수 명사」 → 단수 동사를 씀

(모든 학생이 강당에 앉아 있다.)

Each student is wearing his or her own uniform.
「each+단수 명사」 → 단수 동사를 씀

(각각의 학생은 각자 자신의 교복을 입고 있다.)

1 단수 취급 주어 + 단수 동사

(1) -thing, -body, -one으로 끝나는 부정대명사 + 단수 동사

- **Nothing** is more important than family. (가족보다 더 중요한 것은 없다.)
  -thing
- **Everybody** needs to stay calm during an emergency. (모든 사람은 비상 상황에 침착해야 한다.)
  -body
- If **anyone** needs help, just ask me. (도움이 필요하신 분은 저에게 말씀하세요.)
  -one

(2) to부정사, 명사절, and로 연결되지 않은 동명사 + 단수 동사

- **To understand the problem** is the first step to solving it.
  to부정사

  (문제를 이해하는 것이 그것을 해결하는 첫 번째 단계이다.)

- **That I missed the meeting** was my fault. (내가 회의를 놓친 것은 내 잘못이었다.)
  명사절
- **Running every morning** keeps me healthy. (매일 아침에 달리는 것은 나의 건강을 유지하게 한다.)
  동명사

(3) every나 each를 포함하는 경우 + 단수 동사 ❶

- **Every student** in our school wears a uniform on Mondays.

  (우리 학교의 모든 학생은 월요일마다 교복을 입는다.)

- **Each child** has his or her own unique opinion.

  (각각의 아이는 그 자신만의 고유한 의견을 가지고 있다.)

> **❶ every와 each**
> every와 each 다음에 단수 명사가 나오고 동사도 이에 따라 단수형으로 쓴다.

2 복수 형태 주어 + 단수 동사

(1) 시간, 거리, 무게, 가격 + 단수 동사

- **Two hours** is too short to finish the work. (두 시간은 그 일을 끝내기에 너무 짧다.)
  시간
- **Ten kilometers** is a long distance for a beginner runner. (10킬로미터는 초보 주자에게는 긴 거리다.)
  거리
- **Twenty kilograms** is too much for a small child to lift.
  무게

  (20킬로그램은 어린아이가 들기에는 너무 무겁다.)

- **One hundred dollars** is too much for one meal.
  가격

  (100달러는 한 끼 식사 값으로는 너무 많다.)

(2) -s로 끝나는 질병, 학과, 국가 등 + 단수 동사 ❷

- **Measles** is an infectious disease. (홍역은 전염성 질병이다.)
  -s로 끝나는 질병
- **Ethics** is an important subject in philosophy. (윤리는 철학에서 중요한 과목이다.)
  -s로 끝나는 학과
- **The Philippines** is a beautiful country made up of many islands.
  -s로 끝나는 국가

  (필리핀은 많은 섬으로 이루어진 아름다운 나라다.)

(3) 단일 개념의 A and B + 단수 동사 ❸

- **Tea and sugar** makes a perfect combination. (차와 설탕은 완벽한 조합을 만든다.)

> **❷ -s로 끝나는 질병, 학과, 국가**
> - **질병**: diabetes (당뇨병), mumps (볼거리)
> - **학과**: mathematics (수학), physics (물리학), economics (경제학), linguistics (언어학)
> - **국가**: The United States (미국), The Maldives (몰디브), The Netherlands (네덜란드)

> **❸ 일반적인 경우의 A and B**
> 일반적으로 주어 자리에 and로 연결된 명사가 오면 복수 취급하여 복수 동사가 온다.

■1 단수 취급 주어 + 단수 동사

[01-05] 주어진 동사를 알맞은 형태로 바꾸어 빈칸에 쓰시오. (현재시제로 쓸 것)

01 Every country ________________ its own culture and tradition. (have)

02 To study hard before exams usually ________________ to better grades. (lead)

03 Something about this place ________________ me feel very comfortable. (make)

04 Traveling to new places ________________ you about different cultures. (teach)

05 Each member ________________ to pay the monthly membership fee, which costs 10,000 won. (have)

[06-09] 주어진 우리말과 일치하도록 괄호 안의 말을 배열하시오.

06 너한테 무슨 문제가 있는 거니? (the matter, anything, with, is, you)

➡ ____

07 그가 내게 다시 전화하지 않았다는 것은 예상 밖이었다.

(unexpected, he, call, didn't, that, me, was, back)

➡ ____

08 무언가 매우 중요한 일이 곧 일어날 거야. (soon, important, is going to, something, happen, very)

➡ ____

09 내가 도착했을 때 아무도 집에 없었다. (at home, was, I, when, arrived, nobody)

➡ ____

■2 복수 형태 주어 + 단수 동사

[10-15] 문장에서 틀린 부분을 찾아 밑줄을 긋고 바르게 고치시오.

10 Curry and rice are the restaurant's main dish. ➡ ____________

11 Diabetes affect millions of people every year. ➡ ____________

12 The Philippines are famous for its beautiful islands. ➡ ____________

13 Three miles are too far to walk without a break. ➡ ____________

14 Canada is the biggest producer of maple syrup, and the United States are the biggest consumer. ➡ ____________

15 Physics are the study of matter, energy, and how they interact. ➡ ____________

🦉 **어휘 & 표현**

- **emergency** 비상 상황   · **opinion** 의견   · **distance** 거리   · **infectious** 전염되는   · **mathematics** 수학
- **physics** 물리학   · **ethics** 윤리학   · **philosophy** 철학   · **combination** 조합   · **comfortable** 편안한
- **unexpected** 예상 밖의   · **interact** 상호작용하다

34 DAY

〈 정답과 해설 **p. 135~136** 〉

❸ 여러 가지 주어와 동사의 수 일치

(1) 상관접속사로 연결된 주어

상관접속사	동사의 수 일치	예문
both A and B	복수 동사	• Both the cake and the cookies were a hit at the party. (케이크와 쿠키 모두 파티에서 큰 인기를 끌었다.)
not A but B	B에 동사를 일치시킴	• Not the old computers but the new one is causing the problem. (오래된 컴퓨터들이 아니라 새 컴퓨터가 문제를 일으킨다.)
either A or B		• Either the dog or the cats are responsible for the mess. (어지럽힌 책임은 개나 고양이들 중에 있다.)
neither A nor B		• Neither the employees nor the manager is responsible for this mistake. (직원들도 관리자도 이 실수에 대해 책임이 없다.)
not only A but (also) B		• Not only the architect but also the engineers make key decisions. (건축가뿐만 아니라 엔지니어들도 중요한 결정을 내린다.)
B as well as A		• He as well as his brothers likes swimming. (그의 남동생들뿐만 아니라 그도 수영을 좋아한다.)

(2) 부분을 나타내는 표현이 포함된 주어 ❶ : of 뒤의 명사에 동사의 수 일치

all, some, most, half
part, none, the rest
분수, %(퍼센트)
$\Big\}$ + of + 명사 + 동사 (수 일치)

> **❶ no + 명사**
> no 뒤에 나온 명사에 동사의 수를 일치시킨다.
> • No child is allowed to enter without permission.
> (허락 없이 아이는 들어갈 수 없다.)

• All of the music was composed by one artist.
  (of 뒤에 나온 명사 (단수)) (단수 동사)
  (모든 음악은 한 예술가에 의해 작곡되었다.)

• Most of the city's lights were turned off during Earth Hour.
  (of 뒤에 나온 명사 (복수)) (복수 동사)
  (지구촌 전등 끄기 시간에 도시의 대부분 조명이 꺼졌다.)

• The rest of the books were stored in the basement. (나머지 책들은 지하실에 보관되었다.)
  (of 뒤에 나온 명사 (복수)) (복수 동사)

• 35% of the population of the country comes from different countries.
  (of 뒤에 나온 명사 (단수)) (단수 동사)
  (그 나라의 인구의 35%가 다양한 국가 출신이다.)

(3) 주격 관계대명사절의 선행사와 동사 : 선행사의 수에 일치시킨다.

• The doctor who looks after me explains everything clearly.
  (단수 동사)
  (주격 관계대명사 who의 선행사 (단수))
  (나를 돌봐주는 그 의사는 모든 것을 명확하게 설명한다.)

• The books that are on the desk belong to me. (책상 위에 있는 책들은 내 것이다.)
  (복수 동사)
  (주격 관계대명사 that의 선행사 (복수))

(4) a number of + 복수 동사 : '많은' (복수 취급) → 복수 동사
the number of + 단수 동사 : '~의 수' (단수 취급) → 단수 동사

• A number of people express interest in joining the event.
  (복수 동사)
  (많은 사람들이 그 행사에 참여하겠다고 관심을 보인다.)

• The number of participants in the competition was higher than expected.
  (단수 동사)
  (그 대회에 참가한 사람들의 수는 예상보다 많았다.)

3 **(1) 상관접속사로 연결된 주어와 동사의 수 일치**

[16-20] 주어진 동사를 알맞은 형태로 바꾸어 빈칸에 쓰시오. (현재시제로 쓸 것)

16 Not the dogs but the cat _______________ making that noise. (be)

17 Either you or your brother _______________ about the plan. (know)

18 If both of you _______________ a look at this, you might like it. (take)

19 Neither my father nor my brothers _______________ vegetables. (like)

20 Not only he but also his parents _______________ very proud. (be)

3 **(2) 부분을 나타내는 표현이 포함된 주어와 동사의 수 일치**

[21-30] 괄호 안에서 알맞은 것을 고르시오.

21 No cyclists (use / uses) these roads.

22 Half of the people (is / are) opposing the new rules.

23 All of the articles in this newspaper (is / are) pieces of gossip.

24 No message (has / have) been received from the missing hiker yet.

25 Do you know that ninety percent of a newborn body (is / are) water?

26 Over half of the students (think / thinks) that the mid-term exam was easy.

27 He says that most of the work (has / have) been completed.

28 All of the money that I had (was / were) stolen on the train.

29 Half of the cake (was / were) eaten before the party even started.

30 Two-thirds of their documents (was / were) not recorded correctly.

3 **(3) 주격 관계대명사절의 선행사와 동사, (4) a number of, the number of**

[31-36] 문장에서 틀린 부분을 찾아 밑줄을 긋고 바르게 고치시오.

31 The number of planets in our solar system are eight. ⇒ _______________

32 A number of tourists was waiting in front of the museum. ⇒ _______________

33 She is a good doctor who try her best to help her patients get well. ⇒ _______________

34 All of the teachers who teaches us English came from South Africa. ⇒ _______________

35 A number of companies prevents their workers from smoking in the office.

⇒ _______________

36 Because of global warming, the number of penguins are expected to be reduced.

⇒ _______________

🦉 **어휘 & 표현**

· **responsible** 책임 있는　　· **mess** 어지럽힘, 혼잡　　· **compose** 작곡하다　　· **basement** 지하실　　· **express** 표현하다
· **expect** 예상하다　　· **cyclist** 자전거 타는 사람　　· **oppose** 반대하다　　· **gossip** 소문, 가십　　· **newborn baby** 신생아
· **solar system** 태양계　　· **prevent A from B** A가 B하지 못하게 막다

> **• 시제 일치:** 주절의 상황에 따라 종속절 동사의 시제를 맞춰 쓰는 것을 말한다. ──── 핵심 개념

1 시제 일치의 원칙

(1) 주절이 현재시제 → 종속절은 모든 시제 가능

- I believe that she will succeed in her new job. (나는 그녀가 새 직장에서 성공할 것이라고 믿는다.)
  주절 (현재) / 종속절 (미래)
- I believe that she is succeeding in her new job. (나는 그녀가 새 직장에서 성공하는 중이라고 믿는다.)
  주절 (현재) / 종속절 (현재진행)

(2) 주절이 과거시제 → 종속절은 과거(진행)시제, 과거완료(진행)시제

- I believed that she succeeded in her new job. (나는 그녀가 새 직장에서 성공했다고 믿었다.)
  주절 (과거) / 종속절 (과거)
- I believed that she had succeeded in her new job. (나는 그녀가 새 직장에서 성공했었다고 믿었다.)
  주절 (과거) / 종속절 (과거완료)
- He said that she was crying because she had been waiting for hours.
  주절 (과거) / 종속절 (과거진행) / 종속절 (과거완료진행)
  (그는 그녀가 몇 시간 동안 기다려 왔기 때문에 울고 있다고 말했다.)

2 시제 일치의 예외

(1) 진리, 사실, 습관, 속담❶, 격언을 나타내는 종속절 : 주절의 시제와 관계없이 항상 현재시제로 쓴다.

- They said that there are craters on the moon's surface.
  주절 (과거) / 종속절 (현재)
  (그들은 달 표면에 분화구가 있다고 말했다.)
- He told me that he always gets up early.
  주절 (과거) / 종속절 (현재)
  (그는 내게 그가 항상 일찍 일어난다고 말했다.)

> **❶ 속담 시제의 예외**
> 속담은 대부분 현재시제를 쓰지만 과거시제를 사용하여 과거의 한 사건을 언급하면서 교훈을 줄 때는 과거시제를 쓴다.
> • Rome wasn't built in a day.
> (로마는 하루아침에 이루어진 것이 아니다.)

(2) 역사적인 사실 : 항상 과거시제로 쓴다.

- Lots of people say Alexander Graham Bell invented the telephone. (많은 사람들이 Alexander Graham Bell이 전화기를 발명했다고 말한다.)

(3) 주장, 명령, 충고, 제안, 요구를 나타내는 동사가 주절에 쓰였을 때 :
종속절의 동사 「should+동사원형」에서 should를 생략할 수 있어 **동사원형**으로 쓴다.

- The dentist advised I (should) keep my teeth clean.
  동사원형
  (치과의사는 내가 이를 깨끗이 해야 한다고 충고했다.)

(4) 비교 구문: as나 than 뒤에 나오는 구문의 시제는 앞의 주절의 시제와 상관없이 쓴다.

- It was not so humid yesterday as it is today. (어제는 오늘만큼 습하지 않았다.)
  일치하지 않음
- He ran faster today than he does on a normal day. (그는 평소보다 오늘 더 빨리 달렸다.)
  일치하지 않음

(5) 시간, 조건을 나타내는 부사절❷ : 미래시제 대신 현재시제를 쓴다.

- When you arrive at the airport, you'll meet them.
  시간의 부사절
  (네가 공항에 도착하면, 그들을 만날 것이다.)
- If he comes tomorrow, I'll stay at home.
  조건의 부사절
  (그가 내일 온다면, 나는 집에 있을 것이다.)

> **❷ 시간, 조건을 나타내는 부사절 접속사**
> - **시간 부사절 접속사:** when, while, until, as, after, before, since, as soon as
> - **조건 부사절 접속사:** if, unless, once, in case, as long as

1 시제 일치의 원칙

[01-06] 문장에서 <u>틀린</u> 부분을 찾아 밑줄을 긋고 바르게 고치시오.

01 I thought that the weather will be fine. → ____________________

02 He said that he will not pay for their service. → ____________________

03 He told me that he will leave Korea sooner or later. → ____________________

04 As I visited Rick, I saw that he is painting his house. → ____________________

05 When I was young, I thought my dad is very intelligent. → ____________________

06 I didn't know that he has been at the hospital for three weeks. → ____________________

2 시제 일치의 예외

[07-12] 주어진 동사를 알맞은 형태로 바꾸어 빈칸에 쓰시오. (필요 없는 경우 바꾸지 않아도 됨)

07 I heard that Marie Curie ________________ the Nobel Prize. (win)

08 He claimed that parents ________________ sacrifices for their children. (make)

09 She didn't know that I always ________________ up at 5 o'clock to deliver milk. (get)

10 Before 1543, most people didn't know that the Earth ________________ around the Sun. (go)

11 The teacher told us that Jupiter ________________ the largest planet in our solar system. (be)

12 Some Korean college students don't know that the Korean War ________________ out in 1950. (break)

1 + 2 시제 일치

[13-20] 괄호 안에서 알맞은 것을 고르시오.

13 I asked her what she (do / did) in her free time.

14 Scientists found that Saturn (has / had) nine rings.

15 If he (calls / will call) again, please let me know right away.

16 The doctor insisted that he (do / does) some exercise every day.

17 He told me that he (have been / had been) to Japan several times.

18 When the movie (ends / will end), we will go get something to eat.

19 Did you know that Vatican City (is / was) the smallest country in the world?

20 Many surveys showed almost all parents (want / wanted) their children to go to college.

🦉 **어휘 & 표현**

· **crater** 분화구 · **surface** 표면 · **invent** 발명하다 · **claim** 주장하다 · **sacrifice** 희생 · **deliver** 배달하다
· **Jupiter** 목성 · **solar system** 태양계 · **Saturn** 토성 · **insist** 주장하다

34 DAY

〈 정답과 해설 **p. 137~138** 〉

• **화법**: 다른 사람의 말을 재현하는 방법이다.
　다른 사람의 말을 그대로 전달하는 직접화법과 전달자의 입장에 맞게 바꾸어 전달하는 간접화법이 있다. ───핵심 개념

Jane said to me, *"I love Peter."*
직접화법
(Jane은 내게 "나는 Peter를 사랑해."라고 말했다.)

Jane told me *she loved Peter*. (Jane은 내게 Peter를 사랑한다고 말했다.)
간접화법

1 화법의 개념과 종류

직접화법	간접화법
다른 사람의 말을 그대로 인용하여 전달하는 방식	다른 사람의 말을 (변형하여) 간접적으로 전달하는 방식
① 따옴표("")가 있음 ② 말한 사람이 직접 말한 내용을 그대로 전달함 ③ 문장의 시제와 인칭도 그대로 유지	① 따옴표("")가 없음, 접속사(that 등)가 필요 ② 발화자의 말을 그대로 인용하지 않고 내용을 재구성함 ③ 문장 구조, 시제, 인칭이 변경될 수 있음
• She said, "I need a break." (그녀는 "나는 휴식이 필요해."라고 말했다.)	• She said that she needed a break. (그녀는 휴식이 필요하다고 말했다.)

2 평서문❶ 화법 전환

❶ **평서문**
말하는 이가 사건의 내용을 객관적으로 말하는 문장이다.

직접화법 David said to me, "① I ②③ will ④ see this again tomorrow. ⑤"
(David는 나에게 "나는 이것을 내일 다시 볼 거예요."라고 말했다.)

간접화법 David told me that he would see that again the next day.
(David는 나에게 그것을 다음날 다시 볼 거라고 말했다.)

❷ **that절의 시제**
전달 동사가 과거이고 직접화법이 과거일 때, 간접화법의 that절에는 과거완료시제를 쓴다.

① 전달 동사를 바꾼다.　say(~을 말하다) → say
　　「say to + 사람」(~에게 말하다) → 「tell + 사람」

② 콤마(,)와 인용부호(" ")를 삭제한다. 두 절을 접속사 that으로 연결한다. (단, that은 생략할 수 있다.)

③ that절의 주어는 알맞은 인칭대명사로 바꾼다. I → he(David)

④ that절의 시제❷는 전달 동사(say)의 시제와 일치시킨다. will see → would see

⑤ 시간의 부사 및 지시대명사는 전달자 입장으로 바꾼다. this → that, tomorrow → the next day

직접화법		간접화법
now (지금)		then (그때), at the time (당시에)
today (오늘)		that day (그날)
yesterday (어제)	→	the day before (전날)
tomorrow (내일)		the next [following] day (다음날)
this week (이번 주)		that week (그 주)
next week (다음 주)		the following week (그 다음 주)
last week (지난주)		the week before, the previous week (진주)

직접화법 She said to me, "① I ②③ will ④ go to the store tomorrow. ⑤" (그녀는 나에게 "내일 가게에 갈 거야."라고 말했다.)

간접화법 She told me that she would go to the store the next day. (그녀는 나에게 다음날 가게에 갈 거라고 말했다.)

1 + 2 화법의 개념과 종류, 평서문 화법 전환

[01-04] 직접화법을 간접화법으로 바꿔 빈칸에 알맞은 말을 쓰시오.

01 She said to me, "I am feeling unwell."

➡ She ＿＿＿＿＿ me ＿＿＿＿＿ ＿＿＿＿＿ was feeling unwell.

02 Mom said, "I'm going to the bank now."

➡ Mom said that ＿＿＿＿＿ ＿＿＿＿＿ going to the bank ＿＿＿＿＿.

03 She said to me, "I lost my watch here."

➡ She ＿＿＿＿＿ me she ＿＿＿＿＿ ＿＿＿＿＿ ＿＿＿＿＿ watch ＿＿＿＿＿.

04 They said to us, "We will help you with the project."

➡ They told us ＿＿＿＿＿ ＿＿＿＿＿ ＿＿＿＿＿ help ＿＿＿＿＿ with the project.

[05-08] 간접화법을 직접화법으로 바꿔 빈칸에 알맞은 말을 쓰시오.

05 John said that he would call me later.

➡ John said, "＿＿＿＿＿ ＿＿＿＿＿ call ＿＿＿＿＿ later."

06 The teacher said that the test would be on Friday.

➡ The teacher said, "The test ＿＿＿＿＿ ＿＿＿＿＿ on Friday."

07 He told me that he had been tired the day before.

➡ He said to me, "＿＿＿＿＿ ＿＿＿＿＿ tired ＿＿＿＿＿."

08 Their parents told them they would take them to the amusement park.

➡ Their parents said to them, "＿＿＿＿＿ ＿＿＿＿＿ ＿＿＿＿＿ ＿＿＿＿＿ to the amusement park."

[09-12] 주어진 우리말과 일치하도록 괄호 안에서 알맞은 것을 고르시오.

09 그녀는 이미 숙제를 끝냈다고 말했다.

➡ She said that she (have / had) already finished her homework.

10 그는 나에게 친구를 방문할 거라고 말했다.

➡ He told me that he (is / was) going to visit his friend.

11 그는 "나는 오늘 밤 숙제를 끝낼 거야."라고 말했다.

➡ He said, "I will finish (my / his) homework tonight."

12 Mark는 "나는 다음 주에 할머니, 할아버지를 방문할 계획 중이야."라고 말했다.

➡ Mark said, "(I'm / he's) planning to visit my grandparents next week."

🦉 **어휘 & 표현**

· **unwell** 아픈 　· **amusement park** 놀이공원

〈 정답과 해설 p. 138~139 〉

3 의문문 화법 전환

(1) 의문사가 없는 의문문

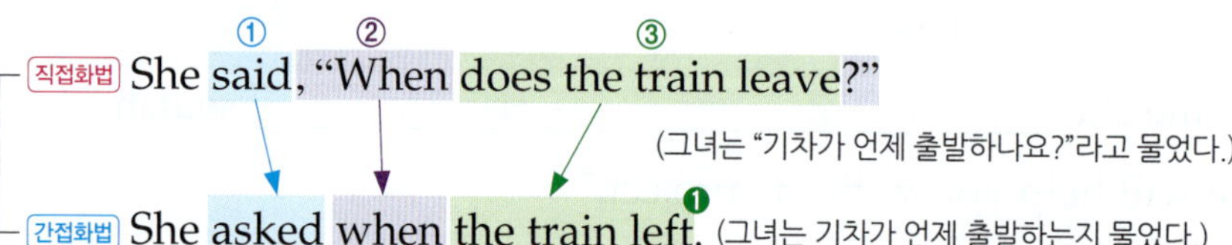

① ②　③
[직접화법] He said, "Are you coming to the party?" (그는 "너는 파티에 오니?"라고 물었다.)

[간접화법] He asked if[whether] I was coming to the party. (그는 내가 파티에 올 것이냐고 물었다.)

① **ask**를 전달 동사로 쓴다.

② **콤마(,)와 인용부호(" ")**, 물음표를 삭제한다. 두 절을 접속사 **if**나 **whether**로 연결한다.

③ 의문문의 어순(「**동사 + 주어**」)을 「**주어 + 동사**」로 바꾼다.

(2) 의문사가 있는 의문문

① ②　③
[직접화법] She said, "When does the train leave?"
(그녀는 "기차가 언제 출발하나요?"라고 물었다.)

[간접화법] She asked when the train left.❶ (그녀는 기차가 언제 출발하는지 물었다.)

① **ask**를 전달 동사로 쓴다.

② **콤마(,)와 인용부호(" ")**, 물음표를 삭제한다. 두 절을 직접화법에 쓰인 의문사를 사용하여 연결한다.

③ 의문사 뒤의 어순을 「**주어 + 동사**」로 바꾼다. (단, 의문사가 주어인 경우 「**의문사+동사**」를 유지한다.)

> ❶ 일반동사 의문문의 화법 전환
>
> 일반동사의 경우, 의문문을 만들 때 사용한 do, does, did를 삭제한다.

4 명령문 화법 전환

① ② ③
[직접화법] He said to me, "Sit down and relax." (그는 나에게 "앉아서 쉬세요."라고 말했다.)

[간접화법] He asked me to sit down and relax. (그는 나에게 앉아서 쉬라고 말했다.)

① ② ③
[직접화법] The teacher said to the students, "Do not read the next chapter."
(선생님은 학생들에게 "다음 장을 읽지 마세요."라고 말씀하셨다.)

[간접화법] The teacher told the students not to read the next chapter.
(선생님은 학생들에게 다음 장을 읽지 말라고 말씀하셨다.)

① 어조에 따라 **tell, ask, advise, order**❷ 등을 전달 동사로 쓴다.

② **콤마(,)와 인용부호(" ")**를 삭제한다.

③ 긍정 명령문은 동사원형을 「**to+동사원형**」로 바꾼다.
부정 명령문은 「**Do not + 동사원형**」을 「**not to+동사원형**」으로 바꾼다.

> ❷ 명령문 어조에 따른 전달 동사
>
> • **일반적인 지시**: tell
> • **충고**: advise
> • **부탁**: ask, beg
> • **명령**: order, command

5 제안문 화법 전환

① ②　③
[직접화법] She said, "Let's go to the beach." (그녀는 "해변에 가자."라고 말했다.)

[간접화법] She suggested going to the beach. (그녀는 해변에 가자고 제안했다.)

① ②　③
[직접화법] He said, "Let's not go outside today." (그는 "오늘 밖에 나가지 말자."라고 말했다.)

[간접화법] He proposed not going outside that day. (그는 그날 밖에 나가지 말자고 제안했다.)

① **suggest, propose** 등을 전달 동사로 쓴다.

② **콤마(,)와 인용부호(" ")**를 삭제한다.

③ 긍정 제안문은 「**Let's + 동사원형**」을 -ing로 바꾼다.
부정 제안문은 「**Let's + not + 동사원형**」을 **not + -ing**로 바꾼다.

3 의문문 화법 전환

[13-17] 직접화법을 간접화법으로 바꿔 쓸 때, 괄호 안에서 알맞은 것을 고르시오.

13 Jane said, "Did you see the new movie?"

→ Jane asked if I (see / had seen) the new movie.

14 He said to me, "Can you help me with the homework?"

→ He asked me whether (could I / I could) help him with the homework.

15 She said, "Can you come to the party tomorrow?"

→ She asked if (I / you) could come to the party the next day.

16 She said to them, "Which book did you read?"

→ She asked them which book (had they read / they had read).

17 The teacher said to us, "How did you solve the problem?"

→ The teacher asked us how we (solve / had solved) the problem.

4 명령문 화법 전환

[18-21] 직접화법은 간접화법으로, 간접화법은 직접화법으로 바꿔 빈칸에 알맞은 말을 쓰시오.

18 He said to me, "Give me the book."

→ He told me ＿＿＿＿＿ ＿＿＿＿＿ ＿＿＿＿＿ the book.

19 She asked me not to forget her birthday.

→ She said to me, "Don't forget ＿＿＿＿＿ birthday."

20 She said, "Don't be late for the meeting."

→ She asked ＿＿＿＿＿ ＿＿＿＿＿ ＿＿＿＿＿ late for the meeting.

21 The teacher ordered the students to write their names on the paper.

→ The teacher ＿＿＿＿＿ ＿＿＿＿＿ the students, "＿＿＿＿＿ ＿＿＿＿＿ names on the paper."

5 제안문 화법 전환

[22-25] 주어진 우리말과 일치하도록 괄호 안의 말을 이용하여 영작하시오.

어휘 & 표현
- **relax** 긴장을 풀다, 쉬다
- **suggest** 제안하다
- **propose** 제안하다
- **station** 역
- **call it a day** 그만하기로 하다

22 그녀는 그만하자고 제안했다. (suggest, call it a day)

→ ＿＿＿＿＿＿＿＿＿＿＿＿＿＿＿＿＿

23 Tom은 "공원에서 산책하자."라고 말했다. (say, take a walk, in the park)

→ ＿＿＿＿＿＿＿＿＿＿＿＿＿＿＿＿＿

24 Dave는 오후 3시에 카페에서 만나자고 제안했다. (suggest, meet at the café at 3 PM)

→ ＿＿＿＿＿＿＿＿＿＿＿＿＿＿＿＿＿

25 그들은 저녁 전에 너무 많이 먹지 말자고 제안했다. (propose, eat too much before dinner)

→ ＿＿＿＿＿＿＿＿＿＿＿＿＿＿＿＿＿

〈 정답과 해설 p. 139~140 〉

[01-02]

두 문장이 같은 뜻이 되도록 빈칸에 알맞은 것을 고르시오.

01

> James said, "I will go shopping."
> = James said that _________ go shopping.

① I will ② I would ③ he will
④ he would ⑤ James will

02

> Maria said to her parents, "I am going to join a new club."
> = Maria told her parents that _________ to join a new club.

① I am going ② I was going
③ she will go ④ she is going
⑤ she was going

[03-07]

빈칸에 알맞은 것을 고르시오.

03

> Each of us _________ pictures of the painter, Pablo Picasso.

① has ② have ③ are
④ is ⑤ were

04

> Taking care of a baby _________ a lot of efforts.

① require ② requires
③ is required ④ have required
⑤ have been required

05

> Three hours _________ enough time for me to finish my homework.

① are ② were ③ has
④ have ⑤ is

06

> Half of the class _________ absent from school.

① are ② is ③ were
④ has ⑤ have

07

> The rest of the pizza _________ for the person who wants to eat more.

① are ② were ③ has
④ have ⑤ is

[08-11]

주어진 우리말과 일치하도록 빈칸에 알맞은 것을 고르시오.

08

> 미국의 10대들 중 반이 자신의 방을 가지고 있다.
> ➡ Half of the teenagers in the U.S. _________ their own bedrooms.

① is ② have ③ are
④ were ⑤ has

09

> 그는 나에게 무슨 요일인지 물었다.
> ➡ He asked me _________________.

① was what day it ② it was what day
③ what it was day ④ what day was it
⑤ what day it was

10

> 그 잔디가 다른 편 잔디보다 푸르다. (남의 떡이 더 커 보인다.)
> ➡ The grass _________ always greener on the other side.

① is   ② are   ③ was
④ will be   ⑤ were

11

> 그녀는 내가 도착하면 그녀에게 전화하라고 나에게 말했다.
> ➡ She _____________________ I arrived.

① told me to call her when
② told her to call me when
③ told me when to call her
④ told her when to call me
⑤ told to call me when her

[12-14] 서술형

빈칸에 공통으로 들어갈 말을 쓰시오.

12

> • The coach said both John and Diana _________ not interested in tennis.
> • Yesterday, the young fans _________ very excited to meet the famous singer.

13

> • A number of people _________ reading books in the library now.
> • The rest of the clothes _________ not mine.

14

> • Playing computer games _________ my hobby.
> • I think that he _________ a cute little guy.

[15-17]

각 빈칸에 들어갈 말이 알맞게 짝지어진 것을 고르시오.

15

> • The security guards as well as I _________ surprised by the loud sound at that time.
> • It is not me but Thomas who _________ you every night.

① was – call   ② was – calls
③ were – call   ④ were – calls
⑤ were – called

16

> My grandmother said to me, "I have a headache today."
> ➡ My grandmother _________ me that she had a headache _________.

① said – today   ② told – that day
③ said to – the next day   ④ told – today
⑤ said – that day

17

> The woman said to me, "Is a pharmacy far from here?"
> ➡ The woman _________ me _________ a pharmacy was far from there.

① said to – where   ② told – if
③ asked – if   ④ asked – where
⑤ said – if

18 고난도

어법상 알맞은 것을 고르시오.

① The rest of the apples is rotten.
② Most of students has made progress this term.
③ Half of my money were gone already.
④ The number of participants are increasing yearly.
⑤ A number of houses were destroyed by the earthquake.

〈 정답과 해설 p. 140~141 〉

19

① Bread and butter was my lunch.
② Two years is a long time for me.
③ Economics is my favorite subject.
④ A number of readers like my new novel.
⑤ Every student in each class study so hard.

20

① Mathematics is difficult but rewarding.
② Everybody says that he looks like me.
③ He came up to the girl who was sitting on the bench.
④ Eighty dollars seem to be a fair price for a good jacket.
⑤ Most of the students are standing in a row in front of the cafeteria.

21

① Pablo said he had visited Seoul once.
② He said he would go camping with us.
③ My grandson said me that he had been sick for days.
④ There is a saying that laughter is the best medicine.
⑤ My roommate said to me, "Are you happy with the present?"

22

① Greg asked me if I could go to the movies.
② She ordered the child not touch the painting.
③ Ann asked me when I could help her with that.
④ My teacher asked me why I hadn't finished my homework.
⑤ My sister asked me what I had done with my computer the day before.

23

① Nobody knows if it will rain tomorrow.
② He found that the door has been unlocked.
③ They'll learn World War II broke out in 1939.
④ My grandfather said that a rolling stone gathers no moss.
⑤ It's the same anywhere in the world that the sun rises in the east and sets in the west.

24

> 많은 학생들이 그의 강의를 듣고 있다.
> ➡ __________ __________ __________ students are listening to his lecture. (number)

25

> 로봇과 AI 중 어느 것도 미래를 확실하게 예측하지 않는다.
> ➡ Neither the robot nor the AI __________ the future with certainty. (predict)

26

The weatherman said that it __________ __________ heavily tomorrow. (will rain)

27

Terry said that he __________ __________ __________ for 25 years. (be married)

28

Peter said that I __________ __________ __________ him the letter. (have to send)

29

My father said that honesty ________________
the best policy. (be)

30

The doctor advised me that I ________________
in bed for a few days. (stay)

31

My teacher said that Russia ________________
the biggest country in the world. (be)

32

I wondered if she __________ __________ to
America before. (be)

[33-34] 고난도

다음 글을 읽고 글의 내용과 일치하도록 빈칸에 알맞게 짝지
은 것을 고르시오.

> (A) Hello, this is Gary. I'm unavailable at the
> moment, so please leave a message after
> the tone. I'll get back to you as soon as
> possible.
> (B) Hi, Gary, it's Owen. I need to see you
> sometime because I'm staying in Seoul
> these days. I'll call you again. Bye.

33

> (A): Gary said that he ________ not available
> at that time, and that he ________ get
> back to the caller soon.

① is – will   ② was – will
③ is – wouldn't   ④ was – would
⑤ was – wouldn't

34

> (B): Owen said that he ______ staying in Seoul,
> so he ______ to meet Gary sometime.

① is – don't need   ② was – need not
③ is – doesn't need   ④ was – need
⑤ was – needed

[35-36]

다음 글을 읽고 물음에 답하시오.

> You will hear a story that ___(A)___ a
> problem. You will have one minute to think
> about how you would solve it. After the first
> beep, you will have one minute to record
> your answer. When you ___(B)___ two short
> beeps, stop recording. Now, let's begin.

35

(A)에 어법상 알맞은 것을 고르시오.

① describe   ② describes
③ describing   ④ to describe
⑤ to describing

36

(B)에 어법상 알맞은 것을 고르시오.

① hear   ② hears
③ heard   ④ will hear
⑤ would hear

[37-38] 고난도

다음 글을 읽고 물음에 답하시오.

> ① Plants and animals have one very
> dangerous enemy. (A) They aren't disease,
> fire or even pollution. ② The most
> dangerous enemy is man. ③ Man is the only
> living creature that have ever caused
> another living creature to become extinct. ④
> Because of man, many other animals are
> nearly extinct. ⑤ If they are not protected,
> they, too, will soon be lost for good.

37 서술형

밑줄 친 (A)를 어법상 바르게 고쳐 쓰시오.

➡ _______________________________

38

어법상 틀린 문장을 고르시오.

①   ②   ③   ④   ⑤

〈 정답과 해설 p. 141~142 〉

39

다음 대화의 ① ~ ⑤ 중 어법상 <u>틀린</u> 것을 고르시오.

> A: Don't you think Columbus ① <u>is</u> great because he knew that the world ② <u>was</u> round back then?
> B: Yes, especially ③ <u>considering</u> the fact that most people at the time thought that the world ④ <u>was</u> flat and you ⑤ <u>would</u> fall off if you sailed too far.

40 수능 맛보기

(A), (B), (C)의 각 네모 안에서 어법에 맞는 표현으로 가장 적절한 것을 고르시오.

> The number of jellyfish attacks (A) <u>is / are</u> increasing worldwide. The climate change as well as overfishing (B) <u>cause / causes</u> an increase in the number of jellyfish. In 2014, about 150 swimmers were stung by jellyfish on a beach in New Hampshire, U.S.A. Jellyfish stings are reported in Korea as well. You should either avoid swimming in the ocean where there (C) <u>is / are</u> a number of jellyfish, or be aware of the proper treatment for jellyfish stings.

	(A)		(B)		(C)
①	is	−	cause	−	are
②	is	−	causes	−	are
③	is	−	causes	−	is
④	are	−	causes	−	are
⑤	are	−	cause	−	is

41 수능 유형

밑줄 친 부분 중 어법상 <u>틀린</u> 것을 고르시오.

> Do you know what sign language is? Do you want to understand what someone ① <u>is</u> saying in sign language? Signing ② <u>is</u> an effective way to communicate among the deaf. Sign language ③ <u>consist</u> of hand gestures, finger spelling, and facial expressions. Most countries have developed ④ <u>their</u> own standard sign languages, but the signs and the spoken languages ⑤ <u>aren't</u> really related.

①   ②   ③   ④   ⑤

42 수능 맛보기

(A), (B), (C)의 각 네모 안에서 어법에 맞는 표현으로 가장 적절한 것을 고르시오.

> I am Jane, a middle school student. Last week, a new student joined my class. My teacher asked the other students in class (A) <u>to help / helping</u> him get used to new school life. I thought if I were him, I would be very nervous. On that day, I found him walking around in the hallway during lunch hour. I asked him if he had eaten lunch. He told me that he (B) <u>couldn't / can't</u> find the cafeteria. I took him to the cafeteria and had a conversation with him. Now, he gets along with other students as well as me. I think if my teacher knew what I did, he would say, "I'm proud of (C) <u>me / you</u>."

	(A)		(B)		(C)
①	to help	−	can't	−	you
②	to help	−	couldn't	−	me
③	to help	−	couldn't	−	you
④	helping	−	couldn't	−	me
⑤	helping	−	can't	−	you

🦉 어휘 & 표현

- **effort** 노력 · **absent** 결석한 · **grass** 풀, 잔디 · **security guard** 보안 요원 · **headache** 두통 · **pharmacy** 약국
- **rotten** 썩은, 부패한 · **progress** 진전 · **destroy** 파괴하다 · **earthquake** 지진 · **rewarding** 보람 있는
- **gather** 모으다 · **moss** 이끼 · **certainty** 확신 · **weatherman** 기상 통보관 · **enemy** 적 · **extinct** 멸종한
- **for good** 영원히 · **jellyfish** 해파리 · **overfishing** (어류) 남획 · **sting** 침, 가시

특수 구문

UNIT 76 도치
倒置 (넘어질 도, 둘 치)
동사가 주어 앞에 오는 형태

UNIT 77 강조
문장에서 동사, 명사 등을 강조하기 위해 쓰는 형태

반복되는 요소 등을
생략하는 형태   같은 것을 표현하는 형태

UNIT 78 생략, 부정 구문, 동격
否定 (아닐 부, 정할 정)
전체 부정과 부분 부정

Near the lake lay a small boat, waiting to be used.
부사구   도치된 주어와 동사
(호숫가 근처에는 사용되기를 기다리는 작은 배가 놓여 있었다.)

They did try their best. (그들은 정말 최선을 다했다.)
동사 강조

While (they were) in Seoul, they visited many places.
부사절의 「주어 + be동사」 생략
(그들은 서울에 있는 동안 많은 곳을 방문했다.)

We do not need all of these tools. (우리가 이 도구들을 모두 필요로 하는 것은 아니다.)
부분 부정

I hate the fact that you lied to me. (나는 네가 나에게 거짓말했다는 사실이 싫다.)
동격절 접속사

 **UNIT 76** 도치 

> **핵심 개념**
> • **도치**: 강조나 부정 등을 위해 동사가 주어 앞에 오는 형태를 도치라고 한다.

Rarely does the princess smile. (그 공주는 좀처럼 웃지 않는다.)
부정어 rarely가 문두에 오면서 「조동사+주어+본동사」의 어순이 됨

A hundred years ago, ***there*** lived a famous clown.
　　　　　　　　　　　there가 문두에 오면서 주어와 동사가 도치됨
　　　　　　　　　　　　　　(몇 백 년 전에 한 유명한 광대가 살았다.)

1 도치의 개념: 영어는 일반적으로 「주어 + 동사」 순으로 오지만,
　　　부정어(구), 부사(구) 등이 강조되어 「주어 + 동사」 앞으로 올 때
　　　「주어 + 동사」가 「동사 + 주어」로 도치된다.

> **❶** little, never 등의 부정어(구)나 「only + 부사(구)」가 문두에 올 경우
>
> 도치되는 동사가 일반동사일 경우, do, did, does가 주어 앞으로 가고, 일반동사는 본동사 자리에 동사원형으로 온다.

2　　부정어(구)
　　　「only + 부사(구)」　+ 조동사 + 주어 + 본동사 ❶　←도치

> 부정어(구): never, no, not, little, nor, seldom, rarely, hardly, scarcely, no sooner 등

• **Never** will we forget the kindness you showed us.
　　부정어　조동사 + 주어 + 본동사
　　　　　　　　　　　　　　(당신이 우리에게 보여준 친절을 우리는 결코 잊지 않을 것이다.)

• **Little** had he prepared for the interview. (그는 면접을 거의 준비하지 않았다.)
　　부정어　조동사 + 주어 + 본동사

• **Seldom** can we get the chance to travel abroad. (우리는 해외여행을 갈 기회를 거의 얻지 못한다.)
　　부정어　조동사 + 주어 + 본동사

• **Only then** did I realize the importance of the situation.
　「only + 부사」　조동사 + 주어 + 본동사
　　　　　　　　　　(그때서야 나는 상황의 중요성을 깨달았다.)

3 there [here]
　　장소, 방향의 부사(구)　+ 자동사 + 주어　←도치

> 자동사: be, come, go, walk, lie, sit, stand, live, appear 등

• **There** appeared a strange light in the sky. (하늘에 이상한 불빛이 나타났다.)
　there　　　　자동사 + 주어

• **Here** begins the story you've all been waiting for. (여러분 모두가 기다리던 이야기가 여기서 시작된다.)
　here　　　자동사 + 주어

• **In the distance** was a ship sailing towards us. (멀리서 우리를 향해 오는 배가 있었다.)
　장소의 부사구　　자동사 + 주어

• **Down the street** came a group of children playing. (길 아래로 아이들이 놀면서 다가왔다.)
　방향의 부사구　　　　자동사 + 주어

> [참고] 주어가 대명사일 때는 주어와 동사를 도치하지 않는다.
>
> • On the hill it stands. (언덕 위에 그것이 있다.)
> 　장소의 부사구　도치되지 않은 대명사 주어 + 동사

4 so + 동사 + 주어,　neither + 동사 + 주어　←도치

• Jane was surprised by the news, and **so** was Tom. (Jane은 그 소식에 놀랐고, Tom도 마찬가지였다.)
　　　　　　　　　　　　　　　　　so　동사 + 주어

• A: I wasn't expecting so many people at the party. (A: 파티에 사람이 이렇게 많을 줄 몰랐어.)

• B: **Neither** was I. (B: 나도 예상 못 했어.)
　neither　동사 + 주어

1 + **2** + **3** 도치

[01-04] 밑줄 친 부분을 강조하는 문장으로 바꿔 쓰시오.

01 The four sisters stood <u>on the grass</u>.

➡ On the grass ____.

02 I could <u>hardly</u> hear what she said.

➡ Hardly ____.

03 Sam feels safe and secure <u>only in his house</u>.

➡ Only in his house ____.

04 I <u>little</u> dreamed that I could meet my favorite actor face to face.

➡ Little ____.

4 so, neither + 동사 + 주어

[05-09] so나 neither를 써서 I가 주어인 대화를 완성하시오. (단, 질문과 동일한 시제를 따를 것)

05 A: I don't like rainy season. B: ___________ ___________ ___________.

06 A: She didn't bring the textbook. B: ___________ ___________ ___________.

07 A: She went to church yesterday. B: ___________ ___________ ___________.

08 A: He is not good at mathematics. B: ___________ ___________ ___________.

09 A: I was nervous before the final exam. B: ___________ ___________ ___________.

1 + **2** + **3** + **4** 도치

[10-15] 문장이나 대화에서 틀린 부분을 찾아 밑줄을 긋고 바르게 고치시오.

10 Never she has finished the work. ➡ ________________

11 A long time ago, there a number of people lived. ➡ ________________

12 Only then he came to know that he didn't bring the umbrella. ➡ ________________

13 A: I didn't want to go to the library.

B: So did I. ➡ ________________

14 A: Do you know where my laptop is?

B: Here are you. ➡ ________________

15 A: I think the movie business in Korea has rapidly progressed.

B: So has I. ➡ ________________

🦉 어휘 & 표현

· **abroad** 해외로	· **importance** 중요성	· **appear** 나타나다	· **sail** 항해하다	· **grass** 풀, 잔디	· **secure** 안심하는
· **face to face** 대면하는	· **business** 산업	· **rapidly** 급격히, 빠르게	· **progress** 발전하다		

〈 정답과 해설 p. 143 〉

 **UNIT 77** 강조 

1 동사 강조: do[does, did] **+ 동사원형** ❶

- They **do know** the answer. (그들은 정말로 답을 알고 있다.)
  do + 동사원형
- This place **does have** good coffee. (여기 커피 정말 맛있다.)
  does + 동사원형
- That's what I **did want** to say. (그것이 내가 정말 말하고 싶었던 것이다.)
  did + 동사원형

2 명사 강조: the very + 명사

- He is **the very man** that the police have arrested. (그가 경찰이 체포한 바로 그 남자이다.)
  the very + 명사

3 비교급 강조: much[far, still, a lot, even] **+ 비교급**

- This book is **much more interesting** than I expected. (이 책은 내가 예상했던 것보다 훨씬 더 재미있다.)
  much + 비교급
- This test is **far more difficult** than the last one. (이번 시험은 지난번 시험보다 훨씬 더 어렵다.)
  far + 비교급

4 부정어 강조: 부정어 + at all[in the least]

- I **didn't** hear the news **at all**. (나는 그 소식을 전혀 듣지 못했다.)
  부정어 didn't + at all
- I'm **not** in the least interested in that topic. (나는 그 주제에 조금도 관심이 없다.)
  부정어 not + in the least

5 의문사 강조: 의문사 + on earth[ever, in the world]

- **What on earth** are you talking about? (도대체 무슨 말을 하는 거니?)
  의문사 what + on earth

6 It ~ that 강조: ~한 사람(것, 곳)은 바로 …이다(였다)

It is[was]와 that 사이에 주어, 목적어, 부사(구) 등 강조하고 싶은 말을 넣어 강조 구문으로 쓴다.

(1) 주어 강조 : that 대신 who 사용

- It was **I** that[who] met Peter in New York last month.
  It was와 that[who] 사이에 주어 I가 옴
  (지난달에 뉴욕에서 Peter를 만났던 사람은 바로 나였다.)

(2) 목적어 강조 : that 대신 who(m) 사용

- It was **Peter** that[who(m)] I met in New York last month.
  It was와 that[who(m)] 사이에 목적어 Peter가 옴
  (지난달에 내가 뉴욕에서 만났던 사람은 바로 Peter였다.)

(3) 장소의 부사(구) 강조 : that 대신 where 사용 ❷

- It was **in New York** that[where] I met Peter last month.
  It was와 that[where] 사이에 부사구 in New York이 옴
  (내가 지난달에 Peter를 만났던 것은 바로 뉴욕에서였다.)

(4) 시간의 부사(구) 강조 : that 대신 when 사용 ❷

- It was **last month** that[when] I met Peter in New York.
  It was와 that[when] 사이에 부사구 last month가 옴
  (내가 뉴욕에서 Peter를 만났던 것은 바로 지난 달이었다.)

(5) 의문사 강조: 의문사 + is[was] it that ~?의 형태로 쓴다.

- **Who** was it that met Peter in New York last month?
  was it that 앞에 의문사 who가 옴
  (지난달에 뉴욕에서 Peter를 만났던 사람은 누구였니?)

---

❶ do, does, did

- 현재시제
  - 3인칭 단수 주어(she, he, it) + does
  - 그 외 주어 + do
- 과거시제
  - 주어 + did

❷ 부사(구) 강조

장소, 시간의 부사(구) 외 다른 부사(구)나 부사절을 강조할 때는 that을 쓴다.

1 + 2 동사, 명사 강조

[01-05] 문장에서 **틀린** 부분을 찾아 밑줄을 긋고 바르게 고치시오.

01 Emily do hope that she knows the answer. ___________

02 I did falling behind schedule this week due to a cold. ___________

03 She does expects to see her old friend at the party. ___________

04 What he said is true. He did made the cake for you. ___________

05 You're the much one that I could see over and over. ___________

3 + 4 + 5 비교급, 부정어, 의문사 강조

[06-11] 빈칸에 알맞은 말을 〈보기〉에서 골라 강조 구문을 완성하시오. (중복 사용 불가)

〈보기〉

| even | on earth | in the least | less | not | who |

06 What _______________ are you doing here?

07 _______________ in the world dares to talk back to me?

08 He was not shocked at the news _______________.

09 She's ambitious, but far _______________ prepared than she should be.

10 These shoes are _______________ more comfortable than the old ones.

11 She does _______________ love children at all and won't take good care of them.

6 It ~ that 강조

[12-16] 밑줄 친 부분을 강조할 때, 빈칸에 알맞은 말을 쓰시오.

12 Brandon wants to sell that car.

➡ It _______________ wants to sell that car.

13 She broke the window last night.

➡ It _______________ she broke the window.

14 I want to go to the concert after the final exam.

➡ It _______________ I want to go to the concert.

15 Susan watched the musical in London.

➡ It _______________ Susan watched the musical.

16 Matthew visited Merlin to ask how to steal Mary's heart.

➡ It _______________ Matthew visited to ask how to steal Mary's heart.

🦉 어휘 & 표현

| · arrest 체포하다 · expect 기대하다 · on earth 도대체 · fall behind schedule 늦어지다 · dare 감히 ~하다 |
| · shocked 충격받은 · ambitious 야망있는 · comfortable 편한 · steal one's heart 마음을 사로잡다 |

〈 정답과 해설 p. 144 〉

 **UNIT 78** 생략, 부정 구문, 동격 

No one is listening. (아무도 듣고 있지 않다.)
전체 부정

Not everyone is listening. (모든 사람이 듣고 있는 것은 아니다.)
부분 부정

1 생략

(1) 반복되는 주어나 동사 생략

- He got up early and (he) went to school. (그는 일찍 일어나서 학교에 갔다.)
  반복되는 주어 생략
- Some people speak in English, and others (speak) in Korean.
  반복되는 동사 생략
  (일부 사람들은 영어로 이야기하고, 다른 사람들은 한국어로 이야기한다.)

(2) 부사절의 「주어+be동사」 생략 ❶

  – 주절의 주어와 같을 때, 주어가 일반적인 it일 때 부사절의 「주어+be동사」는 생략할 수 있다.
- While (I was) in college, I studied Chinese. (대학에 다닐 때, 나는 중국어를 공부했다.)
  부사절의 「주어+be동사」 생략   주어

(3) 관계대명사절의 「주격 관계대명사+be동사」 생략

  –「주격 관계대명사+be동사」 뒤에 분사가 나올 경우 「주격 관계대명사+be동사」는 생략할 수 있다.
- Look at the girl (who is) sitting in the back. (뒷자리에 앉아 있는 여자아이를 봐.)
  관계대명사절의 「주격 관계대명사+be동사」 생략   현재분사

(4) 인사말이나 경고문 등에서의 관용적 생략

- (It's) Nice to meet you. (만나서 반가워.)   · (This is) Out of order. (고장)

> ❶ **감탄문**
> 감탄문의 「주어+be동사」도 생략했을 때 의미가 전달된다면 생략할 수 있다.
> · What a beautiful day (it is)!
> (정말 아름다운 날이야!)

2 부정 구문

전체 부정 '모두[전부] ~이 아니다'	**not + any** [anyone, anything, anywhere] · He did not say anything. (그는 아무 말도 하지 않았다.) (= He said nothing.) **never, no, neither, none, nothing, nowhere** · None of my friends know the truth. (내 친구들 중 아무도 진실을 모른다.)
부분 부정 '모두[전부] ~인 것은 아니다'	**not + all** [every, both, always, necessarily, entirely] · I do not know all of them. (내가 그들 전부를 아는 것은 아니다.) · Expensive things do not always mean the best. (비싼 것이 항상 가장 좋은 것은 아니다.)

3 동격

(1) 명사(구)끼리 동격 : 콤마(,)나 **of**를 사용하여 연결한다.

- Jane, the smartest girl in my class, solved the problem.
  (우리 반에서 가장 똑똑한 여자아이인 Jane이 그 문제를 풀었다.)
- Many tourists visit the city of New York. (많은 관광객들이 뉴욕 시를 방문한다.)

(2) 명사(구)와 절이 동격 : 접속사 **that** ❷을 사용하여 연결한다.

- The police hid the fact that he was alive. (경찰은 그가 살아 있다는 사실을 숨겼다.)

> ❷ **접속사 that**
> 동격의 that절을 이끄는 접속사 that은 간혹 생략하는 경우도 있으나 기본적으로는 생략하지 않는 것이 원칙이다.

1 생략

[01-07] 문장에서 생략할 수 있는 부분에 밑줄을 그으시오.

01 I wish you a happy birthday.

02 I will call you, if it is necessary.

03 Do you know a girl who is named Amy?

04 While I am having breakfast, I always listen to the radio.

05 I was born in New York, and my brother was born in Seoul.

06 These cars were made in Korea and those were made in Japan.

07 There is a standard of communication which is called an Internet Protocol standard.

2 부정 구문

[08-12] 문장을 우리말로 해석하시오.

08 Not all the boys like sports.

➡ ___________________________________

09 I don't always do well on the test.

➡ ___________________________________

10 None of us wanted to join the drama club.

➡ ___________________________________

11 Isn't there anywhere that I can park my car?

➡ ___________________________________

12 You don't necessarily need to make spaghetti using my recipe.

➡ ___________________________________

> **어휘 & 표현**
> · **entirely** 전적으로
> · **tourist** 관광객
> · **name** 이름을 붙이다
> · **standard** 표준, 기준
> · **communication** 의사소통
> · **necessarily** 반드시, 필연적으로
> · **drop out of school** 학교를 그만두다
> · **poverty** 빈곤

3 동격

[13-15] 주어진 우리말과 일치하도록 괄호 안의 말을 바르게 배열하시오.

13 그가 학교를 그만두었다는 사실은 나를 놀라게 했다. (surprised, dropped, that, out of, me, school, he)

➡ The fact ___________________________________.

14 나의 영어 선생님이신 Jones 선생님은 캐나다에서 오셨다. (came, Canada, Mr. Jones, from)

➡ My English teacher, ___________________________________.

15 많은 사람들이 아프리카의 빈곤 문제를 해결하려고 노력한다.

(poverty, solve, Africa, try, of, to, in, the problem)

➡ Lots of people ___________________________________.

〈 정답과 해설 p. 145 〉

[01-03]

빈칸에 알맞은 것을 고르시오.

01

> Hardly ________ skiing last winter.

① I went
② did I go
③ didn't I go
④ do I went
⑤ I didn't go

02

> Rarely ________ ache.

① his shoulder
② his shoulder do
③ do his shoulder
④ his shoulder does
⑤ does his shoulder

03

> I ________ getting up early in the morning.

① do hate
② do hates
③ hate do
④ does hate
⑤ hate does

[04-07]

주어진 우리말과 일치하도록 빈칸에 알맞은 것을 고르시오.

04

> 나는 그렇게 키 큰 소년을 본 적이 없어.
> ➡ Never ________ such a tall boy.

① have I seen
② has I seen
③ seen I have
④ I have seen
⑤ have seen I

05

> 오늘 아침까지만 해도 나는 그 팀이 동계 올림픽에서 금메달을 땄다는 것을 몰랐다.
> ➡ Not until this morning ________ the team won the gold medal in the Winter Olympics.

① knew I
② I knew
③ did I know
④ I don't know
⑤ I didn't know

06

> 너희 둘 다 내일 놀이공원에 가지 않을 것이다.
> ➡ ________ of you will go to the amusement park tomorrow.

① All
② Any
③ Both
④ Either
⑤ Neither

07 고난도

> 나는 강당에 있는 모든 학생들을 다 아는 것은 아니다.
> ➡ I don't know ________ of the students in the auditorium.

① all
② any
③ neither
④ none
⑤ anyone

08 서술형

자연스러운 대화가 되도록 괄호 안의 말을 이용해 문장을 완성하시오.

> A: What's her hobby?
> B: Dancing. She ________ ________ to dance.
>   (do, like)

09 [고난도]

문장에서 생략된 단어들이 모두 짝지어진 것을 고르시오.

> Some birds can fly, but some can't.

① birds, not   ② fly, some
③ birds, fly   ④ birds, can
⑤ birds, can, fly

[10 - 16]

괄호 안에서 알맞은 것을 고르시오.

10

Why (ever / in the least) did you come home so late?

11

Rarely (does he visit / he visits) his grandparents these days.

12

There (they are / are they), coming down the hill.

13

I had eaten only vegetables, but I couldn't lose weight (on earth / at all).

14

When you were talking on the phone, I (do / did) tell you not to sit down on the bench.

15

He hasn't met (both / either) of his cousins. He has met one of them.

16

There's little chance (that / what) he'll win the game.

[17 - 18]

어법상 틀린 것을 고르시오.

17

① Seldom does he eat out.
② Not every girl likes to put on make-up.
③ It was Mike that he gave me some flowers yesterday.
④ It was in this park that I had lost my puppy.
⑤ He did eat the pancake I made 10 minutes ago.

18

① On the hill was it sitting.
② Here comes the dish you've ordered.
③ She strongly believes that he does run very fast.
④ There is a little boy singing across the street.
⑤ Never had I dreamed that he failed the exam.

19 [고난도]

어법상 옳은 것을 고르시오.

① All not Canadians speak English fluently.
② I couldn't find any solution to the problem.
③ The whole town did enjoyed the summer festival.
④ It was very last chance that we had together.
⑤ Mr. White, our English teacher, are very kind.

〈 정답과 해설 p. 145~146 〉

문장에서 **틀린** 부분을 찾아 밑줄을 긋고 바르게 고치시오.

20

Hardly did they knew each other. They didn't seem to have heard about each other.

____

21

It was because Robert was ill who we decided to return.

____

22

How did you know this was very the thing I wanted?

____

23

No sooner I had stepped outside than it started to rain.

____

24

The man was standing in front of us suddenly disappeared.

____

25

At the edge of the frozen lake waits she for someone to return.

____

26

어법상 **틀린** 문장을 고르시오.

> It was only after I had finished my homework that I realized I had been working on the wrong assignment. ① Shocked, I quickly checked the real assignment and found out I had to write an essay, not do math problems! ② So frantic was I that I immediately started writing. ③ Not until halfway through did I realize I didn't know what the topic was. It was only then that I decided to search for it online. ④ Hardly I had started when I found the perfect article! ⑤ It is thanks to that article that I finished my essay just in time.
>
> *frantic 제정신이 아닌

①   ②   ③   ④   ⑤

[27-30] (서술형)

밑줄 친 부분을 강조하는 문장으로 바꿔 쓰시오.

27

A single person <u>never</u> told Sharon the secret.

➡ Never _______________________.

28

William <u>knows</u> the answer.

➡ William _______________________.

29

<u>I</u> showed Mina the letter from Tom.

➡ It was _______________________.

30

I did <u>not</u> learn about African history and culture <u>until high school</u>.

➡ Not until high school _______________

_______________________.

31

밑줄 친 부분 중 생략할 수 <u>없는</u> 것을 고르시오.

① No smoking <u>is allowed here</u>.
② The baby fell down and <u>he</u> cried a lot.
③ I know the woman <u>who</u> is counseling in my school.
④ People in Singapore use a special language <u>which is</u> called 'Singlish.'
⑤ Koreans take off shoes in the house, while Americans don't <u>take off shoes</u>.

32

주어진 문장의 밑줄 친 did와 쓰임이 같은 것을 고르시오.

> Many celebrities <u>did</u> come here for the exhibition.

① They <u>didn't</u> admit their mistake at all.
② He plays better than he <u>did</u> last year.
③ Maria always <u>does</u> the dishes after having dinner.
④ Every student <u>does</u> like his homeroom teacher.
⑤ She doesn't want to move to the suburb, <u>does</u> she?

[33-35]

다음 글을 읽고 물음에 답하시오.

> What is your favorite fruit or vegetable? Do you like cherries or peaches? How about tomatoes or potatoes? If your answer is yes, you should be careful not to eat other parts of those plants. Do you know why? It is other parts of the same plant ___(A)___ may make you sick. People can eat cherries, but the twigs of the cherry tree are poisonous. <u>Peaches are good for people</u>, but the leaves are not supposed to be eaten. So ___(B)___ the leaves and stems of tomato and potato plants.
>
> *twig 잔가지

33

빈칸 (A)에 어법상 알맞은 것을 고르시오.

① what　　② that　　③ who
④ when　　⑤ where

34 （서술형）

밑줄 친 부분을 peaches를 강조하는 문장으로 다시 쓸 때 빈칸에 알맞은 말을 쓰시오.

> __________ __________ peaches that are good for people.

35

빈칸 (B)에 어법상 알맞은 것을 고르시오.

① is　　② was　　③ are
④ be　　⑤ do

[36-41] （서술형）

밑줄 친 부분에서 생략된 것을 넣어 다시 쓰시오.

36

<u>While in high school</u>, I always struggled with punctuality.

➡ ________________________________,
　 I always struggled with punctuality.

37

Some of my family live in Korea and <u>others in China</u>.

➡ Some of my family live in Korea and ______ ________________.

38

A bird in a hand is worth <u>two in the bush</u>.

➡ A bird in a hand is worth ______________ ________________.

〈 정답과 해설 p. 146~148 〉

39

I want to bring it back, if possible.

➡ I want to bring it back, _________________

___________________ .

40

A: Would you like to join us?

B: I'd love to, but I have another plan.

➡ ___________________________________ ,

but I have another plan.

41

The caterpillar builds a small house called a cocoon around himself.

➡ The caterpillar builds a small house _______

___________________ around himself.

[42-44] (수능 유형)

밑줄 친 부분 중 어법상 틀린 것을 고르시오.

42

How do you go to school? I go to school on foot, but ① not all children walk to school. Some children ride bicycles, and others ② ride in a car. But the children ③ are living on the island of 'Ou' don't do any of these. They use long poles ④ called bamboo horses. The water between the islands ⑤ is not deep enough to use a boat, so the children walk on their poles.

①   ②   ③   ④   ⑤

43

① While out of town, how can you water your plants? Here ② useful tips are. Plants ③ which need to be watered every few days can be moved away from sunny windows so that they keep out of direct sunlight. Another way is ④ to place bricks in the two-inch-water-filled tub and set your plants on the bricks. As a last resort, ask a friend to water your plants if he or she ⑤ can.

①   ②   ③   ④   ⑤

44 (고난도)

My driving lessons with Donald were excellent. I always came away from my lessons feeling like I had made progress. When I first began my lessons, I was very nervous about driving and taking a test. But after having lessons with him, never once ① did I feel nervous or worried while ② learning to drive. Only with his help, ③ could I pass the test. Now I'm a very confident driver, and this has been noticed by friends and family. I would recommend Donald as an instructor because not only ④ I learned to drive, but I had a good time doing it. I think he is ⑤ the very instructor that you should have for your driving lesson.

①   ②   ③   ④   ⑤

🦉 어휘 & 표현

- amusement park 놀이공원 ・ auditorium 강당 ・ disappear 사라지다 ・ frozen 얼어붙은 ・ immediately 즉시
- halfway 중간에 ・ article 기사 ・ counsel 상담하다 ・ celebrity 유명 인사 ・ suburb 교외 ・ poisonous 독성의
- stem 줄기 ・ bush 덤불, 관목 ・ struggle with 어려움을 겪다 ・ punctuality 시간 엄수 ・ caterpillar 애벌레
- cocoon 고치 ・ pole 막대 ・ brick 벽돌 ・ last resort 최후의 수단 ・ instructor 강사

실전 모의고사

[01-02]

빈칸에 알맞지 <u>않은</u> 것을 고르시오.

01

> She ___________ some homemade cookies to us.

① gave   ② offered   ③ showed
④ bought   ⑤ brought

02

> I ___________ her leave the office when her shift ended.

① let   ② saw   ③ made
④ allowed   ⑤ noticed

03 (서술형)

빈칸에 공통으로 들어갈 말을 쓰시오.

> • My boss gave a challenging project ___________ me.
> • We expect the meeting ___________ last about an hour.

➡ ___________

04 (고난도)

각 문장과 문장의 형식이 알맞게 짝지어지지 <u>않은</u> 것을 고르시오.

> ⓐ He laughs at funny jokes.
> ⓑ We study together on weekends.
> ⓒ He explained the lesson to the class.
> ⓓ They told us how to fix the problem.
> ⓔ They watched the dog chase a ball in the yard.

① ⓐ – 1형식   ② ⓑ – 2형식
③ ⓒ – 3형식   ④ ⓓ – 4형식
⑤ ⓔ – 5형식

[05-06] (고난도)

주어진 문장과 문장 형식이 같은 것을 고르시오.

05

> He feels confident about his chances of winning the competition.

① He seems tired after the long trip.
② He gave me a gift for my birthday.
③ Tom bought a new phone yesterday.
④ They visited the museum last weekend.
⑤ The teacher found the students studying.

06

> The wind howled through the trees during the storm.

① The news made her upset.
② They offered us a big discount.
③ They arrived at the airport on time.
④ The weather became cold in the evening.
⑤ They are happy with the results of the research.

[07-08]

빈칸에 알맞은 것을 고르시오.

07

> The dog barked ___________ at strangers who came too close to the house.

① loud   ② loudness   ③ loudly
④ be loud   ⑤ be loudly

08

> Losing her job deprived her ___________ financial security.

① to   ② of   ③ for
④ with   ⑤ about

실전 모의고사 **B** 문장의 종류 [UNIT 05~ UNIT 06]

제한 시간 **20분**
맞은 개수 　　　개

[01-02]

빈칸에 알맞은 것을 고르시오.

01

We should leave now, __________?

① aren't we　② don't we　③ haven't we
④ should we　⑤ shouldn't we

02

Can you tell me when __________?

① start the meeting
② starts the meeting
③ the meeting starts
④ does the meeting start
⑤ does start the meeting

03 [서술형]

빈칸에 공통으로 들어갈 말을 쓰시오.

- Can you tell me __________ happened at the event?
- __________ an amazing view this is from the top here!

➡ __________

[04-05] [서술형]

주어진 우리말과 일치하도록 빈칸에 알맞은 말을 쓰시오.

04

이 자료를 제출해, 그러면 처리가 더 빨리 될 거야.
➡ Submit this document, __________ the process will go faster.

05

우리 이번 주말에 너의 조부모님을 뵈러 가는 게 어때?
➡ __________ don't we visit your grandparents this weekend?

[06-07]

주어진 우리말과 일치하도록 괄호 안의 말을 바르게 배열하시오.

06

그는 결과를 받지 못했어요, 그렇죠?
(hasn't, he, has, the results, received, he)

➡ __________

07

이 문제를 해결해, 그렇지 않으면 프로젝트가 지연될 거야. (will, this problem, be delayed, solve, or, the project)

➡ __________

08

〈보기〉의 우리말과 일치하도록 카드를 바르게 배열했을 때, 세 번째에 오는 것을 고르시오.

〈보기〉
그들이 티켓을 가지고 있는지 아세요?

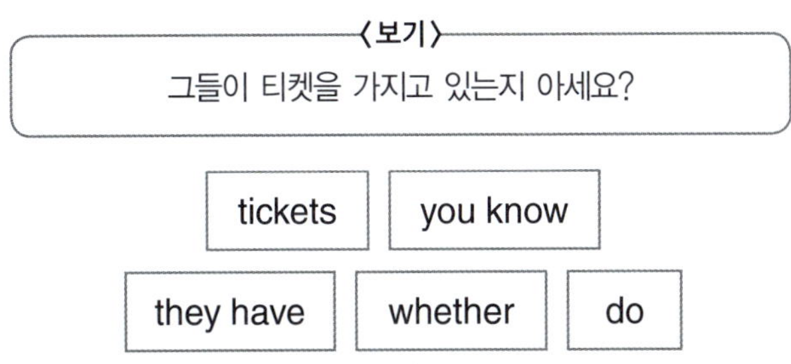

① tickets　② you know　③ they have
④ whether　⑤ do

09 [고난도]

어법상 틀린 것을 고르시오.

① This is the best movie ever, isn't it?
② He doesn't know the answer, does he?
③ Let's go to the beach tomorrow, shall we?
④ They are coming to visit us tomorrow, isn't it?
⑤ You will complete the assignment by tomorrow, won't you?

〈 정답과 해설 p. 148~149 〉

실전 모의고사 C 명사, 관사 UNIT 07~ UNIT 11

제한 시간 20분
맞은 개수 　개

01

빈칸에 알맞은 것을 고르시오.

> There are __________ chairs in the wedding hall for everyone.

① a bar of
② a can of
③ a lot of
④ a loaf of
⑤ a sheet of

02

명사의 복수형으로 옳지 <u>않은</u> 것을 고르시오.

① tooth – teeth
② goose – gooses
③ salmon – salmon
④ mosquito – mosquitoes
⑤ thief – thieves

[03-05]

괄호 안에서 알맞은 것을 고르시오.

03

Micky totally forgot what he learned in (the / ×) politics.

04

Jordan is quite (a / an / the) ambitious person, always aiming for success.

05

(An / The) engineer who designed (a / an) innovative headphone won the Red Dot Design Award.

[06-07] 서술형

주어진 우리말과 일치하도록 괄호 안의 말을 바르게 배열하시오. (필요시 명사의 소유격을 활용할 것)

06

내년의 회의는 파리에서 열릴 예정이다.
(conference, Paris, be held, next year, will, in)

➡ __________________________

07

그 회사의 목표는 환경 보호이다.
(is, environmental protection, the company, the goal, of)

➡ __________________________

08 고난도

빈칸에 들어갈 관사가 나머지 넷과 <u>다른</u> 것을 고르시오.

① I skipped _____ breakfast today.
② He looked up _____ sky to find a hawk.
③ She placed her wallet in _____ showcase.
④ My father heard me telling bad words on _____ phone.
⑤ Neal accidentally broke _____ flowerpot which Ann bought.

09 고난도

밑줄 친 부분 중 어법상 <u>틀린</u> 것을 고르시오.

① Several <u>deer</u> were grazing peacefully.
② The men in the village <u>help</u> rebuild the bridge.
③ One of the main <u>criterions</u> is leadership experience.
④ Tropical woods are home to numerous rare <u>species</u>.
⑤ She always behaves with perfect <u>manners</u> at formal events.

01

어법상 <u>틀린</u> 것을 고르시오.

① None can predict the future.
② Both of the answers was correct.
③ There is something odd about him.
④ I was satisfied with neither of them.
⑤ Anything is possible if you work hard.

02

각 빈칸에 들어갈 말이 알맞게 짝지어진 것을 고르시오.

> • The structure of the cell is similar to ___(A)___ of a factory.
> • ___(B)___ who wait patiently win.

　 (A) 　　 (B) 　　　　 (A) 　　 (B)
① this － It 　　　　② it － Those
③ that － Those 　　④ it － These
⑤ that － These

[03-04]

주어진 우리말과 일치하도록 바르게 영작한 것을 고르시오.

03

> 그녀는 자기도 모르게 손톱을 뜯고 있었다.

① She was picking her nail in herself.
② She was picking her nail by herself.
③ She was picking her nail beside herself.
④ She was picking her nail between herself.
⑤ She was picking her nail in spite of herself.

04

> 그는 그렇게 하는 것이 끔찍하다고 생각했다.

① He found it awful to do so.
② He found awful it to do so.
③ He found so awful to do it.
④ He found awful to do one.
⑤ He found one so awful to do.

[05-06] 고난도

대화의 밑줄 친 부분 중 어법상 <u>틀린</u> 것을 고르시오.

05

> A: Why are you avoiding ① her phone call?
> B: She ② keeps telling me ③ the same story over and over again.
> A: She must need ④ someone to talk to.
> B: I don't mind. I just want to stay ⑤ by oneself.

06

> A: How is ① your job search going?
> B: I found one that pays ② a good deal of money ③ a year.
> A: Really? Where did you find ④ them?
> B: I checked every job posting on the Internet ⑤ myself.

[07-08] 서술형

〈보기〉에 주어진 단어들을 이용하여 빈칸에 알맞은 말을 쓰시오. (필요시 형태를 변형할 것)

07

> 〈보기〉
> it 　　 the 　　 in 　　 river

➡ The beautiful bridge is reflecting __________ ____________.

08

> 〈보기〉
> another 　　 is 　　 other 　　 the 　　 is

➡ I have three notebooks. One is green, _______________ red, and yellow.

〈 정답과 해설 **p. 149~150** 〉

실전 모의고사 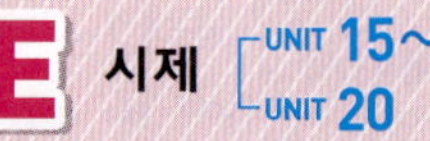 E 시제 [UNIT **15**~ UNIT **20**]

제한 시간 20분
맞은 개수 　　　　 개

[01-02]
빈칸에 알맞은 것을 고르시오.

01

> When I arrived at the party, Jiho was not there. He __________ already.

① went
② has left
③ left
④ will have left
⑤ had left

02

> When Ms. Kim retires next year, she __________ for 40 years.

① taught
② teaches
③ teach
④ has taught
⑤ will have been teaching

03 　고난도
어법상 틀린 것을 고르시오.

① How long have you been driving?
② Did he return your book yesterday?
③ My son has been sleeping since 11 a.m.
④ When you arrive at the airport, I picked you up.
⑤ When I got to the school, the main gate had already been shut.

[04-08]
괄호 안에서 알맞은 것을 고르시오.

04

Emma (is attending / attended) an important business meeting right now.

05

David (completed / completes) his internship at a law firm last summer.

06

They (announce / will announce) the results of the competition tomorrow.

07

Samantha (knows / is knowing) how to solve this type of math problem easily.

08

At 10 p.m. last night, they (are watching / were watching) a documentary.

09 　고난도
주어진 문장의 밑줄 친 부분과 쓰임이 같은 것을 고르시오.

> She had read the book once before the movie came out.

① She had left by the time I arrived.
② The train had left when we departed.
③ I had studied for hours before I slept.
④ By the time I checked my email, he had already replied.
⑤ We had been to that restaurant many times before it moved.

[10-11] 　서술형
주어진 우리말과 일치하도록 괄호 안의 지시대로 빈칸에 알맞은 말을 쓰시오.

10

나는 30분 동안 지하철을 기다리고 있는 중이다.
(현재완료진행시제로)

➡ I __________________ for the subway for half an hour.

11

그녀는 얼마나 오랫동안 영어를 배워오고 있니?
(현재완료진행시제로)

➡ How long __________ she __________ English?

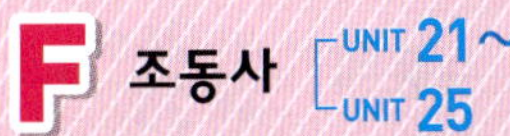

실전 모의고사 **F** 조동사 [UNIT 21~ UNIT 25]

01

주어진 문장의 밑줄 친 do와 쓰임이 같은 것을 고르시오.

> He <u>does</u> his best to stay positive.

① <u>Did</u> they call you last night?
② <u>Do</u> you enjoy playing video games?
③ She <u>does</u> the laundry on weekends.
④ Never <u>did</u> I expect to see you here!
⑤ I <u>do</u> love the way she plays the piano.

[02-05]

주어진 우리말과 일치하도록 〈보기〉에서 알맞은 말을 골라 문장을 완성하시오. (중복 사용 불가)

> 〈보기〉
> may well   ought to
> used to   had better

02

그들은 결정을 내리기 전에 모든 사실을 고려해야 한다.

➡ They ______________ consider all the facts before making a decision.

03

그녀가 직장에서 다음으로 승진할 사람인 것도 당연하다.

➡ She ______________ be the next person to be promoted at work.

04

학생들은 예전엔 무거운 교과서를 들고 다녔지만, 지금은 태블릿을 사용한다.

➡ Students ______________ carry heavy textbooks, but now they use tablets.

05

재킷을 입는 게 좋을 것이다. 밖이 정말 춥다.

➡ You ______________ wear a jacket; it's really cold outside.

[06-07] 서술형

빈칸에 공통으로 들어갈 말을 쓰시오.

06

> • I ___________ play basketball every weekend.
> • We ___________ like to thank everyone who supported us during the event.

➡ _______________

07

> • He used ___________ go for a run every morning, but now he prefers yoga.
> • She was able ___________ convince her boss to approve her idea.

➡ _______________

08 고난도

대화의 밑줄 친 부분 중 어법상 <u>틀린</u> 것을 고르시오.

> A: I ① <u>can't believe</u> I missed my flight!
> B: You ② <u>ought to have misunderstood</u> the departure time.
> A: I ③ <u>should have double-checked</u> the time.
> B: Don't worry, we ④ <u>can get</u> you on the next flight. ⑤ <u>I'll check</u> the next available flight for you.

〈 정답과 해설 **p. 151~152** 〉

실전 모의고사　**G** 수동태　UNIT 26~ UNIT 30

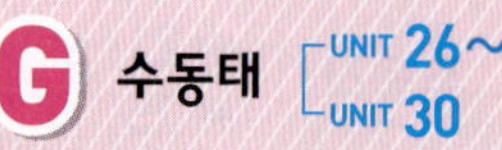

제한 시간 **20분**
맞은 개수　　개

01

두 문장이 같은 뜻이 되도록 빈칸에 알맞은 것을 고르시오.

> Some people are ignoring it when the policemen are checking others.
> = Some people are ignoring it when others __________ by the policemen.

① are checking
② are checked
③ are be checked
④ are been checked
⑤ are being checked

02

주어진 우리말과 일치하도록 바르게 영작한 것을 고르시오.

> 사람들은 Patrick이 유머가 있다고 말한다.

① Patrick says to be humorous.
② Patrick is being said humorous.
③ It says that Patrick is humorous.
④ It is said that Patrick is humorous.
⑤ People are said that Patrick is humorous.

03

대화의 밑줄 친 부분 중 어법상 **틀린** 것을 고르시오.

> A: Who ① gave you this book? Is ② this your birthday present?
> B: Yes. The book ③ was bought ④ to me by ⑤ one of my cousins.

[04-05]

빈칸에 알맞은 것을 고르시오.

04

> The neighbor was heard __________ after midnight.

① sing
② sings
③ is sung
④ singing
⑤ to singing

05

> George will __________ to the woman he met in Paris.

① marry
② marries
③ be married
④ married
⑤ gets married

06 고난도

밑줄 친 부분 중 어법상 **틀린** 것을 고르시오.

① This table is made of wood.
② They were surprised at the shocking news.
③ The store was crowded with many people.
④ This city is well-known to many foreigners.
⑤ The roof of the house was covered of snow.

[07-09] 서술형

주어진 문장을 수동태로 바꿔 쓸 때 빈칸에 알맞은 말을 쓰시오.

07

Will they invite many students this year, too?

➡ Will many students __________ by them this year, too?

08

Jim sent his parents a postcard.

➡ A postcard __________ his parents by Jim.

09

Many people believe that seven is a lucky number.

➡ Seven is __________ a lucky number by many people.

실전 모의고사 H 형용사 UNIT 31~ UNIT 33

제한 시간 20분
맞은 개수   개

[01-02]

연도, 날짜, 시간 등의 영어 표기법이 알맞지 <u>않은</u> 것을 고르시오.

01

① 0.12: zero point one two
② 7월 4일: The 4th of July
③ 9시 45분 : a quarter to nine
④ 2025년 : twenty twenty-five
⑤ ☎ 987–654–3210 : nine eight seven, six five four, three two one zero

02

① 4배: four times
② 6월 10일 : June ten
③ $3\frac{1}{3}$: three and a third
④ 5:30 : half after five
⑤ 8,312: eight thousand three hundred and twelve

[03-06]

주어진 우리말과 일치하도록 〈보기〉에서 알맞은 말을 골라 문장을 완성하시오. (중복 사용 불가)

〈보기〉

a few   few   little   plenty of

03

그는 양말이 많이 있지만, 그 중 어떤 것도 짝이 맞지 않는다.

➡ He has ______________ socks, but none of them match.

04

그녀는 더 이상 그 출세의 길을 쫓는 데 거의 관심이 없다.

➡ She has ______________ interest in pursuing that career path any longer.

05

이 문제의 복잡성을 이해하는 사람은 거의 없다.

➡ ______________ people understand the complexities of this issue.

06

오늘 할 일이 몇 가지 있지만, 대신 낮잠을 잘까 고민 중이다.

➡ I have ______________ things to do today, but I'm considering napping instead.

[07-08] 서술형

어법상 틀린 곳을 찾아 바르게 고치시오.

07

He was exhausted from replying to the number of emails.

➡ ______________ → ______________

08

Talented someone should take the lead in this project.

➡ ______________ → ______________

09 고난도

밑줄 친 형용사의 쓰임이 나머지 넷과 <u>다른</u> 것을 고르시오.

① He gave me a <u>generous</u> gift for my birthday.
② Her voice sounded like a <u>soothing</u> melody.
③ The <u>ancient</u> tree stood in a corner of the forest.
④ This document provided <u>valuable</u> insights into the past.
⑤ The article was <u>informative</u>, giving readers clear explanations.

〈 정답과 해설 p. 152~153 〉

 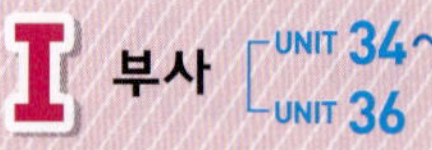

실전 모의고사 Ⅰ 부사 [UNIT 34~ UNIT 36]

제한 시간 **20분**
맞은 개수 □ 개

[01-02]
형용사–부사의 형태가 올바르지 <u>않은</u> 것을 고르시오.

01
① safe – safely ② easy – easily
③ flexible – flexibly ④ specific – specifly
⑤ comfortable – comfortably

02
① true – truly
② quick – quickly
③ basic – basically
④ horrible – horriblely
⑤ probable – probably

03
각 빈칸에 들어갈 말이 알맞게 짝지어진 것을 고르시오.

> W: I need to study ___(A)___ harder to finish this assignment.
> M: Yeah, maybe ___(B)___ into smaller sections.

　　(A)　　　　　(B)
① very – break it down
② very – break down it
③ much – break them down
④ much – break it down
⑤ much – break down it

[04-05] 서술형
어법상 <u>틀린</u> 곳을 찾아 바르게 고치시오.

04

> I hard got any sleep last night because of the noise.

➡ ___________ → ___________

05

> Fog forms usually in the early morning when the temperature is cooler.

➡ ___________ → ___________

06
밑줄 친 부분의 품사가 나머지 넷과 <u>다른</u> 것을 고르시오.

① I didn't drink <u>enough</u> water during the hike.
② He didn't bring <u>enough</u> money to buy the tickets.
③ There's <u>enough</u> space in the garage for both cars.
④ I didn't put on <u>enough</u> sunscreen, so I got sunburned.
⑤ They didn't work hard <u>enough</u> to finish the project on time.

07 서술형 고난도
어법상 <u>틀린</u> 문장을 찾아 바르게 고치시오.

> ⓐ The event happened just an hour ago.
> ⓑ I carefully turned off the stove after cooking.
> ⓒ The kids have already gone to bed, so it's quiet now.
> ⓓ I decided to finish the report instead of putting off it.
> ⓔ Earthquakes sometimes happen without any warning signs.

➡ (1) ___________ 문장
　 (2) ___________ → ___________

실전 모의고사 J 비교급 UNIT 37~ UNIT 40

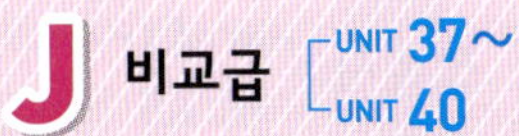

제한 시간 20분
맞은 개수 　　　　개

01

원급, 비교급, 최상급 변화가 알맞게 짝지어지지 <u>않은</u> 것을 고르시오.

① well – better – best
② fast – faster – fastest
③ bad – badder – baddest
④ clever – cleverer – cleverest
⑤ boring – more boring – most boring

02

빈칸에 알맞은 것을 고르시오.

> He was as stubborn as a(n) ___________ when it came to making decisions.

① bee　　　② owl　　　③ mule
④ lark　　　⑤ peacock

[03-05] 서술형

밑줄 친 부분이 맞으면 ○로 표시하고, 틀리면 바르게 고치시오.

03

That was <u>the noisyest</u> party I've ever been to in my life.

➡ ___________________

04

My dog has become <u>much fatter</u> since we switched to a new food.

➡ ___________________

05

He is <u>the hardworkingest</u> member of our team, no question.

➡ ___________________

[06-07]

주어진 우리말과 일치하도록 괄호 안에서 알맞은 것을 고르시오.

06

그는 우리가 갔던 곳 중에서 가장 멀리 떨어져 있다.

➡ He is the (farthest / furthest) from where we went.

07

우리는 그 사건에 대해 더 자세히 알아야 한다.

➡ We need to learn (further / farther) about the incident.

[08-10] 서술형 고난도

어법상 틀린 문장 세 개를 찾아 바르게 고치시오.

> ⓐ He played the piano the best during the recital.
> ⓑ She is one of the best student in the class.
> ⓒ You can join the club so long as you attend the meetings regularly.
> ⓓ He is as twice careful as his colleagues when handling equipment.
> ⓔ This model is inferior than the newer version in terms of performance.

08

➡ (1) ___________ 문장
　(2) ___________ → ___________

09

➡ (1) ___________ 문장
　(2) ___________ → ___________

10

➡ (1) ___________ 문장
　(2) ___________ → ___________

〈 정답과 해설 p. 153~154 〉

실전 모의고사 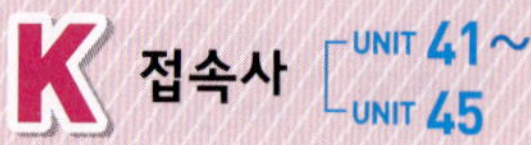 K 접속사 ⎡ UNIT 41 ~ ⎣ UNIT 45

제한 시간 20분
맞은 개수 ☐ 개

[01-02]
두 문장이 같은 뜻이 되도록 빈칸에 알맞은 것을 고르시오.

01

> That she will pass the exam is certain.
> = It is certain ___________ she will pass the exam.

① that　　② what　　③ if
④ whether　　⑤ when

02

> He took the course to get a better job.
> = He took the course ___________ that he could get a better job.

① and　　② but　　③ if
④ so　　⑤ as

[03-04]
빈칸에 공통으로 들어갈 것을 고르시오.

03

> • He saw ___________ the bike and the truck before the car accident.
> • Exercise is good for ___________ body and mind.

① since　　② after　　③ but
④ both　　⑤ either

04

> • I have met many people ___________ I came here.
> • ___________ tomorrow is a holiday, we don't have to go to school.

① since　　② after　　③ once
④ before　　⑤ though

05 고난도
어법상 틀린 것을 고르시오.

① I swim every day so that I can stay healthy.
② As time goes on, the cat is getting bigger and bigger.
③ Even though she is short, she can carry the heavy box.
④ You have to do it until I finish the project.
⑤ I will go there if he will be sick.

[06-08]
주어진 우리말과 일치하도록 괄호 안의 말을 바르게 배열하시오.

06

집중해라, 그러면 너는 의미를 파악할 수 있을 것이다.
(you, can, focus, and, the meaning, grasp)

➡ ___________________________________

____

07

그는 상황을 신중히 분석해서 올바른 결정을 내릴 수 있었다.
(make, so, decision, right, he, the, could)

➡ He analyzed the situation carefully, ______

___________________________________ .

08

그녀는 정직한 평판을 얻었다, 왜냐하면 그녀는 절대 그녀의 원칙을 깬 적이 없었기 때문이다.
(had, never, her, broken, she, for, principles)

➡ She earned a reputation for being honest,

___________________________________ .

실전 모의고사

L 전치사 UNIT 46~ UNIT 50

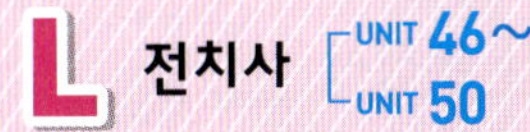

제한 시간 20분
맞은 개수 　　　개

[01-02]

각 빈칸에 들어갈 말이 알맞게 짝지어진 것을 고르시오.

01

> • We drove ___(A)___ the bridge to reach the city.
> • The keys are ___(B)___ the sofa.

　　(A)　　　(B)　　　　　(A)　　　(B)
① into　 − among　 ② across　 − under
③ under − below　 ④ through − under
⑤ across − among

02

> • The cat was taking a nap ___(A)___ the hood of my car.
> • He sat beside me ___(B)___ the concert last night.

　　(A)　　　(B)　　　　　(A)　　　(B)
① on　 − during　 ② among − under
③ up　 − between　 ④ down　 − between
⑤ into − among

[03-05] 서술형

문장에서 틀린 부분을 찾아 바르게 고치시오.

03

Lily is still afraid in insects due to the trauma from her childhood.

➡ ________________ → ________________

04

This is strongly related the company's policy.

➡ ________________ → ________________

05

That road has been notorious to crashes and sinkholes since 2024.

➡ ________________ → ________________

06

어법상 틀린 것을 고르시오.

① The book on the shelf belongs to Rachel.
② He arrived at the airport in the morning.
③ They divided the prize among John and Risa.
④ We discussed the issue thoroughly during the meeting.
⑤ She walked across the bridge without any hesitation.

[07-08]

괄호 안에 주어진 말을 바르게 배열하시오.

07

(were quietly, around, wandering, garden, the)

➡ Our children ________________
________________.

08

(jealous, her, was, friend's, of, success, Margie)

➡ It was certain that ________________
________________.

09 고난도

빈칸에 들어갈 말이 나머지 넷과 다른 것을 고르시오.

① She has lived here ______ five years.
② Does this phone belong ______ you?
③ We are leaving ______ Paris tomorrow.
④ This book is not suitable ______ children.
⑤ I am working ______ her while she is on vacation.

〈 정답과 해설 p. 155~156 〉

실전 모의고사 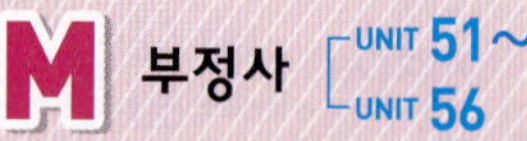 M 부정사 UNIT 51~ UNIT 56

제한 시간 **20분**
맞은 개수 ____ 개

[01-02]
밑줄 친 to부정사의 용법이 나머지 넷과 다른 것을 고르시오.

01
① She hopes to travel Europe.
② His job is to take care of cages.
③ To win a gold medal is not easy.
④ I decided to major in chemical engineering.
⑤ This is a good chance to start learning golf.

02
① I'm very glad to meet you.
② His plan is to study abroad for two years.
③ It's my pleasure to learn foreign languages.
④ Mark recommended me to visit Paris for my vacation.
⑤ I think it is important to choose good TV programs for children.

[03-05]
괄호 안에서 알맞은 것을 고르시오.

03
It was so brave (for / of) you to share this story with us.

04
My coach advised me (not to jump / to not jump) too high.

05
It is important (for / of) drivers to drive slowly on a slippery road.

06 서술형
우리말과 뜻이 같도록 「It ~ to-v」 구문과 괄호 안의 말을 이용하여 문장을 완성하시오.

다른 나라에 있는 친구와 연락을 유지하기는 어렵다.
(not easy, keep in touch with a friend in another country)

➡ ________________________________

____

[07-08]
주어진 우리말과 일치하도록 괄호 안의 말을 바르게 배열하시오.

07
그는 남에게 도움을 청하는 것을 어려워한다.
(it, ask others, difficult, to, for help)
➡ He finds ________________________.

08
Amy는 수영 강좌를 어떻게 신청하는지를 알고 싶어 한다. (how, for the swimming course, to, sign up, to know)
➡ Amy wants ________________________
________________________.

09 고난도
어법상 틀린 것을 고르시오.

① So to speak, it was a rough year.
② I am too tired to continue working.
③ He plans to study abroad next year.
④ He seems to have forgotten about our promise.
⑤ He always makes me to laugh with his jokes.

[01-02] (서술형)

괄호 안의 동사를 알맞은 형태로 바꿔 문장을 완성하시오.

01

He is sorry for ＿＿＿＿＿＿＿ able to give me a hand. (not, be)

02

A: I heard Jason is coming home for Christmas.

B: Yes. We are all looking forward to his ＿＿＿＿＿＿＿. (come)

03

각 빈칸에 들어갈 말이 알맞게 짝지어진 것을 고르시오.

> They look forward to ＿＿(A)＿＿ on the TV talk show for the purpose of ＿＿(B)＿＿ their new album.

	(A)		(B)
①	appear	–	being advertised
②	appear	–	advertising
③	appearing	–	advertise
④	appearing	–	advertising
⑤	appearing	–	being advertised

[04-05] (고난도)

밑줄 친 부분 중 어법상 틀린 것을 고르시오.

04

① I like to eat Thai food every day.
② It is no use trying to excuse yourself.
③ On entering the room, he took off his cap.
④ She couldn't help stay with her sick brother all day.
⑤ He makes a point of doing 30 push-ups every morning.

05

① Jason is far from telling a lie.
② Her suggestion is worth considering.
③ I felt like having a cup of tea in the park.
④ He disappeared without to leave any messages.
⑤ The system prevents others from approaching our documents.

[06-07] (서술형)

주어진 우리말과 일치하도록 〈보기〉의 표현과 괄호 안의 말을 이용하여 빈칸에 알맞은 말을 쓰시오.
(필요시 형태를 변형할 것, 중복 사용 불가)

> 〈보기〉
> feel like   be on the point of

06

그가 무언가를 말하려던 참에 전화가 울렸다.

➡ The telephone rang when he ＿＿＿＿＿＿＿ ＿＿＿＿＿＿＿ something. (say)

07

비가 오고 있어서, Amy는 나가고 싶지 않았다.

➡ Because it was raining, Amy ＿＿＿＿＿＿＿ ＿＿＿＿＿＿＿. (go outside)

08

빈칸에 공통으로 들어갈 알맞은 것을 고르시오.

> • He didn't seem to be used to ＿＿＿＿＿ refused. His heart was broken.
> • Kate is wise enough to keep herself from ＿＿＿＿＿ cheated.

① be   ② being   ③ be have
④ be being   ⑤ her being

〈 정답과 해설 p. 156~157 〉

실전 모의고사 ⓪ 분사 [UNIT 60~ UNIT 63]

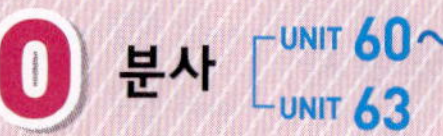

제한 시간 20분
맞은 개수　　　　개

01

밑줄 친 부분의 쓰임이 나머지 넷과 <u>다른</u> 것을 고르시오.

① The <u>boiling</u> water spilled over the pot.
② They talked about <u>going</u> to Jeju Island.
③ The <u>shining</u> sun made the day feel warm.
④ Who is the singer <u>practicing</u> on the stage?
⑤ The <u>burning</u> candle filled the room with scent.

02

밑줄 친 부분 중 어법상 <u>틀린</u> 것을 고르시오.

① The <u>crying</u> child looked for his mother.
② They saw the leaves <u>falling</u> from the trees.
③ The book <u>written</u> in Spanish is on the table.
④ We heard someone <u>singing</u> in the hallway.
⑤ The movie <u>directing</u> by Christopher Nolan was amazing.

[03-04] 서술형

밑줄 친 부분 중 분사구문은 부사절로, 부사절은 분사구문으로 알맞게 바꿔 쓰시오. (분사구문은 접속사를 생략할 것)

03

<u>When we were walking along the road</u>, we found a café.

➡ ＿＿＿＿＿＿＿＿＿＿＿＿＿＿＿＿＿＿,
 we found a café.

04

<u>Having another appointment</u>, they left early.
➡ Because ＿＿＿＿＿＿＿＿＿＿＿＿＿＿＿＿,
 they left early.

05 서술형

주어진 우리말과 일치하도록 〈조건〉에 맞게 영작하시오.

〈조건〉
• With로 문장을 시작할 것
• 동사 fall을 활용할 것
• 4단어로 적을 것

비가 내리고 있어서, 우리는 안에 머물며 쉬기로 했다.

➡ ＿＿＿＿＿＿＿＿＿＿＿＿＿＿＿＿, we decided to stay inside and relax.

[06-08]

괄호 안에서 알맞은 것을 고르시오.

06

(Having studied / Studied having) all night, he finally passed the difficult exam.

07

(Opening / Opened) the box carefully, he found an old photo inside it.

08

(Wanting not / Not wanting) to disturb anyone, she tiptoed across the wooden floor.

09 고난도

밑줄 친 부분을 어법상 알맞은 형태로 바꾼 것끼리 짝지어진 것을 고르시오.

• I was <u>bore</u> during the long documentary film.
• The dog <u>chase</u> a cat ran across the yard.

① boring – chasing　② bored – chased
③ boring – chased　④ bored – chasing
⑤ be bored – chasing

실전 모의고사 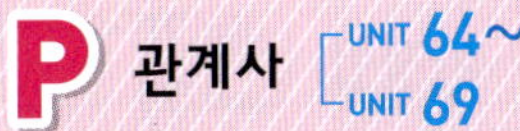 **P** 관계사 UNIT **64~** UNIT **69**

제한 시간 **20분**

맞은 개수 　　 개

01

밑줄 친 부분 중 생략할 수 <u>없는</u> 것을 고르시오.

① The chair on <u>which</u> you are sitting is very old.

② The cat <u>which</u> my sister adopted is very playful.

③ The movie <u>that</u> I was looking forward to was disappointing.

④ The problem <u>that</u> she was struggling with was finally solved.

⑤ The painting <u>which</u> he bought at the auction is worth a fortune.

02

밑줄 친 부분 중 어법상 <u>틀린</u> 것을 고르시오.

① This is the house <u>which</u> I built myself.

② This is the lady <u>whose</u> son is a teacher.

③ I know the man <u>who</u> is playing the guitar.

④ Paul is the class leader <u>whom</u> we have chosen.

⑤ The boys <u>which</u> serve in the restaurant are the owner's sons.

[03-04] 서술형 고난도

ⓐ~ⓔ 중 어법상 <u>틀린</u> 것 두 개를 찾아 기호를 쓰고 바르게 고치시오.

> The woman ⓐ <u>who</u> lives next door is a famous artist. She has a studio ⓑ <u>where</u> is filled with colorful paintings. She has a unique style ⓒ <u>that</u> combines traditional and modern techniques. I can't wait to see her exhibition ⓓ <u>which</u> will open next month. The exhibition will feature the way ⓔ <u>how</u> her works inspired many people.

03

➡ ＿＿＿＿＿＿＿ → ＿＿＿＿＿＿＿

04

➡ ＿＿＿＿＿＿＿ → ＿＿＿＿＿＿＿

05

빈칸에 들어갈 말이 나머지 넷과 <u>다른</u> 것을 고르시오.

① ＿＿＿ you said made me think.

② I can't believe ＿＿＿ I'm hearing.

③ All ＿＿＿ he did was for his family.

④ She showed me ＿＿＿ she bought at the market.

⑤ ＿＿＿ they decided shocked everyone in the room.

06 서술형

두 문장이 같은 뜻이 되도록 빈칸에 알맞은 말을 쓰시오.

No matter who wins the game, we'll still be friends.

= ＿＿＿＿＿＿＿ wins the game, we'll still be friends.

[07-08]

주어진 우리말과 일치하도록 괄호 안의 말을 바르게 배열하시오.

07

이것이 그가 현재 일하고 있는 조직이다.

(the organization, is, he, is, currently working, where, this)

➡ ＿＿＿＿＿＿＿＿＿＿＿＿

＿＿＿＿＿＿＿＿＿＿＿＿

08

그것은 내가 오랫동안 갈망했던 기회였다.

(that, the opportunity, which, I, had longed, for, was)

➡ ＿＿＿＿＿＿＿＿＿＿＿＿

＿＿＿＿＿＿＿＿＿＿＿＿

〈 정답과 해설 **p. 157~159** 〉

01

주어진 문장과 의미가 같은 것을 고르시오.

> Had they listened, they wouldn't be in trouble.

① As they don't listen, they are in trouble.
② As they don't listen, they were in trouble.
③ As they didn't listen, they will be in trouble.
④ As they didn't listen, they were in trouble.
⑤ As they didn't listen, they are in trouble.

02 고난도

어법상 틀린 것을 고르시오.

① I wish I had accepted their suggestion.
② She acts as if she understood everything.
③ Had he noticed the sign, he would've slowed down.
④ If I was the manager, I'd improve the system.
⑤ If it had not been for your support, I couldn't have continued.

[03-04]

각 빈칸에 들어갈 말이 알맞게 짝지어진 것을 고르시오.

03

> Fiona pretends as if her wallet ___(A)___ genuine.
> = ___(B)___, Fiona's wallet is not genuine.

   (A)   (B)
① is   – If
② is   – Though
③ were – In fact
④ were – Once
⑤ were – She wish

04 고난도

> If our teacher had empathy for our stress, she ___(A)___ us such a tricky homework.
> = Since our teacher ___(B)___ empathy for our stress, she gives us such a tricky homework.

    (A)   (B)
① would've not given – doesn't have
② would've not given – didn't have
③ would not give – will not have
④ would not give – doesn't have
⑤ would not give – didn't have

[05-06] 서술형

두 문장이 같은 뜻이 되도록 빈칸에 알맞은 말을 쓰시오.

05

I'm sorry that I didn't answer the phone then.

= I wish ______________________ the phone then.

06

Without your help, I couldn't pass the exam.

= Were ______________________, I couldn't pass the exam.

07 서술형

주어진 문장을 우리말로 해석하시오.

> Had I known the price, I wouldn't have bought the ticket.

➡ ______________________________

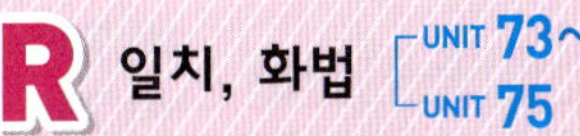

실전 모의고사 **R** 일치, 화법 [UNIT **73**~ UNIT **75**]

제한 시간 **20분**
맞은 개수 [ ] 개

[01-02]

괄호 안에서 알맞은 것을 고르시오.

01

Fifty kilograms (is / are) the limit for this luggage.

02

Not only the singer but also the dancers (perform / performs) live.

03

밑줄 친 부분을 어법상 알맞은 형태로 바꾼 것끼리 짝지어진 것을 고르시오.

> • Either my sister or my parents <u>be</u> picking me up today.
> • The number of tourists visiting the city <u>have</u> increased.

① is – have ② is – has ③ are – have
④ are – has ⑤ are – having

[04-06] 서술형

주어진 우리말과 일치하도록 괄호 안의 단어를 이용하여 빈칸에 알맞은 말을 쓰시오.

04

피시 앤 칩스는 영국에서 인기 있다. (be)

➡ Fish and chips _______________ popular in England.

05

그는 내게 복도에서 뛰지 말라고 말했다. (not, run)

➡ He told me _______________ in the hallway.

06

영화가 시작되면, 나는 핸드폰을 끌 것이다. (start)

➡ When the movie _______________, I will turn off my phone.

[07-08]

직접화법을 간접화법으로 바꿔 쓸 때, 각 빈칸에 알맞은 것을 고르시오.

07

> The teacher said to the students, "Please listen carefully."
> ➡ The teacher ___(A)___ the students ___(B)___ carefully.

  (A)   (B)   (A)   (B)
① tell – to listen ② said – listen
③ said – to listen ④ told – listen
⑤ told – to listen

08

> She said to him, "Can you fix my bike?"
> ➡ She asked him ___(A)___ he could fix ___(B)___ bike.

  (A)   (B)   (A)   (B)
① if – my ② if – her
③ how – my ④ how – her
⑤ if – his

09 고난도

어법상 옳은 것을 <u>모두</u> 고르시오.

> ⓐ Some of the information is outdated.
> ⓑ She asked him what did he want for lunch.
> ⓒ Most of the water are clean enough to drink.
> ⓓ The student who study hard always succeeds.
> ⓔ My sister told me she had already finished dinner.
> ⓕ She believed that true friends are found in difficult times.

➡ _______________

〈 정답과 해설 p. 159~160 〉

실전 모의고사 S 특수 구문 UNIT 76~ UNIT 78

제한 시간 20분
맞은 개수　　　　개

[01-02] (서술형)

밑줄 친 부분을 강조하는 문장으로 바꿔 쓰시오.

01

She has <u>never</u> seen such a thing.

➡ Never _________________________ .

02

They did <u>not</u> realize the truth <u>until the end</u>.

➡ Not until the end _________________ .

[03-04]

주어진 우리말과 일치하도록 바르게 영작한 것을 고르시오.

03

그들 중 어느 누구도 뉴욕에 가 본 적이 없다.

① Anyone has been to New York.
② None of them has been to New York.
③ Anyone of them has been to New York.
④ Neither of them has never been to New York.
⑤ No one of them has never been to New York.

04

모든 학생들이 그 의견에 반대하는 것은 아니다.

① All students are against the opinion.
② Not all students are against the opinion.
③ Every student is not against the opinion.
④ Not every students are not against the opinion.
⑤ Not all students are not against the opinion.

[05-06]

밑줄 친 부분의 쓰임이 나머지 넷과 <u>다른</u> 것을 고르시오.

05

① <u>It</u> is you that can change your life.
② <u>It</u> was at 2 that rain started to fall.
③ <u>It</u> was the stamp that I gave to Jim.
④ <u>It</u> was the man that brought the bird.
⑤ <u>It</u> is difficult for me to solve the math problem.

06

① It was a rose <u>that</u> he gave her yesterday.
② It was on the street <u>that</u> I met him last year.
③ It is so big <u>that</u> I can share it with my sister.
④ It was one year ago <u>that</u> he began to learn how to drive.
⑤ It was with my friends <u>that</u> I saw the picture in the museum.

[07-08] (고난도)

어법상 <u>틀린</u> 것을 고르시오.

07

① Down fell the snow.
② Behind the rock stands a squirrel.
③ Right over my head passed a drone.
④ Seldom does not he visit his parents.
⑤ Just around the corner was the post office.

08

① She does speaks Chinese well.
② I do like to read comic books.
③ I don't like Japanese music at all.
④ This is the very book I have been looking for.
⑤ It is the notebook that you left in my house.

〈부정대명사〉

부정대명사	의미	예문	
one	~ 하나	(1) 앞에 나온 셀 수 있는 명사를 가리키며, 불특정한 것을 나타낸다. • If you have frying pans, can you lend me one? (프라이팬이 있으면, 하나 빌려 주시겠어요?) 앞에 나온 frying pans 중 불특정한 하나 (2) 명사가 복수형일 때는 ones를 쓴다. • Black rocks are on the left and white ones are on the right. 앞에 나온 rocks 중 불특정한 여러 개 (검은 돌들은 왼쪽에 있고 흰 돌들은 오른쪽에 있다.) (3) 일반적인 사람을 나타낼 때도 쓸 수 있다. • One can't always get what one wants. 일반적인 사람　　일반적인 사람 (누구나 자신이 원하는 것을 항상 가질 수는 없다.)	one
another	또 다른 하나 (단수)	• This one is too big for me. Can you show me another? (이것은 제게 너무 커요. 다른 것을 보여주시겠어요?)	one　another 여럿 중 다른 하나
one, another, the other	하나, 또 다른 하나, 나머지 하나	• There are three pens. One is mine, another is my brother's, and the other is my father's. (세 개의 펜이 있다. 하나는 내 것이고, 또 다른 하나는 내 남동생의 것이고, 나머지 하나는 나의 아버지의 것이다.)	one　another　the other 또 다른 하나　나머지 하나
some ~ others	몇몇 …, 나머지 일부 (복수)	• Some like tea, and others like coffee. (어떤 사람들은 차를 좋아하고, 다른 몇몇 사람들은 커피를 좋아한다.) • Some went inside but others went outside. (몇몇은 들어갔고 다른 몇몇 사람들은 나갔다.)	some　others 여럿 중 다른 여럿
some ~ the others	몇몇 …, 나머지 전부 (복수)	• Some of the fruits are oranges, and the others are apples. (과일들 중 일부는 오렌지이고, 나머지 전부는 사과이다.) • Only some work, and the others rest. (몇몇만 일하고 나머지 전부는 쉰다.)	some　the others 여럿 중 나머지 전부

〈동사의 과거-과거분사 불규칙 변화표〉

1 A – A – A형 (원형, 과거, 과거분사가 모두 같은 경우)

뜻	원형	과거	과거분사
내기하다	bet	bet	bet
방송하다	broadcast	broadcast	broadcast
비용이 들다	cost	cost	cost
자르다	cut	cut	cut
치다	hit	hit	hit
다치다	hurt	hurt	hurt
~하게 하다	let	let	let

뜻	원형	과거	과거분사
놓다	put	put	put
그만두다	quit	quit	quit
읽다	read	read	read
재설정하다	reset	reset	reset
놓다	set	set	set
닫다	shut	shut	shut
퍼지다	spread	spread	spread

2 A – B – B형 (과거와 과거분사가 같은 경우)

뜻	원형	과거	과거분사
구부리다	bend	bent	bent
묶다	bind	bound	bound
가져오다	bring	brought	brought
짓다	build	built	built
사다	buy	bought	bought
잡다	catch	caught	caught
거래하다	deal	dealt	dealt
먹이다	feed	fed	fed
느끼다	feel	felt	felt
찾다	find	found	found
얻다	get	got	got, gotten
갈다	grind	ground	ground
가지다	have	had	had
듣다	hear	heard	heard
지니다	hold	held	held
유지하다	keep	kept	kept
놓다, 낳다	lay	laid	laid
인도하다	lead	led	led
떠나다	leave	left	left
빌려주다	lend	lent	lent
잃어버리다	lose	lost	lost

뜻	원형	과거	과거분사
만들다	make	made	made
의미하다	mean	meant	meant
만나다	meet	met	met
지불하다	pay	paid	paid
말하다	say	said	said
팔다	sell	sold	sold
보내다	send	sent	sent
쏘다	shoot	shot	shot
앉다	sit	sat	sat
자다	sleep	slept	slept
냄새를 맡다	smell	smelt	smelt
흘리다	spill	spilt	spilt
소비하다	spend	spent	spent
서다	stand	stood	stood
때리다, 치다	strike	struck	struck
쓸다	sweep	swept	swept
가르치다	teach	taught	taught
말하다	tell	told	told
생각하다	think	thought	thought
이해하다	understand	understood	understood
이기다	win	won	won

3 A − B − A형 (원형과 과거분사가 같은 경우)

뜻	원형	과거	과거분사
되다	become	became	become
오다	come	came	come
극복하다	overcome	overcame	overcome
달리다	run	ran	run

4 A − B − C형 (원형, 과거, 과거분사가 모두 다른 경우)

뜻	원형	과거	과거분사
발생하다	arise	arose	arisen
깨다	awake	awoke	awoken
~이다	be	was, were	been
낳다, 견디다	bear	bore	born(e)
시작하다	begin	began	begun
물다	bite	bit	bitten
불다	blow	blew	blown
깨뜨리다	break	broke	broken
선택하다	choose	chose	chosen
하다	do	did	done
그리다	draw	drew	drawn
마시다	drink	drank	drunk
운전하다	drive	drove	driven
먹다	eat	ate	eaten
떨어지다	fall	fell	fallen
잊다	forget	forgot	forgotten
날다	fly	flew	flown
얼다	freeze	froze	frozen
주다	give	gave	given
가다	go	went	gone

뜻	원형	과거	과거분사
자라다	grow	grew	grown
숨다	hide	hid	hidden
알다	know	knew	known
눕다	lie	lay	lain
타다	ride	rode	ridden
울리다	ring	rang	rung
오르다	rise	rose	risen
보다	see	saw	seen
흔들다	shake	shook	shaken
노래하다	sing	sang	sung
가라앉다	sink	sank	sunk
말하다	speak	spoke	spoken
훔치다	steal	stole	stolen
수영하다	swim	swam	swum
잡다	take	took	taken
찢다	tear	tore	torn
던지다	throw	threw	thrown
깨다	wake	woke	woken
입다	wear	wore	worn
쓰다	write	wrote	written

〈비교급, 최상급 불규칙 변화표〉

원급	비교급	최상급	예문
good 좋은	better 더 좋은, 더 잘	best 가장 좋은, 가장 잘	[비교급] I feel better today than I did yesterday. (나는 어제보다 오늘 기분이 더 좋다.) [최상급] Laughter is the best medicine. (웃음이 가장 좋은 약이다.)
well 잘			[비교급] The changed plan worked better. (수정된 계획이 더 잘 작용했다.)
bad 나쁜	worse 더 나쁜, 더 아픈	worst 가장 나쁜, 가장 아픈	[비교급] The situation is worse than we imagined. (상황은 우리가 상상했던 것보다 더 나쁘다.) [최상급] He had the worst day at work today. (그는 오늘 직장에서 가장 힘든 하루를 보냈다.)
ill 아픈			[최상급] It's the worst flu I've ever had. (내가 앓았던 최고로 아픈 독감이다.)
many [수] 많은	more 더 많은	most 가장 많은	[비교급] There are more people in the park today. (오늘 공원에 더 많은 사람들이 있다.) [최상급] Jack has the most energy in his class. (Jack은 그의 반에서 가장 많은 에너지를 갖고 있다.)
much [양] 많은			
few [수] 적은	fewer 더 적은	fewest 가장 적은	[최상급] David received the fewest votes. (David가 가장 적은 표를 받았다.)
little [양] 적은	less 더 적은	least 가장 적은	[비교급] There was less traffic on the roads. (도로에 교통량이 더 적었다.)
far [거리] 먼, 멀리	farther 더 먼	farthest 가장 먼	[최상급] He threw the ball to the farthest corner. (그는 공을 가장 먼 구석으로 던졌다.)
far [정도] 더욱	further 더 깊이	furthest 가장 깊이	[비교급] Further investigation revealed new evidence. (추가 조사가 새로운 증거를 드러냈다.)
late [시간] 늦은, 늦게	later 이후의	latest 최신의	[비교급] Let's grab a coffee later in the afternoon. (이따 오후에 커피를 마십시다.)
late [순서] 늦은, 늦게	latter 후자의	last 마지막의	[최상급] This is the last train to the city. (이것이 도시로 가는 마지막 기차이다.)
old 오래된, 나이든	older 더 오래된	oldest 가장 오래된	[비교급] My brother is two years older than me. (내 형은 나보다 두 살 더 많다.) [최상급] This building is the oldest building in town. (이 건물은 마을에서 가장 오래된 건물이다.)
old 연상의	elder 더 연상의	eldest 가장 연상의	[비교급] My elder brother is my best friend. (형은 나의 가장 친한 친구이다.) [최상급] She is the eldest child in her family. (그녀는 가족 중에서 맏이다.)

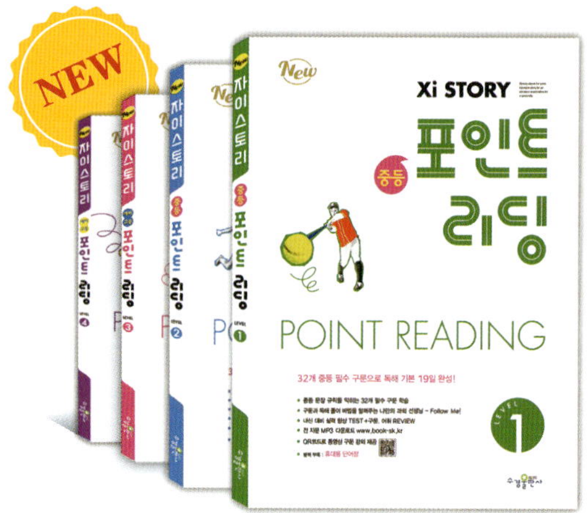

Xi STORY 자이스토리

포인트 리딩

구문 중심 독해   수능 유형 독해

[Level ❶, Level ❷, Level ❸, Level ❹]

"중학교 영어 독해는 포인트 리딩으로 완성한다!"

[Level ❶, Level ❷]

- 32개 중등 필수 구문으로 중등 독해 기초 19일 완성!
- 구문과 독해 풀이 비법을 알려주는 나만의 과외 선생님 - Follow Me!
- 내신 대비 실력 향상 TEST + 구문, 어휘 Review
- DAY별로 3지문씩 공부하는 구문 중심 ACTUAL READING!

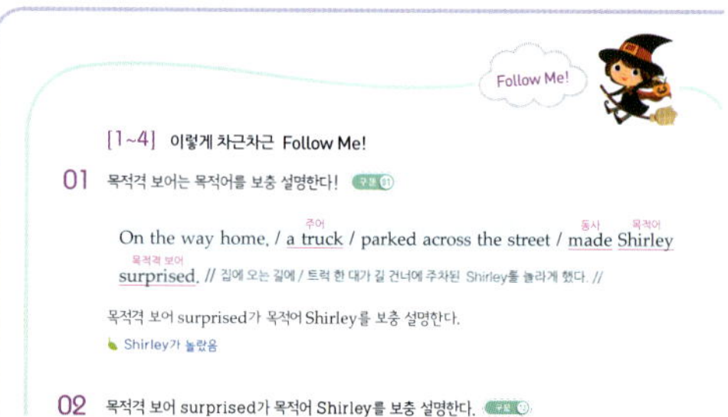

[Level ❸, Level ❹]

- 17개 수능 독해 유형 문제로 예비 고등 영어 독해 20일 완성
- 독해 문제의 풀이 비법을 알려주는 과외 선생님 - Follow Me!
- 내신대비 실력 향상 TEST + 어휘 Review
- 고1 학력평가 기출 지문으로 독해 유형을 익히고 DAY별로 4지문씩 공부하기!

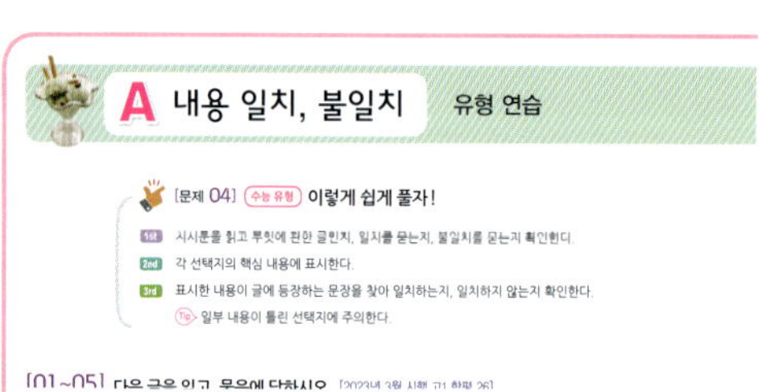

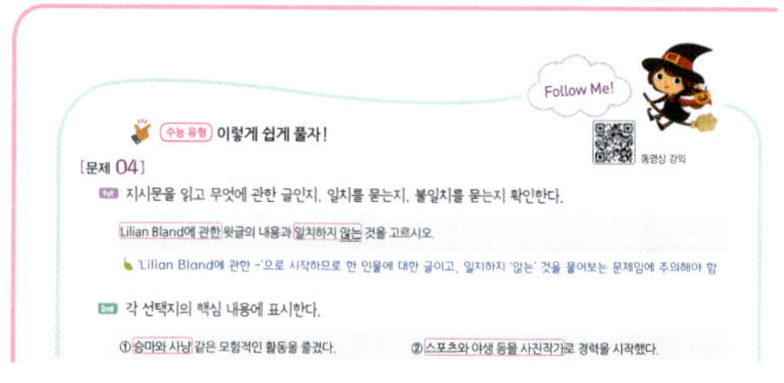

NEW
2022
개정 교육과정

Xistory stands for
eXtra Intensive story for
the University Entrance Examination.

수경출판사

WORKBOOK

[Unit별로 1p씩 개념 확인＋문법 복습 문제 수록]

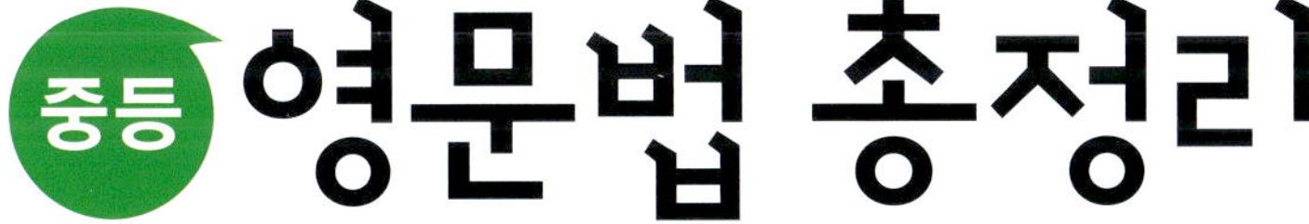

자 이 스 토 리

중등 영문법 총정리

중3

수경출판사

중등 영어 **독해 기본**

[Level 1, Level 2, Level 3]

"중학교 지문으로 수능 독해 유형을 마스터한다!"

* 단계별 수능 독해 학습법

STEP 1 내용 파악하기, STEP 2 중심어와 중심 문장 찾기, STEP 3 글의 흐름 이해하기, STEP 4 글의 내용으로 짐작하기

수능 독해 문제 유형을 지문 이해 순서와 난이도에 따라 4단계로 분류하여
쉽게 이해하고 훈련할 수 있습니다.

① 수능 독해 문제 **유형과 해법 제시!**

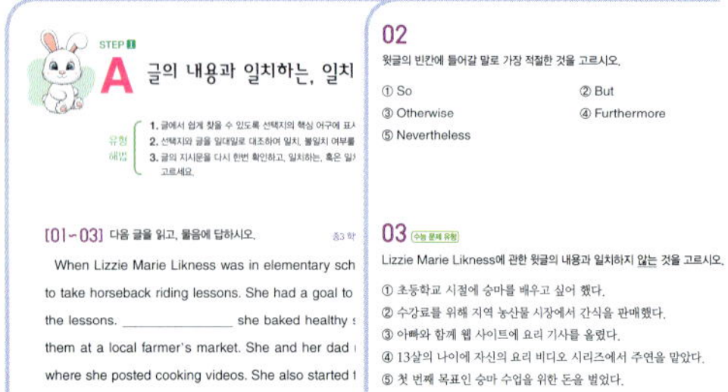

② **직독직해 + 구문 체크** - 완벽한 지문 이해

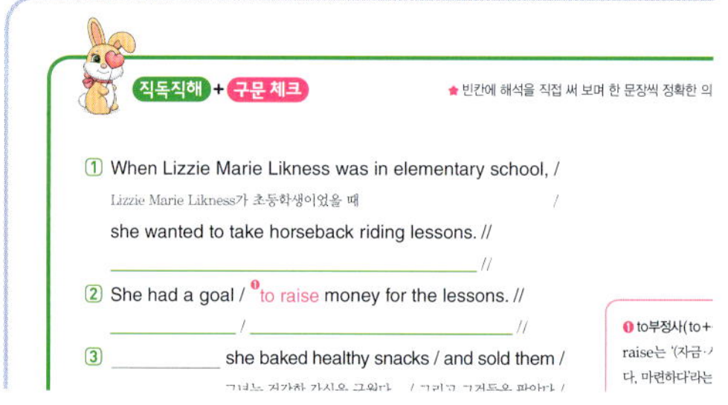

③ 학습한 독해 유형 완성 - **독해 유형 완성 TEST**

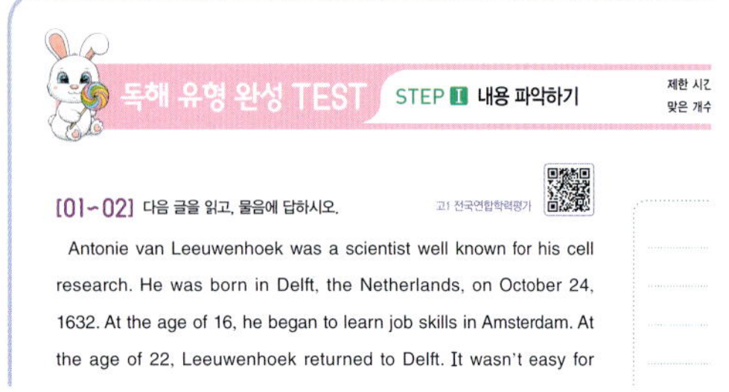

④ 독해 실력 테스트 - **독해 실력 완성 모의고사**

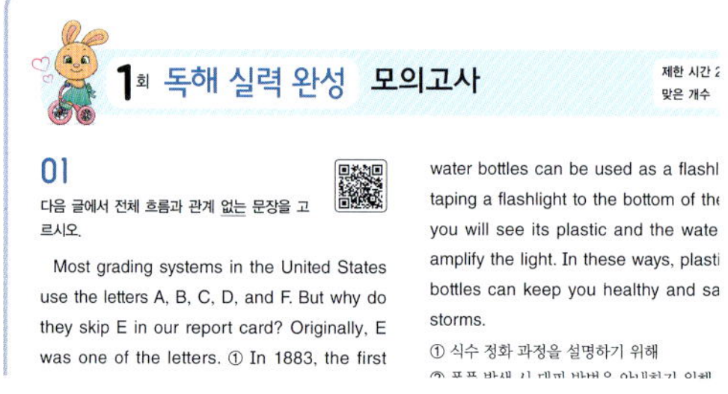

[01-06] 밑줄 친 부분의 품사를 쓰시오.

01 They considered the plan difficult.
　(　　) (　　)　　　　(　　)

02 I know that she is telling the truth.
　　　(　　)(　　)(　　)

03 The clock ticks loudly in the silent room.
　　　　(　　)(　　)　(　　)

04 The news made the audience speechless.
　　　　(　　)　(　　)　(　　)

05 Wow! The sky became dark after the storm.
　(　　)　　　　　　(　　)(　　)

06 They explored the ancient ruins and
　　　　　　　(　　)(　　)

discovered many hidden treasures.
　　　　(　　)

[07-14] 문장에서 주어는 S로, 동사는 V로, 보어는 C로, 목적어는 O로, 수식어는 M으로 표시하시오.

07 The soup tastes spicy and delicious.
　(　　)(　　)　(　　)

08 We visited the museum last weekend.
　(　　)(　　)(　　)　(　　)

09 The wind howls during the heavy storm.
　(　　)(　　)　(　　)

10 She offered him a valuable piece of advice.
　(　　)(　　)(　　)　(　　)

11 The discovery proved the theory incorrect.
　(　　)　(　　)　(　　)　(　　)

12 The baby cried loudly in the middle of the
　(　　)(　　)(　　)　(　　)
night.

13 She became very nervous before the
　(　　)(　　)(　　)(　　)(　　)
presentation.

14 They play soccer at the park every Sunday
　(　　)(　　)(　　)(　　)(　　)
afternoon.

[15-19] 빈칸에 들어갈 말을 〈보기〉에서 골라 문장을 완성하시오. (중복 사용 불가)

〈보기〉
applauds　　quite
under　　us　　difficult

15 The book seems __________ complicated.

16 The audience __________ after the performance.

17 He thought the project too __________ for beginners.

18 They showed __________ the latest innovation in technology.

19 The scientists examined the samples __________ the microscope.

〈 정답 p. 161 〉

[01-06] 빈칸에 들어갈 말을 〈보기〉에서 골라 문장을 완성하시오. (중복 사용 불가)

〈보기〉

tastes	stopped	felt
bloom	sounds	fly

01 She __________ scared of a spider.

02 The flowers ____________ in the spring.

03 The birds ____________ south for the winter.

04 The coffee ____________ bitter without sugar.

05 His story ____________ interesting, but it's hard to believe.

06 The car ____________ suddenly in front of the traffic light.

[07-13] 문장에서 주어는 S로, 동사는 V로, 보어는 C로, 수식어는 M으로 표시하고, 문장의 형식을 쓰시오.

07 The cake smells delicious.
(　　) (　　) (　　)　➡ ____형식

08 We slept for ten hours yesterday.
(　) (　　) (　　) (　　)　➡ ____형식

09 He sings in the choir on Sundays.
(　) (　　) (　　) (　　)　➡ ____형식

10 The dog barks loudly every morning.
(　) (　　) (　　) (　　)　➡ ____형식

11 He became angry when he heard the news.
(　　) (　　) (　　) (　　)　➡ ____형식

12 The movie was exciting from start to finish.
(　　) (　　) (　　) (　　)　➡ ____형식

13 She sighed deeply and nodded slowly.
(　　) (　　) (　　) (　　) (　　)
➡ ____형식

[14-21] 괄호 안에서 알맞은 것을 고르시오.

14 She is very (kind / kindly) to everyone.

15 They meet (frequent / frequently) after work.

16 The sky appears (cloud / cloudy) this morning.

17 The chair feels (comfortable / comfort) to sit in.

18 The cat sleeps (peaceful / peacefully) on the couch.

19 The wind blows (gentle / gently) through the trees.

20 I arrived (at the station / the station) on time in spite of the rain.

21 My phone was ringing (loud / loudly) when I washed the dishes.

〈정답 p. 161〉

[01-05] 〈보기〉와 같이 간접목적어(I.O)와 직접목적어(D.O)를 찾아 쓰시오.

> 〈보기〉
> I will buy you a hamburger.
> ➡ I.O: <u>you</u>　D.O: <u>a hamburger</u>

01 She showed me the data.
➡ I.O: __________　D.O: __________

02 He sent his friend a postcard.
➡ I.O: __________　D.O: __________

03 I bought my sister a necklace.
➡ I.O: __________　D.O: __________

04 He will find my brother his cap.
➡ I.O: __________　D.O: __________

05 I delivered him the cup he ordered.
➡ I.O: __________　D.O: __________

[06-13] 주어진 4형식 문장을 3형식으로 바꿔 쓰시오.

06 I cooked them dinner.
➡ I cooked __________________.

07 She asked him a favor.
➡ She asked __________________.

08 He made me a sandwich.
➡ He made __________________.

09 I bought my mom a present.
➡ I bought __________________.

10 You got me a bottle of juice.
➡ You got __________________.

11 He showed her a rare antique vase.
➡ He showed __________________.

12 The CEO offered them a good partnership.
➡ The CEO offered __________________
__________________.

13 My mother taught the students both English and Math.
➡ My mother taught __________________
__________________.

[14-19] 빈칸에 들어갈 말을 〈보기〉에서 골라 문장을 완성하시오. (중복 사용 불가)

> 〈보기〉
> reminded　　thanked　　discuss
> compared　　accused　　handed

14 He __________ her of cheating.

15 I __________ them after the performance.

16 This picture __________ our class of the field trip.

17 I __________ my new camera with the old one.

18 She __________ me the printed schedule for the trip.

19 Let's __________ the details of the project at tomorrow's meeting.

〈 정답 p. 161 〉

[01-05] 〈보기〉와 같이 목적어(O)와 목적격 보어(O.C)를 찾아 쓰시오.

〈보기〉
I heard you sing a song in the room.
➡ O: <u>you</u>　O.C: <u>sing</u>

01 The baby made her happy.
➡ O: ___________　O.C: ___________

02 The team elected John captain.
➡ O: ___________　O.C: ___________

03 Tom let his son play outside.
➡ O: ___________　O.C: ___________

04 They found the movie interesting.
➡ O: ___________　O.C: ___________

05 The teacher noticed her students answer the questions.
➡ O: ___________　O.C: ___________

[06-12] 괄호 안에서 알맞은 것을 고르시오.

06 The news made him (sad / sadly).

07 He considered the plan (risky / be risky).

08 She called the meeting (succeeded / successful).

09 His performance made me very (proud / proudly).

10 The director wants the team (improve / to improve).

11 We appointed him (manager / managed) of the project.

12 The students found their final test (difficult / difficulty).

[13-19] 주어진 우리말과 일치하도록 괄호 안의 단어를 이용하여 빈칸에 알맞은 말을 쓰시오.

13 나는 그녀에게 천천히 말해달라고 부탁했다.
➡ I asked her ___________ slowly. (speak)

14 엄마는 나에게 내 방을 청소하게 했다.
➡ My mom made me ___________ my room. (clean)

15 우리는 창문이 깨진 것을 발견했다.
➡ We found the window ___________. (break)

16 나는 그녀에게 문을 잠그라고 상기시켰다.
➡ I reminded her ___________ the door. (lock)

17 그녀는 물이 끓는 채로 가스레인지 위에 두었다.
➡ She left the water ___________ on the stove. (boil)

18 나의 부모님은 내가 유학 가도록 격려하셨다.
➡ My parents encouraged me ___________ abroad. (study)

19 그의 실패는 그가 더 열심히 노력하게 만들었다.
➡ His failure drove him ________ harder. (try)

[01-07] 괄호 안에서 알맞은 것을 고르시오.

01 (Don't / Aren't) climb a mountain alone.

02 Hurry up, (and / or) you'll miss the train.

03 (Let / Let's) go to the concert with me tonight.

04 Don't (let / be) them dump their problems on you.

05 Why (don't / do) we have lunch at a nearby restaurant?

06 Work out every day, (and / or) you will lose weight soon.

07 (Finish / To finish) your writing assignment before you go out.

[08-13] 문장을 괄호 안의 지시대로 바꿔 쓰시오.

08 How cute his baby is!
　➡ (평서문으로) ___________________

09 This holiday was so amazing.
　➡ (what을 이용한 감탄문으로) ___________ ___________

10 What pretty dresses she has!
　➡ (평서문으로) ___________________

11 She plays the piano very well.
　➡ (how를 이용한 감탄문으로) ___________ ___________

12 You should not talk during the test.
　➡ (명령문으로) ___________________

13 Let's finish your homework before dinner.
　➡ (명령문으로) ___________________ ___________

[14-19] 주어진 우리말과 일치하도록 괄호 안의 단어를 이용하여 빈칸에 알맞은 말을 쓰시오.

14 그는 참 좋은 선생님이구나! (good teacher)
　➡ What ___________________!

15 항상 너의 친구들에게 배려심 있어라.
　　　　(considerate to, all the time)
　➡ Be ___________________ ___________.

16 방학 동안 여행 가자. (let, go on a trip)
　➡ ___________________ during the vacation.

17 내 생일을 기억하다니 그녀는 정말 다정하네! (sweet)
　➡ How ___________ to remember my birthday!

18 이번 여름에 할아버지 댁에 방문하는 것이 어때?
　　　　(visit, grandfather's house)
　➡ How about ___________________ ___________?

19 우리 저녁 먹고 영화 보는 게 어때?
　　　　(we, watch a movie, after dinner)
　➡ Why don't ___________________ ___________?

〈 정답 p. 161~162 〉

[01-08] 빈칸에 알맞은 부가의문문을 쓰시오.

01 I'm right, _____________?

02 You like this song, _____________?

03 Don't forget to call me, _____________?

04 You've seen that movie, _____________?

05 She is coming to the party, _____________?

06 Let's try that new restaurant, _____________?

07 We were supposed to meet here, _____________?

08 My professors will bring the documents, _____________?

[09-15] 문장을 간접의문문으로 바꾸어 빈칸을 완성하시오.

09 Do you know? + Where is he going?
　➡ Do you know _____________?

10 I wonder. + When will she come back?
　➡ I wonder _____________.

11 I can't understand. + Why did he act that way?
　➡ I can't understand _____________.

12 I don't know. + Did she solve the problem?
　➡ I don't know _____________.

13 Does he want to know? + Why did that happen?
　➡ Does he want to know _____________?

14 Can you tell me? + How can I get to the station?
　➡ Can you tell me _____________?

15 Could you explain? + How does this machine work?
　➡ Could you explain _____________?

[16-21] 틀린 부분을 찾아 밑줄을 긋고 바르게 고치시오.

16 Let's grab some coffee, will you?
　➡ _____________

17 Stop your current task, don't you?
　➡ _____________

18 I'm curious how much does the ticket cost.　➡ _____________

19 We don't know how long does we have to wait.　➡ _____________

20 Let's visit the museum this weekend, shall you?　➡ _____________

21 I don't know whether did she reply to my message.　➡ _____________

〈 정답 p. 162 〉

[01-08] 주어진 명사의 복수형을 쓰시오.

01 man　➡ ______________

02 salmon　➡ ______________

03 house　➡ ______________

04 ox　➡ ______________

05 datum　➡ ______________

06 fox　➡ ______________

07 goose　➡ ______________

08 party　➡ ______________

[09-14] 괄호 안에서 알맞은 것을 고르시오.

09 I saw (a / some) mice eat a piece of cheese.

10 These phenomena (are / is) hard to explain.

11 People in the town (are / is) finding the missing kid.

12 The crisis in the country (are / is) getting worse.

13 I took some (bacterium / bacteria) from the sample for research.

14 We spotted three (moose / mooses) near the lake during our hike in Canada.

[15-18] 밑줄 친 부분에 유의하여 문장을 우리말로 해석하시오.

15 The table is made of <u>wood</u>.

　➡ ________________________________

16 We went hiking in the <u>woods</u>.

　➡ ________________________________

17 Wipe the table with a soft <u>cloth</u>.

　➡ ________________________________

18 She packed all her <u>clothes</u> for the trip.

　➡ ________________________________

[19-23] 밑줄 친 부분이 어법상 옳으면 ○로 표시하고, 틀리면 바르게 고치시오.

19 There are <u>few animals</u> in the mountain.

　➡ ______________

20 All the equipment <u>was</u> tested before the experiment.

　➡ ______________

21 His cattle always <u>grazes</u> peacefully in the field at 6:00 a.m.

　➡ ______________

22 The desert landscape was dotted with many <u>cactuses</u> of various shapes.

　➡ ______________

23 The scientist presented her <u>analyses</u> of the collected data at the conference.

　➡ ______________

〈 정답 p. 162 〉

[01-06] 밑줄 친 명사가 셀 수 있는 명사라면 C(countable), 셀 수 없는 명사라면 UC(uncountable)를 쓰시오.

01 She wore her favorite <u>jeans</u> to the party.

➡ _____________

02 I have always wanted to visit <u>Paris</u> in the spring.

➡ _____________

03 The <u>audience</u> applauded loudly.

➡ _____________

04 He grilled some <u>meat</u> for the family barbecue.

➡ _____________

05 She gained <u>knowledge</u> through years of experience.

➡ _____________

06 I put the message inside my <u>bottle</u>.

➡ _____________

[07-13] 밑줄 친 부분이 어법상 옳으면 ○로 표시하고, 틀리면 바르게 고치시오.

07 <u>Justices</u> must be served.

➡ _____________

08 My parents have showed me <u>a great love</u>.

➡ _____________

09 She gave me <u>an information</u> about the schedule.

➡ _____________

10 She added a <u>spoonful of sugars</u> to his tea.

➡ _____________

11 <u>How many</u> salt do we need to make this menu?

➡ _____________

12 He got <u>a bunch of sticks</u> to start a campfire.

➡ _____________

13 She drank <u>two cup of coffee</u> before going to work.

➡ _____________

[14-19] 빈칸에 들어갈 말을 〈보기〉에서 골라 알맞은 형태로 쓰시오. (중복 사용 불가)

〈보기〉

bottle	piece	sheet
bowl	loaf	jar

14 A _____________ of bread, please.

15 He made me three _____________ of jam.

16 She only needs a _____________ of paper.

17 I drank a _____________ of water an hour ago.

18 Do you want to have two _____________ of cake?

19 There are several _____________ of cereal on the desk.

[01-06] 주어진 단어의 소유격을 빈칸에 쓰시오.

01 I need to return ＿＿＿＿＿＿ book before Christmas. (David)

02 The ＿＿＿＿＿＿ barking kept the neighbors awake all night. (dogs)

03 My ＿＿＿＿＿＿ decision to study abroad surprised everyone. (sister)

04 The ＿＿＿＿＿＿ policy affects all part-time employees. (company)

05 The ＿＿＿＿＿＿ laughter echoed through the playground. (children)

06 I helped carry the ＿＿＿＿＿＿ instruments after the concert. (musicians)

[07-12] 밑줄 친 부분이 어법상 옳으면 ○로 표시하고, 틀리면 바르게 고치시오.

07 The <u>cat</u> eyes glowed in the dark.

➡ ＿＿＿＿＿＿

08 The note on the desk is <u>my sister's</u>.

➡ ＿＿＿＿＿＿

09 I helped her clean <u>children'</u> playroom.

➡ ＿＿＿＿＿＿

10 I skipped reading <u>some pages of the book</u>.

➡ ＿＿＿＿＿＿

11 We attended <u>Mr. and Mrs. Lee</u> anniversary party.

➡ ＿＿＿＿＿＿

12 <u>Women'</u> fashion changes rapidly with each season.

➡ ＿＿＿＿＿＿

[13-19] 주어진 우리말과 일치하도록 괄호 안의 말을 바르게 배열하시오. (필요한 경우 변형할 것)

13 아기의 담요가 유모차에서 떨어졌다. (baby, blanket)

➡ The ＿＿＿＿＿＿ fell off the stroller.

14 여행 가기 전에 차의 엔진을 점검해야 한다. (engine, the car, of)

➡ We should check the ＿＿＿＿＿＿ before going on a trip.

15 우리는 그 화가의 색채 사용에 감탄했다. (color, use, artist, of)

➡ We admired the ＿＿＿＿＿＿ in the painting.

16 그 건물의 지붕은 수리가 필요하다. (the building, roof, of)

➡ The ＿＿＿＿＿＿ needs repair.

17 이건 내 친구의 자전거야, 내 것이 아니야. (my friend, bike)

➡ This is ＿＿＿＿＿＿, not mine.

18 그 소년의 설명은 충분히 명확했다. (explanation, boy)

➡ The ＿＿＿＿＿＿ was clear enough.

19 사람들의 의견들은 매우 달랐다. (people, opinions)

➡ The ＿＿＿＿＿＿ were very different.

〈 정답 p. 162 〉

[01-05] 빈칸에 a나 an, the를 쓰시오.

01 I usually go to the bookstore twice ____________ month.

02 Is there ____________ post office around this area?

03 ____________ cat is loved by many people around the world.

04 Kelly is of ____________ age where she can be more considerate of others.

05 He bought me ____________ bag. The color of ____________ bag is all black.

[06-12] 괄호 안에서 알맞은 것을 모두 고르시오.

06 (An / A / The) sun is much bigger than (an / a / the) earth.

07 (An / A / The) next month is the last summer vacation of middle school.

08 I have been learning to play (an / a / the) violin for a few years.

09 (An / A / The) old sometimes need help from others.

10 The basic shape of this smartphone is (an / a / the) same as that of mine.

11 I just bought (an / a / the) album of Disney songs.

12 (An / A / The) octopus has eight legs.

[13-17] 밑줄 친 부분이 어법상 옳으면 ○로 표시하고, 틀리면 바르게 고치시오.

13 I visited a famous place in Austria, but I don't remember a name.

➡ ____________

14 This is a most expensive present I have ever received from my friend.

➡ ____________

15 You should clean the room at least once the day.

➡ ____________

16 A brave never give up easily.

➡ ____________

17 He wants to be a artist in the future.

➡ ____________

[18-21] 빈칸에 들어갈 말을 〈보기〉에서 골라 문장을 완성하시오. (중복 사용 가능)

〈보기〉
the　　a　　an

18 It was quite ____________ difficult question on the test.

19 When he lost his wallet, he felt like ____________ fool.

20 Susan was successful as ____________ doctor as well as ____________ writer.

21 ____________ marathon was stopped because of a heavy rain, but it began again in half ____________ hour.

〈 정답 p. 162 〉

[01-05] 문장에서 필요 없는 관사를 찾아 밑줄을 그으시오.

01 They like going to the gym to play the badminton.

02 She caught a bad cold and she's been sick in the bed.

03 The emergency team arrived by the helicopter.

04 Brian's mother is at the work, and he's going to the office to see her.

05 The man who escaped is now back in a prison.

[06-12] 우리말과 일치하도록 괄호 안의 말을 이용하여 빈칸에 알맞은 말을 쓰시오. (필요한 경우 변형할 것)

06 그녀는 참 친절한 선생님이다. (kind, such)
→ She is ________________ teacher.

07 나는 아침 식사로 사과 하나를 먹었다.
(eat, apple, for, breakfast)
→ I ________________.

08 공원에 있는 두 마리 개가 공을 쫓고 있었다.
(both, dogs, the)
→ ________________ in the park were chasing after the ball.

09 그는 너무 큰 실수를 해서 사과해야 했다.
(make, a, mistake, such, big)
→ He ________________ that he had to apologize.

10 내게 한 시간을 줄 수 있니? (give, me, hour)
→ Can you ________________?

11 그녀는 그 식당에서 항상 같은 음식을 주문해.
(always order, food, same)
→ She ________________ at that restaurant.

12 내 친구들은 꽤 오랫동안 운동장에서 야구를 했다.
(quite, long, time)
→ My friends played baseball at the playground for ________________.

[13-18] 밑줄 친 부분이 어법상 옳으면 ○로 표시하고, 틀리면 바르게 고치시오.

13 I can speak the Japanese for you.
→ ________________

14 He returned home by taxi last night.
→ ________________

15 He is too tired to go out for a dinner.
→ ________________

16 He is interested in studying physics at school. → ________________

17 Tony has taken part in the competition half a dozen times. → ________________

18 Many children learn to play a tennis at a very young age nowadays.
→ ________________

〈 정답 p. 163 〉

[01-08] 괄호 안에서 알맞은 것을 고르시오.

01 (That / Those) is why I give it back to you.

02 I like this skirt, but (that / those) skirt is cheaper.

03 He doesn't want to hang out with his friends (these / those) days.

04 I don't understand what he is saying. (This / These) embarrasses me.

05 The geographic size of China is much bigger than (that / this) of Korea.

06 Miracles happen only to (that / those) who believe in them.

07 You should believe (this / that); what she just said is not true at all.

08 I can't believe (that / these) buildings survived the earthquake.

[09-14] 밑줄 친 It[it]의 쓰임을 〈보기〉에서 골라 쓰시오.
（중복 사용 가능)

〈보기〉
가주어	비인칭 주어　　앞 문장 전체 대신
	강조 구문　　가목적어

09 It is 5 kilometers from here to the park.

____

10 It was your brother that I came across a week ago.　_______________

11 Your objection makes it impossible to finish this project.　_______________

12 It is not easy to do several things at the same time.　_______________

13 It is slowly getting dark outside as the sun sets behind the horizon.

____

14 The team won the match, and it made everyone happy.　_______________

[15-17] 주어진 우리말과 일치하도록 괄호 안의 말을 바르게 배열하시오.

15 많은 나라들을 여행함으로써 다양한 문화를 경험하는 것은 좋다.
(it, good, many countries, to experience, by traveling, various cultures, is)

➡ _______________________________________

____

16 과학 용어는 일상생활의 그것과 매우 다르다.
(quite, everyday life, is, that, different from, the language of science, of)

➡ _______________________________________

____

17 이 신약은 불면증에 시달리는 사람들을 위한 것이다.
(for, who, insomnia, those, suffer from, is, this new medicine)

➡ _______________________________________

____

[01-06] 괄호 안에서 알맞은 것을 고르시오.

01 Why don't you help (yourself / itself) to some more?

02 Calm down and stop talking to (yourself / myself).

03 The famous movie actress made (herself / himself) at home at the luxury hotel.

04 I enjoyed (myself / yourself) at your birthday party last Saturday.

05 She was looking at (itself / herself) in a mirror before going out for lunch.

06 You need to make (yourself / themselves) understood during the presentation.

[07-11] 주어진 재귀대명사가 들어가기에 알맞은 곳에 ✓ 표 하시오.

07 The ( ) candle ( ) went ( ) out ( ) by ( ). (itself)

08 He ( ) hurt ( ) while ( ) playing ( ) soccer ( ). (himself)

09 She ( ) taught ( ) how to play ( ) the piano ( ). (herself)

10 Amy ( ) introduced ( ) to the new neighbors ( ). (herself)

11 They often ( ) blamed ( ) for ( ) the mistake ( ). (themselves)

[12-17] 빈칸에 알맞은 것을 〈보기〉에서 골라 쓰시오.

(중복 사용 불가)

〈보기〉
by themselves　　in itself
beside himself　　in spite of myself
between ourselves　　by herself

12 Her proposal ____________ is not a problem.

13 She hasn't completed her task ____________.

14 I shouted at my brother ____________ ____________.

15 Henry was ____________ with happiness.

16 Some children go home ____________ after school.

17 ____________, let's keep this story secret for a while.

[18-21] 밑줄 친 부분이 어법상 옳으면 〇로 표시하고, 틀리면 바르게 고치시오.

18 The children <u>himself</u> made this pie.

　➡ ____________

19 I cut <u>me</u> while cooking.

　➡ ____________

20 Remind <u>myself</u> to stay calm before giving your presentation.

　➡ ____________

21 We enjoyed <u>ourselves</u> at the school trip last week.

　➡ ____________

[01-06] 괄호 안에서 알맞은 것을 고르시오.

01 (Some / Each) of the books has a different story.

02 No (one / ones) knows what's going to happen in the far future.

03 He put his phone on the table, but he can't find (one / it) now.

04 Do you have (each / any) questions about today's class?

05 (All / Every) of us need to work together to succeed in this project.

06 I prefer wearing darker jackets to wearing the brighter (one / ones).

[07-12] 주어진 우리말과 일치하도록 괄호 안의 말을 이용하여 빈칸에 알맞은 말을 쓰시오. (필요한 경우 변형할 것)

07 할 말 있어? (anything, say)
➡ Do you have __________________?

08 자리가 전부 다 찼다. (all of, the, seats, taken)
➡ __________________

09 모두가 그 수업을 들을 필요가 있다.
(everyone, need, take this class)
➡ __________________

10 누군가가 우리 대화를 듣고 있었나요?
(be, listening to, anyone)
➡ __________________ our conversation?

11 두 사람 모두 응용 프로그램의 과정을 알았다.
(both of, know)
➡ __________________ the process of the application.

12 아무것도 너의 건강보다 더 중요하지 않다.
(nothing, important)
➡ __________________ than your health.

[13-19] 빈칸에 알맞은 것을 〈보기〉에서 골라 쓰시오.
(중복 사용 불가)

〈보기〉
others　　the others　　another
the other　　some　　each　　all

13 __________ of the tickets were sold out within an hour.

14 __________ room in the hotel has a stunning view of the ocean.

15 One is 123 centimeters long and __________ is 98 centimeters long.

16 She has three notebooks. One is yellow, __________ is green, and the other is red.

17 Some students don't have to take this course for this semester, but __________ do.

18 Many people participated in the contest. __________ of them speak English and the others speak French.

19 Four people out of ten started to get out of the room. Soon it became empty because __________ followed them.

〈 정답 p. 163 〉

[01-07] 괄호 안에서 알맞은 것을 고르시오.

01 He always (forget / forgets) his keys.

02 They (finishes / will finish) the project soon.

03 We (go / went) to the beach last summer.

04 She (has / had) already left when I arrived.

05 We have (knew/ known) each other since 2010.

06 They (will be / were) practicing the performance tomorrow.

07 We (have / had) lived in Seoul before I moved to Busan.

[08-14] 밑줄 친 부분이 어법상 옳으면 ○로 표시하고, 틀리면 바르게 고치시오.

08 <u>Did</u> you ever been to New York?
➡ _____________

09 She <u>studies</u> hard for the exam last night.
➡ _____________

10 The concert <u>will start</u> at 8 p.m. tomorrow.
➡ _____________

11 They <u>will traveling</u> across Europe next summer.
➡ _____________

12 He <u>has</u> cleaned the room before his mom came home.
➡ _____________

13 I forgot to set my alarm, so I <u>am</u> late for work yesterday.
➡ _____________

14 They <u>will launch</u> the new product at the end of this month.
➡ _____________

[15-19] 주어진 우리말과 일치하도록 괄호 안의 단어를 알맞은 형태로 쓰시오. (동사를 시제에 맞게 변형할 것)

15 내 남동생은 지난주에 그의 휴대전화를 고장냈다.
(his, break, phone)
➡ My brother _____________ last week.

16 그 기차는 매일 아침 정확히 9시에 출발한다.
(leave, the train)
➡ _____________ at exactly 9 o'clock every morning.

17 그는 도시의 심한 교통체증 때문에 늦을 것이다.
(will, he, late, be)
➡ _____________ because of the heavy traffic in the city.

18 우리가 역에 도착했을 때, 버스는 떠났었다.
(have, the bus, depart)
➡ _____________ when we reached the station.

19 우리 엄마는 그녀의 친구와 통화하는 중이다.
(talk, on the phone)
➡ My mom _____________ with her friend.

〈 정답 p. 163 〉

E 시제　UNIT 16 현재시제, 과거시제

틀린 개수 ______

[01-08] 괄호 안의 단어를 이용하여 빈칸에 현재시제나 과거시제 형태로 쓰시오.

01 Ice ____________ at 0 degrees Celsius. (melt)

02 He ____________ at 6 a.m. every day. (get up)

03 Actions ____________ louder than words. (speak)

04 He ____________ my call yesterday. (not answer)

05 The train ____________ at 10 a.m. tomorrow. (leave)

06 She ____________ when she heard the sad news. (cry)

07 He always ____________ coffee every morning. (drink)

08 Gutenberg ____________ the printing press around 1440. (invent)

[09-12] 주어진 우리말과 일치하도록 괄호 안의 말을 바르게 배열하시오. (필요한 경우 과거시제 형태로 변형할 것)

09 베를린 장벽은 1989년에 무너졌다.
(the Berlin Wall, fall)

➡ ____________________ in 1989.

10 식물은 광합성을 통해 산소를 생성한다.
(oxygen, through, plants, photosynthesis, produce)

➡ ____________________

11 서울은 1988년에 하계 올림픽을 개최했다.
(the Summer Olympics, Seoul, host)

➡ ____________________ in 1988.

12 알이 부화되기도 전에 닭을 세지 마라.
(they, chickens, your, don't, before, count, hatch)

➡ ____________________

[13-18] 빈칸에 들어갈 말을 〈보기〉에서 골라 알맞은 현재시제나 과거시제 형태로 쓰시오. (중복 사용 불가)

〈보기〉
become	end	deliver
visit	get	drink

13 Michelle will call you when you ____________ home.

14 She always ____________ a cup of tea before bed.

15 As soon as the class ____________, we'll go to lunch.

16 I ____________ Paris during my last summer vacation.

17 The Internet ____________ widely available in the 1990s.

18 Abraham Lincoln ____________ the Gettysburg Address in 1863.

〈 정답 p. 163~164 〉

[01-08] 주어진 동사의 과거형과 과거분사형을 순서대로 쓰시오.

01 spread – _____________ – _____________

02 grind – _____________ – _____________

03 forget – _____________ – _____________

04 bite – _____________ – _____________

05 hit – _____________ – _____________

06 throw – _____________ – _____________

07 bear – _____________ – _____________

08 sweep – _____________ – _____________

[09-14] 빈칸에 들어갈 말을 〈보기〉에서 골라 알맞은 과거시제 형태로 쓰시오. (중복 사용 불가)

> 〈보기〉
> freeze awake overcome
> mean spill cost

09 She _____________ the soup while serving it.

10 The meal _____________ more than I expected.

11 They _____________ the language barrier.

12 She _____________ in panic and couldn't move.

13 The baby _____________ several times last night.

14 What she _____________ was completely different.

[15-18] 주어진 우리말과 일치하도록 괄호 안의 단어를 과거시제 형태로 쓰시오.

15 그녀는 그 소리를 들었을 때 두려움에 떨었다.
(shake, hear)
➡ She _____________ with fear when she _____________ the noise.

16 Sophia는 열쇠들을 자기가 두었던 곳에서 찾았다. (find, leave)
➡ Sophia _____________ her keys where she _____________ them.

17 Smith 씨는 버스를 탈 때 지갑을 잃어버렸다.
(lose, ride)
➡ Mr. Smith _____________ his wallet when he _____________ the bus.

18 그 팀은 승인을 받자마자 프로젝트를 시작했다.
(begin, get)
➡ The team _____________ the project as soon as they _____________ approval.

[19-22] 밑줄 친 부분이 어법상 옳으면 ○로 표시하고, 틀리면 과거시제로 바르게 고치시오.

19 She <u>sell</u> the car because it gave her too many problems.
➡ _____________

20 She <u>felt</u> tired after the long walk.
➡ _____________

21 World War II <u>has ended</u> in 1945.
➡ _____________

22 He <u>tryed</u> to finish his homework on time yesterday.
➡ _____________

〈 정답 p. 164 〉

[01-07] 괄호 안에서 알맞은 것을 고르시오.

01 I am going to (watching / watch) TV tonight.

02 Marry (will travel / traveled) to Japan next month.

03 I am about to eat, so I (will call / called) you later.

04 We are going (learn / to learn) Spanish next semester.

05 I (will wait / have waited) for you while you finish your meal.

06 She is going to cook dinner, and I (will wash / am going wash) the dishes.

07 We (are going to watch / watched) a movie, so bring some popcorn.

[08-12] 문장을 괄호 안의 말을 이용하여 미래시제로 바꿔 쓰시오.

08 Susan is late for school. (be going to)

➡ Susan ______________ late for school.

09 His parents move to a new house. (will)

➡ His parents ______________ to a new house soon.

10 We began the class as soon as the teacher arrived. (will)

➡ We ______________ the class as soon as the teacher arrives.

11 Tom fixes the car. (be going to)

➡ Tom ______________ the car tomorrow.

12 She left the office, so she arrived home. (be about to)

➡ She ______________ the office, so she will arrive home soon.

[13-19] 밑줄 친 부분이 어법상 옳으면 ○로 표시하고, 틀리면 바르게 고치시오.

13 She cried because she <u>lost</u> her phone.

➡ ______________

14 I will join you if I <u>will finish</u> my homework in time.

➡ ______________

15 She <u>will goes</u> to the library tomorrow.

➡ ______________

16 I am going <u>apply</u> for the job, and I hope they will hire me.

➡ ______________

17 We <u>were about leave</u>, but it started snowing.

➡ ______________

18 We will go to the beach if the weather <u>is</u> nice.

➡ ______________

19 They <u>are going to visit</u> us during their next holidays.

➡ ______________

〈 정답 p. 164 〉

[01-05] 괄호 안에서 알맞은 것을 고르시오.

01 He (was working / will be working) this time next Saturday.

02 When you get home, Jimin (going / will be going) to Busan.

03 He (was taking / will be taking) his final exam tomorrow morning.

04 We (were doing / will be doing) our homework when the lights went out.

05 My parents (watch / were watching) the comedy program when I came home.

[06-12] 주어진 단어를 이용하여 알맞은 진행시제로 대화를 완성하시오.

06 A: Where is your brother?
B: He ___________ the window now. (clean)

07 A: Why ___________ you ___________ so hard now? (cry)
B: I lost my wallet on my way to school.

08 A: What was she doing at this time last night?
B: She ___________ a novel. (read)

09 A: Can I visit you around noon?
B: No, I ___________ out for lunch then. Please come after 1 p.m. (go)

10 A: ___________ you ___________ the dishes? (wash)
B: Yes, I am doing it because they are so dirty.

11 A: What ___________ you ___________ when I called you last night? (do)
B: I was watching a movie with my family.

12 A: Were you studying at the café yesterday afternoon?
B: Yes, I ___________ for my English test. (prepare)

[13-17] 주어진 우리말과 일치하도록 괄호 안의 단어를 알맞은 진행시제 형태로 쓰시오.

13 우리 비행기는 내일 출발할 예정이다. (depart)
➡ Our flight ___________ tomorrow.

14 나는 도서관에서 너를 봤어. 너는 수학 시험공부를 하는 중이었니? (study for the math test)
➡ I saw you at the library. ___________ ___________?

15 그들은 회사의 기념일 파티에서 아주 좋은 시간을 보내고 있다. (have a great time)
➡ They ___________ at the company's anniversary party.

16 그는 오늘 저녁에 딸의 보모를 만날 것이다. (see his daughter's babysitter)
➡ He ___________ this evening.

17 나는 요즘 흥미로운 책을 읽고 있다. (read an interesting book)
➡ ___________ these days.

〈 정답 **p. 164** 〉

틀린 개수 ______

[01-04] 두 문장의 의미가 같도록 빈칸에 알맞은 완료시제를 쓰시오.

01 Minsu went to New York, so he is not here now.
= Minsu ____________ to New York.

02 I went back to my seat. Someone stole my bag.
= When I went back to my seat, I found that someone ____________ my bag.

03 She's cooking Bulgogi now. She will finish it by 5 p.m.
= She ______________ cooking Bulgogi by 5 p.m.

04 It was rainy last night. It is still rainy now.
= It ____________ rainy since last night.

[05-12] 밑줄 친 부분이 어법상 옳으면 ○로 표시하고, 틀리면 바르게 고치시오.

05 I <u>have been studying</u> for three hours.
➡ ____________

06 I <u>will have finished</u> the report by tomorrow.
➡ ____________

07 In twenty minutes, he <u>will have working</u> out for one hour.
➡ ____________

08 Kate <u>has repaired</u> her bike three months ago.
➡ ____________

09 We <u>had been studying</u> when the power went out.
➡ ____________

10 I <u>will stay</u> there until I left for Seoul.
➡ ____________

11 He <u>will have finished</u> writing his report by the time his mom comes home.
➡ ____________

12 This book is the most interesting one that I <u>ever read</u>.
➡ ____________

[13-17] 빈칸에 들어갈 말을 〈보기〉에서 골라 알맞은 기호를 쓰시오. (중복 사용 불가)

〈보기〉
ⓐ since 2015
ⓑ she had finished her homework
ⓒ the plane had already taken off
ⓓ she will have been working for 20 years
ⓔ he had been waiting for the job interview

13 He felt nervous because ____________.

14 Before the movie started, ____________.

15 When she retires next year, ____________.

16 When Michael arrived at the airport, ____________.

17 I have been volunteering at the orphanage ____________.

〈정답 p. 164〉

[01-06] 괄호 안에서 알맞은 것을 고르시오.

01 She can (speaks / speak) Spanish very well.

02 (May I / Do I may) go to the party with you?

03 We (should not / should don't) violate the traffic rule.

04 He (has to / have to) memorize the script for the speech contest.

05 (Will you / Do you will) help me revise the handout for the presentation?

06 Because I didn't finish my homework, I (could not go / could go not) to the movies with my friend.

[07-13] 문장을 do동사를 이용하여 괄호 안의 지시대로 바꿔 쓰시오.

07 I participated in the marathon race last week. (부정문으로)

➡ _______________________________

____

08 She never made a mistake during the science experiment. (never를 문두에 써서)

➡ _______________________________

____

09 He thought my brother broke the glass, but I broke. (대동사를 사용하여)

➡ _______________________________

____

10 Sumin wants to have a trip to Europe this summer. (동사를 강조하여)

➡ _______________________________

____

11 They had hamburgers for lunch at the cafeteria. (의문문으로)

➡ _______________________________

____

12 We have an annual meeting at the conference. (부정문으로)

➡ _______________________________

____

13 She likes going to the movies on weekends. (의문문으로)

➡ _______________________________

____

[14-18] 밑줄 친 부분이 어법상 옳으면 ○로 표시하고, 틀리면 바르게 고치시오.

14 She loves me more than you <u>do</u>.

➡ _______________

15 I <u>did told</u> the truth to everyone.

➡ _______________

16 You <u>work must</u> hard to pass the exam.

➡ _______________

17 Juliet <u>wills</u> enter the university next month.

➡ _______________

18 You can <u>making</u> anything with this clay.

➡ _______________

〈 정답 p. 164~165 〉

[01-08] 밑줄 친 조동사의 쓰임으로 알맞은 것에 ✓표 하시오.

01 They <u>may</u> arrive later than expected.

□ 허가 □ 추측

02 The story you told me <u>cannot</u> be true.

□ 추측 □ 허가

03 <u>Could</u> you carry my suitcase upstairs?

□ 허가 □ 요청

04 You <u>can</u> borrow my books if you want.

□ 추측 □ 허가

05 You <u>may</u> leave once you finish your work.

□ 허가 □ 요청

06 <u>Can</u> you lend me your notebook for a while?

□ 추측 □ 요청

07 She <u>can</u> solve complex math problems easily.

□ 가능 □ 허가

08 I <u>could not</u> make a reservation because the seats were all booked.

□ 불가능 □ 불허가

[09-14] 밑줄 친 부분이 어법상 옳으면 ○로 표시하고, 틀리면 바르게 고치시오.

09 I <u>can well</u> follow my parents' plan.

➡ ____________

10 <u>Can I</u> take a look at your photo album?

➡ ____________

11 They <u>may can</u> agree to the company's proposal if negotiation goes well.

➡ ____________

12 You <u>may</u> not enter the building with your pets.

➡ ____________

13 I caught a bad cold last Friday. I <u>can't</u> go to school that day.

➡ ____________

14 I spilt some coffee on my skirt. <u>May</u> you bring me the napkin, please?

➡ ____________

[15-18] 문장의 알맞은 해석을 〈보기〉에서 골라 기호를 쓰시오.

〈보기〉
ⓐ 다 끝났으면 교실을 떠나도 좋아.
ⓑ 네가 필요하면 내 휴대전화를 써도 돼.
ⓒ 그녀는 교통체증 때문에 늦을지도 몰라.
ⓓ 너무 늦었으니 그냥 집에 가는 게 낫겠어.

15 She may be late because of the traffic.

( )

16 You can use my phone if you need it.

( )

17 We may as well go home as it's too late.

( )

18 You may leave the classroom when you're finished.

( )

〈정답 p. 165〉

[01-08] 괄호 안에서 알맞은 것을 고르시오.

01 How (would / will) you like your steak?

02 (May / Will) you open this bottle for me?

03 My brother (will / would) turn eleven next year.

04 I (could / would) rather take a rest than work out.

05 She (must not / not must) follow my direction.

06 He (must / will) have left already; his car isn't here.

07 I thought that Johnson (would / will) have the main role in the play.

08 When he was young, he (might / would) make a paper doll for her sister.

[09-14] 주어진 우리말과 일치하도록 괄호 안의 어구를 이용하여 문장을 완성하시오.

09 너 내일 내 생일 파티에 올래?
(will, my birthday party, tomorrow)
➡ ____________________
____

10 그는 그가 가장 좋아하는 가수의 콘서트에 가고 싶어 한다. (would like, go, his favorite singer's concert)
➡ ____________________
____

11 그녀는 크게 웃고 있다. 그녀는 지금 매우 행복함이 틀림없다. (must, very, happy)
➡ She is laughing a lot. ____________________
____________________ now.

12 너는 오늘 너의 숙제를 제출할 필요가 없다.
(have to, hand in, your assignment)
➡ ____________________
____

13 빗속에 나가느니 차라리 집에 있겠다.
(would rather, stay home, go out)
➡ ____________________
in the rain.

14 너는 운전할 때 반드시 안전벨트를 매야 한다.
(must, wear a seatbelt)
➡ ____________________ while driving.

[15-19] 빈칸에 들어갈 말을 〈보기〉에서 골라 문장을 완성하시오. (중복 사용 불가)

〈보기〉
don't have to　　need not
would　　have to　　must

15 I am very sick. I ____________ go to the hospital.

16 Tomorrow is Sunday. She ____________ go to work.

17 Everybody likes him. He ____________ be a good person.

18 We have enough time. We ____________ hurry.

19 When we were kids, we ____________ play outside until it got dark.

〈정답 p. 165〉

[01-07] 자연스러운 의미가 되도록 빈칸에 알맞은 말을 〈보기〉에서 골라 기호를 쓰시오. (중복 사용 불가)

〈보기〉
ⓐ She ought to study harder.
ⓑ He should clean the floor.
ⓒ You should lose weight.
ⓓ You'd better help her.
ⓔ that he should move to the urban area.
ⓕ or you'll miss the plane.
ⓖ we shall go to the movies.

01 It is necessary (   )

02 He broke the glass cup. (   )

03 You've gained 14 pounds. (   )

04 If you finish your homework, (   )

05 Your mom is carrying a heavy bag.
(   )

06 You'd better leave for the airport now,
(   )

07 Jessy wants to get a higher score in math.
(   )

[08-12] 주어진 어구를 바르게 배열하시오.

08 (had better, stay up, not, you, all night)
➡ __________________________________

09 (insisted, that, I, Jeju-do, to, go, our class)
➡ __________________________________

10 (I, to get, walk, how long, should)
➡ __________________________________
to the museum?

11 (for his health, should, Mike, eating sweets, cut down on)
➡ __________________________________
____

12 (spill, on, the water, you, to, not, ought, your keyboard)
➡ __________________________________
____

[13-17] 밑줄 친 부분이 어법상 옳으면 ○로 표시하고, 틀리면 바르게 고치시오.

13 You had <u>not better</u> cross the river.
➡ __________________

14 He <u>has</u> better drive slowly with kids in his car.
➡ __________________

15 Where <u>do we ought to take</u> the train to go to Busan?
➡ __________________

16 You <u>should not</u> eat too much junk food for your health.
➡ __________________

17 You had better <u>to wear</u> more clothes while going outside.
➡ __________________

〈 정답 p. 165 〉

[01-06] 밑줄 친 부분이 어법상 옳으면 ○로 표시하고, 틀리면 바르게 고치시오.

01 She <u>was used to</u> like coffee.

➡ ______________

02 He must have <u>forget</u> the password.

➡ ______________

03 Did she <u>use to</u> climb a mountain with her father?

➡ ______________

04 He <u>would</u> drink a cup of coffee in the morning.

➡ ______________

05 Antonio <u>was used to</u> play soccer with his friends.

➡ ______________

06 There <u>used to be</u> a cafe next to the post office.

➡ ______________

[07-13] 괄호 안에서 알맞은 것을 고르시오.

07 He (must / should) have failed the driving test.

08 We (might / shall) have offended him without realizing it.

09 There (would / used to) be my favorite cafe, but now I can't find it.

10 He (might / should) have heard this if he hadn't worn headphones.

11 A famous actor just left here. You (should / would) have come earlier.

12 She (cannot / could) have participated in the race. She was sick all day.

13 If I had booked a plane ticket earlier, I (could have traveled / could travel) with you.

[14-17] 주어진 우리말과 일치하도록 괄호 안의 말을 바르게 배열하시오.

14 나는 규칙적으로 운동하곤 했다.

(exercise, used, to, I)

➡ ___________________ regularly.

15 너는 너의 어머니의 의견을 따랐어야 했다.
(have, your mother's opinion, followed, should, you)

➡ ___________________________

____

16 여기는 예전에 쇼핑몰이 아니라 강이 있었다.

(be, used, there, to, a river, here)

➡ ___________________ , not a shopping mall.

17 그녀는 웃고 있었다. 그녀의 친구가 그녀에게 아주 좋은 선물을 줬음에 틀림없다. (have, given, a great gift, her friend, must, to her)

➡ She was smiling. ___________________

___________________ .

〈 정답 p. 165 〉

[01-05] 주어진 능동태 문장을 수동태 문장으로 바꿔 쓰시오.

01 Suji cleans her room.

➡ _______________________________________

02 He missed the school bus.

➡ _______________________________________

03 A stranger took Robert's suitcases.

➡ _______________________________________

____

04 A mechanic repairs my white car.

➡ _______________________________________

05 Jane gave my brother a Christmas gift.

➡ My brother _______________________________

_______________.

[06-10] 주어진 어구를 이용하여 수동태 문장을 완성하시오. (단, 과거형으로 쓸 것)

06 (break, the glass cup, her baby)

Was _______________________________________?

07 (do, the employees of the company)

A lot of work _______________________________

_______________.

08 (this machine, develop)

By whom _______________________________________?

09 (not, wash, my mom)

The dishes _______________________________.

10 (pick, a gentleman)

The magazine _______________________________.

[11-16] 괄호 안에서 알맞은 것을 고르시오.

11 This interesting novel was written (by her / by she).

12 Spanish is spoken (with many people / by many people).

13 (Who / By whom) was the announcement given?

14 The truth (was not told / did not tell) by the lawyer.

15 (Were / Did) many people invited to the exhibition?

16 The movie (was watched by / watched) millions of audiences.

[17-19] 문장을 괄호 안의 지시대로 바꿔 쓰시오.

17 This unique museum was built by the architect. (부정문으로)

➡ _______________________________________

____

18 The famous pieces were played by the orchestra. (의문문으로)

➡ _______________________________________

____

19 Leonardo da Vinci painted the Mona Lisa. (수동태로)

➡ _______________________________________

____

〈 정답 **p. 165~166** 〉

[01-06] 주어진 우리말과 일치하도록 괄호 안의 어구를 이용하여 문장을 완성하시오.

01 저 그림은 내 여동생에 의해 그려졌다.

(draw, my sister)

➡ That picture ___________________.

02 몇 개의 우편물이 집배원에 의해 배달되었다.

(deliver, the postman)

➡ A few pieces of mail ___________________ _______________.

03 이 지역 문화 센터는 주민들에 의해 이용된다.

(use, the neighbors)

➡ This community center _______________ _______________.

04 그 노래는 아름다운 소프라노에 의해 불려졌다.

(sing, the beautiful soprano)

➡ The song ___________________ _______________.

05 이 컴퓨터는 많은 직원들에 의해 접속된다.

(access, many employees)

➡ This computer ___________________ _______________.

06 그 서류들은 그 대표에 의해 서명될 것이다.

(sign, the CEO)

➡ The documents ___________________ _______________.

[07-11] 주어진 능동태 문장을 수동태 문장으로 바꿔 쓰시오.

07 The students are taking a history exam.

➡ ___________________ _______________.

08 I was cooking spaghetti for my family.

➡ ___________________ for my family.

09 The staff are carrying the boxes.

➡ ___________________ _______________.

10 My friends are hearing the noise from outside.

➡ ___________________ _______________.

11 My sister has answered all the questions so far.

➡ ___________________ ___________________ so far.

[12-16] 괄호 안에서 알맞은 것을 고르시오.

12 Jackson (is being chased / being chased) by the police now.

13 The meeting (has often postponed / has often been postponed) by the manager.

14 When I entered the hall, I found that the party (had been started / has been started).

15 The world's first airplane (had been invented / have been inventing) by the Wright Brothers.

16 The series of Harry Potter (has been read / has being read) by readers around the world.

〈 정답 p. 166 〉

[01-05] 문장을 수동태로 고칠 때 빈칸에 알맞은 말을 쓰시오.

01 The workers will paint this building.

→ This building _______________ by the workers.

02 The spectators did not welcome the president.

→ The president _______________ by the spectators.

03 The team members should issue the important agenda.

→ The important agenda _______________ by the team members.

04 The researchers may study the interesting phenomenon.

→ The interesting phenomenon _________ _______________ by the researchers.

05 Others can't use this cup because it belongs to the manager.

→ This cup _______________ by others because it belongs to the manager.

[06-11] 밑줄 친 부분이 어법상 옳으면 ○로 표시하고, 틀리면 바르게 고치시오.

06 The announcement <u>will is</u> addressed by the principal.　→ _______________

07 The next steps <u>should follow</u> by a person in charge.　→ _______________

08 A child <u>ran over</u> by a motorcycle.

→ _______________

09 That action <u>is may be</u> allowed by policy.

→ _______________

10 Will the floor <u>be cleaned</u> by the staff?

→ _______________

11 The science problems <u>have to solve</u> by the students in class.

→ _______________

[12-17] 〈보기〉에 주어진 동사구를 알맞은 형태로 바꾸어 수동태 문장을 완성하시오. (중복 사용 불가)

〈보기〉
take care of　　deal with
put off　　laugh at
give up　　make up of

12 At that time, his idea _______________.

13 The movie festival _______________ various parts.

14 My sick aunt _______________ by her family now.

15 This murder case _______________ by the judge now.

16 The project was so difficult that it _______________ by the other members long ago.

17 Yesterday, the conference _______________ until next week because of the mistake of the host.

〈정답 p. 166〉

[01-06] 주어진 능동태 문장을 수동태 문장으로 바꿔 쓰시오.

01 My boss sent me an e-mail yesterday.
→ An e-mail _________________ by my boss yesterday.

02 Jisu's father bought her a fancy computer.
→ A fancy computer _________________ by her father.

03 The store in this street provides a variety of goods.
→ A variety of goods _________________ _________________ in this street.

04 I offered him a reasonable price.
→ He _________________ by me.

05 The staff gave her the application form.
→ She _________________ by the staff.
→ The application form _________________ by the staff.

06 The students asked the math teacher many difficult questions.
→ The math teacher _________________ _________________ by the students.
→ Many difficult questions _________________ _________________ by the students.

[07-13] 괄호 안에서 알맞은 것을 고르시오.

07 She was made (to tell / tell) the story by her colleagues.

08 David was asked (to join / join) the summer camp.

09 I was (had to repaired / made to repair) the broken machine immediately.

10 Our body shape can be made (better / being better) by working out.

11 The choir (was heard to sing / was heard sing) the beautiful song by me.

12 The players were encouraged (to cheer / cheer) up during the game by their coach.

13 The script for the presentation is expected (to be written / to write) by me.

[14-18] 밑줄 친 부분이 어법상 옳으면 ○로 표시하고, 틀리면 바르게 고치시오.

14 That graceful actress envies for her fame by others.
→ _________________

15 The earth was felt move a lot.
→ _________________

16 A delicious barbecue was cooked for me by my mother.
→ _________________

17 History taught to his sister by Jack.
→ _________________

18 He was made describe the scenery by his parents.
→ _________________

〈 정답 p. 166 〉

[01-07] 괄호 안에서 알맞은 것을 고르시오.

01 This kind of bag (sells / are sold) very well.

02 I (am resembled by / resemble) my old friend.

03 Tom (has / is had) a brand-new smartphone.

04 The pages of that book (is torn / tear) easily.

05 The skin of this fruit (is peel / is peeling) easily.

06 These days, the weather (changes / is changed) frequently.

07 The article (was said / said) that the incident occurred suddenly.

[08-14] 주어진 단어를 이용하여 수동태 문장을 완성하시오.

08 The mug cup is ____________ hot coffee. (fill)

09 France ______________ the Eiffel Tower. (know)

10 The streets ________________ a lot of snow last winter. (cover)

11 I _____________ practicing the guitar every day. (tire)

12 When Tony heard the news, he ________ ______________ it. (please)

13 The team is _____________ people from various countries. (compose)

14 My mother _______________________ my father's health all the time. (concern)

[15-20] 주어진 우리말과 일치하도록 괄호 안의 어구를 이용하여 문장을 완성하시오. (현재시제를 사용할 것)

15 이 잡지는 잘 읽힌다. (read, well)
➡ ______________________________

16 이 식탁은 나무로 만들어졌다.
(table, make, wood)
➡ ______________________________

17 우리의 관계는 우리의 신뢰에 기초를 둔다.
(our relationship, base, our trust)
➡ ______________________________

18 나는 우표를 모으는 것에 관심이 있다.
(interest, collect stamps)
➡ ______________________________

19 Miso는 일본으로 여행 가는 것에 흥분해 있다.
(excite, have a trip to)
➡ ______________________________

20 나는 기말고사에서의 나의 점수에 만족한다.
(satisfy, my scores)
➡ ______________________ in the final exam.

〈 정답 p. 166 〉

[01-08] 밑줄 친 형용사의 종류로 알맞은 것을 〈보기〉에서 골라 기호를 쓰시오. (중복 사용 가능)

〈보기〉
ⓐ 성질·상태 형용사　　ⓑ 수량 형용사
ⓒ 수사 형용사　　　　ⓓ 지시 형용사
ⓔ 소유 형용사　　　　ⓕ 의문 형용사
ⓖ 한정 형용사

01 This is <u>my</u> <u>favorite</u> place to relax.
(　　) (　　)

02 Have you heard about <u>those</u> students?
(　　)

03 He is the <u>third</u> person to arrive at the party.　(　　)

04 I need <u>five</u> <u>more</u> minutes to finish the report. (　　) (　　)

05 I need to find <u>another</u> solution to this problem.　(　　)

06 We have <u>few</u> options left for the weekend trip.　(　　)

07 <u>What</u> color do you prefer for the walls in your room? (　　)

08 It was a <u>challenging</u> task, but we managed to finish it. (　　)

[09-13] 밑줄 친 형용사의 쓰임을 〈보기〉에서 찾아 기호를 쓰시오. (중복 사용 가능)

〈보기〉
ⓐ 명사 수식 (한정적)
ⓑ 주격 보어 (서술적)
ⓒ 목적격 보어 (서술적)

09 She wore an <u>elegant</u> dress.
➡ ____________

10 The children looked <u>tired</u> after the trip.
➡ ____________

11 They considered him <u>trustworthy</u>.
➡ ____________

12 The soup smells <u>delicious</u> and it makes me <u>happy</u>.
➡ ____________

13 They visited a <u>famous</u> museum in Paris.
➡ ____________

[14-17] 괄호 안의 말을 바르게 배열하시오.

14 He made ________________ cookies. (two, tasty, round)

15 They saw a(n) ________________ monkey. (old, big, brown)

16 He bought a ________________ bowl. (round, small, Japanese)

17 She brought ________________ from the box. (and, small, shiny, something)

〈 정답 p. 167 〉

[01-08] 빈칸에 들어갈 말을 〈보기〉에서 골라 알맞은 형태로 쓰시오. (중복 사용 불가)

〈보기〉
> mistake　complaint　employee
> electricity　time　experience
> advice　visitor

01 Few ___________ came to the museum on Monday.

02 Several ___________ were promoted last month.

03 He has a lot of ___________ in customer service.

04 A number of ___________ were found in the report.

05 We still have a great deal of ___________ before the show.

06 They consumed much ___________ to run the air conditioners.

07 He gave me lots of ___________ about how to improve my skills.

08 Plenty of ___________ have been received about the noise.

[09-14] 괄호 안에서 알맞은 것을 고르시오.

09 She needs (a little / a few) relaxation for the next step.

10 There is (many / much) difficulty in this process.

11 (Few / Little) students submitted the assignment on time.

12 I have (a few / a little) minutes to talk with you.

13 (Few / Little) classmates went to the movies yesterday.

14 A (lot / great deal) of volunteers joined the food-sharing event.

[15-20] 밑줄 친 부분이 어법상 옳으면 ○로 표시하고, 틀리면 바르게 고치시오.

15 Any engineers disagreed with the decision to postpone the launch.
➡ ___________

16 The strartup attracted few investors despite its innovative idea.
➡ ___________

17 Sumin wanted to add a little words on the subject.
➡ ___________

18 The rich are not always happy.
➡ ___________

19 He spent a great deal of times studying for the test.
➡ ___________

20 The manager gave us only a few time to prepare before the client meeting.
➡ ___________

〈 정답 p. 167 〉

[01-09] 수를 알맞게 읽으시오.

01 23,690

➡ ______________________

____

02 30.176

➡ ______________________

03 075) 4590-6672

➡ ______________________

____

04 11시 40분

➡ ______________________

05 1874년 2월 3일

➡ ______________________

____

____

06 $7\frac{1}{2}$ ➡ ______________________

07 2.48 ➡ ______________________

08 24,653,829

➡ ______________________

____

____

09 $1\frac{3}{4}$ ➡ ______________________

[10-14] 영어 표현을 숫자로 바꿔 쓰시오.

10 one point three six

➡ ______________

11 six fifteen 또는 a quarter past six

➡ ______________

12 two times 또는 twice

➡ ______________

13 eight and four-fifths

➡ ______________

14 December tenth, two thousand and eight

➡ ______________

[15-18] 문장에서 틀린 부분을 찾아 밑줄을 긋고 바르게 고치시오.

15 The meeting starts at two fifteenth in the afternoon.　➡ ______________

16 The eleventh on November is our wedding anniversary.　➡ ______________

17 The population of your city is about third times as large as that of my city.

➡ ______________

18 Nearly three-fourth of Earth's surface is ocean.　➡ ______________

〈 정답 p. 167 〉

[01-10] 주어진 형용사의 부사형을 쓰시오.

01 quick　　➡ ＿＿＿＿＿＿

02 slow　　➡ ＿＿＿＿＿＿

03 careful　　➡ ＿＿＿＿＿＿

04 loud　　➡ ＿＿＿＿＿＿

05 regular　　➡ ＿＿＿＿＿＿

06 automatic　　➡ ＿＿＿＿＿＿

07 public　　➡ ＿＿＿＿＿＿

08 shy　　➡ ＿＿＿＿＿＿

09 angry　　➡ ＿＿＿＿＿＿

10 brave　　➡ ＿＿＿＿＿＿

[11-22] 밑줄 친 부분이 형용사인지, 부사인지 구분하시오.

11 This bed is too <u>hard</u> to sleep on.
➡ [형용사 / 부사]

12 He studied <u>hard</u> for the exam.
➡ [형용사 / 부사]

13 That's the <u>right</u> answer.
➡ [형용사 / 부사]

14 Turn <u>right</u> at the traffic light.
➡ [형용사 / 부사]

15 The shelf is too <u>low</u> for tall books.
➡ [형용사 / 부사]

16 He spoke <u>low</u>, so others wouldn't hear.
➡ [형용사 / 부사]

17 He exercises <u>daily</u>.
➡ [형용사 / 부사]

18 I read a <u>daily</u> newspaper.
➡ [형용사 / 부사]

19 How <u>long</u> did you stay there?
➡ [형용사 / 부사]

20 It was a <u>long</u> journey.
➡ [형용사 / 부사]

21 Go <u>straight</u> ahead.
➡ [형용사 / 부사]

22 He has <u>straight</u> hair.
➡ [형용사 / 부사]

[23-27] 괄호 안의 형용사를 활용하여 빈칸에 알맞은 부사를 쓰시오.

23 That painting is ＿＿＿＿＿＿ different from the others. (unique)

24 He was ＿＿＿＿＿＿ criticized for his actions during the meeting. (heavy)

25 She was unsure of ＿＿＿＿＿＿ what to say to resolve the conflict. (precise)

26 His health improved ＿＿＿＿＿＿ after starting the new treatment. (steady)

27 ＿＿＿＿＿＿, we had enough money to pay for the emergency repairs. (lucky)

〈 정답 p. 167 〉

[01-07] 밑줄 친 부사가 수식하는 대상을 찾아 〈보기〉와 같이 빈칸에 쓰시오.

> 〈보기〉
> She closed the window gently.
> ➡ 동사 closed

01 The solution seems <u>remarkably</u> simple.

➡ ________________

02 The weather was <u>unusually</u> cold yesterday.

➡ ________________

03 <u>Fortunately</u>, no one was hurt in the car accident yesterday.

➡ ________________

04 I <u>accidentally</u> deleted the file I had been working on all night.

➡ ________________

05 <u>Unfortunately</u>, we missed the flight due to a last-minute delay.

➡ ________________

06 They worked <u>quite</u> efficiently under pressure during the deadline.

➡ ________________

07 They <u>completely</u> forgot the meeting scheduled for Monday morning.

➡ ________________

[08-13] 주어진 부사가 들어가기에 알맞은 곳에 ✓표 하시오.

08 Are you moving to Canada? (really)

09 The brothers argue over small things. (always)

10 These sandwiches are fresh. (very)

11 We need to discuss to reach an agreement. (enough)

12 I need to be patient for harsh circumstances. (enough)

13 He became more confident after winning the award. (much)

[14-16] 주어진 어구를 이용하여 우리말을 영어로 쓰시오.

14 그는 말할 때 종종 다양한 제스처를 사용한다. (often, use, he, various gestures, when, talk, he)

➡ ________________________________

____

15 Tom은 농구선수가 되기에 충분히 키가 크다. (is, Tom, tall, be a basketball player, enough)

➡ ________________________________

____

16 선생님은 칠판에 문제를 천천히 설명했다. (the problem, slowly, the teacher, on the board, explained)

➡ ________________________________

____

〈 정답 **p. 167** 〉

[01-06] 빈칸에 들어갈 말을 〈보기〉에서 골라 문장을 완성하시오. (중복 사용 불가)

> 〈보기〉
> yet　　before　　ago
> very　　already　　much

01 She is much skinnier than she was ten years ___________.

02 Have you started working on your science project ___________?

03 What he just said is the thing I _________ know.

04 The principle of this machine is _________ more complicated than you think.

05 My company produces products faster than ever ___________.

06 He was ___________ surprised by the sudden announcement.

[07-09] 대화의 빈칸에 too, either, neither 중 하나를 쓰시오.

07 A: I love science class.
　　B: I love it ___________!

08 A: I don't like math homework.
　　B: I don't like it ___________.

09 A: Do you want coffee or tea?
　　B: ___________, I'd like some juice.

[10-17] 주어진 우리말과 일치하도록 괄호 안에서 알맞은 것을 고르시오.

10 그녀는 전에 나와 함께 저 영화를 몇 번 봤다.
　➡ She has watched that movie with me several times (before / ago).

11 그는 여전히 버스를 기다리고 있다.
　➡ He is (still / even) waiting for the bus.

12 Tom은 이미 숙제를 다 끝내서 지금 놀아도 된다.
　➡ Tom has (yet / already) finished his homework, so he can play now.

13 그는 아직 어느 대학에 지원할지 결정하지 못했다.
　➡ He hasn't decided which university to apply to (yet / already).

14 이 책은 지난번 책보다 훨씬 더 좋다.
　➡ This book is (much / very) better than the last one.

15 그 질문은 Sam도 답을 모를 만큼 어려웠다.
　➡ The question was so difficult that (even / else) Sam couldn't know the answer.

16 나는 치킨도 안 좋아하고 피자도 안 좋아해.
　➡ I don't like chicken, and I don't like pizza (neither / either).

17 내가 제시간에 못 오면, 다른 누군가가 널 도와줄 거야.
　➡ Someone (even / else) will help you if I can't make it on time.

〈정답 p. 168〉

[01-08] 괄호 안에서 알맞은 것을 고르시오.

01 My friend Minsu runs as fast as (me / my).

02 This building is as big as your house (is / does).

03 The hotel room was as clean as (I / me) expected.

04 This phone is (not as / as not) expensive as it looks.

05 Suji can cook (as well as / as better as) her mother.

06 Your idea about the project is not as simple as (him / his).

07 He speaks English as (fluent / fluently) as a native speaker.

08 My score of the midterm exam was (so not / not so) good as I hoped.

[09-13] 주어진 우리말과 일치하도록 괄호 안의 어구를 이용하여 문장을 완성하시오.

09 그녀는 나의 두 배만큼 많은 치마를 가지고 있다.
(twice, many skirts)
➡ She has ___________________________.

10 Mike는 가능한 한 빨리 그 장소를 떠나고 싶었다.
(soon, possible, want, leave the place)
➡ Mike ___________________________
___________.

11 그녀는 그녀가 원하는 만큼 많은 쿠폰을 얻을 수 있다. (many coupons, get, wish)
➡ She can ___________________________
___________.

12 이 책은 저 책의 약 세 배만큼 많은 그림들이 있다. (that book, many pictures, have, about three times)
➡ This book ___________________________
___________.

13 나는 너를 이해시키기 위해 가능한 한 명확하게 묘사하려고 노력했다.
(clearly, describe, I could, try to)
➡ I ___________________________
to make you understand.

[14-17] 빈칸에 들어갈 말을 〈보기〉에서 골라 문장을 완성하시오. (중복 사용 불가)

〈보기〉
as busy as a bee
as wise as an owl
as stubborn as a donkey
as proud as a peacock

14 My grandfather is ___________________
and always gives great advice.

15 After winning the contest, he walked into the room ___________________.

16 He won't change his mind because he is
___________________.

17 She's been ___________________ all day preparing for the school festival.

[01-10] 형용사와 부사의 비교급과 최상급을 쓰시오.

01 fat　　– ____________ – ____________

02 bad　　– ____________ – ____________

03 little　　– ____________ – ____________

04 carefully　– ____________ – ____________

05 gray　　– ____________ – ____________

06 short　　– ____________ – ____________

07 brave　　– ____________ – ____________

08 helpful　　– ____________ – ____________

09 angry　　– ____________ – ____________

10 comfortable – ____________ – ____________

[11-16] 괄호 안에서 알맞은 것을 고르시오.

11 Mount Everest is (farther / further) from Korea than Mount Fuji.

12 This house is much (older / elder) than the one across the street.

13 There were (fewer / less) stars visible because of the city lights.

14 Before we go (farther / further), let's make the definition clear.

15 We discovered (more / most) gold coins than other participants did.

16 We'll announce the winner at a (later / latter) date.

[17-21] 주어진 우리말과 일치하도록 괄호 안의 단어를 이용하여 빈칸을 완성하시오.

17 오늘은 어제보다 더 바쁘다. (busy)
→ Today is ____________ than yesterday.

18 이번 탐험은 우리가 해온 것 중에서 최악이었다. (bad)
→ This expedition was the ____________ we've ever done.

19 드론은 인간이 할 수 있는 것보다 더 정확하게 목표를 포착할 수 있다. (well)
→ Drones can detect targets ____________ than humans can.

20 그는 섬에서의 삶이 자신이 겪은 것 중 가장 외로웠다고 말했다. (lonely)
→ He said life on the island was the ____________ he had ever experienced.

21 이 문제는 거리에 대한 것이 아니라 훨씬 더 복잡한 무언가다. (complex)
→ This issue is not about distance but something far ____________.

〈 정답 p. 168 〉

[01-05] 주어진 우리말과 일치하도록 괄호 안의 단어를 이용하여 빈칸에 알맞은 말을 쓰시오.

01 Henry는 그의 남동생보다 더 재미있다.
(funny, his brother)
➡ Henry is _____________________.

02 그의 컴퓨터는 내 것보다 훨씬 더 느리다.
(much, slow, mine)
➡ His computer is _________________
_____________.

03 너의 회사는 내 회사보다 더 좋은 체계를 가지고 있다. (a good system)
➡ Your company has ________________
____________.

04 나는 이 프랑스어 강좌가 저 일본어 강좌보다 더 재미있다고 생각한다. (this French course, interesting, that Japanese course)
➡ I think ____________________________
____________________________________.

05 기차로 여행하는 것이 차로 여행하는 것보다 훨씬 더 안전하다. (much, safe, traveling by car)
➡ Traveling by train is ________________
_______________.

[06-11] 주어진 어구를 바르게 배열하여 비교급 문장을 완성하시오.

06 His suitcase is ____________________
____________. (than, three times, bigger, mine)

07 Susan __________________________ as she works out. (thinner, is getting, thinner, and)

08 This strawberry cake is ______________
_____________. (less, than, sweet, this chocolate)

09 English ________________________________
to me. (less, than, Math, difficult, is)

10 He has ________________________________
_____________. (no, two dollars, in, more, than, his wallet)

11 Their service was ____________________
_____________. (inferior, what, I, to, had expected)

[12-16] 밑줄 친 부분이 어법상 옳으면 ○로 표시하고, 틀리면 바르게 고치시오.

12 You are much <u>smart</u> than them.
➡ _____________

13 His sister is <u>very</u> more considerate than him.
➡ _____________

14 I become <u>more forgetful and more forgetful</u> these days.
➡ _____________

15 The more <u>has</u> one, the stingier one gets.
➡ _____________

16 Because he learned how to play the guitar, he got <u>better</u> at it.
➡ _____________

〈 정답 **p. 168** 〉

[01-07] 밑줄 친 부분이 어법상 옳으면 ○로 표시하고, 틀리면 바르게 고치시오.

01 The my eldest sister is more intelligent than my younger sister.

　➡ __________

02 Max is the most short boy in my class.

　➡ __________

03 This is the tallest building of my city.

　➡ __________

04 My friend Christina is the most kindest student in my school.

　➡ __________

05 The Himalaya is the highest mountain in the world.

　➡ __________

06 She answered the most correct in the quiz.

　➡ __________

07 That's the one of the most difficult tasks I've ever completed.

　➡ __________

[08-12] 주어진 어구를 바르게 배열하여 최상급 문장을 완성하시오.

08 King Sejong was __________________ __________________. (of, figures, his time, of, one, the greatest)

09 My teacher is __________________ __________________. (I've, met, ever, that, the, man, most, handsome)

10 His company is __________________ __________________. (car rental businesses, of, one, the, largest)

11 This is __________________ __________________. (seen, scenery, I've, beautiful, the, most, ever)

12 Basketball is __________________ __________________. (of, the fastest, sports, this country, one, growing, in)

[13-17] 두 문장의 의미가 같도록 빈칸에 알맞은 말을 쓰시오.

13 Jimin is the smartest girl in my class.

　➡ Jimin is __________________ any other girl in my class.

14 Meeting her was the best thing in his life.

　➡ There was __________________ than meeting her in his life.

15 This is the longest street in the world.

　➡ __________________ street in the world is longer than this.

16 This song is the most popular musical soundtrack in the world.

　➡ No other musical soundtrack in the world is __________ popular __________ this song.

17 He is more competent than any other man in my company.

　➡ He is the __________________ man in my company.

〈 정답 p. 168 〉

[01-07] 빈칸에 알맞은 등위접속사를 〈보기〉에서 골라 쓰시오. (중복 사용, 복수 정답 가능)

〈보기〉
and　　but　　so　　for　　or

01 He didn't study, ____________ he failed the test.

02 She is very smart, ____________ she can be a little shy.

03 Michael likes reading books ____________ writing stories.

04 Be quiet, ____________ you will get in trouble.

05 He is very talented, ____________ he is still very humble.

06 They are studying English, ____________ they want to travel abroad.

07 You can go to the movies ____________ watch a film at home with us.

[08-13] 주어진 우리말과 일치하도록 괄호 안의 말과 등위접속사를 이용하여 문장을 완성하시오.

08 너는 우리와 함께 가거나 여기 남을 수 있다. (come with us, stay here)
➡ You can ____________________.

09 사실을 말해라, 그렇지 않으면 너는 벌을 받을 것이다. (punish)
➡ Tell the truth, ____________________.

10 그녀는 내게 전화를 하지 않았지만, 메시지는 보냈다. (but, send me, a message)
➡ She didn't call me, ____________ ____________.

11 이 버튼을 눌러라, 그러면 세탁기가 시작될 것이다. (the washing machine, start)
➡ Press this button, ____________ ____________.

12 그녀는 밤새 일했는데도, 보고서를 끝내지 못했다. (yet, can finish, the report)
➡ She worked all night, ____________ ____________.

13 그는 건강한 음식을 먹고 있다, 왜냐하면 살을 빼고 싶기 때문이다. (want to, lose weight)
➡ He is eating healthy foods, ____________ ____________.

[14-16] 〈보기〉와 같이 주어진 문장을 명령문으로 바꿔 쓰시오.

〈보기〉
If you tell me the secret, I will trust you.
➡ Tell me the secret, and I will trust you.

14 If you don't study hard, you will fail the exam.
➡ ____________________

15 If you hurry up, you'll catch the bus.
➡ ____________________

16 If you don't turn off the oven, the food will burn.
➡ ____________________

〈 정답 p. 169 〉

[01-06] 밑줄 친 부분이 어법상 옳으면 ○로 표시하고, 틀리면 바르게 고치시오.

01 The person he likes is not me or you.
➡ _____________

02 You should go there either alone but with others.
➡ _____________

03 Both my sister and my brother goes to the same school with me.
➡ _____________

04 I can help not only James but you.
➡ _____________

05 My friends as well as he takes part in this program.
➡ _____________

06 They are neither kind or diligent.
➡ _____________

[07-13] 괄호 안의 동사를 주어진 시제로 변형하여 빈칸에 쓰시오.

07 Neither Sarah nor her husband _____________ home. (be – 과거)

08 Either he or I _____________ the event. (attend – be going to 미래)

09 Both his courage and his skills _____________ me. (impress – 현재)

10 The coach as well as the players _____________ surprised. (be – 과거)

11 Either the manager or the employees _____________ responsible. (be – 현재)

12 Not only Jane but also her friends _____________ the club. (join – 현재완료)

13 Both Mark and Lisa _____________. (promote – 현재완료 수동)

[14-18] 주어진 우리말과 일치하도록 괄호 안의 말을 이용하여 문장을 완성하시오.

14 우리는 소문이 아니고 사실을 믿어야 한다.
(not ~ but, the rumors, the facts)
➡ We should trust _____________ _____________.

15 그는 공공 부문과 민간 부문 모두에서 일한 적이 있다. (both ~ and, the public, the private, sectors)
➡ He has worked in _____________ _____________.

16 그는 게으르기 때문이 아니라 아팠기 때문에 실패했다. (not ~ but, because, he, lazy, sick)
➡ He failed _____________ _____________.

17 너는 월요일 또는 화요일에 올 수 있다.
(either ~ or, on Monday, on Tuesday)
➡ You can come _____________ _____________.

18 나는 그 소식을 승인할 수도 거부할 수도 없다.
(neither ~ nor, confirm, deny the news)
➡ I can _____________ _____________.

〈 정답 p. 169 〉

[01-07] 괄호 안에서 알맞은 것을 고르시오.

01 It means (if / that) what he said is true.

02 He doesn't know (how / what) I won the game.

03 It's strange (how / that) no one noticed the error.

04 Did you ask her (if / that) she had missed the plane?

05 It is necessary (that / whether) we take more time to think about it.

06 She's wondering (that / whether) the process is going to be changed or not.

07 (What / Whether) Jenny will go abroad this summer is very important to me.

[08-14] 밑줄 친 부분이 어법상 옳으면 ○로 표시하고, 틀리면 바르게 고치시오.

08 It depends on <u>whether</u> she agrees.

　➡ _____________

09 What you said <u>were</u> really helpful.

　➡ _____________

10 That he <u>know</u> the answer surprises me.

　➡ _____________

11 He asked what time <u>does the train arrive</u>.

　➡ _____________

12 <u>If</u> she comes or not doesn't matter to me.

　➡ _____________

13 That they are responsible <u>was</u> proven false.

　➡ _____________

14 The idea <u>how</u> people can fly naturally was absurd.

　➡ _____________

[15-18] 주어진 우리말과 일치하도록 괄호 안의 말을 바르게 배열하시오.

15 네가 한 말이 그녀의 감정을 상하게 했다.
　　　　　(hurt, you, feelings, said, her)
　➡ What _____________________.

16 그녀의 부모님의 걱정은 그녀가 돌아오지 않을까 하는 것이다. (won't, is, she, that, come back)
　➡ Her patents' worry _________________

　_____________.

17 그녀가 그 제안을 받아들이느냐에 따라 달려 있다. (accepts, she, depends on, the offer, whether)
　➡ It _______________________________

　_____________.

18 당신은 우리가 보고서에서 얼마나 많은 정보를 포함시킬 필요가 있는지 결정해야 한다.
　(how much, we, information, need to, in the report, include)
　➡ You should decide _________________

　_____________________________________

　_____________.

〈 정답 p. 169 〉

UNIT 44 부사절을 이끄는 종속접속사

틀린 개수 ______

[01-06] 자연스러운 의미가 되도록 알맞은 기호를 〈보기〉에서 골라 쓰시오. (중복 사용 불가)

〈보기〉

ⓐ he is still my good friend
ⓑ everyone agreed to try it
ⓒ while using this medicine
ⓓ unless you don't know exactly what's inside
ⓔ until it stops raining
ⓕ they can succeed soon

01 Once they overcome their fear, ____________.

02 Don't open the box ____________.

03 Though he often lies, ____________.

04 I will wait at the bus stop ____________.

05 You should not drink alcohol ____________.

06 Although the plan may sound strange, ____________.

[07-10] 주어진 우리말과 일치하도록 괄호 안의 말을 이용하여 문장을 완성하시오. (필요한 경우 변형할 것)

07 나는 방 안을 볼 수 있도록 불을 켰다.
(the light, so that, see inside, the room)
➡ I turned on ____________ ____________.

08 그는 10살 이후로 스키를 연습하고 있다.
(practice skiing, since, he was ten)
➡ He ____________ ____________.

09 그녀는 피곤해짐에 따라 일찍 잠자리에 든다.
(get tired, go to bed, early)
➡ As she ____________ ____________.

10 나는 해외여행을 가기 위해 돈을 저축했다.
(in order, that, might, travel abroad)
➡ I saved money ____________ ____________.

[11-16] 빈칸에 들어갈 말을 〈보기〉에서 골라 쓰시오.
(중복 사용 불가)

〈보기〉

before   although   as soon as
so that   after   as

11 ____________ I disagree, I respect your opinion.

12 ____________ the weather was bad, we canceled the picnic.

13 Finish your science project ____________ the deadline.

14 ____________ the storm, the villagers began rebuilding their homes.

15 ____________ the bell rang, the students ran out of the classroom.

16 She's been studying hard ____________ she could get the highest score.

〈 정답 p. 169 〉

[01-05] 주어진 우리말과 일치하도록 빈칸에 알맞은 것을 〈보기〉에서 골라 쓰시오. (중복 사용 불가)

〈보기〉
for example   on the contrary
in other words   as a result
on the other hand

01 그는 검소하다. 다시 말해, 돈 쓰는 걸 좋아하지 않는다.

→ He's frugal. ____________, he doesn't like to spend money.

02 나는 운동하는 것을 좋아한다. 예를 들어, 자주 축구와 농구를 한다.

→ I like to play sports. ____________, I often play soccer and basketball.

03 그는 시험 공부를 하지 않았다. 그 결과, 낮은 점수를 받았다.

→ He didn't study for the test. ____________, he got a low score.

04 나는 그 영화가 지루할 것이라고 생각했다. 그와는 반대로, 매우 재미있었다.

→ I thought the movie would be boring. ____________, it was very exciting.

05 도시에서 사는 것은 신난다. 한편으로는, 매우 시끄러울 수 있다.

→ Living in the city is exciting. ____________, it can be very noisy.

[06-12] 주어진 우리말과 일치하도록 괄호 안에서 알맞은 것을 고르시오.

06 그는 알람을 맞추지 않았다. 그 결과, 학교에 늦었다.

→ He didn't set an alarm. (Consequently / Nevertheless), he was late for school.

07 나는 중간고사를 열심히 공부하지 못했다. 따라서 나쁜 점수를 받았다.

→ I couldn't study hard for the mid-term exam. (Therefore / However), I got a bad grade.

08 그녀는 피아노를 아주 잘 칠 수 있다. 게다가, 그녀는 바이올린도 연주할 수 있다.

→ She can play the piano very well. (Finally / In addition), she can play the violin.

09 나는 영화 보기를 좋아하지 않았다. 대신에, 드라마 보는 것을 좋아했다.

→ I didn't like watching movies. (Instead / Besides), I loved watching dramas.

10 이제부터 서둘러야 해. 그렇지 않으면, 기차를 놓칠 거야.

→ You must hurry from now on. (Otherwise / In contrast), you'll miss the train.

11 그 영화는 흥미로운 줄거리를 가지고 있었다. 게다가, 배우들의 연기도 훌륭했다.

→ The movie had an interesting story. (Moreover / Consequently), the actors did an excellent job.

12 그녀는 클래식 음악을 좋아한다. 반면에, 그녀의 친구는 힙합을 즐긴다.

→ She likes classical music. (In addition / In contrast), her friend enjoys hip-hop.

〈 정답 p. 169 〉

[01-08] 빈칸에 알맞은 것을 〈보기〉에서 골라 쓰시오.
(중복 사용 불가)

〈보기〉
at　　on　　in　　until
by　　for　　during　　since

01 I've lived here ______________ 2010, and I really love it.

02 I stayed up ____________ midnight, trying to finish my work.

03 The war ended ____________ the 20th century, after many years.

04 The concert is ____________ Saturday night.

05 The deadline is ____________ next Friday, according to the schedule.

06 He was absent ____________ the meeting, which caused confusion.

07 She's been busy ____________ the past few days with school projects.

08 She goes to bed ____________ midnight, after reading an exciting novel.

[09-15] 괄호 안에서 알맞은 것을 고르시오.

09 The movie starts (at / in) an hour, so let's hurry up.

10 We will meet you (at / in) lunchtime in the school cafeteria.

11 She slept (for / during) the movie, because she was exhausted.

12 They will finish the report (within / by) tomorrow, no matter what.

13 Robert has stayed in Japan (for / during) a week, exploring different cities.

14 Elizabeth got married (on / in) Valentine's Day, which was romantic.

15 The machine hasn't worked (from / since) yesterday, which is frustrating.

[16-19] 주어진 우리말과 일치하도록 괄호 안의 말과 전치사를 이용하여 문장을 완성하시오. (필요한 경우 변형할 것)

16 내 생일은 6월 3일이야, 그러니까 잊지 마!
(be, June 3rd)
➡ My birthday ______________, so don't forget!

17 그들은 봄 축제 바로 전, 3월에 여기로 이사 왔다.
(move, March)
➡ They ______________, just before the spring festival.

18 그들은 너무 어두워지기 전에 해질녘까지는 떠나야 한다. (must, leave, sunset)
➡ They ______________, before it gets too dark.

19 우리는 재미있는 이야기를 나누면서 저녁 식사 동안 많이 웃었다. (laugh, a lot, dinner)
➡ We ______________, as we shared funny stories.

〈 정답 p. 169~170 〉

[01-07] 괄호 안에서 알맞은 것을 고르시오.

01 He arrived (at / in) the airport two hours before the flight.

02 I live (at / on) Main Street, (on / in) the heart of the city.

03 The fish swam (below / beside) the surface in the deep ocean.

04 The keys are (on / beneath) the flowerpot where my son can't find them.

05 The bird flew (over / at) the tree and disappeared into the sky.

06 We'll meet (on / in) the park near the fountain (in / by) the lake.

07 The cat is sleeping on the couch (under / above) the warm blanket.

[08-13] 빈칸에 알맞은 것을 〈보기〉에서 골라 쓰시오.
(중복 사용 불가)

〈보기〉

above	below	on
beneath	beside	under

08 There's a small river ___________ the bridge flowing quietly.

09 I saw her ___________ the bus this morning, sitting near the back.

10 The lamp hangs ___________ the table, providing light for the room.

11 Please do not write ___________ this line.

12 The cat is hiding ___________ the bed because of the thunderstorm.

13 The little girl stood ___________ her mother, holding her hand tightly.

[14-18] 주어진 우리말과 일치하도록 괄호 안의 말과 전치사를 이용하여 문장을 완성하시오. (필요한 경우 변형할 것)

14 조별 토론을 위해 여러분의 짝 옆에 앉으세요.
(sit, your partner, next to)
➡ ___________________ for the group discussion.

15 그녀는 그녀의 차를 입구 근처 식당 앞에 주차했다. (park, the restaurant, in front of)
➡ She ___________________
___________, near the entrance.

16 그 비밀은 마을 사람들 사이에 잘 알려져 있었다.
(well-known, the villagers, among)
➡ The secret was ___________________
___________.

17 그 헬리콥터는 건물 위를 몇 분간 날아갔다.
(fly, the building, over)
➡ The helicopter ___________________
for a few minutes.

18 모든 것이 보관된 지하실이 집 아래에 있다.
(a basement, the house, below)
➡ There's ___________________
where everything is stored.

〈 정답 p. 170 〉

[01-08] 빈칸에 알맞은 것을 〈보기〉에서 골라 쓰시오.
(중복 사용 불가)

〈보기〉			
across	around	down	from
into	out of	toward	up

01 This gift is for you, ＿＿＿＿＿＿ all of us.

02 Raindrops slid ＿＿＿＿＿＿ the window during the storm.

03 People ran ＿＿＿＿＿＿ the building as fast as possible because of the fire.

04 A bridge stretches ＿＿＿＿＿＿ the river near the village.

05 Tom looked ＿＿＿＿＿＿ the room for his missing phone.

06 The cat walked ＿＿＿＿＿＿ the room without making a sound.

07 The balloon floated ＿＿＿＿＿＿ into the sky, disappearing from view.

08 My boss walked ＿＿＿＿＿＿ the door with a confused expression.

[09-12] 주어진 우리말과 일치하도록 괄호 안에서 알맞은 것을 고르시오.

09 쥐 한 마리가 벽에 있는 구멍을 통과하여 달렸다.
➡ A mouse ran (across / through) the hole in the wall.

10 그는 아침 일찍 공항으로 떠났다.
➡ He left (for / at) the airport early in the morning.

11 그 조각상은 유리병들로 만들어졌다.
➡ The sculpture was made (of / in) glass bottles.

12 우리는 안전 조치를 개선하는 것에 대해 회의했다.
➡ We had a meeting (at / about) improving safety measures.

[13-16] 주어진 우리말과 일치하도록 괄호 안의 말과 전치사를 이용하여 문장을 완성하시오. (필요한 경우 변형할 것)

13 그 목걸이는 다채로운 유리구슬들로 구성되어 있다. (colorful, glass, beads)
➡ The necklace is composed ＿＿＿＿＿＿ ＿＿＿＿＿＿.

14 우리는 해가 질 무렵 강을 따라 걸으며 경치를 즐겼다. (the river, at sunset)
➡ We walked ＿＿＿＿＿＿＿＿＿, enjoying the view.

15 그녀는 숲에서 하이킹하다가 언덕 아래로 굴러떨어졌다. (fall, the hill)
➡ She ＿＿＿＿＿＿＿ while hiking in the forest.

16 나는 아침을 먹지 않고 학교에 갔다. (eat breakfast)
➡ I went to school ＿＿＿＿＿＿＿ ＿＿＿＿＿＿.

〈 정답 p. 170 〉

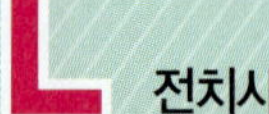

[01-08] 괄호 안에서 알맞은 것을 고르시오.

01 I applied (for / with) a summer internship in New York.

02 Insu is currently looking (at / for) a new job opportunity.

03 Mr. Kim dealt (on / with) the problem very professionally.

04 She is waiting (for / in) her friend in front of the library.

05 I agree (with / of) your idea about the project.

06 My parents believe (in / to) the power of education.

07 You should listen (to / of) your teacher carefully.

08 We depend (at / on) clean water to stay healthy.

[09-12] 주어진 우리말과 일치하도록 괄호 안의 말과 전치사를 이용하여 문장을 완성하시오. (필요한 경우 변형할 것)

09 이 책은 분명 내 남동생의 것이다.
　　　　　　(belong, younger brother)
➡ This book clearly _________________
_________________.

10 그녀는 다가오는 발표에 집중할 필요가 있다.
　　(focus, her, upcoming, presentation)
➡ She needs to _________________
_________________.

11 다른 사람의 작은 실수들을 비웃지 마라.
　　　　　　　　(laugh, someone)
➡ Don't _________________ else's small mistakes.

12 로봇은 결국 노동자를 대신할지도 모른다.
　　　　　(take, the place, workers)
➡ Robots may eventually _____________
_____________.

[13-21] 문장의 빈칸에 알맞은 전치사를 쓰시오.

13 We should take advantage __________ this great opportunity.

14 Don't make fun __________ people who make mistakes.

15 They hired someone to care __________ the garden.

16 Students should make use __________ the school library.

17 She takes pride __________ her painting skills.

18 Can you take the place __________ John in the meeting?

19 I want to take part __________ the school sports day.

20 Please pay attention __________ the safety rules.

21 He made a fool __________ himself during the talent show.

〈 정답 p. 170 〉

[01-08] 빈칸에 알맞은 것을 〈보기〉에서 골라 쓰시오.
(중복 사용 불가)

〈보기〉

afraid of	fond of	jealous of
accustomed to		familiar with
responsible for		known for
	notorious for	

01 He is not yet ____________ waking up early every day.

02 I'm really ____________ eating delicious Korean food because I love spice.

03 He seems confident, but he is actually ____________ speaking in public situations.

04 That politician is ____________ corruption and bribery.

05 The company is well ____________ its creative innovation.

06 He must be ____________ my recent promotion at work.

07 He's mainly ____________ managing the entire budget.

08 She's not ____________ the local customs and traditions since she just moved here.

[09-16] 괄호 안에서 알맞은 것을 고르시오.

09 This question is related (to / of) what we learned yesterday.

10 They are capable (in / of) finishing the project on time.

11 They are poor (with / at) expressing their true feelings.

12 Her opinion is not based (on / under) any real evidence.

13 He was ashamed (with / of) his rude words.

14 They are proud (of / to) their school team's victory.

15 The box was full (in / of) old magazines and papers.

16 My friend is good (at / with) playing the guitar.

[17-22] 문장에서 틀린 부분을 찾아서 밑줄을 긋고 바르게 고쳐 쓰시오.

17 The picnic was canceled because the rain.　➡ ____________

18 Though his cold, he went to school.　➡ ____________

19 Please stay quiet while the movie.　➡ ____________

20 In case fire, leave the building immediately.　➡ ____________

21 He stayed home because of he was sick.　➡ ____________

22 I listened to music during I did my homework.　➡ ____________

〈 정답 p. 170 〉

[01-06] 밑줄 친 부분이 어법상 옳으면 ○로 표시하고, 틀리면 바르게 고치시오.

01 I decided <u>fill</u> in the application form last night.

➡ ______________

02 My goal is <u>to pass</u> the entrance exam.

➡ ______________

03 <u>Speak</u> multiple languages is an advantage.

➡ ______________

04 She promised <u>finish</u> her homework early.

➡ ______________

05 My favorite activity is <u>to swim</u> in the ocean.

➡ ______________

06 It takes effort and time <u>understand</u> others.

➡ ______________

[07-13] 밑줄 친 to부정사가 문장에서 주어, 목적어, 보어 중 어떤 역할을 하는지 쓰시오.

07 <u>To make</u> an omelette is an easy thing.

➡ ______________

08 The first step is <u>to put</u> some salt in it.

➡ ______________

09 Please ask her <u>to call</u> me later.

➡ ______________

10 It is possible <u>to change</u> the original plan.

➡ ______________

11 He described <u>how to install</u> this machine.

➡ ______________

12 She wanted <u>to buy</u> that refrigerator yesterday.

➡ ______________

13 This sample makes it easy <u>to get started</u> on the project.

➡ ______________

[14-17] 주어진 우리말과 일치하도록 괄호 안의 말을 이용하여 문장을 완성하시오. (단, to부정사를 활용할 것)

14 책을 읽는 것은 어휘력을 향상시킨다. (read books, improve)

➡ __________________ vocabulary.

15 경고 신호를 무시한 것은 실수였다. (it, a mistake, ignore)

➡ __________________ the warning signs.

16 그들의 목표는 프로젝트를 제시간에 끝내는 것이다. (finish the project)

➡ Their goal __________________ on time.

17 그녀는 가장 가까운 상점을 어디서 찾을 수 있는지 물었다. (ask, where, find)

➡ She __________________ the nearest store.

〈 정답 p. 170 〉

[01-08] 밑줄 친 부분이 어법상 옳으면 ○로 표시하고, 틀리면 바르게 고치시오.

01 Do you have time <u>talk</u> now?

➡ ______________

02 We want something <u>to eat</u> now.

➡ ______________

03 I found a pen <u>write</u> with during the lecture.

➡ ______________

04 He needs a laptop <u>use</u> for his online classes.

➡ ______________

05 This is a perfect place <u>take</u> photos at sunset.

➡ ______________

06 Do you have any work <u>to finish</u> before Monday?

➡ ______________

07 He needs <u>help someone</u> him with his résumé.

➡ ______________

08 She has a few urgent problems <u>to solve</u> by tomorrow.

➡ ______________

[09-11] 주어진 우리말과 일치하도록 괄호 안의 말을 이용하여 문장을 완성하시오. (필요한 경우 변형할 것)

09 그들은 주말 동안 머물 장소를 찾았다.

(find, a place, stay)

➡ They ____________________ for the weekend.

10 나는 운동 후에 마실 무언가가 필요하다.

(need, something, drink)

➡ I ____________________ after my workout.

11 그 학생들은 시험 전에 낭비할 시간이 없다.

(have, no time, waste)

➡ The students ____________________ before the exam.

[12-16] 두 문장의 뜻이 같도록 빈칸에 알맞은 것을 〈보기〉에서 골라 쓰시오. (중복 사용 불가, 필요한 경우 변형할 것)

〈보기〉

be going to	be able to	intend to
have to	be destined to	

12 If you are to survive, follow my lead.

= If you ____________ survive, follow my lead.

13 She was to become a great artist from a young age.

= She ____________ become a great artist from a young age.

14 All visitors are to show ID at the entrance to attend this meeting.

= All visitors ____________ show ID at the entrance to attend this meeting.

15 The president is to visit Japan next week.

= The president ____________ visit Japan next week.

16 No evidence was to be discovered in the burned building.

= No evidence ____________ be discovered in the burned building.

<단 p. 171 >

[01-08] 밑줄 친 to부정사의 쓰임으로 알맞은 것에 ✓표 하시오.

01 He is so kind <u>to help</u> you.

☐ 결과　☐ 판단의 근거

02 Julie grew up <u>to be</u> a pianist.

☐ 결과　☐ 판단의 근거

03 I was surprised <u>to hear</u> the news.

☐ 조건　☐ 원인, 이유

04 He went to the library <u>to read</u> books.

☐ 목적　☐ 결과

05 You must be crazy <u>to say</u> such a thing.

☐ 조건　☐ 판단의 근거

06 My teacher's handwriting is hard <u>to recognize</u>.

☐ 형용사 수식　☐ 원인, 이유

07 I'm happy <u>to tell</u> you about the amazing result.

☐ 목적　☐ 원인, 이유

08 We need more memory <u>to complete</u> this operation.

☐ 조건　☐ 목적

[09-12] 괄호 안에서 알맞은 것을 고르시오.

09 We were proud (receive / to receive) the award.

10 He was disappointed (failing / to fail) the interview.

11 The news was shocking enough (to / for) leave me speechless.

12 The dress is too expensive for Suji (to buying / to buy) on a budget.

[13-19] 주어진 우리말과 일치하도록 괄호 안의 단어를 알맞은 순서와 형태로 쓰시오.

13 그는 더 많은 책임을 맡을 의향이 있다.

(be willing, take on)

➡ He _____________________ more responsibilities.

14 그 공연은 큰 박수를 받을 만큼 감동적이었다.

(a big applause, enough, get)

➡ The performance was impressive _____________________.

15 날씨가 너무 추워서 코트 없이는 밖으로 나갈 수 없다. (cold, too ~ to, go outside)

➡ The weather is _____________________ without a coat.

16 혼동을 피하기 위해 설명서를 주의 깊게 읽어주세요. (avoid, confusion)

➡ Please read the instructions carefully _____________________.

17 그녀는 그녀의 아기를 깨우지 않기 위해 조용히 말했다. (in order to, wake)

➡ She spoke quietly _____________________ _____________________.

18 그녀는 상자를 열었고, 결과적으로 그것이 비어 있는 것을 알게 되었다. (find, empty)

➡ She opened the box _____________________.

19 그렇게 비싼 차를 산 걸 보니, 그는 분명 부자야.

(buy, such an expensive car)

➡ He must be rich _____________________ _____________________.

<정답 p. 171>

UNIT 54 원형부정사, to부정사의 의미상 주어

틀린 개수 _____

[01-06] 괄호 안에서 알맞은 것을 고르시오.

01 It is easy (of / for) her to make some cookies.

02 It was silly (of / for) him to make small mistakes.

03 It is impossible (of / for) him to do that work alone.

04 It is dangerous (of / for) a baby to sleep on its stomach.

05 It was clever (of / for) you to ask your parents for advice.

06 It was rude (of / for) you to leave without saying good-bye to the elders.

[07-12] 주어진 우리말과 일치하도록 괄호 안의 말을 바르게 배열하시오.

07 그는 휴대폰이 진동하는 것을 느꼈다.
(his, felt, vibrating, phone)
➡ He _________________________.

08 그녀는 동생이 울음을 멈추게 했다.
(to, got, stop, brother, her little)
➡ She _________________ crying.

09 고양이가 물을 좋아하는 건 흔하지 않다.
(like, for, to, common, a cat)
➡ It's not _________________ water.

10 소방관이 안으로 들어간 건 용감했다.
(of, brave, to, the firefighter, go)
➡ It was _________________ inside.

11 선생님은 나에게 사과 편지를 쓰게 하셨다.
(me, write, had, an apology, letter)
➡ My teacher _________________.

12 우리는 선생님이 우리 이름을 크게 말하는 걸 들었다. (the, heard, teacher, say)
➡ We _________________ our names out loud.

[13-16] 밑줄 친 부분이 어법상 옳으면 ○로 표시하고, 틀리면 바르게 고치시오.

13 We made him to apologize for his mistake.
➡ _________________

14 My friend let me to make the final choice.
➡ _________________

15 It was careless for her to say that to her classmates.
➡ _________________

16 I noticed him walked away quietly without saying a word.
➡ _________________

〈 정답 p. 171 〉

[01-06] 두 문장의 뜻이 같도록 빈칸에 알맞은 to부정사를 쓰시오.

01 He pretended that he had done the work.

= He pretended ______________ the work.

02 She promised me she would go shopping with me.

= She promised me __________ shopping with me.

03 It is believed that he won the competition last year.

= He is believed ______________ the competition last year.

04 She hopes that she will have a trip to South America.

= She hopes ______________ a trip to South America.

05 I am the only person who survived the hard training.

= I am the only person ________________ the hard training.

06 I didn't believe that the singer's concert had been canceled.

= I didn't believe the singer's concert ____________________.

[07-14] 괄호 안에서 알맞은 것을 고르시오.

07 He expects his bicycle (to / to be) repaired by Friday.

08 It's important (to not / never to) repeat the same mistake.

09 You need to be more careful (not to be lost / not to lose) this opportunity.

10 The file is (not to share / not to be shared) without permission.

11 She paused for a moment (to gather / to be gathered) her thoughts.

12 She hopes (to visit / to be visited) New York's Central Park one day.

13 I don't want my homework (to finish / to be finished) with my brother's help.

14 He was unlucky to (have blamed / have been blamed) by his colleagues.

[15-18] 문장에서 밑줄 친 to 뒤에 생략된 부분을 쓰시오.

15 Do you want to go on a picnic?
– Yes, I'd like <u>to</u>.　　➡ ____________

16 They tried to solve the problem, but failed <u>to</u>.　　➡ ____________

17 He doesn't need to go there if he doesn't want <u>to</u>.　　➡ ____________

18 She started working for that company, though everyone told her not <u>to</u>.

➡ ________________________

〈 정답 p. 171 〉

[01-04] 〈보기〉와 같이 두 문장이 같은 뜻이 되도록 빈칸에 알맞은 말을 쓰시오.

> ─〈보기〉─
> It seems that he is interested in the project.
> = He seems to be interested in the project.

01 It seems that his sister sticks to a better shape.

➡ His sister ___________________________

___________.

02 It seemed that he had lied about the outcome.

➡ He ___________________________

___________.

> ─〈보기〉─
> The weather seems to get worse later.
> = It seems that the weather will get worse later.

03 She doesn't seem to have noticed the slight change.

➡ It doesn't seem ___________________

___________.

04 He seemed to have lost every bodily function.

➡ It seemed ___________________

___________.

[05-08] 두 문장의 뜻이 같도록 빈칸에 알맞은 말을 쓰시오.

05 It is so early that I can't go home.

= It is too early ___________________.

06 We need creativity to solve problems effectively.

= It takes creativity ___________________

___________.

07 The passwords were too complicated for me to remember.

= The passwords were ___________________

that ___________________ them.

08 This tent is big enough to cover the front yard of my house.

= This tent is __________ that __________

___________.

[09-15] 괄호 안에서 알맞은 것을 고르시오.

09 She was too weak (to endure / not to endure) those hardships.

10 He said sorry to her so that she (could / couldn't) forgive him.

11 To be (frank / frankly) with you, I haven't seen this kind of sight.

12 It takes a lot of effort (maintain / to maintain) a good relationship.

13 To tell you the (true / truth), she didn't make spaghetti by herself.

14 You seem (to have / to had had) many suitcases to carry. I'll help you.

15 It was too dark (us / for us) to notice every detail of the picture.

〈 정답 p. 171 〉

[01-08] 밑줄 친 동명사의 역할을 〈보기〉에서 골라 쓰시오.
(중복 사용 가능)

〈보기〉
주어　　　　보어
동사의 목적어　　전치사의 목적어

01 People avoid <u>looking</u> actual reality in the face.　➡ __________

02 You can help the poor by <u>giving</u> them some money.　➡ __________

03 I am trying to keep <u>doing</u> good things for my friends.　➡ __________

04 <u>Listening</u> to music while studying is not good for you.　➡ __________

05 You shouldn't make a decision without <u>thinking</u> it through.　➡ __________

06 We should consider <u>selecting</u> the topic for the presentation.　➡ __________

07 My favorite hobby is <u>collecting</u> stamps from various countries.　➡ __________

08 <u>Speaking</u> in front of the audience is not an easy job for most people.
　➡ __________

[09-13] 괄호 안에서 알맞은 것을 고르시오.

09 Would you mind (my / I) closing the door?

10 He was excited about (she / her) accepting his offer.

11 I was angry at (not his keeping / his not keeping) the rule.

12 Excuse me for (having not / not having) replied to your e-mail fast.

13 She is afraid of (his / he) leaving her behind in an unfamiliar city.

[14-18] 주어진 우리말과 일치하도록 괄호 안의 말을 바르게 배열하시오.

14 너의 일은 이 우편물들을 분류하는 것이다.
(sorting, is, these pieces of mail)
➡ Your job __________________.

15 내가 네 펜을 빌려도 괜찮을까?
(would, my, mind, borrowing, you)
➡ __________________ your pen?

16 그들은 실수 하나 없이 프로젝트를 끝냈다.
(making, without, mistakes, any)
➡ They finished the project __________
__________________.

17 좋은 분위기를 만드는 방법을 아는 것은 유용한 것이다. (create, is, a good mood, knowing, how to)
➡ __________________
a useful thing.

18 그는 우리 팀 과제를 위해 그가 맡은 부분을 준비하지 않은 것에 대해 미안해해야 한다.
(for, preparing, his part, not)
➡ He should be sorry __________________
__________ for our team project.

〈 정답 p. 171~172 〉

[01-07] 괄호 안에서 알맞은 것을 고르시오.

01 We decided (to travel / traveling) to Canada next month.

02 I promised (to help / helping) my mother make Kimchi.

03 Would you mind (for me to put / my putting) this bag here?

04 They enjoyed (to meet / meeting) each other at the party.

05 He gave up (to become / becoming) a violinist due to economic difficulties.

06 She dislikes (to argue / arguing) in the meeting.

07 I plan (to spend / spending) my holiday in France.

[08-13] 문장을 우리말로 해석하시오.

08 He continues to suggest solutions to his team.

➡ _______________________________

09 She will not forget winning the first prize at the contest last Friday.

➡ _______________________________
____

10 Jenny tries to earn a lot of money from this unique product.

➡ _______________________________
____

11 I remember visiting the zoo with you when we were young.

➡ _______________________________
____

12 This store stopped selling those items last week.

➡ _______________________________
____

13 Jack forgot to write the report with his friends.

➡ _______________________________
____

[14-20] 빈칸에 적절한 말을 〈보기〉에서 골라 알맞은 형태로 바꿔 쓰시오. (중복 사용 불가)

〈보기〉
take　　save　　watch　　get
think　　hide　　answer

14 Don't forget ___________ your umbrella.

15 Stop ___________ about several options and take the necessary action.

16 Please remember ___________ this file before you turn off the computer.

17 He tried ___________ his mistake on purpose.

18 I forgot ___________ your call last night, so you couldn't reach me.

19 I recommend ___________ this documentary on climate change.

20 They risked ___________ caught by sneaking in without tickets.

〈 정답 p. 172 〉

[01-07] 문장에서 틀린 부분을 찾아 밑줄을 긋고 바르게 고치시오.

01 Sorry for break your flower vase.

➡ ___________

02 He doesn't like ordering by other people.

➡ ___________

03 It is no use try to change my mind.

➡ ___________

04 I protected my head to avoid hitting from the ball.

➡ ___________

05 Nobody would enjoy locking up by others in a small room.

➡ ___________

06 Christina is proud of being supporting her sister.

➡ ___________

07 I had trouble to fall asleep last night.

➡ ___________

[08-11] 주어진 우리말과 일치하도록 괄호 안의 말을 이용하여 문장을 완성하시오. (필요한 경우 변형할 것)

08 그는 숲에서 혼자 책을 읽고 싶은 기분이다.
(feel, read)

➡ He ___________ books alone in the woods.

09 전문가들은 피드백을 무시해서 고객을 잃지 말라고 경고한다. (warn, lose)

➡ Experts ___________ customers by ignoring feedback.

10 그 관리자는 기밀 자료를 유출한 혐의로 그녀를 고발했다. (accuse, leak)

➡ The manager ___________ her _____ ___________ confidential data.

11 방에 들어서자마자 그녀는 모두가 조용해지는 것을 눈치챘다. (enter)

➡ ___________ the room, she noticed everyone going quiet.

[12-15] 빈칸에 알맞은 것을 〈보기〉에서 골라 괄호 안의 동사와 함께 쓰시오. (중복 사용 불가, 현재시제로 쓸 것)

〈보기〉
be worth -ing　　cannot help -ing
have difficulty -ing　　be busy -ing

12 We ___________ the beautiful view. (admire)

13 She ___________ to leave on time. (prepare)

14 It ___________ that museum at least once. (visit)

15 They ___________ with each other. (communicate)

〈정답 p. 172〉

[01-07] 괄호 안의 단어를 알맞은 분사 형태로 쓰시오.

01 I saw a (run) woman along the street.
➡ ______________

02 She had her bicycle (repair) a month ago.
➡ ______________

03 I want to know the biggest animal (live) in the sea.
➡ ______________

04 He saw his sister (come) closer to him.
➡ ______________

05 Jackson put the (sign) papers on the desk.
➡ ______________

06 She can read documents (write) in English.
➡ ______________

07 He wants to make this report (shorten) within 10 pages.
➡ ______________

[08-12] 주어진 우리말과 일치하도록 괄호 안의 말을 바르게 배열하시오.

08 울고 있는 아기가 모두를 깨웠다.
(crying, the, woke, baby)
➡ ______________ everyone up.

09 나는 회의실에서 걷고 있는 남자를 안다.
(in the conference room, walking)
➡ I know the man ______________
______________.

10 우리는 밤하늘에 빛나는 별들을 보았다.
(the night sky, shining, the stars, in)
➡ We watched ______________
______________.

11 한국어로 쓰인 편지가 있었다.
(a letter, in Korean, written)
➡ There was ______________.

12 깨진 창문은 수리되어야 한다.
(window, needs to, the broken)
➡ ______________ be fixed.

[13-17] 빈칸에 적절한 말을 〈보기〉에서 골라 알맞은 분사 형태로 쓰시오. (중복 사용 불가)

〈보기〉
miss	play	bake
accept	clean	

13 She is trying to find her ______________ dog in the park.

14 The recommendation letter was ______________ by the professors.

15 I saw a boy ______________ the guitar on the grass.

16 The main hall was ______________ quickly by many workers to prepare for the guests.

17 The cookies ______________ by my mom were delicious.

[01-08] 밑줄 친 부분이 동명사인지 현재분사인지 구분하시오.

01 That <u>crying</u> child looks so sad.

➡ _____________

02 There's a <u>dining</u> room at the end of this hallway.

➡ _____________

03 Can you tell me where the <u>fitting</u> room is?

➡ _____________

04 I want to buy the <u>talking</u> robot.

➡ _____________

05 Who is that <u>sleeping</u> girl on the sofa?

➡ _____________

06 Please put my name on the <u>waiting</u> list.

➡ _____________

07 She read a <u>touching</u> story about friendship.

➡ _____________

08 These sounds are coming from the <u>answering</u> machine.

➡ _____________

[09-12] 문장을 해석하고, 밑줄 친 부분이 동명사인지 현재분사인지 구분하시오.

09 She kept <u>singing</u> even though she was tired.

➡ _____________

➡ [동명사 / 현재분사]

10 Who is the old man <u>standing</u> in front of the door?

➡ _____________

➡ [동명사 / 현재분사]

11 They were <u>playing</u> baseball in the school playground.

➡ _____________

➡ [동명사 / 현재분사]

12 We talked about <u>going</u> to the amusement park.

➡ _____________

➡ [동명사 / 현재분사]

[13-18] 문장에서 틀린 부분을 찾아 밑줄을 긋고 바르게 고치시오.

13 What she told me about the accident was pretty shocked to me.　➡ _____________

14 History is the most interested subject to me.　➡ _____________

15 I was very disappointing with the result of the final match.　➡ _____________

16 The night view of Seoul was so amazed.

➡ _____________

17 She gave a satisfied answer to the question.　➡ _____________

18 I was fascinating due to the beauty of the sunset.　➡ _____________

〈 정답 p. 172 〉

[01-04] 〈보기〉와 같이 분사구문을 이용하여 주어진 문장을 완성하시오.

> 〈보기〉
> If you turn left, you will find the library.
> = Turning left, you will find the library.

01 Because he clearly knew the correct answer, he raised his hand.

➡ ____________________________, he raised his hand.

02 Though she failed the competition, she wasn't disappointed with the result.

➡ ____________________________, she wasn't disappointed with the result.

03 If you work hard, you can complete the task soon.

➡ ______________, you can complete the task soon.

04 Since she felt happy about the news, she called her mom and cried.

➡ ____________________________, she called her mom and cried.

[05-08] 밑줄 친 부분이 어법상 옳으면 ○로 표시하고, 틀리면 바르게 고치시오.

05 He smiling, he said hi to his neighborhood.

➡ ______________

06 Suddenly seeing the police, the thief ran away.

➡ ______________

07 Finishing the final exam, I was satisfied with my score.

➡ ______________

08 Walked along the street, he talked with his friends.

➡ ______________

[09-14] 밑줄 친 분사구문을 부사절로 바꾸어 쓰시오.

09 Reading a magazine, he watched TV.

➡ ____________________________, he watched TV.

10 Very young, she speaks like an adult.

= ____________________________ ______________, she speaks like an adult.

11 Having some time, he decided to wait her more.

= ____________________________, he decided to wait her more.

12 Getting more money, I'll donate some to the poor.

= ____________________________, I'll donate some to the poor.

13 Being tired, she keeps memorizing her lines in the play.

= ____________________________, she keeps memorizing her lines in the play.

14 Feeling extremely tired after work, she went to bed early.

= ____________________________ ______________, she went to bed early.

〈 정답 p. 172~173 〉

[01-08] 괄호 안에서 알맞은 것을 고르시오.

01 (Not knowing / Knowing not) the password, I couldn't enter the building.

02 (Been / Being) seventeen, she started learning French in class.

03 (Spoken / Speaking) of birthdays, mine is coming up next week.

04 Because (having found / not having found) my notebook, I couldn't go home.

05 (Having been left / Having left) the door open, he lost his wallet.

06 (Failed / Having failed) the driving test, she tried one more time.

07 (Not sharing / Sharing not) the details, he worked on it alone.

08 (Considered / Considering) that it's your first attempt, the outcome is impressive.

[09-13] 문장을 분사구문으로 바꾸어 쓰시오.

09 Since the heavy snow blocks traffic, I can't move to other areas.
　➡ ____________________, I can't move to other areas.

10 He was sleeping while the light turned on.
　➡ He was sleeping with ____________
____________.

11 If I speak generally, she is showing good performances.
　➡ ____________, she is showing good performances.

12 Although I didn't give him enough time, he completed the project on time.
　➡ ____________________, he completed the project on time.

13 As the dawn broke, I started packing my stuff to leave.
　➡ With ____________, I started packing my stuff to leave.

[14-18] 문장에서 틀린 부분을 찾아서 밑줄을 긋고 바르게 고치시오.

14 Her having lunch, she is watching TV.
　➡ ____________

15 Lived in China, he visited many regions there.
　➡ ____________

16 Henry was thinking with his arms crossing.
　➡ ____________

17 Comparing with other machines, this one is easy to use.
　➡ ____________

18 Feeling not well, I went home earlier than usual.
　➡ ____________

〈 정답 **p. 173** 〉

[01-04] 빈칸에 알맞은 것을 〈보기〉에서 골라 쓰시오.
(중복 사용 불가)

〈보기〉
who　　which　　whom　　whose

01 The woman ____________ lives next door is a doctor.

02 My uncle is someone ____________ I trust completely.

03 The man ____________ car was stolen is talking to the police.

04 She showed me a picture ____________ she painted herself.

[05-09] 관계대명사가 필요한 곳에 which나 whose를 넣어 문장을 다시 쓰시오.

05 The girl jacket is red is my best friend, Tina.

➡ ____________________________________

06 The present his grandmother gave him is very expensive.

➡ ____________________________________

07 I was very moved by the kindness she showed to me.

➡ ____________________________________

08 At the party, he met a woman dress was all blue.

➡ ____________________________________

09 Here are some options from you can choose.

➡ ____________________________________

[10-15] 관계대명사를 이용하여 주어진 두 문장을 한 문장으로 쓰시오. (who(m), which, whose를 쓸 것)

10 Did you want to get the sunglasses? I bought them yesterday.

➡ ____________________________________

11 I met a lot of people. I saw them at the conference.

➡ ____________________________________

12 She has a brother. He can play basketball very well.

➡ ____________________________________

13 The man is my boss. You saw the man at the party.

➡ ____________________________________

14 We visited a castle. The castle was built in the 18th century.

➡ ____________________________________

15 I taught a boy. His English has improved dramatically.

➡ ____________________________________

〈 정답 p. 173 〉

[01-07] 괄호 안에서 알맞은 것을 고르시오.

01 I'll introduce our new student (that / whom) is from Busan.

02 (What / That) you decide to do next will change your future.

03 He doesn't do something (who / that) people don't like.

04 Who is the old man (whom / that) is standing on the corner?

05 He repeated (what / which) he had heard from others.

06 I saw the girl and her cat (that / which) were running around the park.

07 Fire is the only thing (which / that) scares him.

[08-12] 밑줄 친 부분이 어법상 옳으면 ○로 표시하고, 틀리면 바르게 고치시오.

08 This is the novel that <u>give</u> him pleasure.
➡ ______________

09 What is the last thing <u>that</u> she wants to do?
➡ ______________

10 Tom is an excellent student <u>what</u> deserves an award.
➡ ______________

11 The main point is <u>which</u> you just said.
➡ ______________

12 This story is about <u>that</u> happened to my family.
➡ ______________

[13-18] 주어진 우리말과 일치하도록 관계대명사 that 또는 what과 주어진 말을 이용하여 문장을 완성하시오. (필요한 경우 변형할 것)

13 어젯밤 공연에서 네가 본 것을 말해줘. (see)
➡ Tell me ________________ in the performance last night.

14 그녀는 내가 아프고 혼자였을 때 도와준 친절한 사람이다. (help)
➡ She's the kind woman ______________ when I was sick and alone.

15 네가 프로젝트에 대해 말한 것이 나를 정말 깊이 생각하게 만들었다. (say)
➡ ______________ about the project really made me think deeply.

16 우리가 어젯밤 함께 본 영화는 정말 놀랍고 감동적이었다. (watch)
➡ The movie ______________ together last night was so amazing and touching.

17 그녀가 재난 중에 지역 사회를 위해 한 일은 정말 주목할 만했다. (do)
➡ ______________ for the local community during the disaster was truly remarkable.

18 네가 보호소에서 입양한 그 개와 새는 잘 지내고 있다. (adopt, from the shelter)
➡ The dog and the bird ______________ ______________ are getting along well.

〈 정답 p. 173 〉

[01-08] 문장에서 생략이 가능한 부분을 찾아 쓰시오.
(단, 생략할 부분이 없다면 ×로 표시할 것)

01 I can't understand the sentences that are written here. ➡ ______________

02 Is this the bicycle which your father bought for you? ➡ ______________

03 Please put the bowl back which was used for cooking. ➡ ______________

04 She is the person that invented this machine. ➡ ______________

05 The woman who is washing the dishes is my aunt. ➡ ______________

06 He fell in love with a girl whom he saw once. ➡ ______________

07 The car that was parked outside the building belongs to my friend. ➡ ______________

08 The phone that I bought yesterday has a great camera. ➡ ______________

[09-13] 문장을 우리말로 해석하시오.

09 David gave me a jacket, which was created in a unique style.
➡ ________________________________
____

10 My parents, who have been married for 30 years, still love each other deeply.
➡ ________________________________
____

11 My brother dropped the expensive flower vase which I liked most.
➡ ________________________________
____

12 She is a kind student, who is the leader of our school club.
➡ ________________________________
____

13 He showed me the desirable step of writing, which is an important part.
➡ ________________________________
____

[14-19] 빈칸에 알맞은 것을 〈보기〉에서 골라 쓰시오.
(중복 사용 불가)

〈보기〉

at which	for which	from which
on which	in which	with whom

14 The island ____________ they settled has beautiful beaches.

15 This big company is the one ____________ he worked.

16 The city ____________ she moved was very crowded and noisy.

17 Is that boy your friend ____________ you often go to the movies?

18 The project ____________ we are involved requires careful planning.

19 The conference ____________ we discussed new technologies was very informative.

〈 정답 p. 173~174 〉

[01-07] 괄호 안에서 알맞은 것을 고르시오.

01 My sister likes Chuseok (which / when) she can meet all the cousins.

02 It was the point (during which / at which) she was to meet her big rival.

03 Do you know the day (in / on) which National Central Museum of Korea is closed?

04 This is the city (on which / in which) his mother was born.

05 Please show me the presentation (which / when) he is referring to.

06 Tell me the time (at which / in which) the plane leaves.

07 The quiet town in the mountains (where / that) she was born is famous for apples.

[08-11] 문장에서 틀린 부분을 찾아서 밑줄을 긋고 바르게 고치시오.

08 Can you tell me the way how I can get to the nearest station?

➡ ______________

09 I want to know the reason how he is so popular.

➡ ______________

10 That's the old house by the lake which he grew up with his parents.

➡ ______________

11 There was a turning point in my life that everything changed overnight.

➡ ______________

[12-17] 두 문장의 뜻이 같도록 빈칸에 알맞은 말을 쓰시오.

12 The apartment where I am living is well-known for its access to the subway.
= The apartment ___________ I am living ___________ is well-known for its access to the subway.

13 The company which Sue is working for is a small manufacturing business.
= The company __________ Sue __________ __________ is a small manufacturing business.

14 The city where he was raised has a major tourist attraction.
= The city __________ __________ he was raised has a major tourist attraction.

15 She is a clerk at the place where I got my new closet.
= She is a clerk at the place __________ I got my new closet __________.

16 I like a job in which I can display my abilities.
= I like a job __________ I can display my abilities.

17 This is an island where a lot of residents can settle.
= This is an island __________ __________ a lot of residents can settle.

〈 정답 p. 174 〉

[01-04] 문장에서 생략이 가능한 부분을 찾아 쓰시오.
(단, 생략할 부분이 없다면 ×로 표시할 것)

01 Please explain to her the reason why she should study more.

➡ ___________

02 Show me the way you created this artwork.

➡ ___________

03 Tell me the reason why he didn't join my party.

➡ ___________

04 We met again in Paris in 2019, when both of us had changed a lot.

➡ ___________

[05-09] 빈칸에 알맞은 말을 〈보기〉에서 골라 쓰시오.
(중복 사용 불가)

〈보기〉
| which | who | where | why | when |

05 The artist ___________ painted this mural lives in the building next door.

06 I can't forget the moment ___________ I got accepted to college.

07 That's the bakery ___________ I always buy your favorite bread.

08 I don't understand the reason ___________ he suddenly changed his phone number.

09 She wore the dress ___________ you picked for her birthday party.

[10-13] 두 문장의 뜻이 같도록 알맞은 관계부사를 이용하여 빈칸에 쓰시오.

10 This is a famous library, and here they used to visit for the analysis.

➡ This is a famous library, ___________
___________.

11 His family arrived at 7 o'clock, and then they had a birthday party.

➡ His family arrived at 7 o'clock, ________
___________.

12 They went back to Spain, and there they spent their vacation.

➡ They went back to Spain, ___________
___________.

13 She was in Beijing in 2015, and then her friends visited her.

➡ She was in Beijing in 2015, ___________
___________.

[14-16] 괄호 안의 말을 바르게 배열하시오.

14 (I, well, couldn't, English, speak, when)

➡ There was a time ___________
___________.

15 (so, among, popular, it, the students, is, why)

➡ She told me ___________
___________.

16 (he, where, beautiful, saw, scenery)

➡ Tony loves South Africa, ___________
___________.

〈 정답 p. 174 〉

[01-06] 밑줄 친 복합관계사에 유의하여 〈보기〉와 같이 바꾸어 쓰시오.

> 〈보기〉
> I don't care <u>whatever</u> you buy.
> → I don't care <u>no matter what</u> you buy.

01 <u>Whenever</u> you need a demonstration, just tell me.

➡ ________________________________

________________, just tell me.

02 <u>Whatever</u> she wears, she looks wonderful.

➡ ________________________, she looks

wonderful.

03 <u>Whichever</u> you choose, you should accept the result.

➡ ________________________, you

should accept the result.

04 <u>Whoever</u> needs support with the project, make sure they get it.

➡ ________________________________

________________, make sure they get it.

05 <u>However</u> hard it might be, it'll not take long for him to complete it.

➡ ________________________, it'll

not take long for him to complete it.

06 <u>Whichever</u> group project fits your schedule best, you should join it.

➡ ________________________________

________________, you should join it.

[07-12] 빈칸에 알맞은 것을 〈보기〉에서 골라 쓰시오.

(중복 사용 불가)

> 〈보기〉
> whoever   whichever   whatever
> however   whenever   wherever

07 She always misses him __________ he is.

08 Take __________ seat is still available near the window.

09 __________ she talks to others, she tries to be careful.

10 __________ young they are, it is an unacceptable behavior.

11 Please give this message to __________ arrives at the office first.

12 He eats __________ is on his plate.

[13-17] 괄호 안에서 알맞은 것을 고르시오.

13 (Wherever / Whichever) team wins, it will be a great game.

14 You can call me (at any time / any time) when you want.

15 She can't help solving this math problem, (whatever / however) much she hates it.

16 You can invite (whosever / whomever) you like to the party.

17 However (quickly / quick) he runs, he can't catch up with the fastest runner.

〈 정답 p. 174 〉

[01-07] 괄호 안에서 알맞은 것을 고르시오.

01 If he (listens / listened) to my advice, he wouldn't make that mistake.

02 If she (knows / knew) the details, she would explain everything.

03 If he (was / were) here right now, we could talk about the project.

04 He (talks / will talk) as if he knew everything.

05 I wish my school (started / start) later in the morning so that I could get more sleep than I do now.

06 If I (have / had) more free time this week, I would visit my family more often.

07 Without his help, I (wouldn't / didn't) know how to finish it.

[08-13] 두 문장의 뜻이 같도록 빈칸에 알맞은 말을 쓰시오.

08 As I am not a parent, I ________________ how to raise a child.
 = If I ____________, I would understand how to raise a child.

09 As I don't save money, I ____________ ____________.
 = If I ____________, I could buy a new phone.

10 Without breakfast, I wouldn't have any energy in the morning.
 = If it ____________________, I wouldn't have any energy in the morning.

11 But for ____________, I wouldn't see the board clearly.
 = If ____________ my glasses, I wouldn't see the board clearly.

12 She acts as if ____________.
 = In fact, she doesn't like Tony.

13 He talks as if ____________________ ____________.
 = In fact, he isn't better than his teacher.

[14-17] 주어진 우리말과 일치하도록 괄호 안의 말을 이용하여 문장을 완성하시오.

14 만약 그들이 도움을 요청한다면, 우리는 기꺼이 도와줄 텐데. (be, to ask for help)
 ➡ ____________________________, we would gladly assist them.

15 우리가 더 일찍 만난다면, 함께 일할 수 있을 텐데. (meet, earlier)
 ➡ ____________________, we could work together.

16 만약 그들이 진실을 안다면, 더 잘 이해할 수 있을 텐데. (will, understand)
 ➡ If they knew the truth, they ____________ ____________.

17 깨끗한 물이 없다면 사람들은 건강하게 지낼 수 없을 거야. (will, stay healthy)
 ➡ Without clean water, people ____________ ____________.

〈 정답 p. 174 〉

[01-07] 괄호 안에서 알맞은 것을 고르시오.

01 If you (call / had called) me earlier, I could have picked you up.

02 I wish I (had listened / listened) to my parents before things got worse.

03 If it had not snowed heavily, we (would have gone / would gone) hiking.

04 Without her encouragement, I might not (have tried / try) again.

05 If we had booked the tickets in advance, we might (have gotten / got) better seats.

06 If he had gone to college, he (might had had / might have had) a better job.

07 If she had practiced more, she (would have performed / will perform) better.

[08-13] 두 문장의 뜻이 같도록 빈칸에 알맞은 말을 쓰시오.

08 As he didn't tell me the truth, I __________ ____________.

= If he ______________, I wouldn't have been upset.

09 She cried as if she __________ everything.

= In fact, she didn't lose anything.

10 As you ________________, you couldn't have a great time with him.

= If you had not missed the plane, you ________________________.

11 I wish we ________________ earlier.

= In fact, we arrived at the station late.

12 I wish I ________________________.

= In fact, I didn't tell her how to do it.

13 Without GPS, we ________________ ________________.

= As we had GPS, we didn't get completely lost.

[14-16] 주어진 우리말과 일치하도록 괄호 안의 말을 이용하여 문장을 완성하시오. (필요한 경우 변형할 것)

14 내가 그녀의 생일을 잊지 않았더라면, 내 전화를 무시하지 않았을 텐데. (I, have, not, her birthday, if, forget)

➡ ________________________, she wouldn't have ignored my calls.

15 작년에 수학여행을 갔더라면 좋았을 텐데. (go, I, last year, on the school trip, have)

➡ I wish ________________ ____________.

16 지도가 없었더라면, 그들은 숲에서 길을 잃었을 거야. (get lost, would, in the forest, have, they)

➡ Without the map, ________________ ________________.

〈 정답 p. 175 〉

[01-07] 괄호 안에서 알맞은 것을 고르시오.

01 It's time she (made / makes) a decision.

02 (Was / Were) the weather better, we could go hiking.

03 If they had saved more money, they wouldn't (be / have been) in debt now.

04 (Had / Have) I slept earlier last night, I wouldn't feel so tired now.

05 It's time she (apologized / apologizes) to her friend.

06 (Was / Were) I you, I would take that opportunity.

07 (Had / Have) I studied harder, I would have passed the test.

[08-17] 주어진 우리말과 일치하도록 괄호 안의 말을 이용하여 문장을 완성하시오. (단, 주절에는 will/would를 이용할 것)

08 우리가 카메라를 가져왔더라면, 지금 사진을 찍을 수 있을 텐데. (bring)
→ If we _________________, we could take pictures now.

09 영어를 더 열심히 공부했더라면, 지금 자막 없이 이 영화를 이해할 수 있을 텐데. (understand)
→ If I had studied English harder, I ______ _________________ without subtitles now.

10 그들이 연습을 더 했더라면, 오늘 더 잘할 텐데. (practice more)
→ Had they _____________, they would play better today.

11 그가 더 키가 크다면, 농구팀에 들어갈 수 있을 텐데. (taller)
→ _________ he _________, he could join the basketball team.

12 이제 그는 모두에게 거짓말을 그만해야 해. (should, stop)
→ It's time he _____________ lying to everyone.

13 내 차가 고장이 나지 않았다면 지금쯤 거기 도착했을 텐데. (break down)
→ If _____________________, I would be there by now.

14 내가 네 입장이라면, 다른 결정을 내릴 거야. (make)
→ Were I in your position, I _____________ a different decision.

15 그녀가 그 일자리를 수락했더라면, 지금 뉴욕에 살고 있을 텐데. (take, live)
→ If she _____________ the job offer, she _____________ in New York now.

16 우리가 다른 길로 갔더라면 지금쯤 도착했을 텐데. (take the other road)
→ Had we _____________, we would be there by now.

17 이제 나는 내 기회들을 진지하게 받아들이고, 시간 낭비를 멈춰야 할 때야. (take my opportunities)
→ It's time I _____________________ seriously and stopped wasting time.

〈 정답 p. 175 〉

[01-07] 주어진 동사를 알맞은 형태로 바꾸어 빈칸에 쓰시오. (단, 현재시제로 쓸 것)

01 Not you but he ___________ helping with the work. (be)

02 Every man ___________ his own way of living. (have)

03 A number of people ___________ looking around the exhibition. (be)

04 Neither my mother nor I ___________ jogging in the morning. (like)

05 If both of you ___________ this task, you must feel like an adult. (finish)

06 Each group member ___________ to share the information for the group. (have)

07 Either he or you ___________ the secret of the magician. (know)

[08-12] 주어진 우리말과 일치하도록 괄호 안의 말을 배열하시오.

08 미국은 많은 다양한 인종의 국가이다.
(a, country, is, of, the United States, many, races, different)

➡ _______________________________________

____

09 이 가게에 있는 모든 것은 세일 중이다.
(on sale, everything, is, in, this store)

➡ _______________________________________

10 경제학은 선택에 관한 학문이다.
(the study, of, economics, choices, is)

➡ _______________________________________

11 난 어떤 것이든 가능하다고 말하고 싶어.
(is, say, I, that, possible, want to, anything)

➡ _______________________________________

12 세 시간은 누군가를 기다리기에 너무 길다.
(to, long, someone, three hours, is, too, wait for)

➡ _______________________________________

[13-19] 문장에서 틀린 부분을 찾아서 밑줄을 긋고 바르게 고치시오. (단, 동사의 시제는 유지할 것)

13 Physics are a very difficult subject.

➡ ____________

14 Nobody promote the new product of the company.

➡ ____________

15 The number of employee currently working in this company is approximately 250.

➡ ____________

16 One of your team members are my brother.

➡ ____________

17 Eighty percent of the defective products on the market was recalled immediately.

➡ ____________

18 There are no residents who likes this ugly building.

➡ ____________

19 All the students who takes part in the speech contest should hand in the form.

➡ ____________

〈 정답 p. 175 〉

[01-07] 문장에서 틀린 부분을 찾아 밑줄을 긋고 바르게 고치시오.

01 She thought that I will cook some spicy and sour food.

→ _______________

02 As I visited my grandfather, he is cleaning the back yard.

→ _______________

03 Tommy said that he will not be allowed to leave the team.

→ _______________

04 When she was seven, she thought her father is very handsome.

→ _______________

05 He didn't know that you have stayed in the country for two months.

→ _______________

06 My boss says that Tina had broken her arm, so she can't work today.

→ _______________

07 I told him that I will go there as soon as possible.

→ _______________

[08-15] 주어진 동사를 알맞은 형태로 바꾸어 빈칸에 쓰시오. (필요 없는 경우, 바꾸지 않아도 됨)

08 She thought that she would _______________ with her guests if she had had enough time. (talk)

09 A long time ago, most people didn't believe that the Earth _______________ round. (be)

10 Sujin told me that she always _______________ a cup of coffee every morning. (drink)

11 The doctor advised I _______________ out at least three times a week. (work)

12 Most people say that the Wright Brothers _______________ the airplane. (invent)

13 My father told me that the sun _______________ the only star in our solar system. (be)

14 If it _______________ tomorrow, my sister and I will stay at home. (rain)

15 When he _______________ at the entrance, I'll go out to say hello. (arrive)

[16-20] 괄호 안에서 알맞은 것을 고르시오.

16 When the bell (goes / will go) off, the students will leave the classroom.

17 Minji said she (would have taken / would take) many pictures if she had been there.

18 My sister insisted that I (have / had) regular check-ups to stay healthy.

19 Matthew told me that he (had visited / have visited) Europe many times.

20 He claimed that children (eat / ate) a lot of vegetables to stay healthy.

〈 정답 p. 175 〉

[01-06] 직접화법을 간접화법으로 바꿔 빈칸에 알맞은 말을 쓰시오.

01 He said, "I'm going to start a new job."

→ He said _________ _________ _________ going to start a new job.

02 He said, "Where do you live?"

→ He asked _________ _________ _________.

03 My sister said, "I'm cleaning your room now."

→ My sister said that _________ _________ cleaning _________ room _________.

04 He said, "Let's go for a walk."

→ He suggested _________ _________ go for a walk.

05 Sarah said, "I am meeting my friend today."

→ Sarah said that _________ _________ meeting _________ friend _________ day.

06 John said, "Are you coming with us?"

→ John asked _________ _________ _________ _________ _________ _________.

[07-12] 간접화법을 직접화법으로 바꿔 빈칸에 알맞은 말을 쓰시오.

07 Sumi said that she would visit me the next day.

→ Sumi said, "_________ _________ visit _________ _________."

08 I suggested meeting after work.

→ I said, "Let's _________ _________ _________."

09 They said that they were going to the cinema that night.

→ They said, "_________ _________ going to the cinema _________."

10 They asked why she had left early.

→ They said, "Why _________ _________ _________ _________?"

11 Mira told me that she had been sick the day before.

→ Mira said to me, "_________ _________ sick _________."

12 Chris proposed inviting her to the party.

→ Chris said, "_________ _________ _________ to the party."

[13-17] 주어진 우리말과 일치하도록 괄호 안의 말을 이용하여 문장을 완성하시오. (필요한 경우 변형할 것)

13 John은 "오늘 밤 영화 볼까?"라고 말했다.
(shall, watch a movie)

→ John said, "_________________ _________?"

14 Jane은 "나는 다음 주에 여행을 계획하고 있어."라고 말했다. (plan a trip)

→ Jane said, "_________________ next week."

15 그녀는 충동적으로 행동하지 말자고 제안했다.
(act on impulse)

→ She suggested _________________.

16 경찰관은 그에게 그의 차를 거기에 주차하지 말라고 말했다. (tell, park, there)

→ The policeman _________________ _________.

17 그녀는 "나 정말 운이 좋아!"라고 말했다.
(how, lucky)

→ She said, "_________________!"

〈 정답 p. 175~176 〉

[01-07] 두 문장의 뜻이 같도록 빈칸에 알맞은 말을 쓰시오.

01 I could hardly see what he did.

→ Hardly __________________________.

02 Some museums are near my sister's school.

→ There __________________________
__________________.

03 A cute bird sang on the roof of my house.

→ On the roof of my house __________
__________.

04 He feels comfortable only in his room.

→ Only in his room __________________
__________.

05 The concert had no sooner begun than the power went out.

→ No sooner __________________________
__________________.

06 I have never witnessed such chaos in my entire life.

→ Never __________________________
__________ in my entire life.

07 I little dreamed that I could work with my best friend in the same company.

→ Little __________________________
__________________________.

[08-11] 빈칸에 so 또는 neither를 써서 대화를 완성하시오.

08 A: Sujin didn't review what she learned.

B: __________ did I.

09 A: My brother is not good at playing the guitar.

B: __________ am I.

10 A: He went to the park last week.

B: __________ did I.

11 A: She is incredibly talented at playing the piano.

B: __________ is her sister.

[12-16] 문장에서 틀린 부분을 찾아 밑줄을 긋고 바르게 고치시오.

12 Rarely we have encountered such a difficult problem.

→ __________

13 Not until yesterday I realized the mistake.

→ __________

14 A: They couldn't solve the technical issue on their own.

B: So couldn't we.

→ __________

15 Seldom they visit us during the holiday season.

→ __________

16 Only then she came to believe that he didn't tell a lie.

→ __________

〈 정답 p. 176 〉

[01-06] 빈칸에 알맞은 말을 〈보기〉에서 골라 강조 구문을 완성하시오. (중복 사용 불가)

〈보기〉
does	very	who
on earth	in the least	much

01 What ___________ was going through your mind when you said that?

02 Tom is the one ___________ always stands by me no matter what happens.

03 She is the ___________ person I'd hoped to meet at this conference.

04 He ___________ do his best when he teaches children.

05 I don't agree ___________ with their decision to cancel the event.

06 This test is ___________ more difficult than the last one.

[07-12] 밑줄 친 부분을 강조할 때, 빈칸에 알맞은 말을 쓰시오.

07 He broke the flower vase last Thursday.
➡ It ___________ broke the flower vase last Thursday.

08 Emily wants to buy that skirt.
➡ It ___________ wants to buy that skirt.

09 Robert watched the circus in New Zealand.
➡ It ___________ Robert watched the circus.

10 She wants to join the basketball team of her school.
➡ She ___________ to join the basketball team of her school.

11 We finally decided to take a break at noon.
➡ It ___________ we finally decided to take a break.

12 The conference is being held in New York.
➡ It ___________ the conference is being held.

[13-17] 문장에서 틀린 부분을 찾아 밑줄을 긋고 바르게 고치시오.

13 She did wrote her essay herself.
➡ ___________

14 Why would in the world she want to stay with you?
➡ ___________

15 She is very more talented than anyone else in the class.
➡ ___________

16 He is very the man that cut in line a few minutes ago.
➡ ___________

17 It was at the conference who he met his professor.
➡ ___________

〈 정답 **p. 176** 〉

[01-07] 문장에서 생략할 수 있는 부분에 밑줄을 그으시오.

01 Look at the man who is standing at the front.

02 I lived in Seoul, and my sister lived in Barcelona.

03 There is a book which is about the interesting topic.

04 While she is getting ready to go to work, she always listens to music.

05 I will lend my laptop computer to you, if it is possible.

06 I wish you a Happy New Year.

07 He gathered some friends and he started talking about the issue.

[08-13] 문장을 우리말로 해석하시오.

08 Not all girls like playing with cute dolls.

➡ _______________________________

____

09 None of your classmates want to take part in the presentation.

➡ _______________________________

____

10 She doesn't always win the first prize in the contest.

➡ _______________________________

____

11 The report didn't mention the key issue anywhere.

➡ _______________________________

____

12 It doesn't necessarily mean a bad result.

➡ _______________________________

____

13 She didn't say anything important.

➡ _______________________________

[14-16] 주어진 우리말과 일치하도록 괄호 안의 말을 바르게 배열하시오.

14 우리 반에서 가장 똑똑한 여자아이인 Jenny는 부산에서 왔다. (from, my class, came, in, Busan, the smartest girl)

➡ Jenny, _______________________________

_______________________.

15 그가 고등학교를 마치지 않았다는 사실이 나를 당황하게 했다. (me, high school, didn't, he, that, embarrassed, finish)

➡ The fact _______________________________

_______________________.

16 아무것도 내가 꿈을 이루는 것을 막을 수 없다. (from, nothing, me, can, achieving, stop)

➡ _______________________________ my

dreams.

자이스토리

수학 시리즈

개념은 쉽게, 문제는 빠르게 푼다!

★ 고등 자이스토리 수학

- 촘촘한 유형 분류와 난이도순 기출 문제 배열
- 1등급, 2등급 대비 문제 집중 학습 + 특강 해설
  - ❶ 출제 경향에 따른 개념정리
  - ❷ 출제 유형에 따른 기출문제
  - ❸ 1등급 대비, 2등급 대비 문제만을 위한 풀이 단서 체크
  - ❹ 1등급 심화 특강, My Top Secret
  - ❺ 다양한 풀이법 + 실수, 함정, 주의까지 분석한 입체 첨삭 해설

공통수학 1	고3 수학 I
공통수학 2	고3 수학 II
고2 수학 I	고3 미적분
고2 수학 II	고3 확률과 통계
고2 미적분	고난도 1등급 수학
고2 확률과 통계	(수학 I, 수학 II, 확률과 통계)
기하 (고2, 3)	(수학 I, 수학 II, 미적분)
	전국연합 모의고사 공통수학 1, 2
	연도별 모의고사 고3 수학

★ 중등 자이스토리 수학

- 세분화된 유형 문제로 개념 적용 반복 훈련
- 서술형 문제를 단계별로 익히는 서술형 완전 학습
  - ❶ 개념 다지기+개념 확인 문제 ❷ 학교 시험 유형 익히기
  - ❸ 서술형 다지기 ❹ 고난도 도전 문제
  - ❺ 학교 시험 단원별 모의고사 ❻ 정답 및 해설

중등 수학 1-1, 1-2
2-1, 2-2
3-1, 3-2

자 이 스 토 리

듣기 총정리 모의고사

[중1, 중2, 중3, 고1]

"최신 듣기 유형 분석 + 단계별 모의고사 25회"

EBS 중학 프리미엄 강의 교재
mid.ebs.co.kr *고1 제외

① 듣기 유형 분석 [12~14 유형]

최신 전국 중학 영어 듣기 능력 평가와
고1 전국연합학력평가 유형 완벽 분석

② 잘 틀리는 유형 모의고사 [3회]
+ 듣기 발음 특강 모의고사 [2~3회]

틀리기 쉬운 유형과 발음을 훈련

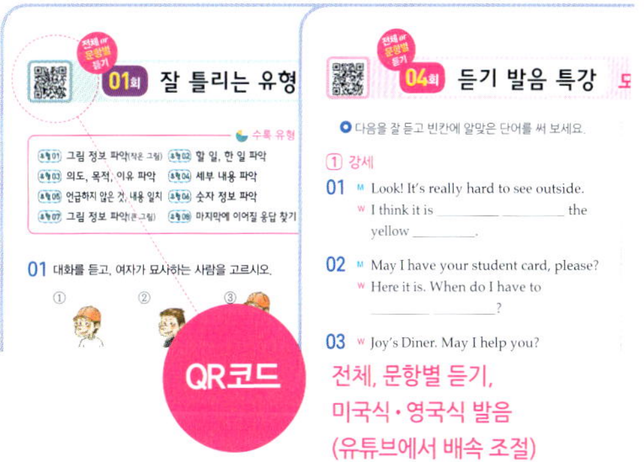

③ 실전+기출 모의고사 [12~16회],
고난도 듣기 실전 모의고사 [3~4회]

최신 기출 문제 유형을 반영한 단계별 모의고사

④ Dictation, 어휘+표현 PREVIEW, REVIEW

표현 체크와 발음 체크로 공부하고 중요한
어휘와 표현들을 익힌다.

학교 시험 유형 훈련과 단계별로 서술형 문제 완성!!

자이스토리 중등 수학

*** 2022 개정교육과정에 꼭 맞춘 자이스토리**

자이스토리와 함께 하면 수학 실력이 하루하루 달라지는
놀라운 경험을 하실 수 있습니다.

[자이스토리 중등 수학 시리즈]

중등 수학 1-1, 1-2
중등 수학 2-1, 2-2
중등 수학 3-1, 3-2

01 개념 다지기 + 개념 확인 문제

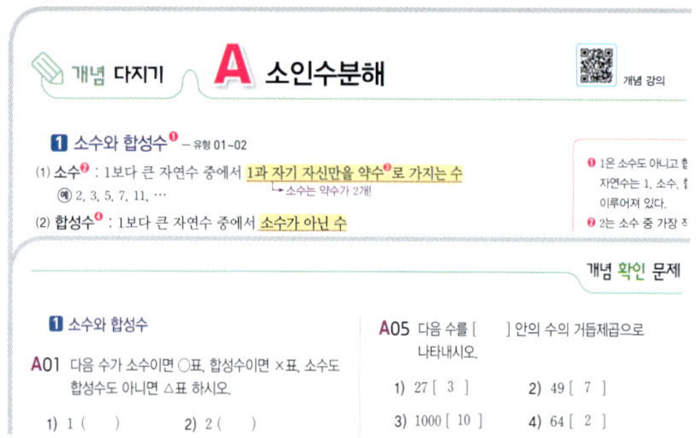

- 각 단원에서 꼭 알아야 하는 개념을 촘촘히 분류해 이해하기 쉽게 설명하였습니다.
- 개념 확인 문제를 풀어보며 개념을 다시 한 번 점검할 수 있습니다.

02 학교 시험 유형 익히기

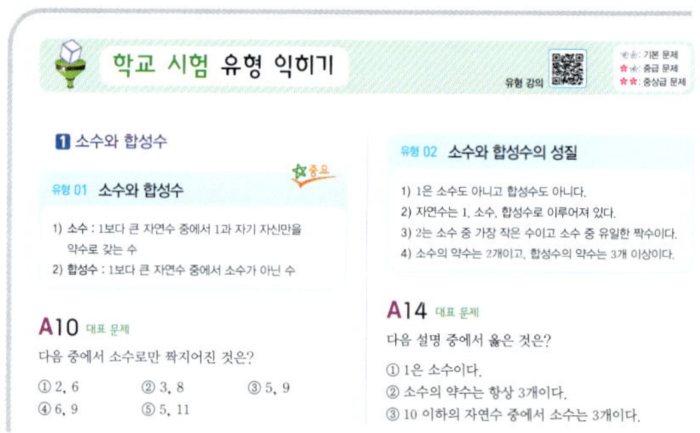

- 학교 시험에 출제되는 모든 유형을 정확히 파악할 수 있습니다.
- 최대 유형 훈련으로 개념을 확장시켜 문제를 쉽게 풀 수 있어 수학 실력이 쑥쑥 오릅니다.

03 서술형 다지기

- 어려워 하는 서술형 문제를 단계별로 익힐 수 있습니다.
- 스스로 서술하는 연습을 충분히 하면 학교 시험 서술형 문제가 쉽게 느껴질 것입니다.

04 고난도 도전 문제

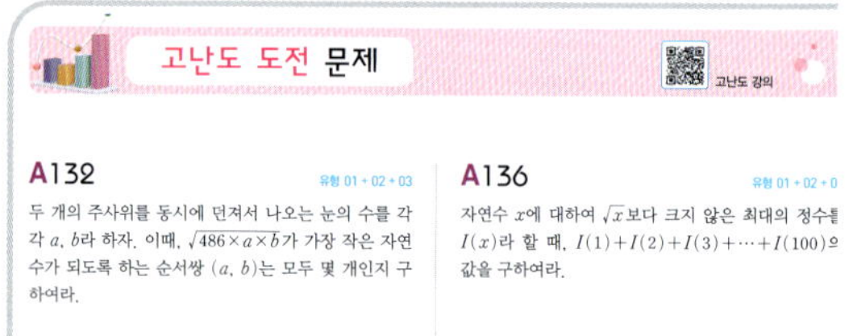

- 여러 개념이 복합된 고난도 문제의 접근 방법을 배우고 익힙니다.
- 수학적 사고력을 확장시켜 학교 시험에서 100점을 받을 수 있습니다.

중·고등 수학 100점을 위한 교재!!

중등 수력충전

수학의 기초 실력 완성
- 쉬운 문제들로 기본 연산력 강화 및 수학 실력 향상
- 풀이 과정을 채워 가면서 스스로 수학의 연산 원리를 터득
- 단원별, 유형별로 문제를 제시하여 부족한 부분 집중 학습

고등 수력충전

기초 개념을 잡는 최적의 시스템
- 기초 연산에 약한 학생들을 위한 적절한 문제
- 기본 개념을 확실히 잡아주는 최적의 시스템
- 유형별로 구성되어 체계화시키기 좋은 구성

수력충전 초·중등 수학개념 총정리

초·중등 수학 개념을 영역별로 총정리하는 필수 개념서!
- 2015 개정 교육과정의 중등 전학년 수학 개념을 한 권으로 총정리 [중등 수학 개념 총정리]
- 필수 개념을 이해하기 쉽게 정리하고, 고등 수학 개념과 연계성 강화
- 개념 완성 테스트 + 영역별 총정리 + 중등·고등 연결 문제로 실력 향상 [초등 수학 개념 총정리]

중등 자이스토리

필수 유형과 서술형 문제 완벽 훈련
- 중등 수학의 모든 개념과 유형의 완벽 학습
- 친근한 대화체 풀이와 단계별 해설로 이해력 향상
- 잘 틀리는 유형의 철저한 대비를 위한 쌍둥이 문제 제시

고등 자이스토리

대한민국 수능 교재 완결판!!
- 수능에 맞춘 유형 분류 및 문항 구성
- 학교시험과 수능 대비를 한 번에 완성 – 고2 자이스토리
- 출제 0순위 개념 정리, 기출 분석에 따른 문항 배치
- 다시는 안 틀리게 하는 입체 첨삭 해설

고등 일등급 수학

학교 시험 + 수능 일등급을 위한 고품격 유형서
- 깔끔하고 순도 높은 명품 문제
- 학교 시험 + 수능 빈출 유형에 대한 완벽한 해법 제시
- 고난도 수능 문제 유형에 대한 가장 효율적인 대비책

해설편

Xi ST🇬🇧RY

고등 영문법 기본

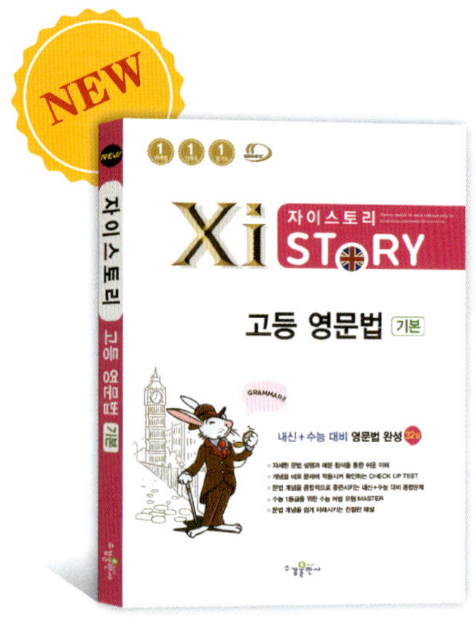

내신＋수능 대비 영문법 완성 32일

- 자세한 문법 설명과 예문 첨삭을 통한 **쉬운 이해**
- 개념을 바로 문제에 적용시켜 확인하는 **CHECK UP TEST**
- 문법 개념을 종합적으로 훈련시키는 **내신＋수능 대비 종합문제**
- 수능 1등급을 위한 **수능 어법 유형 MASTER**
- 문법 개념을 쉽게 이해시키는 **친절한 해설**
- 단원별 개념 설명 ＋ 문제 풀이 **동영상 강의 QR코드**

Step1 예문으로 직접 확인하며 쉽게 이해하는 문법 개념!

Step2 공부한 문법 개념을 확실히 이해시키는 CHECK UP TEST!

Step3 여러 문법 개념을 종합적으로 적용시키는 실전 훈련 종합문제!

Step4 실제 수능에 출제되는 어법 유형을 그대로 구현한 수능 어법 유형 마스터!

📚 자이스토리 중등 영어 시리즈

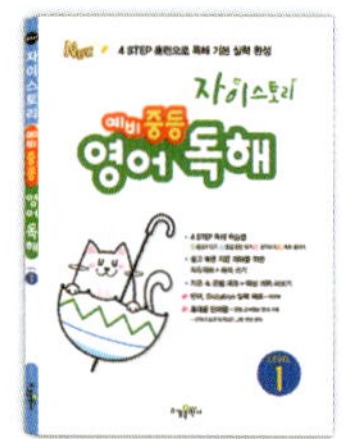

영어 독해 [예비 중등]

Level 1
Level 2

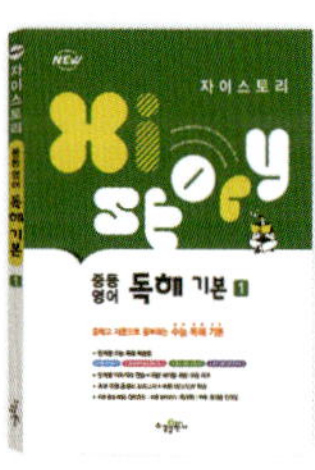

영어 독해 기본

Level 1
Level 2
Level 3

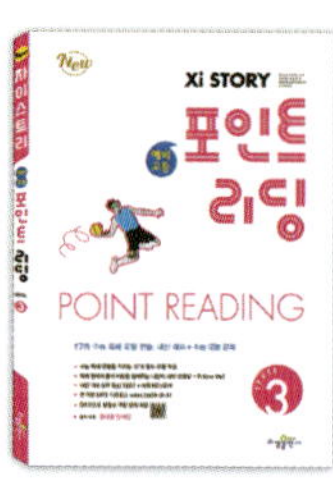

포인트 리딩

Level 1
Level 2
Level 3
Level 4

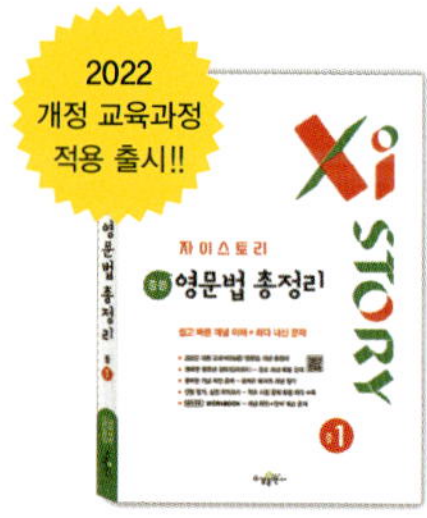

영문법 총정리

중1 / 중2 / 중3

듣기 총정리 모의고사

중1 / 중2

중3 / 고1

차 례

A 문장의 기초

UNIT 01 8품사와 문장의 구성 요소

01 부사, 전치사 **02** 대명사, 형용사 **03** 감탄사, 동사
04 동사, 명사 **05** 동사, 전치사 **06** 접속사, 형용사
07 S, V, C **08** S, V, O, C **09** S, V, O, O
10 V, O, M **11** S, M, V, C **12** S, V, M, M
13 Will you show me the ticket?
14 There are ten songs in his new album.
15 One of my friends was running to school.
16 His parents want him to be a musical star.
17 I enjoy watching horror movies in the dark.

01 정답 **부사, 전치사**
[해석] 나뭇잎 하나가 나무에서 천천히 떨어졌다.
→ slowly는 부사, from은 전치사이다.

02 정답 **대명사, 형용사**
[해석] 역사는 우리에게 많은 것을 가르쳐 준다.
→ us는 대명사, things를 수식하는 many는 형용사이다.

03 정답 **감탄사, 동사**
[해석] 우와! 저기 그림 좀 봐.
→ Wow는 감탄사, Look은 동사이다.

04 정답 **동사, 명사**
[해석] 나는 아침 7시 30분에 학교에 간다.
→ go는 동사, morning은 명사이다.

05 정답 **동사, 전치사**
[해석] 나는 장래에 언론인이 되고 싶다.
→ want는 동사, in은 전치사이다.

06 정답 **접속사, 형용사**
[해석] 가을에 나뭇잎은 빨갛고 노랗게 변한다.
→ and는 접속사, turn의 주격 보어로 온 yellow는 형용사이다.

07 정답 **S, V, C**
[해석] 그 열대 과일은 신맛이 난다.
→ sour는 tastes의 주격 보어이다.

08 정답 **S, V, O, C**
[해석] 내 딸은 나를 행복하게 만들었다.
→ me는 목적어, happy는 목적격 보어이다.

09 정답 **S, V, O, O**
[해석] 김 선생님은 우리에게 한국사를 가르치실 것이다.
→ us는 간접목적어, Korean history는 직접목적어이다.

10 정답 **V, O, M**
[해석] 너의 집 앞에 사과나무를 심어라.
→ 동사로 시작하는 명령문이고, in front of your house는 수식어이다.

11 정답 **S, M, V, C**
[해석] 그녀의 여동생은 마침내 유명한 피아니스트가 되었다.
→ finally는 수식어, a famous pianist는 became의 주격 보어이다.

12 정답 **S, V, M, M**
[해석] 그녀는 버스 정류장에서 오랫동안 기다렸다.
→ for a long time, at the bus stop은 수식어이다.

13 정답 **Will you show me the ticket?**
→ show는 4형식 동사로 간접목적어와 직접목적어를 취한다.

14 정답 **There are ten songs in his new album.**
→ 1형식 문장으로 in his new album은 부사구이다.

15 정답 **One of my friends was running to school.**
→ '학교로 달려가다'는 run to school이라고 쓴다.

16 정답 **His parents want him to be a musical star.**
→ want는 5형식 문장에 쓰일 때 목적격 보어로 to부정사를 취한다.

17 정답 **I enjoy watching horror movies in the dark.**
→ enjoy는 동명사를 목적어로 취한다.

UNIT 02 1형식 문장과 2형식 문장

01 is **02** rises **03** matters
04 are **05** goes
06 a famous singer **07** cooler
08 fell **09** open **10** getting
11 수식어, 주어, 동사, 수식어, 1형식
12 주어, 수식어, 동사, 보어, 2형식
13 주어, 동사, 보어, 수식어, 2형식
14 수식어, 동사, 주어, 수식어, 1형식

01 정답 **is**
[해석] 여기 오늘 밤 콘서트 티켓이 있어요.
→ 1형식 문장으로, 주어 your ticket이 단수로 쓰였으므로 be동사의 단수형 is를 써야 한다.

02 정답 **rises**
[해석] 여름엔 바다 근처에서 해가 일찍 뜬다.
→ 1형식 문장으로, '뜨다, 오르다'를 의미하는 rises가 알맞다.

03 정답 matters

[해석] 네가 행복하기만 하다면 그 외에 다른 것은 문제가 안 된다.

→ nothing과 같은 부정대명사가 주어로 쓰이면 단수 취급하므로 matter에 -s를 붙여야 한다.

04 정답 are

[해석] 지금 공원에 많은 사람들이 있다.

→ 주어 people이 복수로 쓰였으므로 be동사의 복수형 are를 써야 한다.

05 정답 goes

[해석] 그녀의 오빠는 항상 자전거로 학교에 간다.

→ 주어 Her older brother가 단수이므로 goes를 써야 한다.

06 정답 a famous singer

[해석] 그는 유명한 가수가 되었다.

→ 동사 became의 주격 보어로 명사구 a famous singer가 와야 한다.

07 정답 cooler

[해석] 너는 샤워 후에 더 시원하게 느낄 것이다.

→ feel의 주격 보어로는 형용사가 온다. cooler는 형용사의 비교급이고, coolly는 부사이다.

08 정답 fell

[해석] Anna의 아기는 그녀의 등에서 잠들었다.

→ '잠들다'는 fall asleep이라고 쓴다.

09 정답 open

[해석] 책 몇 권이 그의 책상 위에 계속 펼쳐져 있다.

→ keep은 '(어떤 상태를) 유지하다'라는 뜻으로 형용사 보어를 필요로 한다.

10 정답 getting

[해석] 요즘 한국의 날씨는 점점 더 따뜻해지고 있다.

→ 형용사의 비교급 보어를 취해 '점점 ~해지다'라는 의미를 만드는 동사는 get이다.

11 정답 **수식어, 주어, 동사, 수식어, 1형식**

[해석] 〈보기〉 지구는 태양 주위를 돈다.

지난달에 Julie가 호주로 떠났다.

→ 「주어+동사」로 이루어진 1형식 문장이다.

12 정답 **주어, 수식어, 동사, 보어, 2형식**

[해석] 사진 속 사람들은 행복해 보인다.

→ 「주어+동사+보어」로 이루어진 2형식 문장이다.

13 정답 **주어, 동사, 보어, 수식어, 2형식**

[해석] 요가는 너에게 가장 좋은 운동이 될 수 있다.

→ 「주어+동사+보어」로 이루어진 2형식 문장이다.

14 정답 **수식어, 동사, 주어, 수식어, 1형식**

[해석] 모퉁이에 우체국이 있다.

→ 「주어+동사」로 이루어진 1형식 문장이다.

개념 확인 문제 정답 ▶ 문제편 p.21

01 laid **02** with **03** for

04 reach **05** with my sister

06 look up to

07 Could you make some snacks for us?

08 Ms. Lee sent Christmas gifts to her students.

09 Can you show the way to City Hall to me?

10 She cooked a wonderful dinner for her mother.

11 He resembles his grandfather very much.

12 You should tell the king the truth.

또는 You should tell the truth to the king.

13 I'll find you your lost puppy.

또는 I'll find your lost puppy for you.

14 This beautiful scenery reminds me of my hometown.

01 정답 laid

[해석] 그는 가방을 책상 위에 놓았다.

→ '놓다'는 lay이고, 과거형은 laid이다. lied는 '거짓말하다'라는 뜻의 동사 lie의 과거형이다.

02 정답 with

[해석] 회사는 직원들에게 집을 제공할 것이다.

→ provide A with B의 형태로 'A에게 B를 제공하다'라는 뜻으로 쓰인다.

03 정답 for

[해석] 네 쿠키 요리법에 있는 버터 대신 기름을 사용해도 될까?

→ 'A를 B 대신 사용하다'는 substitute A for B라고 쓴다.

04 정답 reach

[해석] 네가 최선을 다한다면 너의 목표에 도달할 수 있다.

→ reach는 '~에 도달하다'라는 뜻의 타동사로 전치사 없이 목적어를 취한다.

05 정답 with my sister

[해석] 나의 엄마는 늘 나와 내 여동생을 비교하신다.

→ 'A와 B를 비교하다'는 compare A with B라고 쓴다.

06 정답 look up to

[해석] 너는 어렸을 때 누구를 우러러봤니?

→ look up은 '올려다보다', look up at은 '쳐다보다', look up to는 '~을 우러러보다'라는 뜻이다.

07 정답 Could you make some snacks for us?

[해석] 당신은 우리에게 간식을 좀 만들어 주실 수 있나요?

→ make는 3형식으로 만들 때 간접목적어 앞에 전치사 for를 쓴다.

08 정답 Ms. Lee sent Christmas gifts to her students.

[해석] 이 선생님은 그녀의 학생들에게 크리스마스 선물을 보냈다.

→ send는 3형식으로 만들 때 간접목적어 앞에 전치사 to를 쓴다.

09 정답 Can you show the way to City Hall to me?

[해석] 너는 나에게 시청으로 가는 길을 알려줄 수 있니?

→ show는 3형식으로 만들 때 간접목적어 앞에 전치사 to를 쓴다.

10 정답 She cooked a wonderful dinner for her mother.

[해석] 그녀는 어머니께 훌륭한 저녁 식사를 요리해 드렸다.

→ cook은 3형식으로 만들 때 간접목적어 앞에 전치사 for를 쓴다.

11 정답 He resembles his grandfather very much.

→ resemble은 타동사로 전치사를 수반하지 않는다.

12 정답 You should tell the king the truth.
또는 You should tell the truth to the king.

→ tell은 「간접목적어+직접목적어」의 어순으로 4형식으로 쓸 수 있고, 「직접목적어+전치사 to+간접목적어」의 어순으로 3형식으로도 쓸 수 있다.

13 정답 I'll find you your lost puppy.
또는 I'll find your lost puppy for you.

→ find는 「간접목적어+직접목적어」의 어순으로 4형식으로 쓸 수 있고, 「직접목적어+전치사 for+간접목적어」의 어순으로 3형식으로도 쓸 수 있다.

14 정답 This beautiful scenery reminds me of my hometown.

→ 'A에게 B를 생각나게 하다'는 remind A of B라고 쓴다.

UNIT 04 5형식 문장

개념 확인 문제 정답　　　▶ 문제편 p.23

01 running　　**02** repaired　　**03** kind
04 shocked　　**05** understood　　**06** amused
07 engaged　　**08** danced → dance 또는 dancing
09 to look → look　　**10** come → to come
11 sat → to sit, was → to be
12 staying → to stay　　**13** to leave → leave
14 chairperson　　**15** touching　　**16** have
17 putting　　**18** encouraged
19 very comfortable　　**20** watched
21 to become

---

01 정답 running

[해석] 그들은 밤새도록 엔진이 돌아가게 놔두었다.

→ 목적어 the engine과의 관계가 능동이므로 현재분사 running이 알맞다.

02 정답 repaired

[해석] 그는 자신의 차를 정비소에서 수리했다.

→ 목적어 his car와의 관계가 수동이므로 과거분사 repaired가 알맞다.

03 정답 kind

[해석] 그 소녀들은 그가 친절하고 관대하다고 생각했다.

→ think의 목적격 보어로 쓰인 형용사 generous와 and로 연결되어 있으므로 형용사 kind로 써야 한다.

04 정답 shocked

[해석] 그 영화는 나를 충격받고 말문이 막힌 상태로 만들었다.

→ 목적어 me와의 관계가 수동이므로 과거분사 shocked가 알맞다.

05 정답 understood

[해석] 그녀는 스페인어가 통하지 않았다.

→ '언어가 통하다'는 의미일 때 make oneself understood를 쓴다.

06 정답 amused

[해석] 보모는 아이들을 몇 시간 동안 계속 즐겁게 해 주었다.

→ 아이들이 즐거움을 느끼는 수동의 관계이므로 목적격 보어로 과거분사를 써야 한다.

07 정답 engaged

[해석] 선생님은 학생들이 토론에 몰입한 상태로 있게 했다.

→ 목적어 the students와의 관계가 수동이므로 과거분사 engaged가 알맞다.

08 정답 danced → dance 또는 dancing

[해석] 나는 그가 거리에서 춤추는 것을 보았다.

→ 지각동사 see의 목적격 보어로는 원형부정사나 현재분사가 온다.

09 정답 to look → look

[해석] 이 드레스는 나를 뚱뚱해 보이게 한다.

→ 사역동사 make의 목적격 보어로는 원형부정사가 온다.

10 정답 come → to come

[해석] 나는 그들이 집에 일찍 올 것이라고 기대하지 않는다.

→ expect의 목적격 보어로는 to부정사가 온다.

11 정답 sat → to sit, was → to be

[해석] 그녀는 그들에게 앉아서 조용히 하라고 명령했다.

→ order는 목적격 보어로 to부정사를 취한다. 목적격 보어가 and에 의해 병렬로 연결되어 있다는 것에 주의해야 한다.

12 정답 staying → to stay

[해석] 그녀의 부모님은 그녀가 늦게까지 집에 안 들어오는 것을 허락하지 않을 것이다.

→ allow는 목적격 보어로 to부정사를 취한다.

13 [정답] to leave → leave

[해석] 그는 그의 학생들이 교실을 떠나도록 허락하지 않을 것이다.

→ 사역동사 let은 목적격 보어로 원형부정사를 취한다.

14 [정답] chairperson

[해석] 우리는 Paul을 의장으로 뽑았다.

→ choose는 목적격 보어로 명사나 형용사를 취한다.

15 [정답] touching

[해석] 그녀는 어떤 손이 그녀의 머리카락을 만지고 있는 것을 느꼈다.

→ 지각동사 feel은 목적격 보어로 원형부정사나 현재분사를 취한다.

16 [정답] have

[해석] 너는 그가 제 마음대로 하게 내버려 두어서는 안 된다.

→ 사역동사 let은 목적격 보어로 원형부정사를 취한다.

17 [정답] putting

[해석] 나는 네가 열쇠를 네 가방에 넣는 것을 봤다.

→ 지각동사 see는 목적격 보어로 원형부정사나 현재분사를 취한다.

18 [정답] encouraged

[해석] 은행은 사람들에게 대출을 받으라고 장려했다.

→ 목적격 보어로 to부정사가 쓰였으므로 encouraged가 알맞다. 사역동사 make의 목적격 보어로는 원형부정사가 와야 한다.

19 [정답] very comfortable

[해석] 우리는 그 좌석이 매우 편안하다는 것을 알았다.

→ find는 목적격 보어로 명사나 형용사를 취한다.

20 [정답] watched

[해석] 어머니는 그녀의 아이들이 놀이터에서 노는 것을 지켜보았다.

→ watch는 목적격 보어로 원형부정사나 현재분사를 취한다.

21 [정답] to become

[해석] 그들은 그가 성공한 감독이 될 거라고 기대하지 않는다.

→ expect는 목적격 보어로 to부정사를 취한다.

A
Unit
01-04

단원 평가 문제 UNIT 01 ~ UNIT 04 ▶문제편 p.24~28

정답

01 ④	02 ③	03 ⑤	04 ①
05 ③	06 ④	07 ④	08 ④
09 ②	10 to play	11 are	12 to join
13 attractive		14 for him	15 fresh
16 called	17 ①	18 ③	19 ⑤
20 ①	21 ⑤	22 marry with → marry	

23 softly → soft 　**24** for → to

25 his good old days → of his good old days

26 being → 삭제 또는 to be　**27** ⑤　**28** ①

29 My boss gave me a challenging project.

30 She made chocolate cookies for her children.

31 My mother doesn't let me stay up late.

32 ②	33 ④	34 ④	35 ⑤	36 ④
37 ⑤	38 ②	39 ②	40 ②	41 ③
42 ③				

---

01 [정답] ④ 　　　　UNIT 03 3형식 문장과 4형식 문장

[해석] 아버지는 ① 민수에게 ② 그에게 ③ 그들에게 ⑤ 내 여동생에게 예쁜 인형들을 사주었다.

→ 4형식 문장의 간접목적어 자리이다. 간접목적어는 명사 또는 대명사의 목적격이 와야 하므로 ④ ours(소유대명사)는 올 수 없다.

02 [정답] ③ 　　　　　　　UNIT 04 5형식 문장

[해석] 그 선생님은 그를 ① 천재 ② 점잖은 ④ 골칫덩어리 ⑤ 좋은 지지자로 여기셨다.

→ 5형식 문장의 목적격 보어 자리이다. 그를 '친절'로 여긴 것은 적절하지 않으므로 ③ kindness 대신에 형용사 형태인 kind가 와야 한다.

03 [정답] ⑤ 　　　　　　　UNIT 04 5형식 문장

[해석] 그는 그 벽을 ① 파랗게 ② 튼튼하게 ③ 높게 ④ 초록색으로 만들었다.

→ 5형식 문장의 목적격 보어 자리이다. 목적격 보어로 부사는 올 수 없으므로 ⑤이 정답이다.

04 [정답] ① 　　　　UNIT 03 3형식 문장과 4형식 문장

[해석] 그녀는 우리에게 집에서 만든 쿠키를 ② 가져왔다 ③ 주었다 ④ 제공했다 ⑤ 보여주었다.

→ buy는 4형식 문장을 3형식 문장으로 전환할 때 간접목적어 앞에 전치사 for를 쓰므로 ①은 올 수 없다.

05 [정답] ③ 　　　　UNIT 02 1형식 문장과 2형식 문장

[해석] 그 개는 낯선 사람들을 보고 크게 짖는다.

→ 「주어 + 동사」로 이루어진 1형식 문장이다. 수식어구가 와야 하므로 '크게'를 의미하는 부사 ③ loudly가 알맞다.

06 [정답] ④ 　　　　UNIT 02 1형식 문장과 2형식 문장

[해석] 그 케이크는 맛있는 냄새가 난다.

→ smells의 보어 자리이다. 보어로는 명사 또는 형용사가 올 수 있으므로 '맛있는'을 의미하는 형용사 ④ delicious가 알맞다.

07 정답 ④　　　　　UNIT **03** 3형식 문장과 4형식 문장

[해석] 나는 오늘 아침에 내 반려동물을 씻겼다.
→ washed의 목적어 자리이다. '내 반려동물'을 의미하는 명사구 ④ my pet이 알맞다.

08 정답 ④　　　　　UNIT **04** 5형식 문장

[해석] 그 감독은 모든 직원들이 그들 자신의 일에 집중하도록 만들었다.
→ 목적격 보어로 원형부정사를 취할 수 있는 동사는 사역동사인 ④ made이다.

09 정답 ②　　　　　UNIT **02** 1형식 문장과 2형식 문장

[해석] 그의 아버지는 그 소식에 놀라 보였다.
→ surprised라는 과거분사를 보어로 취할 수 있는 2형식 동사는 ② appeared이다.

10 정답 to play　　　　　UNIT **04** 5형식 문장

[해석] 그는 내가 밤 11시 넘어서 컴퓨터를 하도록 허락하지 않았다.
→ allow는 5형식 동사로 사용될 때 to부정사를 목적격 보어로 취한다.

11 정답 are　　　　　UNIT **02** 1형식 문장과 2형식 문장

[해석] 지금 교실에 많은 학생들이 있다.
→ 「There+be동사」 구문에서 동사는 뒤의 주어에 일치시키므로, a number of students에 일치시켜 복수형 동사 are가 되어야 한다.

12 정답 to join　　　　　UNIT **04** 5형식 문장

[해석] 그녀는 영어 동아리에 가입하라고 나를 부추겼다.
→ encourage는 목적격 보어로 to부정사를 취한다.

13 정답 attractive　　　　　UNIT **02** 1형식 문장과 2형식 문장

[해석] 산 속의 오래된 집은 매력적으로 보였다.
→ 동사 look은 형용사 보어를 취한다.

14 정답 for him　　　　　UNIT **03** 3형식 문장과 4형식 문장

[해석] 나는 그에게 멋진 차를 사 주고 싶다.
→ buy가 '~에게 …을 사 주다'라는 뜻으로 3형식 문장에 쓰일 때 '~에게'는 「for+목적격」으로 쓴다.

15 정답 fresh　　　　　UNIT **02** 1형식 문장과 2형식 문장

[해석] 이 차가운 음료는 우리를 상쾌하게 만든다.
→ feel 다음에는 보어로 형용사가 온다.

16 정답 called　　　　　UNIT **04** 5형식 문장

[해석] 그녀는 선생님이 그녀의 이름을 부르는 것을 들었다.
→ 그녀의 이름이 그녀의 선생님에 의해 '불리는' 수동의 관계이므로 과거분사로 써야 한다.

17 정답 ①　　　　　UNIT **02** 1형식 문장과 2형식 문장

[해석] 내 남동생은 새로운 직장에 만족한다.
① 그는 긴 여행 후에 피곤해 보인다.
② 그는 내 생일에 나에게 선물을 주었다.
③ Tom은 어제 새 전화기를 샀다.
④ 그들은 지난 주말에 박물관을 방문했다.
⑤ 선생님은 학생들이 도서관에서 공부하고 있는 것을 발견했다.

18 정답 ③　　　　　UNIT **02** 1형식 문장과 2형식 문장

[해석] 그 아이들은 공원에서 재미있게 놀았다.
① 그 소식은 그녀를 속상하게 만들었다.
② 그들은 우리에게 큰 할인을 제공했다.
③ 그들은 공항에 제시간에 도착했다.
④ 저녁에 날씨가 추워졌다.
⑤ 그들은 그 연구 결과에 만족한다.
→ 주어진 문장은 「주어+동사+수식어구」로 이루어진 1형식 문장이다. 이와 같은 구조의 문장은 ③이다. ① 5형식 ② 4형식 ④, ⑤ 2형식

19 정답 ⑤　　　　　UNIT **04** 5형식 문장

[해석] 너는 그들이 더 열심히 일하도록 격려할 수 있다.
① 태양은 동쪽에서 뜬다. ② 그 나무는 점점 더 커졌다.
③ 그녀는 그녀의 아들을 위해 맛있는 케이크를 만들었다.
④ 모든 선수들이 게임에서 최선을 다했다.
⑤ Daniel은 무언가가 그의 팔 위를 기어 다니는 것을 느꼈다.
→ 주어진 문장은 「encourage+목적어+to부정사」의 5형식 구조이다. 이와 같은 구조의 문장은 목적어와 목적격 보어를 동시에 갖는 ⑤이다. ① 1형식 ② 2형식 ③, ④ 3형식

20 정답 ①　　　　　UNIT **03** 3형식 문장과 4형식 문장

[해석] 그 책은 내게 나의 어린 시절을 상기시킨다.
① 아무리 안 좋은 상황에서도 한 가지 긍정적인 측면은 있다.
② 나무의 잎들이 빨갛게 변했다.
③ 어려울 때 친구가 진짜 친구이다.
④ 그녀는 바쁜 거리에서 그녀의 지갑을 도난당했다.
⑤ 강의 오염물질의 양은 증가하고 있다.
→ remind는 전치사구를 수반하는 완전타동사이므로 3형식 문장을 구성한다. 목적어를 취하는 3형식 문장은 ①이다. ②, ③ 2형식 ④ 5형식 ⑤ 1형식

21 정답 ⑤　　　　　UNIT **04** 5형식 문장

[해석] Jessy는 자신이 어느 때보다 더 건강한 것을 알았다.
① 내 이름은 Christopher Lee이다.
② David는 내게 편지를 보내곤 했다.
③ 날씨가 점점 더 더워지고 있다.
④ 매일 아침 Britney는 10킬로미터를 달린다.
⑤ 그녀는 그녀의 아버지가 동화책을 읽어 주는 것을 들었다.
→ 주어진 문장과 ⑤은 5형식 문장이다. ①, ③ 2형식 ② 4형식 ④ 1형식

22 정답 marry with → marry　　　UNIT **03** 3형식 문장과 4형식 문장

[해석] 나는 너와 정말 결혼하고 싶다.
→ marry는 전치사 없이 직접 목적어를 취하는 3형식동사(완전타동사)이다.

23 정답 softly → soft　　　　　UNIT **04** 5형식 문장

[해석] 이 로션은 너의 피부를 부드럽게 만들 것이다.
→ 목적격 보어 위치에 부사는 오지 못하므로 형용사의 형태로 바꾸어야 한다.

24 정답 for → to   **UNIT 03** 3형식 문장과 4형식 문장

[해석] 너는 교수님께 편지를 쓸 거니?

→ write는 3형식 문장에서 「직접목적어+전치사 to+간접목적어」의 형태로 쓴다.

25 정답 his good old days → of his good old days   **UNIT 03** 3형식 문장과 4형식 문장

[해석] 그 그림은 그에게 좋았던 그의 옛 시절을 생각나게 했다.

→ 'A에게 B를 생각나게 하다'는 remind A of B로 쓴다.

26 정답 being → 삭제 또는 to be   **UNIT 04** 5형식 문장

[해석] 나는 그를 긍정적이고 외향적인 사람이라고 생각한다.

→ think는 목적격 보어로 「(to be+)명사/형용사」를 취한다.

27 정답 ⑤   **UNIT 04** 5형식 분상

[해석] 어느 날, Tom의 선생님은 그에게 반 친구인 Jane의 숙제를 도와주라고 부탁했다. Tom은 처음에는 하고 싶지 않았지만, 마음을 바꾸고 그녀를 돕기로 결심했다. Tom은 Jane이 어려운 질문을 하는 것을 들었다. 그는 그것을 설명해 주었고, 그녀는 금방 이해했다. Jane은 행복해하며 "고마워, Tom!"이라고 말했다. Tom은 다른 사람을 돕는 것이 의미 있다는 것을 깨달았기 때문에 미소를 지었다.

→ (A) 목적격 보어로 to부정사 to help가 이어지므로 asked나 said가 가능하지만, said는 자동사로, 뒤에 목적어가 이어질 때는 said to의 형태로 와야 하므로 asked만 가능하다.
(B) 지각동사 heard의 목적격 보어 자리이므로 원형부정사 ask나 현재분사 asking이 가능하다.

28 정답 ①   **UNIT 02** 1형식 문장과 2형식 문장

→ (C) 1형식 문장이므로 부사 quickly가 알맞다.
(D) 2형식 동사로 쓰인 felt의 보어로 형용사 happy가 알맞다.

29 정답 My boss gave me a challenging project.   **UNIT 03** 3형식 문장과 4형식 문장

[해석] 내 상사는 나에게 도전적인 프로젝트를 주었다.

→ 3형식 문장을 4형식 문장으로 바꿀 때, 전치사를 없애고 간접목적어를 직접목적어 앞에 쓴다.

30 정답 She made chocolate cookies for her children.   **UNIT 03** 3형식 문장과 4형식 문장

[해석] 그녀는 자기 아이들에게 초콜릿 쿠키를 만들어 주었다.

→ make는 3형식으로 쓸 때 「직접목적어+전치사 for+간접목적어」의 형태로 쓴다.

31 정답 My mother doesn't let me stay up late.   **UNIT 04** 5형식 문장

[해석] 나의 어머니는 내가 늦게까지 깨어 있는 것을 허락하지 않으신다.

→ allow는 목적격 보어로 to부정사를 취하고, let은 원형부정사를 취한다.

32 정답 ②   **UNIT 02** 1형식 문장과 2형식 문장, **UNIT 04** 5형식 문장

[해석] 어느 맑은 오후, Mia는 그녀의 강아지와 함께 공원에 갔다. 날씨가 완벽해서 산책하기에 좋았다. 강아지와 함께 걷고 있을 때, Mia는 누군가가 자기 이름을 부르는 소리를 들었다. 그것은 그녀의 가장 친한 친구, Lily였다. 그들이 이야기하는 동안, Mia의 강아지가 나비를 쫓았다. Lily는 웃으며 "너의 강아지는 정말 빠르다!"고 말했다. Mia는 미소를 지으며 Lily에게 공을 던지게 했다. 그들은 잠시 함께 놀았다. 나중에 Mia의 엄마는 그녀에게 집에 오라고 전화했다. Mia는 Lily에게 다시 만나자고 약속하고, 둘은 집으로 갔다.

→ ⓐ was의 주격 보어 자리이므로 형용사 nice, sunny, good이 알맞다.

ⓑ 목적격 보어 자리에 원형부정사인 throw가 있으므로 사역동사 make, have, 그리고 준사역동사 help가 알맞다.

33 정답 ④   **UNIT 03** 3형식 문장과 4형식 문장

[해석] ① 그는 나에게 집 열쇠를 건넸다.
② 아기가 엄마를 보고 미소 지었다.
③ 그들은 발표전에 긴장했다.
④ 그녀는 파티를 위해 붉고 초록색인 드레스를 골랐다.
⑤ 쉬는 시간에 소년들은 운동장을 가로질러 소리쳤다.

→ (A)와 ④은 3형식이다. ① 4형식 ②, ⑤ 1형식 ③ 2형식

34 정답 ④   **UNIT 04** 5형식 문장

[해석] 내 자전거가 망가져서 나는 어젯밤에 그것을 수리 맡겼다.

→ 문맥상 '그것이 수리되도록 시킨다'는 의미이고 목적격 보어로 과거분사 repaired가 있으므로 사역동사 had, let, got, made는 모두 쓸 수 있다. hope는 3형식 동사이다.

35 정답 ⑤   **UNIT 02** 1형식 문장과 2형식 문장

[해석] 그 그릇 안의 수프는 ① 맵다 ② 맛있다 ③ 짜다 ④ 시다.

→ taste의 보어로는 형용사만 쓸 수 있다. sweetly는 부사이다.

36 정답 ④   **UNIT 03** 3형식 문장과 4형식 문장

[해석] ① 그들이 우리에게 그 책을 가져다 줄 것이다.
② 그는 그녀에게 질문을 했다.
③ 누가 이 소포를 Jake에게 보냈니?
④ 나의 아버지가 나에게 스마트폰을 사 주셨다.
⑤ 강당을 그들에게 보여 주겠니?

→ ④ buy는 3형식 문장으로 쓸 때 「직접목적어+전치사 for+간접목적어」 형태를 취한다.

37 정답 ⑤   **UNIT 04** 5형식 문장

[해석] ① 나는 그 진실을 알고 싶었다.
② Tom은 그녀에게 그 문제를 설명했다.
③ 너는 그 소식에 대해 궁금해할 것이다.
④ 그는 이웃들에게 몇 가지 질문을 했다.
⑤ 경찰은 그 소년이 그의 부모와 함께 안전한 것을 발견했다.

→ ⑤ 발견 당시 소년의 상태를 나타내는 목적격 보어에 해당하므로, safely는 형용사인 safe로 바뀌어야 한다.

38 정답 ②   **UNIT 02** 1형식 문장과 2형식 문장

[해석] ① 그 소년은 졸린 것 같다.
② 그녀의 최신 가방은 매우 멋져 보인다.
③ 그는 긴 여행 후에 피곤해 보인다.
④ 그녀는 빨간 드레스를 입고 아름다워 보였다.
⑤ 아이들은 영화를 보는 동안 조용히 있었다.

→ ② look, seem, feel, smell, remain 등의 동사가 2형식 동사로 쓰였을 경우 보어의 자리에는 명사나 형용사가 와야 하므로 부사 greatly는 올 수 없다.

39 [정답] ②

UNIT 02 1형식 문장과 2형식 문장, UNIT 03 3형식 문장과 4형식 문장

[해석] 몇몇 사람들은 그들의 자녀들에게 달이 초록색 치즈로 만들어졌다는 이야기를 해 준다. 이 널리 퍼진 통념은 거의 500년 전으로 거슬러 올라갈 수 있다. 사람들은 왜 그런 말을 했을까? 어떤 면에서 보면 달이 치즈를 닮았기 때문이다. 달의 어두운 반점은 치즈의 구멍과 유사하다. 달의 둥근 모양은 우리에게 치즈의 둥근 모양을 떠오르게 한다. 게다가 '초록색 치즈'는 색깔이 초록색이라는 것이 아니라 '젊다'는 의미에서의 초록색이라고 전해져 왔다.

→ (A) say는 자동사이므로 목적어를 취할 수 없으므로 tell이 알맞다. (B) resemble은 타동사이므로 전치사 없이 목적어를 취한다. (C) 'A에게 B를 상기시키다'는 remind A of B라고 쓴다.

40 [정답] ②

UNIT 02 1형식 문장과 2형식 문장

[해석] 나는 교복이 몇 가지 긍정적인 측면을 가지고 있다고 믿는다. 나는 교복을 입으면 깔끔하고 단정해 보인다. 또한 무엇을 입어야 할지 결정하느라 시간을 낭비할 필요가 없기 때문에 나는 아침에 빨리 준비를 한다. 그러나 학생들이 때때로 교복 변화에 의견을 낼 수 있으면 좋을 것이다. 만약 교복 디자인이 매년 변화된다면 교복은 멋진 스타일을 유지할 것이다.

→ (A) look의 보어로는 형용사가 온다. (B) 동사 get ready(준비하다)를 수식해야 하므로 부사 quickly가 필요하다. (C) stay의 보어로는 형용사가 알맞다.

41 [정답] ③

UNIT 04 5형식 문장

[해석] 어느 오후, Sarah의 어머니는 그녀에게 집을 청소하게 했다. Sarah는 하고 싶지 않았지만, 어머니는 그녀에게 그것을 하게 만들었다. 어머니는 청소 후에 그녀에게 아이스크림을 먹으러 가자고 약속했다. 이것은 Sarah가 청소에 대해 나은 기분을 느끼게 했다. 그녀의 남동생 Jack은 그녀가 노래하는 것을 듣고 그것이 웃긴다고 생각했다.

→ 동사 promise는 5형식 문장에서 to부정사를 목적격 보어로 취하는 동사이므로 go를 to go로 고쳐야 한다.

42 [정답] ③

UNIT 02 1형식 문장과 2형식 문장

→ 주격 보어 자리이므로 형용사 ③ funny가 알맞다. 주어 it은 감정을 '느끼는' 것이 아닌 '유발하는' 것이므로 과거분사 ④ excited는 올 수 없다.

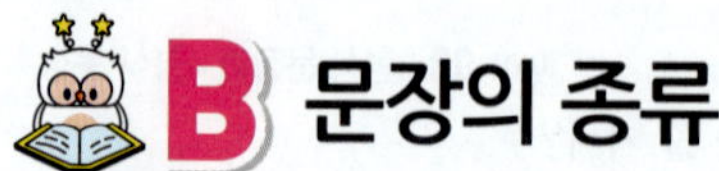

B 문장의 종류

UNIT 05 명령문, 제안문, 감탄문

개념 확인 문제 정답	▶ 문제편 p.31

01 Don't   **02** let   **03** and

04 Let's   **05** or   **06** spending

07 Work   **08** How fast Usain Bolt runs!

09 What a tall building it is!

10 It is a very difficult task.

11 What good things she has in her house!

12 How carefully he takes care of his baby!

13 a good singer she is

14 or you'll be in danger

15 ask him for advice about the problem

16 don't we take a break for a while

01 [정답] Don't
[해석] 그들이 너를 비웃게 두지 마라.
→ 부정 명령문은 Don't[Never]+동사원형 ~으로 쓴다.

02 [정답] let
[해석] 그녀가 햇빛에서 걷게 하지 마.
→ 뒤에 목적어와 목적격 보어가 오므로 사역동사 let을 써야 한다.

03 [정답] and
[해석] 나에게 모든 것을 말해 줘, 그러면 나는 너를 용서할게.
→ 문맥상 '…해라, 그러면 ~'이라는 의미의 명령문, and ~가 알맞다.

04 [정답] Let's
[해석] 그의 새 영화를 보기 위해 극장에 가자.
→ 뒤에 동사원형이 이어지므로 Let's를 써서 제안문으로 만들어야 한다.

05 [정답] or
[해석] 고기를 많이 먹지 마라, 그렇지 않으면 너는 건강하지 못할 것이다.
→ 문맥상 '…해라. 그렇지 않으면 ~'이라는 의미의 명령문, or ~가 알맞다.

06 [정답] spending
[해석] 그 돈을 우리의 여행에 쓰는 게 어때?
→ '~하는 게 어때?'라는 뜻의 표현으로 How about 뒤에 -ing를 쓴다.

07 [정답] Work
[해석] 기말고사에서 좋은 성적을 받기 위해서 열심히 공부해라.
→ 문장에 주어가 없으므로 주어 You를 생략한 명령문으로 만들어야 한다.

08 정답 How fast Usain Bolt runs!

[해석] Usain Bolt는 아주 빨리 달린다.

→ Usain Bolt는 정말 빨리 달리는구나!

→ 부사를 강조하는 감탄문을 쓸 때는 「How+부사(+주어+동사)!」로 쓴다.

09 정답 What a tall building it is!

[해석] 그것은 아주 높은 건물이다.

→ 그것은 정말 높은 건물이구나!

→ What 감탄문은 「What+a(n)+형용사+명사(+주어+동사)!」로 쓴다.

10 정답 It is a very difficult task.

[해석] 그것은 정말 어려운 과제이구나!

→ 그것은 아주 어려운 과제이다.

→ What 감탄문을 평서문으로 바꿀 때는 주어와 동사를 쓴 다음 what을 없애고 형용사 앞에 very를 붙인다.

11 정답 What good things she has in her house!

[해석] 그녀는 집에 아주 좋은 물건들을 가지고 있다.

→ 그녀는 집에 참 좋은 물건들을 가지고 있구나!

→ 「형용사+복수 명사」를 강조하는 감탄문을 만들 때는 「What+형용사+복수 명사(+주어+동사)!」로 쓴다.

12 정답 How carefully he takes care of his baby!

[해석] 그는 그의 아기를 아주 조심스럽게 돌본다.

→ 그는 정말 조심스럽게 그의 아기를 돌보는구나!

→ 부사를 강조하는 감탄문을 쓸 때는 「How+부사(+주어+동사)!」로 쓴다.

13 정답 a good singer she is

→ What 감탄문은 「What+a(n)+형용사+명사(+주어+동사)!」로 쓴다.

14 정답 or you'll be in danger

→ '…해라, 그렇지 않으면 ~'은 명령문, or ~로 쓴다. '위험에 처하다'라는 뜻의 표현은 be in danger이다.

15 정답 ask him for advice about the problem

→ '~하자'라는 뜻의 표현은 「Let's+동사원형 ~」을 쓴다.

16 정답 don't we take a break for a while

→ 제안하는 표현으로 「Why don't we+동사원형 ~?」을 쓴다.

UNIT 06 평서문, 의문문 (부가의문문, 간접의문문)

개념 확인 문제 정답 ▶ 문제편 p.33~35

01 I missed **02** doesn't **03** are planning

04 answer **05** My parents are

06 doesn't **07** did **08** will

09 can't **10** shouldn't **11** shall

12 Don't open the window too wide, will you?

13 You always wake up before 5 a.m. to exercise, don't you?

14 Let's review our notes before the quiz, shall we?

15 You haven't seen my phone anywhere, have you?

16 amn't I → am I not 또는 aren't I

17 aren't → isn't

18 is → aren't

19 I doubt if[whether] he always tells the truth.

20 Who do you think wrote this note?

21 I wonder why he can't take part in the contest.

22 What do you imagine the blue bird looks like?

23 Please tell me when the thief broke into the house.

24 Do you know if[whether] a man donated one million dollars to the orphanage?

25 The movie starts at eight o'clock, doesn't it?

26 I wonder when the teacher will return our test papers.

27 Which team do you think will get the highest score today?

---

01 정답 I missed

[해석] 나는 어젯밤에 막차를 놓쳤다.

→ 평서문은 「주어 + 동사」로 시작한다.

02 정답 doesn't

[해석] 그녀는 붐비는 장소를 전혀 좋아하지 않는다.

→ 일반동사가 쓰인 부정 평서문은 동사 앞에 do not, does not, did not을 쓴다. 주어가 3인칭 단수이므로 doesn't가 와야 한다.

03 정답 are planning

[해석] 그들은 제주도로 여행을 계획하고 있다.

→ 평서문은 「주어 + 동사」로 시작한다. planning만으로는 동사 역할을 할 수 없다.

04 정답 answer

[해석] 그는 내 질문들에 아무 대답도 하지 않았다.

→ 일반동사가 쓰인 부정 평서문은 동사 앞에 do not, does not, did not이 오고 일반동사는 원형으로 온다.

05 [정답] **My parents are**

[해석] 우리 부모님은 지금 거실에 계신다.

→ 평서문은 「주어 + 동사」로 시작한다. 동사 are가 있어야 한다.

06 [정답] **doesn't**

[해석] 그녀는 매운 음식을 정말 즐겨, 그렇지 않니?

→ 평서문의 동사가 일반동사 enjoys이므로 부가의문문에서는 3인칭 단수 부정형인 doesn't로 써야 한다.

07 [정답] **did**

[해석] 그들은 오늘 학교에 안 갔지, 그렇지?

→ 평서문의 동사가 일반동사 didn't go이므로 부가의문문에서는 조동사 did가 와야 한다.

08 [정답] **will**

[해석] 오늘 밤 너무 시끄럽게 하지 마, 알았지?

→ 부정 명령문의 부가의문문은 will you?로 쓴다.

09 [정답] **can't**

[해석] 너는 6시에 역에서 우리를 만날 수 있어, 그렇지 않니?

→ 평서문의 동사가 긍정형 can meet이므로 부가의문문의 동사는 부정형 can't로 써야 한다.

10 [정답] **shouldn't**

[해석] Tom이 무례했던 건 사과해야 해, 그렇지 않아?

→ 평서문의 동사가 조동사 should이므로 부가의문문의 동사는 부정형 shouldn't로 써야 한다.

11 [정답] **shall**

[해석] 영화 끝나고 쇼핑 가자, 어때?

→ Let's ~로 시작하는 제안문의 부가의문문은 shall we?로 쓴다.

12 [정답] **Don't open the window too wide, will you?**

→ '열지 마'라는 의미가 되어야 하므로 Don't open으로 문장이 시작하고, 부정 명령문의 부가의문문인 will you?로 문장이 끝나야 한다.

13 [정답] **You always wake up before 5 a.m. to exercise, don't you?**

→ '항상 일어난다'는 의미가 되어야 하므로 You always wake up으로 문장이 시작하고, 평서문의 동사가 일반동사의 긍정형이었으므로 부가의문문은 don't you?로 문장이 끝나야 한다.

14 [정답] **Let's review our notes before the quiz, shall we?**

→ '~하자'라는 의미가 되어야 하므로 Let's로 문장이 시작하고, 제안문의 부가의문문인 shall we?로 문장이 끝나야 한다.

15 [정답] **You haven't seen my phone anywhere, have you?**

→ '본 적 없다'는 의미가 되어야 하므로 You haven't seen으로 문장이 시작하고, 조동사 haven't의 부가의문문인 have you?로 문장이 끝나야 한다.

16 [정답] **amn't I → am I not 또는 aren't I**

[해석] 나는 너의 친한 친구잖아, 그렇지 않니?

→ I am ~으로 시작하는 문장의 부가의문문은 am I not 또는 aren't I?로 쓴다.

17 [정답] **aren't → isn't**

[해석] 광장 가운데 큰 나무가 한 그루 있어, 그렇지 않니?

→ There is ~로 시작하는 문장의 부가의문문은 isn't there?이다.

18 [정답] **is → aren't**

[해석] 네 휴대폰에 새 메시지들이 있지, 그렇지 않니?

→ There are ~로 시작하는 문장의 부가의문문은 aren't there?이다.

19 [정답] **I doubt if[whether] he always tells the truth.**

[해석] 나는 그가 항상 진실을 말하는 건지 의심스럽다.

→ 의문사가 없는 의문문은 간접의문문으로 만들 때 접속사 if나 whether를 사용하여 주절과 연결하고, 「주어+동사」 순서로 쓴다. 의문문을 만들기 위해 사용된 조동사 Does는 없애고, tell에 인칭을 적용하여 tells로 쓴다.

20 [정답] **Who do you think wrote this note?**

[해석] 너는 누가 이 쪽지를 썼다고 생각하니?

→ think, believe, suppose, imagine 등에 의문사가 있는 의문문이 연결될 때는 의문사가 문장의 맨 앞으로 온다.

21 [정답] **I wonder why he can't take part in the contest.**

[해석] 나는 왜 그가 경연 대회에 참가할 수 없는지 궁금하다.

→ 의문사가 있는 의문문은 간접의문문으로 쓸 때 주절 뒤에 「의문사+주어+동사」 순서로 쓴다.

22 [정답] **What do you imagine the blue bird looks like?**

[해석] 너는 파랑새가 어떻게 생겼다고 상상하니?

→ think, believe, suppose, imagine 등에 의문사가 있는 의문문이 연결될 때는 의문사가 문장의 맨 앞으로 온다.

23 [정답] **Please tell me when the thief broke into the house.**

[해석] 저에게 도둑이 언제 집에 침입했는지 말씀해 주세요.

→ 의문사가 있는 의문문은 간접의문문으로 쓸 때 주절 뒤에 「의문사+주어+동사」 순서로 쓴다.

24 [정답] **Do you know if[whether] a man donated one million dollars to the orphanage?**

[해석] 너는 어떤 남자가 그 고아원에 100만 달러를 기부했다는 것을 아니?

→ 의문사가 없는 의문문은 간접의문문으로 만들 때 접속사 if나 whether를 사용하여 주절과 연결하고, 「주어+동사」 순서로 쓴다.

25 [정답] **The movie starts at eight o'clock, doesn't it?**

→ '영화는 시작한다'는 의미가 되어야 하므로 The movie starts로 문장이 시작하고, 일반동사 starts의 부가의문문인 doesn't it?으로 문장이 끝나야 한다.

26 [정답] I wonder when the teacher will return our test papers.

→ 의문사가 있는 간접의문문은 「의문사+주어+동사」 어순으로 쓴다.

27 [정답] Which team do you think will get the highest score today?

→ think, believe, suppose, imagine 등에 의문사가 있는 의문문이 연결될 때는 의문사가 문장의 맨 앞으로 온다.

단원 평가 문제 UNIT 05 ~ UNIT 06 ▶ 문제편 p.36~38

정답

01 ③　　**02** ②　　**03** ⑤　　**04** ①　　**05** ②
06 ③　　**07** we → they
08 where is the post office → where the post office is
09 or → and　　**10** How → What 또는 babies → 삭제
11 it → there　　**12** do → will 또는 won't
13 ④　　　　**14** I don't know where he is from.
15 How strict your teacher is!
16 This rumor is very hard to believe, isn't it?
17 ④　　**18** ②　　**19** or　　**20** what
21 doesn't　**22** and　　**23** Why don't
24 ②　　**25** ⑤　　**26** ④
27 if, whether　　　　**28** an amazing movie
29 ②

01 [정답] ③　　UNIT 06 평서문, 의문문(부가의문문, 간접의문문)
[해석] 이 휴대폰은 중국에서 만들어졌어, 그렇지 않니?
→ 평서문의 동사가 was이므로 이의 부정형인 wasn't가 부가의문문의 동사가 되어야 하고 주어가 this cell phone이므로 it으로 받아야 한다.

02 [정답] ②　　UNIT 06 평서문, 의문문(부가의문문, 간접의문문)
[해석] 나는 그가 그 역에서 그의 친구를 만났는지 궁금하다.
→ 의문사가 없는 간접의문문을 이끄는 접속사 whether가 필요하다.

03 [정답] ⑤　　UNIT 06 평서문, 의문문(부가의문문, 간접의문문)
[해석] 우리는 이제 떠나야 해, 그렇지 않니?
→ 평서문의 동사가 조동사 should이므로 부가의문문의 동사는 부정형 shouldn't로 써야 한다.

04 [정답] ①　　UNIT 06 평서문, 의문문(부가의문문, 간접의문문)
[해석] 너는 반려동물이 없지, 그렇지?
→ 평서문의 동사가 don't have이므로 부가의문문의 동사는 do로 써야 한다.

05 [정답] ②　　UNIT 05 명령문, 제안문, 감탄문
[해석] 우리 같이 그 공포 영화 보러 가자.
→ '~하자'를 의미하는 제안문을 완성해야 하므로 ② Let's가 와야 한다.

06 [정답] ③　　UNIT 06 평서문, 의문문(부가의문문, 간접의문문)
[해석] 회의가 언제 시작하는지 말해줄 수 있니?
→ 의문사가 있는 간접의문문은 「의문사+주어+동사」 순서로 쓴다.

07 [정답] we → they　UNIT 06 평서문, 의문문(부가의문문, 간접의문문)
[해석] 한국인들은 낯선 사람들을 돕는 것을 꺼리지 않아, 그렇지?
→ 평서문의 주어가 3인칭 복수 주어 Koreans이므로 부가의문문의 주격 대명사는 they로 써야 한다.

08 [정답] where is the post office → where the post office is　UNIT 06 평서문, 의문문(부가의문문, 간접의문문)
[해석] 저에게 우체국이 어디에 있는지 알려주시겠어요?
→ 의문사가 있는 간접의문문은 「의문사+주어+동사」 순서로 쓴다.

09 [정답] or → and　　UNIT 05 명령문, 제안문, 감탄문
[해석] 그 편지를 읽어 봐, 그러면 너는 그녀가 어떤 감정인지 정확히 알게 될 거야.
→ 문맥상 '…해라, 그러면 ~'이라는 의미가 자연스러우므로 명령문, and ~로 써야 한다.

10 [정답] How → What 또는 babies → 삭제　　UNIT 05 명령문, 제안문, 감탄문
[해석] 그들은 참 귀여운 아기들이구나!
→ 형용사 cute 뒤에 명사가 있으므로 What 감탄문으로 쓰거나 babies를 삭제해서 How 감탄문으로 만들어야 한다.

11 [정답] it → there　UNIT 06 평서문, 의문문(부가의문문, 간접의문문)
[해석] 언덕 위에 큰 나무가 있었어, 그렇지 않니?
→ there is로 시작하는 문장은 부가의문문도 isn't there의 형태를 띤다. 앞의 시제가 과거였으므로 wasn't there로 쓴다.

12 [정답] do → will 또는 won't　UNIT 06 평서문, 의문문(부가의문문, 간접의문문)
[해석] 그 책들을 알파벳 순서대로 정리해주세요, 그렇게 해주겠어요?
→ 명령문의 부가의문문은 will you 또는 won't you로 쓴다.

13 [정답] ④　　UNIT 06 평서문, 의문문(부가의문문, 간접의문문)
[해석] 그 남자는 그녀가 선반에서 그 책을 ① 언제 ② 왜 ③ 어떻게 ⑤ 꺼냈는지를 안다.
→ 간접의문문 부분에서 빈칸을 제외하고 주어, 동사, 목적어가 완벽히 갖추어진 문장이므로, 의문대명사인 what은 사용할 수 없다.

14 [정답] I don't know where he is from.　UNIT 06 평서문, 의문문(부가의문문, 간접의문문)
[해석] 나는 그가 어디 출신인지 모른다.
→ 의문사가 있는 간접의문문은 「의문사+주어+동사」 순서로 쓴다.

15 [정답] How strict your teacher is!　UNIT 05 명령문, 제안문, 감탄문
[해석] 네 선생님은 아주 엄격하시다.
→ 네 선생님은 정말 엄격하시구나!
→ How 감탄문은 「How+형용사/부사(+주어+동사)!」로 쓴다.

16 [정답] This rumor is very hard to believe, isn't it?
UNIT **06** 평서문, 의문문(부가의문문, 간접의문문)

[해석] 이 소문은 믿기가 매우 힘들다.

→ 이 소문은 믿기가 매우 힘들어, 그렇지 않니?

→ 평서문의 동사가 is이므로 부가의문문에서는 부정형인 isn't가 되어야 한다. 또한 주어 This rumor는 대명사 it으로 바꾸어야 한다.

17 [정답] ④
UNIT **05** 명령문, 제안문, 감탄문,
UNIT **06** 평서문, 의문문(부가의문문, 간접의문문)

[해석] ① 그 꽃들은 정말 아름답구나!

② Ron은 그 일을 끝내지 못했어, 그렇지 않니?

③ 너의 계획을 절대 그렇게 쉽게 포기하지 마.

④ 도서관에 훌륭한 책들이 있구나!

⑤ 회의 후에 산책을 나가는 게 어때?

→ ④ 감탄문에 의해서 강조되는 부분의 명사가 books이므로 관사 a가 빠져야 한다. ① How 감탄문: 「How+형용사/부사(+주어+동사)!」 ② 평서문의 동사가 couldn't, 주어가 Ron이므로 부가의문문은 could he이다. ③ 부정명령문은 동사원형 앞에 Not이나 Never를 쓴다. ⑤ 제안문은 What about -ing ~?로 쓴다.

18 [정답] ②
UNIT **05** 명령문, 제안문, 감탄문

[해석] ① 그는 참 똑똑하구나!

② 이 사무실은 참 깨끗하구나!

③ 그녀는 정말 사랑스러운 소녀이구나!

④ 너는 정말 멋진 부모님을 가졌구나!

⑤ 너의 집은 정말 멋지구나!

→ ② How 감탄문은 「How+형용사/부사(+주어+동사)!」로 쓴다. ① intelligent 뒤에 수식 받는 명사가 없으므로 How를 사용하여 감탄문을 만들어야 한다. (What → How) / ③, ④ What 감탄문을 만들 때는 「What(+a/an)+형용사+명사(+주어+동사)!」 순서로 쓴다. (is she → she is / do you have → you have) / ⑤ your house가 문장의 주어이므로 it을 중복하여 쓸 수 없다. (your house it is → your house is 또는 it is)

19 [정답] or
UNIT **05** 명령문, 제안문, 감탄문

→ 명령문 다음의 or는 '그렇지 않으면'으로 해석된다.

20 [정답] what
UNIT **06** 평서문, 의문문(부가의문문, 간접의문문)

→ 간접의문문을 이끌면서 '무엇'이라는 의미를 가져야 하므로, 의문사 what이 와야 한다.

21 [정답] doesn't
UNIT **06** 평서문, 의문문(부가의문문, 간접의문문)

→ 평서문의 동사가 일반동사이므로 부가의문문은 조동사 do를 이용하여 doesn't로 표현해야 한다.

22 [정답] and
UNIT **05** 명령문, 제안문, 감탄문

→ '명령문 + and(그러면)' 구문이다.

23 [정답] Why don't
UNIT **05** 명령문, 제안문, 감탄문

→ you 앞에 와서 '~하는 게 어때?'라는 제안문을 완성하려면 Why don't가 와야 한다.

24 [정답] ②
UNIT **06** 평서문, 의문문(부가의문문, 간접의문문)

[해석] • 그 상자들을 내게 가져다줘, 그럴래?

• Sean은 설거지를 하지 않았어, 그렇지?

→ (A) 긍정 명령문의 부가의문문은 긍정의 will 또는 won't you를 쓴다.

(B) 부정 평서문 didn't do의 부가의문문은 긍정의 did he를 쓴다.

25 [정답] ⑤
UNIT **06** 평서문, 의문문(부가의문문, 간접의문문)

[해석] • 우리는 정시에 도착했어, 그렇지 않아?

• 너는 그 영화를 본 적이 없지, 그렇지?

→ (A) 긍정 평서문 were의 부가의문문은 부정의 weren't we를 쓴다.

(B) 조동사 have가 이끄는 부정 평서문의 부가의문문은 긍정의 have you를 쓴다.

26 [정답] ④
UNIT **06** 평서문, 의문문(부가의문문, 간접의문문)

[해석] A: 내일 해변에 가서 햇빛을 즐기자.

B: 정말 멋지네! 네가 선크림을 가져올 거야, 그렇지?

A: 물론이지! 그런데 수건도 가져오는 걸 잊지 마.

B: 고마워! 내일 정말 재미있는 하루가 될 거야!

→ 긍정 평서문이고, 조동사 will이 있으므로 부가의문문은 aren't you가 아닌 won't you가 와야 한다.

27 [정답] if, whether
UNIT **06** 평서문, 의문문(부가의문문, 간접의문문)

[해석] 내 친구 수진이가 우리 집에 와서, 나는 그녀에게 영화를 보고 싶냐고 물었다. 그녀는 적극적으로 "액션 영화를 보자!"라고 했다. 나는 동의했고, 우리는 액션 영화를 보기로 결정했다. 영화는 매우 흥미진진했다. 수진이는 "와! 이렇게 멋진 영화를 보고 있어서 너무 행복해!"라고 외쳤다.

→ 의문사가 없는 간접의문문은 「if[whether] + 주어 + 동사 + ~」 순으로 쓴다. 따라서 빈칸에는 if 또는 whether가 들어갈 수 있다.

28 [정답] an amazing movie
UNIT **05** 명령문, 제안문, 감탄문

→ What 감탄문은 「What+a/an+형용사+명사(+주어+동사)!」로 쓴다.

29 [정답] ②
UNIT **06** 평서문, 의문문(부가의문문, 간접의문문)

[해석] 오늘 아침, 나는 계좌를 개설하기 위해 은행에 갔다. 은행 직원이 다가와서 "도움이 필요하시죠, 그렇지 않아요?"라고 말했다. 나는 계좌를 개설하기 위해 무엇을 해야 하는지 물었다. 그녀는 신분증과 주소 증명이 필요하다고 알려주었다. 그 후, 그녀는 내가 서류를 작성하는 것을 도와주었다. 몇 분 후, 내 계좌가 성공적으로 개설되었다. 나는 "와, 정말 빠르네요!"라고 감탄했다.

→ ② asked의 목적어로 간접의문문이 와야 한다. 간접의문문의 순서는 「의문사+주어+동사」이므로 what I needed로 써야 한다.

 ## C 명사, 관사

UNIT 07 셀 수 있는 명사의 복수형

개념 확인 문제 정답 ▶ 문제편 **p.41~43**

01 집합명사	**02** 보통명사	**03** 보통명사
04 집합명사	**05** thieves	**06** churches
07 lives	**08** galleries	**09** bosses
10 volcanoes	**11** echoes	**12** wheels
13 women	**14** species	**15** analyses
16 teeth	**17** crises	**18** sheep
19 cacti	**20** criteria	**21** cars
22 are	**23** cattle	**24** are
25 ladies	**26** books	**27** is
28 are	**29** boxes	**30** sandwiches
31 ○	**32** diagnoses	**33** clothes
34 woods	**35** goods	**36** custom
37 manners		

---

01 [정답] **집합명사**
[해석] 그 반은 오늘 매우 시끄러웠다.
→ class는 단수 및 복수로 모두 취급하는 집합명사이다.

02 [정답] **보통명사**
[해석] 그 군중은 콘서트에 흥분해 있었다.
→ concert는 셀 수 있는 보통명사이다.

03 [정답] **보통명사**
[해석] 그 팀은 결승전을 대비해 연습하고 있다.
→ match는 셀 수 있는 보통명사이다.

04 [정답] **집합명사**
[해석] 그 소 떼는 들판에서 평화롭게 풀을 뜯고 있었다.
→ cattle은 항상 복수 취급하는 집합명사이다.

05 [정답] **thieves**
[해석] 도둑
→ -f, -fe로 끝나는 명사는 f, fe를 v로 고치고 -es를 붙인다.

06 [정답] **churches**
[해석] 교회
→ -s, -x, -ch, -sh로 끝나는 명사는 뒤에 -es를 붙인다.

07 [정답] **lives**
[해석] 생명
→ -f, -fe로 끝나는 명사는 f, fe를 v로 고치고 -es를 붙인다.

08 [정답] **galleries**
[해석] 미술관
→ 「자음+y」로 끝나는 명사는 y를 i로 고치고 -es를 붙인다.

09 [정답] **bosses**
[해석] 상사
→ -s, -x, -ch, -sh로 끝나는 명사는 뒤에 -es를 붙인다.

---

10 [정답] **volcanoes**
[해석] 화산
→ -o로 끝나는 일부 명사는 -es를 붙인다. (예외: pianos 등은 -s)

11 [정답] **echoes**
[해석] 메아리
→ -o로 끝나는 명사는 뒤에 -es를 붙인다.

12 [정답] **wheels**
[해석] 바퀴
→ 대부분의 명사는 뒤에 -s를 붙인다.

13 [정답] **women**
[해석] 여자
→ woman의 복수형은 women이다.

14 [정답] **species**
[해석] 종(種)
→ 단수형과 복수형이 같은 명사이다.

15 [정답] **analyses**
[해석] 분석
→ analysis의 복수형은 analyses이다.

16 [정답] **teeth**
[해석] 치아
→ tooth의 복수형은 teeth이다.

17 [정답] **crises**
[해석] 위기
→ crisis의 복수형은 crises이다.

18 [정답] **sheep**
[해석] 양
→ 단수형과 복수형이 같은 명사이다.

19 [정답] **cacti**
[해석] 선인장
→ cactus의 복수형은 cacti이다.

20 [정답] **criteria**
[해석] 기준
→ criterion의 복수형은 criteria이다.

21 [정답] **cars**
[해석] 우리는 도로에서 몇 대의 차를 보았다.
→ car는 셀 수 있는 보통명사이며 앞에 several이 있으므로 복수형인 cars로 써야 한다.

22 [정답] **are**
[해석] 경찰이 범죄를 조사하고 있다.
→ police는 복수로만 취급하는 집합명사이므로 복수 주어에 맞는 are로 써야 한다.

23 [정답] **cattle**
[해석] 농장에 여러 마리의 소가 있다.
→ cattle은 복수로만 취급하는 집합명사이므로 뒤에 -s를 붙이지 않는다.

24 [정답] are

[해석] 성직자들은 그 새로운 법에 반대한다.

→ clergy는 복수로만 취급하는 집합명사이므로 복수 주어에 맞는 are로 써야 한다.

25 [정답] ladies

[해석] 그 여성들은 정원에서 커피를 마시고 있다.

→ lady는 셀 수 있는 보통명사이며 뒤에 are가 있으므로 복수형인 ladies로 써야 한다.

26 [정답] books

[해석] 그녀는 서점에서 많은 책을 샀다.

→ book은 셀 수 있는 보통명사이며 앞에 many가 있으므로 복수형인 books로 써야 한다.

27 [정답] is

[해석] 디자이너는 프로젝트를 완료하기 위해 열심히 일하고 있다.

→ 단수 명사가 쓰였으므로 단수 주어에 맞는 is로 써야 한다.

28 [정답] are

[해석] 그 사람들은 그녀의 생일을 위한 깜짝 파티를 계획하고 있다.

→ people은 복수로만 취급하는 집합명사이므로 복수 주어에 맞는 are로 써야 한다.

29 [정답] boxes

[해석] 그들이 도착하기 전에 저 상자들을 정문 앞으로 가져와라.

→ 복수 명사와 함께 쓰이는 those가 앞에 있으므로 box를 복수형인 boxes로 고쳐야 한다.

30 [정답] sandwiches

[해석] 그는 지난 주말 소풍을 위해 샌드위치 몇 개를 샀다.

→ 복수 명사와 함께 쓰이는 several이 앞에 있으므로 sandwich를 복수형인 sandwiches로 고쳐야 한다.

31 [정답] ○

[해석] 그녀의 선반에는 오래된 소설들과 사진 앨범들이 가득 차 있다.

→ 복수 명사 뒤에 쓰이는 be동사 are가 있으므로 shelf의 복수형인 shelves가 알맞게 쓰였다.

32 [정답] diagnoses

[해석] 우리는 지금까지 병원에서 세 가지 다른 진단을 받았다.

→ 세 가지 다른 진단이라고 했으므로 diagnosis를 복수형인 diagnoses로 고쳐야 한다.

33 [정답] clothes

[해석] 이번 주말에 열리는 변장 파티를 위해 옷을 좀 사자.

→ 복수 형태가 될 때 뜻이 달라지는 명사로, cloth는 '천, 직물'을, clothes는 '옷'을 뜻한다. 변장 파티를 위한 옷을 사자는 내용이므로 복수형인 clothes가 알맞다.

34 [정답] woods

[해석] 그는 겨울을 대비해 장작을 모으기 위해 숲에 들어갔나요?

→ 복수 형태가 될 때 뜻이 달라지는 명사로, wood는 재료로서의 '나무', woods는 '숲'을 뜻한다. 숲이라는 장소로 들어갔는지 물었으므로 복수형인 woods가 알맞다.

35 [정답] goods

[해석] 중국은 세계 최대의 명품 시장이 되었다.

→ 복수 형태가 될 때 뜻이 달라지는 명사로, good은 '선(善)', goods는 '상품, 물품'을 뜻한다. 명품 시장에 관한 내용이므로 복수형인 goods가 알맞다.

36 [정답] custom

[해석] 발렌타인데이에 초콜릿을 주는 풍습은 일본에서 처음으로 유행하기 시작했다.

→ 복수 형태가 될 때 뜻이 달라지는 명사로, custom은 '풍습, 관습', customs는 '세관'을 뜻한다. 초콜릿을 주는 풍습에 관한 내용이므로 단수형 custom이 알맞다.

37 [정답] manners

[해석] 그녀는 식사 중에 팔꿈치를 식탁에 올리는 것은 예절에 어긋난다고 내게 말했다.

→ 복수 형태가 될 때 뜻이 달라지는 명사로, manner는 '방식', manners는 '예절'을 뜻한다. 식사 예절에 관한 내용이므로 복수형 manners가 알맞다.

UNIT 08 셀 수 없는 명사의 복수형

개념 확인 문제 정답 ▶ 문제편 p.43~45

01 water, air, sugar, milk, salt

02 ambition, courage, freedom, happiness, wisdom

03 Paris, New York, Amazon, Seoul, London

04 clothing, jewelry, furniture, machinery

05 ○ **06** ○

07 new machinery **08** Kindness

09 Korea **10** milk

11 requires **12** furniture

13 loafs → loaves **14** a → 삭제

15 slice → slices **16** bottle → a bottle

17 sauces → sauce **18** a → a pair of

19 good deals → a good deal

20 bunch **21** a **22** meat

23 jars **24** three **25** bar

26 We need a great deal of bread and milk to feed them.

27 There are six bars of soap in a box.

28 Three avocado hamburgers, a milkshake, and two colas

29 I'd like a coffee and a cheesecake

01 정답 water, air, sugar, milk, salt
[해석] 물, 공기, 설탕, 우유, 소금
→ 재료나 물질들을 나타내므로 물질명사이다.

02 정답 ambition, courage, freedom, happiness, wisdom
[해석] 야망, 용기, 자유, 행복, 지혜
→ 눈에 보이지 않는 추상적인 개념을 나타내므로 추상명사이다.

03 정답 Paris, New York, Amazon, Seoul, London
[해석] 파리, 뉴욕, 아마존, 서울, 런던
→ 세상에 하나뿐인 것의 이름을 나타내므로 고유명사이다.

04 정답 clothing, jewelry, furniture, machinery
[해석] 옷, 보석, 가구, 기계
→ 여러 개의 개체가 모여 하나의 집합이나 단체를 형성할 때 사용되는 집합명사이다.

05 정답 O
[해석] 우리는 다음 주말에 제주도로 여행을 간다.
→ Jeju Island는 셀 수 없는 고유명사이다.

06 정답 O
[해석] 그 의자는 철로 만들어져서 매우 무겁다.
→ iron은 셀 수 없는 물질명사이다.

07 정답 new machinery
[해석] 그 공장은 생산을 위해 새 기계류를 사용한다.
→ machinery는 셀 수 없는 집합명사로 관사 a와 함께 쓰지 않는다.

08 정답 Kindness
[해석] 친절은 세상을 살기 더 나은 곳으로 만든다.
→ kindness는 셀 수 없는 추상명사로 관사 a와 함께 쓰지 않는다.

09 정답 Korea
[해석] 12월은 보통 한국에서 매우 추운 달이다.
→ Korea는 셀 수 없는 고유명사로 관사 a와 함께 쓰지 않는다.

10 정답 milk
[해석] 그녀는 남동생을 위해 컵에 우유를 따랐다.
→ milk는 셀 수 없는 물질명사로 -s가 붙지 않는다.

11 정답 requires
[해석] 성공은 노력, 인내, 그리고 결단력을 필요로 한다.
→ success는 셀 수 없는 추상명사로 단수 취급한다. 따라서 동사도 3인칭 단수형인 requires가 와야 한다.

12 정답 furniture
[해석] 거실에는 현대적이고 편안한 가구가 있다.
→ furniture는 셀 수 없는 집합명사로 -s가 붙지 않는다.

13 정답 loafs → loaves
[해석] 그녀는 스테이크를 만들기 위해 소고기 두 덩어리를 샀다.
→ loaf의 복수형은 loaves이다.

14 정답 a → 삭제
[해석] 그녀는 화장에 많은 시간을 투자한다.
→ '많은'은 plenty of라고 한다.

15 정답 slice → slices
[해석] 나는 샌드위치를 만들기 위해 치즈 몇 장이 필요하다.
→ slice는 셀 수 있는 명사이므로 several 뒤에서는 복수로 써야 한다. 셀 수 없는 명사의 수량을 나타낼 때 단위명사를 복수형으로 쓴다.

16 정답 bottle → a bottle
[해석] 슈퍼마켓에 가서 소금 한 병 사 올래?
→ bottle은 셀 수 있는 명사이므로 '한 병의'는 a bottle of라고 한다.

17 정답 sauces → sauce
[해석] 간장 한 숟가락을 넣고 10분 동안 끓여라.
→ sauce처럼 셀 수 없는 명사의 수량을 나타낼 때는 명사 뒤에 -s를 붙이지 않고 단위명사를 복수형으로 쓴다.

18 정답 a → a pair of
[해석] 어린 소년이 가위로 많은 종이를 자르며 방을 어지럽혔다.
→ 가위는 같은 모양의 두 부분으로 이루어진 것이므로 a pair of scissors라고 한다.

19 정답 good deals → a good deal
[해석] 우주여행에 엄청난 돈을 기꺼이 쓰려는 사람들이 많다.
→ '엄청난 양의'는 a good deal of라고 한다.

20 정답 bunch
[해석] 네가 나에게 예쁜 튤립 한 다발을 가져다줬구나!
→ 앞에 a가 있으므로 단수형으로 써야 한다.

21 정답 a
[해석] 프린터에서 찢어진 종이 한 장을 빼줘.
→ sheet은 단수형이므로 부정관사 a가 알맞다.

22 정답 meat
[해석] 시장에서 고기를 몇 파운드나 샀니?
→ 고기는 셀 수 없으므로 단위명사 뒤에 단수형으로 와야 한다.

23 정답 jars
[해석] 아침 식사 전에 딸기잼 두 병을 열어야 해.
→ jar는 셀 수 있는 명사이므로 '두 병'은 two jars of라고 한다.

24 정답 three
[해석] 그녀는 매운 국수 세 그릇을 내주고 차도 함께 권했다.
→ bowls는 복수형이므로 three가 알맞다.

25 정답 bar
[해석] 냉장고 뒤쪽에서 초콜릿 바 하나를 찾았어. 누가 그것을 거기에 놨지?
→ bar는 셀 수 있는 명사이므로 '바 하나'는 a bar of라고 한다.

26 [정답] We need a great deal of bread and milk to feed them.

→ a great deal of는 '많은 양의'라는 뜻으로, 셀 수 없는 명사와 함께 쓴다.

27 [정답] There are six bars of soap in a box.

→ '비누 여섯 개'는 six bars of soap이라고 한다.

28 [정답] Three avocado hamburgers, a milkshake, and two colas

→ milkshake, cola는 셀 수 없는 명사지만, 주문할 때는 a, two, three 등으로 나타낼 수 있다.

29 [정답] I'd like a coffee and a cheesecake

→ coffee, cheesecake는 셀 수 없는 명사지만, 주문할 때는 a, two, three 등으로 나타낼 수 있다.

UNIT 09 명사의 소유격

개념 확인 문제 정답 ▶ 문제편 p.47

01 doctors' **02** teachers' **03** team's
04 company's **05** professor's **06** children's
07 edges' → edges of
08 parents's → parents' 또는 parent's
09 athletes → athletes' 또는 athlete's
10 girls of → girls' 또는 girl's
11 pages' → pages of **12** color's → color of
13 The boys' bicycles **14** The travelers' luggage
15 The price of the product
16 the facility of the pool **17** Eric's (plan)

01 [정답] doctors'

[해석] 의사들의 회의가 다음 주에 있다.

→ -s로 끝나는 복수 명사의 소유격은 뒤에 '를 붙여 표현한다.

02 [정답] teachers'

[해석] 교사들의 회의가 연기되었다.

→ -s로 끝나는 복수 명사의 소유격은 뒤에 '를 붙여 표현한다.

03 [정답] team's

[해석] 그 팀의 성과는 뛰어났다.

→ 단수 명사의 소유격은 뒤에 's를 붙여 표현한다. 여기서 team은 하나의 집합체로서 '팀'을 나타내므로 단수 명사로 취급한다.

04 [정답] company's

[해석] 그 회사의 정책이 최근에 바뀌었다.

→ 단수 명사의 소유격은 뒤에 's를 붙여 표현한다.

05 [정답] professor's

[해석] 그 교수님의 강의는 매우 유익했다.

→ 단수 명사의 소유격은 뒤에 's를 붙여 표현한다.

06 [정답] children's

[해석] 아이들의 웃음소리가 홀을 가득 채웠다.

→ -s로 끝나지 않는 복수 명사의 소유격은 뒤에 's를 붙여 표현한다.

07 [정답] edges' → edges of

[해석] 지붕의 가장자리가 무너지기 직전이다.

→ roof는 무생물 명사이므로 「of+명사」로 소유격을 나타낸다.

08 [정답] parents's → parents' 또는 parent's

[해석] 부모님의 조언은 믿기지 않을 만큼 유용했다.

→ parents는 -s로 끝나는 복수 명사이므로 뒤에 '를 붙여야 한다. 또는 단수 명사 parent로 고치고 뒤에 's를 붙일 수도 있다.

09 [정답] athletes → athletes' 또는 athlete's

[해석] 그 선수(들)의 유니폼이 라커룸에 있다.

→ athletes는 -s로 끝나는 복수 명사이므로 뒤에 '를 붙여야 한다. 또는 단수 명사 athlete로 고치고 뒤에 's를 붙일 수도 있다.

10 [정답] girls of → girls' 또는 girl's

[해석] 그 소녀(들)의 드레스가 옷장에 걸려 있다.

→ girls는 -s로 끝나는 복수 명사이므로 뒤에 '를 붙여야 한다. 또는 단수 명사 girl로 고치고 뒤에 's를 붙일 수도 있다.

11 [정답] pages' → pages of

[해석] 그 책의 페이지들은 노랗게 변하기 시작했다.

→ book은 무생물 명사이므로 「of+명사」로 소유격을 나타낸다. 문장의 동사가 복수형인 have이므로 복수 명사 pages는 그대로 두고 뒤에 ' 대신 of를 붙여야 한다.

12 [정답] color's → color of

[해석] 그 가죽 부츠의 색은 나에게 너무 밝다.

→ boots는 무생물 명사이므로 「of+명사」로 소유격을 나타낸다. 문장의 동사가 단수형인 is이므로 단수 명사 color는 그대로 두고 뒤에 's 대신 of를 붙여야 한다.

13 [정답] The boys' bicycles

→ -s로 끝나는 복수 명사의 소유격은 뒤에 '를 붙여 표현한다.

14 [정답] The travelers' luggage

→ -s로 끝나는 복수 명사의 소유격은 뒤에 '를 붙여 표현한다.

15 [정답] The price of the product

→ 무생물 명사의 소유격은 「of+명사」로 표현한다.

16 [정답] the facility of the pool

→ 무생물 명사의 소유격은 「of+명사」로 표현한다.

17 [정답] Eric's (plan)

→ 반복해서 나오는 경우, 소유격 뒤의 명사는 생략할 수 있다.

정답

01 ④	**02** ②	**03** works
04 The fish's fins	**05** many	
06 The oxen's yokes	**07** woods	
08 kids'	**09** ④	
10 three boxes of	**11** several pieces of	
12 five bars of	**13** two slices of	
14 ten pairs of	**15** The men's jackets	
16 The mice's nests	**17** The geese's migration	

18 It costs a huge amount of money to fix the house.

19 He eased his hunger with a loaf of bread.

20 two glasses of milk and two cheese sandwiches

21 ②	**22** ④

---

01 정답 ④　　UNIT 08 셀 수 없는 명사의 복수형

[해석] 반려동물을 기르는 것은 당신에게 많은 즐거움을 준다.

→ pleasure는 셀 수 없는 명사이므로 a great many와 함께 쓸 수 없다.

02 정답 ②　　UNIT 07 셀 수 있는 명사의 복수형

[해석] Nick은 쓰지 않는 한 쌍의 ① 신발 ③ 양말 ④ 장갑 ⑤ 젓가락을 버렸다.

→ ② glass는 단수형이므로, 쌍을 이루는 명사를 셀 때 쓰이는 a pair of와 함께 쓸 수 없다.

03 정답 works　　UNIT 07 셀 수 있는 명사의 복수형

[해석] 나는 미켈란젤로의 삶과 작품들에 관한 정보를 좀 구해야 한다.

→ '예술 작품'을 의미할 때는 works라고 한다.

04 정답 The fish's fins　　UNIT 09 명사의 소유격

[해석] 물고기들의 지느러미는 효율적으로 헤엄치는 데 도움이 된다.

→ -s로 끝나지 않는 복수 명사의 소유격은 뒤에 's를 붙여 표현한다.

05 정답 many　　UNIT 07 셀 수 있는 명사의 복수형

[해석] 서류들에는 많은 오류가 있다.

→ error는 셀 수 있는 명사이므로 many로 수식해야 한다.

06 정답 The oxen's yokes　　UNIT 09 명사의 소유격

[해석] 소들의 멍에가 헛간에 보관되어 있다.

→ -s로 끝나지 않는 복수 명사의 소유격은 뒤에 's를 붙여 표현한다.

07 정답 woods　　UNIT 07 셀 수 있는 명사의 복수형

[해석] 오래전에 사람들은 숲속에 사악한 것들이 산다고 믿었다.

→ '숲'을 의미할 때는 woods라고 한다.

08 정답 kids'　　UNIT 09 명사의 소유격

[해석] 그 아이들의 농담이 모두를 몇 시간 동안 웃게 했다.

→ -s로 끝나는 복수 명사의 소유격은 '를 붙여 표현한다.

09 정답 ④　　UNIT 07 셀 수 있는 명사의 복수형

[해석] • Carrie는 친근한 방식으로 인사했다.

• 그 가게는 신발과 가방 같은 가죽 상품을 취급한다.

• 영국에 도착해서 당신은 세관을 통과해야 할 것이다.

→ in a friendly manner는 '친근한 방식으로'라는 뜻이다. goods는 '상품', good은 '선, 좋음'이라는 뜻이다. customs는 '세관', custom은 '관습, 풍습'이라는 뜻이다.

10 정답 three boxes of　　UNIT 08 셀 수 없는 명사의 복수형

[해석] 나는 슈퍼마켓에 가서 시리얼 세 상자를 샀다.

→ cereal은 a box of로 센다.

11 정답 several pieces of　　UNIT 08 셀 수 없는 명사의 복수형

[해석] 나에게 그것에 관한 정보를 몇 개 주겠니?

→ information은 a piece of를 이용하여 세고 단위 명사를 복수로 써서 수량을 나타낸다.

12 정답 five bars of　　UNIT 08 셀 수 없는 명사의 복수형

[해석] 그는 초콜릿을 좋아해서 매일 초콜릿을 5개씩 먹는다.

→ 초콜릿은 a bar of로 센다.

13 정답 two slices of　　UNIT 08 셀 수 없는 명사의 복수형

[해석] 나는 두 장의 햄을 내 샌드위치에 얹었다.

→ ham은 셀 수 없는 명사로 a slice of를 이용해 센다.

14 정답 ten pairs of　　UNIT 07 셀 수 있는 명사의 복수형

[해석] 그녀는 청바지 입는 것을 좋아한다. 그녀는 현재 10벌의 청바지를 가지고 있다.

→ jeans는 같은 모양의 두 부분으로 이루어진 것이므로 a pair of를 이용해 센다.

15 정답 The men's jackets　　UNIT 09 명사의 소유격

→ -s로 끝나지 않는 복수 명사의 소유격은 뒤에 's를 붙여 표현한다.

16 정답 The mice's nests　　UNIT 09 명사의 소유격

→ -s로 끝나지 않는 복수 명사의 소유격은 뒤에 's를 붙여 표현한다.

17 정답 The geese's migration　　UNIT 09 명사의 소유격

→ -s로 끝나지 않는 복수 명사의 소유격은 뒤에 's를 붙여 표현한다.

18 정답 It costs a huge amount of money to fix the house.　　UNIT 08 셀 수 없는 명사의 복수형

→ money는 셀 수 없는 명사로 a huge amount of를 이용해 센다.

19 정답 He eased his hunger with a loaf of bread.　　UNIT 08 셀 수 없는 명사의 복수형

→ '빵 한 덩어리'는 a loaf of bread라고 한다.

20 정답 two glasses of milk and two cheese sandwiches

UNIT 07 셀 수 있는 명사의 복수형, UNIT 08 셀 수 없는 명사의 복수형

→ milk는 셀 수 없는 명사이며 두 잔을 주문했으므로 two glasses of milk로 쓴다. sandwich는 셀 수 있는 보통명사이며 두 개를 주문했다고 했으므로 two cheese sandwiches로 쓴다.

21 정답 ②　　UNIT 07 셀 수 있는 명사의 복수형

[해석] 어느 날 아침, 한 그룹의 사람들이 깊은 숲으로 모험을 떠났다. 그들이 숲속을 탐험하던 중, 나뭇잎 아래에서 재빨리 기어

가는 쥐 가족을 만났다. 늑대들은 멀리서 울고 있었고, 사슴들은 강가에서 평화롭게 풀을 뜯고 있었다. 갑자기, 새 떼가 날개를 퍼덕이며 조화를 이루며 노래를 불렀다. 그룹의 남자들은 더 좋은 경치를 보기 위해 더 높은 곳에 올라가기로 했고, 반면에 여자들은 여우 한 마리가 덤불 근처에서 노는 모습을 지켜보며 그 아래에 머물렀다.

→ ② mouse의 복수형은 mice다.

22 정답 ④ UNIT 07 셀 수 있는 명사의 복수형

→ (A) leaf의 복수형은 leaves, (B) fox의 복수형은 foxes이다.

UNIT 10 부정관사(a, an)와 정관사(the)

개념 확인 문제 정답			▶ 문제편 p.51
01 a	**02** a	**03** a	**04** an
05 a	**06** A	**07** The	**08** the
09 the, the	**10** a, The	**11** The, the	**12** the
13 A, the, the		**14** an → the	**15** a → the
16 an → the	**17** the → a	**18** a → the	

01 정답 a
[해석] 나는 아버지와 일주일에 한 번 하이킹을 간다.
→ '일주일에 한 번'은 once a week라고 한다.

02 정답 a
[해석] 실례지만, 버스 정류장이 어디 있나요?
→ 특정한 버스 정류장이 아니라 아무 버스 정류장 한 곳을 의미하므로 a를 쓴다.

03 정답 a
[해석] 그 그림에서 뒤로 물러나라. 조금 떨어져서 보면 더 잘 보인다.
→ '조금 떨어져서'는 at a distance라고 하고, 이때의 a는 some의 의미이다.

04 정답 an
[해석] Emily와 나는 동갑이라서 우리는 상당히 빠르게 아주 친한 친구가 되었다.
→ '동갑의'는 of an age라고 한다.

05 정답 a
[해석] 그는 새 안경이 갖고 싶어서 고의로 안경을 깼다.
→ 안경을 셀 때는 a pair of, two pairs of 등으로 센다.

06 정답 A
[해석] 5월과 6월 사이에 피는 장미는 모든 꽃들의 여왕이라고 불린다.
→ 종족 전체를 나타낼 때는 단수 명사 앞에 a나 the를 쓴다.

07 정답 The
[해석] 사자는 밀림의 왕으로 알려져 있다.
→ 종족 전체를 나타낼 때 부정관사와 정관사 모두를 쓸 수 있지만 명사의 첫 소리 발음이 자음이므로 부정관사를 쓸 때는 An이 아닌 A가 와야 한다.

08 정답 the
[해석] 참 아름답구나! 하늘에서 반짝이는 별들을 봐.
→ sky같이 유일한 사물에는 the를 붙인다.

09 정답 the, the
[해석] 사실은 달이 지구 주위를 돈다는 것이다.
→ 세상에서 유일한 것 앞에는 정관사 the를 쓴다.

10 정답 a, The
[해석] 나는 도서관에서 어떤 남자를 만났다. 그 남자는 유명한 작가였다.
→ 앞 문장에서는 불특정한 어떤 사람을 만났다는 의미이므로 a를 써야 하고, 뒤 문장에서는 앞 문장에서 말한 바로 그 남자를 말하는 것이므로 The를 쓴다.

11 정답 The, the
[해석] 컵에 담긴 차는 너무 뜨거워서 나는 입천장을 데었다.
→ tea는 셀 수 없는 명사이고 전치사구 in the cup의 수식을 받고 있으므로 The를 쓴다. of my mouth의 수식을 받는 roof 앞에도 정관사 the를 쓴다.

12 정답 the
[해석] 나는 공부에 집중할 수가 없어. 라디오를 좀 꺼 주겠니?
→ 말하는 사람끼리 서로 알고 있는 라디오를 말하므로 the를 써야 한다.

13 정답 A, the, the
[해석] 침팬지는 가장 영리한 동물로 알려져 있는데, 인간과 거의 같은 지능을 가지고 있다.
→ 첫소리가 자음이므로 A를 쓰고, 최상급, same 앞에는 the를 쓴다.

14 정답 an → the
[해석] 우리는 실직자들을 위한 일자리를 만들기를 바란다.
→ '~한 사람들'의 의미일 때는 형용사 앞에 the를 쓴다.

15 정답 a → the
[해석] 그는 값비싼 호텔에 묵었지만 이름을 기억하지 못한다.
→ 앞에서 언급된 호텔의 이름을 가리키는 것이므로 name 앞에 the를 써야 한다.

16 정답 an → the
[해석] 너는 그 지역에 익숙하니? 그 근처에서 최고의 음식점은 어디야?
→ 말하는 사람끼리 서로 알고 있는 특정한 지역을 말하는 것이므로 area 앞의 부정관사 an을 정관사 the로 고쳐야 한다.

17 정답 the → a
[해석] 나는 하루에 물 8잔 이상을 마시려고 애쓰지만 그것은 꽤 어렵다.
→ '하루에'는 a day라고 한다. 이때의 a는 per의 의미이다.

18 정답 a → the
[해석] 나는 수백 명의 음악가들을 알고 지냈지만, 그는 내가 지금까지 만난 최고의 음악가이다.
→ 최상급 앞에는 the를 쓴다.

개념 확인 문제 정답　　　▶ 문제편 p.53

01 So expensive a gift makes me uncomfortable.
02 He stayed at his cousin's house quite a long time.
03 She has taken part in singing contests half a dozen times.
04 I've never seen such a strong woman in my life.
05 This is too good a secret recipe to share.
06 the (step)　　**07** A (last summer), the (bus)
08 the (work)　　**09** the (bed), the (days)
10 the (basketball)
11 a (high school), a (college)
12 an　　**13** ×, a　　**14** a, a　　**15** ×, ×
16 The, an

---

01 [정답] So expensive a gift makes me uncomfortable.
→ 「so+형용사+부정관사+명사」 순서로 쓴다.

02 [정답] He stayed at his cousin's house quite a long time.
→ 「quite+부정관사(+형용사)+명사」 순서로 쓴다.

03 [정답] She has taken part in singing contests half a dozen times.
→ half는 「half+관사+명사」 순서로 쓰는데, 여섯 번은 half a dozen times라고 한다.

04 [정답] I've never seen such a strong woman in my life.
→ 「such+부정관사(+형용사)+명사」 순서로 쓴다.

05 [정답] This is too good a secret recipe to share.
→ 「too+형용사+부정관사+명사」 순서로 쓴다.

06 [정답] the (step)
[해석] 너는 막 지시를 한 단계씩 따라했다.
→ 관용적인 표현인 '한 걸음 한 걸음'은 관사 없이 step by step으로 표현한다.

07 [정답] A (last summer), the (bus)
[해석] 지난여름에 나는 기차와 버스로 유럽 횡단 여행을 했다.
→ '지난여름'은 관사 없이 last summer라고 한다. by 뒤에 오는 교통수단은 관사 없이 쓴다.

08 [정답] the (work)
[해석] 우리 아빠는 직장에 계시고 나는 그를 만나러 사무실에 갈 것이다.
→ '직장에 있다'는 be at work라고 한다.

09 [정답] the (bed), the (days)
[해석] 그는 지독한 감기에 걸려서 며칠 동안 아파서 누워 있다.
→ '아파서 누워 있다'는 be sick in bed라고 하며 '며칠 동안'은 for days라고 한다.

10 [정답] the (basketball)
[해석] 내 친구와 나는 농구를 하기 위해 학교 운동장에서 만났다.
→ 운동 경기 이름 앞에는 관사를 쓰지 않는다.

11 [정답] a (high school), a (college)
[해석] 나는 고등학교 3학년이라서 내년에 대학에 갈 것이다.
→ 고등학교에 공부를 하기 위해 재학 중이라는 의미이므로 in high school로 써야 하며 '대학에 가다, 대학에 다니다'는 go to college로 쓴다.

12 [정답] an
[해석] 내가 신분증을 잃어버렸을 때, 나는 멍청이가 된 기분이었다.
→ idiot은 셀 수 있는 명사이므로 앞에 부정관사를 써야 한다. 첫 소리가 모음으로 시작하는 명사이므로 an을 쓴다.

13 [정답] ×, a
[해석] 봄에는 많은 사람들이 소풍을 간다.
→ 일반적인 계절 이름 앞에는 관사를 쓰지 않는다. '소풍을 가다'는 go on a picnic이라고 한다.

14 [정답] a, a
[해석] 그녀는 변호사이자 정치인으로 모두 성공했다.
→ 직업 이름 앞에는 부정관사를 쓴다.

15 [정답] ×, ×
[해석] 나는 남미를 대대적으로 여행할 계획을 세우고 있기 때문에 스페인어를 배우고 싶다.
→ 언어 이름과 대륙 이름 앞에는 관사를 쓰지 않는다.

16 [정답] The, an
[해석] 그 경기는 갑작스러운 소나기 때문에 중단되었지만, 30분 후에 다시 시작되었다.
→ 비 때문에 중단된 경기는 특정한 경기이므로 정관사 the를 쓰고, '30분'은 half an hour라고 한다.

정답

01 bed	**02** a	**03** What a
04 such an interesting job		**05** 관사 없음
06 The	**07** ②	**08** ④
09 ③		**10** the → a
11 Sun → the Sun		**12** a → the
13 ⑤	**14** ②	
15 I take an English lesson four times a week.		
16 the last step for your promotion		
17 a hidden treasure in an old box		
18 ⑤　**19** ④　**20** ③　**21** ①　**22** ⑤		
23 ⑤　**24** ③　**25** ③　**26** ①		

01 정답 bed　　　UNIT 11 주의해야 할 관사의 쓰임
[해석] 일어날 시간이다.
→ '일어나다'라는 관용표현은 get out of bed라고 한다.

02 정답 a　　　UNIT 10 부정관사(a, an)와 정관사(the)
[해석] 그녀는 빨간 드레스를 입고 있다.
→ 뒤에 나오는 단어의 첫소리가 자음으로 시작하므로 a를 쓴다.

03 정답 What a　　　UNIT 11 주의해야 할 관사의 쓰임
[해석] 그는 내게 "너는 참 좋은 차를 가지고 있구나!"라고 말했다.
→ 「what+부정관사(+형용사)+명사」 순서로 쓴다.

04 정답 such an interesting job
　　　UNIT 11 주의해야 할 관사의 쓰임
[해석] 그것은 하기에 아주 흥미로운 일처럼 보인다.
→ 「such+부정관사(+형용사)+명사」 순서로 쓴다.

05 정답 관사 없음　　　UNIT 11 주의해야 할 관사의 쓰임
[해석] 그녀는 MIT에서 컴퓨터공학을 공부하고 있다.
→ 학문의 이름 앞에는 관사를 쓰지 않는다.

06 정답 The　　　UNIT 10 부정관사(a, an)와 정관사(the)
[해석] 국제연합(UN)은 수십 년 동안 국제 외교에서 중요한 역할을 해왔다.
→ 유일한 국제기구이므로 정관사(the)를 써야 한다.

07 정답 ②　　　UNIT 11 주의해야 할 관사의 쓰임
[해석] 이것은 나에게는 너무 어려운 문제다. 나는 그것을 아직 풀지 못했다.
→ too는 「too+형용사+부정관사+명사」 순서로 쓴다.

08 정답 ④　　　UNIT 10 부정관사(a, an)와 정관사(the)
[해석] 하루에 세 번씩 약을 먹어라.
① 내게 잠깐만 시간을 주세요.
② 같은 깃털을 가진 새들은 함께 모인다. (유유상종)
③ 선반 위에 요리책 한 권이 있다.
④ 당신은 일주일에 두 번 이 프로그램을 사용할 수 있다.
⑤ 말은 대개 신성한 동물로 묘사된다.

→ 주어진 문장과 ④의 a는 '~마다'를 의미하는 관사로 사용되었다. ①은 '얼마간의', ②은 '같은', ③은 '하나의', ⑤은 종족 전체를 나타내는 a로 사용되었다.

09 정답 ③　　　UNIT 10 부정관사(a, an)와 정관사(the)
[해석] 그 부부는 항상 거리를 두고 걷는다.
① 우리는 난민 문제에 대해 같은 생각이다.
② 나팔꽃은 아침에 핀다.
③ 그녀는 잠깐 밖에 나갔을 것이다.
④ 이 차는 한 시간에 240킬로미터를 달릴 수 있다.
⑤ 네가 나간 동안 Bill이라는 사람이 너를 만나러 왔다.
→ 주어진 문장과 ③의 a는 some과 같은 의미로 쓰였다. ①은 '같은', ②은 종족 전체, ④은 '~마다', ⑤은 '어떤'을 나타내는 a로 쓰였다.

10 정답 the → a　　　UNIT 10 부정관사(a, an)와 정관사(the)
[해석] 내가 병원에 갔을 때, 의사는 나에게 매일 사과 한 개를 먹으라고 조언했다.
→ '하루에 사과 한 개'는 an apple a day와 같이 표현한다.

11 정답 Sun → the Sun　UNIT 10 부정관사(a, an)와 정관사(the)
[해석] 지구는 어떤 예외도 없이 매일 태양 주위를 돈다.
→ 세상에서 유일한 것을 나타내는 명사 앞에는 the를 쓴다.

12 정답 a → the　　　UNIT 10 부정관사(a, an)와 정관사(the)
[해석] 우리는 항상 노인을 존경해야 한다.
→ 노인을 나타내려면 「the+형용사」의 형태인 the elderly로 쓴다. 따라서 a를 the로 고쳐야 한다.

13 정답 ⑤　　　UNIT 11 주의해야 할 관사의 쓰임
[해석] ① 너는 점심으로 무엇을 먹었니?
② 꽃병이 우연히 깨졌다.
③ 너는 전에 배구를 해 본 적이 있니?
④ 그는 3년 동안 수감되었다.
⑤ 나는 어머니가 전화 통화하시는 것을 들었다.
→ ⑤ '전화 통화하다'는 talk on the phone이라고 한다. ① for lunch: 점심 식사로 ② by accident: 우연히 ③ 운동 경기 이름은 관사 없이 쓴다. ④ be sent to prison: 감옥에 가다

14 정답 ②　　　UNIT 10 부정관사(a, an)와 정관사(the)
[해석] A: 너는 어떻게 돈을 받니?
B: 음, 회사가 나에게 한 달에 한 번 최저 임금만 줘.
→ 빈칸 앞에 once가 있으므로 '한 달에 한 번'을 뜻하려면 a month가 와야 한다. 여기서 a는 per(~마다, ~당)와 같은 의미로 쓰였다.

15 정답 I take an English lesson four times a week.
　　　UNIT 10 부정관사(a, an)와 정관사(the)
→ '일주일에 네 번'은 four times a week라고 한다.

16 정답 the last step for your promotion
　　　UNIT 10 부정관사(a, an)와 정관사(the)
→ last 앞에는 정관사 the를 써야 하므로 '승진을 위한 마지막 단계'는 the last step for your promotion이라고 한다.

17 정답 a hidden treasure in an old box
　　　UNIT 10 부정관사(a, an)와 정관사(the)
→ 정해지지 않은 막연한 보물과 오래된 상자는 부정관사 a나 an을 써서 a hidden treasure와 an old box로 쓴다.

18 정답 ⑤　　　　　　　　　　　UNIT **11** 주의해야 할 관사의 쓰임

[해석] ① 나의 사촌은 정말 예쁜 소녀이다.
② Brown은 정말 똑똑한 소년이다.
③ 내 막내 동생은 꽤 잘생긴 소년이다.
④ 이것은 놓치기에는 너무나 좋은 기회이다.
⑤ 모든 종이들이 바닥에 흩어져있다.
→ ⑤「all+관사+명사」의 어순이 옳으므로 ⑤은 All the paper가 되어야 한다.
① a very+형용사+명사 ② such+a(n)+형용사+명사 ③ quite+a(n)+형용사+명사 ④ too+형용사+a(n)+명사

19 정답 ④　　　　　　UNIT **10** 부정관사(a, an)와 정관사(the),
　　　　　　　　　　　　　　UNIT **11** 주의해야 할 관사의 쓰임

[해석] ① 탁자 위에 지루한 책이 한 권 있다.
② 그의 의견은 한 편으로는 이치에 맞는다.
③ 나는 맛있는 점심을 먹어서 배가 부르다.
④ 나는 늦어서 택시를 타고 거기에 갔다.
⑤ 이솝 우화에서 뱀은 대개 사악한 것으로 묘사된다.
→ ④「by+교통수단」에서는 교통수단 앞에 관사를 붙이지 않는다.
① 책 한 권이 있는 것이므로 a ② in a sense: 한 편으로는 ③ lunch 앞에 형용사 good이 있으므로 a 가능 ⑤ 종족 전체를 가리키는 A

20 정답 ③　　　　　　UNIT **10** 부정관사(a, an)와 정관사(the),
　　　　　　　　　　　　　　UNIT **11** 주의해야 할 관사의 쓰임

[해석] ① 내가 사랑하는 유일한 사람은 너이다.
② 우리는 가난한 사람들을 무시해서는 안 된다.
③ 그는 한가할 때 보통 축구를 한다.
④ 태양은 항성이고 달은 위성이다.
⑤ 나의 결혼기념일은 너의 결혼기념일과 똑같다.
→ ③ 운동경기인 명사 앞에는 정관사 the를 붙이지 않는다.
① the only는 '유일한'의 뜻 ②「the+형용사」: ~한 사람들 ④ 세상에 유일무이한 것이므로 the ⑤ same 앞에 붙여서 '같은'의 뜻

21 정답 ①　　　　　　　UNIT **10** 부정관사(a, an)와 정관사(the)

[해석] 그는 자격증을 유지하기 위해 일주일마다 한 번씩 온라인 교육과정을 이수하도록 요구받았다.
→ 문장에서 a week은 '일주일마다'라는 의미로 사용되었으므로 ① per와 의미가 같다.

22 정답 ⑤　　　　　　　UNIT **10** 부정관사(a, an)와 정관사(the)

[해석] 독수리는 다른 많은 새들과 달리, 멀리서도 먹이를 발견할 수 있다.
→ 문장에서 An eagle은 '독수리'라는 전체 집단을 나타내므로 ⑤ The eagle과 의미가 같다.

23 정답 ⑤　　　　　　　UNIT **10** 부정관사(a, an)와 정관사(the)

[해석] 구조대가 사고 후 부상자들을 도왔다.
→ 사람을 지칭하는 형용사 앞에 정관사 the를 써 '~하는 사람들'이라는 의미를 나타낼 수 있다.

24 정답 ③　　　　　　　　　UNIT **11** 주의해야 할 관사의 쓰임

[해석] Elvis Aaron Presley는 미국의 가수이자 배우였다. 20세기 가장 중요한 문화적 아이콘의 하나로서 간주되어 그는 종종 King of Rock이라고 언급된다. 1954년 7월 5일 그는 첫 싱글 앨범을 녹음했고 그것은 대중음악에 거대한 영향을 미쳤다. 그 이후에 그는 팝, 컨트리, 블루스, 가스펠을 포함한 많은 장르에서 상업적으로 성공을 거두었고 음악계의 역사에서 베스트셀러 솔로 아티스트가 되었다.
→ such 다음에는「a[an]+형용사+명사」의 어순이 와야 하므로 ③ such a tremendous effect on으로 배열해야 한다.

25 정답 ③　　　　　　　　　UNIT **11** 주의해야 할 관사의 쓰임

[해석] 많은 사람이 긴장을 풀고 근육통을 완화하는 데 도움이 되는 사우나, 스파, 온수 욕조를 즐긴다. 그러나 명심해야 할 것이 있다. 뜨거운 물은 혈액이 몸으로 빠르게 흐르게 만들어서 뇌에는 충분한 혈액이 도달하지 않게 만들기 때문에 뜨거운 물에 오래 있으면 어지러움을 느낄 수 있다. 사람들이 긴 목욕 후에 일어설 때 어지러움을 느끼고 기절할 수 있다. 이는 넘어져서 바닥에 부딪힐 수 있는 결과를 초래할 수 있다. 뜨거운 욕조에 들어가고 나올 때 조심해라, 그리고 기절하거나 다른 문제가 생길 경우를 대비해 다른 사람과 함께 있어라.
→ ③ water는 셀 수 없는 명사이므로 부정관사 a를 삭제하고 such hot water로 써야 한다. 필요에 따라 such 대신 정관사 the를 써서 the hot water로 나타낼 수도 있다.

26 정답 ①　　　　　　　　　UNIT **10** 부정관사(a, an)와 정관사(the)

→ (A) 우리 몸 안의 뇌, 즉 정해진 것을 언급하므로 정관사 the를 써야 한다. (B) 특정한 목욕이 아닌 '긴 목욕'을 가리키므로 부정관사 a를 써야 한다.

D 대명사

UNIT **12** 지시대명사 this (these), that (those), it

> **개념 확인 문제 정답**　　　　　▶ 문제편 p.59
>
> | | | | |
> |---|---|---|---|
> | **01** that | **02** This | **03** those | **04** this |
> | **05** that | **06** these | **07** that | **08** That |
> | **09** 비인칭주어 | **10** 가주어 | **11** 강조 구문 | **12** 가목적어 |
> | **13** 강조 구문 | **14** 비인칭주어 | **15** 앞에 나온 단수 명사 대신 | |
> | **16** ⓓ | **17** ⓒ | **18** ⓐ | **19** ⓔ |
> | **20** ⓑ | | | |

01 정답 that

[해석] 그는 실수를 하고 그것은 아주 잦다.
→ 앞에 나온 절 전체, 즉 실수를 하는 일은 아주 자주 일어난다는 뜻이므로 that을 써야 한다.

02 정답 **This**

[해석] 그는 아직 집에 오지 않았다. 이것이 나를 걱정하게 한다.

→ 앞에 나온 절을 대신하므로 This를 써야 한다.

03 정답 **those**

[해석] 나는 그들이 결코 용서 받을 수 없는 사람들이라고 생각한다.

→ '~한 사람들'은 those who라고 한다.

04 정답 **this**

[해석] 그가 내게 말한 것은 이것인데, 그는 영국으로 가고 싶어 한다는 것이다.

→ 뒤에 나온 절을 대신할 때는 this를 사용한다.

05 정답 **that**

[해석] 내 딸의 정신 연령은 그녀의 친구들의 것보다 더 높다.

→ 앞에 나온 명사구 mental age를 대신하는 that을 써야 한다.

06 정답 **these**

[해석] 결혼을 하지 않은 사람들의 숫자는 요즘 증가해 왔다.

→ '요즘'은 these days라고 한다.

07 정답 **that**

[해석] 칠레를 강타한 지진은 아이티의 그것보다 훨씬 더 강력했다.

→ 앞에 나온 the earthquake를 대신하는 말이므로 that이 알맞다.

08 정답 **That**

[해석] 그녀는 과체중이고 무릎 통증이 있다. 그것이 그녀가 살을 빼고 싶어 하는 이유이다.

→ '그것이 ~한 이유이다'는 That is why ~라고 한다.

09 정답 **비인칭주어**

[해석] 오늘은 7월 14일이다.

→ 날짜를 나타내는 비인칭주어 it이다.

10 정답 **가주어**

[해석] 미래를 예측하는 것은 어렵다.

→ It은 가주어, to predict 이하가 진주어이다.

11 정답 **강조 구문**

[해석] 내가 어제 방문했던 사람은 바로 그녀의 여동생이었다.

→ It was ~ that … 강조 구문으로 visited의 목적어 her sister가 강조되었다.

12 정답 **가목적어**

[해석] 짙은 안개는 운전하는 것을 어렵게 한다.

→ it은 makes의 가목적어이고 to drive가 진목적어이다.

13 정답 **강조 구문**

[해석] 우리가 미래의 세계를 창조하는 날은 바로 오늘이다.

→ It is ~ that … 강조 구문으로 부사 today가 강조되었다.

14 정답 **비인칭주어**

[해석] 우리가 동굴에 더 깊이 들어갈수록 더 어두워졌다.

→ 명암을 나타내는 비인칭주어이다.

15 정답 **앞에 나온 단수 명사 대신**

[해석] 나의 가족은 수족관에 갔는데, 그곳은 매우 붐볐다.

→ it은 the aquarium을 대신하는 지시대명사이다.

16 정답 ⓓ

[해석] 내 성적들은 내 쌍둥이 동생의 성적들보다 훨씬 더 낮았다.

→ 앞에 나온 명사구 my grades를 대신하는 those를 사용한다.

17 정답 ⓒ

[해석] 그가 다음 주 경주에 참가하는 것은 불가능하다.

→ 의미상의 주어가 있는 가주어, 진주어 구문이다.

18 정답 ⓐ

[해석] 우리에게 그 이야기를 읽으라고 하셨던 분은 바로 우리 영어 선생님이었다.

→ It was ~ that … 강조 구문으로 주어 our English teacher가 강조되었다.

19 정답 ⓔ

[해석] 나는 노인들에게 무례한 사람들이 싫다.

→ '~한 사람들'은 those who로 쓴다.

20 정답 ⓑ

[해석] 그녀가 그곳에 가는 데는 약 2시간이 걸릴 것이다.

→ '~하는 데 (시간이) 걸리다'는 「It takes+시간+to부정사」로 쓴다. for her는 의미상의 주어이다.

UNIT 13 재귀대명사

개념 확인 문제 정답　　　▶ 문제편 **p.61**

01 I ✔ built 또는 house ✔ and
02 teacher ✔　　**03** thrill ✔
04 she ✔ repaired 또는 glue ✔
05 we ✔ built 또는 our dog ✔
06 mom ✔ taught 또는 math ✔
07 yourself　　**08** yourself　　**09** himself
10 herself　　**11** yourself　　**12** myself
13 him　　**14** them　　**15** for himself
16 by itself　　**17** in spite of myself
18 beside himself　　　　**19** in itself
20 Between ourselves

01 정답 **I ✔ built 또는 house ✔ and**

[해석] 내가 이 집을 직접 지었고, 나의 가족이 지난달에 그곳으로 이사했다.

→ myself는 주어 I를 강조하는 재귀대명사이므로 I 뒤에 쓰거나 I가 쓰인 절이 끝나는 house 뒤에 쓸 수 있다.

02 정답 teacher ✓

[해석] Jessica는 바로 그녀의 담임선생님 본인과 이야기를 하고 싶어 했다.

→ himself는 이 문장에서 her homeroom teacher 당사자를 강조하는 용법으로 쓰였다.

03 정답 thrill ✓

[해석] 놀이공원에서 롤러코스터를 타는 것은 스릴 그 자체이다.

→ 보어 a thrill을 강조하여 '스릴 그 자체'라는 의미로 쓰였다.

04 정답 she ✓ repaired 또는 glue ✓

[해석] 구두 굽이 부러졌지만 그녀는 직접 그것을 접착제로 수리했다.

→ herself는 주어 she를 강조하는 재귀대명사이므로 she 뒤에 쓰거나 she가 쓰인 절이 끝나는 glue 뒤에 쓸 수 있다.

05 정답 we ✓ built 또는 our dog ✓

[해석] 개집을 사는 대신에 우리는 직접 우리 개를 위해 개집을 만들어 주었다.

→ ourselves는 주어 we를 강조하는 재귀대명사이므로 we 뒤에 쓰거나 문장 끝인 our dog 뒤에 쓸 수 있다.

06 정답 mom ✓ taught 또는 math ✓

[해석] 나는 수학을 잘하지 않아서 엄마가 직접 나에게 수학을 가르쳐 주셨다.

→ herself는 mom을 강조하는 재귀대명사이므로 mom 뒤에 쓰거나 mom이 쓰인 절이 끝나는 math 뒤에 쓸 수 있다.

07 정답 yourself

[해석] 네가 원하는 것은 무엇이든지 마음껏 먹을 수 있다.

→ '마음껏 먹다'는 help oneself to로 주어 you와 help의 목적어가 같은 사람을 가리키므로 재귀대명사 yourself를 써야 한다.

08 정답 yourself

[해석] 당신에게 간단히 자기소개를 해 달라고 부탁해도 될까요?

→ 내가 상대방에게 자기소개를 해 달라고 부탁하는 것이므로 yourself를 써야 한다.

09 정답 himself

[해석] 그는 자신의 생일을 축하하려고 새 재킷을 샀다.

→ 주어 He와 bought의 간접목적어가 같은 사람을 가리키므로 재귀대명사 himself를 써야 한다.

10 정답 herself

[해석] 그녀는 빙판에 넘어졌지만 전혀 다치지 않았다.

→ hurt의 목적어와 주어 she가 일치하므로 재귀대명사 herself를 써야 한다.

11 정답 yourself

[해석] 그것은 네 잘못이 아니다. 나는 네가 네 자신을 탓해서는 안 된다고 생각한다.

→ 주어 you와 같은 사람이므로 yourself를 써야 한다.

12 정답 myself

[해석] 내 남동생이 나를 화나게 했지만, 나는 진정하려고 애썼다.

→ 주어 I와 같은 사람을 가리키므로 myself가 알맞다.

13 정답 him

[해석] Peter에 대해서는 걱정하지 마. 그의 엄마가 그를 잘 보살필 거야.

→ take care of의 목적어는 Peter로 문장의 주어 His mom과 다른 사람이므로 Peter를 목적격 대명사 him으로 써야 한다.

14 정답 them

[해석] Wendy는 어디에 안경을 두었는지 잊어버려서 그녀는 그것을 찾고 있는 중이었다.

→ Wendy가 찾는 것은 her glasses로 문장의 주어 she와 일치하지 않는다. 따라서 목적격 대명사 them을 써야 한다.

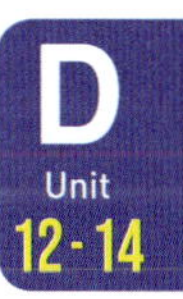

15 정답 for himself

[해석] 그 배우는 혼자 힘으로 액션 장면들을 연기하고 싶어 했다.

→ '혼자 힘으로'는 for oneself라고 한다.

16 정답 by itself

[해석] 나는 누가 들어오는 것을 보지 못했다. 나는 문이 저절로 열렸다고 생각한다.

→ '저절로'는 by oneself라고 한다.

17 정답 in spite of myself

[해석] 나는 무심코 Melissa의 비밀을 폭로했다.

→ '무심코, 자기도 모르게'는 in spite of oneself라고 한다.

18 정답 beside himself

[해석] 그를 혼자 내버려 둬. 그는 화가 나서 제정신이 아니야.

→ '제정신이 아닌'은 beside oneself라고 한다.

19 정답 in itself

[해석] 두뇌 자체는 아무런 통증을 느끼지 않는다.

→ '본래, 그 자체가'는 in itself라고 한다.

20 정답 Between ourselves

[해석] 우리끼리 하는 이야기지만, 학교를 같이 다녔을 때 그는 그녀를 좋아했어.

→ '우리끼리 하는 이야기지만'은 between ourselves라고 한다.

개념 확인 문제 정답 ▶ 문제편 p.63~67

01 one **02** one **03** ones **04** one

05 ones **06** ones **07** One, another

08 the others **09** Some **10** the other

11 others **12** one **13** One

14 Some, the others

15 One, another, the other

16 any **17** some **18** any **19** any

20 any **21** some **22** some **23** nobody

24 anybody **25** anybody **26** Somebody

27 something **28** anyone

29 Nothing **30** anything **31** each **32** was

33 each **34** guest **35** was **36** options

37 All of the boys are in the playground.

38 Both of these jackets aren't[are not] expensive.

39 All of us have to make more effort

40 Both **41** all **42** Every **43** Each

---

01 정답 one

[해석] 나는 택시를 타야 해서 한 대 불렀다.

→ 정해진 택시가 아니라 아무 택시나 한 대를 의미하므로 one 을 써야 한다.

02 정답 one

[해석] 나는 지갑을 잃어버려서 새것을 사야 한다.

→ 잃어버린 지갑을 가리키는 것이 아니고 불특정한 지갑을 가리키는 것이므로 one을 써야 한다.

03 정답 ones

[해석] 작은 고추는 종종 큰 고추보다 더 맵다.

→ 불특정한 복수 명사 peppers를 대신해야 하므로 ones를 써야 한다.

04 정답 one

[해석] 이 책이 흥미롭지 않다면 다른 것을 읽어라.

→ another book을 가리키므로 단수 대명사 one을 써야 한다.

05 정답 ones

[해석] 요즈음 어린아이들은 스마트 기기에 중독된 것 같다.

→ '어린아이들'의 의미일 때 the young ones를 쓴다. 복수 동사 seem이 쓰였으므로 one은 쓸 수 없다.

06 정답 ones

[해석] 다른 것들이 동일하다면 대부분의 사람들은 더 값이 싼 물건들을 선호한다.

→ 불특정한 '더 싼 물건들'의 의미일 때 the cheaper ones 를 쓴다.

07 정답 One, another

[해석] 나에게는 세 명의 아들이 있다. 한 명은 교사이고, 다른 한 명은 비행기 조종사이고, 나머지 한 명은 사업가이다.

→ 셋 중에서 각각을 가리킬 때 one, another, the other로 쓴다.

08 정답 the others

[해석] 다섯 조각의 케이크가 있다. 내가 한 조각을 먹었고, 그가 나머지를 먹었다.

→ 셋 이상 중에서 하나는 one이고, 나머지는 the others로 가리킨다.

09 정답 Some

[해석] 나는 엄마께 꽃을 사 드렸다. 그것들 중 일부는 흰색이고, 나머지는 빨간색이다.

→ 여럿 중에서 몇 개는 some이고, 나머지 전부는 the others로 가리킨다. 빈칸 뒤에 복수 동사 are가 쓰였으므로 one은 쓸 수 없다.

10 정답 the other

[해석] 그는 두 개의 유용한 공구를 가져왔다. 하나는 망치이고, 다른 하나는 드라이버이다.

→ 둘 중에서 하나와 다른 하나는 one, the other로 나타낸다.

11 정답 others

[해석] 세계의 일부 사람들은 영어를 그들의 제1언어로 사용하고, 다른 일부 사람들은 그것을 제2언어로 사용한다.

→ 여럿 중에서 몇몇은 ~, 다른 몇몇은 …을 가리킬 때 some ~, others …로 나타낸다.

12 정답 one

→ 불특정한 모자 하나를 나타내므로 one이 알맞다.

13 정답 One

→ 일반적인 사람을 나타낼 때 one을 쓸 수 있다.

14 정답 Some, the others

→ 여럿 중에서 몇몇은 some이고, 나머지 전부는 the others로 가리킨다.

15 정답 One, another, the other

→ 셋 중에서 각각을 가리킬 때 one, another, the other로 쓴다.

16 정답 any

[해석] 우리는 등산을 위한 물을 전혀 가져오지 않았다.

→ 부정문에서 '아무것도'의 의미를 표현할 때 any를 쓴다.

17 정답 some

[해석] 나는 몇몇 연습 문제를 풀었지만, 나머지는 건너뛰었다.

→ 긍정문에서 '몇몇'의 의미를 표현할 때 some을 쓴다.

18 정답 any

[해석] 너 창문으로 들어오는 빛이 조금이라도 보이니?

→ 의문문에서 '어떤'의 의미를 표현할 때 any를 쓴다.

19 정답 any

[해석] Marie가 쿠키를 구웠지만, 나는 아무것도 먹지 못했다.

→ 부정문에서 '아무것도'의 의미를 표현할 때 any를 쓴다.

20 정답 any

[해석] 앞쪽에 자리가 남아 있나요? — 아니요, 모두 찼어요.

→ 의문문에서 '어떤'의 의미를 표현할 때 any를 쓴다.

21 정답 some

[해석] 상자에서 몇몇 도구가 없는 것 같아.

→ 긍정문에서 '일부'의 의미를 표현할 때 some을 쓴다.

22 정답 some

[해석] 모든 아이들이 게임에 참여했지만, 몇몇은 일찍 나갔다.

→ 긍정문에서 '몇몇'의 의미를 표현할 때 some을 쓴다.

23 정답 nobody

[해석] 나는 여러 번 초인종을 눌렀지만, 아무도 응답하지 않았다.

→ 빈칸 앞에 but이 있으므로 '아무도 ~않다'라는 뜻으로 부정의 의미를 나타내는 nobody를 쓴다.

24 정답 anybody

[해석] 우리가 계획 중인 깜짝 파티에 대해 아무에게도 말하지 마.

→ not과 함께 쓰여 '아무도 ~않다'를 의미하는 anybody를 쓴다.

25 정답 anybody

[해석] 이 무거운 상자를 드는 걸 도와줄 사람이 근처에 있나요?

→ 의문문에서 '누군가'를 의미하는 anybody를 쓴다.

26 정답 Somebody

[해석] 아마 누군가가 회의 중에 테이블 위에 휴대전화를 두고 갔을 것이다.

→ 긍정문에서 '누군가'를 의미하는 somebody를 쓴다.

27 정답 something

[해석] A: 나 지금 배가 너무 고파!

B: 그러면 나가기 전에 뭐라도 좀 먹어.

→ 긍정문에서 '무언가'를 의미하는 something을 쓴다.

28 정답 anyone

[해석] A: 너 아무한테도 말 안 했어, 맞지?

B: 당연히 아니야! 난 절대 그런 건 안 해.

→ 긍정문에서 '아무나'를 의미하는 anyone을 쓴다.

29 정답 Nothing

[해석] A: 오래된 지하실에서 무엇을 찾았니?

B: 아무것도. 완전 어둡고 텅 비었었어.

→ 부정문에서 '아무것도 ~아닌'을 의미하는 nothing을 쓴다.

30 정답 anything

[해석] A: 내가 서랍장에서 우연히 발견한 걸 봐봐!

B: 와, 여기로 이사 온 이후로 저런 건 본 적도 없어!

→ never와 함께 쓰여 '아무것도 ~않다'를 의미하는 anything을 쓴다.

31 정답 each

[해석] 우리는 행사 후에 아이들 각각에게 작은 선물을 주었다.

→ 「of + 복수 명사」 앞에는 대명사 each가 와야 한다. every는 형용사로만 쓰인다.

32 정답 was

[해석] 학생들 각자가 다른 교실로 배정되었다.

→ each는 단수 취급하므로 동사 was가 알맞다.

33 정답 each

[해석] 나는 각가 기사들을 읽었지만, 단 하나만 인상 깊었다.

→ 「of + 복수 명사」 앞에는 대명사 each가 와야 한다. every는 형용사로만 쓰인다.

34 정답 guest

[해석] Bella는 모든 손님을 따뜻한 미소와 악수로 맞이했다.

→ every는 항상 단수 명사와 함께 쓰인다.

35 정답 was

[해석] 모두가 아이디어를 발표하라는 요청을 받았지만, 아무도 대답하지 않았다.

→ everyone은 단수 취급하므로 단수형인 was가 알맞다.

36 정답 options

[해석] 네가 준 각각의 선택지가 나름대로 타당해 보인다.

→ 「each + of + 복수 명사」 형태이므로 복수 명사인 options가 알맞다.

37 정답 All of the boys are in the playground.

→ all of 뒤에 셀 수 있는 명사가 나올 때는 복수 명사로 쓰고, 동사도 복수형으로 쓴다. 관사는 명사의 앞에 온다.

38 정답 Both of these jackets aren't[are not] expensive.

→ '~의 둘 다'는 both of ~라고 한다.

39 정답 All of us have to make more effort

→ all 뒤에 인칭대명사가 올 경우 of를 꼭 써야 하므로 All of us로 쓴다.

40 정답 Both

→ '두 ~ 모두'는 「both + 복수 명사」로 쓴다.

41 정답 all

→ '모든'을 의미하는 all과 every 중에서 빈칸의 대명사 자리에 올 수 있는 것은 all이다.

42 정답 Every

→ 빈칸 뒤에 단수 명사가 있고 '모든'을 나타내야 하므로 every가 와야 한다.

43 정답 Each

→ '각각의 ~'는 「each + of + 복수 명사」 형태로 나타내므로 each를 써야 한다.

정답

01 ④	**02** One	**03** those	**04** ones
05 it	**06** Anyone	**07** Each	**08** All
09 someone	**10** ④	**11** ⑤	**12** that
13 itself	**14** some	**15** that	**16** by itself
17 ②	**18** ③		

19 It was this morning that Johnson had a car accident.

20 I don't have anything to do tonight.
또는 I have nothing to do tonight.

21 some enjoy working out, the others prefer to exercise

22 This → These　　**23** him → himself

24 this → it　　**25** some → any

26 it → 삭제　　**27** ①　　**28** ①

29 ③　**30** ④　**31** ⑤　**32** ③

33 Between **34** beside　**35** for　**36** of

37 in　**38** ④　**39** ②　**40** the other

41 one　**42** Both of the women were French.

43 It was his uncle that I met yesterday.

44 This music makes it possible for me to forget everything.

45 You can come to my house and make yourself at home.　**46** ③　　**47** ②

01　정답 ④　　UNIT 14 부정대명사

[해석] ① 어떤 도움이 필요하면 내게 전화해.
② 이번 주말에 어떤 계획이 있니?
③ 어떤 아이라도 그 원리를 이해할 수 있다.
④ 케이크를 좀 더 먹을래?
⑤ 병에 물이 하나도 없다.
→ 의문문에서는 대개 any를 쓰지만 권유나 긍정의 대답을 기대하는 의문문에서는 some을 쓴다.

02　정답 One　　UNIT 14 부정대명사

[해석] 탁자 위에 세 개의 사과가 있었다. 한 개는 여기 있다. 나머지는 어디에 있는가?
→ 셋 이상 중 하나는 one이고, 나머지는 the others로 가리킨다.

03　정답 those　UNIT 12 지시대명사 this (these), that (those), it

[해석] 그 시험에 합격하는 사람들의 비결은 무엇일까?
→ '~한 사람들'은 those who라고 한다.

04　정답 ones　　UNIT 14 부정대명사

[해석] 젓가락을 바닥에 떨어뜨렸어요. 저에게 새것을 가져다주시겠어요?
→ 불특정한 젓가락을 가리키고 chopsticks는 복수형을 써야 하므로 ones가 알맞다.

05　정답 it　　UNIT 12 지시대명사 this (these), that (those), it

[해석] 네가 초대하고 싶은 사람이 바로 그녀니?
→ her를 강조하는 「It is[was] ~ that …」 강조 구문이므로 it이 알맞다.

06　정답 Anyone　　UNIT 14 부정대명사

[해석] 사진 찍는 것에 관심이 있는 사람은 누구나 우리 동아리에 가입할 수 있다.
→ 긍정문에는 대개 someone을 쓰지만, '어떤 사람이라도'라는 의미로 쓰일 때는 anyone을 쓴다.

07　정답 Each　　UNIT 14 부정대명사

[해석] 우리들 각각은 기차를 타기 전에 엄마에게 입맞춤을 할 것이다.
→ 빈칸 뒤에 단수 동사 is가 있으므로 all은 쓸 수 없고 each를 써야 한다. each는 항상 단수 취급하지만, all of는 뒤에 복수 명사가 오면 복수 취급한다.

08　정답 All　　UNIT 14 부정대명사

[해석] 그의 돈 전부를 기차에서 도둑맞았다.
→ '그의 돈 전부'라는 의미의 all of his money가 알맞다. all of 뒤에 셀 수 없는 명사가 오면 단수 취급한다.

09　정답 someone　　UNIT 14 부정대명사

[해석] 문 뒤에 누군가가 있는 것 같다.
→ 긍정문에는 someone을 쓴다.

10　정답 ④　　UNIT 13 재귀대명사

[해석] 〈보기〉 그 변호사는 서류를 확인할 것을 스스로에게 상기시켰다.
① 그녀는 직접 자신의 실수를 인정했다.
② 우리는 그 프로젝트를 직접 완수했다.
③ 그는 개회 연설을 직접 했다.
④ 그 개는 자신의 귀 뒤를 긁었다.
⑤ 그들은 전체 행사를 직접 조직했다.
→ 〈보기〉와 ④의 재귀대명사는 주어와 목적어가 같은 재귀 용법으로 쓰였다. 나머지는 모두 강조 용법으로 쓰였다.

11　정답 ⑤　　UNIT 12 지시대명사 this (these), that (those), it

[해석] • 이 그림에서 별들의 위치는 실제 하늘의 그것과 유사하다.
• 사전 등록한 사람들만 참여할 수 있다.
→ 첫 문장에서는 the position을 대신해야 하므로 that이 필요하다. / '~한 사람들'은 those who로 표현한다.

12　정답 that　　UNIT 12 지시대명사 this (these), that (those), it

[해석] 나는 그 책들을 통독하려고 애썼지만, 그것은 쉽지 않았다.
→ 앞 문장 전체를 대신할 때는 that을 쓴다.

13　정답 itself　　UNIT 13 재귀대명사

[해석] 그의 존재 자체가 나에게는 고문이었다.
→ His presence를 강조해야 하므로 itself가 알맞다.

14　정답 some　　UNIT 14 부정대명사

[해석] 쿠키를 좀 더 먹을래?
→ 의문문에서는 대개 any를 쓰지만 권유나 긍정의 대답을 기대하는 의문문에서는 some을 쓴다.

15 정답 that　　　UNIT **12** 지시대명사 this (these), that (those), it
[해석] 기린의 목은 사슴의 그것보다 훨씬 더 길다.
→ 앞에 나온 단수 명사를 대신할 때는 that을 사용한다.

16 정답 by itself　　　UNIT **13** 재귀대명사
[해석] 전자레인지는 몇 초 후에 저절로 작동하기 시작할 것이다.
→ by itself는 '저절로'라는 뜻이고, in itself는 '그 자체가, 본래'라는 뜻이다.

17 정답 ②　　　UNIT **13** 재귀대명사
[해석] ① Peter는 자기 자신을 부끄러워한다.
② 학생들은 벽을 직접 다시 칠했다.
③ Jenny는 약속을 어기지 말자고 혼잣말을 했다.
④ 청중에게 자기소개를 하는 것이 어떠세요?
⑤ 그는 성공적인 연설을 한 것에 대해 자기 자신을 매우 자랑스러워했다.
→ ②은 주어를 강조하는 강조 용법의 재귀대명사로 생략 가능하다. ①, ③, ⑤은 전치사의 목적어, ④은 동사의 목적어로 쓰인 재귀 용법의 재귀대명사로 생략할 수 없다.

18 정답 ③　　　UNIT **12** 지시대명사 this (these), that (those), it
[해석] 그가 부탁하는 것은 물 한 잔이다.
① 오늘은 일요일이다.
② 여기에서 그리 멀지 않다.
③ 내가 그녀를 만난 날은 바로 어제였다.
④ 우리 자신을 건강하게 유지하는 것은 중요하다.
⑤ 이것은 그 지도를 그리는 것을 가능하게 할 것이다.
→ 주어진 문장과 ③의 It은 「It is[was] ~ that …」 강조 구문에 쓰인 It이다. ①, ② 비인칭주어 ④ 가주어 ⑤ 가목적어

19 정답 It was this morning that Johnson had a car accident.
　　　UNIT **12** 지시대명사 this (these), that (those), it
[해석] Johnson은 오늘 아침 자동차 사고를 당했다.
→ Johnson이 자동차 사고를 당한 때는 바로 오늘 아침이었다.
→ 부사(구)를 강조할 때는 「It is[was] ~ that …」 강조 구문을 쓴다. 과거시제 문장이므로 be동사는 was로 써야 한다.

20 정답 I don't have anything to do tonight. 또는 I have nothing to do tonight.　　　UNIT **14** 부정대명사
[해석] 나는 오늘 밤에 할 일이 있다.
→ 나는 오늘 밤에 할 일이 아무것도 없다.
→ 부정문에서는 something이 아니라 anything을 써야 한다. not ~ anything은 nothing으로 쓸 수 있다.

21 정답 some enjoy working out, the others prefer to exercise　　　UNIT **14** 부정대명사
[해석] 우리 팀의 17명 중에서, 6명은 아침에 운동하는 것을 즐기는 반면, 11명은 저녁에 운동하는 것을 선호한다.
→ 우리 팀의 17명 중에서, 몇몇은 아침에 운동하는 것을 즐기는 반면, 나머지는 저녁에 운동하는 것을 선호한다.
→ 17명 중 6명은 some으로, 나머지 전부인 11명은 the others로 나타낼 수 있다.

22 정답 This → These
　　　UNIT **12** 지시대명사 this (these), that (those), it
[해석] 이 장난감들은 아이들에게 인기 있어요. 그것들을 사지 않으면 당신은 그것을 후회할 거예요.
→ toys는 복수이므로 this가 아니라 these로 써야 한다.

23 정답 him → himself　　　UNIT **13** 재귀대명사
[해석] Jack은 면도를 하다가 베였다.
→ '베이다'는 cut oneself라고 쓴다.

24 정답 this → it
　　　UNIT **12** 지시대명사 this (these), that (those), it
[해석] 인터넷은 정보를 찾는 것을 더 쉽게 만들었다.
→ 가목적어 역할을 하는 it을 써야 한다.

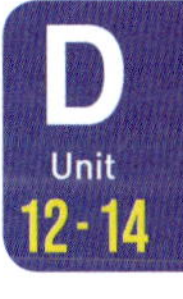

25 정답 some → any　　　UNIT **14** 부정대명사
[해석] 그는 어떤 실수도 하지 않았다.
→ 부정문이므로 some이 아니라 any를 써야 한다.

26 정답 it → 삭제
　　　UNIT **12** 지시대명사 this (these), that (those), it
[해석] 나를 건강하게 만든 것은 바로 규칙적인 운동이었다.
→ 「It is[was] ~ that …」 강조 구문에서 주어 regular exercise가 강조되고 있으므로 that 뒤의 it은 불필요하다.

27 정답 ①　　　UNIT **12** 지시대명사 this (these), that (those), it
[해석] 식량을 위해 동물을 죽이는 것은 불가피해 보이지만, 단순히 목숨을 빼앗는 즐거움을 위해 동물을 사냥하는 것은 용인될 수 없다.
→ 진주어가 to hunt 이하이므로 가주어 it이 필요하다.

28 정답 ①　　　UNIT **12** 지시대명사 this (these), that (those), it
[해석] 오늘 날씨는 아름답고, 나는 이번 주 내내 날씨가 이렇게 유지될 것이라고 믿고 싶다.
→ 앞에 나온 단수 명사 weather를 대신하는 대명사 it이 필요하다.

29 정답 ③　　　UNIT **14** 부정대명사
[해석] A: 제가 샐러드를 조금 더 먹을 수 있을까요?
B: 물론입니다만, 추가로 돈을 더 내셔야 합니다.
→ 권유, 부탁, 긍정의 대답을 기대하는 의문문에서는 any 대신 some을 사용한다.

30 정답 ④　　　UNIT **14** 부정대명사
[해석] A: 저는 이 셔츠가 무척 마음에 들지만 너무 꽉 끼네요.
B: 다른 사이즈 한번 입어보시겠어요?
→ 여러 대상 중 하나를 제외한 불특정한 다른 하나는 another로 나타낸다. 입어본 옷이 아닌 다른 것을 입어보는 상황이므로 ④ another가 들어가야 한다.

31 정답 ⑤　　　UNIT **14** 부정대명사
[해석] A: 나는 오늘 회의가 두 개 있어.
B: 나는 하나만 있지만, 그 다른 회의에는 함께 할게.
→ 대상이 둘일 때 나머지 하나는 the other로 나타낸다. B가 가진 회의 하나를 제외한 나머지 하나의 회의를 뜻하므로 ⑤ the other가 들어가야 한다.

32 정답 ③　　　UNIT **12** 지시대명사 this (these), that (those), it

[해석] 〈보기〉 하늘은 스스로 돕는 자를 돕는다.

① 나는 저것들이 내 귀걸이라고 생각한다.

② 네가 나에게 빌려준 저 책들은 정말 유용했다.

③ 이기적인 행동은 우리 주변의 사람들에게 정말 큰 피해를 입히기 쉽다.

④ 그의 올해 판매량은 작년의 그것과 비교했을 때 많이 올랐다.

⑤ 몇 가지 프로젝트들이 진행 중인 것으로 알고 있습니다. 그것들에 대해 이야기해 주시겠습니까?

→ 〈보기〉와 ③에서 those는 '~하는 사람들'을 의미한다. ①, ④, ⑤은 지시대명사, ②은 지시형용사로 those가 사용되었다.

33 정답 Between　　　UNIT **13** 재귀대명사

[해석] 우리끼리 이야기이지만 나는 그녀와 친구가 되는 것을 원하지 않아.

→ '우리끼리 이야기이지만'을 의미하는 표현은 between ourselves이다.

34 정답 beside　　　UNIT **13** 재귀대명사

[해석] 그가 그 소식을 들었을 때 그 소년은 두려움으로 제정신이 아니었다.

→ '제정신이 아닌'을 의미하는 표현은 beside oneself이다.

35 정답 for　　　UNIT **13** 재귀대명사

[해석] 나는 내 동생이 숙제를 하는 것을 도와주지 않았는데 왜냐하면 나는 그가 그것을 혼자 힘으로 하기를 원했기 때문이다.

→ '혼자 힘으로'를 의미하는 표현은 for oneself이다.

36 정답 of　　　UNIT **13** 재귀대명사

[해석] 문이 저절로 열렸을 때 모두가 충격을 받았다.

→ '저절로'를 의미하는 표현은 of itself이다.

37 정답 in　　　UNIT **13** 재귀대명사

[해석] 그와 몇 마디 이야기를 나누는 것 그 자체가 대단한 영광이다.

→ '그 자체가'를 의미하는 표현은 in itself이다.

38 정답 ④　　　UNIT **13** 재귀대명사

[해석] ① 내가 직접 이 음식을 요리했다.

② 그 여자는 순수함 자체이다.

③ 나는 직접 그를 보고 싶다.

④ 그 소녀는 아무 이유도 없이 그녀 자신을 싫어한다.

⑤ 그녀가 직접 아기를 돌보고 있다.

→ ④의 herself는 문장의 목적어 역할을 하는 재귀 용법으로 사용되었고 나머지는 모두 재귀대명사의 생략이 가능한 강조 용법으로 사용되었다.

39 정답 ②　　　UNIT **12** 지시대명사 this (these), that (those), it

[해석] ① 나를 매우 좋아하는 것은 바로 그녀이다.

② 네가 열심히 공부하는 것은 중요하다.

③ 네가 거리에서 만났던 것은 우리 엄마였다.

④ 내가 그를 우연히 만났던 것은 어제였다.

⑤ 그녀가 그녀의 남자친구를 만났던 것은 커피숍에서였다.

→ ②의 it은 가주어이고 나머지는 모두 「It is[was] ~ that …」 강조 구문의 it이다.

40 정답 the other　　　UNIT **14** 부정대명사

[해석] A: 이 두 커피 메이커의 차이점이 무엇인가요?

B: 음, 이것이 다른 하나에 비해 사용하기에 좀 더 어렵습니다.

→ 둘 중에서 다른 하나를 지칭하고 있으므로 the other가 적절하다.

41 정답 one　　　UNIT **14** 부정대명사

[해석] A: 내 디지털 카메라가 잘 작동하지 않아.

B: 새로운 것을 하나 사지 그래?

→ 앞에 언급된 명사와 같은 종류이면서 정해지지 않은 하나를 지칭할 때 one을 쓴다.

42 정답 Both of the women were French.　　　UNIT **14** 부정대명사

→ 「all, both, each+of+관사+명사」의 어순이므로 주어는 Both of the women의 순서로 써야 한다.

43 정답 It was his uncle that I met yesterday.

UNIT **12** 지시대명사 this (these), that (those), it

→ '그의 삼촌'을 강조하므로 「It is[was] ~ that …」 강조 구문을 써서 It was his uncle that …의 순서로 써야 한다.

44 정답 This music makes it possible for me to forget everything.

UNIT **12** 지시대명사 this (these), that (those), it

→ 가목적어 it과 진목적어인 to부정사가 있으므로 makes it possible ~ to forget의 순서로 써야 한다.

45 정답 You can come to my house and make yourself at home.　　　UNIT **13** 재귀대명사

→ '집에 있는 것처럼 편하게 지내다'를 의미하는 make oneself at home을 써야 한다.

46 정답 ③　　　UNIT **14** 부정대명사

[해석] 다른 사람이 당신을 학교나 다른 곳에 좀 늦게 데리러 온 적이 있는가? NASA 우주비행사 Chris Baker는 이번 주에 비슷한 상황에 놓였다. Chris는 7월부터 국제 우주 정거장(ISS)에서 살고 있었다. 그는 우주 왕복선 디스커버리호를 타고 지구로 돌아올 예정이었지만, 그의 귀환은 지연되었다. 디스커버리호가 화요일 정해진 시간에 발사될 수 없었던 것은 바로 뇌우 때문이었다. 디스커버리호가 그를 집으로 데려다주기 위해 도착할 때까지, Chris와 다른 다섯 명의 우주비행사들은 현재 국제 우주 정거장에서 살고 있다.

→ (A), (B) 의문문에는 any-를 써야 한다. (C) '다른' 우주비행사들을 나타내려면 other를 써야 한다.

47 정답 ②　　　UNIT **12** 지시대명사 this (these), that (those), it,
UNIT **13** 재귀대명사

→ ⓐ Chris Baker '스스로가' 그 상황에 놓이게 되었다는 것을 나타내므로 himself가 와야 한다. ⓑ due to thunderstorms를 강조하는 「It was ~ that …」 강조 구문이므로 It이 와야 한다.

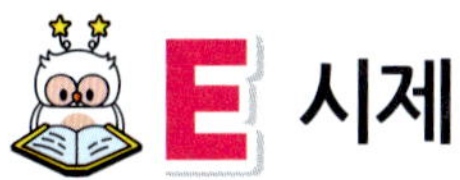 ## E 시제

개념 확인 문제 정답 ▶ 문제편 p.75

01 현재진행 **02** 현재완료 **03** 과거 **04** 미래완료
05 과거진행 **06** 미래진행 **07** 현재완료진행
08 circulated → circulates **09** will → will be
10 had → have **11** have → has 또는 had
12 was → had **13** has visited
14 graduated **15** will[are going to] travel
16 were having **17** participates
18 will be watching

---

01 정답 **현재진행**

[해석] 아이들은 밖에서 놀고 있다.
→ 「are + -ing」의 형태이므로 현재진행시제이다.

02 정답 **현재완료**

[해석] 우리는 여기서 5년 동안 살았다.
→ 「have + 과거분사」의 형태이므로 현재완료시제이다.

03 정답 **과거**

[해석] 나는 지난 주말에 할머니를 방문했다.
→ 일반동사 visit의 과거형인 visited가 왔으므로 과거시제이다.

04 정답 **미래완료**

[해석] 나는 오후 7시까지 숙제를 끝냈을 것이다.
→ 「will have + 과거분사」의 형태이므로 미래완료시제이다.

05 정답 **과거진행**

[해석] 그는 친구가 방문했을 때 공부하고 있었다.
→ 「was + -ing」의 형태이므로 과거진행시제이다.

06 정답 **미래진행**

[해석] 그는 내일 오후에 축구를 하고 있을 것이다.
→ will be -ing의 형태이므로 미래진행시제이다.

07 정답 **현재완료진행**

[해석] 우리는 너를 한 시간 넘게 기다리고 있다.
→ have been -ing의 형태이므로 현재완료진행시제이다.

08 정답 circulated → circulates

[해석] 혈액은 몸을 순환한다.
→ 불변의 진리는 현재시제로 나타내므로 과거형인 circulated를 현재형인 circulates로 고쳐야 한다.

09 정답 will → will be

[해석] 나는 네가 도착할 때까지 기다리고 있을 것이다.
→ '네가 도착하는' 미래의 특정 시간에 기다리고 있을 것임을 나타내려면 미래진행시제를 써서 will을 will be로 고쳐야 한다.

10 정답 had → have

[해석] 2028년까지 그들은 새로운 다리를 건설했을 것이다.
→ '2028년'이라는 미래의 특정 시점까지 건설이 완료될 것임을 나타내려면 미래완료시제를 써야 하므로 had를 have로 고쳐야 한다.

11 정답 have → has 또는 had

[해석] 그녀는 한 시간 동안 피아노를 연습해오고 있다[있었다].
→ 주어가 3인칭 단수이므로 have를 has 또는 had로 고쳐야 한다.

12 정답 was → had

[해석] 그는 나가기 전에 2시간 동안 공부했었다.
→ 주어가 3인칭 단수이고 완료시제와 함께 쓰이는 for가 있으며 '그가 나가기 전'이라는 과거 시점 이전에 일어난 일을 나타내므로 was를 had로 고쳐야 한다.

13 정답 has visited

→ 과거부터 현재까지 세 번에 걸친 과거의 경험을 나타내므로 현재완료시제를 써서 has visited로 표현한다.

14 정답 graduated

→ 2020년이라는 과거의 시점에 일어난 일을 나타내므로 과거시제로 써야 한다. graduate의 과거형은 graduated이다.

15 정답 will[are going to] travel

→ 다음 여름이라는 미래의 시점에 일어날 일을 나타내므로 미래시제를 써서 will[are going to] travel로 표현한다.

16 정답 were having

→ 과거의 특정 시간에 진행 중이었던 일을 나타내므로 과거진행시제를 써서 were + having으로 표현한다.

17 정답 participates

→ 매 학기 반복되는 일을 나타내므로 현재시제가 와야 한다. 주어가 3인칭 단수이므로 -s가 붙은 participates로 표현한다.

18 정답 will be watching

→ 미래의 특정 시간에 진행될 동작을 나타내므로 미래완료시제를 써서 will be watching으로 표현한다.

UNIT 16 현재시제, 과거시제

01 정답 flows
[해석] 강의 물은 바다로 흐른다.
→ 주어가 3인칭 단수 현재시제일 때 대부분의 동사는 원형에 -s를 붙인다.

02 정답 tries
[해석] 지금 그녀는 제시간에 숙제를 끝내려고 한다.
→ 「자음+y」로 끝나는 동사는 y를 i로 바꾸고 -es를 붙인다.

03 정답 departs
[해석] 도시 관광버스는 중앙역에서 매시간 출발한다.
→ 주어가 3인칭 단수 현재시제일 때 대부분의 동사는 원형에 -s를 붙인다.

04 정답 astonishes
[해석] 그가 역사에 대해 얼마나 많이 아는지가 항상 나를 놀라게 한다.
→ -sh로 끝나는 동사는 -es를 붙인다.

05 정답 analyzes
[해석] 그녀는 매번 발표를 준비할 때 데이터를 신중하게 분석한다.
→ 주어가 3인칭 단수 현재시제일 때 대부분의 동사는 원형에 -s를 붙인다.

06 정답 developed
[해석] Albert Einstein은 상대성 이론을 개발했다.
→ 과거의 역사적인 사실은 항상 과거시제로 쓴다.

07 정답 planned
[해석] 우리는 지난주에 우리의 휴가 계획을 세웠다.
→ last week라는 과거에 이미 동작이 끝났으므로 과거시제로 쓴다.

08 정답 saved
[해석] 그녀는 분명히 새벽 전에 보고서를 저장했다.
→ before dawn이라는 과거에 이미 동작이 끝났으므로 과거시제로 쓴다.

09 정답 cleaned
[해석] 그 학생들은 어제 그들의 교실을 청소했다.
→ yesterday라는 과거에 이미 동작이 끝났으므로 과거시제로 쓴다.

10 정답 answered
[해석] 그녀는 어젯밤에 모든 질문에 정확하게 대답했다.
→ last night이라는 과거에 이미 동작이 끝났으므로 과거시제로 쓴다.

11 정답 discovered
[해석] Christopher Columbus는 1492년에 아메리카를 발견했다.
→ 과거의 역사적인 사실은 항상 과거시제로 쓴다.

12 정답 spends time with his family
→ 현재의 습관을 나타내므로 현재시제로 쓴다.

13 정답 recommended a new horror movie
→ yesterday라는 과거에 이미 동작이 끝났으므로 과거시제로 쓴다.

14 정답 develops a new recipe
→ 반복되는 사실을 나타내므로 현재시제로 쓴다.

15 정답 reads the newspaper every morning
→ 현재의 습관을 나타내므로 현재시제로 쓴다.

16 정답 moved to a new house
→ last month라는 과거에 이미 동작이 끝났으므로 과거시제로 쓴다.

UNIT 17 동사의 과거−과거분사 불규칙 변화표

49 wrote, written 50 bore, born(e)
51 broke, broken 52 shook, shaken
53 wore, worn 54 drank, drunk 55 ran, run
56 rose, risen 57 overcame, overcome
58 smelt, smelt 59 sat, sat 60 stood, stood
61 woke, woken 62 hit, hit 63 bit, bitten
64 tore, torn 65 read 66 sunk
67 led 68 began 69 stole
70 wore

01 [정답] bet, bet
[해석] 내기하다
→ bet은 원형, 과거, 과거분사가 모두 같은 동사이다.

02 [정답] heard, heard
[해석] 듣다
→ hear는 과거와 과거분사가 같은 동사이다.

03 [정답] quit, quit
[해석] 그만두다
→ quit은 원형, 과거, 과거분사가 모두 같은 동사이다.

04 [정답] found, found
[해석] 찾다
→ find는 과거와 과거분사가 같은 동사이다.

05 [정답] reset, reset
[해석] 재설정하다
→ reset은 원형, 과거, 과거분사가 모두 같은 동사이다.

06 [정답] caught, caught
[해석] 잡다
→ catch는 과거와 과거분사가 같은 동사이다.

07 [정답] bent, bent
[해석] 구부리다
→ bend는 과거와 과거분사가 같은 동사이다.

08 [정답] laid, laid
[해석] 놓다, 낳다
→ lay는 과거와 과거분사가 같은 동사이다.

09 [정답] hurt, hurt
[해석] 다치다
→ hurt는 원형, 과거, 과거분사가 모두 같은 동사이다.

10 [정답] left, left
[해석] 떠나다
→ leave는 과거와 과거분사가 같은 동사이다.

11 [정답] bound, bound
[해석] 묶다
→ bind는 과거와 과거분사가 같은 동사이다.

12 [정답] sold, sold
[해석] 팔다
→ sell은 과거와 과거분사가 같은 동사이다.

13 [정답] dealt, dealt
[해석] 거래하다
→ deal은 과거와 과거분사가 같은 동사이다.

14 [정답] fed, fed
[해석] 먹이다
→ feed는 과거와 과거분사가 같은 동사이다.

15 [정답] meant, meant
[해석] 의미하다
→ mean은 과거와 과거분사가 같은 동사이다.

16 [정답] ground, ground
[해석] 갈다
→ grind는 과거와 과거분사가 같은 동사이다.

17 [정답] held, held
[해석] 지니다
→ hold는 과거와 과거분사가 같은 동사이다.

18 [정답] shot, shot
[해석] 쏘다
→ shoot은 과거와 과거분사가 같은 동사이다.

19 [정답] shut, shut
[해석] 닫다
→ shut은 원형, 과거, 과거분사가 모두 같은 동사이다.

20 [정답] spread, spread
[해석] 퍼지다
→ spread는 원형, 과거, 과거분사가 모두 같은 동사이다.

21 [정답] brought, brought
[해석] 가져오다
→ bring은 과거와 과거분사가 같은 동사이다.

22 [정답] spilt, spilt
[해석] 흘리다
→ spill은 과거와 과거분사가 같은 동사이다.

23 [정답] struck, struck
[해석] 때리다, 치다
→ strike는 과거와 과거분사가 같은 동사이다.

24 [정답] led, led
[해석] 인도하다
→ lead는 과거와 과거분사가 같은 동사이다.

25 [정답] lost, lost
[해석] 잃어버리다
→ lose는 과거와 과거분사가 같은 동사이다.

26 [정답] won, won
[해석] 이기다
→ win은 과거와 과거분사가 같은 동사이다.

27 [정답] hit
[해석] 공이 벽에 세게 부딪힌[혔]다.
→ hit은 원형, 과거, 과거분사가 모두 같은 동사이다.

E
Unit
15-20

28 정답 hurt

[해석] 그녀는 조깅하다가 발목을 다친[쳤]다.

→ hurt는 원형, 과거, 과거분사가 모두 같은 동사이다.

29 정답 bent

[해석] 그는 손으로 금속을 구부린[렸]다.

→ bend의 과거형은 bent이다.

30 정답 swept

[해석] 그들은 학교 끝나고 차고를 쓴[쓸었]다.

→ sweep의 과거형은 swept이다.

31 정답 paid

[해석] 그는 그 게임에 모든 돈을 지불한[했]다.

→ pay의 과거형은 paid이다.

32 정답 broadcast

[해석] 그 채널은 그 경기를 생중계한[했]다.

→ broadcast는 원형, 과거, 과거분사가 모두 같은 동사이다.

33 정답 smelt

[해석] 우리는 복도에서 이상한 냄새를 맡는[았]다.

→ smell의 과거형은 smelt이다.

34 정답 spent

[해석] 그녀는 혼자서 지하실을 청소하며 주말을 보낸[냈]다.

→ spend의 과거형은 spent이다.

35 정답 did, done

[해석] 하다

→ do는 원형, 과거, 과거분사가 모두 다른 동사이다.

36 정답 cost, cost

[해석] 비용이 들다

→ cost는 원형, 과거, 과거분사가 모두 같은 동사이다.

37 정답 ate, eaten

[해석] 먹다

→ eat은 원형, 과거, 과거분사가 모두 다른 동사이다.

38 정답 paid, paid

[해석] 지불하다

→ pay는 과거와 과거분사가 같은 동사이다.

39 정답 rang, rung

[해석] 울리다

→ ring은 원형, 과거, 과거분사가 모두 다른 동사이다.

40 정답 chose, chosen

[해석] 선택하다

→ choose는 원형, 과거, 과거분사가 모두 다른 동사이다.

41 정답 bought, bought

[해석] 사다

→ buy는 과거와 과거분사가 같은 동사이다.

42 정답 taught, taught

[해석] 가르치다

→ teach는 과거와 과거분사가 같은 동사이다.

43 정답 arose, arisen

[해석] 발생하다

→ arise는 원형, 과거, 과거분사가 모두 다른 동사이다.

44 정답 sent, sent

[해석] 보내다

→ send는 과거와 과거분사가 같은 동사이다.

45 정답 let, let

[해석] ～하게 하다

→ let은 원형, 과거, 과거분사가 모두 같은 동사이다.

46 정답 built, built

[해석] 짓다

→ build는 과거와 과거분사가 같은 동사이나.

47 정답 threw, thrown

[해석] 던지다

→ throw는 원형, 과거, 과거분사가 모두 다른 동사이다.

48 정답 awoke, awoken

[해석] 깨다

→ awake는 원형, 과거, 과거분사가 모두 다른 동사이다.

49 정답 wrote, written

[해석] 쓰다

→ write는 원형, 과거, 과거분사가 모두 다른 동사이다.

50 정답 bore, born(e)

[해석] 낳다, 견디다

→ bear는 원형, 과거, 과거분사가 모두 다른 동사이다.

51 정답 broke, broken

[해석] 깨뜨리다

→ break는 원형, 과거, 과거분사가 모두 다른 동사이다.

52 정답 shook, shaken

[해석] 흔들다

→ shake는 원형, 과거, 과거분사가 모두 다른 동사이다.

53 정답 wore, worn

[해석] 입다

→ wear는 원형, 과거, 과거분사가 모두 다른 동사이다.

54 정답 drank, drunk

[해석] 마시다

→ drink는 원형, 과거, 과거분사가 모두 다른 동사이다.

55 정답 ran, run

[해석] 달리다

→ run은 원형과 과거분사가 같은 동사이다.

56 정답 rose, risen

[해석] 오르다

→ rise는 원형, 과거, 과거분사가 모두 다른 동사이다.

57 정답 overcame, overcome

[해석] 극복하다

→ overcome은 원형과 과거분사가 같은 동사이다.

58 정답 smelt, smelt

[해석] 냄새를 맡다

→ smell은 과거와 과거분사가 같은 동사이다.

59 정답 sat, sat

[해석] 앉다

→ sit은 과거와 과거분사가 같은 동사이다.

60 정답 stood, stood

[해석] 서다

→ stand는 과거와 과거분사가 같은 동사이다.

61 정답 woke, woken

[해석] 깨다

▸ wake는 원형, 과기, 과기분사가 모두 다른 동사이다.

62 정답 hit, hit

[해석] 치다

→ hit은 원형, 과거, 과거분사가 모두 같은 동사이다.

63 정답 bit, bitten

[해석] 물다

→ bite는 원형, 과거, 과거분사가 모두 다른 동사이다.

64 정답 tore, torn

[해석] 찢다

→ tear는 원형, 과거, 과거분사가 모두 다른 동사이다.

65 정답 read

→ read는 원형, 과거, 과거분사가 모두 같은 동사이다. '읽었다'라고 했으므로 과거형인 read로 써야 한다.

66 정답 sunk

→ sink는 원형, 과거, 과거분사가 모두 다른 동사이다. 현재완료시제가 쓰였으므로 과거분사인 sunk로 써야 한다.

67 정답 led

→ lead는 과거와 과거분사가 같은 동사이다. '이끌었다'라고 했으므로 과거형인 led로 써야 한다.

68 정답 began

→ begin은 원형, 과거, 과거분사가 모두 다른 동사이다. '시작했다'라고 했으므로 과거형인 began으로 써야 한다.

69 정답 stole

→ steal은 원형, 과거, 과거분사가 모두 다른 동사이다. '훔쳤다'라고 했으므로 과거형인 stole로 써야 한다.

70 정답 wore

→ wear는 원형, 과거, 과거분사가 모두 다른 동사이다. '입었다'라고 했으므로 과거형인 wore로 써야 한다.

UNIT 18 미래시제

> **개념 확인 문제 정답** ▶ 문제편 **p.83**
>
> **01** to leave **02** to run **03** finish **04** be
> **05** going **06** to move **07** will not forget
> **08** are about to launch **09** is going to study
> **10** will announce **11** was about to unveil
> **12** was going to buy
> **13** will confirm → confirms
> **14** will strike → strikes **15** is going to set → sets
> **16** will worsen → worsens

01 정답 to leave

[해석] 나는 공항으로 떠나려고 한다.

→ 즉시 일어날 미래를 나타낼 때는 「be about to+동사원형」을 쓴다.

02 정답 to run

[해석] 그는 내년에 선거에 출마할 것이다.

→ 미래에 일어날 계획된 일을 나타낼 때는 「be going to+동사원형」을 쓴다.

03 정답 finish

[해석] 그들은 금요일까지 프로젝트를 끝낼 것이다.

→ 미래에 일어날 일이나 의지를 나타낼 때는 「will+동사원형」을 써야 하므로 finish가 와야 한다.

04 정답 be

[해석] 우리는 회의에 참석할 수 없을 것이다.

→ 미래에 일어날 일이나 의지를 나타낼 때는 「will+동사원형」을 써야 하므로 be가 와야 한다.

05 정답 going

[해석] 그녀는 곧 팀장으로 승진할 예정이다.

→ 미래에 일어날 계획된 일을 나타낼 때는 「be going to+동사원형」을 쓴다.

06 정답 to move

[해석] 나는 다음 달에 새 아파트로 이사하려고 한다.

→ 즉시 일어날 미래를 나타낼 때는 「be about to+동사원형」을 쓴다.

07 정답 will not forget

→ 미래에 일어날 일이나 의지를 나타낼 때는 「will+동사원형」을 쓴다. 부정형은 will과 동사원형 사이에 not을 쓴다.

08 정답 are about to launch

→ 즉시 일어날 미래를 나타낼 때는 「be about to+동사원형」을 쓴다.

09 정답 is going to study

→ 미래에 일어날 계획된 일을 나타낼 때는 「be going to+동사원형」을 쓴다.

10 정답 will announce
→ 미래에 일어날 일이나 의지를 나타낼 때는 「will+동사원형」
을 쓴다.

11 정답 was about to unveil
→ 즉시 일어날 미래를 나타낼 때는 「be about to+동사원형」
을 쓴다.

12 정답 was going to buy
→ 과거를 기준으로 미래에 일어날 계획된 일을 나타내고 있으
므로 「be going to+동사원형」에서 be동사 자리에 was가 오
는 것이 알맞다.

13 정답 will confirm → confirms
[해석] 그녀가 일정을 확인하자마자, 나는 표를 예약할 것이
다.
→ as soon as는 시간의 부사절 접속사이다. 시간의 부사절에
서는 현재시제로 미래를 나타내므로 will confirm을
confirms로 고쳐야 한다.

14 정답 will strike → strikes
[해석] 시계가 정오를 알리면, 학생들은 강당을 떠날 것이다.
→ 시간의 부사절에서는 현재시제로 미래를 나타내므로 will
strike를 strikes로 고쳐야 한다.

15 정답 is going to set → sets
[해석] 해가 지기 전에, 등산객들은 하산할 것이다.
→ 시간의 부사절에서는 현재시제로 미래를 나타내므로 is
going to set을 sets로 고쳐야 한다.

16 정답 will worsen → worsens
[해석] 저녁에 날씨가 나빠지면 야외 콘서트는 취소될 것이
다.
→ 조건의 부사절에서는 현재시제로 미래를 나타내므로 will
worsen을 worsens로 고쳐야 한다.

단원 평가 문제 UNIT 15 ~ UNIT 18 ▶ 문제편 p.84~85

정답

01 ④	02 ③	03 ③	04 ①	05 ②
06 ①	07 ④	08 ③	09 is	10 was
11 made	12 ③	13 ②	14 ③	15 ⑤
16 ①				

01 정답 ④ UNIT 17 동사의 과거–과거분사 불규칙 변화표
[해석] ① 말하다 ② 닫다 ③ 놓다 ④ 짓다 ⑤ 서다
→ ④ build는 과거와 과거분사가 같은 동사이다. (build-built-
built)
① speak - spoke - spoken ② shut - shut - shut ③ put -
put - put ⑤ stand - stood - stood

02 정답 ③ UNIT 17 동사의 과거–과거분사 불규칙 변화표
[해석] ① 숨다 ② 빌리다 ③ 얼다 ④ 잡다 ⑤ 퍼지다
→ ③ freeze는 원형, 과거, 과거분사가 모두 다른 동사이다.
(freeze-froze-frozen)
① hide - hid - hidden ② lend - lent - lent ④ catch -
caught - caught ⑤ spread - spread - spread

03 정답 ③ UNIT 16 현재시제, 과거시제
[해석] • 그녀는 매일 아침 샤워를 한다.
• 공항까지 가는 데 약 한 시간이 걸린다.
→ 습관과 일반적인 사실을 나타내고 주어가 She와 It이므로 3인칭
단수 현재형인 takes가 들어가야 한다.

04 정답 ① UNIT 18 미래시제
[해석] A: 내가 집에 도착하면 너에게 바로 문서들을 보내줄게.
B: 좋아, 너의 이메일을 기다릴게.
→ 집에 도착하는 시점에 문서를 보내고 이메일을 기다리겠다는 것이
므로, 미래시제를 나타내는 will이 들어가야 한다.

05 정답 ② UNIT 16 현재시제, 과거시제
[해석] • 우리는 어제 오후 3시에 회의를 했다.
• 우리는 지난 주말에 예술 박람회에서 좋은 시간을 보냈다.
→ yesterday와 last weekend라는 과거에 이미 끝난 동작을 나
타내므로 have의 과거형인 had가 들어가야 한다.

06 정답 ① UNIT 16 현재시제, 과거시제, UNIT 18 미래시제
[해석] ① 기차는 5분 후에 출발할 것이다.
② 그는 30대 시절에 영어를 가르쳤다.
③ 어제의 문자는 내게 큰 의미가 있었다.
④ 나는 그 회의에서 많은 새로운 사람들을 만났다.
⑤ 내가 이 수학 문제를 푸는 데 거의 한 시간이 걸릴 것이다.
→ ① 주어가 3인칭 단수이므로 가까운 미래를 나타내는 현재시제로
쓰려면 leaves, 미래시제로 쓰려면 will leave로 고쳐야 한다.

07 정답 ④ UNIT 16 현재시제, 과거시제
[해석] ① 그는 어제 5킬로미터를 뛰었다.
② 그녀는 다음 주에 새로운 팀에 합류할 것이다.
③ 나는 지난주에 친구에게 편지를 썼다.
④ 그녀는 요즘 버스를 타고 출근한다.
⑤ 너는 그 나라에 여행하려면 비자가 필요할 거야.
→ ④ these days가 쓰여 최근의 규칙적인 습관임을 나타내므로
was taking을 현재시제인 takes로 고쳐야 한다.

08 정답 ③ UNIT 16 현재시제, 과거시제
[해석] 남: 그녀는 지금 E. I. 소프트웨어 회사에서 일해.
여: 오, 정말? 나는 같은 회사의 마케팅 부서에서 일해.
→ (A) 주어가 3인칭 단수인 she이고 현재를 나타내는 now가 쓰였
으므로 works로 쓴다.
(B) 주어가 I이므로 동사원형인 work로 쓴다.

09 정답 is UNIT 16 현재시제, 과거시제
[해석] 지구는 태양으로부터 세 번째 행성이다.
→ 불변의 진리는 항상 현재시제로 쓴다.

10 정답 was   UNIT **16** 현재시제, 과거시제

[해석] 최초의 성공적인 백신은 1796년에 Edward Jenner에 의해 개발되었다.

→ 과거의 역사적인 사실은 항상 과거시제로 쓴다.

11 정답 made   UNIT **16** 현재시제, 과거시제

[해석] Wright 형제는 1903년에 첫 번째 동력 비행을 했다.

→ 과거의 역사적인 사실은 항상 과거시제로 쓴다.

12 정답 ③   UNIT **16** 현재시제, 과거시제

[해석] Flora는 아름다운 목소리를 ① 가지고 있다 ② 가졌다 ④ 듣는다 ⑤ 들었다.

→ 주어가 3인칭 단수이므로 동사원형인 hear는 알맞지 않다.

13 정답 ②   UNIT **18** 미래시제

[해석] 신사 숙녀 여러분, 뮤지컬 *Frankenstein*이 곧 시작됩니다.

→ ② 가까운 미래를 나타낼 때, 동사 자리에 starting이 단독으로 쓰일 수 없다.

14 정답 ③   UNIT **16** 현재시제, 과거시제

[해석] 2003년에 고고학자들은 4,000년 된 피라미드를 이집트에서 발견했다.

→ 과거의 역사적인 사실은 항상 과거시제로 써야 하므로 과거형인 ③ discovered가 들어가야 한다.

15 정답 ⑤   UNIT **17** 동사의 과거–과거분사 불규칙 변화표

[해석] 2시간 전에 Lily와 그녀의 개는 공원으로 산책하러 갔다. 그들은 아름다운 꽃을 발견하고 그것을 냄새 맡기 위해 멈췄다. 갑자기, Lily의 개가 나비를 쫓아 달려갔다. 그녀는 웃으며 그를 쫓아갔다. 잠시 후, 그들은 나무 아래에서 쉬며 평화로운 오후를 즐겼다. 집으로 가는 길에, Lily는 그것이 그들이 겪었던 최고의 산책이었다고 생각했다.

→ Two hours ago가 쓰여 과거 시점을 나타내므로 (A)에는 go 의 과거형인 went, (B)에는 stop의 과거형인 stopped가 들어가야 한다.

16 정답 ①   UNIT **17** 동사의 과거–과거분사 불규칙 변화표

→ ① run의 과거형은 ran이다.

UNIT **19** 진행시제

> **개념 확인 문제 정답**   ▶ 문제편 p.87
>
> **01** will be flying   **02** will be working
> **03** was surfing   **04** was working
> **05** went
> **06** I think that they are not telling the truth.
> **07** When I entered his room, he was having snacks.
> **08** Water consists of hydrogen and oxygen.
> **09** I've[I have] never seen this food before, but it tastes really good.
> **10** were, doing, was watching
> **11** are, wearing   **12** is talking   **13** Are, having

01 정답 will be flying

[해석] 네가 집에 올 때면, 나는 동해를 날고 있을 것이다.

→ 시간의 부사절에서 현재시제가 미래시제를 대신하고 있으므로 주절에는 미래진행시제를 쓰는 것이 알맞다.

02 정답 will be working

[해석] 다음 주 이맘때 당신은 새 직장에서 일하고 있을 것이다.

→ 미래의 특정 시점에 일어나는 동작을 나타내므로 미래진행시제를 사용한다.

03 정답 was surfing

[해석] Tom은 내가 도착했을 때 인터넷 검색을 하고 있었다.

→ 과거에 진행 중이었던 동작을 나타낸다.

04 정답 was working

[해석] 혼자 일하고 있었던 동안에 나는 이상한 소리를 들었다.

→ 과거에 진행 중이었던 동작을 나타낸다.

05 정답 went

[해석] James와 나는 지난 일요일에 영화를 보러 갔지만, 별로 재미있지 않았다.

→ 진행시제를 쓰면 but 이후의 내용과 문맥이 자연스럽지 않으므로 과거시제를 써야 한다.

06 정답 I think that they are not telling the truth.

→ think가 '생각하다'라는 뜻의 상태동사로 쓰일 때는 진행형으로 쓰지 않는다. that절의 동사 tell은 현재진행시제의 부정형으로 쓴다.

07 정답 When I entered his room, he was having snacks.

→ have가 '먹다'라는 뜻으로 쓰일 때는 진행형으로 사용할 수 있다. 과거의 일이므로 과거진행시제를 사용한다.

08 정답 Water consists of hydrogen and oxygen.

→ 상태동사 consist of는 진행형으로 쓰지 않는다.

09 정답 I've[I have] never seen this food before, but it tastes really good.

→ 주어의 의지가 포함되지 않은 지각동사 taste는 진행형으로 쓰지 않는다.

10 정답 were, doing, was watching

[해석] A: 너는 어제 이 시간에 무엇을 하고 있었니?
B: TV를 보고 있었어.

→ 과거의 특정 시점에 하고 있던 일을 물어보는 것이므로 과거진행시제를 사용한다.

11 정답 are, wearing

[해석] A: 너는 왜 그런 낡은 옷을 입고 있니?
B: 울타리와 지붕에 페인트칠을 하려고.

→ B가 앞으로 할 일을 말하고 있으므로 A는 지금 왜 그런 옷을 입고 있느냐는 뜻으로 현재진행시제로 묻는 것이 자연스럽다.

12 정답 is talking

[해석] A: Barbara는 어디에 있나요?
B: 그녀는 지금 통화 중이에요.
→ right now가 있으므로 현재 진행 중인 일이 되도록 현재진행시제를 써야 한다.

13 정답 Are, having

[해석] A: 좋은 시간 보내고 있니?
B: 응, 나는 매우 즐겁게 보내고 있어.
→ 현재진행시제로 대답하고 있으므로 질문도 현재진행시제를 써야 한다. have가 '시간을 보내다'라는 뜻으로 쓰일 때는 진행형으로 사용할 수 있다.

UNIT 20 완료시제

개념 확인 문제 정답　　　▶ 문제편 p.89~91

01 met　**02** have texted　**03** left
04 have called　**05** ②　**06** ③　**07** ②
08 ③　**09** ①　**10** ④　**11** ①　**12** ④
13 announced　**14** have explored
15 haven't visited　**16** has shown
17 have been seeing　**18** has gone
19 has been studying　**20** has been
21 has received　**22** ⓓ　**23** ⓒ　**24** ⓑ
25 ⓐ　**26** ⓕ　**27** ⓖ　**28** ⓔ
29 be finishing → have finished
30 finish → have finished
31 cook → have been cooking 또는 have cooked
32 be working → have been working
　　또는 have worked
33 be waiting → have been waiting

---

01 정답 met
→ yesterday는 명백한 과거 시점이므로 과거시제인 met으로 써야 한다.

02 정답 have texted
→ 과거에 일어난 일이 현재까지 이어짐을 나타내는 since가 있으므로 현재완료시제인 have texted로 써야 한다.

03 정답 left
→ in 2020는 명백한 과거 시점이므로 과거시제인 left로 써야 한다.

04 정답 have called
→ 과거에 일어난 일이 현재까지 이어짐을 나타내는 so far가 있으므로 현재완료시제인 have called로 써야 한다.

05 정답 ②
[해석] 너는 가족과 함께 해외여행을 해 본 적이 있니?
→ '여행하다'라는 동작을 해 본 적이 있음을 나타내는 〈경험〉 용법의 현재완료시제 문장이다. ever는 〈경험〉을 나타내는 현재완료시제와 자주 함께 쓰인다.

06 정답 ③
[해석] 그녀는 지금 막 발표 자료 수정을 마쳤다.
→ '마치다'라는 동작이 현재 완료되었음을 나타내는 〈완료〉 용법의 현재완료시제 문장이다. just는 〈완료〉를 나타내는 현재완료시제와 자주 함께 쓰인다.

07 정답 ②
[해석] 나는 그런 감동적인 연설은 들어본 적이 없어.
→ '듣다'라는 동작을 해 본 적이 있음을 나타내는 〈경험〉 용법의 현재완료시제 문장이다. never는 〈경험〉을 나타내는 현재완료시제와 자주 함께 쓰인다.

08 정답 ③
[해석] 그 파일 지우지 마! 나 아직 변경 사항을 저장하지 않았어.
→ '저장하다'라는 동작이 현재 완료되지 않았음을 나타내는 〈완료〉 용법의 현재완료시제 문장이다. yet은 〈완료〉를 나타내는 현재완료시제와 자주 함께 쓰인다.

09 정답 ①
[해석] 우리는 한 시간 넘게 기다려 왔어. 이제 그냥 가자.
→ '기다리다'라는 동작을 계속해 오고 있음을 나타내는 〈계속〉 용법의 현재완료시제 문장이다. for는 〈계속〉을 나타내는 현재완료시제와 자주 함께 쓰인다.

10 정답 ④
[해석] 봐! 화산이 폭발했어, 그래서 하늘이 연기로 가득해.
→ 화산이 폭발한 결과, 현재 하늘이 연기로 가득함을 나타내는 〈결과〉 용법의 현재완료시제 문장이다.

11 정답 ①
[해석] 우리 할아버지는 십대 때부터 희귀 동전을 수집해 오셨다.
→ '수집하다'라는 동작을 계속해 오고 있음을 나타내는 〈계속〉 용법의 현재완료시제 문장이다. since는 〈계속〉을 나타내는 현재완료시제와 자주 함께 쓰인다.

12 정답 ④
[해석] 그가 또 창문을 깼다고? 그의 부모님은 틀림없이 화나실 거야.
→ 창문을 깬 결과, 부모님이 화나실 것임을 나타내는 〈결과〉 용법의 현재완료시제 문장이다.

13 정답 announced
[해석] 어제 정부는 산불 피해 지역을 위한 새로운 계획을 발표했다.
→ yesterday는 명백한 과거 시점이므로 과거시제인 announced로 써야 한다.

14 정답 have explored
[해석] 많은 문화권의 예술가들이 수십 년 동안 정체성과 갈등을 탐구해왔다.
→ 예술가들이 수십 년 동안 탐구한 것을 나타내는 현재완료시제 have explored로 써야 한다.

15 정답 haven't visited

[해석] Issac은 아직 그 지역에 있는 고대 궁전 유적을 방문하지 못했다.

→ '방문하다'라는 동작을 해 본 적이 없음을 나타내는 〈경험〉 용법의 현재완료시제 문장이다. yet은 〈경험〉을 나타내는 현재완료시제와 자주 함께 쓰인다.

16 정답 has shown

[해석] 정말 멋진 경기야! 그 팀은 지금까지 최고의 경기력을 보여주고 있어.

→ '보여주다'라는 동작을 계속해 오고 있음을 나타내는 〈계속〉 용법의 현재완료시제 문장이다. so far는 〈계속〉을 나타내는 현재완료시제와 자주 함께 쓰인다.

17 정답 have been seeing

[해석] 나는 고등학생이었을 때부터 민수를 만나 오고 있다.

→ 현재완료진행시제이므로 「have been + -ing」 형태인 have been seeing으로 써야 한다.

18 정답 has gone

[해석] Jane은 시드니에 갔다.

→ 현재완료시제이고 주어가 3인칭 단수인 Jane이므로 「has + 과거분사」 형태인 has gone으로 써야 한다.

19 정답 has been studying

[해석] 그녀는 오늘 아침부터 지금까지 시험 공부를 하고 있다.

→ 현재완료진행시제이고 주어가 3인칭 단수인 She이므로 「has been + -ing」 형태인 has been studying으로 써야 한다.

20 정답 has been

[해석] 어제 이후로 날씨가 흐리다.

→ 현재완료시제이고 주어가 3인칭 단수인 It이므로 「has + 과거분사」 형태인 has been으로 써야 한다.

21 정답 has received

[해석] Tony는 여러 번 건강 검진을 받았다.

→ 현재완료시제이고 주어가 3인칭 단수인 Tony이므로 「has + 과거분사」 형태인 has received로 써야 한다.

22 정답 ⓓ

[해석] 그녀는 아주 많은 일을 해 오고 있었기 때문에 피곤했다.

→ 일을 많이 한 것은 과거 이전부터 과거까지 계속되어 온 일이므로 과거완료진행시제로 표현한다.

23 정답 ⓒ

[해석] 그가 역에 도착했을 때 기차는 벌써 떠나고 있었다.

→ 기차가 떠나고 있는 것은 그가 역에 도착하기 전부터 그가 역에 도착한 순간까지 계속되고 있는 일이므로 과거완료진행시제로 표현한다.

24 정답 ⓑ

[해석] Jimmy는 그 영화를 이미 보았기 때문에 영화를 보러가지 않았다.

→ 영화를 보러가지 않은 것에 대한 이유가 들어가야 하므로, 그때보다 더 이전에 '영화를 이미 보았기 때문'이라고 하는 과거완료시제인 ⓑ와 연결하는 것이 알맞다.

25 정답 ⓐ

[해석] 제주도로 이사한 때까지 나는 부산에서 살았다.

→ 제주도로 이사하기 이전부터 제주도로 이사한 과거의 시점까지 부산에서 계속 살았다는 것이므로 ⓐ와 연결하는 것이 알맞다.

26 정답 ⓕ

[해석] 그는 차를 수리하고 있었고, 그것은 마침내 작동했다.

→ 차가 작동하기 전까지 차를 수리한 것이므로 과거완료진행시제로 표현한다.

27 정답 ⓖ

[해석] 열심히 공부했지만 시험은 여전히 어려웠다.

→ 시험을 보기 전에 열심히 공부했던 것이므로 과거완료시제로 표현한다.

28 정답 ⓔ

[해석] 편지를 끝내자마자 나는 그것을 부쳤다.

→ 편지를 부치기 전에 편지를 쓴 것이므로 과거완료시제로 표현한다.

29 정답 be finishing → have finished

[해석] 오후 2시까지 그는 숙제를 끝낼 것이다.

→ by 2 p.m.이라는 미래의 특정 시점까지 숙제를 끝낼 것이라는 의미이므로 미래완료시제로 써야 한다.

30 정답 finish → have finished

[해석] 그들은 선생님이 돌아오실 때까지 공부를 끝낼 것이다.

→ by the time 이후는 미래의 특정 시점을 나타내므로 주절의 동사는 미래완료시제로 써야 한다.

31 정답 cook → have been cooking **또는** have cooked

[해석] 당신이 도착할 무렵이면 나는 두 시간 동안 요리를 하고 있을 것이다.

→ by the time은 '~할 무렵에는'이라는 뜻으로 미래의 시간을 나타내는 부사절을 이끈다. 따라서 미래완료진행시제로 미래에 계속될 일을 말하는 have been cooking이나 미래완료시제인 have cooked로 써야 한다.

32 정답 be working → have been working **또는** have worked

[해석] 그때면 그는 20년 동안 이 공장에서 일하고 있을 것이다.

→ 미래의 특정한 때인 by then과 함께 계속되는 기간을 나타내는 for 20 years가 있다. 따라서 미래완료진행시제로 미래에 계속될 일을 말하는 have been working이나 미래완료시제인 have worked로 써야 한다.

33 정답 be waiting → have been waiting

[해석] 10분 후면 나는 두 시간 동안 그를 기다리고 있게 될 것이다.

→ 미래의 특정 시점까지 계속되는 일을 말하므로 미래완료진행시제를 써야 한다.

정답

01 ②	**02** have been walking
03 tastes	**04** have you studied
05 had already left	**06** will be watching
07 have used	**08** had seen
09 was washing	**10** had missed
11 have been married, will have been married	
12 ②　　**13** ③	**14** likes　**15** consists
16 bought	**17** will have been
18 has known	**19** ⑤　　**20** ②
21 has been	**22** will have finished
23 has lived	**24** has gone
25 have already swum	**26** am thinking
27 ②　　**28** ⑤	**29** have been waiting
30 had been driving	**31** ④　　**32** ②

---

01 정답 ② — UNIT 19 진행시제

[해석] 나는 Bill이 다음 주에 ① 한국을 떠난다는 ③ 한국에 온다는 ④ 한국을 여행한다는 ⑤ 한국으로 이사온다는 것을 믿을 수 없다.
→ 이동을 나타내는 동사(go, come, depart, arrive, leave)가 현재진행시제로 쓰이면 가까운 미래를 나타낼 수 있다. ② 과거분사인 gone을 going으로 고쳐야 한다.

02 정답 have been walking — UNIT 20 완료시제

[해석] 나는 그때 이후로 운동 삼아 걸어오고 있다.
→ 그때 이후로 계속 걷고 있다는 뜻이므로 현재완료진행시제가 알맞다.

03 정답 tastes — UNIT 19 진행시제

[해석] 그 케이크는 맛이 아주 좋다.
→ 주어의 의지가 포함되지 않은 지각동사 taste는 진행형으로 쓰지 않는다.

04 정답 have you studied — UNIT 20 완료시제

[해석] 너는 얼마나 오랫동안 중국어를 공부했니?
→ how long은 기간을 묻는 표현이므로 과거부터 현재까지 〈계속〉의 의미가 있는 현재완료시제를 쓴다.

05 정답 had already left — UNIT 20 완료시제

[해석] 그는 공항에 도착했었지만 그의 비행기는 이미 떠났다.
→ 공항에 도착한 것보다 비행기가 떠난 것이 먼저 일어난 일이므로 과거완료시제를 쓴다.

06 정답 will be watching — UNIT 19 진행시제

[해석] 나는 밤 10시에서 11시까지 TV를 볼 것이다. 그러니 10시 30분에 나는 TV를 보는 중일 것이다.
→ 미래에 진행 중일 일을 나타내므로 미래진행시제를 써야 한다.

07 정답 have used — UNIT 20 완료시제

[해석] 이것들은 내가 12살 때부터 사용해 온 사전들이다.
→ 12살 때부터 사용해 온 사전이라는 의미이므로 현재완료시제를 써야 한다.

08 정답 had seen — UNIT 20 완료시제

[해석] 나는 전에 그를 본 적이 있었기 때문에 그를 쉽게 찾을 수 있었다.
→ 그를 찾았던 것보다 그를 본 것이 먼저 일어난 일이므로 과거완료시제를 써야 한다.

09 정답 was washing — UNIT 19 진행시제

[해석] 전화벨이 울렸을 때 Emma는 머리를 감고 있었다.
→ 전화벨이 울리던 과거에 진행 중이던 동작이므로 과거진행시제를 써야 한다.

10 정답 had missed — UNIT 20 완료시제

[해석] 우리는 버스를 놓쳤던 것을 알게 되어서 다음 버스를 기다렸다.
→ 버스를 놓친 것을 알게 된 것보다 버스를 놓친 것이 먼저 일어난 일이므로 과거완료시제를 써야 한다.

11 정답 have been married, will have been married — UNIT 20 완료시제

[해석] Tony와 Julie는 결혼한지 10년이 되었다. 내년에 그들은 결혼한지 11년이 될 것이다.
→ 첫 번째 빈칸에는 현재까지 결혼한 기간이 얼마나 되는지를 나타내므로 현재완료시제를 써야 한다. 두 번째 빈칸에는 내년, 즉 미래 시점까지 계속될 일을 말하므로 미래완료시제를 써야 한다.

12 정답 ② — UNIT 20 완료시제

[해석] A: 드디어 네가 나에게 말했던 영화를 봤어. 그 영화가 소설을 바탕으로 한 거 알고 있니?
B: 응, 나는 전에 그것을 읽었어.
→ 과거에 소설을 읽은 경험은 현재까지 영향을 준 것이므로 현재완료시제를 쓴다.

13 정답 ③ — UNIT 20 완료시제

[해석] 그녀는 그 미술관을 한 번 방문했다.
① 그들은 5년 동안 이곳에서 살았다.
② 그는 교실 열쇠를 잃어버렸다.
③ Tom은 돌고래 쇼를 한 번도 본 적이 없다.
④ 그녀는 막 방 청소를 끝냈다.
⑤ 나는 2010년 이후로 가난한 사람들을 위한 집을 짓는 일을 도왔다.
→ 주어진 문장과 ③은 〈경험〉, ①과 ⑤은 〈계속〉, ②은 〈결과〉, ④은 〈완료〉 용법으로 쓰였다.

14 정답 likes — UNIT 19 진행시제

[해석] Kevin은 그의 삼촌과 테니스를 치는 것을 좋아한다.
→ 상태동사 like는 진행형으로 쓰지 않으므로 현재시제로 고쳐야 한다.

15 정답 consists UNIT **19** 진행시제

[해석] 나의 가족은 작은 강아지를 포함하여 5명이다.
→ 상태동사 consist of는 진행형으로 쓰지 않는다.

16 정답 bought UNIT **20** 완료시제

[해석] 그들은 20년 전에 산 집에서 여전히 산다.
→ twenty years ago라는 명백한 과거 시점을 나타내는 부사구가 있으므로 과거시제로 고쳐야 한다.

17 정답 will have been UNIT **20** 완료시제

[해석] 만약 내가 호주를 한 번 더 여행한다면, 나는 거기에 세 번 가게 될 것이다.
→ 미래에 완료되는 일을 말하므로 미래완료시제로 고쳐야 한다.

18 정답 has known UNIT **20** 완료시제

[해석] 그는 네가 학교에 입학한 이후로 너를 알고 있다.
→ 상태동사 know는 진행형으로 쓰지 않으므로 현재완료시제로 고쳐야 한다.

19 정답 ⑤ UNIT **20** 완료시제

[해석] • 나는 내가 어렸을 때 이후로 영어를 배워오고 있다.
• 그의 엄마가 도착했었을 때 Sean은 밖에서 두 시간 동안 노는 중이었다.
→ 현재완료진행시제와 함께 쓰며 '~한 이후로'를 의미하는 접속사는 since이며 '~동안'을 의미하는 전치사는 for이다.

20 정답 ② UNIT **20** 완료시제

[해석] 나는 내가 그녀를 직접 만났을 때까지 그녀에 대해 아는 것이 없었다.
→ 그녀를 만난 것이 과거 시점이고 그 시점까지 그녀에 대해 아는 것이 없었다는 것이므로 과거완료시제인 ② had known이 적절하다.

21 정답 has been UNIT **20** 완료시제

[해석] 그녀는 한 시간 전에 통화를 하고 있었다. 그녀는 아직도 통화 중이다. → 그녀는 한 시간 동안 통화를 하고 있다.
→ 과거인 한 시간 전부터 현재까지 계속 통화하고 있는 일을 나타내므로 현재완료진행시제인 has been talking으로 써야 한다.

22 정답 will have finished UNIT **20** 완료시제

[해석] Chris는 아버지의 차를 세차하고 있다. 그가 세차를 끝내는 데 한 시간 정도 걸릴 것이다. → Chris는 약 한 시간 후에는 아버지 차의 세차를 끝냈을 것이다.
→ 아버지 차의 세차를 하는 것이 미래의 특정 시점까지 계속되므로 미래완료시제인 will have finished로 써야 한다.

23 정답 has lived UNIT **20** 완료시제

[해석] 내 사촌은 2년 전에 시카고로 떠났다. 그는 지금도 여전히 거기에 산다. → 내 사촌은 2년 동안 시카고에서 살고 있다.
→ 과거인 2년 전에 시카고로 떠나서 지금까지 계속되고 있는 일을 나타내므로 현재완료시제인 has lived로 써야 한다.

24 정답 has gone UNIT **20** 완료시제

[해석] Jenny는 도서관에 갔다. 그녀는 아직 돌아오지 않았다.
→ Jenny는 도서관에 갔다.
→ 과거에 도서관에 가서 현재 아직 돌아오지 않은 상태이므로 현재완료시제인 has gone으로 써야 한다.

25 정답 have already swum UNIT **20** 완료시제

[해석] A: 너는 체육관에서 수영을 할 거니?
B: 아니야. 나는 이번 주에 이미 체육관에서 수영했어.
A: 정말이야? 언제?
B: 나는 이틀 전에 거기에서 수영을 했어.
→ 이번 주에 이미 수영을 한 상황이므로 현재완료형이 되어야 한다.

26 정답 am thinking UNIT **19** 진행시제

[해석] A: 너 틀림없이 무슨 문제가 있구나. 무슨 일이야?
B: 나는 나의 미래에 대해 생각하고 있어. 나는 미래가 괜찮을지 확신하지 못하겠어.
→ 지금 미래에 관해 생각 중인 상황이므로 현재진행형이 사용되어야 한다.

27 정답 ② UNIT **20** 완료시제

[해석] ① 그는 지난주부터 아파왔다.
② 그 아기는 이제 막 걷기 시작했다.
③ 그들은 결혼한 지 30년이다.
④ 우리는 우리가 학교에 다닐 때 이후로 친구였다.
⑤ 나는 이 회사에서 10년 동안 일해왔다.
→ ②은 현재완료의 용법 중 〈완료〉를 나타내고 나머지는 모두 〈계속〉을 나타낸다.

28 정답 ⑤ UNIT **20** 완료시제

[해석] A: 너는 미국에 가본 적이 있니?
B: 아니. 거기에 가본 적이 전혀 없어. 너는 어때?
A: 나는 미국에 세 번 가봤어. 우리 삼촌이 거기에 살고 계시거든. 그는 10년 동안 거기에 살고 계셔.
→ ⑤ 삼촌이 미국에 10년 동안 살고 있는 상황이므로 현재완료시제인 has lived가 적절하다. ① 경험을 묻는 현재완료시제에 강조하는 ever가 포함됐다. ② 경험을 나타내는 현재완료시제에 부정을 의미하는 never가 들어갔다. ③ What about you?는 '너는 어때?'라고 묻는 표현이다. ④ 경험을 말하면서 '세 번'을 의미하는 표현이다.

29 정답 have been waiting UNIT **20** 완료시제

→ 20분 동안 과거부터 현재까지 버스를 기다리는 중이었으므로 현재완료진행시제인 have been waiting으로 써야 한다.

30 정답 had been driving UNIT **20** 완료시제

→ 몇 시간 동안 과거 이전부터 과거까지 운전하고 있었으므로 과거완료진행시제인 had been driving으로 써야 한다.

31 정답 ④ UNIT **20** 완료시제

[해석] 저는 당신의 조언이 필요해요. 저는 13살짜리 제 딸이 아주 걱정스러워요. 그 아이는 아주 건강하게 보였는데, 최근에 다이어트를 하기로 결심했어요. 3주가 넘는 기간 동안 그 아이는 과일이랑 물만 먹고 있어요. 그 결과 몸무게가 아주 많이 줄었고 아이는 이것에 만족하고 있어요. 저는 딸아이가 예전에 훨씬 더 좋아 보였다고 생각해요. 이제 그 아이는 피곤해 보이고 아파 보여요. 저는 그 아이가 다시 정상적으로 먹기 시작하도록 설득하고 싶어요.
→ (A) 3주가 넘는 기간 동안(For over three weeks) 계속되고 있는 일을 말하므로 현재완료진행시제가 알맞다. (B) 3주 이전부터 지금까지 계속 몸무게가 줄어든 것이므로 현재완료시제가 알맞다. (C) 몸무게가 줄어든 지금보다 이전에(before) 더 좋아 보인 것이므로 과거시제인 looked가 알맞다.

E Unit **15·20**

32 [정답] ②

[해석] Jane은 지난 몇 년 동안 많은 나라를 여행했다. 그녀가 이탈리아에 가기 전에, 그녀는 항상 콜로세움을 보고 싶어 했다. 마침내 로마에 도착했을 때, 그녀는 이미 콜로세움 티켓을 예약해 두었다. 그녀는 고대 유적지를 탐험하고 많은 사진을 찍었다. 여행을 마쳤을 때쯤에, 그녀는 로마 역사에 대해 많은 것을 배웠다. 그녀는 로마의 여러 곳을 방문했지만, 콜로세움은 분명 그녀 여행의 하이라이트였다.
→ ② Jane이 Italy에 가기 전부터 Colosseum을 보고 싶었던 것이므로, 과거완료시제인 had always wanted로 써야 한다.

F 조동사

UNIT 21 조동사의 특징과 조동사 do

> **개념 확인 문제 정답** ▶ 문제편 p.97
>
> **01** Will you **02** prepare **03** be able to
> **04** talk **05** should not
> **06** could not travel
> **07** Does Paul go to church every Sunday?
> **08** We didn't go to the station by taxi.
> **09** Did his nephew stay with him for a long time?
> **10** Rarely does my older brother go out.
> **11** I do know what I should do.
> **12** She earns as much money as he does.
> **13** going → go **14** travels → travel
> **15** does → do **16** trusted → trust

01 [정답] Will you
[해석] 너는 이번 금요일에 Jenny의 파티에 갈 거니?
→ 조동사의 의문문은 「조동사+주어+동사원형 ~?」 순서로 쓴다.

02 [정답] prepare
[해석] 그들은 수업 첫날에 대한 준비를 해야 한다.
→ 조동사 should 뒤에는 동사원형이 와야 한다.

03 [정답] be able to
[해석] 그는 나에게 그가 이 컴퓨터를 고칠 수 있다고 말했다.
→ 조동사 뒤에 조동사가 올 경우, 그 대체 어구를 쓰므로 be able to가 알맞다.

04 [정답] talk
[해석] 그 앵무새는 많은 단어들을 기억할 수 있고 그의 주인과 이야기할 수 있다.
→ 조동사 can 뒤에 나오는 동사원형 memorize와 병렬로 연결되어야 하므로 동사원형 talk를 써야 한다.

05 [정답] should not
[해석] 너는 다른 사람과 너의 개인 정보를 공유해서는 안 된다.
→ 조동사의 부정문은 조동사 뒤에 not을 쓴다.

06 [정답] could not travel
[해석] 화산 분출 때문에 그들은 그 나라로 여행할 수 없었다.
→ 조동사의 부정문은 조동사 뒤에 not을 쓴다.

07 [정답] Does Paul go to church every Sunday?
[해석] Paul은 매주 일요일마다 교회에 간다.
→ Paul은 매주 일요일마다 교회에 가니?
→ 일반동사 의문문에는 조동사 do를 쓴다. 주어 Paul이 3인칭 단수이므로 조동사 does를 맨 앞에 쓰고 주어와 동사의 순서로 의문문을 쓴다.

08 [정답] We didn't go to the station by taxi.
[해석] 우리는 택시를 타고 역에 갔다.
→ 우리는 택시를 타고 역에 가지 않았다.
→ 일반동사 부정문에는 조동사 do를 쓰는데, 주어진 문장의 시제가 과거이므로 didn't를 사용한다.

09 [정답] Did his nephew stay with him for a long time?
[해석] 그의 조카는 오랫동안 그와 함께 머물렀다.
→ 그의 조카가 오랫동안 그와 함께 머물렀니?
→ 과거시제 문장이므로 「Did+주어+동사원형 ~?」의 순서로 의문문을 만든다.

10 [정답] Rarely does my older brother go out.
[해석] 나의 형은 거의 외출하지 않는다.
→ 부정어 rarely가 문두로 나오면 주어와 동사가 도치되는데, 동사가 일반동사일 때는 조동사 do를 사용한다. 주어 my older brother가 3인칭 단수이므로 does를 주어 앞에 쓰고, 주어 뒤에는 동사원형을 써야 한다.

11 [정답] I do know what I should do.
[해석] 나는 내가 해야 하는 것을 안다.
→ 나는 내가 해야 하는 것을 정말로 안다.
→ 동사를 강조할 때는 조동사 do를 동사 앞에 쓴다.

12 [정답] She earns as much money as he does.
[해석] 그녀는 그가 버는 것만큼 돈을 번다.
→ 반복되는 동사는 조동사 do로 대신할 수 있다. earns가 반복되므로 he 뒤의 earns를 does로 대신한다.

13 [정답] going → go
[해석] 너는 네가 원하는 곳은 어디든 가도 된다.
→ 조동사 may 뒤에는 동사원형을 써야 한다.

14 [정답] travels → travel
[해석] 그는 내년에 세계 일주를 할 것이다.
→ 조동사 will 뒤에는 동사원형을 써야 한다.

15 [정답] does → do
[해석] 내 남동생이 Jessica에 대해 나보다 더 많이 안다.
→ 반복되는 동사는 조동사 do로 대신할 수 있다. I는 1인칭이므로 does가 아니라 do를 써야 한다.

16 정답 trusted → trust

[해석] 그는 그녀를 정말로 믿었다. 그녀는 그에게 또는 다른 사람에게도 결코 거짓말을 하지 않았다.

→ 동사를 강조하는 조동사 do 뒤에는 동사원형이 와야 한다.

UNIT 22 can (could), may (might)

개념 확인 문제 정답　　　　　　▶ 문제편 p.99

01 능력　　**02** 요청　　**03** 추측　　**04** 불가

05 너는 그에게 선물을 주는 것이 낫다.

06 내가 좀 더 편한 시간에 너에게 전화해도 될까?

07 그녀는 항상 늦는다. 그가 화를 내는 것도 당연하다.

08 당신은 이 건물 안에서 언제든 담배를 피워서는 안 된다.

09 새해에도 평안하시고 행복하시길 바랍니다.

10 May → Can 또는 Could　**11** can → be able to

12 can't → couldn't　　**13** can → may 또는 might

01 정답 능력

[해석] 그는 5개 국어 이상을 할 수 있다.

→ can은 '~할 수 있다'는 뜻의 능력을 나타낸다.

02 정답 요청

[해석] 내가 MP3 파일을 다운로드 받는 것을 도와주겠니?

→ Could you ~?는 '~해 주겠니?'라는 뜻으로 요청을 나타낸다.

03 정답 추측

[해석] 그곳에서 네가 본 사람이 Jane일 리 없다.

→ cannot be는 '~일 리 없다'라는 뜻으로 추측을 나타낸다.

04 정답 불가

[해석] 그 가구는 너무 무거워서 그는 혼자서 그것을 옮길 수 없었다.

→ could not은 '~할 수 없었다'는 뜻으로 불가능을 나타낸다.

05 정답 너는 그에게 선물을 주는 것이 낫다.

→ may[might] as well은 '~하는 것이 낫다'라는 뜻의 표현이다.

06 정답 내가 좀 더 편한 시간에 너에게 전화해도 될까?

→ May I ~?는 '내가 ~해도 될까?'라는 뜻으로 허가를 구할 때 쓴다.

07 정답 그녀는 항상 늦는다. 그가 화를 내는 것도 당연하다.

→ may[might] well은 '~하는 것도 당연하다'라는 뜻의 표현이다.

08 정답 당신은 이 건물 안에서 언제든 담배를 피워서는 안 된다.

→ may not은 '~해서는 안 된다'는 불허의 뜻을 나타낸다.

09 정답 새해에도 평안하시고 행복하시길 바랍니다.

→ may는 기원하는 말에 쓸 수 있다.

10 정답 May → Can 또는 Could

[해석] 우리는 곧 이륙할 것입니다. 안전벨트를 매 주시겠어요?

→ 요청할 때는 Can you ~?나 Could you ~?를 쓴다.

11 정답 can → be able to

[해석] 그 우주 과학자는 우리가 조만간 화성으로 여행을 갈 수 있을 거라고 말한다.

→ 조동사는 두 개를 연이어 쓸 수 없으므로 will 뒤의 can을 같은 의미의 표현인 be able to로 바꾸어 써야 한다.

12 정답 can't → couldn't

[해석] 어제는 영하 10도였다. 너무 추워서 우리는 밖에 나갈 수 없었다.

→ 과거의 일을 언급하고 있고, 주절에 과거 동사 was가 쓰였으므로 that절의 조동사도 과거형으로 써야 한다.

13 정답 can → may 또는 might

[해석] Mike의 삼촌이 복권에 당첨됐어. Mike가 매주 복권을 사는 것도 당연해.

→ '~하는 것도 당연하다'라는 뜻의 표현은 may[might] well이다.

UNIT 23 will (would), must (have to)

개념 확인 문제 정답　　　　　　▶ 문제편 p.101

01 would　　**02** would　　**03** Will

04 would　　**05** would　　**06** have to

07 must　　**08** not have to　**09** need not

10 must not

11 I would like to take part in the contest.

12 You didn't have to finish the work today.

13 She must doubt if it is possible.

14 Will you come to my house for dinner?

01 정답 would

[해석] 그녀는 그들이 집에 갈 거라고 생각했다.

→ 주절에 과거 동사가 쓰였으므로 that절의 조동사도 과거형으로 써야 한다.

02 정답 would

[해석] 그녀는 그와 헤어지고 싶어 한다.

→ '~하고 싶다'는 would like to라고 쓴다.

03 정답 Will

[해석] 나 대신 컴퓨터 좀 켜 줄래?

→ '~해 주겠니?'라고 요청할 때는 Will you ~?를 쓴다.

04 정답 would

[해석] 나는 그것을 포기하느니 차라리 그에게 도움을 요청하겠다.

→ 'B하느니 차라리 A하겠다'는 would rather A than B라고 쓴다.

05 정답 would

[해석] 그는 사용자 설명서를 읽지 않으려고 하더니 결국 토스터를 고장 냈다.

→ and 뒤에 연결된 문장에 과거 동사 broke가 쓰였으므로 and 앞에도 will의 과거형 would를 써야 한다.

06 정답 have to

[해석] 내가 이 신청서를 다시 작성해야 하니?

→ '내가 ~해야 되니?'라는 뜻의 의무를 나타내는 표현으로 Must I ~?, Need I ~?, Do I have to ~?를 쓴다.

07 정답 must

[해석] 그녀는 오늘 기운이 넘친다. 그녀는 기분이 좋은 게 틀림없다.

→ 강한 추측을 나타낼 때는 must를 쓴다.

08 정답 not have to

[해석] 그는 매우 부자였다. 그는 생계를 위해 일을 할 필요가 없었다.

→ '~할 필요가 없다'는 don't have to나 need not으로 쓴다.

09 정답 need not

[해석] Tom은 그의 병에서 회복했다. 그는 더 이상 병원에 갈 필요가 없다.

→ '~할 필요가 없다'는 의미의 need not을 쓴다.

10 정답 must not

[해석] 여기에 주차하면 경찰이 당신에게 딱지를 끊을 거예요. 당신은 여기에 주차해서는 안 돼요.

→ '~해서는 안 된다'는 금지의 표현은 must not으로 쓴다.

11 정답 I would like to take part in the contest.

→ '~하고 싶다'는 would like to로 쓴다.

12 정답 You didn't have to finish the work today.

→ '~할 필요가 없었다'는 didn't have to로 쓴다.

13 정답 She must doubt if it is possible.

→ '~임에 틀림없다'는 추측의 의미를 나타낼 때는 must를 쓴다.

14 정답 Will you come to my house for dinner?

→ 요청할 때는 Will you ~?나 Would you ~?를 쓴다.

UNIT 24 shall, should, ought to, had better (not)

개념 확인 문제 정답 　▶ 문제편 p.103

01 ⓐ　**02** ⓑ　**03** ⓔ　**04** ⓒ　**05** ⓓ

06 It's necessary that we attend the meeting.

07 All the evidence suggests that he is innocent.

08 My family doctor insisted that I stay in bed.

09 have → had　**10** to clean → clean

11 have → had　**12** not better → better not

13 to go → go　**14** not better → better not

01 정답 ⓐ

[해석] 나는 금요일까지 이 프로젝트를 끝낼 것이다.

→ shall은 의도를 나타낸다.

02 정답 ⓑ

[해석] 운전 중에 당신은 안전벨트를 매야 한다.

→ 운전하는 사람에게 해 줄 충고로 알맞은 것을 골라야 한다.

03 정답 ⓔ

[해석] 그녀는 나에게 실망했다. 내가 무엇을 해야 할까?

→ shall은 의도를 나타낸다.

04 정답 ⓒ

[해석] 그는 늘 학교에 지각한다. 그는 좀 더 일찍 일어나야 한다.

→ 학교에 늘 지각하는 사람에게 해 줄 충고로 알맞은 것을 골라야 한다.

05 정답 ⓓ

[해석] Jenny는 살을 빼고 싶어 한다. 그녀는 운동을 더 많이 해야 한다.

→ 살을 빼고 싶어 하는 사람에게 해 줄 충고로 알맞은 것을 골라야 한다.

06 정답 It's necessary that we attend the meeting.

[해석] 우리가 회의에 참석하는 것이 필요하다.

→ 주절에 필요를 나타내는 형용사 necessary가 쓰이면, that절의 동사는 「(should+) 동사원형」으로 쓴다.

07 정답 All the evidence suggests that he is innocent.

[해석] 모든 증거는 그가 무죄임을 암시한다.

→ suggest가 '암시하다'라는 뜻을 나타내므로, that절의 동사는 문맥에 맞게 is로 쓴다.

08 정답 My family doctor insisted that I stay in bed.

[해석] 내 주치의는 내가 누워 있어야 한다고 주장했다.

→ 주절에 주장을 나타내는 동사 insist가 쓰이면, that절의 동사는 「(should+) 동사원형」으로 쓴다.

09 정답 have → had

[해석] 저 구름을 봐. 너는 우산을 가져오는 게 좋겠어.

→ '~하는 게 좋다'라는 뜻의 조동사는 had better이다.

10 정답 to clean → clean

[해석] 네 방은 엉망이구나. 너는 방을 청소하는 게 좋겠어.
→ 조동사 had better 뒤에는 동사원형이 와야 한다.

11 정답 have → had

[해석] 우리는 지금 출발하는 게 좋겠어, 그렇지 않으면 기차를 놓칠 거야.
→ '~하는 게 좋다'라는 뜻의 조동사는 had better이다.

12 정답 not better → better not

[해석] 너는 회의에 늦지 않는 게 좋겠다.
→ had better의 부정문은 had better not으로 쓴다.

13 정답 to go → go

[해석] 너 창백해 보여. 병원에 가 보는 게 좋을 것 같아.
→ 조동사 had better 뒤에는 동사원형이 와야 한다.

14 정답 not better → better not

[해석] 너는 전화를 받지 않는 게 좋겠어.
→ had better의 부정문은 had better not으로 쓴다.

UNIT **25** used to, would, 조동사 + have + 과거분사

개념 확인 문제 정답　　　　▶ 문제편 p.105

01 ○
02 used to → was[became, got] used to
　　또는 eating → eat
03 was used to → used to
04 would → used to　　**05** must
06 should　　**07** may
08 cannot have seen
09 might have been changed
10 나는 좀 더 주의했어야 했다.
11 내가 어렸을 때는 여름이 지금만큼 덥지 않았다.
12 그는 기분이 좋아 보였다. 영화가 재미있었던 것이 틀림없다.
13 우리는 벌써 30분째 기다리고 있다. 우리는 자리를 예약했어야 했다.
14 이 지역은 예전에는 아파트 단지가 아니라 넓은 들판이었다.
15 그는 그 영화를 봤을지도 모른다.

---

01 정답 ○

[해석] 때때로 나는 그와 야구를 하곤 했다.
→ 과거의 반복적인 습관을 나타낼 때는 would를 사용한다.

02 정답 used to → was[became, got] used to
　　　또는 eating → eat

[해석] 내 미국인 친구는 젓가락으로 음식을 먹는 데 익숙해졌다. / 내 미국인 친구는 젓가락으로 음식을 먹곤 했다.
→ '~하곤 했다'라는 뜻의 조동사 used to 뒤에는 동사원형이 오고, '~하는 데 익숙해지다'라는 뜻의 be[become, get] used to 뒤에는 명사나 동명사가 온다.

03 정답 was used to → used to

[해석] 그녀는 일요일마다 아이들에게 영어를 가르치곤 했다.
→ 과거의 반복적인 습관을 나타낼 때는 used to를 쓴다.

04 정답 would → used to

[해석] 그는 70세임에도 불구하고 젊었을 때만큼 혈기가 왕성하다.
→ 과거에 계속된 상태를 나타낼 때는 used to를 쓴다.

05 정답 must

[해석] 그녀는 귀걸이 한 짝을 잃어버렸다. 그녀는 어딘가에 그것을 떨어뜨렸음에 틀림없다.
→ 과거의 일에 대한 추측은 must have p.p.로 표현한다.

06 정답 should

[해석] 너는 대통령을 만날 수 있는 기회를 놓쳤어. 너는 여기 왔어야 했어.
→ 과거에 이루지 못한 일에 대한 후회나 유감은 should have p.p.를 쓴다.

07 정답 may

[해석] 만약 그녀가 비행기 표를 구했더라면 그녀는 어제 집으로 떠났을지도 모른다.
→ 과거의 사실과 반대되는 일을 가정하고 있으므로 '~할 수 있었을 텐데'라는 뜻의 could have p.p.나 '~했을지도 모른다'는 뜻의 may[might] have p.p.를 써야 한다.

08 정답 cannot have seen

[해석] 너는 거기서 그녀를 보았을 리가 없어. 그녀는 그때 나와 함께 여기에 있었어.
→ '~했을 리가 없다'라는 뜻의 과거에 대한 추측은 cannot have p.p.를 사용한다.

09 정답 might have been changed

[해석] 그들이 그 나라를 정복했더라면 세계의 역사는 바뀌었을지도 모른다.
→ 과거의 사실과 반대되는 일을 가정하고 있으므로 '~했을지도 모른다'는 뜻의 might have p.p.를 써야 한다. should have p.p.는 과거에 이루지 못한 일에 대한 후회나 유감을 나타낼 때 쓴다.

10 정답 나는 좀 더 주의했어야 했다.

→ should have p.p.는 '~했어야 했다'라는 뜻으로 과거에 이루지 못한 일에 대한 후회나 유감을 나타낼 때 쓴다.

11 정답 내가 어렸을 때는 여름이 지금만큼 덥지 않았다.

→ used to는 과거에 계속된 상태를 나타낼 때 쓴다.

12 정답 그는 기분이 좋아 보였다. 영화가 재미있었던 것이 틀림없다.

→ must have p.p.는 '~했음에 틀림없다'라는 뜻으로 과거의 일에 대한 확실한 추측을 나타낼 때 쓴다.

13 정답 우리는 벌써 30분째 기다리고 있다. 우리는 자리를 예약했어야 했다.

→ ought to have p.p.는 '~했어야 했다'라는 뜻으로 과거에 이루지 못한 일에 대한 후회나 유감을 나타낼 때 쓴다.

14 [정답] 이 지역은 예전에는 아파트 단지가 아니라 넓은 들판
이었다.

→ used to는 '예전에는 ~이었다'라는 뜻으로 과거에 계속된
상태를 나타낸다.

15 [정답] 그는 그 영화를 봤을지도 모른다.

→ may have p.p.는 '~했을지도 모른다'라는 뜻을 나타낸다.

단원 평가 문제 UNIT 21 ～ UNIT 25 ▶ 문제편 p.106~110

정답

01 ⑤	**02** ①	**03** ②	**04** cannot
05 must	**06** cannot	**07** cannot	**08** must
09 ②	**10** ③	**11** might	**12** has to
13 will	**14** had better not		**15** cannot
16 used to	**17** must have had		
18 must come		**19** should sleep	
20 ⑤	**21** ②	**22** go	**23** shall
24 should	**25** ②	**26** ③	**27** ⑤
28 ②	**29** ②		

30 They did encourage her to reveal her true feelings.

31 She isn't able to force her son to eat what he doesn't like.

32 The students don't have to wear their uniform on Saturday.

33 ⑤　**34** ⑤　**35** should have come

36 don't have to get up 또는 need not get up

37 should [had better] not eat 또는 ought not to eat

38 ⑤	**39** ⑤	**40** ④	**41** ②	**42** ②
43 ③	**44** ②	**45** ⑤	**46** ④	

01 [정답] ⑤ 　　　UNIT 23 will (would), must (have to)
[해석] A: 정말 무서운 개군요!
B: 당신은 무서워할 필요가 없어요. 그 개는 절대 사람을 물지
않거든요.
→ '~할 필요가 없다'라는 의미를 나타내는 조동사 표현으로 적절한
것은 don't have to이다.

02 [정답] ① 　　　UNIT 22 can (could), may (might)
[해석] A: 저는 오늘 기분이 최악이에요. 미팅은 몇 시에 끝나죠?
B: 당신은 지금 집에 가서 쉬어도 괜찮아요.
→ '집에 가서 쉬어도 괜찮다'라는 허가를 나타내는 상황에 적절한 조
동사는 can이다.

03 [정답] ② UNIT 25 used to, would, 조동사 + have + 과거분사
[해석] A: 그는 시험에서 또 만점을 받았어.
B: ① 그는 밤새 공부하는 게 좋겠어.
② 그는 밤새 공부했음에 틀림없어.

③ 그가 밤새 공부했을 리가 없어.
④, ⑤ 그는 밤새 공부했어야 했어.
→ 시험에서 만점을 받은 사람에 대해 밤새 공부했을 거라고 추측하
는 것이 문맥상 어울린다. must have p.p.는 '~했음에 틀림없다'라
는 뜻으로 과거의 일에 대한 강한 추측을 나타낼 때 쓴다.

04 [정답] cannot 　　　UNIT 22 can (could), may (might)
[해석] Jenny는 이탈리아에 갔다. 그녀는 지금 한국에 있을 리가
없다.
→ '~일 리가 없다'는 부정의 추측은 cannot으로 나타낸다.

05 [정답] must 　　　UNIT 23 will (would), must (have to)
[해석] 그녀는 화장을 하고 있다. 그녀는 외출을 할 것임에 틀림없
다.
→ '~임에 틀림없다'는 뜻으로 강한 추측을 나타낼 때는 must를 쓴
다.

06 [정답] cannot 　　　UNIT 22 can (could), may (might)
[해석] Joe는 한 시간 전에 브런치를 먹었다. 그는 배가 고플 리가
없다.
→ '~일 리가 없다'는 뜻의 cannot이 알맞다.

07 [정답] cannot
　　　UNIT 25 used to, would, 조동사 + have + 과거분사
[해석] Peter는 어제 아팠다. 그가 숙제를 했을 리가 없다.
→ '~했을 리가 없다'는 뜻으로 과거 사실에 대한 부정의 추측은
cannot have p.p.로 쓴다.

08 [정답] must 　　　UNIT 23 will (would), must (have to)
[해석] 그는 하루 종일 걸었다. 그는 지금 피곤할 것임에 틀림없
다.
→ '~임에 틀림없다'는 뜻의 must가 알맞다.

09 [정답] ② UNIT 24 shall, should, ought to, had better (not)
[해석] ① 나는 나의 오랜 친구를 돕고 싶다.
② 너는 다시는 그녀를 만나지 않는 것이 좋겠다.
③ 나의 사촌 Jane은 일본 음식에 익숙하다.
④ 그녀는 의사의 충고를 듣지 않을 것이다.
⑤ 너는 내일 아침에 일찍 일어날 필요가 없다.
→ ② had better not 다음에는 동사원형이 나와야 한다. ①
「would like to+동사원형」: ~하고 싶다 ③ 「be used to+명사」: ~
에 익숙하다 ④ 주어의 고집을 나타내는 조동사 would ⑤ 「don't
have to+동사원형」: ~할 필요가 없다

10 [정답] ③ 　　　UNIT 22 can (could), may (might)
[해석] ① 나는 가족과 시간을 보내는 것을 정말 즐긴다.
② 너는 항상 나를 의지할 수 있다.
③ 그들은 다음 주 회의에 참석할 수 없다.
④ 그는 가능한 한 빨리 너에게 회신할 것이다.
⑤ 우리는 날씨에 대해 걱정할 필요 없다; 괜찮을 것이다.
→ ③ can을 대신하는 어구는 be able to이다. 따라서 to attend
로 고쳐야 한다. ① 강조를 위한 조동사 do ② '가능'의 can ④ 미래의
당위적인 행동을 나타내는 shall ⑤ 불필요를 나타내는 need not

11 [정답] might 　　　UNIT 22 can (could), may (might)
[해석] 그녀는 그 반지가 가짜일지도 모른다고 생각했다.
→ '~일지도 모른다'라는 추측의 의미를 나타내는 might가 알맞다.

12 정답 has to　　　　UNIT **23** will (would), must (have to)

[해석] David는 혼자 힘으로 숙제를 해야 한다.

→ 의무를 나타낼 때는 조동사 have to를 사용한다. 주어가 3인칭 단수이므로 has to를 써야 한다.

13 정답 will　　　　UNIT **23** will (would), must (have to)

[해석] 우리는 내년에 고등학생이 될 것이다.

→ '~일 것이다'라는 의미의 미래를 나타내는 조동사 will을 쓴다.

14 정답 had better not
　　　　UNIT **25** used to, would, 조동사 + have + 과거분사

[해석] 너는 허락 없이 그 방에 들어가지 않는 것이 좋겠다.

→ without permission이라는 말이 있으므로 빈칸에는 had better not이 들어가야 한다.

15 정답 cannot　　　　UNIT **22** can (could), may (might)

[해석] 나는 내 지갑을 찾을 수가 없다. 내가 어딘가에서 그것을 떨어뜨린 것이 틀림없다.

→ '~할 수 없다'는 불가능의 뜻을 나타낼 때는 cannot을 쓴다.

16 정답 used to
　　　　UNIT **25** used to, would, 조동사 + have + 과거분사

[해석] 내가 어렸을 때 나의 아버지는 일요일 오후마다 요리를 하시곤 했다.

→ 과거의 규칙적인 습관은 used to로 나타낸다.

17 정답 must have had
　　　　UNIT **25** used to, would, 조동사 + have + 과거분사

[해석] A: 나는 왜 John이 어젯밤 파티에 오지 않았는지 궁금해.
B: 타당한 이유가 아니면 그가 파티를 놓쳤을 리 없어. 그는 뭔가 일이 생겼음에 틀림없어.

→ 과거 일에 대한 강한 추측은 must have p.p.로 쓴다.

18 정답 must come　　　　UNIT **23** will (would), must (have to)

[해석] A: 우리가 길을 잃은 것 같아.
B: 알아. 우리는 어떻게 해야 할까?
A: 나도 모르겠어. 우리가 선생님 말씀을 듣지 않았어. 우리는 그의 말을 들었어야 했는데.
B: 지난 일을 가지고 후회하지 마. 누군가가 와서 우리를 도와줄 것임에 틀림없어.

→ '~임에 틀림없다'의 강한 추측은 조동사 must를 이용해서 표현한다.

19 정답 should sleep
　　　　UNIT **24** shall, should, ought to, had better (not)

[해석] A: Tom이 심각한 건강 문제가 있어.
B: 그게 사실이니? 그는 전에는 괜찮아 보였는데.
A: 근데 최근에 그는 밤에 잠을 자지 않았어. 의사는 그가 밤에 잠을 자야 한다고 주장했지만, 그는 의사의 충고를 따르지 않았어.
B: 그가 건강상의 문제가 있는 것은 당연해.

→ 주절에 주장을 나타내는 동사 insist가 사용되었으므로 종속절에 당위의 의미를 표현하는 조동사 should가 사용되어야 한다.

20 정답 ⑤　　　　UNIT **22** can (could), may (might)

[해석] ① 나의 형은 스페인어를 할 수 있다.
② 누가 이 질문에 답할 수 있니?
③ 그는 100미터를 13초 안에 달릴 수 있다.
④ 그들은 네가 이 책을 나르는 것을 도와줄 수 있다.
⑤ John은 괜찮아 보이지 않는다. 그는 아플지도 모른다.

→ ⑤의 can은 '~일지 모른다, ~일 수 있다'라는 추측의 의미로 쓰였고, 나머지는 모두 '~할 수 있다'는 능력·가능의 의미로 쓰였다.

21 정답 ②　　　　UNIT **23** will (would), must (have to)

[해석] ① 당신은 이곳에서 조용히 해야 한다.
② 김 씨는 좋은 선생님임에 틀림없다.
③ 너는 너의 부모님께 당장 전화해야 한다.
④ 너는 하루에 적어도 두 번 물을 마셔야 한다.
⑤ 모든 학생들은 규칙을 준수하고 따라야 한다.

→ ②은 조동사 must의 의미 중 '강한 추측'을 나타내고 나머지는 모두 '당위'를 나타낸다.

22 정답 go　　　UNIT **25** used to, would, 조동사 + have + 과거분사

[해석] A: 나는 예전에 매일 아침 헬스장에 가곤 했는데, 시간이 지나면서 그 습관을 잃어버렸어.
B: 그런 일은 늘 있지.

→ 문맥상 '~하곤 했다'를 의미해야 하므로 go가 알맞다.

23 정답 shall
　　　　UNIT **24** shall, should, ought to, had better (not)

[해석] A: 내일 발표에 대해 무엇을 해야 할지 잘 모르겠어.
B: 걱정 마. 너는 잘 할 거야! 잘 준비했잖아.

→ 문맥상 '~할 것이다'를 의미해야 하므로 shall이 알맞다.

24 정답 should
　　　　UNIT **25** used to, would, 조동사 + have + 과거분사

[해석] A: 나는 그림 그리기 같은 새로운 취미를 시작할까 생각 중이야.
B: 좋은 생각이야! 넌 그걸 더 빨리 했어야 했어.

→ '~했어야 했다'를 의미하는 것은 should have p.p.이다.

25 정답 ②　　　　UNIT **21** 조동사의 특징과 조동사 do

[해석] 그들은 아무에게도 비밀번호를 공유해서는 안 된다.

→ 조동사의 부정문은 조동사 뒤에 not을 붙인다.

26 정답 ③　　UNIT **24** shall, should, ought to, had better (not)

[해석] 당신은 도로의 경고 표지판을 무시하지 않는 것이 좋다.

→ had better의 부정은 had better 뒤에 not을 붙인다.

27 정답 ⑤　　　UNIT **25** used to, would, 조동사 + have + 과거분사

[해석] ① 너는 우선 경찰에 전화를 하는 게 좋겠어.
② 그가 숙제하는 것을 도와줘도 되나요?
③ 너는 그녀가 여기로 돌아오게 해야 한다.
④ 그가 미국에 살았던 것은 사실일지도 모른다.
⑤ 그녀는 아침에 일찍 일어나곤 했다.

→ ⑤ 조동사 used to 뒤에는 동사원형이 와야 한다. (got → get)

28 정답 ②　UNIT **24** shall, should, ought to, had better (not)

[해석] ① 그녀는 세 개의 언어를 유창하게 할 수 있다.
② 우리는 내일까지 이 프로젝트를 끝내야 한다.
③ 너는 그 결정을 재고하는 것이 낫다.
④ 나는 그가 그의 소비에 더 신경 쓰기를 주장한다.
⑤ 그들은 지름길로 갔었다면 더 일찍 도착했을 것이다.

→ 의무를 의미하는 조동사는 ought to이다. (ought → ought to)

29 [정답] ②   UNIT **25** used to, would, 조동사 + have + 과거분사
→ '~했음에 틀림없다'를 의미하는 표현은 must have p.p.이다.

30 [정답] They did encourage her to reveal her true feelings.   UNIT **21** 조동사의 특징과 조동사 do

[해석] 그들은 솔직한 심정을 밝히도록 그녀를 부추겼다.
→ 그들은 솔직한 심정을 밝히도록 그녀를 정말로 부추겼다.
→ 동사를 강조할 때는 조동사 do를 쓴다. 과거동사가 쓰였으므로 조동사는 과거형인 did를 쓰고, encouraged는 동사원형으로 쓴다.

31 [정답] She isn't able to force her son to eat what he doesn't like.   UNIT **22** can (could), may (might)

[해석] 그녀는 아들에게 그가 좋아하지 않는 것을 먹도록 강요할 수 없다.
→ 조동사 can은 be able to로 바꾸어 쓸 수 있다.

32 [정답] The students don't have to wear their uniform on Saturday.   UNIT **23** will (would), must (have to)

[해석] 학생들은 토요일에 교복을 입을 필요가 없다.
→ '~할 필요가 없다'는 뜻의 조동사 need not은 don't have to로 바꾸어 쓸 수 있다.

33 [정답] ⑤   UNIT **25** used to, would, 조동사 + have + 과거분사
[해석] ① 부탁 하나 해도 될까요?
② 나는 방을 예약하고 싶다.
③ 너는 보고서를 제출할 필요가 없다.
④ 그녀는 초콜릿 케이크를 만들 수 있다.
⑤ 그들은 부모님에게 사실을 말했어야 했다.
그들은 부모님에게 사실을 말했을지도 모른다.
→ ⑤ should have p.p.는 '~했어야 했다'라는 뜻으로 과거에 이루지 못한 일에 대한 후회나 유감을 나타낼 때 쓰는 반면, may have p.p.는 '~했을지도 모른다'라는 뜻으로 과거의 사실에 대한 추측을 나타낼 때 쓴다.

34 [정답] ⑤   UNIT **23** will (would), must (have to)
[해석] ① 그녀는 뉴욕에 살곤 했다.
② 너는 우산을 가져가야 한다. ③ 너는 규칙을 지켜야 한다.
④ 나는 내일 체육관에 갈지도 모른다.
⑤ 운전 중에 전화기를 사용할 필요는 없다.
운전 중에 전화기를 사용하지 않는 것이 좋다.
→ ⑤ don't have to는 '~할 필요 없다'를, had better not은 '~하지 않는 편이 좋겠다'를 의미한다.

35 [정답] should have come
   UNIT **25** used to, would, 조동사 + have + 과거분사
[해석] A: 어젯밤에 파티에 못 갔어. 파티는 어땠니?
B: 환상적이었어. 너는 파티에 왔어야 했어.
→ 과거에 하지 않은 일에 대한 후회나 유감은 should have p.p.로 쓴다.

36 [정답] don't have to get up 또는 need not get up
   UNIT **23** will (would), must (have to)
[해석] A: 정신 차리고 일어나! 7시야.
B: 오늘은 일을 안 해서 일찍 일어날 필요가 없어.
→ '~할 필요가 없다'는 don't have to나 need not으로 쓴다.

37 [정답] should [had better] not eat 또는 ought not to eat
   UNIT **24** shall, should, ought to, had better (not)
[해석] A: 나는 건강을 위해 인스턴트 식품을 그만 먹기로 결심했어.
B: 잘했어. 너는 인스턴트 식품을 더 이상 먹지 않는 게 좋아.
→ 문맥상 '~하지 않는 게 좋다'는 뜻이 적절하므로 충고를 나타내는 should, ought to, had better를 사용한 부정문을 써야 한다.

38 [정답] ⑤   UNIT **22** can (could), may (might)
[해석] A: Mary가 일본어를 잘 하니?
B: 아니, 그녀는 일본어를 잘하지 않아. 그녀는 겨우 일 년 동안 그것을 공부했어.
A: 그런데 그녀는 이번 겨울에 일본에 갈 거잖아. 맞지?
B: 맞아. 그게 바로 그녀가 일본어를 매우 잘 하고 싶어 하기를 원하는 이유야.
→ ⑤ can과 be able to는 모두 가능을 나타내는 표현이고 둘 중 하나만 사용하는 것이 적절하다.

39 [정답] ⑤   UNIT **25** used to, would, 조동사 + have + 과거분사
[해석] A: 나는 어디에서도 내 열쇠를 찾을 수 없어!
B: 너는 아마 사무실에 두고 왔을 거야.
A: 오, 그럴 것 같아. 떠나기 전에 확인했어야 했는데.
B: 걱정 마, 우리가 돌아가서 그것들을 가져올 수 있어.
A: 잠깐, 나는 아마 차에 두고 왔을 거야.
B: 그럴 수도 있겠네. 우선 차부터 확인해 보자.
→ ⑤ '~했을지도 모른다'를 의미하는 표현은 may[might] have p.p.이다.

40 [정답] ④   UNIT **24** shall, should, ought to, had better (not)
[해석] 너는 너의 의사가 네게 해준 조언을 따라야만 한다.
→ '~해야만 한다'라는 당위를 나타내는 조동사 ought to와 의미가 같은 조동사는 should이다.

41 [정답] ②   UNIT **23** will (would), must (have to)
[해석] 원하지 않으면 당신은 제 전화를 받을 필요가 없습니다.
→ '~할 필요가 없다'를 의미하는 don't have to와 같은 표현은 need not이다.

42 [정답] ②   UNIT **25** used to, would, 조동사 + have + 과거분사
[해석] 나는 너의 답장을 받지 못했어. 그것이 내 스팸 폴더에 들어갔을 수도 있어.
→ may have p.p.(~했을지도 모른다)와 바꿔 쓸 수 있는 것은 might have p.p.이다.

43 [정답] ③   UNIT **21** 조동사의 특징과 조동사 do
[해석] 나는 이번 일요일에 콘서트에 정말 가고 싶어.
① 너는 스톱워치를 가지고 있니?
② Sally, 너 설거지 했니?
③ 그녀는 어젯밤에 정말로 숙제를 했다.
④ 나는 그렇게 이상한 사람을 결코 본 적이 없었다.
⑤ 너는 카메라를 가져올 필요가 없다.
→ 주어진 문장과 ③의 do동사는 동사를 강조하는 용법으로 쓰였다.
① 의문문에 쓰인 조동사 ② '~하다'라는 뜻의 일반동사 ④ 도치 구문에 쓰인 조동사 ⑤ 부정문에 쓰인 조동사

44 정답 ② UNIT **24** shall, should, ought to, had better (not)

[해석] 70세가 되신 나의 할머니는 항상 내가 무엇을 해야 하고 무엇을 하지 말아야 하는지를 나에게 말씀하신다. 할머니는 항상 찬장 문을 닫아 두어야 한다고 주장하신다. 할머니는 내가 찬장 문을 열어 두면 우리 가족에게 불운을 가져오게 될 거라고 말씀하신다. 어려서 이것을 들었을 때 나는 그것이 미신적인 것과 관련이 있다고 생각했다. 지금 나는 그것이 나에게 좋은 습관을 기르게 해 주었다는 것을 안다.

→ ② 주절에 주장을 나타내는 동사 insist가 쓰였으므로 that절의 동사는 「should+동사원형」으로 써야 한다. (should be)

45 정답 ⑤ UNIT **24** shall, should, ought to, had better (not)

[해석] Tom은 비행기를 타는 걸 좋아하지 않지만, 다음 주 출장 때문에 비행기를 타야 할 것이다. 그의 동료는 함께 갈 수 있었지만, 가족 행사 때문에 참석하지 못한다. Tom은 차로 가고 싶지만, 그 여행은 차로 가기엔 너무 멀다. 그는 가장 좋은 가격을 얻기 위해 곧 항공편을 예약해야 한다. 그는 늦고 싶지 않기 때문에 계획보다 더 일찍 출발해야 한다. 그는 다가오는 바쁜 한 주를 준비하며 "나는 여행 중에 집중하는 게 좋겠어."라고 생각했다.

→ had better 뒤에는 동사원형이 와야 하므로 to stay를 stay로 고쳐야 한다.

46 정답 ④ UNIT **25** used to, would, 조동사 + have + 과거분사

→ '그의 동료가 같이 갈 수도 있었는데'라는 의미가 되어야 하므로 ④ could have joined가 알맞다.

G 수동태

UNIT **26** 수동태의 개념 및 형태

개념 확인 문제 정답 ▶ 문제편 p.113

01 They were fired by the company.
02 His grandparents were visited by him.
03 The dangerous work is done by robots.
04 The last train was missed by her.
05 The front seat was taken by the young man.
06 Lots of buildings were destroyed by the earthquake.
07 not **08** is not
09 by him **10** were not arrested
11 was not broken **12** was the picture taken
13 was that window broken
14 this house designed by you

---

01 정답 They were fired by the company.

[해석] 그 회사는 그들을 해고했다.

→ 그들은 그 회사에 의해 해고되었다.

→ 능동태 문장의 목적어 them을 주격 they로 바꾸고, 동사 fired는 「be동사+과거분사」로 바꾼다. 수동태 문장의 주어가 복수이므로 be동사는 were를 써야 한다.

02 정답 His grandparents were visited by him.

[해석] 그는 그의 조부모님을 방문했다.

→ 그의 조부모님은 그의 방문을 받았다.

→ 수동태 문장의 주어는 복수 His grandparents이므로 be동사는 were를 써야 한다. 능동태 문장의 주어 He를 목적격 him으로 바꾸어 by 뒤에 쓴다.

03 정답 The dangerous work is done by robots.

[해석] 로봇들이 그 위험한 일을 한다.

→ 그 위험한 일은 로봇들에 의해 행해진다.

→ 능동태 문장의 목적어 the dangerous work가 수동태 문장의 주어가 된다.

04 정답 The last train was missed by her.

[해석] 그녀는 마지막 열차를 놓쳤다.

→ 마지막 열차는 그녀에 의해 놓쳐졌다.

→ 수동태 문장의 주어가 단수 명사 The last train이므로 be동사는 was를 써야 한다.

05 정답 The front seat was taken by the young man.

[해석] 젊은 남자가 앞자리를 차지했다.

→ 앞자리는 젊은 남자에 의해 차지되었다.

→ 능동태 문장의 목적어 the front seat가 수동태 문장의 주어가 된다.

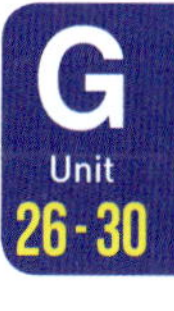

06 정답 Lots of buildings were destroyed by the earthquake.

[해석] 그 지진이 많은 건물들을 파괴했다.

→ 많은 건물들이 그 지진으로 파괴되었다.

→ 능동태 문장의 목적어 lots of buildings가 수동태 문장의 주어가 되고 「be동사+과거분사」의 수동태 동사는 주어의 수에 맞추어 복수형 were를 쓴다.

07 정답 not

[해석] 이 메시지는 어젯밤 내가 보낸 것이 아니다.

→ 수동태의 부정문은 「be동사 + not + 과거분사」로 쓴다.

08 정답 is not

[해석] 그 방은 Jane이 매일 청소하지 않는다.

→ 수동태의 부정문은 「be동사 + not + 과거분사」로 쓴다.

09 정답 by him

[해석] 그 기계는 그에 의해 개발되지 않았다.

→ 수동태 문장의 행위자는 「by+목적격」으로 나타낸다.

10 정답 were not arrested

[해석] 그 용의자는 경찰에 의해 체포되지 않았다.

→ 수동태의 부정문은 「be동사+not+과거분사」로 써야 한다.

11 정답 was not broken

[해석] 그 유리는 Nick에 의해 깨지지 않았다.

→ 뒤에 「by+목적격」, 즉 수동태 문장의 행위자가 나와 있으므로 수동태 동사의 부정형인 was not broken이 알맞다.

12 [정답] was the picture taken

[해석] 어디에서 그 사진이 찍혔니?

→ 사진은 찍혔던 것이므로 was taken으로 표현한다. 수동태 문장의 주어 the picture는 의문문에서 be동사와 과거분사 사이에 위치해야 한다.

13 [정답] was that window broken

[해석] 저 창문은 누구에 의해 깨졌니?

→ '저 창문이 깨졌다'라는 뜻의 수동태 문장은 that window was broken이다. 의문문에서 주어는 be동사와 과거분사 사이에 위치한다.

14 [정답] this house designed by you

[해석] 이 집은 당신에 의해 설계되었나요?

→ design의 수동태 과거형으로 was designed를 쓴다.

UNIT 27 수동태의 시제

개념 확인 문제 정답 ▶ 문제편 p.115

01 This water is drunk by the villagers.

02 The email was written by the police officers.

03 English is spoken by many people around the world.

04 The document will[are going to] be printed later.

05 The roof of my house is being painted by two men.

06 Empty boxes were being collected by an old woman.

07 Symphonies are being played by the famous pianist.

08 Hot food was being served by the waitress.

09 Cheerful songs are being sung by the students.

10 had been invited   **11** has used

12 have been supplied   **13** had been cooked

14 has usually been spent

15 had been canceled

01 [정답] This water is drunk by the villagers.

→ 주어 This water는 3인칭 단수 명사이므로 수동태의 be동사도 3인칭 단수형인 is를 써야 한다. '마시다'라는 뜻의 drink의 과거분사는 drunk이다.

02 [정답] The email was written by the police officers.

→ 주어 The email이 단수이고, '쓰여졌다'는 과거시제로 표현해야 하므로 be동사는 was를 사용해야 한다. write의 과거분사는 written이다.

03 [정답] English is spoken by many people around the world.

→ 주어 English가 3인칭 단수 명사이므로 수동태의 be동사도 3인칭 단수형인 is를 써야 한다. speak의 과거분사는 spoken이다.

04 [정답] The documents will[are going to] be printed later.

→ 미래시제 수동태가 되어야 하므로 will[are going to] be printed로 오는 것이 알맞다.

05 [정답] The roof of my house is being painted by two men.

[해석] 두 명의 남자가 우리 집 지붕을 페인트칠하고 있다.

→ 우리 집 지붕은 두 명의 남자에 의해 페인트칠 되고 있다.

→ 진행시제 수동태는 「be동사+being+과거분사」로 쓴다. 현재진행시제이고, 단수 명사 the roof of my house가 주어이므로 is being painted가 수동태 동사가 된다.

06 [정답] Empty boxes were being collected by an old woman.

[해석] 한 노부인이 빈 상자들을 모으고 있었다.

→ 빈 상자들이 한 노부인에 의해 모아지고 있었다.

→ 과거진행시제이고, 복수 명사 empty boxes가 주어이므로 were being collected가 수동태 동사가 된다.

07 [정답] Symphonies are being played by the famous pianist.

[해석] 유명한 피아니스트가 교향곡을 연주하고 있다.

→ 교향곡은 유명한 피아니스트에 의해 연주되고 있다.

→ 현재진행시제이고, 복수 명사 symphonies가 주어이므로 are being played가 수동태 동사가 된다.

08 [정답] Hot food was being served by the waitress.

[해석] 그 종업원은 뜨거운 음식을 제공하고 있었다.

→ 뜨거운 음식은 그 종업원에 의해 제공되고 있었다.

→ 과거진행시제이고, 단수 명사 hot food가 주어이므로 was being served가 수동태 동사가 된다.

09 [정답] Cheerful songs are being sung by the students.

[해석] 학생들이 경쾌한 노래를 부르고 있다.

→ 경쾌한 노래가 학생들에 의해 불려지고 있다.

→ 현재진행시제이고, 복수 명사 cheerful songs가 주어이므로 are being sung이 수동태 동사가 된다.

10 [정답] had been invited

[해석] 몇몇 친구들이 나에 의해 그 파티에 초대받았다.

→ 완료시제 수동태는 「have[has]/had been+과거분사」로 쓴다.

11 [정답] has used

[해석] 그 목수는 탁자를 만들기 위해 견고한 나무를 사용해 왔다.

→ 목수가 나무를 사용하는 능동의 관계이므로 능동태 동사를 써야 한다.

12 [정답] have been supplied

[해석] 이 제품들은 그의 회사에 의해 공급되어져 왔다.

→ 현재완료시제 수동태는 「have/has been+과거분사」로 쓴다.

13 정답 had been cooked

[해석] 스테이크는 너무 오래 요리되어서 아주 질겼다.

→ 스테이크가 질긴 것보다 스테이크가 요리된 것이 먼저 일어난 일이므로 과거완료시제 수동태를 써야 한다.

14 정답 has usually been spent

[해석] 그녀의 용돈은 대개 간식에 쓰여 왔다.

→ 용돈은 누군가에 의해 '쓰이는' 수동의 관계이므로 수동태가 쓰여야 한다. 현재완료 수동태에서 빈도부사는 have[has]와 been 사이에 위치한다.

15 정답 had been canceled

[해석] 극장에 도착했을 때 우리는 영화가 취소되었다는 것을 알았다.

→ 우리가 극장에 도착한 것보다 영화가 취소된 것이 먼저 일어난 일이므로 과거완료 수동태를 써야 한다.

UNIT 28 조동사와 동사구의 수동태

개념 확인 문제 정답 ▶ 문제편 p.117

01 can't be seen **02** may be heard
03 Helmets should be worn
04 was not provided **05** will be taught
06 is made up of **07** was laughed at
08 been run over **09** be filled in
10 been put off **11** is → 삭제
12 are → be **13** stop → be stopped
14 dealt → dealt with

01 정답 can't be seen

[해석] 우리는 밤에 태양을 볼 수 없다.

→ 태양은 밤에 우리에게 보여질 수 없다.

→ 조동사 수동태는 「조동사+be+과거분사」로 쓴다.

02 정답 may be heard

[해석] 당신은 '삐' 소리를 들을지도 모른다.

→ '삐' 소리는 당신에게 들릴지도 모른다.

→ 조동사 수동태는 「조동사+be+과거분사」로 쓴다.

03 정답 Helmets should be worn

[해석] 근로자들은 헬멧을 착용해야 한다.

→ 헬멧은 근로자들에 의해 착용되어져야 한다.

→ 능동태의 목적어 helmets가 수동태 문장의 주어가 되어야 한다. wear의 과거분사는 worn이다.

04 정답 was not provided

[해석] 그들은 해결책을 제공하지 않았다.

→ 해결책은 그들에 의해 제공되지 않았다.

→ 조동사 do가 쓰인 문장을 수동태로 바꿀 때는 do를 쓰지 않고 be동사를 쓴다. 과거시제 부정문이고, 단수 명사 the solution이 주어이므로 동사는 「was not+과거분사」의 형태로 써야 한다.

05 정답 will be taught

[해석] 그들은 이 학교의 학생들에게 영어로 가르칠 것이다.

→ 이 학교의 학생들은 그들에 의해 영어로 배울 것이다.

→ 조동사 수동태는 「조동사+be+과거분사」로 쓴다.

06 정답 is made up of

[해석] 운전 면허 시험은 필기 시험과 주행 시험으로 구성된다.

→ '~으로 구성되다'는 be made up of라고 쓴다.

07 정답 was laughed at

[해석] 어제 그의 우스꽝스러운 모자는 그의 반 친구들에 의해 놀림을 받았다.

→ Yesterday라는 과거를 나타내는 부사가 있으므로 수동태 동사는 과거형으로 써야 한다.

08 정답 been run over

[해석] 경찰관은 과속하는 차량에 의해 사슴이 치였다고 보고했다.

→ 동사구의 수동태는 동사구를 하나로 취급하여 수동태로 바꾼다. 보고한 것보다 치인 것이 먼저 일어난 일이므로 「had been+과거분사」의 과거완료 수동태로 써야 한다.

09 정답 be filled in

[해석] 이 서식의 모든 빈칸이 채워져야 한다.

→ 빈칸 앞에 조동사 should가 있으므로 be동사는 동사원형 be로 써야 한다.

10 정답 been put off

[해석] 폭우 때문에 그들의 경기는 미뤄졌지만, 다음 날 경기가 치러졌다.

→ 다음 날 경기가 치러진 것은 과거의 일이고, 경기가 미뤄진 것은 그보다 더 먼저 일어난 일이므로 「had been+과거분사」의 과거완료 수동태로 써야 한다.

11 정답 is → 삭제

[해석] 소포는 우편집배원에 의해 배달될 수 있다.

→ 조동사 수동태는 「조동사+be+과거분사」로 쓰므로, can 앞의 be동사 is는 삭제해야 한다.

12 정답 are → be

[해석] 셰익스피어의 희곡들 중 하나가 그들에 의해 상연될 것이다.

→ 조동사 뒤에 나오는 be동사는 원형으로 써야 한다.

13 정답 stop → be stopped

[해석] 대부분의 사람들이 이 프로젝트가 그들에 의해 바로 중단되어야 한다고 생각한다.

→ 프로젝트는 누군가에 의해 중단되는 수동의 의미여야 하므로 수동태로 써야 한다. 조동사 수동태는 「조동사+be+과거분사」로 쓴다.

14 정답 dealt → dealt with

[해석] 우리의 고객 불만 사항들은 그 부서에 의해 다뤄진다.

→ '~을 다루다'는 deal with이고, 수동태 문장에 쓰일 때는 be dealt with ~의 형태로 쓴다.

정답

01 ③	**02** ⑤	**03** was injured
04 was not taken	**05** ③	
06 are grown	**07** are being caught	
08 was wrapped	**09** was being bought	
10 run → run over	**11** from → by	
12 asked → was asked	**13** listened → listened to	
14 ⑤		
15 Her bakery was broken into by someone.		
16 She is going to be interviewed by me.		
17 ③	**18** ③	

---

01 정답 ③　　　　　　　　　　　UNIT **27** 수동태의 시제

[해석] 이 시는 1788년에 Robert Burns에 의해 쓰였다.
→ 시가 '쓰이는' 것이므로 수동이고, 과거를 나타내는 부사구인 in 1788이 있으므로 과거시제의 수동태로 표현되어야 한다.

02 정답 ⑤　　　　　　　UNIT **26** 수동태의 개념 및 형태

[해석] 누구에 의해 그 골동품 차가 구매되었니?
→ 빈칸 뒷부분의 문장에서 수동태의 행위자가 나타나지 않았으므로, 「by+행위자」에 해당하는 By whom이 정답이다.

03 정답 was injured　　　　　　UNIT **27** 수동태의 시제

→ 과거에 사고에서 '부상당한' 것이므로, 과거시제의 수동태를 써야 한다.

04 정답 was not taken　　　　　UNIT **27** 수동태의 시제

→ 과거시제 수동태의 부정은 be동사 다음에 not을 위치시킨다.

05 정답 ③　　　　　　　　　　　UNIT **27** 수동태의 시제

[해석] 그 어머니는 아기의 울음소리를 듣지 않았다.
→ 아기의 울음소리는 그 어머니에 의해 들리지 않았다.
→ 능동태 문장의 목적어가 the baby's cry이므로 이것이 수동태 문장의 주어가 되고, 과거시제의 부정문이므로 수동태로 전환 시 「wasn't + 과거분사」의 형태가 되어야 한다.

06 정답 are grown　　　　　UNIT **26** 수동태의 개념 및 형태

[해석] 다양한 꽃들이 그녀에 의해 풀밭에서 재배된다.
→ 꽃들이 그녀에 의해 '재배되는' 수동의 의미이므로 수동태 are grown으로 써야 한다.

07 정답 are being caught　　　　UNIT **27** 수동태의 시제

[해석] 물고기 몇 마리가 두 명의 소년들에 의해 잡히고 있다.
→ 물고기들은 '잡히는' 수동의 의미여야 한다. 현재진행 수동태는 「be동사의 현재형 + being + 과거분사」의 형태로 쓴다.

08 정답 was wrapped　　　　　UNIT **27** 수동태의 시제

[해석] 각각의 포도송이는 노란 종이에 싸여 있었다.
→ 포도가 종이에 싸여 있는 것이므로 수동태 동사를 써야 한다. 주어가 each bunch로 단수이므로 수동태의 be동사는 3인칭 과거 단수형인 was를 써야 한다.

09 정답 was being bought　　　　UNIT **27** 수동태의 시제

[해석] 사과 한 봉지가 한 여자에 의해 구입되고 있었다.
→ 사과가 여자에 의해 구입되는 것이므로 수동태 동사를 써야 한다. 과거진행 수동태는 「be동사의 과거형+being+과거분사」 형태로 쓰는데, 주어가 a bag이므로 3인칭 과거 단수형인 was를 써야 한다.

10 정답 run → run over　　UNIT **28** 조동사와 동사구의 수동태

[해석] 그녀가 그녀의 개를 산책시키는 동안, 그녀는 한 남자가 차에 치이는 것을 보았다.
→ '차가 치다'는 run over라고 쓴다.

11 정답 from → by　　　　UNIT **26** 수동태의 개념 및 형태

[해석] 나는 선생님께 나의 부주의함에 대해 야단맞았다.
→ 수동태 문장에서 행위자 앞에 쓰는 전치사는 by이다.

12 정답 asked → was asked　　UNIT **26** 수동태의 개념 및 형태

[해석] 할아버지께 부탁을 받았을 때, 나는 "예, 할아버지가 돌아오실 때까지 제가 그녀를 돌볼게요."라고 대답했다.
→ 내가 부탁을 받은 것이고 asked 뒤에 「by+행위자」가 있으므로 asked를 수동태 형태로 고쳐야 한다.

13 정답 listened → listened to
　　　　　　　　　　UNIT **28** 조동사와 동사구의 수동태

[해석] 그는 교실에서 누구에 의해서도 수용되지 않았다.
→ 동사구는 수동태가 되어도 전치사를 그대로 수반하여야 한다.

14 정답 ⑤　　UNIT **26** 수동태의 개념 및 형태, UNIT **27** 수동태의 시제

[해석] ① 그의 방은 파란색과 노란색으로 칠해졌다.
② 그 결과는 Eric이 당장 듣게 하는 게 좋다.
③ 장미가 자라도록 잡초가 뽑혀야 한다.
④ 그 질문들은 자정까지 답변될 것이다.
⑤ 저녁이 지어졌을 때 John이 먹으라고 나를 불렀다.
→ ⑤ 저녁은 누군가에 의해 '지어지는' 수동의 의미여야 하므로 made가 was made로 바뀌어야 옳은 문장이 된다.
① was painted는 과거시제 수동태 ② had better 뒤에 동사원형인 be, be told는 「be동사+ 과거분사」의 형태 ③ 「have to + 동사원형」에서 동사원형인 be, be pulled는 「be동사 + 과거분사」의 형태 ④ are going to be answered는 미래시제 수동태

15 정답 Her bakery was broken into by someone.
　　　　　　　　　　UNIT **28** 조동사와 동사구의 수동태

→ '~에 침입하다'는 break into이고, 수동태로 쓰면 be broken into ~가 된다.

16 정답 She is going to be interviewed by me.
　　　　　　　　　　　　　UNIT **27** 수동태의 시제

→ be going to와 수동태 동사가 연결되면 「be going to + be + 과거분사」로 쓴다.

17 정답 ③　　　　　UNIT **28** 조동사와 동사구의 수동태

[해석] 비가 그친 후, 우리는 무지개를 볼지도 모른다.
→ 비가 그친 후, 무지개가 보일지도 모른다.
→ 조동사가 있는 문장의 수동태는 「조동사+be+과거분사」로 쓴다.

18 정답 ③　　UNIT **26** 수동태의 개념 및 형태, UNIT **27** 수동태의 시제

[해석] '거북선'이라고도 알려진 한국의 거북선은 세계 역사상 최초의 철갑선이다. 거북처럼 생겼기 때문에 그것은 거북선이라고

불린다. 이순신 장군이 이 대단한 전함을 발명한 위대한 인물로 여겨진다. 거북선에는 진보된 무기가 있었다. 그것들은 일본 해군과의 전투에서 사용되었고, 전쟁에서 많은 승리를 이끌었다.
→ ③ 이순신 장군이 위대한 인물로 여겨지는, 즉 수동의 의미이므로 수동태 동사가 사용되어야 한다. 현재에도 그렇게 여겨지는 것이므로 be동사를 현재형으로 쓰는 것에 유의해야 한다.
(considered → is considered)
① '~로 알려진'은 known as ② '~로 불리다'는 의미로 수동태에 쓰인 과거분사 ④ 거북선이 무기를 가지고 있던 것이므로 능동태, have는 수동태로 쓰이지 않음 ⑤ were used는 과거시제 수동태

UNIT 29 4형식, 5형식의 수동태

개념 확인 문제 정답 ▶ 문제편 p.121~123

01 A lot of homework was given to us by our English teacher. / We were given a lot of homework by our English teacher.

02 An interesting storybook was read to young children by the librarian.

03 A doll was made for me by my mother.

04 English and math are taught to them by Ella's older brother. / They are taught English and math by Ella's older brother.

05 A brand-new smartphone was bought for me by him.

06 She was awarded

07 was given to the teacher

08 was bought for him

09 Better conditions were offered

10 were passed to　　11 was prepared for

12 was made for　　13 was inquired of

14 She was made　　15 He was made to wash

16 He was seen making

17 The players were helped to improve

18 to take　　19 strong　　20 watching

21 to buy　　22 think　　23 is called

24 were heard to sing　　25 to work

26 for → to　　27 call → to call　　28 him → to him

29 run → to run 또는 running

30 requires → is required

31 dance → to dance 또는 dancing

32 feeling → felt

---

01 [정답] A lot of homework was given to us by our English teacher. / We were given a lot of homework by our English teacher.
[해석] 우리 영어 선생님은 우리에게 많은 숙제를 내주셨다.

→ give가 사용된 4형식 문장은 직접목적어와 간접목적어를 둘 다 수동태의 주어로 쓸 수 있다. 직접목적어가 주어가 될 때 간접목적어는 수동태 동사 뒤에 「to+목적격」으로 쓴다.

02 [정답] An interesting storybook was read to young children by the librarian.
[해석] 그 사서는 어린아이들에게 흥미로운 동화책을 읽어 주었다.

→ read가 사용된 4형식 문장은 직접목적어만 수동태의 주어로 쓸 수 있다. 직접목적어가 주어가 될 때 간접목적어는 수동태 동사 뒤에 「to+목적격」으로 쓴다.

03 [정답] A doll was made for me by my mother.
[해석] 어머니는 나에게 인형을 만들어 주셨다.

→ make가 사용된 4형식 문장은 직접목적어만 수동태의 주어로 쓸 수 있다. 직접목적어가 주어가 될 때 간접목적어는 수동태 동사 뒤에 「for+목적격」으로 쓴다.

04 [정답] English and math are taught to them by Ella's older brother. / They are taught English and math by Ella's older brother.
[해석] Ella의 오빠가 그들에게 영어와 수학을 가르친다.

→ teach가 사용된 4형식 문장은 직접목적어와 간접목적어를 둘 다 수동태의 주어로 쓸 수 있다. 직접목적어가 주어가 될 때 간접목적어는 수동태 동사 뒤에 「to+목적격」으로 쓴다.

05 [정답] A brand-new smartphone was bought for me by him.
[해석] 그가 나에게 최신 스마트폰을 사 주었다.

→ buy가 사용된 4형식 문장은 직접목적어만 수동태의 주어로 쓸 수 있다. 직접목적어가 주어가 될 때 간접목적어는 수동태 동사 뒤에 「for+목적격」으로 쓴다.

06 [정답] She was awarded
[해석] 학교는 그녀에게 특별상을 수여했다.
→ 그녀는 학교에 의해 특별상을 받았다.
→ 직접목적어인 a special prize가 수동태 문장의 동사 자리 뒤에 그대로 왔으므로 간접목적어인 she를 주어로 써야 한다.

07 [정답] was given to the teacher
[해석] 학생들은 선생님에게 감동적인 편지를 드렸다.
→ 감동적인 편지가 학생들에 의해 선생님에게 주어졌다.
→ give는 직접목적어가 주어가 될 때 간접목적어를 수동태 동사 뒤에 「to+목적격」으로 쓴다.

08 [정답] was bought for him
[해석] 그의 아버지는 그에게 새 자전거를 사 주셨다.
→ 새 자전거가 그를 위해 그의 아버지에 의해 구매되었다.
→ buy가 사용된 4형식 문장은 직접목적어만 수동태의 주어로 쓸 수 있다. 직접목적어가 주어가 될 때 간접목적어는 수동태 동사 뒤에 「for+목적격」으로 쓴다.

09 [정답] Better conditions were offered
[해석] 회사는 근로자들에게 더 나은 근무 환경을 제공했다.
→ 더 나은 근무 환경이 회사에 의해 근무자들에게 주어졌다.

→ offer의 간접목적어인 the workers가 수동태 동사 뒤에
「to+목적격」으로 왔으므로 직접목적어인 better conditions
를 주어로 써야 한다.

10 정답 **were passed to**
→ pass는 직접목적어가 주어가 될 때 간접목적어를 수동태 동
사 뒤에 「to+목적격」으로 쓴다.

11 정답 **was prepared for**
→ prepare는 직접목적어가 주어가 될 때 간접목적어를 수동
태 동사 뒤에 「for+목적격」으로 쓴다.

12 정답 **was made for**
→ make는 직접목적어가 주어가 될 때 간접목적어를 수동태
동사 뒤에 「for+목적격」으로 쓴다.

13 정답 **was inquired of**
→ inquire는 직접목적어가 주어가 될 때 간접목적어를 수동
태 동사 뒤에 「of+목적격」으로 쓴다.

14 정답 **She was made**
[해석] 우리는 그녀를 그룹의 리더로 만들었다.
→ 그녀는 우리에 의해 그룹의 리더가 되었다.
→ 5형식 문장에서 make의 목적격 보어로 쓰인 명사는 수동
태 문장에서 동사 뒤에 그대로 온다.

15 정답 **He was made to wash**
[해석] 그녀는 그에게 차를 세차하게 했다.
→ 그는 그녀에 의해 차를 세차하게 되었다.
→ 사역동사 make의 5형식 문장을 수동태로 고칠 때, 목적격
보어로 쓰인 동사원형은 to부정사로 바뀐다.

16 정답 **He was seen making**
[해석] 그녀는 그가 맛있는 샌드위치를 만드는 것을 보았다.
→ 그가 맛있는 샌드위치를 만드는 것이 그녀에 의해 목격
되었다.
→ 지각동사 see의 5형식 문장을 수동태로 고칠 때, 목적격 보
어로 쓰인 현재분사는 동사 뒤에 그대로 온다.

17 정답 **The players were helped to improve**
[해석] 코치는 선수들이 그들의 기술을 향상시키도록 도왔
다. → 선수들은 코치에 의해 그들의 기술을 향상시키는 것
을 도움받았다.
→ 준사역동사 help의 5형식 문장을 수동태로 고칠 때, 목적격
보어로 쓰인 동사원형은 to부정사로 바뀐다.

18 정답 **to take**
[해석] 나는 나의 선생님에 의해 그 경주에 참가하도록 권장
받았다.
→ 5형식 문장에서 encourage의 목적격 보어로 쓰인 to부
정사는 수동태 문장에서 동사 뒤에 그대로 온다.

19 정답 **strong**
[해석] 우리는 건강에 좋은 음식을 먹음으로써 튼튼해질 수
있다.
→ 5형식 문장에서 make의 목적격 보어로 쓰인 형용사는 수
동태 문장에서 동사 뒤에 그대로 온다.

20 정답 **watching**
[해석] 많은 사람들이 그녀에 의해 콘서트를 보는 것이 목격
되었다.
→ 5형식 문장에서 지각동사 see의 목적격 보어로 쓰인 현재
분사는 수동태 문장에서 동사 뒤에 그대로 온다.

21 정답 **to buy**
[해석] 그 고객은 판매원에 의해 이 컴퓨터를 사도록 권유받
았다.
→ recommend는 5형식 문장에서 recommend A to-v
로 쓰이며, 수동태 문장에서는 A is recommended to-v가
되어야 하므로 him은 필요 없다.

22 정답 **think**
[해석] 경찰은 그가 유죄라고 생각한다.
→ 생각하는 행위자가 경찰이므로 능동태 동사를 써야 한다.

23 정답 **is called**
[해석] 그 섬은 좋은 경치 때문에 지상 낙원이라고 불린다.
→ 섬이 사람들에 의해 지상 낙원이라고 '불리는' 수동의 관계이
므로 수동태 동사를 써야 한다.

24 정답 **were heard to sing**
[해석] 그들이 노래 부르는 것이 우리에게 들렸다.
→ 지각동사 hear의 5형식 문장을 수동태로 고칠 때, 목적격
보어로 쓰인 동사원형은 to부정사로 바뀐다.

25 정답 **to work**
[해석] 직원들은 주말에 일하도록 강요받았다.
→ 사역동사 make의 5형식 문장을 수동태로 고칠 때, 목적격
보어로 쓰인 동사원형은 to부정사로 바뀐다.

26 정답 **for → to**
[해석] 그 문자 메시지는 Sara에 의해 엉뚱한 사람에게 보내
질 것이다.
→ send가 사용된 4형식 문장이 수동태가 될 때 간접목적어는
수동태 동사 뒤에 「to+목적격」으로 써야 한다.

27 정답 **call → to call**
[해석] 우리는 그 남자에 의해 경찰을 부르도록 요청받았다.
→ 5형식 문장에서 ask의 목적격 보어로 쓰인 to부정사는 수
동태 문장에서도 동사 뒤에 to부정사 형태 그대로 쓴다.

28 정답 **him → to him**
[해석] 내 사진첩은 나의 부모님에 의해 그에게 보여졌다.
→ show가 사용된 4형식 문장이 수동태가 될 때 간접목적어
는 수동태 동사 뒤에 「to+목적격」으로 써야 한다.

29 정답 **run → to run 또는 running**
[해석] 두 명의 수상한 남자들이 그 건물 밖으로 달려 나오는
것이 목격되었다.
→ 지각동사 watch의 5형식 문장을 수동태로 고칠 때, 목적
격 보어로 쓰인 동사원형은 to부정사로 바뀐다. (분사는 형태
유지)

30 정답 **requires → is required**
[해석] 그 보고서는 선생님에 의해 다음 주 월요일까지 끝내
지도록 요구된다.

→ 보고서는 누군가에 의해 끝내지는 것이 요구되는 것이므로 is required가 되어야 한다.

31 정답 dance → to dance 또는 dancing
[해석] 그녀는 그들에 의해 파티에서 춤추는 것이 목격되었다.
→ 지각동사 watch의 5형식 문장을 수동태로 고칠 때, 목적격 보어로 쓰인 동사원형은 to부정사로 바뀐다. (분사는 형태 유지)

32 정답 feeling → felt
[해석] 바람이 나무들 사이로 불어 오는 것이 나에 의해 느껴진다.
→ 지각동사 feel의 5형식 문장을 수동태로 고칠 때, 동사 feel은 「be + 과거분사」 형태로 바꿔야 하므로 feeling을 felt로 써야 한다.

UNIT 30 주의해야 할 수동태와 관용표현

개념 확인 문제 정답 ▶ 문제편 p.125

01 had **02** opened **03** says
04 resembles **05** reads **06** don't cut
07 is peeling **08** was worried about
09 were surprised at[by] **10** interested in
11 is known to **12** be satisfied with
13 were married 또는 got married
14 Jane was pleased with her friend's decision.
15 Ice cream sells well on such a hot day.
16 His eyes are filled with tears.
17 Italy is known for spaghetti and pizza.
18 The top of the bookcase is covered with dust.
19 is said that fresh fruit is good for our health / is said to be good for our health

01 정답 had
[해석] 나는 Michael의 삼촌이 멋진 요트를 가지고 있다고 들었다.
→ '가지고 있다'라는 뜻으로 쓰인 have는 수동형으로 쓸 수 없다.

02 정답 opened
[해석] 바람이 전혀 없었는데도 불구하고, 문이 저절로 열렸다.
→ open은 '열리다'라는 뜻의 자동사로 쓰일 때 능동의 형태로 수동의 의미를 나타낸다.

03 정답 says
[해석] 표지판을 봐. 수영 금지라고 쓰여 있어.
→ say가 '~라고 쓰여 있다'라는 의미로 쓰일 때 능동의 형태로 수동의 의미를 나타낸다.

04 정답 resembles
[해석] 내 여동생은 할머니를 닮았다.
→ resemble은 수동태로 쓸 수 없는 동사이다.

05 정답 reads
[해석] 그 기사는 아주 잘 읽힌다.
→ read는 '읽히다'라는 뜻의 자동사로 쓰일 때 능동의 형태로 수동의 의미를 나타낸다.

06 정답 don't cut
[해석] 가위가 무뎌서 아주 잘 잘리지 않는다.
→ cut은 '잘리다'라는 뜻의 자동사로 쓰일 때 능동의 형태로 수동의 의미를 나타낸다.

07 정답 is peeling
[해석] 그 벽의 페인트칠이 벗겨지고 있다.
→ peel은 '벗겨지다'라는 뜻의 자동사로 쓰일 때 능동의 형태로 수동의 의미를 나타낸다.

08 정답 was worried about
[해석] 고등학교에 다녔을 때 그녀는 살이 찌는 것에 대해 걱정했다.
→ '~에 대해 걱정하다'는 be worried about이라고 쓴다. 과거를 나타내는 부사절이 있으므로 과거시제로 써야 한다.

09 정답 were surprised at[by]
[해석] 2018년에 우리는 동계 올림픽의 결과에 놀랐다.
→ '~에 놀라다'는 be surprised at 또는 be surprised by라고 쓴다. In 2018이라는 과거를 나타내는 부사구가 있으므로 과거시제로 써야 한다.

10 정답 interested in
[해석] 너는 사진 찍는 것에 관심이 있니?
→ '~에 관심이 있다'는 be interested in이라고 쓴다. 의문문이라서 be동사가 문장 앞으로 나왔으므로 빈칸에는 interested in만 써야 한다.

11 정답 is known to
[해석] 요가가 건강에 좋다는 사실은 많은 사람들에게 알려져 있다.
→ '~에게 알려져 있다'는 be known to라고 쓴다.

12 정답 be satisfied with
[해석] 학생들 모두 방과 후 프로그램들에 만족할 것이다.
→ '~에 만족하다'는 be satisfied with라고 쓴다. 빈칸 앞에 조동사가 있으므로 뒤에 오는 be동사는 원형인 be로 써야 한다.

13 정답 were married 또는 got married
[해석] 나의 부모님은 2000년 봄에 결혼하셨다.
→ '~와 결혼하다'는 be[get] married to라고 쓰지만, 이 문장에서는 결혼을 한 두 사람이 문장 앞에 나와 있으므로 '결혼하다'라는 뜻의 be married나 get married만 쓰면 된다. 과거를 나타내는 부사구 in the spring of 2000이 있으므로 be나 get을 과거시제로 써야 한다.

14 정답 Jane was pleased with her friend's decision.
→ '~에 기뻐하다'는 be pleased with라고 쓴다.

15 정답 Ice cream sells well on such a hot day.
→ sell은 '팔리다'라는 뜻의 자동사로 쓰일 때 능동의 형태로 수동의 의미를 나타낸다.

16 정답 His eyes are filled with tears.
→ '~으로 가득하다'는 be filled with라고 쓴다.

17 정답 Italy is known for spaghetti and pizza.
→ '~으로 유명하다'는 be known for라고 쓴다.

18 정답 The top of the bookcase is covered with dust.
→ '~으로 덮여 있다'는 be covered with라고 쓴다.

19 정답 is said that fresh fruit is good for our health / is said to be good for our health
→ 동사 say의 목적어가 that절인 경우, 가주어 it이나 that절의 주어를 수동태의 주어로 할 수 있다. 「It + be동사 + 과거분사 + that ~」, 「that절의 주어 + be동사 + 과거분사 + to부정사 ~」 형태로 쓴다.

단원 평가 문제  UNIT 29 ~ UNIT 30 ▶ 문제편 p.126~128

정답

01 ③　　**02** was bought for me
03 was given some lessons
04 ③　　**05** was named Henry
06 was found to approach 또는 approaching
07 ④　　**08** by → about　**09** by → with
10 ②　**11** ④　**12** ②　**13** ②　**14** ⑤
15 of　**16** with　**17** about **18** to　**19** in
20 ④
21 It is believed that fresh vegetables are good for our health.
22 She was made to type the document by me.
23 He was heard playing the violin along with other friends.
24 ③　　**25** ①　　**26** were given to me

---

01 정답 ③　　UNIT 29 4형식, 5형식의 수동태
→ 지각동사의 수동태에서는 목적격 보어로 사용된 동사원형이 수동태 문장에서 to부정사로 바뀌어야 하므로 seen to jog가 적절하다.

02 정답 was bought for me　UNIT 29 4형식, 5형식의 수동태
[해석] 우리 삼촌은 좋은 자전거를 내게 사 주셨다.
→ buy를 이용한 4형식 문장은 수동태로 전환시 간접목적어 앞에 전치사 for를 위치시켜야 한다.

03 정답 was given some lessons
UNIT 29 4형식, 5형식의 수동태
[해석] 그 선생님은 내게 몇 가지 교훈을 주셨다.
→ 간접목적어를 수동태의 주어로 하는 경우 직접목적어는 「be동사 + 과거분사」 뒤에 온다.

04 정답 ③　　UNIT 30 주의해야 할 수동태와 관용표현
[해석] ① 그녀는 그 선물에 기뻤다.
② 사람들은 그 결과에 만족스러워했다.
③ 정부는 오염에 대해 걱정한다.
④ 그 창고는 먼지로 가득 차 있다.
⑤ 그 마을은 흰 눈으로 덮여 있었다.
→ ③ '~에 대해 걱정하다'는 be worried about으로 나타내므로 about이 들어가고 나머지는 모두 전치사 with가 필요하다.
① be pleased with: ~에 기뻐하다 ② be satisfied with: ~에 만족하다 ④ be filled with: ~로 가득하다 ⑤ be covered with: ~로 덮여 있다

05 정답 was named Henry　UNIT 29 4형식, 5형식의 수동태
→ 동사 name은 목적어 뒤에 이름에 해당하는 명사를 목적격 보어로 가지고, 이는 수동태로 바뀌어도 그대로 동사 뒤에 온다.

06 정답 was found to approach 또는 approaching
UNIT 29 4형식, 5형식의 수동태
→ 목적어에 해당하는 태풍이 수동태 주어로 나왔으므로 동사는 was found가 되고, '다가오고 있다'는 의미의 목적격 보어가 필요하므로 to approach 또는 approaching이 들어가야 한다.

07 정답 ④　　UNIT 30 주의해야 할 수동태와 관용표현
[해석] 사람들은 그 제품이 Joy의 가게에 있다고 말한다.
→ say 등의 동사가 that절을 목적어로 취할 때 that절을 수동태의 주어로 삼거나, that절 안의 주어를 수동태로 삼아 「be said + to부정사」의 형태를 취할 수 있다.

08 정답 by → about　UNIT 30 주의해야 할 수동태와 관용표현
[해석] 최근에 많은 청소년들이 살이 찌는 것에 대해 걱정한다.
→ '~에 대해 걱정하다'는 be concerned about이라고 쓴다.

09 정답 by → with　UNIT 30 주의해야 할 수동태와 관용표현
[해석] 티틀리스 산은 일 년 내내 눈으로 덮여 있다.
→ '~으로 덮여 있다'는 be covered with라고 쓴다.

10 정답 ②　　UNIT 30 주의해야 할 수동태와 관용표현
[해석] ① 그 도넛은 설탕으로 덮여 있다.
② 나는 이 일에 싫증이 난다.
③ 그는 가수 겸 배우로 알려져 있다.
④ 그들은 그들의 결정에 만족했다.
⑤ 너는 한국 전통 춤에 관심이 있니?
→ ② '~에 싫증이 나다'는 be tired of이다. (am tired → am tired of)
① be covered with: ~로 덮여 있다 ③ be known as: ~로 알려져 있다 ④ be satisfied with: ~에 만족하다 ⑤ be interested in: ~에 관심이 있다

11 정답 ④　　UNIT 30 주의해야 할 수동태와 관용표현
[해석] ① 나의 언니는 나와 닮았다.
② 모든 거리가 눈으로 덮여 있었다.
③ 그 개들은 그녀에 의해 돌보아졌다.
④ 그녀의 새 앨범은 많은 팬들에 의해 기대되고 있다.
⑤ 비록 어려운 어휘가 있긴 해도 이 책은 잘 읽힌다.
→ ① resemble은 수동태로 쓸 수 없다. (is resembled by → resembles)

② '~으로 덮여 있다'는 be covered with로 쓴다. (were covered by → were covered with) ③ 동사구 take care of(~을 돌보다)의 수동태는 be taken care of이다. (were taken care → were taken care of) ⑤ read는 '읽히다'라는 뜻의 자동사로 쓰일 때 능동의 형태로 수동의 의미를 나타낸다. (is read → reads)

12 [정답] ② UNIT 30 주의해야 할 수동태와 관용표현

[해석] ① 창문은 Sean에 의해 깨졌다.
② 그 영화는 사람들에게 사랑받아 왔다.
③ 그 책은 나의 남동생에 의해 찢겼다.
④ 그 케이크는 Jake에게 먹혔다.
⑤ 그 쇼는 그 배우에 의해 제작되었다.
→ 수동데에시 행위자가 they, we, people 같은 일반인이거나 언급하지 않아도 알 수 있을 때는 「by+행위자」가 생략될 수 있다.

13 [정답] ② UNIT 29 4형식, 5형식의 수동태

[해석] • 그 이메일은 Mike에 의해 그녀에게 보내졌다.
• 치즈케이크는 James의 엄마에 의해 그를 위해 만들어졌다.
→ 4형식 문장을 수동태로 바꿀 때 능동태 문장의 간접목적어는 수동태 동사 뒤에 「전치사+목적격」으로 써야 한다. send는 전치사로 to를 쓰고, make는 for를 쓴다.

14 [정답] ⑤ UNIT 29 4형식, 5형식의 수동태

[해석] ① 그가 무엇을 했니? → 무엇이 그에 의해 행해졌니?
② 우리는 그를 우리 반의 반장으로 선출했다.
→ 그는 우리에 의해 우리 반의 반장으로 선출되었다.
③ 그녀는 그녀의 어머니의 그림을 그리고 있다.
→ 그녀의 어머니의 그림이 그녀에 의해 그려지고 있다.
④ 버스가 노부인을 치었다. → 노부인이 버스에 치였다.
⑤ 나의 아버지는 나에게 책을 한 권 사 주셨다.
→ ⑤ buy가 사용된 4형식 문장은 직접목적어만을 수동태의 주어로 쓸 수 있다. 직접목적어가 주어가 될 때 간접목적어는 수동태 동사 뒤에 「for+목적격」으로 쓴다. (A book was bought for me by my father.)
① 「be동사+과거분사」 형태인 was done이다.
② 5형식 문장의 목적격보어가 수동태 문장에서도 그대로 쓰인다.
③ 수동태의 현재진행시제인 「be동사 + being + 과거분사」 형태이다.
④ 동사구 run over는 하나의 단위로 취급해 수동태로 바꾼다.

15 [정답] of UNIT 30 주의해야 할 수동태와 관용표현

[해석] 그 팀은 10명의 선수로 구성되어 있다.
→ '~으로 구성되어 있다'는 be composed of이다.

16 [정답] with UNIT 30 주의해야 할 수동태와 관용표현

[해석] 나는 여행 가이드로서 내 직업에 만족하지 않는다.
→ '~에 만족하다'는 be satisfied with이다.

17 [정답] about UNIT 30 주의해야 할 수동태와 관용표현

[해석] 그녀는 내일 학교에서 그녀의 큰 발표에 대해 단지 걱정하고 있다.
→ '~에 대해 걱정하다'는 be worried about이다.

18 [정답] to UNIT 30 주의해야 할 수동태와 관용표현

[해석] 그는 그가 꿈꿔왔던 여자와 결혼했다.
→ '~와 결혼하다'는 be married to이다.

19 [정답] in UNIT 30 주의해야 할 수동태와 관용표현

[해석] Jerome은 어떤 운동에도 관심이 없다.
→ '~에 관심이 있다'는 be interested in이다.

20 [정답] ④ UNIT 30 주의해야 할 수동태와 관용표현

[해석] • 제 고양이가 당신에 의해 한 시간 동안 돌보아질 수 있습니까?
• 그 병은 우유로 가득 차 있다.
→ '~을 돌보다'를 의미하는 look after, '~로 가득 차 있다'를 의미하는 be filled with기 수동형으로 사용된 경우이다.

21 [정답] It is believed that fresh vegetables are good for our health. UNIT 30 주의해야 할 수동태와 관용표현

→ 동사 believe의 목적어가 that절인 경우 가주어 it을 수동태의 주어로 할 수 있다.

22 [정답] She was made to type the document by me. UNIT 29 4형식, 5형식의 수동태

→ 사역동사 make의 목적어와 목적격 보어의 관계가 수동임에 유의하여 문장을 완성한다.

23 [정답] He was heard playing the violin along with other friends. UNIT 29 4형식, 5형식의 수동태

→ 지각동사 hear가 수동형으로 사용되어 뒤에 현재분사가 주격 보어로 나오고 있음에 유의하여 문장을 완성한다.

24 [정답] ③ UNIT 29 4형식, 5형식의 수동태

[해석] 나는 건강한 습관을 몇 개 가지고 있는데, 그것은 어머니와 근처 산을 등산하는 것을 포함한다. 등산하는 이유를 질문받으면 나는 산에 관한 모든 것을 좋아하기 때문이라고 말한다. 산에 가면, 나는 깨끗한 공기와 산에서 부는 산들바람을 누리는 것을 허락받는다. 다람쥐가 나무 위아래로 오르내리는 것이 보일 수 있다. 무엇보다도 등산을 마쳤을 때 나는 결국 해냈다는 느낌을 받는다.
→ ③ 목적격 보어가 to부정사인 경우, 수동태 문장에서도 그대로 오므로 to enjoy가 알맞다.

25 [정답] ① UNIT 30 주의해야 할 수동태와 관용표현

[해석] 어머니께서 예쁜 케이크를 구우셨다. 그것은 다채로운 초콜릿과 사탕 조각으로 장식되었다. 내 생일을 축하하기 위해 엄마에 의해 케이크 위에 몇 개의 촛불이 놓였다. 친구들은 파티 중에 나에게 선물을 주었다. 파티는 모두가 즐겼고, 많은 사진이 찍혔다. 파티가 끝난 후, 집은 가족에 의해 청소되었다. 모든 사람에게 감사의 마음을 표현하기 위해 감사의 편지가 나에 의해 작성될 것이다.
→ ① '~로 장식되다'는 be decorated with로 나타내므로 by를 with로 고쳐야 한다.

26 [정답] were given to me UNIT 29 4형식, 5형식의 수동태

→ give가 사용된 4형식 문장에서 직접목적어가 주어가 될 때 간접목적어는 수동태 동사 뒤에 「to+목적격」으로 쓴다.

H 형용사

개념 확인 문제 정답 ▶ 문제편 **p.131**

01 의문 형용사 **02** 수량 형용사
03 소유 형용사, 수사 형용사
04 지시 형용사, 성질·상태 형용사 **05** 한정 형용사
06 ⓐ, ⓒ **07** ⓐ, ⓑ **08** ⓐ, ⓑ, ⓑ
09 ⓐ, ⓒ **10** ⓒ **11** ⓐ, ⓑ
12 ⓐ, ⓑ **13** ⓒ
14 His four playful rabbits
15 something very light and simple
16 a small round wooden table
17 Our three spacious balconies

---

01 정답 **의문 형용사**
[해석] 기차는 몇 시에 출발하나요?
→ What은 질문을 할 때 사용되는 의문 형용사이다.

02 정답 **수량 형용사**
[해석] 내가 이 일을 끝내려면 조금 시간이 필요하다.
→ a little은 명사의 수나 양을 나타내는 수량 형용사이다.

03 정답 **소유 형용사, 수사 형용사**
[해석] 이번이 내가 파리를 방문하는 첫 번째이다.
→ my는 명사가 소유하는 것임을 나타내는 소유 형용사이고, first는 명사의 정확한 순서를 나타내는 수사 형용사이다.

04 정답 **지시 형용사, 성질·상태 형용사**
[해석] 이 책은 유익한 정보를 담고 있다.
→ This는 명사가 특정한 것임을 나타내는 지시 형용사이고, valuable은 명사의 성질이나 상태를 나타내는 성질·상태 형용사이다.

05 정답 **한정 형용사**
[해석] 그 학급의 모든 학생이 시험에 합격했다.
→ Every는 명사의 의미를 한정하는 한정 형용사이다.

06 정답 **ⓐ, ⓒ**
[해석] 나쁜 날씨는 우리를 걱정스럽게 했다.
→ bad는 명사 weather를 수식하는 한정적 쓰임으로, worried는 목적격 보어 자리에서 서술적 쓰임으로 쓰였다.

07 정답 **ⓐ, ⓑ**
[해석] 모퉁이에 있는 그 큰 도서관은 조용했다.
→ large는 명사 library를 수식하는 한정적 쓰임으로, quiet는 주격 보어 자리에서 서술적 쓰임으로 쓰였다.

08 정답 **ⓐ, ⓑ, ⓑ**
[해석] 그 어린 소녀는 명랑하고 에너지가 넘쳤다.
→ young은 명사 girl을 수식하는 한정적 쓰임으로, cheerful과 energetic은 주격 보어 자리에서 서술적 쓰임으로 쓰였다.

09 정답 **ⓐ, ⓒ**
[해석] 그 위험한 경험은 나를 혼란스럽게 만들었다.
→ dangerous는 명사 experience를 수식하는 한정적 쓰임으로, confused는 목적격 보어 자리에서 서술적 쓰임으로 쓰였다.

10 정답 **ⓒ**
[해석] 그녀의 공연은 관객들을 놀라게 만들었다.
→ amazed는 목적격 보어 자리에서 서술적 쓰임으로 쓰였다.

11 정답 **ⓐ, ⓑ**
[해석] 공원 근처에 있는 그 작은 카페는 친근했다.
→ small은 명사 café를 수식하는 한정적 쓰임으로, welcoming은 주격 보어 자리에서 서술적 쓰임으로 쓰였다.

12 정답 **ⓐ, ⓑ**
[해석] 문 옆에 서 있는 그 키 큰 남자는 진지했다.
→ tall은 명사 man을 수식하는 한정적 쓰임으로, serious는 주격 보어 자리에서 서술적 쓰임으로 쓰였다.

13 정답 **ⓒ**
[해석] 그의 승진 소식은 모두를 자랑스럽게 만들었다.
→ proud는 목적격 보어 자리에서 서술적 쓰임으로 쓰였다.

14 정답 **His four playful rabbits**
[해석] 그의 네 마리 장난기 많은 토끼들은 항상 깡충깡충 뛰어다닌다.
→ '인칭대명사의 소유격 → 수량 형용사 → 일반 형용사'의 순서이다.

15 정답 **something very light and simple**
[해석] 나는 매우 담백하고 가벼운 식사를 하고 싶다.
→ -thing/-body/-one으로 끝나는 대명사는 형용사가 그 뒤에 위치한다.

16 정답 **a small round wooden table**
[해석] 그녀는 거실에 작은 둥근 나무 테이블을 샀다.
→ 일반 형용사는 '크기 → 모양 → 재료'의 순서이다.

17 정답 **Our three spacious balconies**
[해석] 우리의 세 개의 넓은 발코니는 항상 아침 커피를 마시기에 완벽하다.
→ '인칭대명사의 소유격 → 수량 형용사 → 일반 형용사'의 순서이다.

개념 확인 문제 정답 ▶ 문제편 p.133

01 any **02** Many **03** a few
04 A great deal of **05** were
06 volunteers **07** ○ **08** effort
09 a great deal of, a lot of, lots of 등
10 much **11** Few **12** any
13 a little **14** a few **15** deal
16 children **17** experience

01 [정답] any
→ 의문문에서 '어떤 ~라도'를 뜻하는 것은 any이다.

02 [정답] Many
→ scientists는 셀 수 있는 명사의 복수형이고 '많은'을 나타내야 하므로 many를 써야 한다.

03 [정답] a few
→ drops는 셀 수 있는 명사의 복수형이고 '몇, 약간'을 나타내야 하므로 a few를 써야 한다.

04 [정답] A great deal of
→ patience는 셀 수 없는 명사이고 '많은'을 나타내야 하므로 a great deal of를 써야 한다.

05 [정답] were
[해석] 어제 도로에는 많은 차들이 있었다.
→ 주어로 복수 명사 cars가 왔기 때문에 단수 동사 was는 복수 동사 were로 고쳐야 한다.

06 [정답] volunteers
[해석] 우리는 행사에 도울 많은 자원봉사자가 필요하다.
→ plenty of는 '많은'을 의미하기 때문에 셀 수 있는 명사가 뒤에 올 때는 복수 형태로 와야 한다.

07 [정답] ○
[해석] 많은 사람들이 어젯밤 콘서트에 참석했다.
→ a number of는 셀 수 있는 명사를 수식하므로 people 앞에 온 것은 알맞다.

08 [정답] effort
[해석] 그 일을 완수하는 데 많은 노력이 필요하다.
→ a great deal of는 셀 수 없는 명사를 수식하므로 단수 형태인 effort가 와야 한다.

09 [정답] a great deal of, a lot of, lots of 등
[해석] 나는 발표 준비에 많은 시간을 보냈다.
→ a number of는 셀 수 있는 명사를 수식하므로 time 앞에 올 수 없다. a number of를 a great deal of, a lot of, lots of 등으로 고쳐야 한다.

10 [정답] much
[해석] 너는 돈이 얼마나 필요하니?
→ money는 셀 수 없는 명사이므로 much를 써야 한다.

11 [정답] Few
[해석] 그의 발표를 이해할 수 있는 사람들은 거의 없다.
→ people은 셀 수 있는 명사의 복수형이므로 few와 함께 쓴다.

12 [정답] any
[해석] 당신은 회의 전에 어떤 질문이라도 있었나요?
→ 의문문에서 '어떤 ~라도'를 뜻하는 것은 any이다.

13 [정답] a little
[해석] 그녀는 회의가 시작되기 전에 약간의 시간이 있다.
→ time은 셀 수 없는 명사이므로 a little을 써야 한다.

14 [정답] a few
[해석] 버스가 도착하기 전에 몇 분이 남았다.
→ minutes는 셀 수 있는 명사의 복수형이므로 a few와 함께 쓴다.

15 [정답] deal
[해석] 디자인에서 세부 사항에 많은 주의가 기울여졌다.
→ attention은 셀 수 없는 명사이므로 a great deal of를 써야 한다.

16 [정답] children
[해석] 오후에 많은 아이들이 공원에서 놀고 있었다.
→ lots of는 '많은'을 의미하기 때문에 셀 수 있는 명사가 뒤에 올 때는 복수 형태로 와야 한다.

17 [정답] experience
[해석] 부상자들은 종종 육체적 고통 외에도 정신적 외상을 겪는다.
→ 「the+형용사」는 복수 취급하므로 experience가 알맞다.

개념 확인 문제 정답 ▶ 문제편 p.135~137

01 third **02** seventh **03** fifteenth
04 sixtieth **05** tenth **06** thirty
07 ninety-nine **08** one hundred
09 forty-four **10** sixteen
11 two-thirds **12** six point zero seven
13 four-ninths **14** (zero) point two five
15 three hundred (and) fifty-seven
16 one and three-fifths **17** three point one four
18 five-eighths
19 forty-two thousand three hundred (and) fifty
20 seven and two-sevenths **21** ninth
22 one-millionth **23** Two-thirds **24** eighty-seven
25 (zero) point three three
26 seven times **27** five to six
28 ten to ten **29** twelve thirty
30 six forty-five **31** four twenty
32 a quarter after three
33 February (the) fourteenth 또는 the fourteenth of February
34 March (the) third 또는 the third of March
35 December (the) twenty-fourth
또는 the twenty-fourth of December
36 January (the) fourth, seventeen eighty-six 또는 the fourth of January, seventeen eighty-six
37 three four eight zero, nine nine two seven
38 zero one zero, two three four five, six seven eight nine
39 area code zero five one, two four six eight, one three five seven
40 21th → 21st **41** triple → three
42 dollar → dollars **43** fourth → four
44 on → of

01 정답 third
[해석] 3 → 3번째
→ 기수 three를 서수로 바꿀 때는 third로 쓴다.

02 정답 seventh
[해석] 7 → 7번째
→ 기수 seven을 서수로 바꿀 때는 seventh로 쓴다.

03 정답 fifteenth
[해석] 15 → 15번째
→ 기수 fifteen을 서수로 바꿀 때는 fifteenth로 쓴다.

04 정답 sixtieth
[해석] 60 → 60번째
→ 기수 sixty를 서수로 바꿀 때는 sixtieth로 쓴다.

05 정답 tenth
[해석] 10 → 10번째
→ 기수 ten을 서수로 바꿀 때는 tenth로 쓴다.

06 정답 thirty
[해석] 30번째 → 30
→ 서수 thirtieth의 기수는 thirty이다.

07 정답 ninety-nine
[해석] 99번째 → 99
→ 서수 ninety-ninth의 기수는 ninety-nine이다.

08 정답 one hundred
[해석] 100번째 → 100
→ 서수 one hundredth의 기수는 one hundred이다.

09 정답 forty-four
[해석] 44번째 → 44
→ 서수 forty-fourth의 기수는 forty-four이다.

10 정답 sixteen
[해석] 16번째 → 16
→ 서수 sixteenth의 기수는 sixteen 뒤에 times이다.

11 정답 two-thirds
→ 분자는 기수 two로, 분모는 분자가 2 이상이므로 서수 thirds로 읽는다.

12 정답 six point zero seven
→ 소수점까지는 기수 six로, 소수점은 point로, 소수점 이하는 한 자리씩 zero seven이라고 읽는다.

13 정답 four-ninths
→ 분자는 기수 four로, 분모는 분자가 2 이상이므로 서수 ninths로 읽는다.

14 정답 (zero) point two five
→ 소수점까지는 기수 zero로, 소수점은 point로, 소수점 이하는 한 자리씩 two five로 읽는다. point 앞의 zero는 생략 가능하다.

15 정답 three hundred (and) fifty-seven
→ 세 자리씩 천 단위로 끊어 읽고, hundred 뒤의 and는 생략할 수 있다.

16 정답 one and three-fifths
→ one을 먼저 읽고, 분자는 기수 three, 분모는 분자가 2 이상이므로 서수 fifths로 읽는다.

17 정답 three point one four
→ 소수점까지는 기수 three로, 소수점은 point로, 소수점 이하는 한 자리씩 one four로 읽는다.

18 정답 five-eighths
→ 분자는 기수 five로, 분모는 분자가 2 이상이므로 서수 eighths로 읽는다.

19 정답 forty-two thousand three hundred (and) fifty
→ 세 자리씩 천 단위로 끊어 읽고, hundred 뒤의 and는 생략할 수 있다.

20 정답 seven and two-sevenths
→ seven을 먼저 읽고, 분자는 기수 two, 분모는 분자가 2 이상이므로 서수 sevenths로 읽는다.

21 정답 ninth
→ first, second, third를 제외하고 서수는 기수에 -th를 붙여 나타낸다.

22 정답 one-millionth
→ 분수를 쓸 때는 분자는 기수로, 분모는 서수로 쓴다.

23 정답 Two-thirds
→ 분자는 기수 two로, 분모는 분자가 2 이상이므로 서수 thirds로 쓴다.

24 정답 eighty-seven
→ 기수 eighty-seven으로 읽는다.

25 정답 (zero) point three three
→ 소수점까지는 기수 zero로, 소수점은 point로, 소수점 이하는 한 자리씩 three three로 읽는다. point 앞의 zero는 생략 가능하다.

26 정답 seven times
→ 1배(once), 2배(twice)를 제외한 배수는 「기수+times」로 나타낸다.

27 정답 five to six
→ 5:55는 five fifty-five, five to six로 표현한다. five fifty는 5:50이다.

28 정답 ten to ten
→ 9:50는 nine fifty, ten to ten으로 표현한다. nine fifteen은 9:15이다.

29 정답 twelve thirty
→ 12:30는 twelve thirty, a half past[after] twelve로 표현한다. a half past one은 1:30이다.

30 정답 six forty-five
→ 6:45는 six forty-five, a quarter to seven으로 표현한다. a quarter to six는 5:45이다.

31 정답 four twenty
→ 4:20는 four twenty로 표현한다. twenty past five는 5:20이다.

32 정답 a quarter after three
→ 3:15는 three fifteen, a quarter past[after] three로 표현한다. a quarter past four는 4:15이다.

33 정답 February (the) fourteenth 또는 the fourteenth of February
→ 날짜를 읽을 때는 '월'은 명칭으로, '일'은 서수로 읽는다. 월을 먼저 쓰기도 하고 일을 먼저 쓸 수도 있다.

34 정답 March (the) third 또는 the third of March
→ 날짜를 읽을 때는 '월'은 명칭으로, '일'은 서수로 읽는다. 월을 먼저 쓰기도 하고 일을 먼저 쓸 수도 있다.

35 정답 December (the) twenty-fourth 또는 the twenty-fourth of December
→ 날짜를 읽을 때는 '월'은 명칭으로, '일'은 서수로 읽는다. 월을 먼저 쓰기도 하고 일을 먼저 쓸 수도 있다.

36 정답 January (the) fourth, seventeen eighty-six 또는 the fourth of January, seventeen eighty-six
→ 날짜를 읽을 때는 '월'은 명칭으로, '일'은 서수로 읽는다. 월을 먼저 쓰기도 하고 일을 먼저 쓸 수도 있다. 연도는 두 자리씩 끊어 읽는다.

37 정답 three four eight zero, nine nine two seven
→ 전화번호는 한 자리씩 기수로 읽는다.

38 정답 zero one zero, two three four five, six seven eight nine
→ 전화번호는 한 자리씩 기수로 읽는다.

39 정답 area code zero five one, two four six eight, one three five seven
→ 전화번호는 한 자리씩 기수로 읽는다. 지역 번호는 area code를 붙여 읽는다.

40 정답 21th → 21st
[해석] 나는 1999년 7월 21일을 잊지 않을 것이다.
→ 21은 서수로 twenty-first로 읽고, 21st라고 쓴다.

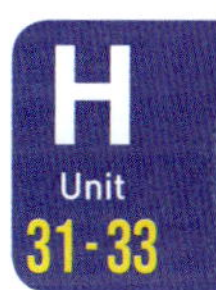

41 정답 triple → three
[해석] 나의 삼촌은 내 나이의 세 배이다.
→ '~ 배'는 「기수+times」라고 쓴다.

42 정답 dollar → dollars
[해석] 이 가게의 대부분의 품목의 가격은 9.99달러이다.
→ 2달러 이상일 때는 dollar에 -s를 붙인다.

43 정답 fourth → four
[해석] 브라질의 인구는 한국 인구의 대략 네 배이다.
→ '~ 배'는 「기수+times」라고 쓴다.

44 정답 on → of
[해석] 12월 12일은 내 딸의 생일이다.
→ 날짜는 「일+of+월」로 읽으며, '일'은 「the+서수」로 읽는다.

정답

01 ① **02** ② **03** ④ **04** four-sevenths

05 (zero) point four nine three

06 one hundred (and) eight point five

07 six million, three hundred (and) twenty-nine thousand, seven hundred (and) sixty-five

08 five five three, eight nine two five

09 eleven five 또는 five after[past] eleven

10 ① **11** some **12** interesting things

13 something cheaper **14** much **15** ②

16 The **17** a **18** 없음 **19** ④

20 ④ **21** ① **22** ④

23 this large old wooden chest

24 three cute little black puppies

25 a black leather jacket **26** 서술적 **27** 한정적

28 서술적 **29** 한정적 **30** ② **31** ②

32 ② **33** ① **34** ⑤

35 Three-fourth → Three-fourths

36 unexpected something → something unexpected

37 any → some **38** ② **39** ① **40** ②

41 ⑤ **42** ③ **43** many

44 She packed her large brown bag. **45** ④

---

01 [정답] ① UNIT 33 수사 형용사의 표현
→ ① 분수를 읽을 때 분자가 2 이상의 복수일 때만 분모에 복수형 -s를 붙인다.

02 [정답] ② UNIT 33 수사 형용사의 표현
→ ② 1배, 2배를 제외한 배수는 「기수+times」로 나타낸다.

03 [정답] ④ UNIT 33 수사 형용사의 표현
→ ④ '11시 30분'은 eleven thirty나 half past eleven이라고 읽는다.

04 [정답] four-sevenths UNIT 33 수사 형용사의 표현
→ 분수의 분자는 기수로, 분모는 서수로 읽는다. 분자가 2 이상이면 분모에 복수형 -s를 붙여 읽는다.

05 [정답] (zero) point four nine three UNIT 33 수사 형용사의 표현
→ 소수는 소수점까지는 정수처럼 읽고, 소수점은 point로, 소수점 이하는 하나씩 읽는다. point 앞의 zero는 생략 가능하다.

06 [정답] one hundred (and) eight point five UNIT 33 수사 형용사의 표현
→ 소수는 소수점까지는 정수처럼 읽고, 소수점은 point로, 소수점 이하는 하나씩 읽는다.

07 [정답] six million, three hundred (and) twenty-nine thousand, seven hundred (and) sixty-five UNIT 33 수사 형용사의 표현
→ 정수는 콤마가 붙어 있는 대로 세 자리씩 끊어서 읽는다. hundred 단위 뒤에는 and를 넣어야 하지만, 구어에서는 생략하는 것이 일반적이다.

08 [정답] five five three, eight nine two five UNIT 33 수사 형용사의 표현
→ 전화번호는 한 자리씩 기수로 읽는다.

09 [정답] eleven five 또는 five after[past] eleven UNIT 33 수사 형용사의 표현
→ 시각은 '시'와 '분'을 끊어서 읽고, '~이 지난'이라는 뜻의 after[past]를 사용할 수도 있다.

10 [정답] ① UNIT 32 부정 수량 형용사
[해석] • 오늘 콘서트에는 사람이 거의 없다. 그렇게 많이 붐비지 않는다.
• 버스가 오기까지 아직 시간이 많이 남았으니, 너무 걱정하지 마.
→ (A) 셀 수 있는 명사인 people을 수식하며, '거의 없는'을 의미하는 것은 few이다.
(B) 셀 수 없는 명사인 time을 수식하며 '많은'을 의미하는 것은 lots of이다.

11 [정답] some UNIT 32 부정 수량 형용사
[해석] 나는 숙제를 하는 데 약간의 도움이 필요하다.
→ help는 셀 수 없는 명사이므로 some을 써야 한다.

12 [정답] interesting things UNIT 31 형용사의 종류, 쓰임, 어순
[해석] 이 책에서 나는 초콜릿에 관한 흥미로운 것들을 발견할 수 있었다.
→ anything, something, everything 등의 대명사를 꾸며주는 형용사는 대명사 뒤에 오지만, thing을 꾸며 주는 형용사는 thing 앞에 온다.

13 [정답] something cheaper UNIT 31 형용사의 종류, 쓰임, 어순
[해석] 저에게 더 싼 것을 보여 주시겠어요?
→ -thing으로 끝나는 대명사를 꾸며 주는 형용사는 -thing 뒤에 온다.

14 [정답] much UNIT 32 부정 수량 형용사
[해석] 나는 자동판매기에 넣을 잔돈을 많이 가지고 있다.
→ change(잔돈)는 셀 수 없는 명사이므로 much와 함께 쓴다.

15 [정답] ② UNIT 32 부정 수량 형용사
[해석] ① 나는 그것에 대해 거의 알지 못한다.
② 매년 많은 학생들이 대학에 간다.
③ 그는 몸이 아주 약해서 한 달에 몇 번씩 학교에 결석한다.
④ 콘서트홀에 아주 많은 사람들이 있었다.
⑤ 그 초고층 빌딩을 짓는 데 아주 많은 돈이 들었다.
→ ② the number of는 '~의 수'라는 뜻이고, '많은'이라는 뜻은 a number of로 써야 한다. ① 셀 수 없는 명사를 수식하는 little ③ '몇 번'을 나타낼 때 뒤의 times를 수식하는 several ④ 셀 수 있는 명사 people을 수식하는 a great many ⑤ 셀 수 없는 명사 money를 수식하는 a great amount of

16 정답 The　　　　　　　　　　UNIT **32** 부정 수량 형용사

[해석] A: 어제 경기장은 얼마나 붐볐나요?
B: 참석자 수가 예상보다 많았어요.
→ 단수 동사 was가 있고 '~의 수'를 나타내야 하므로 the number of로 쓴다. a number of는 복수 명사와 쓰이고 '많은'을 뜻한다.

17 정답 a　　　　　　　　　　UNIT **32** 부정 수량 형용사

[해석] A: 많은 지원자들이 자격 조건을 충족했나요?
B: 아니요, 필요한 경력을 가진 사람은 거의 없었어요.
→ only a few는 few와 마찬가지로 '거의 없는' 상태를 강조한다.

18 정답 없음　　　　　　　　　　UNIT **32** 부정 수량 형용사

[해석] A: 그 발표에 왜 전혀 반응하지 않았어요?
B: 그들이 말하는 것에 거의 관심이 없었어요.
→ 셀 수 없는 명사 interest를 수식하며, 관심이 '거의 없었음'을 나타내려면 관사 없이 little만 써야 한다.

19 정답 ④　　　　　　　　　　UNIT **31** 형용사의 종류, 쓰임, 어순

[해석] ① 그는 멋진 둥근 오크 나무 탁자를 가지고 있다.
② 그녀는 이 값비싼 긴 빨간색 드레스를 원한다.
③ 이 큰 둥근 의자는 너의 것이니?
④ 저 새 갈색 가죽 가방은 얼마니?
⑤ 그 작은 오래된 식당은 40년의 역사를 가지고 있다.
→ ④ 형용사는 관사, 지시형용사, 소유격 뒤에 「의견+크기+나이+모양+색깔+국적+재료+분사」 순서로 명사 앞에 쓴다. ① a round nice oak → a nice round oak ② expensive this long red → this expensive long red ③ this round large → this large round ⑤ The old small → The small old

20 정답 ④　　　　　　　　　　UNIT **31** 형용사의 종류, 쓰임, 어순

[해석] ① 나는 공원에서 귀엽고 폭신한 흰 강아지를 보았다.
② 오래되고 녹슨 금속 자전거가 마당에 놓여 있었다.
③ 그들은 지난주에 현대적이고 세련된 검은색 차를 샀다.
④ 그는 그녀에게 아름답고 파란 실크 스카프를 선물로 주었다.
⑤ 그녀는 내가 알아야 할 중요한 것을 숨기고 있었다.
→ ④ 형용사는 관사, 지시형용사, 소유격 뒤에 「의견+크기+나이+모양+색깔+국적+재료+분사」 순서로 명사 앞에 쓴다. ① a white cute fluffy puppy → a cute fluffy white puppy ② The metal old rusty bike → The old rusty metal bike ③ a black modern sleek car → a sleek modern black car ⑤ important something → something important

21 정답 ①　　　　　　　　　　UNIT **33** 수사 형용사의 표현

[해석] 행사는 5시 반까지 마칠 예정이지만, 일부 활동은 조금 더 오래 걸릴 수도 있다.
→ a half past five는 5시 반을 의미하므로 ① five thirty로 바꿔 쓸 수 있다.

22 정답 ④　　　　　　　　　　UNIT **32** 부정 수량 형용사

[해석] 여러 나라들이 평화 협정에 서명했다.
→ A number of는 '많은'을 의미하며 셀 수 있는 명사를 수식하므로 ④ Plenty of로 바꿔 쓸 수 있다.

23 정답 this large old wooden chest　　UNIT **31** 형용사의 종류, 쓰임, 어순

[해석] 나는 다락에서 이 오래된 커다란 나무 상자를 찾았다.
→ 「지시형용사+크기+나이+재료」 순서로 쓴다.

24 정답 three cute little black puppies　　UNIT **31** 형용사의 종류, 쓰임, 어순

[해석] 내 개 Molly는 귀엽고 작은 세 마리의 검은색 강아지를 낳았다.
→ 「수량형용사+의견+크기+색깔」 순서로 쓴다.

25 정답 a black leather jacket　　UNIT **31** 형용사의 종류, 쓰임, 어순

[해석] 그는 모자가 달린 회색 셔츠 위에 검은색 가죽 재킷을 입고 있었다.
→ 형용사는 관사 뒤에 「색깔+재료」 순서로 명사 앞에 쓴다.

26 정답 서술적　　　　　　　　　　UNIT **31** 형용사의 종류, 쓰임, 어순

[해석] 케이크가 너무 맛있어 보여서 나는 빨리 맛보고 싶다.
→ delicious가 주격 보어로 쓰였다.

27 정답 한정적　　　　　　　　　　UNIT **31** 형용사의 종류, 쓰임, 어순

[해석] 따뜻한 날씨는 공원에서 피크닉을 즐기기에 완벽했다.
→ warm이 명사 weather를 수식하고 있다.

28 정답 서술적　　　　　　　　　　UNIT **31** 형용사의 종류, 쓰임, 어순

[해석] 선생님은 실제 예시를 사용하여 수업을 흥미롭게 만들었다.
→ interesting이 목적격 보어로 쓰였다.

29 정답 한정적　　　　　　　　　　UNIT **31** 형용사의 종류, 쓰임, 어순

[해석] 그 영화는 우리를 긴장하게 만든 흥미진진한 줄거리를 가지고 있었다.
→ thrilling이 명사 plot을 수식하고 있다.

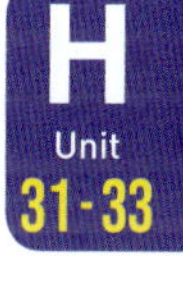

30 정답 ②　　　　　　　　　　UNIT **32** 부정 수량 형용사

[해석] 지진 이후, 지역 전역에 일부 피해가 보고되었다. 구조팀들이 급파되었지만, 처음 몇 시간 동안은 지원이 거의 없었다. 왜냐하면 대부분의 도로와 다리들도 손상되었기 때문이었다. 이 혼란스러운 상황은 특히 노인들과 아이들에게 큰 우려를 불러일으켰다.
→ (A) damage는 셀 수 없는 명사이므로 some이 와야 한다.
(B) 셀 수 없는 명사 support를 수식하며, 뒤 문장에서 도로와 다리들도 손상되었다고 했으므로 지원이 '거의 없었음'을 나타내는 little이 와야 한다.

31 정답 ②　　　　　　　　　　UNIT **32** 부정 수량 형용사

→ (C)는 셀 수 없는 명사 concern을 수식하므로, 셀 수 있는 명사를 수식하는 many는 적절하지 않다.

32 정답 ②　　　　　　　　　　UNIT **32** 부정 수량 형용사

[해석] 그는 단 일주일의 연습 기간 동안 ＿＿＿＿ 진전을 이루었다.
→ progress는 셀 수 없는 명사이므로 ② a few는 올 수 없다.

33 정답 ①　　　　　　　　　　UNIT **33** 수사 형용사의 표현

[해석] 보고서에 따르면, 도시 인구의 10분의 ＿＿＿＿이 50세 미만이다.
→ 분자가 2 이상일 때만 분모에 -s를 붙이므로, ① one은 -tenths 앞에 올 수 없다.

34 정답 ⑤   UNIT **32** 부정 수량 형용사

[해석] 어제 새 회사 정책에 대해 많은 _______이 있었다.
① 의견들 ② 걱정들 ③ 질문들 ④ 불평들
→ many는 셀 수 있는 명사를 수식하므로 셀 수 없는 명사 ⑤ information은 올 수 없다.

35 정답 Three-fourth → Three-fourths
       UNIT **33** 수사 형용사의 표현

[해석] 작업의 4분의 3이 완료되었지만, 나머지는 아직 남아 있다.
→ 분수를 읽을 때 분자가 2 이상의 복수면 분모에 복수형 -s를 붙인다.

36 정답 unexpected something → something unexpected   UNIT **31** 형용사의 종류, 쓰임, 어순

[해석] 그녀는 받은 편지함에서 예상치 못한 것을 발견했다.
→ -thing으로 끝나는 대명사를 꾸며 주는 형용사는 -thing 뒤에 온다.

37 정답 any → some   UNIT **32** 부정 수량 형용사

[해석] 나가기 전에 차 한 잔 드실래요?
→ 권유의 의문문에서 '약간의, 조금의'를 뜻하는 것은 some이다.

38 정답 ②   UNIT **32** 부정 수량 형용사

[해석] A: 저는 코딩에 대한 경험이 거의 없지만 배우고 싶어요.
B: 걱정 마세요, 조금만 연습하면 금방 자신감이 생길 거예요.
→ 셀 수 없는 명사 experience 앞에서 '거의 없는'을 의미해야 하므로 정답은 ② little이다.

39 정답 ①   UNIT **32** 부정 수량 형용사

[해석] A: 점심 전에 이 일을 끝내기 위해 몇 분이 더 필요해요.
B: 걱정 마세요. 기다릴게요.
→ 셀 수 있는 명사의 복수형 minutes 앞에서 '조금의'를 의미해야 하므로 정답은 ① a few이다.

40 정답 ②   UNIT **31** 형용사의 종류, 쓰임, 어순

[해석] ① 그녀는 빨간 드레스를 입고 파티에 갔다.
② 해질 무렵 하늘이 정말 분홍색으로 보인다.
③ 그는 도시에 있는 작은 아파트에 살고 있다.
④ 해변의 하얀 모래는 정말 편안하게 해주었다.
⑤ 밝은 태양은 해변을 더욱 아름답게 보이게 만들었다.
→ 나머지는 모두 명사를 수식하는 한정적 쓰임으로 쓰였지만, ②은 주격 보어 자리에서 서술적 쓰임으로 쓰였다.

41 정답 ⑤   UNIT **31** 형용사의 종류, 쓰임, 어순

[해석] ① 넓은 강은 카누 타기에 완벽하다.
② 모두가 게임을 시작할 준비가 되었다.
③ 케이크는 커 보이지만 놀랍게도 가볍다.
④ 그녀는 모두가 탈락한 뒤에 혼자 남았다.
⑤ 배가 그렇게 고프지 않아서 작은 커피를 샀다.
→ 나머지는 모두 주격 보어 자리에서 서술적 쓰임으로 쓰였지만, ⑤은 명사를 수식하는 한정적 쓰임으로 쓰였다.

42 정답 ③   UNIT **31** 형용사의 종류, 쓰임, 어순

[해석] 3살의 영국 남자아이, William Potter는 멘사에 가입했다. IQ 140의 이 천재 어린이는 다른 아이들처럼 밖에서 노는 것을 좋아한다. 하지만 그에게는 특별한 점이 있다. 24개월 때 그는 20까지 셀 수 있었고, 모든 색상과 알파벳을 알았다. "그가 겨우 18개월이었을 때, 어린이 영화 속 몇몇 임의의 캐릭터들을 기억하는 모습을 보고 깜짝 놀랐어요,"라고 그의 어머니는 말했다. 지금 그는 지도 읽기와 컴퓨터에서 어려운 단어 퍼즐을 푸는 것을 즐긴다. 이것은 배움에 흥미를 가진 많은 어린 학습자에게 인상적일 것이다.
→ -thing/-body/-one으로 끝나는 대명사는 형용사가 그 뒤에 위치하므로 ③ something special로 고쳐야 한다.

43 정답 many   UNIT **32** 부정 수량 형용사

→ 셀 수 있는 명사 learner를 수식하므로, 셀 수 없는 명사를 수식하는 much는 적절하지 않다.

44 정답 She packed her large brown bag.
       UNIT **31** 형용사의 종류, 쓰임, 어순

[해석] 비 오는 오후에 Sarah는 자신의 프로젝트를 하기 위해 도서관에 가기로 결심했다. 그녀는 그녀의 큰 갈색 가방을 챙겼다. 그 도서관에는 공간을 더 편안하게 느껴지게 해주는 살아 있는 식물이 놓인 조용한 구역이 있었다. 읽기 시작하면서 그녀는 연구에 도움이 될 몇 개의 유용한 기사들을 발견했다. 몇 시간 동안 집중해서 작업한 후, 그녀는 자신의 진전에 대해 성취감과 큰 행복을 느꼈다.
→ '인칭대명사의 소유격 → 일반형용사'의 순서이고, 일반형용사는 '크기 → 색깔'의 순서이므로 「주어+동사」 뒤에 her large brown bag으로 쓰는 것이 알맞다.

45 정답 ④   UNIT **33** 부정 수량 형용사

→ (A) 한정적 쓰임의 형용사 자리이므로 live가 알맞다. (B) 셀 수 있는 명사 articles를 수식해야 하므로 a few가 알맞다. (C) 셀 수 없는 명사 happiness를 수식해야 하므로 a great deal of가 알맞다.

I 부사

개념 확인 문제 정답　　　▶ 문제편 p.145~147

01 near, ⓑ	**02** soon, ⓐ	**03** never, ⓔ
04 smoothly, ⓒ	**05** very, ⓓ	**06** slyly
07 truly	**08** dully	**09** easily
10 sillily	**11** quietly	**12** actually
13 gently	**14** happily	**15** subtly
16 classically	**17** smoothly	**18** suddenly
19 psychically	**20** probably	**21** steadily
22 publicly	**23** automatically	**24** basically
25 fortunately	**26** truly	**27** fully
28 shyly	**29** smoothly	**30** publicly
31 부사	**32** 형용사	**33** 형용사
34 부사	**35** 형용사	**36** 부사
37 near	**38** highly	**39** shortly
40 hardly	**41** late	**42** 부사
43 형용사	**44** 부사	**45** 형용사
46 부사	**47** 형용사	**48** 부사
49 형용사	**50** 부사	

01 [정답] near, ⓑ
[해석] 그녀가 가까이 기울이자, 난 그녀의 향수를 맡을 수 있었다.
→ 부사 near는 '가까이'라는 장소를 나타낸다.

02 [정답] soon, ⓐ
[해석] 그녀는 곧 자신만의 빵집을 열 계획이다.
→ 부사 soon은 '곧'이라는 시간을 나타낸다.

03 [정답] never, ⓔ
[해석] 나는 서둘러야 할 때는 절대 아침 식사를 하지 않는다.
→ 부사 never는 '절대 ~하지 않는'이라는 빈도를 나타낸다.

04 [정답] smoothly, ⓒ
[해석] 그 로봇은 부드럽게 유리 바닥을 가로질러 움직였다.
→ 부사 smoothly는 '부드럽게'라는 방법을 나타낸다.

05 [정답] very, ⓓ
[해석] 그 교복은 그 학생에게 너무 비쌌다.
→ 부사 very는 '너무'라는 정도를 나타낸다.

06 [정답] slyly
[해석] 교활한 → 교활하게
→ sly의 부사는 slyly이다.

07 [정답] truly
[해석] 진실한 → 진실하게
→ -ue로 끝나는 형용사는 ue를 uly로 고쳐 부사를 만든다.

08 [정답] dully
[해석] 둔한 → 둔하게
→ -ll로 끝나는 형용사는 -y를 붙여 부사를 만든다.

09 [정답] easily
[해석] 쉬운 → 쉽게
→ 「자음+y」로 끝나는 형용사는 y를 ily로 고쳐 부사를 만든다.

10 [정답] sillily
[해석] 바보 같은 → 바보같이
→ 「자음+y」로 끝나는 형용사는 y를 ily로 고쳐 부사를 만든다.

11 [정답] quietly
[해석] 조용한 → 조용히
→ 대부분의 경우 형용사에 -ly를 붙여 부사를 만든다.

12 [정답] actually
[해석] 실제의 → 실제로
→ 대부분의 경우 형용사에 -ly를 붙여 부사를 만든다.

13 [정답] gently
[해석] 부드러운 → 부드럽게
→ -le로 끝나는 형용사는 le를 ly로 고쳐 부사를 만든다.

14 [정답] happily
[해석] 행복한 → 행복하게
→ 「자음+y」로 끝나는 형용사는 y를 ily로 고쳐 부사를 만든다.

15 [정답] subtly
[해석] 미묘한 → 미묘하게
→ -le로 끝나는 형용사는 le를 ly로 고쳐 부사를 만든다.

16 [정답] classically
[해석] 고전적인 → 고전적으로
→ -ic로 끝나는 형용사는 -ally를 붙여 부사를 만든다.

17 [정답] smoothly
[해석] 매끄러운 → 매끄럽게
→ 대부분의 경우 형용사에 -ly를 붙여 부사를 만든다.

18 [정답] suddenly
[해석] 갑작스러운 → 갑자기
→ 대부분의 경우 형용사에 -ly를 붙여 부사를 만든다.

19 [정답] psychically
[해석] 심령의 → 심령적으로
→ -ic로 끝나는 형용사는 -ally를 붙여 부사를 만든다.

20 [정답] probably
[해석] 있을 법한 → 아마도
→ -le로 끝나는 형용사는 le를 ly로 고쳐 부사를 만든다.

21 [정답] steadily
[해석] 꾸준한 → 꾸준히
→ 「자음+y」로 끝나는 형용사는 y를 ily로 고쳐 부사를 만든다.

22 [정답] publicly
[해석] 공적인 → 공개적으로
→ public의 부사는 publicly이다.

23 [정답] automatically

[해석] 자동의 → 자동적으로

→ -ic로 끝나는 형용사는 -ally를 붙여 부사를 만든다.

24 [정답] basically

[해석] 기본적인 → 기본적으로

→ -ic로 끝나는 형용사는 -ally를 붙여 부사를 만든다.

25 [정답] fortunately

[해석] 운이 좋은 → 운 좋게

→ 대부분의 경우 형용사에 -ly를 붙여 부사를 만든다.

26 [정답] truly

[해석] 그는 자신이 실수했다는 것을 진심으로 인정했다.

→ -ue로 끝나는 형용사는 ue를 uly로 고쳐 부사를 만든다. honesty는 '정직'을 뜻하는 명사이다.

27 [정답] fully

[해석] 그 식당은 크리스마스 당일에 예약이 꽉 찼다.

→ -ll로 끝나는 형용사는 -y를 붙여 부사를 만든다.

28 [정답] shyly

[해석] 그녀는 복도에서 새 학생에게 수줍게 말을 걸었다.

→ shy의 부사는 shyly이다. friendly는 '친절한'을 뜻하는 형용사이다.

29 [정답] smoothly

[해석] 비가 내린 뒤 강은 계곡을 따라 매끄럽게 흘렀다.

→ 대부분의 경우 형용사에 -ly를 붙여 부사를 만든다.

30 [정답] publicly

[해석] 그녀는 기자회견에서 자신의 실수에 대해 공개적으로 사과했다.

→ public의 부사는 publicly이다.

31 [정답] 부사

[해석] 독수리가 하늘 높이 날았다.

→ high는 형용사와 부사의 형태가 동일하다. 이 문장에서는 부사로 쓰였다.

32 [정답] 형용사

[해석] 그녀는 일찍 일어나는 사람이다.

→ early는 형용사와 부사의 형태가 동일하다. 이 문장에서는 형용사로 쓰였다.

33 [정답] 형용사

[해석] 우리는 모두를 위한 충분한 음식이 없다.

→ enough는 형용사와 부사의 형태가 동일하다. 이 문장에서는 형용사로 쓰였다.

34 [정답] 부사

[해석] 기차가 늦게 도착했다.

→ late는 형용사와 부사의 형태가 동일하다. 이 문장에서는 부사로 쓰였다.

35 [정답] 형용사

[해석] 그는 빠르게 달리는 사람이다.

→ fast는 형용사와 부사의 형태가 동일하다. 이 문장에서는 형용사로 쓰였다.

36 [정답] 부사

[해석] 가까이 와서 한 번 봐.

→ near는 형용사와 부사의 형태가 동일하다. 이 문장에서는 부사로 쓰였다.

37 [정답] near

[해석] 사냥꾼은 소리 하나 없이 가까이 움직였다.

→ 부사 near는 '가까이', nearly는 '거의'라는 뜻이다.

38 [정답] highly

[해석] 그 영화는 국제 평론가들 사이에서 대단히 높이 평가되었다.

→ 부사 high는 '높이', highly는 '대단히'라는 뜻이다.

39 [정답] shortly

[해석] 회의가 시작된 직후 그녀가 합류할 것이다.

→ 부사 short는 '짧게', shortly는 '곧'이라는 뜻이다.

40 [정답] hardly

[해석] 그녀는 속보에 정신이 팔려 음식을 거의 손대지 않았다.

→ 부사 hard는 '열심히', hardly는 '거의 ~않다'라는 뜻이다.

41 [정답] late

[해석] 그는 눈에 띄지 않기 위해 평소보다 늦게 나타났다.

→ 부사 late는 '늦게', lately는 '최근에'라는 뜻이다.

42 [정답] 부사

[해석] 그는 마지막 버스를 잡기 위해 빠르게 달렸다.

→ fast는 형용사와 부사의 형태가 같다. 이 문장에서는 부사로 쓰였다.

43 [정답] 형용사

[해석] 그것은 급커브에 조종이 뛰어난 빠른 차다.

→ fast는 형용사와 부사의 형태가 같다. 이 문장에서는 형용사로 쓰였다.

44 [정답] 부사

[해석] 나는 뒤에 다른 약속이 있어서 오래 머물지 않았다.

→ long은 형용사와 부사의 형태가 같다. 이 문장에서는 부사로 쓰였다.

45 [정답] 형용사

[해석] 우리는 여름 행사 계획을 논의하는 긴 회의를 했다.

→ long은 형용사와 부사의 형태가 같다. 이 문장에서는 형용사로 쓰였다.

46 [정답] 부사

[해석] 의사 선생님이 곧 진료하실 예정이니, 여기서 기다리세요.

→ 부사 short는 '짧게', shortly는 '곧'이라는 뜻이다.

47 [정답] 형용사

[해석] 그는 시상식이 시작하기 전에 짧은 연설을 했다.

→ 형용사 short는 '짧은'을 뜻한다.

48 [정답] 부사

[해석] 작은 디테일을 또렷하게 보고 싶다면 가까이 오세요.

→ near는 형용사와 부사의 형태가 같다. 이 문장에서는 부사로 쓰였다.

49 정답 형용사

[해석] 가까운 건물이 폭풍 이후 수리로 폐쇄되었다.

→ near는 형용사와 부사의 형태가 같다. 이 문장에서는 형용사로 쓰였다.

50 정답 부사

[해석] 그녀는 지루하고 긴 강의 중에 거의 잠들 뻔했다.

→ 부사 near는 '가까이', nearly는 '거의'라는 뜻이다.

UNIT 35 부사의 역할 및 위치

개념 확인 문제 정답 ▶ 문제편 p.149

01 Fortunately, 문장 전체

02 incredibly, 형용사 difficult

03 Luckily, 문장 전체 **04** eagerly, 동사 waited

05 absolutely, 형용사 fantastic

06 creatively, 동사 decorated

07 hard, 동사 worked **08** are✓icy

09 trained✓for **10** it ✓again

11 문장 맨 뒤

12 He always finishes his work before the deadline.

13 Deforestation is never a sustainable solution for land development.

14 They have usually been very supportive of each other during tough times.

01 정답 Fortunately, 문장 전체

[해석] 다행히도, 우리는 잃어버린 열쇠를 찾았다.

→ 부사 Fortunately가 문장 전체를 수식하고 있다.

02 정답 incredibly, 형용사 difficult

[해석] 그건 정말로 어려운 도전이었다.

→ 부사 incredibly가 뒤에 오는 형용사 difficult를 수식하고 있다.

03 정답 Luckily, 문장 전체

[해석] 운 좋게도, 그녀는 회의에 딱 맞춰 도착했다.

→ 부사 Luckily가 문장 전체를 수식하고 있다.

04 정답 eagerly, 동사 waited

[해석] 아이들은 서커스가 시작되기를 간절히 기다렸다.

→ 부사 eagerly가 앞에 온 동사 waited를 수식하고 있다.

05 정답 absolutely, 형용사 fantastic

[해석] 그 콘서트는 시작부터 끝까지 정말 환상적이었다.

→ 부사 absolutely가 뒤에 오는 형용사 fantastic을 수식하고 있다.

06 정답 creatively, 동사 decorated

[해석] 그 예술가는 다채로운 벽화로 벽을 창의적으로 장식했다.

→ 부사 creatively가 뒤에 오는 동사 decorated를 수식하고 있다.

07 정답 hard, 동사 worked

[해석] 그들은 마감 전에 프로젝트를 완료하기 위해 열심히 일했다.

→ 부사 hard가 앞에 온 동사 worked를 수식하고 있다.

08 정답 are✓icy

[해석] 오늘 아침에는 거리가 정말 얼어 있다.

→ 형용사를 꾸며 주는 부사는 꾸며 주는 단어 앞에 오므로 icy 앞에 really를 써야 한다.

09 정답 trained✓for

[해석] 나는 그 시합을 위해 충분히 훈련하지 못했다.

→ 부사 enough는 꾸며 주는 단어 뒤에 오므로 trained 뒤에 enough를 써야 한다.

10 정답 it ✓again

[해석] 히터가 작동하지 않으면, 다시 켜 보세요.

→ 「타동사+부사」의 목적어가 대명사일 때, 부사는 목적어 뒤에 온다.

11 정답 문장 맨 뒤

[해석] 이런 큰 문제들은 무섭지만, 하나씩 나눠서 생각해봅시다.

→ 「타동사+부사」의 목적어가 대명사일 때, 부사는 목적어 뒤에 온다.

12 정답 He always finishes his work before the deadline.

→ '항상'을 의미하는 빈도부사는 always이다. 빈도부사는 조동사와 be동사 뒤, 일반동사 앞에 오므로, always가 일반동사 finishes 앞에 와야 한다.

13 정답 Deforestation is never a sustainable solution for land development.

→ '절대, 결코'를 의미하는 빈도부사는 never이다. 빈도부사는 조동사와 be동사 뒤, 일반동사 앞에 오므로, never가 be동사 is 뒤에 와야 한다.

14 정답 They have usually been very supportive of each other during tough times.

→ '보통, 대개'를 의미하는 빈도부사는 usually이다. 빈도부사는 조동사와 be동사 뒤, 일반동사 앞에 오므로, usually가 조동사 have 뒤에 와야 한다.

UNIT 36 그 밖의 중요 부사

개념 확인 문제 정답 ▶ 문제편 p.151

01 before **02** ago **03** either **04** too

05 Neither **06** before **07** ago **08** very

09 else **10** yet **11** even **12** already

13 much **14** yet **15** Even **16** very

17 already **18** else

01 정답 before

[해석] 나는 전에 이 동상을 어딘가에서 본 적이 있다.
→ 완료시제와 함께 '~ 전에'라는 뜻으로 before를 쓴다.

02 정답 ago

[해석] 그는 세 달 전에 비행기 표를 예약했다.
→ 과거시제와 함께 '~ 전에'라는 뜻으로 ago를 쓴다.

03 정답 either

[해석] A: 나는 매운 음식을 좋아하지 않아. 그건 내 위를 아프게 해.
B: 나도 매운 음식을 좋아하지 않아. 나는 더 순한 맛을 선호해.
→ either는 부정문에 '또한, 역시'라는 의미를 더할 때 쓰는 부사이다.

04 정답 too

[해석] A: 오늘 회의는 건너뛸 거야. 그냥 기분이 안 좋아서.
B: 나도 같은 생각이야. 나도 회의를 건너뛸지도 몰라.
→ too는 긍정문에 '또한, 역시'라는 의미를 더할 때 쓰는 부사이다.

05 정답 Neither

[해석] A: 나는 새 웹사이트 디자인이 마음에 안 들어. 둘러보기가 너무 어려워.
B: 나도 그래. 옛날 것보다 훨씬 더 혼란스러워.
→ not ~ either는 neither로 바꿔쓸 수 있다.

06 정답 before

[해석] 그녀는 그녀가 그를 전에 결코 본 적이 없다고 말했다.
→ 완료시제와 함께 쓰여 '~ 전에'를 의미하는 부사는 before이다.

07 정답 ago

[해석] 한국 전쟁은 60년도 더 전에 끝났다.
→ 과거시제와 함께 쓰여 '~ 전에'를 의미하는 부사는 ago이다.

08 정답 very

[해석] 그의 이야기는 언제나 매우 흥미롭다.
→ 원급의 형용사나 부사는 very가 꾸며준다.

09 정답 else

[해석] 디저트로 다른 거 드시겠어요?
→ else는 수식하려는 말의 뒤에 쓰여 '또 다른, 그 밖에'라는 의미를 더할 때 쓰는 부사, 형용사이다.

10 정답 yet

[해석] 나는 아직 이번 달 월급을 받지 못했다.
→ 부정문에 사용되어 '아직'이라는 의미를 가지는 부사는 yet이다.

11 정답 even

[해석] 그것이 얼마나 힘들었을지 상상도 할 수 없다.
→ even은 강조하려는 말의 앞에 쓰여 '~도, ~조차'라는 의미를 더할 때 쓰는 부사이다.

12 정답 already

[해석] 내가 도착했을 때 그는 이미 그의 숙제를 끝냈다.
→ 긍정문에서 사용되어 '이미, 벌써' 등을 의미하는 부사는 already이다.

13 정답 much

[해석] 그 블록버스터 영화는 내가 생각했던 것보다 훨씬 더 재미있었다.
→ 비교급을 꾸며 주는 부사는 much이다.

14 정답 yet

[해석] 나는 아버지로부터 아직 엽서를 받지 못했다.
→ '아직'이라는 뜻으로 부정문에 쓰이는 부사는 yet이다.

15 정답 Even

[해석] 심지어 선생님도 그의 영리한 대답에 놀랐다.
→ even은 강조하려는 말의 앞에 쓰여 '~도, ~조차'라는 의미를 더할 때 쓰는 부사이다.

16 정답 very

[해석] 우리는 의사의 조언을 아주 주의 깊게 들어야 한다.
→ 형용사나 부사의 원급을 꾸며 주는 부사는 very이다.

17 정답 already

[해석] 나는 기차역에 갔는데, 기차가 이미 떠났다.
→ 긍정문에서 '이미, 벌써'의 의미로 쓰이는 것은 already이다.

18 정답 else

[해석] 그들은 안 좋은 리뷰를 보고 다른 곳에 호텔을 예약했다.
→ else는 수식하려는 말의 뒤에 쓰여 '또 다른, 그 밖에'라는 의미를 더할 때 쓰는 부사이다.

단원 평가 문제   UNIT 34 ~ UNIT 36   ▶ 문제편 p.152~156

정답

01 ⑤	**02** ④	**03** ①	**04** yet	**05** loudly
06 ago	**07** much	**08** ④	**09** ①	**10** ⑤
11 ③	**12** ②	**13** ⑤	**14** ⑤	**15** ③
16 ③	**17** near → nearly		**18** short → shortly	
19 ①	**20** ⑤	**21** ⓓ, ⓗ	**22** ⓔ, ⓖ	**23** ⓑ, ⓕ
24 ⓐ, ⓒ	**25** up	**26** off	**27** ②	**28** ④
29 ③	**30** ①	**31** ④	**32** ③	**33** ②
34 ②	**35** ④	**36** ④	**37** ②	**38** ④
39 can often hear	**40** usually sleep			
41 were never	**42** always occurs		**43** ①	

01 정답 ⑤   UNIT 34 부사의 형태

[해석] ① 수줍은 – 수줍게 ② 멋진 – 멋지게 ③ 진실된 – 정말로 ④ 무거운 – 무겁게 ⑤ 주의 깊은 – 조심스럽게

→ ⑤ careful은 대부분의 형용사처럼 -ly를 붙여 부사를 만든다. ①
shy - shyly ② nice - nicely ③ true - truly ④ heavy - heavily

02 정답 ④　　　　　　　　　　　UNIT 34 부사의 형태
[해석] ① 고귀한 – 고귀하게 ② 간단한 – 간단하게 ③ 유일한 –
유일하게 ④ 정확한 – 정확하게 ⑤ 끔찍한 – 끔찍하게
→ ④ precise는 대부분의 형용사처럼 -ly를 붙여 부사를 만든다. ①
noble - nobly ② simple - simply ③ unique - uniquely ⑤
terrible - terribly

03 정답 ①　　　　　　　　　　　UNIT 34 부사의 형태
[해석] ① 교활한 – 교활하게 ② 기본적인 – 기본적으로 ③ 화난
– 화를 내며 ④ 공공의 – 공식적으로 ⑤ 환상적인 – 환상적으
로
→ ① sly는 「자음 + y」로 끝나는 형용사처럼 y를 ily로 고치는 것이
아니라 형용사에 ly를 붙여 부사를 만든다. ② basic - basically ③
angry - angrily ④ public - publicly ⑤ fantastic - fantastically

04 정답 yet　　　　　　　　　　UNIT 36 그 밖의 중요 부사
[해석] 그는 아직 떠날 준비가 되지 않았다.
→ already(이미)는 긍정문에, yet(아직)은 부정문과 의문문에 쓴
다.

05 정답 loudly　　　　　　　　　UNIT 34 부사의 형태
[해석] 팀이 골을 넣은 후 군중은 크게 환호했다.
→ cheered를 수식하는 부사 loudly가 와야 한다.

06 정답 ago　　　　　　　　　　UNIT 36 그 밖의 중요 부사
[해석] 폭풍은 오늘 아침 훨씬 일찍, 대략 3시간 전에 시작되었다.
→ 과거시제와 함께 쓰여 '~ 전에'를 뜻하는 것은 ago이다.

07 정답 much　　　　　　　　　UNIT 36 그 밖의 중요 부사
[해석] 신선한 과일과 채소는 가공식품보다 훨씬 더 영양가가 높
다.
→ 비교급 more nutritious를 수식하는 것은 much이다.

08 정답 ④　　　　　　　　　　　UNIT 34 부사의 형태
[해석] ① 그녀는 아름답게 노래한다.
② 그는 매일 열심히 일한다.
③ 그녀는 우아하게 춤을 추고 있었다.
④ 아이들은 밖에서 행복하게 놀았다.
⑤ 해는 저녁에 천천히 진다.
→ ④ 동사 played를 수식해야 하므로 형용사 happy를 부사
happily로 고쳐야 한다.

09 정답 ①　　　　　　　　　　　UNIT 34 부사의 형태
[해석] ① 그는 진심으로 사과했다.
② 개가 크게 짖었다.
③ 그는 파티에 늦게 도착했다.
④ 선생님은 매우 명확하게 말했다.
⑤ 그들은 조용히 거리를 걷고 있었다.
→ ① 동사 apologized를 수식해야 하므로 형용사 sincere를 부
사 sincerely로 고쳐야 한다.

10 정답 ⑤　　　　　　　　　UNIT 35 부사의 역할 및 위치
[해석] ① 나는 겨울에 대개 스키를 타러 간다.
② 그녀는 항상 8시 버스를 탄다.

③ 나는 네가 나에게 했던 말을 결코 잊지 않겠다.
④ Susan은 이 비싼 차를 살만큼 충분히 부자이다.
⑤ 나는 이 음악을 들을 때 항상 너를 생각하겠다.
→ ⑤ 빈도부사는 be동사와 조동사의 뒤, 일반동사의 앞에 와야 하므
로 will always think of의 어순이 옳다.

11 정답 ③　　　　　　　　　UNIT 35 부사의 역할 및 위치
[해석] A: 이봐, 불 좀 켜줄래? 여기 점점 어두워지고 있어.
B: 물론! 내가 불을 켤게. 이제 됐다!
→ 「타동사+부사」의 목적어가 대명사일 경우, 목적어는 타동사와 부
사 사이에 온다. 따라서 목적어 them을 on의 앞에 써야 한다. 목적
어가 the lights이므로 대명사 it이 아닌 them이 와야 한다.

12 정답 ②　　　　　　　　　UNIT 36 그 밖의 중요 부사
[해석] A: 나는 그 책을 일주일 전에 다 읽었고, 정말 멋졌어.
B: 나는 몇 주 전에 읽었는데, 별로 재미있지 않았어.
→ 과거시제와 함께 쓰여 '~ 전에'를 뜻하는 것은 ② ago이다.

13 정답 ⑤　　　UNIT 35 부사의 역할 및 위치, UNIT 36 그 밖의 중요 부사
[해석] ⓐ 나는 항상 집에서 내 열쇠들을 잊어버린다.
ⓑ 그녀는 나보다 훨씬 더 건강하게 먹는다.
ⓒ 나는 아직 숙제를 끝내지 못했다.
ⓓ 나는 2주 전에 그녀를 봤고, 우리는 좋은 대화를 나눴다.
ⓔ 다행히도, 전력은 짧은 정전 후에 다시 공급되었다.
→ 부사가 문장 전체를 수식할 때는 일반적으로 맨 앞에 오므로 ⑤이
정답이다.

14 정답 ⑤　　　　　　　　　UNIT 36 그 밖의 중요 부사
[해석] 나는 그 노래를 전에 들었지만, 가사가 기억이 나지 않는
다.
→ 완료시제와 함께 쓰여 '~ 전에'를 뜻하는 것은 ⑤ before이다.

15 정답 ③　　　　　　　　　UNIT 35 부사의 역할 및 위치
[해석] 이 운동장은 나의 모든 친구들이 축구와 야구를 하기에 충
분히 크다.
→ enough는 형용사나 부사를 뒤에서 수식한다.

16 정답 ③　　　　　　　　　UNIT 35 부사의 역할 및 위치
[해석] 아무리 불행할지라도, 우리는 행복이 멀리 있지 않음을 항
상 기억해야 한다.
→ 빈도부사는 be동사와 조동사의 뒤, 일반동사의 앞에 위치해야 하
므로 조동사 should와 일반동사 remember 사이에 오는 것이 적
절하다.

17 정답 near → nearly　　　　　　UNIT 34 부사의 형태
[해석] 이 지역에서는 주차 공간을 찾는 것이 거의 불가능하다.
→ near는 '가까운, 가까이'를, nearly는 '거의'를 의미한다. 문맥상
'거의'가 알맞다.

18 정답 short → shortly　　　　　UNIT 34 부사의 형태
[해석] 저는 곧 떠날 예정이니, 회의를 마무리해 주세요.
→ short는 '짧은, 짧게'를, shortly는 '곧'을 의미한다. 문맥상 '곧'이
알맞다.

19 정답 ①　　　　　　　　　UNIT 35 부사의 역할 및 위치
[해석] ① Bob은 거의 제시간에 도착하는 법이 없다.
② 나는 항상 너를 생각하고 있었어.

I
Unit
34·36

③ 그녀는 결코 다시 걷지 않을 거라고 생각한다.
④ 내 컴퓨터는 때때로 고장이 난다.
⑤ 너는 남동생과 종종 싸우니?
→ ① 빈도부사는 be동사와 조동사 뒤, 일반동사 앞에 위치한다. ② have been always → have always been ③ never will walk → will never walk ④ sometimes are → are sometimes ⑤ have often → often have

20 [정답] ⑤　　　　UNIT 35 부사의 역할 및 위치
[해석] ① 나는 거의 아침을 거르지 말아야 한다.
② 그는 보통 직장에서 매우 바쁘다.
③ 그녀는 저녁 후에 절대 디저트를 먹지 않는다.
④ 나는 항상 회의에 제시간에 있어야 한다.
⑤ 그는 가끔 점심을 가져오는 것을 잊는다.
→ 빈도부사는 be동사와 조동사 뒤, 일반동사 앞에 위치한다. ① rarely should skip → should rarely skip ② usually is → is usually ③ eats never → never eats ④ always must be → must always be

21 [정답] ⓓ, ⓗ　　　　UNIT 35 부사의 역할 및 위치
[해석] ⓓ 그는 매주 일요일에 어머니께 전화하는 것을 항상 기억을 한다.
ⓗ 나는 패스트푸드를 거의 먹지 않는데 집에서 만든 음식을 더 선호하기 때문이다.
→ 뒤에 오는 동사 ⓓ remembers, ⓗ eat을 수식하고 있다.

22 [정답] ⓔ, ⓖ　　　　UNIT 35 부사의 역할 및 위치
[해석] ⓔ 이 시기에 비해 날씨가 놀랍도록 따뜻하다.
ⓖ 그 영화는 정말 훌륭했고, 모두가 그것을 좋아했다.
→ 뒤에 오는 형용사 ⓔ warm, ⓖ fantastic을 수식하고 있다.

23 [정답] ⓑ, ⓕ　　　　UNIT 35 부사의 역할 및 위치
[해석] ⓑ 지구의 기온이 놀라울 만큼 빠르게 상승하고 있다.
ⓕ 그들은 프로젝트를 제시간에 끝내기 위해 믿을 수 없을 만큼 열심히 일했다.
→ 뒤에 오는 부사 ⓑ fast, ⓕ hard를 수식하고 있다.

24 [정답] ⓐ, ⓒ　　　　UNIT 35 부사의 역할 및 위치
[해석] ⓐ 다행히, 우리는 어두워지기 전에 길을 되찾았다.
ⓒ 다행스럽게도, 사고 중에 다친 사람은 없었다.
→ 문장 맨 앞에서 문장 전체를 수식하고 있다.

25 [정답] up　　　　UNIT 35 부사의 역할 및 위치
[해석] • 그녀는 걸으면서 떨어뜨린 책을 줍기 위해 멈췄다.
• 퍼즐을 해결하려고 몇 시간 동안 시도한 후, 그녀는 그만두기로 결정했다.
→ 「타동사+부사」 형태인 pick up은 '줍다'를, give up은 '포기하다'를 뜻한다. 따라서 공통으로 들어갈 말은 up이다.

26 [정답] off　　　　UNIT 35 부사의 역할 및 위치
[해석] • 타이머가 울리면 오븐을 꺼주세요.
• 나는 너무 바빠서 계속 헬스장 가는 것을 미루고 있다.
→ 「타동사+부사」 형태인 turn off는 '끄다', put off는 '미루다'를 뜻한다. 따라서 공통으로 들어갈 말은 off이다.

27 [정답] ②　　　　UNIT 34 부사의 형태
[해석] ① 나는 어젯밤 충분한 잠을 자지 못했다.
② 그는 시험에 합격할 만큼 충분히 공부하지 않았다.
③ 그녀는 소풍을 위한 충분한 음식을 가져오지 않았다.
④ 차에는 우리 모두가 탈 수 있을 만큼 충분한 공간이 있다.
⑤ 나는 여행을 위해 충분한 옷을 싸지 않았고, 그래서 더 사야 했다.
→ 나머지는 모두 형용사로 쓰였고, ②은 부사로 쓰였다.

28 [정답] ④　　　　UNIT 34 부사의 형태
[해석] ① 이것은 어려운 문제이다.
② 그는 어려운 결정을 마주했다.
③ 오늘은 직장에서 힘든 하루였다.
④ 그는 프로젝트에서 열심히 일했다.
⑤ 그 재료는 너무 단단해서 구부릴 수 없다.
→ 나머지는 모두 형용사로 쓰였고, ④은 부사로 쓰였다.

29 [정답] ③　　　　UNIT 34 부사의 형태
[해석] ① 그는 프로젝트를 일찍 끝냈다.
② 우리는 교통 체증을 피하기 위해 일찍 떠났다.
③ 우리는 오늘 이른 저녁을 먹었다.
④ 그 상점은 일요일에 일찍 열린다.
⑤ 기차는 오늘 아침 일찍 출발했다.
→ 나머지는 모두 부사로 쓰였고, ③은 형용사로 쓰였다.

30 [정답] ①　　　　UNIT 34 부사의 형태
[해석] ① 치타는 육지에서 가장 빠른 동물이다.
② 차는 교차로를 빠르게 지나쳤다.
③ 나는 빠르게 타이핑할 수 있지만, 여전히 몇 가지 실수를 한다.
④ 폭풍은 빠르게 이동했고, 우리는 준비할 시간이 거의 없었다.
⑤ 그는 결정을 빠르게 내렸고, 계약을 빨리 성사시켰다.
→ 나머지는 모두 부사로 쓰였고, ①은 형용사로 쓰였다.

31 [정답] ④　　　　UNIT 35 부사의 역할 및 위치
[해석] 그녀는 바닥에 있는 연필을 보고 시험에 사용하기 위해 그것을 집었다.
→ 「타동사+부사」의 목적어가 대명사일 경우, 목적어는 타동사와 부사 사이에 온다. 따라서 부사 up을 대명사 목적어 it 뒤에 써야 한다.

32 [정답] ③　　　　UNIT 35 부사의 역할 및 위치
[해석] 그 수프는 아기가 안전하게 먹기에는 충분히 뜨겁지 않았다.
→ enough는 형용사나 부사를 뒤에서 수식한다. 따라서 hot 뒤에 와야 한다.

33 [정답] ②　　　　UNIT 35 부사의 역할 및 위치
[해석] 그녀는 신청서를 발견하고 마감 기한 전에 그것을 작성했다.
→ 「타동사+부사」의 목적어가 대명사일 경우, 목적어는 타동사와 부사 사이에 온다. 따라서 it을 out의 앞에 써야 한다.

34 [정답] ②　　　　UNIT 35 부사의 역할 및 위치
[해석] 여: 3일 전 밤에 밖에서 큰 소리가 났어. 그 소리 들었니?
남: 응, 소음 때문에 깨서 그 이후에는 거의 잠을 잘 수 없었어. 무슨 일이 일어났는지 아니?

→ (A) 과거시제와 함께 '~ 전에'라는 뜻으로 쓸 수 있는 부사는 ago 이다. (B) 문맥상 '거의 잠을 잘 수 없었다'는 뜻이 되어야 하므로 빈도부사로 hardly를 써야 한다. 빈도부사는 조동사 뒤에 위치한다.

35 [정답] ④　　　　　　　　　UNIT 34 부사의 형태

[해석] 여: 새로 나온 영화 봤어? 요즘 모두 그 영화에 대해 이야기하고 있어.

남: 응, 그 영화가 아주 추천받는다고 들었어. 이번 주말에 볼 계획이야.

→ (A) late는 '늦은, 늦게'를, lately는 '최근에'를 의미한다. 문맥상 '최근에'가 알맞다. (B) high는 '높은, 높게'를, highly는 '매우'를 의미한다. 문맥상 '매우, 아주'가 알맞다.

36 [정답] ④　　　　　　　　　UNIT 36 그 밖의 중요 부사

[해석] ① 나는 아직 아침을 먹지 않았다.

② 우리는 점심 먹고 다른 곳에 갈 수 있다.

③ 그는 나에게 전화하지 않았고, 나도 그에게 전화하지 않았다.

④ 나는 파티에 가지 않았고, 그녀도 가지 않았다.

⑤ 내가 마침내 도착했을 때 그들은 이미 집을 떠난 상태였다.

→ ④ neither는 not ~ either를 대신하는 말이므로 she didn't either로 쓰거나 neither did she가 와야 한다.

37 [정답] ②　　　　　　　　　UNIT 36 그 밖의 중요 부사

→ 긍정문, 의문문, 부정문에서 '여전히, 아직도'를 뜻하는 부사는 still이다.

38 [정답] ④　　　　　　　　　UNIT 36 그 밖의 중요 부사

→ 부정문에서 '또한, 역시'를 뜻하는 부사는 either이다. 동사가 be동사이므로 wasn't either로 오는 것이 알맞다.

39 [정답] can often hear　　　　UNIT 35 부사의 역할 및 위치

→ '자주, 종종'을 의미하는 빈도부사는 often이다. 빈도부사는 조동사와 be동사 뒤, 일반동사 앞에 오므로, often이 조동사 can 뒤에 오는 것이 알맞다.

40 [정답] usually sleep　　　　UNIT 35 부사의 역할 및 위치

→ '보통'을 의미하는 빈도부사는 usually이다. 빈도부사는 조동사와 be동사 뒤, 일반동사 앞에 오므로, usually가 일반동사 sleep 앞에 오는 것이 알맞다.

41 [정답] were never　　　　UNIT 35 부사의 역할 및 위치

→ '절대 ~ 않다'를 의미하는 빈도부사는 never이다. 빈도부사는 조동사와 be동사 뒤, 일반동사 앞에 오므로, never가 be동사 were 뒤에 오는 것이 알맞다.

42 [정답] always occurs　　　　UNIT 35 부사의 역할 및 위치

→ '항상'을 의미하는 빈도부사는 always이다. 빈도부사는 조동사와 be동사 뒤, 일반동사 앞에 오므로, always가 일반동사 occurs 앞에 오는 것이 알맞다.

43 [정답] ①　　　　　　　　　UNIT 35 부사의 역할 및 위치

[해석] Sarah는 바쁜 일정 때문에 친구들을 거의 보지 못했다. 외로움을 느꼈지만, 그녀는 친구들과 더 많은 시간을 보내기 위한 방법을 찾는 것을 포기하지 않았다. 운 좋게도, 어느 주말에 그녀의 친구들이 하이킹 여행에 초대했다. 그녀는 이것이 그들이 놓친 시간을 보충할 충분한 기회라는 것을 알았다. Sarah는 그들이 드디어 함께 시간을 보낼 수 있게 되어 기뻤다.

→ 빈도부사는 조동사와 be동사 뒤, 일반동사 앞에 위치한다. 따라서 seldom saw의 어순으로 와야 한다.

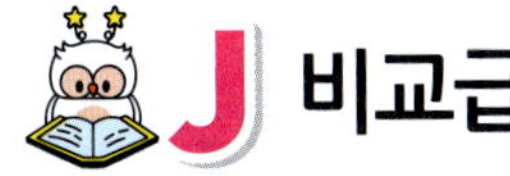

J 비교급

UNIT 37 원급

<table>
<tr><td colspan="4">개념 확인 문제 정답　　　　　▶ 문제편 p.159</td></tr>
<tr><td>01 well</td><td>02 I</td><td>03 as many as</td><td>04 not so</td></tr>
<tr><td>05 as</td><td>06 ⓑ</td><td>07 ⓓ</td><td>08 ⓐ　　09 ⓔ</td></tr>
<tr><td colspan="4">10 ⓒ</td></tr>
<tr><td colspan="4">11 is as stubborn as a mule, so she doesn't listen to anyone</td></tr>
<tr><td colspan="4">12 looked as happy as a lark on the day of his graduation</td></tr>
<tr><td colspan="4">13 was as brave as a lion when he entered the burning building</td></tr>
<tr><td colspan="4">14 is as smart as a fox when it comes to solving tricky problems</td></tr>
<tr><td colspan="4">15 is as busy as a bee even on the weekend</td></tr>
</table>

01 [정답] well

[해석] 그 회사는 지난해만큼 잘하고 있지 않다.

→ 동사 is doing을 꾸며 주는 말이므로 부사 well이 알맞다.

02 [정답] I

[해석] 그 소식을 들은 후 그녀는 나만큼 흥분했다.

→ as 뒤의 비교 대상이 주어질 경우 be동사는 생략 가능하다.

03 [정답] as many as

[해석] 그녀는 매주 무려 세 권만큼 많은 책을 읽는다.

→ books는 셀 수 있는 명사의 복수형이므로 many를 사용하여 원급을 나타낸다.

04 [정답] not so

[해석] 그의 새 영화는 그의 이전 영화들만큼 흥미롭지 않다.

→ '…만큼 ~하지 않은'은 「not as[so]+형용사[부사]의 원급+as」로 표현한다.

05 [정답] as

[해석] Jamie의 눈은 그의 어머니의 눈만큼 크다.

→ '…만큼 ~한'은 「as+형용사의 원급+as」로 표현한다.

06 [정답] ⓑ

[해석] 그는 내가 가진 돈의 세 배를 가지고 있다.

→ 배수사를 이용한 원급은 「배수사+as+형용사[부사]의 원급+as」로 표현한다.

07 [정답] ⓓ

[해석] 너는 가능한 한 빨리 집에 가는 게 좋겠다.

→ '가능한 한 ~한[하게]'은 「as+형용사[부사]의 원급+as+주어+can[could]」으로 표현한다.

08 [정답] ⓐ

[해석] 나는 버스를 타기 위해 가능한 한 빠르게 달리려고 노력했다.

→ 가능한 한 빨리 달리려고 한 이유가 나오도록 목적을 나타내는 to부정사와 연결한다.

09 [정답] ⓔ

[해석] 영어는 스페인어보다 두 배나 많은 단어를 가지고 있다.

→ 배수사를 이용한 원급은 「배수사+as+형용사의 원급+명사+as」로 표현한다.

10 [정답] ⓒ

[해석] 원숭이는 가능한 한 많은 바나나를 잡으려고 애썼다.

→ ⓓ의 could 뒤에는 catch가 생략되어 있다.

11 [정답] is as stubborn as a mule, so she doesn't listen to anyone

→ '아주 고집이 센'은 as stubborn as a mule로 표현한다.

12 [정답] looked as happy as a lark on the day of his graduation

→ '아주 즐거운'은 as happy as a lark으로 표현한다.

13 [정답] was as brave as a lion when he entered the burning building

→ '아주 용감한'은 as brave as a lion으로 표현한다.

14 [정답] is as smart as a fox when it comes to solving tricky problems

→ '아주 약삭빠른'은 as smart as a fox로 표현한다.

15 [정답] is as busy as a bee even on the weekend

→ '아주 바쁜'은 as busy as a bee로 표현한다.

UNIT 38 비교급, 최상급 형태

개념 확인 문제 정답 ▶ 문제편 p.161~163

01 sunnier, sunniest   **02** lazier, laziest

03 humbler, humblest

04 more flexible, most flexible

05 lovelier, loveliest

06 more logical, most logical

07 funnier, funniest   **08** busier, busiest

09 more responsible, most responsible

10 bigger, biggest

11 more annoying, most annoying

12 happier, happiest   **13** wetter, wettest

14 more intelligent, most intelligent

15 closer, closest   **16** thinner, thinnest

17 gentler, gentlest   **18** colder, coldest

19 more challenging, most challenging

20 ruder, rudest   **21** bravest

22 quicker   **23** more respectful

24 simplest 또는 most simple

25 harder   **26** noblest

27 quieter   **28** most accurate

29 more flexible   **30** old, elder

31 better, best   **32** worse, worst

33 more, most   **34** few, fewest

35 far, farther   **36** far, furthest

37 late, latest   **38** late, last

39 less, least   **40** worse, worst

41 old, oldest

42 He became lazier after the vacation ended.

43 Neptune is the farthest planet in our solar system.

44 ○   **45** ○   **46** ○

47 Drinking water is better than drinking soda for staying healthy.

48 ○   **49** ○

50 He acted the most carefully in the dangerous situation to stay safe.

51 The ground is wetter than usual due to last night's heavy rainfall.

---

01 [정답] sunnier, sunniest

[해석] 맑은, 더 맑은, 가장 맑은

→ 원급이 「자음+y」로 끝나는 경우 y를 i로 고치고 -er을 붙여 비교급을, -est를 붙여 최상급을 만든다.

02 [정답] lazier, laziest

[해석] 게으른, 더 게으른, 가장 게으른

→ 원급이 「자음+y」로 끝나는 경우 y를 i로 고치고 -er을 붙여
비교급을, -est를 붙여 최상급을 만든다.

03 [정답] humbler, humblest
[해석] 겸손한, 더 겸손한, 가장 겸손한
→ 원급이 -e로 끝나는 경우 -r을 붙여 비교급을, -st를 붙여 최
상급을 만든다.

04 [정답] more flexible, most flexible
[해석] 유연한, 더 유연한, 가장 유연한
→ 2음절 이상의 단어는 앞에 more를 붙여 비교급을, most
를 붙여 최상급을 만든다.

05 [정답] lovelier, loveliest
[해석] 사랑스러운, 더 사랑스러운, 가장 사랑스러운
→ 원급이 「자음+y」로 끝나는 경우 y를 i로 고치고 -er을 붙여
비교급을, -est를 붙여 최상급을 만든다.

06 [정답] more logical, most logical
[해석] 논리적인, 더 논리적인, 가장 논리적인
→ 2음절 이상의 단어는 앞에 more를 붙여 비교급을, most
를 붙여 최상급을 만든다.

07 [정답] funnier, funniest
[해석] 웃긴, 더 웃긴, 가장 웃긴
→ 원급이 「자음+y」로 끝나는 경우 y를 i로 고치고 -er을 붙여
비교급을, -est를 붙여 최상급을 만든다.

08 [정답] busier, busiest
[해석] 바쁜, 더 바쁜, 가장 바쁜
→ 원급이 「자음+y」로 끝나는 경우 y를 i로 고치고 -er을 붙여
비교급을, -est를 붙여 최상급을 만든다.

09 [정답] more responsible, most responsible
[해석] 책임감 있는, 더 책임감 있는, 가장 책임감 있는
→ 2음절 이상의 단어는 앞에 more를 붙여 비교급을, most
를 붙여 최상급을 만든다.

10 [정답] bigger, biggest
[해석] 큰, 더 큰, 가장 큰
→ 원급이 「단모음+단자음」으로 끝나는 경우 끝 자음을 한 번
더 쓰고 -er을 붙여 비교급을, -est를 붙여 최상급을 만든다.

11 [정답] more annoying, most annoying
[해석] 짜증나는, 더 짜증나는, 가장 짜증나는
→ 분사는 앞에 more를 붙여 비교급을, most를 붙여 최상급
을 만든다.

12 [정답] happier, happiest
[해석] 행복한, 더 행복한, 가장 행복한
→ 원급이 「자음+y」로 끝나는 경우 y를 i로 고치고 -er을 붙여
비교급을, -est를 붙여 최상급을 만든다.

13 [정답] wetter, wettest
[해석] 젖은, 더 젖은, 가장 젖은
→ 원급이 「단모음+단자음」으로 끝나는 경우 끝 자음을 한 번
더 쓰고 -er을 붙여 비교급을, -est를 붙여 최상급을 만든다.

14 [정답] more intelligent, most intelligent
[해석] 똑똑한, 더 똑똑한, 가장 똑똑한
→ 2음절 이상의 단어는 앞에 more를 붙여 비교급을, most
를 붙여 최상급을 만든다.

15 [정답] closer, closest
[해석] 가까운, 더 가까운, 가장 가까운
→ 원급이 -e로 끝나는 경우 -r을 붙여 비교급을, -st를 붙여 최
상급을 만든다.

16 [정답] thinner, thinnest
[해석] 얇은, 더 얇은, 가장 얇은
→ 원급이 「단모음+단자음」으로 끝나는 경우 끝 자음을 한 번
더 쓰고 -er을 붙여 비교급을, -est를 붙여 최상급을 만든다.

17 [정답] gentler, gentlest
[해석] 부드러운, 더 부드러운, 가장 부드러운
→ 원급이 -e로 끝나는 경우 -r을 붙여 비교급을, -st를 붙여 최
상급을 만든다.

18 [정답] colder, coldest
[해석] 추운, 더 추운, 가장 추운
→ 대부분의 경우 원급에 -er을 붙여 비교급을, -est를 붙여 최
상급을 만든다.

19 [정답] more challenging, most challenging
[해석] 도전적인, 더 도전적인, 가장 도전적인
→ 분사는 앞에 more를 붙여 비교급을, most를 붙여 최상급
을 만든다.

20 [정답] ruder, rudest
[해석] 무례한, 더 무례한, 가장 무례한
→ 원급이 -e로 끝나는 경우 -r을 붙여 비교급을, -st를 붙여 최
상급을 만든다.

21 [정답] bravest
→ 원급이 -e로 끝나는 경우 -st를 붙여 최상급을 만든다.

22 [정답] quicker
→ 대부분의 경우 원급에 -er을 붙여 비교급을 만든다.

23 [정답] more respectful
→ 2음절 이상의 단어는 앞에 more를 붙여 비교급을 만든다.

24 [정답] simplest 또는 most simple
→ simple은 두 개의 비교급을 갖는 형용사이다.

25 [정답] harder
→ 대부분의 경우 원급에 -er을 붙여 비교급을 만든다.

26 [정답] noblest
→ 원급이 -e로 끝나는 경우 -st를 붙여 최상급을 만든다.

27 [정답] quieter
→ 대부분의 경우 원급에 -er을 붙여 비교급을 만든다.

28 [정답] most accurate
→ 2음절 이상의 단어는 앞에 most를 붙여 최상급을 만든다.

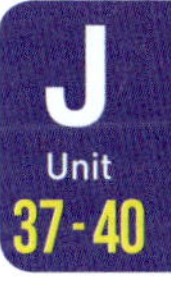

29 [정답] more flexible
→ 2음절 이상의 단어는 앞에 more를 붙여 비교급을 만든다.

30 [정답] old, elder
[해석] 연상의, 더 연상의, 가장 연상의
→ old가 '연상의'를 뜻할 때 비교급은 elder, 최상급은 eldest이다.

31 [정답] better, best
[해석] 좋은, 더 좋은, 가장 좋은
→ good의 비교급은 better, 최상급은 best이다.

32 [정답] worse, worst
[해석] 나쁜, 더 나쁜, 가장 나쁜
→ bad의 비교급은 worse, 최상급은 worst이다.

33 [정답] more, most
[해석] 많은, 더 많은, 가장 많은
→ many의 비교급은 more, 최상급은 most이다.

34 [정답] few, fewest
[해석] 적은, 더 적은, 가장 적은
→ few의 비교급은 fewer, 최상급은 fewest이다.

35 [정답] far, farther
[해석] 먼, 더 먼, 가장 먼
→ far가 '(거리가) 먼' 것을 뜻할 때 비교급은 farther, 최상급은 farthest이다.

36 [정답] far, furthest
[해석] 더욱, 더 깊이, 가장 깊이
→ far가 '(정도가) 더'를 뜻할 때 비교급은 further, 최상급은 furthest이다.

37 [정답] late, latest
[해석] 늦은, 이후의, 최신의
→ late가 '(시간이) 늦은' 것을 뜻할 때 비교급은 later, 최상급은 latest이다.

38 [정답] late, last
[해석] 늦은, 후자의, 마지막의
→ late가 '(순서가) 늦은' 것을 뜻할 때 비교급은 latter, 최상급은 last이다.

39 [정답] less, least
[해석] 적은, 더 적은, 가장 적은
→ little의 비교급은 less, 최상급은 least이다.

40 [정답] worse, worst
[해석] 아픈, 더 아픈, 가장 아픈
→ ill의 비교급은 worse, 최상급은 worst이다.

41 [정답] old, oldest
[해석] 오래된, 더 오래된, 가장 오래된
→ old가 '오래된'을 뜻할 때 비교급은 older, 최상급은 oldest이다.

42 [정답] He became lazier after the vacation ended.
[해석] 그는 방학이 끝난 뒤 더 게을러졌다.
→ 원급이 「자음+y」로 끝나는 경우 y를 i로 고치고 -er을 붙여 비교급을 만든다.

43 [정답] Neptune is the farthest planet in our solar system.
[해석] 해왕성은 태양계에서 가장 멀리 있는 행성이다.
→ '(거리가) 먼'을 의미하는 far의 최상급은 farthest이다. furthest는 '(정도가) 더'를 뜻하는 far의 최상급이다.

44 [정답] ○
[해석] 세계에서 가장 인기 있는 스포츠는 축구다.
→ 2음절 이상의 단어는 앞에 most를 붙여 최상급을 만든다.

45 [정답] ○
[해석] 그 길은 지도에서 보이는 것보다 더 좁다.
→ 대부분의 경우 원급에 -er을 붙여 비교급을 만든다.

46 [정답] ○
[해석] 고양이는 어떤 상황에서는 개보다 더 친근할 수 있다.
→ friendly는 friendlier와 more friendly 두 개의 비교급을 갖는 형용사이다.

47 [정답] Drinking water is better than drinking soda for staying healthy.
[해석] 건강을 위해서는 탄산음료를 마시는 것보다 물을 마시는 게 더 낫다.
→ good의 비교급은 better이다.

48 [정답] ○
[해석] 가장 적게 공부한 학생이 가장 낮은 점수를 받았다.
→ little의 최상급은 least이고, low의 최상급은 -est를 붙인 lowest이다.

49 [정답] ○
[해석] 숲은 우리가 더 깊이 걸어갈수록 더 빽빽해졌다.
→ 대부분의 경우 원급에 -er을 붙여 비교급을 만들고, 원급이 -e로 끝나는 경우 -r을 붙여 비교급을 만든다.

50 [정답] He acted the most carefully in the dangerous situation to stay safe.
[해석] 그는 위험한 상황에서 가장 조심스럽게 행동하여 안전을 지켰다.
→ 「형용사+ly」 형태의 부사는 앞에 most를 붙여 최상급을 만들기 때문에, most carefully로 고쳐야 적절하다.

51 [정답] The ground is wetter than usual due to last night's heavy rainfall.
[해석] 그 땅은 어젯밤의 폭우로 인해 평소보다 더 젖어 있다.
→ 원급이 「단모음+단자음」으로 끝나는 경우 끝 자음을 한 번 더 쓰고 -er을 붙여 비교급을 만들기 때문에, wetter로 고쳐야 적절하다.

개념 확인 문제 정답 ▶ 문제편 p.165

01 more diligent than Steve
02 less popular than baseball
03 much more expensive than mine
04 a bigger population than Busan
05 more stylish than the old model
06 twice bigger than mine
07 Which is more comfortable
08 the more questions they have
09 is going to get cooler and cooler
10 is becoming worse and worse
11 no more than a beginner
12 five times harder than the previous one
13 prior to launching

01 [정답] more diligent than Steve
→ '~보다 더 부지런한'은 more diligent than으로 쓴다.

02 [정답] less popular than baseball
→ '~보다 덜 …한[하게]'은 「less+형용사[부사]의 원급+than」으로 쓴다.

03 [정답] much more expensive than mine
→ much는 비교급 앞에서 '훨씬'이라는 뜻으로 비교급의 의미를 강조한다.

04 [정답] a bigger population than Busan
→ '~보다 …한 -를 가지고 있다'는 「have(+a[an])+형용사의 비교급+명사+than ~」으로 표현한다.

05 [정답] more stylish than the old model
→ '~보다 더 세련된'은 more stylish than으로 쓴다.

06 [정답] twice bigger than mine
[해석] 그의 발은 내 것보다 두 배 더 크다.
→ 비교급을 이용한 배수사 표현은 「배수사 비교급 than」으로 표현한다.

07 [정답] Which is more comfortable
[해석] 이 소파와 저 의자 중 어느 것이 더 편한가요?
→ 'A와 B 중 어느 쪽이 더 ~한가?'는 「What[Who, Which] ~ 비교급, A or B?」로 표현한다.

08 [정답] the more questions they have
[해석] 학생들은 더 많이 배울수록, 더 많은 질문을 한다.
→ '~할수록 더 …한'은 「the+비교급, the+비교급」으로 표현한다.

09 [정답] is going to get cooler and cooler
[해석] 날씨가 매일 점점 더 서늘해질 것이다.
→ '점점 더 ~한'은 「비교급+and+비교급」으로 표현한다.

10 [정답] is becoming worse and worse
→ '점점 더 ~한'은 「비교급+and+비교급」으로 표현한다.

11 [정답] no more than a beginner
→ '겨우, 단지, ~ 이하의'는 no more than으로 표현한다.

12 [정답] five times harder than the previous one
→ 비교급을 이용한 배수사 표현은 「배수사 비교급+than」으로 표현한다.

13 [정답] prior to launching
→ prior처럼 라틴어에서 온 단어들은 to로 비교 대상을 나타낸다.

개념 확인 문제 정답 ▶ 문제편 p.167

01 of → in
02 The → 삭제
03 the most fastest → the fastest
04 more → the most
05 diligentest → most diligent
06 One of the shortest men in the world
07 one of my most cherished books
08 the most foolish thing you've ever done
09 the most boring movie I've ever watched
10 higher than
11 the nearest
12 No (other), than
13 as[so], as

01 [정답] of → in
[해석] 그는 이 나라에서 가장 큰 회사를 가지고 있다.
→ 최상급의 비교 범위를 나타낼 때 장소를 나타내는 단수 명사가 나오면 앞에 in을 쓴다.

02 [정답] The → 삭제
[해석] 나의 큰 오빠는 삼촌보다 나이가 많다.
→ 최상급 앞에 소유격이 있을 때는 최상급 앞에 the를 붙이지 않는다.

03 [정답] the most fastest → the fastest
[해석] 너희 학교에서 가장 빠른 남자아이는 누구니?
→ fast의 최상급은 fastest이다.

04 [정답] more → the most
[해석] 부모가 되는 것은 세상에서 가장 어려운 일이다.
→ 비교 범위로 in the world가 나와 있으므로 최상급을 써야 한다.

05 [정답] diligentest → most diligent
[해석] 나는 내 남자 친구가 우리 동네에서 가장 부지런한 소년이라고 생각한다.
→ diligent는 최상급으로 만들 때 most를 앞에 붙인다.

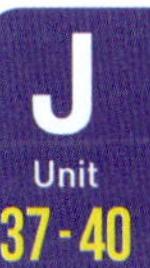

06 정답 One of the shortest men in the world

[해석] 세계에서 가장 작은 사람들 중 한 명은 29인치이다.

→ '가장 ~한 것 중 하나'는 「one of the+최상급+복수 명사」의 형태로 쓴다.

07 정답 one of my most cherished books

[해석] '호밀밭의 파수꾼'은 내가 가장 소중하게 여기는 책들 중 하나이다.

→ '가장 ~한 것 중 하나'는 「one of the+최상급+복수 명사」의 형태로 쓰며 소유격이 올 때는 the를 붙이지 않는다.

08 정답 the most foolish thing you've ever done

[해석] 네가 지금까지 한 일들 중 가장 어리석은 일은 무엇이니?

→ '(지금까지) ~한 것 중 가장 …한'은 「the+최상급+명사(+that)+주어+have[has] (ever)+과거분사」로 쓴다.

09 정답 the most boring movie I've ever watched

[해석] 그것은 내가 지금까지 본 것 중 가장 지루한 영화이다.

→ '(지금까지) ~한 것 중 가장 …한'은 「the+최상급+명사(+that)+주어+have[has] (ever)+과거분사」로 쓴다.

10 정답 higher than

[해석] 히말라야는 세계에서 가장 높은 산맥이다.

→ 히말라야는 세상의 어떤 다른 산맥보다도 더 높다.

→ 「비교급+than any other+단수 명사」로 최상급의 의미를 나타낼 수 있다.

11 정답 the nearest

[해석] 수성은 우리 태양계에서 다른 어떤 행성보다도 태양에 더 가깝다.

→ 수성은 우리 태양계에서 태양에 가장 가까운 행성이다.

→ 「비교급+than any other+단수 명사」는 비교급을 이용한 최상급 표현이므로 빈칸에 「the+최상급」을 써야 한다.

12 정답 No (other), than

[해석] 모기는 세계에서 가장 위험한 곤충이다.

→ 세상의 어떤 곤충도 모기보다 더 위험하지 않다.

→ 비교급 more dangerous가 있으므로 비교급을 이용한 최상급 표현 「No (other)+단수 명사+비교급+than」의 형태로 써야 한다.

13 정답 as[so], as

[해석] 부르즈 칼리파는 세계에서 가장 높은 건물이다.

→ 세계의 어떤 다른 건물도 부르즈 칼리파만큼 높지 않다.

→ 빈칸 사이에 형용사의 원급 tall이 있으므로 원급을 이용한 최상급 표현 「No (other)+단수 명사+as[so]+원급+as」의 형태로 써야 한다.

정답

01 ①	**02** ②	**03** ③	**04** ②	**05** ②
06 other animal		**07** nothing better		**08** ④
09 ⑤	**10** ④	**11** ⑤	**12** ⑤	
13 merrier		**14** many	**15** more slowly	
16 ⑤	**17** ③	**18** ⑤	**19** ④	**20** ⑤

21 ③　**22** most expensive → the most expensive

23 more well → better　**24** could → can

25 large as → as large as 또는 larger than

26 fat → fattest　**27** as → than

28 more → the more　**29** happily → happy

30 ③

31 Nothing is more important than keeping kids safe in school. 또는 Keeping kids safe in school is more important than any other thing.

32 There are fewer jobs than we need.

33 The more you read, the more knowledgeable you become.

34 Andy is the most intelligent student in my class.

35 clever　**36** of　**37** farther　**38** he is

39 wiser and wiser

40 twice as many books as Cindy

41 faster than any other sprinter in the world

42 ③　**43** ②　**44** ③

---

01 정답 ①　　　　UNIT 37 원급

[해석] 나는 우리 형만큼 키가 크다.

→ 원급 비교에서 as와 as 사이에는 형용사나 부사의 원급이 들어가야 한다.

02 정답 ②　　　　UNIT 39 비교급

[해석] 사자는 호랑이보다 힘이 세지 않다.

→ 비교의 전치사 than 앞에는 형용사나 부사의 비교급이 들어가야 한다.

03 정답 ③　　　　UNIT 40 최상급

[해석] 저 주차장은 이 지역에서 가장 크다.

→ '이 지역에서'라는 범위가 나왔고 앞에 the가 있으므로 최상급이 들어가야 한다.

04 정답 ②　　　　UNIT 39 비교급

[해석] 새로 나온 햄버거는 그것이 다른 것들보다 지방이 적기 때문에 인기가 있다.

→ 빈칸 뒤에 than이 있으므로 빈칸에는 비교급이 들어가야 한다.

05 정답 ②　　　　UNIT 39 비교급

[해석] 이 의자는 너의 소파보다 훨씬 더 편안하다.

→ very는 형용사나 부사의 원급을 수식하는 부사이다.

06 [정답] other animal　　　　　　　UNIT **40** 최상급

[해석] 호랑이는 세상에서 가장 위험한 동물이다.

→ 세상의 어떤 동물도 호랑이보다 더 위험하지 않다.

→ 최상급을 「no other+단수 명사」로 표현할 수 있다.

07 [정답] nothing better　　　　　　UNIT **40** 최상급

[해석] 우리 남편을 만난 것은 내 인생에서 최고의 일이었다.

→ 내 인생에서 우리 남편을 만난 것보다 더 좋은 것은 없었다.

→ 최상급을 「There was nothing 비교급+than」 표현으로 바꿔 쓸 수 있다.

08 [정답] ④　　　　　　　　　　　UNIT **37** 원급

[해석] 내 방은 네 방만큼 깨끗하지 않다.

→ 내 방은 네 방보다 덜 깨끗하다.

→ 「not as[so]+형용사+as ~」 표현을 이용한 '내 방은 네 방만큼 깨끗하지 않다'는 '내 방은 네 방보다 덜 깨끗하다'로 바꾸어 쓸 수 있으므로 less와 than이 빈칸에 들어가야 한다.

09 [정답] ⑤　　　　　　　　　　　UNIT **39** 비교급

[해석] 가격이 더 저렴해짐에 따라, 사람들은 그것을 더 많이 살 것이다.

→ 가격이 더 저렴할수록, 사람들은 그것들을 더 많이 살 것이다.

→ '가격이 더 저렴해짐에 따라 사람들은 그것들을 더 많이 살 것이다'는 '가격이 더 저렴할수록 사람들은 그것들을 더 많이 살 것이다.'로 바꾸어 쓸 수 있다. '~할수록 더 …하다'는 뜻의 「The+비교급 ~, the+비교급 …」 구문을 이용하여 The cheaper와 the more가 들어가야 한다.

10 [정답] ④　　　　　　　　　　　UNIT **40** 최상급

[해석] Rachel은 우리 반에서 가장 빠른 학생이다.

→ 우리 반에서 Rachel보다 더 빠른 학생은 없다.

→ 'Rachel은 우리 반에서 가장 빠른 학생이다'는 최상급 표현이 쓰였으므로 「no+단수 명사+동사+비교급+than ~」을 이용해 '우리 반에서 어떤 학생도 Rachel보다 빠르지 않다'로 바꾸어 쓸 수 있다. No와 faster than이 빈칸에 들어가야 한다.

11 [정답] ⑤　　　　　　　　　　　UNIT **40** 최상급

[해석] ① 뱀은 사자만큼 위험하지는 않다.

② 수학은 영어보다 훨씬 더 어렵다.

③ 이것은 내가 이제껏 타본 가장 빠른 기차이다.

④ 이 다리는 저 다리보다 세 배나 더 짧다.

⑤ Lim은 세상에서 가장 유명한 영화감독 중 한 명이다.

→ ⑤ '가장 ~한 것 중 하나'는 「one of the+최상급+복수 명사」로 표현하므로 ⑤의 director는 복수 명사 directors로 고쳐야 한다. ① 「not as+형용사+as」: ~만큼 …하지 않은 ② a lot은 비교급 more difficult를 강조하는 부사 ③ 최상급 표현인 the fastest ④ 「배수사+비교급+than」: ~보다 몇 배 더 …한

12 [정답] ⑤　　　　　　　　　　　UNIT **40** 최상급

[해석] ① Dave는 그가 할 수 있는 한 빨리 달렸다.

② 나에게 편지를 가능한 빨리 보내주세요.

③ 날씨가 점점 더 더워지고 있다.

④ 그녀의 어린 여동생은 모든 소녀들 중에서 가장 똑똑하다.

⑤ 나일강은 세계의 어떤 다른 강보다도 더 길다.

→ ⑤ 비교급 than 뒤에는 「any other+단수 명사」가 와서 최상급을 나타내야 하므로 rivers는 단수 명사 river가 되어야 한다. ①

「as+형용사[부사]의 원급+as+one could」: ~가 가능한 …한[하게]
② as soon as possible: 가능한 빨리 ③ 「비교급+and+비교급」: 점점 더 ~한 ④ 앞의 최상급 표현의 범위를 표현하는 「of+복수 명사」

13 [정답] merrier　　　　　　　　　UNIT **39** 비교급

[해석] A: 엄마, 제가 파티에 친구들 몇 명을 초대해도 돼요?

B: 물론이지. 더 많을수록 더 즐거운 법이니까.

→ '~할수록 더 …한'은 「the+형용사[부사]의 비교급(+주어+동사), the+형용사[부사]의 비교급(+주어+동사)」로 쓰는데, 비교급 뒤의 주어와 동사는 생략될 수 있으므로 빈칸에는 merry의 비교급 merrier를 쓰면 된다.

14 [정답] many　　　　　　　　　　UNIT **37** 원급

[해석] A: 결혼식에 손님들이 많았니?

B: 글쎄, 내가 기대했던 것만큼 손님들이 많지는 않았어.

→ 빈칸 전후로 as ~ as가 있으므로 빈칸에는 many의 원급을 그대로 써서 원급 비교 문장을 만들어야 한다.

15 [정답] more slowly　　　　　　　UNIT **39** 비교급

[해석] A: 너는 말을 너무 빨리 하고 있어. 나는 네가 무슨 말을 하고 있는지 거의 알아들을 수가 없어.

B: 너는 내가 더 천천히 말하기를 원하니?

→ 지금 말하는 것보다 더 천천히 말한다는 의미여야 하므로 빈칸에는 slowly의 비교급을 써야 한다. 비교급 문장에서 than 이하는 종종 생략되며, slowly의 비교급은 more를 앞에 붙여 만든다.

16 [정답] ⑤　　　　　　　　　　　UNIT **39** 비교급

[해석] 나는 지난 학기보다 훨씬 더 좋은 성적을 받을 것이라고 생각한다.

① 두 명의 선수가 완전히 대등했다.

② 그녀는 고른 이를 드러내 보이며 미소 지었다.

③ 2, 4, 6은 짝수이다.

④ 그 남자아이조차도 길에 쓰레기를 버렸다.

⑤ 버스를 타는 것이 그곳으로 가기에 훨씬 더 빠르다.

→ 주어진 문장과 ⑤의 even은 '훨씬'이라는 의미로 비교급을 강조하는 부사로 쓰였다. ① 대등한 ② 고른 ③ even number: 짝수 ④ (심지어) ~까지도

17 [정답] ③　　　　　　　　　　　UNIT **37** 원급

→ 「배수사+as+형용사[부사]의 원급+as」의 어순이 되어야 하므로 ③이 알맞다.

18 [정답] ⑤　　　　　　　　　　　UNIT **40** 최상급

→ '가장 ~한 것 중 하나'는 「one of the+최상급+복수 명사」의 구문을 이용하여 표현한다.

19 [정답] ④　　　　　　　　　　　UNIT **40** 최상급

[해석] Chris는 우리 반에서 가장 웃기는 학생이다.

① 우리 반의 어떤 이도 Chris보다 더 웃기지 않다.

② 우리 반에서 어떤 학생도 Chris보다 더 웃기지 않다.

③ 우리 반에서 어떤 학생도 Chris만큼 웃기지 않다.

④ Chris는 우리 반의 다른 어떤 학생만큼 웃기지 않다.

⑤ Chris는 우리 반의 다른 어떤 학생보다 더 웃기다.

→ 최상급 표현은 「비교급+than any other+단수 명사」나 「No (other)+단수 명사+동사+as+원급+as」 또는 「No (other)+단수 명사+동사+비교급+than」으로 바꾸어 쓸 수 있다.

20 [정답] ⑤ UNIT **39** 비교급

[해석] ① 가능한 한 많이 쓰레기를 주워라.

② 사람들은 전만큼 행복하지 않다.

③ 상황이 작년보다 더 나빠졌다.

④ 중국은 세계에서 가장 붐비는 나라 중 하나이다.

⑤ 벌써 새벽 2시야. 너는 좀 더 일찍 돌아왔어야 해.

→ ⑤ early의 비교급 earlier가 알맞게 쓰였다. ① '가능한 한 ~ 한 [하게]'은 「as+형용사[부사]의 원급+as+주어+can[could]」으로 표현한다. (as you do → as you can) ② 비교 구문에서 as와 as 사이에는 형용사나 부사의 원급이 온다. (happier → happy) ③ bad의 비교급은 worse이다. (badder → worse) ④ '가장 ~한 것 중 하나'는 「one of the+최상급+복수 명사」의 형태로 쓴다. (country → countries)

21 [정답] ③ UNIT **37** 원급

[해석] 그의 손목시계는 내 것보다 훨씬 더 좋다.

→ 내 손목시계는 그의 것보다 덜 좋다.

→ 내 손목시계는 그의 것만큼 좋지 않다.

→ 첫 번째 빈칸 뒤에는 than이 있으므로 '…보다 덜 ~한'의 뜻으로 「less+형용사[부사]의 원급+than」을 써야 한다. 두 번째 빈칸 뒤에는 as가 있으므로 '…만큼 ~하지 않은'이라는 뜻으로 「not as[so]+형용사[부사]의 원급+as」를 써야 한다.

22 [정답] most expensive → the most expensive UNIT **40** 최상급

[해석] 이곳은 내가 지금까지 가 본 곳 중 가장 비싼 식당이다.

→ 경험을 나타내는 현재완료 문장의 수식을 받는 것은 최상급이다. 최상급 앞에는 the를 쓴다.

23 [정답] more well → better UNIT **38** 비교급, 최상급 형태

[해석] 나는 다른 학생들보다 모든 문제에 더 잘 대답했다.

→ well의 비교급은 better이다.

24 [정답] could → can UNIT **37** 원급

[해석] 나는 가능한 한 많은 책을 읽고 싶다.

→ 주절의 시제가 현재(want)이므로 as 뒤에 나온 동사도 현재형으로 써야 한다.

25 [정답] large as → as large as 또는 larger than UNIT **37** 원급

[해석] 서울의 인구는 부산의 인구보다 약 4배만큼 많다.

→ 배수사 비교 표현은 「배수사+as+형용사[부사]의 원급+as」나 「배수사+형용사[부사]의 비교급+than」으로 쓴다.

26 [정답] fat → fattest UNIT **40** 최상급

[해석] 1,215파운드가 나가는 그 여자는 세계에서 가장 뚱뚱한 여자들 중 한 명이다.

→ '가장 ~한 것 중 하나'는 「one of the+최상급+복수 명사」의 형태로 쓴다.

27 [정답] as → than UNIT **39** 비교급

[해석] 올해 우리는 작년보다 외식하는 데 더 적은 돈을 썼다.

→ 앞에 less가 있으므로 비교의 의미를 가지는 전치사는 than이 알맞다.

28 [정답] more → the more UNIT **39** 비교급

[해석] 내가 그 문제에 대해 생각할수록 그것은 더 어렵게 느껴진다.

→ '~할수록 더 …하다'는 「The+비교급 ~, the+비교급 …」의 구문이므로 more difficult가 the more difficult가 되어야 한다.

29 [정답] happily → happy UNIT **37** 원급

[해석] 그녀는 꼬리가 두 개 달린 개처럼 행복해 보인다.

→ 주격 보어 자리에 원급 비교 구문이 걸려있으므로 as와 as 사이에 부사가 아니라 형용사가 들어가야 한다.

30 [정답] ③ UNIT **37** 원급

[해석] ① 가능한 한 크게 말해라.

→ 네가 할 수 있는 한 크게 말해라.

② 이 강은 세상에서 가장 큰 강이다.

→ 세상에서 어떤 강도 이 강보다 크지 않다.

③ 그 역은 내가 생각했던 것보다 가까이 있었다.

→ 그 역은 내가 생각했던 것만큼 멀리 있었다.

④ 여전히 춥지만, 어제는 더 추웠다.

→ 어제만큼 춥지는 않다.

⑤ 목성은 태양계에서 가장 큰 행성이다.

→ 목성은 태양계에서 어떤 다른 행성보다 더 크다.

→ ③에서 '그 역은 내가 생각했던 것보다 가까이 있었다'라는 문장을 고치면 '그 역은 내가 생각했던 것보다 멀리 있지 않았다'가 되어야 하므로 The station was not as far as I thought.가 되어야 한다. ① 「as+부사의 원급+as possible」 = 「as+부사의 원급+as+one can」 ② 최상급 표현 「no+단수 명사+동사+비교급+than ~」 ④ 「not as+형용사+as」: ~만큼 …하지 않은 ⑤ 최상급 표현 「~+동사+비교급+than any other+단수 명사」

31 [정답] Nothing is more important than keeping kids safe in school. 또는 Keeping kids safe in school is more important than any other thing. UNIT **40** 최상급

[해석] 학교에서 아이들을 안전하게 지키는 것은 가장 중요한 일이다.

→ 비교급을 이용한 최상급 표현은 「No (other)+단수 명사+동사+비교급+than」, 「비교급+than any other+단수 명사」의 형태로 쓴다.

32 [정답] There are fewer jobs than we need. UNIT **39** 비교급

[해석] 우리가 필요로 하는 것만큼 많은 직업이 없다.

→ 원급 비교의 부정인 「not as+형용사[부사]의 원급+as」 구문을 비교급을 이용한 표현으로 써야 하므로 '우리가 필요로 하는 것보다 더 적은 직업이 있다.'라는 뜻의 비교급 문장으로 써야 한다.

33 [정답] The more you read, the more knowledgeable you become. UNIT **39** 비교급

[해석] 네가 더 많이 읽을수록 너는 더 아는 것이 많아진다.

→ '~할수록 더 …한'은 「the+형용사[부사]의 비교급(+주어+동사), the+형용사[부사]의 비교급(+주어+동사)」로 쓴다.

34 [정답] Andy is the most intelligent student in my class. UNIT **40** 최상급

[해석] 우리 반의 어떤 학생도 Andy만큼 똑똑하지 않다.

→ 「No (other)+단수 명사+동사+as+원급+as」는 원급을 이용한 최상급 표현이다. 최상급은 「the+형용사[부사]의 최상급」으로 표현한다.

35 [정답] clever　　　　　　　　　UNIT 37 원급

[해석] 그는 생긴 것만큼 영리하지 않다.

→ not so ~ as가 있으므로 형용사의 원급을 써야 한다.

36 [정답] of　　　　　　　　　UNIT 40 최상급

[해석] Jennifer는 그 소녀들 중에서 가장 관대하다.

→ 최상급 뒤에 「of+복수 명사」를 써서 비교 범위를 나타낸다.

37 [정답] farther　　　　　　　　　UNIT 39 비교급

[해석] 출입구 앞에 서 있지 마. 좀 더 뒤로 물러서 주겠니?

→ 문맥상 앞에 a bit가 있으므로 far의 비교급인 farther를 쓴다.

38 [정답] he is　　　　　　　　　UNIT 39 비교급

[해석] 아무도 이 나라에서 그보다 부유하지 않다.

→ 그와 다른 사람들의 부유함을 비교하는 것이므로 than 뒤의 시제도 앞과 일치시켜 현재로 써야 한다.

39 [정답] wiser and wiser　　　　　　　　　UNIT 39 비교급

[해석] 나이가 들수록 그녀는 점점 더 현명해졌다.

→ '점점 더 ~해지다'는 「become+비교급+and+비교급」으로 나타낼 수 있고, wise의 비교급은 wiser로 쓴다.

40 [정답] twice as many books as Cindy　　　　UNIT 37 원급

→ 배수사 twice가 as ~ as … 원급 비교 앞에 위치함에 유의하여 쓴다.

41 [정답] faster than any other sprinter in the world

UNIT 40 최상급

→ 최상급의 의미를 표현하는 「비교급+than any other+단수 명사」의 구문을 이용하여 문장을 완성한다.

42 [정답] ③　　　　　　　　　UNIT 39 비교급

[해석] 바다는 특히 더 깊은 곳에서 매우 차가울 수 있다. 바다 깊숙이 잠수하는 다이버들은 이것을 염두에 두어야 한다. 수면에서는 물이 더 따뜻해 보이지만, 잠수하면 할수록 기온은 점점 더 낮아진다. 실제로, 그들이 더 깊이 갈수록 물은 점점 더 차가워진다. 바다의 가장 깊은 부분이 가장 차갑다. 온도와 함께, 물의 압력도 강해진다. 바다의 가장 깊은 지점에서의 압력은 가장 강하고, 적절한 장비 없이 이 압력은 위험할 수 있다. 따라서 다이버들은 극한의 환경에서 자신의 안전을 보장할 수 있기 위해 가장 안전한 보호 장비를 착용해야만 한다.

→ ③ 「the+비교급, the+비교급 (점점 ~할수록 점점 더 …한)」 구문으로, deeper가 되어야 한다.

43 [정답] ②　　　　　　　　　UNIT 39 비교급

[해석] 최근 지구에서 이상한 일들이 발생하고 있다. 파키스탄에서는 7월 이후 홍수가 나라의 거의 3분의 1을 덮쳐 적어도 1,500명이나 되는 사망자를 초래했고 400만 명 이상이 집을 떠나야 했다. 러시아에서는 폭염으로 광범위한 가뭄과 통제할 수 없는 산불이 발생했다. 여름 기온은 러시아 모스크바에서 정상보다 평균 30도 더 높다. 그린란드에서는 더위로 인해 페터만 빙하에서 맨해튼 섬 크기의 4배에 달하는 거대한 얼음덩어리가 갈라졌다. 이는 지금까지 기록된 가장 큰 빙하 붕괴이다. 과학자들은 지구온난화로 인해 이런 극단적인 기후 현상이 앞으로 훨씬 더 심각할 수 있다고 경고하고 있다.

→ '~만큼이나, ~ 이상의'를 뜻하는 비교급 표현은 no less than이다.

44 [정답] ③　　　　　　　　　UNIT 37 원급

→ 배수사의 원급 비교 구문이므로 ③ as four times big as를 four times as big as로 써야 한다.

K 접속사

UNIT 41 등위접속사

> **개념 확인 문제 정답**　　　▶ 문제편 p.175
>
> **01** now　　**02** she failed　　**03** but
> **04** for　　**05** yet　　**06** so
> **07** yet　　**08** so　　**09** and
> **10** or　　**11** for　　**12** yet
> **13** yet[but] it was really interesting
> **14** for she was sick
> **15** and you will improve your skills
> **16** Finish your dinner, or

01 [정답] now

[해석] 당신은 지금이나 나중에 가게에 갈 수 있다.

→ 등위접속사 or로 부사 later와 연결되는 것은 부사 now이다.

02 [정답] she failed

[해석] 그녀는 공부하지 않아서 시험에 떨어졌다.

→ 등위접속사 so로 절 She didn't study와 연결되는 것은 절 she failed the test이다.

03 [정답] but

[해석] 그는 재능이 있지만, 충분히 연습하지 않는다.

→ 앞뒤의 반대되는 내용을 연결하는 것은 등위접속사 but이다.

04 [정답] for

[해석] 그는 출근하지 않았다, 왜냐하면 그는 심각하게 아팠기 때문이다.

→ '왜냐하면 그가 심각하게 아팠기 때문이다'라고 하는 것이 가장 적절하므로 for가 와야 한다.

05 [정답] yet

[해석] 나는 피곤했지만 프로젝트를 끝내기 위해 밤을 새웠다.

→ 앞뒤의 반대되는 내용을 연결하는 것은 등위접속사 yet이다.

06 [정답] so

[해석] 그녀는 파인애플 피자를 좋아하지 않아서 항상 감자 피자를 고른다.

→ '파인애플 피자를 좋아하지 않아서 항상 감자 피자를 고른다'라고 하는 것이 가장 적절하므로 so가 와야 한다.

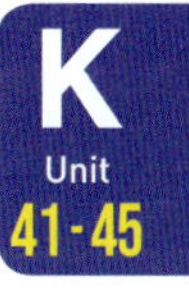

07 [정답] yet

[해석] 그 업무는 불가능해 보였지만, 그녀는 마침내 그것을 해내는 데 성공했다.

→ 앞뒤의 반대되는 내용을 연결하는 것은 등위접속사 yet이다.

08 [정답] so

[해석] 나는 기운이 다 빠져서 일찍 잠자리에 들었다.

→ '기운이 다 빠져서 일찍 잠자리에 들었다'라고 하는 것이 가장 적절하므로 so가 와야 한다.

09 [정답] and

[해석] 해가 빛나고, 새들이 노래하고 있었다.

→ '해가 빛난다'와 '새들이 노래하고 있었다'라는 대등한 내용을 연결하므로 and가 와야 한다.

10 [정답] or

[해석] 평상복 또는 더 격식 있는 것을 원하시나요?

→ '평상복 또는 더 격식 있는 것'이라고 하는 것이 가장 적절하므로 or가 와야 한다.

11 [정답] for

[해석] 나는 우산을 챙겼다, 왜냐하면 비가 올 것 같았기 때문이다.

→ '왜냐하면 비가 올 것 같았기 때문이다'라고 하는 것이 가장 적절하므로 for가 와야 한다.

12 [정답] yet

[해석] 그녀는 경험이 부족했지만, 상황에 잘 대처했다.

→ '경험이 부족했다'라는 것과 '상황에 잘 대처했다'라는 반대되는 내용이 연결되어야 하므로 yet이 와야 한다.

13 [정답] yet[but] it was really interesting

→ '하지만 정말 흥미로웠다'라고 하는 것이 가장 적절하므로 yet[but] it was really interesting으로 써야 한다.

14 [정답] for she was sick

→ '왜냐하면 그녀는 아팠기 때문이다'라고 하는 것이 가장 적절하므로 for she was sick으로 써야 한다.

15 [정답] and you will improve your skills

→ Practice every day 뒤에 and를 붙여 '~해라, 그러면'을 의미하는 명령문을 완성한다.

16 [정답] Finish your dinner, or

→ '~해라, 그렇지 않으면'을 의미하려면 명령문 Finish your dinner 뒤에 or를 붙인다.

UNIT 42 상관접속사

> **개념 확인 문제 정답** ▶ 문제편 p.177
>
> **01** Neither **02** Either **03** but **04** but also
> **05** Both **06** like **07** are **08** is
> **09** help **10** is **11** deliver **12** accepts
> **13** but → or **14** or → but **15** are → is **16** or → nor
> **17** is → are **18** also → but (also)

01 [정답] Neither

[해석] John도 그의 친구들도 올바른 답을 가지고 있지 않다.

→ 'A와 B 둘 다 ~아닌'은 neither A nor B로 쓴다.

02 [정답] Either

[해석] 어머니나 아버지 중 한 분이 시장에 가신다.

→ 'A나 B 둘 중 하나'는 either A or B로 쓴다.

03 [정답] but

[해석] 빨간 드레스가 아니라 파란 드레스가 너에게 더 잘 어울린다.

→ 'A가 아니라 B'는 not A but B로 쓴다.

04 [정답] but also

[해석] 나뿐만 아니라 내 친구들도 회의에 참석한다.

→ 'A뿐만 아니라 B도'는 not only A but also B로 쓴다.

05 [정답] Both

[해석] 팀과 코치 모두 그 시합을 위한 준비가 되었다.

→ 'A와 B 둘 다'는 both A and B로 쓴다.

06 [정답] like

[해석] 선생님과 작가 모두 그 아이디어를 좋아한다.

→ both A and B가 주어로 쓰이면 뒤에 항상 복수 동사가 온다. 따라서 복수형인 like가 적절하다.

07 [정답] are

[해석] 케이크가 아니라 쿠키가 후식으로 제공된다.

→ not A but B가 주어로 쓰이면 B에 동사의 수를 일치시킨다. 따라서 cookies에 맞는 동사 are가 적절하다.

08 [정답] is

[해석] 역사 그 자체가 아니라, 그것의 의미가 중요한 것이다.

→ not A but B가 주어로 쓰이면 B에 동사의 수를 일치시킨다. 따라서 its meaning에 맞는 동사 is가 적절하다.

09 [정답] help

[해석] 내 형 또는 내 친구들이 프로젝트를 도와준다.

→ either A or B가 주어로 쓰이면 B에 동사의 수를 일치시킨다. 따라서 my friends에 맞는 동사 help가 적절하다.

10 [정답] is

[해석] 그의 형들뿐만 아니라 Tom도 스페인어 배우는 것에 관심이 있다.

→ B as well as A가 주어로 쓰이면 B에 동사의 수를 일치시킨다. 따라서 Tom에 맞는 동사 is가 적절하다.

11 [정답] deliver

[해석] 교과서에서는 글뿐만 아니라 그림들도 의미를 전달한다.

→ not only A but also B가 주어로 쓰이면 B에 동사의 수를 일치시킨다. 따라서 pictures에 맞는 동사 deliver가 적절하다.

12 [정답] accepts

[해석] 선수들도 감독도 경기 결과를 받아들이지 않는다.

→ neither A nor B가 주어로 쓰이면 B에 동사의 수를 일치시킨다. 따라서 the coach에 맞는 동사 accepts가 적절하다.

13 [정답] but → or

[해석] 나는 그가 중국 사람 아니면 일본 사람임이 틀림없다고 생각한다.

→ 'A나 B 둘 중 하나'는 either A or B로 쓴다.

14 [정답] or → but

[해석] 내가 원하는 것은 네가 소유한 것이 아니라 너이다.

→ 'A가 아니라 B'는 not A but B로 쓴다.

15 [정답] are → is

[해석] 그의 형들뿐만 아니라 그도 운동을 잘한다.

→ B as well as A는 B에 동사를 일치시킨다.

16 [정답] or → nor

[해석] 그의 의사는 그에게 담배를 피우는 것과 술을 마시는 것 둘 다 허용하지 않는다.

→ 'A와 B 둘 다 ~아닌'은 neither A nor B로 쓴다.

17 [정답] is → are

[해석] 영어와 중국어 둘 다 홍콩에서 쓰인다.

→ both A and B는 복수 취급하므로 복수 동사를 쓴다.

18 [정답] also → but (also)

[해석] 영국과 미국뿐만 아니라 호주와 뉴질랜드도 영어를 그들의 제1언어로 사용한다.

→ 'A뿐만 아니라 B도'는 not only A but also B로 쓰는데, but 뒤의 also는 생략될 수 있다.

UNIT 43 명사절을 이끄는 종속접속사

> **개념 확인 문제 정답** ▶ 문제편 p.179
>
> **01** 주어   **02** 보어   **03** 진목적어
> **04** 목적어   **05** 진주어   **06** Whether
> **07** if   **08** who   **09** that
> **10** that   **11** How   **12** if
> **13** It doesn't matter whether you leave or not.
>   또는 It doesn't matter whether or not you leave.
> **14** He knows how much I care about him.
> **15** It is not certain that they broke the law.
> **16** Don't you really wonder what Felix said to me?

01 [정답] 주어

[해석] 그녀가 언제 도착할지는 아직 알려지지 않았다.

→ When이 이끄는 명사절이 문장에서 주어로 쓰였다.

02 [정답] 보어

[해석] 중요한 것은 그녀가 제안을 받아들일지 여부이다.

→ whether가 이끄는 명사절이 문장에서 보어로 쓰였다.

03 [정답] 진목적어

[해석] 그들은 그가 메시지에 답하지 않은 것이 이상하다고 생각했다.

→ 가목적어 it이 동사 found의 목적어로 쓰였으므로 목적격 보어 뒤에 온 that절은 진목적어이다.

04 [정답] 목적어

[해석] 나는 그들이 그 프로젝트에 관심이 있는지에 대해 걱정된다.

→ whether가 이끄는 명사절이 전치사 about의 목적어로 쓰였다.

05 [정답] 진주어

[해석] 혁신팀의 결과가 정확하다는 것은 여전히 불분명하다.

→ 가주어 it이 쓰였으므로 문장 끝에 온 that절은 진주어이다.

06 [정답] Whether

[해석] 그녀가 올지 안 올지는 중요하지 않다.

→ if가 이끄는 명사절은 주어 자리에는 쓸 수 없다.

07 [정답] if

[해석] 나는 그가 은퇴를 할지 안 할지를 알고 싶다.

→ 뒤에 or not이 있으므로 if를 써야 한다. if 바로 뒤에 or not은 쓸 수 없지만, if절의 끝에 쓰는 것은 가능하다.

08 [정답] who

[해석] 그들은 누가 선거에서 이기든지 상관 안 한다.

→ 의문사절의 동사 wins의 주어 역할을 해야 하므로 주격 의문대명사 who를 써야 한다.

09 [정답] that

[해석] 너의 반려동물이 죽었다는 사실을 바꿀 수는 없다.

→ 문맥상 '~라는 것'이라는 의미인 목적어절을 이끄는 접속사 that이 알맞다.

10 [정답] that

[해석] 네가 최선을 다했다는 것이 중요하다.

→ 진주어절을 이끄는 접속사가 와야 하므로 that이 알맞다.

11 [정답] How

[해석] 그가 어떻게 제시간에 왔는지가 미스터리이다.

→ 문맥상 방법을 묻는 의문사 how가 알맞다.

12 [정답] if

[해석] 그녀가 그에게 그가 조부모님께 전화했는지를 물어봤니?

→ 의문시 되는 사실을 이끄는 접속사는 if이다.

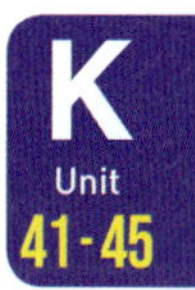

13 [정답] It doesn't matter whether you leave or not. 또는 It doesn't matter whether or not you leave.

→ '~인지 아닌지'는 whether ~ or not으로 표현한다.

14 [정답] He knows how much I care about him.

→ knows의 목적어로 의문사 how much가 이끄는 절을 쓴다.

15 [정답] It is not certain that they broke the law.

→ 가주어 it, 진주어 that절을 쓴다.

16 [정답] Don't you really wonder what Felix said to me?

→ wonder의 목적어로 의문사 what이 이끄는 절을 쓴다.

UNIT 44 부사절을 이끄는 종속접속사

개념 확인 문제 정답 ▶ 문제편 p.181

01 ⓒ **02** ⓐ **03** ⓕ **04** ⓑ **05** ⓓ

06 ⓔ **07** As the days get longer

08 As it rained a lot **09** since she had a cold

10 although she didn't win the contest

11 such an interesting novel that

12 because **13** as soon as

14 Although **15** If

16 so that

---

01 [정답] ⓒ

[해석] 갑자기 비가 오기 시작했을 때 나는 버스 정류장에 걸어가고 있었다.

→ 접속사 when은 '~할 때'라는 뜻으로 시간의 부사절을 이끈다.

02 [정답] ⓐ

[해석] 학교로 가기 전에 네 가방을 챙겼는지 꼭 확인해.

→ 접속사 before는 '~ 전에'라는 뜻으로 시간의 부사절을 이끈다.

03 [정답] ⓕ

[해석] 일단 선택하고 나면 너는 네 결정에 대해 마음을 바꿀 수 없다.

→ 접속사 once는 '일단 ~하면'이라는 뜻이다.

04 [정답] ⓑ

[해석] 나는 휴가 동안 많이 쉬었다.

→ 접속사 while은 '~하는 동안'이라는 뜻으로 시간의 부사절을 이끈다.

05 [정답] ⓓ

[해석] 만약 열차가 연착되지 않는다면 나는 7시에 그곳에 도착할 것이다.

→ unless는 '만약 ~하지 않는다면'의 의미이다.

06 [정답] ⓔ

[해석] 그들은 아이스크림 트럭을 잡을 수 있기 위해 빠르게 달렸다.

→ in order that은 '~하기 위해'라는 뜻으로 목적의 부사절을 이끈다.

07 [정답] As the days get longer

→ as는 '~함에 따라'라는 뜻의 접속사로 쓰이고, '(점점) ~해지다'는 「get+비교급」으로 표현한다.

08 [정답] As it rained a lot

→ as는 이유의 접속사로 쓰인다. 주절의 시제가 과거이므로 as절의 시제도 과거로 써야 한다.

09 [정답] since she had a cold

→ since는 '~ 이래로, 이후로'라는 뜻의 시간의 접속사로 쓰이고, 이때 since절에는 주로 과거형이 쓰인다.

10 [정답] although she didn't win the contest

→ although는 '비록 ~일지라도'라는 뜻으로 양보의 부사절을 이끈다.

11 [정답] such an interesting novel that

→ '매우 ~해서 …하다'라는 뜻으로 such ~ that을 쓸 때는 「such + a(n) + 형용사 + 명사 + that + 주어 + 동사」 형태로 쓴다.

12 [정답] because

[해석] 나는 감기에 걸렸기 때문에 놀이공원에 갈 수 없었다.

→ because는 '~하기 때문에'라는 뜻으로 이유의 부사절을 이끈다.

13 [정답] as soon as

[해석] 엄마를 보자마자 어린 소년은 와락 울음을 터뜨렸다.

→ as soon as는 '~하자마자'라는 뜻으로 시간의 부사절을 이끈다.

14 [정답] Although

[해석] 그들이 우리에게 무언가를 말하더라도, 우리는 우리가 믿는 것을 고수할 것이다.

→ Although는 '비록 ~일지라도'라는 뜻으로 양보의 부사절을 이끈다.

15 [정답] If

[해석] 네가 매일 열심히 공부하면 좋은 성적을 받을 수 있을 거야.

→ if는 '~한다면'이라는 뜻으로 조건의 부사절을 이끈다.

16 [정답] so that

[해석] 그는 우리가 그 문제들을 풀 수 있도록 우리에게 충분한 시간을 주었다.

→ so that은 '~하도록'이라는 뜻으로 목적의 부사절을 이끈다.

개념 확인 문제 정답 ▸ 문제편 p.183

01 In contrast	**02** However
03 On the other hand	**04** As a result
05 Therefore	**06** Finally
07 However	**08** In addition
09 Consequently	**10** For example
11 In other words	

01 [정답] In contrast
→ In contrast는 '그와는 반대로'를 의미하는 접속부사이다.

02 [정답] However
→ However는 '그러나'를 뜻하는 접속부사이다.

03 [정답] On the other hand
→ On the other hand는 '반면에'를 의미하는 접속부사이다.

04 [정답] As a result
→ As a result는 '그 결과'를 의미하는 접속부사이다.

05 [정답] Therefore
→ Therefore는 '그러므로'를 의미하는 접속부사이다.

06 [정답] Finally
→ Finally는 '결국'을 의미하는 접속부사이다.

07 [정답] However
→ However는 '그러나'를 의미하는 접속부사이다.

08 [정답] In addition
→ In addition은 '게다가'를 의미하는 접속부사이다.

09 [정답] Consequently
→ Consequently는 '그 결과'를 의미하는 접속부사이다.

10 [정답] For example
→ For example은 '예를 들면'을 의미하는 접속부사이다.

11 [정답] In other words
→ In other words는 '다시 말해서'를 의미하는 접속부사이다.

단원 평가 문제 UNIT **41** ~ UNIT **45** ▸ 문제편 p.184~190

정답

01 ②　**02** ③　**03** ①　**04** ⑤　**05** ①
06 how long you have been waiting
07 that the task is not easy
08 as soon as I get back home
09 so wise that everyone wants to get some advice from him
10 ⑤
11 I'll let you know as soon as I get the news.
또는 As soon as I get the news, I'll let you know.
12 Jessica and Amy are not so close although they've known each other for a long time.
또는 Although they've known each other for a long time, Jessica and Amy are not so close.
13 The planes were redirected to other airports because there was heavy fog at the airport.
또는 Because there was heavy fog at the airport, the planes were redirected to other airports.
14 Three buses went by in the opposite direction while I was waiting at the bus stop.
또는 While I was waiting at the bus stop, three buses went by in the opposite direction.
15 We will refund your payment right away if you are not satisfied with our service for any reason.
또는 If you are not satisfied with our service for any reason, we will refund your payment right away.
16 He speaks with such a convincing voice that everyone is impressed.
17 as well as　**18** ③　**19** such　**20** Who
21 either **22** whether　**23** unless **24** Once
25 ②　**26** ①　**27** ③　**28** ④　**29** ②
30 so → because 또는 since
31 because of → because
32 In other words → For example 또는 For instance
33 ①　**34** ②　**35** ④　**36** or → and
37 smoking → smokes　**38** that → so that
39 Although → When 또는 As　**40** ⑤　**41** ③
42 ①　**43** ⑤　**44** ②　**45** ①　**46** ⑤
47 ②　**48** yet　**49** or　**50** As a result
51 For instance　**52** as soon as
53 but 또는 yet　**54** both, and　**55** ③
56 so that　**57** started running in circles
58 ③

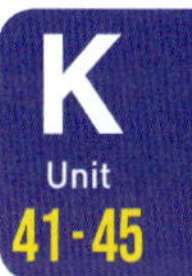

01 [정답] ②   UNIT **45** 접속부사

[해석] 우리는 최근에 메뉴를 개편했다. 게다가, 우리는 채식 옵션을 추가했다.

→ 메뉴를 개편한 것에 덧붙여 채식 옵션을 추가했다는 추가적인 정보를 나타내므로 '게다가'를 의미하는 접속부사 Besides를 써야 한다.

02 [정답] ③   UNIT **41** 등위접속사

[해석] 그 프로젝트는 지연되었다, 왜냐하면 우리는 자재를 제시간에 받지 못했기 때문이다.

→ 그 프로젝트가 지연된 이유를 나타내는 등위접속사 for를 써야 한다.

03 [정답] ①   UNIT **41** 등위접속사

[해석] 내게 즉시 전화해, 그렇지 않으면 나는 회의에 늦을 거야.

→ '명령문 + or'은 '~해라, 그렇지 않으면 …'을 뜻한다.

04 [정답] ⑤   UNIT **43** 명사절을 이끄는 종속접속사

[해석] 네 답이 '좋다'인지 아니면 '싫다'인지 가능한 한 빨리 내게 알려 줘.

→ '~인지 (아닌지)'라는 뜻으로 명사절을 이끄는 접속사는 if와 whether이다.

05 [정답] ①   UNIT **44** 부사절을 이끄는 종속접속사

[해석] (A) 축구 경기가 시작되기 전에 선수들은 몸을 풀었다.
(B) 나는 일하는 동안 방해받고 싶지 않아.
(C) 너는 네가 이 실험을 함께 하기를 원하는지 질문을 받을 것이다.

→ (A) before는 '~ 전에', (B) while은 '~하는 동안', (C) if는 '~인지 (아닌지)'의 뜻이다.

06 [정답] how long you have been waiting
     UNIT **43** 명사절을 이끄는 종속접속사

→ 의문사가 명사절을 이끌 때는 「의문사 + 주어 + 동사」 순서로 쓴다.

07 [정답] that the task is not easy
     UNIT **43** 명사절을 이끄는 종속접속사

→ know의 목적어절로 that절을 쓴다.

08 [정답] as soon as I get back home
     UNIT **44** 부사절을 이끄는 종속접속사

→ '~하자마자'는 as soon as로 쓴다.

09 [정답] so wise that everyone wants to get some advice from him UNIT **44** 부사절을 이끄는 종속접속사

→ '매우 ~해서 …하다'는 「so + 형용사/부사 + that + 주어 + 동사」로 쓴다.

10 [정답] ⑤   UNIT **44** 부사절을 이끄는 종속접속사

[해석] 날씨가 점점 더 더워짐에 따라 많은 사람들이 시원한 마실 것을 찾고 있다.
① 풍선들이 터졌을 때 아기가 울기 시작했다.
② 경보가 울렸을 때 강도는 그의 차 안으로 급히 뛰어들었다.
③ 대학생이었을 때 그는 도전을 요하는 일들을 해 보고 싶어 했다.
④ 너도 알다시피 스키와 스노보드 타기는 여러 가지 면에서 다르다.
⑤ 과학 기술이 빠르게 발전함에 따라 사람들은 변화에 적응하려고 노력한다.

→ 주어진 문장과 ⑤의 as는 '~함에 따라'라는 비례의 의미로 쓰였다.
①, ②, ③ ~할 때(시간) ④ ~대로(양태)

11 [정답] I'll let you know as soon as I get the news. **또는** As soon as I get the news, I'll let you know.   UNIT **44** 부사절을 이끄는 종속접속사

[해석] 내가 소식을 받자마자 너에게 알려줄게.

→ as soon as는 '~하자마자'라는 뜻이다. 부사절은 주절 앞이나 뒤에 쓸 수 있다.

12 [정답] Jessica and Amy are not so close although they've known each other for a long time. **또는** Although they've known each other for a long time, Jessica and Amy are not so close.
     UNIT **44** 부사절을 이끄는 종속접속사

[해석] Jessica와 Amy는 오랫동안 서로 알고 지냈음에도 불구하고 아주 친하지는 않다.

→ although는 '(비록) ~하더라도'라는 뜻으로 양보의 부사절을 이끈다.

13 [정답] The planes were redirected to other airports because there was heavy fog at the airport. **또는** Because there was heavy fog at the airport, the planes were redirected to other airports.   UNIT **44** 부사절을 이끄는 종속접속사

[해석] 공항에 심한 안개가 끼었기 때문에 비행기들은 다른 공항으로 항로를 돌렸다.

→ because는 '~ 때문에'라는 뜻으로 이유, 원인의 부사절을 이끈다.

14 [정답] Three buses went by in the opposite direction while I was waiting at the bus stop. **또는** While I was waiting at the bus stop, three buses went by in the opposite direction.   UNIT **44** 부사절을 이끄는 종속접속사

[해석] 내가 버스 정류장에서 기다리고 있었던 동안 세 대의 버스가 반대 방향에서 지나갔다.

→ while은 '~하는 동안'이라는 뜻으로 시간의 부사절을 이끈다.

15 [정답] We will refund your payment right away if you are not satisfied with our service for any reason. **또는** If you are not satisfied with our service for any reason, we will refund your payment right away.
     UNIT **44** 부사절을 이끄는 종속접속사

[해석] 어떤 이유에서든 저희 서비스에 만족하지 못하신다면 즉시 지불하신 돈을 환불해드릴 것입니다.

→ if는 '(만약) ~이라면'이라는 뜻으로 조건의 부사절을 이끈다.

16 [정답] He speaks with such a convincing voice that everyone is impressed.
     UNIT **44** 부사절을 이끄는 종속접속사

[해석] 그는 아주 설득력 있는 목소리로 말해서 모든 사람들이 감명을 받는다.
→ '아주 ~해서 …하다'라는 뜻으로 such를 쓸 때는 「such + a(n) + 형용사 + 명사 + that + 주어 + 동사」 형태로 쓴다.

17 정답 as well as　　　　UNIT **42** 상관접속사
[해석] 미술관들은 골동품뿐만 아니라 현대 미술 작품도 전시한다.
→ 'A뿐만 아니라 B도'라는 뜻의 not only A but (also) B는 B as well as A로 바꾸어 쓸 수 있다.

18 정답 ③　　　　UNIT **42** 상관접속사
[해석] ① 그는 키가 크지도 작지도 않다.
② 너뿐만 아니라 Linda도 아름답다.
③ 이탈리아 음식점이나 프랑스 음식점 중 하나가 좋다.
④ 그의 어머니와 아버지 둘 다 그 프로그램에 참가하고 있다.
⑤ 키위뿐만 아니라 딸기도 비타민 C를 많이 포함하고 있다.
→ ③ either A or B는 B에 동사를 일치시킨다. (are → is) ① neither A nor B: A도 B도 아닌 ② not only A but also B는 B에 동사를 일치시키므로 is는 알맞다. ④ Both A and B는 복수로 취급하므로 are는 알맞다. ⑤ B as well as A는 B에 동사를 일치시키므로 contains는 알맞다.

19 정답 such　　　　UNIT **44** 부사절을 이끄는 종속접속사
[해석] 그것은 아주 지루한 영화라서 나는 그것을 보다가 잠이 들었다.
→ 뒤에 「a+형용사+명사」가 있으므로 such를 써야 한다.

20 정답 Who　　　　UNIT **43** 명사절을 이끄는 종속접속사
[해석] 누가 옳은지는 확실하지 않다.
→ is right의 주어 역할을 하면서 주어절도 이끌어야 하므로 의문사 Who가 알맞다.

21 정답 either　　　　UNIT **42** 상관접속사
[해석] 나는 점심으로 치즈버거나 피자 둘 중 하나를 원한다.
→ 'A나 B 둘 중 하나'는 either A or B라고 쓴다.

22 정답 whether　　　　UNIT **43** 명사절을 이끄는 종속접속사
[해석] Joseph이 우리에게 동의했는지 아닌지를 들었니?
→ 뒤에 or not이 있으므로 '~인지 아닌지'의 뜻이 되도록 whether를 써야 한다.

23 정답 unless　　　　UNIT **44** 부사절을 이끄는 종속접속사
[해석] 나는 방해받고 싶지 않으니까 중요한 일이 아니라면 나에게 전화하지 마.
→ 문맥상 '중요한 일이 아니라면'이라는 뜻이 되도록 unless를 써야 한다.

24 정답 Once　　　　UNIT **44** 부사절을 이끄는 종속접속사
[해석] 당신이 일단 자전거 타는 법을 배우면, 절대 그것을 잊지 않는다.
→ once는 '일단 ~하면'이라는 뜻으로 조건의 부사절을 이끈다.

25 정답 ②　　　　UNIT **44** 부사절을 이끄는 종속접속사
[해석] 그가 나타나자마자 나는 게임을 시작할 것이다.
→ 시간을 나타내는 부사절에서는 현재가 미래를 대신한다.

26 정답 ①　　　　UNIT **42** 상관접속사
[해석] 나는 내 컴퓨터를 고치든지 새로 사든지 할 것이다.
→ 'A 또는 B'는 either A or B로 쓴다.

27 정답 ③　　　　UNIT **42** 상관접속사
[해석] 나는 나를 행복하고 성공하게 도울 것을 찾고 있다.
→ 'A와 B 둘 다'라는 뜻의 both A and B에서 A와 B는 문법상 대등한 어구가 와야 한다.

28 정답 ④　　　　UNIT **42** 상관접속사
[해석] 우리 마을에서는 플라스틱뿐만 아니라 종이컵도 재활용이 되지 않는다.
→ Neither A nor B에서 동사는 B에 일치시킨다.

29 정답 ②　　　　UNIT **43** 명사절을 이끄는 종속접속사
[해석] 우리는 그녀가 그의 프러포즈를 받아들일 것을 기대하지 않았다.
→ 문맥상 목적어절을 이끄는 접속사 that이 필요하다.

30 정답 so → because 또는 since　　　　UNIT **41** 등위접속사
→ '비행기를 놓친 것'의 이유가 '대합실에서 잠들었던 것'이므로 so를 because이나 since로 고쳐야 한다.

31 정답 because of → because
　　　　UNIT **44** 부사절을 이끄는 종속접속사
→ 뒤에 절이 이어지므로 전치사 because of를 접속사 because로 고쳐야 한다.

32 정답 In other words → For example 또는 For instance　　　　UNIT **41** 등위접속사
→ '예를 들면'을 의미하는 접속부사는 for example 또는 for instance이다.

33 정답 ①　　　　UNIT **43** 명사절을 이끄는 종속접속사
[해석] 그가 키가 큰지 안 큰지는 나에게 중요하지 않다.
→ whether A or B는 'A이든 B이든'이라는 의미로 주어, 보어절을 이끌 수 있으므로 It으로 시작하는 문장으로 바꿔도 whether를 쓸 수 있다.

34 정답 ②　　　　UNIT **44** 부사절을 이끄는 종속접속사
[해석] 네가 포기하지 않는다면 너의 꿈을 이룰 것이다.
→ if ~ not은 '만약 ~하지 않는다면'의 뜻으로 unless로 바꾸어 쓸 수 있다.

35 정답 ④　　　　UNIT **42** 상관접속사
[해석] 그녀는 수영할 수 있고, 다이빙도 할 수 있다. (= 그녀는 수영할 수 있을 뿐만 아니라 다이빙할 수 있다.)
→ 'A뿐만 아니라 B도'라는 뜻은 B as well as A로 쓴다.

36 정답 or → and　　　　UNIT **42** 상관접속사
[해석] 우리 부모님은 클래식 음악과 대중 음악을 둘 다 좋아하신다.
→ both A and B는 'A와 B 둘 다'라는 뜻이다.

37 정답 smoking → smokes　　　　UNIT **42** 상관접속사
[해석] 그의 삼촌은 술도 안 드시고 담배도 안 피우신다.
→ neither A nor B에서 A와 B는 문법상 대등한 어구가 와야 한다.

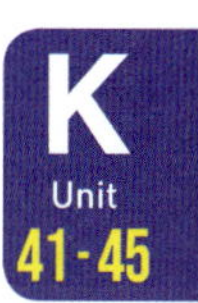

38 정답 that → so that　　　UNIT **44** 부사절을 이끄는 종속접속사

[해석] 우리는 감기에 걸리지 않기 위해서 따뜻한 옷을 입었다.

→ 「so that+주어+동사」는 '~하기 위해서'라는 뜻으로 쓰인다.

39 정답 Although → When 또는 As　　　UNIT **44** 부사절을 이끄는 종속접속사

[해석] 내가 창문을 열었을 때, 시원한 바람이 방 안으로 들어왔다.

→ '~할 때'라는 뜻을 나타내야 하므로 When 또는 As가 와야 한다.

40 정답 ⑤　　　UNIT **43** 명사절을 이끄는 종속접속사

[해석] ① 그가 오디션을 통과하지 못했다는 것이 모두를 실망시켰다.

② 그의 최종 목표는 그의 팀이 내셔널리그에서 우승하는 것이다.

③ 누가 그 감독이 고작 100만 달러로 이 영화를 만들었다고 상상할 수 있겠는가?

④ 그가 그때 그곳에 없었다는 것은 놀랍지 않았다.

⑤ David는 그의 할아버지가 그에게 주었던 시계를 잃어버렸다.

→ ⑤은 목적격 관계대명사이고 나머지는 모두 명사절을 이끄는 접속사이다. ① 주어 ② 보어 ③ 목적어 ④ 진주어

41 정답 ③　　　UNIT **44** 부사절을 이끄는 종속접속사

[해석] • 어제 내가 전화하지 않아서 화가 난 거야?

• 날씨가 추워서 나는 감기에 걸렸다.

→ 이유를 나타내는 접속사는 as이다.

42 정답 ①　　　UNIT **43** 명사절을 이끄는 종속접속사,
　　　UNIT **44** 부사절을 이끄는 종속접속사

[해석] • 나는 그녀가 올해 내 생일을 기억할지 궁금하다.

• 이 도로가 폐쇄되어 있다면 다른 길을 찾아야 한다.

→ if는 '~인지 아닌지'를 뜻하는 명사절 접속사로 쓰일 수 있고, '~한다면'을 뜻하는 조건의 부사절 접속사로도 쓰일 수 있다.

43 정답 ⑤　　　UNIT **43** 명사절을 이끄는 종속접속사

[해석] ① 학생들은 시험이 끝났다고 생각했다.

② 나는 그녀가 곧 여기에 올 것이라는 것을 안다.

③ 이것은 내가 많이 좋아하는 강아지이다.

④ 너는 그녀가 동계올림픽에서 금메달을 땄다는 것을 믿을 수 있니?

⑤ 내가 뉴스에서 들었던 것은 일본에서 지진이 일어났다는 것이었다.

→ that이 주격 보어절을 이끌고 있으므로 이때 that은 생략할 수 없다. ①, ②, ④은 목적어절을 이끄는 접속사, ③은 관계사로 생략할 수 있다.

44 정답 ②　　　UNIT **42** 상관접속사

[해석] ① 그들은 네가 한국에 방문할 때 너를 서울로 데려갈 것이다.

② 너는 여기에서 중국 음식이나 일본 음식을 주문할 수 있다.

③ 나는 발생한 일에 당황했을 뿐 아니라 꽤 충격을 받았다.

④ 나는 그 영화가 너에게 너무 지루할지 아닐지는 확신할 수가 없다.

⑤ 너의 정답이 맞는 것은 사실이다.

→ ② 'A 또는 B'는 either A or B로 쓴다. neither A nor B는 'A와 B 둘 다 아닌'으로 쓰인다. ① '~할 때'의 뜻을 나타내는 종속접속사 when ③ not only A but (also) B: A뿐만 아니라 B도 ④ 명사절을 이끄는 접속사 if ⑤ 진주어절을 이끄는 접속사 that

45 정답 ①　　　UNIT **44** 부사절을 이끄는 종속접속사

[해석] ① 네가 달린다면 늦지 않을 것이다.

② 잊기 전에 그것을 지금 당장 해라.

③ 우리가 영화를 보는 동안에 그는 잠이 들었다.

④ 내일은 개교기념일이므로 나는 학교에 갈 필요가 없다.

⑤ 내가 공원에서 그를 만났던 건 어제였다.

→ ① unless는 '~하지 않으면'의 뜻이므로 문맥상 맞으려면 '~ 한다면'의 뜻인 if를 써야 한다. ② '~ 전에'라는 뜻을 나타내는 종속접속사 before ③ '~ 동안에'라는 뜻을 나타내는 종속접속사 while ④ 이유를 나타내는 종속접속사 as ⑤ It was ~ that … 강조 구문에서 쓰인 that

46 정답 ⑤　　　UNIT **42** 상관접속사

[해석] ① Tom과 Lisa는 둘 다 여기 있다.

② 나도 그도 초대받지 못했다.

③ 너나 그 중 한 명이 주도권을 잡는다.

④ 개들뿐만 아니라 고양이도 정기 검진이 필요하다.

⑤ 그의 친구들이 아니라 John 자신이 그 실수에 책임이 있었다.

→ not A but B가 주어로 쓰이면 B에 동사의 수를 일치시킨다. 따라서 John에 맞는 동사 was가 적절하다.

47 정답 ②　　　UNIT **43** 명사절을 이끄는 종속접속사

[해석] ① 내일은 비가 올 것이다.

② 그녀가 화가 났다는 것은 분명하다.

③ 자정이었지만 나는 깨어 있었다.

④ 거기까지 가는 데 30분 정도 걸린다.

⑤ 계절이 바뀌면서 날씨가 따뜻해지고 있다.

→ ② It은 가주어이며 진주어는 that she is upset이다. ① 날씨를 ③ 때를 ④ 시간이 ~ 걸리다 ⑤ 날씨를 나타내는 비인칭 주어이다.

48 정답 yet　　　UNIT **41** 등위접속사

[해석] 그는 열심히 공부했지만, 원하는 결과를 얻지 못했다.

→ 열심히 공부했음에도 원하는 결과를 얻지 못했다는 반대되는 내용을 나타내므로, 등위접속사 yet이 들어가야 한다.

49 정답 or　　　UNIT **41** 등위접속사

[해석] 오늘 밤에는 소설을 읽는 게 좋은가요, 아니면 영화를 보는 게 좋은가요?

→ 소설을 읽는 것과 영화를 보는 것 중 하나를 선택하므로, 등위접속사 or가 들어가야 한다.

50 정답 As a result　　　UNIT **45** 접속부사

[해석] Lena는 수년간 추상화를 연습했다. 그 결과, 그녀의 작품은 현재 여러 현대 미술관에 전시되어 있다.

→ 뒤 문장은 Lena가 추상화를 연습한 결과를 나타내므로 '그 결과'를 의미하는 As a result가 가장 알맞다.

51 [정답] For instance
UNIT 45 접속부사

[해석] 온라인 학습은 몇 가지 경우에 효과적일 수 있다. 예를 들면, 학생들은 자신만의 속도로 강의를 복습할 수 있다.
→ 뒤 문장은 온라인 학습이 효과적인 경우의 예시를 나타내므로 '예를 들면'을 의미하는 For instance가 알맞다.

52 [정답] as soon as
UNIT 44 부사절을 이끄는 종속접속사

→ as soon as는 '~하자마자'라는 뜻으로 쓴다.

53 [정답] but 또는 yet
UNIT 41 등위접속사

→ 뒤의 절(he still remained well-dressed)이 앞의 절과 반대되는 내용이므로 but 또는 yet이 들어가야 한다.

54 [정답] both, and
UNIT 42 상관접속사

→ '연극의 연출과 연기 둘 다'라고 헸으므로 both A and B의 형태로 쓴다.

55 [정답] ③
UNIT 44 부사절을 이끄는 종속접속사

[해석] 나는 내 강아지 Kelly를 잃어버렸다. 나는 모든 곳을 찾아봤는데도 그것을 찾을 수 없어서 눈물을 흘렸다. 나는 동네에 모두 붙일 수 있도록 많은 양의 포스터를 만들었다. 다음날 나는 전화 한 통을 받았다. 전화를 건 사람이 "제가 푸들 한 마리를 찾았는데요, 그것이 당신 개인 것을 어떻게 알죠?"라고 말했다. 나는 "그것을 증명할 좋은 방법이 있어요. 그 푸들에게 '징글벨'을 휘파람 불어주세요."라고 말했다. 잠시 후에 그는 다시 전화기를 들고 말했다. "강아지가 빙글빙글 돌며 뛰기 시작했어요." "그러면 틀림없이 Kelly예요!"라고 나는 말했다.
→ ⓐ 문맥상 '모든 곳을 찾아봤는데도 강아지를 찾을 수 없었다'라는 내용이므로, 양보를 나타내는 Though가 들어가야 한다.
ⓑ 뒤의 절(I shed tears)이 앞의 상황에 따른 결과를 나타내므로 so가 들어가야 한다.

56 [정답] so that
UNIT 44 부사절을 이끄는 종속접속사

→ '~하도록'이라는 목적을 나타내는 접속사 so that을 써야 한다.

57 [정답] started running in circles
UNIT 44 부사절을 이끄는 종속접속사

→ 마지막 부분에 The dog started running in circles.라고 했으므로 The dog를 It으로 바꿔 쓰면 된다.

58 [정답] ③
UNIT 43 명사절을 이끄는 종속접속사, UNIT 44 부사절을 이끄는 종속접속사

[해석] 대체적으로 무당벌레와 매미 같은 곤충들은 죽을 때 다리를 가슴에 말아 올린 채 등을 바닥에 대고 눕는다. 그것들은 다리를 세 쌍, 총 6개를 가지고 있다. 그것들은 많은 다리를 갖고 있어서 몸무게를 균등하게 분산시키고 쉽게 움직일 수 있다. 죽기 시작할 때 그것들의 다리 근육이 수축한다. 다리가 몸무게를 더 이상 지탱할 수 없을 때 곤충들은 뒤집어지기 시작한다.
→ ③ '매우 ~해서 …하다'는 「such+명사(구)+that+주어+동사」로 표현한다. 따라서 if는 that으로 고쳐야 한다. ①, ⑤ '~할 때'의 뜻을 나타내는 부사절 종속접속사 when ② '~를 가지고'의 뜻을 나타내는 전치사 with ④ '~할 때'의 뜻을 나타내는 부사절 종속접속사 as

---

L 전치사

UNIT 46 시간을 나타내는 전치사

<table>
<tr><td colspan="4">개념 확인 문제 정답   ▶ 문제편 p.193~195</td></tr>
<tr><td>01 at</td><td>02 during</td><td>03 for</td><td>04 during</td></tr>
<tr><td>05 on</td><td>06 in</td><td>07 from</td><td>08 during</td></tr>
<tr><td>09 since</td><td>10 for</td><td>11 from</td><td>12 since</td></tr>
<tr><td>13 during</td><td>14 on</td><td>15 for</td><td>16 at</td></tr>
<tr><td>17 by</td><td>18 within</td><td>19 until</td><td>20 until</td></tr>
<tr><td>21 by</td><td>22 within</td><td></td><td></td></tr>
<tr><td colspan="4">23 before her long business trip</td></tr>
<tr><td colspan="4">24 after the final exam</td></tr>
<tr><td colspan="4">25 Before the medical checkup</td></tr>
<tr><td colspan="4">26 After the performance</td></tr>
<tr><td>27 by</td><td>28 within</td><td>29 until</td><td>30 before</td></tr>
</table>

01 [정답] at
[해석] 기차는 정확히 7시 45분에 도착할 예정이니, 늦지 마.
→ 정확한 시간을 말하므로 at이 적절하다.

02 [정답] during
[해석] 그 가게는 평일마다 점심시간 동안 문을 닫는다는 걸 기억해.
→ 특정 기간 안에 일어나는 일이므로 during이 적절하다.

03 [정답] for
[해석] 그들은 꽁꽁 언 날씨에 밖에서 한 시간을 기다리고 있었다.
→ 기다린 시간의 길이를 나타내므로 for가 적절하다.

04 [정답] during
[해석] 오늘 교통 혼잡 시간 동안 정말 비극적인 교통사고가 있었어!
→ 특정 기간 안에 일어난 일이므로 during이 적절하다.

05 [정답] on
[해석] 내 생일이 공휴일 바로 다음 날인 1월 2일이라는 거 믿을 수 있겠니?
→ 특정한 날짜를 말하므로 on이 적절하다.

06 [정답] in
[해석] 복원 프로젝트 전체가 예정대로 2주 안에 완료될 것이다.
→ 특정 기간 '이내'를 말하므로 in이 적절하다.

07 [정답] from
[해석] 정확히 오전 9시부터 11시 30분까지 시험을 치르세요.
→ 「from A to B」 형태로 '9시부터'를 나타내야 하므로 from이 적절하다.

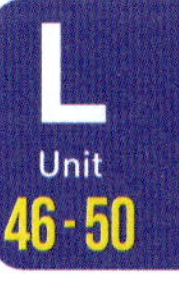

08 정답 during

[해석] 그는 기조연설 중에 잠들었다.

→ 기조연설이라는 특정 기간 안에 일어난 일이므로 during이 적절하다.

09 정답 since

[해석] 그녀는 2019년 이후로 대사관에서 일해 오고 있다.

→ 현재완료시제와 함께 쓰여 2019년 이후로 '일한다'는 행위가 지속됨을 나타내므로 since가 적절하다.

10 정답 for

[해석] 나는 3년 동안 환경법을 공부해 왔다.

→ 3년이라는 구체적인 길이의 시간을 나타내므로 for가 적절하다.

11 정답 from

→ '다음 주부터'를 나타내야 하므로 from이 적절하다.

12 정답 since

→ 현재완료시제와 함께 쓰여 폐막식 이후로 '연락하다'라는 행위가 지속되었는지를 물었으므로 since가 적절하다.

13 정답 during

→ 회의라는 특정 기간 안에 일어난 일이므로 during이 적절하다.

14 정답 on

→ Saturday 앞에 빈칸이 있으므로 요일 앞에 쓰이는 on이 적절하다.

15 정답 for

→ 며칠이라는 길이의 시간을 나타내므로 for가 적절하다.

16 정답 at

→ 정확한 시간을 말하므로 at이 적절하다.

17 정답 by

[해석] 모든 행사 참가자는 늦어도 오전 9시 30분까지 체크인을 완료해야 합니다.

→ 9시 30분까지 행위가 완료되어야 함을 나타내므로 by가 적절하다.

18 정답 within

[해석] 요청을 받은 후 48시간 이내에 보고서를 제출해야 합니다.

→ 48시간 이내에 행위가 완료되어야 함을 나타내므로 within이 적절하다.

19 정답 until

[해석] 우리는 정오까지 짧은 휴식을 가질 예정이니, 제시간에 자리로 돌아오세요.

→ 정오까지 행위가 지속될 것임을 나타내므로 until이 적절하다.

20 정답 until

[해석] 그녀는 최종 승인을 받기 위해 자정까지 기다렸지만, 아무런 메시지도 오지 않았다.

→ 자정까지 행위가 지속되었음을 나타내므로 until이 적절하다.

21 정답 by

[해석] 마감일까지 모든 비자 서류를 완료하셨나요?

→ 마감일까지 행위가 완료되었는지를 물었으므로 by가 적절하다.

22 정답 within

[해석] 당신은 계약을 확보하려면 출판사의 제안에 7일 이내에 응답해야 한다.

→ 7일 이내에 행위가 완료되어야 함을 나타내므로 within이 적절하다.

23 정답 before her long business trip

→ 긴 출장 '전'이라고 했으므로 before her long business trip으로 쓴다.

24 정답 after the final exam

→ 기말고사 '후'라고 했으므로 after the final exam으로 쓴다.

25 정답 Before the medical checkup

→ 건강검진 '전'이라고 했으므로 Before the medical checkup으로 쓴다.

26 정답 After the performance

→ 공연 '후'라고 했으므로 After the performance로 쓴다.

27 정답 by

→ 금요일까지 행위가 완료되어야 함을 나타내므로 by가 적절하다.

28 정답 within

→ 1분기 '이내'를 나타내므로 within이 적절하다.

29 정답 until

→ 새벽까지 행위가 지속되었음을 나타내므로 until이 적절하다.

30 정답 before

→ 수술 '전'이라고 했으므로 before가 적절하다.

UNIT 47 장소를 나타내는 전치사

개념 확인 문제 정답 ▶ 문제편 p.197~199

01 in **02** on **03** at **04** over

05 above **06** over **07** in **08** at

09 over **10** on **11** above

12 The ancient remains are often found beneath the modern city.

13 The little black cat is sleeping under the wooden table.

14 next to **15** in front of **16** between

17 between **18** among **19** among

20 between **21** on, under **22** over

23 on, beside 또는 next to 또는 by **24** in

01 정답 in

[해석] 해가 진 뒤엔 숲속에서 길을 잃지 마.
수천 개의 인공위성이 현재 우주에서 추적되고 있다.
→ in은 넓은 장소나 지역, 우주나 하늘에 있는 상태를 나타낸다.

02 정답 on

[해석] 고대 지도는 돌 테이블 위에 펼쳐져 있었다.
청동 조각상이 받침대 위에 당당히 서 있었다.
→ on은 표면에 접촉한 상태를 나타낸다.

03 정답 at

[해석] 깃발이 성의 가장 높은 탑 위치에 게양되었다.
중앙 아치 바로 그 지점에 조각된 문장이 있다.
→ at은 비교적 좁은 장소나 지점을 나타낸다.

04 정답 over

[해석] A: 방금 해변 위로 날아가는 비행기 봤어?
B: 응, 너무 낮게 떠서 거기 착륙할 줄 알았어!
→ 비행기가 해변 가까이 위를 지나간다고 했으므로 over가 적절하다.

05 정답 above

[해석] A: 와, 저 그림이 좀 너무 높이 걸려 있는 것 같아.
B: 맞아. 선반보다 훨씬 위에 있네. 자세한 걸 보기도 힘들어.
→ 그림이 선반보다 떨어진 위에 있다고 했으므로 above가 적절하다.

06 정답 over

[해석] A: 산 위에 있는 저 이상한 구름은 뭐야?
B: 그냥 반대편에서 밀려오는 안개같아.
→ 덮여 있듯 산 위에 있는 구름을 나타내므로 over가 적절하다.

07 정답 in

[해석] 나는 식물원 안에서 서성이는 낯선 사람을 발견했다.
→ 넓은 장소 안이므로 in이 적절하다.

08 정답 at

[해석] 정오쯤 역사 자료관 앞에서 만날까요?
→ 역사 자료관 앞이라는 지점이므로 at이 적절하다.

09 정답 over

[해석] 큐레이터에게 저 장식품을 기둥 위에 둘 수 있는지 여쭤보세요.
→ 장식품을 기둥 '위에' 둘 수 있는지를 나타내는 것이 자연스러우므로 over가 적절하다.

10 정답 on

[해석] 입구 근처 벽에 붙은 세부적인 지도가 있다.
→ 벽의 표면 위에 붙은 것이므로 on이 적절하다.

11 정답 above

[해석] 드론은 보안 목적을 위해 전시장 위를 떠다니고 있을 것이다.
→ 전시장 위쪽에 떠다니고 있음을 나타내므로 above가 적절하다.

12 정답 The ancient remains are often found beneath the modern city.

→ 현대적인 도시와 '접촉하여 아래에' 있는 것이므로 the modern city 앞에 beneath를 쓴다.

13 정답 The little black cat is sleeping under the wooden table.

→ 위치상 나무 탁자 '아래에서' 자고 있는 것이므로 the wooden table 앞에 under를 쓴다.

14 정답 next to

→ 책상 '옆에'라고 했으므로 next to가 적절하다.

15 정답 in front of

→ 경찰서 '앞'이라고 했으므로 in front of가 적절하다.

16 정답 between

[해석] 남북한 사이의 긴장은 2018년에 감소했었다.
→ 두 한국(남한과 북한) '사이'라고 했으므로 between이 적절하다.

17 정답 between

[해석] 비밀의 문은 두 책장 사이에 있었다.
→ 두 책장 '사이'라고 했으므로 between이 적절하다.

18 정답 among

[해석] 중간고사 이후에 모든 학생들 사이에서 걱정이 퍼졌다.
→ 모든 학생들 '사이'라고 했으므로 among이 적절하다.

19 정답 among

[해석] 내 미어캣은 수많은 옷 사이에서 그의 장난감을 찾고 있었다.
→ 수많은 옷 '사이'라고 했으므로 among이 적절하다.

20 정답 between

[해석] 한 남자가 고양이와 여자 사이에 앉아 있다.
→ 고양이와 여자 '사이에' 앉아 있는 것이므로 between이라고 쓴다.

21 정답 on, under

[해석] 네 명의 아이들이 나무 아래 돗자리 위에 있다.
→ '돗자리 위에'는 on the mat라고 쓰고, '나무 밑에'는 under the tree라고 쓴다.

22 정답 over

[해석] 모자를 쓴 여자가 개울 위에 있는 다리를 걸어서 건넌다.
→ 다리는 개울 위쪽에 걸려 있는 것이므로 over를 쓴다.

23 정답 on, beside **또는** next to **또는** by

[해석] 고양이 한 마리가 벤치 옆 잔디밭 위에서 자고 있다.
→ '잔디밭 위에'는 on the grass라고 쓰고, '~ 옆에'는 beside, next to, by로 쓴다.

24 정답 in

[해석] 물고기들이 개울 속에서 헤엄치고 있다.
→ '~ 속에, 안에'는 in으로 쓴다.

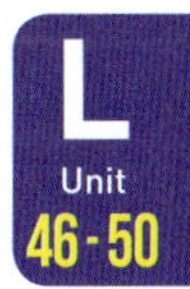

개념 확인 문제 정답   ▶ 문제편 p.201~205

01 down	**02** into	**03** out of	**04** up
05 along	**06** off	**07** onto	**08** for
09 across	**10** toward	**11** with	**12** by
13 in	**14** for	**15** of	**16** in
17 as	**18** by	**19** with	**20** with
21 for	**22** by	**23** without	
24 instead of	**25** due to	**26** except	
27 According to	**28** except for	**29** due to	
30 against	**31** by	**32** such as	
33 like	**34** by	**35** across	
36 without	**37** out of	**38** including	
39 like			

01 정답 down
[해석] 그녀는 한 손에 서류철을 들고 계단을 내려가고 있었다.
→ 계단을 내려가는 것이므로 down이 적절하다.

02 정답 into
[해석] 그가 방 안으로 들어갔을 때, 그는 놀라운 무언가를 보았다.
→ 방 안으로 들어가는 것이므로 into가 적절하다.

03 정답 out of
[해석] 두더지 한 마리가 흙 밖으로 나왔다.
→ 흙 밖으로 나온 것이므로 out of가 적절하다.

04 정답 up
[해석] 나의 할아버지는 난간 없이는 계단을 올라갈 수 없다.
→ 계단을 올라가는 것이므로 up이 적절하다.

05 정답 along
[해석] 새끼 펭귄들이 어미를 따라 걷고 있다.
→ 어미를 따라 걷는 것이므로 along이 적절하다.

06 정답 off
[해석] 내 딸은 병원에 있다, 왜냐하면 어제 자전거에서 떨어졌기 때문이다.
→ 자전거에서 떨어진 것이므로 off가 적절하다.

07 정답 onto
→ 접시 위로 떨어뜨리는 것이므로 onto가 적절하다.

08 정답 for
→ 군산이라는 정확한 목적지를 향하는 것이므로 for가 적절하다.

09 정답 across
→ 강을 가로지르는 것이므로 across가 적절하다.

10 정답 toward
→ 지평선 쪽을 향하는 것이므로 toward가 적절하다.

11 정답 with
[해석] 그녀는 밝은 미소를 가진 남자와 함께 있었다.
→ 밝은 미소를 가진 것이므로 with가 적절하다.

12 정답 by
[해석] 우리는 휴가 동안에 기차로 도시를 여행했다.
→ 기차로 여행한 것이므로 by가 적절하다.

13 정답 in
[해석] 빨간 옷을 입은 여자가 나의 가장 친한 친구인 Tina이다.
→ 빨간 옷을 입은 것이므로 in이 적절하다.

14 정답 for
[해석] 그는 열심히 일한 것 때문에 상을 받았다.
→ '~ 때문에'를 나타내는 for가 적절하다.

15 정답 of
[해석] 그녀는 작년에 심각한 병으로 세상을 떠났다.
→ '~(으)로'를 나타내는 of가 적절하다.

16 정답 in
[해석] 파란 재킷을 입고 있는 남자는 우리의 새 코치이다.
→ '~을 입고 있는'을 나타내는 in이 적절하다.

17 정답 as
[해석] 그는 동물 보호소에서 자원봉사자로 일하고 있다.
→ '~로(서)'를 나타내는 as가 적절하다.

18 정답 by
[해석] 그 그림은 프랑스 출신의 유명한 화가에 의해 그려졌다.
→ '~에 의해'를 나타내는 by가 적절하다.

19 정답 with
[해석] 그녀는 매일 오후에 뒷마당에서 강아지와 함께 논다.
→ '~와 함께'를 나타내는 with가 적절하다.

20 정답 with
[해석] 나는 내 친구와 함께 콘서트에 갔다.
James는 열쇠로 문을 열었다.
→ '~와 함께'라는 의미와 '~로'라는 도구의 의미 둘 다를 나타낼 수 있는 전치사는 with이다.

21 정답 for
[해석] 그녀는 친절함 때문에 칭찬을 받았다.
그는 오늘 아침 파리를 향해 떠났다.
→ '~ 때문에'라는 목적과 '~을 향해'라는 방향 둘 다를 나타낼 수 있는 전치사는 for이다.

22 정답 by
[해석] • 이 책은 유명한 작가에 쓰여졌다.
• 그들은 신용카드로 지불했다.
→ '~에 의해'라는 의미와 '~로'라는 수단의 의미 둘 다를 나타낼 수 있는 전치사는 by이다.

23 [정답] without

[해석] • 그는 그의 친구들 없이 점심을 먹었다.

• 그녀는 질문에 대답하지 않고 걸어나갔다.

→ '~ 없이'라는 의미와 '~하지 않고'라는 의미 둘 다를 나타낼 수 있는 전치사는 without이다.

24 [정답] instead of

[해석] 그녀는 커피 대신에 주스를 마셨다.

→ '~ 대신에'를 나타내는 instead of가 적절하다.

25 [정답] due to

[해석] 폭설 때문에 경기가 취소되었다.

→ '~ 때문에'를 나타내는 due to가 적절하다.

26 [정답] except

[해석] 그 박물관은 월요일을 제외하고 매일 연다.

→ '~를 제외하고'를 나타내는 except가 적절하다.

27 [정답] According to

[해석] 기상 예보에 따르면 내일 날씨는 맑을 것이다.

→ '~에 따르면'을 나타내는 according to가 적절하다.

28 [정답] except for

[해석] 그는 모든 사람에게 친절했지만, 그 낯선 사람만은 예외였다.

→ '~을 제외하고'를 나타내는 except for가 적절하다.

29 [정답] due to

[해석] 그 도시는 심각한 대기 오염 때문에 경고를 받았다.

→ '~ 때문에'를 나타내는 due to가 적절하다.

30 [정답] against

[해석] 많은 과학자들이 그 이론에 공개적으로 반대해 왔다.

→ '~에 반대하여'를 나타내는 against가 적절하다.

31 [정답] by

[해석] 그 데이터는 당신이 설치한 새 소프트웨어에 의해 분석되었나요?

→ 소프트웨어라는 수단을 나타내는 by가 적절하다.

32 [정답] such as

[해석] 아이들은 사과, 배, 체리와 같은 과일을 가져왔다.

→ '~와 같은'을 나타내는 such as가 적절하다.

33 [정답] like

[해석] 그 아이는 변장 파티에서 영화 캐릭터처럼 옷을 입었다.

→ 영화 캐릭터처럼 옷을 입은 것이므로 like가 적절하다.

34 [정답] by

→ 작가에 '의해' 쓰여진 것이므로 by가 적절하다.

35 [정답] across

→ 길을 '가로질러' 달린 것이므로 across가 적절하다.

36 [정답] without

→ 컴퓨터 '없이는'이라는 뜻이므로 without이 적절하다.

37 [정답] out of

→ 창문 '밖으로'라고 했으므로 out of가 적절하다.

38 [정답] including

→ 남동생을 '포함하여'라고 했으므로 including이 적절하다.

39 [정답] like

→ 프로 가수'처럼' 노래한다고 했으므로 like가 적절하다.

UNIT 49 동사 + 전치사

개념 확인 문제 정답 ▶ 문제편 p.207

01 to	02 for	03 on	04 to	05 for
06 for	07 on	08 for	09 to	10 of
11 from	12 at	13 on	14 with	15 of
16 to	17 of	18 of	19 to	20 in
21 with	22 in			

01 [정답] to

[해석] 나는 공부할 때 음악을 듣는 것을 좋아한다.

→ '~을 듣다'는 listen to로 나타낸다.

02 [정답] for

[해석] 나는 지난주에 과학 캠프를 신청했다.

→ '~을 신청하다'는 apply for로 나타낸다.

03 [정답] on

[해석] 식물은 자라기 위해 햇빛과 물에 의존한다.

→ '~에 의존하다'는 depend on으로 나타낸다.

04 [정답] to

[해석] 정크 푸드를 너무 많이 먹으면 비만으로 이어질 수 있다.

→ '~로 이어지다'는 lead to로 나타낸다.

05 [정답] for

[해석] 그들은 교실 밖에서 선생님을 기다렸다.

→ '~을 기다리다'는 wait for로 나타낸다.

06 [정답] for

[해석] 그녀는 잃어버린 열쇠들을 찾으려고 노력하고 있다.

→ '~을 찾다'는 look for로 나타낸다.

07 [정답] on

[해석] 시끄러울 때 공부에 집중하는 것은 어렵다.

→ '~에 집중하다'는 focus on으로 나타낸다.

08 [정답] for

[해석] 그는 유학을 위해 장학금을 신청했다.

→ '~에 지원하다'는 apply for로 나타낸다.

09 [정답] to

[해석] 수면 부족은 건강 문제로 이어질 수 있다.

→ '~로 이어지다'는 lead to로 나타낸다.

10 정답 of

[해석] 그들은 카페의 무료 와이파이를 이용했다.

→ '~을 이용하다'는 take advantage of로 나타낸다.

11 정답 from

[해석] 그는 작년에 심장마비로 죽었다.

→ '~로 죽다'는 die from으로 나타낸다.

12 정답 at

[해석] 단지 다르다는 이유로 사람들을 비웃지 마라.

→ '~을 비웃다'는 laugh at으로 나타낸다.

13 정답 on

[해석] 나는 밖에 나가기 전에 자외선 차단제를 발라야 한다.

→ '~을 바르다'는 put on으로 나타낸다.

14 정답 with

[해석] 그녀는 지난주에 도입된 새 정책에 동의한다.

→ '~에 동의하다'는 agree with로 나타낸다.

15 정답 of

[해석] 내 남동생은 매일 아침 우리 강아지를 돌본다.

→ '~을 돌보다'는 take care of로 나타낸다.

16 정답 to

[해석] 저 빨간 자전거는 내 사촌 것이다.

→ '~에 속하다'는 belong to로 나타낸다.

17 정답 of

[해석] 너는 이 기회를 배움에 이용해야 한다.

→ '~을 이용하다'는 take advantage of로 나타낸다.

18 정답 of

[해석] 오래된 상자들을 보관용으로 활용하자.

→ '~을 이용[활용]하다'는 make use of로 나타낸다.

19 정답 to

[해석] 아기는 알록달록한 장난감에 주의를 기울였다.

→ '~에 주의를 기울이다'는 pay attention to로 나타낸다.

20 정답 in

[해석] 그는 다른 사람을 돕는 것에 자부심을 느낀다.

→ '~을 자랑하다'는 take pride in으로 나타낸다.

21 정답 with

[해석] 그는 직장에서의 많은 스트레스를 처리해야 했다.

→ '~을 다루다, 처리하다'는 deal with로 나타낸다.

22 정답 in

[해석] 네 자신을 믿는 것이 중요하다.

→ '~을 믿다'는 believe in으로 나타낸다.

UNIT 50 형용사 + 전치사, 주의해야 할 전치사

개념 확인 문제 정답 ▶ 문제편 p.209

01 for **02** of **03** for **04** of **05** to

06 at **07** on **08** from **09** to **10** with

11 for **12** of

13 In case → In case of **14** during → while

15 In case → In case of **16** because → because of

17 despite → though[although]

18 because → because of

19 In spite of → Though[Although]

20 During → While

---

01 정답 for

[해석] 나는 행사를 조직하는 데 책임이 있다.

→ '~에 책임이 있다'는 be responsible for로 나타낸다.

02 정답 of

[해석] 그는 파티에서 자신의 옷차림을 부끄러워했다.

→ '~을 부끄러워하다'는 be ashamed of로 나타낸다.

03 정답 for

[해석] 파리는 아름다운 건축물로 유명하다.

→ '~로 유명하다'는 be famous for로 나타낸다.

04 정답 of

[해석] 이 기계는 많은 양의 데이터를 처리할 수 있다.

→ '~을 할 수 있다'는 be capable of로 나타낸다.

05 정답 to

[해석] 그 이름은 나에게 익숙하지만 어디서 들었는지는 기억이 안 난다.

→ '~에게 익숙하다'는 be familiar to로 나타낸다.

06 정답 at

[해석] 나는 이름을 기억하는 것을 잘 못한다.

→ '~을 못하다'는 be poor at으로 나타낸다.

07 정답 on

[해석] 이 책은 실제 사건을 바탕으로 만들어졌다.

→ '~에 근거하다'는 be based on으로 나타낸다.

08 정답 from

[해석] 내 의견은 네 것과 다르다.

→ '~와 다르다'는 be different from으로 나타낸다.

09 정답 to

[해석] 그는 늦게까지 깨어 있는 데 익숙하다.

→ '~에 익숙해지다'는 be accustomed to로 나타낸다.

10 정답 with

[해석] 나는 이런 종류의 문제에 친숙하다.

→ '~에 친숙하다'는 be familiar with로 나타낸다.

11 정답 for

[해석] 그는 친절한 선생님으로 알려져 있다.

→ '~로 알려지다'는 be known for로 나타낸다.

12 정답 of

[해석] 나는 깊은 물에서 수영하는 것이 무섭다.

→ '~을 두려워하다'는 be afraid of로 나타낸다.

13 정답 In case → In case of

[해석] 기술적 결함이 발생할 경우, 예비 발전기가 작동할 것이다.

→ in case 뒤에는 절이 나와야 하므로 같은 뜻의 전치사 in case of로 고쳐야 한다.

14 정답 during → while

[해석] 위원회가 회의 중일 때 보고서를 제출하시오.

→ during 뒤에는 명사가 나와야 하므로 같은 뜻의 접속사 while로 고쳐야 한다.

15 정답 In case → In case of

[해석] 예기치 못한 지연이 있을 경우, 상사에게 알려주세요.

→ in case 뒤에는 절이 나와야 하므로 같은 뜻의 전치사 in case of로 고쳐야 한다.

16 정답 because → because of

[해석] 갑작스러운 정전 때문에 공연이 취소되었다.

→ because 뒤에는 절이 나와야 하므로 같은 뜻의 전치사 because of로 고쳐야 한다.

17 정답 despite → though[although]

[해석] 증거에 신빙성이 없는데도 판사가 그것을 인정했나요?

→ despite 뒤에는 명사가 나와야 하므로 같은 뜻의 접속사 though[although]로 고쳐야 한다.

18 정답 because → because of

[해석] 기상 조건 때문에 회의가 연기되었다.

→ because 뒤에는 절이 나와야 하므로 같은 뜻의 전치사 because of로 고쳐야 한다.

19 정답 In spite of → Though[Although]

[해석] 그는 피곤했지만 계속 일했다.

→ in spite of 뒤에는 명사가 와야 하므로 같은 뜻의 접속사 Though[Although]로 고쳐야 한다.

20 정답 During → While

[해석] 그녀가 발표를 하는 동안, 나는 메모를 했다.

→ during 뒤에는 명사가 와야 하므로 같은 뜻의 접속사 while로 고쳐야 한다.

단원 평가 문제 UNIT 46 ~ UNIT 50

▶ 문제편 p.210~216

정답

01 ③	02 ③	03 ①	04 ④	05 ②

06 for **07** within **08** against

09 with **10** by **11** by **12** in **13** like

14 from **15** about

16 Five boys are swimming across the stream.

17 One of her friends became a famous singer.

18 There is a small park between the two buildings.

19 The service will be stopped until[till] midnight.

20 ⑤ **21** ⑤ **22** ④ **23** ○ **24** into

25 ○ **26** by **27** from **28** for **29** ①

30 ② **31** ② **32** ④ **33** ⑤ **34** ④

35 since **36** between **37** with **38** on

39 from **40** at **41** ① On → By ② until → by

42 ① by → of ② to → for **43** at **44** for

45 on **46** to **47** ⑤ **48** depended on

49 took part in the environmental campaign

50 ashamed of **51** ② **52** ③ **53** ③

54 ③,⑤ **55** ①,② **56** ③ **57** ④

58 They arrived early at the international terminal.

59 She had a quarrel with her brother.

60 The room was already full of students

61 ③ **62** ③ **63** ⑤ **64** at, on, at

65 ③ **66** can lead to serious health problems

67 ②

68 ⓐ The opening hours of the museum is from 9 AM to 6 PM

ⓑ People often take pictures in front of the glass pyramid

---

01 정답 ③ UNIT 46 시간을 나타내는 전치사, UNIT 49 동사+전치사

[해석] • 그는 당뇨병으로 고생한다.

• 나는 다음 주부터 이곳에서 살 예정이다.

→ '~로 고통 받다'는 suffer from으로 쓰고, 시작 시점을 나타낼 때도 전치사 from을 쓴다.

02 정답 ③ UNIT 46 시간을 나타내는 전치사

[해석] • 우리는 여름에 휴가를 갈 것이다.

• 그녀는 3시간 안에 과제를 끝냈다.

→ 계절 앞에 쓰이고 특정 시간 '이내'를 나타내므로 전치사 in을 쓴다.

03 정답 ① UNIT 46 시간을 나타내는 전치사, UNIT 48 방향 및 기타 전치사

[해석] • 그들은 오전 8시까지 공항에 있어야 한다.

• 그는 매일 전철로 출근한다.

→ '8시까지'라는 기한과 교통수단을 나타내므로 전치사 by를 쓴다.

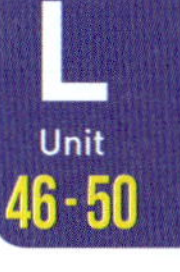

04 [정답] ④　　　　　　　　　UNIT **46** 시간을 나타내는 전치사

[해석] • Smith는 발표 중에 긴장을 느꼈다.
• Hana는 점심시간 동안 요가를 연습했다.
→ 특정한 사건이나 기간 안에 일어난 일을 나타내므로 전치사 during을 쓴다.

05 [정답] ②　　　　　　　　　UNIT **46** 시간을 나타내는 전치사

[해석] ① 그녀는 정오까지 그를 기다렸다.
② 음악 축제는 가을에 개최되었다.
③ 한 남자가 숲을 통과하여 걷고 있다.
④ 우리는 10시에 만나기로 되어 있다.
⑤ 내 휴가가 폭설 때문에 망쳐질 수 있다.
→ ② 숫자를 포함하지 않은 특정 기간을 나타낼 때는 during을 써야 한다.
① '~할 때까지'의 뜻을 나타내는 until ③ '~을 통과하여'라는 뜻을 나타내는 through ④ '~에'라는 뜻으로 시각을 나타내는 at ⑤ '~ 때문에'라는 뜻으로 뒤에 명사(구)가 나오는 because of

06 [정답] for　　　　　　　　　UNIT **48** 방향 및 기타 전치사

[해석] 죄송하지만 저를 위해 문을 잡아주시겠어요?
→ '~을 위해'라는 뜻으로 전치사 for를 써야 한다.

07 [정답] within　　　　　　　　UNIT **46** 시간을 나타내는 전치사

[해석] 온라인 구매는 대부분 그것을 수령한 날로부터 7일 이내에 환불될 수 있다.
→ '(시간) 안에'는 within으로 표현한다.

08 [정답] against　　　　　　　UNIT **48** 방향 및 기타 전치사

[해석] 이 건물에서 담배를 피우는 것은 위법이다.
→ '~에 위반되는'은 against로 쓴다.

09 [정답] with　　　　　　　　　UNIT **48** 방향 및 기타 전치사

[해석] 인도에서는 오른손으로 먹어야 한다.
→ '~을 가지고'라는 뜻으로 도구를 나타내는 전치사는 with이다.

10 [정답] by　　　　　　　　　　UNIT **48** 방향 및 기타 전치사

[해석] 우리가 이 소포를 오늘 항공우편으로 보내면 당신은 금요일 이전에 그것을 받으실 겁니다.
→ 교통, 배송 수단을 말할 때는 by를 쓴다.

11 [정답] by　　　　　　　　　　UNIT **46** 시간을 나타내는 전치사

[해석] 협정에 따르면 그 나라는 2020년까지 수천 톤의 쌀을 수입해야 한다.
→ 쌀 수입을 완료해야 하는 시점을 나타내므로 by를 쓴다.

12 [정답] in　　　　　　　　　　UNIT **48** 방향 및 기타 전치사

[해석] 너는 영어로 의사소통을 할 수 있니?
→ 언어 수단에는 전치사 in을 쓴다.

13 [정답] like　　　　　　　　　UNIT **48** 방향 및 기타 전치사

[해석] 웃을 때 그녀의 웃음소리는 어린 소녀처럼 들린다.
→ '~처럼 들리다'는 sound like라고 쓴다.

14 [정답] from　　　　　　　　　UNIT **48** 방향 및 기타 전치사

[해석] 그 화장지는 재활용 종이로 만들어진다.
→ 원재료가 화학적 변화를 겪을 때는 from을 쓴다.

15 [정답] about　　　　　　　　UNIT **48** 방향 및 기타 전치사

[해석] 그는 해양 동물에 관한 다큐멘터리를 보는 것을 즐긴다.
→ '~에 대해, ~에 관해'라는 뜻의 전치사는 about이다.

16 [정답] Five boys are swimming across the stream.
　　　　　　　　　　　　UNIT **48** 방향 및 기타 전치사

[해석] 다섯 명의 소년이 개울을 헤엄쳐 건너고 있다.
→ '헤엄쳐서 건너다'는 swim across라고 한다.

17 [정답] One of her friends became a famous singer.
　　　　　　　　　　　　UNIT **48** 방향 및 기타 전치사

[해석] 그녀의 친구들 중 한 명이 유명한 가수가 되었다.
→ '~의'라는 뜻으로 소유를 나타내는 전치사는 of이다.

18 [정답] There is a small park between the two buildings.　　UNIT **47** 장소를 나타내는 전치사

[해석] 두 건물 사이에 작은 공원이 있다.
→ '(둘) 사이에'는 between으로 표현한다.

19 [정답] The service will be stopped until[till] midnight.　　UNIT **46** 시간을 나타내는 전치사

[해석] 그 서비스는 자정까지 중단될 것이다.
→ 자정까지 계속 중단된다는 의미이므로 전치사 until[till]을 사용해야 한다.

20 [정답] ⑤　　　　　　　　　UNIT **47** 장소를 나타내는 전치사

[해석] • 그 도로는 아직 공사 중이다.
• Lisa는 세 명의 소녀들 중에서 가장 키가 크다.
→ '공사 중'은 under construction이라고 하고, 셋 이상에서 '~ 사이에, 중에'라는 의미를 나타낼 때는 among을 쓴다. between은 둘 사이를 나타낼 때 쓴다.

21 [정답] ⑤　　　　　　　　　UNIT **46** 시간을 나타내는 전치사

[해석] Kelly는 밤하늘의 별을 바라보는 것을 좋아한다. 저녁을 먹고 나서 그녀는 10분 동안 하늘을 올려다보며 잔디밭에 누워 있다.
→ 숫자를 포함하는 구체적인 기간을 나타낼 때는 전치사 for를 쓴다.

22 [정답] ④　　　　　　　　　UNIT **46** 시간을 나타내는 전치사,
　　　　　　　　　　　　UNIT **47** 장소를 나타내는 전치사

[해석] ① 지금 교실에 있는 사람은 아무도 없다.
② 우리는 여름에 많은 종류의 과일을 먹는다.
③ 내 남동생과 나는 둘 다 7월에 태어났다.
④ 죄송하지만 우리는 일요일에는 문을 닫습니다.
⑤ 현금으로 내면 할인을 받을 수 있다.
→ ④ 요일 앞에는 on을 써야 하고, 나머지에는 모두 in을 쓴다.

23 [정답] ○　　　　　　　　　UNIT **48** 방향 및 기타 전치사

[해석] 그녀는 눈가를 제외한 얼굴을 가리고 있었다.
→ except for는 '~을 제외하고'라는 뜻의 전치사이다.

24 [정답] into　　　　　　　　　UNIT **49** 동사+전치사

[해석] 비가 눈으로 바뀌었다.
→ '~으로 바꾸다'라는 뜻은 change into로 쓴다.

25 [정답] ○　　　　　　　　　UNIT **46** 시간을 나타내는 전치사

[해석] 그들은 크리스마스 휴가 동안 할아버지를 방문해야 할 것이다.
→ 숫자를 포함하지 않은 특정 기간을 말할 때는 during을 쓴다.

26 정답 by　　　　　　　　　　　UNIT **48** 방향 및 기타 전치사

[해석] 그는 휴대 전화를 가지고 있지 않기 때문에 우리는 그에게 이메일로만 연락할 수 있다.
→ 연락 수단을 나타낼 때는 by를 쓴다.

27 정답 from　　　　　　　　　　UNIT **46** 시간을 나타내는 전치사

[해석] 그는 대개 오전 9시부터 오후 6시까지 사무실에 있다.
→ 'A부터 B까지'는 from A to B로 표현한다.

28 정답 for　　　　　　　　　　　UNIT **48** 방향 및 기타 전치사

[해석] 저에게 당신을 만날 기회를 주셔서 감사합니다.
→ '~에 대해 감사하다'는 thank for ~라고 한다.

29 정답 ①　　　　　　　　　　UNIT **47** 장소를 나타내는 전치사

[해석] 내가 도착했을 때 아버지는 문 ② 옆에, ③ 뒤에, ④ 가까이에, ⑤ 앞에 서 있었다.
→ ① on은 접촉한 표면 위에 있음을 나타내므로 문 '위에' 서 있다는 표현은 어색하다.

30 정답 ②
　　　UNIT **46** 시간을 나타내는 전치사, UNIT **47** 장소를 나타내는 전치사

[해석] 아이들이 소나무 ① 근처에서 ③ 뒤에서 ④ 주변에서 ⑤ 가까이에서 놀고 있다.
→ ② from은 '~부터'라는 의미이므로 이 문장에서의 쓰임이 어색하다.

31 정답 ②　　　　　　　　　　UNIT **48** 방향 및 기타 전치사

[해석] 그들은 그 가게에 가기 위해 거리 ① 위를 ③ 를 따라 ④ 를 가로질러 ⑤ 를 통과해서 걸었다.
→ ② in은 '안에, 안으로'라는 의미이므로 이 문장에서의 쓰임이 어색하다.

32 정답 ④　　UNIT **46** 시간을 나타내는 전치사, UNIT **49** 동사+전치사

[해석] A: 이 문제를 다루실 수 있나요?
B: 물론이죠! 하지만 저는 다음 몇 시간 동안 바쁠 거예요.
→ ④ deal with는 '~을 다루다'라는 뜻이므로 첫 번째 빈칸에는 with, 다음 몇 시간 '동안'이라는 뜻이므로 두 번째 빈칸에는 for가 와야 한다.

33 정답 ⑤　　　　　　　　　　UNIT **47** 장소를 나타내는 전치사

[해석] A: 개가 문 앞에 앉아서 나가려고 기다리고 있어.
B: 나는 고양이가 소파 뒤에 숨어서 개에게 다가가는 걸 봤어!
→ ⑤ 개가 문 '앞에' 있음을 나타내므로 첫 번째 빈칸에는 in front of, 고양이가 소파 '뒤에' 있음을 나타내므로 두 번째 빈칸에는 behind가 와야 한다.

34 정답 ④　　　　　　　　　　UNIT **48** 방향 및 기타 전치사

[해석] A: 우리는 오두막에 가기 위해 숲을 통과해서 차를 몰았어.
B: 멋지다! 너희는 강도 건너갔어?
→ ④ 숲을 '통과해서' 갔다고 했으므로 첫 번째 빈칸에는 through, 강을 '가로질러' 건넜음을 나타내야 하므로 두 번째 빈칸에는 across가 와야 한다.

35 정답 since　　　　　　　　　　UNIT **46** 시간을 나타내는 전치사

[해석] 그는 지난달 이래로 열심히 일해왔다.
→ since는 '~이래로'라는 뜻으로 쓰인다.

36 정답 between　　　　　　　　　UNIT **47** 장소를 나타내는 전치사

[해석] 그녀는 Tom과 Jenny 사이에 서 있었다.
→ 'A와 B 사이에'는 between A and B로 쓴다.

37 정답 with　　　　　　　　　　UNIT **48** 방향 및 기타 전치사

[해석] 너의 책상은 종이와 공책들로 꽉 차 있다.
→ '~로'는 with를 쓴다.

38 정답 on　　　　　　　　　　　　UNIT **49** 동사+전치사

[해석] 발표자는 청중에게 발표 내용에 집중하라고 요청했다.
→ '~에 집중하다'는 focus on으로 나타낸다.

39 정답 from　　　　　　　　　　UNIT **47** 장소를 나타내는 전치사

[해석] 부상당한 새는 지붕에서 날아 숲속으로 사라졌다.
→ 출발 지점을 나타낼 때는 from을 쓴다.

40 정답 at　　　　　　　　　　　UNIT **46** 시간을 나타내는 전치사

[해석] 세미나는 오전 9시 30분 정각에 시작됩니다. 그러니 늦지 마세요.
→ 특정한 시각을 나타낼 때는 at을 쓴다.

41 정답 ① On → By ② until → by
　　　　　　　　　　　　UNIT **46** 시간을 나타내는 전치사

[해석] 내일 이맘때쯤 우리는 뉴욕에 있을 겁니다. 그러니 그 일을 오늘 6시까지 끝내주실 수 있나요?
→ '이맘때쯤'이라고 할 때는 by this time이라고 하며, '~을 언제까지 끝내다'라는 완료의 의미일 때는 「by+정해진 시간」으로 쓴다. until은 '그때까지 계속 한다'는 의미이다.

42 정답 ① by → of ② to → for
　　　　　　UNIT **50** 형용사+전치사, 주의해야 할 전치사

[해석] 그녀는 회의 중 자신의 행동을 부끄러워했지만, 뒤따른 혼란에 대해 자신에게도 책임이 있다는 것을 알고 있었다.
→ '~을 부끄러워하다'를 나타낼 때는 be ashamed of를 써야 하므로 by를 of로 고쳐 쓴다. '~에 책임이 있다'를 나타낼 때는 be responsible for를 써야 하므로 to를 for로 고쳐 쓴다.

43 정답 at　　　　　UNIT **50** 형용사+전치사, 주의해야 할 전치사

[해석] 그녀는 다른 사람들 앞에서 노래하는 것을 항상 잘해 왔다.
→ '~을 잘하다'는 be good at으로 나타낸다.

44 정답 for　　　　　　　　　　　　UNIT **49** 동사+전치사

[해석] 우리는 버스를 30분 동안 기다렸다.
→ '~을 기다리다'는 wait for로 나타낸다.

45 정답 on　　　　　　　　　　　　UNIT **49** 동사+전치사

[해석] 그는 그 일을 끝내기 위해 팀에 의존했다.
→ '~에 의존하다'는 depend on으로 나타낸다.

46 정답 to　　　　　　　　　　　　UNIT **49** 동사+전치사

[해석] 나는 선택을 하기 전에 너의 조언을 들었다.
→ '~을 듣다'는 listen to로 나타낸다.

47 정답 ⑤　　　　UNIT **50** 형용사+전치사, 주의해야 할 전치사

[해석] ① 나는 추리소설 읽는 것을 좋아한다.
② 그녀는 언니의 재능을 질투한다.
③ 우리는 우리 팀의 성장을 자랑스럽게 생각한다.
④ 그들은 일찍 일어나는 데 익숙하다.

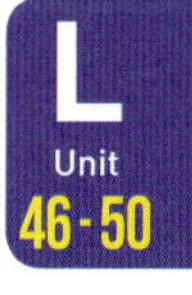

⑤ 그는 어려운 수학 문제를 풀 수 있다.

→ ⑤ '~을 할 수 있다'는 be capable of로 나타내므로 to를 of로 고쳐야 한다.

48 정답 **depended on**　　　UNIT **49** 동사+전치사

[해석] 그의 시험 성공은 그가 얼마나 공부했는지에 달려 있었다.

→ '~에 달려 있다'는 depend on으로 나타낸다.

49 정답 **took part in the environmental campaign**
　　　UNIT **49** 동사+전치사

[해석] 그들은 지난 주말 환경 캠페인에 참여했다.

→ '~에 참여하다'는 take part in으로 나타낸다.

50 정답 **ashamed of**
　　　UNIT **50** 형용사+전치사, 주의해야 할 전치사

[해석] 나는 나의 부주의한 실수를 정말 부끄러워했다.

→ '~을 부끄러워하다'는 be ashamed of로 나타낸다.

51 정답 ②　　　UNIT **49** 동사+전치사

[해석] ① 그녀는 동료에게 사과했다.

② 그녀는 그 문제를 다루기로 동의했다.

③ 우리는 가장 가까운 역까지 걸었다.

④ 나는 교수님께 시험에 대해 이야기했다.

⑤ 그는 공지를 주의 깊게 들었다.

→ ②의 to는 address와 함께 to부정사로 쓰였다. 나머지는 모두 '~에게'라는 뜻의 전치사로 쓰였다.

52 정답 ③　　　UNIT **48** 방향 및 기타 전치사

[해석] ① 나는 너의 잠재력 중 약 90%를 믿는다.

② 그는 커튼에서 약 5피트 떨어진 곳에 서 있었다.

③ 이번 달 예산에 대해 이야기하자.

④ 그들은 친척 약 10명과 함께 왔다.

⑤ 그녀는 숙제에 약 3시간을 쓴다.

→ ③의 about은 '~에 대해'라는 뜻의 전치사로 쓰였다. 나머지는 모두 '약, 대략'이라는 뜻의 부사로 쓰였다.

53 정답 ③　　　UNIT **50** 형용사+전치사, 주의해야 할 전치사

[해석] 그녀는 행사를 조직하는 것과 사람들과 일하는 것을 정말 잘한다.

→ '~을 잘하다'는 be good at으로 나타낸다.

54 정답 ③, ⑤　　　UNIT **47** 장소를 나타내는 전치사,
　　　UNIT **50** 형용사+전치사, 주의해야 할 전치사

[해석] ① 그녀는 도움을 받기 위해 팀원들에게 의존한다.

② 고양이는 아무도 보지 않을 때 책상 위로 뛰어올랐다.

③ 우리는 1시간 전에 기차역에 도착했다.

④ 시험은 월요일 아침에 예정되어 있다.

⑤ 나는 너의 성과가 자랑스럽다.

→ ③ 기차역이라는 지점에 도착했음을 나타내야 하므로 on을 at으로 고쳐야 한다. ⑤ '~을 자랑스러워하다'는 be proud of로 나타내야 하므로, on을 of로 고쳐야 한다.

55 정답 ①, ②　　　UNIT **46** 시간을 나타내는 전치사,
　　　UNIT **48** 방향 및 기타 전치사

[해석] ① 그는 어젯밤 독일로 떠났다.

② 나는 두 시간 넘게 기다렸다.

③ 이 편지는 나의 조부모님을 위한 것이다.

④ 그것은 개인적인 성장을 위해 중요하다.

⑤ 그녀는 초대 손님들을 위해 저녁을 준비했다.

→ ①에서 for는 '~을 향해'라는 뜻으로 방향을 나타낸다. ②에서 for는 기간을 나타낸다. 나머지는 모두 for가 '~을 위해'라는 뜻으로 쓰였다.

56 정답 ③　　　UNIT **49** 동사+전치사

[해석] ① 가방이 바닥 위에 있다.

② 그는 거리를 가로질러 뛰어갔다.

③ 그녀는 심각한 병으로 인해 죽었다.

④ 그것은 철과 플라스틱으로 만들어졌다.

⑤ 우리는 빗속에서 버스를 기다렸다.

→ die of는 '~로 인해 죽다'라는 뜻으로 원인을 나타내는 표현이다.

57 정답 ④　　　UNIT **48** 방향 및 기타 전치사

[해석] 그녀는 조용히 박물관에 들어갔다.

① 그녀는 박물관에서 빠르게 나왔다.

② 그녀는 박물관 위를 천천히 걸었다.

③ 그녀는 박물관 건물을 뛰어넘었다.

④ 그녀는 조용히 박물관 안으로 걸어 들어갔다.

⑤ 그녀는 조심스럽게 박물관 아래로 움직였다.

→ enter는 '들어가다'라는 뜻이므로, '안으로'를 나타내는 into가 함께 쓰여야 한다.

58 정답 **They arrived early at the international terminal.**　　　UNIT **47** 장소를 나타내는 전치사

→ '~에 도착하다'는 arrive at으로 나타낸다. at 뒤에 장소를 쓴다.

59 정답 **She had a quarrel with her brother.**
　　　UNIT **48** 방향 및 기타 전치사

→ 남동생과 말다툼을 벌였다고 했으므로 with her brother로 쓴다.

60 정답 **The room was already full of students**
　　　UNIT **50** 형용사+전치사, 주의해야 할 전치사

→ '~로 가득 차 있다'는 「be full of + 명사」로 나타낸다. 부사 already는 be동사와 full 사이에 위치한다.

61 정답 ③　　　UNIT **46** 시간을 나타내는 전치사

[해석] 유미는 겨울 동안 호주에 갈 예정이기 때문에 불안해했다. '나는 친구도 없이 무인도에 있는 사람처럼 혼자일 거야. 나는 그곳에서 무엇을 해야 할지 모르겠어.'라고 그녀는 생각했다. 호주로 떠나기 전에 유미는 그 나라에 대해 더 알고 싶었다. 그녀는 인터넷 검색을 했고, 다행히 아주 좋은 웹사이트를 찾았다. 그 사이트에서 그녀는 그곳의 사람들과 연락을 하기 위한 링크를 찾아서 이메일을 보냈다. 곧 그녀는 도움이 되는 답장을 받았다.

→ (A) 숫자를 포함하지 않은 특정 기간을 말할 때는 during을 쓴다. (B) 뒤에 명사 someone이 왔으므로 접속사 as if가 아니라 전치사 just like가 적절하다. (C) 동사가 전치사의 목적어로 올 때 동명사가 와야 한다.

62 정답 ③　　　UNIT **46** 시간을 나타내는 전치사,
UNIT **47** 장소를 나타내는 전치사, UNIT **48** 방향 및 기타 전치사

[해석] Emily는 조용히 교실에 들어갔고, 그녀가 아무도 방해하지 않기를 바랐다. 그녀는 칠판 바로 앞에 자리를 잡고 정중하게 미소 지었다. 수업은 오전 9시에 시작되기로 예정되어 있었고, 선생님은 제시간에 도착했다.

→ (A) 교실 '안으로' 들어갔음을 나타내므로 into가 적절하다. (B) 칠판 바로 '앞'을 나타내므로 in front of로 쓴다. (C) 정확한 시간을 말하므로 at이 적절하다.

63 [정답] ⑤　　　　　　UNIT 50 형용사+전치사, 주의해야 할 전치사

[해석] 생일 파티!
누구를 위해: Miya Edwards / 날짜: 8월 18일 / 시각: 저녁 6시 45분 / 장소: David 레스토랑 / 협찬: ABC Society
Sophie Yu에게 010 – 1234 – 5678로 회신해 주세요.
① Miya는 그녀의 생일을 기다리고 있다.
② 사람들은 파티에서 저녁을 먹을 수 있다.
③ ABC Society는 파티의 주최자이다.
④ Sophie Yu는 파티를 관리하는 책임이 있다.
⑤ Miya는 파티가 그녀의 친구들로 붐비기를 원할지도 모른다.
→ ⑤ '~로 붐비다'는 be crowded with로 나타낸다. 따라서 in을 with로 고쳐야 한다.

64 [정답] at, on, at　　　UNIT 46 시간을 나타내는 전치사, UNIT 47 장소를 나타내는 전치사

[해석] Miya를 위한 생일 파티는 David 레스토랑에서 8월 18일 저녁 6시 45분에 열릴 것이다.
→ 「at+작은 장소」이므로 David restaurant 앞에는 at, 「on+날짜」이므로 August 18th 앞에는 on, 「at+시각」이므로 6:45 p.m. 앞에는 at이 적절하다.

65 [정답] ③　　　　　　UNIT 49 동사+전치사

[해석] 좋은 수면의 질은 전반적인 건강과 웰빙을 유지하는 데 필수적이다. 나쁜 수면은 심장 질환과 당뇨병 같은 심각한 건강 문제를 초래할 수 있다. 수면의 질을 향상시키기 위해서는 잠자기 전에 카페인을 피하는 것이 중요하다. 많은 사람들이 불면증에 시달리며, 이는 잠들기 어렵게 만든다. 규칙적으로 운동하는 것은 밤에 더 잘 잘 수 있도록 도와준다. 스크린에서 나오는 빛은 밤늦게 사용할 경우 수면에 방해가 될 수 있다. 차갑고 조용한 환경에서 자는 것은 당신의 수면 질을 개선할 수 있다.
→ '~을 겪다'는 struggle with로 나타낸다. 따라서 ③ of를 with로 고쳐야 한다.

66 [정답] can lead to serious health problems
UNIT 49 동사+전치사

→ '~로 이끌다', '~로 이어지다'는 lead to로 나타낸다.

67 [정답] ②　　　　　　UNIT 48 방향 및 기타 전치사

[해석] 루브르 박물관은 프랑스 파리에 위치해 있다. 이 박물관은 세계에서 가장 유명한 박물관 중 하나이다. 박물관에는 Leonardo da Vinci와 Vincent van Gogh 같은 유명한 예술가들의 작품을 포함한 방대한 예술 컬렉션이 있다. 많은 방문객들이 매일 루브르에 와서 그 명작들을 감상한다. 박물관의 개장 시간은 오전 9시부터 오후 6시까지이며, 화요일은 제외이다. 모나리자는 박물관 내의 특별한 전시실에 전시되어 있다. 사람들은 종종 박물관의 유리 피라미드 앞에서 사진을 찍곤 하는데, 이 피라미드는 현대적인 건축물이다.
→ ② Leonardo da Vinci와 Vincent van Gogh '같은' 유명한 예술가들을 언급하므로 from을 like로 고쳐야 한다.

68 [정답] ⓐ The opening hours of the museum is from 9 AM to 6 PM
ⓑ People often take pictures in front of the glass pyramid
UNIT 46 시간을 나타내는 전치사, UNIT 47 장소를 나타내는 전치사

→ ⓐ 'A부터 B까지'는 from A to B로 나타낸다. ⓑ '~앞에'는 in front of로 나타낸다.

 M 부정사

UNIT 51 to부정사의 명사적 용법

> **개념 확인 문제 정답**　　　　　　▶ 문제편 p.219
>
> 01 주어　02 보어　03 주어　04 목적어
> 05 목적어　06 보어　07 목적어　08 to accept
> 09 to skip　10 to save　11 to move
> 12 It is essential to plan　13 it easy to understand
> 14 tell me where to find
> 15 how to reset the password
> 16 it important to invest

01 [정답] 주어

[해석] 외국어에 통달하는 것은 어려운 일이다.
→ To master는 동사 is의 주어 역할을 한다.

02 [정답] 보어

[해석] 내 직업은 중학교 학생들을 위한 책을 만드는 것이다.
→ to make는 is의 주격 보어로 쓰였다.

03 [정답] 주어

[해석] 물 없이 사막에서 살아남는 것은 불가능하다.
→ It이 가주어이고 to survive가 진주어이다.

04 [정답] 목적어

[해석] 부실한 식습관은 건강을 유지하는 것을 어렵게 만들 것이다.
→ make의 목적어로 가목적어 it과 진목적어 to stay가 쓰였다.

05 [정답] 목적어

[해석] 그의 부모는 그에게 분노를 조절하는 방법을 가르쳐야 한다.
→ how to control은 teach의 직접목적어로 쓰였다.

06 [정답] 보어

[해석] 그는 그녀가 영어 말하기 대회에 참가하기를 원한다.
→ to take는 wants의 목적격 보어로 쓰였다.

07 [정답] 목적어

[해석] 그녀는 그녀의 반 친구들 중 한 명과 집을 같이 쓰기로 결정했다.
→ to share는 동사 decided의 목적어로 쓰였다.

08 정답 to accept

[해석] 그들은 새 계약 조건을 받아들이기를 거부했다.

→ refuse는 to부정사를 목적어로 취하는 동사이다.

09 정답 to skip

[해석] 그녀는 이미 충분히 배가 불러서 후식을 건너뛰기로 선택했다.

→ choose는 to부정사를 목적어로 취하는 동사이다.

10 정답 to save

[해석] 우리는 돈을 모아서 새로운 게임기를 사려고 계획하고 있다.

→ plan은 to부정사를 목적어로 취하는 동사이다.

11 정답 to move

[해석] 그들은 더 나은 기회를 위해 더 큰 도시로 이사하기로 결정했다.

→ decide는 to부정사를 목적어로 취하는 동사이다.

12 정답 It is essential to plan

→ 문장의 주어 to plan for your future가 문장 뒤로 보내진 가주어-진주어 구문이다.

13 정답 it easy to understand

→ 문장의 목적어 to understand the problem이 문장 뒤로 보내진 가목적어-진목적어 구문이다.

14 정답 tell me where to find

→ '어디에서 ~할지'는 「where + to부정사」로 표현한다.

15 정답 how to reset the password

→ '어떻게 ~할지'는 「how + to부정사」로 표현한다.

16 정답 it important to invest

→ 문장의 목적어 to invest in renewable energy가 문장 뒤로 보내진 가목적어-진목적어 구문이다.

UNIT 52 to부정사의 형용사적 용법

개념 확인 문제 정답 ▶ 문제편 **p.221**

01 desk to work at
02 place to live
03 pet to bring her
04 work to finish
05 book to read
06 There is nothing to be afraid of.
07 They have little to eat.
08 I need a piece of paper to write on.
09 She wants to borrow a pen to write with.
10 He has lots of friends to play with
11 was destined to marry him as her parents wished
12 is going to visit the headquarters tomorrow
13 have to follow the rules during the exam
14 are able to cancel the event

01 정답 desk to work at

[해석] 나는 내 사무실에서 일할 책상이 필요하다.

→ a desk를 to work at이 뒤에서 수식한다. 이때 a desk는 전치사 at의 목적어이므로 at은 to work 뒤에 와야 한다.

02 정답 place to live

[해석] 그는 대학 근처에 살 곳을 찾았다.

→ a place를 to live가 뒤에서 수식한다.

03 정답 pet to bring her

[해석] 그녀는 집에서 그녀에게 행복을 가져다줄 반려동물을 원한다.

→ a pet을 to bring이 뒤에서 수식한다.

04 정답 work to finish

[해석] 그는 마감일 전에 끝낼 일이 많다.

→ work를 to finish가 뒤에서 수식한다.

05 정답 book to read

[해석] 나는 다음 주 휴가 동안 읽을 책이 필요하다.

→ a book을 to read가 뒤에서 수식한다.

06 정답 There is nothing to be afraid of.

→ afraid는 형용사이므로 to부정사로 쓸 때 be가 필요하다.

07 정답 They have little to eat.

→ to부정사는 명사를 뒤에서 수식한다. little은 '거의 없음'이라는 뜻의 명사로 쓸 수 있다.

08 정답 I need a piece of paper to write on.

→ 수식받는 명사 a piece of paper와 수식하는 to부정사 write의 관계에서 a piece of paper는 write의 목적어가 될 수 없으므로 write 뒤에 전치사 on을 반드시 써야 한다.

09 정답 She wants to borrow a pen to write with.

→ 수식받는 명사 a pen과 수식하는 to부정사 write의 관계에서 a pen은 write의 목적어가 될 수 없으므로 write 뒤에 전치사 with를 반드시 써야 한다.

10 정답 He has lots of friends to play with

→ 수식받는 명사 friends와 수식하는 to부정사 play의 관계에서 friends는 play의 목적어가 될 수 없으므로 play 뒤에 '~와 같이'라는 뜻의 전치사 with를 반드시 써야 한다.

11 정답 was destined to marry him as her parents wished

[해석] 그녀는 부모님의 바람대로 그와 결혼할 운명이었다.

→ 「be동사+to부정사」는 '운명'의 의미를 나타낼 수 있다.

12 정답 is going to visit the headquarters tomorrow

[해석] CEO는 내일 본사를 방문할 예정이다.

→ 「be동사+to부정사」는 '예정'의 의미를 나타낼 수 있다.

13 정답 have to follow the rules during the exam

[해석] 학생들은 시험 중 규칙을 따라야 한다.

→ 「be동사+to부정사」는 '의무'의 의미를 나타낼 수 있다.

14 정답 are able to cancel the event

[해석] 그들은 그 행사를 취소할 가능성이 있다.

→ 「be동사+to부정사」는 '가능'의 의미를 나타낼 수 있다.

개념 확인 문제 정답　　　　▶ 문제편 p.223

01 판단의 근거　　**02** 결과　　**03** 형용사 수식

04 원인, 이유　　**05** 목적　　**06** 목적

07 그는 그 상자를 들 만큼 강하지 않다. (형용사 수식)

08 우리는 교통체증을 피하기 위해 일찍 떠나야 한다. (목적)

09 저렇게 소리치는 것을 보니 그녀는 신이 났나 보다. (판단의 근거)

10 나의 할머니께서는 고향을 떠나게 되어 슬퍼하셨다. (원인, 이유)

11 나는 컴퓨터를 고치려고 했지만 결국 더 나쁘게 만들었다. (결과)

12 upset to find out

13 excited to be promoted

14 to help, dogs

01 정답 **판단의 근거**

[해석] 그렇게 말하다니 그녀는 아주 똑똑하다.

→ '~을 보니, ~하다니'로 해석하며, 판단의 근거를 나타내고 있다.

02 정답 **결과**

[해석] 나의 할머니는 91세까지 사셨다.

→ 「live to be+나이」는 '~세까지 살다'라는 뜻으로 to부정사 결과 구문이다.

03 정답 **형용사 수식**

[해석] 이 컴퓨터 프로그램은 사용하기에 쉽다.

→ to use가 형용사 easy를 수식하고 있다. '~하기에'로 해석된다.

04 정답 **원인, 이유**

[해석] 나는 결승 경기를 직접 보게 되어 흥분된다.

→ to부정사 앞에 감정을 나타내는 형용사가 있고, '~하게 되어'로 해석되므로 감정의 원인을 나타낸다.

05 정답 **목적**

[해석] 그 탐정은 깨어 있기 위해 커피를 많이 마셨다.

→ '~하기 위해'라는 뜻의 목적을 나타낸다.

06 정답 **목적**

[해석] 부모들은 서로를 더 잘 알기 위해 자녀들과 더 많이 대화해야 한다.

→ '~하기 위해'라는 뜻의 목적을 나타낸다.

07 정답 **그는 그 상자를 들 만큼 강하지 않다. (형용사 수식)**

→ to lift가 strong enough를 수식하며 무엇하기에 충분히 강하지 않은지를 나타낸다.

08 정답 **우리는 교통체증을 피하기 위해 일찍 떠나야 한다. (목적)**

→ to avoid가 '피하기 위해'라는 목적을 나타낸다.

09 정답 **저렇게 소리치는 것을 보니 그녀는 신이 났나 보다. (판단의 근거)**

→ to shout가 excited라고 판단한 근거를 나타낸다.

10 정답 **나의 할머니께서는 고향을 떠나게 되어 슬퍼하셨다. (원인, 이유)**

→ to leave가 감정의 형용사 sad의 원인을 나타낸다.

11 정답 **나는 컴퓨터를 고치려고 했지만 결국 더 나쁘게 만들었다. (결과)**

→ to make가 결과를 나타낸다.

12 정답 **upset to find out**

→ to find out이 감정의 형용사 upset의 원인을 나타낸다.

13 정답 **excited to be promoted**

→ to be promoted가 감정의 형용사 excited의 원인을 나타낸다.

14 정답 **to help, dogs**

→ to help가 '돕기 위해'라는 목적을 나타낸다.

단원 평가 문제　UNIT 51 ~ UNIT 53　▶ 문제편 p.224~225

정답

01 주어　**02** 목적어　**03** 주어　**04** 보어　**05** 보어

06 ④　**07** ⑤　**08** ②　**09** ⑤　**10** ②

11 ⑤

12 It is difficult to solve this matter alone.

13 It is not a good idea to skip breakfast.

14 It is often dangerous to ride a motorbike.

15 ④　**16** ②　**17** ④　**18** ③

01 정답 **주어**　　UNIT 51 to부정사의 명사적 용법

[해석] 이 구역 주변에 주차하는 것은 힘들다.

→ It은 가주어이고, to park around this area는 이 문장의 진주어이다.

02 정답 **목적어**　　UNIT 51 to부정사의 명사적 용법

[해석] 우리는 그 작가를 다시 만나기를 기대했다.

→ 동사 expected의 목적어로 쓰였고 명사적 용법에 해당한다.

03 정답 **주어**　　UNIT 51 to부정사의 명사적 용법

[해석] 나는 진실을 조사하는 것이 우리의 의무라고 생각한다.

→ think의 목적어절에 가주어 it이 왔고, to investigate는 진주어이다.

04 정답 **보어**　　UNIT 51 to부정사의 명사적 용법

[해석] 역사를 공부하는 이유는 과거로부터 배우기 위함이다.

→ 동사 is의 보어로 쓰였고 명사적 용법에 해당한다.

05 정답 **보어**　　UNIT 51 to부정사의 명사적 용법

[해석] 우리가 기억해야만 하는 유일한 것은 우리가 지금 가지고 있는 것에 감사하는 것이다.

→ 동사 is의 보어로 쓰였고 명사적 용법에 해당한다.

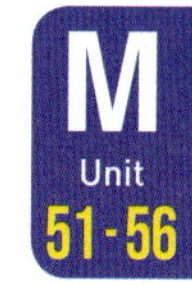

06 정답 ④   UNIT **53** to부정사의 부사적 용법

[해석] 그녀는 그곳에서 그를 보게 되어 놀랐다.
→ ④ to see가 감정의 형용사 surprised의 원인을 나타낸다.

07 정답 ⑤   UNIT **51** to부정사의 명사적 용법

[해석] 저녁으로 무엇을 먹을지가 아직 결정되지 않았다.
→ '저녁으로 무엇을 먹을지'가 주어가 되어야 하는 문장이므로 ⑤「의문사 + to부정사」가 와야 한다.

08 정답 ②   UNIT **51** to부정사의 명사적 용법

[해석] 안전벨트를 착용하지 않고 운전하는 것은 위험하다.
→ 주어 자리에 가주어 It이 왔고, 진주어 ② to drive가 보어 뒤에 오는 것이 알맞다.

09 정답 ⑤   UNIT **51** to부정사의 명사적 용법

[해석] ① 그녀는 다른 사람을 돕게 되어 기쁘다.
② 그녀는 너무 피곤해서 외출할 수 없었다.
③ 그는 시험에 합격하기 위해 열심히 공부했다.
④ 그들은 축구를 하기 위해 공원에 갔다.
⑤ 나는 내일 박물관을 방문할 계획이다.
→ ⑤은 동사(plan)의 목적어로 쓰인 명사적 용법이고 나머지는 모두 부사적 용법이다.

10 정답 ②   UNIT **52** to부정사의 형용사적 용법

[해석] ① 그녀의 제안은 휴식을 취하는 것이다.
② 나는 오늘 끝내야 할 일이 많다.
③ 다른 사람을 돕는 것은 고귀한 일이다.
④ 우리는 그가 금요일까지 보고서를 마칠 것으로 기대한다.
⑤ 너는 공항으로 언제 출발하는지를 알고 있니?
→ ②은 명사(a lot of work)를 수식하는 형용사적 용법이고 나머지는 모두 명사적 용법이다.

11 정답 ⑤   UNIT **53** to부정사의 부사적 용법

[해석] ① 나는 곧 너를 만나기를 희망한다.
② Minju는 추리 소설을 읽는 것을 좋아한다.
③ 그들은 이번 주말에 등산을 가기로 결정했다.
④ Jane은 피아노를 치는 법을 배우고 싶어 한다.
⑤ 그는 파티에서 친구들을 만나서 기뻤다.
→ ⑤은 원인을 나타내는 부사적 용법이고, 나머지는 모두 명사적 용법이다.

12 정답 It is difficult to solve this matter alone.
      UNIT **51** to부정사의 명사적 용법

→ solve 이하가 진주어 to부정사가 되고, 주격 보어에 해당하는 difficult가 It is 다음에 오는 구조로 쓴다.

13 정답 It is not a good idea to skip breakfast.
      UNIT **51** to부정사의 명사적 용법

→ skip 이하가 진주어 to부정사가 되고, 주격 보어에 해당하는 a good idea가 It is not 다음에 오는 구조로 써야 한다.

14 정답 It is often dangerous to ride a motorbike.
      UNIT **51** to부정사의 명사적 용법

→ ride 이하가 진주어 to부정사가 되고, often dangerous가 It is 다음에 오는 구조로 써야 한다.

15 정답 ④   UNIT **53** to부정사의 부사적 용법

→ He tiptoed into the room in order not to disturb anyone.으로 쓸 수 있으므로 ⓒ에는 ④ not이 들어간다.

16 정답 ②   UNIT **51** to부정사의 명사적 용법

[해석] ① 여러분 모두를 만나서 반갑습니다.
② 잘 말하는 것보다 잘 행동하는 것이 더 낫다.
③ 그녀는 첫 번째 기차를 타기 위해 일찍 일어났다.
④ 이 과정을 등록하려면 무엇을 해야 하나요?
⑤ 우리는 좋은 결과를 얻기 위해 매우 열심히 일했다.
→ ②의 to do는 가주어 ~ 진주어 구문에서 진주어 자리에 온 명사적 용법의 to부정사이다.

17 정답 ④   UNIT **53** to부정사의 부사적 용법

[해석] 나는 나의 어머니가 세상에서 가장 지혜로운 여성이라고 말할 수 있지만, 때때로 잊어버리시곤 한다. 몇 주 전, 어머니와 나는 외출할 준비가 되어 있었다. 어머니께서는 나를 역까지 태워다 주기 위해 주차장에서 기다리겠다고 말씀하셨다. 하지만 내가 내려갔을 때, 어머니는 어디에도 계시지 않았다. 결국 나는 기차를 놓치지 않기 위해 제시간에 역에 도착하려 버스를 타야 했다. 어머니께 전화를 시도했지만, 어머니의 전화는 꺼져 있었다.
→ ④ 목적을 나타내는 to부정사는 so as[in order] to로 바꿔쓸 수 있으며, 이때 부정 표현은 so as[in order] not to이다.
①, ⑤ 명사적 용법의 to부정사 ②, ③ 부사적 용법의 to부정사

18 정답 ③   UNIT **51** to부정사의 명사적 용법

[해석] 6개월 전에 Evan은 한국어를 공부하기 위해 한국에 왔다. Evan은 여름옷을 충분히 가져오지 않았기 때문에 티셔츠와 반바지를 좀 사야 했다. 하지만 그는 어디로 쇼핑을 가야 할지 알지 못했다. 그는 몇 명의 한국 친구들에게 어디에서 품질 좋은 옷을 싼 가격에 살 수 있는지 물었다. 그들은 할인 매장을 추천해 주었고 그에게 그가 원한다면 그들과 같이 가자고 말했다.
→ ③ know는 「의문사+to부정사」를 목적어로 취할 수 있다. 따라서 장소를 나타내는 의문사 where를 사용하여 where to go라고 써야 한다.
① 부사적 용법의 to부정사 ② needed의 목적어인 to부정사 ④ 목적어절을 이끄는 의문사 where ⑤ told의 목적격 보어인 to부정사

UNIT **54** 원형부정사, to부정사의 의미상 주어

01 I heard her yell
02 I didn't see him leave the building.
03 Enough sunlight will let the plants grow better.
04 helped the team to clean up
05 for   **06** of   **07** for   **08** for   **09** for
10 of   **11** of   **12** of them → for them
13 to print → print   **14** to get → get 또는 getting
15 invest → to invest **16** for you → of you
17 to singing → sing 또는 singing
18 clean → to clean

01 정답 **I heard her yell**

[해석] 나는 그녀가 몇 분 전에 소리 지르는 것을 들었다.

→ '~이 …하는 것을 듣다'는 「hear+목적어+원형부정사」로 쓴다.

02 정답 **I didn't see him leave the building.**

[해석] 나는 그가 건물에서 나가는 것을 보지 못했다.

→ '~이 …하는 것을 보다'는 「see+목적어+원형부정사」로 쓴다.

03 정답 **Enough sunlight will let the plants grow better.**

[해석] 충분한 햇빛은 그 식물들이 더 잘 자라게 해 줄 것이다.

→ '~이 …하게 해 주다'는 「let+목적어+원형부정사」로 쓴다.

04 정답 **helped the team to clean up**

[해석] 자원봉사자들은 큰 행사가 끝난 후 팀이 청소하도록 도왔다.

→ '~이 …하는 것을 돕다'는 「help+목적어+원형부정사 또는 to부정사」로 쓴다.

05 정답 **for**

[해석] 그가 글씨를 잘 쓰는 것은 어렵다.

→ to부정사의 의미상 주어는 「for + 목적격」으로 쓴다.

06 정답 **of**

[해석] 네가 그렇게 쉬운 시험에서 떨어지다니 어리석었다.

→ foolish는 사람의 성질을 나타내는 형용사이므로 의미상 주어는 「of + 목적격」으로 쓴다.

07 정답 **for**

[해석] 그들이 자녀를 학대하는 것은 괜찮지 않다.

→ to부정사의 의미상 주어는 「for + 목적격」으로 쓴다.

08 정답 **for**

[해석] 그들이 내일까지 돌아오는 것은 불가능하다.

→ to부정사의 의미상 주어는 「for + 목적격」으로 쓴다.

09 정답 **for**

[해석] 나는 주말에 일찍 일어나는 것이 정말 어렵다.

→ to부정사의 의미상 주어는 「for + 목적격」으로 쓴다.

10 정답 **of**

[해석] 그가 그의 친구의 실수를 용서하는 것은 아주 관대했다.

→ generous는 사람의 성격을 나타내는 형용사이므로 의미상 주어는 「of + 목적격」으로 쓴다.

11 정답 **of**

[해석] 그녀가 모든 일을 너에게 남겨 두고 집에 간 것은 이기적이었다.

→ selfish는 사람의 성격을 나타내는 형용사이므로 의미상 주어는 「of + 목적격」으로 쓴다.

12 정답 **of them → for them**

[해석] 그들이 앞으로 나아갈 때이다.

→ to부정사의 의미상 주어는 「for + 목적격」으로 쓴다.

13 정답 **to print → print**

[해석] 그녀는 조수에게 모든 보고서를 출력하게 했다.

→ 사역동사는 목적격 보어로 원형부정사를 취하므로 print가 알맞다.

14 정답 **to get → get 또는 getting**

[해석] 너는 몇 명의 사람들이 그 차에 타는 것을 보았니?

→ 지각동사 see는 목적격 보어로 원형부정사나 현재분사를 취한다.

15 정답 **invest → to invest**

[해석] 그가 금에 그의 돈을 투자한 것은 아주 영리했다.

→ 진주어 역할을 하는 것은 to부정사나 that절이다. to부정사의 의미상 주어 of him이 있으므로 invest는 to부정사의 형태로 써야 한다.

16 정답 **for you → of you**

[해석] 네가 그것을 다시 생각해 보기 위해 시간을 좀 가진 것은 현명했다.

→ wise는 사람의 성질을 나타내는 형용사이므로 의미상 주어는 「of + 목적격」으로 쓴다.

17 정답 **to singing → sing 또는 singing**

[해석] 나는 내가 가장 좋아하는 가수가 'I Had a Dream'이라는 노래를 부르는 것을 들었다.

→ 지각동사 listen to는 목적격 보어로 원형부정사나 현재분사를 취한다.

18 정답 **clean → to clean**

[해석] 캠프 지도자가 아이들이 저녁 먹기 전에 방을 청소하게 했다.

→ get은 목적격 보어로 원형부정사가 아닌 to부정사를 취하므로 clean을 to clean으로 고쳐야 한다.

UNIT 55 to부정사의 시제, 부정, 수동태, 대부정사

개념 확인 문제 정답 ▶ 문제편 p.229

01 to catch **02** to have done **03** to win
04 to have won **05** to call **06** to have come
07 not to **08** to be called **09** never to
10 to be **11** not to fail
12 not to have been hurt **13** to enter
14 go hiking **15** take a picture with him
16 believe it **17** do the work
18 open the window **19** make curry and rice

01 정답 **to catch**

[해석] 나는 제시간에 기차를 타기를 바란다.

→ 주절은 현재시제이고 that절에 미래시제가 쓰였으므로 to부정사는 단순부정사 형태로 써야 한다.

02 [정답] to have done

[해석] 아무도 그가 그런 일을 했으리라고 믿지 않았다.

→ 종속절의 시제가 주절보다 한 시제 앞선 과거완료이므로 to부정사는 「to have+과거분사」 형태의 완료부정사로 써야 한다.

03 [정답] to win

[해석] 그녀는 금메달을 따서 기뻤다.

→ 주절과 종속절의 시제가 같으므로 to부정사는 「to+동사원형」 형태로 써야 한다.

04 [정답] to have won

[해석] 그는 두 번 상을 탄 유일한 사람이다.

→ 종속절의 시제가 주절보다 한 시제 앞서므로 to부정사를 「to have+과거분사」 형태의 완료부정사로 써야 한다.

05 [정답] to call

[해석] 그는 내게 다시 전화하겠다고 약속했지만 할 수 없었다.

→ 주절과 종속절의 시제가 같으므로 to부정사는 「to+동사원형」으로 쓴다.

06 [정답] to have come

[해석] 그들은 가짜 명품 가방이 중국에서 만들어졌다고 생각했다.

→ 종속절의 시제가 주절보다 한 시제 앞선 과거완료이므로 to부정사를 「to have+과거분사」 형태의 완료부정사로 써야 한다.

07 [정답] not to

[해석] 너는 기차를 놓치지 않기 위해서 서둘러야 한다.

→ 문맥상 '기차를 놓치지 않기 위해서'라는 뜻이 적절하므로 「not + to부정사」로 써야 한다.

08 [정답] to be called

[해석] 나는 내 이름이 불려지기를 기다리고 있었다.

→ 수동의 의미이므로 to부정사의 수동태인 to be called가 알맞다.

09 [정답] never to

[해석] 성급히 결론을 내리지 않도록 주의하라.

→ to부정사의 부정은 「not + to부정사」나 「never + to부정사」로 쓴다.

10 [정답] to be

[해석] 우리가 어떤 질문의 답변을 받을 수 있을 거라고 기대할 수 있겠는가?

→ 「to be+과거분사」 형태의 to부정사의 수동태로 써야 한다.

11 [정답] not to fail

[해석] 그는 시험에 떨어지지 않으려고 열심히 공부했다.

→ to부정사의 부정은 「not + to부정사」로 쓴다.

12 [정답] not to have been hurt

[해석] 네가 심각하게 부상을 입지 않아서 다행이었다.

→ hurt 뒤에 목적어가 없으므로 수동태로 쓰인 not to have been hurt가 알맞다.

13 [정답] to enter

[해석] 한국에서 대부분의 학생들은 좋은 대학에 들어가기를 바란다.

→ 능동의 의미이므로 to enter가 알맞다.

14 [정답] go hiking

[해석] 너는 하이킹을 가고 싶니? – 응, 그리고 싶어.

→ 반복되는 to부정사의 go hiking이 생략되어 있다.

15 [정답] take a picture with him

[해석] 네가 원한다면 너는 그와 사진을 찍을 수 있다.

→ 반복되는 take a picture with him이 생략되어 있다.

16 [정답] believe it

[해석] 그것을 믿기 어려웠지만 믿지 않는 것은 어리석은 일일 것이다.

→ 반복되는 to부정사의 believe it이 생략되어 있다.

17 [정답] do the work

[해석] 너는 원하지 않으면 그 일을 할 필요가 없다.

→ 반복되는 to부정사의 do the work가 생략되어 있다.

18 [정답] open the window

[해석] 내가 그에게 그러지 말라고 했음에도 불구하고 그는 창문을 열었다.

→ 상반되는 내용을 though로 연결하고 있으므로 앞에 나온 open the window가 생략되어 있음을 알 수 있다.

19 [정답] make curry and rice

[해석] 나는 카레라이스를 만들고 싶었지만 만드는 방법을 몰랐다.

→ 반복되는 to부정사의 make curry and rice가 생략되어 있다.

UNIT 56 to부정사의 관용표현

개념 확인 문제 정답 ▶ 문제편 p.231

01 It seems that you take a different view.

02 It seems that you know a lot about him.

03 It doesn't seem that he was rich.

04 It seemed that she had misunderstood the question.

05 It seemed that they had had a good time in Disneyland.

06 to cancel   **07** warm enough

08 so small, can be put

09 so nervous, couldn't make

10 so   **11** short   **12** to be sure

13 worse

01 [정답] It seems that you take a different view.

[해석] 너는 다른 견해를 가진 것 같다.

→ seem 뒤에 단순부정사가 쓰였으므로 that절에는 seems 와 같은 시제인 현재시제를 써야 한다.

02 정답 It seems that you know a lot about him.

[해석] 너는 그에 대해 많이 아는 것 같다.

→ seem 뒤에 단순부정사가 쓰였으므로 that절에는 seems 와 같은 시제인 현재시제를 써야 한다.

03 정답 It doesn't seem that he was rich.

[해석] 그는 부자였던 것 같지 않다.

→ doesn't seem 뒤에 완료부정사가 쓰였으므로 that절에 는 doesn't seem보다 한 시제 앞선 과거시제를 써야 한다.

04 정답 It seemed that she had misunderstood the question.

[해석] 그녀는 질문을 오해했던 것 같았다.

→ seemed 뒤에 완료부정사가 쓰였으므로 that절에는 seemed보다 한 시제 앞선 과거완료시제를 써야 한다.

05 정답 It seemed that they had had a good time in Disneyland.

[해석] 그들은 디즈니랜드에서 즐거운 시간을 보냈던 것 같 았다.

→ seemed 뒤에 완료부정사가 쓰였으므로 that절에는 seemed보다 한 시제 앞선 과거완료시제를 써야 한다.

06 정답 to cancel

[해석] 너무 늦어서 나는 비행기를 취소할 수 없다.

→ '너무 ~해서 …할 수 없다'라는 뜻의 「so ~ that + 주어 + can't + 동사원형」은 too ~ to부정사로 바꾸어 쓸 수 있다.

07 정답 warm enough

[해석] 물이 아주 따뜻해서 우리는 수영을 할 수 있다.

→ '…할 정도로 충분히 ~하다'라는 뜻의 「so ~ that+주어 +can+동사원형」은 「enough + to부정사」로 바꾸어 쓸 수 있 다.

08 정답 so small, can be put

[해석] 그녀의 애완동물은 주머니에 들어갈 정도로 작다.

→ '…할 정도로 충분히 ~하다'라는 뜻의 「enough+to부정 사」는 「so ~ that+주어+can+동사원형」으로 바꾸어 쓸 수 있 다.

09 정답 so nervous, couldn't make

[해석] 그는 너무 긴장해서 사람들 앞에서 연설을 할 수 없었다.

→ '너무 ~해서 …할 수 없다'라는 뜻의 too ~ to부정사는 「so ~ that+주어+can't[couldn't]+동사원형」으로 바꾸어 쓸 수 있다. 주절의 시제가 과거이므로 that절의 동사도 과거형으로 써야 한다.

10 정답 so

[해석] 그 아이디어는, 말하자면, 시대를 앞서 있었다.

→ '말하자면'은 so to speak으로 쓴다.

11 정답 short

[해석] 요약하면 그것은 전부 내 잘못이었다.

→ '요약하면'은 to make a long story short로 쓴다.

12 정답 to be sure

[해석] 그는 확실히 머리가 좋기는 하지만 매우 게으르기도 하다.

→ '확실히'는 to be sure라고 쓴다.

13 정답 worse

[해석] 지붕 여기저기에 물이 샜다. 설상가상으로 비가 오기 시작했다.

→ '설상가상으로'는 to make matters worse라고 쓴다.

단원 평가 문제 UNIT 54 ~ UNIT 56 ▶ 문제편 p.232~236

정답

01 ④ 02 ① 03 ⑤ 04 ① 05 ③
06 ⑤ 07 ②

08 It seemed that the room had been cleaned.

09 We were asked not[never] to vote for him.

10 He is too foolish to do such a thing.

11 to be served 12 go 13 keep

14 sing 15 to be downloaded

16 ④ 17 ⑤ 18 ③

19 for he → for him 20 for him → of him

21 ④ 22 To make matters worse

23 to tell the truth 24 so to speak

25 not to mention 26 too, to

27 small enough 28 ④

29 ③ 30 ④ 31 ④

32 She seems to be quite busy now.

33 Her secretary seemed to make a big mistake.

34 We hope for everyone to arrive on time.

35 finish his homework first

36 work in a group

37 ② 38 ③ 39 ③ 40 ③ 41 ③

42 ②

01 정답 ④ UNIT 55 to부정사의 시제, 부정, 수동태, 대부정사

[해석] 매니저는 아이들이 복도에서 뛰어다니지 말도록 정중하게 요청했다.

→ to부정사의 부정형은 「not/never + to부정사」이다.

02 정답 ① UNIT 54 원형부정사, to부정사의 의미상 주어

[해석] 그 선수는 기자들을 한 시간 넘게 기다리게 했다.

→ 사역동사 make는 목적격 보어로 원형부정사가 와야 한다.

03 정답 ⑤ UNIT 54 원형부정사, to부정사의 의미상 주어

[해석] 우리의 야구팀 코치는 우리가 규칙적으로 운동을 하게 한 다 / 운동을 하는 것을 본다.

→ 목적격 보어로 원형부정사 exercise가 있으므로 to부정사를 목 적격 보어로 취하는 allows는 쓸 수 없다.

04 정답 ①　　　　　　　UNIT **54** 원형부정사, to부정사의 의미상 주어

[해석] 네가 생각하는 바를 말하는 것은 무례하다 / 조심스럽지
못하다 / 어리석다 / 배려심이 없다.
→ to부정사의 의미상 주어로 「of + 목적격」이 사용되었으므로 빈칸
에는 사람의 성격이나 성질을 나타내는 형용사가 들어가야 한다.

05 정답 ③　　　　　　　UNIT **54** 원형부정사, to부정사의 의미상 주어

[해석] 그는 지진 중에 땅이 흔들리는 것을 ① 보았다 ② 느꼈다
④ 보았다 ⑤ 알아차렸다.
→ 목적격 보어로 원형부정사(shake)가 왔으므로 지각동사 또는 사
역동사만 올 수 있으며, knew는 올 수 없다.

06 정답 ⑤　　　　　　　UNIT **54** 원형부정사, to부정사의 의미상 주어

[해석] 그들이 그 문제를 빠르게 푸는 것은 ① 쉬웠다 ② 필요했
다 ③ 어려웠다 ④ 중요했다.
→ 성질이나 성격을 나타내는 형용사 뒤에 to부정사의 의미상 주어
는 「of + 목적격」을 써야 하므로 for them 앞에 ⑤ thoughtless
(배려심 없는)는 올 수 없다.

07 정답 ②　　　　　　UNIT **55** to부정사의 시제, 부정, 수동태, 대부정사

[해석] 영어를 배우는 가장 좋은 방법 중 하나는 영어로 된 책을
더 많이 읽는 것이다.
→ 동사 is의 보어로 쓰이는 명사적 용법의 to부정사가 와야 하며 목
적어가 있으므로 능동태가 맞다.

08 정답 It seemed that the room had been cleaned.
　　　　　　　　　　　　UNIT **56** to부정사의 관용표현

[해석] 그 방은 청소된 것 같았다.
→ seemed 뒤에 완료부정사가 쓰였으므로 that절에는 seemed
보다 한 시제 앞선 과거완료시제를 써야 한다.

09 정답 We were asked not[never] to vote for him.
　　　　　　　　　UNIT **55** to부정사의 시제, 부정, 수동태, 대부정사

[해석] 우리는 그에게 투표하지 말라는 요청을 받았다.
→ to부정사의 부정은 「not + to부정사」나 「never + to부정사」로
쓴다.

10 정답 He is too foolish to do such a thing.
　　　　　　　　　　　　UNIT **56** to부정사의 관용표현

[해석] 그는 너무 어리석어서 그런 일을 할 수 없다.
→ '너무 ~해서 …할 수 없다'라는 뜻의 「so ~ that +주어+can't+동
사원형」은 too ~ to부정사로 바꾸어 쓸 수 있다.

11 정답 to be served
　　　　　　　　　UNIT **55** to부정사의 시제, 부정, 수동태, 대부정사

[해석] 나는 안내받기를 기다리는 중이다.
→ 내가 안내받기를 기다리는 '수동'의 입장이므로 to부정사의 수동
태를 써야 한다.

12 정답 go　　　　　UNIT **54** 원형부정사, to부정사의 의미상 주어

[해석] 나의 부모님은 내가 밤에 외출하는 것을 절대 허락하지 않
으신다.
→ 사역동사 let의 목적격 보어로는 원형부정사가 쓰인다.

13 정답 keep　　　　UNIT **54** 원형부정사, to부정사의 의미상 주어

[해석] 많은 운동이 내가 몸매를 유지하는 것을 도와준다.
→ help의 목적격 보어로는 원형부정사나 to부정사가 쓰인다.

14 정답 sing　　　UNIT **54** 원형부정사, to부정사의 의미상 주어

[해석] 나는 오디션에서 Joe가 아름다운 노래를 부르는 것을 들었
다.
→ 지각동사 hear의 목적격 보어로는 원형부정사나 현재분사가 쓰
인다.

15 정답 to be downloaded
　　　　　　UNIT **55** to부정사의 시제, 부정, 수동태, 대부정사

[해석] Jessie는 영화 몇 편을 다운로드 받기를 원한다.
→ 영화는 누군가에 의해 '다운로드 되어지는' 것이므로 to부정사의
수동태를 써야 한다.

16 정답 ④　　　　　UNIT **54** 원형부정사, to부정사의 의미상 주어

[해석] ① 그녀가 지금 우리에게 전화를 다시 하는 것은 불가능하
다.
② 내가 이렇게 일찍 일어나는 것은 정말 힘들었다.
③ 내가 글씨를 잘 쓰는 것은 어렵다.
④ 그가 너의 실수를 용서해주다니 아주 관대했어.
⑤ 그들이 과제를 늦게 제출하는 것은 안 된다.
→ ④ 「It is + 형용사 + for + 목적격 + to부정사」 구문에서 형용사
가 사람의 성질, 성격을 나타내는 경우 for 대신 of를 써야 한다. 나머
지는 모두 for가 들어간다.

17 정답 ⑤　　　　　UNIT **54** 원형부정사, to부정사의 의미상 주어

[해석] ① 우리는 내년에 다시 만나기를 기대한다.
② 그들은 내일 나를 수족관으로 데려가기로 약속했다.
③ 너는 여름 방학에 무언가를 할 계획이니?
④ 나는 그들이 이 프로젝트를 더 빨리 끝내기 위해 스터디 그룹
을 조직하기를 바란다.
⑤ 나는 네가 샀던 책이 숙제를 쉽게 하는 것을 도와줄 거라 확
신한다.
→ ⑤ help는 목적격 보어로 to부정사나 원형부정사가 온다. ①, ②,
③, ④ expect, promise, plan, want 모두 목적어로 to부정사를
취한다.

18 정답 ③　　　　　UNIT **54** 원형부정사, to부정사의 의미상 주어

[해석] ① 우리는 Sam의 개가 어젯밤에 짖는 것을 들었다.
② Rebecca가 자신의 우산을 다시 두고 왔다니 정말 어리석구
나.
③ 사실, Yumi는 경연대회에서 이길 것을 결코 기대하지 않았
다.
④ Cathy는 대표로 선출되어 매우 놀랐다.
⑤ 그는 수리공이 되도록 빨리 엘리베이터를 고치도록 시켰다.
→ ③ expect는 목적어로 to부정사를 취한다. ① 「지각동사+목적어
+목적격 보어」에서 목적격 보어 자리에는 원형부정사나 현재분사가
온다. ② 「It is + 형용사 + for + 목적격 + to부정사」 구문에서 형용
사가 사람의 성질, 성격을 나타내는 경우 for 대신 of를 써야 한다.
④ '선출된다'는 수동의 의미이므로 to부정사의 수동태를 써야 한다.
⑤ 사역동사 get은 목적격 보어 자리에 분사나 to부정사를 취한다.

19 정답 for he → for him
UNIT **54** 원형부정사, to부정사의 의미상 주어

[해석] 진수는 수학을 아주 잘하는 나의 반 친구이다. 어제, 나는 수학 문제를 푸는 데 어려움이 있어서, 그에게 물어보았다. 그가 그 문제를 푸는 것은 아주 쉬워보였다. 그는 어떻게 그 답을 얻었는지 나에게 친절하게 설명해주었다. 그가 나를 도와주는 걸 보니 참 착하다.

→ 「It is + 형용사 + for + 목적격 + to부정사」 구문에서 for 뒤에 대명사가 올 때 목적격으로 와야 한다.

20 정답 for him → of him
UNIT **54** 원형부정사, to부정사의 의미상 주어

→ 「It is + 형용사 + for + 목적격 + to부정사」 구문에서 형용사가 사람의 성질, 성격을 나타내는 경우 for 대신 of를 써야 한다.

21 정답 ④
UNIT **56** to부정사의 관용표현

[해석] 기온이 너무 높아서 사람들이 한낮에 일을 할 수 없다.

→ '너무 ~해서 …할 수 없다'라는 뜻의 「so ~ that + 주어 + can't + 동사원형」은 too ~ to부정사로 바꾸어 쓸 수 있다. 주절과 that절의 주어가 다르므로 to부정사 앞에는 「for + 목적격」의 의미상 주어를 써야 한다.

22 정답 To make matters worse UNIT **56** to부정사의 관용표현
[해석] 나는 여행 동안 멀미로 고생했다. 설상가상으로, 나는 지갑을 잃어버렸다.

→ to make matters worse는 '설상가상으로'라는 뜻이다.

23 정답 to tell the truth
UNIT **56** to부정사의 관용표현
[해석] 나는 자신 있는 척 했다. 하지만 사실, 나는 이 일을 감당할 수 있을지 모르겠다.

→ to tell the truth는 '사실'이라는 의미이다.

24 정답 so to speak
UNIT **56** to부정사의 관용표현
[해석] 박 선생님은 말하자면 걸어다니는 사전이다. 그녀는 모든 것을 알고 있다.

→ so to speak은 '말하자면'이라는 뜻이다.

25 정답 not to mention
UNIT **56** to부정사의 관용표현
[해석] James는 부자이고 관대한 것은 말할 것도 없다!

→ not to mention은 '말할 것도 없는'이라는 뜻이다.

26 정답 too, to
UNIT **56** to부정사의 관용표현
[해석] 그는 너무 아파서 학교에 갈 수 없었다.

→ 「too + 형용사/부사 + to부정사」는 「so + 형용사/부사 + 주어 + can't[couldn't]」로 바꿔 쓸 수 있다.

27 정답 small enough
UNIT **56** to부정사의 관용표현
[해석] 나의 카메라는 네 주머니에 가지고 다닐 수 있을 만큼 작다.

→ 「형용사/부사 + enough + to부정사」는 「so + 형용사/부사 + 주어 + can[could]」으로 바꿔 쓸 수 있다.

28 정답 ④
UNIT **56** to부정사의 관용표현
[해석] 그녀는 화가 났던 것처럼 보인다.

→ 주절의 시제보다 종속절의 시제가 앞서므로 완료부정사(to have+과거분사)를 써야 한다.

29 정답 ③
UNIT **56** to부정사의 관용표현
[해석] 그가 말할 기회는 없는 것 같다.

→ 주절의 seems와 that절의 doesn't have의 시제가 같으므로 to부정사는 단순부정사의 부정 형태로 써야 한다.

30 정답 ④
UNIT **56** to부정사의 관용표현
[해석] 관객들은 그 연극에 감동을 받은 듯 보였다.

→ 주절의 seemed와 종속절 was의 시제가 같으므로 to부정사는 단순부정사의 수동태 형태로 써야 한다.

31 정답 ④
UNIT **56** to부정사의 관용표현
[해석] 나는 John이 자신의 결정에 책임을 질 만큼 나이를 먹었다고 생각한다.

→ 「형용사/부사 + enough + to부정사」는 '~할 만큼 …하다'는 의미이다.

32 정답 She seems to be quite busy now.
UNIT **56** to부정사의 관용표현
[해석] 〈보기〉 나는 시험 날짜를 잊어버렸던 것이 창피했다.
그녀는 지금 꽤 바쁜 것 같다.

→ 주절의 시제와 종속절의 시제가 같으므로 단순부정사를 써야 한다.

33 정답 Her secretary seemed to make a big mistake.
UNIT **56** to부정사의 관용표현
[해석] 그녀의 비서는 큰 실수를 저지르는 것 같았다.

→ 주절의 시제와 종속절의 시제가 같으므로 단순부정사를 써야 한다.

34 정답 We hope for everyone to arrive on time.
UNIT **54** 원형부정사, to부정사의 의미상 주어
[해석] 우리는 모두가 제 시간에 도착하기를 희망한다.

→ to부정사의 의미상 주어가 주절의 주어와 다른 경우 「for + 목적격」으로 나타낸다.

35 정답 finish his homework first
UNIT **54** 원형부정사, to부정사의 의미상 주어

[해석] Tim: 컴퓨터 게임해도 돼요?
엄마: 아니, 안 된단다. 너는 숙제를 먼저 해야 해.
Tim: 알겠어요.

→ 사역동사는 목적격 보어로 원형부정사를 취한다.

36 정답 work in a group
UNIT **54** 원형부정사, to부정사의 의미상 주어

[해석] Lisa: 저 혼자 해도 되나요? 저는 혼자 할 때 항상 더 잘해요.

Jackson 선생님: 안 된단다. 오늘은 그룹 활동을 해야 해.

→ 사역동사는 목적격 보어로 원형부정사를 취한다.

37 정답 ②
UNIT **54** 원형부정사, to부정사의 의미상 주어
[해석] • 나는 나의 남동생이 영화 티켓을 예매하도록 시켰다.
• 김 선생님은 우리가 현재의 사회적 문제들에 관한 발표를 하도록 시켰다.
• 고맙게도, 그 경찰관은 우리가 그 장소를 찾는 것을 도와주었다.

→ (A) 사역동사는 목적격 보어로 원형부정사를 취한다. (B) get은 목적격 보어로 to부정사가 와야 한다. (C) help는 목적격 보어로 원형부정사와 to부정사가 가능하다.

38 정답 ③　　　UNIT 55 to부정사의 시제, 부정, 수동태, 대부정사

[해석] ① 나는 오늘 밤 나가지 않기로 결심했다.
② 의사는 그녀에게 휴식을 취하라고 충고했다.
③ Brian은 그녀의 농담에 웃지 않으려 했다.
④ 그는 그 돈을 훔쳤던 것으로 여겨진다.
⑤ 그들은 내가 너희와 캠핑을 가는 것을 허락하지 않을 것이다.
→ ③ Brian이 그녀의 농담에 웃지 않으려 노력한 것이므로 능동태인 to laugh가 와야 한다.

39 정답 ③　　　UNIT 54 원형부정사, to부정사의 의미상 주어

[해석] ① 그녀는 내가 울타리를 칠하도록 했다.
② 나는 집이 지금 흔들리는 것을 느낀다.
③ Tom이 저 집으로 침입하는 것을 누군가가 보았니?
④ 우리는 어젯밤에 누가 초인종을 누르는 것을 들었다.
⑤ Jenny는 내가 영어로 보고서를 쓰는 것을 도울 것이다.
→ 「지각동사+목적어+목적격 보어」에서 목적격 보어 자리에는 원형부정사나 현재분사가 올 수 있고, 사역동사는 목적격 보어에 원형부정사만 취한다. help만 원형부정사와 to부정사가 가능하다. 따라서 to break는 break로 고쳐야 한다.

40 정답 ③　　　UNIT 56 to부정사의 관용표현

[해석] ① 나는 학교에 가는 데 30분이 걸린다.
② 그녀는 모두에게 존경받는 것 같다.
③ 그는 소위 말해서 팀의 중심축이다.
④ 이 책은 유명한 작가가 쓴 것으로 알려져 있다.
⑤ 그 영화는 나중에 다시 볼 만큼 충분히 재미있었다.
→ ③ to부정사를 활용한 관용표현으로, '말하자면'은 so to speak으로 표현한다.

41 정답 ③　　　UNIT 55 to부정사의 시제, 부정, 수동태, 대부정사

[해석] 휴대폰을 현명하게 사용하는 것은 여러분의 건강과 학업에 중요하다. 공부를 위해서가 아니라면 수업 중에 휴대폰을 사용하는 것은 좋지 않다. 게임이나 소셜 미디어에 중독되지 않는 것은 여러분의 미래의 성공에 필요하다. 수업 중에는 휴대폰을 치워두어야 학생들이 학업에 집중할 수 있다. 여러분의 휴대폰을 책임감 있게 어떻게 사용해야 할지를 배우는 것은 여러분의 학업과 사회생활을 향상시키는데 도움이 될 수 있다.
→ to부정사의 부정은 to 앞에 not 또는 never를 써야 하므로 ③ To not get은 Not to get으로 써야 한다.

42 정답 ②　　　UNIT 54 원형부정사, to부정사의 의미상 주어

[해석] 백야를 경험하는 것은 독특하고 흥미로운 사건이다. St. Petersburg와 같은 곳에서는 여름 동안 태양이 몇 주 동안 지지 않는다. 백야 동안 하늘이 항상 밝아서 잠을 자는 것이 어렵다. 백야는 지구의 기울기와 태양에 대한 지구의 위치로 인해 발생한다. 이 현상을 이해하기 위해서 우리는 지구의 자전과 공전을 공부할 필요가 있다. 북부 지역에서는 백야를 축제와 함께 기념한다고 한다.
→ 성질이나 성격을 나타내는 형용사 뒤에 오는 경우를 제외하고 대부분의 to부정사는 「for + 목적격」을 의미상 주어로 취한다. 따라서 ② of us를 for us로 고쳐야 한다.

N 동명사

UNIT 57 동명사

개념 확인 문제 정답　　　▶ 문제편 p.239

01 동사의 목적어　**02** 전치사의 목적어　**03** 전치사의 목적어
04 주어　　　　　**05** 동사의 목적어　**06** 주어
07 보어　**08** her　**09** his　**10** her
11 his not inviting　**12** not knowing
13 Shaking hands is a way of greeting someone.
14 went to the mountain instead of going to the sea
15 Would you mind my asking your opinion?
16 You should excuse her not going there.

01 정답 **동사의 목적어**

[해석] 나는 예전만큼 걷기를 즐기지 않는다.
→ walking은 동사 enjoy의 목적어로 쓰였다.

02 정답 **전치사의 목적어**

[해석] 너는 독서를 많이 함으로써 영어 실력을 향상시킬 수 있다.
→ reading은 전치사 by의 목적어로 쓰였다.

03 정답 **전치사의 목적어**

[해석] 근로자들은 초과 근무를 해야 하는 것에 불평했다.
→ being은 전치사 of의 목적어로 쓰였다.

04 정답 **주어**

[해석] 새로운 사람들을 만나는 것이 어떤 사람들에게는 어렵다.
→ Meeting은 동사 is의 주어로 쓰였다.

05 정답 **동사의 목적어**

[해석] 나는 그녀에게 잘 보이려고 노력하는 것을 포기해야 할 것 같다.
→ trying은 동사 give up의 목적어로 쓰였다.

06 정답 **주어**

[해석] 체스를 하는 것은 아이들이 수학에서 뛰어난 실력을 보이는 것을 도와준다고 한다.
→ playing은 that절에서 동사 helps의 주어로 쓰였다.

07 정답 **보어**

[해석] 내 직업에서 내가 가장 좋아하는 것은 많은 나라들을 여행하는 것이다.
→ traveling은 동사 is의 보어로 쓰였다.

08 정답 **her**

[해석] 나는 그녀가 변호사가 된 것을 믿을 수 없다.
→ 동명사의 의미상 주어는 소유격이나 목적격으로 쓴다.

09 정답 **his**

[해석] 나는 그가 상을 받는 것에 흥분했다.
→ 동명사의 의미상 주어는 소유격이나 목적격으로 쓴다.

10 정답 her

[해석] 그는 그녀가 축구 규칙에 대한 질문을 하는 것에 질렸다.
→ 동명사의 의미상 주어는 소유격이나 목적격으로 쓴다.

11 정답 his not inviting

[해석] 나는 그가 나를 그의 생일 파티에 초대하지 않은 것을 이해할 수 없다.
→ 동명사의 의미상 주어는 동명사 앞에 쓰며, 동명사를 부정형으로 쓸 때는 동명사 바로 앞에 not이나 never를 쓴다.

12 정답 not knowing

[해석] 읽고 쓰는 방법을 모르는 것보다 더 큰 가난은 없다.
→ 문맥상 읽고 쓰는 방법을 모르는 것이 가장 큰 가난이라는 뜻이므로 동명사 knowing의 부정형으로 써야 한다.

13 정답 Shaking hands is a way of greeting someone.

→ 동명사구 shaking hands를 주어로 쓴다.

14 정답 went to the mountain instead of going to the sea

→ 전치사구 instead of 뒤에 동명사를 쓴다.

15 정답 Would you mind my asking your opinion?

→ 동사 mind는 동명사를 목적어로 취하며 동명사의 의미상 주어는 소유격이나 목적격으로 쓴다.

16 정답 You should excuse her not going there.

→ 동명사의 의미상 주어는 동명사 앞에 쓰고, 동명사의 부정형은 동명사 바로 앞에 not이나 never를 쓴다.

UNIT 58 동사의 목적어로 쓰이는 동명사, to부정사

개념 확인 문제 정답 ▶ 문제편 **p.241**

01 to meet **02** speaking **03** telling
04 to climb **05** my smoking **06** hiring
07 to buy
08 나는 오늘 저녁 늦게 너에게 다시 전화하는 것을 기억할 것이다.
09 나는 어젯밤에 파티에서 너를 만났던 것을 결코 잊지 않을 것이다.
10 그 상담가는 그가 말하고 있는 것에 계속 귀 기울이고 있었다.
11 Chris는 이 라디오를 고치려고 열심히 노력하고 있지만, 그것은 쉽지 않아 보인다.
12 shaking **13** writing **14** to bring
15 to be **16** feeding

---

01 정답 to meet

[해석] 우리는 일요일에 다시 만나는 데 동의했다.
→ agree는 to부정사를 목적어로 취한다.

02 정답 speaking

[해석] 그 여자아이들은 Lisa를 욕하는 것을 인정했다.
→ admit은 동명사를 목적어로 취한다.

03 정답 telling

[해석] 그는 부모님에게 그 소식을 말하는 것을 미루었다.
→ delay는 동명사를 목적어로 취한다.

04 정답 to climb

[해석] 그들은 올해 안에 한라산을 등반하기로 마음먹었다.
→ decide는 to부정사를 목적어로 취한다.

05 정답 my smoking

[해석] 제가 이 방에서 담배를 피워도 될까요?
→ mind는 동명사를 목적어로 취하며, 동명사의 의미상 주어는 목적격이나 소유격으로 동명사 앞에 쓴다.

06 정답 hiring

[해석] 공장주는 더 많은 일꾼들을 고용하는 것을 고려하고 있다.
→ consider는 동명사를 목적어로 취한다.

07 정답 to buy

[해석] 나의 아버지는 이번 크리스마스 때 나에게 테디 베어를 사 주기로 약속하셨다.
→ promise는 to부정사를 목적어로 취한다.

08 정답 나는 오늘 저녁 늦게 너에게 다시 전화하는 것을 기억할 것이다.

→ 「remember+to부정사」는 '(앞으로) ~할 것을 기억하다'라는 뜻이다.

09 정답 나는 어젯밤에 파티에서 너를 만났던 것을 결코 잊지 않을 것이다.

→ 「forget+동명사」는 '(과거에) ~한 것을 잊다'라는 뜻이다.

10 정답 그 상담가는 그가 말하고 있는 것에 계속 귀 기울이고 있었다.

→ continue는 to부정사나 동명사를 목적어로 취할 수 있고, '계속 ~하다'로 해석한다.

11 정답 Chris는 이 라디오를 고치려고 열심히 노력하고 있지만, 그것은 쉽지 않아 보인다.

→ 「try+to부정사」는 '~하려고 노력하다'라는 뜻이다.

12 정답 shaking

[해석] 식사하는 동안 다리를 떠는 것을 멈춰.
→ '~하는 것을 멈추다'라는 뜻으로, stop의 목적어로 쓰이는 것은 동명사이다.

13 정답 writing

[해석] 나는 작년에 그녀에게 편지를 썼던 것을 기억한다.
→ 작년의 일을 말하고 있으므로 '(과거에) ~한 것을 기억하다'라는 뜻으로 「remember+동명사」를 써야 한다.

14 정답 to bring

[해석] 너의 교과서를 가져오는 것을 잊지 마.
→ '(앞으로) ~할 것을 잊다'는 「forget+to부정사」로 쓴다.

15 정답 **to be**

[해석] 사람들은 항상 다이어트를 하려고 노력하지만 그들 중 많은 이들이 실패한다.

→ '~하려고 노력하다'는 「try+to부정사」라고 쓰며, '다이어트를 하다'는 be on a diet라고 한다.

16 정답 **feeding**

[해석] 그녀는 그녀의 개에게 먹이를 준 것을 잊어버리고 그릇에 개 사료를 다시 채웠다.

→ 사료를 다시 채웠다는 말이 and 뒤에 나오므로 and 앞은 그녀가 사료를 준 것을 잊어버렸다는 의미가 되어야 한다. '(과거에) ~한 것을 잊다'는 「forget+동명사」로 쓴다.

UNIT **59** 전치사의 목적어로 쓰인 동명사, 관용표현

개념 확인 문제 정답 ▶ 문제편 p.243

01 without apologizing **02** used, for analyzing

03 believe in acting

04 were in favor of reducing

05 by exploring **06** instead of following

07 needs reviewing

08 was worth staying

09 It is no use running

10 is looking forward to speaking

11 insisted on taking

12 was afraid of being judged

---

01 정답 **without apologizing**

→ '~하지 않고'는 without -ing로 표현한다.

02 정답 **used, for analyzing**

→ '~하는 데 …을 쓰다'는 use … for -ing로 표현한다.

03 정답 **believe in acting**

→ '~을 믿다'는 believe in -ing로 표현한다.

04 정답 **were in favor of reducing**

→ '~에 찬성하다'는 be in favor of -ing로 표현한다.

05 정답 **by exploring**

→ '~함으로써'는 by -ing로 표현한다.

06 정답 **instead of following**

→ '~하는 대신에'는 instead of -ing로 표현한다.

07 정답 **needs reviewing**

→ '~될 필요가 있다'는 need[want] -ing로 표현한다.

08 정답 **was worth staying**

→ '~할 가치가 있다'는 be worth -ing로 표현한다.

09 정답 **It is no use running**

→ '~해도 소용없다'는 It is no use -ing로 표현한다.

10 정답 **is looking forward to speaking**

→ '~하기를 고대하다'는 look forward to -ing로 표현한다.

11 정답 **insisted on taking**

→ '~을 주장하다, 고집하다'는 insist on -ing로 표현한다.

12 정답 **was afraid of being judged**

→ '~을 두려워하다'는 be afraid of -ing로 표현한다.

단원 평가 문제 UNIT **57** ~ UNIT **59** ▶ 문제편 p.244~248

정답

01 ③ **02** ③ **03** ③ **04** ②

05 to testify **06** to find **07** reading **08** going

09 being **10** hearing **11** sharing **12** eating

13 turning **14** ④ **15** ② **16** ②

17 ③ **18** ⑤ **19** learning **20** going

21 not turning **22** talking **23** reading

24 to speak **25** to sign **26** making

27 our[us] going to the movies

28 meeting her the other day

29 travelling around the world

30 Wearing uniforms while you are at work

31 ① **32** ② **33** ③ **34** ⑤

35 kept researching **36** succeeded in raising

37 is focusing on providing

38 making a mistake during the singing contest

39 talking loudly on your cell phones, to take all your belongings with you

40 to walk → walking

41 studying not → not[never] studying

42 create → creating

43 ④ **44** ② **45** ④ **46** ④ **47** ③

---

01 정답 ③ UNIT **58** 동사의 목적어로 쓰이는 동명사, to부정사

[해석] James는 혼자 프로그램 설치하는 것을 멈추고 Jack에게 도움을 청하기로 결정했다.

→ '~하는 것을 멈추다'라는 의미는 stop 다음에 동명사를 써서 표현한다.

02 정답 ③ UNIT **59** 전치사의 목적어로 쓰인 동명사, 관용표현

[해석] 우리는 공연장에 음식을 가지고 온 것을 사과하지 않을 수 없었다.

→ '~하지 않을 수 없다'는 cannot help -ing로 쓴다.

03 정답 ③　　　　UNIT **59** 전치사의 목적어로 쓰인 동명사, 관용표현
[해석] 몇몇 사람들은 미래를 예측하는 데 관심이 있다.
→ '~하는 데 관심이 있다'는 be interested in -ing로 쓴다.

04 정답 ②　　　　UNIT **58** 동사의 목적어로 쓰이는 동명사, to부정사
[해석] 그 배의 선장은 빙하와 부딪히는 것을 피하기 위해 노력했다.
→ avoid는 목적어로 동명사를 취한다.

05 정답 to testify
　　　　UNIT **58** 동사의 목적어로 쓰이는 동명사, to부정사
[해석] 그는 법정에서 증언하는 것을 거부했다.
→ refuse는 to부정사를 목적어로 취한다.

06 정답 to find　　UNIT **58** 동사의 목적어로 쓰이는 동명사, to부정사
[해석] 나는 이 가게에서 이것을 발견할 것이라고 기대하지 않았다.
→ expect는 to부정사를 목적어로 취한다.

07 정답 reading　　UNIT **58** 동사의 목적어로 쓰이는 동명사, to부정사
[해석] 너는 저 잡지를 다 읽었니?
→ finish는 동명사를 목적어로 취한다.

08 정답 going　　UNIT **58** 동사의 목적어로 쓰이는 동명사, to부정사
[해석] 그는 다음 주까지 외과 의사를 만나는 것을 연기하고 싶어 한다.
→ put off는 동명사를 목적어로 취한다.

09 정답 being　　　　　　　　　　UNIT **57** 동명사
[해석] Emma는 가수가 되는 것을 꿈꾸지만, 그녀는 노래를 아주 잘 부르지는 못한다.
→ 전치사의 목적어로는 동명사가 와야 한다.

10 정답 hearing　　UNIT **59** 전치사의 목적어로 쓰인 동명사, 관용표현
[해석] 화재 경보가 울리는 것을 듣자마자 가장 가까운 비상구로 걸어가십시오.
→ '~하자마자'는 on -ing로 쓴다.

11 정답 sharing　　UNIT **59** 전치사의 목적어로 쓰인 동명사, 관용표현
[해석] 시간이 지남에 따라 나는 여동생과 내 방을 같이 쓰는 것에 익숙해졌다.
→ '~하는 데 익숙하다'라는 뜻의 get used to 뒤에는 동명사를 써야 한다.

12 정답 eating　　UNIT **58** 동사의 목적어로 쓰이는 동명사, to부정사
[해석] Sandra는 우리가 홍콩에 있는 동안 Jumbo 레스토랑에서 식사를 할 것을 추천했다.
→ recommend는 동명사를 목적어로 취한다.

13 정답 turning　　UNIT **58** 동사의 목적어로 쓰이는 동명사, to부정사
[해석] A: 너 난방기 끄는 거 또 잊었지?
B: 무슨 소리 하는 거야? 나는 확실히 난방기를 껐어. 나는 분명히 그것을 끈 것을 기억해.
→ B가 확실히 난방기를 껐다고 말하고 있으므로 '(과거에) ~한 것을 기억하다'라는 뜻으로 remember 뒤에 동명사 turning을 써야 한다.

14 정답 ④　　　　UNIT **58** 동사의 목적어로 쓰이는 동명사, to부정사
[해석] ① 고양이는 쥐를 잡으려고 노력했다.
② 많은 사람들이 결혼하지 않는 것을 선택한다.
③ 그는 계속해서 내가 말한 모든 것을 무시했다.
④ Ryan은 책을 연재물로 쓰는 것을 포기했다.
⑤ 그 공무원은 그 문제를 조사하겠다고 약속했다.
→ ④ give up은 동명사를 목적어로 취한다. (to write → writing) ①「try+to부정사」: ~하려고 노력하다 ② choose의 목적어인 to부정사 ③「continue+to부정사」: ~하는 것을 계속하다 ⑤ promise의 목적어인 to부정사

15 정답 ②　　　　UNIT **58** 동사의 목적어로 쓰이는 동명사, to부정사
[해석] ① 나는 약 1년 전에 담배를 끊었다.
② 그녀는 경영학을 전공하기로 마음먹었다.
③ 우리와 함께 테이블을 쓰는 게 어떠세요?
④ 그는 젊었을 때 낚시를 즐겨했다.
⑤ 그들은 유령의 집에서 소리를 지르기 시작했다.
→ ② decide는 목적어로 to부정사를 취한다. (majoring → to major) ① quit의 목적어인 동명사 ③ mind의 목적어인 동명사 ④ enjoy의 목적어인 동명사 ⑤ begin의 목적어인 동명사

16 정답 ②　　　　UNIT **59** 전치사의 목적어로 쓰인 동명사, 관용표현
[해석] ① 나는 젓가락을 사용하는 데 익숙하다.
② 그는 웃음을 터뜨리지 않을 수 없었다.
③ 나는 곧 너를 보기를 기대하고 있다.
④ 그녀는 밤에 운전하는 데 익숙하다.
⑤ 그는 학생들을 가르치는 것을 자랑스럽게 생각한다.
→ ② '~하지 않을 수 없다'는 「cannot help -ing」로 쓰므로 burst를 bursting으로 고쳐야 한다. ① be used to -ing: ~하는 데 익숙하다 ③ look forward to -ing: ~하기를 고대하다 ④ be accustomed to -ing: ~하는 데 익숙하다 ⑤ be proud of -ing: ~을 자랑스럽게 생각하다

17 정답 ③　　　　UNIT **58** 동사의 목적어로 쓰이는 동명사, to부정사
[해석] 많은 회사들이 결혼한 여성을 고용하는 것을 ① 시작했다 ② 그만두었다 ④ 꺼렸다 ⑤ 고려했다는 것이 화젯거리가 되어 왔다.
→ 빈칸 뒤에 동명사 hiring이 있으므로 동명사를 목적어로 취하는 began, stopped, minded, considered는 쓸 수 있으나 to부정사를 목적어로 취하는 decided는 쓸 수 없다.

18 정답 ⑤　　　　UNIT **58** 동사의 목적어로 쓰이는 동명사, to부정사
[해석] 우리 부모님은 내가 장기자랑쇼에 나가는 것에 대해 말하는 것을 ① 피하셨다 ② 계속하셨다 ③ 멈추셨다 ④ 시작하셨다.
→ want는 to부정사를 목적어로 취한다.

19 정답 learning　　UNIT **59** 전치사의 목적어로 쓰인 동명사, 관용표현
[해석] 너는 계속 중국어를 배우고 싶니?
→ '계속 ~하다'는 go on -ing로 쓴다.

20 정답 going　　UNIT **59** 전치사의 목적어로 쓰인 동명사, 관용표현
[해석] 나는 여름휴가 중에 해변에 가고 싶다.
→ '~하고 싶다'라는 뜻은 feel like -ing로 쓴다.

21 정답 not turning   UNIT **57** 동명사

[해석] 소리를 높이지 않아도 되겠니?

→ mind는 동명사를 목적어로 취하며, 동명사의 부정형은 동명사 앞에 not을 쓴다.

22 정답 talking   UNIT **59** 전치사의 목적어로 쓰인 동명사, 관용표현

[해석] 나의 엄마는 많은 시간을 전화 통화하는 데 쓰신다.

→ '~하는 데 시간을 쓰다'는 「spend+시간+-ing」로 쓴다.

23 정답 reading   UNIT **59** 전치사의 목적어로 쓰인 동명사, 관용표현

[해석] 이 신문에는 읽을 만한 가치가 있는 기사가 없다.

→ '~할 가치가 있다'는 be worth -ing로 쓴다.

24 정답 to speak   UNIT **58** 동사의 목적어로 쓰이는 동명사, to부정사

[해석] Amy는 말다툼 이후로 나와 말하는 것을 거부해 왔다.

→ refuse는 to부정사를 목적어로 취한다.

25 정답 to sign   UNIT **58** 동사의 목적어로 쓰이는 동명사, to부정사

[해석] 뉴스 보도에 따르면, 두 회사는 계약에 사인하기로 동의했다.

→ agree는 to부정사를 목적어로 취한다.

26 정답 making   UNIT **58** 동사의 목적어로 쓰이는 동명사, to부정사

[해석] 거울 앞에서 연설하는 것을 연습하는 것은 네가 말하기 대회에서 잘 할 수 있게 도와줄 것이다.

→ practice는 동명사를 목적어로 취한다.

27 정답 our[us] going to the movies   UNIT **58** 동사의 목적어로 쓰이는 동명사, to부정사

[해석] Eric은 우리에게 극장에 가자고 제안했다.

→ suggest는 동명사를 목적어로 취한다.

28 정답 meeting her the other day   UNIT **58** 동사의 목적어로 쓰이는 동명사, to부정사

[해석] 그는 일전에 그녀를 만났던 것을 기억하지 못한다.

→ '(과거에) ~한 것을 기억하지 못하다'라고 할 때는 not remember 뒤에 동명사를 써야 한다.

29 정답 travelling around the world   UNIT **58** 동사의 목적어로 쓰이는 동명사, to부정사

[해석] 나의 꿈은 내가 너무 늙기 전에 전 세계를 여행하는 것이다.

→ 보어 자리에 오는 to부정사를 동명사로 바꿔 쓸 수 있다.

30 정답 Wearing uniforms while you are at work   UNIT **58** 동사의 목적어로 쓰이는 동명사, to부정사

[해석] 직장에서 제복을 입는 것은 필요하다.

→ 진주어인 to부정사를 동명사로 바꿔 쓸 수 있다.

31 정답 ①   UNIT **57** 동명사

[해석] ① 나는 기타 치는 법을 배우고 있다.

② 그의 관심사는 자신의 재산을 보호하는 것이다.

③ 나의 취미는 패션 잡지를 읽는 것이다.

④ 그의 바람은 자신의 손자들을 다시 보는 것이다.

⑤ 그녀의 목표는 유명한 작곡가가 되는 것이다.

→ ①은 현재진행시제에 쓰인 현재분사이고, 나머지는 모두 문장의 보어로 쓰인 동명사이다.

32 정답 ②   UNIT **57** 동명사

[해석] ① 너의 공부습관을 바꾸는 것은 쉽지 않을 것이다.

② 여행에서 돌아온 후, 우리는 해산물 빠에야의 맛을 잊을 수 없었다.

③ 컴퓨터 게임을 너무 많이 하는 것은 너의 눈을 피로하게 할 수 있다.

④ 균형 잡힌 식사를 하는 것은 체중을 줄이는 데 도움이 될 수 있다.

⑤ Ted는 바이올린을 연주하는 것 뿐만 아니라 그림 그리는 것도 좋아한다.

→ ②은 After we returned로 바꿔 쓸 수 있는 현재분사이고, 나머지는 모두 동명사이다.

33 정답 ③   UNIT **58** 동사의 목적어로 쓰이는 동명사, to부정사

[해석] ① 나는 파리에서 건축학을 공부하는 것을 선택했다.

② 그녀는 행복하지 않은 척했다.

③ 그는 그의 친구들을 집으로 초대하는 것을 꺼린다.

④ Sarah는 외국에서 사는 것을 원한다.

⑤ 기차에서 내릴 준비를 하십시오.

→ ③ mind는 동명사를 목적어로 취한다. choose, pretend, want, prepare는 모두 to부정사를 목적어로 취하는 동사이다. ① studying → to study ② being → to be ④ living → to live ⑤ getting → to get

34 정답 ⑤   UNIT **59** 전치사의 목적어로 쓰인 동명사, 관용표현

[해석] ① 우리는 그들에게 장난감을 몇 개 보내기로 약속했다.

② 나의 여동생은 단 것을 먹는 것을 절대 포기하지 않는다.

③ 누군가의 감정을 다치게 하는 것을 피하도록 노력해라.

④ 그는 그들을 위협하는 것을 부인했다.

⑤ 나는 그녀를 방문하기를 학수고대한다.

→ ⑤ look forward to -ing는 '~하기를 고대하다'라는 뜻이다. promise는 to부정사, give up, avoid, deny는 동명사를 목적어로 취한다. ① sending → to send ② to eat → eating ③ to hurt → hurting ④ to threaten → threatening

35 정답 kept researching   UNIT **59** 전치사의 목적어로 쓰인 동명사, 관용표현

→ '계속 ~하다'는 keep -ing로 표현한다.

36 정답 succeeded in raising   UNIT **59** 전치사의 목적어로 쓰인 동명사, 관용표현

→ '~에서 성공하다'는 succeed in -ing로 표현한다.

37 정답 is focusing on providing   UNIT **59** 전치사의 목적어로 쓰인 동명사, 관용표현

→ '~에 집중하다'는 focus on -ing로 표현한다.

38 정답 making a mistake during the singing contest   UNIT **59** 전치사의 목적어로 쓰인 동명사, 관용표현

[해석] Mike: 수미, 왜 표정이 어둡니?

수미: 나는 노래대회 때 내가 실수를 할까봐 걱정이 돼.

수미는 무엇에 대해 걱정하고 있는가?

→ 수미는 노래대회 때 실수를 하는 것에 대해 걱정하고 있다.

→ 전치사 뒤에 올 수 있는 것은 동명사이므로 making ~로 써야 한다.

39 [정답] **talking loudly on your cell phones,
to take all your belongings with you**

UNIT **58** 동사의 목적어로 쓰이는 동명사, to부정사

[해석] 기차에서
1. 휴대폰으로 크게 통화하지 마세요.
→ 휴대폰으로 크게 통화하는 것을 멈추세요.
2. 자신의 소지품을 모두 챙겨가셔야 합니다.
→ 자신의 소지품을 모두 챙겨가는 것을 잊지 마십시오.
→ '~하는 것을 멈추다'는 stop -ing로 쓴다. / '~할 것을 잊다'는 「forget+to부정사」로 쓴다.

40 [정답] **to walk → walking**

UNIT **58** 동사의 목적어로 쓰이는 동명사, to부정사

[해석] Sam은 매일 강을 따라 걷는 것을 즐긴다.
→ enjoy의 목적어로 동명사가 와야 한다.

41 [정답] **studying not → not[never] studying**

UNIT **57** 동명사

[해석] Mary는 시험을 위해 충분히 공부하지 않은 것을 후회한다.
→ 동명사의 부정형은 앞에 not 또는 never를 써야 한다.

42 [정답] **create → creating**

UNIT **59** 전치사의 목적어로 쓰인 동명사, 관용표현

[해석] 우리는 모두를 위한 더 나은 미래를 만들 수 있다.
→ '~을 할 수 있다'를 뜻하는 be capable of 뒤에는 동명사가 온다.

43 [정답] **④**

UNIT **59** 전치사의 목적어로 쓰인 동명사, 관용표현

[해석] (A) 나는 당신으로부터 최종 결정에 대한 소식을 듣기를 고대한다.
(B) 그녀는 이런 곤경에서 벗어나는 것에 익숙하다.
(C) 그 국회의원은 쌀을 수입하는 것에 찬성했다.
→ (A) '~하기를 고대하다'는 look forward to -ing라고 쓴다.
(B) 전치사 to의 목적어로는 동명사가 와야 하고, 그녀가 '벗어나는' 능동의 의미여야 하므로 getting을 써야 한다.
(C) '~에 찬성하다'는 be in favor of -ing라고 쓴다.

44 [정답] **②**

UNIT **58** 동사의 목적어로 쓰이는 동명사, to부정사

[해석] ① 그는 비판받는 것을 피하려고 한다.
② 나는 지금 막 너의 기사를 다 읽었다.
③ 김 박사님은 나에게 커피 마시는 것을 중단하라고 말했다.
④ 그들은 그들의 엄마가 그들에게 말한 것을 하는 것을 잊어버렸다.
⑤ 몇 달 내로 외국어를 배우기를 기대하지 마라.
→ ② finish는 목적어로 동명사를 취한다. (to read → reading)
① avoid의 목적어인 동명사 ③ stop -ing: ~하는 것을 멈추다
④「forget+to부정사」: ~할 것을 잊다 ⑤ expect의 목적어인 to부정사

45 [정답] **④**

UNIT **58** 동사의 목적어로 쓰이는 동명사, to부정사

[해석] • 나는 그가 마라톤을 완주하는 것을 포기하지 않을 것이라고 믿는다.
• Vicky는 건강해지기 위해 패스트푸드를 먹지 않기로 결심했다.
• 그 기사는 이 단편 이야기가 출판될 가치가 있다고 말한다.

→ (A) give up -ing: ~하는 것을 포기하다 (B) quit -ing: ~하는 것을 그만두다 (C) be worth -ing: ~할 가치가 있다.

46 [정답] **④**

UNIT **57** 동명사

[해석] 김연아는 2010년 밴쿠버 동계 올림픽 피겨 스케이팅에서 금메달을 딴 한국의 피겨 스케이트 선수이다. 다리 부상과 경제적 문제로 고생했지만, 그녀는 올림픽에서 금메달리스트가 될 때까지 결코 포기하지 않았다. 언젠가 그녀의 어머니는 그녀가 항상 울곤 했다고 말했다. 그것은 메달을 딸 때까지 그녀가 계속 스케이트를 타는 것이 얼마나 스트레스를 받는 일이었는지를 보여 준다. 올림픽에서 프리 스케이팅 프로그램을 연기하고 나서 그녀는 "(경기에서) 처음으로 울었는데, 왜 그랬는지 아직도 모르겠어요."라고 말했다. 그녀가 이전에 흘렸던 눈물이 그녀를 피겨 스케이팅에서 한국의 첫 번째 올림픽 챔피언으로 만들었다.
→ ④ 명사는 목적어를 취할 수 없지만 동명사는 목적어를 취할 수 있다. her free-skating program을 목적어로 취해야 하므로 performance를 동명사 performing으로 고쳐야 한다. ① 분사구문 ②「used+to부정사」: ~하곤 했다 ③ go on -ing: 계속 ~하다 ⑤ 과거보다 앞선 시제로 쓰인 과거완료

47 [정답] **③**

UNIT **58** 동사의 목적어로 쓰이는 동명사, to부정사

[해석] 제주올레길은 자연을 좋아하는 사람에게 환상적인 장소이다. 경치 좋은 길을 걷는 것은 제주도의 숨 막히는 풍경을 즐길 수 있는 기회를 제공한다. 많은 사람들이 제주도의 해안선과 시골 풍경의 아름다움을 경험하기 위해 이 길을 하이킹하는 것을 선택한다. 다양한 길을 탐험하는 것이 자연과 연결되고 평화를 찾는 데 도움이 된다고 한다. 제주를 여행할 계획이라면 이 유명한 길을 걸어보는 기회를 놓치지 마라. 여유롭게 산책하는 것이나, 더 긴 구간에 도전하는 것, 그 어떤 방식으로든 이 길은 모두에게 맞는 무언가를 제공한다.
→ ③ choose는 to부정사를 목적어로 취하는 동사이므로 hiking을 to hike로 고쳐야 한다.

⑩ 분사

UNIT 60 분사의 종류와 역할

<table>
<tr><td colspan="3">개념 확인 문제 정답   ▶ 문제편 p.251</td></tr>
<tr><td>01 lying</td><td>02 missing</td><td>03 made</td></tr>
<tr><td>04 uploaded</td><td>05 cooked</td><td>06 driving</td></tr>
<tr><td>07 placed</td><td>08 shining</td><td>09 carrying</td></tr>
<tr><td>10 injured</td><td>11 sitting</td><td>12 chased</td></tr>
<tr><td>13 sleeping</td><td>14 arrested</td><td>15 repairing</td></tr>
<tr><td>16 listening</td><td>17 ⓐ</td><td>18 ⓐ</td></tr>
<tr><td>19 ⓒ</td><td>20 ⓑ</td><td>21 ⓒ</td></tr>
</table>

01 정답 lying

[해석] 나무 아래 누워 있는 고양이는 졸려 보인다.

→ cat을 수식하는 현재분사 lying으로 고쳐야 한다.

02 정답 missing

[해석] 경찰은 미아를 찾고 있다.

→ child를 수식하는 현재분사 missing으로 고쳐야 한다.

03 정답 made

[해석] 많은 사람들이 중국에서 만들어진 제품을 사용한다.

→ products를 수식하는 과거분사 made로 고쳐야 한다.

04 정답 uploaded

[해석] 네 블로그에 올린 내 사진들을 삭제해 주겠니?

→ photos를 수식하는 과거분사 uploaded로 고쳐야 한다.

05 정답 cooked

[해석] 어떤 사람들은 요리된 채소가 날것보다 훨씬 더 낫다고 말한다.

→ vegetables를 수식하는 과거분사 cooked로 고쳐야 한다.

06 정답 driving

[해석] 그 차를 운전하고 있는 남자는 우리의 선생님이다.

→ '차를 운전하고 있다'는 능동의 의미여야 하므로 현재분사 driving이 알맞다.

07 정답 placed

[해석] 나는 탁자에 몇 권의 책들이 놓여져 있는 것을 봤다.

→ 책들이 '놓여져 있다'는 수동의 의미여야 하므로 과거분사 placed가 알맞다.

08 정답 shining

[해석] 그녀는 파티에서 빛나는 목걸이를 했다.

→ '빛나는'이라는 능동의 의미여야 하므로 현재분사 shining이 알맞다.

09 정답 carrying

[해석] 큰 상자를 옮기고 있는 소년은 내 남동생이다.

→ '옮기고 있는'이라는 능동의 의미여야 하므로 현재분사 carrying이 알맞다.

10 정답 injured

[해석] 그들은 사고 후에 다친 사람들을 도왔다.

→ '다친'이라는 수동의 의미여야 하므로 과거분사 injured가 알맞다.

11 정답 sitting

[해석] 벤치에 앉아 있는 그 여자아이는 내 사촌이다.

→ '앉아 있다'는 능동의 의미여야 하므로 현재분사 sitting이 알맞다.

12 정답 chased

[해석] 그는 아이들 무리에게 쫓기고 있는 개를 봤다.

→ '쫓기고 있는' 수동의 의미여야 하므로 과거분사 chased가 알맞다.

13 정답 sleeping

[해석] 소파에서 자고 있는 소녀는 누구니?

→ '소파에서 자고 있는'이라는 능동과 진행의 의미여야 하므로 현재분사 sleeping이 알맞다.

14 정답 arrested

[해석] 나는 경찰에 체포된 남자를 보았다.

→ 남자가 경찰에게 체포를 당한 수동의 의미여야 하므로 수동의 의미를 갖는 과거분사 arrested가 알맞다.

15 정답 repairing

[해석] Tina는 그가 내 시계를 고치고 있는 것을 보았다.

→ '그가 고치고 있는' 것이므로 능동과 진행의 의미를 나타내도록 repairing이 와야 한다.

16 정답 listening

[해석] 그녀는 이어폰을 낀 채로 음악을 듣고 있었다.

→ 그녀가 음악을 듣는 능동의 의미여야 하므로 현재분사 listening이 와야 한다.

17 정답 ⓐ

[해석] 그 굴뚝에서 피어오르는 연기는 짙다.

→ 현재분사 rising이 명사를 수식한다.

18 정답 ⓐ

[해석] 그 콘서트장은 신난 팬들로 가득 찼다.

→ 과거분사 excited가 명사를 수식한다.

19 정답 ⓒ

[해석] 그녀는 전문 스타일리스트에게 머리를 잘랐다.

→ 과거분사 cut이 목적어 her hair의 행위를 보충 설명하는 목적격 보어로 쓰였다.

20 정답 ⓑ

[해석] 그 영화는 너무 흥미로워서 나는 그것을 두 번 봤다.

→ 현재분사 interesting이 주어의 상태를 보충 설명하는 주격 보어로 쓰였다.

21 정답 ⓒ

[해석] 나는 그 로봇이 어떤 인간의 도움도 없이 스스로 조립하는 것을 봤다.

→ 현재분사 assembling이 목적어 the robot의 행위를 보충 설명하는 목적격 보어로 쓰였다.

UNIT 61 현재분사와 동명사, 감정을 나타내는 분사

개념 확인 문제 정답 ▶ 문제편 **p.253**

01 a　　**02** a　　**03** b

04 현재분사　　**05** 동명사　　**06** 동명사

07 현재분사　　**08** 동명사　　**09** 현재분사

10 She told us an amazing story about her trip.

11 We were surprised to hear that he is leaving.

12 She likes watching exciting movies in the evening.

13 Everyone was disappointed when the concert was canceled.

14 I checked out the manuals, but they were very confusing.

---

01 정답 a

[해석] a. 저쪽에 서 있는 여자는 누구니?
b. 한 장소에 오래 서 있는 것은 힘든 일임에 틀림없다.
→ 첫 번째 문장의 standing 이하는 woman을 수식하는 현재분사구이고, 두 번째 문장의 standing은 주어 역할을 하는 동명사이다.

02 정답 a

[해석] a. 나는 내 아들이 수영장에서 수영하고 있는 것을 보았다.
b. 내가 가장 좋아하는 여름 활동은 수영하기이다.
→ 첫 번째 문장의 swimming은 지각동사 see의 목적격 보어로 쓰인 현재분사이고, 두 번째 문장의 swimming은 보어로 쓰인 동명사이다.

03 정답 b

[해석] a. 그녀의 꿈은 훌륭한 소설을 쓰는 것이다.
b. 내가 그녀의 방에 들어갔을 때 그녀는 영어로 일기를 쓰고 있었다.
→ 첫 번째 문장의 writing은 보어로 쓰인 동명사이고, 두 번째 문장의 writing은 was와 과거진행시제를 이루는 현재분사이다.

04 정답 현재분사

[해석] 자고 있는 아기들은 매우 평화로워 보인다.
→ sleeping은 babies를 수식하는 역할을 하는 현재분사이다.

05 정답 동명사

[해석] 네 침낭을 가져오는 것을 잊지 마.
→ sleeping bag은 '침낭'이라는 뜻의 동명사 어구이다.

06 정답 동명사

[해석] 이 건물에 흡연실이 있니?
→ smoking room은 '흡연실'이라는 뜻으로 동명사 어구이다.

07 정답 현재분사

[해석] 다음의 예는 우리에게 그것이 어떻게 작동하는지를 보여 줄 것이다.
→ following은 example을 수식하는 역할을 하는 현재분사이다.

08 정답 동명사

[해석] 너는 돋보기를 쓰고 있는 남자가 누구인지 아니?
→ reading glasses는 '돋보기'라는 뜻의 동명사 어구이다.

09 정답 현재분사

[해석] 그는 그의 분야를 속속들이 안다. 그는 걸어다니는 사전이다.
→ walking은 dictionary를 수식하는 역할을 하는 현재분사이다.

10 정답 She told us an amazing story about her trip.

→ 이야기가 '놀라운' 것이므로 현재분사 amazing을 쓴다.

11 정답 We were surprised to hear that he is leaving.

→ 우리가 '놀란' 것이므로 과거분사 surprised를 쓴다.

12 정답 She likes watching exciting movies in the evening.

→ 영화가 '신나는' 것이므로 현재분사 exciting을 쓴다.

13 정답 Everyone was disappointed when the concert was canceled.

→ 모두가 '실망한' 것이므로 과거분사 disappointed를 쓴다.

14 정답 I checked out the manuals, but they were very confusing.

→ 설명서가 '혼란스러운' 것이므로, 현재분사 confusing을 쓴다.

단원 평가 문제　UNIT 60 ~ UNIT 61　▶ 문제편 p.254~257

정답

01 called　**02** ③　**03** ③　**04** ③

05 ②　**06** ②　**07** injured　**08** fallen

09 leading　**10** called　**11** playing　**12** closed

13 permitting　**14** blowing　**15** kidnapped

16 named　**17** ①　**18** ①　**19** ④

20 ②　**21** waiting　**22** doing　**23** found

24 overlooking　**25** filled　**26** ending

27 ②　**28** ④　**29** ②　**30** ②　**31** ④

32 written　**33** injured　**34** playing

35 accommodating

36 at the baby smiling at me

37 work at a company founded 100 years ago

38 ⑤　**39** ③　**40** ⑤

01 정답 called   UNIT **60** 분사의 종류와 역할

[해석] 그들은 태블릿 PC라고 불리는 놀라운 기계를 팔기 시작했다.
→ '불리는'이라는 의미의 수동형이므로 과거분사 called가 와야 한다.

02 정답 ③   UNIT **60** 분사의 종류와 역할

[해석] 너는 문자 Q로 시작하는 어떤 단어를 말할 수 있니?
→ '시작하는'이라는 의미의 능동형이므로 현재분사가 와야 한다.

03 정답 ③   UNIT **60** 분사의 종류와 역할

[해석] 우리는 이 칼을 날카롭게 만들어야 할 필요가 있다. 그것은 너무 무디다.
→ 칼이 '날카롭게 되는' 수동의 의미이므로 과거분사가 와야 한다.

04 정답 ③   UNIT **60** 분사의 종류와 역할

[해석] 이것은 독일에서 온 여행객들을 위해 번역된 책인가요?
→ '번역된'이라는 의미의 수동형이므로 과거분사가 와야 한다.

05 정답 ②   UNIT **60** 분사의 종류와 역할

[해석] 나는 올해 올림픽에 참가하는 16세의 테니스 선수를 인터뷰하고 싶다.
→ '참가하는'이라는 의미의 능동형이므로 현재분사가 와야 한다.

06 정답 ②   UNIT **60** 분사의 종류와 역할

[해석] 최근에 출간된 많은 패션 잡지들 중에 이것이 최고이다.
→ '출간된'이라는 의미의 수동형이므로 과거분사가 와야 한다.

07 정답 injured   UNIT **60** 분사의 종류와 역할

[해석] 부상당한 군인들이 많다.
→ '부상당한'이라는 의미의 수동형이므로 과거분사가 와야 한다.

08 정답 fallen   UNIT **60** 분사의 종류와 역할

[해석] 어제 우리는 공원에서 낙엽 위를 걸었다.
→ '떨어진'이라는 의미의 수동형이므로 과거분사가 와야 한다.

09 정답 leading   UNIT **60** 분사의 종류와 역할

[해석] 이것이 인도의 선도 기업들의 목록이다.
→ '선도하는'이라는 의미의 능동형이므로 현재분사가 와야 한다.

10 정답 called   UNIT **60** 분사의 종류와 역할

[해석] 그녀는 어디선가 자신의 이름이 불리는 것을 들었다.
→ '불리는'이라는 의미의 수동형이므로 과거분사가 와야 한다.

11 정답 playing   UNIT **60** 분사의 종류와 역할

[해석] Kelly는 테니스를 하다가 손목을 삐었다.
→ Kelly가 테니스를 하는 것이므로 능동의 의미를 갖는 현재분사 playing이 알맞다.

12 정답 closed   UNIT **60** 분사의 종류와 역할

[해석] 그 소녀는 눈을 감은 채 음악을 들었다.
→ 눈이 감겨지는 수동의 관계이므로 과거분사 closed가 알맞다.

13 정답 permitting   UNIT **60** 분사의 종류와 역할

[해석] 날씨가 허락하면 우리는 벽을 페인트칠할 것이다.
→ 날씨가 허락하는 것이므로 능동의 의미를 갖는 현재분사 permitting이 알맞다.

14 정답 blowing   UNIT **60** 분사의 종류와 역할

[해석] 바다로부터 불어오는 차가운 바람이 있었다.
→ 바람이 '불어오는' 상태를 나타내므로 현재분사를 쓴다.

15 정답 kidnapped   UNIT **60** 분사의 종류와 역할

[해석] 경찰은 납치당한 소년을 찾기 위해 엄청난 노력을 기울이고 있다.
→ 누군가로부터 '납치당한'이라는 수동의 의미이므로 과거분사가 와야 한다.

16 정답 named   UNIT **60** 분사의 종류와 역할

[해석] 나는 "신에게 바쳐진"이라는 뜻을 의미하는 Isabella라고 이름 붙여진 친구가 하나 있다.
→ '이름 붙여진'이라는 수동의 의미이므로 과거분사가 와야 한다.

17 정답 ①   UNIT **61** 현재분사와 동명사, 감정을 나타내는 분사

[해석] ① 침낭이 왜 필요한 거야?
② 그는 터널을 통과하고 있는 차를 보았다.
③ 길을 건너고 있는 두 명의 여자들이 있다.
④ 우리는 자고 있는 아기를 깨우고 싶지 않았다.
⑤ 그들은 무대에서 연습하고 있는 가수를 안다.
→ ①의 sleeping bag은 '침낭'이라는 뜻으로, 이때 sleeping은 동명사이다. 나머지는 현재분사이다.

18 정답 ①   UNIT **61** 현재분사와 동명사, 감정을 나타내는 분사

[해석] ① 낯선 사람들을 향해 짖는 개가 한 마리 있다.
② 영어를 유창하게 말하는 것은 쉽지 않다.
③ 그는 다른 사람들의 감정을 아주 잘 읽는다.
④ 내가 창문을 모두 열어도 될까요?
⑤ 어린이 병원에서 봉사활동을 하는 것은 멋진 경험이었다.
→ ①은 앞의 명사 a dog를 수식하는 현재분사이고 나머지는 모두 동명사이다.

19 정답 ④   UNIT **60** 분사의 종류와 역할

[해석] ① 나는 내 가방에서 잃어버린 열쇠를 찾았다.
② 깨진 꽃병이 탁자 위에 있었다.
③ 어제 보낸 편지는 중요했다.
④ 그는 축구하다가 다리를 부러뜨렸다.
⑤ 피곤한 노동자들이 교대 근무 후에 휴식을 취했다.
→ ④ broken은 현재완료로 사용되었고, 나머지 문장들에서 과거분사는 형용사로 사용되어 명사를 수식하거나 상태를 나타내고 있다.

20 정답 ②   UNIT **60** 분사의 종류와 역할

[해석] ① 그 파손된 차는 견인됐다.
② 그녀는 시드니를 세 번 방문했다.
③ 완성된 제품은 배송 준비가 되어 있다.
④ 그들은 조각된 나무 조각상을 봤다.
⑤ 그는 면접에서 다듬어진 신발을 자랑했다.
→ ② visited는 과거분사가 현재완료로 사용되었고, 나머지 모두는 과거분사가 형용사로 사용되어 명사를 수식하고 있다.

21 정답 waiting   UNIT **60** 분사의 종류와 역할

[해석] 우리는 택시를 기다리면서 서 있었다.
→ 우리가 택시를 기다리는 것이므로 능동의 의미인 현재분사 waiting으로 써야 한다.

22 정답 doing   UNIT **60** 분사의 종류와 역할

[해석] David는 태권도를 하다가 허리를 다쳤다.
→ David가 태권도를 하는 것이므로 능동의 의미인 현재분사 doing으로 써야 한다.

23 [정답] found UNIT 60 분사의 종류와 역할

[해석] 소파 밑에서 발견된 열쇠는 Jake의 것이다.

→ 열쇠가 소파 밑에서 발견되는 수동의 관계이므로 과거분사 found로 써야 한다.

24 [정답] overlooking UNIT 60 분사의 종류와 역할

[해석] 나는 아름다운 정원이 내려다보이는 아파트에 산다.

→ overlook은 '(건물 등이) 바라보다, 내려다보다'라는 뜻의 동사이다. 아파트가 정원을 내려다보는 능동의 관계이므로 현재분사 overlooking을 써야 한다.

25 [정답] filled UNIT 60 분사의 종류와 역할

[해석] 사과 주스가 가득 담긴 유리잔이 탁자 위에 있었다.

→ 사과 주스는 유리잔에 담겨지는 수동의 관계이므로 과거분사 filled로 써야 한다.

26 [정답] ending UNIT 60 분사의 종류와 역할

[해석] 나의 아내는 우리 남자 아기가 '준'으로 끝나는 이름을 갖기를 원한다.

→ end는 '끝나다'라는 뜻의 자동사이므로 능동의 의미를 갖는 현재분사 ending을 써야 한다.

27 [정답] ② UNIT 60 분사의 종류와 역할

[해석] ① 흐르는 물은 매우 차갑다.

② 나는 발아래에서 차가 움직이는 걸 느꼈다.

③ 청소된 사무실은 훨씬 더 좋아 보였다.

④ 우리는 커플이 파티에서 춤추는 것을 지켜봤다.

⑤ 침대에서 울고 있는 아기는 주의가 필요하다.

→ ② the car가 움직이는 능동의 의미를 지녀야 하므로 현재분사 moving을 써야 한다.

28 [정답] ④ UNIT 60 분사의 종류와 역할

[해석] ① 짖고 있는 개가 모두를 깨웠다.

② 우리는 개울에서 흐르는 물을 즐겼다.

③ 우리 어머니가 초대한 손님들이 늦게 도착했다.

④ 그녀는 운동장에서 공이 튀는 것을 지켜봤다.

⑤ 프랑스어로 번역된 설명은 명확했다.

→ ④ the ball이 움직이는 능동의 의미를 지녀야 하므로 현재분사 bouncing 또는 원형부정사 bounce를 써야 한다.

29 [정답] ② UNIT 60 분사의 종류와 역할

[해석] ① 그는 그 연극에 놀랐다.

② 그 소음은 나에게 매우 거슬린다.

③ Jessy는 점수에 만족하지 않았다.

④ 나는 모든 종류의 영화를 보는 데 흥미가 있다.

⑤ 내비게이션은 너무 헷갈려서 도움이 되지 않았다.

→ ② 감정을 느끼게 하는 사물이나 대상은 현재분사, 감정을 느끼는 것은 과거분사를 사용해 표현하므로 annoyed가 아니라 annoying이 되어야 한다.

30 [정답] ② UNIT 60 분사의 종류와 역할

[해석] ① 나는 네게 말해줄 놀라운 소식이 있다.

② 그녀는 결과에 실망했다.

③ 그가 의사가 되었다니 놀랍다.

④ 그것은 모험에 관한 흥미진진한 영화이다.

⑤ 선생님의 설명은 아주 흥미롭다.

→ ② 감정을 느끼게 하는 사물이나 대상은 현재분사, 감정을 느끼는 것은 과거분사를 사용해 표현하므로 disappointing이 아니라 disappointed가 되어야 한다.

31 [정답] ④ UNIT 60 분사의 종류와 역할

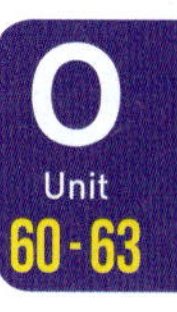

[해석] ① 나는 어머니가 전화 통화하시는 것을 들었다.

② 박물관에서 도난당한 그림은 아직 발견되지 않았다.

③ 오늘 아침에 버스가 거리에 주차되어 있는 차들과 충돌했다.

④ 정비소에는 아주 숙련된 엔지니어들이 몇 명 있다.

⑤ 그는 축구 선수로 뛰었던 시절에 대한 가장 재미있는 이야기를 내게 해 주었다.

→ ④ '노련한, 경험 많은'이라는 뜻으로 사람을 수식할 때는 수동의 의미를 갖는 experienced를 써야 한다.

32 [정답] written UNIT 60 분사의 종류와 역할

[해석] 나는 책을 찾고 있어. 그것은 John Grisham에 의해 쓰였어.

→ 나는 John Grisham에 의해 쓰인 책을 찾고 있어.

→ 책은 John Grisham에 의해 '쓰인' 수동의 관계이므로 과거분사 written을 써야 한다.

33 [정답] injured UNIT 60 분사의 종류와 역할

[해석] 그 노부인은 사고로 다쳤다. 그녀는 병원으로 실려 갔다.

→ 사고로 다친 그 노부인은 병원으로 실려 갔다.

→ 노부인이 다친 것이므로 수동의 의미를 갖는 과거분사 injured를 써야 한다.

34 [정답] playing UNIT 60 분사의 종류와 역할

[해석] 공원에 아이들이 몇 명 있다. 그들은 숨바꼭질을 하고 있다.

→ 공원에 숨바꼭질을 하고 있는 아이들이 몇 명 있다.

→ 아이들이 숨바꼭질을 하고 있는 것이므로 능동의 의미를 갖는 현재분사 playing을 써야 한다.

35 [정답] accommodating UNIT 60 분사의 종류와 역할

[해석] 새로운 영화관이 도심부에 막 개장했다. 그 영화관은 200명의 사람들을 수용한다.

→ 200명의 사람들을 수용하는 새로운 영화관이 도심부에 막 개장했다.

→ 영화관이 200명의 사람들을 수용하는 주체이므로 능동의 의미를 갖는 현재분사 accommodating을 써야 한다.

36 [정답] at the baby smiling at me UNIT 60 분사의 종류와 역할

→ '미소 짓고 있는'이라는 의미의 능동형이므로 명사 the baby를 현재분사 smiling이 뒤에서 수식하는 구조로 쓴다.

37 [정답] work at a company founded 100 years ago UNIT 60 분사의 종류와 역할

→ '설립된'이라는 의미의 수동형이므로 과거분사 founded가 명사 a company를 뒤에서 수식하는 구조로 쓴다.

38 [정답] ⑤ UNIT 61 현재분사와 동명사, 감정을 나타내는 분사

[해석] ① 나는 오색빛깔의 단풍잎이 떨어지는 것을 보았다.

② 너는 왼손잡이들을 위해 만들어진 가위를 받았니?

③ 사용하지 않을 때는 전등을 꺼놔야 한다.

④ 나는 처음으로 놀이공원을 가게 되어 너무 기뻤다.

⑤ 우리는 서울에서 열리는 개막식에 참석할 것이다.

→ '개막식'은 동명사를 사용하여 opening ceremony로 표현한다. ① to fall → fall[falling] ② making → made ③ turn off → be turned off ④ exciting → excited

39 정답 ③　　　　　UNIT 60 분사의 종류와 역할

[해석] 콜라 같은 탄산음료가 치아에 해롭다는 것이 알려져 왔다. 산은 그 성분 중 하나이다. 그것은 에나멜이라고 불리는 보호 코팅을 부식시켜 결국에는 치아의 표면을 약하게 한다. 게다가 탄산음료 속의 당은 극히 크기가 작아서 표면에 더 오래 남아 있을 수 있다. 결국 치아 조직 전체가 설탕이 든 탄산음료에 의해 약해진다.

→ ③ 보호막이 에나멜이라고 불리는 것이므로 수동의 의미를 지닌 과거분사 called가 들어가야 한다. ① 과거분사 known을 사용하여 만든 수동태 ② 전치사의 목적어로 온 동명사 ④ Because it is extremely small을 분사구문으로 바꾼 것 ⑤ 과거분사 weakened를 사용하여 만든 수동태

40 정답 ⑤　　　　　UNIT 60 분사의 종류와 역할

[해석] Antoni Gaudí(안토니 가우디)는 스페인의 유명한 건축가였으며, 자연에서 영감을 받은 그의 독특한 스타일로 잘 알려져 있다. 그의 스타일은 복잡한 곡선과 유기적인 형태로 특징지어졌으며, 환경과의 조화를 이뤄내는 느낌을 자아냈다. 가우디는 바르셀로나에서 많은 대표적인 건축물들을 설계했으며, 그중에는 사그라다 파밀리아, 카사 바트요, 파르크 구엘 등이 있다. 그의 작품들은 현재 유네스코 세계문화유산으로 보호받고 있다. 예를 들어, 가우디에 의해 설계된 사그라다 파밀리아와 파르크 구엘은 1984년에 유네스코 세계문화유산으로 등재되었다. 또한, 카사 바트요와 카사 밀라는 그들의 독특한 디자인으로 인정받아 2005년에 포함되었다.

→ ⑤ '독특한 디자인으로 인정받아'라는 내용을 의미해야 하므로 현재분사 recognizing을 수동 또는 완료를 의미하는 과거분사 recognized로 고쳐야 한다.

UNIT 62 분사구문

개념 확인 문제 정답　　　▶ 문제편 p.259

01 Being tired　　02 Winning the game
03 Winning the prize
04 Wanting to travel to America
05 Although[(Even) Though] he is out of breath
06 Because[As, Since] she felt sick
07 While[As] we had lunch
08 While[As] she patted him on the shoulder
09 I → 삭제　　　10 Talked → Talking
11 Accept → Accepting　　12 To go → Going
13 Gotten → Getting　　14 and → 삭제

---

01 정답 Being tired

[해석] 피곤해서 나는 일찍 집에 왔다.

→ 부사절의 접속사와 주어 I를 생략하고, be동사를 Being으로 바꾸어 분사구문으로 만든다.

02 정답 Winning the game

[해석] 그 경기에 이기면 너는 16강에 들 수 있다.

→ 부사절의 접속사와 주어 you를 생략하고, 동사 win을 Winning으로 바꾸어 분사구문으로 만든다.

03 정답 Winning the prize

[해석] 상을 탔음에도 불구하고, 그는 그것에 만족하지 않았다.

→ 부사절의 접속사와 주어 he를 생략하고, 동사 won을 Winning으로 바꾸어 분사구문으로 만든다.

04 정답 Wanting to travel to America

[해석] 그는 미국으로 여행을 가고 싶어서 영어를 열심히 공부한다.

→ 부사절의 접속사와 주어 he를 생략하고, 동사 wants를 Wanting으로 바꾸어 분사구문으로 만든다.

05 정답 Although[(Even) Though] he is out of breath

[해석] 숨이 차는데도 불구하고 그는 계속 달린다.

→ 주절과 분사구문의 내용이 상반되므로 분사구문을 양보의 부사절로 만든다. 주절의 시제가 현재이므로 부사절의 시제도 현재시제로 쓴다.

06 정답 Because[As, Since] she felt sick

[해석] 아파서 그녀는 학교를 조퇴했다.

→ 분사구문이 원인, 주절이 결과에 해당하므로 이유의 접속사 because, as, since를 사용하여 부사절을 만든다.

07 정답 While[As] we had lunch

[해석] 점심을 먹으면서 우리는 휴가 계획에 대해 이야기했다.

→ 동시동작을 나타내므로 접속사 while이나 as를 이용하여 부사절로 바꾼다. 주절에 과거시제 동사가 쓰였으므로 부사절의 시제도 과거로 일치시킨다.

08 정답 While[As] she patted him on the shoulder

[해석] 그녀는 그의 어깨를 두드리면서 기운을 북돋워 주려고 노력했다.

→ 동시동작을 나타내므로 접속사 while이나 as를 이용하여 부사절로 바꾼다. 동사를 주절의 시제에 맞추어 과거시제로 쓴다.

09 정답 I → 삭제

[해석] 아침을 먹은 후에 나는 학교에 갔다.

→ 분사구문에서 부사절의 주어와 주절의 주어가 같으면 부사절의 주어를 생략하므로 주어 I를 생략하고 Eating만 써야 한다.

10 정답 Talked → Talking

[해석] 전화 통화를 하면서 그녀는 간식을 먹었다.

→ 동시동작을 나타내도록 Talked를 현재분사 Talking으로 바꾸어 분사구문으로 만든다.

11 정답 Accept → Accepting
[해석] 내 제안을 받아들인다면 너는 많은 돈을 벌 것이다.
→ 조건을 나타내는 분사구문이므로 Accept를 현재분사 Accepting으로 고쳐야 한다.

12 정답 To go → Going
[해석] 한 블록을 더 가면 너는 역을 볼 수 있을 것이다.
→ 조건을 나타내는 분사구문이므로 To go를 현재분사 Going으로 고쳐야 한다.

13 정답 Gotten → Getting
[해석] 나쁜 결과를 받아서 나는 매우 실망했다.
→ 분사구문의 분사는 능동의 의미를 갖는 현재분사로 써야 한다.

14 정답 and → 삭제
[해석] 버스를 기다리다가 나는 지갑을 집에 두고 왔다는 것을 알았다.
→ 분사구문과 주절 사이에 접속사는 필요하지 않다.

UNIT 63 주의해야 할 분사구문

> **개념 확인 문제 정답**　　　　▶ 문제편 p.261
>
> **01** Not feeling　　**02** eaten
> **03** Being　　**04** Not having met
> **05** Having arrived　　**06** Not knowing
> **07** Having burnt　　**08** the radio turned on
> **09** The water (being) cut off
> **10** He not arriving yet　　**11** Frankly speaking
> **12** night approaching
> **13** Knowing not → Not knowing
> **14** Traveled → Traveling　　**15** His having → Having
> **16** crossing → crossed　　**17** failing → failed

01 정답 Not feeling
[해석] 몸이 좋지 않아서 나는 초대를 거절했다.
→ 분사구문의 부정형은 분사 앞에 not을 쓴다.

02 정답 eaten
[해석] 매일 사과 한 개를 먹게 되면 당신은 건강을 증진시킬 수 있다.
→ 사과는 사람에 의해 먹히는 수동의 관계이므로 과거분사 eaten이 알맞다. eaten 앞에 being이 생략된 것이다.

03 정답 Being
[해석] 여우에게 아첨을 받고서 어리석은 까마귀는 노래를 부르기 시작했다.
→ 수동 분사구문은 「being[having been]+과거분사」 형태로 쓰므로 Being이 알맞다.

04 정답 Not having met
[해석] 그녀를 전에 만난 적이 없어서 나는 쉽게 그녀를 알아볼 수 없었다.
→ 문맥상 그녀를 쉽게 알아볼 수 없는 이유는 그녀를 이전에 만난 적이 없기 때문이므로 완료형 분사구문을 부정 형태로 써야 한다.

05 정답 Having arrived
[해석] 커피숍에 도착했을 때 그는 그의 여자 친구가 가 버린 것을 발견했다.
→ 여자 친구가 가 버린 것을 발견한 것보다 먼저 커피숍에 도착한 것이므로 완료형 분사구문으로 쓴다.

06 정답 Not knowing
[해석] 경기의 규칙을 모르기 때문에 나는 경기를 즐길 수 없었다.
→ 경기를 즐길 수 없는 이유는 경기의 규칙을 모르기 때문이므로 분사구문의 부정 형태로 써야 한다.

07 정답 Having burnt
[해석] 집을 다 태우고 나서야 불이 제어되었다.
→ 불이 집을 태우는 능동의 의미이므로 능동태 완료형 분사구문을 써야 한다.

08 정답 the radio turned on
[해석] 그녀는 라디오를 켠 채로 잠이 들었다.
→ 부사절을 「with+명사+분사」의 분사구문으로 바꾼다. 라디오는 누군가에 의해 켜진 수동의 관계이므로 the radio 뒤에 과거분사 turned를 쓴다.

09 정답 The water (being) cut off
[해석] 단수 중이어서 나는 샤워를 할 수 없다.
→ 부사절과 주절의 주어가 다르므로 분사구문에 주어를 써야 한다. 수동 분사구문의 being은 생략할 수 있다.

10 정답 He not arriving yet
[해석] 그가 아직 도착하지 않았음에도 우리는 파티를 시작했다.
→ 부사절과 주절의 주어가 다르므로 분사구문에 주어를 써 주어야 한다. 분사의 부정형은 분사 앞에 not을 써야 하므로 He not arriving yet으로 쓴다.

11 정답 Frankly speaking
[해석] 솔직히 말해서 그 일은 그의 능력을 넘어서는 것 같다.
→ '솔직히 말해서'라는 뜻의 분사구문의 관용적 표현은 frankly speaking이라고 쓴다.

12 정답 night approaching
[해석] 밤이 다가오면서 밝은 별들이 하늘에 나타났다.
→ 부사절을 「with+명사+분사」의 분사구문으로 바꾼다. approached는 능동의 의미를 갖는 현재분사 approaching으로 써야 한다.

13 정답 Knowing not → Not knowing
[해석] 무엇을 해야 할지 몰라서 그는 가만히 서 있었다.
→ 분사구문의 부정형은 분사 앞에 not을 쓴다.

14 정답 Traveled → Traveling
[해석] 호주에서 여행을 하면서 나는 캥거루 고기를 먹어 보았다.

→ 내가 여행을 한 것이므로 Traveled를 능동의 의미인 현재 분사 Traveling으로 써야 한다.

15 [정답] His having → Having
[해석] 그는 커피 한 잔을 마시면서 신문을 보고 있다.
→ 부사절과 주절의 주어가 같으므로 분사 앞의 His는 삭제해야 한다.

16 [정답] crossing → crossed
[해석] 그녀는 다리를 꼰 채 스마트폰을 확인하고 있었다.
→ 다리가 꼬이는 수동의 관계이므로 과거분사 crossed로 써야 한다.

17 [정답] failing → failed
[해석] 시험에 두 번 떨어져서 그는 다시 그것을 시도하지 않기로 결정했다.
→ 완료형 분사구문은 「having+과거분사」 형태로 쓴다.

단원 평가 문제　UNIT 62 ~ UNIT 63　▶ 문제편 p.262~266

정답

01 ④	**02** ⑤	**03** Frankly speaking
04 While going	**05** Being	**06** Not talking
07 ④	**08** ②	**09** ④　　**10** ④

11 Feeling tired　**12** Walking my dog
13 Being an hour late　**14** Not knowing
15 Having　**16** ③　**17** ⑤　**18** ①
19 ②　**20** ②　**21** your back turned
22 Checking in the hotel
23 Having seen the advertisement
24 There being no empty seats on the train
25 ②　**26** ⑤　**27** Sitting
28 Because[As, Since] it started raining[to rain]
29 checking　**30** pointing　**31** Judging from
32 ⑤　**33** ②　**34** ②　**35** ④　**36** ⑤
37 With the baby crying
38 ④　**39** ①　**40** ⑤

01 [정답] ④　UNIT 63 주의해야 할 분사구문
[해석] A: 파리는 처음이니?
B: 아니, 2년 전에 와봐서 길은 알아.
→ 2년 전에 방문한 것은 과거의 일이므로 「having+과거분사」의 완료형 분사구문으로 써야 한다.

02 [정답] ⑤　UNIT 63 주의해야 할 분사구문
[해석] A: 유명한 감독에 의해 연출된 그 영화는 멋진 장면들로 가득했어.
B: 그거 정말 멋지게 들리네!

→ 분사구문에서 '영화가 감독에 의해 연출된 상태'로 완료된 동작을 설명할 때 수동태 형태 Having been directed가 와야 한다.

03 [정답] Frankly speaking　UNIT 63 주의해야 할 분사구문
[해석] 솔직히 말해서 이것은 말도 안 된다.
→ '솔직히 말해서'라는 뜻의 분사구문의 관용적 표현은 frankly speaking으로 쓴다.

04 [정답] While going　UNIT 62 분사구문
[해석] 역에 가는 동안 나는 내 친구 중의 한 명을 만났다.
→ 내가 역에 가고 있었던 것이므로 능동의 의미를 갖는 현재분사 going이 알맞다. 부사절을 분사구문으로 만들 때 분사구문의 의미를 정확하게 나타내기 위해 접속사를 생략하지 않을 수도 있다.

05 [정답] Being　UNIT 62 분사구문
[해석] 16살밖에 안 됐기 때문에 나는 운전면허증을 취득할 수 없다.
→ 분사구문이 주절의 시제와 일치하므로 Being이 알맞다.

06 [정답] Not talking　UNIT 63 주의해야 할 분사구문
[해석] 많이 이야기하지 않아도 우리는 상대방이 무슨 생각을 하는지 알 수 있다.
→ 분사구문을 부정형으로 쓸 때 not을 분사 앞에 쓴다.

07 [정답] ④　UNIT 62 분사구문
[해석] 기사를 다 쓴 후에, 나는 뉴욕으로 떠났다.
→ 분사구문에서 주절과 종속절의 주어가 같고, 시제가 같으면, -ing 형태로 쓸 수 있고, 뜻을 명확히 하기 위해 접속사를 생략하지 않을 수 있다.

08 [정답] ②　UNIT 62 분사구문
[해석] 창밖을 내다보았을 때, 그녀는 하늘에 번개가 번쩍이는 것을 보았다.
→ 분사구문에 주어가 없고 Looking으로 시작하므로 주절과 종속절의 주어와 시제가 같고, '~할 때'를 나타내는 접속사가 필요하므로 ② When she looked out the window가 알맞다.

09 [정답] ④　UNIT 63 주의해야 할 분사구문
→ 분사구문의 관용적 표현인 '솔직히 말하자면'은 frankly speaking으로 쓴다.

10 [정답] ④　UNIT 62 분사구문
[해석] • 놀라서 그녀는 휴대폰을 떨어뜨리고 뒤로 물러섰다.
• 무거운 박스를 들고 있었기 때문에 남자는 문을 열기 어려웠다.
→ '놀란'이라는 의미로 감정을 느끼는 것이므로 수동형인 과거분사를 써야 하고, '나르고 있는'이라는 능동의 의미이므로 현재분사를 써야 한다.

11 [정답] Feeling tired　UNIT 62 분사구문
[해석] 피곤했기 때문에, 그녀는 침대에 누웠다.
→ 종속절과 주절의 주어가 she로 같으므로 주어를 생략하고 시제도 같으므로 종속절의 동사를 Feeling으로 변형시킨다.

12 [정답] Walking my dog　UNIT 62 분사구문
[해석] 개를 산책시키는 동안 나는 우연히 내 옛 친구를 만났다.
→ 종속절과 주절의 주어가 I로 같으므로 주어를 생략하고 시제도 같으므로 종속절의 진행형 동사에서 Walking만 남긴다.

13 [정답] Being an hour late   UNIT **62** 분사구문

[해석] 한 시간이나 늦었음에도 불구하고 그녀는 사과의 한 마디를 하지 않았다.

→ 종속절과 주절의 주어가 she로 같으므로 주어를 생략하고 시제도 같으므로 종속절의 동사를 Being으로 변형시킨다.

14 [정답] Not knowing   UNIT **63** 주의해야 할 분사구문

[해석] 어디로 가야할지 몰랐기 때문에, 나는 길을 묻기 위해 멈추었다.

→ 종속절과 주절의 주어가 I로 같으므로 주어를 생략하고 시제도 같으므로 종속절의 동사를 knowing으로 변형시킨다. 또한, 분사구문의 부정문은 분사 앞에 not 또는 never를 붙여야 하므로 Not knowing이 알맞다.

15 [정답] Having   UNIT **62** 분사구문

[해석] 나와 식사를 마친 후, Elly는 집으로 돌아갔다.

→ 종속절과 주절의 주어가 같고 시제도 같으므로 종속절의 동사를 Having으로 변형시킨다. 또한, Elly라는 고유명사가 있으므로 주절의 주어를 Elly로 써 준다.

16 [정답] ③   UNIT **62** 분사구문

[해석] ① 가난함에도 불구하고, 그녀는 미소를 절대 잃지 않는다.

② 나이가 어림에도 불구하고, 그녀는 세계적으로 유명한 화가이다.

③ 소파에서 신문을 읽으면서, 나는 편안함을 느꼈다.

④ 어린아이에 의해 쓰여졌음에도 불구하고, 그 기사는 잘 쓰이고 설득력이 있었다.

⑤ 퍼즐을 어떻게 풀지 모름에도 불구하고, 그는 그것에 대해 아는 척한다.

→ ③은 동시동작을 나타내는 분사구문이고, 나머지는 양보의 의미를 지닌 분사구문이다.

17 [정답] ⑤   UNIT **62** 분사구문

[해석] 하루 종일 일을 하느라 피곤했음에도 불구하고 그는 여행 가방을 싸는 것을 멈출 수 없었다.

→ 피곤했는데도 불구하고 여행 가방을 계속 쌌다고 했으므로 양보의 접속사를 이용하여 절로 바꾸는 것이 알맞다.

18 [정답] ①   UNIT **62** 분사구문

[해석] 버스에서 내렸을 때 나는 내 가방을 두고 온 것을 알아차렸다.

→ '버스를 내린 순간'을 강조하는 순차적인 의미로 접속사 When이 이끄는 부사절 ①이 가장 적절하다.

19 [정답] ②   UNIT **62** 분사구문

[해석] 나는 과제를 제출한 후, 컴퓨터 게임을 했다.

→ '과제를 제출한 후'라는 의미가 가장 적절하므로 접속사 After가 이끄는 부사절 ②이 가장 적절하다.

20 [정답] ②   UNIT **62** 분사구문

[해석] 무슨 말을 해야 할지 몰라서 모두 침묵을 지켰다.

→ '무엇을 말해야 할지 몰라서'라는 원인이나 이유를 설명하기 위해서는 접속사 as가 이끄는 ②이 가장 적절하다.

21 [정답] your back turned   UNIT **63** 주의해야 할 분사구문

[해석] 등을 돌린 채 말하지 않는 게 좋다.

→ 부사절의 주어를 with의 목적어로 쓰고, is turned를 분사 being turned로 바꾸어야 하는데 with 분사구문에서 being은 생략한다.

22 [정답] Checking in the hotel   UNIT **62** 분사구문

[해석] 호텔에 입실 수속을 한 후, 나는 엄마에게 전화를 걸었다.

→ 부사절과 주절의 주어, 시제가 일치하므로 접속사, 주어를 생략하고, checked를 현재분사 checking으로 쓰면 된다.

23 [정답] Having seen the advertisement   UNIT **63** 주의해야 할 분사구문

[해석] 광고를 보았기 때문에 그는 그 축제에 대해 알고 있다.

→ 부사절과 주절의 주어는 같고 시제는 한 시제 앞서므로 접속사, 주어를 생략하고 saw를 완료형 분사구문 「having+과거분사」로 쓰면 된다.

24 [정답] There being no empty seats on the train   UNIT **63** 주의해야 할 분사구문

[해석] 기차에 빈자리가 없다면 너는 계속 서 있어야 한다.

→ 부사절에 there is 구문이 쓰이면 there를 생략하지 않고 그대로 쓴 다음 be동사를 being으로 쓴다.

25 [정답] ②   UNIT **62** 분사구문

→ 종속절의 접속사를 생략하고, 주절의 주어와 종속절의 주어가 the book으로 같으므로 주어를 생략한다. '쓰여진' 것이므로 수동형인데 이 경우 Being을 생략할 수 있으므로 Written in English가 알맞다.

26 [정답] ⑤   UNIT **62** 분사구문

→ 종속절의 접속사를 생략하고, 주절의 주어와 종속절의 주어가 I로 같으므로 주어를 생략한다. 또한, 분사구문의 부정문은 분사 앞에 not 또는 never를 붙이고, '어디로 ~할지'는 「where+to부정사」로 쓴다.

27 [정답] Sitting   UNIT **62** 분사구문

→ 동시동작을 나타내는 분사구문이다.

28 [정답] Because[As, Since] it started raining[to rain]   UNIT **62** 분사구문

→ 이유의 접속사 Because[As, Since]를 써서 부사절을 완성한다.

29 [정답] checking   UNIT **62** 분사구문

→ 시간을 나타내는 접속사 After를 의미 전달을 위해 생략하지 않았으므로 뒤에 분사구문이 이어지도록 한다. '~을 확인하다'라는 뜻의 check를 이용해 쓴다. 빈칸이 1개이므로 make sure 등은 쓸 수 없다.

30 [정답] pointing   UNIT **62** 분사구문

→ 손가락으로 '가리키고 있는' 것이 능동의 의미이므로 현재분사를 써서 분사구문을 완성한다.

31 [정답] Judging from   UNIT **63** 주의해야 할 분사구문

→ '~으로 판단하건대'라는 뜻의 분사구문의 관용적 표현은 judging from이다.

32 [정답] ⑤   UNIT **62** 분사구문

[해석] ① 빨리 어두워졌기 때문에 우리는 서둘러야 했다.

② 크게 짖으면서 그 개는 나에게 달려왔다.

③ 아팠기 때문에, 나는 오늘 출근을 하지 못했다.

④ 네가 비협조적이기 때문에, 우리는 이 프로젝트를 제시간에 끝낼 수 없다.

⑤ Jack은 생일날 선물을 받아서 기분이 매우 좋았다.

→ ⑤ Jack이 생일에 선물을 받는 것이므로 현재분사를 과거분사로 고쳐야 한다. (Being giving → Given) ① 주어가 주절과 다르므로 It, 시제는 과거로 같으므로 getting으로 쓴 분사구문 ② 주어가 주절의 주어와 같아서 생략하고 시제도 과거로 같은 분사구문 Barking loudly ③ 주어가 주절의 주어 I와 같아서 생략하고 시제도 과거로 같은 분사구문 Being sick ④ 주어가 주절과 다르므로 You, 시제는 과거로 같으므로 being으로 쓴 분사구문

33 [정답] ② UNIT **63** 주의해야 할 분사구문

[해석] ① 입에 음식이 가득한 채로 말을 하지 않도록 해라.

② James는 팔짱을 낀 채 말을 하고 있었다.

③ 그녀는 얼굴에 눈물을 흘리며 말했다.

④ 너는 TV를 켜 둔 채로 종종 잠을 자니?

⑤ 그는 자신의 등을 벽에 기댄 채 무언가를 생각하고 있었다.

→ 「with+명사+분사」는 '~한 채, ~하고서'라는 의미로 동시 동작을 나타낸다. ②의 arms는 동작을 받는 수동의 의미를 가지므로 crossing을 과거분사인 crossed로 써야 한다. 나머지는 모두 알맞은 형태로 '~한 채, ~하고서'라는 의미를 나타내고 있다.

34 [정답] ② UNIT **62** 분사구문

[해석] 노예의 아들로 태어났기 때문에 John은 배울 기회가 많지 않았다. 그러나 그는 평생 11개의 학위를 취득했고, 6개의 언어를 배웠다. 그는 배우는 것을 결코 멈추지 않았다. 그는 "배우는 것은 항상 나에게 아주 큰 즐거움입니다."라고 말했다.

→ (A) Because he was born as ~의 부사절을 분사구문으로 바꾼 것이므로 Being born이나 Born으로 시작해야 한다.
(B) 문맥상 '배우는 것을 멈추지 않았다'라는 의미가 되어야 하므로 stop의 목적어로 동명사를 써야 한다.

35 [정답] ④ UNIT **63** 주의해야 할 분사구문

[해석] ① 사람들은 맹렬하게 타는 불을 지켜보았다.

② 당신은 'Miracle'이라고 불리는 건물을 알고 있나요?

③ 당신의 나라에서 말해지는 첫 번째 언어는 무엇인가요?

④ 개가 사납게 짖는 가운데 그들은 집을 나섰다.

⑤ 질문을 받는 사람 대부분은 설문에 답하기를 망설였다.

→ ④ 「with+명사+분사」는 '~한 채, ~하고서'라는 의미로 동시 동작을 나타낸다. 개가 '짖는' 것이므로 현재분사 barking이 오는 것은 알맞다. ① '타고 있는 불'을 의미해야 하므로 현재분사를 써야 한다. (burned → burning) ② '~라는 이름으로 불리는'을 의미해야 하므로 과거분사를 써야 한다. (calling → called) ③ '말해지는 첫 번째 언어'를 의미해야 하므로 과거분사를 써야 한다. (speaking → spoken) ⑤ '질문을 받은 사람'을 의미해야 하므로 과거분사를 써야 한다. (questioning → questioned)

36 [정답] ⑤ UNIT **63** 주의해야 할 분사구문

[해석] ① 빨간 불일 때는 길을 건널 수 없다.

② 비가 와서 우리는 집에 있기로 결정했다.

③ 보청기가 없어서 John은 내가 말하는 것을 들을 수 없었다.

④ 그 여자는 머리카락이 바람에 날리는 채로 벤치에 앉아 있다.

⑤ 그의 억양으로 판단하건대 박 선생님은 호주 출신임이 분명하다.

→ ⑤ 일반인을 주어로 하는 분사구문에서는 주어가 생략된다. judging from은 '~로 판단하건대'라는 뜻이다. ① 주절의 you가 빨간 불로 바뀌는 것이 아니므로 분사구문의 주어가 필요하다. (Turning red → The light turning red) ② 날씨를 나타내는 분사구문의 주어 It이 필요하다. (Being rainy → It being rainy) ③ 문맥상 보청기가 없어서 못 듣는 것이므로 분사구문의 부정형으로 써야 한다. (Having not → Not having) ④ blow는 '날리다'라는 뜻의 자동사로 쓰이므로 과거분사 blown을 blowing으로 써야 한다.

37 [정답] With the baby crying UNIT **63** 주의해야 할 분사구문

→ 아기가 '우는' 능동의 관계이므로 현재분사 crying을 쓴 With the baby crying이 알맞다.

38 [정답] ④ UNIT **63** 주의해야 할 분사구문

[해석] ⓐ 무슨 말을 해야 할지 몰라서, 나는 그냥 고개만 끄덕였다.

ⓑ 생일 얘기 나와서 말인데, 내 생일은 다음 주야!

ⓒ 모두가 보고 있는 상황에서 그는 실수를 했다.

→ ④ 분사구문의 관용적 표현은 주어가 you가 아닌 일반인일 때 생략하고 쓰는 표현이다.

39 [정답] ① UNIT **63** 주의해야 할 분사구문

[해석] Ronald Reagan이 캘리포니아의 주지사로 있었을 때 그는 멕시코시티에서 연설을 했다. 연설을 마친 후, 그는 자리에 앉았다. 하지만 청중이 그에게 박수갈채를 보내지 않아서 그는 당혹스러웠다. 다음 연설자가 스페인 어로 말을 했는데, Reagan은 그 연설을 이해하지 못했다. 그리고 그 연사는 매 단락마다 박수갈채를 받았다. 자존심을 지키기 위해 Reagan은 다른 누구보다도 앞서 그리고 다른 누구보다도 오래 박수를 치기 시작했다. 그러자 미국 대사가 그에게 다가가 조용히 말했다. "주지사님, 제가 주지사님이라면 그렇게 하지 않겠어요. 그는 주지사님의 연설을 스페인 어로 통역하고 있는 겁니다."

→ ① 종속절(분사구문 부분)과 주절의 주어는 같고 시제는 다르다. 따라서 「having+과거분사」 형태의 완료형 분사구문으로 써야 하므로 Having finished가 알맞다. ② felt의 보어로 쓰인 과거분사 ③ 수동태를 만드는 과거분사 ④ started의 목적어로 쓰인 동명사 ⑤ 현재진행시제를 만드는 현재분사

40 [정답] ⑤ UNIT **62** 분사구문

[해석] 영국 콘월에 있는 Eden Project는 자연과 어울리도록 설계된 독특한 생물 군계들의 모음이다. 이곳은 인간과 환경의 관계를 보여주며, 다양한 기후에서 온 수천 종의 식물들을 보유하고 있다. 옛 점토 채석장에 지어진 이 생물 군계는 땅에서 자연스럽게 자라는 것으로 보인다. 방문객들은 생기가 넘치는 식물들과 나무들로 둘러싸여 있는 울창한 열대 우림을 걷는다. 육각형 패널로 만들어진 투명한 돔은 햇빛을 받아들여 다양한 생태계에 이상적인 조건을 만들어 준다.

→ ⑤ 투명한 돔이 만드는 것이 아니라 '만들어진' 것이므로 과거분사 made가 와야 한다.

 **관계사**

UNIT 64 관계대명사

> **개념 확인 문제 정답**   ▶ 문제편 **p.269**

01 who   **02** whose   **03** whom
04 which   **05** who(m) you called is my boss
06 who solved the problem is very smart
07 whose coach was fired is struggling this season
08 주격 관계대명사   **09** 소유격 관계대명사
10 목적격 관계대명사

01 정답 who

[해석] 나는 인턴 한 명을 고용했다. 그 인턴은 중국어로 유창하게 말한다.
→ 나는 중국어로 유창하게 말하는 인턴을 고용했다.
→ The intern은 an intern을 가리키므로 사람을 선행사로 하는 주격 관계대명사 who로 바꾸어 두 문장을 연결한다.

02 정답 whose

[해석] 그녀는 앵무새 한 마리를 입양했다. 그것의 깃털은 밝은 녹색과 파란색이다.
→ 그녀는 깃털이 밝은 녹색과 파란색인 앵무새를 입양했다.
→ Its는 a parrot's를 가리키므로 소유격 관계대명사 whose로 바꾸어 두 문장을 연결한다.

03 정답 whom

[해석] 그는 손님들을 맞이했다. 그는 그들을 여름휴가 동안 만났다.
→ 그는 여름휴가 동안 만났던 손님들을 맞이했다.
→ them은 the guests를 가리키므로 사람을 선행사로 하는 목적격 관계대명사 whom으로 바꾸어 두 문장을 연결한다.

04 정답 which

[해석] 그 상자에는 사탕이 많이 들어 있었다. 그것은 오늘 아침에 나에게 배달되었다. → 오늘 아침에 나에게 배달되었던 상자에는 사탕이 많이 들어 있었다.
→ It은 The box를 가리키므로 사물을 선행사로 하는 주격 관계대명사 which로 바꾸어 두 문장을 연결한다.

05 정답 who(m) you called is my boss

[해석] 그 사람은 내 상사이다. 당신은 그에게 전화했다.
→ 당신이 전화한 그 사람은 내 상사이다.
→ him은 my boss를 가리키므로 사람을 선행사로 하는 목적격 관계대명사 who(m)으로 바꾸어 두 문장을 연결한다.

06 정답 who solved the problem is very smart

[해석] 그 학생은 매우 똑똑하다. 그는 그 문제를 풀었다.
→ 문제를 푼 학생은 매우 똑똑하다.
→ He는 The student를 가리키므로 사람을 선행사로 하는 주격 관계대명사 who로 바꾸어 두 문장을 연결한다.

07 정답 whose coach was fired is struggling this season

[해석] 그 팀은 이번 시즌에 어려움을 겪고 있다. 그것의 감독은 해임되었다. → 감독이 해임된 그 팀은 이번 시즌에 어려움을 겪고 있다.
→ Its는 the team's를 가리키므로 소유격 관계대명사 whose로 바꾸어 두 문장을 연결한다.

08 정답 **주격 관계대명사**

[해석] 이상한 소음을 내는 그 차는 수리가 필요하다.
→ 선행사 The car가 관계대명사절에서 주어 역할을 한다.

09 정답 **소유격 관계대명사**

[해석] 그녀는 다리가 심하게 부러진 고양이를 발견했다.
→ whose가 선행사의 소유 관계를 나타내는 소유격 관계대명사로 쓰였다.

10 정답 **목적격 관계대명사**

[해석] 나는 1950년에 할아버지가 쓰신 편지를 발견했다.
→ 선행사 a letter가 관계대명사절에서 목적어 역할을 한다.

UNIT 65 관계대명사 that, what

> **개념 확인 문제 정답**   ▶ 문제편 **p.271**

01 that   **02** that   **03** whose
04 that   **05** that   **06** that
07 that   **08** what he is saying
09 what you have in your hand
10 What he wants
11 what I asked you to do
12 what he had found in the stream
13 whom → who 또는 that
14 that → what
15 what → that 또는 which
16 That → What
17 what → that 또는 which
18 whom → that

01 정답 that

[해석] 나무 뒤에 있는 그것은 무엇이니?
→ 의문사 who, which, what으로 시작하는 의문문에서는 that을 관계대명사로 쓴다.

02 정답 that

[해석] 너는 너에게 미소 짓고 있는 남자를 아니?
→ 선행사가 사람이고 관계사절에서 is smiling의 주어 역할을 해야 하므로 주격 관계대명사 that을 쓸 수 있다.

03 정답 whose

[해석] 우리 엄마는 남편이 의사인 친구가 한 명 있다.
→ 관계사 뒤에 명사 husband가 나오므로 소유격 관계대명사 whose가 필요하다.

04 [정답] that

[해석] 반짝이는 것이 모두 금은 아니라는 속담이 있다.

→ all이 선행사인 경우에는 that을 관계대명사로 쓴다.

05 [정답] that

[해석] 너는 내가 식욕을 잃게 하는 것을 아니?

→ 선행사가 anything인 경우에는 that을 관계대명사로 쓴다.

06 [정답] that

[해석] 너는 네가 공항에서 태웠던 남자를 기억할 수 있니?

→ 선행사가 사람인 the man이고, 관계사절에서 picked up의 목적어 역할을 해야 하므로 that을 쓸 수 있다.

07 [정답] that

[해석] 분홍색 옷을 차려 입은 Mina와 그녀의 개는 사람들의 시선을 끌었다.

→ 선행사가 「사람+동물」인 경우에는 that을 관계대명사로 쓴다.

08 [정답] what he is saying

→ '그가 하고 있는 말'은 what he is saying이라고 쓴다.

09 [정답] what you have in your hand

→ '네 손에 가지고 있는 것'은 what you have in your hand라고 쓴다.

10 [정답] What he wants

→ 주어 he가 3인칭 단수이므로 동사 want에 -s를 붙여야 한다.

11 [정답] what I asked you to do

→ 5형식 문장에서 ask의 목적격 보어로 to부정사를 써야 한다.

12 [정답] what he had found in the stream

→ 그가 내게 준 것보다 개울에서 찾은 것이 더 먼저 일어난 일이므로 주절의 시제보다 한 시제 앞선 과거완료시제로 써야 한다.

13 [정답] whom → who 또는 that

[해석] 음악에 관심 있는 사람은 누구나 환영이다.

→ anyone이 관계사절에서 동사 is의 주어 역할을 해야 하므로 주격 관계대명사 who나 that을 써야 한다.

14 [정답] that → what

[해석] 나는 내가 했던 일에 대해 정말로 미안함을 느낀다.

→ 관계대명사의 선행사가 없으므로 that을 선행사를 포함한 관계대명사 what으로 고쳐야 한다.

15 [정답] what → that 또는 which

[해석] 내가 엄마와 한 약속들은 지켜지지 않았다.

→ 앞에 선행사 The promises가 있고 관계대명사절에서 목적어 역할을 하므로 what을 목적격 관계대명사 that 또는 which로 고쳐야 한다.

16 [정답] That → What

[해석] 우리에게 필요한 것은 가위 한 벌과 색종이 세 장이다.

→ 관계대명사의 선행사가 없으므로 That을 선행사를 포함한 관계대명사 What으로 고쳐야 한다.

17 [정답] what → that 또는 which

[해석] 그는 1,000달러가 나가는 시계를 가지고 있다.

→ 선행사 a watch가 있으므로 what을 주격 관계대명사 that이나 which로 고쳐야 한다.

18 [정답] whom → that

[해석] 그녀는 내가 면접을 했던 마지막 사람이었다.

→ the last가 선행사를 수식하고 있으므로 관계대명사로 that을 써야 한다.

UNIT 66 관계대명사의 계속적 용법과 생략

개념 확인 문제 정답		▶ 문제편 p.273
01 who	**02** whom	**03** which
04 and it	**05** which	**06** which
07 who is	**08** which	**09** whom
10 that is	**11** 없음	**12** which was
13 with which	**14** with whom	**15** from which
16 for which	**17** on which	

01 [정답] who

[해석] 우리는 관광 가이드를 만났는데, 그[그녀]는 그 성 근처에 산다.

→ the tour guide에 관한 추가 정보를 덧붙이는 관계대명사의 계속적 용법이므로 관계대명사 who 또는 「접속사 + 대명사」를 써야 한다.

02 [정답] whom

[해석] Lisa는 Ethan에게 전화를 걸었는데, 그녀는 그를 수년간 보지 못했었다.

→ Ethan에 관한 추가 정보를 덧붙이는 관계대명사의 계속적 용법이므로 관계대명사 whom을 쓰거나 「접속사 + 대명사」를 써야 한다.

03 [정답] which

[해석] 우리 아버지는 나를 Aiden이라 이름 지으셨는데, 그것은 '작은 불꽃'을 뜻한다.

→ 관계대명사 that은 계속적 용법으로 쓸 수 없으므로 which를 써야 한다.

04 [정답] and it

[해석] 그녀가 내게 바이올린을 보여 주었고, 그것은 1984년에 만들어졌다.

→ 관계대명사 that은 계속적 용법으로 쓸 수 없으므로 「접속사 + 대명사」로 이를 바꿔쓸 수 있다.

05 [정답] which

[해석] 그는 숙제를 잊었고, 그것은 선생님을 매우 놀라게 했다.
→ 앞 문장 전체를 선행사로 받아 추가 설명을 덧붙이는 관계대명사의 계속적 용법이다. 관계대명사 that은 계속적 용법으로 쓸 수 없다.

06 [정답] which

[해석] 설거지를 하는 동안 나는 컵을 깼는데, 그것은 우리 엄마가 가장 좋아하시는 것이다.
→ the cup에 관한 추가 정보를 덧붙이는 관계대명사의 계속적 용법이므로 관계대명사 which 또는 「접속사 + 대명사」를 써야 한다.

07 [정답] who is

[해석] 출입구에서 신문을 읽고 있는 남자는 나의 삼촌이다.
→ 「주격 관계대명사+be동사」는 생략할 수 있다.

08 [정답] which

[해석] 그것이 도서관 사서가 우리에게 읽으라고 추천했던 책이니?
→ 목적격 관계대명사 which는 생략할 수 있다.

09 [정답] whom

[해석] 나는 내가 어렸을 때 큰 신세를 졌던 분을 찾고 있다.
→ 목적격 관계대명사 whom은 생략할 수 있다.

10 [정답] that is

[해석] 호주에서 사람들은 '스트라인'이라고 불리는 특별한 호주식 영어를 사용한다.
→ 「주격 관계대명사+be동사」는 생략할 수 있다.

11 [정답] 없음

[해석] Robert Edwin Peary는 북극을 탐험한 최초의 미국인이었다.
→ 주격 관계대명사는 단독으로 생략할 수 없다.

12 [정답] which was

[해석] 그 학자는 2,000년 전에 쓰인 편지를 해독하려고 애써왔다.
→ 「주격 관계대명사+be동사」는 생략할 수 있다.

13 [정답] with which

[해석] 나는 가지고 쓸 수 있는 연필이 필요하다.
→ 연필은 가지고 쓰는 것이므로 도구를 나타내는 전치사 with를 관계대명사 which 앞에 써야 한다.

14 [정답] with whom

[해석] 너는 학교 축제에 함께 갈 친구가 있니?
→ '~와 함께 가다'는 go with라고 한다. 선행사가 a friend로 사람이므로 빈칸에는 with whom이 필요하다.

15 [정답] from which

[해석] 이곳이 네가 졸업한 대학교이니?
→ '~을 졸업하다'는 graduate from이라고 한다.

16 [정답] for which

[해석] 그들이 일하는 회사는 재정적인 문제를 가지고 있다.
→ '~을 위해 일하다'는 work for라고 한다.

17 [정답] on which

[해석] 아파트 단지가 지어졌던 부지는 크지 않았다.
→ 아파트 단지는 부지 위에 지어지는(was built on the site) 것이므로 on which가 알맞다.

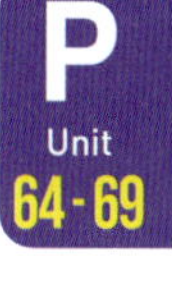

단원 평가 문제 UNIT 64 ~ UNIT 66 ▶문제편 p.274~277

정답

01 ①	**02** ④	**03** ①	**04** that
05 what	**06** which	**07** whom	**08** ②
09 ④	**10** ③	**11** ①	**12** What
13 who	**14** whom	**15** which	**16** ①

17 novel written → novel which[that] was written

18 museum we → museum which[that] we

19 boy sitting → boy who[that] was sitting

20 ④   **21** which she is afraid of

22 of which she is afraid   **23** ④

24 which made me miss the first class

25 which meant he had to stay there

26 which was very thankful

27 ①   **28** ④

29 She owns a company whose products are sold in more than fifty countries worldwide.

30 She didn't tell me what happened at the meeting.

31 The very comedy novel that I was looking for is really exciting.

32 The boy who is wearing glasses is Tom.

33 What kept me from attending the meeting

34 that we are discussing is very important

35 ⑤   **36** ①   **37** ②

01 [정답] ① UNIT 64 관계대명사

[해석] 그 환자는 의사를 만났다.
+ 그는 심장 수술을 전문으로 한다.
→ 그 환자는 심장 수술을 전문으로 하는 의사를 만났다.
→ 선행사가 사람이고, 관계사절의 주어 자리이므로 주격 관계대명사 who를 써야 한다.

02 [정답] ④ UNIT 64 관계대명사

[해석] 그 작가는 오늘 강연을 한다.
+ 그녀의 책은 베스트셀러가 되었다.
→ 책이 베스트셀러가 된 작가가 오늘 강연을 한다.
→ 선행사가 사람이고, 관계대명사가 소유격을 대신하므로 소유격 관계대명사 whose를 써야 한다.

03 정답 ①   UNIT **64** 관계대명사

[해석] 나는 여동생이 두 명 있는데, 그들은 초등학생이다.
나는 두 명의 여동생이 있는데, 그들은 초등학생이다.
→ 선행사가 사람이고, 콤마 뒤 빈칸이 있으며 관계사절의 주어 자리이므로 계속적 용법의 주격 관계대명사 who를 써야 한다.

04 정답 that   UNIT **65** 관계대명사 that, what

[해석] 그녀는 잘못되는 일은 어느 것이든 다른 사람을 탓한다.
→ anything이 선행사인 경우에는 관계대명사 that을 쓴다.

05 정답 what   UNIT **65** 관계대명사 that, what

[해석] 솔직히 말해서 나는 생일에 엄마에게 받은 것이 마음에 들지 않았다.
→ 선행사가 없으므로 선행사를 포함한 관계대명사 what이 맞다.

06 정답 which   UNIT **66** 관계대명사의 계속적 용법과 생략

[해석] 그는 나에게 몇 가지 충고를 해 주었는데, 나는 그것에 귀기울이지 않았다.
→ 관계대명사 that은 계속적 용법으로 쓸 수 없다.

07 정답 whom   UNIT **64** 관계대명사

[해석] 그녀가 돌봤던 환자가 나아졌다.
→ 전치사 of의 목적어 역할을 해야 하므로 목적격 관계대명사 whom이 알맞다.

08 정답 ②   UNIT **66** 관계대명사의 계속적 용법과 생략

[해석] 그녀가 내가 말했던 친절한 소녀이다.
→ 관계대명사 who나 that 앞에는 전치사를 쓸 수 없다.

09 정답 ④   UNIT **64** 관계대명사

[해석] 소방관이 위험에 처한 나이 든 여자를 구했다.
→ 선행사가 사람이고 소유격이 와야 하므로 whose가 알맞다.

10 정답 ③   UNIT **64** 관계대명사

[해석] 나는 내가 갖고 싶었던 파란 재킷을 샀다.
→ 선행사가 사물이고 have의 목적어가 필요하므로 목적격 관계대명사 which를 써야 한다.

11 정답 ①   UNIT **65** 관계대명사 that, what

[해석] 네가 먹고 싶은 것을 메뉴에서 골라라.
→ 선행사가 없으므로 선행사를 포함한 관계대명사 what이 알맞다.

12 정답 What   UNIT **65** 관계대명사 that, what

[해석] 내가 우선 알고 싶었던 것은 시간이 얼마나 걸릴지였다.
→ 선행사가 없으므로 선행사를 포함한 관계대명사 what이 알맞다.

13 정답 who   UNIT **64** 관계대명사

[해석] 은행을 턴 남자는 복면을 쓰고 있었다.
→ 선행사로 사람 the man이 쓰였고, robbed의 주어 역할을 해야 하므로 주격 관계대명사 who가 필요하다.

14 정답 whom   UNIT **64** 관계대명사
     UNIT **66** 관계대명사의 계속적 용법과 생략

[해석] 내가 소개받은 여자는 매우 도움이 되었다.
→ 선행사가 사람인 the woman이고 전치사 to의 목적어 역할을 해야 하므로 목적격 관계대명사 whom을 써야 한다. 전치사가 관계대명사 앞에 올 때는 whom 대신 who를 쓸 수 없다.

15 정답 which   UNIT **64** 관계대명사
     UNIT **66** 관계대명사의 계속적 용법과 생략

[해석] 상태가 매우 좋은 우리 아버지의 차는 10년 전에 만들어졌다.
→ 선행사로 사물인 car가 왔으므로 which를 관계대명사로 쓴다. 계속적 용법이 아니더라도 콤마 뒤에는 that을 쓰지 않는다.

16 정답 ①   UNIT **65** 관계대명사 that, what

[해석] ① 이 사람이 그가 사랑에 빠졌던 여자이다.
② 나는 그들이 나에게 말했던 것을 기억하고 싶지 않다.
③ 비행기는 1시간 더 지연되었고, 그것이 나를 곤경에 빠뜨렸다.
④ 이것은 내가 2주 전에 잃어버렸던 것과 똑같은 휴대폰이다.
⑤ 네가 아는 그 남자와 그 개가 정문 앞에서 너를 기다리고 있다.
→ ① 관계대명사 that 앞에는 전치사를 쓸 수 없다. ② 선행사를 포함하는 관계대명사 what ③ 계속적 용법의 관계대명사 which ④ 목적격 관계대명사 that ⑤ 선행사 The man and the dog를 받는 목적격 관계대명사 that

17 정답 novel written → novel which[that] was written
     UNIT **66** 관계대명사의 계속적 용법과 생략

[해석] 그녀는 유명한 작가에 의해 쓰인 소설을 읽었다.
→ the novel 뒤에 「주격 관계대명사+be동사」가 생략되어 있다.

18 정답 museum we → museum which[that] we
     UNIT **66** 관계대명사의 계속적 용법과 생략

[해석] 우리가 지난달에 방문했던 박물관은 지금은 문을 닫았다.
→ museum 뒤에 목적격 관계대명사가 생략되어 있다.

19 정답 boy sitting → boy who[that] was sitting
     UNIT **66** 관계대명사의 계속적 용법과 생략

[해석] 내 옆에 앉아 있었던 남자아이는 쉬지도 않고 계속 재잘거렸다.
→ boy 뒤에 「주격 관계대명사+be동사」가 생략되어 있다.

20 정답 ④   UNIT **65** 관계대명사 that, what

[해석] ① 내가 원하는 전부는 네가 나와 함께 있는 것이다.
② 이곳은 내가 과거에 일했던 회사이다.
③ 아이들에게 미소 짓고 있는 남자는 이 학교의 선생님이다.
④ 너는 나쁜 날씨 때문에 현장 학습이 취소될 거라는 말을 들었니?
⑤ 사람들이 가장 흥미를 느끼는 TV 프로그램이 무엇이니?
→ ④의 that은 목적어절을 이끄는 접속사이고, 나머지는 모두 관계대명사이다.

21 정답 which she is afraid of
     UNIT **65** 관계대명사 that, what

→ '~을 두려워하다'는 be afraid of라고 쓴다. 전치사 of는 관계대명사 앞에 써도 된다.

22 정답 of which she is afraid
     UNIT **65** 관계대명사 that, what

→ '~을 두려워하다'는 be afraid of라고 쓴다. 전치사 of는 관계대명사 앞에 써도 된다.

23 [정답] ④   UNIT **66** 관계대명사의 계속적 용법과 생략

[해석] ① 이것은 우리 아버지가 내 생일에 사 주셨던 카메라이다.

② 너는 영어로 쓰인 책을 읽어 본 적이 있니?

③ 너는 빨간 신발을 신고 있는 여자아이를 아니?

④ 오늘 아침에 열 명의 학생들이 늦게 왔고, 그것은 선생님을 정말 짜증나게 했다.

⑤ 세종대왕은 내가 한국 역사에서 가장 존경하는 인물이다.

→ ①, ⑤ 목적격 관계대명사, ②, ③「주격 관계대명사+be동사」는 생략할 수 있다. 계속적 용법으로 쓰인 관계대명사는 생략할 수 없다.

24 [정답] which made me miss the first class

UNIT **66** 관계대명사의 계속적 용법과 생략

[해석] 나는 학교에 늦었는데, 그것이 내가 1교시를 놓치게 만들었다.

→ 앞 문장 전체를 받는 관계대명사 which를 써서 연결해야 한다.

25 [정답] which meant he had to stay there

UNIT **66** 관계대명사의 계속적 용법과 생략

[해석] Joseph은 마지막 기차를 놓쳤는데, 그것은 그가 거기에서 머물러야 했다는 것을 의미했다.

→ 계속적 용법의 관계대명사 which는 앞 문장 전체 또는 일부를 선행사로 취할 수 있다.

26 [정답] which was very thankful

UNIT **66** 관계대명사의 계속적 용법과 생략

[해석] Judy는 나에게 돈을 좀 빌려줬는데, 그것은 매우 고마운 것이었다.

→ 앞 문장 전체를 받는 관계대명사 which를 써서 연결해야 한다.

27 [정답] ①   UNIT **65** 관계대명사 that, what

[해석] ① 나는 그가 원하는 것을 모른다.

② 그는 내가 말했던 그 사람이다.

③ 너는 정말 중요한 것에 집중해야 한다.

④ 내가 산 휴대전화가 고장났다.

⑤ 주인이 이사 간 그 개는 지금 보호소에 있다.

→ ① 관계대명사 앞에 선행사가 없으므로 선행사를 포함하는 what으로 고치거나 which 앞에 선행사 the thing을 써야 한다.

28 [정답] ④   UNIT **64** 관계대명사

[해석] ① 이것은 내가 살던 집이다.

② 나는 하루 종일 자는 것을 좋아하는 고양이가 있다.

③ 이 책을 쓴 사람을 알고 있니?

④ 차를 도난당한 남자가 경찰에 신고했다.

⑤ 이것은 내가 도서관에서 빌린 책이다.

→ ④ 관계대명사 뒤에 명사가 나오므로 which를 소유격 관계대명사 whose로 고쳐야 한다.

29 [정답] She owns a company whose products are sold in more than fifty countries worldwide.

UNIT **64** 관계대명사, UNIT **65** 관계대명사 that, what

[해석] • 그녀는 회사를 소유하고 있다.

• 그 회사의 제품은 전 세계 50개국 이상에서 판매된다.

→ 그녀는 제품이 전 세계 50개국 이상에서 판매되는 회사를 소유하고 있다.

→ 관계대명사가 소유격을 대신하므로 소유격 관계대명사 whose를 써야 한다.

30 [정답] She didn't tell me what happened at the meeting.   UNIT **65** 관계대명사 that, what

[해석] • 그녀는 내게 그 일을 말하지 않았다.

• 그 일은 회의에서 일어났다.

→ 그녀는 회의에서 일어난 그 일을 내게 말하지 않았다.

→ 선행사가 the thing이고 이를 관계대명사 which[that]와 함께 쓸 때, 선행사를 포함하는 관계대명사 what으로 바꿔쓸 수 있다.

31 [정답] The very comedy novel that I was looking for is really exciting.   UNIT **65** 관계대명사 that, what

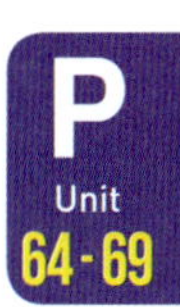

[해석] • 바로 그 코미디 소설은 정말 재미있다.

• 나는 바로 그 코미디 소설을 찾고 있었다.

→ 내가 찾고 있었던 바로 그 코미디 소설은 정말 재미있다.

→ 선행사에 the very가 있으므로 관계대명사 that을 써야 한다.

32 [정답] The boy who is wearing glasses is Tom.

UNIT **64** 관계대명사, UNIT **65** 관계대명사 that, what

→ 선행사가 the boy이고, 주어 역할을 해야 하므로 주격 관계대명사 who를 써야 한다.

33 [정답] What kept me from attending the meeting

UNIT **65** 관계대명사 that, what

→ 선행사가 없고, 주어 역할을 하면서 '날 회의에 참석하지 못하게 한 것'을 나타내야 하므로 선행사를 포함하는 주격 관계대명사 what을 써야 한다.

34 [정답] that we are discussing is very important

UNIT **65** 관계대명사 that, what

→ 선행사에 서수인 The last가 있고, 목적어 역할을 해야 하므로 목적격 관계대명사 that을 써야 한다.

35 [정답] ⑤   UNIT **64** 관계대명사, UNIT **65** 관계대명사 that, what

[해석] 너의 선생님이 너를 싫어하게끔 하는 것을 잘 생각해 봐라. 네가 아침에 인사를 하지 않아서 그런가? 수업 중에 네가 소음을 내서 그런가? 만약 그렇다면, 너의 나쁜 습관을 고치고 수업에 더 집중해 봐라. 더해서, 친구들에게 물어보라. 그들도 그녀가 그들을 싫어한다고 생각하는가? 만약 그들이 너에게 동의한다면, 너의 선생님은 그냥 기쁘게 하기 어려운 까다로운 선생님일 뿐이다.

→ (A) 전치사 about 뒤에 선행사가 없으므로 선행사를 포함하는 관계대명사 what이 와야 한다.

(B) 사람인 a tough teacher가 선행사이므로 주격 관계대명사 who나 that이 와야 한다.

36 [정답] ①   UNIT **65** 관계대명사 that, what

[해석] ① 나는 그녀가 나에게 진실을 말했다고 믿는다.

② Sally는 모두가 좋아하는 학생이다.

③ 너는 하늘에 있는 저 작은 별을 볼 수 있니?

④ 내 할아버지는 저 건물에서 일하고 있다.

⑤ 이곳은 내가 내 반지를 산 가게이다.

→ ⓐ의 that은 목적어절을 이끄는 접속사로 쓰였으며 ①의 that도 목적어절을 이끄는 접속사로 쓰였다. ②, ⑤은 목적격 관계대명사, ③, ④은 지시형용사로 쓰였다.

37 정답 ②

[해석] 십대의 청력 손상은 큰 문제이다. 많은 십대들이 음악을 듣거나 영상을 보기 위해 무선이든 아니든 이어폰을 사용하는데, 그것이 십대들을 일종의 청력 손상으로 이끈다. 전문가들은 십대들이 청력 손상을 피하기 위해 청취 기계의 소리를 줄여야 한다고 충고한다. 그들이 소리를 더 높여야 하기 때문에 사람이 붐비는 지역에서 그런 기구를 사용하는 것은 더 위험할 수 있다. 그것이 바로 그들이 예정보다 더 일찍 보청기를 끼기 쉬운 이유이다.

→ ② 관계대명사 that은 계속적 용법으로 사용할 수 없고, which를 써야 한다. (that → which) ① 단수 주어에 맞는 동사 is ③ advise의 목적격 보어인 to부정사 ④ 가주어 It, 진주어는 to use 이하 ⑤ 뒤의 than과 함께 비교급을 나타내는 earlier

UNIT 67 관계부사

개념 확인 문제 정답 ▶ 문제편 p.279

01 when   **02** at which   **03** in which
04 when   **05** which   **06** at which
07 when   **08** on which   **09** where
10 in which   **11** where, is working
12 which 또는 that, at 또는 in
13 the way in how → how 또는 the way 또는 the way in which
14 what → why 또는 for which
15 which → why 또는 for which
16 how → why 또는 for which
17 the way how → the way 또는 how 또는 the way in which

---

01 정답 when

[해석] 내가 런던에 도착한 계절은 겨울이었다.
→ 선행사 The season이 시간을 나타내므로 관계부사 when이 알맞다.

02 정답 at which

[해석] 너는 기차가 도착하는 시간을 아니?
→ 시각과 같이 쓰는 전치사는 at이므로 at which가 알맞다.

03 정답 in which

[해석] 1914년은 1차 세계대전이 발발한 해였다.
→ 년도와 같이 쓰는 전치사는 in이므로 in which가 알맞다.

04 정답 when

[해석] 그녀는 아들이 처음으로 '엄마'라고 말한 순간을 기억한다.
→ 관계부사는 전치사와 함께 쓰이지 않으므로 when이 알맞다.

05 정답 which

[해석] 네가 지금 낭비하고 있는 시간을 되돌릴 수 없다는 것을 명심해라.
→ 선행사 time이 동사 are wasting의 목적어 역할을 하므로 목적격 관계대명사 which가 알맞다.

06 정답 at which

[해석] 나는 내가 처음으로 초밥을 먹었던 그 순간을 잊을 수 없다.
→ the moment와 같이 쓰는 전치사는 at이므로 at which 이다.

07 정답 when

[해석] 크리스마스는 기독교도들이 예수의 탄생을 기리는 휴일이다.
→ 관계사절에 주어, 동사, 목적어가 모두 나와 있으므로 관계부사 when이 알맞다.

08 정답 on which

[해석] 이곳이 너희 아버지가 일하시는 층이다.
→ '층'을 나타내는 the floor는 on과 함께 쓰므로 「전치사+관계대명사」 on which를 써야 한다. that은 전치사 다음에 쓸 수 없다.

09 정답 where

[해석] 나는 많은 사람들을 만날 수 있는 도시로 갔다.
→ 장소 명사 the city를 선행사로 하는 「전치사+관계대명사」를 대신할 수 있는 것은 관계부사 where이다.

10 정답 in which

[해석] 내가 태어난 곳에는 몇몇 고대 유적들이 있다.
→ '~에서 태어나다'는 be born in이라고 한다. 「전치사+관계대명사」로 쓸 때 that은 쓸 수 없으므로 in which로 써야 한다.

11 정답 where, is working

[해석] Tom이 일하는 백화점은 이 도시에서 가장 큰 상점이다.
→ 선행사가 장소인 the department store이므로 관계부사 where를 써야 한다. 동사 뒤의 전치사는 삭제해야 한다.

12 정답 which 또는 that, at 또는 in

[해석] 그들이 머물고 있는 호텔은 우아한 실내 디자인으로 유명하다.
→ '호텔에 머물다'는 stay at[in] a hotel이라고 한다. the hotel을 선행사로 해야 하므로 관계대명사 which나 that을 쓸 수 있으며, 동사 뒤에 전치사 at 또는 in을 써야 한다.

13 정답 the way in how → how 또는 the way 또는 the way in which

[해석] 이것이 내가 살을 뺀 방법이다.
→ 관계부사 how는 선행사 the way와 함께 쓸 수 없으며 관계부사 앞에는 전치사를 쓰지 않는다. 따라서 how나 the way만 쓰거나 how를 「전치사+관계대명사」로 바꾸어 the way in which로 써야 한다.

14 [정답] what → why **또는** for which

[해석] 네가 이 자판기를 사용하지 않는 이유를 나한테 알려줘.

→ 관계사절에서 관계대명사 what을 뺀 나머지 부분에 주어, 동사, 목적어가 모두 있으므로 what은 관계부사 why 또는 for which로 고쳐야 한다.

15 [정답] which → why **또는** for which

[해석] 나한테 네가 억만장자가 되고 싶어 하는 이유를 말해 줘.

→ 선행사가 the reason일 때는 관계부사 why를 쓰고, 관계부사 why는 for which로 바꾸어 쓸 수 있다.

16 [정답] how → why **또는** for which

[해석] 나힌테 네가 니타나지 않았던 이유를 말해 주겠니?

→ 선행사가 the reason일 때는 관계부사 why를 쓰고, 관계부사 why는 for which로 바꾸어 쓸 수 있다.

17 [정답] the way how → the way **또는** how **또는** the way in which

[해석] 나는 그가 시험에 합격한 방법을 너에게 말하지 않을 거라고 확신한다.

→ 관계부사 how는 선행사 the way와 함께 쓸 수 없으므로 둘 중 하나를 삭제하거나 how를 in which로 바꾸어 써야 한다.

UNIT 68 관계부사의 계속적 용법과 생략

개념 확인 문제 정답　　▶ 문제편 p.281

01 when we started to have dinner
02 where I spent my childhood
03 when the accident happened
04 where we notice two polar bears swimming
05 nowhere I would feel comfortable
06 the hospital she was born in
07 why you didn't tell him the truth
08 when I have to show up in front of him
09 you are always sleepy and tired
10 where　　**11** why　　**12** when
13 which　　**14** who

01 [정답] when we started to have dinner

[해석] 우리는 8시에 집에 왔는데, 그때 우리는 저녁식사를 시작했다.

→ 시간을 나타내는 8 o'clock을 선행사로 하는 계속적 용법의 관계부사 when을 써야 한다.

02 [정답] where I spent my childhood

[해석] 나는 부산으로 다시 돌아가기로 결정했는데, 그곳에서 나는 어린 시절을 보냈다.

→ 장소를 나타내는 Busan을 선행사로 하는 계속적 용법의 관계부사 where를 써야 한다.

03 [정답] when the accident happened

[해석] 나는 아직도 2008년 3월 3일을 분명하게 기억하는데, 그때 사고가 일어났다.

→ 시간을 나타내는 March 3, 2008을 선행사로 하는 계속적 용법의 관계부사 when을 써야 한다.

04 [정답] where we notice two polar bears swimming

[해석] 우리의 배는 빙하 근처로 가고 있고, 이곳에서 우리는 두 마리의 북극곰이 헤엄치고 있는 것을 목격한다.

→ 장소를 나타내는 the glacier를 선행사로 하는 계속적 용법의 관계부사 where를 써야 한다.

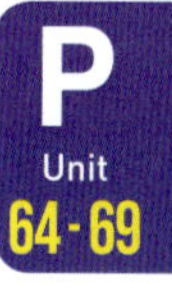

05 [정답] nowhere I would feel comfortable

[해석] 여기는 내가 편하게 느낄 수 있는 곳이 아니다.

→ nowhere를 선행사로 하는 관계부사 where가 생략되었나.

06 [정답] the hospital she was born in

[해석] 저곳이 그녀가 태어난 병원이다.

→ the hospital을 선행사로 하는 목적격 관계대명사가 생략되었고, 전치사 in이 동사 뒤에 남은 형태이다.

07 [정답] why you didn't tell him the truth

[해석] 네가 그에게 사실을 말하지 않았던 이유를 내게 말해 줘.

→ 관계부사 why로 시작하는 관계부사절을 쓴다. 선행사 the reason이 생략되었다.

08 [정답] when I have to show up in front of him

[해석] 나는 내가 그 앞에 나타나야 하는 때를 알고 싶다.

→ 관계부사 when으로 시작하는 관계부사절을 쓴다. 선행사 the time이 생략되었다.

09 [정답] you are always sleepy and tired

[해석] 네가 항상 졸리고 피곤한 이유는 무엇이니?

→ the reason을 선행사로 하는 관계부사 why가 생략되었다.

10 [정답] where

[해석] 이곳은 고흐의 작품이 전시되는 박물관이다.

→ 완전한 절을 이끌며 선행사 the museum이 장소를 나타내므로 관계부사 where가 알맞다.

11 [정답] why

[해석] 그것이 많은 학생들이 온라인 수업을 선택하는 이유이다.

→ 완전한 절을 이끌며 선행사 the reason이 이유를 나타내므로 관계부사 why가 알맞다.

12 [정답] when

[해석] 우리는 결과가 발표될 그날을 기다리고 있다.

→ 완전한 절을 이끌며 선행사 the day가 시간을 나타내므로 관계부사 when이 알맞다.

13 [정답] which

[해석] 그는 야간에도 4K 화질로 촬영할 수 있는 카메라를 샀다.

→ 선행사가 사물인 a camera이고 관계사절의 주어가 없으므로 주격 관계대명사 which가 알맞다.

14 [정답] who

[해석] 노벨상을 받은 그 과학자는 지금 우리 학교에서 강의
하신다.

→ 선행사가 사람인 The scientist이고 관계사절의 주어가 없
으므로 주격 관계대명사 who가 알맞다.

UNIT 69 복합관계대명사, 복합관계부사

> **개념 확인 문제 정답**   ▶ 문제편 p.283
>
> **01** anyone who wants it
> **02** anything that you want
> **03** anything that you want
> **04** No matter who is right or wrong
> **05** No matter what happens
> **06** Anyone whose keys were left
> **07** wherever   **08** when   **09** where
> **10** Whenever   **11** However   **12** how

01 [정답] anyone who wants it

[해석] 너는 원하는 사람이면 누구에게나 그 옷을 줄 수 있
다.

→ '~하는 사람 누구에게나'라는 의미로 쓰였으므로 anyone
who로 바꾸어 쓸 수 있다.

02 [정답] anything that you want

[해석] 이 색상들 중에서 당신이 원하는 어느 것이든 고르세
요.

→ '~하는 것은 어느 것이나'라는 의미로 쓰였으므로 anything
that으로 바꾸어 쓸 수 있다.

03 [정답] anything that you want

[해석] 그는 네가 원하는 것은 무엇이든 너에게 사줄 것이다.

→ '~하는 것은 무엇이나'라는 의미로 쓰였으므로 anything
that으로 바꾸어 쓸 수 있다.

04 [정답] No matter who is right or wrong

[해석] 누가 옳고 그르든 너희는 서로 싸움을 해서는 안 된
다.

→ '누가 ~하더라도'라는 의미이므로 no matter who가 맞
다.

05 [정답] No matter what happens

[해석] 무슨 일이 일어나더라도 그는 그 어린 소녀를 보호할
것이다.

→ '무엇을 ~하더라도'라는 의미로 쓰였으므로 no matter
what으로 바꾸어 쓸 수 있다.

06 [정답] Anyone whose keys were left

[해석] 카운터 위에 열쇠를 놓고 간 사람은 문 닫기 전에 가
지러 오세요.

→ 명사절에 쓰인 복합관계대명사 whosever는 anyone
whose로 바꿀 수 있다.

07 [정답] wherever

[해석] 너는 네가 원하는 곳 어디에서나 머물러도 된다.

→ to는 대부정사로 뒤에 stay가 생략되어 있으므로 장소를 나
타내는 복합관계부사 wherever가 알맞다.

08 [정답] when

[해석] 언제 시작하든, 배우기에 늦은 때는 없다.

→ '언제 ~하더라도'를 의미하는 양보의 부사절을 완성하는
when이 알맞다.

09 [정답] where

[해석] 어디에 살든, 요즘은 인터넷 접속이 필수다.

→ '어디에서 ~하더라도'를 의미하는 양보의 부사절을 완성하
는 where가 알맞다.

10 [정답] Whenever

[해석] 그들이 너에게 문제를 가지고 올 때는 언제든 그들에
게 탈출구가 있다는 것을 알려 주어라.

→ 부사절을 이끌어야 하고, 문맥상 '~할 때는 언제든지'라는 뜻
으로 연결되어야 하므로 복합관계부사 whenever가 알맞다.

11 [정답] However

[해석] 아무리 많이 벌더라도 그는 오르는 집값을 따라잡을
수 없었다.

→ 빈칸 뒤에 부사 much가 있으므로 however를 써서 '아무
리 많이 벌더라도'의 의미를 만드는 것이 적절하다.

12 [정답] how

[해석] 그가 아무리 조심해서 운전해도, 사고는 여전히 가끔
난다.

→ '아무리 ~하더라도'를 의미하는 양보의 부사절을 완성하는
how가 알맞다.

단원 평가 문제 UNIT 67 ~ UNIT 69

▶ 문제편 p.284~288

정답

01 ④ **02** ① **03** ① **04** ① **05** ①
06 on which **07** how **08** However
09 whenever **10** is where → is the place where
11 the reason you → the reason why you
12 is when → is the time when
13 and there **14** no matter who
15 ① **16** ② **17** ④ **18** ③ **19** ②
20 ③ **21** ① **22** ③ **23** ④ **24** ③
25 ① **26** ③ **27** Wherever
28 whenever **29** However **30** whichever
31 Whosever **32** ③ **33** ④
34 is the reason why I didn't attend the meeting
35 the night when the alien first contacted him
36 the place where you first saw the movie
37 ④ **38** when **39** where **40** However
41 ④ **42** ⑤ **43** ④

---

01 정답 ④ UNIT 69 복합관계대명사, 복합관계부사
[해석] 그것을 좋아하는 사람 누구에게나 그것을 주어라.
→ 복합관계대명사 whoever가 명사절에 쓰였으므로 anyone who가 알맞다.

02 정답 ① UNIT 69 복합관계대명사, 복합관계부사
[해석] 그는 지위가 높은 사람 누구에게나 아첨한다.
→ 명사절에 쓰인 복합관계대명사 whosever는 anyone whose로 바꿀 수 있다.

03 정답 ① UNIT 69 복합관계대명사, 복합관계부사
[해석] 네가 어디를 가든 나는 너를 위해 거기에 있을게.
→ no matter where는 복합관계부사 wherever로 바꿀 수 있다.

04 정답 ① UNIT 69 복합관계대명사, 복합관계부사
[해석] 이유가 무엇이든지 간에 고래들이 뛰어오를 때 배 위에 착지하는 일은 드물다.
→ whatever는 '~가 무엇이든지 간에'라는 의미이므로 no matter what으로 바꾸어 쓸 수 있다.

05 정답 ① UNIT 67 관계부사
[해석] 네가 돌아올 때 쯤 나는 그 일을 끝냈을 것이다.
→ 선행사가 the time이므로 관계부사 when을 써야 한다.

06 정답 on which UNIT 67 관계부사
[해석] 나는 쓸 수 있는 종이 한 장이 필요하다.
→ 글씨는 종이 위에(on) 쓰는 것이므로 on which가 알맞다.

07 정답 how UNIT 67 관계부사
[해석] 나에게 은행으로 가는 방법을 말해 주겠니?
→ 문맥상 은행에 가는 방법을 나타내는 관계부사 how가 맞다.

---

08 정답 However UNIT 69 복합관계대명사, 복합관계부사
[해석] 이 방이 아무리 좋아도 나는 내 방이 더 좋다.
→ 뒤에 형용사 good이 있으므로 However를 쓰는 것이 알맞다.

09 정답 whenever UNIT 69 복합관계대명사, 복합관계부사
[해석] 만약 배가 고프다면 너는 원할 때마다 약간의 음식을 먹을 수 있다.
→ '네가 원할 때마다'의 의미가 되어야 하므로 whenever가 맞다.

10 정답 is where → is the place where
UNIT 68 관계부사의 계속적 용법과 생략
[해석] 이곳이 우리가 와이파이를 사용할 수 있는 곳이다.
→ 관계부사 where 앞에 선행사 the place가 생략되었다.

11 정답 thc reason you → the reason why you
UNIT 68 관계부사의 계속적 용법과 생략
[해석] 네가 미국에 가고 싶은 이유는 무엇이니?
→ the reason 뒤에 관계부사 why가 생략되어 있다.

12 정답 is when → is the time when
UNIT 68 관계부사의 계속적 용법과 생략
[해석] 이때가 수박이 가장 맛있는 시기이다.
→ 관계부사 when의 선행사 the time이 생략되어 있다.

13 정답 and there UNIT 68 관계부사의 계속적 용법과 생략
[해석] 나는 이탈리아에 갔는데, 거기서 유명한 K-pop 가수를 우연히 만났다.
→ 콤마 뒤에 관계부사 where가 나오는 계속적 용법으로 쓰였으므로 and there로 바꿔 쓸 수 있다.

14 정답 no matter who UNIT 69 복합관계대명사, 복합관계부사
[해석] 나는 그들이 누구든 만나고 싶지 않다.
→ 복합관계대명사 whoever가 양보의 부사절일 때 no matter who로 바꿔 쓸 수 있다.

15 정답 ① UNIT 67 관계부사
[해석] 나는 그들이 역으로 떠났던 시간을 모른다.
→ 선행사 the time이 시간을 나타내므로 관계부사는 when을 써야 한다.

16 정답 ② UNIT 67 관계부사
[해석] 모든 학생들이 왕이 살았던 궁에 도착했다.
→ 선행사 the palace가 장소이므로 관계부사 where 또는 in which로 쓸 수 있다.

17 정답 ④ UNIT 67 관계부사
[해석] 나는 그들이 화가 난 이유를 안다.
→ 관계부사가 why이므로 선행사는 이유를 나타내는 the reason이 알맞다.

18 정답 ③ UNIT 67 관계부사
[해석] 우리의 삶을 좋거나 나쁘게 만드는 것은 우리가 어떻게 마음먹느냐에 달려 있다.
→ 빈칸 뒤에 주어, 동사, 목적어가 있으므로 빈칸에는 관계부사가 들어가야 하는데, 문맥상 how가 알맞다.

19 정답 ② UNIT 69 복합관계대명사, 복합관계부사
[해석] ① 너는 네가 좋아하는 것은 무엇이든지 해도 된다.

② 너와 함께 오는 사람은 누구든지 환영이다.

③ 그들이 어떤 것을 선택하든지 나는 그것을 그들에게 줄 것이다.

④ 네가 어디를 가더라도 여권을 챙기는 것을 잊지 마.

⑤ 내가 아무리 열심히 공부해도 우리 부모님은 만족하지 않으셨다.

→ ② 동사 comes의 주어 역할을 해야 하므로 목적격 복합관계대명사 whomever가 아니라 주격 whoever를 써야 한다. ① '~하는 것은 무엇이든지'를 나타내는 복합관계대명사 ③ '어느 것을 ~하든지'를 나타내는 복합관계대명사 ④ '어디를 ~하더라도'를 나타내는 복합관계부사 ⑤ '아무리 ~하더라도'를 나타내는 복합관계부사

20 [정답] ③   UNIT **67** 관계부사

[해석] ① 너는 시험이 언제 시작했는지 아니?

② 아무도 아기가 울고 있는 이유를 모른다.

③ 그가 키가 커진 방법을 나에게 말해줘.

④ 우리가 많은 골동품을 봤던 그 박물관은 대단했다.

⑤ 내가 맛있는 스파게티를 먹었던 그 레스토랑의 이름은 무엇이니?

→ ③ 선행사가 방법을 나타내는 the way일 때는 관계부사 how와 선행사 the way 중 한 개만 써야 한다. ① 선행사 the time에 맞는 관계부사 when ② 선행사 the reason에 맞는 관계부사 why ④ 선행사 The museum에 맞는 관계부사 where ⑤ 선행사 the restaurant에 맞는 관계부사 where

21 [정답] ①   UNIT **67** 관계부사

[해석] ① 그녀가 떠날 날은 아직 정해지지 않았다.

② 나는 우리가 북유럽을 여행했던 그 여름을 절대 잊지 못할 것이다.

③ Van Gogh의 작품이 전시된 그 박물관은 많은 관광객을 끌어모은다.

④ 결말이 모두를 놀라게 했던 그 소설은 베스트셀러가 되었다.

⑤ 모든 것이 이해되기 시작했던 그 순간을 그녀는 마침내 찾았다.

→ ① 시간을 나타내는 선행사 the day가 있으므로 which를 on which나 when으로 고쳐야 한다.

22 [정답] ③   UNIT **67** 관계부사

[해석] 너는 내게 그가 그의 숙제를 끝낼 시간을 / 그들이 사는 곳을 / 네가 그 문제를 푼 방법을 / 이것이 왜 내게 벌어지고 있는지 말해 줄 수 있니?

→ ③ '너는 내게 ~을 말해줄 수 있니?'의 뜻이 되어야 하므로 빈칸에 목적어가 올 수 있는데 선택지가 모두 관계부사와 관련 있다. 따라서 「관계부사+주어+동사」의 어순이 와야 한다.

23 [정답] ④   UNIT **69** 복합관계대명사, 복합관계부사

[해석] 그는 ① 언제 우리를 방문하든지 ② 고객을 만날 때 ③ 파티에 참석할 때마다 ⑤ 언제 여행에서 돌아오든지 선물을 들고 다닌다.

→ ④ whenever는 at any time when으로 바꿔쓸 수 있다. 따라서 time과 he 사이에 관계부사 when을 써야 한다.

24 [정답] ③   UNIT **69** 복합관계대명사, 복합관계부사

[해석] ① 시험이 있었던 ② 민감한 자료가 저장되어 있던 ④ 몇 시간 동안 아무도 들어가지 않았던 ⑤ Hall 박사가 프로젝트를 수행했던 그 실험실은 아무 공지 없이 폐쇄되었다.

→ ③ 장소를 나타내는 선행사가 앞에 있으므로 시간을 나타내는 복합관계부사 whenever가 뒤에 오는 것은 적절하지 않다.

25 [정답] ①   UNIT **68** 관계부사의 계속적 용법과 생략

[해석] ① 이 기계가 어떻게 작동하는지 설명해 줄 수 있니?

② 그가 왜 떠났는지 이유를 말해줄 수 있어?

③ 모든 것이 변한 순간이 바로 이때였다.

④ 왜 회의가 취소되었는지 궁금하다.

⑤ 이곳은 내가 어린 시절의 대부분을 보낸 마을이다.

→ ① how는 관계부사로 the way 또는 how 둘 중 하나를 생략해야 하는데, 이미 앞에 선행사가 생략되었으므로 how는 생략할 수 없다.

26 [정답] ③   UNIT **68** 관계부사의 계속적 용법과 생략

[해석] ① 내가 그 프로젝트를 끝내지 못한 이유는 시간이 부족했기 때문이다.

② 우리가 자주 놀던 공원 기억나?

③ 나는 피자를 발명한 나라를 방문하고 싶다.

④ 우리가 파리로 여행 갔던 때를 기억하니?

⑤ 여기가 내가 축구를 하곤 했었던 장소이다.

→ ③은 주격 관계대명사이므로 생략할 수 없다.

27 [정답] Wherever   UNIT **69** 복합관계대명사, 복합관계부사

[해석] Tom이 어디에 살더라도, 우리는 그를 아주 많이 그리워할 것이다.

→ '어디에서 ~하더라도'라는 뜻으로 연결되어야 하고 부사절을 이끌어야 하므로 복합관계부사 wherever를 써야 한다.

28 [정답] whenever   UNIT **69** 복합관계대명사, 복합관계부사

[해석] 그는 곤경에 처할 때마다 진정하려고 노력한다.

→ 부사절을 이끌고 '~할 때는 언제든지'라는 뜻으로 연결되어야 하므로 복합관계부사 whenever가 알맞다.

29 [정답] However   UNIT **69** 복합관계대명사, 복합관계부사

[해석] 규칙이 아무리 바람직스럽지 않더라도 너는 그것을 따라야 한다.

→ '아무리 ~하더라도'라는 의미의 양보의 부사절이 되어야 하므로 복합관계부사 however가 들어가야 한다.

30 [정답] whichever   UNIT **69** 복합관계대명사, 복합관계부사

[해석] 그녀는 원하는 것은 어느 것이나 고를 수 있다.

→ ' ~하는 것은 어느 것이나'라는 뜻의 복합관계대명사 whichever를 써야 한다.

31 [정답] Whosever   UNIT **69** 복합관계대명사, 복합관계부사

[해석] 계속 울리는 전화의 주인은 전화를 꺼주세요.

→ '~하는 것이 누구의 것이든지'라는 뜻의 복합관계대명사 whosever가 알맞다.

32 [정답] ③   UNIT **67** 관계부사

[해석] 나는 그 장소를 좋아한다. 나는 그곳에서 태어났다.

→ 나는 내가 태어난 장소를 좋아한다.

→ 관계부사 where를 쓰면 전치사 in은 삭제해야 한다. (born in → born)

33 [정답] ④   UNIT **68** 관계부사의 계속적 용법과 생략

[해석] 그녀는 여전히 그 순간을 기억한다. 그녀는 그 순간에 유성을 보았다.

→ 그녀는 유성을 보았던 그 순간을 여전히 기억한다.

→ 관계부사는 「전치사+관계대명사」로 바꿔쓸 수 있으므로 at when을 at which로 고치거나 at을 생략해야 한다.

34 [정답] is the reason why I didn't attend the meeting
    UNIT **67** 관계부사

→ 선행사가 the reason이고, 이유를 나타내야 하므로 관계부사 why를 써야 한다.

35 [정답] the night when the alien first contacted him
    UNIT **67** 관계부사

→ 선행사가 the night이고, 시간을 나타내야 하므로 관계부사 when을 써야 한다.

36 [정답] the place where you first saw the movie
    UNIT **67** 관계부사

→ 선행사가 the place이고, 장소를 나타내야 하므로 관계부사 where를 써야 한다.

37 [정답] ④   UNIT **68** 관계부사의 계속적 용법과 생략

[해석] • 그들이 화석을 발견한 그 박물관은 한때 왕족의 욕실이었다.

• 그녀는 그녀의 마을이 모래 속으로 사라진 해를 기억한다.

• 그것이 학자들이 아직도 그의 마지막 이론에 대해 논의하는 이유이다.

• 그는 항상 공정하게 경쟁하고, 그것이 그가 경쟁자들 사이에서 존중받는 이유이다.

• 그들은 새벽에 최신 업데이트를 배포했고, 그때 그들은 오류들을 수정하는 것을 마쳤다.

→ ④ 관계부사 why는 계속적 용법으로 쓰일 수 없다. 계속적 용법으로 쓰일 수 있는 관계부사로는 when과 where가 있다.

38 [정답] when   UNIT **67** 관계부사

[해석] • 그때가 폭풍우 전에 하늘이 이상한 녹색 빛으로 변하는 시간이다.

• Hana는 갑자기 정전이 났던 정확한 순간을 기억한다.

→ 두 문장 모두 빈칸 앞에 시간을 나타내는 선행사가 있으므로 관계부사 when이 와야 한다.

39 [정답] where   UNIT **67** 관계부사

[해석] • 여기는 우리가 월식을 같이 봤던 방이다.

• 그녀는 반짝이는 조각상을 봤던 장소를 방문했다.

→ 두 문장 모두 장소를 나타내는 선행사가 있으므로 관계부사 where가 와야 한다.

40 [정답] However   UNIT **69** 복합관계대명사, 복합관계부사

[해석] • 이상해 보였을지라도, 그들은 그 거울을 만졌다.

• 큰 소리가 있었다. 하지만, 아무도 그것이 무엇이었는지 확인하지 않았다.

→ 첫 번째 문장에는 빈칸 뒤에 형용사가 있고 '이상해 보였을지라도'라는 뜻이 되어야 하므로 복합관계부사 However가 와야 한다. 두 번째 문장에는 반대되는 내용을 나타내는 접속부사 However가 와야 한다.

41 [정답] ④   UNIT **69** 복합관계대명사, 복합관계부사

[해석] 우리가 처음 서로 마주쳤던 그 카페가 이제 확장되어 도심 한가운데에 우아한 새 지점을 열었다. 나는 우리가 그곳에 몇 시간 동안 앉아있던 순간과 모든 것을 상의했던 방식을 자주 그리워한다. 우리는 새로 열린 지점을 언제든지 방문할 수 있지만, 원래의 그 장소가 가진 분위기 있는 매력을 그리워할 수도 있을 것이다. 아무리 시간이 많이 지나도, 그곳의 커피의 잊을 수 없는 맛은 여전히 우리의 기억 속에 남을 것이다. 어디를 가더라도, 그 특별한 장소의 추억은 내 마음에 남아 있다.

→ ④ 뒤에 형용사 much가 있고 '아무리 시간이 많이 지나도'라고 해석하는 것이 적절하므로 However much ~ 형태가 되어야 한다. 따라서 Whoever를 However로 고쳐야 한다.

42 [정답] ⑤   UNIT **67** 관계부사

[해석] ① 보통 하루를 어떻게 시작하나요?

② 오늘 밤 별들이 정말 아름다워 보여요!

③ 그녀는 기계가 어떻게 작동하는지 자세히 설명했다.

④ 나는 그 해커가 보안 시스템을 얼마나 자주 침해하려 했는지 궁금하다.

⑤ 이것이 전통이 한 세대에서 다음 세대로 전해지는 방식이다.

→ @는 상의했던 '방식'을 나타내는 관계부사로 쓰였다. ⑤의 how는 '전통이 전해지는 방식'을 나타내므로 마찬가지로 관계부사 how가 쓰였다.

① 의문문을 이끄는 의문사 how ② 감탄문을 이끄는 how ③ 「의문사 + to부정사」 ④ 간접의문문을 이끄는 의문사 how

43 [정답] ④   UNIT **67** 관계부사, UNIT **69** 복합관계대명사, 복합관계부사

[해석] 나는 미국에서 유아교육을 공부했다. 나는 유치원 한 곳에서 교생으로 근무했는데, 그곳에서 유치원 선생님들로부터 교수법을 배웠다. 비록 내가 한국인으로서, 그들에게는 외국인이었지만 나는 우리가 정말 잘 지냈다고 느꼈다. 나는 6세 반 중 하나에 속해 있었다. 그 반에 Kelly라는 아이가 있었다. 그녀는 미국에서 태어나고 자란 중국계 미국인 여자아이였다. 어느 날 그 반의 남자아이가 내게 "선생님이 Kelly의 엄마예요?"라고 물었다. 나는 나이를 얼마나 먹었을지라도, 아이들이 다른 인종을 구별할 수 있다는 것을 알게 되었다.

→ (A) 뒤에 주어, 동사, 목적어가 나와 있으므로 장소를 나타내는 kindergarten을 선행사로 갖는 관계부사 where가 적절하다.

(B) 동사 was born의 주어 역할을 해야 하므로 주격 관계대명사 who를 써야 한다.

(C) 뒤에 형용사 old가 있으므로 however가 적절하다.

Q 가정법

개념 확인 문제 정답 ▶ 문제편 p.291

01 don't apologize, were

02 speaks, weren't[were not]

03 weren't[were not], doesn't visit

04 she doesn't like him **05** as if he were a teacher

06 for the trainer

07 were lying on the beach

08 it were not for his alarm clock

09 knew **10** were not raining

11 were not for you **12** allowed

---

01 정답 **don't apologize, were**

[해석] 내가 너의 입장이 아니라서, 나는 그녀에게 사과하지 않는다.

→ 내가 너의 입장이라면, 그녀에게 사과할 것이다.

→ 가정법 문장의 긍정/부정은 현재 사실과 반대되므로 직설법 문장의 am not은 가정법 문장에서 were로, 가정법 문장의 would apologize는 직설법 문장에서 don't apologize로 바꿔쓸 수 있다.

02 정답 **speaks, weren't[were not]**

[해석] 그녀는 매우 소심해서, 반 친구들 앞에서 절대 말을 하지 않는다.

→ 만약 그녀가 매우 소심하지 않았다면, 반 친구들 앞에서 말했을 것이다.

→ 가정법 문장의 if절에서 be동사는 주어에 상관없이 were로 쓴다. 따라서 직설법 문장의 is는 weren't[were not]로 바꿔야 한다. 가정법 문장의 would speak은 직설법 문장에서 doesn't speak으로 바꿔쓸 수 있는데, 빈칸 앞에 부정어 never가 있으므로 speaks로 쓴다.

03 정답 **weren't[were not], doesn't visit**

[해석] 그가 9월에 바쁘지 않다면, 부모님을 더 자주 방문할 텐데.

→ 그는 9월에 바빠서 부모님을 더 자주 방문하지 않는다.

→ 가정법 문장의 if절에서 be동사는 주어에 상관없이 were로 쓴다. 따라서 직설법 문장의 is는 weren't[were not]로 바꿔야 한다. 가정법 문장의 would visit은 직설법 문장에서 doesn't visit으로 바꿔쓸 수 있다.

04 정답 **she doesn't like him**

[해석] 그녀는 그를 좋아하는 것처럼 행동한다.

→ 사실 그녀는 그를 좋아하지 않는다.

→ 주절에 현재시제가 왔고, as if절에 가정법 과거가 쓰였으므로 as if절의 내용을 현재시제로 써야 한다.

05 정답 **as if he were a teacher**

[해석] 사실 그는 그 학교 선생님이 아니다.

→ 그는 마치 그 학교 선생님인 것처럼 말한다.

→ 주절의 시제와 동일한 현재 사실과 반대되는 일을 사실인 척 나타내므로 as if 가정법 과거로 써야 한다.

06 정답 **for the trainer**

[해석] 훈련사가 없다면, 내 강아지는 그렇게 활발하지 않을 것이다.

→ 「If it were not for + 명사(구)」는 「But for + 명사(구)」로 바꿔쓸 수 있다.

07 정답 **were lying on the beach**

[해석] 내가 해변에 누워 있는 대신 교실에 앉아 있는 것이 유감이다.

→ 내가 교실에 앉아 있는 대신 해변에 누워 있다면 좋을 텐데.

→ 현재의 일에 대한 유감이나 아쉬움을 나타낼 때는 I wish 뒤에 가정법 과거를 쓴다.

08 정답 **it were not for his alarm clock**

[해석] 그의 알람 시계가 없다면, 그는 매일 첫 수업을 놓칠 것이다.

→ 가정법 과거 문장의 if절을 대신하는 「Without + 명사(구)」는 「If it were not for + 명사(구)」로 바꿔쓸 수 있다.

09 정답 **knew**

→ 가정법 과거 문장의 if절에는 동사의 과거형을 써야 하므로 knew가 알맞다.

10 정답 **were not raining**

→ 가정법 과거 문장의 if절에서 be동사는 주어에 상관없이 were로 쓴다. '비가 오지 않는다면'을 나타내야 하므로 were not raining이 알맞다.

11 정답 **were not for you**

→ '~이 없다면'은 without이나 but for, if it were not for를 쓴다. 빈칸 앞에 If it이 있으므로 were not for you가 알맞다.

12 정답 **allowed**

→ 현재의 일에 대한 아쉬움을 나타내므로 「I wish + 가정법 과거」 형태로 써야 한다. allow의 과거형인 allowed가 알맞다.

개념 확인 문제 정답 ▶ 문제편 p.293

01 had invited, have gone
02 had submitted, not have failed
03 had responded, not have missed
04 had witnessed   **05** had guided
06 had known   **07** had formulated
08 had hidden
09 wouldn't[would not] have survived
10 would have failed
11 wouldn't[would not] have met

01 정답 **had invited, have gone**
[해석] 그들이 나를 초대하지 않았기 때문에, 나는 결혼식에 가지 않았다. → 그들이 나를 초대했다면 결혼식에 갔을 텐데.
→ 직설법 문장이 과거시제이므로 부사절의 didn't invite를 had invited로, 주절의 didn't go를 would have gone 으로 바꿔 쓴다.

02 정답 **had submitted, not have failed**
[해석] 그녀는 기말 과제를 제출하지 않아서 과목을 낙제했다.
→ 그녀가 기말 과제를 제출했다면 그 과목을 낙제하지 않았을 텐데.
→ 직설법 문장이 과거시제이므로 부사절의 didn't submit 을 had submitted로, 주절의 failed를 wouldn't[would not] have failed로 바꿔 쓴다.

03 정답 **had responded, not have missed**
[해석] 그는 즉시 응답하지 않아서 그 기회를 놓쳤다.
→ 그가 즉시 응답했다면 그 기회를 놓치지 않았을 텐데.
→ 직설법 문장이 과거시제이므로 부사절의 didn't respond 를 had responded로, 주절의 missed를 wouldn't [would not] have missed로 바꿔 쓴다.

04 정답 **had witnessed**
[해석] 나는 어젯밤 별들의 바다를 목격하지 않았던 것을 후회한다.
→ 내가 어젯밤 별들의 바다를 목격했더라면 좋았을 텐데.
→ 직설법 문장이 I regret that ~으로 시작하고 과거시제이므로 that절의 didn't witness를 had witnessed로 바꿔 쓴다.

05 정답 **had guided**
[해석] 지난 탐험 중에 내 직감이 더 명확히 나를 이끌지 못한 것을 후회한다.
→ 지난 탐험 중에 내 직감이 더 명확히 나를 이끌었으면 좋았을 텐데.
→ 직설법 문장이 I regret that ~으로 시작하고 과거시제이므로 that절의 didn't guide를 had guided로 바꿔 쓴다.

06 정답 **had known**
[해석] 그는 마치 양자 물리학을 완벽히 알고 있었던 것처럼 말했다.
→ 과거 사실과 반대되는 일을 나타내므로 had known이 알맞다.

07 정답 **had formulated**
[해석] 그녀는 마치 자신이 그 이론들을 직접 만들었던 것처럼 철학자들과 토론했다.
→ 과거 사실과 반대되는 일을 나타내므로 had formulated 가 알맞다.

08 정답 **had hidden**
[해석] 그는 마치 그 사고에 대해 무언가를 숨기고 있었던 것처럼 보였다.
→ 과거 사실과 반대되는 일을 나타내므로 had hidden이 알맞다.

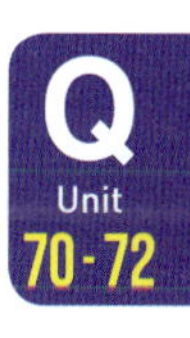

09 정답 **wouldn't[would not] have survived**
→ 과거 사실과 반대되는 일을 가정하므로 주절에는 wouldn't[would not] have survived가 알맞다.

10 정답 **would have failed**
→ 과거 사실과 반대되는 일을 가정하므로 주절에는 would have failed가 알맞다.

11 정답 **wouldn't[would not] have met**
→ 과거 사실과 반대되는 일을 가정하므로 주절에는 wouldn't[would not] have met이 알맞다.

개념 확인 문제 정답 ▶ 문제편 p.295

01 ⓓ   **02** ⓑ   **03** ⓔ   **04** ⓒ   **05** ⓐ
06 Were, would assess
07 Had, been, wouldn't[would not] have mistaken
08 Were, would be
09 Had, brought, wouldn't[would not] have gotten
10 time   **11** should   **12** to   **13** that

01 정답 **ⓓ**
[해석] 내가 Helen과 결혼했더라면 나는 지금 런던에 살고 있을 텐데.
→ 과거의 사실이 현재에 미치는 영향을 나타낼 때 if절은 가정법 과거완료로 쓰고, 주절은 가정법 과거로 쓴다. Helen과 결혼을 하지 않은 일이 현재 미치는 영향으로 알맞은 것과 연결해야 한다.

02 정답 **ⓑ**
[해석] 그가 일찍 잠자리에 들었다면 지금 피곤하지 않을 텐데.
→ 일찍 잠자리에 들지 않은 것이 현재 미치는 영향이 알맞다.

03 정답 ⓔ

[해석] 네가 우산을 가져왔다면 너는 지금 산성비에 대해 걱정할 필요가 없을 텐데.
→ 우산을 가져오지 않은 일이 현재 미치는 영향이 알맞다.

04 정답 ⓒ

[해석] 그녀가 파리에 갔다면 그녀는 프랑스어를 말할 수 있을 텐데.
→ 그녀가 파리에 가지 않은 결과로 생긴 현재 일이 알맞다.

05 정답 ⓐ

[해석] 택시를 탔더라면 그들은 지금쯤 여기 있을 텐데.
→ 택시를 타지 않아 생긴 현재 일로 알맞은 것을 골라야 한다.

06 정답 Were, would assess

→ if절의 빈칸 뒤에 동사 없이 주어 I와 명사 a botanist가 이어지므로 if가 생략되고 주어와 be동사가 도치된 문장이다. 현재 사실과 반대되는 일을 가정하므로 if절에는 Were, 주절에는 would assess가 알맞다.

07 정답 Had, been, wouldn't[would not] have mistaken

→ if절의 두 빈칸 사이에 주어 he가 있고, 과거 사실과 반대되는 일을 가정하므로, if절에는 Had와 been, 주절에는 wouldn't[would not] have mistaken이 알맞다.

08 정답 Were, would be

→ if절의 빈칸 뒤에 동사 없이 주어 this information과 형용사 true가 이어지므로 if가 생략되고 주어와 be동사가 도치된 문장이다. 현재 사실과 반대되는 일을 가정하므로 if절에는 Were, 주절에는 would be가 알맞다.

09 정답 Had, brought, wouldn't[would not] have gotten

→ if절의 두 빈칸 사이에 주어 we가 있고, 과거 사실과 반대되는 일을 가정하므로, if절에는 Had와 brought, 주절에는 wouldn't[would not] have gotten이 알맞다.

10 정답 time

[해석] 그들이 집으로 떠날 때이다.
→ It's와 they left 사이에 빈칸이 있으므로 '~할 때이다'라는 뜻을 나타내는 「It's time (that) + 가정법 과거」 형태로 쓰는 것이 알맞다.

11 정답 should

[해석] 그가 그의 가족을 위해 무언가 해야 할 때이다.
→ 「It's time (that) + 가정법 과거」는 「It's time (that) + 주어 + should + 동사원형」으로 바꿔쓸 수 있다.

12 정답 to

[해석] 사람들이 잠들기 전 스마트폰을 내려놓아야 할 때이다.
→ It's time과 동사 put 사이에 빈칸이 있으므로 '~할 때이다'라는 뜻을 나타내는 「It's time to+동사원형」 형태로 쓰는 것이 알맞다.

13 정답 that

[해석] 네가 진지하게 공부를 시작할 때이다.
→ It's time과 주어 you 사이에 빈칸이 있으므로 '~할 때이다'라는 뜻을 나타내는 「It's time (that)+가정법 과거」 형태로 쓰는 것이 알맞다.

단원 평가 문제 UNIT 70 ~ UNIT 72
▶ 문제편 p.296~300

정답

01 ②	**02** ②	**03** ②	**04** ①	**05** ②
06 ③	**07** ④	**08** ②	**09** ③	**10** ①
11 ③	**12** ⑤	**13** for	**14** had	

15 had been　**16** Without　**17** had been
18 went　**19** But　**20** ⑤
21 were　**22** didn't eat
23 would have happened
24 were　**25** would advise **26** joined
27 ⑤　**28** not for　**29** had finished
30 got　**31** had taken, would be
32 I had had the apple pie then.
33 had let him help you, you could have completed the task.
34 will be → were　**35** were, would
36 ②　**37** ①
38 you were watching a movie
39 could see　**40** ⑤　**41** ⑤
42 ④　**43** If I brought an umbrella
44 If she had asked me twice　**45** ③

01 정답 ② UNIT 70 가정법 과거

[해석] 네가 산에 간다면 기분이 더 좋아질 텐데.
→ 가정법 과거 문장의 if절 동사는 과거형으로 쓴다.

02 정답 ② UNIT 71 가정법 과거완료

[해석] 비가 멈췄었다면 우리는 등산을 갔었을 텐데.
→ 가정법 과거완료 문장의 주절 동사는 「would[could, might, should]+have+과거분사」로 쓴다.

03 정답 ② UNIT 72 가정법의 다양한 형태

[해석] 내가 너라면 나는 영어를 열심히 공부할 텐데.
→ 가정법 과거 문장의 if절의 동사가 were인 경우 접속사 if를 생략하고 맨 앞에 쓸 수 있다.

04 정답 ① UNIT 70 가정법 과거

[해석] 나의 수학 선생님이 없다면 나는 시험에 실패할 것이다.
→ '~이 없다면'은 without이나 but for, if it were not for를 써서 나타낸다.

05 [정답] ②   UNIT **72** 가정법의 다양한 형태

[해석] 너는 즉석식품을 먹는 것을 그만둘 때이다.

→ '~할 때이다'라는 뜻의 It's time 뒤에는 동사의 과거형이 알맞다.

06 [정답] ③   UNIT **70** 가정법 과거, UNIT **71** 가정법 과거완료

[해석] A: 너 어제 도서관에 갔니?

B: 아니. 날씨가 너무 추웠어. 날씨가 춥지 않았더라면 거기에 갔을 거야.

A: 그래, 오늘도 아직 추워. 날씨가 더 따뜻해지면 좋을 텐데.

→ B는 과거 사실과 반대되는 일을 가정하고 있으므로 가정법 과거완료로 써야 하고, A는 현재의 일에 대한 유감을 나타내므로 가정법 과거를 써야 한다.

07 [정답] ④   UNIT **70** 가정법 과거

[해석] 우리 엄마는 오늘 너무 바쁘셔서 나와 놀지 못하신다.

= 우리 엄마가 오늘 너무 바쁘지 않으시면 나와 놀아주실 텐데.

→ 현재 사실의 반대이므로 가정법 과거 문장으로 써야 한다.

08 [정답] ②   UNIT **70** 가정법 과거

[해석] 그는 마치 내가 집안일 하는 것을 도와주는 것처럼 말한다.

= 사실 그는 내가 집안일 하는 것을 도와주지 않는다.

→ 주절과 동일한 시제의 반대되는 일을 사실인 척 말하므로 「as if+가정법 과거」를 써야 한다.

09 [정답] ③   UNIT **70** 가정법 과거

[해석] ① 그가 파티에 오면 좋을 텐데.

② 그녀는 그녀가 나보다 더 나이가 많은 것처럼 말한다.

③ 내가 너라면 이 재킷을 살 텐데.

④ 네가 서두르면 그를 만날 수 있을 텐데.

⑤ 그 소년은 그의 장난감을 잃어버렸던 것처럼 보였다.

→ ③ 가정법 과거이므로 「If + 주어 + were[동사의 과거형] ~, 주어 + 조동사의 과거형 + 동사원형」이 맞다.

① comes → came, ② is → were ④ can → could, ⑤ loses → had lost

10 [정답] ①   UNIT **70** 가정법 과거

[해석] ① 내가 그 버튼을 누르면 무슨 일이 벌어질까?

② 너의 도움이 없다면 우리는 그것을 끝내지 못했을 텐데.

③ 내가 돈이 많았다면 나는 너에게 노트북을 사주었을 텐데.

④ 우리가 10시에 떠난다면 우리는 시간에 맞춰 도착할 텐데.

⑤ 내가 너와 함께 콘서트에 갈 수 있으면 좋을 텐데.

→ ①은 가정법 과거의 의문문 형태이므로 「조동사의 과거형 + 동사원형 + if + 주어 + were[동사의 과거형] ~?」으로 알맞게 썼다.

② With → Without, ③ have → had had, ④ will → would, ⑤ can → could

11 [정답] ③   UNIT **70** 가정법 과거

[해석] ① 너는 마치 네가 그와 친한 것처럼 말했다.

② 내가 그녀의 이메일을 보았다면 나는 그녀에게 메시지를 보냈을 텐데.

③ 내가 만약 학교를 청소할 필요가 없다면 나는 집에 더 일찍 갈 수 있을 텐데.

④ 내가 오토바이가 있다면 좋을 텐데.

⑤ 네가 그것을 안다면 거기에 가지 않을 텐데.

→ ③은 가정법 과거 문장이므로 「If + 주어 + were[동사의 과거형] ~, 주어 + 조동사의 과거형 + 동사원형」으로 알맞게 썼다.

① are → were, ② will send → would have sent, ④ have → had, ⑤ know → knew

12 [정답] ⑤   UNIT **72** 가정법의 다양한 형태

[해석] ① 내가 너라면 사실을 말할 텐데.

② 시간이 있다면 그는 식사를 거르지 않을 텐데.

③ 서두르면 우리는 기차를 탈 수 있을 텐데.

④ 그녀가 건강했더라면 경주를 끝마쳤을 텐데. (그녀가 건강하다면 경기를 끝마칠 텐데.)

⑤ 그가 내 충고를 따랐었더라면 그는 지금 더 성공적일 텐데.

→ ⑤ 혼합 가정법 문장으로 과거에 하지 않은 일이 현재 미치는 영향을 언급하고 있다.

① will → would ② won't → wouldn't ③ hurried → had hurried 또는 have caught → catch ④ were → had been 또는 have finished → finish

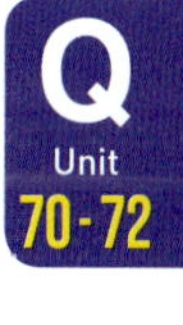

13 [정답] for   UNIT **71** 가정법 과거완료

[해석] 나의 선생님이 안 계셨다면 나는 소설을 쓸 수 없었을 것이다.

→ '~이 없었다면'은 if it had not been for라고 쓴다.

14 [정답] had   UNIT **70** 가정법 과거

[해석] 그들은 매우 배가 고프다고 말한다. 그들이 먹을 것을 가지고 있다면 좋을 텐데.

→ '그들이 배가 고프다'는 것은 현재의 사실이므로 현재의 일에 대한 유감이나 아쉬움을 말할 때는 I wish 뒤에 가정법 과거를 쓴다.

15 [정답] had been   UNIT **71** 가정법 과거완료

[해석] 그는 아프리카에 가 본 적이 없다. 하지만 그는 마치 전에 그곳에 가봤던 것처럼 말한다.

→ 과거에 하지 않았던 경험을 가정하여 말해야 하므로 가정법 과거완료를 써야 한다.

16 [정답] Without   UNIT **71** 가정법 과거완료

[해석] 전기가 없었다면 그들의 삶이 훨씬 더 어려웠을 텐데.

→ 문맥상 '전기가 없었다면'이 어울리므로 without을 써야 한다.

17 [정답] had been   UNIT **71** 가정법 과거완료

[해석] Mike의 생일날 그의 여자 친구는 해외에 있었다. 그녀가 그와 같이 있었으면 좋았을 텐데.

→ 과거 Mike의 생일에 이루지 못한 일에 대한 아쉬움을 나타내야 하므로 가정법 과거완료를 써야 한다.

18 [정답] went   UNIT **72** 가정법의 다양한 형태

[해석] 그들이 산책할 때이다.

→ '~할 때이다'라는 뜻의 It's time 뒤에는 동사의 과거형을 써야 한다.

19 [정답] But   UNIT **71** 가정법 과거완료

[해석] 그들의 지원이 없었다면 그는 선거에서 이길 수 없었을 것이다.

→ 뒤에 for가 있으므로 But을 써야 한다. '~이 없(었)다면'이라는 뜻으로 if절을 대신하여 without이나 but for를 쓸 수 있다.

20 [정답] ⑤   UNIT **70** 가정법 과거, UNIT **72** 가정법의 다양한 형태

[해석] 물이 있기 때문에 생명체가 지구에 존재할 수 있다.
①~④ 물이 없다면 어떤 생명체도 지구에 존재할 수 없을 텐데.
⑤ 물이 없었다면 어떤 생명체도 지금 지구에 존재할 수 없을 텐데.
→ 현재의 사실과 반대되는 일을 가정할 때는 가정법 과거를 쓴다. ⑤는 혼합 가정법 문장이다.

21 [정답] were   UNIT **70** 가정법 과거

[해석] 그녀가 배가 고프다면 너와 점심을 먹을 텐데.
→ 주절의 동사가 would be having이므로 if절은 가정법 과거로 써야 한다. 가정법 과거 문장의 if절의 동사는 과거형으로 쓰며, be동사는 주어의 인칭이나 수에 상관없이 were로 쓴다.

22 [정답] didn't eat   UNIT **70** 가정법 과거

[해석] 너는 사탕을 너무 많이 먹고 있어. 네가 사탕을 너무 많이 먹지 않으면 좋을 텐데.
→ 현재의 일에 대한 유감을 나타낼 때는 I wish 뒤에 가정법 과거를 쓴다.

23 [정답] would have happened   UNIT **71** 가정법 과거완료

[해석] 일본이 진주만을 침략하지 않았더라면 어떤 일이 일어났을까?
→ 과거의 사실과 반대되는 일을 가정하고 있으므로 가정법 과거완료로 문장을 완성해야 한다. 가정법 과거완료의 주절 동사는 「would [could, might, should] + have + 과거분사」 형태로 쓴다.

24 [정답] were   UNIT **70** 가정법 과거

[해석] 그는 고작 열다섯 살이지만 마치 노인인 것처럼 걷는다.
→ 주절과 동일한 현재 사실과 반대되는 일을 가정하고 있으므로 as if 뒤에 가정법 과거를 써야 한다.

25 [정답] would advise   UNIT **70** 가정법 과거

[해석] 내가 의사라면 너에게 담배를 끊으라고 충고할 텐데.
→ 현재의 사실과 반대되는 일을 가정하므로 가정법 과거로 써야 한다. 가정법 과거 문장의 주절 동사는 「would[could, might, should] + 동사원형」으로 쓴다.

26 [정답] joined   UNIT **70** 가정법 과거

[해석] 네가 우리 댄스 동아리에 가입하면 우리는 일등상을 탈 텐데.
→ 주절에 가정법 과거가 쓰였으므로 if절의 동사는 과거형으로 써야 한다.

27 [정답] ⑤   UNIT **71** 가정법 과거완료

[해석] 그들이 이른 기차를 타지 않았기 때문에 그들은 제시간에 도착하지 못했다. → ⑤ 그들이 이른 기차를 탔다면 제시간에 도착했을 텐데.
→ 과거 사실과 반대되는 일을 가정할 때는 가정법 과거완료를 쓴다.

28 [정답] not for   UNIT **70** 가정법 과거

[해석] 녀의 노력이 없다면 우리는 그 일을 하지 못할 텐데.
→ 주절에 가정법 과거가 쓰였으므로 if절의 동사도 과거형으로 쓴다. '~이 없다면'은 if it were not for라고 쓴다. if를 생략하고 주어와 동사를 도치시켜 Were it not for라고 써도 된다.

29 [정답] had finished   UNIT **72** 가정법의 다양한 형태

[해석] 나는 어제 숙제를 끝내지 못했기 때문에 지금 쉴 수 없다.
→ 내가 어제 숙제를 끝냈더라면 지금 쉴 수 있을 텐데.
→ 혼합 가정법 문장이다. if절은 과거의 사실과 반대되는 가정을 해야 하므로 가정법 과거완료로 써야 한다.

30 [정답] got   UNIT **72** 가정법의 다양한 형태

[해석] 그가 일어날 때이다.
→ '~할 때이다'라는 뜻의 It's time 뒤에는 동사의 과거형이 알맞다.

31 [정답] had taken, would be   UNIT **72** 가정법의 다양한 형태

[해석] 내 트레이너의 충고를 받아들이지 않았기 때문에 나는 지금 몸매가 좋지 않다. → 내 트레이너의 충고를 받아들였다면 나는 지금 몸매가 좋을 텐데.
→ 과거에 하지 않았던 일이 현재에 미치는 영향을 언급하므로 if절은 가정법 과거완료, 주절은 가정법 과거인 혼합 가정법 문장이다.

32 [정답] I had had the apple pie then.   UNIT **71** 가정법 과거완료

→ 과거에 이루지 못한 일에 대한 아쉬움을 나타내므로 I wish 뒤에 가정법 과거완료를 써야 한다.

33 [정답] had let him help you, you could have completed the task.   UNIT **71** 가정법 과거완료

→ 과거 사실과 반대되는 일을 가정하고 있으므로 「If + 주어 + had + 과거분사 ~, 주어 + would[could, might, should] + have + 과거분사 ~」의 가정법 과거완료 문장으로 써야 한다.

34 [정답] will be → were   UNIT **70** 가정법 과거

[해석] Alison에게,
안녕하세요, 저는 23살 여자입니다. 저는 부모님과 문제가 있어요. 저는 법을 전공했지만, 화가입니다. 저는 그림 그리기를 좋아하고 제 직업을 사랑합니다. 불행하게도 저의 부모님께서는 제가 변호사가 되면 좋을 텐데 하세요. 솔직히 말씀드리면 저는 법에 관심이 없고 유명한 화가가 되고 싶어요. 어떻게 해야 할까요?
Maria로부터
→ 「I wish + 가정법 과거」 문장이 되어야 하므로 were로 고쳐야 한다.

35 [정답] were, would   UNIT **70** 가정법 과거

→ 가정법 과거이므로 if절에는 were, 주절에는 would가 맞다.

36 [정답] ②   UNIT **70** 가정법 과거

[해석] 너의 제일 친한 친구 Susan이 파티에 갈 생각에 흥분해 있지만, 그녀의 드레스와 화장은 끔찍하다. Susan은 당신에게 자신이 괜찮게 보이냐고 묻는다. 당신은 그녀에게 무엇이라고 말하겠는가? 당신이 그녀에게 사실을 말하지 않으면 그녀의 감정은 다치지 않을 텐데. 잠깐! 이런 식으로 생각해보자. 사실을 말하는 것은 그녀에게 상황을 더 좋게 만들 두 번째 기회를 주는 것을 의미할 수도 있다. 예를 들어 그녀는 집에 가서 드레스를 바꿔 입고 화장을 고칠 수도 있다.
① 내가 너라면 나는 그와 함께 거기에 갈 텐데.
② 나는 그녀가 나에게 화가 났는지를 알 수 없다.
③ 네가 나라면 너는 무엇을 할래?

④ 내가 일본에 있다면 나는 이모 결혼식에 참석할 수 있을 텐데.
⑤ 내가 충분한 시간이 있다면 놀이공원에 갈 텐데.
→ ⓐ는 명사절을 이끄는 접속사 if이다. ②만 if의 쓰임이 같고 나머지는 모두 가정법의 if이다.

37 정답 ①
UNIT **70** 가정법 과거

→ '당신이 그녀에게 사실을 말하지 않으면 그녀의 감정은 다치지 않을 텐데'라는 의미의 가정법 과거가 맞다. if절의 동사는 과거형, 부정의 의미를 나타내야 하므로 didn't tell이 알맞다.

38 정답 you were watching a movie
UNIT **70** 가정법 과거

[해석] 당신은 주로 몇 시에 잠자리에 드는가? 당신은 꿈을 많이 꾸는가? 당신의 답이 '그렇다'라면 당신은 이 사실을 알게 되면 놀랄 것이다. 당신이 꿈을 꿀 때, 당신의 눈은 마치 당신이 영화 한 편을 보고 있는 것처럼 움직인다. 과학자들은 그것을 "REM(빠른 눈의 움직임)"이라고 부른다. 다음에 당신이 누군가 자고 있는 것을 보았을 때, 그 또는 그녀의 눈이 움직이는지 아닌지를 확인해 봐라. 그것들이 움직인다면 당신은 그 사람이 꿈을 꾸고 있다는 것을 알 것이다. 당신이 직접 그것을 보면 좋을 텐데.
→ 「as if + 주어 + 동사의 과거형」은 가정법 과거의 의미를 나타낸다.

39 정답 could see
UNIT **70** 가정법 과거

→ 「I wish + 가정법 과거」가 되어야 하므로 could see로 써야 한다.

40 정답 ⑤
UNIT **70** 가정법 과거

→ 가정법 과거는 「If + 주어 + were[동사의 과거형] ~, 주어 + 조동사의 과거형 + 동사원형」으로 쓴다.

41 정답 ⑤
UNIT **70** 가정법 과거

→ 가정법 과거는 「If + 주어 + were[동사의 과거형] ~, 주어 + 조동사의 과거형 + 동사원형」으로 쓴다.

42 정답 ④
UNIT **70** 가정법 과거

→ 가정법 과거는 「If + 주어 + were[동사의 과거형] ~, 주어 + 조동사의 과거형 + 동사원형」으로 쓴다.

43 정답 If I brought an umbrella
UNIT **70** 가정법 과거

[해석] 나는 우산을 가져오지 않아서 영화를 보러 갈 수 없다.
→ 만약 내가 우산을 가져왔으면 나는 영화를 보러 갈 수 있을 텐데.
→ 가정법 과거이므로 if절은 「If + 주어 + 동사의 과거형 ~」이다.

44 정답 If she had asked me twice
UNIT **71** 가정법 과거완료

[해석] 그녀가 나에게 두 번 묻지 않아서 나는 그녀를 돕지 않았다. → 그녀가 나에게 두 번 물었다면 나는 그녀를 도왔을 텐데.
→ 가정법 과거완료이므로 if절은 「If + 주어 + had + 과거분사 ~」이다.

45 정답 ③
UNIT **70** 가정법 과거

[해석] 당신의 아이들이 공공장소에서 화를 내고 통제할 수 없는 상태가 된다면 어떻게 하겠는가? 어느 날 나는 집에 가는 길에 한 여자와 그녀의 어린 아들을 보았다. 남자아이는 사탕을 달라고 큰 소리로 울고 있었지만 그의 엄마는 그것을 주려고 하지 않았다. 나를 신경 쓰이게 했던 것은 엄마의 태도였다. 그녀는 "그

만해! 그만!"이라고 계속 그에게 소리치고 있었다. 그러나 그는 엄마의 말이 들리지 않는 것처럼 행동했다. 울음과 고함소리가 점점 더 커졌고 그는 멈추려고 하지 않았다. 집으로 돌아와 나는 그 여자와 그녀의 어린 아들에 대해 생각했다. 만일 내가 그녀였다면 나는 그에게 소리를 지르지 않았을 것이고 그가 조용해질 때까지 기다렸을 것이다.
→ ③ 과거에 보였던 아이의 행동을 나타내는 문장이므로 주절의 시제와 같이 as if절의 동사도 과거형인 didn't hear로 써야 주절과 같은 시제의 반대되는 일을 가정하는 표현이 된다.
① 현재 일어나지 않은 일에 대해 가정하므로 가정법 과거 ② 조동사 would 뒤의 동사원형 ④ 앞에 주어와 be동사가 생략됨 ⑤ 과거의 사실과 반대되는 일을 가정하므로 가정법 과거완료

R 일치, 화법

R Unit **73 - 75**

UNIT **73** 주어와 동사의 수 일치

개념 확인 문제 정답 ▶ 문제편 p.303~305

01 has	**02** leads	**03** makes
04 teaches	**05** has	

06 Is anything the matter with you?
07 That he didn't call me back was unexpected.
08 Something very important is going to happen soon.
09 Nobody was at home when I arrived.

10 are → is	**11** affect → affects	
12 are → is	**13** are → is	
14 두 번째 are → is	**15** are → is	
16 is	**17** knows	**18** take
19 like	**20** are	**21** use
22 are	**23** are	**24** has
25 is	**26** think	**27** has
28 was	**29** was	**30** were
31 are → is	**32** was → were	**33** try → tries
34 teaches → teach	**35** prevents → prevent	
36 are → is		

01 정답 has
[해석] 모든 나라는 자신들의 문화와 전통을 가지고 있다.
→ every 뒤에는 단수 명사와 단수 동사가 온다.

02 정답 leads
[해석] 시험 전에 열심히 공부하는 것은 보통 더 좋은 성적을 가져다준다.
→ to부정사는 단수 취급하므로 단수 동사 leads가 알맞다.

03 [정답] makes

[해석] 이 장소의 무언가가 나를 아주 편안하게 만들어준다.

→ something이 주어일 때는 단수 동사를 쓴다.

04 [정답] teaches

[해석] 새로운 곳을 여행하는 것은 당신에게 다양한 문화를 가르친다.

→ 동명사는 단수 취급하므로 단수 동사 teaches가 알맞다.

05 [정답] has

[해석] 각각의 회원은 월 회비를 내야 하는데 만 원이다.

→ each 뒤에는 단수 명사와 단수 동사가 온다.

06 [정답] Is anything the matter with you?

→ anything이 주어일 때는 단수 동사를 쓴다.

07 [정답] That he didn't call me back was unexpected.

→ 명사절이 주어일 때는 단수 동사를 쓴다.

08 [정답] Something very important is going to happen soon.

→ 부정대명사 something은 단수 취급한다.

09 [정답] Nobody was at home when I arrived.

→ -body로 끝나는 부정대명사가 주어일 때는 단수 동사를 쓴다.

10 [정답] are → is

[해석] 카레라이스는 그 음식점의 주된 요리이다.

→ curry and rice는 '카레라이스'이며, 단일 개념으로 단수 취급한다.

11 [정답] affect → affects

[해석] 당뇨병은 매년 수백만 명에게 영향을 미친다.

→ 질병 이름은 -s로 끝나더라도 단수 취급한다.

12 [정답] are → is

[해석] 필리핀은 그것의 아름다운 섬들로 유명하다.

→ 나라 이름은 -s로 끝나더라도 단수 취급한다.

13 [정답] are → is

[해석] 3마일은 쉬지 않고 걷기엔 너무 먼 거리다.

→ 거리는 -s로 끝나더라도 단수 취급한다.

14 [정답] 두 번째 are → is

[해석] 캐나다는 메이플 시럽의 최대 생산국이고, 미국은 최대 소비자이다.

→ 나라 이름은 -s로 끝나더라도 단수 취급한다.

15 [정답] are → is

[해석] 물리학은 물질, 에너지, 그리고 그것들의 상호작용에 관한 학문이다.

→ 과목 이름은 -s로 끝나더라도 단수 취급한다.

16 [정답] is

[해석] 개들이 아니라 고양이가 그 소리를 내고 있다.

→ not A but B는 B에 동사를 일치시킨다.

17 [정답] knows

[해석] 너나 너의 남동생 둘 중 하나는 그 계획에 대해 알고 있다.

→ either A or B가 주어로 쓰이면 B에 동사를 일치시킨다.

18 [정답] take

[해석] 너희 둘 다 이것을 본다면 그것을 마음에 들어할 것이다.

→ both of you가 주어일 때는 복수 동사를 쓴다.

19 [정답] like

[해석] 나의 아버지도 나의 남동생들도 채소를 좋아하지 않는다.

→ neither A nor B가 주어로 쓰이면 B에 동사를 일치시킨다.

20 [정답] are

[해석] 그뿐만 아니라 그의 부모님도 매우 자랑스러워한다.

→ not only A but also B가 주어로 쓰이면 B에 동사를 일치시킨다.

21 [정답] use

[해석] 이 도로를 이용하는 자전거 타는 사람들은 없다.

→ no 뒤에 오는 명사에 수를 일치시키므로 cyclists에 맞게 동사도 복수형으로 쓴다.

22 [정답] are

[해석] 사람들의 절반이 새로운 규칙들에 반대하고 있다.

→ 「half of+명사」가 주어로 쓰이면 of 뒤에 나온 명사에 동사의 수를 일치시킨다.

23 [정답] are

[해석] 이 신문의 모든 기사가 가십 거리들이다.

→ All of 뒤의 명사가 the articles이므로 복수 동사를 써야 한다.

24 [정답] has

[해석] 실종된 등산객에게서 아무런 메시지도 받지 못했다.

→ no 뒤에 오는 명사에 수를 일치시키므로 message에 맞는 단수 동사 has가 알맞다.

25 [정답] is

[해석] 갓난아기의 몸의 약 90%가 물이라는 것을 아니?

→ 부분을 나타내는 표현인 「~%+of+명사」가 주어일 때는 of 뒤에 나온 명사에 동사의 수를 일치시킨다.

26 [정답] think

[해석] 절반이 넘는 학생들이 중간고사가 쉬웠다고 생각한다.

→ 「half of+명사」가 주어로 쓰이면 of 뒤에 나온 명사에 동사의 수를 일치시킨다.

27 [정답] has

[해석] 그는 일의 대부분이 완성되었다고 말한다.

→ 부분을 나타내는 표현인 「most of+명사」가 주어일 때는 of 뒤에 나온 명사에 동사의 수를 일치시킨다.

28 정답 was

[해석] 내가 가지고 있던 돈은 모두 기차에서 도둑맞았다.

→ 부분을 나타내는 표현인 「all of+명사」가 주어일 때는 of 뒤에 나온 명사에 동사의 수를 일치시킨다. money는 셀 수 없는 명사로 단수 취급한다.

29 정답 was

[해석] 파티가 시작되기도 전에 케이크의 절반이 먹혔다.

→ 부분을 나타내는 표현인 「half of+명사」가 주어일 때는 of 뒤에 나온 명사에 동사의 수를 일치시킨다.

30 정답 were

[해석] 그들의 문서의 2/3가 정확하게 기록되지 않았다.

→ 부분을 나타내는 표현인 「분수+of+명사」가 주어일 때는 of 뒤에 나온 명사에 동사의 수를 일치시킨다.

31 정답 are → is

[해석] 우리 태양계의 행성의 개수는 8개이다.

→ the number of는 '~의 수'라는 뜻으로 단수 동사가 온다.

32 정답 was → were

[해석] 많은 관광객들이 박물관 앞에서 기다리고 있었다.

→ a number of는 '많은'이라는 뜻으로 「a number of + 복수 명사」가 주어일 때는 항상 복수 취급한다.

33 정답 try → tries

[해석] 그녀는 그녀의 환자들이 건강을 회복하도록 돕기 위해 최선을 다하는 좋은 의사이다.

→ 주격 관계대명사절에서 동사는 선행사에 일치시키므로 a good doctor에 맞추어 3인칭 단수 동사를 사용해야 한다.

34 정답 teaches → teach

[해석] 우리에게 영어를 가르쳐주시는 선생님들은 모두 남아프리카에서 오셨다.

→ 주격 관계대명사절에서 동사는 선행사에 일치시킨다. 「all of + 복수 명사」는 복수 취급하므로 복수형 동사 teach를 써야 한다.

35 정답 prevents → prevent

[해석] 많은 회사들이 직원들이 사무실 안에서 흡연하는 것을 금지한다.

→ a number of는 '많은'이라는 뜻으로 「a number of+복수 명사」가 주어일 때는 항상 복수 취급한다.

36 정답 are → is

[해석] 지구 온난화 때문에 펭귄의 수가 줄어들 것이라고 예상된다.

→ 「the number of+복수 명사」가 주어일 때는 단수 취급한다.

UNIT **74** 시제 일치

개념 확인 문제 정답 ▶ 문제편 **p.307**

01 will → would **02** will → would **03** will → would
04 is → was **05** is → was **06** has → had
07 won **08** (should) make
09 get **10** goes **11** is
12 broke **13** did **14** has
15 calls **16** do **17** had been
18 ends **19** is **20** wanted

01 정답 will → would

[해석] 나는 날씨가 맑을 거라고 생각했다.

→ 주절의 시제가 과거이므로 종속절의 시제도 과거가 맞다.

02 정답 will → would

[해석] 그는 그들의 서비스에 대해서 값을 지불하지 않겠노라고 말했다.

→ 주절의 시제가 과거이므로 종속절의 시제도 과거가 맞다.

03 정답 will → would

[해석] 그는 내게 그가 조만간 한국을 떠날 것이라고 말했다.

→ 주절의 시제가 과거이므로 종속절의 시제도 과거가 맞다.

04 정답 is → was

[해석] Rick을 방문했을 때 나는 그가 그의 집을 페인트 칠하고 있는 것을 보았다.

→ 주절의 시제가 과거이므로 종속절의 시제도 과거가 맞다.

05 정답 is → was

[해석] 내가 어렸을 때, 나는 아빠가 매우 똑똑하다고 생각했다.

→ 주절의 시제가 과거이므로 종속절의 시제도 과거가 맞다.

06 정답 has → had

[해석] 나는 그가 3주 동안 병원에 있었다는 것을 몰랐다.

→ 주절의 시제가 과거이므로 종속절의 시제는 과거나 과거완료이다.

07 정답 won

[해석] 나는 Marie Curie가 노벨상을 탔다고 들었다.

→ 과거의 역사적인 사실은 항상 과거시제로 쓴다.

08 정답 (should) make

[해석] 그는 부모가 그들의 자녀를 위해 희생해야 한다고 주장했다.

→ 주장을 나타내는 동사 claim이 주절에 쓰였을 때, that절이 '~해야 한다'는 당위의 의미이면 that절의 동사를 「(should+)동사원형」으로 쓴다.

09 정답 get

[해석] 그녀는 내가 우유를 배달하기 위해 항상 5시에 일어난다는 것을 몰랐다.

→ 현재 반복되는 습관은 현재시제로 나타낸다.

10 정답 goes

[해석] 1543년 이전에 대부분의 사람들은 지구가 태양 주위를 돈다는 것을 몰랐다.
→ 불변의 진리는 항상 현재시제로 쓴다.

11 정답 is

[해석] 선생님은 우리에게 목성이 우리의 태양계에서 가장 큰 행성이라고 말씀하셨다.
→ 불변의 진리는 항상 현재시제로 쓴다.

12 정답 broke

[해석] 몇몇 한국 대학생들은 한국 전쟁이 1950년에 발발했다는 것을 모른다.
→ 과거의 역사적인 사실은 항상 과거시제로 쓴다.

13 정답 did

[해석] 나는 그녀에게 여가 시간에 무엇을 했냐고 물었다.
→ 주절의 시제가 과거이므로 종속절의 시제도 과거가 맞다.

14 정답 has

[해석] 과학자들은 토성에 9개의 고리가 있다는 것을 발견했다.
→ 불변의 진리는 항상 현재시제로 쓴다.

15 정답 calls

[해석] 그가 다시 전화하면 내게 바로 알려 주세요.
→ 조건을 나타내는 부사절에서는 미래시제 대신 현재시제를 쓴다.

16 정답 do

[해석] 의사는 그가 매일 운동을 좀 해야 한다고 주장했다.
→ 주장을 나타내는 동사 insist가 주절에 쓰였을 때, that절이 '~해야 한다'는 당위의 의미이면 that절의 동사를 「(should+) 동사원형」으로 쓴다.

17 정답 had been

[해석] 그는 내게 그가 일본에 몇 번 다녀온 적이 있다고 말했다.
→ 주절의 시제가 과거이므로 종속절의 시제는 과거나 과거완료이다.

18 정답 ends

[해석] 영화가 끝나면 우리는 먹으러 갈 것이다.
→ 시간을 나타내는 부사절에서는 미래시제 대신 현재시제를 쓴다.

19 정답 is

[해석] 너는 바티칸 시국이 세계에서 가장 작은 나라라는 것을 알았니?
→ 현재의 사실은 현재시제로 쓴다.

20 정답 wanted

[해석] 많은 설문 조사들이 거의 모든 부모들이 그들의 자녀가 대학에 가기를 원한다는 것을 보여 주었다.
→ 주절의 시제가 과거이므로 종속절의 시제도 과거가 맞다.

UNIT **75** 화법

개념 확인 문제 정답 ▶ 문제편 p.309~311

01 told, that she   **02** she was, then
03 told, had lost her, there
04 that they would, us   **05** I will, you
06 will be   **07** I was, yesterday
08 We will take you   **09** had
10 was   **11** my   **12** I'm
13 had seen   **14** I could   **15** I
16 they had read   **17** had solved
18 to give him   **19** my
20 not to be   **21** said to, Write your
22 She suggested calling it a day.
23 Tom said, "Let's take a walk in the park."
24 Dave suggested meeting at the cafe at 3 PM.
25 They proposed not eating too much before dinner.

01 정답 told, that she

[해석] 그녀는 나에게 "나는 몸이 좋지 않아."라고 말했다.
→ 그녀는 나에게 몸이 좋지 않다고 말했다.
→ said to는 told로 바꾼 후, 시제와 인칭을 주절과 일치시켜야 한다.

02 정답 she was, then

[해석] 엄마는 "지금 은행에 갈 거야."라고 말했다.
→ 엄마는 그때 은행에 갈 거라고 말했다.
→ 시제와 인칭을 주절과 일치시키고 now는 then으로 바꾸어야 한다.

03 정답 told, had lost her, there

[해석] 그녀는 나에게 "여기서 내 시계를 잃어버렸어."라고 말했다.
→ 그녀는 나에게 그곳에서 시계를 잃어버렸다고 말했다.
→ 시제를 한 시제 앞선 과거완료시제로 바꾸어야 하고, here는 there로 바꾸어야 한다.

04 정답 that they would, us

[해석] 그들은 우리에게 "우리는 너희를 프로젝트와 관련해서 도와줄 거야."라고 말했다. → 그들은 우리에게 프로젝트와 관련해서 도와줄 거라고 말했다.
→ 시제와 인칭을 주절과 일치시켜야 한다.

05 정답 I will, you

[해석] John은 나중에 내게 전화할 거라고 말했다.
→ John은 "내가 나중에 네게 전화할게."라고 말했다.
→ he는 I로, would는 will로, me는 대상이 되는 you로 바꿔야 한다.

06 정답 will be

[해석] 선생님은 시험이 금요일에 있을 거라고 말했다.

→ 선생님은 "시험은 금요일에 있을 거야."라고 말했다.

→ would be는 주절의 시제가 과거이기 때문에 바뀐 것으로, 직접화법에서 will be로 바꿔야 한다.

07 정답 I was, yesterday

[해석] 그는 나에게 그가 전날 피곤했다고 말했다.

→ 그는 나에게 "나는 어제 피곤했어."라고 말했다.

→ he는 I로, had been은 말하는 시점에서 과거를 나타내므로 was로, the day before는 yesterday로 바꿔야 한다.

08 정답 We will take you

[해석] 그들의 부모님은 그들에게 놀이공원에 데려갈 거라고 말했다. → 그들의 부모님은 그들에게 "우리는 너희를 놀이공원에 데려갈 거야."라고 말했다.

→ 주절과 종속절의 주어가 같은 사람을 가리키므로 직접화법에서는 인용문의 주어로 We를 써야 한다.

09 정답 had

→ 말하는 시점인 과거보다 먼저 일어난 일이므로 과거완료시제 had already finished가 알맞다.

10 정답 was

→ 주절과 시제 일치를 해야 하므로 was가 알맞다.

11 정답 my

→ 직접화법에서 그가 '내 숙제'를 끝낼 것이라고 말하는 것이므로 my가 알맞다.

12 정답 I'm

→ 직접화법에서 Mark가 '나는 계획 중이야'라고 말하는 것이므로 I'm planning이 오는 것이 알맞다.

13 정답 had seen

[해석] Jane은 "너 그 새 영화 봤어?"라고 말했다.

→ Jane은 내가 그 새 영화를 봤는지 물었다.

→ 의문사가 없는 의문문을 간접화법으로 바꿀 때 종속절 앞에 if 또는 whether를 쓰고, 어순을 「주어+동사」로 바꾼다. 직접화법의 과거시제에 맞춰 간접화법에서 had seen으로 바꾸는 것이 알맞다.

14 정답 I could

[해석] 그는 나에게 "숙제 좀 도와줄 수 있어?"라고 말했다.

→ 그는 나에게 숙제를 도와줄 수 있는지 물었다.

→ 의문사가 없는 의문문을 간접화법으로 바꿀 때 종속절 앞에 if 또는 whether를 쓰고, 어순을 「주어+동사」로 바꾼다. 직접화법의 you는 간접화법에서 I로, 직접화법의 can은 과거시제에 맞춰 could로 바꾸는 것이 알맞다.

15 정답 I

[해석] 그녀는 "너 내일 파티에 올 수 있어?"라고 말했다.

→ 그녀는 내가 다음 날 파티에 올 수 있는지 물었다.

→ 직접화법의 you는 간접화법에서 I로 바꾼다.

16 정답 they had read

[해석] 그녀는 그들에게 "어떤 책 읽었어?"라고 말했다.

→ 그녀는 그들에게 어떤 책을 읽었는지 물었다.

→ 의문사가 있는 의문문을 간접화법으로 바꿀 때는 의문사 뒤의 어순을 「주어+동사」로 바꾼다. 의문사절의 시제는 주절의 시제보다 앞섰으므로 과거완료시제(had read)로 바꾼다.

17 정답 had solved

[해석] 선생님은 우리에게 "그 문제 어떻게 풀었니?"라고 물으셨다.

→ 선생님은 우리가 그 문제를 어떻게 풀었는지 물으셨다.

→ 의문사가 있는 의문문을 간접화법으로 바꿀 때는 의문사 뒤의 어순을 「주어+동사」로 바꾼다. 의문사절의 시제는 주절의 시제보다 앞섰으므로 과거완료시제(had solved)로 바꾼다.

18 정답 to give him

[해석] 그는 나에게 "그 책을 줘."라고 말했다.

→ 그는 나에게 그 책을 달라고 말했다.

→ 긍정 명령문을 간접화법으로 바꿀 때는 to부정사의 형태로 바꾼다. 직접화법의 me는 간접화법 주절의 주어인 him으로 바꾼다.

19 정답 my

[해석] 그녀는 나에게 자신의 생일을 잊지 말라고 요청했다.

→ 그녀는 나에게 "내 생일 잊지 마."라고 말했다.

→ 주어인 She가 '자신의' 생일을 말하는 것이므로 간접화법의 her를 직접화법에서 my로 바꾼다.

20 정답 not to be

[해석] 그녀는 "회의에 늦지 마."라고 말했다.

→ 그녀는 회의에 늦지 말라고 요청했다.

→ 부정 명령문을 간접화법으로 바꿀 때는 「not to+동사원형」의 형태로 바꾼다.

21 정답 said to, Write your

[해석] 선생님은 학생들에게 종이에 이름을 쓰라고 지시했다.

→ 선생님은 학생들에게 "종이에 이름을 쓰세요."라고 말했다.

→ 간접화법의 ordered ~ to write ~은 직접화법의 명령문으로 쓸 수 있다. ordered는 said to가 되고, 긍정 명령문인 Write your names ~가 오는 것이 알맞다.

22 정답 She suggested calling it a day.

→ 긍정 제안문을 간접화법으로 쓸 때 전달 동사는 suggest나 propose로 하고, Let's 뒤에 오는 동사원형을 -ing의 형태로 바꾼다.

23 정답 Tom said, "Let's take a walk in the park."

→ 긍정 제안문의 직접화법은 「주어 + said, "Let's + 동사원형 ~."」형태로 쓴다.

24 정답 Dave suggested meeting at the cafe at 3 PM.

→ 긍정 제안문을 간접화법으로 쓸 때 전달 동사는 suggest나 propose로 하고, Let's 뒤에 오는 동사원형을 -ing의 형태로 바꾼다.

25 정답 They proposed not eating too much before dinner.

→ 부정 제안문을 간접화법으로 쓸 때 전달 동사는 suggest나 propose로 하고, Let's 뒤에 오는 동사원형을 not -ing의 형태로 바꾼다.

단원 평가 문제 UNIT 73 ~ UNIT 75   ▶ 문제편 p.312~316

정답

01 ④	02 ⑤	03 ①	04 ②	05 ⑤
06 ②	07 ⑤	08 ②	09 ⑤	10 ①
11 ①	12 were	13 are	14 is	15 ④
16 ②	17 ③	18 ⑤	19 ⑤	20 ④
21 ③	22 ②	23 ②		

24 A number of　25 predicts
26 would rain　27 had been married
28 had to send　29 is　30 stay
31 is　32 had been　33 ④　34 ⑤
35 ②　36 ①　37 It isn't　38 ③　39 ②
40 ②　41 ③　42 ③

01 정답 ④　　　　　　　　　　　UNIT 75 화법
[해석] James는 "나는 쇼핑을 갈 거야."라고 말했다.
→ 주절의 동사가 said로 과거이므로 동사인 will이 would로, I는 James를 의미하므로 he로 바꿔야 한다.

02 정답 ⑤　　　　　　　　　　　UNIT 75 화법
[해석] Maria는 부모님께 "저는 새 동아리에 가입할 거예요."라고 말했다.
→ 간접화법 that절의 주어는 Maria이므로 she를 써야 하고, 주절의 동사가 과거이므로 was going을 써야 한다.

03 정답 ①　　　　　　　　UNIT 73 주어와 동사의 수 일치
[해석] 우리들 각자는 화가인 Pablo Picasso의 그림들을 가지고 있다.
→ Each of us가 주어이므로 동사는 단수로 쓰고 문맥상 '가지고 있다'는 의미가 있으므로 has가 알맞다.

04 정답 ②　　　　　　　　UNIT 73 주어와 동사의 수 일치
[해석] 아이를 돌보는 것은 많은 노력이 요구된다.
→ 동명사구는 단수 취급하고, 의미상 수동태로 쓸 수 없다.

05 정답 ⑤　　　　　　　　UNIT 73 주어와 동사의 수 일치
[해석] 세 시간은 내가 숙제를 끝내는 데 충분한 시간이다.
→ 시간을 나타내는 명사는 단수 취급한다.

06 정답 ②　　　　　　　　UNIT 73 주어와 동사의 수 일치
[해석] 학생들의 절반이 학교에 결석했다
→ 「half of+단수 명사」는 명사에 동사의 수를 일치시켜 단수로 취급하고, be absent from은 '~에 결석하다'라는 뜻이다.

07 정답 ⑤　　　　　　　　UNIT 73 주어와 동사의 수 일치
[해석] 나머지 피자는 더 먹고 싶은 사람을 위한 것이다.
→ 「The rest of+단수 명사」는 단수 취급한다.

08 정답 ②　　　　　　　　UNIT 73 주어와 동사의 수 일치
→ 「half of+복수 명사」는 명사에 동사의 수를 일치시켜 복수 취급한다.

09 정답 ⑤　　　　　　　　　　　UNIT 75 화법
→ 의문문을 간접화법으로 바꿀 때는 평서문의 어순으로 바꿔야 한다.

10 정답 ①　　　　　　　　　　　UNIT 74 시제 일치
→ 속담이나 격언은 특별한 경우가 아니면 현재를 써야 하며, the grass는 단수이므로 ① is가 알맞다.

11 정답 ①　　　　　　　　　　　UNIT 75 화법
→ 그녀에게 전화할 것을 내게 말한 것이므로 ① told me to call her when이 알맞다.

12 정답 were　　　　　　　UNIT 73 주어와 동사의 수 일치
[해석] • 코치는 John과 Diana가 둘 다 테니스에 관심이 없다고 말했다.
• 어제 어린 팬들이 그 유명한 가수를 만나서 매우 흥분했다.
→ both A and B는 복수로 취급하고, fans도 복수이므로 were로 쓴다.

13 정답 are　　　　　　　UNIT 73 주어와 동사의 수 일치
[해석] • 많은 사람들이 지금 도서관에서 책을 읽고 있다.
• 나머지 옷들은 내 것이 아니다.
→ 「a number of+복수 명사」는 복수로 취급하고, 「the rest of+복수 명사」도 명사에 수를 일치시켜 복수로 취급한다. 두 문장의 시제가 현재이므로 are가 알맞다.

14 정답 is　　　　UNIT 73 주어와 동사의 수 일치, UNIT 74 시제 일치
[해석] • 컴퓨터 게임을 하는 것은 내 취미이다.
• 나는 그가 귀여운 어린 남자라고 생각한다.
→ 동명사구 Playing computer games가 주어이므로 단수 취급해서 첫 번째 빈칸에 is가 들어간다. 주절의 동사가 think로 현재시제이므로 종속절의 시제로 무엇이든 쓸 수 있지만 공통으로 들어가야 하므로 역시 is가 알맞다.

15 정답 ④　　　　　　　　UNIT 73 주어와 동사의 수 일치
[해석] • 나뿐만 아니라 보안 요원들도 그때 그 커다란 소리에 놀랐다.
• 네게 매일 밤 전화하는 사람은 내가 아니라 Thomas이다.
→ B as well as A가 주어로 쓰이면 B에 동사를 일치시킨다. 주격 관계대명사 뒤의 동사는 선행사의 수에 일치시키므로 두 번째 문장은 Thomas에 동사의 수를 일치시킨다.

16 정답 ②　　　　　　　　　　　UNIT 75 화법
[해석] 우리 할머니는 나에게 "오늘 나는 머리가 아프구나."라고 말씀하셨다.
→ 직접화법을 간접화법으로 바꿀 때, 주절의 동사인 said to는 told로 바꾸고, today는 that day로 바꾼다.

17 정답 ③   UNIT **75** 화법

[해석] 그 여자는 나에게 "약국이 여기에서 멀어요?"라고 말했다.
→ 간접화법으로 바꿀 때 접속사 if나 whether를 쓰고 전달동사 said to는 asked로 바꿔 쓰고 here는 there로 바꾼다.

18 정답 ⑤   UNIT **73** 주어와 동사의 수 일치

[해석] ① 나머지 사과들이 썩었다.
② 대부분의 학생들은 이번 기간에 발전했다.
③ 내 돈의 절반이 이미 사라졌다.
④ 참가자 수가 해마다 증가하고 있다.
⑤ 많은 집들이 지진에 의해 파괴되었다.
→ ⑤ a number of는 복수로 취급하므로 동사 were는 알맞게 쓰였다. ① is → are, ② has → have, ③ were → was, ④ are → is

19 정답 ⑤   UNIT **73** 주어와 동사의 수 일치

[해석] ① 버터 바른 **빵**이 내 점심 식사였다.
② 2년은 내게 긴 시간이다.
③ 경제학은 내가 가장 좋아하는 과목이다.
④ 많은 독자들이 나의 새 소설을 좋아한다.
⑤ 각 교실의 모든 학생이 아주 열심히 공부한다.
→ ⑤ every는 단수 명사, 단수 동사와 함께 쓰인다. (study → studies)
① 단일 개념은 단수 취급 ② 시간 단위는 단수 취급 ③ 학문명은 단수 취급 ④「a number of+복수 명사」는 복수 취급

20 정답 ④   UNIT **73** 주어와 동사의 수 일치

[해석] ① 수학은 어렵지만 보람 있다.
② 모든 사람들이 그가 나를 닮았다고 말한다.
③ 그는 벤치에 앉아 있는 그 소녀에게 다가갔다.
④ 80달러는 좋은 재킷 가격으로 적당한 것 같다.
⑤ 대부분의 학생들이 구내식당 앞에서 줄 서 있다.
→ ④ 금액은 복수형이라도 단수 취급하므로 seem 대신 seems를 써야 한다.
① 학문명은 단수 취급하므로 is가 알맞게 쓰였다. ② everybody는 단수 취급하므로 동사 says는 알맞다. ③ 선행사가 the girl로 단수이므로 관계사절의 was는 알맞다. ⑤「most of+복수 명사」는 복수 취급하므로 are는 알맞다.

21 정답 ③   UNIT **75** 화법

[해석] ① Pablo는 서울을 한 번 방문했다고 말했다.
② 그는 우리와 함께 캠핑을 가겠다고 말했다.
③ 내 손자가 며칠 동안 아팠었다고 내게 말했다.
④ 웃음이 최고의 명약이라는 말이 있다.
⑤ 내 룸메이트는 "너는 선물이 마음에 드니?"라고 내게 말했다.
→ ③ 간접화법에서 said me로 쓸 수는 없고 told me로 써야 한다.
① 과거시제에 이어지는 과거완료시제 ② will이 아닌 would ④ 격언에 알맞은 현재시제 ⑤ 직접화법 의문문

22 정답 ②   UNIT **75** 화법

[해석] ① Greg는 나에게 영화를 보러 갈 수 있는지 물었다.
② 그녀는 그 아이에게 그림을 만지지 말라고 명령했다.
③ Ann은 나에게 내가 언제 그것에 대해 그녀를 도울 수 있는지 물었다.
④ 나의 선생님은 나에게 왜 숙제를 끝내지 않았는지 물으셨다.
⑤ 내 여동생이 나에게 전날 컴퓨터로 무엇을 했었는지 물었다.
→ ② 명령문을 간접화법으로 바꿀 때는 명령문의 동사를 to부정사로 바꿔야 하므로 touch를 to touch로 고쳐야 한다.
① 의문사가 없는 의문문을 간접화법으로 바꾸면서 접속사 if를 썼다.
③, ④, ⑤ 의문사가 있는 의문문을 간접화법으로 바꾸면서 전달동사를 asked로 쓰고 인용문을「의문사+주어+동사」순서로 썼다.

23 정답 ②   UNIT **74** 시제 일치

[해석] ① 아무도 내일 비가 올지 모른다.
② 그는 문이 잠겨 있지 않았다는 것을 알았다.
③ 그들은 제2차 세계 대전이 1939년에 발발했다고 배울 것이다.
④ 나의 할아버지께서는 구르는 돌에는 이끼가 끼지 않는다고 말씀하셨다.
⑤ 해가 동쪽에서 뜨고 서쪽에서 지는 것은 세계 어디에서든 같다.
→ ② 주절의 시제가 과거이므로 종속절의 시제는 과거나 과거완료로 써야 한다. (has been → had been)
① 주절의 시제가 현재이므로 종속절의 시제는 무엇이든 쓸 수 있다.
③ 역사적인 사실은 항상 과거시제로 쓴다. ④, ⑤ 변하지 않는 진리는 주절의 시제와 관계없이 항상 현재시제로 쓴다.

24 정답 A number of   UNIT **73** 주어와 동사의 수 일치

→「a number of+복수 명사」는 '많은 ~'의 뜻이며 복수로 취급한다.

25 정답 predicts   UNIT **73** 주어와 동사의 수 일치

→ neither A nor B가 주어로 쓰이면 B에 동사의 수를 일치시킨다. 따라서 the AI에 맞는 동사 predicts가 적절하다.

26 정답 would rain   UNIT **74** 시제 일치

[해석] 기상 통보관은 내일 폭우가 내릴 거라고 말했다.
→ 주절의 시제가 과거이므로 조동사 will도 시제를 일치시켜 과거형인 would로 써야 한다.

27 정답 had been married   UNIT **74** 시제 일치

[해석] Terry는 그가 결혼 25년째라고 말했다.
→ 주절의 시제가 과거이므로 종속절의 시제는 과거나 과거완료를 써야 하는데, 과거 이전부터 말하는 시점의 과거까지 계속되어 온 일을 말하므로 과거완료시제를 써야 한다.

28 정답 had to send   UNIT **74** 시제 일치

[해석] Peter는 내가 그에게 편지를 보내야 한다고 말했다.
→ 주절이 과거이므로 종속절의 시제도 과거로 일치시켜야 한다. 조동사 have to의 과거형은 had to로 쓴다.

29 정답 is   UNIT **74** 시제 일치

[해석] 나의 아버지는 정직이 최선의 방책이라고 말씀하셨다.
→ 속담은 항상 현재시제로 쓴다.

30 정답 stay   UNIT **74** 시제 일치

[해석] 의사는 나에게 며칠 동안 누워 있어야 한다고 충고했다.
→ 충고를 나타내는 동사 advise가 주절에 쓰일 때, that절이 '~해야 한다'라는 당위의 의미이면 that절의 동사를「(should+)동사원형」으로 쓴다.

R
Unit
73-75

31 정답 is   UNIT **74** 시제 일치

[해석] 나의 선생님은 러시아가 세계에서 가장 큰 나라라고 말씀하셨다.

→ 현재의 사실을 나타낼 때는 현재시제를 쓴다.

32 정답 had been   UNIT **74** 시제 일치

[해석] 나는 그녀가 전에 미국에 가 본 적이 있는지 궁금했다.

→ 주절의 시제가 과거이므로 종속절의 시제는 과거나 과거완료를 써야 하는데, 과거의 경험을 말하므로 과거완료시제를 써야 한다.

33 정답 ④   UNIT **74** 시제 일치

[해석] (A) 여보세요, 저는 Gary입니다. 저는 현재 전화를 받을 수 없습니다, 그러니 삐 소리 후에 메시지를 남겨주세요. 제가 가능한 빨리 연락드릴게요.
(B) 안녕, Gary, 나 Owen이야. 내가 요즘 서울에 머무르고 있어서 언젠가 너를 봐야겠어. 내가 다시 전화할게. 안녕.
(A): Gary는 그 당시에 전화를 받을 수 없었고 그는 곧 전화를 건 사람에게 전화를 걸겠다고 말했다.

→ 주절의 시제가 said로 과거이므로 종속절의 시제도 과거로 맞추고, 동사는 모두 긍정형으로 써야 한다.

34 정답 ⑤   UNIT **74** 시제 일치

[해석] (B): Owen은 그가 서울에 머무르고 있어서 Gary를 한 번 만날 필요가 있다고 말했다.

→ 주절의 동사가 said로 과거이므로 종속절의 시제도 과거로 써야 한다.

35 정답 ②   UNIT **73** 주어와 동사의 수 일치

[해석] 당신은 문제를 묘사하는 이야기를 들을 것이다. 당신은 그 문제를 해결하는 방법에 관해서 생각할 시간을 1분 가질 것이다. 첫 번째 삐 소리가 난 뒤에 당신은 당신의 답을 녹음할 1분의 시간을 가질 것이다. 두 개의 짧은 삐 소리가 날 때, 녹음을 멈춰라. 자, 이제 시작하자.

→ 선행사가 a story이므로 관계대명사절의 동사는 3인칭 단수인 주어에 일치시켜 단수 동사인 describes가 알맞다.

36 정답 ①   UNIT **74** 시제 일치

→ 시간의 부사절에서는 현재시제가 미래시제를 대신하므로 ① hear가 알맞다.

37 정답 It isn't   UNIT **73** 주어와 동사의 수 일치

[해석] 식물과 동물들은 매우 위험한 적 하나를 가지고 있다. 그것은 질병이나 화재, 심지어 오염도 아니다. 가장 위험한 적은 인간이다. 인간은 다른 생명체를 멸종시킨 적이 있는 유일한 생명체이다. 인간 때문에 많은 다른 동물들은 거의 멸종 상태이다. 만약 그들이 보호되지 않는다면 그들도 곧 영원히 사라질 것이다.

→ one very dangerous enemy는 단수이므로 They 대신 It이, 단수 주어에 일치시켜서 aren't 대신 isn't가 알맞다.

38 정답 ③   UNIT **73** 주어와 동사의 수 일치

→ 관계대명사 that 뒤의 동사는 선행사인 the only living creature와 수를 일치시켜야 하므로 ③의 have는 has로 고쳐야 한다.

39 정답 ②   UNIT **74** 시제 일치

[해석] A: 콜럼버스는 그 당시에 세계가 둥글다는 것을 알았으니 대단한 것 같지 않니?
B: 응, 특히 그 당시 대부분의 사람들이 세상이 평평해서 너무 멀리 항해를 하면 떨어질 거라고 생각했던 것을 고려하면 말이야.

→ ② 불변의 진리는 현재시제로 쓴다. (was → is)
① 불변의 진리를 발견해서 대단하다는 것이므로 현재시제는 알맞다. ③ '~을 고려할 때'라는 분사구문으로 알맞게 쓰였다. ④ 과거에 그렇게 생각한 것이므로 과거시제가 알맞다. ⑤ 가정법 과거의 주절에 알맞은 시제로 쓰였다.

40 정답 ②   UNIT **73** 주어와 동사의 수 일치

[해석] 해파리의 공격 횟수가 전 세계적으로 증가하고 있다. 남획뿐만 아니라 기후 변화도 해파리 숫자의 증가를 야기한다. 2014년에 약 150명의 수영객들이 미국 뉴햄프셔의 한 해변에서 해파리에 쏘였다. 해파리의 쏘기 공격은 한국에서도 보도된다. 해파리가 많은 바다에서 수영하는 것을 피하거나 해파리 쏘기 공격에 대한 적절한 치료법에 대해 알고 있어야 한다.

→ (A) 「the number of+복수 명사」가 주어일 때는 단수 취급한다.
(B) B as well as A가 주어로 쓰이면 B에 동사를 일치시킨다.
(C) 「a number of+복수 명사」가 주어일 때는 복수 취급한다.

41 정답 ③   UNIT **73** 주어와 동사의 수 일치

[해석] 당신은 수어가 무엇인지 아는가? 당신은 누군가가 수어로 말하는 것을 이해하고 싶은가? 수어는 청각 장애인들 사이에서 효과적인 의사소통 방법이다. 수어는 손동작, 손가락 철자 표현, 그리고 표정으로 이루어져 있다. 대부분의 나라들은 자신만의 표준 수어를 발전시켰지만, 수어와 구어는 실제로 관련이 없다.

→ ③ Sign language는 단수로 취급하므로, 동사 역시 단수 동사인 consists가 와야 한다.

42 정답 ③   UNIT **75** 화법

[해석] 나는 Jane이고 중학생이다. 지난주에 새로운 학생이 우리 반에 들어왔다. 선생님은 반의 다른 학생들에게 그가 새 학교생활에 익숙해지도록 도와주라고 하셨다. 나는 내가 만일 그라면 매우 긴장될 거라고 생각했다. 그날 나는 점심시간에 그가 복도에서 서성이는 것을 발견했다. 나는 그에게 점심을 먹었냐고 물었다. 그는 나에게 식당을 찾을 수가 없다고 말했다. 나는 그를 식당으로 데려갔고 그와 대화를 나누었다. 이제 그는 나뿐만 아니라 다른 학생들과도 잘 지낸다. 선생님께서 내가 한 일을 아신다면 "나는 네가 자랑스럽구나."라고 말씀하실 것이다.

→ (A) 동사 asked의 목적격 보어는 to부정사로 써야 한다.
(B) 간접화법에서 전달동사 told가 과거이므로 인용문 동사의 시제는 과거로 써야 한다.
(C) 직접화법이므로 목적어는 you가 알맞다.

S 특수 구문

UNIT 76 도치

개념 확인 문제 정답 ▶ 문제편 p.319

01 stood the four sisters
02 could I hear what she said
03 does Sam feel safe and secure
04 did I dream that I could meet my favorite actor face to face
05 Neither do I
06 Neither did I
07 So did I
08 Neither am I
09 So was I
10 she has → has she
11 a number of people lived → lived a number of people
12 he came → did he come
13 So → Neither
14 are you → you are
15 has → do

---

01 [정답] stood the four sisters
[해석] 네 명의 자매가 풀밭 위에 서 있었다.
→ 자동사 stand가 쓰인 문장에서 장소의 부사구가 문두로 나오면 주어와 동사가 도치된다.

02 [정답] could I hear what she said
[해석] 나는 그녀가 한 말을 거의 알아들을 수 없었다.
→ 부정어 hardly가 문두로 나오면 주어와 동사가 도치된다.

03 [정답] does Sam feel safe and secure
[해석] Sam은 오직 그의 집에서만 안전하다고 느낀다.
→ 「only+부사(구)」가 문두로 나오면 주어와 동사가 도치된다.

04 [정답] did I dream that I could meet my favorite actor face to face
[해석] 나는 내가 가장 좋아하는 배우를 직접 대면할 수 있으리라고는 꿈도 꾸지 못했다.
→ 부정어 little이 문두로 나오면 주어와 동사가 도치되고 일반동사이므로 did를 사용한다.

05 [정답] Neither do I
[해석] A: 난 비 오는 계절을 좋아하지 않아. B: 나도 그래.
→ A의 동사가 don't like로 부정이므로 동의 표현을 쓸 때는 Neither를 써야 한다. 주어와 동사는 도치되어 do I 순으로 온다.

06 [정답] Neither did I
[해석] A: 그녀는 교과서를 가져오지 않았어. B: 나도 그랬어.
→ A의 동사가 didn't bring으로 부정이므로 동의 표현을 쓸 때는 Neither를 써야 한다. 주어와 동사는 도치되어 did I 순으로 온다.

07 [정답] So did I
[해석] A: 그녀는 어제 교회에 갔어. B: 나도 그랬어.
→ A의 동사가 went로 긍정이므로 동의 표현을 쓸 때는 So를 써야 한다. 주어와 동사는 도치되어 did I 순으로 온다.

08 [정답] Neither am I
[해석] A: 그는 수학을 잘하지 못해. B: 나도 그래.
→ A의 동사가 is not으로 부정이므로 동의 표현을 쓸 때는 Neither를 써야 한다. 주어와 동사는 도치되어 am I 순으로 온다.

09 [정답] So was I
[해석] A: 난 기말 시험 전에 초조했어. B: 나도 그랬어.
→ A의 동사가 was로 긍정이므로 동의 표현을 쓸 때는 So를 써야 한다. 주어와 동사는 도치되어 was I 순으로 온다.

10 [정답] she has → has she
[해석] 그녀는 결코 그 일을 끝낸 적이 없다.
→ 부정어 never가 문두로 나오면 주어와 동사가 도치된다.

11 [정답] a number of people lived → lived a number of people
[해석] 오래전에 많은 사람들이 살았다.
→ there가 문두로 오고 자동사 live가 쓰였으므로 주어와 동사가 도치된다.

12 [정답] he came → did he come
[해석] 그제서야 그는 우산을 가져오지 않았다는 것을 알게 되었다.
→ 「only+부사(구)」가 문두로 오면 주어와 동사가 도치되고 동사가 일반동사일 경우 do, did, does가 주어 앞으로 간다. 동사가 came으로 과거이므로 did he come으로 써야 한다.

13 [정답] So → Neither
[해석] A: 난 도서관에 가고 싶지 않았어. B: 나도 그랬어.
→ A의 동사가 didn't want로 부정이므로 동의 표현을 쓸 때는 Neither를 써야 한다.

14 [정답] are you → you are
[해석] A: 내 노트북이 어디에 있는지 아니? B: 여기 있어.
→ 대명사가 주어일 때는 here가 문두로 와도 도치가 일어나지 않는다.

15 [정답] has → do
[해석] A: 나는 한국의 영화 산업이 빠르게 발전해 왔다고 생각해. B: 나도 그래.
→ A의 주절 동사가 일반동사인 think이므로 '나도 그렇다.'는 의미의 동의 표현을 쓸 때는 do동사를 써야 한다.

<table><tr><td>

개념 확인 문제 정답   ▶ 문제편 **p.321**

01 do → does   **02** falling → fall

03 expects → expect   **04** made → make

05 much → very   **06** on earth   **07** Who

08 in the least   **09** less   **10** even

11 not

12 is Brandon that[who]

13 was last night that[when]

14 is after the final exam that[when]

15 was in London that[where]

16 was Merlin that[who(m)]

</td></tr></table>

01 [정답] do → does

[해석] Emily는 그 답을 알기를 정말로 원한다.

→ 일반동사인 hope를 강조하는데 주어인 Emily가 3인칭 단수이므로 does를 써야 한다.

02 [정답] falling → fall

[해석] 나는 이번 주에 감기 때문에 정말 일정에 뒤처졌다.

→ 일반동사를 강조하는 did가 쓰였으므로 falling을 동사원형인 fall로 고쳐야 한다.

03 [정답] expects → expect

[해석] 그녀는 파티에서 그녀의 오랜 친구를 보기를 정말로 기대한다.

→ 일반동사를 강조하는 does가 쓰였으므로 expects를 동사원형인 expect로 고쳐야 한다.

04 [정답] made → make

[해석] 그가 한 말은 사실이야. 그가 너를 위해 그 케이크를 정말로 만들었어.

→ 일반동사를 강조하기 위해 do동사를 쓰면, do 뒤에 나오는 본동사는 동사원형으로 쓴다.

05 [정답] much → very

[해석] 너는 내가 몇 번이고 계속 볼 수 있는 바로 그 사람이야.

→ '바로 그 ~'라는 뜻으로 명사를 강조할 때는 the very를 쓴다. 따라서 much를 very로 고쳐야 한다.

06 [정답] on earth

[해석] 너는 도대체 여기에서 무엇을 하고 있니?

→ 의문사를 강조할 때는 의문사 뒤에 on earth를 쓴다.

07 [정답] Who

[해석] 도대체 누가 감히 내게 말대꾸하니?

→ 의문사를 강조하는 in the world가 있으므로 그 앞에 의문사 Who를 쓴다.

08 [정답] in the least

[해석] 그는 그 소식에 전혀 충격을 받지 않았다.

→ 부정어를 강조할 때는 in the least를 쓴다.

09 [정답] less

[해석] 그녀는 야망은 있지만, 마땅히 그래야 할 만큼 준비가 되어 있지는 않다.

→ 비교급을 강조하는 far가 있으므로 그 뒤에 less를 쓴다.

10 [정답] even

[해석] 이 신발들은 오래된 것들보다 훨씬 더 편안하다.

→ 비교급인 more comfortable을 강조할 때 앞에 even을 쓸 수 있다.

11 [정답] not

[해석] 그녀는 아이들을 전혀 사랑하지 않고 그들을 잘 돌보지 않을 것이다.

→ 부정어를 강조할 때는 not at all을 쓴다.

12 [정답] is Brandon that[who]

[해석] Brandon은 저 차를 팔고 싶어 한다.

→ 저 차를 팔고 싶어 하는 사람은 바로 Brandon이다.

→ 주어인 Brandon은 사람이므로 강조하려면 that이나 who를 써야 한다.

13 [정답] was last night that[when]

[해석] 그녀는 어젯밤에 그 창문을 깼다.

→ 그녀가 그 창문을 깬 것은 바로 어젯밤이었다.

→ last night은 시간의 부사구이므로 강조하려면 that[when]을 써야 한다.

14 [정답] is after the final exam that[when]

[해석] 나는 기말고사 후에 콘서트로 가고 싶다.

→ 내가 콘서트로 가고 싶은 것은 바로 기말고사 후다.

→ 강조 구문에서 현재시제이므로 is를 써야 하고, after the final exam은 시간의 부사구이므로 강조하기 위해서 that[when]을 써야 한다.

15 [정답] was in London that[where]

[해석] Susan은 London에서 그 뮤지컬을 봤다.

→ Susan이 뮤지컬을 본 것은 바로 런던에서였다.

→ 강조 구문에서 과거시제이므로 was를 써야 하고, in London은 장소의 부사구이므로 강조하기 위해서 that[where]를 써야 한다.

16 [정답] was Merlin that[who(m)]

[해석] Matthew는 Mary의 마음을 사로잡을 방법을 묻기 위해 Merlin을 찾아갔다.

→ Matthew가 Mary의 마음을 사로잡을 방법을 묻기 위해 찾아간 사람은 바로 Merlin이었다.

→ 강조 구문에서 과거시제이므로 was를 써야 하고, Merlin은 목적어이므로 강조하기 위해서 that[who(m)]을 써야 한다.

개념 확인 문제 정답 ▶ 문제편 p.323

01 I wish you a **02** it is **03** who is
04 I am **05** in Seoul 앞의 was born
06 in Japan 앞의 were made **07** which is
08 모든 남자아이들이 운동을 좋아하는 것은 아니다.
09 내가 항상 시험을 잘 보는 것은 아니다.
10 우리 중 아무도 연극 동아리에 가입하고 싶어하지 않았다.
11 제 차를 주차할 수 있는 곳이 아무데도 없나요?
12 너는 꼭 내 요리법을 사용해서 스파게티를 만들 필요는 없다.
13 that he dropped out of school surprised me
14 Mr. Jones, came from Canada
15 try to solve the problem of poverty in Africa

01 [정답] I wish you a
[해석] 생일 축하해.
→ I wish you a는 흔히 생략된다.

02 [정답] it is
[해석] 필요하면 너한테 전화할게.
→ 주어가 일반적인 it일 때 부사절에서 「주어+be동사」는 생략할 수 있다.

03 [정답] who is
[해석] 너는 Amy라는 이름의 여자아이를 아니?
→ 「주격 관계대명사+be동사」는 생략할 수 있다.

04 [정답] I am
[해석] 아침을 먹는 동안 나는 항상 라디오를 듣는다.
→ 주절의 주어와 같을 때 부사절에서 「주어+be동사」는 생략할 수 있다.

05 [정답] in Seoul 앞의 was born
[해석] 나는 뉴욕에서 태어났고, 내 남동생은 서울에서 태어났다.
→ and 뒤에 반복되는 동사 was born은 생략할 수 있다.

06 [정답] in Japan 앞의 were made
[해석] 이 자동차들은 한국에서 만들어졌고, 저것들은 일본에서 만들어졌다.
→ and 뒤에 반복되는 동사 were made는 생략할 수 있다.

07 [정답] which is
[해석] 인터넷 프로토콜 스탠다드라고 불리는 통신 규범이 있다.
→ 「주격 관계대명사+be동사」는 생략할 수 있다.

08 [정답] 모든 남자아이들이 운동을 좋아하는 것은 아니다.
→ not all은 '모두가 ~인 것은 아닌'이라는 뜻으로 부분 부정 표현이다.

09 [정답] 내가 항상 시험을 잘 보는 것은 아니다.
→ not always는 '항상 ~인 것은 아닌'이라는 뜻으로 부분 부정이다.

10 [정답] 우리 중 아무도 연극 동아리에 가입하고 싶어하지 않았다.
→ none은 '아무도 ~ 않는'이라는 뜻으로 전체 부정 표현이다.

11 [정답] 제 차를 주차할 수 있는 곳이 아무데도 없나요?
→ not ~ anywhere는 '아무데도 ~ 없는'이라는 뜻으로 전체 부정 표현으로 쓰인다.

12 [정답] 너는 꼭 내 요리법을 사용해서 스파게티를 만들 필요는 없다.
→ not necessarily는 '반드시[꼭] ~인 것은 아닌'이라는 뜻으로 부분 부정 표현으로 쓰인다.

13 [정답] that he dropped out of school surprised me
→ the fact 뒤에 동격절이 나올 때는 접속사 that을 사용한다.

14 [정답] Mr. Jones, came from Canada
→ 명사(구)끼리 동격을 이룰 때는 콤마를 사용하여 연결한다.

15 [정답] try to solve the problem of poverty in Africa
→ 명사(구)끼리 동격을 이룰 때는 전치사 of를 사용하여 연결할 수 있다.

S
Unit
76-78

단원 평가 문제 UNIT 76 ~ UNIT 78 ▶ 문제편 p.324~328

정답

01 ② **02** ⑤ **03** ① **04** ① **05** ③
06 ⑤ **07** ① **08** does like **09** ③
10 ever **11** does he visit **12** they are
13 at all **14** did **15** both **16** that
17 ③ **18** ① **19** ②
20 knew → know **21** who → that
22 very the → the very **23** I had → had I
24 was → 삭제 또는 who[that] was
25 waits she → she waits **26** ④
27 did a single person tell Sharon the secret
28 does know the answer
29 I that[who] showed Mina the letter from Tom
30 did I learn about African history and culture
31 ③ **32** ④ **33** ② **34** It is **35** ③
36 While I was in high school
37 others live in China **38** two birds in the bush
39 if it is possible **40** I'd love to join you
41 which[that] is called a cocoon
42 ③ **43** ② **44** ④

01 [정답] ② UNIT 76 도치
[해석] 작년 겨울에 나는 거의 스키를 타러 가지 못했다.
→ 부정어 hardly가 문두로 나오면 「조동사+주어+본동사」 순으로 도치된다.

02 [정답] ⑤   UNIT **76** 도치

[해석] 그의 어깨는 좀처럼 아프지 않다.

→ 부정어구인 rarely가 문두로 나오면 주어와 동사가 도치된다. 주어인 his shoulder가 3인칭 단수이므로 does가 필요하다.

03 [정답] ①   UNIT **77** 강조

[해석] 나는 아침에 일찍 일어나는 것을 정말 싫어한다.

→ 일반동사를 강조할 때 do동사를 쓰며, 주어가 I이므로 do 뒤에 나오는 본동사는 동사원형으로 쓴다.

04 [정답] ①   UNIT **76** 도치

→ 부정어 never가 문두로 나오면 주어와 동사가 도치된다.

05 [정답] ③   UNIT **76** 도치

→ 부정어 not이 문두로 나오면 did I know로 써야 한다.

06 [정답] ⑤   UNIT **78** 생략, 부정 구문, 동격

→ 동사에 부정의 뜻이 없기 때문에 부정의 뜻을 포함한 말이 필요하므로 Neither가 알맞다.

07 [정답] ①   UNIT **78** 생략, 부정 구문, 동격

→ not all은 부분 부정을 나타내는 표현이고, 앞에 이미 부정을 의미하는 not이 있으므로 뒤에 부정의 말은 올 수 없다.

08 [정답] does like   UNIT **77** 강조

[해석] A: 그녀의 취미는 무엇이니?

B: 춤추기야. 그녀는 춤추기를 정말 좋아해.

→ 일반동사를 강조할 때는 do를 사용하며, 인칭과 시제에 따라 「do[does, did]+동사원형」의 형태가 된다.

09 [정답] ③   UNIT **78** 생략, 부정 구문, 동격

[해석] 어떤 새들은 날 수 있지만, 어떤 새들은 날 수 없다.

→ some 뒤에 중복되는 명사 birds, can't 뒤에 중복되는 동사 fly가 생략되었다.

10 [정답] ever   UNIT **77** 강조

[해석] 너는 도대체 왜 이렇게 집에 늦게 왔니?

→ 의문사를 강조할 때 의문사 뒤에 ever를 쓸 수 있다.

11 [정답] does he visit   UNIT **76** 도치

[해석] 그는 요즘 좀처럼 그의 조부모님을 방문하지 않는다.

→ 부정어 rarely가 문두로 나오면 주어와 동사가 도치된다.

12 [정답] they are   UNIT **76** 도치

[해석] 그들이 저기에 있는데, 언덕을 내려오고 있다.

→ there가 문두에 있어도 대명사가 주어일 때는 도치되지 않는다.

13 [정답] at all   UNIT **77** 강조

[해석] 나는 채소만 먹어 왔지만 전혀 살을 뺄 수 없었다.

→ 부정문을 강조할 때는 at all을 쓴다.

14 [정답] did   UNIT **77** 강조

[해석] 네가 전화 통화를 하고 있었을 때, 나는 너에게 벤치에 앉지 말라고 정말로 말했다.

→ 일반동사를 강조할 때는 do동사를 사용하는데, 부사절이 과거시제이므로 주절도 과거시제로 일치시켜야 한다.

15 [정답] both   UNIT **78** 생략, 부정 구문, 동격

[해석] 그가 그의 사촌을 둘 다 만난 적은 없다. 그는 그들 중 한 명을 만났다.

→ 뒤에 한 명만 만났다는 말이 있으므로 not ~ both로 '둘 다 ~은 아닌'이라는 의미의 부분 부정 표현을 써야 한다.

16 [정답] that   UNIT **78** 생략, 부정 구문, 동격

[해석] 그가 경기에 이길 가능성은 거의 없다.

→ 동격절을 이끄는 접속사 that을 써야 한다.

17 [정답] ③   UNIT **77** 강조

[해석] ① 그는 좀처럼 외식을 하지 않는다.

② 모든 여자아이가 화장하는 것을 좋아하는 것은 아니다.

③ 어제 나에게 꽃을 준 사람은 Mike였다.

④ 내가 강아지를 잃어버렸던 것은 바로 이 공원에서였다.

⑤ 그는 내가 10분 전에 만들었던 팬케이크를 정말 먹었다.

→ ③ It ~ that ... 강조 구문에서 주어 Mike를 강조하고 있으므로 뒤에 또 he가 나올 수는 없다.

① seldom이 문두로 나가면서 주어와 동사가 도치되었다. ② not 뒤에 every를 써서 부분 부정을 나타낼 수 있다. ④ It ~ that ... 강조 구문에서 in this park가 강조되었다. ⑤ 동사 eat를 did가 강조하고 있다.

18 [정답] ①   UNIT **76** 도치

[해석] ① 언덕 위에 그것은 앉아 있었다.

② 네가 주문했던 요리가 나온다.

③ 그녀는 그가 정말 빨리 달린다고 강하게 믿는다.

④ 길 건너편에서 노래를 하는 한 작은 소년이 있다.

⑤ 나는 그가 시험에 실패할 것이라는 것은 꿈에도 생각하지 못했다.

→ ① 장소의 부사구가 문두로 나와도 대명사가 주어일 때는 주어와 동사를 도치하지 않는다.

② here가 문두로 나가면서 주어와 동사가 도치되었다. ③ 동사 run을 강조하는 does가 왔다. ④「주격 관계대명사 + be동사」가 생략되었다. ⑤ 부정어 never가 문두로 나가면서 주어와 동사가 도치되었다.

19 [정답] ②   UNIT **78** 생략, 부정 구문, 동격

[해석] ① 모든 캐나다인이 영어를 유창하게 하는 것은 아니다.

② 나는 그 문제에 대한 어떤 해결책도 찾지 못했다.

③ 마을 전체가 여름 축제를 정말로 즐겼다.

④ 그것은 우리가 함께한 바로 마지막 기회였다.

⑤ 영어 선생님이신 White 씨는 매우 친절하다.

→ ② 전체 부정을 나타내는 표현인 not any가 알맞게 쓰였다.

① All not → Not all ③ enjoyed → enjoy ④ very → the very ⑤ are → is

20 [정답] knew → know   UNIT **76** 도치

[해석] 그들은 서로를 거의 몰랐다. 그들은 서로에 대해 들어본 적이 없는 것 같았다.

→ 부정어 hardly가 문두로 나오면 주어와 동사가 도치되는데, 조동사 do 뒤에 나오는 본동사는 동사원형으로 쓴다.

21 [정답] who → that   UNIT **77** 강조

[해석] 우리가 돌아가기로 결정한 것은 Robert가 아팠기 때문이었다.

→ 부사절 because Robert was ill이 강조되는 것이므로 접속사 that을 써야 한다.

22 정답 very the → the very　　　　　　　UNIT **77** 강조

[해석] 너는 어떻게 이것이 내가 원하는 바로 그 물건이라는 것을 알았니?

→ 명사를 강조할 때는 the very를 강조하려는 명사 앞에 쓴다.

23 정답 I had → had I　　　　　　　UNIT **76** 도치

[해석] 내가 밖에 나오자마자 비가 오기 시작했다.

→ 부정어구 no sooner가 문두에 오면 주어와 동사가 도치된다.

24 정답 was → 삭제 또는 who[that] was
　　　　　　　UNIT **78** 생략, 부정 구문, 동격

[해석] 우리 앞에 서 있던 남자가 갑자기 사라졌다.

→ 관계대명사절에서 주격 관계대명사를 생략할 때는 「주격 관계대명사+be동사」를 함께 생략해야 힌다.

25 정답 waits she → she waits　　　　　　　UNIT **76** 도치

[해석] 얼어붙은 호수 가장자리에 그녀는 누군가가 돌아오기를 기다린다.

→ 주어가 대명사일 때는 장소의 부사구가 문두에 오더라도 주어와 동사는 도치되지 않는다.

26 정답 ④　　　　　　　UNIT **76** 도치

[해석] 나는 숙제를 끝낸 후에야 내가 잘못된 과제를 하고 있었다는 것을 깨달았다. ① 깜짝 놀란 나는 급히 진짜 과제를 확인했고, 내가 수학 문제를 푸는 것이 아니라 에세이를 써야 한다는 것을 알게 되었다! ② 나는 정신없이 바로 글쓰기를 시작했다. ③ 내가 에세이의 중반쯤 왔을 때야 그 주제가 무엇인지 전혀 모른다는 것을 깨달았다. 그때서야 나는 인터넷에서 그 주제를 찾아보기로 결심했다. ④ 내가 검색을 시작하자마자 그 주제에 딱 맞는 완벽한 기사를 찾았다! ⑤ 그 기사 덕분에 나는 에세이를 간신히 제시간에 끝낼 수 있었다.

→ ④ 부정어 hardly가 문두에 왔으므로 주어와 동사는 도치되어야 한다. 따라서 I had를 had I라고 써야 한다.

27 정답 did a single person tell Sharon the secret
　　　　　　　UNIT **76** 도치

[해석] 단 한 사람도 Sharon에게 비밀을 말하지 않았다.

→ never가 문두에 나오면 주어와 동사가 도치된다.

28 정답 does know the answer　　　　　　　UNIT **77** 강조

[해석] William은 정말로 그 답을 알고 있다.

→ 동사를 강조할 때는 do를 본동사 앞에 쓴다. 주어가 3인칭이고 현재시제이므로 does가 알맞다. 그 뒤에 오는 knows는 원형인 know로 바꾸어야 한다.

29 정답 I that[who] showed Mina the letter from Tom
　　　　　　　UNIT **77** 강조

[해석] 나는 미나에게 Tom으로부터 온 편지를 보여 주었다.

→ 주어를 강조할 때는 It is[was] ~ that[who] ... 강조 구문을 쓸 수 있다. 이 문장에서 주어는 I이다.

30 정답 did I learn about African history and culture
　　　　　　　UNIT **76** 도치

[해석] 나는 고등학교 때까지 아프리카의 역사와 문화에 대해서 배우지 않았다.

→ 부정어 not이 포함된 어구가 문두로 나오면 주어와 동사가 도치된다. 일반동사의 과거형이 쓰였으므로 조동사 do의 과거형 did를 쓰고, 주어 I 뒤의 본동사 learn은 동사원형으로 써야 한다.

31 정답 ③　　　　　　　UNIT **78** 생략, 부정 구문, 동격

[해석] ① 이곳에서는 흡연이 허용되지 않습니다.

② 아기는 넘어져서 많이 울었다.

③ 나는 우리 학교에서 상담을 해 주는 여자를 안다.

④ 싱가포르 사람들은 '싱글리시'라고 불리는 특별한 언어를 사용한다.

⑤ 한국인들은 집안에서 신발을 벗는 반면에 미국인들은 신발을 벗지 않는다.

→ ③ 주격 관계대명사만 단독으로 생략할 수는 없다.

① 경고문에서 관용적으로 생략할 수 있는 부분이다. ② 앞의 주어와 같으므로 생략할 수 있다. ④ 주격 관계대명사와 be동사는 함께 생략 가능하다. ⑤ 반복되는 말이므로 생략할 수 있다.

32 정답 ④　　　　　　　UNIT **77** 강조

[해석] 많은 유명 인사들이 전시회를 위해 이곳에 정말로 왔다.

① 그들은 그들의 실수를 전혀 인정하지 않았다.

② 그는 작년에 했던 것보다 더 잘한다.

③ Maria는 저녁을 먹은 후 항상 설거지를 한다.

④ 모든 학생이 그의 담임선생님을 정말 좋아한다.

⑤ 그녀는 교외로 이사 가고 싶어 하지 않아, 그렇지?

→ 주어진 문장과 ④은 일반동사를 강조하기 위해 쓰인 조동사이다.

① 부정문에 쓰인 조동사 ② 대동사(= played) ③ 일반동사(~하다) ⑤ 부가의문문에 쓰인 조동사

33 정답 ②　　　　　　　UNIT **77** 강조

[해석] 당신이 가장 좋아하는 과일이나 채소는 무엇인가? 당신은 체리나 복숭아를 좋아하는가? 토마토나 감자는 어떤가? 만약 당신의 답이 yes라면, 당신은 그 식물들의 다른 부분들을 먹지 않도록 조심해야 한다. 왜 그런지 아는가? 당신을 아프게 만들지도 모르는 것이 바로 같은 식물의 다른 부분들이다. 사람들은 체리를 먹을 수 있지만 체리나무의 잔가지는 독성이 있다. 복숭아는 사람들에게 좋지만, 그 잎은 먹지 않아야 한다. 토마토와 감자 식물의 잎과 줄기도 그렇다.

→ other parts of the same plant를 강조하는 문장으로 It ~ that ... 강조 구문을 사용했다. 강조하는 대상이 사람이나 시간, 장소의 부사구가 아니므로 ③ who, ④ when, ⑤ where는 올 수 없다.

34 정답 It is　　　　　　　UNIT **77** 강조

→ 강조하는 부분을 It과 that 사이에 놓는다. peaches가 복수라고 해서 동사를 복수형에 맞춰서 쓰는 것은 맞지 않다.

35 정답 ③　　　　　　　UNIT **76** 도치

→ so가 문두에 올 때 주어와 동사가 도치된다. 주어가 복수 명사이며 앞에 are로 be동사가 쓰였으므로 빈칸에도 are를 쓴다.

36 정답 While I was in high school
　　　　　　　UNIT **78** 생략, 부정 구문, 동격

[해석] 고등학생이었을 때, 나는 늘 시간 엄수에 어려움을 겪었다.

→ 부사절과 주절의 주어가 일치할 때 부사절의 「주어+be동사」는 생략할 수 있다.

37 정답 others live in China　　　UNIT **78** 생략, 부정 구문, 동격

[해석] 내 가족 중 일부는 한국에 살고 다른 가족들은 중국에 산다.

→ and 뒤에 반복되는 동사는 생략할 수 있다.

S Unit 76-78

38 [정답] two birds in the bush   UNIT **78** 생략, 부정 구문, 동격

[해석] 손 안에 있는 한 마리의 새가 덤불 속에 있는 두 마리의 새보다 가치 있다.

→ 반복되는 명사 birds가 생략되어 있다.

39 [정답] if it is possible   UNIT **78** 생략, 부정 구문, 동격

[해석] 가능하다면 나는 그것을 돌려주고 싶다.

→ '가능하다면'의 if it is possible에서 it is는 생략할 수 있다.

40 [정답] I'd love to join you   UNIT **78** 생략, 부정 구문, 동격

[해석] A: 너 우리와 함께 할래?

B: 그러고 싶지만 나는 다른 계획이 있어.

→ 대부정사 to 뒤에는 A의 to 이하에 쓰인 join you가 생략됐다.

41 [정답] which[that] is called a cocoon   UNIT **78** 생략, 부정 구문, 동격

[해석] 애벌레는 자신 주위에 '고치'라고 불리는 작은 집을 짓는다.

→ 「주격 관계대명사+be동사」는 생략할 수 있다.

42 [정답] ③   UNIT **78** 생략, 부정 구문, 동격

[해석] 당신은 학교에 어떻게 가는가? 나는 걸어서 학교에 가지만, 모든 아이들이 걸어서 학교에 가는 것은 아니다. 어떤 아이들은 자전거를 타고, 다른 아이들은 차를 타고 간다. 하지만 Ou 섬에 사는 아이들은 이 중 어떤 것도 하지 않는다. 그들은 '대나무 말'이라고 불리는 긴 막대를 사용한다. 섬들 사이의 물은 배를 사용할 만큼 깊지 않아서, 아이들은 막대를 타고 걷는다.

→ ③ 관계대명사절에서 주격 관계대명사를 생략할 때는 「주격 관계대명사＋be동사」를 함께 생략해야 한다. 따라서 주격 관계대명사만 생략하고 남은 are living을 who[that] are living 또는 living으로 고쳐야 한다.

43 [정답] ②   UNIT **78** 생략, 부정 구문, 동격

[해석] 도시를 떠나 있는 동안, 당신은 식물에 어떻게 물을 줄 수 있을까? 여기에 유용한 조언이 있다. 며칠마다 물을 주어야 하는 식물들은 직사광선을 피할 수 있도록 햇빛이 비치는 창문으로부터 치워 두어야 한다. 또 다른 방법은 2인치의 물로 채워진 욕조에 벽돌을 넣고 그 벽돌 위에 식물을 두는 것이다. 마지막 수단으로, 친구가 해 줄 수 있다면 친구에게 당신의 식물에 물을 주도록 부탁하라.

→ ② there, here 또는 장소, 방향의 부사구가 문두에 올 때, 「자동사 + 주어」 순으로 온다. 따라서 are useful tips의 순서로 와야 한다.

44 [정답] ④   UNIT **76** 도치

[해석] Donald와 함께 한 운전 수업은 정말 좋았다. 나는 항상 운전이 늘었다는 느낌을 받으면서 수업에서 돌아왔다. 처음 수업을 시작했을 때, 나는 운전하고 시험 보는 것에 매우 긴장을 했다. 하지만 그와 같이 수업을 한 후에 운전을 배우면서 한 번도 긴장을 하거나 걱정을 한 적이 없었다. 그의 도움 덕분에 나는 시험에 합격할 수 있었다. 이제 나는 매우 자신감 있게 운전을 하고 친구들과 가족도 이것을 알아보았다. 나는 내가 운전을 배웠을 뿐만 아니라 배우면서 좋은 시간을 보냈기 때문에 Donald를 운전 강사로 추천한다. 나는 그가 당신이 운전 연수를 받는 데 필요한 바로 그 강사라고 생각한다.

→ ④ 부정어 not이 포함된 not only가 문두에 나오면 주어와 동사가 도치된다. (I learned → did I learn)

정답

01 ④	02 ④	03 to	04 ②	05 ①
06 ③	07 ③	08 ②		

01 [정답] ④   UNIT **03** 3형식 문장과 4형식 문장

[해석] 그녀는 집에서 만든 쿠키를 우리에게 ① 주었다 ② 제공했다 ③ 보여주었다 ⑤ 가져왔다.

→ ④ buy는 4형식 문장을 3형식 문장으로 전환할 때 전치사 for를 쓴다.

02 [정답] ④   UNIT **04** 5형식 문장

[해석] 교대 근무가 끝났을 때, 나는 그녀가 사무실을 ①, ③ 떠나게 했다 ②, ⑤ 떠나는 것을 보았다.

→ ④ 목적격 보어 자리에 원형부정사 leave가 왔으므로 to부정사를 취하는 allowed는 올 수 없다.

• shift 교대 근무 (시간)

03 [정답] to   UNIT **03** 3형식 문장과 4형식 문장, UNIT **04** 5형식 문장

[해석] • 내 상사는 나에게 도전적인 프로젝트를 주었다.

• 회의는 약 한 시간 정도 소요될 것으로 예상된다.

→ give는 4형식 문장을 3형식 문장으로 전환할 때 전치사 to를 쓰고, expect는 5형식 문장에 쓰일 때 목적격 보어로 to부정사를 취한다. 따라서 정답은 to이다.

04 [정답] ②   UNIT **02** 1형식 문장과 2형식 문장

[해석] ⓐ 그는 재미있는 농담에 웃는다.

ⓑ 우리는 주말에 함께 공부한다.

ⓒ 그는 수업을 학생들에게 설명했다.

ⓓ 그들은 우리가 문제를 어떻게 해결할 수 있는지 말했다.

ⓔ 그들은 마당에서 개가 공을 쫓는 것을 지켜봤다.

→ ⓑ together는 부사로, 2형식이 아닌 1형식 문장이다.

• chase 쫓다

05 [정답] ①   UNIT **02** 1형식 문장과 2형식 문장

[해석] 그는 경쟁에서 이길 가능성에 대해 자신감을 느낀다.

① 그는 긴 여행 후에 피곤해 보인다.

② 그는 내 생일에 나에게 선물을 주었다.

③ Tom은 어제 새 전화기를 샀다.

④ 그들은 지난 주말에 박물관을 방문했다.

⑤ 선생님은 학생들이 공부하고 있는 것을 발견했다.

→ 주어진 문장과 ①은 「주어+동사+주격 보어」로 이루어진 2형식 문장이다. ②은 4형식, ③, ④은 3형식, ⑤은 5형식 문장이다.

06 [정답] ③   UNIT **02** 1형식 문장과 2형식 문장

[해석] 폭풍 동안 바람은 나무 사이로 윙윙거렸다.

① 그 소식은 그녀를 속상하게 만들었다.

② 그들은 우리에게 큰 할인을 제공했다.

③ 그들은 공항에 제시간에 도착했다.

④ 저녁에 날씨가 추워졌다.

⑤ 그들은 그 연구 결과에 만족한다.

→ 주어진 문장과 ③은 「주어+동사」로 이루어진 1형식 문장이다. ①은 5형식, ②은 4형식, ④, ⑤은 2형식 문장이다.
· howl 울부짖다 · discount 할인

07 정답 ③　　　　　　　　　UNIT 02 1형식 문장과 2형식 문장
[해석] 그 개는 집에 너무 가까이 다가온 낯선 사람들에게 크게 짖었다.
→ 「주어+동사」로 이루어진 1형식 문장이며, 그 외의 것은 모두 수식어이므로 ③ 부사(loudly)가 적절하다.

08 정답 ②　　　　　　　　　UNIT 03 3형식 문장과 4형식 문장
[해석] 실직으로 인해 그녀는 재정적 안정성을 잃었다.
→ deprive A of B는 'A에게서 B를 박탈하다'를 뜻한다.
· financial 재정적인 · security 안정성

B 실전 모의고사　　　　　▶ 문제편 p.331

정답

01 ⑤	**02** ③	**03** w[W]hat
04 and	**05** Why	

06 He hasn't received the results, has he?
07 Solve this problem, or the project will be delayed.
08 ④　　　**09** ④

01 정답 ⑤　　　　　　　　　UNIT 06 평서문, 의문문
[해석] 우리는 이제 떠나야 하지, 그렇지 않니?
→ 긍정 평서문이므로 부가의문문은 부정문이 되어야 하고, 조동사 should가 쓰였으므로 ⑤ shouldn't we가 알맞다.

02 정답 ③　　　　　　　　　UNIT 06 평서문, 의문문
[해석] 회의가 언제 시작하는지 내게 말해줄 수 있니?
→ 직접목적어로 간접의문문이 왔다. 간접의문문의 어순은 「의문사+주어+동사」이므로 ③이 알맞다.

03 정답 w[W]hat　　　UNIT 05 명령문, 제안문, 감탄문,
　　　　　　　　　　　　　　UNIT 06 평서문, 의문문
[해석] · 그 행사에서 무슨 일이 있었는지 제게 말해줄 수 있나요?
· 여기 꼭대기에서 보는 정말 멋진 경치네요!
→ tell의 직접목적어로 간접의문문이 왔다. 간접의문문을 이끄는 의문사 자리이므로 what이 와야 한다. 명사 view를 수식하는 what 감탄문이다. 따라서 빈칸에 공통으로 들어갈 말은 w[W]hat이다.

04 정답 and　　　　　　　　UNIT 05 명령문, 제안문, 감탄문
→ 「명령문, and ~」 구문을 완성해야 하므로 and가 오는 것이 알맞다.
· process 진행, 처리

05 정답 Why　　　　　　　　UNIT 05 명령문, 제안문, 감탄문
→ don't와 함께 쓰여 '~하는 게 어때?'를 완성하는 것은 why이다.

06 정답 He hasn't received the results, has he?
　　　　　　　　　　　　　　UNIT 06 평서문, 의문문
→ 부정 평서문의 주어가 He이고 동사가 hasn't received이므로 부가의문문으로 has he?가 와야 한다.

---

07 정답 Solve this problem, or the project will be delayed.　　　UNIT 05 명령문, 제안문, 감탄문
→ 「명령문, or ~」 구문을 완성해야 하므로 Solve this problem, or the project will be delayed.의 순서로 오는 것이 알맞다.
· delay 지연시키다

08 정답 ④　　　　　　　　　UNIT 06 평서문, 의문문
→ know의 목적어로 간접의문문이 왔다. 의문사가 없는 간접의문문의 어순은 「if[whether]+주어+동사」이므로 Do you know whether they have tickets?의 순서가 되어야 한다.

09 정답 ④　　　　　　　　　UNIT 06 평서문, 의문문
[해석] ① 이것은 지금까지 본 영화 중 최고죠, 그렇지 않나요?
② 그는 답을 몰라요, 그렇죠?
③ 내일 해변에 갑시다, 어때요?
④ 그들은 내일 우리를 방문하러 올 거죠, 그렇지 않나요?
⑤ 당신은 내일까지 과제를 끝낼 거죠, 그렇지 않나요?
→ ④ 긍정 평서문의 주어가 They이고 동사가 are이므로 부가의문문 aren't they?가 와야 한다.
· complete 완료하다 · assignment 과제

C 실전 모의고사　　　　　▶ 문제편 p.332

정답

01 ③	**02** ②	**03** ×	**04** an

05 The, an
06 Next year's conference will be held in Paris.
07 The goal of the company is environmental protection.
08 ①　　　**09** ③

01 정답 ③　　　　　　　　　UNIT 08 셀 수 없는 명사의 복수형
[해석] 결혼식장에는 모두를 위한 많은 의자가 있다.
→ a lot of는 셀 수 있는 명사와 셀 수 없는 명사 모두를 수식할 수 있다.

02 정답 ②　　　　　　　　　UNIT 07 셀 수 있는 명사의 복수형
[해석] ① 이 ② 거위 ③ 연어 ④ 모기 ⑤ 도둑
→ goose의 복수형은 geese이다.

03 정답 ×　　　　　　　　　UNIT 11 주의해야 할 관사의 쓰임
[해석] Micky는 정치학에서 배운 것을 완전히 잊었다.
→ politics와 같은 학문명 앞에는 관사를 쓰지 않는다.
· politics 정치학

04 정답 an　　　　　　　　　UNIT 11 주의해야 할 관사의 쓰임
[해석] Jordan은 항상 성공을 목표로 하는 꽤 야망 있는 사람이다.
→ 「quite+부정관사(+형용사)+명사」의 구조이고, 뒤의 형용사가 모음으로 시작하므로 부정관사 an이 와야 한다.
· ambitious 야망이 있는 · aim for ~을 목표로 하다

05 정답 The, an　　　　　UNIT **10** 부정관사와 정관사

[해석] 혁신적인 헤드폰을 설계한 그 엔지니어는 레드닷 디자인 상을 받았다.

→ 명사 engineer가 수식어구로 한정되므로 앞에 정관사 the가 와야 한다. headphone을 꾸미는 형용사가 모음으로 시작하므로 부정관사 an이 와야 한다.

· innovative 혁신적인

06 정답 Next year's conference will be held in Paris.　　　　　UNIT **09** 명사의 소유격

→ 시간을 나타내는 명사의 소유격은 뒤에 's를 붙여 표현한다.

· be held (행사 등이) 열리다

07 정답 The goal of the company is environmental protection.　　　　　UNIT **09** 명사의 소유격

→ 무생물 명사의 소유격은 「of+명사」로 표현한다.

· environmental 환경의　· goal 목표

08 정답 ①　　　　　UNIT **10** 부정관사와 정관사

[해석] ① 나는 오늘 아침 식사를 걸렀다.
② 그는 매 한 마리를 찾기 위해 하늘을 올려다봤다.
③ 그녀는 그녀의 지갑을 진열장에 놓았다.
④ 아버지는 내가 전화로 나쁜 말을 하는 것을 들으셨다.
⑤ Neal은 실수로 Ann이 산 화분을 깨뜨렸다.

→ ① 식사 앞에는 관사를 쓰지 않는다. 나머지 빈칸에는 모두 정관사 the가 들어가야 한다.

· hawk 매　· showcase 진열장　· accidentally 실수로

09 정답 ③　　　　　UNIT **07** 셀 수 있는 명사의 복수형

[해석] ① 사슴 몇 마리가 평화롭게 풀을 뜯고 있었다.
② 그 마을의 남자들은 다리를 다시 세우는 것을 돕는다.
③ 주요 기준 중 하나는 리더십 경험이다.
④ 열대림은 수많은 희귀한 종들의 서식지이다.
⑤ 그녀는 공식 행사에서 항상 완벽한 예절로 행동한다.

→ ③ criterion의 복수형은 criteria이다.

· graze 풀을 뜯다　· criterion 기준　· tropical 열대의
· formal 공식적인

D 실전 모의고사　　　▶ 문제편 p.333

정답

01 ②	**02** ③	**03** ⑤	**04** ①	**05** ⑤
06 ④	**07** itself in the river			
08 another is, the other is				

01 정답 ②　　　　　UNIT **14** 부정대명사

[해석] ① 미래를 예측할 수 있는 사람은 없다.
② 두 개의 답변 모두 맞았다.
③ 그에게 뭔가 이상한 점이 있다.
④ 나는 그것들 중 어떤 것도 만족스럽지 않았다.
⑤ 열심히 노력하면 무엇이든 가능하다.

→ ② both는 복수로 취급하므로 단수형 동사인 was를 복수형인 were로 고쳐야 한다.

· predict 예측하다　· odd 이상한

02 정답 ③　　　　　UNIT **12** 지시대명사 this (these), that (those), it

[해석] · 세포의 구조는 공장의 구조와 비슷하다.
· 인내심 있게 기다리는 자들이 이긴다.

→ 앞에 나온 단수 명사인 structure를 대신해야 하므로 that이 와야 한다. '~한 사람들'은 those who로 표현한다.

· structure 구조　· cell 세포　· patiently 인내심 있게

03 정답 ⑤　　　　　UNIT **13** 재귀대명사

→ '자기도 모르게'는 in spite of oneself로 표현한다.

· pick one's nail ~의 손톱을 뜯다

04 정답 ①　　　　　UNIT **12** 지시대명사 this (these), that (those), it

→ to do가 이끄는 명사구를 대신하여 가목적어 it이 쓰였으므로 found it awful to do so의 순서로 써야 한다.

· awful 끔찍한

05 정답 ⑤　　　　　UNIT **13** 재귀대명사

[해석] A: 왜 너는 그녀의 전화를 피하고 있니?
B: 그녀는 내게 계속해서 똑같은 이야기를 반복해서 말하고 있어.
A: 그녀는 이야기 할 누군가가 필요함에 틀림없어.
B: 신경 안 써. 나는 단지 혼자 있고 싶단 말이야.

→ ⑤ by oneself는 '혼자'라는 뜻이다. 문장의 주어인 I와 같은 대상을 나타내므로 oneself를 myself로 고쳐야 한다.
① her는 뒤의 phone call에 대한 소유격 대명사이다. ② keep v-ing는 '계속 ~하다'라는 뜻이다. ③ same의 앞에는 정관사 the를 써야 한다. ④ 앞의 someone을 수식하는 to부정사의 형용사적 용법이다.

· avoid 피하다　· mind 상관하다

06 정답 ④　　　　　UNIT **12** 지시대명사 this (these), that (those), it

[해석] A: 너의 구직활동은 어떻게 되어가고 있니?
B: 일 년에 많은 돈을 주는 자리를 찾았어.
A: 정말이야? 어디서 그것을 찾았는데?
B: 인터넷에 올라와 있는 모든 채용공고를 직접 확인했지.

→ ④ 앞에 나온 one을 다시 가리키려면 them을 it으로 고쳐야 한다. ① your는 뒤의 job search에 대한 소유격 대명사이다. ② 셀 수 없는 명사 money 앞에 붙어서 '많은'의 뜻을 나타내는 a good deal of이다. ③ '일 년에'를 의미하는 표현은 a year이다. ⑤ 문장의 끝에 붙어서 강조 용법으로 쓰인 재귀대명사이다.

· job search 구직활동　· job posting 채용공고

07 정답 itself in the river　　　　　UNIT **13** 재귀대명사

[해석] 아름다운 다리가 강에 그것을 반사하고 있다.

→ 강에 다리가 반사되어 비치는 모습이므로 재귀대명사를 이용하여 문장을 완성한다.

· reflect 반사하다

08 정답 another is, the other is　　　　　UNIT **14** 부정대명사

[해석] 나는 세 개의 공책을 가지고 있다. 하나는 녹색이고, 다른 하나는 빨간색, 그리고 또 다른 하나는 노란색이다.

→ 셋 중에서 하나를 one으로 지칭할 때, 다른 하나는 another, 나머지 하나는 the other가 된다.

정답

01 ⑤	**02** ⑤	**03** ④	**04** is attending
05 completed	**06** will announce		
07 knows	**08** were watching		
09 ⑤	**10** have been waiting		
11 has, been learning			

01 정답 ⑤ UNIT 20 완료시제

[해석] 내가 파티에 도착했을 때 지호는 거기에 없었다. 그는 이미 가버렸다.

→ I가 파티에 간 시점이 과거이고 지호는 그 전에 이미 가버린 상황이므로 과거완료시제가 사용되어야 한다.

02 정답 ⑤ UNIT 20 완료시제

[해석] 김 선생님이 내년에 은퇴할 때 그녀는 40년 동안 가르친 것이 될 것이다.

→ 미래의 특정 시점까지 계속되는 일을 나타내는 상황이므로 미래완료진행시제가 사용되어야 한다.

· retire 은퇴하다

03 정답 ④ UNIT 18 미래시제

[해석] ① 당신은 얼마 동안 운전을 해왔습니까?

② 그가 어제 너의 책을 돌려주었니?

③ 나의 아들은 오전 11시부터 자고 있는 중이다.

④ 네가 공항에 도착할 때, 내가 데리러 갈 것이다.

⑤ 내가 학교에 도착했을 때 정문은 이미 닫혀 있었다.

→ ④ 시간을 나타내는 부사절의 미래시제는 현재시제로 나타내므로, 주절의 동사인 picked를 will pick으로 고쳐야 한다.

① 현재완료진행시제인 have been driving ② 과거시제 의문문 ③ 현재완료진행시제인 has been sleeping ⑤ 정문이 닫힌 것이 학교에 도착한 것보다 앞선 과거완료시제

· return 반납하다

04 정답 is attending UNIT 19 진행시제

[해석] Emma는 지금 중요한 사업 회의에 참석 중이다.

→ 현재진행시제와 함께 쓰이는 right now가 있으므로 is attending이 알맞다.

· attend 참석하다

05 정답 completed UNIT 16 현재시제, 과거시제

[해석] David는 지난여름에 한 법률 사무소에서 인턴십을 마쳤다.

→ 과거의 한 시점을 나타내는 last summer가 있으므로 과거시제인 completed가 알맞다.

· law firm 법률 사무소

06 정답 will announce UNIT 18 미래시제

[해석] 그들은 경연 결과를 내일 발표할 것이다.

→ 미래 시점을 나타내는 tomorrow가 있으므로 미래시제인 will announce가 알맞다.

· competition 경연

07 정답 knows UNIT 19 진행시제

[해석] Samantha는 이 유형의 수학 문제를 어떻게 쉽게 풀 수 있는지를 안다.

→ 상태를 나타내는 동사인 know는 진행시제와 함께 쓰일 수 없다. 따라서 현재시제인 knows가 알맞다.

08 정답 were watching UNIT 19 진행시제

[해석] 어젯밤 10시에, 그들은 다큐멘터리를 보고 있었다.

→ 과거의 한 시점에 다큐멘터리를 보고 있었음을 나타내야 하므로 과거진행시제인 were watching이 알맞다.

09 정답 ⑤ UNIT 20 완료시제

[해석] 그녀는 영화가 나오기 전에 그 책을 한 번 읽었었다.

① 내가 도착했을 때, 그녀는 이미 떠났었다.

② 우리가 출발했을 때, 기차는 이미 떠났었다.

③ 나는 자기 전에 몇 시간 동안 공부했었다.

④ 내가 이메일을 확인했을 때, 그는 이미 답장을 보냈었다.

⑤ 그 식당이 이전하기 전에 우리는 여러 번 그곳에 갔었다.

→ 주어진 문장은 과거완료시제의 〈경험〉 용법을 나타내므로 ⑤가 정답이다.

10 정답 have been waiting UNIT 20 완료시제

→ 과거부터 지금까지 계속되는 일을 나타내는 상황에는 현재완료진행형이 사용되어야 하며 '~ 동안'을 의미하는 전치사는 for이다.

11 정답 has, been learning UNIT 20 완료시제

→ 과거부터 지금까지 계속되는 일을 나타내는 상황에는 현재완료진행형이 사용되어야 한다.

실전 모의고사 D~F

정답

01 ③	**02** ought to	**03** may well
04 used to	**05** had better	**06** would
07 to	**08** ②	

01 정답 ③ UNIT 21 조동사의 특징과 조동사 do

[해석] 그는 긍정적으로 유지하기 위해 최선을 다한다.

① 그들이 어젯밤에 너에게 전화했니?

② 너는 비디오 게임 하는 것을 즐기니?

③ 그녀는 주말마다 빨래를 한다.

④ 나는 너를 여기서 만날 줄은 전혀 예상하지 못했어!

⑤ 나는 그녀가 피아노를 연주하는 방식을 정말 좋아해.

→ 주어진 문장과 ③은 '하다'를 의미하는 동사 do이다. 나머지는 모두 조동사로 쓰인 do이다.

· positive 긍정적인 · laundry 빨래

02 정답 ought to UNIT 24 shall, should, ought to, had better (not)

→ '~해야 한다'를 의미하는 조동사는 ought to이다.

· make a decision 결정하다

03 정답 may well　　　　　UNIT **22** can (could), may (might)

→ '~하는 것도 당연하다'를 의미하는 것은 may well이다.

• promote 승진하다

04 정답 used to
　　　　UNIT **25** used to, would, 조동사 + have + 과거분사

→ '~하곤 했다'를 의미하는 것은 used to이다.

• textbook 교과서

05 정답 had better
　　　UNIT **24** shall, should, ought to, had better (not)

→ '~하는 편이 좋겠다'를 의미하는 것은 had better이다.

06 정답 would　　　　UNIT **23** will (would), must (have to)
　　　　UNIT **25** used to, would, 조동사 + have + 과거분사

[해석] • 나는 매주 주말마다 농구를 하곤 했다.
• 우리는 행사 동안 우리를 지지해 준 모든 분들께 감사드리고 싶습니다.

→ '~하곤 했다'를 의미하는 조동사는 would이다. would like to 는 '~하고 싶다'를 의미한다.

• support 지지하다

07 정답 to　　UNIT **25** used to, would, 조동사 + have + 과거분사

[해석] • 그는 매일 아침마다 뛰곤 했지만, 지금은 요가를 선호한다.
• 그녀는 상사를 설득하여 자신의 아이디어를 승인받을 수 있었다.

→ used는 to와 함께 쓰이면 '~하곤 했다'를 의미한다. can을 대신하는 어구는 be able to이다.

• convince 설득하다 • approve 승인하다

08 정답 ②　　UNIT **25** used to, would, 조동사 + have + 과거분사

[해석] A: 저는 비행기를 놓쳤다는 게 믿기지 않아요!
B: 당신은 출발 시간을 잘못 이해했음에 틀림없어요.
A: 저는 시간을 다시 한 번 확인했어야 했어요.
B: 걱정 마세요, 당신을 다음 비행기에 태울 수 있을 거예요. 제가 가능한 다음 비행기를 확인해 볼게요.

→ ② '~했음에 틀림없다'를 의미하는 표현은 must have + 과거분사이다. should[ought to] have + 과거분사는 '~했어야 했다'를 의미한다.

• departure time 출발 시각 • double-check 다시 한 번 확인하다 • available 이용 가능한

G 실전 모의고사

정답

01 ⑤	**02** ④	**03** ④	**04** ④	**05** ③
06 ⑤	**07** be invited		**08** was sent to	
09 believed to be				

01 정답 ⑤　　　　　　　　　　　UNIT **27** 수동태의 시제

[해석] 어떤 사람들은 경찰이 다른 사람들을 조사하고 있을 때 그것을 무시하고 있다. = 어떤 사람들은 다른 사람들이 경찰에 의해 조사받고 있을 때 그것을 무시하고 있다.

→ 다른 사람들이 경찰에 의해 '조사받고 있는' 상황이므로 수동태의 현재진행시제가 적절하다.

• ignore 무시하다

02 정답 ④　　　UNIT **30** 주의해야 할 수동태와 관용표현

→ 동사 say의 목적어가 that절이므로 Patrick is said to be humorous.나 It is said that Patrick is humorous.로 나타낼 수 있다.

• humorous 유머가 있는

03 정답 ④　UNIT **27** 수동태의 시제, UNIT **28** 4형식, 5형식의 수동태

[해석] A: 누가 너에게 이 책을 줬니? 이것이 네 생일 선물이야?
B: 응. 이 책은 내 사촌 중 하나가 나에게 사준 거야.

→ ④동사 buy는 수동태가 될 때 for 간접목적어를 수반하는 동사이다. ① 과거형인 gave ② 앞에서 말한 this book을 받는 지시대명사 this ③ 과거시제 수동태 ⑤「one of+복수 명사」: ~ 중 하나

04 정답 ④　　　　　　UNIT **29** 4형식, 5형식의 수동태

[해석] 그 이웃이 자정 이후에 노래를 부르는 것이 들렸다.

→ 지각동사의 목적격 보어는 원형부정사나 분사가 가능한데 수동태로 전환될 시 원형부정사는 to부정사로 바꿔 쓰고, 분사는 그대로 쓴다.

05 정답 ③　　　　　　UNIT **28** 조동사와 동사구의 수동태

[해석] George는 파리에서 만난 여자와 결혼할 것이다.

→ '~와 결혼하다'는 be married to라고 쓴다.

06 정답 ⑤　　　　UNIT **30** 주의해야 할 수동태와 관용표현

[해석] ① 이 탁자는 나무로 만들어졌다.
② 그들은 충격적인 소식에 놀랐다.
③ 그 가게는 많은 사람들로 가득했다.
④ 이 도시는 많은 외국인들에게 잘 알려져 있다.
⑤ 그 집의 지붕은 눈으로 덮여 있었다.

→ ⑤ '~으로 덮여 있다'는 be covered with라고 쓴다.

① be made of: ~로 만들어지다 ② be surprised at: ~에 놀라다 ③ be crowded with: ~로 가득하다 ④ be well-known to: ~에게 잘 알려지다

• foreigner 외국인 • roof 지붕

07 정답 be invited　　　　UNIT **26** 수동태의 개념 및 형태

[해석] 그들은 올해에도 역시 많은 학생들을 초대할까?

→ 많은 학생들이 올해에도 역시 그들에 의해 초대될까?

→ 원래 문장에서 목적어였던 many students가 주어가 된 수동태 문장이므로「be동사 + 과거분사」가 들어가야 한다.

08 정답 was sent to　　　　　**UNIT 29** 4형식, 5형식의 수동태

[해석] Jim은 그의 부모님께 엽서를 보냈다.
→ 엽서가 Jim에 의해 그의 부모님께 보내졌다.
→ 4형식 동사 send가 수동태로 전환될 때 be sent to의 구조를
취한다.
· postcard 엽서

09 정답 believed to be　　　**UNIT 30** 주의해야 할 수동태와 관용표현

[해석] 많은 사람들은 7이 행운의 숫자라고 믿는다.
→ 7은 많은 사람들에 의해 행운의 숫자라고 믿어진다.
→ 동사 believe의 목적어가 that절인 경우 that절의 주어를 수동
태의 주어로 할 수 있다.

H 실전 모의고사　　　▶ 문제편 p.337

정답

01 ③	**02** ②	**03** plenty of	**04** little
05 Few	**06** a few	**07** the → a	
08 Talented someone → Someone talented			
09 ⑤			

01 정답 ③　　　　　**UNIT 33** 수사 형용사의 표현

→ a quarter to nine은 8시 45분이다. 9시 45분은 a quarter
to ten, nine forty-five 등으로 표현한다.

02 정답 ②　　　　　**UNIT 33** 수사 형용사의 표현

→ 6월 10일은 June (the) tenth 또는 the tenth of June으로
읽는다.

03 정답 plenty of　　　　　**UNIT 32** 부정 수량 형용사

→ '많은'을 의미하는 것은 plenty of이다.
· match (색깔 등이 서로) 맞다

04 정답 little　　　　　**UNIT 32** 부정 수량 형용사

→ 셀 수 없는 명사 interest 앞에서 '거의 없다'를 의미해야 하므로
little이 와야 한다.
· pursue 추구하다

05 정답 Few　　　　　**UNIT 32** 부정 수량 형용사

→ 셀 수 있는 명사 people 앞에서 '거의 없다'를 의미해야 하므로
few가 와야 한다.
· complexity 복잡성

06 정답 a few　　　　　**UNIT 32** 부정 수량 형용사

→ 셀 수 있는 명사 things 앞에서 '조금의'를 의미해야 하므로 a
few가 와야 한다.
· nap 낮잠을 자다

07 정답 the → a　　　　　**UNIT 32** 부정 수량 형용사

[해석] 그는 많은 이메일에 답장하는 것에 지쳐 있었다.
→ 셀 수 있는 명사 emails 앞에서 '많은'을 나타내려면 a number
of로 써야 한다.

08 정답 Talented someone → Someone talented
　　　　　UNIT 31 형용사의 종류, 쓰임, 어순

[해석] 재능 있는 누군가가 이 프로젝트를 주도해야 한다.
→ -thing/-body/-one으로 끝나는 대명사는 형용사가 그 뒤에 위
치하므로 Talented someone을 Someone talented로 고쳐야
한다.

09 정답 ⑤　　　　　**UNIT 31** 형용사의 종류, 쓰임, 어순

[해석] ① 그는 내 생일에 나에게 후한 선물을 주었다.
② 그녀의 목소리는 편안한 멜로디처럼 들렸다.
③ 그 고대 나무는 숲의 한 구석에 서 있었다.
④ 이 문서는 과거에 대한 귀중한 통찰을 제공했다.
⑤ 그 기사는 유익해서 독자들에게 명확한 설명을 제공했다.
→ 나머지는 모두 명사를 수식하는 한정적 쓰임으로 쓰였지만, ⑤은
주격 보어 자리에서 서술적 쓰임으로 쓰였다.
· soothe 달래다 · insight 통찰(력) · informative 유익한
· explanation 설명

I 실전 모의고사　　　▶ 문제편 p.338

정답

01 ④	**02** ④	**03** ④	**04** hard → hardly
05 forms usually → usually forms			**06** ⑤
07 (1) ⓓ (2) off it → it off			

01 정답 ④　　　　　**UNIT 34** 부사의 형태

[해석] ① 안전한 – 안전하게 ② 쉬운 – 쉽게 ③ 유연한 – 유연
하게 ④ 구체적인 – 구체적으로 ⑤ 편안한 – 편안하게
→ ④ -ic로 끝나는 형용사는 -ally를 붙여 부사를 만든다. 따라서
specifically가 알맞다.

02 정답 ④　　　　　**UNIT 34** 부사의 형태

[해석] ① 참된 – 참으로 ② 빠른 – 빠르게 ③ 기본적인 – 기본
적으로 ④ 끔찍한 – 형편없게 ⑤ 있을 것 같은 – 아마도
→ ④ -le로 끝나는 형용사는 le를 ly로 고쳐 부사를 만든다. 따라서
horribly가 알맞다.

03 정답 ④　　　　　**UNIT 35** 부사의 역할 및 위치

[해석] 여: 나는 이 과제를 끝내기 위해 훨씬 더 열심히 공부해야 해.
남: 응, 아마 작은 부분으로 나누는 게 좋을 거야.
→ (A) 비교급을 수식하는 부사는 much이다. (B) 「타동사+부사」의
목적어가 대명사일 경우, 목적어는 타동사와 부사 사이에 온다. 따라
서 목적어 it을 down의 앞에 써야 한다. 목적어가 this
assignment이므로 대명사 it이 와야 한다.
· section 부분

04 정답 hard → hardly　　　　　**UNIT 34** 부사의 형태

[해석] 나는 어젯밤 소음 때문에 거의 잠을 못 잤다.
→ hard는 '열심히, 어려운, 딱딱한'을, hardly는 '거의 ~않는'을 의
미한다. 문맥상 거의 잠을 못 잔 것이므로 hard를 hardly로 고쳐야
한다.

05 정답 forms usually → usually forms

UNIT **35** 부사의 역할 및 위치

[해석] 안개는 보통 기온이 더 낮을 때 이른 아침에 형성된다.
→ 빈도부사는 조동사 뒤, 일반동사 앞에 위치한다. 따라서 usually 는 일반동사 forms 앞에 와야 한다.
・temperature 기온, 온도

06 정답 ⑤

UNIT **34** 부사의 형태

[해석] ① 나는 하이킹 중에 충분한 물을 마시지 않았다.
② 그는 티켓을 살 만큼 충분한 돈을 가져오지 않았다.
③ 차고에는 두 대의 차가 들어갈 충분한 공간이 있다.
④ 나는 충분한 자외선 차단제를 바르지 않아서 햇볕에 탔다.
⑤ 그들은 프로젝트를 제시간에 끝낼 만큼 충분히 열심히 일하지 않았다.
→ 나머지는 모두 형용사로 쓰였고, ⑤은 부사로 쓰였다.
・garage 차고 ・sunscreen 자외선 차단제

07 정답 (1) ⓓ (2) off it → it off

UNIT **35** 부사의 역할 및 위치

[해석] ⓐ 그 사건은 바로 한 시간 전에 일어났다.
ⓑ 나는 요리한 후 조심스럽게 가스레인지를 껐다.
ⓒ 아이들이 이미 자러 갔으므로 지금은 조용하다.
ⓓ 나는 그 보고서를 미루는 대신 끝내기로 결심했다.
ⓔ 지진은 때때로 어떤 경고 없이 발생한다.
→ 「타동사+부사」의 목적어가 대명사일 경우, 목적어는 타동사와 부사 사이에 온다. 따라서 목적어 it을 off의 앞에 써서 putting it off 가 되어야 한다.
・put off ~을 미루다 ・earthquake 지진

J 실전 모의고사

▶ 문제편 p.339

정답

01 ③	**02** ③	**03** the noisiest
04 ○	**05** the most hardworking	
06 farthest	**07** further	
08 (1) ⓑ (2) student → students		
09 (1) ⓓ (2) as twice → twice as		
10 (1) ⓔ (2) than → to		

01 정답 ③

UNIT **38** 비교급, 최상급 형태

[해석] ① 잘, 더 잘, 가장 잘
② 빠른, 더 빠른, 가장 빠른
③ 나쁜, 더 나쁜, 가장 나쁜
④ 영리한, 더 영리한, 가장 영리한
⑤ 지루한, 더 지루한, 가장 지루한
→ bad는 불규칙을 따르는 형용사로, 비교급은 worse, 최상급은 worst이다.

02 정답 ③

UNIT **37** 원급

[해석] 그는 결정을 내릴 때만 되면 아주 고집이 셌다.
→ '아주 고집이 센'은 as stubborn as a donkey[mule]로 표현한다.
・stubborn 고집이 센

03 정답 the noisiest

UNIT **38** 비교급, 최상급 형태

[해석] 그건 내가 인생에서 가본 가장 시끄러운 파티였다.
→ 원급이 「자음+y」로 끝나는 경우 y를 i로 고치고 -est를 붙여 최상급을 만들므로 the noisiest로 고쳐야 적절하다.

04 정답 ○

UNIT **38** 비교급, 최상급 형태

[해석] 내 강아지는 우리가 새로운 음식으로 바꾼 이후로 더 뚱뚱해졌다.
→ 원급이 「단모음+단자음」으로 끝나는 경우 끝 자음을 한 번 더 쓰고 -er를 붙여 비교급을 만든다. much는 비교급을 수식할 수 있다.
・switch 바꾸다

05 정답 the most hardworking

UNIT **38** 비교급, 최상급 형태

[해석] 그는 의심의 여지가 없이 우리 팀에서 가장 성실한 구성원이다.
→ 2음절 이상의 단어는 앞에 most를 붙여 최상급을 만들므로, the most hardworking으로 고쳐야 적절하다.
・hardworking 근면한, 열심히 하는

06 정답 farthest

UNIT **38** 비교급, 최상급 형태

→ far가 '(거리가) 먼' 것을 뜻할 때 최상급은 farthest이다.

07 정답 further

UNIT **38** 비교급, 최상급 형태

→ far가 '(정도가) 더'를 뜻할 때 비교급은 further이다.

08 정답 (1) ⓑ (2) student → students

UNIT **40** 최상급

[해석] ⓐ 그는 연주회에서 피아노를 가장 잘 쳤다.
ⓑ 그녀는 반에서 가장 뛰어난 학생 중 한 명이다.
ⓒ 정기적으로 회의에 참석하기만 하면 동아리에 가입할 수 있다.
ⓓ 그는 장비를 다룰 때 동료들보다 두 배만큼 조심한다.
ⓔ 이 모델은 성능 면에서 최신 버전보다 열등하다.
→ 최상급 뒤에 비교 대상이 나올 때는 복수 명사가 와야 하므로 student를 students로 고쳐야 한다.
・recital 발표회, 연주회 ・regularly 정기적으로
・equipment 기구, 장비 ・inferior 열등한

09 정답 (1) ⓓ (2) as twice → twice as

UNIT **37** 원급

→ 배수사를 이용한 원급은 「배수사+as+형용사[부사]의 원급+as」로 표현하므로 as twice를 twice as로 고쳐야 한다.

10 정답 (1) ⓔ (2) than → to

UNIT **39** 비교급

→ inferior처럼 라틴어에서 온 단어들의 비교급은 to로 비교 대상을 나타낸다. 따라서 than을 to로 고쳐야 한다.

정답

01 ①　**02** ④　**03** ④　**04** ①　**05** ⑤
06 Focus, and you can grasp the meaning.
07 so he could make the right decision
08 for she had never broken her principles

---

01 [정답] ①　　　　　UNIT **43** 명사절을 이끄는 종속접속사
[해석] 그녀가 시험에 합격할 것이 확실하다.
→ It은 가주어이고, 진주어절을 이끄는 접속사가 와야 하므로 that이 알맞다.

02 [정답] ④　　　　　UNIT **44** 부사절을 이끄는 종속접속사
[해석] 그는 더 좋은 직업을 갖기 위해서 그 과정을 수강했다.
→ so that은 '~하도록, ~하기 위해서'라는 뜻의 목적의 부사절을 이끈다.

03 [정답] ④　　　　　　　　UNIT **42** 상관접속사
[해석] • 그는 자동차 사고 전에 자전거와 트럭 둘 다 보았다.
• 운동은 육체와 정신 둘 다에 좋다.
→ 문맥상 'A와 B 둘 다'라는 뜻이 되도록 both A and B가 들어가야 한다.

04 [정답] ①　　　　　UNIT **44** 부사절을 이끄는 종속접속사
[해석] • 나는 여기에 온 이래로 많은 사람들을 만났다.
• 내일은 휴일이기 때문에 우리는 학교에 가지 않아도 된다.
→ since는 '~ 이래로'라는 뜻의 시간을 나타내기도 하고, '~ 때문에'라는 뜻의 이유를 나타내기도 한다.

05 [정답] ⑤　　　　　UNIT **44** 부사절을 이끄는 종속접속사
[해석] ① 나는 건강을 유지할 수 있도록 매일 수영을 한다.
② 시간이 지날수록 그 고양이는 점점 커지고 있다.
③ 그녀는 키가 작지만, 무거운 상자를 운반할 수 있다.
④ 내가 그 프로젝트를 끝낼 때까지 너는 그것을 해야 해.
⑤ 그가 아프다면 내가 거기에 갈게.
→ ⑤ 조건의 부사절인 if 절에서는 현재시제로 써야 하므로 will be가 아니라 is가 알맞다.
① so that ~: 그래서 ~하도록 ② '~함에 따라'라는 뜻의 종속접속사 as ③ '~하더라도'라는 뜻의 종속접속사 even though ④ '~할 때까지'라는 뜻의 종속접속사 until
• stay healthy 건강을 유지하다

06 [정답] Focus, and you can grasp the meaning.
UNIT **41** 등위접속사
→ Focus 뒤에 and를 붙여 '~해라, 그러면'을 의미하는 명령문을 완성한다.
• grasp 파악하다

07 [정답] so he could make the right decision
UNIT **41** 등위접속사
→ 뒤의 절이 결과를 나타내므로 등위접속사 so를 써서 so he could make ~의 순서로 써야 한다.
• analyze 분석하다

08 [정답] for she had never broken her principles
UNIT **41** 등위접속사
→ 뒤의 절이 원인이나 이유를 나타내므로 등위접속사 for를 써서 for she had never broken ~의 순서로 써야 한다.
• principle 원칙 • earn 얻다 • reputation 평판

정답

01 ②　　　**02** ①　　　**03** in → of
04 related → related to　　**05** to → for　**06** ③
07 were quietly wandering around the garden
08 Margie was jealous of her friend's success
09 ②

---

01 [정답] ②　　　UNIT **47** 장소를 나타내는 전치사
　　　　　　　　　UNIT **48** 방향 및 기타 전치사
[해석] (A) 우리는 도시로 가기 위해 다리를 가로질러 차를 몰았다.
(B) 열쇠들은 소파 밑에 있다.
→ (A) '가로질러'는 across로 나타낸다.
(B) '~ 밑에'는 under로 나타낸다.

02 [정답] ①　　　UNIT **46** 시간을 나타내는 전치사
　　　　　　　　　UNIT **47** 장소를 나타내는 전치사
[해석] (A) 그 고양이는 내 차의 덮개 위에서 낮잠을 자고 있었다.
(B) 그는 어젯밤 콘서트 동안 내 옆에 앉았다.
→ (A) '~ 위에'는 on으로 나타낸다.
(B) 특정 기간 '동안'은 during으로 나타낸다.
• take a nap 낮잠을 자다

03 [정답] in → of　　UNIT **50** 형용사+전치사, 주의해야 할 전치사
[해석] Lily는 어린 시절 그녀의 트라우마로 인해 여전히 곤충을 무서워한다.
→ '~을 두려워하다'는 be afraid of로 쓴다. 따라서 in을 of로 고쳐야 한다.
• childhood 어린 시절

04 [정답] related → related to
UNIT **50** 형용사+전치사, 주의해야 할 전치사
[해석] 이것은 회사의 정책과 크게 연관되어 있다.
→ '~와 관련 있다'는 be related to로 쓴다. 따라서 related 뒤에 to가 와야 한다.
• policy 정책

05 [정답] to → for　　UNIT **50** 형용사+전치사, 주의해야 할 전치사
[해석] 그 길은 2024년 이래로 사고와 싱크홀로 악명이 높았다.
→ '~로 악명 높다'는 be notorious for로 쓴다. 따라서 to를 for로 고쳐야 한다.
• notorious 악명 높은 • crash 사고

06 [정답] ③   **UNIT 46** 시간을 나타내는 전치사
                     UNIT 47 장소를 나타내는 전치사

[해석] ① 선반 위에 있는 그 책은 Rachel의 것이다.
② 그는 아침에 공항에 도착했다.
③ 그들은 John과 Risa 사이에서 상품을 나누었다.
④ 우리는 회의 동안에 그 문제를 철저히 논의했다.
⑤ 그녀는 주저함 없이 다리를 건넜다.
→ ③ among은 셋 이상 사이를 나타내므로 둘 사이를 나타내는 between으로 고쳐야 한다.
① belong to: ~에 속하다 ② in: 비교적 긴 시간 앞 ④ during: ~ 동안 ⑤ without: ~ 없이
• thoroughly 철저히 • hesitation 망설임, 주저함

07 [정답] were quietly wandering around the garden
                     UNIT 48 방향 및 기타 전치사

[해석] 우리 아이들은 정원 주변에서 조용히 돌아다니고 있었다.
→ 정원 '주변'을 나타내야 하므로 around the garden의 순서로 쓴다.
• wander 돌아다니다

08 [정답] Margie was jealous of her friend's success
          UNIT 50 형용사+전치사, 주의해야 할 전치사

[해석] Margie가 그녀의 친구의 성공을 질투했음이 확실했다.
→ '~을 질투하다'는 be jealous of로 쓴다. 따라서 Margie was jealous of ~의 순서로 쓴다.

09 [정답] ②   **UNIT 50** 형용사+전치사, 주의해야 할 전치사

[해석] ① 그녀는 여기에서 5년 동안 살았다.
② 이 휴대폰이 네 것이니?
③ 우리는 내일 파리로 떠난다.
④ 이 책은 어린이들에게 적합하지 않다.
⑤ 나는 그녀가 휴가 중일 때 그녀를 위해 일하고 있다.
→ ② '~에 속하다'는 belong 뒤에 전치사가 to가 온다.
① 5년 '동안', ③ 파리를 '향해', ④ 어린이들을 '위해', ⑤ 그녀를 '위해'를 나타내므로 나머지는 모두 for가 와야 한다.
• suitable 적절한

M 실전 모의고사
▶ 문제편 p.342

정답

01 ⑤   **02** ①   **03** of   **04** not to jump
05 for
06 It is not easy to keep in touch with a friend in another country.
07 it difficult to ask others for help
08 to know how to sign up for the swimming course
09 ⑤

---

01 [정답] ⑤   **UNIT 52** to부정사의 형용사적 용법

[해석] ① 그녀는 유럽을 여행하기를 희망한다.
② 그의 직업은 새장을 관리하는 것이다.
③ 금메달을 따는 것은 쉽지 않다.
④ 나는 화학 공학을 전공하기로 결심했다.
⑤ 이번이 골프를 배우기 시작할 좋은 기회이다.
→ ⑤은 명사(chance)를 수식하는 형용사적 용법이고 나머지는 모두 명사적 용법이다.
• take care of ~을 관리하다[돌보다] • major in ~을 전공하다
• chemical engineering 화학 공학

02 [정답] ①   **UNIT 53** to부정사의 부사적 용법

[해석] ① 너를 만나서 매우 반가워.
② 그의 계획은 2년 동안 외국에서 공부하는 것이다.
③ 외국어를 배우는 것은 나의 즐거움이다.
④ Mark는 나에게 휴가 동안 파리를 방문할 것을 추천했다.
⑤ 나는 아이들을 위한 좋은 TV 프로그램을 선택하는 것이 중요하다고 생각한다.
→ ①은 감정의 원인을 나타내는 부사적 용법이고, 나머지는 모두 명사적 용법이다.
• abroad 해외로 • recommend 추천하다

03 [정답] of   **UNIT 54** 원형부정사, to부정사의 의미상 주어

[해석] 네가 우리와 함께 이 이야기를 공유하다니 매우 용감했어.
→ brave는 사람의 성질을 나타내는 형용사이므로 의미상 주어는 「of + 목적격」으로 쓴다.

04 [정답] not to jump
         UNIT 55 to부정사의 시제, 부정, 수동태, 대부정사

[해석] 나의 코치는 나에게 너무 높이 뛰어오르지 말라고 충고했다.
→ to부정사의 부정은 「not + to부정사」로 쓴다.

05 [정답] for   **UNIT 54** 원형부정사, to부정사의 의미상 주어

[해석] 운전자들은 미끄러운 도로에서 천천히 운전하는 것이 중요하다.
→ 성질이나 성격을 나타내는 형용사 뒤에 오는 경우를 제외하고 대부분의 to부정사는 「for + 목적격」을 의미상 주어로 취한다.
• slippery 미끄러운

06 [정답] It is not easy to keep in touch with a friend in another country.
         UNIT 51 to부정사의 명사적 용법

→ 주어 자리에 가주어 it을 쓰고, 진주어인 keep 이하는 to부정사로서 뒤로 보낸다.
• keep in touch 연락을 유지하다

07 [정답] it difficult to ask others for help
         UNIT 51 to부정사의 명사적 용법

→ 5형식의 목적어가 to부정사인 경우 가목적어 it으로 채우고 진목적어는 문장의 뒤로 이동시킨다.

08 [정답] to know how to sign up for the swimming course
         UNIT 51 to부정사의 명사적 용법

→ 「how + to부정사」는 '어떻게 ~ 할지'로 해석한다.

09 정답 ⑤　　　　　　　　UNIT **54** 원형부정사, to부정사의 의미상 주어

[해석] ① 말하자면, 힘든 한 해였다.

② 나는 너무 피곤해서 일을 계속할 수 없다.

③ 그는 내년에 유학할 계획이다.

④ 그는 우리의 약속을 잊었던 것 같다.

⑤ 그는 항상 그의 농담으로 나를 웃게 만든다.

→ ⑤ 사역동사 make는 목적격 보어로 원형부정사가 오므로 to laugh를 laugh로 고쳐야 한다.

N 실전 모의고사

▶ 문제편 p.343

정답

01 not being　　**02** coming　　**03** ④

04 ④　　**05** ④　　**06** was on the point of saying

07 didn't feel like going outside　　**08** ②

01 정답 not being　　　　　　　　UNIT **57** 동명사

[해석] 그는 나를 도와줄 수 없음을 미안해한다.

→ 동명사의 부정은 앞에 not을 쓴다.

02 정답 coming　　UNIT **59** 전치사의 목적어로 쓰인 동명사, 관용표현

[해석] A: 나는 Jason이 크리스마스에 집에 올 거라고 들었어.

B: 그래. 우리 모두 그가 오기를 고대하고 있어.

→ '~하기를 고대하다'라는 뜻은 look forward to -ing로 쓴다.

03 정답 ④　　UNIT **59** 전치사의 목적어로 쓰인 동명사, 관용표현

[해석] 그들은 자신들의 새로운 앨범을 홍보하려는 목적으로 TV 토크쇼에 나오기를 학수고대하고 있다.

→ (A) '~하는 것을 고대하다'는 look forward to -ing로 쓴다.

(B) '~하려는 목적으로'는 for the purpose of -ing로 쓴다.

04 정답 ④　　UNIT **59** 전치사의 목적어로 쓰인 동명사, 관용표현

[해석] ① 나는 매일 태국 음식을 먹고 싶다.

② 변명하려고 애써 봤자 소용없다.

③ 방에 들어오자마자 그는 모자를 벗었다.

④ 그녀는 하루 종일 아픈 남동생과 함께 있지 않을 수 없었다.

⑤ 그는 매일 아침 30번의 팔 굽혀 펴기를 하는 것을 규칙으로 삼는다.

→ ④ '~하지 않을 수 없다'는 cannot help -ing로 쓴다. (stay → staying)

① like는 to부정사와 동명사 모두를 목적어로 취함 ② It is no use -ing: ~해봐야 소용없다 ③ on -ing: ~하자마자 ⑤ make a point of -ing: ~하는 것을 규칙으로 삼다

・excuse oneself 변명하다

05 정답 ④　　　　　　　　　　UNIT **57** 동명사

[해석] ① Jason은 거짓말하는 것과는 거리가 멀다.

② 그녀의 제안은 고려할 가치가 있다.

③ 나는 공원에서 차 한 잔 마시고 싶은 기분이었다.

④ 그는 아무런 메시지도 남기지 않고 사라졌다.

⑤ 그 시스템은 다른 사람들이 우리의 문서에 접근하는 것을 방지한다.

→ ④ 전치사 without의 목적어 자리이므로 동명사가 와야 한다. (to leave → leaving)

① far from -ing: ~하는 것과 거리가 멀다 ② be worth -ing: ~할 가치가 있다 ③ feel like -ing: ~하고 싶다 ⑤ prevent A from -ing: A가 ~하는 것을 막다

・suggestion 제안　・disappear 사라지다

・approach 접근하다　・document 문서

06 정답 was on the point of saying

UNIT **59** 전치사의 목적어로 쓰인 동명사, 관용표현

→ '~하려던 참이다'는 be on the point of -ing로 쓴다.

07 정답 didn't feel like going outside

UNIT **59** 전치사의 목적어로 쓰인 동명사, 관용표현

→ '~하고 싶다'는 feel like -ing로 쓴다.

08 정답 ②　　UNIT **59** 전치사의 목적어로 쓰인 동명사, 관용표현

[해석] ・그는 거절당하는 것에 익숙하지 않은 것 같았다. 그는 상심했다.

・Kate는 사기를 당하지 않을 만큼 현명하다.

→ '~하는 데 익숙하다'는 be used to -ing라고 하고, 'A가 ~하는 것을 막다'는 keep A from -ing라고 한다. 거절당하는 것에 익숙하지 않고, 속임을 당하는 것을 막을 수 있을 정도로 현명한 것이므로 to와 from 뒤에는 동명사의 수동태, 「being+과거분사」가 와야 한다.

・refuse 거절하다　・cheat 속이다, 사기치다

O 실전 모의고사

▶ 문제편 p.344

정답

01 ②　　**02** ⑤　　**03** Walking along the road

04 they had another appointment

05 With the rain falling　　**06** Having studied

07 Opening　　**08** Not wanting　　**09** ④

01 정답 ②　　UNIT **61** 현재분사와 동명사, 감정을 나타내는 분사

[해석] ① 끓는 물이 냄비 밖으로 넘쳤다.

② 그들은 제주도에 가는 것에 대해 이야기했다.

③ 빛나는 태양이 그날을 따뜻하게 느껴지게 했다.

④ 무대에서 연습하고 있는 가수가 누구야?

⑤ 타고 있는 촛불이 방 안을 향기로 가득 채웠다.

→ ②의 going은 전치사 about의 목적어로 쓰인 동명사이다. 나머지는 모두 현재분사이다.

・spill over 넘치다　・scent 향기

02 정답 ⑤　　　　　　　　UNIT **60** 분사의 종류와 역할

[해석] ① 우는 아이가 엄마를 찾았다.

② 그들은 나무에서 떨어지는 나뭇잎을 보았다.

③ 스페인어로 쓰인 책이 책상 위에 있다.

④ 우리는 복도에서 누군가가 노래하는 것을 들었다.

⑤ Christopher Nolan이 감독한 영화는 정말 훌륭했다.

→ ⑤ 'Christopher Nolan이 감독한 영화'이므로 영화는 수동을 의미하는 과거분사 directed의 수식을 받아야 한다.
· direct 감독하다

03 [정답] Walking along the road　　　UNIT **62** 분사구문
[해석] 길을 따라 걷다가, 우리는 한 카페를 발견했다.
→ 주절과 동일한 부사절의 주어 we를 없애고, 주절과 시제가 같으므로 Walking이 분사구문을 이끄는 것이 알맞다.

04 [정답] they had another appointment
　　　　　　　　　　　　　　　　UNIT **62** 분사구문
[해석] 그들은 다른 약속이 있었기 때문에 일찍 떠났다.
→ Having이 분사구문을 이끌고 있으므로 주절과 주어, 시제가 같다. 따라서 부사절의 주어, 동사로 they had가 오는 것이 알맞다.
· appointment 약속

05 [정답] With the rain falling　　UNIT **63** 주의해야 할 분사구문
→ 비가 '내리는' 능동의 관계이므로 현재분사 falling을 쓴 With the rain falling이 알맞다.

06 [정답] Having studied　　　UNIT **63** 주의해야 할 분사구문
[해석] 밤새 공부한 후에, 그는 결국 그 어려운 시험을 통과했다.
→ 부사절의 시제가 주절보다 앞설 때, 「having + 과거분사」 형태의 완료형 분사구문을 쓴다.

07 [정답] Opening　　　　　　　UNIT **62** 분사구문
[해석] 그 상자를 조심스럽게 열자, 그는 안에서 오래된 사진 한 장을 발견했다.
→ 주절의 주어 '그'가 상자를 연 것이므로 능동의 의미의 현재분사 Opening이 분사구문을 이끄는 것이 알맞다.

08 [정답] Not wanting　　　UNIT **63** 주의해야 할 분사구문
[해석] 누구에게도 방해가 되지 않기 위해, 그녀는 나무 바닥을 살금살금 걸었다.
→ 분사구문의 부정형은 분사 앞에 not이나 never를 쓴다.
· disturb 방해하다 · tiptoe 살금살금 걷다

09 [정답] ④　　　UNIT **61** 현재분사와 동명사, 감정을 나타내는 분사
[해석] · 나는 긴 다큐멘터리 영화를 보는 동안 지루했다.
· 고양이를 쫓고 있는 개가 마당을 가로질러 달렸다.
→ 내가 '지루함을 느끼는' 것이므로 과거분사 bored가, 개가 '쫓는' 것이므로 현재분사 chasing이 오는 것이 알맞다.

P 실전 모의고사　　　▶ 문제편 p.345

정답

01 ①　　　**02** ⑤　　　**03** ⓑ, which 또는 that
04 ⓔ, 삭제 또는 that, in which
05 ③　　　**06** Whoever
07 This is the organization where he is currently working.
08 That was the opportunity for which I have longed. 또는 That was the opportunity which I have longed for.

01 [정답] ①　　　UNIT **66** 관계대명사의 계속적 용법과 생략
[해석] ① 당신이 앉아 있는 의자는 매우 낡았다.
② 내 여동생이 입양한 고양이는 매우 장난기가 많다.
③ 내가 기대했던 영화는 실망스러웠다.
④ 그녀가 고군분투하던 문제는 마침내 해결되었다.
⑤ 그가 경매에서 산 그림은 엄청난 가치를 지니고 있다.
→ ①「전치사+관계대명사」 구조에서 관계대명사만 생략할 수는 없고, 전치사가 관계사절의 동사 뒤에 위치해야 관계대명사를 생략할 수 있다.
· adopt 입양하다 · playful 장난기 많은 · auction 경매
· fortune 재산, 부

02 [정답] ⑤　　　　　　　　　　UNIT **64** 관계대명사
[해석] ① 이것은 내가 직접 지은 집이다.
② 이분은 아들이 선생님인 여성이다.
③ 나는 기타를 치고 있는 남자를 안다.
④ Paul은 우리가 선택한 반장이다.
⑤ 레스토랑에서 일하는 소년들은 주인의 아들들이다.
→ ⑤ 선행사가 사람인 The boys이고 주격 관계대명사가 와야 하므로 who를 써야 한다.

03 [정답] ⓑ, which 또는 that
　　　　　　　　UNIT **64** 관계대명사, UNIT **67** 관계부사
[해석] 옆집에 사는 그 여성은 유명한 예술가이다. 그녀는 색색의 그림들로 가득 찬 스튜디오를 가지고 있다. 그녀는 전통적인 기법과 현대적인 기법을 결합한 독특한 스타일을 가지고 있다. 나는 다음 달에 열릴 그녀의 전시회를 빨리 보고 싶다. 그 전시회는 그녀의 작품이 많은 사람들에게 영감을 준 방법을 선보일 것이다.
→ 선행사가 a studio이고 ⓑ where 뒤에 주어가 없는 관계사절이 이어지므로 주격 관계대명사 which 또는 that으로 고쳐야 한다.
· combine 결합하다 · traditional 전통적인 · exhibition 전시회 · feature 특징으로 하다 · inspire 영감을 주다

04 [정답] ⓔ, 삭제 또는 that, in which　　　UNIT **67** 관계부사
→ ⓔ how 앞에 이미 선행사 the way가 있으므로 how를 삭제하거나 that, in which로 바꿔야 한다.

05 [정답] ③　　　　　UNIT **65** 관계대명사 that, what
[해석] ① 네가 말한 것은 나를 생각하게 했다.
② 나는 지금 듣고 있는 걸 믿을 수가 없다.
③ 그가 한 모든 것은 가족을 위한 것이었다.
④ 그녀는 시장에서 산 것을 나에게 보여 주었다.
⑤ 그들이 결정한 것은 방 안의 모두를 놀라게 했다.
→ 나머지는 모두 선행사를 포함하며 명사절을 이끄는 관계대명사 what이 와야 하고, ③은 선행사 All을 수식하는 목적격 관계대명사 that이 와야 한다.

06 [정답] Whoever　　UNIT **69** 복합관계대명사, 복합관계부사
[해석] 경기에서 누가 이기든 우리는 여전히 친구야.
→ 양보의 부사절 no matter who ~는 복합관계대명사 whoever로 바꿔쓸 수 있다.

07 [정답] This is the organization where he is currently working.　　　UNIT **67** 관계부사

→ 장소의 선행사 the organization을 꾸미는 관계부사 where를 써서 the organization where he ~의 순서로 써야 한다.
• organization 조직 • currently 현재

08 정답 That was the opportunity for which I had longed. **또는** That was the opportunity which I had longed for.
UNIT 66 관계대명사의 계속적 용법과 생략
→ 관계사절의 동사구 long for를 그대로 쓰거나, 전치사 for를 선행사 the opportunity와 which의 사이에 쓸 수 있다.
• opportunity 기회 • long for 갈망하다

Q 실전 모의고사 ▶ 문제편 p.346

정답

01 ⑤　　**02** ④　　**03** ③　　**04** ④
05 I had answered　　**06** it not for your help
07 내가 가격을 알았었다면, 나는 그 티켓을 사지 않았을 텐데.

01 정답 ⑤ **UNIT 72 가정법의 다양한 형태**
[해석] 그들이 말을 들었더라면, 곤경에 처하지 않을 텐데.
→ if절은 if가 생략된 가정법 과거완료, 주절은 가정법 과거이므로 혼합 가정법 문장이다. 이를 직설법 문장으로 바꾸려면 부사절은 과거시제(didn't), 주절은 현재시제(are)로 써야 한다.

02 정답 ④ **UNIT 70 가정법 과거**
[해석] ① 내가 그들의 제안을 받아들였으면 좋을 텐데.
② 그녀는 마치 모든 걸 다 아는 것처럼 행동한다.
③ 그가 그 표지판을 봤더라면 속도를 줄였을 텐데.
④ 내가 매니저라면 그 시스템을 개선할 텐데.
⑤ 네가 도와주지 않았다면 나는 계속하지 못했을 것이다.
→ ④ 가정법 문장에서 if절의 be동사는 were로 써야 한다.
① I wish 가정법 과거완료 ② as if 가정법 과거 ③ if가 생략된 가정법 과거완료 ⑤「without + 명사(구)」가정법 과거완료
=「if it had not been for」

03 정답 ③ **UNIT 70 가정법 과거**
[해석] Fiona는 그녀의 지갑이 진품인 척한다.
= 사실, Fiona의 지갑은 진품이 아니다.
→ (A) 직설법 문장의 동사가 현재시제이므로 as if절의 동사는 과거시제가 알맞다.
(B) as if 문장을 직설법으로 바꿀 때, 앞에 접속부사 In fact를 쓴다.
• pretend ~인 척하다 • genuine 진짜의

04 정답 ④ **UNIT 70 가정법 과거**
[해석] 우리 선생님이 우리의 스트레스에 공감한다면, 그녀는 우리에게 그런 까다로운 숙제는 주지 않으실 텐데.
= 우리 선생님은 우리의 스트레스에 공감하지 않기 때문에, 그녀는 우리에게 그런 까다로운 숙제를 주신다.
→ (A) 직설법 문장의 주절에 현재시제가 쓰였으므로 가정법 문장의 주절에는「would + 동사원형」을 써야 한다.

(B) 가정법 문장의 if절에 had가 있지만, 이는 가정법 과거완료를 나타내는 조동사 had가 아니라 과거시제 동사 had이다. 따라서 직설법 문장 부사절의 동사는 현재시제가 알맞다.
• empathy 공감 • tricky 까다로운

05 정답 I had answered **UNIT 71 가정법 과거완료**
[해석] 내가 그때 전화를 받지 못해서 유감이다.
= 내가 그때 전화를 받았으면 좋을 텐데.
→ 가정법 과거완료이므로「I wish + 주어 + had + 과거분사 ~」이다.

06 정답 it not for your help **UNIT 70 가정법 과거**
[해석] 너의 도움이 없다면 나는 시험에 합격하지 못할 텐데.
→ 가정법 과거를 나타낼 때 Without이나 But for, If it were not for를 쓸 수 있다. 이때 If it were not for에서 If를 생략하여 Were it not for로 쓸 수도 있다.

07 정답 내가 가격을 알았었다면, 나는 그 티켓을 사지 않았을 텐데. **UNIT 72 가정법의 다양한 형태**
→ 가정법 과거완료 문장에서 if가 생략되면서 주어와 동사가 도치된 문장이다.

R 실전 모의고사 ▶ 문제편 p.347

정답

01 is　　**02** perform　　**03** ④
04 is　　**05** not to run　　**06** starts
07 ⑤　　**08** ②　　**09** ⓐ, ⓔ, ⓕ

01 정답 is **UNIT 73 주어와 동사의 수 일치**
[해석] 50킬로그램은 이 수하물의 제한이다.
→ 무게를 나타내는 명사는 단수 취급한다.
• luggage 수하물

02 정답 perform **UNIT 73 주어와 동사의 수 일치**
[해석] 가수뿐만 아니라 무용수들도 라이브 공연을 한다.
→ not only A but also B가 주어로 쓰이면 B에 동사를 일치시킨다. B가 the dancers로 복수이므로 perform이 알맞다.

03 정답 ④ **UNIT 73 주어와 동사의 수 일치**
[해석] • 오늘은 내 여동생이나 부모님께서 나를 데리러 오신다.
• 그 도시를 방문하는 관광객 수가 증가했다.
→ either A or B가 주어로 쓰이면 B에 동사를 일치시킨다. B가 my parents로 복수이므로 are가 알맞다.「the number of+복수명사」가 주어일 때는 단수 취급한다. 따라서 has가 알맞다.

04 정답 is **UNIT 73 주어와 동사의 수 일치**
→ fish and chips는 '피시 앤 칩스'이며, 단일 개념으로 단수 취급한다.

05 정답 not to run **UNIT 75 화법**
→ 부정 명령문을 간접화법으로 바꿀 때는「not to+동사원형」의 형태로 바꾼다.

06 정답 starts   UNIT **74** 시제 일치

→ 조건을 나타내는 부사절에서는 미래시제 대신 현재시제를 쓴다.

07 정답 ⑤   UNIT **75** 화법

[해석] 선생님은 학생들에게 "주의 깊게 들으세요."라고 말했다.

→ 선생님은 학생들에게 주의 깊게 들으라고 말했다.

→ 긍정 명령문을 간접화법으로 바꿀 때 전달 동사는 어조에 따라 tell, order, advise 등으로 바꾸고, 동사원형은 to부정사의 형태로 바꾼다.

08 정답 ②   UNIT **75** 화법

[해석] 그녀는 그에게 "제 자전거를 고칠 수 있나요?"라고 말했다.

→ 그녀는 그에게 자신의 자전거를 고칠 수 있는지 물었다.

→ 의문사가 없는 의문문을 간접화법으로 바꿀 때 종속절 앞에 if 또는 whether를 쓰고, 어순을 「주어+동사」로 바꾼다. 직접화법의 my는 간접화법의 주어인 her로 바꾸는 것이 알맞다.

09 정답 ⓐ, ⓔ, ⓕ   UNIT **73** 주어와 동사의 수 일치, UNIT **75** 화법

[해석] ⓐ 정보 중 일부는 구식이다.

ⓑ 그녀는 그에게 점심으로 무엇을 먹고 싶은지 물었다.

ⓒ 물의 대부분은 마시기에 충분히 깨끗하다.

ⓓ 열심히 공부하는 학생은 항상 성공한다.

ⓔ 내 여동생은 나에게 이미 저녁을 먹었다고 말했다.

ⓕ 그녀는 진정한 친구는 어려운 시기에 나타난다고 믿었다.

→ ⓑ 의문사가 포함된 의문문을 간접 화법으로 바꿀 때는 「의문사+주어+동사」의 순으로 쓴다. (what did he want → what he wanted) ⓒ 부분을 나타내는 표현인 「most+of+명사」가 주어일 때는 of 뒤에 나온 명사에 동사의 수를 일치시킨다. water는 셀 수 없는 명사로 단수 취급한다. (are → is) ⓓ 주격 관계대명사절에서 동사는 선행사에 일치시키므로 The student에 맞추어 3인칭 단수 동사를 써야 한다. (study → studies)

· outdated 구식인

S 실전 모의고사
▶ 문제편 p.348

정답

01 has she seen such a thing

02 did they realize the truth   **03** ②   **04** ②

05 ⑤   **06** ③   **07** ④   **08** ①

01 정답 has she seen such a thing   UNIT **76** 도치

[해석] 결코 그녀는 그런 것을 본 적이 없다.

→ never, hardly, no, not, little 등의 부정어구가 문장 맨 앞으로 올 때, 주어와 동사에 도치가 일어난다. 따라서 조동사 has와 주어 she가 도치되어야 한다.

02 정답 did they realize the truth   UNIT **76** 도치

[해석] 그들은 끝날 때까지 진실을 깨닫지 못했다.

→ not until, never, hardly 등의 부정어구가 문장 맨 앞으로 올 때, 주어와 동사에 도치가 일어난다. 따라서 조동사 did와 주어 they가 도치되어야 한다.

03 정답 ②   UNIT **78** 생략, 부정 구문, 동격

→ none of는 '~ 중 어느 누구도'의 뜻이고, 이 표현이 전체 부정을 나타내기 때문에 다른 부정어는 필요하지 않다.

04 정답 ②   UNIT **78** 생략, 부정 구문, 동격

→ not all은 '모두가 ~인 것은 아닌'이라는 뜻으로 부분 부정을 나타낸다.

05 정답 ⑤   UNIT **77** 강조

[해석] ① 너의 인생을 바꿀 수 있는 것은 바로 너이다.

② 비가 오기 시작한 것은 2시였다.

③ 내가 Jim에게 주었던 것은 우표였다.

④ 새를 가져온 것은 그 남자였다.

⑤ 내가 그 수학 문제를 푸는 것은 어렵다.

→ ⑤ to solve가 진주어이고, it은 가주어로 쓰였다. 나머지는 모두 It ~ that … 강조 구문의 it이다.

06 정답 ③   UNIT **77** 강조

[해석] ① 그가 어제 그녀에게 주었던 것은 바로 장미 한 송이였다.

② 내가 그를 작년에 만났던 것은 바로 그 거리에서였다.

③ 그것은 너무 커서 나는 내 여동생과 나눌 수 있다.

④ 그가 운전하는 법을 배우기 시작한 것은 바로 1년 전이었다.

⑤ 내가 박물관에서 그 그림을 보았던 것은 바로 내 친구들과 함께였다.

→ ③ '너무 ~해서 …하다'라는 뜻의 so ~ that …구문으로 쓰인 that이고, 나머지는 모두 It ~ that … 강조 구문의 that이다.

07 정답 ④   UNIT **76** 도치

[해석] ① 눈이 내렸다.

② 바위 뒤에 다람쥐 한 마리가 서 있다.

③ 드론 한 대가 내 머리 바로 위로 지나갔다.

④ 그는 그의 부모님을 좀처럼 방문하지 않는다.

⑤ 모퉁이를 돌면 우체국이 있었다.

→ ④ 강조하는 말이 앞으로 나오면 주어와 동사가 도치된다. 부정어 seldom이 강조를 위해 문두로 나왔기 때문에 not을 또 쓰면 안 된다. ① 부사 down이 앞으로 나오면서 주어 the snow와 동사 fell이 도치되었다. ② 부사구가 앞으로 나오면서 주어 a squirrel과 동사 stands가 도치되었다. ③ 부사구가 앞으로 나오면서 주어 a drone과 동사 passed가 도치되었다. ⑤ 부사구가 앞으로 나오면서 주어 the post office와 동사 was가 도치되었다.

· squirrel 다람쥐

08 정답 ①   UNIT **77** 강조

[해석] ① 그녀는 중국어를 정말 잘 한다.

② 나는 만화책 읽기를 정말로 좋아한다.

③ 나는 일본 음악을 전혀 좋아하지 않는다.

④ 이것이 바로 내가 찾아왔던 그 책이다.

⑤ 네가 우리 집에 놓고 간 것은 바로 그 공책이다.

→ ① does가 이미 3인칭 단수 현재를 표현하고 있으므로 speaks가 아니라 speak로 써야 한다. ② 동사 like를 do가 강조하고 있다. ③ not ~ at all은 '전혀 ~ 아니다'의 뜻을 나타낸다. ④ the very가 뒤의 명사 book을 강조한다. ⑤ It ~ that … 강조 구문에서 the notebook이 강조되고 있다.

A 문장의 기초

UNIT 01 8품사와 문장의 구성 요소 ▶ p.2

01 대명사, 동사, 형용사   02 접속사, 대명사, 동사
03 동사, 부사, 형용사   04 동사, 명사, 형용사
05 감탄사, 형용사, 전치사   06 명사, 접속사, 형용사
07 S, V, C   08 S, V, O, M
09 S, V, M   10 S, V, O, O
11 S, V, O, C   12 S, V, M, M
13 S, V, M, C, M   14 S, V, O, M, M
15 quite   16 applauds   17 difficult
18 us   19 under

UNIT 02 1형식 문장과 2형식 문장 ▶ p.3

01 felt   02 bloom   03 fly
04 tastes   05 sounds   06 stopped
07 S, V, C, 2   08 S, V, M, M, 1
09 S, V, M, M, 1   10 S, V, M, M, 1
11 S, V, C, M, 2   12 S, V, C, M, 2
13 S, V, M, V, M, 1   14 kind
15 frequently   16 cloudy
17 comfortable   18 peacefully
19 gently   20 at the station
21 loudly

UNIT 03 3형식 문장과 4형식 문장 ▶ p.4

01 me, the data   02 his friend, a postcard
03 my sister, a necklace
04 my brother, his cap
05 him, the cup he ordered
06 dinner for them

07 a favor of him
→ ask, require, inquire 등이 3형식 문장으로 쓰일 때, 간접목적어 앞에는 전치사 of가 온다.
08 a sandwich for me
09 a present for my mom
10 a bottle of juice for me
11 a rare antique vase to her
12 a good partnership to them
13 both English and Math to the students
14 accused   15 thanked   16 reminded
17 compared   18 handed   19 discuss

UNIT 04 5형식 문장 ▶ p.5

01 her, happy   02 John, captain
03 his son, play (outside)
04 the movie, interesting
05 her students, answer (the questions)
06 sad   07 risky   08 successful
09 proud   10 to improve   11 manager
12 difficult   13 to speak   14 clean
15 broken   16 to lock   17 boiling
18 to study   19 to try

B 문장의 종류

UNIT 05 명령문, 제안문, 감탄문 ▶ p.6

01 Don't   02 or   03 Let's
04 let   05 don't   06 and
07 Finish   08 His baby is very cute.
09 What an amazing holiday this was!
10 She has very pretty dresses.
11 How well she plays the piano!

12 Don't talk during the test.

13 Finish your homework before dinner.

14 a good teacher he is

15 considerate to your friends all the time

16 Let's go on a trip　　**17** sweet she is

18 visiting grandfather's house this summer

19 we watch a movie after dinner

UNIT 06 평서문, 의문문 (부가의문문, 간접의문문) ▶ p.7

01 am I not 또는 aren't I　　**02** don't you

03 will you　**04** haven't you　**05** isn't she

06 shall we　**07** weren't we　**08** won't they

09 where he is going

10 when she will come back

11 why he acted that way

12 whether[if] she solved the problem

13 why that happened

14 how I can get to the station

15 how this machine works

16 will you → shall we　**17** don't → will

18 does the ticket cost → the ticket costs

19 does → 삭제　　**20** you → we

21 did she reply → she replied

C 명사, 관사

UNIT 07 셀 수 있는 명사의 복수형　　▶ p.8

01 men　　**02** salmon　　**03** houses

04 oxen　　**05** data　　**06** foxes

07 geese　　**08** parties　　**09** some

10 are

→ '현상'을 뜻하는 phenomenon의 복수형은 phenomena이다.

11 are　　**12** is　　**13** bacteria

14 moose

---

15 그 탁자는 나무로 만들어졌다.

16 우리는 숲속으로 하이킹을 갔다.

17 부드러운 천으로 탁자를 닦으세요.

18 그녀는 여행을 위해 옷을 모두 챙겼다.

19 ○　　**20** ○　　**21** graze

22 cacti　　**23** ○

UNIT 08 셀 수 없는 명사의 복수형　　▶ p.9

01 C　　**02** UC　　**03** C

04 UC　　**05** UC　　**06** C

07 Justice　　**08** great love　　**09** information

10 a spoonful of sugar　　**11** How much

12 ○　　**13** two cups of coffee

14 loaf　　**15** jars　　**16** sheet

17 bottle　　**18** pieces　　**19** bowls

UNIT 09 명사의 소유격　　▶ p.10

01 David's　　**02** dogs'　　**03** sister's

04 company's　**05** children's　**06** musicians'

07 The cat's　　**08** ○　　**09** children's

10 ○　　**11** Mr. and Mrs. Lee's

12 Women's fashion　　**13** baby's blanket

14 engine of the car　　**15** artist's use of color

16 roof of the building　　**17** my friend's bike

18 boy's explanation　　**19** people's opinions

UNIT 10 부정관사 (a, an)와 정관사 (the)　　▶ p.11

01 a　　**02** a　　**03** A[The]

04 an　　**05** a, the　　**06** The, the

07 The　　**08** the　　**09** The

10 the　　**11** an　　**12** An, The

13 the　　**14** the　　**15** a

16 The　　**17** an　　**18** a

19 a　　**20** a, a　　**21** The, an

UNIT 11 주의해야 할 관사의 쓰임 ▸ p.12

01 the (badminton) 02 the (bed)
03 the (helicopter) 04 the (work)
05 a (prison) 06 such a kind
07 ate an apple for breakfast
08 Both the dogs
09 made such a big mistake
10 give me an hour
11 always orders the same food
12 quite a long time
→ 「what, such, quite + 부정관사 (+ 형용사) + 명사」의 어순을 따른다.
13 Japanese 14 ○ 15 for dinner
16 ○ 17 ○ 18 tennis

D 대명사

UNIT 12 지시대명사 this (these), that (those), it ▸ p.13

01 That 02 that 03 these
04 This 05 that 06 those
07 this 08 these 09 비인칭 주어
10 강조 구문 11 가목적어 12 가주어
13 비인칭 주어 14 앞 문장 전체 대신
15 It is good to experience various cultures by traveling many countries.
16 The language of science is quite different from that of everyday life.
17 This new medicine is for those who suffer from insomnia.

UNIT 13 재귀대명사 ▸ p.14

01 yourself 02 yourself 03 herself
04 myself 05 herself 06 yourself
07 by (✓) 08 hurt (✓) while
09 taught (✓) how to play
10 introduced (✓) to 11 blamed (✓) for
12 in itself 13 by herself

14 in spite of myself 15 beside himself
16 by themselves 17 Between ourselves
18 themselves 19 myself
20 yourself 21 ○

UNIT 14 부정대명사 ▸ p.15

01 Each 02 one 03 it
04 any 05 All 06 ones
07 anything to say
08 All of the seats are taken.
09 Everyone needs to take this class.
10 Was anyone listening to
11 Both of them knew
12 Nothing is more important
13 All 14 Each 15 the other
16 another 17 others 18 Some
19 the others

E 시제

UNIT 15 시제의 종류 ▸ p.16

01 forgets 02 will finish 03 went
04 had 05 known 06 will be
07 had 08 Have 09 studied
10 ○ 11 will be traveling 또는 will travel
12 had 13 was 14 ○
15 broke his phone 16 The train leaves
17 He will be late
18 The bus had departed
19 is talking on the phone

UNIT 16 현재시제, 과거시제 ▸ p.17

01 melts 02 gets up 03 speak
04 didn't answer 05 leaves

06 cried   07 drinks   08 invented

09 The Berlin Wall fell

10 Plants produce oxygen through photosynthesis.

11 Seoul hosted the Summer Olympics

12 Don't count your chickens before they hatch.

13 get   14 drinks   15 ends

16 visited   17 became   18 delivered

UNIT 17 동사의 과거–과거분사 불규칙 변화표 ▶ p.18

01 spread, spread   02 ground, ground

03 forgot, forgotten   04 bit, bitten

05 hit, hit   06 threw, thrown

07 bore, born(e)   08 swept, swept

09 spilled[spilt]   10 cost

11 overcame   12 froze   13 awoke

14 meant   15 shook, heard

16 found, left   17 lost, rode   18 began, got

19 sold   20 ○   21 ended

22 tried

UNIT 18 미래시제 ▶ p.19

01 watch   02 will travel   03 will call

04 to learn   05 will wait   06 will wash

07 are going to watch   08 is going to be

09 will move   10 will begin

11 is going to fix   12 is about to leave

13 ○   14 finish   15 will go

16 to apply   17 were about to

18 ○   19 ○

UNIT 19 진행시제 ▶ p.20

01 will be working   02 will be going

03 will be taking   04 were doing

05 were watching   06 is cleaning

07 are, crying   08 was reading

09 will be going   10 Are, washing

11 were, doing   12 was preparing

13 is departing

14 Were you studying for the math test

15 are having a great time

16 is seeing his daughter's babysitter

17 I am reading an interesting book

UNIT 20 완료시제 ▶ p.21

01 has gone   02 had stolen

03 will have finished   04 has been

05 ○   06 ○

07 will have been   08 repaired

09 ○

10 had stayed 또는 stayed

11 ○   12 have ever read

13 ⓔ   14 ⓑ   15 ⓓ   16 ⓒ   17 ⓐ

F 조동사

UNIT 21 조동사의 특징과 조동사 do ▶ p.22

01 speak   02 May I   03 should not

04 has to   05 Will you   06 could not go

07 I didn't participate in the marathon race last week.

08 Never did she make a mistake during the science experiment.
→ 부정어구 도치는 「부정어구 + do[does, did] + 주어 + 동사원형」의 어순을 따른다.

09 He thought my brother broke the glass, but I did.

10 Sumin does want to have a trip to Europe this summer.

11 Did they have hamburgers for lunch at the cafeteria?

12 We don't have an annual meeting at the conference.

13 Does she like going to the movies on weekends?

14 ○

15 did tell 또는 did 삭제

16 must work

17 will

18 make

UNIT 22 can (could), may (might) ▸ p.23

01 추측
02 추측
03 요청

04 허가
05 허가
06 요청

07 가능
08 불가능

09 may well 또는 might well

10 ○
11 be able to
12 ○

13 couldn't[could not]
14 Can 또는 Could

15 ©
16 ⓑ
17 ⓓ
18 ⓐ

UNIT 23 will (would), must (have to) ▸ p.24

01 would
02 Will
03 will

04 would
05 must not
06 must

07 would
08 would

09 Will you come to my birthday party tomorrow?

10 He would like to go to his favorite singer's concert.

11 She must be very happy

12 You don't have to hand in your assignment today.

13 I would rather stay home than go out

14 You must wear a seatbelt

15 have to
16 need not
17 must

18 don't have to
19 would

UNIT 24 shall, should, ought to, had better (not) ▸ p.25

01 ⓔ
02 ⓑ
03 ©
04 ⓖ
05 ⓓ

06 ⓕ
07 ⓐ

08 You had better not stay up all night.

09 I insisted that our class go to Jeju-do.

10 How long should I walk to get

11 Mike should cut down on eating sweets for his health.

12 You ought not to spill the water on your keyboard.

13 better not
14 had

15 ought we to take
→ ought to의 의문문은 「ought + 주어 + to + 동사원형」의 어순을 따른다.

16 ○
17 wear

UNIT 25 used to, would, 조동사+have+과거분사 ▸ p.26

01 used to
02 forgotten
03 ○

04 ○
05 used to
06 ○

07 must
08 might
09 used to

10 might
11 should
12 cannot

13 could have traveled

14 I used to exercise

15 You should have followed your mother's opinion.

16 There used to be a river here

17 Her friend must have given a great gift to her

G 수동태

UNIT 26 수동태의 개념 및 형태 ▸ p.27

01 Suji's room is cleaned by her.

02 The school bus was missed by him.

03 Robert's suitcases were taken by a stranger.

04 My white car is repaired by a mechanic.

05 was given a Christmas gift by Jane

06 the glass cup broken by her baby

07 was done by the employees of the company

08 was this machine developed

09 were not washed by my mom

10 was picked by a gentleman

11 by her **12** by many people

13 By whom **14** was not told

15 Were **16** was watched by

17 This unique museum wasn't[was not] built by the architect.

18 Were the famous pieces played by the orchestra?

19 The Mona Lisa was painted by Leonardo da Vinci.

UNIT 27 수동태의 시제 ▸ p.28

01 was drawn by my sister

02 were delivered by the postman

03 is used by the neighbors

04 was sung by the beautiful soprano

05 is accessed by many employees

06 will be signed by the CEO

07 A history exam is being taken by the students.

08 Spaghetti was being cooked by me

09 The boxes are being carried by the staff.

10 The noise from outside is being heard by my friends.

11 All the questions have been answered by my sister

12 is being chased

13 has often been postponed

14 had been started

15 had been invented **16** has been read

UNIT 28 조동사와 동사구의 수동태 ▸ p.29

01 will be painted **02** was not welcomed

03 should be issued **04** may be studied

05 can't be used **06** will be

07 should be followed **08** was run over

09 may be **10** ○

11 have to be solved **12** was laughed at

---

13 is made up of

14 is (being) taken care of

15 is (being) dealt with

16 was given up **17** was put off

UNIT 29 4형식, 5형식의 수동태 ▸ p.30

01 was sent to me **02** was bought for Jisu

03 are provided by the store

04 was offered a reasonable price

05 was given the application form, was given to her

06 was asked many difficult questions, were asked of the math teacher

07 to tell **08** to join

09 made to repair **10** better

11 was heard to sing **12** to cheer

13 to be written **14** is envied

15 to move **16** ○

17 was taught **18** to describe

UNIT 30 주의해야 할 수동태와 관용표현 ▸ p.31

01 sells **02** resemble **03** has

04 tear
 → tear는 수동태의 의미를 포함하고 있으므로 「be동사+과거분사」로 쓰지 않도록 해야 한다.

05 is peeling **06** changes **07** said

08 filled with **09** is known for

10 were covered with **11** am tired of

12 was pleased with **13** composed of

14 is concerned about

15 This magazine reads well.

16 This table is made of wood.

17 Our relationship is based on our trust.

18 I am interested in collecting stamps.

19 Miso is excited about having a trip to Japan.

20 I am satisfied with my scores

H 형용사

UNIT 31 형용사의 종류, 쓰임, 어순 ▶ p.32

01 ⓔ, ⓐ   **02** ⓓ   **03** ⓒ
04 ⓒ, ⓑ   **05** ⓖ   **06** ⓑ
07 ⓕ   **08** ⓐ   **09** ⓐ
10 ⓑ   **11** ⓒ   **12** ⓑ, ⓒ
13 ⓐ   **14** two tasty round
15 big old brown
16 small round Japanese
17 something small and shiny

UNIT 32 부정 수량 형용사 ▶ p.33

01 visitors   **02** employees   **03** experience
04 mistakes   **05** time   **06** electricity
07 advice   **08** complaints   **09** a little
10 much   **11** Few   **12** a few
13 Few   **14** lot   **15** Some
16 ○   **17** a few   **18** ○
19 a great deal of time   **20** only a little

UNIT 33 수사 형용사의 표현 ▶ p.34

01 twenty-three thousand six hundred (and) ninety
02 thirty point one seven six
03 area code zero seven five, four five nine zero, six six seven two
04 eleven forty 또는 twenty to twelve
05 February (the) third, eighteen seventy-four 또는 the third of February, eighteen seventy-four
06 seven and a[one] half
07 two point four eight
08 twenty-four million six hundred (and) fifty-three thousand eight hundred (and) twenty-nine
09 one and three-fourths

10 1.36   **11** 6시 15분   **12** 2배
13 $8\frac{4}{5}$ **14** 2008년 12월 10일
15 fifteenth → fifteen   **16** on → of
17 third → three
18 three-fourth → three-fourths
→ 분자가 2 이상이면 분모에 -s를 붙인다.

I 부사

UNIT 34 부사의 형태 ▶ p.35

01 quickly   **02** slowly   **03** carefully
04 loudly   **05** regularly
06 automatically   **07** publicly
08 shyly   **09** angrily   **10** bravely
11 형용사   **12** 부사   **13** 형용사
14 부사   **15** 형용사   **16** 부사
17 부사   **18** 형용사   **19** 부사
20 형용사   **21** 부사   **22** 형용사
23 uniquely   **24** heavily   **25** precisely
26 steadily   **27** Luckily

UNIT 35 부사의 역할 및 위치 ▶ p.36

01 형용사 simple   **02** 형용사 cold
03 문장 전체   **04** 동사 deleted
05 문장 전체   **06** 부사 efficiently
07 동사 forgot   **08** you ✓ moving
09 brothers ✓ argue   **10** are ✓ fresh
11 discuss ✓ to   **12** patient ✓ for
13 became ✓ more
14 He often uses various gestures when he talks.
15 Tom is tall enough to be a basketball player.
16 The teacher slowly explained the problem on the board.

| UNIT **36** 그 밖의 중요 부사 | ▶ p.37 |

01 ago	**02** yet	**03** already
04 much	**05** before	**06** very
07 too	**08** either	**09** Neither
10 before	**11** still	**12** already
13 yet	**14** much	**15** even
16 either	**17** else	

J 비교급

| UNIT **37** 원급 | ▶ p.38 |

01 me	**02** is	**03** I
04 not as	**05** as well as	
06 his	**07** fluently	**08** not so

09 twice as many skirts as I have

10 wanted to leave the place as soon as possible

11 get as many coupons as she wishes

12 has about three times as many pictures as that book
→ '…의 몇 배 ~한[하게]'는 「배수사 + as + 원급 + as」로 표현한다.

13 tried to describe as clearly as I could

14 as wise as an owl

15 as proud as a peacock

16 as stubborn as a donkey

17 as busy as a bee

| UNIT **38** 비교급, 최상급 형태 | ▶ p.39 |

01 fatter, fattest   **02** worse, worst

03 less, least

04 more carefully, most carefully

05 grayer, grayest   **06** shorter, shortest

07 braver, bravest

08 more helpful, most helpful

09 angrier, angriest

10 more comfortable, most comfortable

11 farther	**12** older	**13** fewer
14 further	**15** more	**16** later
17 busier	**18** worst	**19** better
20 loneliest	**21** more complex	

| UNIT **39** 비교급 | ▶ p.40 |

01 funnier than his brother

02 much slower than mine

03 a better system than my company

04 this French course is more interesting than that Japanese course

05 much safer than traveling by car

06 three times bigger than mine

07 is getting thinner and thinner

08 less sweet than this chocolate

09 is less difficult than Math

10 no more than two dollars in his wallet

11 inferior to what I had expected

12 smarter

13 much[even, still, far, a lot 등]

14 more and more forgetful

15 one has   **16** ○

| UNIT **40** 최상급 | ▶ p.41 |

01 My eldest sister	**02** shortest	
03 in	**04** kindest	**05** ○
06 the most correctly		**07** one

08 one of the greatest figures of his time

09 the most handsome man that I've ever met

10 one of the largest car rental businesses

11 the most beautiful scenery I've ever seen

12 one of the fastest growing sports in this country

13 smarter than   **14** nothing better

15 No (other)   **16** as, as

17 most competent

K 접속사

UNIT 41 등위접속사 ▶ p.42

01 so 또는 for 02 and 또는 but 03 and 또는 or

04 or 05 and 또는 but 06 and 또는 for

07 or 08 come with us or stay here

09 or you'll be punished

10 but she sent me a message

11 and the washing machine will start

12 yet she couldn't finish the report

13 for he wants to lose weight

14 Study hard, or you will fail the exam.

15 Hurry up, and you'll catch the bus.

16 Turn off the oven, or the food will burn.

UNIT 42 상관접속사 ▶ p.43

01 but 02 or 03 go

04 ○ 05 take 06 nor

07 was 08 am going to attend

09 impress 10 was 11 are

12 have joined 13 have been promoted

14 not the rumors but the facts

15 both the public and the private sectors

16 not because he was lazy but because he was sick

17 either on Monday or on Tuesday

18 neither confirm nor deny the news

UNIT 43 명사절을 이끄는 종속접속사 ▶ p.44

01 that 02 how 03 that

04 if 05 that 06 whether

07 Whether 08 ○ 09 was

10 knows 11 the train arrives

12 Whether 13 ○ 14 that

UNIT 44 부사절을 이끄는 종속접속사 ▶ p.45

01 ⓕ 02 ⓓ 03 ⓐ

04 ⓔ 05 ⓒ 06 ⓑ

07 the light so that I could see inside the room

08 has practiced skiing since he was ten

09 gets tired, she goes to bed early

10 in order that I might travel abroad
→ '~하도록, ~하기 위하여'를 뜻하는 목적의 부사절 접속사는 so that, in order that이다.

11 Although 12 As 13 before

14 After 15 As soon as 16 so that

UNIT 45 접속부사 ▶ p.46

01 In other words 02 For example

03 As a result 04 On the contrary

05 On the other hand 06 Consequently

07 Therefore 08 In addition 09 Instead

10 Otherwise 11 Moreover 12 In contrast

L 전치사

UNIT 46 시간을 나타내는 전치사 ▶ p.47

01 since 02 until 03 in

04 on 05 by 06 during

07 for 08 at 09 in

10 at 11 during 12 by

13 for 14 on 15 since

16 is on June 3rd

17 moved here in March

18 must leave by sunset

19 laughed a lot during dinner

UNIT 47 장소를 나타내는 전치사 ▸ p.48

01 at **02** on, in **03** below

04 beneath
→ beneath는 접촉하여 아래에, below는 조금 떨어져 아래에를 뜻하는 전치사이다.

05 over **06** in, by

07 under **08** beneath **09** on

10 above **11** below **12** under

13 beside **14** Sit next to your partner

15 parked her car in front of the restaurant

16 well-known among the villagers

17 flew over the building

18 a basement below the house

UNIT 48 방향 및 기타 전치사 ▸ p.49

01 from **02** down **03** out of

04 across **05** around **06** into

07 up **08** toward **09** through

10 for **11** of **12** about

13 of colorful glass beads

14 along the river at sunset

15 fell down the hill

16 without eating breakfast

UNIT 49 동사＋전치사 ▸ p.50

01 for **02** for **03** with

04 for **05** with **06** in

07 to **08** on

09 belongs to my younger brother

10 focus on her upcoming presentation

11 laugh at someone

---

12 take the place of workers

13 of **14** of **15** for

16 of **17** in **18** of

19 in **20** to **21** of

UNIT 50 형용사＋전치사, 주의해야 할 전치사 ▸ p.51

01 accustomed to **02** fond of

03 afraid of **04** notorious for

05 known for **06** jealous of

07 responsible for **08** familiar with

09 to **10** of **11** at

12 on **13** of **14** of

15 of **16** at

17 because → because of

18 Though → Despite[In spite of]

19 while → during

20 In case → In case of

21 because of → because

22 during → while

M 부정사

UNIT 51 to부정사의 명사적 용법 ▸ p.52

01 to fill **02** ○

03 To speak 또는 Speaking
→ 동사가 주어 자리에 올 때, to부정사나 동명사 형태로 올 수 있다.

04 to finish **05** ○

06 to understand **07** 주어

08 보어 **09** 보어 **10** 주어

11 목적어 **12** 목적어 **13** 목적어

14 To read books improves

15 It was a mistake to ignore

16 is to finish the project

17 asked where to find

| UNIT **52** to부정사의 형용사적 용법 | | ▸ p.53 |

01 to talk	**02** ○	**03** to write
04 to use	**05** to take	**06** ○
07 someone to help		**08** ○

09 found a place to stay
10 need something to drink
11 have no time to waste
12 intend to   **13** was destined to
14 have to   **15** is going to
16 was able to

| UNIT **53** to부정사의 부사적 용법 | | ▸ p.54 |

01 판단의 근거	**02** 결과	**03** 원인, 이유
04 목적	**05** 판단의 근거	**06** 형용사 수식
07 원인, 이유	**08** 목적	**09** to receive
10 to fail	**11** to	**12** to buy

13 is willing to take on
14 enough to get a big applause
15 too cold to go outside
16 to avoid confusion
17 in order not to wake her baby
　→ 「in order[so as] to + 동사원형」의 부정은 「in order[so as] + not to + 동사원형」으로 나타낸다.
18 to find it empty
19 to buy such an expensive car

| UNIT **54** 원형부정사, to부정사의 의미상 주어 | | ▸ p.55 |

01 for	**02** of	**03** for
04 for	**05** of	**06** of

07 felt his phone vibrating
08 got her little brother to stop
09 common for a cat to like
10 brave of the firefighter to go
11 had me write an apology letter
12 heard the teacher say
13 apologize   **14** make
15 of her   **16** walk 또는 walking

| UNIT **55** to부정사의 시제, 부정, 수동태, 대부정사 | ▸ p.56 |

01 to have done	**02** to go
03 to have won	**04** to have

05 to have survived
06 to have been canceled   **07** to be
08 never to   **09** not to lose
10 not to be shared   **11** to gather
12 to visit   **13** to be finished
14 have been blamed   **15** go on a picnic
16 solve the problem   **17** go there
18 start working for that company

| UNIT **56** to부정사의 관용표현 | ▸ p.57 |

01 seems to stick to a better shape
02 seemed to have lied about the outcome
03 that she noticed the slight change
04 that he had lost every bodily function
05 for me to go home
06 for us to solve problems effectively
07 so complicated, I couldn't remember
08 so big, it can cover the front yard of my house
09 to endure   **10** could   **11** frank
12 to maintain **13** truth   **14** to have
15 for us

N 동명사

| UNIT **57** 동명사 | ▸ p.58 |

01 동사의 목적어	**02** 전치사의 목적어
03 동사의 목적어	**04** 주어
05 전치사의 목적어	**06** 동사의 목적어
07 보어	**08** 주어
09 my	**10** her
11 his not keeping	**12** not having
13 his	

14 is sorting these pieces of mail

15 Would you mind my borrowing

16 without making any mistakes

17 Knowing how to create a good mood is

18 for not preparing his part

UNIT 58 동사의 목적어로 쓰이는 동명사, to부정사 ▶ p.59

01 to travel 02 to help 03 my putting

04 meeting 05 becoming 06 arguing

07 to spend

08 그는 그의 팀에 해결책을 계속 제시한다.

09 그녀는 지난 금요일에 대회에서 1등상을 받았던 것을 잊지 않을 것이다.

10 Jenny는 이 독특한 제품으로 많은 돈을 벌려고 노력한다.

11 나는 우리가 어렸을 때 너와 함께 동물원을 방문했던 것을 기억한다.

12 이 가게는 지난주에 저 물건들을 파는 것을 그만두었다.

13 Jack은 그의 친구들과 함께 그 보고서를 써야 할 것을 잊었다.

14 to take 15 thinking 16 to save

17 to hide 18 to answer 19 watching

20 getting

UNIT 59 전치사의 목적어로 쓰인 동명사, 관용표현 ▶ p.60

01 break → breaking

02 ordering → being ordered

03 try → trying 04 hitting → being hit

05 locking → being locked

06 being supporting → supporting 또는 being supported by

07 to fall → falling

08 feels like reading

09 warn against losing

10 accused, of leaking 11 On entering

12 cannot help admiring

13 is busy preparing 14 is worth visiting

15 have difficulty communicating
→ '~하는 데 어려움을 겪다'는 have difficulty[trouble] (in) -ing로 표현한다.

O 분사

UNIT 60 분사의 종류와 역할 ▶ p.61

01 running 02 repaired 03 living

04 coming 05 signed 06 written

07 shortened 08 The crying baby woke

09 walking in the conference room

10 the stars shining in the night sky

11 a letter written in Korean

12 The broken window needs to

13 missing 14 accepted 15 playing

16 cleaned 17 baked

UNIT 61 현재분사와 동명사, 감정을 나타내는 분사 ▶ p.62

01 현재분사 02 동명사 03 동명사

04 현재분사 05 현재분사 06 동명사

07 현재분사 08 동명사

09 그녀는 피곤했지만 계속 노래를 불렀다., 동명사

10 문 앞에 서 있는 그 나이 든 남자는 누구야?, 현재분사

11 그들은 학교 운동장에서 야구를 하는 중이었다., 현재분사

12 우리는 놀이공원에 가는 것에 대해 이야기했다., 동명사

13 shocked → shocking

14 interested → interesting

15 disappointing → disappointed

16 amazed → amazing

17 satisfied → satisfying

18 fascinating → fascinated

UNIT 62 분사구문 ▶ p.63

01 Clearly knowing the correct answer

02 Failing the competition

03 Working hard

04 Feeling happy about the news

05 Smiling 06 ○

07 ○		**08** Walking	

09 While[As] he read a magazine

10 Although[Even though, Though] she is very young

11 Because[As, Since] he had some time

12 If[After, When] I get more money

13 Although[Even though, Though] she is tired

14 Because[As, Since] she felt extremely tired after work

UNIT 63 주의해야 할 분사구문 ▶ p.64

01 Not knowing **02** Being

03 Speaking **04** not having found

05 Having left **06** Having failed

07 Not sharing **08** Considering

09 The heavy snow blocking traffic

10 the light turned on **11** Generally speaking

12 I not giving him enough time

13 the dawn breaking

14 Her having → Having

15 Lived → Living

16 crossing → crossed

17 Comparing → Compared

18 Feeling not → Not feeling

P 관계사

UNIT 64 관계대명사 ▶ p.65

01 who **02** whom

03 whose **04** which

05 The girl whose jacket is red is my best friend, Tina.

06 The present which his grandmother gave him is very expensive.

07 I was very moved by the kindness which she showed to me.

08 At the party, he met a woman whose dress was all blue.

09 Here are some options from which you can choose.

10 Did you want to get the sunglasses which I bought yesterday?

11 I met a lot of people who(m) I saw at the conference.
→ who와 whom은 모두 목적격으로 쓰일 수 있다. 단, 전치사 뒤에 올 때는 who가 올 수 없다.

12 She has a brother who can play basketball very well.

13 The man who(m) you saw at the party is my boss.

14 We visited a castle which was built in the 18th century.

15 I taught a boy whose English has improved dramatically.

UNIT 65 관계대명사 that, what ▶ p.66

01 that **02** What **03** that

04 that **05** what **06** that

07 that **08** gives[gave] **09** ○

10 that[who] **11** what **12** what

13 what you saw **14** that helped me

15 What you said **16** that we watched

17 What she did

18 that you adopted from the shelter

UNIT 66 관계대명사의 계속적 용법과 생략 ▶ p.67

01 that are **02** which **03** which was

04 ×
→ 주격 관계대명사는 단독으로 생략할 수 없다.

05 who is **06** whom

07 that was **08** that

09 David는 내게 재킷을 주었는데, 그것은 독특한 스타일로 만들어졌다.

10 내 부모님은 결혼한 지 30년이 되셨는데, 여전히 서로를 깊이 사랑하신다.

11 내 남동생이 내가 가장 좋아했던 비싼 꽃병을 떨어뜨렸다.

12 그녀는 친절한 학생인데, 그녀는 우리 학교 동아리의 회장이다.

13 그는 나에게 글쓰기의 바람직한 단계를 보여주었는데, 그것은 중요한 부분이다.

14 on which **15** for which **16** from which

17 with whom **18** in which **19** at which

---

01 when **02** at which **03** on

04 in which **05** which

06 at which
→ 시각과 같이 쓰는 전치사는 at이므로 at which가 알맞다.

07 where

08 the way how → the way 또는 how 또는 the way in which

09 how → why 또는 for which 또는 삭제

10 which → where **11** that → when

12 which[that], in **13** where, is working

14 in which **15** which[that], at

16 where **17** on which

---

01 the reason 또는 why **02** ×

03 the reason 또는 why **04** ×

05 who **06** when **07** where

08 why **09** which

10 where they used to visit for the analysis

11 when they had a birthday party

12 where they spent their vacation

13 when her friends visited her

---

14 when I couldn't speak English well

15 why it is so popular among the students

16 where he saw beautiful scenery

---

01 No matter when you need a demonstration

02 No matter what she wears

03 No matter which you choose

04 No matter who needs support with the project

05 No matter how hard it might be

06 No matter which group project fits your schedule best

07 wherever **08** whichever **09** Whenever

10 However **11** whoever **12** whatever

13 Whichever **14** at any time **15** however

16 whomever **17** quickly

Q 가정법

01 listened **02** knew **03** were

04 talks **05** started **06** had

07 wouldn't

08 don't understand, were a parent

09 can't buy a new phone, saved money

10 were not for breakfast

11 my glasses, it were not for

12 she liked Tony

13 he were better than his teacher

14 If they were to ask for help
→ 「be동사 + to부정사」는 '예정, 가능, 의도, 의무, 운명'의 의미를 나타낸다.

15 If we met earlier

16 would understand better

17 wouldn't stay healthy

UNIT 71 가정법 과거완료 ▸ p.72

01 had called 02 had listened
03 would have gone 04 have tried
05 have gotten 06 might have had
07 would have performed
08 was upset, had told me the truth
09 had lost
10 missed the plane, could have had a great time with him
11 had arrived at the station
12 had told her how to do it
13 would have gotten completely lost
14 If I hadn't forgotten her birthday
15 I had gone on the school trip last year
16 they would have gotten lost in the forest

UNIT 72 가정법의 다양한 형태 ▸ p.73

01 made 02 Were 03 be
04 Had 05 apologized 06 Were
07 Had 08 had brought the camera
09 would understand this movie
10 practiced more 11 Were, taller
12 should stop
13 my car hadn't broken down
14 would make
15 had taken, would live
16 taken the other road
17 took my opportunities
→ '~해야 할 때이다'를 뜻하는 표현은 「It's time (that) + 가정법 과거」, 「It's time to + 동사원형」, 「It's time (that) + 주어 + should + 동사원형」으로 표현한다.

UNIT 73 주어와 동사의 수 일치 ▸ p.74

01 is 02 has 03 are
04 like 05 finish 06 has
07 know
08 The United States is a country of many different races.
09 Everything in this store is on sale.
10 Economics is the study of choices.
11 I want to say that anything is possible.
12 Three hours is too long to wait for someone.
13 are → is
14 promote → promotes
15 employee → employees
16 are → is 17 was → were
18 likes → like 19 takes → take

UNIT 74 시제 일치 ▸ p.75

01 will → would 02 is → was
03 will → would 04 is → was
05 have → had 06 had → has
07 will → would 08 have talked
09 is 10 drinks
11 (should) work 12 invented
13 is 14 rains
15 arrives 16 goes
17 would have taken 18 have
19 had visited 20 eat

UNIT 75 화법 ▸ p.76

01 that he was 02 where I lived
03 she was, my, then 04 that we
05 she was, her, that

06 if[whether] I was coming with them

07 I will, you tomorrow

08 meet after work   **09** We are, tonight

10 did she leave early   **11** I was, yesterday

12 Let's invite her

13 Shall we watch a movie tonight

14 I am planning a trip

15 not acting on impulse

16 told him not to park his car there

17 How lucky I am

S 특수 구문

UNIT 76 도치　　　▶ p.77

01 could I see what he did

02 are some museums near my sister's school

03 sang a cute bird

04 does he feel comfortable

05 had the concert begun than the power went out

06 have I witnessed such chaos

07 did I dream that I could work with my best friend in the same company

08 Neither   **09** Neither

10 So   **11** So

12 we have → have we

13 I realized → did I realize

14 So couldn't → Neither could

15 they visit → do they visit

16 she came → did she come

UNIT 77 강조　　　▶ p.78

01 on earth   **02** who   **03** very

04 does   **05** in the least   **06** much

07 was he that[who]

08 is Emily that[who]

09 was in New Zealand that[where]

10 does want

11 was at noon that[when]

12 is in New York that[where]

13 wrote → write

14 would in the world → in the world would
→ 의문사 강조는 의문사 바로 뒤에 on earth[ever, in the world]를 쓴다.

15 very → much, far, still, a lot, even 등

16 very the → the very

17 who → that[where]

UNIT 78 생략, 부정 구문, 동격　　　▶ p.79

01 who is   **02** lived

03 which is   **04** she is

05 it is   **06** I wish you a

07 he

08 모든 여자아이들이 귀여운 인형을 가지고 노는 것을 좋아하는 것은 아니다.

09 너의 반 친구들 중 아무도 발표에 참가하고 싶어 하지 않는다.

10 그녀가 항상 대회에서 1등 상을 받는 것은 아니다.

11 그 보고서는 어디에서도 그 핵심 문제를 언급하지 않았다.
→ '모두[전부] ~이 아니다'를 뜻하는 전체 부정은 not + any[anyone, anything, anywhere]로 표현한다.

12 그것이 반드시 나쁜 결과를 의미하는 것은 아니다.

13 그녀는 중요한 건 아무것도 말하지 않았다.
→ '모두[전부] ~이 아니다'를 뜻하는 전체 부정은 not + any[anyone, anything, anywhere]로 표현한다.

14 the smartest girl in my class, came from Busan

15 that he didn't finish high school embarrassed me

16 Nothing can stop me from achieving

판매량 **1**위, 만족도 **1**위, 추천도서 **1**위!!

쉬운 개념 이해와 정확한 연산력을 키운다!!

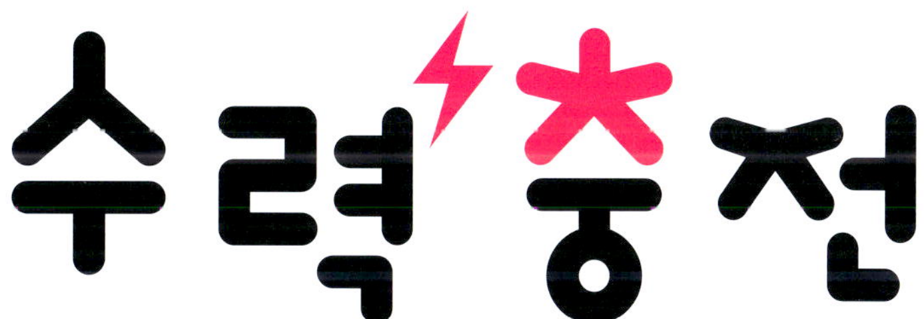

★ 수력충전이 꼭 필요한 학생들

- 계산력이 약해서 시험에서 실수가 잦은 학생
- 개념 이해가 어려워 자신감이 없는 학생
- 부족한 단원을 빠르게 보충하려는 학생
- 스스로 원리를 터득하기 원하는 학생
- 수학의 전체적인 흐름을 잡기 원하는 학생
- 선행 학습을 하고 싶은 학생

1 쉬운 개념 이해와 다양한 문제의 풀이를 따라가면서 수학의 연산 원리를 이해하는 교재!!

2 매일매일 반복하는 연산학습으로 기본 개념을 자연스럽고 완벽하게 이해하는 교재!!

3 단원별, 유형별 다양한 문제 접근 방법으로 부족한 부분의 문제를 집중 학습할 수 있는 교재!!

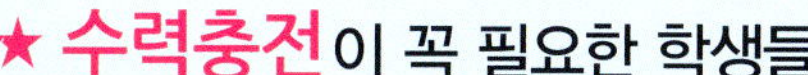
★ 수력충전 시리즈

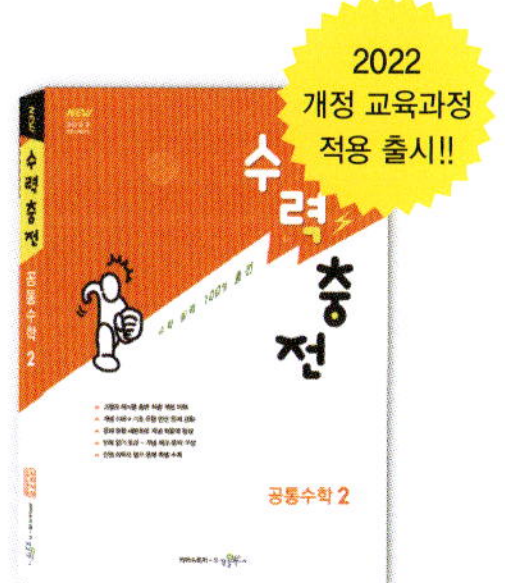

초등 수력충전 [기본]

초등 수학 1–1, 2 / 초등 수학 2–1, 2
초등 수학 3–1, 2 / 초등 수학 4–1, 2
초등 수학 5–1, 2 / 초등 수학 6–1, 2

중등 수력충전

중등 수학 1–1, 2
중등 수학 2–1, 2
중등 수학 3–1, 2

고등 수력충전

공통수학 1, 공통수학 2
대수 / 미적분 Ⅰ / 확률과 통계

자이스토리 국어 비문학, 문학, 문법, 어휘 시리즈

자이스토리 중학 국어 시리즈

중학 국어 비문학 독해 1, 2, 3 (예비 고등)

- 문해력 + 어휘 체크 문제
- 4단계 독해 STEP별 아주 특별한 문제
- 다양한 유형의 어휘력 향상 TEST, 배경지식, 어휘 총정리 + 어휘 특별 TEST
- 독해 STEP에 따른 단계별 독해 훈련

  STEP ❶ 핵심어 찾기, 중심 문장 찾기 [3일]　　STEP ❸ 글의 구조 파악하기, 주제 찾기 [5일]
  STEP ❷ 문단 요약하기, 문단 간의 관계 파악하기 [4일]　　STEP ❹ 실력 향상 TEST [8일]

중학 국어 문학 독해 + 문학 용어 1, 2, 3

갈래별 STEP에 따른 단계별 독해 훈련

〈시〉
STEP
❶ 화자, 중심 대상 찾기
❷ 상황, 정서, 태도 파악하기
❸ 표현상 특징 파악하기

〈소설·극〉
STEP
❶ 중심인물, 배경 파악하기
❷ 중심 사건, 갈등 파악하기
❸ 서술상 특징 파악하기

〈수필〉
STEP
❶ 중심 대상 찾기
❷ 글쓴이의 생각, 태도 파악하기
❸ 서술상 특징 파악하기

중학 국어 독해력 완성 1, 2, 3 [비문학]

- 독해 STEP에 따른 단계별 독해 훈련
- 지문과 문제 접근법을 알려 주는 Follow Me!
- 다양한 유형의 어휘 테스트와 배경지식

자이스토리 중학 국어 문법 기본, 문법 완성

- 2022 개정 중학 교과서 문법 개념 총정리
- 쉬운 개념 정리 + 다양한 예문의 개념 확인 문제
- 문법 개념 동영상 강의 QR코드
- 최다 내신 문제와 서술형 문제 수록
- **특별 부록**: [문법 개념 테스트] – 공부한 개념 복습 문제

중학 국어 문해력을 키우는 어휘 1, 2

- (읽기, 듣기·말하기·쓰기 교과서 어휘 + 용어 수록)
  영역별·주제별 핵심 어휘
- (문학) 교과서 필수 작품
- (문법) 교과서 필수 개념

자 이 스 토 리

예비 중등 **영어 독해**

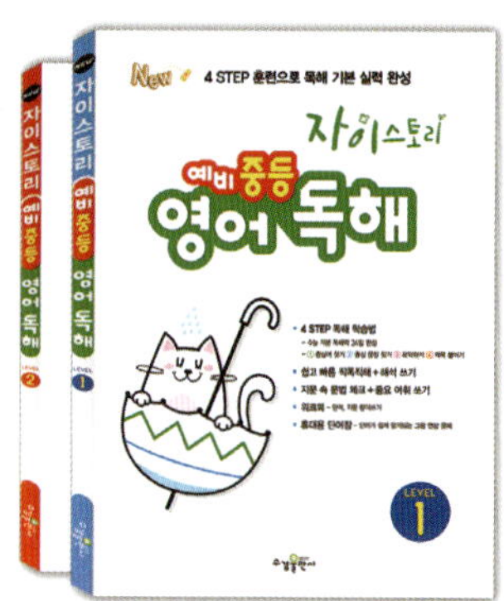

[Level 1, Level 2]

"중등 영어 독해를 계단식으로 탄탄하게 다진다!"

★ 계단식 독해 학습법 (4 STEP)

계단식 독해 학습법을 익히면 길고 어려운 중학교 영어 지문도
쉽게 이해할 수 있는 독해 능력을 기를 수 있습니다.

① 중심어 찾기 ② 중심 문장 찾기 ③ 요약하기 ④ 제목 붙이기

---

① 다양한 지문으로 기초부터 **계단식 독해 학습**

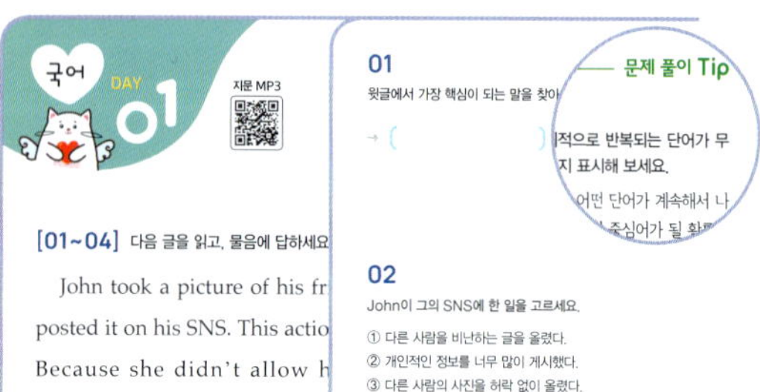

② 쉽고 빠른 지문 이해가 가능한
〔직독직해 + 해석 쓰기〕

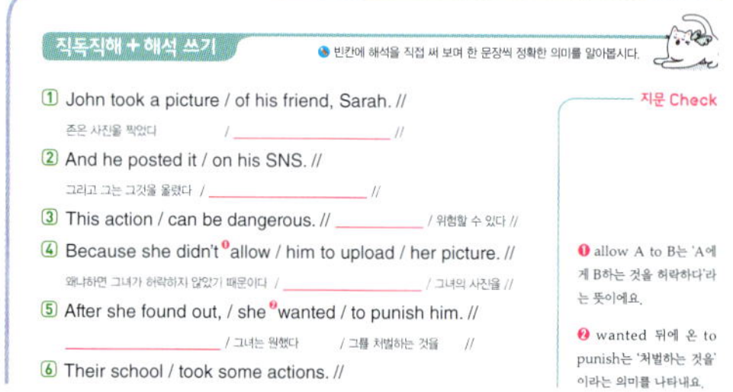

③ 지문 속 **문법 체크 + 중요 어휘 쓰기!**

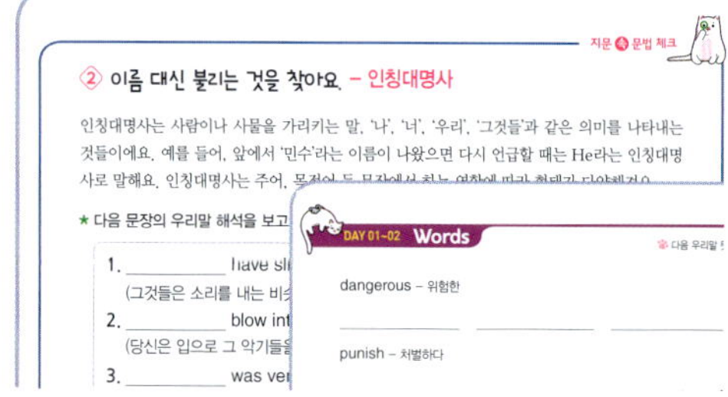

④ 5일 독해 학습을 총정리하는 **Review Test!**

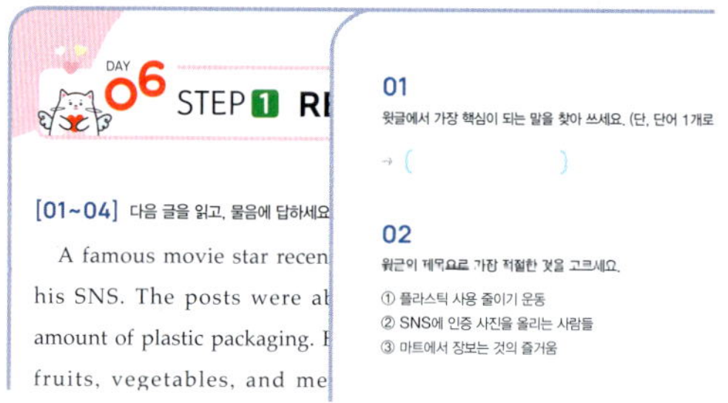